Crime in America's Top-Rated Cities: A Statistical Profile

1997 - 1998
2nd Edition

Rhoda Garoogian, *Managing Editor*
Andrew Garoogian, *Associate Editor*
Jacqueline Diaz, *Research Assistant*

Universal Reference Publications

Crime in America's Top-Rated Cities: A Statistical Profile 1997-98
ISBN 1-881220-37-0

Printed and bound in the United States of America.

Universal Reference Publications, 1355 W. Palmetto Park Road, Suite 315, Boca Raton, FL 33486
Toll-Free: 1-800-377-7551, Phone: (561) 997-7557, Fax: (561) 997-6756, Web: www.citystats.com

Preface

Crime may be down in 1996 according to figures released by the Federal Bureau of Investigation but certainly not out. Homicide rates took a sharp drop in some cities (Boston, Dallas, Denver) but showed increases in other cities (Washington, Atlanta, Miami). Experts caution that even with the latest decline, crime remains an urgent issue for most Americans and seems to always appear near the top of surveys asking Americans to name the most important issues facing the nation. The public says that reducing crime is a top priority for Congress but they also want their legislators and law enforcement officials at all levels of government to develop effective strategies to further reduce crime and ensure safe and thriving communities. To better allocate our resources to fight crime, it is important that the decision makers be properly informed about the statistics on crime.

With information as the key, the editors decided to add to their *America's Top-Rated Cities* series, the present publication, *Crime in America's Top-Rated Cities: A Statistical Profile*, which is now in its second edition. This compendium again focuses on those American cities (75 in all) which have been cited in various magazine surveys *(Entrepreneur, Fortune, Home Office Computing, Money, Site Selection* and others*)* as being the best places for business and/or living.

Arrangement

Crime In America's Top-Rated Cities includes statistics for the past 20 years (1977-1996) in all major crime categories: violent crimes (murder, rape, robbery, aggravated assault), property crimes (burglary, larceny, theft, motor vehicle theft) and total crime. Each table compares numbers of crimes and crime rates for the city, suburbs, metro area and U.S. Graphs showing crime trends are included for violent, property and total crimes as a means of offering the user an added perspective from which to study crime.

Conveniently arranged by city, the handbook also contains statistics on hate crimes, illegal drugs, correctional facilities, shock incarceration programs, curfews, inmates and HIV/AIDS, the death penalty, law enforcement personnel, handgun/alcohol/hate crime laws, anti-crime programs and the chances of becoming a victim.

Audience

Crime in America's Top-Rated Cities has been designed for individuals relocating, business persons, general researchers, the press, law enforcement officials as well as students of criminal justice who use public, academic and special libraries.

Crime Index Offenses

All the crimes covered in this book are Crime Index offenses as defined by the FBI Uniform Crime Reporting Program and include the following categories: murder and non-negligent manslaughter, forcible rape, robbery, aggravated assault, burglary, larceny-theft and motor vehicle theft. The classification of all Crime Index offenses is based solely on police investigation as opposed to the determination of a court, medical examiner, coroner, jury, or other judicial body.

The crime statistics contained in the *FBI Uniform Crime Reports* were contributed by state and local law enforcement agencies. Population size is the only correlate of crime used in that publication. The reader is, therefore, cautioned against comparing statistical data between cities or metro areas because many factors contribute to the numbers and types of crimes reported: population density, population characteristics, economic conditions (median income, poverty rates, job availability), climate, strength of law enforcement agencies and crime reporting practices of the citizenry, among others.

No attempt has been made to provide rankings of cities based on their crime rates; we leave those compilations to the news media. Rankings are but one factor in our understanding of crime and as stated by the FBI, "often create misleading perceptions which adversely affect cities along with their residents."

Appendices

Appendix A defines Metropolitan Statistical Areas (MSA). The reader is urged to consult this section if he/she is interested in the statistics for MSA or suburban areas as the MSA definitions for most of the cities have changed at least once since 1977. Appendix B lists city Police Departments. Appendix C defines the different types of crimes covered in this book and an explanation of terms for the table on laws relating to alcohol use and driving.

Sources

In addition to materials provided by private and public agencies, numerous library resources were also consulted including the *FBI Uniform Crime Reports, Sourcebook of Criminal Justice Statistics, Bureau of the Census publications, FBI Law Enforcement Bulletin, Police Chief* and other periodical and newspaper sources. In all cases, every table, chart, etc. is properly cited with the appropriate reference.

Acknowledgments

The editors wish to thank all of those individuals who responded to our requests for information. Especially helpful were the various city police departments and reference specialists in the National Criminal Justice Reference Service and the Federal Bureau of Investigation.

Mission Statement

The mission of Universal Reference Publications is to develop a series of comprehensive but affordable statistical reference handbooks about America's best cities. Towards that end we have also published the four-volume *America's Top-Rated Cities, America's Top-Rated Smaller Cities* (cities under 100,000 population) and *Health & Environment in America's Top-Rated Cities.*

Although every effort has been made to gather the most current and most accurate information information, discrepancies may occur due to the changing nature in the way private and governmental agencies compile and interpret statistical data.

We welcome your comments and suggestions for improving the coverage and presentation of data in future editions of *Crime in America's Top-Rated Cities.*

The editors,
Rhoda & Andrew Garoogian

Table of Contents

Atlanta, Georgia 41

Austin, Texas 51

Baltimore, Maryland 61

Boston, Massachusetts 71

Colorado Springs, Colorado 121

Columbus, Ohio 131

Dallas, Texas 141

Denver, Colorado 151

Jacksonville, Florida 281

Kansas City, Missouri 291

Knoxville, Tennessee 301

Lansing, Michigan 311

Las Vegas, Nevada 321

Lexington, Kentucky 331

Los Angeles, California 341

Lubbock, Texas 351

Madison, Wisconsin. 361

Manchester, New Hampshire. 371

Miami, Florida 381

Milwaukee, Wisconsin. 391

Minneapolis, Minnesota 401

Mobile, Alabama 411

Nashville, Tennessee 421

New Orleans, Louisiana. 431

New York, New York 441

Norfolk, Virginia 451

Oakland, California 461

Omaha, Nebraska 471

Orlando, Florida 481

Philadelphia, Pennsylvania 491

Phoenix, Arizona 501

Pittsburgh, Pennsylvania 511

Sacramento, California 561

Saint Louis, Missouri 571

Saint Paul, Minnesota 581

Salt Lake City, Utah 591

San Antonio, Texas 601

San Diego, California 611

San Francisco, California 621

San Jose, California 631

Seattle, Washington 641

Sioux Falls, South Dakota 651

Springfield, Missouri 661

Stamford, Connecticut 671

Tacoma, Washington 681

Tallahassee, Florida 691

Tampa, Florida 701

Topeka, Kansas. 711

Abilene, Texas

OVERVIEW

The total crime rate for the city increased 21.4% between 1977 and 1996. During that same period, the violent crime rate increased 220.2% and the property crime rate increased 13.6%.

Among violent crimes, the rates for: Murders decreased 41.9%; Forcible Rapes increased 67.0%; Robberies increased 94.7%; and Aggravated Assaults increased 464.7%.

Among property crimes, the rates for: Burglaries decreased 0.9%; Larceny-Thefts increased 17.1%; and Motor Vehicle Thefts increased 37.3%.

ANTI-CRIME PROGRAMS

Information not available at time of publication.

CRIME RISK

Your Chances of Becoming a Victim[1]

Area	Any Crime	Violent Crime					Property Crime			
		Any	Murder	Forcible Rape[2]	Robbery	Aggrav. Assault	Any	Burglary	Larceny -Theft	Motor Vehicle Theft
City	1:19	1:192	1:16,360	1:895	1:909	1:287	1:21	1:102	1:29	1:467

Note: (1) Figures have been calculated by dividing the population of the city by the number of crimes reported to the FBI during 1996 and are expressed as odds (eg. 1:20 should be read as 1 in 20). (2) Figures have been calculated by dividing the female population of the city by the number of forcible rapes reported to the FBI during 1996. The female population of the city was estimated by calculating the ratio of females to males reported in the 1990 Census and applying that ratio to 1996 population estimate.
Source: FBI Uniform Crime Reports 1996

CRIME STATISTICS

Total Crimes and Total Crime Rates: 1977 - 1996

Year	Number				Rate per 100,000 population			
	City	Suburbs[2]	MSA[1]	U.S.	City	Suburbs[3]	MSA[1]	U.S.
1977	4,107	706	4,813	10,984,500	4,293.5	2,143.6	3,742.8	5,077.6
1978	4,584	655	5,239	11,209,000	4,749.5	1,712.6	3,887.6	5,140.3
1979	4,794	734	5,528	12,249,500	4,808.8	2,050.9	4,080.3	5,565.5
1980	5,488	775	6,263	13,408,300	5,586.8	1,894.9	4,501.5	5,950.0
1981	5,687	692	6,379	13,423,800	5,559.8	1,624.8	4,403.1	5,858.2
1982	6,249	713	6,962	12,974,400	5,899.3	1,616.6	4,640.3	5,603.6
1983	6,285	428	6,713	12,108,600	5,765.9	2,941.6	5,433.3	5,175.0
1984	5,813	322	6,135	11,881,800	5,325.8	2,239.5	4,966.6	5,031.3
1985	6,511	344	6,855	12,431,400	5,849.1	2,337.1	5,438.9	5,207.1
1986	7,435	394	7,829	13,211,900	6,588.5	2,526.0	6,095.2	5,480.4
1987	7,518	315	7,833	13,508,700	6,643.6	2,396.5	6,201.7	5,550.0
1988	6,612	325	6,937	13,923,100	6,002.9	2,535.7	5,641.5	5,664.2
1989	6,695	322	7,017	14,251,400	6,080.8	2,514.6	5,709.3	5,741.0
1990	5,739	299	6,038	14,475,600	5,381.0	2,299.8	5,046.2	5,820.3
1991	6,451	334	6,785	14,872,900	5,922.2	2,515.6	5,552.1	5,897.8
1992	5,410	299	5,709	14,438,200	4,880.2	2,213.0	4,590.4	5,660.2
1993	5,474	284	5,758	14,144,800	4,966.3	2,235.3	4,684.1	5,484.4
1994	6,131	295	6,426	13,989,500	5,457.5	2,278.2	5,128.9	5,373.5
1995	6,049	328	6,377	13,862,700	5,395.8	2,712.5	5,134.6	5,275.9
1996	5,971	355	6,326	13,473,600	5,213.8	2,874.0	4,986.0	5,078.9

Notes: (1) Metropolitan Statistical Area - see Appendix A for areas included; (2) calculated by the editors using the following formula: (number of crimes in the MSA minus number of crimes in the city); (3) calculated by the editors using the following formula: ((number of crimes in the MSA minus number of crimes in the city) ÷ (population of the MSA minus population of the city)) x 100,000; n/a not avail.
Source: U.S. Department of Justice, FBI Uniform Crime Reports, 1977 - 1996

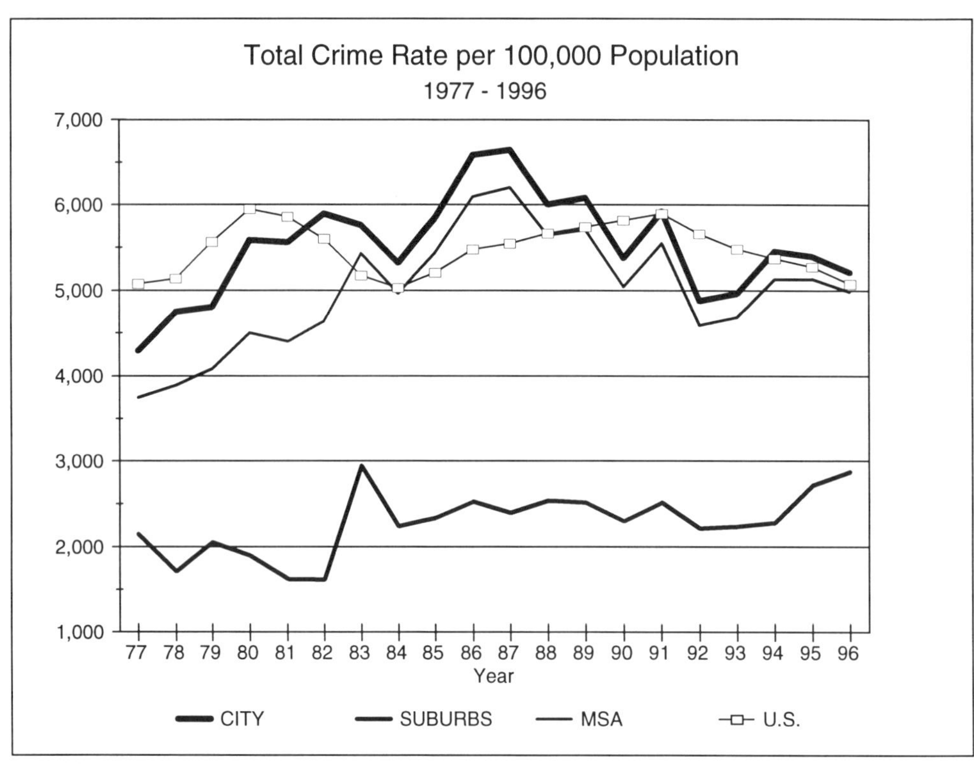

Note: Missing line segments indicate data not available.

Violent Crimes and Violent Crime Rates: 1977 - 1996

Year	Number				Rate per 100,000 population			
	City	Suburbs[2]	MSA[1]	U.S.	City	Suburbs[3]	MSA[1]	U.S.
1977	156	68	224	1,029,580	163.1	206.5	174.2	475.9
1978	247	70	317	1,085,550	255.9	183.0	235.2	497.8
1979	239	57	296	1,208,030	239.7	159.3	218.5	548.9
1980	251	55	306	1,344,520	255.5	134.5	219.9	596.6
1981	381	71	452	1,361,820	372.5	166.7	312.0	594.3
1982	449	94	543	1,322,390	423.9	213.1	361.9	571.1
1983	374	55	429	1,258,090	343.1	378.0	347.2	537.7
1984	339	29	368	1,273,280	310.6	201.7	297.9	539.2
1985	355	31	386	1,328,800	318.9	210.6	306.3	556.6
1986	506	37	543	1,489,170	448.4	237.2	422.7	617.7
1987	561	20	581	1,484,000	495.8	152.2	460.0	609.7
1988	679	22	701	1,566,220	616.5	171.6	570.1	637.2
1989	740	35	775	1,646,040	672.1	273.3	630.6	663.1
1990	914	31	945	1,820,130	857.0	238.4	789.8	731.8
1991	870	21	891	1,911,770	798.7	158.2	729.1	758.1
1992	859	20	879	1,932,270	774.9	148.0	706.8	757.5
1993	890	25	915	1,926,020	807.5	196.8	744.3	746.8
1994	721	38	759	1,857,670	641.8	293.5	605.8	713.6
1995	696	39	735	1,798,790	620.8	322.5	591.8	684.6
1996	598	45	643	1,682,280	522.2	364.3	506.8	634.1

Notes: Violent crimes include murder, forcible rape, robbery and aggravated assault; n/a not available; (1) Metropolitan Statistical Area - see Appendix A for areas included; (2) calculated by the editors using the following formula: (number of crimes in the MSA minus number of crimes in the city); (3) calculated by the editors using the following formula: ((number of crimes in the MSA minus number of crimes in the city) ÷ (population of the MSA minus population of the city)) x 100,000
Source: U.S. Department of Justice, FBI Uniform Crime Reports, 1977 - 1996

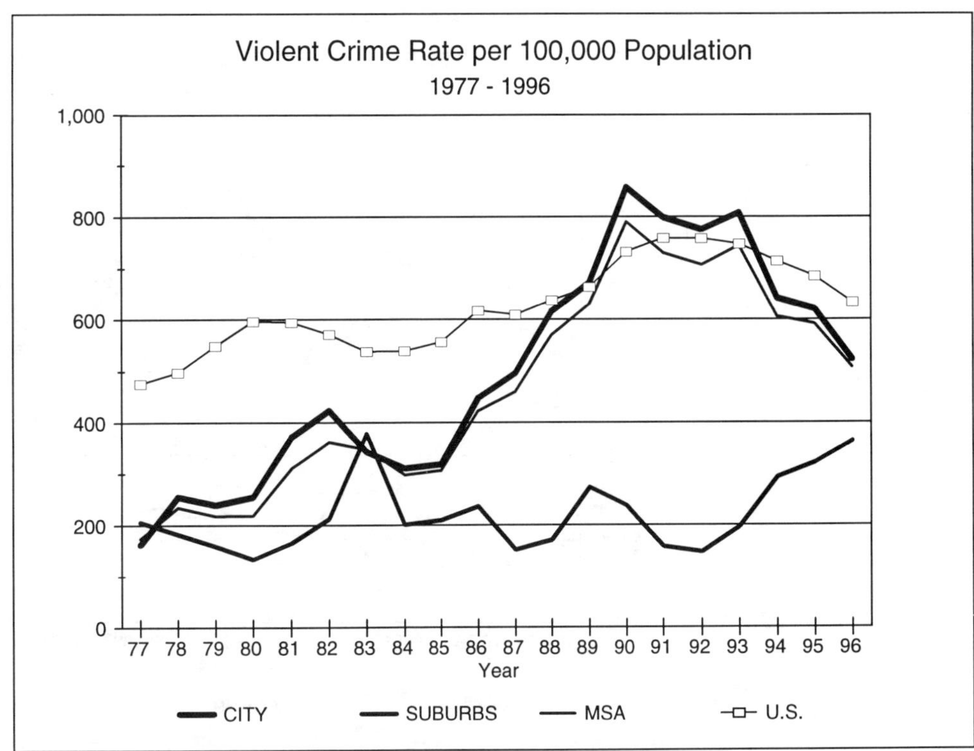

Note: Missing line segments indicate data not available.

Property Crimes and Property Crime Rates: 1977 - 1996

Year	Number				Rate per 100,000 population			
	City	Suburbs[2]	MSA[1]	U.S.	City	Suburbs[3]	MSA[1]	U.S.
1977	3,951	638	4,589	9,955,000	4,130.4	1,937.1	3,568.7	4,601.7
1978	4,337	585	4,922	10,123,400	4,493.6	1,529.6	3,652.4	4,642.5
1979	4,555	677	5,232	11,041,500	4,569.1	1,891.6	3,861.8	5,016.6
1980	5,237	720	5,957	12,063,700	5,331.3	1,760.4	4,281.6	5,353.3
1981	5,306	621	5,927	12,061,900	5,187.4	1,458.1	4,091.1	5,263.9
1982	5,800	619	6,419	11,652,000	5,475.5	1,403.5	4,278.4	5,032.5
1983	5,911	373	6,284	10,850,500	5,422.8	2,563.6	5,086.1	4,637.4
1984	5,474	293	5,767	10,608,500	5,015.3	2,037.8	4,668.7	4,492.1
1985	6,156	313	6,469	11,102,600	5,530.2	2,126.5	5,132.7	4,650.5
1986	6,929	357	7,286	11,722,700	6,140.1	2,288.8	5,672.4	4,862.6
1987	6,957	295	7,252	12,024,700	6,147.9	2,244.4	5,741.7	4,940.3
1988	5,933	303	6,236	12,356,900	5,386.5	2,364.0	5,071.4	5,027.1
1989	5,955	287	6,242	12,605,400	5,408.7	2,241.3	5,078.7	5,077.9
1990	4,825	268	5,093	12,655,500	4,524.0	2,061.4	4,256.4	5,088.5
1991	5,581	313	5,894	12,961,100	5,123.5	2,357.5	4,823.0	5,139.7
1992	4,551	279	4,830	12,505,900	4,105.3	2,065.0	3,883.7	4,902.7
1993	4,584	259	4,843	12,218,800	4,158.9	2,038.6	3,939.7	4,737.6
1994	5,410	257	5,667	12,131,900	4,815.7	1,984.7	4,523.1	4,660.0
1995	5,353	289'	5,642	12,063,900	4,775.0	2,390.0	4,542.8	4,591.3
1996	5,373	310	5,683	11,791,300	4,691.6	2,509.7	4,479.2	4,444.8

Notes: Property crimes include burglary, larceny-theft and motor vehicle theft; n/a not available; (1) Metropolitan Statistical Area - see Appendix A for areas included; (2) calculated by the editors using the following formula: (number of crimes in the MSA minus number of crimes in the city); (3) calculated by the editors using the following formula: ((number of crimes in the MSA minus number of crimes in the city) ÷ (population of the MSA minus population of the city)) x 100,000
Source: U.S. Department of Justice, FBI Uniform Crime Reports, 1977 - 1996

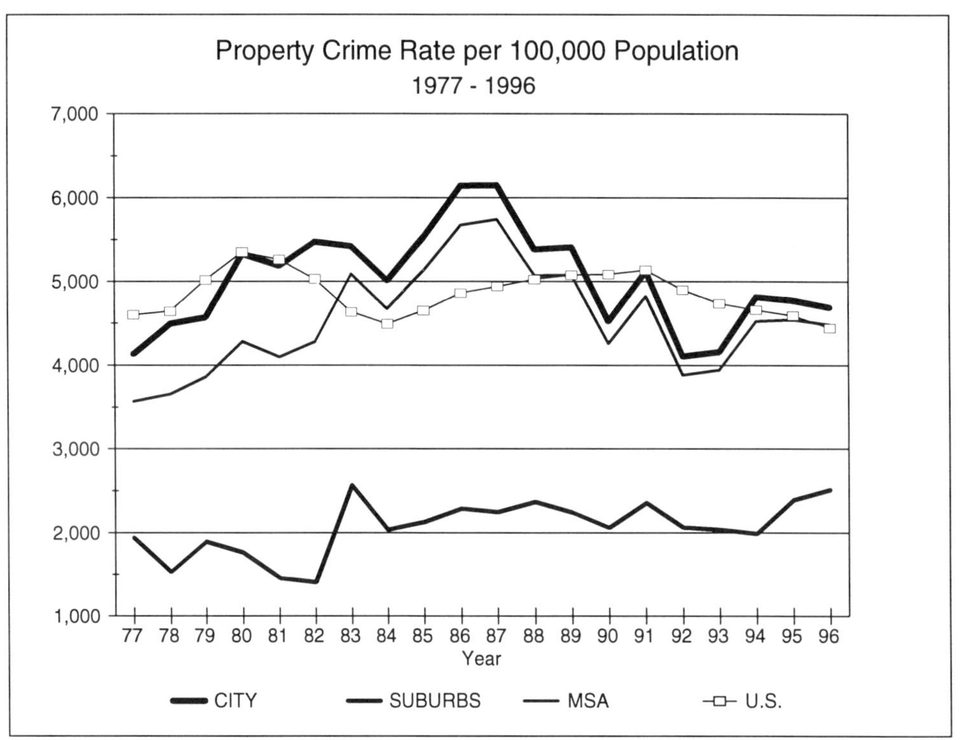

Note: Missing line segments indicate data not available.

Murders and Murder Rates: 1977 - 1996

Year	Number				Rate per 100,000 population			
	City	Suburbs[2]	MSA[1]	U.S.	City	Suburbs[3]	MSA[1]	U.S.
1977	10	3	13	19,120	10.5	9.1	10.1	8.8
1978	7	2	9	19,560	7.3	5.2	6.7	9.0
1979	9	2	11	21,460	9.0	5.6	8.1	9.7
1980	12	1	13	23,040	12.2	2.4	9.3	10.2
1981	14	6	20	22,520	13.7	14.1	13.8	9.8
1982	12	6	18	21,010	11.3	13.6	12.0	9.1
1983	7	2	9	19,310	6.4	13.7	7.3	8.3
1984	5	1	6	18,690	4.6	7.0	4.9	7.9
1985	8	2	10	18,980	7.2	13.6	7.9	7.9
1986	12	2	14	20,610	10.6	12.8	10.9	8.6
1987	5	1	6	20,100	4.4	7.6	4.8	8.3
1988	4	1	5	20,680	3.6	7.8	4.1	8.4
1989	7	1	8	21,500	6.4	7.8	6.5	8.7
1990	7	1	8	23,440	6.6	7.7	6.7	9.4
1991	15	1	16	24,700	13.8	7.5	13.1	9.8
1992	4	2	6	23,760	3.6	14.8	4.8	9.3
1993	8	0	8	24,530	7.3	0.0	6.5	9.5
1994	6	0	6	23,330	5.3	0.0	4.8	9.0
1995	5	0	5	21,610	4.5	0.0	4.0	8.2
1996	7	1	8	19,650	6.1	8.1	6.3	7.4

Notes: (1) Metropolitan Statistical Area - see Appendix A for areas included; (2) calculated by the editors using the following formula: (number of crimes in the MSA minus number of crimes in the city); (3) calculated by the editors using the following formula: ((number of crimes in the MSA minus number of crimes in the city) ÷ (population of the MSA minus population of the city)) x 100,000; n/a not avail.
Source: U.S. Department of Justice, FBI Uniform Crime Reports, 1977 - 1996

Forcible Rapes and Forcible Rape Rates: 1977 - 1996

Year	Number				Rate per 100,000 population			
	City	Suburbs[2]	MSA[1]	U.S.	City	Suburbs[3]	MSA[1]	U.S.
1977	33	3	36	63,500	34.5	9.1	28.0	29.4
1978	42	3	45	67,610	43.5	7.8	33.4	31.0
1979	33	9	42	76,390	33.1	25.1	31.0	34.7
1980	39	6	45	82,990	39.7	14.7	32.3	36.8
1981	50	8	58	82,500	48.9	18.8	40.0	36.0
1982	61	14	75	78,770	57.6	31.7	50.0	34.0
1983	32	4	36	78,920	29.4	27.5	29.1	33.7
1984	85	8	93	84,230	77.9	55.6	75.3	35.7
1985	36	1	37	88,670	32.3	6.8	29.4	37.1
1986	48	4	52	91,460	42.5	25.6	40.5	37.9
1987	32	2	34	91,110	28.3	15.2	26.9	37.4
1988	64	1	65	92,490	58.1	7.8	52.9	37.6
1989	69	2	71	94,500	62.7	15.6	57.8	38.1
1990	92	7	99	102,560	86.3	53.8	82.7	41.2
1991	64	0	64	106,590	58.8	0.0	52.4	42.3
1992	89	0	89	109,060	80.3	0.0	71.6	42.8
1993	75	5	80	106,010	68.0	39.4	65.1	41.1
1994	90	7	97	102,220	80.1	54.1	77.4	39.3
1995	80	9	89	97,470	71.4	74.4	71.7	37.1
1996	66	7	73	95,770	57.6	56.7	57.5	36.1

Notes: (1) Metropolitan Statistical Area - see Appendix A for areas included; (2) calculated by the editors using the following formula: (number of crimes in the MSA minus number of crimes in the city); (3) calculated by the editors using the following formula: ((number of crimes in the MSA minus number of crimes in the city) ÷ (population of the MSA minus population of the city)) x 100,000; n/a not avail.
Source: U.S. Department of Justice, FBI Uniform Crime Reports, 1977 - 1996

Robberies and Robbery Rates: 1977 - 1996

Year	Number				Rate per 100,000 population			
	City	Suburbs[2]	MSA[1]	U.S.	City	Suburbs[3]	MSA[1]	U.S.
1977	54	7	61	412,610	56.5	21.3	47.4	190.7
1978	78	10	88	426,930	80.8	26.1	65.3	195.8
1979	69	8	77	480,700	69.2	22.4	56.8	218.4
1980	67	4	71	565,840	68.2	9.8	51.0	251.1
1981	119	9	128	592,910	116.3	21.1	88.4	258.7
1982	130	13	143	553,130	122.7	29.5	95.3	238.9
1983	125	7	132	506,570	114.7	48.1	106.8	216.5
1984	94	3	97	485,010	86.1	20.9	78.5	205.4
1985	96	3	99	497,870	86.2	20.4	78.5	208.5
1986	176	7	183	542,780	156.0	44.9	142.5	225.1
1987	198	3	201	517,700	175.0	22.8	159.1	212.7
1988	169	3	172	542,970	153.4	23.4	139.9	220.9
1989	173	3	176	578,330	157.1	23.4	143.2	233.0
1990	187	1	188	639,270	175.3	7.7	157.1	257.0
1991	216	5	221	687,730	198.3	37.7	180.8	272.7
1992	136	0	136	672,480	122.7	0.0	109.4	263.6
1993	134	3	137	659,870	121.6	23.6	111.4	255.9
1994	119	4	123	618,950	105.9	30.9	98.2	237.7
1995	131	3	134	580,510	116.9	24.8	107.9	220.9
1996	126	1	127	537,050	110.0	8.1	100.1	202.4

Notes: (1) Metropolitan Statistical Area - see Appendix A for areas included; (2) calculated by the editors using the following formula: (number of crimes in the MSA minus number of crimes in the city); (3) calculated by the editors using the following formula: ((number of crimes in the MSA minus number of crimes in the city) ÷ (population of the MSA minus population of the city)) x 100,000; n/a not avail.
Source: U.S. Department of Justice, FBI Uniform Crime Reports, 1977 - 1996

Aggravated Assaults and Aggravated Assault Rates: 1977 - 1996

Year	Number				Rate per 100,000 population			
	City	Suburbs[2]	MSA[1]	U.S.	City	Suburbs[3]	MSA[1]	U.S.
1977	59	55	114	534,350	61.7	167.0	88.7	247.0
1978	120	55	175	571,460	124.3	143.8	129.9	262.1
1979	128	38	166	629,480	128.4	106.2	122.5	286.0
1980	133	44	177	672,650	135.4	107.6	127.2	298.5
1981	198	48	246	663,900	193.6	112.7	169.8	289.7
1982	246	61	307	669,480	232.2	138.3	204.6	289.2
1983	210	42	252	653,290	192.7	288.7	204.0	279.2
1984	155	17	172	685,350	142.0	118.2	139.2	290.2
1985	215	25	240	723,250	193.1	169.8	190.4	302.9
1986	270	24	294	834,320	239.3	153.9	228.9	346.1
1987	326	14	340	855,090	288.1	106.5	269.2	351.3
1988	442	17	459	910,090	401.3	132.6	373.3	370.2
1989	491	29	520	951,710	446.0	226.5	423.1	383.4
1990	628	22	650	1,054,860	588.8	169.2	543.2	424.1
1991	575	15	590	1,092,740	527.9	113.0	482.8	433.3
1992	630	18	648	1,126,970	568.3	133.2	521.0	441.8
1993	673	17	690	1,135,610	610.6	133.8	561.3	440.3
1994	506	27	533	1,113,180	450.4	208.5	425.4	427.6
1995	480	27	507	1,099,210	428.2	223.3	408.2	418.3
1996	399	36	435	1,029,810	348.4	291.5	342.9	388.2

Notes: (1) Metropolitan Statistical Area - see Appendix A for areas included; (2) calculated by the editors using the following formula: (number of crimes in the MSA minus number of crimes in the city); (3) calculated by the editors using the following formula: ((number of crimes in the MSA minus number of crimes in the city) ÷ (population of the MSA minus population of the city)) x 100,000; n/a not avail.
Source: U.S. Department of Justice, FBI Uniform Crime Reports, 1977 - 1996

Burglaries and Burglary Rates: 1977 - 1996

Year	Number				Rate per 100,000 population			
	City	Suburbs[2]	MSA[1]	U.S.	City	Suburbs[3]	MSA[1]	U.S.
1977	944	249	1,193	3,071,500	986.9	756.0	927.7	1,419.8
1978	932	236	1,168	3,128,300	965.7	617.1	866.7	1,434.6
1979	1,006	250	1,256	3,327,700	1,009.1	698.5	927.1	1,511.9
1980	1,473	311	1,784	3,795,200	1,499.5	760.4	1,282.3	1,684.1
1981	1,269	233	1,502	3,779,700	1,240.6	547.1	1,036.7	1,649.5
1982	1,363	248	1,611	3,447,100	1,286.7	562.3	1,073.8	1,488.8
1983	1,425	182	1,607	3,129,900	1,307.3	1,250.9	1,300.7	1,337.7
1984	1,526	119	1,645	2,984,400	1,398.1	827.7	1,331.7	1,263.7
1985	1,623	166	1,789	3,073,300	1,458.0	1,127.8	1,419.4	1,287.3
1986	2,351	189	2,540	3,241,400	2,083.3	1,211.7	1,977.5	1,344.6
1987	2,607	145	2,752	3,236,200	2,303.8	1,103.2	2,178.9	1,329.6
1988	2,223	155	2,378	3,218,100	2,018.2	1,209.3	1,933.9	1,309.2
1989	2,486	160	2,646	3,168,200	2,257.9	1,249.5	2,152.9	1,276.3
1990	1,647	113	1,760	3,073,900	1,544.2	869.2	1,470.9	1,235.9
1991	1,808	107	1,915	3,157,200	1,659.8	805.9	1,567.0	1,252.0
1992	1,439	80	1,519	2,979,900	1,298.1	592.1	1,221.4	1,168.2
1993	1,089	88	1,177	2,834,800	988.0	692.6	957.5	1,099.2
1994	1,250	88	1,338	2,712,800	1,112.7	679.6	1,067.9	1,042.0
1995	1,044	110	1,154	2,593,800	931.3	909.7	929.2	987.1
1996	1,120	123	1,243	2,501,500	978.0	995.8	979.7	943.0

Notes: (1) Metropolitan Statistical Area - see Appendix A for areas included; (2) calculated by the editors using the following formula: (number of crimes in the MSA minus number of crimes in the city); (3) calculated by the editors using the following formula: ((number of crimes in the MSA minus number of crimes in the city) ÷ (population of the MSA minus population of the city)) x 100,000; n/a not avail.
Source: U.S. Department of Justice, FBI Uniform Crime Reports, 1977 - 1996

Larceny-Thefts and Larceny-Theft Rates: 1977 - 1996

Year	Number				Rate per 100,000 population			
	City	Suburbs[2]	MSA[1]	U.S.	City	Suburbs[3]	MSA[1]	U.S.
1977	2,858	370	3,228	5,905,700	2,987.8	1,123.4	2,510.3	2,729.9
1978	3,155	321	3,476	5,991,000	3,268.9	839.3	2,579.4	2,747.4
1979	3,308	399	3,707	6,601,000	3,318.2	1,114.9	2,736.2	2,999.1
1980	3,492	347	3,839	7,136,900	3,554.9	848.4	2,759.3	3,167.0
1981	3,722	341	4,063	7,194,400	3,638.8	800.7	2,804.5	3,139.7
1982	4,102	313	4,415	7,142,500	3,872.5	709.7	2,942.7	3,084.8
1983	4,231	173	4,404	6,712,800	3,881.5	1,189.0	3,564.5	2,868.9
1984	3,592	158	3,750	6,591,900	3,291.0	1,098.9	3,035.8	2,791.3
1985	4,116	133	4,249	6,926,400	3,697.5	903.6	3,371.3	2,901.2
1986	4,225	145	4,370	7,257,200	3,744.0	929.6	3,402.2	3,010.3
1987	4,099	139	4,238	7,499,900	3,622.3	1,057.5	3,355.4	3,081.3
1988	3,487	127	3,614	7,705,900	3,165.8	990.9	2,939.1	3,134.9
1989	3,181	114	3,295	7,872,400	2,889.2	890.3	2,680.9	3,171.3
1990	2,912	151	3,063	7,945,700	2,730.3	1,161.4	2,559.9	3,194.8
1991	3,534	193	3,727	8,142,200	3,244.3	1,453.6	3,049.8	3,228.8
1992	2,946	185	3,131	7,915,200	2,657.5	1,369.3	2,517.5	3,103.0
1993	3,323	156	3,479	7,820,900	3,014.8	1,227.9	2,830.1	3,032.4
1994	3,918	160	4,078	7,879,800	3,487.6	1,235.6	3,254.8	3,026.7
1995	4,095	171	4,266	7,997,700	3,652.8	1,414.2	3,434.9	3,043.8
1996	4,008	184	4,192	7,894,600	3,499.7	1,489.6	3,304.0	2,975.9

Notes: (1) Metropolitan Statistical Area - see Appendix A for areas included; (2) calculated by the editors using the following formula: (number of crimes in the MSA minus number of crimes in the city); (3) calculated by the editors using the following formula: ((number of crimes in the MSA minus number of crimes in the city) ÷ (population of the MSA minus population of the city)) x 100,000; n/a not avail.
Source: U.S. Department of Justice, FBI Uniform Crime Reports, 1977 - 1996

Motor Vehicle Thefts and Motor Vehicle Theft Rates: 1977 - 1996

Year	Number				Rate per 100,000 population			
	City	Suburbs[2]	MSA[1]	U.S.	City	Suburbs[3]	MSA[1]	U.S.
1977	149	19	168	977,700	155.8	57.7	130.6	451.9
1978	250	28	278	1,004,100	259.0	73.2	206.3	460.5
1979	241	28	269	1,112,800	241.7	78.2	198.6	505.6
1980	272	62	334	1,131,700	276.9	151.6	240.1	502.2
1981	315	47	362	1,087,800	308.0	110.4	249.9	474.7
1982	335	58	393	1,062,400	316.3	131.5	261.9	458.8
1983	255	18	273	1,007,900	233.9	123.7	221.0	430.8
1984	356	16	372	1,032,200	326.2	111.3	301.2	437.1
1985	417	14	431	1,102,900	374.6	95.1	342.0	462.0
1986	353	23	376	1,224,100	312.8	147.5	292.7	507.8
1987	251	11	262	1,288,700	221.8	83.7	207.4	529.4
1988	223	21	244	1,432,900	202.5	163.8	198.4	582.9
1989	288	13	301	1,564,800	261.6	101.5	244.9	630.4
1990	266	4	270	1,635,900	249.4	30.8	225.6	657.8
1991	239	13	252	1,661,700	219.4	97.9	206.2	659.0
1992	166	14	180	1,610,800	149.7	103.6	144.7	631.5
1993	172	15	187	1,563,100	156.0	118.1	152.1	606.1
1994	242	9	251	1,539,300	215.4	69.5	200.3	591.3
1995	214	8	222	1,472,400	190.9	66.2	178.7	560.4
1996	245	3	248	1,395,200	213.9	24.3	195.5	525.9

Notes: (1) Metropolitan Statistical Area - see Appendix A for areas included; (2) calculated by the editors using the following formula: (number of crimes in the MSA minus number of crimes in the city); (3) calculated by the editors using the following formula: ((number of crimes in the MSA minus number of crimes in the city) ÷ (population of the MSA minus population of the city)) x 100,000; n/a not avail.
Source: U.S. Department of Justice, FBI Uniform Crime Reports, 1977 - 1996

HATE CRIMES

Criminal Incidents by Bias Motivation

Area	Race	Ethnicity	Religion	Sexual Orientation
Abilene	0	0	0	0

Notes: Figures include both violent and property crimes. Law enforcement agencies must have submitted data for at least one quarter of calendar year 1995 to be included in this report, therefore figures shown may not represent complete 12-month totals; n/a not available
Source: U.S. Department of Justice, FBI Uniform Crime Reports, Hate Crime Statistics 1995

LAW ENFORCEMENT

Full-Time Law Enforcement Employees

Jurisdiction	Police Employees			Police Officers per 100,000 population
	Total	Officers	Civilians	
Abilene	227	170	57	148.4

Notes: Data as of October 31, 1996
Source: U.S. Department of Justice, FBI Uniform Crime Reports, 1996

CORRECTIONS

Federal Correctional Facilities

Type	Year Opened	Security Level	Sex of Inmates	Rated Capacity	Population on 7/1/95	Number of Staff
None listed						

Notes: Data as of 1995
Source: Bureau of Justice Statistics, Sourcebook of Criminal Justice Statistics Online

City/County/Regional Correctional Facilities

Name	Year Opened	Year Renov.	Rated Capacity	1995 Pop.	Number of COs[1]	Number of Staff	ACA[2] Accred.
Taylor Co Jail	1984	1987	292	n/a	n/a	n/a	No

Notes: Data as of April 1996; (1) Correctional Officers; (2) American Correctional Assn. Accreditation
Source: American Correctional Association, 1996-1998 National Jail and Adult Detention Directory

Private Adult Correctional Facilities

Name	Date Opened	Rated Capacity	Present Pop.	Security Level	Facility Construct.	Expans. Plans	ACA[1] Accred.
None listed							

Notes: Data as of December 1996; (1) American Correctional Association Accreditation
Source: University of Florida, Center for Studies in Criminology and Law, Private Adult Correctional Facility Census, 10th Ed., March 15, 1997

Characteristics of Shock Incarceration Programs

Jurisdiction	Year Program Began	Number of Camps	Average Num. of Inmates	Number of Beds	Program Length	Voluntary/ Mandatory
Texas	1989	2	250	500 male; 20 female	75 to 90 days	Mandatory

Note: Data as of July 1996;
Source: Sourcebook of Criminal Justice Statistics Online

DEATH PENALTY

Death Penalty Statistics

State	Prisoners Executed		Prisoners Under Sentence of Death					Avg. No. of Years on Death Row[4]
	1930-1995	1996[1]	Total[2]	White[3]	Black[3]	Hisp.	Women	
Texas	401	3	404	241	158	68	6	6.5

Notes: Data as of 12/31/95 unless otherwise noted; (1) Data as of 7/31/97; (2) Includes persons of other races; (3) Includes people of Hispanic origin; (4) Covers prisoners sentenced 1974 through 1995
Source: Bureau of Justice Statistics, Capital Punishment 1995 (released 12/96); Death Penalty Information Center Web Site, 9/30/97

Capital Offenses and Methods of Execution

Capital Offenses in Texas	Minimum Age for Imposition of Death Penalty	Mentally Retarded Excluded	Methods of Execution[1]
Criminal homicide with 1 of 8 aggravating circumstances.	17	No	Lethal injection

Notes: Data as of 12/31/95 unless otherwise noted; (1) Data as of 7/31/97
Source: Bureau of Justice Statistics, Capital Punishment 1995 (released 12/96); Death Penalty Information Center Web Site, 9/30/97

LAWS

Statutory Provisions Relating to the Purchase, Ownership and Use of Handguns

Jurisdiction	Instant Background Check	Federal Waiting Period Applies[1]	State Waiting Period (days)	License or Permit to Purchase	Regis-tration	Record of Sale Sent to Police	Concealed Carry Law
Texas	No	Yes[a]	No	No	No	No	Yes[b]

Note: Data as of 1996; (1) The Federal 5-day waiting period for handgun purchases applies to states that don't have instant background checks, waiting period requirements, or licensing procedures exempting them from the Federal requirement; (a) The Federal waiting period does not apply to a person holding a valid permit or license to carry a firearm, issued within 5 years of proposed purchase; (b) "Shall issue" permit system, liberally administered discretion by local authorities over permit issuance, or no permit required
Source: Sourcebook of Criminal Justice Statistics Online

Statutory Provisions Relating to Alcohol Use and Driving

Jurisdiction	Drinking Age	Blood Alcohol Concentration Levels as Evidence in State Courts[1]		Open Container Law[1]	Anti-Consump-tion Law[1]	Dram Shop Law[1]
		Illegal per se at 0.10%	Presumption at 0.10%			
Texas	21	Yes	No	No	Yes[a]	Yes[b]

Note: Data as of January 1, 1997; (1) See Appendix C for an explanation of terms; (a) Applies to drivers only; (b) Statutory law has limited dram shop actions
Source: Sourcebook of Criminal Justice Statistics Online

Statutory Provisions Relating to Hate Crimes

Jurisdiction	Bias-Motivated Violence and Intimidation						Institutional Vandalism
		Criminal Penalty					
	Civil Action	Race/ Religion/ Ethnicity	Sexual Orientation	Mental/ Physical Disability	Gender	Age	
Texas	No	No	No	No	No	No	Yes

Source: Anti-Defamation League, 1997 Hate Crimes Laws

Albuquerque, New Mexico

OVERVIEW

The total crime rate for the city increased 37.4% between 1977 and 1996. During that same period, the violent crime rate increased 78.8% and the property crime rate increased 32.8%.

Among violent crimes, the rates for: Murders increased 53.3%; Forcible Rapes increased 23.6%; Robberies increased 80.7%; and Aggravated Assaults increased 86.5%.

Among property crimes, the rates for: Burglaries decreased 6.2%; Larceny-Thefts increased 28.0%; and Motor Vehicle Thefts increased 309.4%.

ANTI-CRIME PROGRAMS

Programs include:

- Safe Streets '97—major new program to address crime through increased ticketing and traffic control, both treeway s and major arterials, as well as neighborhood streets.
- Crime Prevention Through Environmental Design (CPTED) Neighborhoods—retrofiting neighborhoods with major crime problems by using CPTED principles to reduce crime.
- Crime-Free, Multi-Housing Program which attempts to reduce crime in public and private multi-housing complexes through a several-step certification process.
  Albuquerque Police Department, 6/97

CRIME RISK

Your Chances of Becoming a Victim[1]

Area	Any Crime	Violent Crime					Property Crime			
		Any	Murder	Forcible Rape[2]	Robbery	Aggrav. Assault	Any	Burglary	Larceny -Theft	Motor Vehicle Theft
City	1:9	1:68	1:6,096	1:586	1:214	1:112	1:10	1:47	1:16	1:61

Note: (1) Figures have been calculated by dividing the population of the city by the number of crimes reported to the FBI during 1996 and are expressed as odds (eg. 1:20 should be read as 1 in 20).
(2) Figures have been calculated by dividing the female population of the city by the number of forcible rapes reported to the FBI during 1996. The female population of the city was estimated by calculating the ratio of females to males reported in the 1990 Census and applying that ratio to 1996 population estimate.
Source: FBI Uniform Crime Reports 1996

CRIME STATISTICS

Total Crimes and Total Crime Rates: 1977 - 1996

Year	Number				Rate per 100,000 population			
	City	Suburbs[2]	MSA[1]	U.S.	City	Suburbs[3]	MSA[1]	U.S.
1977	23,955	4,216	28,171	10,984,500	8,232.0	4,039.2	7,125.1	5,077.6
1978	22,866	4,626	27,492	11,209,000	7,751.2	4,305.2	6,831.1	5,140.3
1979	27,341	5,382	32,723	12,249,500	9,049.7	4,659.2	7,835.3	5,565.5
1980	29,326	3,265	32,591	13,408,300	8,918.1	2,721.7	7,261.8	5,950.0
1981	30,614	5,925	36,539	13,423,800	9,088.6	4,821.9	7,948.1	5,858.2
1982	29,214	6,154	35,368	12,974,400	8,468.8	4,889.9	7,512.1	5,603.6
1983	29,250	4,390	33,640	12,108,600	8,235.7	4,728.3	7,508.8	5,175.0
1984	31,408	5,098	36,506	11,881,800	8,813.4	5,279.3	8,059.9	5,031.3
1985	33,158	5,471	38,629	12,431,400	9,286.6	5,435.6	8,439.8	5,207.1
1986	35,516	6,332	41,848	13,211,900	9,751.9	6,168.2	8,963.9	5,480.4
1987	37,008	5,896	42,904	13,508,700	9,954.9	5,403.2	8,922.1	5,550.0
1988	38,972	3,502	42,474	13,923,100	10,305.3	3,154.8	8,682.7	5,664.2
1989	38,344	3,994	42,338	14,251,400	9,964.6	3,427.3	8,445.0	5,741.0
1990	38,721	6,291	45,012	14,475,600	10,064.3	6,564.0	9,366.2	5,820.3
1991	40,433	3,689	44,122	14,872,900	10,284.4	3,767.2	8,984.8	5,897.8
1992	38,014	8,446	46,460	14,438,200	9,467.3	3,959.2	7,556.3	5,660.2
1993	39,025	8,512	47,537	14,144,800	9,581.7	3,825.1	7,547.8	5,484.4
1994	n/a	n/a	n/a	13,989,500	n/a	n/a	n/a	5,373.5
1995	n/a	n/a	49,505	13,862,700	n/a	n/a	7,521.9	5,275.9
1996	48,253	7,291	55,544	13,473,600	11,307.5	3,008.0	8,301.1	5,078.9

Notes: (1) Metropolitan Statistical Area - see Appendix A for areas included; (2) calculated by the editors using the following formula: (number of crimes in the MSA minus number of crimes in the city); (3) calculated by the editors using the following formula: ((number of crimes in the MSA minus number of crimes in the city) ÷ (population of the MSA minus population of the city)) x 100,000; n/a not avail.
Source: U.S. Department of Justice, FBI Uniform Crime Reports, 1977 - 1996

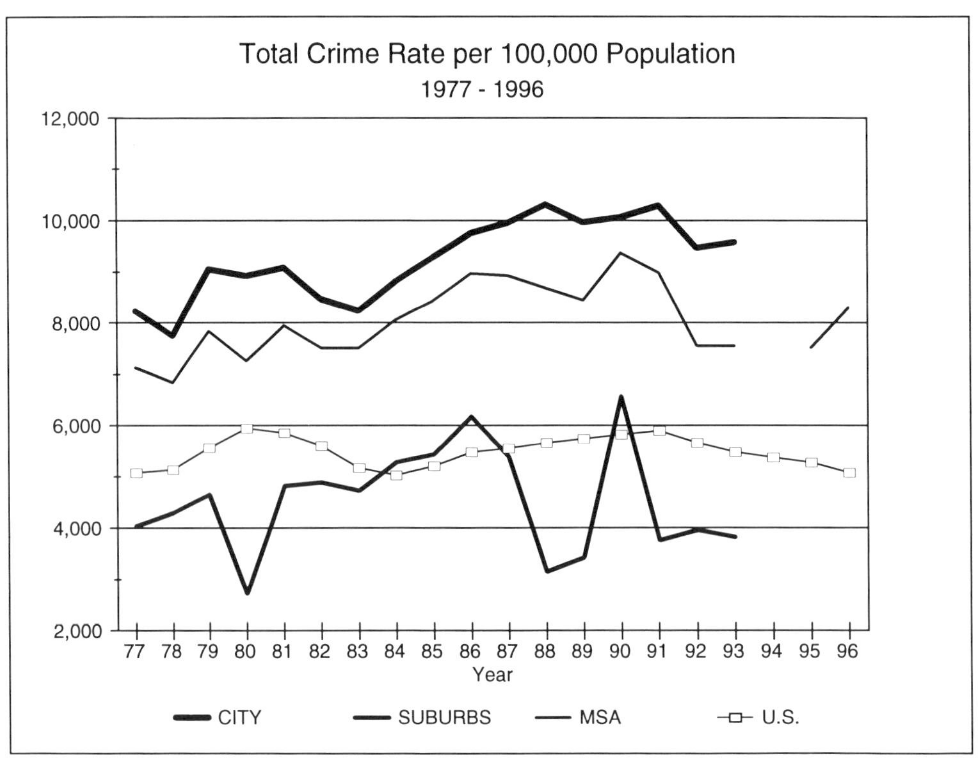

Note: Missing line segments indicate data not available.

Violent Crimes and Violent Crime Rates: 1977 - 1996

Year	Number				Rate per 100,000 population			
	City	Suburbs[2]	MSA[1]	U.S.	City	Suburbs[3]	MSA[1]	U.S.
1977	2,390	466	2,856	1,029,580	821.3	446.5	722.4	475.9
1978	2,434	471	2,905	1,085,550	825.1	438.3	721.8	497.8
1979	2,679	515	3,194	1,208,030	886.7	445.8	764.8	548.9
1980	3,008	169	3,177	1,344,520	914.7	140.9	707.9	596.6
1981	2,985	908	3,893	1,361,820	886.2	738.9	846.8	594.3
1982	2,659	938	3,597	1,322,390	770.8	745.3	764.0	571.1
1983	2,954	479	3,433	1,258,090	831.7	515.9	766.3	537.7
1984	3,615	503	4,118	1,273,280	1,014.4	520.9	909.2	539.2
1985	4,105	595	4,700	1,328,800	1,149.7	591.2	1,026.9	556.6
1986	4,292	761	5,053	1,489,170	1,178.5	741.3	1,082.4	617.7
1987	3,845	646	4,491	1,484,000	1,034.3	592.0	933.9	609.7
1988	4,275	264	4,539	1,566,220	1,130.4	237.8	927.9	637.2
1989	4,696	304	5,000	1,646,040	1,220.4	260.9	997.3	663.1
1990	5,121	765	5,886	1,820,130	1,331.0	798.2	1,224.8	731.8
1991	5,591	293	5,884	1,911,770	1,422.1	299.2	1,198.2	758.1
1992	6,168	1,188	7,356	1,932,270	1,536.1	556.9	1,196.4	757.5
1993	6,696	1,325	8,021	1,926,020	1,644.1	595.4	1,273.6	746.8
1994	n/a	n/a	n/a	1,857,670	n/a	n/a	n/a	713.6
1995	n/a	n/a	5,788	1,798,790	n/a	n/a	879.4	684.6
1996	6,267	973	7,240	1,682,280	1,468.6	401.4	1,082.0	634.1

Notes: Violent crimes include murder, forcible rape, robbery and aggravated assault; n/a not available; (1) Metropolitan Statistical Area - see Appendix A for areas included; (2) calculated by the editors using the following formula: (number of crimes in the MSA minus number of crimes in the city); (3) calculated by the editors using the following formula: ((number of crimes in the MSA minus number of crimes in the city) ÷ (population of the MSA minus population of the city)) x 100,000
Source: U.S. Department of Justice, FBI Uniform Crime Reports, 1977 - 1996

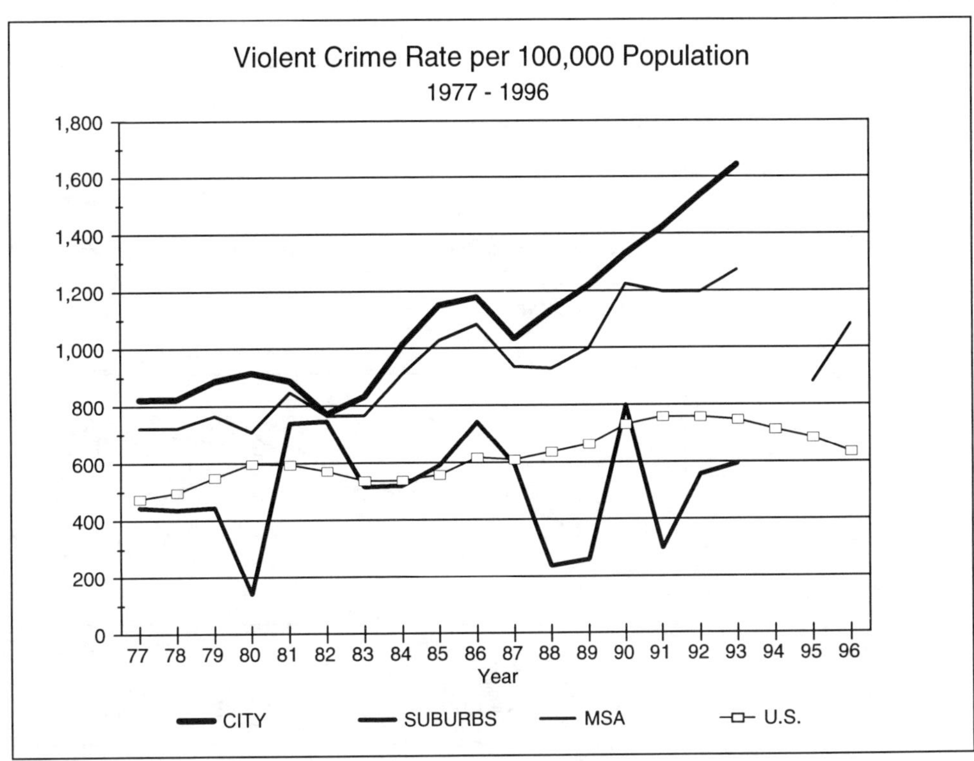

Note: Missing line segments indicate data not available.

Property Crimes and Property Crime Rates: 1977 - 1996

Year	Number				Rate per 100,000 population			
	City	Suburbs[2]	MSA[1]	U.S.	City	Suburbs[3]	MSA[1]	U.S.
1977	21,565	3,750	25,315	9,955,000	7,410.7	3,592.8	6,402.8	4,601.7
1978	20,432	4,155	24,587	10,123,400	6,926.1	3,866.9	6,109.3	4,642.5
1979	24,662	4,867	29,529	11,041,500	8,163.0	4,213.4	7,070.6	5,016.6
1980	26,318	3,096	29,414	12,063,700	8,003.4	2,580.8	6,554.0	5,353.3
1981	27,629	5,017	32,646	12,061,900	8,202.4	4,082.9	7,101.3	5,263.9
1982	26,555	5,216	31,771	11,652,000	7,697.9	4,144.6	6,748.1	5,032.5
1983	26,296	3,911	30,207	10,850,500	7,403.9	4,212.4	6,742.5	4,637.4
1984	27,793	4,595	32,388	10,608,500	7,799.0	4,758.5	7,150.8	4,492.1
1985	29,053	4,876	33,929	11,102,600	8,136.9	4,844.5	7,412.9	4,650.5
1986	31,224	5,571	36,795	11,722,700	8,573.4	5,426.9	7,881.5	4,862.6
1987	33,163	5,250	38,413	12,024,700	8,920.6	4,811.2	7,988.1	4,940.3
1988	34,697	3,238	37,935	12,356,900	9,174.8	2,917.0	7,754.8	5,027.1
1989	33,648	3,690	37,338	12,605,400	8,744.3	3,166.4	7,447.7	5,077.9
1990	33,600	5,526	39,126	12,655,500	8,733.3	5,765.8	8,141.5	5,088.5
1991	34,842	3,396	38,238	12,961,100	8,862.3	3,468.0	7,786.6	5,139.7
1992	31,846	7,258	39,104	12,505,900	7,931.2	3,402.3	6,359.9	4,902.7
1993	32,329	7,187	39,516	12,218,800	7,937.7	3,229.7	6,274.2	4,737.6
1994	n/a	n/a	n/a	12,131,900	n/a	n/a	n/a	4,660.0
1995	36,818	6,899	43,717	12,063,900	8,772.2	2,893.5	6,642.5	4,591.3
1996	41,986	6,318	48,304	11,791,300	9,838.9	2,606.6	7,219.0	4,444.8

Notes: Property crimes include burglary, larceny-theft and motor vehicle theft; n/a not available; (1) Metropolitan Statistical Area - see Appendix A for areas included; (2) calculated by the editors using the following formula: (number of crimes in the MSA minus number of crimes in the city); (3) calculated by the editors using the following formula: ((number of crimes in the MSA minus number of crimes in the city) ÷ (population of the MSA minus population of the city)) x 100,000
Source: U.S. Department of Justice, FBI Uniform Crime Reports, 1977 - 1996

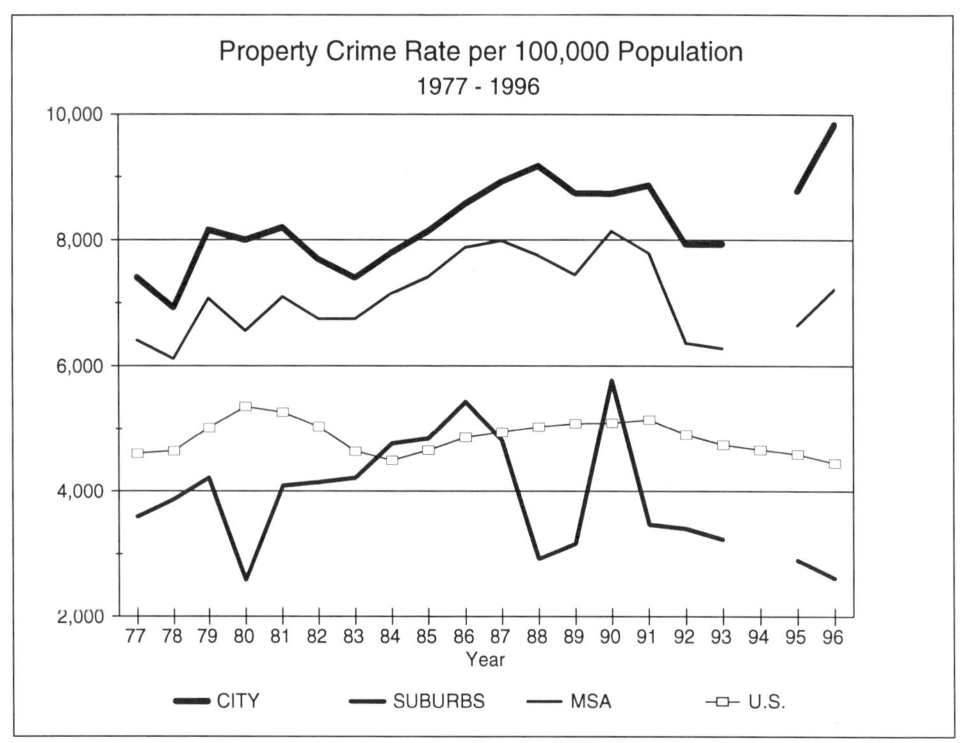

Note: Missing line segments indicate data not available.

Murders and Murder Rates: 1977 - 1996

Year	Number				Rate per 100,000 population			
	City	Suburbs[2]	MSA[1]	U.S.	City	Suburbs[3]	MSA[1]	U.S.
1977	31	6	37	19,120	10.7	5.7	9.4	8.8
1978	37	11	48	19,560	12.5	10.2	11.9	9.0
1979	47	18	65	21,460	15.6	15.6	15.6	9.7
1980	50	8	58	23,040	15.2	6.7	12.9	10.2
1981	45	17	62	22,520	13.4	13.8	13.5	9.8
1982	26	16	42	21,010	7.5	12.7	8.9	9.1
1983	24	7	31	19,310	6.8	7.5	6.9	8.3
1984	28	7	35	18,690	7.9	7.2	7.7	7.9
1985	42	10	52	18,980	11.8	9.9	11.4	7.9
1986	49	16	65	20,610	13.5	15.6	13.9	8.6
1987	48	18	66	20,100	12.9	16.5	13.7	8.3
1988	49	11	60	20,680	13.0	9.9	12.3	8.4
1989	41	10	51	21,500	10.7	8.6	10.2	8.7
1990	34	16	50	23,440	8.8	16.7	10.4	9.4
1991	51	3	54	24,700	13.0	3.1	11.0	9.8
1992	42	12	54	23,760	10.5	5.6	8.8	9.3
1993	50	7	57	24,530	12.3	3.1	9.1	9.5
1994	n/a	n/a	n/a	23,330	n/a	n/a	n/a	9.0
1995	53	11	64	21,610	12.6	4.6	9.7	8.2
1996	70	25	95	19,650	16.4	10.3	14.2	7.4

Notes: (1) Metropolitan Statistical Area - see Appendix A for areas included; (2) calculated by the editors using the following formula: (number of crimes in the MSA minus number of crimes in the city); (3) calculated by the editors using the following formula: ((number of crimes in the MSA minus number of crimes in the city) ÷ (population of the MSA minus population of the city)) x 100,000; n/a not avail.
Source: U.S. Department of Justice, FBI Uniform Crime Reports, 1977 - 1996

Forcible Rapes and Forcible Rape Rates: 1977 - 1996

Year	Number				Rate per 100,000 population			
	City	Suburbs[2]	MSA[1]	U.S.	City	Suburbs[3]	MSA[1]	U.S.
1977	207	59	266	63,500	71.1	56.5	67.3	29.4
1978	187	55	242	67,610	63.4	51.2	60.1	31.0
1979	215	53	268	76,390	71.2	45.9	64.2	34.7
1980	225	26	251	82,990	68.4	21.7	55.9	36.8
1981	213	55	268	82,500	63.2	44.8	58.3	36.0
1982	199	69	268	78,770	57.7	54.8	56.9	34.0
1983	206	38	244	78,920	58.0	40.9	54.5	33.7
1984	210	64	274	84,230	58.9	66.3	60.5	35.7
1985	238	51	289	88,670	66.7	50.7	63.1	37.1
1986	247	52	299	91,460	67.8	50.7	64.0	37.9
1987	211	53	264	91,110	56.8	48.6	54.9	37.4
1988	190	32	222	92,490	50.2	28.8	45.4	37.6
1989	178	60	238	94,500	46.3	51.5	47.5	38.1
1990	222	52	274	102,560	57.7	54.3	57.0	41.2
1991	261	48	309	106,590	66.4	49.0	62.9	42.3
1992	294	70	364	109,060	73.2	32.8	59.2	42.8
1993	259	119	378	106,010	63.6	53.5	60.0	41.1
1994	n/a	n/a	n/a	102,220	n/a	n/a	n/a	39.3
1995	296	74	370	97,470	70.5	31.0	56.2	37.1
1996	375	85	460	95,770	87.9	35.1	68.7	36.1

Notes: (1) Metropolitan Statistical Area - see Appendix A for areas included; (2) calculated by the editors using the following formula: (number of crimes in the MSA minus number of crimes in the city); (3) calculated by the editors using the following formula: ((number of crimes in the MSA minus number of crimes in the city) ÷ (population of the MSA minus population of the city)) x 100,000; n/a not avail.
Source: U.S. Department of Justice, FBI Uniform Crime Reports, 1977 - 1996

Robberies and Robbery Rates: 1977 - 1996

Year	Number				Rate per 100,000 population			
	City	Suburbs[2]	MSA[1]	U.S.	City	Suburbs[3]	MSA[1]	U.S.
1977	754	89	843	412,610	259.1	85.3	213.2	190.7
1978	694	114	808	426,930	235.3	106.1	200.8	195.8
1979	815	80	895	480,700	269.8	69.3	214.3	218.4
1980	993	12	1,005	565,840	302.0	10.0	223.9	251.1
1981	1,107	124	1,231	592,910	328.6	100.9	267.8	258.7
1982	926	103	1,029	553,130	268.4	81.8	218.6	238.9
1983	909	79	988	506,570	255.9	85.1	220.5	216.5
1984	1,215	84	1,299	485,010	340.9	87.0	286.8	205.4
1985	1,247	124	1,371	497,870	349.2	123.2	299.5	208.5
1986	1,248	134	1,382	542,780	342.7	130.5	296.0	225.1
1987	987	107	1,094	517,700	265.5	98.1	227.5	212.7
1988	928	28	956	542,970	245.4	25.2	195.4	220.9
1989	1,032	31	1,063	578,330	268.2	26.6	212.0	233.0
1990	1,030	132	1,162	639,270	267.7	137.7	241.8	257.0
1991	1,307	23	1,330	687,730	332.4	23.5	270.8	272.7
1992	1,460	68	1,528	672,480	363.6	31.9	248.5	263.6
1993	1,552	79	1,631	659,870	381.1	35.5	259.0	255.9
1994	n/a	n/a	n/a	618,950	n/a	n/a	n/a	237.7
1995	1,623	125	1,748	580,510	386.7	52.4	265.6	220.9
1996	1,998	72	2,070	537,050	468.2	29.7	309.4	202.4

Notes: (1) Metropolitan Statistical Area - see Appendix A for areas included; (2) calculated by the editors using the following formula: (number of crimes in the MSA minus number of crimes in the city); (3) calculated by the editors using the following formula: ((number of crimes in the MSA minus number of crimes in the city) ÷ (population of the MSA minus population of the city)) x 100,000; n/a not avail.
Source: U.S. Department of Justice, FBI Uniform Crime Reports, 1977 - 1996

Aggravated Assaults and Aggravated Assault Rates: 1977 - 1996

Year	Number				Rate per 100,000 population			
	City	Suburbs[2]	MSA[1]	U.S.	City	Suburbs[3]	MSA[1]	U.S.
1977	1,398	312	1,710	534,350	480.4	298.9	432.5	247.0
1978	1,516	291	1,807	571,460	513.9	270.8	449.0	262.1
1979	1,602	364	1,966	629,480	530.3	315.1	470.7	286.0
1980	1,740	123	1,863	672,650	529.1	102.5	415.1	298.5
1981	1,620	712	2,332	663,900	480.9	579.4	507.3	289.7
1982	1,508	750	2,258	669,480	437.1	595.9	479.6	289.2
1983	1,815	355	2,170	653,290	511.0	382.4	484.4	279.2
1984	2,162	348	2,510	685,350	606.7	360.4	554.2	290.2
1985	2,578	410	2,988	723,250	722.0	407.3	652.8	302.9
1986	2,748	559	3,307	834,320	754.5	544.5	708.4	346.1
1987	2,599	468	3,067	855,090	699.1	428.9	637.8	351.3
1988	3,108	193	3,301	910,090	821.8	173.9	674.8	370.2
1989	3,445	203	3,648	951,710	895.3	174.2	727.7	383.4
1990	3,835	565	4,400	1,054,860	996.8	589.5	915.6	424.1
1991	3,972	219	4,191	1,092,740	1,010.3	223.6	853.4	433.3
1992	4,372	1,038	5,410	1,126,970	1,088.8	486.6	879.9	441.8
1993	4,835	1,120	5,955	1,135,610	1,187.1	503.3	945.5	440.3
1994	n/a	n/a	n/a	1,113,180	n/a	n/a	n/a	427.6
1995	n/a	n/a	3,606	1,099,210	n/a	n/a	547.9	418.3
1996	3,824	791	4,615	1,029,810	896.1	326.3	689.7	388.2

Notes: (1) Metropolitan Statistical Area - see Appendix A for areas included; (2) calculated by the editors using the following formula: (number of crimes in the MSA minus number of crimes in the city); (3) calculated by the editors using the following formula: ((number of crimes in the MSA minus number of crimes in the city) ÷ (population of the MSA minus population of the city)) x 100,000; n/a not avail.
Source: U.S. Department of Justice, FBI Uniform Crime Reports, 1977 - 1996

Burglaries and Burglary Rates: 1977 - 1996

Year	Number				Rate per 100,000 population			
	City	Suburbs[2]	MSA[1]	U.S.	City	Suburbs[3]	MSA[1]	U.S.
1977	6,568	1,475	8,043	3,071,500	2,257.0	1,413.2	2,034.3	1,419.8
1978	6,191	1,528	7,719	3,128,300	2,098.6	1,422.0	1,918.0	1,434.6
1979	7,298	1,640	8,938	3,327,700	2,415.6	1,419.8	2,140.2	1,511.9
1980	8,081	817	8,898	3,795,200	2,457.4	681.1	1,982.6	1,684.1
1981	9,074	1,818	10,892	3,779,700	2,693.9	1,479.5	2,369.3	1,649.5
1982	7,980	1,750	9,730	3,447,100	2,313.3	1,390.5	2,066.6	1,488.8
1983	7,733	1,352	9,085	3,129,900	2,177.3	1,456.2	2,027.9	1,337.7
1984	8,686	1,737	10,423	2,984,400	2,437.4	1,798.8	2,301.2	1,263.7
1985	9,186	2,196	11,382	3,073,300	2,572.7	2,181.8	2,486.8	1,287.3
1986	9,746	2,725	12,471	3,241,400	2,676.0	2,654.5	2,671.3	1,344.6
1987	9,965	2,321	12,286	3,236,200	2,680.5	2,127.0	2,554.9	1,329.6
1988	11,042	1,399	12,441	3,218,100	2,919.8	1,260.3	2,543.2	1,309.2
1989	9,672	1,541	11,213	3,168,200	2,513.5	1,322.3	2,236.6	1,276.3
1990	9,497	2,715	12,212	3,073,900	2,468.4	2,832.8	2,541.1	1,235.9
1991	10,348	1,393	11,741	3,157,200	2,632.1	1,422.5	2,390.9	1,252.0
1992	8,705	2,345	11,050	2,979,900	2,168.0	1,099.3	1,797.2	1,168.2
1993	8,199	2,263	10,462	2,834,800	2,013.1	1,017.0	1,661.1	1,099.2
1994	n/a	n/a	n/a	2,712,800	n/a	n/a	n/a	1,042.0
1995	8,362	2,069	10,431	2,593,800	1,992.3	867.8	1,584.9	987.1
1996	9,037	1,667	10,704	2,501,500	2,117.7	687.8	1,599.7	943.0

Notes: (1) Metropolitan Statistical Area - see Appendix A for areas included; (2) calculated by the editors using the following formula: (number of crimes in the MSA minus number of crimes in the city); (3) calculated by the editors using the following formula: ((number of crimes in the MSA minus number of crimes in the city) ÷ (population of the MSA minus population of the city)) x 100,000; n/a not avail.
Source: U.S. Department of Justice, FBI Uniform Crime Reports, 1977 - 1996

Larceny-Thefts and Larceny-Theft Rates: 1977 - 1996

Year	Number				Rate per 100,000 population			
	City	Suburbs[2]	MSA[1]	U.S.	City	Suburbs[3]	MSA[1]	U.S.
1977	13,833	2,052	15,885	5,905,700	4,753.6	1,966.0	4,017.7	2,729.9
1978	12,910	2,378	15,288	5,991,000	4,376.3	2,213.1	3,798.7	2,747.4
1979	15,613	2,912	18,525	6,601,000	5,167.8	2,520.9	4,435.7	2,999.1
1980	16,808	2,115	18,923	7,136,900	5,111.3	1,763.1	4,216.4	3,167.0
1981	16,984	2,848	19,832	7,194,400	5,042.2	2,317.7	4,313.9	3,139.7
1982	17,214	3,143	20,357	7,142,500	4,990.1	2,497.4	4,323.8	3,084.8
1983	17,087	2,331	19,418	6,712,800	4,811.0	2,510.6	4,334.3	2,868.9
1984	17,485	2,593	20,078	6,591,900	4,906.5	2,685.2	4,432.9	2,791.3
1985	17,935	2,399	20,334	6,926,400	5,023.1	2,383.5	4,442.6	2,901.2
1986	19,490	2,498	21,988	7,257,200	5,351.5	2,433.4	4,709.8	3,010.3
1987	20,913	2,586	23,499	7,499,900	5,625.5	2,369.9	4,886.7	3,081.3
1988	20,950	1,630	22,580	7,705,900	5,539.7	1,468.4	4,615.9	3,134.9
1989	21,670	1,937	23,607	7,872,400	5,631.5	1,662.2	4,708.8	3,171.3
1990	22,130	2,493	24,623	7,945,700	5,752.0	2,601.2	5,123.6	3,194.8
1991	22,024	1,771	23,795	8,142,200	5,602.0	1,808.5	4,845.5	3,228.8
1992	20,236	4,491	24,727	7,915,200	5,039.7	2,105.2	4,021.6	3,103.0
1993	20,552	4,425	24,977	7,820,900	5,046.1	1,988.5	3,965.8	3,032.4
1994	n/a	n/a	n/a	7,879,800	n/a	n/a	n/a	3,026.7
1995	23,461	4,367	27,828	7,997,700	5,589.8	1,831.6	4,228.3	3,043.8
1996	25,961	4,229	30,190	7,894,600	6,083.6	1,744.8	4,511.9	2,975.9

Notes: (1) Metropolitan Statistical Area - see Appendix A for areas included; (2) calculated by the editors using the following formula: (number of crimes in the MSA minus number of crimes in the city); (3) calculated by the editors using the following formula: ((number of crimes in the MSA minus number of crimes in the city) ÷ (population of the MSA minus population of the city)) x 100,000; n/a not avail.
Source: U.S. Department of Justice, FBI Uniform Crime Reports, 1977 - 1996

Motor Vehicle Thefts and Motor Vehicle Theft Rates: 1977 - 1996

Year	Number				Rate per 100,000 population			
	City	Suburbs[2]	MSA[1]	U.S.	City	Suburbs[3]	MSA[1]	U.S.
1977	1,164	223	1,387	977,700	400.0	213.7	350.8	451.9
1978	1,331	249	1,580	1,004,100	451.2	231.7	392.6	460.5
1979	1,751	315	2,066	1,112,800	579.6	272.7	494.7	505.6
1980	1,429	164	1,593	1,131,700	434.6	136.7	354.9	502.2
1981	1,571	351	1,922	1,087,800	466.4	285.6	418.1	474.7
1982	1,361	323	1,684	1,062,400	394.5	256.7	357.7	458.8
1983	1,476	228	1,704	1,007,900	415.6	245.6	380.4	430.8
1984	1,622	265	1,887	1,032,200	455.2	274.4	416.6	437.1
1985	1,932	281	2,213	1,102,900	541.1	279.2	483.5	462.0
1986	1,988	348	2,336	1,224,100	545.9	339.0	500.4	507.8
1987	2,285	343	2,628	1,288,700	614.7	314.3	546.5	529.4
1988	2,705	209	2,914	1,432,900	715.3	188.3	595.7	582.9
1989	2,306	212	2,518	1,564,800	599.3	181.9	502.3	630.4
1990	1,973	318	2,291	1,635,900	512.8	331.8	476.7	657.8
1991	2,470	232	2,702	1,661,700	628.3	236.9	550.2	659.0
1992	2,905	422	3,327	1,610,800	723.5	197.8	541.1	631.5
1993	3,578	499	4,077	1,563,100	878.5	224.2	647.3	606.1
1994	n/a	n/a	n/a	1,539,300	n/a	n/a	n/a	591.3
1995	4,995	463	5,458	1,472,400	1,190.1	194.2	829.3	560.4
1996	6,988	422	7,410	1,395,200	1,637.5	174.1	1,107.4	525.9

Notes: (1) Metropolitan Statistical Area - see Appendix A for areas included; (2) calculated by the editors using the following formula: (number of crimes in the MSA minus number of crimes in the city); (3) calculated by the editors using the following formula: ((number of crimes in the MSA minus number of crimes in the city) ÷ (population of the MSA minus population of the city)) x 100,000; n/a not avail.
Source: U.S. Department of Justice, FBI Uniform Crime Reports, 1977 - 1996

HATE CRIMES

Criminal Incidents by Bias Motivation

Area	Race	Ethnicity	Religion	Sexual Orientation
Albuquerque	9	1	2	2

Notes: Figures include both violent and property crimes. Law enforcement agencies must have submitted data for at least one quarter of calendar year 1995 to be included in this report, therefore figures shown may not represent complete 12-month totals; n/a not available
Source: U.S. Department of Justice, FBI Uniform Crime Reports, Hate Crime Statistics 1995

LAW ENFORCEMENT

Full-Time Law Enforcement Employees

Jurisdiction	Police Employees			Police Officers per 100,000 population
	Total	Officers	Civilians	
Albuquerque	1,253	895	358	209.7

Notes: Data as of October 31, 1996
Source: U.S. Department of Justice, FBI Uniform Crime Reports, 1996

Number of Police Officers by Race

Race	Police Officers				Index of Representation[1]		
	1983		1992				
	Number	Pct.	Number	Pct.	1983	1992	% Chg.
Black	14	2.5	16	2.1	0.96	0.67	-30.2
Hispanic[2]	184	32.8	262	34.2	0.97	0.99	2.1

Notes: (1) The index of representation is calculated by dividing the percent of black/hispanic police officers by the percent of corresponding blacks/hispanics in the local population. An index approaching 1.0 indicates that a city is closer to achieving a representation of police officers equal to their proportion in the local population; (2) Hispanic officers can be of any race
Source: Bureau of Justice Statistics, Sourcebook of Criminal Justice Statistics, 1994

CORRECTIONS

Federal Correctional Facilities

Type	Year Opened	Security Level	Sex of Inmates	Rated Capacity	Population on 7/1/95	Number of Staff
None listed						

Notes: Data as of 1995
Source: Bureau of Justice Statistics, Sourcebook of Criminal Justice Statistics Online

City/County/Regional Correctional Facilities

Name	Year Opened	Year Renov.	Rated Capacity	1995 Pop.	Number of COs[1]	Number of Staff	ACA[2] Accred.
Bernalillo City/County Satellite Jail	1978	1983	752	995	343	442	No
Bernalillo Co Detention Ctr	1978	1983	665	n/a	n/a	n/a	No

Notes: Data as of April 1996; (1) Correctional Officers; (2) American Correctional Assn. Accreditation
Source: American Correctional Association, 1996-1998 National Jail and Adult Detention Directory

Private Adult Correctional Facilities

Name	Date Opened	Rated Capacity	Present Pop.	Security Level	Facility Construct.	Expans. Plans	ACA[1] Accred.
None listed							

Notes: Data as of December 1996; (1) American Correctional Association Accreditation
Source: University of Florida, Center for Studies in Criminology and Law, Private Adult Correctional Facility Census, 10th Ed., March 15, 1997

Characteristics of Shock Incarceration Programs

Jurisdiction	Year Program Began	Number of Camps	Average Num. of Inmates	Number of Beds	Program Length	Voluntary/ Mandatory
New Mexico did not have a shock incarceration program as of July 1996						

Source: Sourcebook of Criminal Justice Statistics Online

DEATH PENALTY

Death Penalty Statistics

State	Prisoners Executed		Prisoners Under Sentence of Death					Avg. No. of Years on Death Row[4]
	1930-1995	1996[1]	Total[2]	White[3]	Black[3]	Hisp.	Women	
New Mexico	8	0	3	3	0	2	0	n/c

Notes: Data as of 12/31/95 unless otherwise noted; n/c not calculated on fewer than 10 inmates; (1) Data as of 7/31/97; (2) Includes persons of other races; (3) Includes people of Hispanic origin; (4) Covers prisoners sentenced 1974 through 1995
Source: Bureau of Justice Statistics, Capital Punishment 1995 (released 12/96); Death Penalty Information Center Web Site, 9/30/97

Capital Offenses and Methods of Execution

Capital Offenses in New Mexico	Minimum Age for Imposition of Death Penalty	Mentally Retarded Excluded	Methods of Execution[1]
First-degree murder (Section 30-2-1 A, NMSA).	18	No	Lethal injection

Notes: Data as of 12/31/95 unless otherwise noted; (1) Data as of 7/31/97
Source: Bureau of Justice Statistics, Capital Punishment 1995 (released 12/96); Death Penalty Information Center Web Site, 9/30/97

LAWS

Statutory Provisions Relating to the Purchase, Ownership and Use of Handguns

Jurisdiction	Instant Background Check	Federal Waiting Period Applies[1]	State Waiting Period (days)	License or Permit to Purchase	Regis- tration	Record of Sale Sent to Police	Concealed Carry Law
New Mexico	No	Yes	No	No	No	No	Yes[a]

Note: Data as of 1996; (1) The Federal 5-day waiting period for handgun purchases applies to states that don't have instant background checks, waiting period requirements, or licensing procedures exempting them from the Federal requirement; (a) No permit system exists and concealed carry is prohibited
Source: Sourcebook of Criminal Justice Statistics Online

Statutory Provisions Relating to Alcohol Use and Driving

Jurisdiction	Drinking Age	Blood Alcohol Concentration Levels as Evidence in State Courts[1]		Open Container Law[1]	Anti-Consumption Law[1]	Dram Shop Law[1]
		Illegal per se at 0.10%	Presumption at 0.10%			
New Mexico	21	(a)	No	Yes	Yes	Yes

Note: Data as of January 1, 1997; (1) See Appendix C for an explanation of terms; (a) 0.08%
Source: Sourcebook of Criminal Justice Statistics Online

Statutory Provisions Relating to Curfews

Jurisdiction	Year Enacted	Latest Revision	Age Group(s)	Curfew Provisions
Albuquerque	1994	-	16 and under	11 pm to 5 am every night

Note: Data as of February 1996
Source: Sourcebook of Criminal Justice Statistics Online

Statutory Provisions Relating to Hate Crimes

Jurisdiction	Bias-Motivated Violence and Intimidation						Institutional Vandalism
	Civil Action	Criminal Penalty					
		Race/ Religion/ Ethnicity	Sexual Orientation	Mental/ Physical Disability	Gender	Age	
New Mexico	No	No	No	No	No	No	Yes

Source: Anti-Defamation League, 1997 Hate Crimes Laws

Amarillo, Texas

OVERVIEW

The total crime rate for the city increased 41.1% between 1977 and 1996. During that same period, the violent crime rate increased 96.5% and the property crime rate increased 36.8%.

Among violent crimes, the rates for: Murders decreased 54.3%; Forcible Rapes increased 20.4%; Robberies increased 101.5%; and Aggravated Assaults increased 111.7%.

Among property crimes, the rates for: Burglaries decreased 21.0%; Larceny-Thefts increased 64.0%; and Motor Vehicle Thefts increased 20.7%.

ANTI-CRIME PROGRAMS

Information not available at time of publication.

CRIME RISK

Your Chances of Becoming a Victim[1]

Area	Any Crime	Violent Crime					Property Crime			
		Any	Murder	Forcible Rape[2]	Robbery	Aggrav. Assault	Any	Burglary	Larceny -Theft	Motor Vehicle Theft
City	1:12	1:120	1:15,615	1:1,261	1:514	1:170	1:14	1:81	1:17	1:250

Note: (1) Figures have been calculated by dividing the population of the city by the number of crimes reported to the FBI during 1996 and are expressed as odds (eg. 1:20 should be read as 1 in 20). (2) Figures have been calculated by dividing the female population of the city by the number of forcible rapes reported to the FBI during 1996. The female population of the city was estimated by calculating the ratio of females to males reported in the 1990 Census and applying that ratio to 1996 population estimate.
Source: FBI Uniform Crime Reports 1996

CRIME STATISTICS

Total Crimes and Total Crime Rates: 1977 - 1996

Year	Number				Rate per 100,000 population			
	City	Suburbs[2]	MSA[1]	U.S.	City	Suburbs[3]	MSA[1]	U.S.
1977	8,312	534	8,846	10,984,500	5,812.6	3,260.7	5,550.4	5,077.6
1978	8,874	592	9,466	11,209,000	6,162.5	4,021.5	5,963.9	5,140.3
1979	9,102	656	9,758	12,249,500	6,072.1	5,160.9	6,000.9	5,565.5
1980	9,698	621	10,319	13,408,300	6,501.4	2,546.9	5,945.8	5,950.0
1981	9,751	555	10,306	13,423,800	6,277.7	2,185.9	5,702.8	5,858.2
1982	11,160	641	11,801	12,974,400	6,938.0	2,437.9	6,305.7	5,603.6
1983	11,202	672	11,874	12,108,600	6,767.5	2,483.7	6,165.7	5,175.0
1984	9,949	716	10,665	11,881,800	6,119.7	2,696.7	5,639.2	5,031.3
1985	10,843	779	11,622	12,431,400	6,502.7	2,773.0	5,964.9	5,207.1
1986	13,865	810	14,675	13,211,900	8,159.4	2,834.5	7,392.8	5,480.4
1987	12,949	810	13,759	13,508,700	7,757.9	2,751.5	7,007.3	5,550.0
1988	13,390	863	14,253	13,923,100	8,013.6	2,872.0	7,229.9	5,664.2
1989	13,793	950	14,743	14,251,400	8,233.8	3,097.9	7,439.1	5,741.0
1990	13,643	822	14,465	14,475,600	8,655.9	2,746.2	7,712.7	5,820.3
1991	12,768	850	13,618	14,872,900	7,931.5	2,780.6	7,109.5	5,897.8
1992	13,745	928	14,673	14,438,200	8,390.0	2,983.1	7,527.1	5,660.2
1993	13,868	930	14,798	14,144,800	8,444.0	2,983.5	7,573.0	5,484.4
1994	13,546	951	14,497	13,989,500	8,092.3	2,993.5	7,279.0	5,373.5
1995	13,293	950	14,243	13,862,700	7,905.8	2,913.8	7,095.1	5,275.9
1996	14,088	857	14,945	13,473,600	8,201.7	2,573.2	7,287.6	5,078.9

Notes: (1) Metropolitan Statistical Area - see Appendix A for areas included; (2) calculated by the editors using the following formula: (number of crimes in the MSA minus number of crimes in the city); (3) calculated by the editors using the following formula: ((number of crimes in the MSA minus number of crimes in the city) ÷ (population of the MSA minus population of the city)) x 100,000; n/a not avail.
Source: U.S. Department of Justice, FBI Uniform Crime Reports, 1977 - 1996

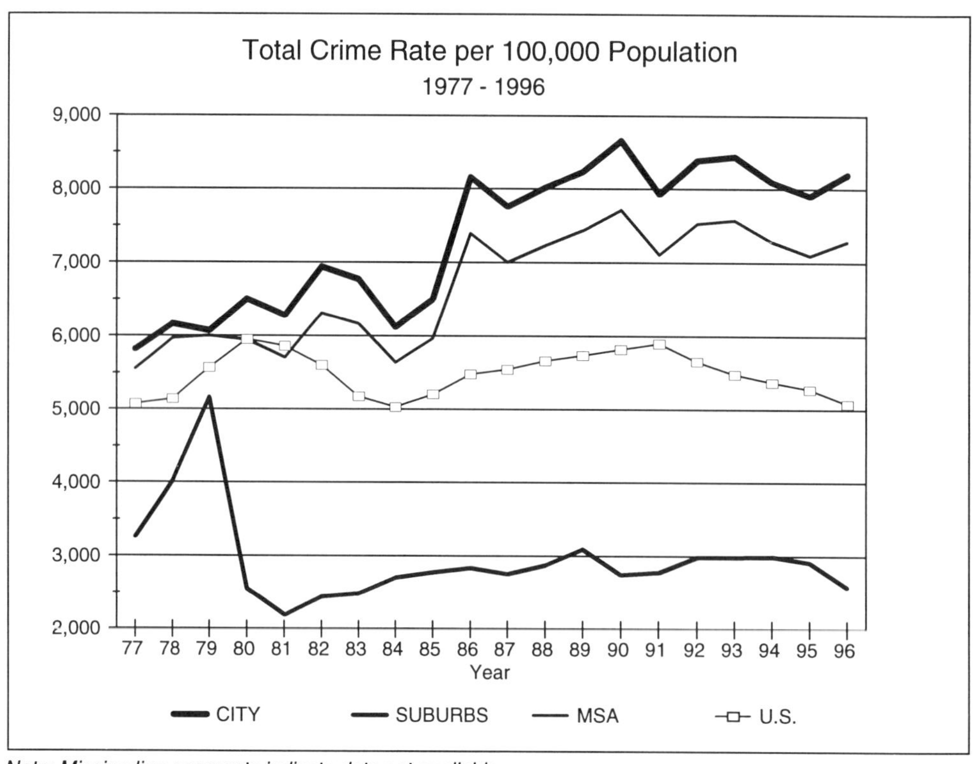

Note: Missing line segments indicate data not available.

Violent Crimes and Violent Crime Rates: 1977 - 1996

Year	Number				Rate per 100,000 population			
	City	Suburbs[2]	MSA[1]	U.S.	City	Suburbs[3]	MSA[1]	U.S.
1977	605	45	650	1,029,580	423.1	274.8	407.8	475.9
1978	696	52	748	1,085,550	483.3	353.2	471.3	497.8
1979	681	35	716	1,208,030	454.3	275.4	440.3	548.9
1980	739	38	777	1,344,520	495.4	155.8	447.7	596.6
1981	793	57	850	1,361,820	510.5	224.5	470.3	594.3
1982	865	55	920	1,322,390	537.8	209.2	491.6	571.1
1983	844	59	903	1,258,090	509.9	218.1	468.9	537.7
1984	718	52	770	1,273,280	441.6	195.8	407.1	539.2
1985	759	48	807	1,328,800	455.2	170.9	414.2	556.6
1986	887	41	928	1,489,170	522.0	143.5	467.5	617.7
1987	842	47	889	1,484,000	504.5	159.7	452.8	609.7
1988	923	49	972	1,566,220	552.4	163.1	493.1	637.2
1989	960	42	1,002	1,646,040	573.1	137.0	505.6	663.1
1990	926	82	1,008	1,820,130	587.5	274.0	537.5	731.8
1991	906	89	995	1,911,770	562.8	291.1	519.5	758.1
1992	1,134	82	1,216	1,932,270	692.2	263.6	623.8	757.5
1993	1,129	73	1,202	1,926,020	687.4	234.2	615.1	746.8
1994	1,261	91	1,352	1,857,670	753.3	286.4	678.8	713.6
1995	1,380	99	1,479	1,798,790	820.7	303.7	736.8	684.6
1996	1,428	73	1,501	1,682,280	831.3	219.2	731.9	634.1

Notes: Violent crimes include murder, forcible rape, robbery and aggravated assault; n/a not available; (1) Metropolitan Statistical Area - see Appendix A for areas included; (2) calculated by the editors using the following formula: (number of crimes in the MSA minus number of crimes in the city); (3) calculated by the editors using the following formula: ((number of crimes in the MSA minus number of crimes in the city) ÷ (population of the MSA minus population of the city)) x 100,000
Source: U.S. Department of Justice, FBI Uniform Crime Reports, 1977 - 1996

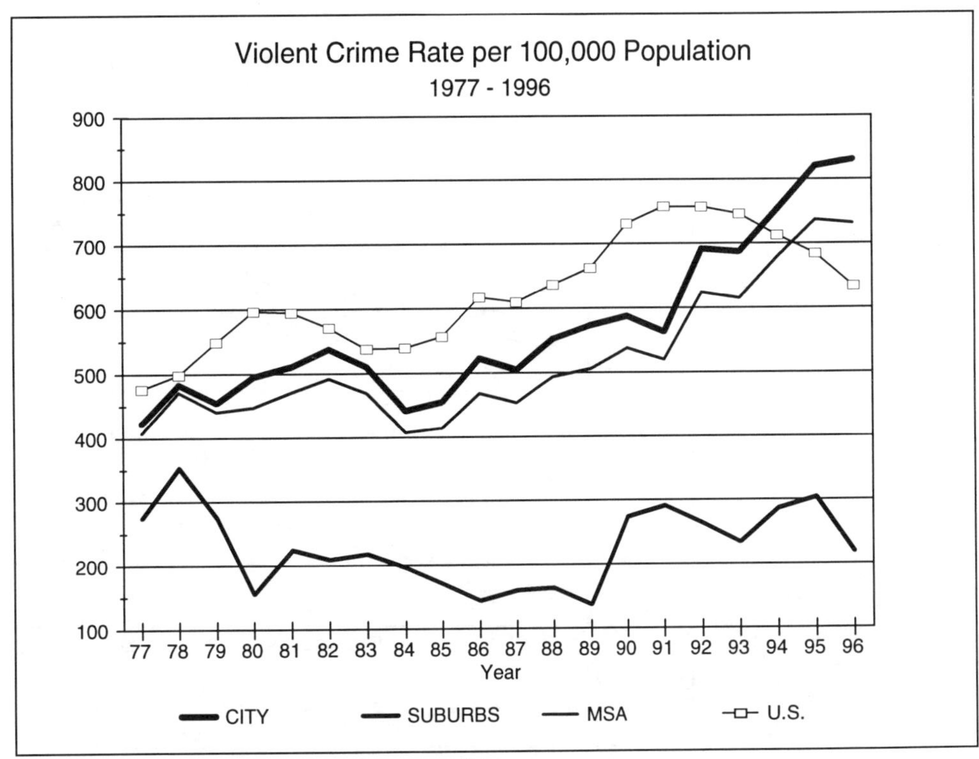

Note: Missing line segments indicate data not available.

Property Crimes and Property Crime Rates: 1977 - 1996

Year	Number				Rate per 100,000 population			
	City	Suburbs[2]	MSA[1]	U.S.	City	Suburbs[3]	MSA[1]	U.S.
1977	7,707	489	8,196	9,955,000	5,389.5	2,985.9	5,142.5	4,601.7
1978	8,178	540	8,718	10,123,400	5,679.2	3,668.2	5,492.7	4,642.5
1979	8,421	621	9,042	11,041,500	5,617.8	4,885.5	5,560.5	5,016.6
1980	8,959	583	9,542	12,063,700	6,006.0	2,391.0	5,498.1	5,353.3
1981	8,958	498	9,456	12,061,900	5,767.2	1,961.4	5,232.5	5,263.9
1982	10,295	586	10,881	11,652,000	6,400.2	2,228.7	5,814.1	5,032.5
1983	10,358	613	10,971	10,850,500	6,257.6	2,265.7	5,696.8	4,637.4
1984	9,231	664	9,895	10,608,500	5,678.1	2,500.8	5,232.0	4,492.1
1985	10,084	731	10,815	11,102,600	6,047.5	2,602.2	5,550.7	4,650.5
1986	12,978	769	13,747	11,722,700	7,637.4	2,691.1	6,925.3	4,862.6
1987	12,107	763	12,870	12,024,700	7,253.4	2,591.9	6,554.6	4,940.3
1988	12,467	814	13,281	12,356,900	7,461.2	2,708.9	6,736.8	5,027.1
1989	12,833	908	13,741	12,605,400	7,660.8	2,960.9	6,933.5	5,077.9
1990	12,717	740	13,457	12,655,500	8,068.4	2,472.3	7,175.3	5,088.5
1991	11,862	761	12,623	12,961,100	7,368.7	2,489.5	6,590.0	5,139.7
1992	12,611	846	13,457	12,505,900	7,697.8	2,719.5	6,903.3	4,902.7
1993	12,739	857	13,596	12,218,800	7,756.6	2,749.4	6,957.9	4,737.6
1994	12,285	860	13,145	12,131,900	7,339.0	2,707.0	6,600.2	4,660.0
1995	11,913	851	12,764	12,063,900	7,085.1	2,610.2	6,358.3	4,591.3
1996	12,660	784	13,444	11,791,300	7,370.3	2,354.0	6,555.7	4,444.8

Notes: Property crimes include burglary, larceny-theft and motor vehicle theft; n/a not available; (1) Metropolitan Statistical Area - see Appendix A for areas included; (2) calculated by the editors using the following formula: (number of crimes in the MSA minus number of crimes in the city); (3) calculated by the editors using the following formula: ((number of crimes in the MSA minus number of crimes in the city) ÷ (population of the MSA minus population of the city)) x 100,000
Source: U.S. Department of Justice, FBI Uniform Crime Reports, 1977 - 1996

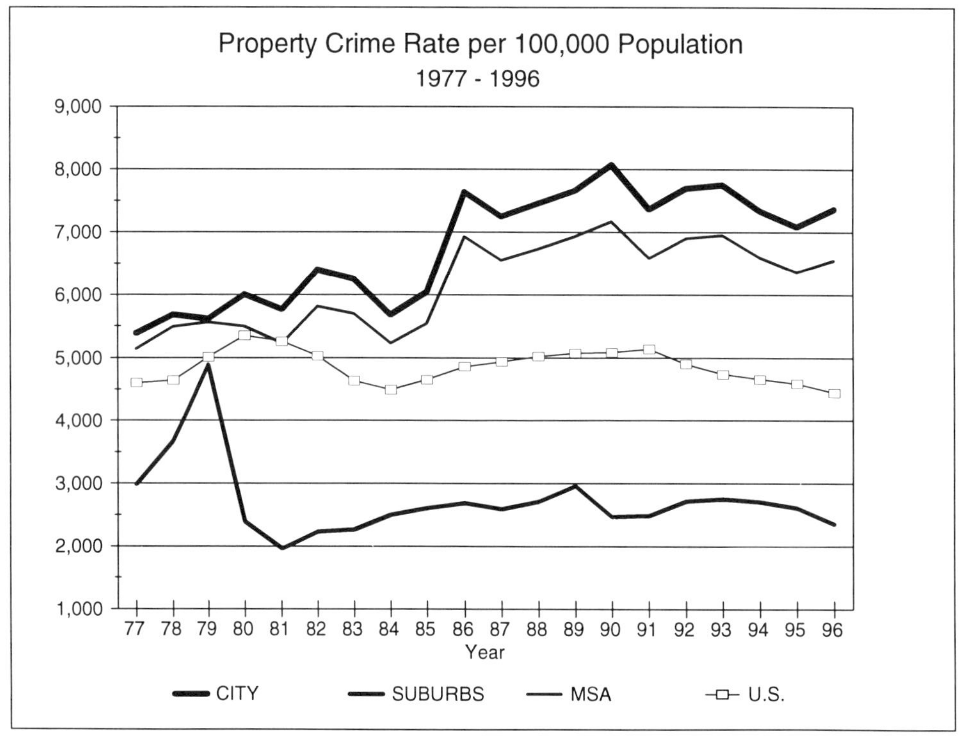

Note: Missing line segments indicate data not available.

Murders and Murder Rates: 1977 - 1996

Year	Number				Rate per 100,000 population			
	City	Suburbs[2]	MSA[1]	U.S.	City	Suburbs[3]	MSA[1]	U.S.
1977	20	1	21	19,120	14.0	6.1	13.2	8.8
1978	13	0	13	19,560	9.0	0.0	8.2	9.0
1979	16	3	19	21,460	10.7	23.6	11.7	9.7
1980	17	3	20	23,040	11.4	12.3	11.5	10.2
1981	15	0	15	22,520	9.7	0.0	8.3	9.8
1982	22	3	25	21,010	13.7	11.4	13.4	9.1
1983	18	3	21	19,310	10.9	11.1	10.9	8.3
1984	22	0	22	18,690	13.5	0.0	11.6	7.9
1985	17	2	19	18,980	10.2	7.1	9.8	7.9
1986	21	2	23	20,610	12.4	7.0	11.6	8.6
1987	18	2	20	20,100	10.8	6.8	10.2	8.3
1988	16	3	19	20,680	9.6	10.0	9.6	8.4
1989	15	2	17	21,500	9.0	6.5	8.6	8.7
1990	22	2	24	23,440	14.0	6.7	12.8	9.4
1991	15	5	20	24,700	9.3	16.4	10.4	9.8
1992	17	0	17	23,760	10.4	0.0	8.7	9.3
1993	11	1	12	24,530	6.7	3.2	6.1	9.5
1994	25	1	26	23,330	14.9	3.1	13.1	9.0
1995	16	3	19	21,610	9.5	9.2	9.5	8.2
1996	11	1	12	19,650	6.4	3.0	5.9	7.4

Notes: (1) Metropolitan Statistical Area - see Appendix A for areas included; (2) calculated by the editors using the following formula: (number of crimes in the MSA minus number of crimes in the city); (3) calculated by the editors using the following formula: ((number of crimes in the MSA minus number of crimes in the city) ÷ (population of the MSA minus population of the city)) x 100,000; n/a not avail.
Source: U.S. Department of Justice, FBI Uniform Crime Reports, 1977 - 1996

Forcible Rapes and Forcible Rape Rates: 1977 - 1996

Year	Number				Rate per 100,000 population			
	City	Suburbs[2]	MSA[1]	U.S.	City	Suburbs[3]	MSA[1]	U.S.
1977	49	4	53	63,500	34.3	24.4	33.3	29.4
1978	49	10	59	67,610	34.0	67.9	37.2	31.0
1979	43	2	45	76,390	28.7	15.7	27.7	34.7
1980	47	3	50	82,990	31.5	12.3	28.8	36.8
1981	62	8	70	82,500	39.9	31.5	38.7	36.0
1982	50	4	54	78,770	31.1	15.2	28.9	34.0
1983	52	6	58	78,920	31.4	22.2	30.1	33.7
1984	52	8	60	84,230	32.0	30.1	31.7	35.7
1985	59	9	68	88,670	35.4	32.0	34.9	37.1
1986	81	6	87	91,460	47.7	21.0	43.8	37.9
1987	71	11	82	91,110	42.5	37.4	41.8	37.4
1988	58	8	66	92,490	34.7	26.6	33.5	37.6
1989	79	10	89	94,500	47.2	32.6	44.9	38.1
1990	75	11	86	102,560	47.6	36.7	45.9	41.2
1991	80	6	86	106,590	49.7	19.6	44.9	42.3
1992	103	6	109	109,060	62.9	19.3	55.9	42.8
1993	89	15	104	106,010	54.2	48.1	53.2	41.1
1994	106	10	116	102,220	63.3	31.5	58.2	39.3
1995	84	11	95	97,470	50.0	33.7	47.3	37.1
1996	71	9	80	95,770	41.3	27.0	39.0	36.1

Notes: (1) Metropolitan Statistical Area - see Appendix A for areas included; (2) calculated by the editors using the following formula: (number of crimes in the MSA minus number of crimes in the city); (3) calculated by the editors using the following formula: ((number of crimes in the MSA minus number of crimes in the city) ÷ (population of the MSA minus population of the city)) x 100,000; n/a not avail.
Source: U.S. Department of Justice, FBI Uniform Crime Reports, 1977 - 1996

Robberies and Robbery Rates: 1977 - 1996

Year	Number				Rate per 100,000 population			
	City	Suburbs[2]	MSA[1]	U.S.	City	Suburbs[3]	MSA[1]	U.S.
1977	138	4	142	412,610	96.5	24.4	89.1	190.7
1978	158	2	160	426,930	109.7	13.6	100.8	195.8
1979	140	9	149	480,700	93.4	70.8	91.6	218.4
1980	186	4	190	565,840	124.7	16.4	109.5	251.1
1981	167	13	180	592,910	107.5	51.2	99.6	258.7
1982	223	11	234	553,130	138.6	41.8	125.0	238.9
1983	186	13	199	506,570	112.4	48.0	103.3	216.5
1984	164	5	169	485,010	100.9	18.8	89.4	205.4
1985	162	4	166	497,870	97.2	14.2	85.2	208.5
1986	275	3	278	542,780	161.8	10.5	140.0	225.1
1987	250	3	253	517,700	149.8	10.2	128.9	212.7
1988	258	5	263	542,970	154.4	16.6	133.4	220.9
1989	271	3	274	578,330	161.8	9.8	138.3	233.0
1990	248	1	249	639,270	157.3	3.3	132.8	257.0
1991	265	4	269	687,730	164.6	13.1	140.4	272.7
1992	278	4	282	672,480	169.7	12.9	144.7	263.6
1993	208	5	213	659,870	126.6	16.0	109.0	255.9
1994	237	7	244	618,950	141.6	22.0	122.5	237.7
1995	242	8	250	580,510	143.9	24.5	124.5	220.9
1996	334	7	341	537,050	194.4	21.0	166.3	202.4

Notes: (1) Metropolitan Statistical Area - see Appendix A for areas included; (2) calculated by the editors using the following formula: (number of crimes in the MSA minus number of crimes in the city); (3) calculated by the editors using the following formula: ((number of crimes in the MSA minus number of crimes in the city) ÷ (population of the MSA minus population of the city)) x 100,000; n/a not avail.
Source: U.S. Department of Justice, FBI Uniform Crime Reports, 1977 - 1996

Aggravated Assaults and Aggravated Assault Rates: 1977 - 1996

Year	Number				Rate per 100,000 population			
	City	Suburbs[2]	MSA[1]	U.S.	City	Suburbs[3]	MSA[1]	U.S.
1977	398	36	434	534,350	278.3	219.8	272.3	247.0
1978	476	40	516	571,460	330.6	271.7	325.1	262.1
1979	482	21	503	629,480	321.5	165.2	309.3	286.0
1980	489	28	517	672,650	327.8	114.8	297.9	298.5
1981	549	36	585	663,900	353.4	141.8	323.7	289.7
1982	570	37	607	669,480	354.4	140.7	324.3	289.2
1983	588	37	625	653,290	355.2	136.8	324.5	279.2
1984	480	39	519	685,350	295.3	146.9	274.4	290.2
1985	521	33	554	723,250	312.4	117.5	284.3	302.9
1986	510	30	540	834,320	300.1	105.0	272.0	346.1
1987	503	31	534	855,090	301.4	105.3	272.0	351.3
1988	591	33	624	910,090	353.7	109.8	316.5	370.2
1989	595	27	622	951,710	355.2	88.0	313.9	383.4
1990	581	68	649	1,054,860	368.6	227.2	346.0	424.1
1991	546	74	620	1,092,740	339.2	242.1	323.7	433.3
1992	736	72	808	1,126,970	449.3	231.4	414.5	441.8
1993	821	52	873	1,135,610	499.9	166.8	446.8	440.3
1994	893	73	966	1,113,180	533.5	229.8	485.0	427.6
1995	1,038	77	1,115	1,099,210	617.3	236.2	555.4	418.3
1996	1,012	56	1,068	1,029,810	589.2	168.1	520.8	388.2

Notes: (1) Metropolitan Statistical Area - see Appendix A for areas included; (2) calculated by the editors using the following formula: (number of crimes in the MSA minus number of crimes in the city); (3) calculated by the editors using the following formula: ((number of crimes in the MSA minus number of crimes in the city) ÷ (population of the MSA minus population of the city)) x 100,000; n/a not avail.
Source: U.S. Department of Justice, FBI Uniform Crime Reports, 1977 - 1996

Burglaries and Burglary Rates: 1977 - 1996

Year	Number				Rate per 100,000 population			
	City	Suburbs[2]	MSA[1]	U.S.	City	Suburbs[3]	MSA[1]	U.S.
1977	2,229	168	2,397	3,071,500	1,558.7	1,025.8	1,504.0	1,419.8
1978	2,387	172	2,559	3,128,300	1,657.6	1,168.4	1,612.3	1,434.6
1979	2,515	191	2,706	3,327,700	1,677.8	1,502.6	1,664.1	1,511.9
1980	2,705	222	2,927	3,795,200	1,813.4	910.5	1,686.5	1,684.1
1981	2,903	170	3,073	3,779,700	1,869.0	669.6	1,700.4	1,649.5
1982	3,372	198	3,570	3,447,100	2,096.3	753.1	1,907.6	1,488.8
1983	2,904	196	3,100	3,129,900	1,754.4	724.4	1,609.7	1,337.7
1984	2,457	194	2,651	2,984,400	1,511.3	730.7	1,401.7	1,263.7
1985	2,689	249	2,938	3,073,300	1,612.6	886.4	1,507.9	1,287.3
1986	3,653	238	3,891	3,241,400	2,149.7	832.9	1,960.2	1,344.6
1987	3,200	262	3,462	3,236,200	1,917.2	890.0	1,763.2	1,329.6
1988	3,532	266	3,798	3,218,100	2,113.8	885.2	1,926.5	1,309.2
1989	3,370	261	3,631	3,168,200	2,011.7	851.1	1,832.2	1,276.3
1990	3,262	194	3,456	3,073,900	2,069.6	648.1	1,842.7	1,235.9
1991	2,354	194	2,548	3,157,200	1,462.3	634.6	1,330.2	1,252.0
1992	2,722	264	2,986	2,979,900	1,661.5	848.6	1,531.8	1,168.2
1993	2,739	235	2,974	2,834,800	1,667.7	753.9	1,522.0	1,099.2
1994	2,168	181	2,349	2,712,800	1,295.2	569.7	1,179.4	1,042.0
1995	2,419	234	2,653	2,593,800	1,438.7	717.7	1,321.6	987.1
1996	2,116	176	2,292	2,501,500	1,231.9	528.4	1,117.6	943.0

Notes: (1) Metropolitan Statistical Area - see Appendix A for areas included; (2) calculated by the editors using the following formula: (number of crimes in the MSA minus number of crimes in the city); (3) calculated by the editors using the following formula: ((number of crimes in the MSA minus number of crimes in the city) ÷ (population of the MSA minus population of the city)) x 100,000; n/a not avail.
Source: U.S. Department of Justice, FBI Uniform Crime Reports, 1977 - 1996

Larceny-Thefts and Larceny-Theft Rates: 1977 - 1996

Year	Number				Rate per 100,000 population			
	City	Suburbs[2]	MSA[1]	U.S.	City	Suburbs[3]	MSA[1]	U.S.
1977	5,004	301	5,305	5,905,700	3,499.3	1,837.9	3,328.6	2,729.9
1978	5,270	330	5,600	5,991,000	3,659.7	2,241.7	3,528.2	2,747.4
1979	5,469	380	5,849	6,601,000	3,648.5	2,989.5	3,596.9	2,999.1
1980	5,730	328	6,058	7,136,900	3,841.3	1,345.2	3,490.6	3,167.0
1981	5,587	298	5,885	7,194,400	3,596.9	1,173.7	3,256.5	3,139.7
1982	6,394	346	6,740	7,142,500	3,975.0	1,315.9	3,601.4	3,084.8
1983	6,909	373	7,282	6,712,800	4,173.9	1,378.6	3,781.2	2,868.9
1984	6,233	430	6,663	6,591,900	3,834.0	1,619.5	3,523.1	2,791.3
1985	6,864	423	7,287	6,926,400	4,116.4	1,505.8	3,740.0	2,901.2
1986	8,656	474	9,130	7,257,200	5,094.0	1,658.7	4,599.4	3,010.3
1987	8,396	453	8,849	7,499,900	5,030.1	1,538.8	4,506.7	3,081.3
1988	8,367	503	8,870	7,705,900	5,007.5	1,673.9	4,499.3	3,134.9
1989	8,884	605	9,489	7,872,400	5,303.4	1,972.9	4,788.0	3,171.3
1990	8,876	509	9,385	7,945,700	5,631.4	1,700.5	5,004.1	3,194.8
1991	9,020	520	9,540	8,142,200	5,603.3	1,701.1	4,980.5	3,228.8
1992	9,297	535	9,832	7,915,200	5,674.9	1,719.8	5,043.7	3,103.0
1993	9,351	560	9,911	7,820,900	5,693.7	1,796.5	5,072.0	3,032.4
1994	9,575	614	10,189	7,879,800	5,720.1	1,932.7	5,115.9	3,026.7
1995	8,883	562	9,445	7,997,700	5,283.0	1,723.8	4,705.0	3,043.8
1996	9,857	553	10,410	7,894,600	5,738.5	1,660.4	5,076.2	2,975.9

Notes: (1) Metropolitan Statistical Area - see Appendix A for areas included; (2) calculated by the editors using the following formula: (number of crimes in the MSA minus number of crimes in the city); (3) calculated by the editors using the following formula: ((number of crimes in the MSA minus number of crimes in the city) ÷ (population of the MSA minus population of the city)) x 100,000; n/a not avail.
Source: U.S. Department of Justice, FBI Uniform Crime Reports, 1977 - 1996

Motor Vehicle Thefts and Motor Vehicle Theft Rates: 1977 - 1996

Year	Number				Rate per 100,000 population			
	City	Suburbs[2]	MSA[1]	U.S.	City	Suburbs[3]	MSA[1]	U.S.
1977	474	20	494	977,700	331.5	122.1	310.0	451.9
1978	521	38	559	1,004,100	361.8	258.1	352.2	460.5
1979	437	50	487	1,112,800	291.5	393.4	299.5	505.6
1980	524	33	557	1,131,700	351.3	135.3	320.9	502.2
1981	468	30	498	1,087,800	301.3	118.2	275.6	474.7
1982	529	42	571	1,062,400	328.9	159.7	305.1	458.8
1983	545	44	589	1,007,900	329.3	162.6	305.8	430.8
1984	541	40	581	1,032,200	332.8	150.7	307.2	437.1
1985	531	59	590	1,102,900	318.4	210.0	302.8	462.0
1986	669	57	726	1,224,100	393.7	199.5	365.7	507.8
1987	511	48	559	1,288,700	306.1	163.1	284.7	529.4
1988	568	45	613	1,432,900	339.9	149.8	310.9	582.9
1989	579	42	621	1,564,800	345.6	137.0	313.3	630.4
1990	579	37	616	1,635,900	367.4	123.6	328.5	657.8
1991	488	47	535	1,661,700	303.1	153.8	279.3	659.0
1992	592	47	639	1,610,800	361.4	151.1	327.8	631.5
1993	649	62	711	1,563,100	395.2	198.9	363.9	606.1
1994	542	65	607	1,539,300	323.8	204.6	304.8	591.3
1995	611	55	666	1,472,400	363.4	168.7	331.8	560.4
1996	687	55	742	1,395,200	400.0	165.1	361.8	525.9

Notes: (1) Metropolitan Statistical Area - see Appendix A for areas included; (2) calculated by the editors using the following formula: (number of crimes in the MSA minus number of crimes in the city); (3) calculated by the editors using the following formula: ((number of crimes in the MSA minus number of crimes in the city) ÷ (population of the MSA minus population of the city)) x 100,000; n/a not avail.
Source: U.S. Department of Justice, FBI Uniform Crime Reports, 1977 - 1996

HATE CRIMES

Criminal Incidents by Bias Motivation

Area	Race	Ethnicity	Religion	Sexual Orientation
Amarillo	1	0	0	0

Notes: Figures include both violent and property crimes. Law enforcement agencies must have submitted data for at least one quarter of calendar year 1995 to be included in this report, therefore figures shown may not represent complete 12-month totals; n/a not available
Source: U.S. Department of Justice, FBI Uniform Crime Reports, Hate Crime Statistics 1995

LAW ENFORCEMENT

Full-Time Law Enforcement Employees

Jurisdiction	Police Employees			Police Officers per 100,000 population
	Total	Officers	Civilians	
Amarillo	319	244	75	142.1

Notes: Data as of October 31, 1996
Source: U.S. Department of Justice, FBI Uniform Crime Reports, 1996

CORRECTIONS

Federal Correctional Facilities

Type	Year Opened	Security Level	Sex of Inmates	Rated Capacity	Population on 7/1/95	Number of Staff
None listed						

Notes: Data as of 1995
Source: Bureau of Justice Statistics, Sourcebook of Criminal Justice Statistics Online

City/County/Regional Correctional Facilities

Name	Year Opened	Year Renov.	Rated Capacity	1995 Pop.	Number of COs[1]	Number of Staff	ACA[2] Accred.
None listed							

Notes: Data as of April 1996; (1) Correctional Officers; (2) American Correctional Assn. Accreditation
Source: American Correctional Association, 1996-1998 National Jail and Adult Detention Directory

Private Adult Correctional Facilities

Name	Date Opened	Rated Capacity	Present Pop.	Security Level	Facility Construct.	Expans. Plans	ACA[1] Accred.
None listed							

Notes: Data as of December 1996; (1) American Correctional Association Accreditation
Source: University of Florida, Center for Studies in Criminology and Law, Private Adult Correctional Facility Census, 10th Ed., March 15, 1997

Characteristics of Shock Incarceration Programs

Jurisdiction	Year Program Began	Number of Camps	Average Num. of Inmates	Number of Beds	Program Length	Voluntary/ Mandatory
Texas	1989	2	250	500 male; 20 female	75 to 90 days	Mandatory

Note: Data as of July 1996;
Source: Sourcebook of Criminal Justice Statistics Online

DEATH PENALTY

Death Penalty Statistics

State	Prisoners Executed		Prisoners Under Sentence of Death					Avg. No. of Years on Death Row[4]
	1930-1995	1996[1]	Total[2]	White[3]	Black[3]	Hisp.	Women	
Texas	401	3	404	241	158	68	6	6.5

Notes: Data as of 12/31/95 unless otherwise noted; (1) Data as of 7/31/97; (2) Includes persons of other races; (3) Includes people of Hispanic origin; (4) Covers prisoners sentenced 1974 through 1995
Source: Bureau of Justice Statistics, Capital Punishment 1995 (released 12/96); Death Penalty Information Center Web Site, 9/30/97

Capital Offenses and Methods of Execution

Capital Offenses in Texas	Minimum Age for Imposition of Death Penalty	Mentally Retarded Excluded	Methods of Execution[1]
Criminal homicide with 1 of 8 aggravating circumstances.	17	No	Lethal injection

Notes: Data as of 12/31/95 unless otherwise noted; (1) Data as of 7/31/97
Source: Bureau of Justice Statistics, Capital Punishment 1995 (released 12/96); Death Penalty Information Center Web Site, 9/30/97

LAWS

Statutory Provisions Relating to the Purchase, Ownership and Use of Handguns

Jurisdiction	Instant Background Check	Federal Waiting Period Applies[1]	State Waiting Period (days)	License or Permit to Purchase	Regis-tration	Record of Sale Sent to Police	Concealed Carry Law
Texas	No	Yes[a]	No	No	No	No	Yes[b]

Note: Data as of 1996; (1) The Federal 5-day waiting period for handgun purchases applies to states that don't have instant background checks, waiting period requirements, or licensing procedures exempting them from the Federal requirement; (a) The Federal waiting period does not apply to a person holding a valid permit or license to carry a firearm, issued within 5 years of proposed purchase; (b) "Shall issue" permit system, liberally administered discretion by local authorities over permit issuance, or no permit required
Source: Sourcebook of Criminal Justice Statistics Online

Statutory Provisions Relating to Alcohol Use and Driving

Jurisdiction	Drinking Age	Blood Alcohol Concentration Levels as Evidence in State Courts[1]		Open Container Law[1]	Anti-Consump-tion Law[1]	Dram Shop Law[1]
		Illegal per se at 0.10%	Presumption at 0.10%			
Texas	21	Yes	No	No	Yes[a]	Yes[b]

Note: Data as of January 1, 1997; (1) See Appendix C for an explanation of terms; (a) Applies to drivers only; (b) Statutory law has limited dram shop actions
Source: Sourcebook of Criminal Justice Statistics Online

Statutory Provisions Relating to Curfews

Jurisdiction	Year Enacted	Latest Revision	Age Group(s)	Curfew Provisions
Amarillo	1995	-	16 and under	Midnight to 6 am every night

Note: Data as of February 1996
Source: Sourcebook of Criminal Justice Statistics Online

Statutory Provisions Relating to Hate Crimes

Jurisdiction	Bias-Motivated Violence and Intimidation						Institutional Vandalism
		Criminal Penalty					
	Civil Action	Race/ Religion/ Ethnicity	Sexual Orientation	Mental/ Physical Disability	Gender	Age	
Texas	No	No	No	No	No	No	Yes

Source: Anti-Defamation League, 1997 Hate Crimes Laws

Ann Arbor, Michigan

OVERVIEW

The total crime rate for the city decreased 44.0% between 1977 and 1996. During that same period, the violent crime rate decreased 5.4% and the property crime rate decreased 46.1%.

Among violent crimes, the rates for: Murders increased 0.0%; Forcible Rapes increased 27.7%; Robberies decreased 26.9%; and Aggravated Assaults increased 4.1%.

Among property crimes, the rates for: Burglaries decreased 56.7%; Larceny-Thefts decreased 41.8%; and Motor Vehicle Thefts decreased 57.3%.

ANTI-CRIME PROGRAMS

Information not available at time of publication.

CRIME RISK

Your Chances of Becoming a Victim[1]

Area	Any Crime	Violent Crime					Property Crime			
		Any	Murder	Forcible Rape[2]	Robbery	Aggrav. Assault	Any	Burglary	Larceny -Theft	Motor Vehicle Theft
City	1:23	1:269	1:109,939	1:1,505	1:973	1:426	1:26	1:137	1:33	1:550

Note: (1) Figures have been calculated by dividing the population of the city by the number of crimes reported to the FBI during 1996 and are expressed as odds (eg. 1:20 should be read as 1 in 20).
(2) Figures have been calculated by dividing the female population of the city by the number of forcible rapes reported to the FBI during 1996. The female population of the city was estimated by calculating the ratio of females to males reported in the 1990 Census and applying that ratio to 1996 population estimate.
Source: FBI Uniform Crime Reports 1996

CRIME STATISTICS

Total Crimes and Total Crime Rates: 1977 - 1996

Year	Number				Rate per 100,000 population			
	City	Suburbs[2]	MSA[1]	U.S.	City	Suburbs[3]	MSA[1]	U.S.
1977	8,092	8,136	16,228	10,984,500	7,634.0	5,709.2	6,530.2	5,077.6
1978	7,446	8,047	15,493	11,209,000	7,091.4	5,260.5	6,005.7	5,140.3
1979	8,313	9,824	18,137	12,249,500	7,852.4	6,547.0	7,087.0	5,565.5
1980	8,587	10,685	19,272	13,408,300	8,574.6	6,719.4	7,436.3	5,950.0
1981	8,414	10,109	18,523	13,423,800	8,426.6	6,375.9	7,168.3	5,858.2
1982	n/a	n/a	n/a	12,974,400	n/a	n/a	n/a	5,603.6
1983	n/a	n/a	n/a	12,108,600	n/a	n/a	n/a	5,175.0
1984	9,638	8,811	18,449	11,881,800	9,230.7	5,794.5	7,193.4	5,031.3
1985	9,193	8,662	17,855	12,431,400	8,525.3	5,746.9	6,905.6	5,207.1
1986	10,619	10,675	21,294	13,211,900	9,790.6	6,867.5	8,068.9	5,480.4
1987	10,269	10,159	20,428	13,508,700	9,478.8	6,524.0	7,736.3	5,550.0
1988	9,518	9,162	18,680	13,923,100	8,674.5	5,809.4	6,984.9	5,664.2
1989	8,641	9,474	18,115	14,251,400	7,939.9	6,047.1	6,823.0	5,741.0
1990	9,212	9,794	19,006	14,475,600	8,405.7	5,753.8	6,792.5	5,820.3
1991	6,991	12,152	19,143	14,872,900	6,329.6	7,083.8	6,788.4	5,897.8
1992	6,301	16,987	23,288	14,438,200	5,663.2	4,434.4	4,711.0	5,660.2
1993	n/a	n/a	n/a	14,144,800	n/a	n/a	n/a	5,484.4
1994	5,489	n/a	n/a	13,989,500	4,968.1	n/a	n/a	5,373.5
1995	5,414	15,431	20,845	13,862,700	4,947.7	3,805.4	4,048.1	5,275.9
1996	4,696	16,744	21,440	13,473,600	4,271.5	4,109.9	4,144.3	5,078.9

Notes: (1) Metropolitan Statistical Area - see Appendix A for areas included; (2) calculated by the editors using the following formula: (number of crimes in the MSA minus number of crimes in the city); (3) calculated by the editors using the following formula: ((number of crimes in the MSA minus number of crimes in the city) ÷ (population of the MSA minus population of the city)) x 100,000; n/a not avail.
Source: U.S. Department of Justice, FBI Uniform Crime Reports, 1977 - 1996

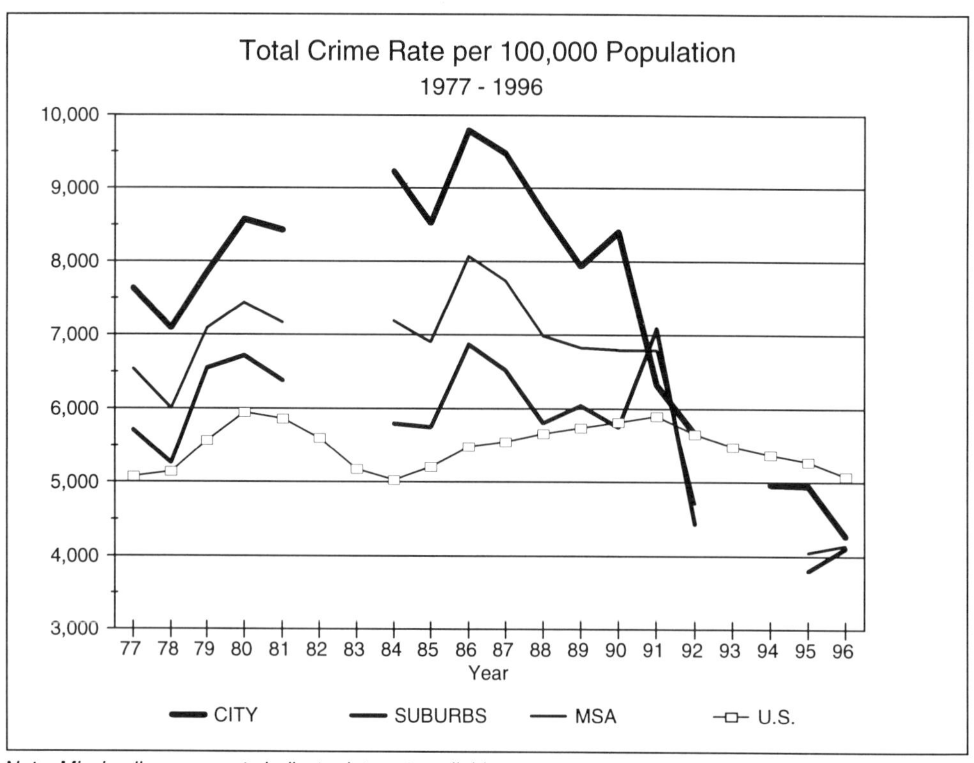

Note: Missing line segments indicate data not available.

Violent Crimes and Violent Crime Rates: 1977 - 1996

Year	Number				Rate per 100,000 population			
	City	Suburbs[2]	MSA[1]	U.S.	City	Suburbs[3]	MSA[1]	U.S.
1977	417	693	1,110	1,029,580	393.4	486.3	446.7	475.9
1978	386	739	1,125	1,085,550	367.6	483.1	436.1	497.8
1979	503	930	1,433	1,208,030	475.1	619.8	559.9	548.9
1980	478	945	1,423	1,344,520	477.3	594.3	549.1	596.6
1981	431	854	1,285	1,361,820	431.6	538.6	497.3	594.3
1982	n/a	n/a	n/a	1,322,390	n/a	n/a	n/a	571.1
1983	n/a	n/a	n/a	1,258,090	n/a	n/a	n/a	537.7
1984	586	903	1,489	1,273,280	561.2	593.9	580.6	539.2
1985	635	1,130	1,765	1,328,800	588.9	749.7	682.6	556.6
1986	749	1,448	2,197	1,489,170	690.6	931.5	832.5	617.7
1987	675	1,117	1,792	1,484,000	623.1	717.3	678.7	609.7
1988	875	1,145	2,020	1,566,220	797.5	726.0	755.3	637.2
1989	656	1,207	1,863	1,646,040	602.8	770.4	701.7	663.1
1990	580	1,210	1,790	1,820,130	529.2	710.9	639.7	731.8
1991	613	1,344	1,957	1,911,770	555.0	783.5	694.0	758.1
1992	596	1,613	2,209	1,932,270	535.7	421.1	446.9	757.5
1993	n/a	n/a	n/a	1,926,020	n/a	n/a	n/a	746.8
1994	552	n/a	n/a	1,857,670	499.6	n/a	n/a	713.6
1995	472	1,424	1,896	1,798,790	431.3	351.2	368.2	684.6
1996	409	1,471	1,880	1,682,280	372.0	361.1	363.4	634.1

Notes: Violent crimes include murder, forcible rape, robbery and aggravated assault; n/a not available; (1) Metropolitan Statistical Area - see Appendix A for areas included; (2) calculated by the editors using the following formula: (number of crimes in the MSA minus number of crimes in the city); (3) calculated by the editors using the following formula: ((number of crimes in the MSA minus number of crimes in the city) ÷ (population of the MSA minus population of the city)) x 100,000
Source: U.S. Department of Justice, FBI Uniform Crime Reports, 1977 - 1996

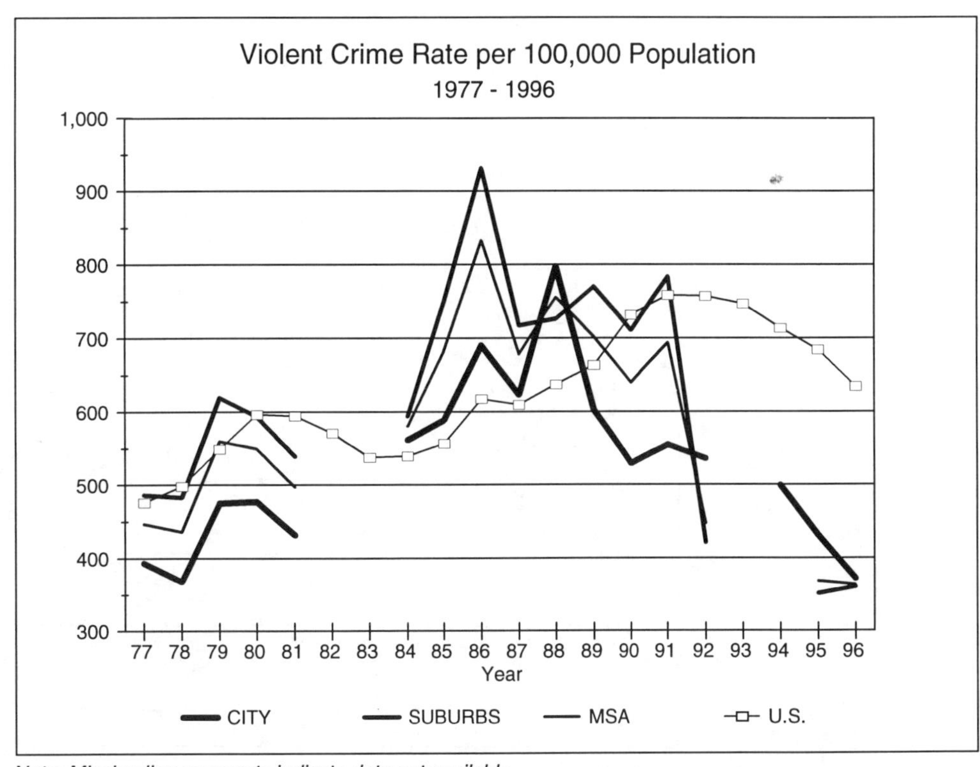

Note: Missing line segments indicate data not available.

Property Crimes and Property Crime Rates: 1977 - 1996

Year	Number				Rate per 100,000 population			
	City	Suburbs[2]	MSA[1]	U.S.	City	Suburbs[3]	MSA[1]	U.S.
1977	7,675	7,443	15,118	9,955,000	7,240.6	5,222.9	6,083.5	4,601.7
1978	7,060	7,308	14,368	10,123,400	6,723.8	4,777.4	5,569.6	4,642.5
1979	7,810	8,894	16,704	11,041,500	7,377.3	5,927.2	6,527.1	5,016.6
1980	8,109	9,740	17,849	12,063,700	8,097.3	6,125.1	6,887.2	5,353.3
1981	7,983	9,255	17,238	12,061,900	7,994.9	5,837.3	6,671.1	5,263.9
1982	n/a	n/a	n/a	11,652,000	n/a	n/a	n/a	5,032.5
1983	n/a	n/a	n/a	10,850,500	n/a	n/a	n/a	4,637.4
1984	9,052	7,908	16,960	10,608,500	8,669.4	5,200.6	6,612.8	4,492.1
1985	8,558	7,532	16,090	11,102,600	7,936.4	4,997.1	6,223.0	4,650.5
1986	9,870	9,227	19,097	11,722,700	9,100.0	5,936.0	7,236.4	4,862.6
1987	9,594	9,042	18,636	12,024,700	8,855.8	5,806.7	7,057.7	4,940.3
1988	8,643	8,017	16,660	12,356,900	7,877.0	5,083.3	6,229.6	5,027.1
1989	7,985	8,267	16,252	12,605,400	7,337.1	5,276.7	6,121.3	5,077.9
1990	8,632	8,584	17,216	12,655,500	7,876.5	5,042.9	6,152.7	5,088.5
1991	6,378	10,808	17,186	12,961,100	5,774.6	6,300.3	6,094.4	5,139.7
1992	5,705	15,374	21,079	12,505,900	5,127.5	4,013.4	4,264.1	4,902.7
1993	5,393	14,377	19,770	12,218,800	4,890.4	3,652.5	3,923.4	4,737.6
1994	4,937	n/a	n/a	12,131,900	4,468.4	n/a	n/a	4,660.0
1995	4,942	14,007	18,949	12,063,900	4,516.4	3,454.2	3,679.9	4,591.3
1996	4,287	15,273	19,560	11,791,300	3,899.4	3,748.9	3,780.9	4,444.8

Notes: Property crimes include burglary, larceny-theft and motor vehicle theft; n/a not available; (1) Metropolitan Statistical Area - see Appendix A for areas included; (2) calculated by the editors using the following formula: (number of crimes in the MSA minus number of crimes in the city); (3) calculated by the editors using the following formula: ((number of crimes in the MSA minus number of crimes in the city) ÷ (population of the MSA minus population of the city)) x 100,000
Source: U.S. Department of Justice, FBI Uniform Crime Reports, 1977 - 1996

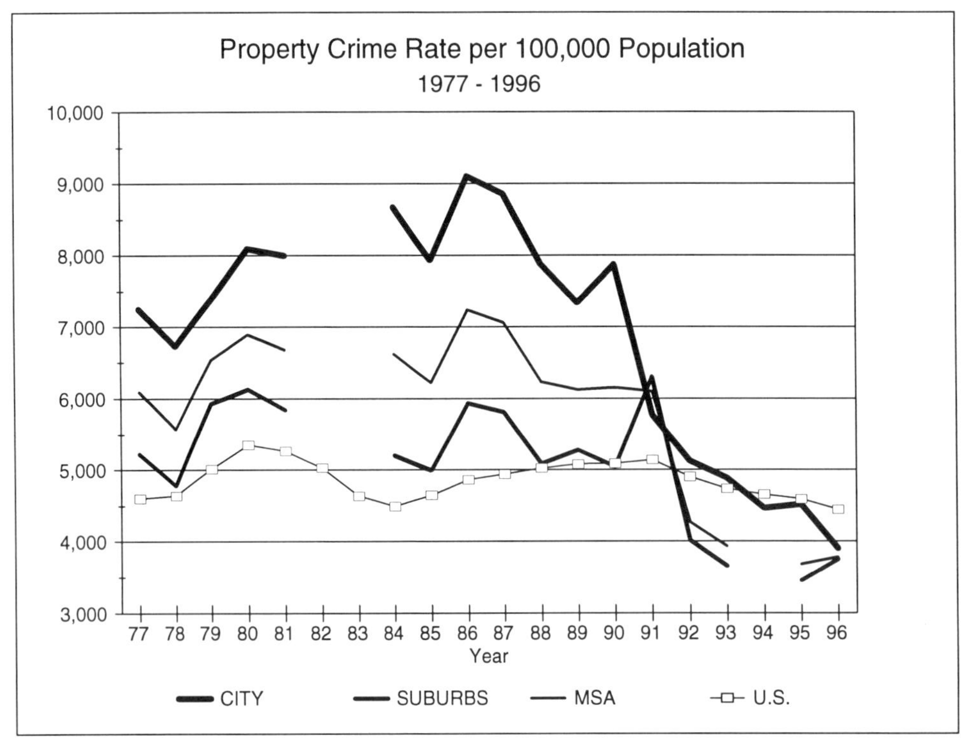

Note: Missing line segments indicate data not available.

Murders and Murder Rates: 1977 - 1996

Year	Number				Rate per 100,000 population			
	City	Suburbs[2]	MSA[1]	U.S.	City	Suburbs[3]	MSA[1]	U.S.
1977	1	7	8	19,120	0.9	4.9	3.2	8.8
1978	5	15	20	19,560	4.8	9.8	7.8	9.0
1979	1	7	8	21,460	0.9	4.7	3.1	9.7
1980	4	9	13	23,040	4.0	5.7	5.0	10.2
1981	3	13	16	22,520	3.0	8.2	6.2	9.8
1982	n/a	n/a	n/a	21,010	n/a	n/a	n/a	9.1
1983	n/a	n/a	n/a	19,310	n/a	n/a	n/a	8.3
1984	1	20	21	18,690	1.0	13.2	8.2	7.9
1985	4	11	15	18,980	3.7	7.3	5.8	7.9
1986	3	11	14	20,610	2.8	7.1	5.3	8.6
1987	4	17	21	20,100	3.7	10.9	8.0	8.3
1988	0	11	11	20,680	0.0	7.0	4.1	8.4
1989	3	4	7	21,500	2.8	2.6	2.6	8.7
1990	1	7	8	23,440	0.9	4.1	2.9	9.4
1991	2	8	10	24,700	1.8	4.7	3.5	9.8
1992	1	10	11	23,760	0.9	2.6	2.2	9.3
1993	2	14	16	24,530	1.8	3.6	3.2	9.5
1994	4	n/a	n/a	23,330	3.6	n/a	n/a	9.0
1995	3	11	14	21,610	2.7	2.7	2.7	8.2
1996	1	9	10	19,650	0.9	2.2	1.9	7.4

Notes: (1) Metropolitan Statistical Area - see Appendix A for areas included; (2) calculated by the editors using the following formula: (number of crimes in the MSA minus number of crimes in the city); (3) calculated by the editors using the following formula: ((number of crimes in the MSA minus number of crimes in the city) ÷ (population of the MSA minus population of the city)) x 100,000; n/a not avail.
Source: U.S. Department of Justice, FBI Uniform Crime Reports, 1977 - 1996

Forcible Rapes and Forcible Rape Rates: 1977 - 1996

Year	Number				Rate per 100,000 population			
	City	Suburbs[2]	MSA[1]	U.S.	City	Suburbs[3]	MSA[1]	U.S.
1977	28	76	104	63,500	26.4	53.3	41.8	29.4
1978	31	70	101	67,610	29.5	45.8	39.2	31.0
1979	22	88	110	76,390	20.8	58.6	43.0	34.7
1980	29	84	113	82,990	29.0	52.8	43.6	36.8
1981	42	99	141	82,500	42.1	62.4	54.6	36.0
1982	n/a	n/a	n/a	78,770	n/a	n/a	n/a	34.0
1983	n/a	n/a	n/a	78,920	n/a	n/a	n/a	33.7
1984	51	123	174	84,230	48.8	80.9	67.8	35.7
1985	37	157	194	88,670	34.3	104.2	75.0	37.1
1986	44	185	229	91,460	40.6	119.0	86.8	37.9
1987	59	115	174	91,110	54.5	73.9	65.9	37.4
1988	66	161	227	92,490	60.2	102.1	84.9	37.6
1989	54	169	223	94,500	49.6	107.9	84.0	38.1
1990	63	195	258	102,560	57.5	114.6	92.2	41.2
1991	50	204	254	106,590	45.3	118.9	90.1	42.3
1992	50	276	326	109,060	44.9	72.0	65.9	42.8
1993	n/a	n/a	n/a	106,010	n/a	n/a	n/a	41.1
1994	42	n/a	n/a	102,220	38.0	n/a	n/a	39.3
1995	43	180	223	97,470	39.3	44.4	43.3	37.1
1996	37	214	251	95,770	33.7	52.5	48.5	36.1

Notes: (1) Metropolitan Statistical Area - see Appendix A for areas included; (2) calculated by the editors using the following formula: (number of crimes in the MSA minus number of crimes in the city); (3) calculated by the editors using the following formula: ((number of crimes in the MSA minus number of crimes in the city) ÷ (population of the MSA minus population of the city)) x 100,000; n/a not avail.
Source: U.S. Department of Justice, FBI Uniform Crime Reports, 1977 - 1996

Robberies and Robbery Rates: 1977 - 1996

Year	Number				Rate per 100,000 population			
	City	Suburbs[2]	MSA[1]	U.S.	City	Suburbs[3]	MSA[1]	U.S.
1977	149	171	320	412,610	140.6	120.0	128.8	190.7
1978	116	184	300	426,930	110.5	120.3	116.3	195.8
1979	150	240	390	480,700	141.7	159.9	152.4	218.4
1980	112	216	328	565,840	111.8	135.8	126.6	251.1
1981	96	161	257	592,910	96.1	101.5	99.5	258.7
1982	n/a	n/a	n/a	553,130	n/a	n/a	n/a	238.9
1983	n/a	n/a	n/a	506,570	n/a	n/a	n/a	216.5
1984	96	189	285	485,010	91.9	124.3	111.1	205.4
1985	143	233	376	497,870	132.6	154.6	145.4	208.5
1986	217	337	554	542,780	200.1	216.8	209.9	225.1
1987	180	270	450	517,700	166.1	173.4	170.4	212.7
1988	213	303	516	542,970	194.1	192.1	192.9	220.9
1989	152	268	420	578,330	139.7	171.1	158.2	233.0
1990	125	249	374	639,270	114.1	146.3	133.7	257.0
1991	148	241	389	687,730	134.0	140.5	137.9	272.7
1992	161	283	444	672,480	144.7	73.9	89.8	263.6
1993	129	307	436	659,870	117.0	78.0	86.5	255.9
1994	153	n/a	n/a	618,950	138.5	n/a	n/a	237.7
1995	132	270	402	580,510	120.6	66.6	78.1	220.9
1996	113	318	431	537,050	102.8	78.1	83.3	202.4

Notes: (1) Metropolitan Statistical Area - see Appendix A for areas included; (2) calculated by the editors using the following formula: (number of crimes in the MSA minus number of crimes in the city); (3) calculated by the editors using the following formula: ((number of crimes in the MSA minus number of crimes in the city) ÷ (population of the MSA minus population of the city)) x 100,000; n/a not avail.
Source: U.S. Department of Justice, FBI Uniform Crime Reports, 1977 - 1996

Aggravated Assaults and Aggravated Assault Rates: 1977 - 1996

Year	Number				Rate per 100,000 population			
	City	Suburbs[2]	MSA[1]	U.S.	City	Suburbs[3]	MSA[1]	U.S.
1977	239	439	678	534,350	225.5	308.1	272.8	247.0
1978	234	470	704	571,460	222.9	307.2	272.9	262.1
1979	330	595	925	629,480	311.7	396.5	361.4	286.0
1980	333	636	969	672,650	332.5	400.0	373.9	298.5
1981	290	581	871	663,900	290.4	366.4	337.1	289.7
1982	n/a	n/a	n/a	669,480	n/a	n/a	n/a	289.2
1983	n/a	n/a	n/a	653,290	n/a	n/a	n/a	279.2
1984	438	571	1,009	685,350	419.5	375.5	393.4	290.2
1985	451	729	1,180	723,250	418.2	483.7	456.4	302.9
1986	485	915	1,400	834,320	447.2	588.6	530.5	346.1
1987	432	715	1,147	855,090	398.8	459.2	434.4	351.3
1988	596	670	1,266	910,090	543.2	424.8	473.4	370.2
1989	447	766	1,213	951,710	410.7	488.9	456.9	383.4
1990	391	759	1,150	1,054,860	356.8	445.9	411.0	424.1
1991	413	891	1,304	1,092,740	373.9	519.4	462.4	433.3
1992	384	1,044	1,428	1,126,970	345.1	272.5	288.9	441.8
1993	336	1,124	1,460	1,135,610	304.7	285.6	289.7	440.3
1994	353	n/a	n/a	1,113,180	319.5	n/a	n/a	427.6
1995	294	963	1,257	1,099,210	268.7	237.5	244.1	418.3
1996	258	930	1,188	1,029,810	234.7	228.3	229.6	388.2

Notes: (1) Metropolitan Statistical Area - see Appendix A for areas included; (2) calculated by the editors using the following formula: (number of crimes in the MSA minus number of crimes in the city); (3) calculated by the editors using the following formula: ((number of crimes in the MSA minus number of crimes in the city) ÷ (population of the MSA minus population of the city)) x 100,000; n/a not avail.
Source: U.S. Department of Justice, FBI Uniform Crime Reports, 1977 - 1996

Burglaries and Burglary Rates: 1977 - 1996

Year	Number				Rate per 100,000 population			
	City	Suburbs[2]	MSA[1]	U.S.	City	Suburbs[3]	MSA[1]	U.S.
1977	1,789	1,805	3,594	3,071,500	1,687.7	1,266.6	1,446.2	1,419.8
1978	1,683	1,821	3,504	3,128,300	1,602.9	1,190.4	1,358.3	1,434.6
1979	1,892	2,004	3,896	3,327,700	1,787.2	1,335.5	1,522.4	1,511.9
1980	1,882	2,490	4,372	3,795,200	1,879.3	1,565.9	1,687.0	1,684.1
1981	1,922	2,238	4,160	3,779,700	1,924.9	1,411.6	1,609.9	1,649.5
1982	n/a	n/a	n/a	3,447,100	n/a	n/a	n/a	1,488.8
1983	n/a	n/a	n/a	3,129,900	n/a	n/a	n/a	1,337.7
1984	1,990	2,061	4,051	2,984,400	1,905.9	1,355.4	1,579.5	1,263.7
1985	1,562	1,943	3,505	3,073,300	1,448.5	1,289.1	1,355.6	1,287.3
1986	1,753	2,078	3,831	3,241,400	1,616.2	1,336.8	1,451.7	1,344.6
1987	1,718	2,019	3,737	3,236,200	1,585.8	1,296.6	1,415.2	1,329.6
1988	1,671	1,602	3,273	3,218,100	1,522.9	1,015.8	1,223.8	1,309.2
1989	1,503	1,569	3,072	3,168,200	1,381.1	1,001.5	1,157.1	1,276.3
1990	1,453	1,627	3,080	3,073,900	1,325.8	955.8	1,100.7	1,235.9
1991	1,251	1,908	3,159	3,157,200	1,132.6	1,112.2	1,120.2	1,252.0
1992	1,164	3,058	4,222	2,979,900	1,046.2	798.3	854.1	1,168.2
1993	1,101	2,911	4,012	2,834,800	998.4	739.5	796.2	1,099.2
1994	943	n/a	n/a	2,712,800	853.5	n/a	n/a	1,042.0
1995	1,083	2,878	3,961	2,593,800	989.7	709.7	769.2	987.1
1996	804	2,892	3,696	2,501,500	731.3	709.9	714.4	943.0

Notes: (1) Metropolitan Statistical Area - see Appendix A for areas included; (2) calculated by the editors using the following formula: (number of crimes in the MSA minus number of crimes in the city); (3) calculated by the editors using the following formula: ((number of crimes in the MSA minus number of crimes in the city) ÷ (population of the MSA minus population of the city)) x 100,000; n/a not avail.
Source: U.S. Department of Justice, FBI Uniform Crime Reports, 1977 - 1996

Larceny-Thefts and Larceny-Theft Rates: 1977 - 1996

Year	Number				Rate per 100,000 population			
	City	Suburbs[2]	MSA[1]	U.S.	City	Suburbs[3]	MSA[1]	U.S.
1977	5,435	4,930	10,365	5,905,700	5,127.4	3,459.5	4,170.9	2,729.9
1978	4,897	4,693	9,590	5,991,000	4,663.8	3,067.9	3,717.5	2,747.4
1979	5,516	5,812	11,328	6,601,000	5,210.4	3,873.3	4,426.4	2,999.1
1980	5,908	6,311	12,219	7,136,900	5,899.4	3,968.8	4,714.8	3,167.0
1981	5,721	6,164	11,885	7,194,400	5,729.5	3,887.8	4,599.5	3,139.7
1982	n/a	n/a	n/a	7,142,500	n/a	n/a	n/a	3,084.8
1983	n/a	n/a	n/a	6,712,800	n/a	n/a	n/a	2,868.9
1984	6,646	5,145	11,791	6,591,900	6,365.1	3,383.6	4,597.4	2,791.3
1985	6,497	4,893	11,390	6,926,400	6,025.1	3,246.3	4,405.2	2,901.2
1986	7,534	6,276	13,810	7,257,200	6,946.3	4,037.5	5,233.0	3,010.3
1987	7,378	6,197	13,575	7,499,900	6,810.3	3,979.7	5,141.0	3,081.3
1988	6,523	5,619	12,142	7,705,900	5,944.9	3,562.8	4,540.2	3,134.9
1989	6,066	5,929	11,995	7,872,400	5,573.8	3,784.4	4,517.9	3,171.3
1990	6,811	6,170	12,981	7,945,700	6,214.9	3,624.8	4,639.2	3,194.8
1991	4,725	8,110	12,835	8,142,200	4,278.0	4,727.6	4,551.5	3,228.8
1992	4,256	11,413	15,669	7,915,200	3,825.2	2,979.4	3,169.7	3,103.0
1993	4,032	10,525	14,557	7,820,900	3,656.2	2,673.9	2,888.9	3,032.4
1994	3,786	n/a	n/a	7,879,800	3,426.7	n/a	n/a	3,026.7
1995	3,644	9,918	13,562	7,997,700	3,330.2	2,445.8	2,633.8	3,043.8
1996	3,283	10,962	14,245	7,894,600	2,986.2	2,690.7	2,753.5	2,975.9

Notes: (1) Metropolitan Statistical Area - see Appendix A for areas included; (2) calculated by the editors using the following formula: (number of crimes in the MSA minus number of crimes in the city); (3) calculated by the editors using the following formula: ((number of crimes in the MSA minus number of crimes in the city) ÷ (population of the MSA minus population of the city)) x 100,000; n/a not avail.
Source: U.S. Department of Justice, FBI Uniform Crime Reports, 1977 - 1996

Motor Vehicle Thefts and Motor Vehicle Theft Rates: 1977 - 1996

Year	Number				Rate per 100,000 population			
	City	Suburbs[2]	MSA[1]	U.S.	City	Suburbs[3]	MSA[1]	U.S.
1977	451	708	1,159	977,700	425.5	496.8	466.4	451.9
1978	480	794	1,274	1,004,100	457.1	519.1	493.9	460.5
1979	402	1,078	1,480	1,112,800	379.7	718.4	578.3	505.6
1980	319	939	1,258	1,131,700	318.5	590.5	485.4	502.2
1981	340	853	1,193	1,087,800	340.5	538.0	461.7	474.7
1982	n/a	n/a	n/a	1,062,400	n/a	n/a	n/a	458.8
1983	n/a	n/a	n/a	1,007,900	n/a	n/a	n/a	430.8
1984	416	702	1,118	1,032,200	398.4	461.7	435.9	437.1
1985	499	696	1,195	1,102,900	462.8	461.8	462.2	462.0
1986	583	873	1,456	1,224,100	537.5	561.6	551.7	507.8
1987	498	826	1,324	1,288,700	459.7	530.4	501.4	529.4
1988	449	796	1,245	1,432,900	409.2	504.7	465.5	582.9
1989	416	769	1,185	1,564,800	382.2	490.8	446.3	630.4
1990	368	787	1,155	1,635,900	335.8	462.3	412.8	657.8
1991	402	790	1,192	1,661,700	364.0	460.5	422.7	659.0
1992	285	903	1,188	1,610,800	256.1	235.7	240.3	631.5
1993	260	941	1,201	1,563,100	235.8	239.1	238.3	606.1
1994	208	n/a	n/a	1,539,300	188.3	n/a	n/a	591.3
1995	215	1,211	1,426	1,472,400	196.5	298.6	276.9	560.4
1996	200	1,419	1,619	1,395,200	181.9	348.3	312.9	525.9

Notes: (1) Metropolitan Statistical Area - see Appendix A for areas included; (2) calculated by the editors using the following formula: (number of crimes in the MSA minus number of crimes in the city); (3) calculated by the editors using the following formula: ((number of crimes in the MSA minus number of crimes in the city) ÷ (population of the MSA minus population of the city)) x 100,000; n/a not avail.
Source: U.S. Department of Justice, FBI Uniform Crime Reports, 1977 - 1996

HATE CRIMES

Criminal Incidents by Bias Motivation

Area	Race	Ethnicity	Religion	Sexual Orientation
Ann Arbor	5	1	1	0

Notes: Figures include both violent and property crimes. Law enforcement agencies must have submitted data for at least one quarter of calendar year 1995 to be included in this report, therefore figures shown may not represent complete 12-month totals; n/a not available
Source: U.S. Department of Justice, FBI Uniform Crime Reports, Hate Crime Statistics 1995

LAW ENFORCEMENT

Full-Time Law Enforcement Employees

Jurisdiction	Police Employees			Police Officers per 100,000 population
	Total	Officers	Civilians	
Ann Arbor	239	181	58	164.6

Notes: Data as of October 31, 1996
Source: U.S. Department of Justice, FBI Uniform Crime Reports, 1996

CORRECTIONS

Federal Correctional Facilities

Type	Year Opened	Security Level	Sex of Inmates	Rated Capacity	Population on 7/1/95	Number of Staff
None listed						

Notes: Data as of 1995
Source: Bureau of Justice Statistics, Sourcebook of Criminal Justice Statistics Online

City/County/Regional Correctional Facilities

Name	Year Opened	Year Renov.	Rated Capacity	1995 Pop.	Number of COs[1]	Number of Staff	ACA[2] Accred.
Washtenaw Co Jail	1978	--	281	n/a	n/a	n/a	No

Notes: Data as of April 1996; (1) Correctional Officers; (2) American Correctional Assn. Accreditation
Source: American Correctional Association, 1996-1998 National Jail and Adult Detention Directory

Private Adult Correctional Facilities

Name	Date Opened	Rated Capacity	Present Pop.	Security Level	Facility Construct.	Expans. Plans	ACA[1] Accred.
None listed							

Notes: Data as of December 1996; (1) American Correctional Association Accreditation
Source: University of Florida, Center for Studies in Criminology and Law, Private Adult Correctional Facility Census, 10th Ed., March 15, 1997

Characteristics of Shock Incarceration Programs

Jurisdiction	Year Program Began	Number of Camps	Average Num. of Inmates	Number of Beds	Program Length	Voluntary/ Mandatory
Michigan	1988	1	319	360	90 days	Voluntary

Note: Data as of July 1996;
Source: Sourcebook of Criminal Justice Statistics Online

DEATH PENALTY

Michigan did not have the death penalty as of July 31, 1997.
Source: Death Penalty Information Center Web Site, 9/30/97

LAWS

Statutory Provisions Relating to the Purchase, Ownership and Use of Handguns

Jurisdiction	Instant Background Check	Federal Waiting Period Applies[1]	State Waiting Period (days)	License or Permit to Purchase	Regis- tration	Record of Sale Sent to Police	Concealed Carry Law
Michigan	No	No	No	Yes[a]	Yes	Yes	Yes[b]

Note: Data as of 1996; (1) The Federal 5-day waiting period for handgun purchases applies to states that don't have instant background checks, waiting period requirements, or licensing procedures exempting them from the Federal requirement; (a) A handgun purchaser must obtain a license to purchase from local law enforcement, and within 10 days present to such official the license and handgun purchased to obtain a certificate of inspection; (b) Restrictively administered discretion by local authorities over permit issuance, or permits are unavailable and carrying is prohibited in most circumstances
Source: Sourcebook of Criminal Justice Statistics Online

Statutory Provisions Relating to Alcohol Use and Driving

Jurisdiction	Drinking Age	Blood Alcohol Concentration Levels as Evidence in State Courts[1]		Open Container Law[1]	Anti- Consump- tion Law[1]	Dram Shop Law[1]
		Illegal per se at 0.10%	Presumption at 0.10%			
Michigan	21	Yes	(a)	Yes	Yes	Yes

Note: Data as of January 1, 1997; (1) See Appendix C for an explanation of terms; (a) Presumption of driving while impaired at 0.07%; presumption of driving under the influence at 0.10%
Source: Sourcebook of Criminal Justice Statistics Online

Statutory Provisions Relating to Hate Crimes

Jurisdiction	Bias-Motivated Violence and Intimidation						Institutional Vandalism
	Civil Action	Criminal Penalty					
		Race/ Religion/ Ethnicity	Sexual Orientation	Mental/ Physical Disability	Gender	Age	
Michigan	Yes	Yes	No	No	Yes	No	No

Source: Anti-Defamation League, 1997 Hate Crimes Laws

Atlanta, Georgia

OVERVIEW

The total crime rate for the city increased 56.1% between 1977 and 1996. During that same period, the violent crime rate increased 82.1% and the property crime rate increased 50.9%.

Among violent crimes, the rates for: Murders increased 43.2%; Forcible Rapes decreased 22.4%; Robberies increased 44.6%; and Aggravated Assaults increased 133.3%.

Among property crimes, the rates for: Burglaries decreased 14.0%; Larceny-Thefts increased 66.1%; and Motor Vehicle Thefts increased 195.6%.

ANTI-CRIME PROGRAMS

Programs include:

- COMNET—provides a communication link which allows private sector security direct contact with police services through Atlanta's Emergency Communications Center.
- C.O.P.S.M.O.R.E. (The Community Oriented Policing Services/Making Officer Redeployment Effective)—police officers are provided with portable microcomputers in their patrol cars. The microcomputers give the officers quicker access to information on suspects, crime patterns, and community resources.
- Auto Safety Awareness Campaign—fliers are placed on cars to warn the driver that he or she has left valuables in the car, failed to lock the door, etc.
- The Georgia Unified Firearm Injury Notification System—affectionately called "Cops & Docs" links hospital emergency rooms' knowledge of gunshot injuries with police reports of incidents. It is helpful in the search for wounded fugitives, to identify fun assaults and to monitor rates of firearm violence.
- Operation Jail & Tell—enhances uniformed visibility and vigorous undercover operations and uses every legal means to curb drug and vice activity through a method of public embarrassment. Perpetrators' names are broadcast via the City Cable Channel.
- Youth Crime Gun Interdiction Project—tracks the use and possession of firearms by persons under age 18 in an effort to reduce the illegal supply of firearms to young people.
- Neighborhood Watch/Business Watch—residents of a neighborhood receive crime prevention information from the police and report suspicious activity to the police.
- Truancy and Curfew Enforcement—focuses on truancy and curfew violations in an effort to prevent school children who run the risk of becoming crime victims or perpetrators.
  Atlanta Police Department, 6/97

CRIME RISK

Your Chances of Becoming a Victim[1]

Area	Any Crime	Violent Crime						Property Crime			
		Any	Murder	Forcible Rape[2]	Robbery	Aggrav. Assault	Any	Burglary	Larceny -Theft	Motor Vehicle Theft
City	1:6	1:30	1:2,108	1:552	1:86	1:50	1:7	1:39	1:11	1:45

Note: (1) Figures have been calculated by dividing the population of the city by the number of crimes reported to the FBI during 1996 and are expressed as odds (eg. 1:20 should be read as 1 in 20). (2) Figures have been calculated by dividing the female population of the city by the number of forcible rapes reported to the FBI during 1996. The female population of the city was estimated by calculating the ratio of females to males reported in the 1990 Census and applying that ratio to 1996 population estimate.
Source: FBI Uniform Crime Reports 1996

CRIME STATISTICS

Total Crimes and Total Crime Rates: 1977 - 1996

Year	Number				Rate per 100,000 population			
	City	Suburbs[2]	MSA[1]	U.S.	City	Suburbs[3]	MSA[1]	U.S.
1977	45,597	60,885	106,482	10,984,500	10,934.5	4,171.1	5,673.9	5,077.6
1978	53,870	74,919	128,789	11,209,000	13,301.2	5,142.6	6,917.3	5,140.3
1979	58,724	86,935	145,659	12,249,500	13,879.4	6,030.5	7,811.4	5,565.5
1980	59,394	92,938	152,332	13,408,300	14,058.6	5,850.9	7,575.2	5,950.0
1981	60,569	97,327	157,896	13,423,800	13,903.9	5,942.2	7,614.8	5,858.2
1982	56,964	88,878	145,842	12,974,400	12,914.0	5,359.0	6,946.2	5,603.6
1983	48,413	84,994	133,407	12,108,600	10,791.2	4,721.1	5,932.0	5,175.0
1984	48,632	88,112	136,744	11,881,800	10,979.1	4,691.6	5,891.5	5,031.3
1985	57,505	107,817	165,322	12,431,400	13,182.7	5,389.6	6,784.7	5,207.1
1986	63,068	122,261	185,329	13,211,900	14,153.0	5,983.3	7,446.0	5,480.4
1987	66,891	138,456	205,347	13,508,700	15,557.7	6,352.7	7,869.4	5,550.0
1988	78,087	153,984	232,071	13,923,100	17,547.8	6,730.2	8,491.6	5,664.2
1989	88,241	175,295	263,536	14,251,400	20,690.4	7,455.6	9,487.7	5,741.0
1990	75,793	169,442	245,235	14,475,600	19,236.0	6,945.0	8,653.9	5,820.3
1991	76,398	164,576	240,974	14,872,900	18,953.3	6,598.2	8,317.0	5,897.8
1992	71,275	174,695	245,970	14,438,200	17,347.1	6,493.9	7,931.9	5,660.2
1993	69,914	175,051	244,965	14,144,800	17,353.7	6,201.6	7,594.5	5,484.4
1994	66,280	173,770	240,050	13,989,500	16,118.5	6,070.9	7,333.0	5,373.5
1995	69,011	176,625	245,636	13,862,700	17,067.7	5,896.2	7,224.7	5,275.9
1996	70,521	195,001	265,522	13,473,600	17,070.2	6,375.1	7,647.7	5,078.9

Notes: (1) Metropolitan Statistical Area - see Appendix A for areas included; (2) calculated by the editors using the following formula: (number of crimes in the MSA minus number of crimes in the city); (3) calculated by the editors using the following formula: ((number of crimes in the MSA minus number of crimes in the city) ÷ (population of the MSA minus population of the city)) x 100,000; n/a not avail.
Source: U.S. Department of Justice, FBI Uniform Crime Reports, 1977 - 1996

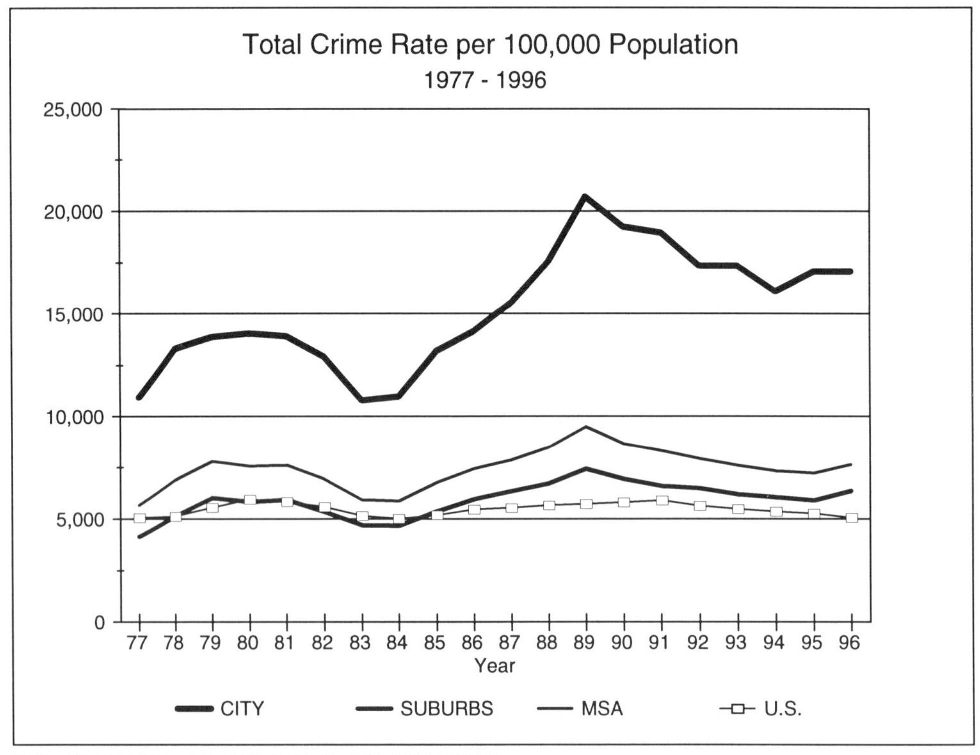

Note: Missing line segments indicate data not available.

Violent Crimes and Violent Crime Rates: 1977 - 1996

Year	Number				Rate per 100,000 population			
	City	Suburbs[2]	MSA[1]	U.S.	City	Suburbs[3]	MSA[1]	U.S.
1977	7,595	3,489	11,084	1,029,580	1,821.3	239.0	590.6	475.9
1978	8,845	4,563	13,408	1,085,550	2,184.0	313.2	720.1	497.8
1979	10,715	5,671	16,386	1,208,030	2,532.5	393.4	878.8	548.9
1980	11,075	5,870	16,945	1,344,520	2,621.5	369.5	842.6	596.6
1981	10,579	5,964	16,543	1,361,820	2,428.5	364.1	797.8	594.3
1982	10,486	4,618	15,104	1,322,390	2,377.2	278.4	719.4	571.1
1983	9,326	5,509	14,835	1,258,090	2,078.7	306.0	659.6	537.7
1984	10,525	5,502	16,027	1,273,280	2,376.1	293.0	690.5	539.2
1985	11,610	6,486	18,096	1,328,800	2,661.5	324.2	742.6	556.6
1986	13,162	8,260	21,422	1,489,170	2,953.7	404.2	860.7	617.7
1987	12,893	8,421	21,314	1,484,000	2,998.7	386.4	816.8	609.7
1988	15,911	10,312	26,223	1,566,220	3,575.5	450.7	959.5	637.2
1989	16,852	11,873	28,725	1,646,040	3,951.4	505.0	1,034.1	663.1
1990	16,097	12,811	28,908	1,820,130	4,085.4	525.1	1,020.1	731.8
1991	16,289	12,334	28,623	1,911,770	4,041.1	494.5	987.9	758.1
1992	15,856	13,301	29,157	1,932,270	3,859.1	494.4	940.2	757.5
1993	16,281	13,519	29,800	1,926,020	4,041.2	478.9	923.9	746.8
1994	14,684	13,031	27,715	1,857,670	3,571.0	455.3	846.6	713.6
1995	14,744	12,725	27,469	1,798,790	3,646.5	424.8	807.9	684.6
1996	13,699	13,427	27,126	1,682,280	3,316.0	439.0	781.3	634.1

Notes: Violent crimes include murder, forcible rape, robbery and aggravated assault; n/a not available; (1) Metropolitan Statistical Area - see Appendix A for areas included; (2) calculated by the editors using the following formula: (number of crimes in the MSA minus number of crimes in the city); (3) calculated by the editors using the following formula: ((number of crimes in the MSA minus number of crimes in the city) ÷ (population of the MSA minus population of the city)) x 100,000
Source: U.S. Department of Justice, FBI Uniform Crime Reports, 1977 - 1996

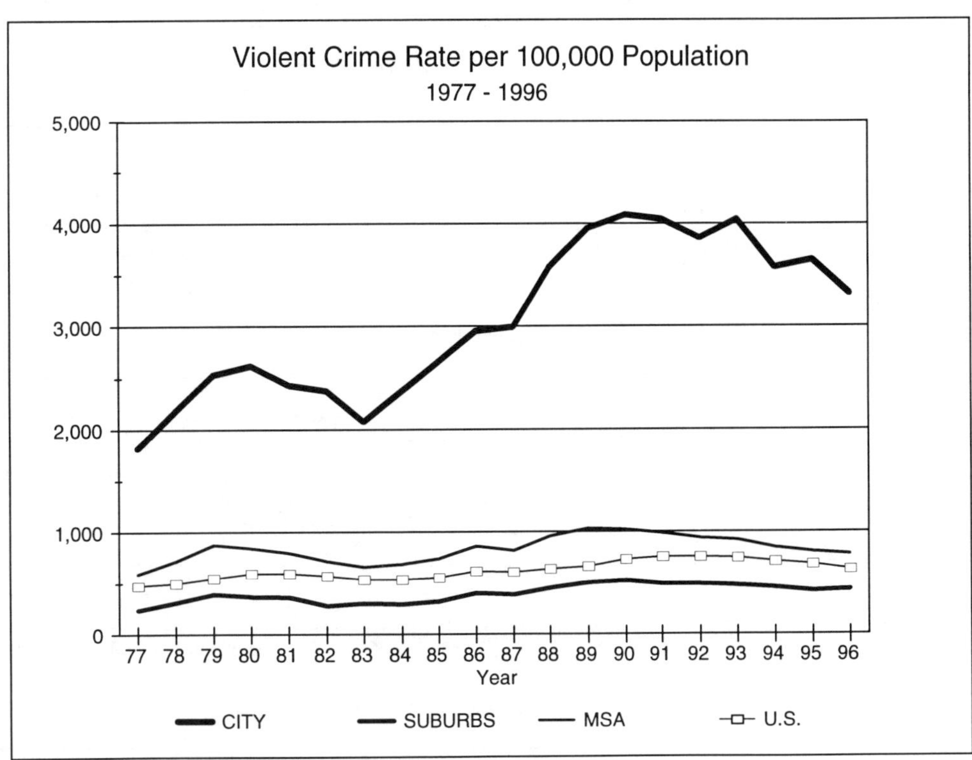

Note: Missing line segments indicate data not available.

Property Crimes and Property Crime Rates: 1977 - 1996

Year	Number				Rate per 100,000 population			
	City	Suburbs[2]	MSA[1]	U.S.	City	Suburbs[3]	MSA[1]	U.S.
1977	38,002	57,396	95,398	9,955,000	9,113.2	3,932.0	5,083.3	4,601.7
1978	45,025	70,356	115,381	10,123,400	11,117.3	4,829.4	6,197.1	4,642.5
1979	48,009	81,264	129,273	11,041,500	11,346.9	5,637.1	6,932.7	5,016.6
1980	48,319	87,068	135,387	12,063,700	11,437.2	5,481.3	6,732.6	5,353.3
1981	49,990	91,363	141,353	12,061,900	11,475.4	5,578.0	6,817.0	5,263.9
1982	46,478	84,260	130,738	11,652,000	10,536.8	5,080.5	6,226.8	5,032.5
1983	39,087	79,485	118,572	10,850,500	8,712.4	4,415.1	5,272.4	4,637.4
1984	38,107	82,610	120,717	10,608,500	8,603.0	4,398.7	5,201.0	4,492.1
1985	45,895	101,331	147,226	11,102,600	10,521.2	5,065.3	6,042.0	4,650.5
1986	49,906	114,001	163,907	11,722,700	11,199.3	5,579.1	6,585.3	4,862.6
1987	53,998	130,035	184,033	12,024,700	12,559.0	5,966.4	7,052.6	4,940.3
1988	62,176	143,672	205,848	12,356,900	13,972.3	6,279.5	7,532.1	5,027.1
1989	71,389	163,422	234,811	12,605,400	16,739.0	6,950.6	8,453.5	5,077.9
1990	59,696	156,631	216,327	12,655,500	15,150.6	6,419.9	7,633.8	5,088.5
1991	60,109	152,242	212,351	12,961,100	14,912.2	6,103.7	7,329.1	5,139.7
1992	55,419	161,394	216,813	12,505,900	13,488.0	5,999.5	6,991.7	4,902.7
1993	53,633	161,532	215,165	12,218,800	13,312.5	5,722.7	6,670.6	4,737.6
1994	51,596	160,739	212,335	12,131,900	12,547.5	5,615.6	6,486.4	4,660.0
1995	54,267	163,900	218,167	12,063,900	13,421.2	5,471.4	6,416.8	4,591.3
1996	56,822	181,574	238,396	11,791,300	13,754.3	5,936.2	6,866.4	4,444.8

Notes: Property crimes include burglary, larceny-theft and motor vehicle theft; n/a not available; (1) Metropolitan Statistical Area - see Appendix A for areas included; (2) calculated by the editors using the following formula: (number of crimes in the MSA minus number of crimes in the city); (3) calculated by the editors using the following formula: ((number of crimes in the MSA minus number of crimes in the city) ÷ (population of the MSA minus population of the city)) x 100,000
Source: U.S. Department of Justice, FBI Uniform Crime Reports, 1977 - 1996

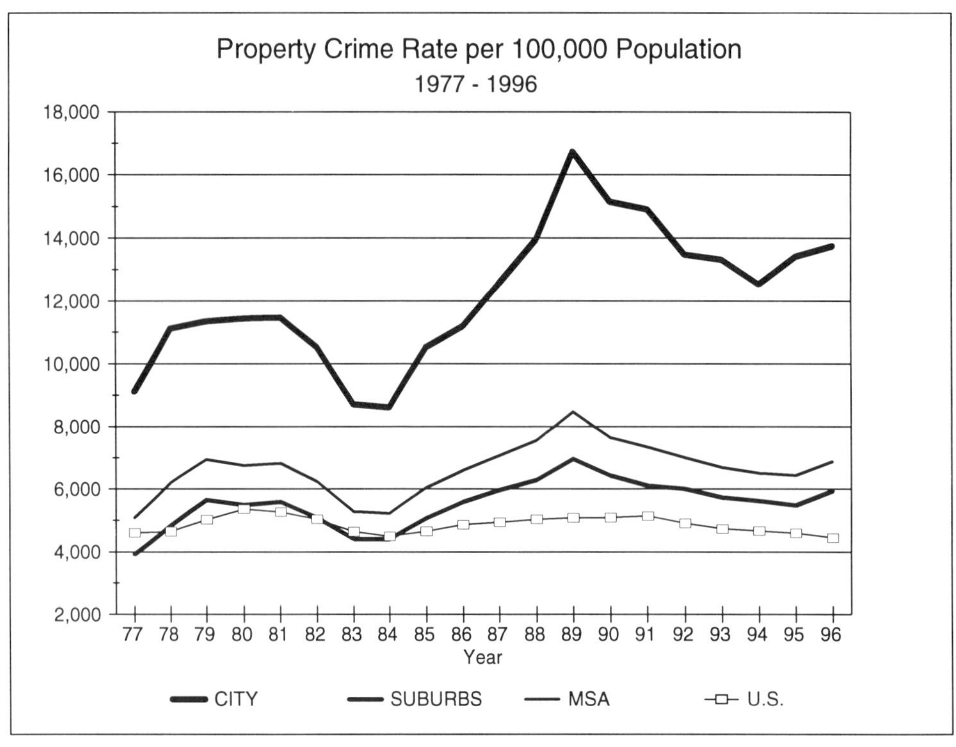

Note: Missing line segments indicate data not available.

Murders and Murder Rates: 1977 - 1996

Year	Number				Rate per 100,000 population			
	City	Suburbs[2]	MSA[1]	U.S.	City	Suburbs[3]	MSA[1]	U.S.
1977	138	74	212	19,120	33.1	5.1	11.3	8.8
1978	144	114	258	19,560	35.6	7.8	13.9	9.0
1979	231	145	376	21,460	54.6	10.1	20.2	9.7
1980	201	89	290	23,040	47.6	5.6	14.4	10.2
1981	182	142	324	22,520	41.8	8.7	15.6	9.8
1982	152	113	265	21,010	34.5	6.8	12.6	9.1
1983	141	87	228	19,310	31.4	4.8	10.1	8.3
1984	135	80	215	18,690	30.5	4.3	9.3	7.9
1985	145	121	266	18,980	33.2	6.0	10.9	7.9
1986	186	144	330	20,610	41.7	7.0	13.3	8.6
1987	207	154	361	20,100	48.1	7.1	13.8	8.3
1988	217	175	392	20,680	48.8	7.6	14.3	8.4
1989	246	167	413	21,500	57.7	7.1	14.9	8.7
1990	231	156	387	23,440	58.6	6.4	13.7	9.4
1991	205	172	377	24,700	50.9	6.9	13.0	9.8
1992	198	196	394	23,760	48.2	7.3	12.7	9.3
1993	203	191	394	24,530	50.4	6.8	12.2	9.5
1994	191	189	380	23,330	46.4	6.6	11.6	9.0
1995	184	172	356	21,610	45.5	5.7	10.5	8.2
1996	196	149	345	19,650	47.4	4.9	9.9	7.4

Notes: (1) Metropolitan Statistical Area - see Appendix A for areas included; (2) calculated by the editors using the following formula: (number of crimes in the MSA minus number of crimes in the city); (3) calculated by the editors using the following formula: ((number of crimes in the MSA minus number of crimes in the city) ÷ (population of the MSA minus population of the city)) x 100,000; n/a not avail.
Source: U.S. Department of Justice, FBI Uniform Crime Reports, 1977 - 1996

Forcible Rapes and Forcible Rape Rates: 1977 - 1996

Year	Number				Rate per 100,000 population			
	City	Suburbs[2]	MSA[1]	U.S.	City	Suburbs[3]	MSA[1]	U.S.
1977	510	350	860	63,500	122.3	24.0	45.8	29.4
1978	592	489	1,081	67,610	146.2	33.6	58.1	31.0
1979	656	611	1,267	76,390	155.0	42.4	67.9	34.7
1980	671	582	1,253	82,990	158.8	36.6	62.3	36.8
1981	644	552	1,196	82,500	147.8	33.7	57.7	36.0
1982	613	525	1,138	78,770	139.0	31.7	54.2	34.0
1983	619	457	1,076	78,920	138.0	25.4	47.8	33.7
1984	632	608	1,240	84,230	142.7	32.4	53.4	35.7
1985	683	615	1,298	88,670	156.6	30.7	53.3	37.1
1986	681	745	1,426	91,460	152.8	36.5	57.3	37.9
1987	636	779	1,415	91,110	147.9	35.7	54.2	37.4
1988	721	944	1,665	92,490	162.0	41.3	60.9	37.6
1989	691	997	1,688	94,500	162.0	42.4	60.8	38.1
1990	695	1,168	1,863	102,560	176.4	47.9	65.7	41.2
1991	638	936	1,574	106,590	158.3	37.5	54.3	42.3
1992	627	1,221	1,848	109,060	152.6	45.4	59.6	42.8
1993	492	875	1,367	106,010	122.1	31.0	42.4	41.1
1994	422	886	1,308	102,220	102.6	31.0	40.0	39.3
1995	441	987	1,428	97,470	109.1	32.9	42.0	37.1
1996	392	884	1,276	95,770	94.9	28.9	36.8	36.1

Notes: (1) Metropolitan Statistical Area - see Appendix A for areas included; (2) calculated by the editors using the following formula: (number of crimes in the MSA minus number of crimes in the city); (3) calculated by the editors using the following formula: ((number of crimes in the MSA minus number of crimes in the city) ÷ (population of the MSA minus population of the city)) x 100,000; n/a not avail.
Source: U.S. Department of Justice, FBI Uniform Crime Reports, 1977 - 1996

Robberies and Robbery Rates: 1977 - 1996

Year	Number				Rate per 100,000 population			
	City	Suburbs[2]	MSA[1]	U.S.	City	Suburbs[3]	MSA[1]	U.S.
1977	3,354	1,166	4,520	412,610	804.3	79.9	240.8	190.7
1978	4,119	1,674	5,793	426,930	1,017.0	114.9	311.1	195.8
1979	5,189	2,362	7,551	480,700	1,226.4	163.8	404.9	218.4
1980	4,733	2,239	6,972	565,840	1,120.3	141.0	346.7	251.1
1981	4,507	2,459	6,966	592,910	1,034.6	150.1	335.9	258.7
1982	3,999	1,795	5,794	553,130	906.6	108.2	276.0	238.9
1983	3,552	1,899	5,451	506,570	791.7	105.5	242.4	216.5
1984	4,029	1,694	5,723	485,010	909.6	90.2	246.6	205.4
1985	4,792	2,240	7,032	497,870	1,098.5	112.0	288.6	208.5
1986	5,428	3,566	8,994	542,780	1,218.1	174.5	361.4	225.1
1987	5,100	3,633	8,733	517,700	1,186.2	166.7	334.7	212.7
1988	5,972	4,510	10,482	542,970	1,342.0	197.1	383.5	220.9
1989	6,796	5,112	11,908	578,330	1,593.5	217.4	428.7	233.0
1990	6,109	5,255	11,364	639,270	1,550.4	215.4	401.0	257.0
1991	6,479	5,625	12,104	687,730	1,607.4	225.5	417.8	272.7
1992	5,824	5,654	11,478	672,480	1,417.5	210.2	370.1	263.6
1993	6,045	5,862	11,907	659,870	1,500.5	207.7	369.1	255.9
1994	5,343	5,188	10,531	618,950	1,299.4	181.2	321.7	237.7
1995	5,260	4,641	9,901	580,510	1,300.9	154.9	291.2	220.9
1996	4,805	5,361	10,166	537,050	1,163.1	175.3	292.8	202.4

Notes: (1) Metropolitan Statistical Area - see Appendix A for areas included; (2) calculated by the editors using the following formula: (number of crimes in the MSA minus number of crimes in the city); (3) calculated by the editors using the following formula: ((number of crimes in the MSA minus number of crimes in the city) ÷ (population of the MSA minus population of the city)) x 100,000; n/a not avail.
Source: U.S. Department of Justice, FBI Uniform Crime Reports, 1977 - 1996

Aggravated Assaults and Aggravated Assault Rates: 1977 - 1996

Year	Number				Rate per 100,000 population			
	City	Suburbs[2]	MSA[1]	U.S.	City	Suburbs[3]	MSA[1]	U.S.
1977	3,593	1,899	5,492	534,350	861.6	130.1	292.6	247.0
1978	3,990	2,286	6,276	571,460	985.2	156.9	337.1	262.1
1979	4,639	2,553	7,192	629,480	1,096.4	177.1	385.7	286.0
1980	5,470	2,960	8,430	672,650	1,294.8	186.3	419.2	298.5
1981	5,246	2,811	8,057	663,900	1,204.2	171.6	388.6	289.7
1982	5,722	2,185	7,907	669,480	1,297.2	131.7	376.6	289.2
1983	5,014	3,066	8,080	653,290	1,117.6	170.3	359.3	279.2
1984	5,729	3,120	8,849	685,350	1,293.4	166.1	381.3	290.2
1985	5,990	3,510	9,500	723,250	1,373.2	175.5	389.9	302.9
1986	6,867	3,805	10,672	834,320	1,541.0	186.2	428.8	346.1
1987	6,950	3,855	10,805	855,090	1,616.5	176.9	414.1	351.3
1988	9,001	4,683	13,684	910,090	2,022.7	204.7	500.7	370.2
1989	9,119	5,597	14,716	951,710	2,138.2	238.1	529.8	383.4
1990	9,062	6,232	15,294	1,054,860	2,299.9	255.4	539.7	424.1
1991	8,967	5,601	14,568	1,092,740	2,224.6	224.6	502.8	433.3
1992	9,207	6,230	15,437	1,126,970	2,240.8	231.6	497.8	441.8
1993	9,541	6,591	16,132	1,135,610	2,368.2	233.5	500.1	440.3
1994	8,728	6,768	15,496	1,113,180	2,122.5	236.4	473.4	427.6
1995	8,859	6,925	15,784	1,099,210	2,191.0	231.2	464.2	418.3
1996	8,306	7,033	15,339	1,029,810	2,010.5	229.9	441.8	388.2

Notes: (1) Metropolitan Statistical Area - see Appendix A for areas included; (2) calculated by the editors using the following formula: (number of crimes in the MSA minus number of crimes in the city); (3) calculated by the editors using the following formula: ((number of crimes in the MSA minus number of crimes in the city) ÷ (population of the MSA minus population of the city)) x 100,000; n/a not avail.
Source: U.S. Department of Justice, FBI Uniform Crime Reports, 1977 - 1996

Burglaries and Burglary Rates: 1977 - 1996

Year	Number				Rate per 100,000 population			
	City	Suburbs[2]	MSA[1]	U.S.	City	Suburbs[3]	MSA[1]	U.S.
1977	12,295	19,588	31,883	3,071,500	2,948.4	1,341.9	1,698.9	1,419.8
1978	15,185	23,505	38,690	3,128,300	3,749.4	1,613.4	2,078.1	1,434.6
1979	16,111	25,736	41,847	3,327,700	3,807.8	1,785.3	2,244.2	1,511.9
1980	16,812	27,623	44,435	3,795,200	3,979.4	1,739.0	2,209.7	1,684.1
1981	17,458	29,264	46,722	3,779,700	4,007.6	1,786.7	2,253.3	1,649.5
1982	15,134	26,146	41,280	3,447,100	3,430.9	1,576.5	1,966.1	1,488.8
1983	12,501	23,907	36,408	3,129,900	2,786.5	1,327.9	1,618.9	1,337.7
1984	10,813	23,334	34,147	2,984,400	2,441.1	1,242.4	1,471.2	1,263.7
1985	12,192	28,459	40,651	3,073,300	2,795.0	1,422.6	1,668.3	1,287.3
1986	13,454	32,454	45,908	3,241,400	3,019.2	1,588.3	1,844.4	1,344.6
1987	14,927	35,479	50,406	3,236,200	3,471.8	1,627.9	1,931.7	1,329.6
1988	15,556	37,271	52,827	3,218,100	3,495.8	1,629.0	1,933.0	1,309.2
1989	17,202	38,895	56,097	3,168,200	4,033.5	1,654.3	2,019.6	1,276.3
1990	15,519	37,880	53,399	3,073,900	3,938.7	1,552.6	1,884.4	1,235.9
1991	13,861	35,997	49,858	3,157,200	3,438.7	1,443.2	1,720.8	1,252.0
1992	13,065	37,534	50,599	2,979,900	3,179.8	1,395.2	1,631.7	1,168.2
1993	13,168	35,048	48,216	2,834,800	3,268.5	1,241.7	1,494.8	1,099.2
1994	12,136	30,612	42,748	2,712,800	2,951.3	1,069.5	1,305.9	1,042.0
1995	11,694	28,522	40,216	2,593,800	2,892.1	952.1	1,182.8	987.1
1996	10,471	32,577	43,048	2,501,500	2,534.6	1,065.0	1,239.9	943.0

Notes: (1) Metropolitan Statistical Area - see Appendix A for areas included; (2) calculated by the editors using the following formula: (number of crimes in the MSA minus number of crimes in the city); (3) calculated by the editors using the following formula: ((number of crimes in the MSA minus number of crimes in the city) ÷ (population of the MSA minus population of the city)) x 100,000; n/a not avail.
Source: U.S. Department of Justice, FBI Uniform Crime Reports, 1977 - 1996

Larceny-Thefts and Larceny-Theft Rates: 1977 - 1996

Year	Number				Rate per 100,000 population			
	City	Suburbs[2]	MSA[1]	U.S.	City	Suburbs[3]	MSA[1]	U.S.
1977	22,549	32,412	54,961	5,905,700	5,407.4	2,220.5	2,928.6	2,729.9
1978	25,874	40,032	65,906	5,991,000	6,388.6	2,747.9	3,539.8	2,747.4
1979	27,424	47,405	74,829	6,601,000	6,481.6	3,288.4	4,012.9	2,999.1
1980	27,502	51,871	79,373	7,136,900	6,509.7	3,265.5	3,947.1	3,167.0
1981	28,966	55,084	84,050	7,194,400	6,649.3	3,363.1	4,053.5	3,139.7
1982	27,818	51,495	79,313	7,142,500	6,306.5	3,104.9	3,777.5	3,084.8
1983	23,566	49,075	72,641	6,712,800	5,252.8	2,725.9	3,230.0	2,868.9
1984	24,110	52,077	76,187	6,591,900	5,443.0	2,772.9	3,282.5	2,791.3
1985	29,372	62,878	92,250	6,926,400	6,733.4	3,143.1	3,785.9	2,901.2
1986	30,380	69,480	99,860	7,257,200	6,817.5	3,400.3	4,012.1	3,010.3
1987	31,559	79,915	111,474	7,499,900	7,340.1	3,666.7	4,272.0	3,081.3
1988	37,306	90,326	127,632	7,705,900	8,383.5	3,947.9	4,670.1	3,134.9
1989	42,660	105,487	148,147	7,872,400	10,002.8	4,486.5	5,333.5	3,171.3
1990	33,020	99,195	132,215	7,945,700	8,380.3	4,065.7	4,665.6	3,194.8
1991	35,237	98,993	134,230	8,142,200	8,741.8	3,968.8	4,632.8	3,228.8
1992	33,903	105,299	139,202	7,915,200	8,251.4	3,914.3	4,488.9	3,103.0
1993	31,249	106,808	138,057	7,820,900	7,756.5	3,783.9	4,280.1	3,032.4
1994	30,888	111,527	142,415	7,879,800	7,511.6	3,896.3	4,350.5	3,026.7
1995	34,221	112,206	146,427	7,997,700	8,463.5	3,745.7	4,306.8	3,043.8
1996	37,104	125,647	162,751	7,894,600	8,981.3	4,107.7	4,687.7	2,975.9

Notes: (1) Metropolitan Statistical Area - see Appendix A for areas included; (2) calculated by the editors using the following formula: (number of crimes in the MSA minus number of crimes in the city); (3) calculated by the editors using the following formula: ((number of crimes in the MSA minus number of crimes in the city) ÷ (population of the MSA minus population of the city)) x 100,000; n/a not avail.
Source: U.S. Department of Justice, FBI Uniform Crime Reports, 1977 - 1996

Motor Vehicle Thefts and Motor Vehicle Theft Rates: 1977 - 1996

Year	Number				Rate per 100,000 population			
	City	Suburbs[2]	MSA[1]	U.S.	City	Suburbs[3]	MSA[1]	U.S.
1977	3,158	5,396	8,554	977,700	757.3	369.7	455.8	451.9
1978	3,966	6,819	10,785	1,004,100	979.3	468.1	579.3	460.5
1979	4,474	8,123	12,597	1,112,800	1,057.4	563.5	675.6	505.6
1980	4,005	7,574	11,579	1,131,700	948.0	476.8	575.8	502.2
1981	3,566	7,015	10,581	1,087,800	818.6	428.3	510.3	474.7
1982	3,526	6,619	10,145	1,062,400	799.4	399.1	483.2	458.8
1983	3,020	6,503	9,523	1,007,900	673.2	361.2	423.4	430.8
1984	3,184	7,199	10,383	1,032,200	718.8	383.3	447.3	437.1
1985	4,331	9,994	14,325	1,102,900	992.9	499.6	587.9	462.0
1986	6,072	12,067	18,139	1,224,100	1,362.6	590.5	728.8	507.8
1987	7,512	14,641	22,153	1,288,700	1,747.2	671.8	849.0	529.4
1988	9,314	16,075	25,389	1,432,900	2,093.1	702.6	929.0	582.9
1989	11,527	19,040	30,567	1,564,800	2,702.8	809.8	1,100.5	630.4
1990	11,157	19,556	30,713	1,635,900	2,831.6	801.5	1,083.8	657.8
1991	11,011	17,252	28,263	1,661,700	2,731.7	691.7	975.5	659.0
1992	8,451	18,561	27,012	1,610,800	2,056.8	690.0	871.1	631.5
1993	9,216	19,676	28,892	1,563,100	2,287.5	697.1	895.7	606.1
1994	8,572	18,600	27,172	1,539,300	2,084.6	649.8	830.0	591.3
1995	8,352	23,172	31,524	1,472,400	2,065.6	773.5	927.2	560.4
1996	9,247	23,350	32,597	1,395,200	2,238.3	763.4	938.9	525.9

Notes: (1) Metropolitan Statistical Area - see Appendix A for areas included; (2) calculated by the editors using the following formula: (number of crimes in the MSA minus number of crimes in the city); (3) calculated by the editors using the following formula: ((number of crimes in the MSA minus number of crimes in the city) ÷ (population of the MSA minus population of the city)) x 100,000; n/a not avail.
Source: U.S. Department of Justice, FBI Uniform Crime Reports, 1977 - 1996

HATE CRIMES

Criminal Incidents by Bias Motivation

Area	Race	Ethnicity	Religion	Sexual Orientation
Atlanta	18	1	2	17

Notes: Figures include both violent and property crimes. Law enforcement agencies must have submitted data for at least one quarter of calendar year 1995 to be included in this report, therefore figures shown may not represent complete 12-month totals; n/a not available
Source: U.S. Department of Justice, FBI Uniform Crime Reports, Hate Crime Statistics 1995

ILLEGAL DRUGS

Drug Use by Adult Arrestees

Sex	Percent Testing Positive by Urinalysis (%)				
	Any Drug[1]	Cocaine	Marijuana	Opiates	Multiple Drugs
Male	80	59	37	3	20
Female	77	63	26	3	18

Notes: The catchment area is the entire city; (1) Includes cocaine, opiates, marijuana, methadone, phencyclidine (PCP), benzodiazepines, methaqualone, propoxyphene, barbiturates & amphetamines
Source: National Institute of Justice, 1996 Drug Use Forecasting, Annual Report on Adult and Juvenile Arrestees (released June 1997)

LAW ENFORCEMENT

Full-Time Law Enforcement Employees

Jurisdiction	Police Employees			Police Officers per 100,000 population
	Total	Officers	Civilians	
Atlanta	1,967	1,467	500	355.1

Notes: Data as of October 31, 1996
Source: U.S. Department of Justice, FBI Uniform Crime Reports, 1996

Number of Police Officers by Race

Race	Police Officers 1983		Police Officers 1992		Index of Representation[1]		
	Number	Pct.	Number	Pct.	1983	1992	% Chg.
Black	602	45.8	668	54.6	0.69	0.81	17.4
Hispanic[2]	9	0.7	0	0.0	0.43	0.00	-100.0

Notes: (1) The index of representation is calculated by dividing the percent of black/hispanic police officers by the percent of corresponding blacks/hispanics in the local population. An index approaching 1.0 indicates that a city is closer to achieving a representation of police officers equal to their proportion in the local population; (2) Hispanic officers can be of any race
Source: Bureau of Justice Statistics, Sourcebook of Criminal Justice Statistics, 1994

CORRECTIONS

Federal Correctional Facilities

Type	Year Opened	Security Level	Sex of Inmates	Rated Capacity	Population on 7/1/95	Number of Staff
U.S. Penitentiary[1]	1902	High	Male	1,509	2,190	721

Notes: Data as of 1995; (1) A minimum security satellite camp is operated adjacent to this facility.
Source: Bureau of Justice Statistics, Sourcebook of Criminal Justice Statistics Online

City/County/Regional Correctional Facilities

Name	Year Opened	Year Renov.	Rated Capacity	1995 Pop.	Number of COs[1]	Number of Staff	ACA[2] Accred.
Fulton County Jail	1989	--	2,278	2,278	n/a	564	No
Fulton County-Atlanta City Detention Center	1995	--	1,078	1,117	213	328	No
Fulton County-Atlanta Correctional Center	1943	1988	400	n/a	n/a	n/a	No
Fulton County-Bellwood Correctional Institution	1972	1983	240	n/a	n/a	n/a	No

Notes: Data as of April 1996; (1) Correctional Officers; (2) American Correctional Assn. Accreditation
Source: American Correctional Association, 1996-1998 National Jail and Adult Detention Directory

Private Adult Correctional Facilities

Name	Date Opened	Rated Capacity	Present Pop.	Security Level	Facility Construct.	Expans. Plans	ACA[1] Accred.
None listed							

Notes: Data as of December 1996; (1) American Correctional Association Accreditation
Source: University of Florida, Center for Studies in Criminology and Law, Private Adult Correctional Facility Census, 10th Ed., March 15, 1997

Characteristics of Shock Incarceration Programs

Georgia did not have a shock incarceration program as of July 1996

Source: Sourcebook of Criminal Justice Statistics Online

INMATES AND HIV/AIDS

HIV Testing Policies for Inmates

Jurisdiction	All Inmates at Some Time	All Convicted Inmates at Admission	Random Samples While in Custody	High-risk Groups	Upon Inmate Request	Upon Court Order	Upon Involvement in Incident
Fulton Co.[1]	No	Yes	No	No	Yes	No	No

Notes: (1) All facilities reported following the same testing policy or authorities reported the policy to be jurisdiction-wide
Source: HIV in Prisons and Jails, 1993 (released August 1995)

Inmates Known to be Positive for HIV

Jurisdiction	Number of Jail Inmates in Facilities Providing Data	Type of HIV Infection/AIDS Cases				HIV/AIDS Cases as a Percent of Tot. Custody Pop.
		Total	Asymptomatic	Symptomatic	Confirmed AIDS	
Fulton Co.[1]	2,702	n/a	n/a	n/a	n/a	n/a

Note: (1) Jurisdiction did not provide data on HIV/AIDS cases; n/a not available
Source: HIV in Prisons and Jails, 1993 (released August, 1995)

DEATH PENALTY

Death Penalty Statistics

State	Prisoners Executed		Prisoners Under Sentence of Death					Avg. No. of Years on Death Row[4]
	1930-1995	1996[1]	Total[2]	White[3]	Black[3]	Hisp.	Women	
Georgia	386	2	98	55	43	1	0	7.6

Notes: Data as of 12/31/95 unless otherwise noted; (1) Data as of 7/31/97; (2) Includes persons of other races; (3) Includes people of Hispanic origin; (4) Covers prisoners sentenced 1974 through 1995
Source: Bureau of Justice Statistics, Capital Punishment 1995 (released 12/96); Death Penalty Information Center Web Site, 9/30/97

Capital Offenses and Methods of Execution

Capital Offenses in Georgia	Minimum Age for Imposition of Death Penalty	Mentally Retarded Excluded	Methods of Execution[1]
Murder; kidnaping with bodily injury or ransom where the victim dies; aircraft hijacking; treason.	17	No	Electrocution

Notes: Data as of 12/31/95 unless otherwise noted; (1) Data as of 7/31/97
Source: Bureau of Justice Statistics, Capital Punishment 1995 (released 12/96); Death Penalty Information Center Web Site, 9/30/97

LAWS

Statutory Provisions Relating to the Purchase, Ownership and Use of Handguns

Jurisdiction	Instant Background Check	Federal Waiting Period Applies[1]	State Waiting Period (days)	License or Permit to Purchase	Regis-tration	Record of Sale Sent to Police	Concealed Carry Law
Georgia	Yes[a]	No	No	No	No	No	Yes[b]

Note: Data as of 1996; (1) The Federal 5-day waiting period for handgun purchases applies to states that don't have instant background checks, waiting period requirements, or licensing procedures exempting them from the Federal requirement; (a) Concealed firearm carry permit holders are exempt from Instant Check; (b) "Shall issue" permit system, liberally administered discretion by local authorities over permit issuance, or no permit required
Source: Sourcebook of Criminal Justice Statistics Online

Statutory Provisions Relating to Alcohol Use and Driving

Jurisdiction	Drinking Age	Blood Alcohol Concentration Levels as Evidence in State Courts[1]		Open Container Law[1]	Anti-Consump-tion Law[1]	Dram Shop Law[1]
		Illegal per se at 0.10%	Presumption at 0.10%			
Georgia	21	Yes	(a)	Yes[b]	No	Yes

Note: Data as of January 1, 1997; (1) See Appendix C for an explanation of terms; (a) 0.08%; (b) Applies to drivers only
Source: Sourcebook of Criminal Justice Statistics Online

Statutory Provisions Relating to Curfews

Jurisdiction	Year Enacted	Latest Revision	Age Group(s)	Curfew Provisions
Atlanta	1992	1994	16 and under	11 pm to 6 am weekday nights midnight to 6 am weekend nights

Note: Data as of February 1996
Source: Sourcebook of Criminal Justice Statistics Online

Statutory Provisions Relating to Hate Crimes

Jurisdiction	Bias-Motivated Violence and Intimidation						Institutional Vandalism
	Civil Action	Criminal Penalty					
		Race/ Religion/ Ethnicity	Sexual Orientation	Mental/ Physical Disability	Gender	Age	
Georgia	No	No	No	No	No	No	Yes

Source: Anti-Defamation League, 1997 Hate Crimes Laws

Austin, Texas

OVERVIEW

The total crime rate for the city increased 7.9% between 1977 and 1996. During that same period, the violent crime rate increased 82.2% and the property crime rate increased 3.7%.

Among violent crimes, the rates for: Murders decreased 27.5%; Forcible Rapes decreased 13.3%; Robberies increased 61.5%; and Aggravated Assaults increased 142.9%.

Among property crimes, the rates for: Burglaries decreased 37.2%; Larceny-Thefts increased 18.4%; and Motor Vehicle Thefts increased 79.5%.

ANTI-CRIME PROGRAMS

Among the newest and most successful programs are:

- District Representative Program—a one-year pilot program dedicated to long-term problem solving. Under this program, one officer is assigned to each district in the sector. The mission is to use problem-solving skills to find long-term solutions to recurring crime problems in the district and to act as a liaison between the community and the patrol officers.
- Bait Vehicle Program—vehicles are being equipped with a state-of-the-art satellite tracking system that allows officers to immediately follow the path of the stolen vehicle and arrest the thief.
- Gang Suppression Unit—works in conjunction with Operations, Investigations and Operations Support and the community to handle crimes perpetrated by known gang members. The Gang Suppression Unit's primary mission is to improve public safety through the interdiction of street gang activity by employing a proactive response to crimes committed by gang members.
- Crime Net—focuses on providing multi-faceted responses to deeply rooted neighborhood problems that cannot be solved by patrol officers alone.
  Austin Police Department 7/97

CRIME RISK

Your Chances of Becoming a Victim[1]

Area	Any Crime	Violent Crime					Property Crime			
		Any	Murder	Forcible Rape[2]	Robbery	Aggrav. Assault	Any	Burglary	Larceny -Theft	Motor Vehicle Theft
City	1:13	1:141	1:13,437	1:996	1:391	1:252	1:14	1:71	1:20	1:145

Note: (1) Figures have been calculated by dividing the population of the city by the number of crimes reported to the FBI during 1996 and are expressed as odds (eg. 1:20 should be read as 1 in 20).
(2) Figures have been calculated by dividing the female population of the city by the number of forcible rapes reported to the FBI during 1996. The female population of the city was estimated by calculating the ratio of females to males reported in the 1990 Census and applying that ratio to 1996 population estimate.
Source: FBI Uniform Crime Reports 1996

CRIME STATISTICS

Total Crimes and Total Crime Rates: 1977 - 1996

Year	Number				Rate per 100,000 population			
	City	Suburbs[2]	MSA[1]	U.S.	City	Suburbs[3]	MSA[1]	U.S.
1977	23,536	6,431	29,967	10,984,500	7,286.7	5,044.0	6,652.0	5,077.6
1978	24,719	6,669	31,388	11,209,000	7,748.9	4,323.9	6,632.6	5,140.3
1979	27,237	7,110	34,347	12,249,500	8,064.8	4,622.7	6,987.7	5,565.5
1980	30,066	7,923	37,989	13,408,300	8,754.7	4,183.5	7,129.9	5,950.0
1981	30,867	8,511	39,378	13,423,800	8,631.5	4,315.8	7,097.5	5,858.2
1982	31,811	8,753	40,564	12,974,400	8,589.9	4,286.0	7,060.1	5,603.6
1983	29,812	9,318	39,130	12,108,600	7,822.8	4,434.0	6,618.3	5,175.0
1984	31,821	10,569	42,390	11,881,800	8,260.1	4,691.7	6,943.4	5,031.3
1985	39,044	12,478	51,522	12,431,400	9,605.7	4,906.4	7,797.0	5,207.1
1986	45,856	14,760	60,616	13,211,900	11,070.4	5,694.1	9,001.0	5,480.4
1987	44,338	14,946	59,284	13,508,700	9,442.8	5,717.3	8,110.5	5,550.0
1988	50,673	15,305	65,978	13,923,100	10,840.9	5,659.0	8,941.6	5,664.2
1989	50,028	15,455	65,483	14,251,400	10,669.1	5,398.5	8,671.1	5,741.0
1990	54,543	15,168	69,711	14,475,600	11,714.0	4,800.8	8,919.3	5,820.3
1991	53,715	16,007	69,722	14,872,900	11,295.2	4,960.6	8,734.5	5,897.8
1992	52,964	18,554	71,518	14,438,200	10,943.5	4,690.3	8,131.1	5,660.2
1993	51,468	18,216	69,684	14,144,800	10,252.2	4,371.0	7,584.5	5,484.4
1994	40,632	17,379	58,011	13,989,500	7,941.0	4,091.6	6,194.9	5,373.5
1995	42,586	16,844	59,430	13,862,700	8,131.9	3,674.3	6,051.2	5,275.9
1996	42,278	17,518	59,796	13,473,600	7,865.9	3,760.7	5,960.0	5,078.9

Notes: (1) Metropolitan Statistical Area - see Appendix A for areas included; (2) calculated by the editors using the following formula: (number of crimes in the MSA minus number of crimes in the city); (3) calculated by the editors using the following formula: ((number of crimes in the MSA minus number of crimes in the city) ÷ (population of the MSA minus population of the city)) x 100,000; n/a not avail.
Source: U.S. Department of Justice, FBI Uniform Crime Reports, 1977 - 1996

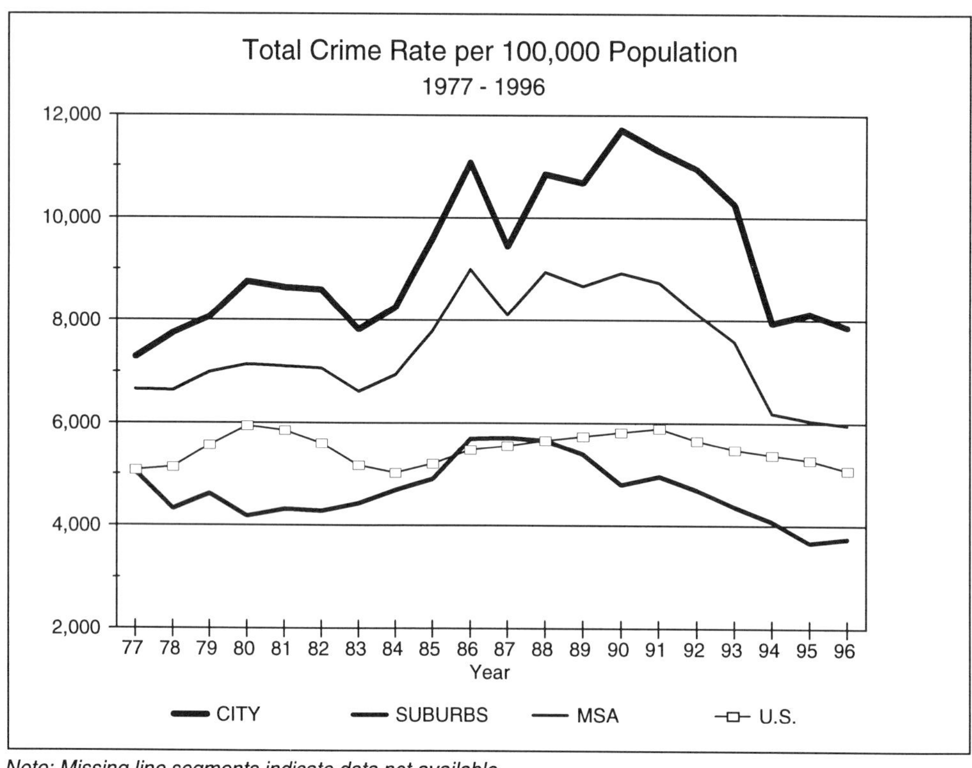

Note: Missing line segments indicate data not available.

Violent Crimes and Violent Crime Rates: 1977 - 1996

Year	Number				Rate per 100,000 population			
	City	Suburbs[2]	MSA[1]	U.S.	City	Suburbs[3]	MSA[1]	U.S.
1977	1,260	379	1,639	1,029,580	390.1	297.3	363.8	475.9
1978	1,413	347	1,760	1,085,550	442.9	225.0	371.9	497.8
1979	1,495	408	1,903	1,208,030	442.7	265.3	387.2	548.9
1980	1,723	508	2,231	1,344,520	501.7	268.2	418.7	596.6
1981	1,545	625	2,170	1,361,820	432.0	316.9	391.1	594.3
1982	1,532	656	2,188	1,322,390	413.7	321.2	380.8	571.1
1983	1,534	809	2,343	1,258,090	402.5	385.0	396.3	537.7
1984	1,648	815	2,463	1,273,280	427.8	361.8	403.4	539.2
1985	2,363	1,063	3,426	1,328,800	581.3	418.0	518.5	556.6
1986	2,667	1,213	3,880	1,489,170	643.9	467.9	576.1	617.7
1987	2,313	1,016	3,329	1,484,000	492.6	388.7	455.4	609.7
1988	2,508	951	3,459	1,566,220	536.6	351.6	468.8	637.2
1989	2,605	1,005	3,610	1,646,040	555.5	351.1	478.0	663.1
1990	3,326	1,086	4,412	1,820,130	714.3	343.7	564.5	731.8
1991	2,968	1,078	4,046	1,911,770	624.1	334.1	506.9	758.1
1992	2,850	1,752	4,602	1,932,270	588.9	442.9	523.2	757.5
1993	3,011	1,842	4,853	1,926,020	599.8	442.0	528.2	746.8
1994	3,249	1,798	5,047	1,857,670	635.0	423.3	539.0	713.6
1995	4,050	1,642	5,692	1,798,790	773.4	358.2	579.6	684.6
1996	3,821	1,405	5,226	1,682,280	710.9	301.6	520.9	634.1

Notes: Violent crimes include murder, forcible rape, robbery and aggravated assault; n/a not available; (1) Metropolitan Statistical Area - see Appendix A for areas included; (2) calculated by the editors using the following formula: (number of crimes in the MSA minus number of crimes in the city); (3) calculated by the editors using the following formula: ((number of crimes in the MSA minus number of crimes in the city) ÷ (population of the MSA minus population of the city)) x 100,000
Source: U.S. Department of Justice, FBI Uniform Crime Reports, 1977 - 1996

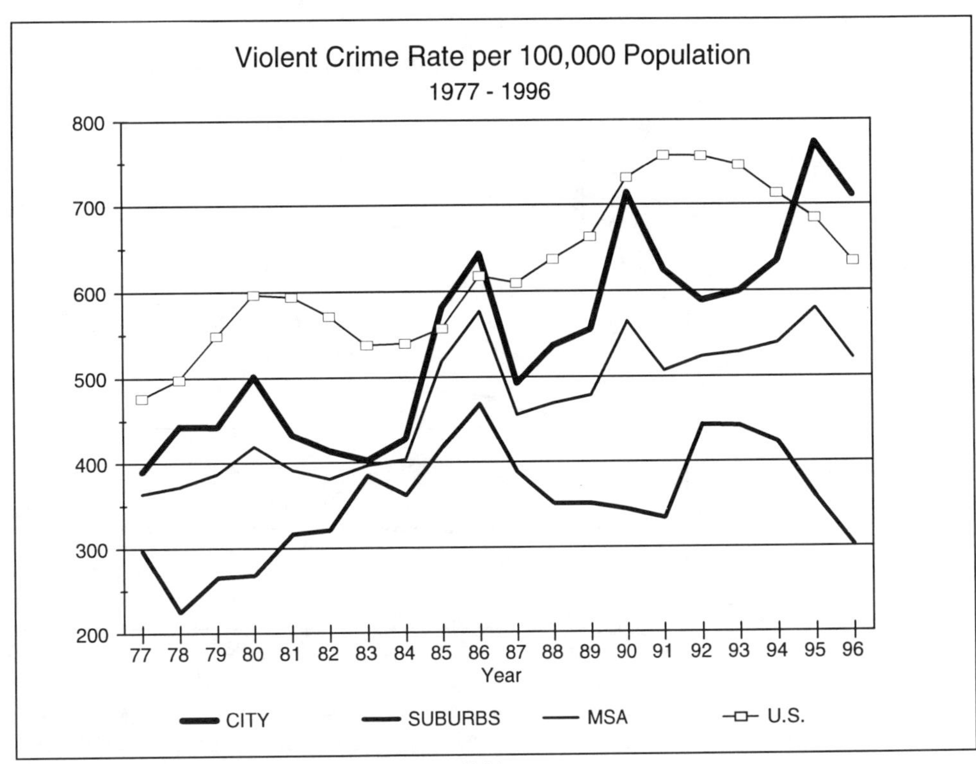

Note: Missing line segments indicate data not available.

Property Crimes and Property Crime Rates: 1977 - 1996

Year	Number				Rate per 100,000 population			
	City	Suburbs[2]	MSA[1]	U.S.	City	Suburbs[3]	MSA[1]	U.S.
1977	22,276	6,052	28,328	9,955,000	6,896.6	4,746.7	6,288.1	4,601.7
1978	23,306	6,322	29,628	10,123,400	7,306.0	4,098.9	6,260.7	4,642.5
1979	25,742	6,702	32,444	11,041,500	7,622.1	4,357.4	6,600.6	5,016.6
1980	28,343	7,415	35,758	12,063,700	8,253.0	3,915.3	6,711.2	5,353.3
1981	29,322	7,886	37,208	12,061,900	8,199.5	3,998.8	6,706.4	5,263.9
1982	30,279	8,097	38,376	11,652,000	8,176.2	3,964.8	6,679.3	5,032.5
1983	28,278	8,509	36,787	10,850,500	7,420.3	4,049.0	6,222.0	4,637.4
1984	30,173	9,754	39,927	10,608,500	7,832.3	4,329.9	6,540.0	4,492.1
1985	36,681	11,415	48,096	11,102,600	9,024.3	4,488.4	7,278.5	4,650.5
1986	43,189	13,547	56,736	11,722,700	10,426.6	5,226.1	8,424.9	4,862.6
1987	42,025	13,930	55,955	12,024,700	8,950.2	5,328.7	7,655.0	4,940.3
1988	48,165	14,354	62,519	12,356,900	10,304.4	5,307.4	8,472.8	5,027.1
1989	47,423	14,450	61,873	12,605,400	10,113.5	5,047.4	8,193.0	5,077.9
1990	51,217	14,082	65,299	12,655,500	10,999.7	4,457.0	8,354.8	5,088.5
1991	50,747	14,929	65,676	12,961,100	10,671.0	4,626.5	8,227.6	5,139.7
1992	50,114	16,802	66,916	12,505,900	10,354.7	4,247.4	7,607.9	4,902.7
1993	48,457	16,374	64,831	12,218,800	9,652.4	3,929.0	7,056.3	4,737.6
1994	37,383	15,581	52,964	12,131,900	7,306.0	3,668.2	5,656.0	4,660.0
1995	38,536	15,202	53,738	12,063,900	7,358.5	3,316.1	5,471.6	4,591.3
1996	38,457	16,113	54,570	11,791,300	7,155.0	3,459.1	5,439.1	4,444.8

Notes: Property crimes include burglary, larceny-theft and motor vehicle theft; n/a not available; (1) Metropolitan Statistical Area - see Appendix A for areas included; (2) calculated by the editors using the following formula: (number of crimes in the MSA minus number of crimes in the city); (3) calculated by the editors using the following formula: ((number of crimes in the MSA minus number of crimes in the city) ÷ (population of the MSA minus population of the city)) x 100,000
Source: U.S. Department of Justice, FBI Uniform Crime Reports, 1977 - 1996

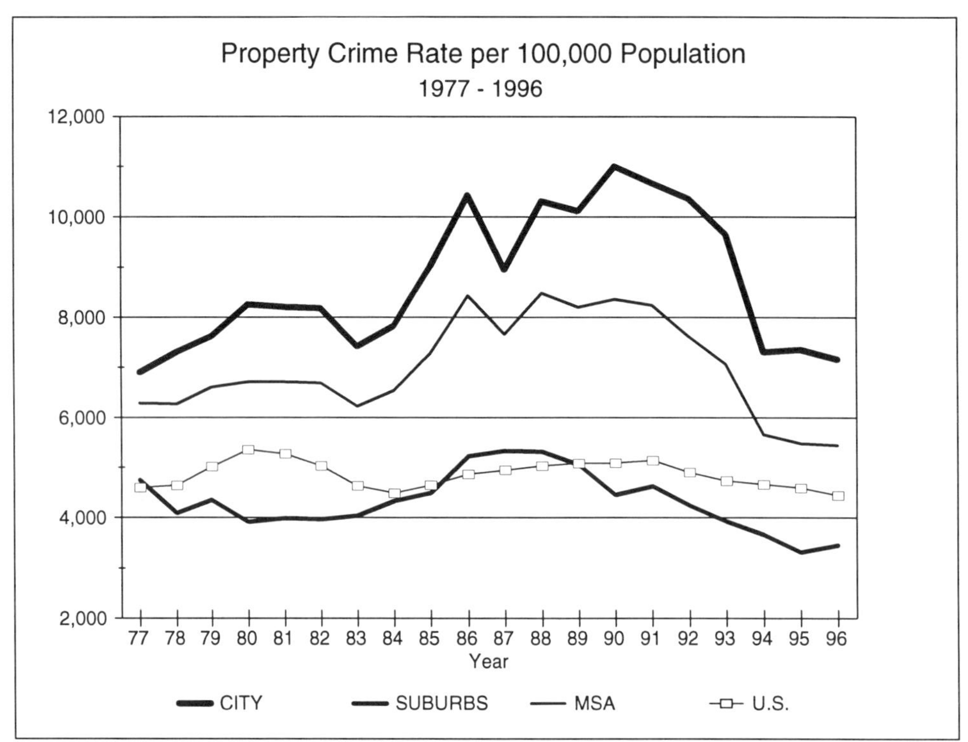

Note: Missing line segments indicate data not available.

Murders and Murder Rates: 1977 - 1996

Year	Number				Rate per 100,000 population			
	City	Suburbs[2]	MSA[1]	U.S.	City	Suburbs[3]	MSA[1]	U.S.
1977	33	6	39	19,120	10.2	4.7	8.7	8.8
1978	35	15	50	19,560	11.0	9.7	10.6	9.0
1979	43	15	58	21,460	12.7	9.8	11.8	9.7
1980	43	11	54	23,040	12.5	5.8	10.1	10.2
1981	39	10	49	22,520	10.9	5.1	8.8	9.8
1982	57	22	79	21,010	15.4	10.8	13.7	9.1
1983	58	21	79	19,310	15.2	10.0	13.4	8.3
1984	59	12	71	18,690	15.3	5.3	11.6	7.9
1985	52	23	75	18,980	12.8	9.0	11.4	7.9
1986	48	14	62	20,610	11.6	5.4	9.2	8.6
1987	39	3	42	20,100	8.3	1.1	5.7	8.3
1988	43	14	57	20,680	9.2	5.2	7.7	8.4
1989	31	20	51	21,500	6.6	7.0	6.8	8.7
1990	46	11	57	23,440	9.9	3.5	7.3	9.4
1991	49	12	61	24,700	10.3	3.7	7.6	9.8
1992	37	15	52	23,760	7.6	3.8	5.9	9.3
1993	37	18	55	24,530	7.4	4.3	6.0	9.5
1994	37	15	52	23,330	7.2	3.5	5.6	9.0
1995	46	9	55	21,610	8.8	2.0	5.6	8.2
1996	40	14	54	19,650	7.4	3.0	5.4	7.4

Notes: (1) Metropolitan Statistical Area - see Appendix A for areas included; (2) calculated by the editors using the following formula: (number of crimes in the MSA minus number of crimes in the city); (3) calculated by the editors using the following formula: ((number of crimes in the MSA minus number of crimes in the city) ÷ (population of the MSA minus population of the city)) x 100,000; n/a not avail.
Source: U.S. Department of Justice, FBI Uniform Crime Reports, 1977 - 1996

Forcible Rapes and Forcible Rape Rates: 1977 - 1996

Year	Number				Rate per 100,000 population			
	City	Suburbs[2]	MSA[1]	U.S.	City	Suburbs[3]	MSA[1]	U.S.
1977	187	48	235	63,500	57.9	37.6	52.2	29.4
1978	194	48	242	67,610	60.8	31.1	51.1	31.0
1979	216	45	261	76,390	64.0	29.3	53.1	34.7
1980	237	58	295	82,990	69.0	30.6	55.4	36.8
1981	263	60	323	82,500	73.5	30.4	58.2	36.0
1982	235	46	281	78,770	63.5	22.5	48.9	34.0
1983	240	55	295	78,920	63.0	26.2	49.9	33.7
1984	264	89	353	84,230	68.5	39.5	57.8	35.7
1985	489	96	585	88,670	120.3	37.7	88.5	37.1
1986	388	124	512	91,460	93.7	47.8	76.0	37.9
1987	284	126	410	91,110	60.5	48.2	56.1	37.4
1988	247	153	400	92,490	52.8	56.6	54.2	37.6
1989	235	152	387	94,500	50.1	53.1	51.2	38.1
1990	280	154	434	102,560	60.1	48.7	55.5	41.2
1991	276	201	477	106,590	58.0	62.3	59.8	42.3
1992	294	206	500	109,060	60.7	52.1	56.8	42.8
1993	271	231	502	106,010	54.0	55.4	54.6	41.1
1994	249	231	480	102,220	48.7	54.4	51.3	39.3
1995	308	186	494	97,470	58.8	40.6	50.3	37.1
1996	270	141	411	95,770	50.2	30.3	41.0	36.1

Notes: (1) Metropolitan Statistical Area - see Appendix A for areas included; (2) calculated by the editors using the following formula: (number of crimes in the MSA minus number of crimes in the city); (3) calculated by the editors using the following formula: ((number of crimes in the MSA minus number of crimes in the city) ÷ (population of the MSA minus population of the city)) x 100,000; n/a not avail.
Source: U.S. Department of Justice, FBI Uniform Crime Reports, 1977 - 1996

Robberies and Robbery Rates: 1977 - 1996

Year	Number				Rate per 100,000 population			
	City	Suburbs[2]	MSA[1]	U.S.	City	Suburbs[3]	MSA[1]	U.S.
1977	512	60	572	412,610	158.5	47.1	127.0	190.7
1978	635	69	704	426,930	199.1	44.7	148.8	195.8
1979	577	85	662	480,700	170.8	55.3	134.7	218.4
1980	678	101	779	565,840	197.4	53.3	146.2	251.1
1981	669	116	785	592,910	187.1	58.8	141.5	258.7
1982	635	119	754	553,130	171.5	58.3	131.2	238.9
1983	665	98	763	506,570	174.5	46.6	129.1	216.5
1984	768	97	865	485,010	199.4	43.1	141.7	205.4
1985	1,076	100	1,176	497,870	264.7	39.3	178.0	208.5
1986	1,124	133	1,257	542,780	271.4	51.3	186.7	225.1
1987	985	151	1,136	517,700	209.8	57.8	155.4	212.7
1988	1,018	123	1,141	542,970	217.8	45.5	154.6	220.9
1989	1,019	127	1,146	578,330	217.3	44.4	151.7	233.0
1990	1,461	131	1,592	639,270	313.8	41.5	203.7	257.0
1991	1,555	162	1,717	687,730	327.0	50.2	215.1	272.7
1992	1,450	181	1,631	672,480	299.6	45.8	185.4	263.6
1993	1,555	193	1,748	659,870	309.7	46.3	190.3	255.9
1994	1,542	239	1,781	618,950	301.4	56.3	190.2	237.7
1995	1,336	178	1,514	580,510	255.1	38.8	154.2	220.9
1996	1,376	199	1,575	537,050	256.0	42.7	157.0	202.4

Notes: (1) Metropolitan Statistical Area - see Appendix A for areas included; (2) calculated by the editors using the following formula: (number of crimes in the MSA minus number of crimes in the city); (3) calculated by the editors using the following formula: ((number of crimes in the MSA minus number of crimes in the city) ÷ (population of the MSA minus population of the city)) x 100,000; n/a not avail.
Source: U.S. Department of Justice, FBI Uniform Crime Reports, 1977 - 1996

Aggravated Assaults and Aggravated Assault Rates: 1977 - 1996

Year	Number				Rate per 100,000 population			
	City	Suburbs[2]	MSA[1]	U.S.	City	Suburbs[3]	MSA[1]	U.S.
1977	528	265	793	534,350	163.5	207.8	176.0	247.0
1978	549	215	764	571,460	172.1	139.4	161.4	262.1
1979	659	263	922	629,480	195.1	171.0	187.6	286.0
1980	765	338	1,103	672,650	222.8	178.5	207.0	298.5
1981	574	439	1,013	663,900	160.5	222.6	182.6	289.7
1982	605	469	1,074	669,480	163.4	229.6	186.9	289.2
1983	571	635	1,206	653,290	149.8	302.2	204.0	279.2
1984	557	617	1,174	685,350	144.6	273.9	192.3	290.2
1985	746	844	1,590	723,250	183.5	331.9	240.6	302.9
1986	1,107	942	2,049	834,320	267.2	363.4	304.3	346.1
1987	1,005	736	1,741	855,090	214.0	281.5	238.2	351.3
1988	1,200	661	1,861	910,090	256.7	244.4	252.2	370.2
1989	1,320	706	2,026	951,710	281.5	246.6	268.3	383.4
1990	1,539	790	2,329	1,054,860	330.5	250.0	298.0	424.1
1991	1,088	703	1,791	1,092,740	228.8	217.9	224.4	433.3
1992	1,069	1,350	2,419	1,126,970	220.9	341.3	275.0	441.8
1993	1,148	1,400	2,548	1,135,610	228.7	335.9	277.3	440.3
1994	1,421	1,313	2,734	1,113,180	277.7	309.1	292.0	427.6
1995	2,360	1,269	3,629	1,099,210	450.6	276.8	369.5	418.3
1996	2,135	1,051	3,186	1,029,810	397.2	225.6	317.6	388.2

Notes: (1) Metropolitan Statistical Area - see Appendix A for areas included; (2) calculated by the editors using the following formula: (number of crimes in the MSA minus number of crimes in the city); (3) calculated by the editors using the following formula: ((number of crimes in the MSA minus number of crimes in the city) ÷ (population of the MSA minus population of the city)) x 100,000; n/a not avail.
Source: U.S. Department of Justice, FBI Uniform Crime Reports, 1977 - 1996

Burglaries and Burglary Rates: 1977 - 1996

Year	Number				Rate per 100,000 population			
	City	Suburbs[2]	MSA[1]	U.S.	City	Suburbs[3]	MSA[1]	U.S.
1977	7,243	2,237	9,480	3,071,500	2,242.4	1,754.5	2,104.3	1,419.8
1978	6,886	2,261	9,147	3,128,300	2,158.6	1,465.9	1,932.9	1,434.6
1979	7,766	2,274	10,040	3,327,700	2,299.5	1,478.5	2,042.6	1,511.9
1980	7,216	2,394	9,610	3,795,200	2,101.2	1,264.1	1,803.6	1,684.1
1981	7,875	2,346	10,221	3,779,700	2,202.1	1,189.6	1,842.2	1,649.5
1982	8,774	2,584	11,358	3,447,100	2,369.2	1,265.3	1,976.8	1,488.8
1983	7,966	2,517	10,483	3,129,900	2,090.3	1,197.7	1,773.0	1,337.7
1984	8,389	3,057	11,446	2,984,400	2,177.6	1,357.0	1,874.8	1,263.7
1985	10,261	3,427	13,688	3,073,300	2,524.4	1,347.5	2,071.5	1,287.3
1986	12,454	4,140	16,594	3,241,400	3,006.6	1,597.1	2,464.1	1,344.6
1987	11,417	4,268	15,685	3,236,200	2,431.5	1,632.6	2,145.8	1,329.6
1988	11,990	4,384	16,374	3,218,100	2,565.1	1,621.0	2,219.1	1,309.2
1989	11,160	4,248	15,408	3,168,200	2,380.0	1,483.8	2,040.3	1,276.3
1990	11,371	3,773	15,144	3,073,900	2,442.1	1,194.2	1,937.6	1,235.9
1991	11,591	4,190	15,781	3,157,200	2,437.3	1,298.5	1,977.0	1,252.0
1992	10,208	4,559	14,767	2,979,900	2,109.2	1,152.5	1,678.9	1,168.2
1993	8,453	4,213	12,666	2,834,800	1,683.8	1,010.9	1,378.6	1,099.2
1994	7,047	4,213	11,260	2,712,800	1,377.2	991.9	1,202.4	1,042.0
1995	7,521	3,847	11,368	2,593,800	1,436.2	839.2	1,157.5	987.1
1996	7,575	4,060	11,635	2,501,500	1,409.3	871.6	1,159.7	943.0

Notes: (1) Metropolitan Statistical Area - see Appendix A for areas included; (2) calculated by the editors using the following formula: (number of crimes in the MSA minus number of crimes in the city); (3) calculated by the editors using the following formula: ((number of crimes in the MSA minus number of crimes in the city) ÷ (population of the MSA minus population of the city)) x 100,000; n/a not avail.
Source: U.S. Department of Justice, FBI Uniform Crime Reports, 1977 - 1996

Larceny-Thefts and Larceny-Theft Rates: 1977 - 1996

Year	Number				Rate per 100,000 population			
	City	Suburbs[2]	MSA[1]	U.S.	City	Suburbs[3]	MSA[1]	U.S.
1977	13,796	3,507	17,303	5,905,700	4,271.2	2,750.6	3,840.9	2,729.9
1978	15,079	3,793	18,872	5,991,000	4,727.0	2,459.2	3,987.9	2,747.4
1979	16,390	4,106	20,496	6,601,000	4,853.0	2,669.6	4,169.8	2,999.1
1980	19,558	4,674	24,232	7,136,900	5,695.0	2,468.0	4,548.0	3,167.0
1981	19,838	5,187	25,025	7,194,400	5,547.4	2,630.2	4,510.5	3,139.7
1982	20,114	5,178	25,292	7,142,500	5,431.4	2,535.5	4,402.0	3,084.8
1983	18,889	5,621	24,510	6,712,800	4,956.6	2,674.7	4,145.5	2,868.9
1984	20,097	6,180	26,277	6,591,900	5,216.8	2,743.4	4,304.1	2,791.3
1985	24,308	7,358	31,666	6,926,400	5,980.3	2,893.2	4,792.1	2,901.2
1986	28,469	8,783	37,252	7,257,200	6,872.9	3,388.3	5,531.6	3,010.3
1987	28,486	9,038	37,524	7,499,900	6,066.8	3,457.3	5,133.5	3,081.3
1988	34,056	9,298	43,354	7,705,900	7,285.9	3,437.9	5,875.5	3,134.9
1989	33,556	9,468	43,024	7,872,400	7,156.2	3,307.2	5,697.1	3,171.3
1990	35,955	9,556	45,511	7,945,700	7,721.9	3,024.5	5,823.0	3,194.8
1991	34,417	9,840	44,257	8,142,200	7,237.2	3,049.4	5,544.3	3,228.8
1992	35,336	11,244	46,580	7,915,200	7,301.2	2,842.4	5,295.9	3,103.0
1993	35,647	11,243	46,890	7,820,900	7,100.7	2,697.8	5,103.6	3,032.4
1994	26,403	10,451	36,854	7,879,800	5,160.1	2,460.5	3,935.6	3,026.7
1995	27,434	10,606	38,040	7,997,700	5,238.6	2,313.5	3,873.2	3,043.8
1996	27,187	11,218	38,405	7,894,600	5,058.2	2,408.3	3,827.9	2,975.9

Notes: (1) Metropolitan Statistical Area - see Appendix A for areas included; (2) calculated by the editors using the following formula: (number of crimes in the MSA minus number of crimes in the city); (3) calculated by the editors using the following formula: ((number of crimes in the MSA minus number of crimes in the city) ÷ (population of the MSA minus population of the city)) x 100,000; n/a not avail.
Source: U.S. Department of Justice, FBI Uniform Crime Reports, 1977 - 1996

Motor Vehicle Thefts and Motor Vehicle Theft Rates: 1977 - 1996

Year	Number				Rate per 100,000 population			
	City	Suburbs[2]	MSA[1]	U.S.	City	Suburbs[3]	MSA[1]	U.S.
1977	1,237	308	1,545	977,700	383.0	241.6	343.0	451.9
1978	1,341	268	1,609	1,004,100	420.4	173.8	340.0	460.5
1979	1,586	322	1,908	1,112,800	469.6	209.4	388.2	505.6
1980	1,569	347	1,916	1,131,700	456.9	183.2	359.6	502.2
1981	1,609	353	1,962	1,087,800	449.9	179.0	353.6	474.7
1982	1,391	335	1,726	1,062,400	375.6	164.0	300.4	458.8
1983	1,423	371	1,794	1,007,900	373.4	176.5	303.4	430.8
1984	1,687	517	2,204	1,032,200	437.9	229.5	361.0	437.1
1985	2,112	630	2,742	1,102,900	519.6	247.7	415.0	462.0
1986	2,266	624	2,890	1,224,100	547.1	240.7	429.1	507.8
1987	2,122	624	2,746	1,288,700	451.9	238.7	375.7	529.4
1988	2,119	672	2,791	1,432,900	453.3	248.5	378.2	582.9
1989	2,707	734	3,441	1,564,800	577.3	256.4	455.6	630.4
1990	3,891	753	4,644	1,635,900	835.7	238.3	594.2	657.8
1991	4,739	899	5,638	1,661,700	996.5	278.6	706.3	659.0
1992	4,570	999	5,569	1,610,800	944.3	252.5	633.2	631.5
1993	4,357	918	5,275	1,563,100	867.9	220.3	574.1	606.1
1994	3,933	917	4,850	1,539,300	768.7	215.9	517.9	591.3
1995	3,581	749	4,330	1,472,400	683.8	163.4	440.9	560.4
1996	3,695	835	4,530	1,395,200	687.5	179.3	451.5	525.9

Notes: (1) Metropolitan Statistical Area - see Appendix A for areas included; (2) calculated by the editors using the following formula: (number of crimes in the MSA minus number of crimes in the city); (3) calculated by the editors using the following formula: ((number of crimes in the MSA minus number of crimes in the city) ÷ (population of the MSA minus population of the city)) x 100,000; n/a not avail.
Source: U.S. Department of Justice, FBI Uniform Crime Reports, 1977 - 1996

HATE CRIMES

Criminal Incidents by Bias Motivation

Area	Race	Ethnicity	Religion	Sexual Orientation
Austin	21	6	0	11

Notes: Figures include both violent and property crimes. Law enforcement agencies must have submitted data for at least one quarter of calendar year 1995 to be included in this report, therefore figures shown may not represent complete 12-month totals; n/a not available
Source: U.S. Department of Justice, FBI Uniform Crime Reports, Hate Crime Statistics 1995

LAW ENFORCEMENT

Full-Time Law Enforcement Employees

Jurisdiction	Police Employees			Police Officers per 100,000 population
	Total	Officers	Civilians	
Austin	1,352	935	417	174.0

Notes: Data as of October 31, 1996
Source: U.S. Department of Justice, FBI Uniform Crime Reports, 1996

Number of Police Officers by Race

Race	Police Officers				Index of Representation[1]		
	1983		1992				
	Number	Pct.	Number	Pct.	1983	1992	% Chg.
Black	43	7.1	81	9.8	0.57	0.78	36.8
Hispanic[2]	73	12.0	123	14.8	0.64	0.64	0.0

Notes: (1) The index of representation is calculated by dividing the percent of black/hispanic police officers by the percent of corresponding blacks/hispanics in the local population. An index approaching 1.0 indicates that a city is closer to achieving a representation of police officers equal to their proportion in the local population; (2) Hispanic officers can be of any race
Source: Bureau of Justice Statistics, Sourcebook of Criminal Justice Statistics, 1994

CORRECTIONS

Federal Correctional Facilities

Type	Year Opened	Security Level	Sex of Inmates	Rated Capacity	Population on 7/1/95	Number of Staff
None listed						

Notes: Data as of 1995
Source: Bureau of Justice Statistics, Sourcebook of Criminal Justice Statistics Online

City/County/Regional Correctional Facilities

Name	Year Opened	Year Renov.	Rated Capacity	1995 Pop.	Number of COs[1]	Number of Staff	ACA[2] Accred.
Travis County Jail	1986	--	479	n/a	n/a	n/a	No

Notes: Data as of April 1996; (1) Correctional Officers; (2) American Correctional Assn. Accreditation
Source: American Correctional Association, 1996-1998 National Jail and Adult Detention Directory

Private Adult Correctional Facilities

Name	Date Opened	Rated Capacity	Present Pop.	Security Level	Facility Construct.	Expans. Plans	ACA[1] Accred.
Travis Co. Comm. Justice Center	3/97	1,000	n/a	Min/Med	New	None	Will be sought

Notes: Data as of December 1996; (1) American Correctional Association Accreditation
Source: University of Florida, Center for Studies in Criminology and Law, Private Adult Correctional Facility Census, 10th Ed., March 15, 1997

Characteristics of Shock Incarceration Programs

Jurisdiction	Year Program Began	Number of Camps	Average Num. of Inmates	Number of Beds	Program Length	Voluntary/ Mandatory
Texas	1989	2	250	500 male; 20 female	75 to 90 days	Mandatory

Note: Data as of July 1996;
Source: Sourcebook of Criminal Justice Statistics Online

INMATES AND HIV/AIDS

HIV Testing Policies for Inmates

Jurisdiction	All Inmates at Some Time	All Convicted Inmates at Admission	Random Samples While in Custody	High-risk Groups	Upon Inmate Request	Upon Court Order	Upon Involvement in Incident
Travis Co.	No	No	No	No	Yes	Yes	No

Source: HIV in Prisons and Jails, 1993 (released August 1995)

Inmates Known to be Positive for HIV

Jurisdiction	Number of Jail Inmates in Facilities Providing Data	Type of HIV Infection/AIDS Cases				HIV/AIDS Cases as a Percent of Tot. Custody Pop.
		Total	Asymp-tomatic	Symp-tomatic	Confirmed AIDS	
Travis Co.[1]	806	15	1	8	6	1.9

Note: (1) Some but not all facilities reported data on HIV/AIDS cases. Excludes inmates in facilities that did not report data.
Source: HIV in Prisons and Jails, 1993 (released August, 1995)

DEATH PENALTY

Death Penalty Statistics

State	Prisoners Executed		Prisoners Under Sentence of Death					Avg. No. of Years on Death Row[4]
	1930-1995	1996[1]	Total[2]	White[3]	Black[3]	Hisp.	Women	
Texas	401	3	404	241	158	68	6	6.5

Notes: Data as of 12/31/95 unless otherwise noted; (1) Data as of 7/31/97; (2) Includes persons of other races; (3) Includes people of Hispanic origin; (4) Covers prisoners sentenced 1974 through 1995
Source: Bureau of Justice Statistics, Capital Punishment 1995 (released 12/96); Death Penalty Information Center Web Site, 9/30/97

Capital Offenses and Methods of Execution

Capital Offenses in Texas	Minimum Age for Imposition of Death Penalty	Mentally Retarded Excluded	Methods of Execution[1]
Criminal homicide with 1 of 8 aggravating circumstances.	17	No	Lethal injection

Notes: Data as of 12/31/95 unless otherwise noted; (1) Data as of 7/31/97
Source: Bureau of Justice Statistics, Capital Punishment 1995 (released 12/96); Death Penalty Information Center Web Site, 9/30/97

LAWS

Statutory Provisions Relating to the Purchase, Ownership and Use of Handguns

Jurisdiction	Instant Background Check	Federal Waiting Period Applies[1]	State Waiting Period (days)	License or Permit to Purchase	Regis-tration	Record of Sale Sent to Police	Concealed Carry Law
Texas	No	Yes[a]	No	No	No	No	Yes[b]

Note: Data as of 1996; (1) The Federal 5-day waiting period for handgun purchases applies to states that don't have instant background checks, waiting period requirements, or licensing procedures exempting them from the Federal requirement; (a) The Federal waiting period does not apply to a person holding a valid permit or license to carry a firearm, issued within 5 years of proposed purchase; (b) "Shall issue" permit system, liberally administered discretion by local authorities over permit issuance, or no permit required
Source: Sourcebook of Criminal Justice Statistics Online

Statutory Provisions Relating to Alcohol Use and Driving

Jurisdiction	Drinking Age	Blood Alcohol Concentration Levels as Evidence in State Courts[1]		Open Container Law[1]	Anti-Consump-tion Law[1]	Dram Shop Law[1]
		Illegal per se at 0.10%	Presumption at 0.10%			
Texas	21	Yes	No	No	Yes[a]	Yes[b]

Note: Data as of January 1, 1997; (1) See Appendix C for an explanation of terms; (a) Applies to drivers only; (b) Statutory law has limited dram shop actions
Source: Sourcebook of Criminal Justice Statistics Online

Statutory Provisions Relating to Curfews

Jurisdiction	Year Enacted	Latest Revision	Age Group(s)	Curfew Provisions
Austin	1994	-	16 and under	11:30 pm to 6 am school nights 12:30 am to 6 am weekend nights 12:30 am to 6 am summer nights 10 pm to 6 am every night in club dist.[1] 9 pm to 6 am school days

Note: Data as of Feb. 1996; (1) A well-known section of Guadelupe Street near the University of Texas
Source: Sourcebook of Criminal Justice Statistics Online

Statutory Provisions Relating to Hate Crimes

Jurisdiction	Bias-Motivated Violence and Intimidation						Institutional Vandalism
		Criminal Penalty					
	Civil Action	Race/ Religion/ Ethnicity	Sexual Orientation	Mental/ Physical Disability	Gender	Age	
Texas	No	No	No	No	No	No	Yes

Source: Anti-Defamation League, 1997 Hate Crimes Laws

Baltimore, Maryland

OVERVIEW

The total crime rate for the city increased 43.4% between 1977 and 1996. During that same period, the violent crime rate increased 53.3% and the property crime rate increased 40.7%.

Among violent crimes, the rates for: Murders increased 115.0%; Forcible Rapes increased 44.1%; Robberies increased 54.2%; and Aggravated Assaults increased 51.1%.

Among property crimes, the rates for: Burglaries increased 8.9%; Larceny-Thefts increased 44.1%; and Motor Vehicle Thefts increased 102.3%.

ANTI-CRIME PROGRAMS

Programs include:

- V.C.T.F. (Violent Crimes Task Force)—In August 1992 the Task Force was formed to impact violent crime by means of street enforcement, investigations, and involvement with community organizations. The goal of the V.C.T.F. is to identify and target criminals. As a result of its implementation the number of shootings in the most violent areas were reduced by 40%.
- E.C.H.O. (Emergency Cooperative Housecleaning Operation)—Initiated in 1993 to make public housing areas a better place for its residents to live.
- In November 1993 the Domestic Violence Unit was formed. Its purpose is to intervene in domestic incidents before they deteriorate and result in serious injury or death.
- C.O.P.S. (Community Oriented Police Services)—Grants have been awarded to add 76 additional officers on the street for community policing.
- G.R.E.A.T. (Gang Resistance Education and Training)—Grant for 9 officers to receive specialized training in instruction of gang awareness which is then presented to all 6th and 7th graders.
- Vehicle Theft Grant—To aid in vehicle theft prevention and reduce vehicle theft by sharing data with other law enforcement agencies. *Baltimore Police Department, Planning and Research Division, 9/97*

CRIME RISK

Your Chances of Becoming a Victim[1]

Area	Any Crime	Violent Crime					Property Crime			
		Any	Murder	Forcible Rape[2]	Robbery	Aggrav. Assault	Any	Burglary	Larceny -Theft	Motor Vehicle Theft
City	1:8	1:37	1:2,184	1:595	1:69	1:88	1:11	1:48	1:18	1:64

Note: (1) Figures have been calculated by dividing the population of the city by the number of crimes reported to the FBI during 1996 and are expressed as odds (eg. 1:20 should be read as 1 in 20). (2) Figures have been calculated by dividing the female population of the city by the number of forcible rapes reported to the FBI during 1996. The female population of the city was estimated by calculating the ratio of females to males reported in the 1990 Census and applying that ratio to 1996 population estimate.
Source: FBI Uniform Crime Reports 1996

CRIME STATISTICS

Total Crimes and Total Crime Rates: 1977 - 1996

Year	Number				Rate per 100,000 population			
	City	Suburbs[2]	MSA[1]	U.S.	City	Suburbs[3]	MSA[1]	U.S.
1977	67,287	70,927	138,214	10,984,500	8,369.0	5,275.5	6,433.1	5,077.6
1978	69,463	71,023	140,486	11,209,000	8,770.6	5,273.9	6,568.8	5,140.3
1979	73,744	76,988	150,732	12,249,500	9,324.0	5,671.5	7,016.1	5,565.5
1980	76,704	85,075	161,779	13,408,300	9,776.8	6,163.5	7,473.0	5,950.0
1981	77,563	84,803	162,366	13,423,800	9,726.6	6,044.6	7,379.0	5,858.2
1982	72,906	78,355	151,261	12,974,400	9,134.1	5,579.8	6,867.9	5,603.6
1983	68,667	70,593	139,260	12,108,600	8,524.5	4,891.1	6,192.6	5,175.0
1984	65,363	71,689	137,052	11,881,800	8,288.4	4,874.6	6,066.2	5,031.3
1985	66,121	73,776	139,897	12,431,400	8,574.9	4,932.7	6,171.7	5,207.1
1986	66,273	81,577	147,850	13,211,900	8,458.1	5,367.5	6,418.8	5,480.4
1987	65,553	79,527	145,080	13,508,700	8,570.2	5,125.4	6,262.8	5,550.0
1988	70,021	82,420	152,441	13,923,100	9,166.5	5,168.6	6,463.4	5,664.2
1989	71,373	80,063	151,436	14,251,400	9,352.6	4,954.8	6,365.6	5,741.0
1990	77,989	83,160	161,149	14,475,600	10,596.1	5,051.8	6,764.8	5,820.3
1991	85,068	90,885	175,953	14,872,900	11,371.2	5,431.7	7,266.8	5,897.8
1992	90,114	90,405	180,519	14,438,200	11,927.5	5,350.1	7,382.3	5,660.2
1993	91,920	86,856	178,776	14,144,800	12,540.8	5,037.2	7,275.4	5,484.4
1994	92,783	87,718	180,501	13,989,500	12,552.2	5,045.6	7,285.1	5,373.5
1995	94,855	89,910	184,765	13,862,700	13,318.4	5,085.2	7,449.4	5,275.9
1996	85,982	89,344	175,326	13,473,600	12,001.2	5,023.2	7,026.9	5,078.9

Notes: (1) Metropolitan Statistical Area - see Appendix A for areas included; (2) calculated by the editors using the following formula: (number of crimes in the MSA minus number of crimes in the city); (3) calculated by the editors using the following formula: ((number of crimes in the MSA minus number of crimes in the city) ÷ (population of the MSA minus population of the city)) x 100,000; n/a not avail.
Source: U.S. Department of Justice, FBI Uniform Crime Reports, 1977 - 1996

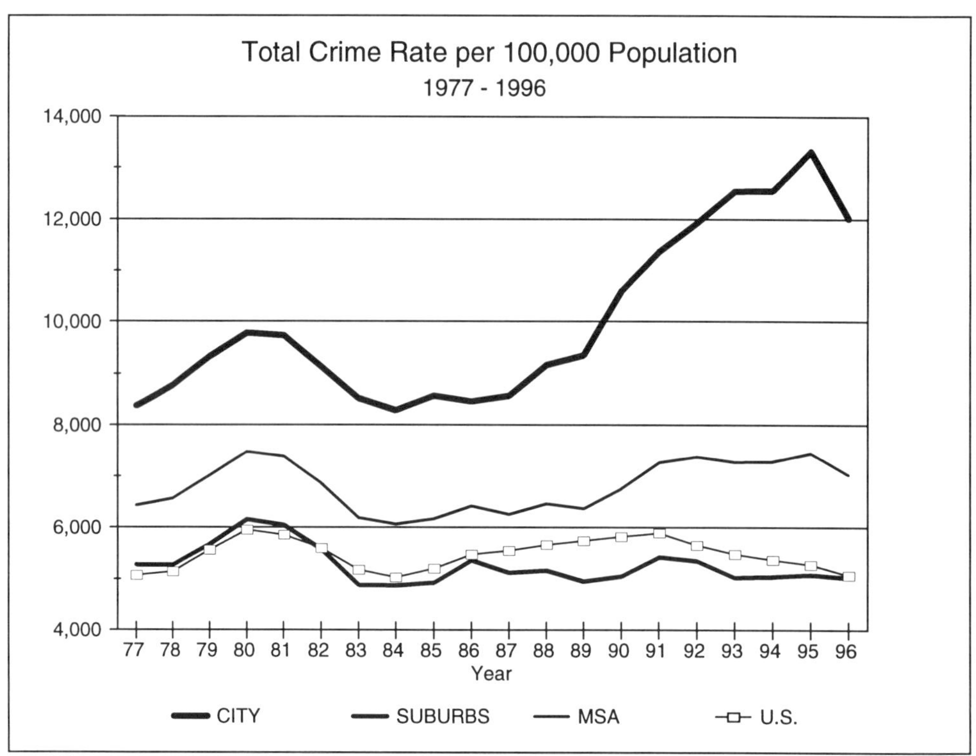

Note: Missing line segments indicate data not available.

Violent Crimes and Violent Crime Rates: 1977 - 1996

Year	Number				Rate per 100,000 population			
	City	Suburbs[2]	MSA[1]	U.S.	City	Suburbs[3]	MSA[1]	U.S.
1977	14,283	6,598	20,881	1,029,580	1,776.5	490.8	971.9	475.9
1978	14,659	7,199	21,858	1,085,550	1,850.9	534.6	1,022.0	497.8
1979	15,523	7,854	23,377	1,208,030	1,962.7	578.6	1,088.1	548.9
1980	16,571	8,575	25,146	1,344,520	2,112.2	621.2	1,161.6	596.6
1981	17,737	8,885	26,622	1,361,820	2,224.3	633.3	1,209.9	594.3
1982	16,683	9,158	25,841	1,322,390	2,090.1	652.2	1,173.3	571.1
1983	16,132	8,677	24,809	1,258,090	2,002.7	601.2	1,103.2	537.7
1984	15,581	9,012	24,593	1,273,280	1,975.8	612.8	1,088.5	539.2
1985	15,498	10,162	25,660	1,328,800	2,009.9	679.4	1,132.0	556.6
1986	15,229	10,146	25,375	1,489,170	1,943.6	667.6	1,101.6	617.7
1987	14,295	8,701	22,996	1,484,000	1,868.9	560.8	992.7	609.7
1988	14,721	9,830	24,551	1,566,220	1,927.1	616.4	1,041.0	637.2
1989	15,618	10,451	26,069	1,646,040	2,046.5	646.8	1,095.8	663.1
1990	17,942	10,314	28,256	1,820,130	2,437.7	626.5	1,186.1	731.8
1991	19,032	11,357	30,389	1,911,770	2,544.0	678.7	1,255.0	758.1
1992	21,799	11,442	33,241	1,932,270	2,885.3	677.1	1,359.4	757.5
1993	21,945	11,377	33,322	1,926,020	2,994.0	659.8	1,356.1	746.8
1994	20,951	11,166	32,117	1,857,670	2,834.4	642.3	1,296.3	713.6
1995	21,495	11,638	33,133	1,798,790	3,018.1	658.2	1,335.9	684.6
1996	19,507	11,365	30,872	1,682,280	2,722.7	639.0	1,237.3	634.1

Notes: Violent crimes include murder, forcible rape, robbery and aggravated assault; n/a not available; (1) Metropolitan Statistical Area - see Appendix A for areas included; (2) calculated by the editors using the following formula: (number of crimes in the MSA minus number of crimes in the city); (3) calculated by the editors using the following formula: ((number of crimes in the MSA minus number of crimes in the city) ÷ (population of the MSA minus population of the city)) x 100,000
Source: U.S. Department of Justice, FBI Uniform Crime Reports, 1977 - 1996

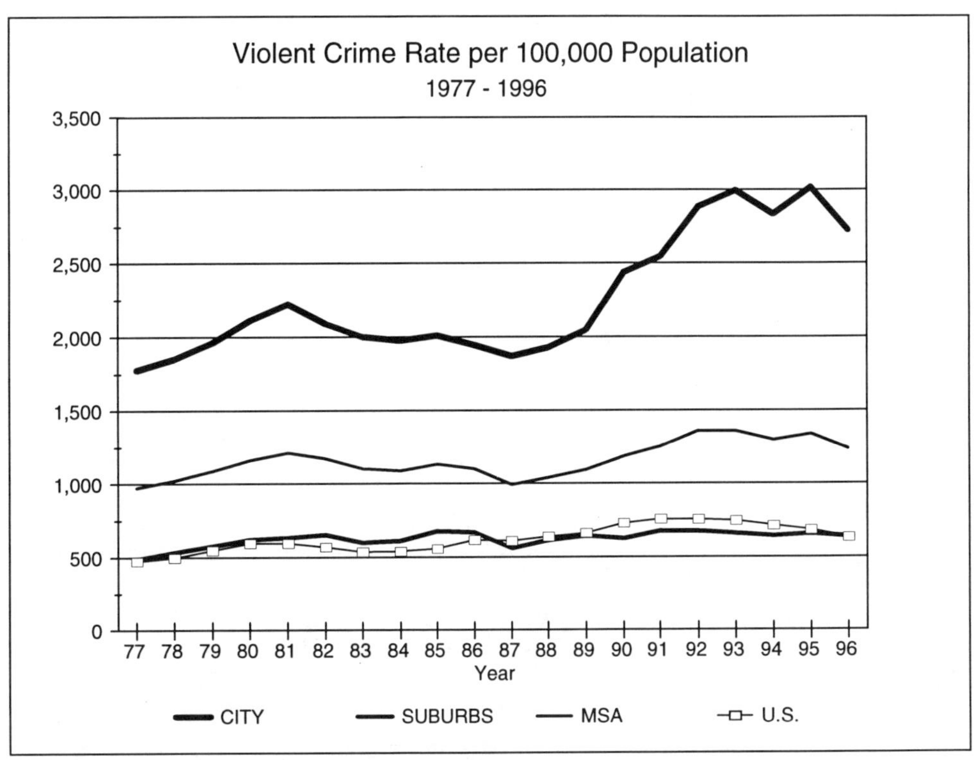

Note: Missing line segments indicate data not available.

Property Crimes and Property Crime Rates: 1977 - 1996

Year	Number				Rate per 100,000 population			
	City	Suburbs[2]	MSA[1]	U.S.	City	Suburbs[3]	MSA[1]	U.S.
1977	53,004	64,329	117,333	9,955,000	6,592.5	4,784.7	5,461.2	4,601.7
1978	54,804	63,824	118,628	10,123,400	6,919.7	4,739.3	5,546.8	4,642.5
1979	58,221	69,134	127,355	11,041,500	7,361.4	5,092.9	5,928.0	5,016.6
1980	60,133	76,500	136,633	12,063,700	7,664.6	5,542.3	6,311.4	5,353.3
1981	59,826	75,918	135,744	12,061,900	7,502.4	5,411.3	6,169.1	5,263.9
1982	56,223	69,197	125,420	11,652,000	7,043.9	4,927.6	5,694.6	5,032.5
1983	52,535	61,916	114,451	10,850,500	6,521.8	4,289.9	5,089.4	4,637.4
1984	49,782	62,677	112,459	10,608,500	6,312.7	4,261.8	4,977.7	4,492.1
1985	50,623	63,614	114,237	11,102,600	6,565.1	4,253.3	5,039.7	4,650.5
1986	51,044	71,431	122,475	11,722,700	6,514.5	4,699.9	5,317.2	4,862.6
1987	51,258	70,826	122,084	12,024,700	6,701.3	4,564.6	5,270.1	4,940.3
1988	55,300	72,590	127,890	12,356,900	7,239.4	4,552.2	5,422.5	5,027.1
1989	55,755	69,612	125,367	12,605,400	7,306.0	4,308.1	5,269.8	5,077.9
1990	60,047	72,846	132,893	12,655,500	8,158.4	4,425.2	5,578.6	5,088.5
1991	66,036	79,528	145,564	12,961,100	8,827.2	4,752.9	6,011.7	5,139.7
1992	68,315	78,963	147,278	12,505,900	9,042.2	4,673.0	6,022.9	4,902.7
1993	69,975	75,479	145,454	12,218,800	9,546.8	4,377.4	5,919.3	4,737.6
1994	71,832	76,552	148,384	12,131,900	9,717.8	4,403.4	5,988.8	4,660.0
1995	73,360	78,272	151,632	12,063,900	10,300.3	4,427.0	6,113.5	4,591.3
1996	66,475	77,979	144,454	11,791,300	9,278.4	4,384.2	5,789.6	4,444.8

Notes: Property crimes include burglary, larceny-theft and motor vehicle theft; n/a not available; (1) Metropolitan Statistical Area - see Appendix A for areas included; (2) calculated by the editors using the following formula: (number of crimes in the MSA minus number of crimes in the city); (3) calculated by the editors using the following formula: ((number of crimes in the MSA minus number of crimes in the city) ÷ (population of the MSA minus population of the city)) x 100,000
Source: U.S. Department of Justice, FBI Uniform Crime Reports, 1977 - 1996

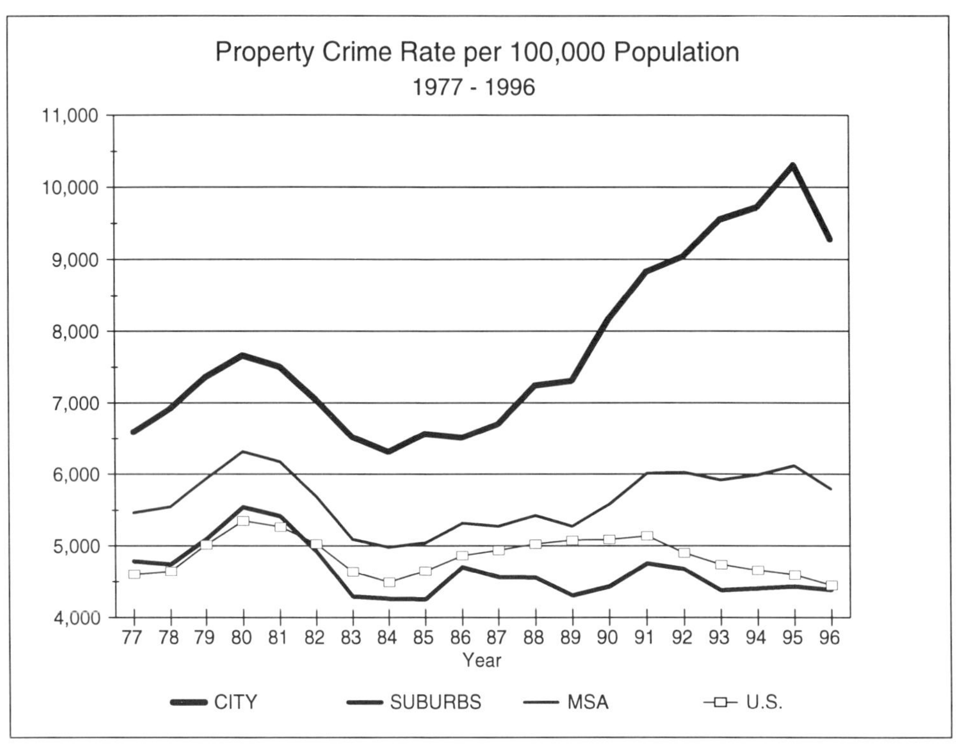

Note: Missing line segments indicate data not available.

Murders and Murder Rates: 1977 - 1996

Year	Number				Rate per 100,000 population			
	City	Suburbs[2]	MSA[1]	U.S.	City	Suburbs[3]	MSA[1]	U.S.
1977	171	48	219	19,120	21.3	3.6	10.2	8.8
1978	197	54	251	19,560	24.9	4.0	11.7	9.0
1979	245	49	294	21,460	31.0	3.6	13.7	9.7
1980	216	55	271	23,040	27.5	4.0	12.5	10.2
1981	228	69	297	22,520	28.6	4.9	13.5	9.8
1982	227	67	294	21,010	28.4	4.8	13.3	9.1
1983	201	57	258	19,310	25.0	3.9	11.5	8.3
1984	215	53	268	18,690	27.3	3.6	11.9	7.9
1985	213	48	261	18,980	27.6	3.2	11.5	7.9
1986	240	63	303	20,610	30.6	4.1	13.2	8.6
1987	226	74	300	20,100	29.5	4.8	13.0	8.3
1988	234	59	293	20,680	30.6	3.7	12.4	8.4
1989	262	77	339	21,500	34.3	4.8	14.2	8.7
1990	305	66	371	23,440	41.4	4.0	15.6	9.4
1991	304	55	359	24,700	40.6	3.3	14.8	9.8
1992	335	73	408	23,760	44.3	4.3	16.7	9.3
1993	353	70	423	24,530	48.2	4.1	17.2	9.5
1994	321	58	379	23,330	43.4	3.3	15.3	9.0
1995	325	67	392	21,610	45.6	3.8	15.8	8.2
1996	328	66	394	19,650	45.8	3.7	15.8	7.4

Notes: (1) Metropolitan Statistical Area - see Appendix A for areas included; (2) calculated by the editors using the following formula: (number of crimes in the MSA minus number of crimes in the city); (3) calculated by the editors using the following formula: ((number of crimes in the MSA minus number of crimes in the city) ÷ (population of the MSA minus population of the city)) x 100,000; n/a not avail.
Source: U.S. Department of Justice, FBI Uniform Crime Reports, 1977 - 1996

Forcible Rapes and Forcible Rape Rates: 1977 - 1996

Year	Number				Rate per 100,000 population			
	City	Suburbs[2]	MSA[1]	U.S.	City	Suburbs[3]	MSA[1]	U.S.
1977	499	382	881	63,500	62.1	28.4	41.0	29.4
1978	554	319	873	67,610	69.9	23.7	40.8	31.0
1979	564	363	927	76,390	71.3	26.7	43.1	34.7
1980	560	391	951	82,990	71.4	28.3	43.9	36.8
1981	565	354	919	82,500	70.9	25.2	41.8	36.0
1982	550	327	877	78,770	68.9	23.3	39.8	34.0
1983	497	292	789	78,920	61.7	20.2	35.1	33.7
1984	564	358	922	84,230	71.5	24.3	40.8	35.7
1985	592	426	1,018	88,670	76.8	28.5	44.9	37.1
1986	660	464	1,124	91,460	84.2	30.5	48.8	37.9
1987	595	430	1,025	91,110	77.8	27.7	44.2	37.4
1988	517	381	898	92,490	67.7	23.9	38.1	37.6
1989	541	459	1,000	94,500	70.9	28.4	42.0	38.1
1990	687	529	1,216	102,560	93.3	32.1	51.0	41.2
1991	701	542	1,243	106,590	93.7	32.4	51.3	42.3
1992	749	570	1,319	109,060	99.1	33.7	53.9	42.8
1993	668	553	1,221	106,010	91.1	32.1	49.7	41.1
1994	637	525	1,162	102,220	86.2	30.2	46.9	39.3
1995	683	505	1,188	97,470	95.9	28.6	47.9	37.1
1996	641	482	1,123	95,770	89.5	27.1	45.0	36.1

Notes: (1) Metropolitan Statistical Area - see Appendix A for areas included; (2) calculated by the editors using the following formula: (number of crimes in the MSA minus number of crimes in the city); (3) calculated by the editors using the following formula: ((number of crimes in the MSA minus number of crimes in the city) ÷ (population of the MSA minus population of the city)) x 100,000; n/a not avail.
Source: U.S. Department of Justice, FBI Uniform Crime Reports, 1977 - 1996

Robberies and Robbery Rates: 1977 - 1996

Year	Number				Rate per 100,000 population			
	City	Suburbs[2]	MSA[1]	U.S.	City	Suburbs[3]	MSA[1]	U.S.
1977	7,563	1,408	8,971	412,610	940.7	104.7	417.6	190.7
1978	8,097	1,441	9,538	426,930	1,022.3	107.0	446.0	195.8
1979	8,482	1,621	10,103	480,700	1,072.4	119.4	470.3	218.4
1980	10,020	1,816	11,836	565,840	1,277.2	131.6	546.7	251.1
1981	10,715	2,174	12,889	592,910	1,343.7	155.0	585.8	258.7
1982	9,347	1,898	11,245	553,130	1,171.0	135.2	510.6	238.9
1983	9,167	1,986	11,153	506,570	1,138.0	137.6	495.9	216.5
1984	8,002	1,729	9,731	485,010	1,014.7	117.6	430.7	205.4
1985	7,771	1,756	9,527	497,870	1,007.8	117.4	420.3	208.5
1986	7,989	2,022	10,011	542,780	1,019.6	133.0	434.6	225.1
1987	7,466	2,080	9,546	517,700	976.1	134.1	412.1	212.7
1988	7,396	2,370	9,766	542,970	968.2	148.6	414.1	220.9
1989	7,966	2,621	10,587	578,330	1,043.8	162.2	445.0	233.0
1990	9,477	2,421	11,898	639,270	1,287.6	147.1	499.5	257.0
1991	10,770	3,120	13,890	687,730	1,439.6	186.5	573.6	272.7
1992	12,263	3,316	15,579	672,480	1,623.1	196.2	637.1	263.6
1993	12,376	3,256	15,632	659,870	1,688.5	188.8	636.2	255.9
1994	11,275	3,225	14,500	618,950	1,525.3	185.5	585.2	237.7
1995	11,353	3,701	15,054	580,510	1,594.1	209.3	607.0	220.9
1996	10,393	3,686	14,079	537,050	1,450.6	207.2	564.3	202.4

Notes: (1) Metropolitan Statistical Area - see Appendix A for areas included; (2) calculated by the editors using the following formula: (number of crimes in the MSA minus number of crimes in the city); (3) calculated by the editors using the following formula: ((number of crimes in the MSA minus number of crimes in the city) ÷ (population of the MSA minus population of the city)) x 100,000; n/a not avail.
Source: U.S. Department of Justice, FBI Uniform Crime Reports, 1977 - 1996

Aggravated Assaults and Aggravated Assault Rates: 1977 - 1996

Year	Number				Rate per 100,000 population			
	City	Suburbs[2]	MSA[1]	U.S.	City	Suburbs[3]	MSA[1]	U.S.
1977	6,050	4,760	10,810	534,350	752.5	354.0	503.1	247.0
1978	5,811	5,385	11,196	571,460	733.7	399.9	523.5	262.1
1979	6,232	5,821	12,053	629,480	788.0	428.8	561.0	286.0
1980	5,775	6,313	12,088	672,650	736.1	457.4	558.4	298.5
1981	6,229	6,288	12,517	663,900	781.1	448.2	568.9	289.7
1982	6,559	6,866	13,425	669,480	821.7	488.9	609.6	289.2
1983	6,267	6,342	12,609	653,290	778.0	439.4	560.7	279.2
1984	6,800	6,872	13,672	685,350	862.3	467.3	605.2	290.2
1985	6,922	7,932	14,854	723,250	897.7	530.3	655.3	302.9
1986	6,340	7,597	13,937	834,320	809.1	499.9	605.1	346.1
1987	6,008	6,117	12,125	855,090	785.5	394.2	523.4	351.3
1988	6,574	7,020	13,594	910,090	860.6	440.2	576.4	370.2
1989	6,849	7,294	14,143	951,710	897.5	451.4	594.5	383.4
1990	7,473	7,298	14,771	1,054,860	1,015.3	443.3	620.1	424.1
1991	7,257	7,640	14,897	1,092,740	970.1	456.6	615.2	433.3
1992	8,452	7,483	15,935	1,126,970	1,118.7	442.8	651.7	441.8
1993	8,548	7,498	16,046	1,135,610	1,166.2	434.8	653.0	440.3
1994	8,718	7,358	16,076	1,113,180	1,179.4	423.2	648.8	427.6
1995	9,134	7,365	16,499	1,099,210	1,282.5	416.6	665.2	418.3
1996	8,145	7,131	15,276	1,029,810	1,136.9	400.9	612.2	388.2

Notes: (1) Metropolitan Statistical Area - see Appendix A for areas included; (2) calculated by the editors using the following formula: (number of crimes in the MSA minus number of crimes in the city); (3) calculated by the editors using the following formula: ((number of crimes in the MSA minus number of crimes in the city) ÷ (population of the MSA minus population of the city)) x 100,000; n/a not avail.
Source: U.S. Department of Justice, FBI Uniform Crime Reports, 1977 - 1996

Burglaries and Burglary Rates: 1977 - 1996

Year	Number				Rate per 100,000 population			
	City	Suburbs[2]	MSA[1]	U.S.	City	Suburbs[3]	MSA[1]	U.S.
1977	15,257	17,371	32,628	3,071,500	1,897.6	1,292.0	1,518.7	1,419.8
1978	15,793	17,216	33,009	3,128,300	1,994.1	1,278.4	1,543.4	1,434.6
1979	16,915	18,580	35,495	3,327,700	2,138.7	1,368.7	1,652.2	1,511.9
1980	17,659	22,037	39,696	3,795,200	2,250.8	1,596.5	1,833.7	1,684.1
1981	18,446	21,488	39,934	3,779,700	2,313.2	1,531.6	1,814.9	1,649.5
1982	16,315	17,972	34,287	3,447,100	2,044.0	1,279.8	1,556.8	1,488.8
1983	14,547	16,546	31,093	3,129,900	1,805.9	1,146.4	1,382.6	1,337.7
1984	13,837	16,561	30,398	2,984,400	1,754.6	1,126.1	1,345.5	1,263.7
1985	13,872	16,888	30,760	3,073,300	1,799.0	1,129.1	1,357.0	1,287.3
1986	14,321	18,871	33,192	3,241,400	1,827.7	1,241.6	1,441.0	1,344.6
1987	13,475	16,733	30,208	3,236,200	1,761.7	1,078.4	1,304.0	1,329.6
1988	14,251	16,986	31,237	3,218,100	1,865.6	1,065.2	1,324.4	1,309.2
1989	14,315	16,652	30,967	3,168,200	1,875.8	1,030.5	1,301.7	1,276.3
1990	14,753	16,667	31,420	3,073,900	2,004.4	1,012.5	1,319.0	1,235.9
1991	16,230	16,879	33,109	3,157,200	2,169.5	1,008.8	1,367.4	1,252.0
1992	16,298	16,909	33,207	2,979,900	2,157.2	1,000.7	1,358.0	1,168.2
1993	17,901	16,171	34,072	2,834,800	2,442.3	937.8	1,386.6	1,099.2
1994	15,897	14,531	30,428	2,712,800	2,150.6	835.8	1,228.1	1,042.0
1995	16,569	14,710	31,279	2,593,800	2,326.4	832.0	1,261.1	987.1
1996	14,802	14,545	29,347	2,501,500	2,066.0	817.8	1,176.2	943.0

Notes: (1) Metropolitan Statistical Area - see Appendix A for areas included; (2) calculated by the editors using the following formula: (number of crimes in the MSA minus number of crimes in the city); (3) calculated by the editors using the following formula: ((number of crimes in the MSA minus number of crimes in the city) ÷ (population of the MSA minus population of the city)) x 100,000; n/a not avail.
Source: U.S. Department of Justice, FBI Uniform Crime Reports, 1977 - 1996

Larceny-Thefts and Larceny-Theft Rates: 1977 - 1996

Year	Number				Rate per 100,000 population			
	City	Suburbs[2]	MSA[1]	U.S.	City	Suburbs[3]	MSA[1]	U.S.
1977	31,560	41,815	73,375	5,905,700	3,925.4	3,110.1	3,415.2	2,729.9
1978	33,137	41,900	75,037	5,991,000	4,184.0	3,111.3	3,508.6	2,747.4
1979	34,537	45,073	79,610	6,601,000	4,366.8	3,320.4	3,705.6	2,999.1
1980	36,854	49,010	85,864	7,136,900	4,697.4	3,550.7	3,966.3	3,167.0
1981	36,066	49,173	85,239	7,194,400	4,522.8	3,505.0	3,873.8	3,139.7
1982	35,456	46,406	81,862	7,142,500	4,442.1	3,304.6	3,716.9	3,084.8
1983	33,528	40,972	74,500	6,712,800	4,162.2	2,838.8	3,312.8	2,868.9
1984	30,530	41,551	72,081	6,591,900	3,871.4	2,825.3	3,190.5	2,791.3
1985	30,732	41,661	72,393	6,926,400	3,985.5	2,785.5	3,193.7	2,901.2
1986	29,850	46,091	75,941	7,257,200	3,809.6	3,032.6	3,296.9	3,010.3
1987	30,319	47,151	77,470	7,499,900	3,963.8	3,038.8	3,344.2	3,081.3
1988	32,606	47,839	80,445	7,705,900	4,268.5	3,000.0	3,410.8	3,134.9
1989	33,267	45,256	78,523	7,872,400	4,359.2	2,800.7	3,300.7	3,171.3
1990	35,383	47,342	82,725	7,945,700	4,807.4	2,875.9	3,472.7	3,194.8
1991	39,213	52,860	92,073	8,142,200	5,241.7	3,159.1	3,802.6	3,228.8
1992	40,717	52,798	93,515	7,915,200	5,389.3	3,124.6	3,824.3	3,103.0
1993	41,451	50,282	91,733	7,820,900	5,655.2	2,916.1	3,733.1	3,032.4
1994	42,402	51,993	94,395	7,879,800	5,736.4	2,990.7	3,809.8	3,026.7
1995	45,619	54,696	100,315	7,997,700	6,405.3	3,093.6	4,044.5	3,043.8
1996	40,522	55,324	95,846	7,894,600	5,656.0	3,110.5	3,841.4	2,975.9

Notes: (1) Metropolitan Statistical Area - see Appendix A for areas included; (2) calculated by the editors using the following formula: (number of crimes in the MSA minus number of crimes in the city); (3) calculated by the editors using the following formula: ((number of crimes in the MSA minus number of crimes in the city) ÷ (population of the MSA minus population of the city)) x 100,000; n/a not avail.
Source: U.S. Department of Justice, FBI Uniform Crime Reports, 1977 - 1996

Motor Vehicle Thefts and Motor Vehicle Theft Rates: 1977 - 1996

Year	Number				Rate per 100,000 population			
	City	Suburbs[2]	MSA[1]	U.S.	City	Suburbs[3]	MSA[1]	U.S.
1977	6,187	5,143	11,330	977,700	769.5	382.5	527.4	451.9
1978	5,874	4,708	10,582	1,004,100	741.7	349.6	494.8	460.5
1979	6,769	5,481	12,250	1,112,800	855.9	403.8	570.2	505.6
1980	5,620	5,453	11,073	1,131,700	716.3	395.1	511.5	502.2
1981	5,314	5,257	10,571	1,087,800	666.4	374.7	480.4	474.7
1982	4,452	4,819	9,271	1,062,400	557.8	343.2	420.9	458.8
1983	4,460	4,398	8,858	1,007,900	553.7	304.7	393.9	430.8
1984	5,415	4,565	9,980	1,032,200	686.7	310.4	441.7	437.1
1985	6,019	5,065	11,084	1,102,900	780.6	338.7	489.0	462.0
1986	6,873	6,469	13,342	1,224,100	877.2	425.6	579.2	507.8
1987	7,464	6,942	14,406	1,288,700	975.8	447.4	621.9	529.4
1988	8,443	7,765	16,208	1,432,900	1,105.3	486.9	687.2	582.9
1989	8,173	7,704	15,877	1,564,800	1,071.0	476.8	667.4	630.4
1990	9,911	8,837	18,748	1,635,900	1,346.6	536.8	787.0	657.8
1991	10,593	9,789	20,382	1,661,700	1,416.0	585.0	841.8	659.0
1992	11,300	9,256	20,556	1,610,800	1,495.7	547.8	840.6	631.5
1993	10,623	9,026	19,649	1,563,100	1,449.3	523.5	799.6	606.1
1994	13,533	10,028	23,561	1,539,300	1,830.8	576.8	950.9	591.3
1995	11,172	8,866	20,038	1,472,400	1,568.6	501.5	807.9	560.4
1996	11,151	8,110	19,261	1,395,200	1,556.4	456.0	772.0	525.9

Notes: (1) Metropolitan Statistical Area - see Appendix A for areas included; (2) calculated by the editors using the following formula: (number of crimes in the MSA minus number of crimes in the city); (3) calculated by the editors using the following formula: ((number of crimes in the MSA minus number of crimes in the city) ÷ (population of the MSA minus population of the city)) x 100,000; n/a not avail.
Source: U.S. Department of Justice, FBI Uniform Crime Reports, 1977 - 1996

HATE CRIMES

Criminal Incidents by Bias Motivation

Area	Race	Ethnicity	Religion	Sexual Orientation
Baltimore	4	0	0	0

Notes: Figures include both violent and property crimes. Law enforcement agencies must have submitted data for at least one quarter of calendar year 1995 to be included in this report, therefore figures shown may not represent complete 12-month totals; n/a not available
Source: U.S. Department of Justice, FBI Uniform Crime Reports, Hate Crime Statistics 1995

LAW ENFORCEMENT

Full-Time Law Enforcement Employees

Jurisdiction	Police Employees			Police Officers per 100,000 population
	Total	Officers	Civilians	
Baltimore	3,658	3,081	577	430.0

Notes: Data as of October 31, 1996
Source: U.S. Department of Justice, FBI Uniform Crime Reports, 1996

Number of Police Officers by Race

Race	Police Officers				Index of Representation[1]		
	1983		1992				
	Number	Pct.	Number	Pct.	1983	1992	% Chg.
Black	537	17.6	851	30.2	0.32	0.51	59.4
Hispanic[2]	10	0.3	14	0.5	0.30	0.40	33.3

Notes: (1) The index of representation is calculated by dividing the percent of black/hispanic police officers by the percent of corresponding blacks/hispanics in the local population. An index approaching 1.0 indicates that a city is closer to achieving a representation of police officers equal to their proportion in the local population; (2) Hispanic officers can be of any race
Source: Bureau of Justice Statistics, Sourcebook of Criminal Justice Statistics, 1994

CORRECTIONS

Federal Correctional Facilities

Type	Year Opened	Security Level	Sex of Inmates	Rated Capacity	Population on 7/1/95	Number of Staff
None listed						

Notes: Data as of 1995
Source: Bureau of Justice Statistics, Sourcebook of Criminal Justice Statistics Online

City/County/Regional Correctional Facilities

Name	Year Opened	Year Renov.	Rated Capacity	1995 Pop.	Number of COs[1]	Number of Staff	ACA[2] Accred.
Baltimore City Detention Ctr	1859	1968	2,014	n/a	n/a	n/a	No
Baltimore City Graves Street Work Release Center	1983	--	99	n/a	n/a	n/a	No
Baltimore City Women's Detention Center	1968	1988	671	n/a	n/a	n/a	No
Baltimore O'Brien House Work Release Center	1950	--	45	n/a	n/a	n/a	No

Notes: Data as of April 1996; (1) Correctional Officers; (2) American Correctional Assn. Accreditation
Source: American Correctional Association, 1996-1998 National Jail and Adult Detention Directory

Private Adult Correctional Facilities

Name	Date Opened	Rated Capacity	Present Pop.	Security Level	Facility Construct.	Expans. Plans	ACA[1] Accred.
None listed							

Notes: Data as of December 1996; (1) American Correctional Association Accreditation
Source: University of Florida, Center for Studies in Criminology and Law, Private Adult Correctional Facility Census, 10th Ed., March 15, 1997

Characteristics of Shock Incarceration Programs

Jurisdiction	Year Program Began	Number of Camps	Average Num. of Inmates	Number of Beds	Program Length	Voluntary/ Mandatory
Maryland	1990	1	272	200	180 days	Voluntary

Note: Data as of July 1996;
Source: Sourcebook of Criminal Justice Statistics Online

INMATES AND HIV/AIDS

HIV Testing Policies for Inmates

Jurisdiction	All Inmates at Some Time	All Convicted Inmates at Admission	Random Samples While in Custody	High-risk Groups	Upon Inmate Request	Upon Court Order	Upon Involvement in Incident
Baltimore Co.[1]	No	No	No	No	Yes	No	No

Notes: (1) All facilities reported following the same testing policy or authorities reported the policy to be jurisdiction-wide
Source: HIV in Prisons and Jails, 1993 (released August 1995)

Inmates Known to be Positive for HIV

Jurisdiction	Number of Jail Inmates in Facilities Providing Data	Type of HIV Infection/AIDS Cases				HIV/AIDS Cases as a Percent of Tot. Custody Pop.
		Total	Asymp-tomatic	Symp-tomatic	Confirmed AIDS	
Baltimore Co.	3,112	79	38	36	5	2.5

Source: HIV in Prisons and Jails, 1993 (released August, 1995)

DEATH PENALTY

Death Penalty Statistics

State	Prisoners Executed		Prisoners Under Sentence of Death					Avg. No. of Years on Death Row[4]
	1930-1995	1996[1]	Total[2]	White[3]	Black[3]	Hisp.	Women	
Maryland	69	0	13	2	11	0	0	8.0

Notes: Data as of 12/31/95 unless otherwise noted; (1) Data as of 7/31/97; (2) Includes persons of other races; (3) Includes people of Hispanic origin; (4) Covers prisoners sentenced 1974 through 1995
Source: Bureau of Justice Statistics, Capital Punishment 1995 (released 12/96); Death Penalty Information Center Web Site, 9/30/97

Capital Offenses and Methods of Execution

Capital Offenses in Maryland	Minimum Age for Imposition of Death Penalty	Mentally Retarded Excluded	Methods of Execution[1]
First-degree murder, either premeditated or during the commission of a felony, provided that certain death eligibility requirements are satisfied.	18	No	Lethal injection; lethal gas

Notes: Data as of 12/31/95 unless otherwise noted; (1) Data as of 7/31/97
Source: Bureau of Justice Statistics, Capital Punishment 1995 (released 12/96); Death Penalty Information Center Web Site, 9/30/97

LAWS

Statutory Provisions Relating to the Purchase, Ownership and Use of Handguns

Jurisdiction	Instant Background Check	Federal Waiting Period Applies[1]	State Waiting Period (days)	License or Permit to Purchase	Regis-tration	Record of Sale Sent to Police	Concealed Carry Law
Maryland	No	No	7	No	No	Yes	Yes[a]

Note: Data as of 1996; (1) The Federal 5-day waiting period for handgun purchases applies to states that don't have instant background checks, waiting period requirements, or licensing procedures exempting them from the Federal requirement; (a) Restrictively administered discretion by local authorities over permit issuance, or permits are unavailable and carrying is prohibited in most circumstances
Source: Sourcebook of Criminal Justice Statistics Online

Statutory Provisions Relating to Alcohol Use and Driving

Jurisdiction	Drinking Age	Blood Alcohol Concentration Levels as Evidence in State Courts[1]		Open Container Law[1]	Anti-Consump-tion Law[1]	Dram Shop Law[1]
		Illegal per se at 0.10%	Presumption at 0.10%			
Maryland	21	Yes	(a)	Yes[b]	Yes[c]	No

Note: Data as of January 1, 1997; (1) See Appendix C for an explanation of terms; (a) An alcohol concentration equal to or greater than 0.07% but less than 0.10% constitutes prima facie evidence of driving while under the influence; (b) Limited application; (c) Applies to drivers only
Source: Sourcebook of Criminal Justice Statistics Online

Statutory Provisions Relating to Curfews

Jurisdiction	Year Enacted	Latest Revision	Age Group(s)	Curfew Provisions
Baltimore	1976	1994	16 and under	11 pm to 6 am weekday nights midnight to 6 am weekend nights 9 am to 2:30 pm school days

Note: Data as of February 1996
Source: Sourcebook of Criminal Justice Statistics Online

Statutory Provisions Relating to Hate Crimes

Jurisdiction	Bias-Motivated Violence and Intimidation						Institutional Vandalism
	Civil Action	Criminal Penalty					
		Race/ Religion/ Ethnicity	Sexual Orientation	Mental/ Physical Disability	Gender	Age	
Maryland	No	Yes	No	No	No	No	Yes

Source: Anti-Defamation League, 1997 Hate Crimes Laws

Boston, Massachusetts

OVERVIEW

The total crime rate for the city decreased 25.4% between 1977 and 1996. During that same period, the violent crime rate increased 8.7% and the property crime rate decreased 30.9%.

Among violent crimes, the rates for: Murders decreased 11.6%; Forcible Rapes increased 13.5%; Robberies decreased 31.4%; and Aggravated Assaults increased 77.5%.

Among property crimes, the rates for: Burglaries decreased 61.8%; Larceny-Thefts increased 11.2%; and Motor Vehicle Thefts decreased 51.6%.

ANTI-CRIME PROGRAMS

Among numerous programs:

- G.R.E.A.T. (Gang Resistance Education & Awareness Training Program)—Officers teach gang resistance and character building tools in schools.
- Y.V.S.F. (Youth Violence Strike Force)—Multi-agency coordinated task force designed to attack youth violence problems, e.g. serving outstanding felony warrants on youthful offenders wanted for violent or gun-related offenses.
- Senior Citizen Response Program—An officer is assigned to conduct crime prevention programs and other activities to aid senior citizens.
- D.A.R.E. (Drug Abuse Resistance Education)—An educational program offered to school children on the hazards of drug abuse.
- Uniform Bicycle Directed Patrol Program—Bike patrols act in place of foot beat officers. The night bicycle program has proven to be very successful in the area of drug arrests.
- Neighborhood Crime Watch Program— neighbors learn to work together with police to make their street free of drug houses, to conduct resident patrols, and to report suspicious activity.
- Mini Strike Force—Special units act as a roving operation in and out of various neighborhoods which creates the effect of an always present atmosphere among the criminal element.
- Whistle Alert!—Neighbors "armed" with whistles can signal other neighbors anytime they feel threatened for they will be helped by other participants. The whistle has become the universal language in neighborhoods where many languages are spoken.
  Boston Police Department, 9/97

CRIME RISK

Your Chances of Becoming a Victim[1]

Area	Any Crime	Violent Crime					Property Crime			
		Any	Murder	Forcible Rape[2]	Robbery	Aggrav. Assault	Any	Burglary	Larceny -Theft	Motor Vehicle Theft
City	1:12	1:60	1:9,365	1:697	1:159	1:106	1:16	1:109	1:26	1:60

Note: (1) Figures have been calculated by dividing the population of the city by the number of crimes reported to the FBI during 1996 and are expressed as odds (eg. 1:20 should be read as 1 in 20). (2) Figures have been calculated by dividing the female population of the city by the number of forcible rapes reported to the FBI during 1996. The female population of the city was estimated by calculating the ratio of females to males reported in the 1990 Census and applying that ratio to 1996 population estimate.
Source: FBI Uniform Crime Reports 1996

CRIME STATISTICS

Total Crimes and Total Crime Rates: 1977 - 1996

Year	Number				Rate per 100,000 population			
	City	Suburbs[2]	MSA[1]	U.S.	City	Suburbs[3]	MSA[1]	U.S.
1977	66,995	123,609	190,604	10,984,500	10,840.6	4,542.4	5,708.0	5,077.6
1978	65,366	121,592	186,958	11,209,000	10,949.1	4,450.1	5,615.4	5,140.3
1979	70,231	138,111	208,342	12,249,500	11,713.3	5,096.6	6,295.3	5,565.5
1980	75,755	132,411	208,166	13,408,300	13,465.6	5,009.3	6,493.3	5,950.0
1981	79,643	127,532	207,175	13,423,800	14,054.3	4,706.5	6,323.3	5,858.2
1982	74,039	123,944	197,983	12,974,400	13,040.6	4,565.4	6,031.3	5,603.6
1983	67,302	91,846	159,148	12,108,600	11,879.2	4,175.7	5,753.6	5,175.0
1984	63,555	85,172	148,727	11,881,800	11,244.9	3,753.6	5,247.5	5,031.3
1985	68,073	88,394	156,467	12,431,400	11,877.4	3,895.5	5,505.0	5,207.1
1986	69,007	82,028	151,035	13,211,900	12,019.9	3,607.0	5,302.8	5,480.4
1987	67,417	78,753	146,170	13,508,700	11,706.7	3,466.9	5,133.3	5,550.0
1988	66,578	81,979	148,557	13,923,100	11,480.5	3,588.8	5,186.7	5,664.2
1989	70,003	89,273	159,276	14,251,400	12,067.5	3,901.3	5,552.8	5,741.0
1990	68,057	93,859	161,916	14,475,600	11,850.8	4,062.7	5,613.2	5,820.3
1991	62,039	95,358	157,397	14,872,900	10,837.4	4,141.7	5,475.0	5,897.8
1992	56,399	187,493	243,892	14,438,200	9,845.8	4,087.7	4,727.0	5,660.2
1993	55,555	108,833	164,388	14,144,800	10,030.3	3,833.0	4,844.6	5,484.4
1994	53,078	98,973	152,051	13,989,500	9,534.0	3,469.1	4,459.4	5,373.5
1995	52,278	96,182	148,460	13,862,700	9,492.8	3,337.1	4,324.6	5,275.9
1996	44,711	85,034	129,745	13,473,600	8,092.2	2,941.7	3,768.2	5,078.9

Notes: (1) Metropolitan Statistical Area - see Appendix A for areas included; (2) calculated by the editors using the following formula: (number of crimes in the MSA minus number of crimes in the city); (3) calculated by the editors using the following formula: ((number of crimes in the MSA minus number of crimes in the city) ÷ (population of the MSA minus population of the city)) x 100,000; n/a not avail.
Source: U.S. Department of Justice, FBI Uniform Crime Reports, 1977 - 1996

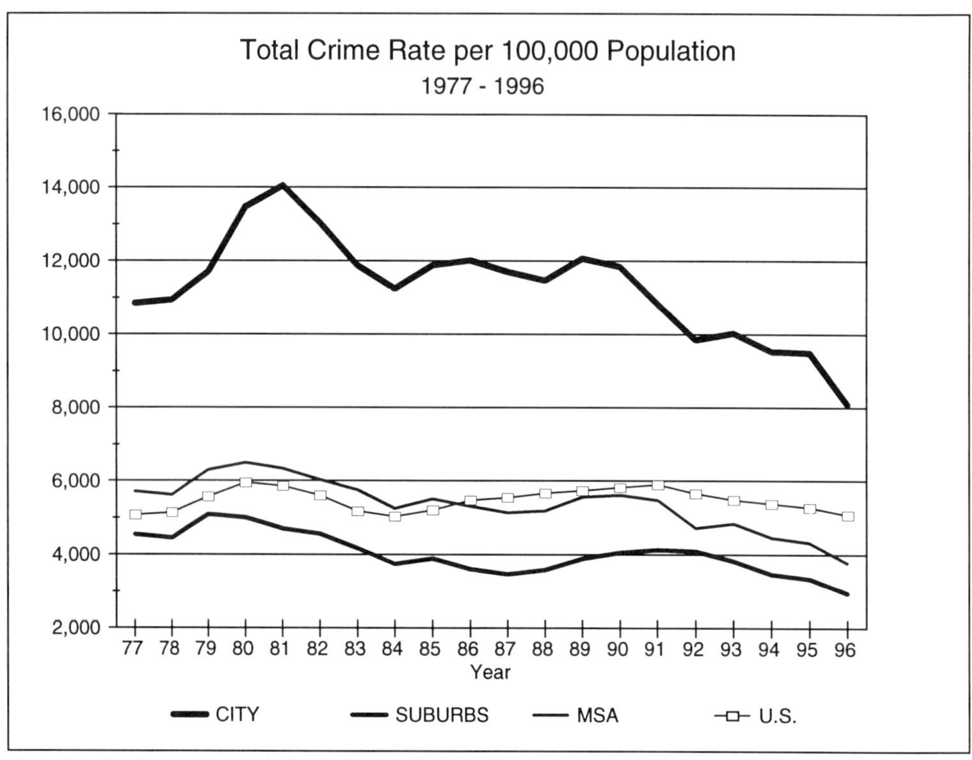

Note: Missing line segments indicate data not available.

Violent Crimes and Violent Crime Rates: 1977 - 1996

Year	Number				Rate per 100,000 population			
	City	Suburbs[2]	MSA[1]	U.S.	City	Suburbs[3]	MSA[1]	U.S.
1977	9,422	7,795	17,217	1,029,580	1,524.6	286.5	515.6	475.9
1978	10,035	8,780	18,815	1,085,550	1,680.9	321.3	565.1	497.8
1979	11,392	10,059	21,451	1,208,030	1,900.0	371.2	648.2	548.9
1980	12,478	10,824	23,302	1,344,520	2,218.0	409.5	726.9	596.6
1981	14,071	11,094	25,165	1,361,820	2,483.1	409.4	768.1	594.3
1982	10,970	11,358	22,328	1,322,390	1,932.2	418.4	680.2	571.1
1983	11,365	9,277	20,642	1,258,090	2,006.0	421.8	746.3	537.7
1984	10,557	7,200	17,757	1,273,280	1,867.9	317.3	626.5	539.2
1985	11,887	6,975	18,862	1,328,800	2,074.0	307.4	663.6	556.6
1986	12,395	7,233	19,628	1,489,170	2,159.0	318.1	689.1	617.7
1987	11,954	7,323	19,277	1,484,000	2,075.8	322.4	677.0	609.7
1988	12,175	8,454	20,629	1,566,220	2,099.4	370.1	720.2	637.2
1989	12,919	9,844	22,763	1,646,040	2,227.0	430.2	793.6	663.1
1990	13,664	11,258	24,922	1,820,130	2,379.3	487.3	864.0	731.8
1991	11,829	12,098	23,927	1,911,770	2,066.4	525.5	832.3	758.1
1992	11,672	23,746	35,418	1,932,270	2,037.6	517.7	686.5	757.5
1993	10,843	15,523	26,366	1,926,020	1,957.7	546.7	777.0	746.8
1994	10,664	12,747	23,411	1,857,670	1,915.5	446.8	686.6	713.6
1995	9,569	12,560	22,129	1,798,790	1,737.6	435.8	644.6	684.6
1996	9,154	10,847	20,001	1,682,280	1,656.8	375.2	580.9	634.1

Notes: Violent crimes include murder, forcible rape, robbery and aggravated assault; n/a not available; (1) Metropolitan Statistical Area - see Appendix A for areas included; (2) calculated by the editors using the following formula: (number of crimes in the MSA minus number of crimes in the city); (3) calculated by the editors using the following formula: ((number of crimes in the MSA minus number of crimes in the city) ÷ (population of the MSA minus population of the city)) x 100,000
Source: U.S. Department of Justice, FBI Uniform Crime Reports, 1977 - 1996

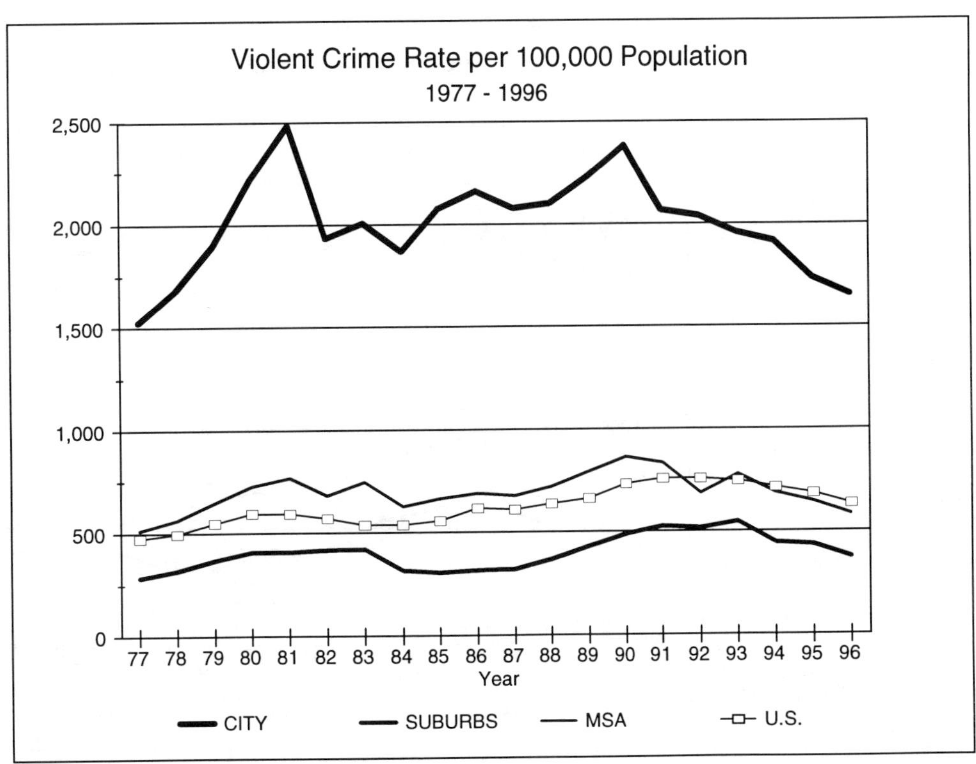

Note: Missing line segments indicate data not available.

Property Crimes and Property Crime Rates: 1977 - 1996

Year	Number				Rate per 100,000 population			
	City	Suburbs[2]	MSA[1]	U.S.	City	Suburbs[3]	MSA[1]	U.S.
1977	57,573	115,814	173,387	9,955,000	9,316.0	4,255.9	5,192.4	4,601.7
1978	55,331	112,812	168,143	10,123,400	9,268.2	4,128.7	5,050.3	4,642.5
1979	58,839	128,052	186,891	11,041,500	9,813.3	4,725.4	5,647.2	5,016.6
1980	63,277	121,587	184,864	12,063,700	11,247.6	4,599.8	5,766.4	5,353.3
1981	65,572	116,438	182,010	12,061,900	11,571.3	4,297.1	5,555.2	5,263.9
1982	63,069	112,586	175,655	11,652,000	11,108.4	4,147.0	5,351.1	5,032.5
1983	55,937	82,569	138,506	10,850,500	9,873.3	3,753.9	5,007.3	4,637.4
1984	52,998	77,972	130,970	10,608,500	9,377.0	3,436.3	4,621.0	4,492.1
1985	56,186	81,419	137,605	11,102,600	9,803.3	3,588.1	4,841.4	4,650.5
1986	56,612	74,795	131,407	11,722,700	9,860.9	3,289.0	4,613.6	4,862.6
1987	55,463	71,430	126,893	12,024,700	9,631.0	3,144.5	4,456.4	4,940.3
1988	54,403	73,525	127,928	12,356,900	9,381.1	3,218.7	4,466.5	5,027.1
1989	57,084	79,429	136,513	12,605,400	9,840.5	3,471.1	4,759.2	5,077.9
1990	54,393	82,601	136,994	12,655,500	9,471.5	3,575.4	4,749.2	5,088.5
1991	50,210	83,260	133,470	12,961,100	8,771.0	3,616.3	4,642.7	5,139.7
1992	44,727	163,747	208,474	12,505,900	7,808.2	3,570.0	4,040.5	4,902.7
1993	44,712	93,310	138,022	12,218,800	8,072.7	3,286.3	4,067.6	4,737.6
1994	42,414	86,226	128,640	12,131,900	7,618.5	3,022.3	3,772.8	4,660.0
1995	42,709	83,622	126,331	12,063,900	7,755.2	2,901.3	3,680.0	4,591.3
1996	35,557	74,187	109,744	11,791,300	6,435.4	2,566.4	3,187.3	4,444.8

Notes: Property crimes include burglary, larceny-theft and motor vehicle theft; n/a not available; (1) Metropolitan Statistical Area - see Appendix A for areas included; (2) calculated by the editors using the following formula: (number of crimes in the MSA minus number of crimes in the city); (3) calculated by the editors using the following formula: ((number of crimes in the MSA minus number of crimes in the city) ÷ (population of the MSA minus population of the city)) x 100,000
Source: U.S. Department of Justice, FBI Uniform Crime Reports, 1977 - 1996

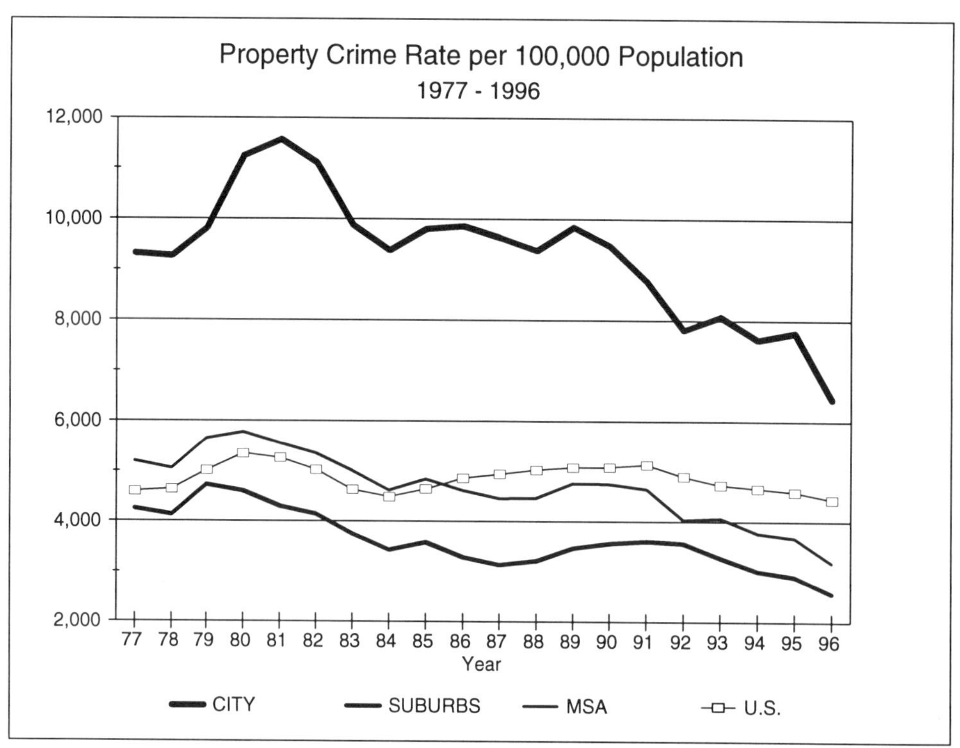

Note: Missing line segments indicate data not available.

Murders and Murder Rates: 1977 - 1996

Year	Number				Rate per 100,000 population			
	City	Suburbs[2]	MSA[1]	U.S.	City	Suburbs[3]	MSA[1]	U.S.
1977	75	44	119	19,120	12.1	1.6	3.6	8.8
1978	72	82	154	19,560	12.1	3.0	4.6	9.0
1979	92	62	154	21,460	15.3	2.3	4.7	9.7
1980	92	74	166	23,040	16.4	2.8	5.2	10.2
1981	100	49	149	22,520	17.6	1.8	4.5	9.8
1982	93	80	173	21,010	16.4	2.9	5.3	9.1
1983	90	32	122	19,310	15.9	1.5	4.4	8.3
1984	82	34	116	18,690	14.5	1.5	4.1	7.9
1985	87	46	133	18,980	15.2	2.0	4.7	7.9
1986	105	45	150	20,610	18.3	2.0	5.3	8.6
1987	76	39	115	20,100	13.2	1.7	4.0	8.3
1988	93	35	128	20,680	16.0	1.5	4.5	8.4
1989	99	34	133	21,500	17.1	1.5	4.6	8.7
1990	143	32	175	23,440	24.9	1.4	6.1	9.4
1991	113	49	162	24,700	19.7	2.1	5.6	9.8
1992	73	107	180	23,760	12.7	2.3	3.5	9.3
1993	98	47	145	24,530	17.7	1.7	4.3	9.5
1994	85	48	133	23,330	15.3	1.7	3.9	9.0
1995	96	40	136	21,610	17.4	1.4	4.0	8.2
1996	59	38	97	19,650	10.7	1.3	2.8	7.4

Notes: (1) Metropolitan Statistical Area - see Appendix A for areas included; (2) calculated by the editors using the following formula: (number of crimes in the MSA minus number of crimes in the city); (3) calculated by the editors using the following formula: ((number of crimes in the MSA minus number of crimes in the city) ÷ (population of the MSA minus population of the city)) x 100,000; n/a not avail.
Source: U.S. Department of Justice, FBI Uniform Crime Reports, 1977 - 1996

Forcible Rapes and Forcible Rape Rates: 1977 - 1996

Year	Number				Rate per 100,000 population			
	City	Suburbs[2]	MSA[1]	U.S.	City	Suburbs[3]	MSA[1]	U.S.
1977	408	346	754	63,500	66.0	12.7	22.6	29.4
1978	475	399	874	67,610	79.6	14.6	26.3	31.0
1979	464	389	853	76,390	77.4	14.4	25.8	34.7
1980	484	447	931	82,990	86.0	16.9	29.0	36.8
1981	531	417	948	82,500	93.7	15.4	28.9	36.0
1982	366	427	793	78,770	64.5	15.7	24.2	34.0
1983	367	380	747	78,920	64.8	17.3	27.0	33.7
1984	460	375	835	84,230	81.4	16.5	29.5	35.7
1985	532	362	894	88,670	92.8	16.0	31.5	37.1
1986	516	394	910	91,460	89.9	17.3	31.9	37.9
1987	550	406	956	91,110	95.5	17.9	33.6	37.4
1988	558	404	962	92,490	96.2	17.7	33.6	37.6
1989	483	376	859	94,500	83.3	16.4	29.9	38.1
1990	539	399	938	102,560	93.9	17.3	32.5	41.2
1991	486	386	872	106,590	84.9	16.8	30.3	42.3
1992	537	1,197	1,734	109,060	93.7	26.1	33.6	42.8
1993	480	581	1,061	106,010	86.7	20.5	31.3	41.1
1994	453	511	964	102,220	81.4	17.9	28.3	39.3
1995	379	479	858	97,470	68.8	16.6	25.0	37.1
1996	414	480	894	95,770	74.9	16.6	26.0	36.1

Notes: (1) Metropolitan Statistical Area - see Appendix A for areas included; (2) calculated by the editors using the following formula: (number of crimes in the MSA minus number of crimes in the city); (3) calculated by the editors using the following formula: ((number of crimes in the MSA minus number of crimes in the city) ÷ (population of the MSA minus population of the city)) x 100,000; n/a not avail.
Source: U.S. Department of Justice, FBI Uniform Crime Reports, 1977 - 1996

Robberies and Robbery Rates: 1977 - 1996

Year	Number				Rate per 100,000 population			
	City	Suburbs[2]	MSA[1]	U.S.	City	Suburbs[3]	MSA[1]	U.S.
1977	5,655	2,309	7,964	412,610	915.0	84.9	238.5	190.7
1978	5,635	2,411	8,046	426,930	943.9	88.2	241.7	195.8
1979	6,600	3,012	9,612	480,700	1,100.8	111.1	290.4	218.4
1980	7,526	3,304	10,830	565,840	1,337.8	125.0	337.8	251.1
1981	9,248	3,802	13,050	592,910	1,632.0	140.3	398.3	258.7
1982	6,531	3,525	10,056	553,130	1,150.3	129.8	306.3	238.9
1983	6,713	2,539	9,252	506,570	1,184.9	115.4	334.5	216.5
1984	5,539	1,995	7,534	485,010	980.0	87.9	265.8	205.4
1985	6,232	2,097	8,329	497,870	1,087.4	92.4	293.0	208.5
1986	6,225	2,139	8,364	542,780	1,084.3	94.1	293.7	225.1
1987	5,408	1,993	7,401	517,700	939.1	87.7	259.9	212.7
1988	5,233	1,992	7,225	542,970	902.4	87.2	252.3	220.9
1989	5,866	2,487	8,353	578,330	1,011.2	108.7	291.2	233.0
1990	6,022	2,790	8,812	639,270	1,048.6	120.8	305.5	257.0
1991	4,784	2,777	7,561	687,730	835.7	120.6	263.0	272.7
1992	4,765	4,691	9,456	672,480	831.8	102.3	183.3	263.6
1993	4,081	2,790	6,871	659,870	736.8	98.3	202.5	255.9
1994	4,245	2,317	6,562	618,950	762.5	81.2	192.5	237.7
1995	3,597	2,348	5,945	580,510	653.2	81.5	173.2	220.9
1996	3,470	1,783	5,253	537,050	628.0	61.7	152.6	202.4

Notes: (1) Metropolitan Statistical Area - see Appendix A for areas included; (2) calculated by the editors using the following formula: (number of crimes in the MSA minus number of crimes in the city); (3) calculated by the editors using the following formula: ((number of crimes in the MSA minus number of crimes in the city) ÷ (population of the MSA minus population of the city)) x 100,000; n/a not avail.
Source: U.S. Department of Justice, FBI Uniform Crime Reports, 1977 - 1996

Aggravated Assaults and Aggravated Assault Rates: 1977 - 1996

Year	Number				Rate per 100,000 population			
	City	Suburbs[2]	MSA[1]	U.S.	City	Suburbs[3]	MSA[1]	U.S.
1977	3,284	5,096	8,380	534,350	531.4	187.3	251.0	247.0
1978	3,853	5,888	9,741	571,460	645.4	215.5	292.6	262.1
1979	4,236	6,596	10,832	629,480	706.5	243.4	327.3	286.0
1980	4,376	6,999	11,375	672,650	777.8	264.8	354.8	298.5
1981	4,192	6,826	11,018	663,900	739.7	251.9	336.3	289.7
1982	3,980	7,326	11,306	669,480	701.0	269.8	344.4	289.2
1983	4,195	6,326	10,521	653,290	740.4	287.6	380.4	279.2
1984	4,476	4,796	9,272	685,350	791.9	211.4	327.1	290.2
1985	5,036	4,470	9,506	723,250	878.7	197.0	334.5	302.9
1986	5,549	4,655	10,204	834,320	966.5	204.7	358.3	346.1
1987	5,920	4,885	10,805	855,090	1,028.0	215.0	379.5	351.3
1988	6,291	6,023	12,314	910,090	1,084.8	263.7	429.9	370.2
1989	6,471	6,947	13,418	951,710	1,115.5	303.6	467.8	383.4
1990	6,960	8,037	14,997	1,054,860	1,211.9	347.9	519.9	424.1
1991	6,446	8,886	15,332	1,092,740	1,126.0	385.9	533.3	433.3
1992	6,297	17,751	24,048	1,126,970	1,099.3	387.0	466.1	441.8
1993	6,184	12,105	18,289	1,135,610	1,116.5	426.3	539.0	440.3
1994	5,881	9,871	15,752	1,113,180	1,056.4	346.0	462.0	427.6
1995	5,497	9,693	15,190	1,099,210	998.2	336.3	442.5	418.3
1996	5,211	8,546	13,757	1,029,810	943.1	295.6	399.5	388.2

Notes: (1) Metropolitan Statistical Area - see Appendix A for areas included; (2) calculated by the editors using the following formula: (number of crimes in the MSA minus number of crimes in the city); (3) calculated by the editors using the following formula: ((number of crimes in the MSA minus number of crimes in the city) ÷ (population of the MSA minus population of the city)) x 100,000; n/a not avail.
Source: U.S. Department of Justice, FBI Uniform Crime Reports, 1977 - 1996

Burglaries and Burglary Rates: 1977 - 1996

Year	Number				Rate per 100,000 population			
	City	Suburbs[2]	MSA[1]	U.S.	City	Suburbs[3]	MSA[1]	U.S.
1977	14,793	34,939	49,732	3,071,500	2,393.7	1,283.9	1,489.3	1,419.8
1978	15,064	33,965	49,029	3,128,300	2,523.3	1,243.1	1,472.6	1,434.6
1979	15,662	37,940	53,602	3,327,700	2,612.2	1,400.1	1,619.7	1,511.9
1980	17,032	37,317	54,349	3,795,200	3,027.5	1,411.8	1,695.3	1,684.1
1981	16,694	36,644	53,338	3,779,700	2,945.9	1,352.3	1,628.0	1,649.5
1982	14,286	31,269	45,555	3,447,100	2,516.2	1,151.8	1,387.8	1,488.8
1983	11,471	22,349	33,820	3,129,900	2,024.7	1,016.1	1,222.7	1,337.7
1984	11,446	20,032	31,478	2,984,400	2,025.2	882.8	1,110.6	1,263.7
1985	11,470	20,419	31,889	3,073,300	2,001.3	899.9	1,122.0	1,287.3
1986	10,485	18,557	29,042	3,241,400	1,826.3	816.0	1,019.7	1,344.6
1987	10,412	17,121	27,533	3,236,200	1,808.0	753.7	966.9	1,329.6
1988	9,163	17,043	26,206	3,218,100	1,580.0	746.1	915.0	1,309.2
1989	9,882	18,281	28,163	3,168,200	1,703.5	798.9	981.8	1,276.3
1990	10,238	19,105	29,343	3,073,900	1,782.7	827.0	1,017.2	1,235.9
1991	10,029	20,186	30,215	3,157,200	1,751.9	876.7	1,051.0	1,252.0
1992	8,718	41,985	50,703	2,979,900	1,521.9	915.4	982.7	1,168.2
1993	7,982	22,271	30,253	2,834,800	1,441.1	784.4	891.6	1,099.2
1994	6,799	19,642	26,441	2,712,800	1,221.3	688.5	775.5	1,042.0
1995	6,671	18,337	25,008	2,593,800	1,211.3	636.2	728.5	987.1
1996	5,052	15,447	20,499	2,501,500	914.4	534.4	595.3	943.0

Notes: (1) Metropolitan Statistical Area - see Appendix A for areas included; (2) calculated by the editors using the following formula: (number of crimes in the MSA minus number of crimes in the city); (3) calculated by the editors using the following formula: ((number of crimes in the MSA minus number of crimes in the city) ÷ (population of the MSA minus population of the city)) x 100,000; n/a not avail.
Source: U.S. Department of Justice, FBI Uniform Crime Reports, 1977 - 1996

Larceny-Thefts and Larceny-Theft Rates: 1977 - 1996

Year	Number				Rate per 100,000 population			
	City	Suburbs[2]	MSA[1]	U.S.	City	Suburbs[3]	MSA[1]	U.S.
1977	21,353	54,487	75,840	5,905,700	3,455.2	2,002.3	2,271.2	2,729.9
1978	20,620	53,315	73,935	5,991,000	3,453.9	1,951.2	2,220.7	2,747.4
1979	23,121	63,204	86,325	6,601,000	3,856.2	2,332.4	2,608.4	2,999.1
1980	25,225	61,984	87,209	7,136,900	4,483.8	2,345.0	2,720.3	3,167.0
1981	27,137	58,242	85,379	7,194,400	4,788.8	2,149.4	2,605.9	3,139.7
1982	27,079	59,326	86,405	7,142,500	4,769.5	2,185.2	2,632.2	3,084.8
1983	26,419	43,816	70,235	6,712,800	4,663.1	1,992.1	2,539.2	2,868.9
1984	24,333	41,678	66,011	6,591,900	4,305.3	1,836.8	2,329.0	2,791.3
1985	26,938	43,714	70,652	6,926,400	4,700.1	1,926.5	2,485.8	2,901.2
1986	26,553	40,784	67,337	7,257,200	4,625.1	1,793.4	2,364.2	3,010.3
1987	26,791	40,268	67,059	7,499,900	4,652.2	1,772.7	2,355.0	3,081.3
1988	28,542	42,130	70,672	7,705,900	4,921.7	1,844.3	2,467.4	3,134.9
1989	30,794	46,343	77,137	7,872,400	5,308.4	2,025.2	2,689.2	3,171.3
1990	29,642	47,850	77,492	7,945,700	5,161.6	2,071.2	2,686.5	3,194.8
1991	26,726	47,757	74,483	8,142,200	4,668.7	2,074.2	2,590.9	3,228.8
1992	24,598	95,188	119,786	7,915,200	4,294.2	2,075.3	2,321.6	3,103.0
1993	24,798	53,727	78,525	7,820,900	4,477.2	1,892.2	2,314.2	3,032.4
1994	24,375	53,094	77,469	7,879,800	4,378.3	1,861.0	2,272.0	3,026.7
1995	26,002	53,719	79,721	7,997,700	4,721.5	1,863.8	2,322.3	3,043.8
1996	21,234	48,206	69,440	7,894,600	3,843.1	1,667.6	2,016.7	2,975.9

Notes: (1) Metropolitan Statistical Area - see Appendix A for areas included; (2) calculated by the editors using the following formula: (number of crimes in the MSA minus number of crimes in the city); (3) calculated by the editors using the following formula: ((number of crimes in the MSA minus number of crimes in the city) ÷ (population of the MSA minus population of the city)) x 100,000; n/a not avail.
Source: U.S. Department of Justice, FBI Uniform Crime Reports, 1977 - 1996

Motor Vehicle Thefts and Motor Vehicle Theft Rates: 1977 - 1996

Year	Number				Rate per 100,000 population			
	City	Suburbs[2]	MSA[1]	U.S.	City	Suburbs[3]	MSA[1]	U.S.
1977	21,427	26,388	47,815	977,700	3,467.2	969.7	1,431.9	451.9
1978	19,647	25,532	45,179	1,004,100	3,291.0	934.4	1,357.0	460.5
1979	20,056	26,908	46,964	1,112,800	3,345.0	993.0	1,419.1	505.6
1980	21,020	22,286	43,306	1,131,700	3,736.3	843.1	1,350.8	502.2
1981	21,741	21,552	43,293	1,087,800	3,836.6	795.4	1,321.4	474.7
1982	21,704	21,991	43,695	1,062,400	3,822.8	810.0	1,331.1	458.8
1983	18,047	16,404	34,451	1,007,900	3,185.4	745.8	1,245.5	430.8
1984	17,219	16,262	33,481	1,032,200	3,046.6	716.7	1,181.3	437.1
1985	17,778	17,286	35,064	1,102,900	3,101.9	761.8	1,233.7	462.0
1986	19,574	15,454	35,028	1,224,100	3,409.5	679.6	1,229.8	507.8
1987	18,260	14,041	32,301	1,288,700	3,170.8	618.1	1,134.4	529.4
1988	16,698	14,352	31,050	1,432,900	2,879.4	628.3	1,084.1	582.9
1989	16,408	14,805	31,213	1,564,800	2,828.5	647.0	1,088.2	630.4
1990	14,513	15,646	30,159	1,635,900	2,527.2	677.2	1,045.5	657.8
1991	13,455	15,317	28,772	1,661,700	2,350.4	665.3	1,000.8	659.0
1992	11,411	26,574	37,985	1,610,800	1,992.1	579.4	736.2	631.5
1993	11,932	17,312	29,244	1,563,100	2,154.3	609.7	861.8	606.1
1994	11,240	13,490	24,730	1,539,300	2,019.0	472.8	725.3	591.3
1995	10,036	11,566	21,602	1,472,400	1,822.4	401.3	629.3	560.4
1996	9,271	10,534	19,805	1,395,200	1,678.0	364.4	575.2	525.9

Notes: (1) Metropolitan Statistical Area - see Appendix A for areas included; (2) calculated by the editors using the following formula: (number of crimes in the MSA minus number of crimes in the city); (3) calculated by the editors using the following formula: ((number of crimes in the MSA minus number of crimes in the city) ÷ (population of the MSA minus population of the city)) x 100,000; n/a not avail.
Source: U.S. Department of Justice, FBI Uniform Crime Reports, 1977 - 1996

HATE CRIMES

Criminal Incidents by Bias Motivation

Area	Race	Ethnicity	Religion	Sexual Orientation
Boston	114	33	3	14

Notes: Figures include both violent and property crimes. Law enforcement agencies must have submitted data for at least one quarter of calendar year 1995 to be included in this report, therefore figures shown may not represent complete 12-month totals; n/a not available
Source: U.S. Department of Justice, FBI Uniform Crime Reports, Hate Crime Statistics 1995

LAW ENFORCEMENT

Full-Time Law Enforcement Employees

Jurisdiction	Police Employees			Police Officers per 100,000 population
	Total	Officers	Civilians	
Boston	2,926	2,218	708	401.4

Notes: Data as of October 31, 1996
Source: U.S. Department of Justice, FBI Uniform Crime Reports, 1996

Number of Police Officers by Race

Race	Police Officers				Index of Representation[1]		
	1983		1992				
	Number	Pct.	Number	Pct.	1983	1992	% Chg.
Black	248	13.3	404	20.5	0.59	0.80	35.6
Hispanic[2]	40	2.1	84	4.3	0.33	0.39	18.2

Notes: (1) The index of representation is calculated by dividing the percent of black/hispanic police officers by the percent of corresponding blacks/hispanics in the local population. An index approaching 1.0 indicates that a city is closer to achieving a representation of police officers equal to their proportion in the local population; (2) Hispanic officers can be of any race
Source: Bureau of Justice Statistics, Sourcebook of Criminal Justice Statistics, 1994

CORRECTIONS

Federal Correctional Facilities

Type	Year Opened	Security Level	Sex of Inmates	Rated Capacity	Population on 7/1/95	Number of Staff
None listed						

Notes: Data as of 1995
Source: Bureau of Justice Statistics, Sourcebook of Criminal Justice Statistics Online

City/County/Regional Correctional Facilities

Name	Year Opened	Year Renov.	Rated Capacity	1995 Pop.	Number of COs[1]	Number of Staff	ACA[2] Accred.
Suffolk County Jail	1990	1994	555	553	339	439	Yes

Notes: Data as of April 1996; (1) Correctional Officers; (2) American Correctional Assn. Accreditation
Source: American Correctional Association, 1996-1998 National Jail and Adult Detention Directory

Private Adult Correctional Facilities

Name	Date Opened	Rated Capacity	Present Pop.	Security Level	Facility Construct.	Expans. Plans	ACA[1] Accred.
None listed							

Notes: Data as of December 1996; (1) American Correctional Association Accreditation
Source: University of Florida, Center for Studies in Criminology and Law, Private Adult Correctional Facility Census, 10th Ed., March 15, 1997

Characteristics of Shock Incarceration Programs

Jurisdiction	Year Program Began	Number of Camps	Average Num. of Inmates	Number of Beds	Program Length	Voluntary/ Mandatory
Massachusetts did not have a shock incarceration program as of July 1996						

Source: Sourcebook of Criminal Justice Statistics Online

INMATES AND HIV/AIDS

HIV Testing Policies for Inmates

Jurisdiction	All Inmates at Some Time	All Convicted Inmates at Admission	Random Samples While in Custody	High-risk Groups	Upon Inmate Request	Upon Court Order	Upon Involvement in Incident
Boston[1]	No	No	No	No	Yes	No	Yes

Notes: (1) All facilities reported following the same testing policy or authorities reported the policy to be jurisdiction-wide
Source: HIV in Prisons and Jails, 1993 (released August 1995)

Inmates Known to be Positive for HIV

Jurisdiction	Number of Jail Inmates in Facilities Providing Data	Type of HIV Infection/AIDS Cases				HIV/AIDS Cases as a Percent of Tot. Custody Pop.
		Total	Asymptomatic	Symptomatic	Confirmed AIDS	
Boston	1,727	83	0	36	47	4.8

Source: HIV in Prisons and Jails, 1993 (released August, 1995)

DEATH PENALTY

Massachusetts did not have the death penalty as of July 31, 1997.
Source: Death Penalty Information Center Web Site, 9/30/97

LAWS

Statutory Provisions Relating to the Purchase, Ownership and Use of Handguns

Jurisdiction	Instant Background Check	Federal Waiting Period Applies[1]	State Waiting Period (days)	License or Permit to Purchase	Registration	Record of Sale Sent to Police	Concealed Carry Law
Massachusetts	No	No	7	Yes[a]	No	Yes	Yes[b]

Note: Data as of 1996; (1) The Federal 5-day waiting period for handgun purchases applies to states that don't have instant background checks, waiting period requirements, or licensing procedures exempting them from the Federal requirement; (a) Firearm owners must possess a Firearms Owner's ID Card (FID) or a license to carry.; (b) Restrictively administered discretion by local authorities over permit issuance, or permits are unavailable and carrying is prohibited in most circumstances
Source: Sourcebook of Criminal Justice Statistics Online

Statutory Provisions Relating to Alcohol Use and Driving

Jurisdiction	Drinking Age	Blood Alcohol Concentration Levels as Evidence in State Courts[1]		Open Container Law[1]	Anti-Consumption Law[1]	Dram Shop Law[1]
		Illegal per se at 0.10%	Presumption at 0.10%			
Massachusetts	21	No	(a)	No	Yes[b]	(c)

Note: Data as of January 1, 1997; (1) See Appendix C for an explanation of terms; (a) 0.08%; (b) Applies to drivers only; (c) Adopted via case law decisions
Source: Sourcebook of Criminal Justice Statistics Online

Statutory Provisions Relating to Hate Crimes

Jurisdiction	Bias-Motivated Violence and Intimidation						Institutional Vandalism
	Civil Action	Criminal Penalty					
		Race/ Religion/ Ethnicity	Sexual Orientation	Mental/ Physical Disability	Gender	Age	
Massachusetts	Yes	Yes	No	No	No	No	Yes

Source: Anti-Defamation League, 1997 Hate Crimes Laws

Charlotte, North Carolina

OVERVIEW

The total crime rate for the city increased 24.3% between 1977 and 1996. During that same period, the violent crime rate increased 112.2% and the property crime rate increased 14.8%.

Among violent crimes, the rates for: Murders decreased 19.5%; Forcible Rapes increased 37.3%; Robberies increased 125.7%; and Aggravated Assaults increased 116.8%.

Among property crimes, the rates for: Burglaries decreased 25.3%; Larceny-Thefts increased 29.8%; and Motor Vehicle Thefts increased 121.8%.

ANTI-CRIME PROGRAMS

The Charlotte-Mecklenburg County police department is developing a comprehensive strategic information and automated records management system called Knowledge-Based Community Oriented Policing System, or KB-COPS. The database will be designed with modules for offense reports, property and evidence, investigations, crime scene search, crime lab analysis, field interviews and a juvenile component, among others. KB-COPS is scheduled to be fully operational in October 1999. *Governing, 7/97*

Charlotte is one of the recipients of the National Institute of Justice's award to receive funding for projects to improve police-citizen cooperation. The project: "Future Alert and Contact Network". This program will develop a network which will allow the police to predict community problems and allow beat officers to be more proactive in community policing. *National Institute of Justice Journal, 6/97*

CRIME RISK

Your Chances of Becoming a Victim[1]

Area	Any Crime	Violent Crime					Property Crime			
		Any	Murder	Forcible Rape[2]	Robbery	Aggrav. Assault	Any	Burglary	Larceny -Theft	Motor Vehicle Theft
City	1:10	1:62	1:7,804	1:952	1:214	1:93	1:12	1:54	1:18	1:133

Note: (1) Figures have been calculated by dividing the population of the city by the number of crimes reported to the FBI during 1996 and are expressed as odds (eg. 1:20 should be read as 1 in 20).
(2) Figures have been calculated by dividing the female population of the city by the number of forcible rapes reported to the FBI during 1996. The female population of the city was estimated by calculating the ratio of females to males reported in the 1990 Census and applying that ratio to 1996 population estimate.
Source: FBI Uniform Crime Reports 1996

CRIME STATISTICS

Total Crimes and Total Crime Rates: 1977 - 1996

Year	Number				Rate per 100,000 population			
	City	Suburbs[2]	MSA[1]	U.S.	City	Suburbs[3]	MSA[1]	U.S.
1977	22,996	14,074	37,070	10,984,500	7,768.9	4,617.8	6,170.3	5,077.6
1978	23,119	13,121	36,240	11,209,000	7,732.1	4,323.3	6,015.0	5,140.3
1979	22,984	13,582	36,566	12,249,500	7,646.8	4,401.4	6,002.8	5,565.5
1980	26,208	15,485	41,693	13,408,300	8,432.6	4,819.6	6,596.1	5,950.0
1981	29,646	15,346	44,992	13,423,800	9,366.7	4,690.2	6,989.7	5,858.2
1982	32,987	16,965	49,952	12,974,400	10,304.6	5,126.5	7,672.5	5,603.6
1983	31,485	29,806	61,291	12,108,600	9,726.5	4,367.5	6,091.6	5,175.0
1984	32,767	30,168	62,935	11,881,800	9,869.8	4,335.7	6,123.3	5,031.3
1985	33,087	31,457	64,544	12,431,400	9,856.4	4,426.4	6,168.4	5,207.1
1986	35,381	32,191	67,572	13,211,900	10,413.3	4,476.9	6,381.9	5,480.4
1987	39,609	33,307	72,916	13,508,700	11,107.5	4,609.1	6,756.3	5,550.0
1988	43,979	36,006	79,985	13,923,100	11,870.4	4,863.6	7,200.7	5,664.2
1989	49,341	40,059	89,400	14,251,400	13,241.9	5,315.1	7,937.5	5,741.0
1990	49,862	42,576	92,438	14,475,600	12,593.5	5,557.1	7,954.4	5,820.3
1991	50,902	44,074	94,976	14,872,900	12,642.8	5,655.7	8,035.9	5,897.8
1992	51,489	41,311	92,800	14,438,200	12,590.5	5,222.4	7,733.5	5,660.2
1993	49,758	39,819	89,577	14,144,800	11,767.0	4,927.5	7,277.0	5,484.4
1994	51,057	35,135	86,192	13,989,500	9,686.0	4,849.6	6,886.5	5,373.5
1995	52,110	33,725	85,835	13,862,700	9,576.5	4,579.9	6,703.2	5,275.9
1996	53,518	35,551	89,069	13,473,600	9,659.1	4,753.3	6,841.0	5,078.9

Notes: (1) Metropolitan Statistical Area - see Appendix A for areas included; (2) calculated by the editors using the following formula: (number of crimes in the MSA minus number of crimes in the city); (3) calculated by the editors using the following formula: ((number of crimes in the MSA minus number of crimes in the city) ÷ (population of the MSA minus population of the city)) x 100,000; n/a not avail.
Source: U.S. Department of Justice, FBI Uniform Crime Reports, 1977 - 1996

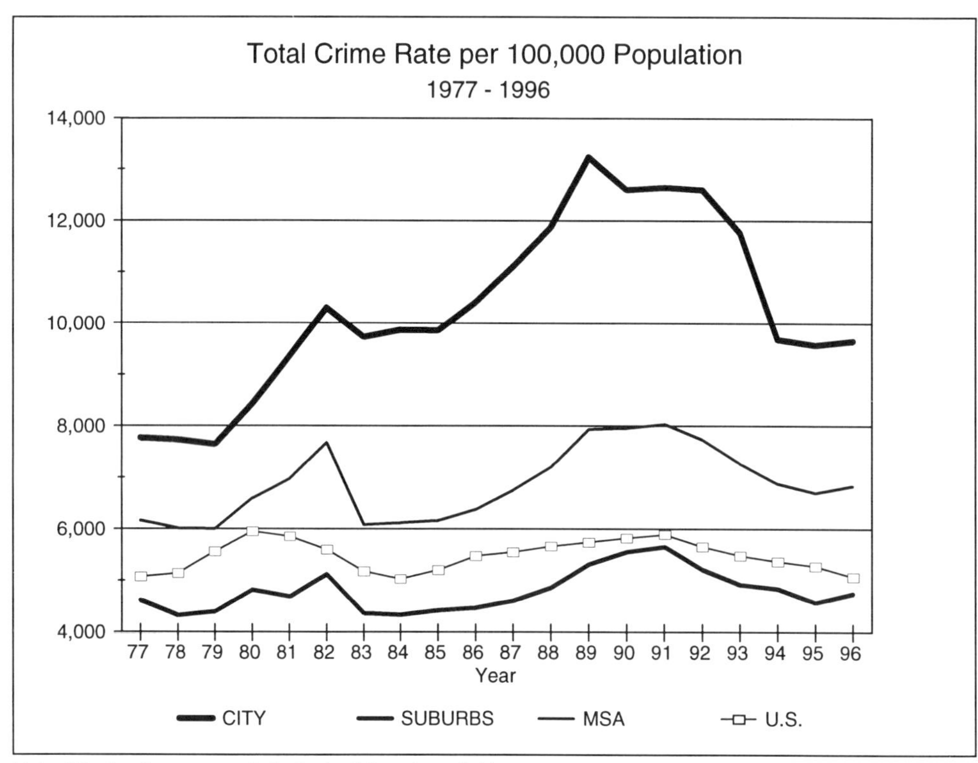

Note: Missing line segments indicate data not available.

Violent Crimes and Violent Crime Rates: 1977 - 1996

Year	Number				Rate per 100,000 population			
	City	Suburbs[2]	MSA[1]	U.S.	City	Suburbs[3]	MSA[1]	U.S.
1977	2,245	1,558	3,803	1,029,580	758.4	511.2	633.0	475.9
1978	2,435	1,612	4,047	1,085,550	814.4	531.1	671.7	497.8
1979	2,485	1,634	4,119	1,208,030	826.8	529.5	676.2	548.9
1980	2,759	1,709	4,468	1,344,520	887.7	531.9	706.9	596.6
1981	3,166	1,253	4,419	1,361,820	1,000.3	383.0	686.5	594.3
1982	4,100	1,055	5,155	1,322,390	1,280.8	318.8	791.8	571.1
1983	4,267	2,370	6,637	1,258,090	1,318.2	347.3	659.6	537.7
1984	4,431	2,627	7,058	1,273,280	1,334.7	377.6	686.7	539.2
1985	4,575	2,879	7,454	1,328,800	1,362.9	405.1	712.4	556.6
1986	5,487	3,277	8,764	1,489,170	1,614.9	455.7	827.7	617.7
1987	5,992	3,173	9,165	1,484,000	1,680.3	439.1	849.2	609.7
1988	6,815	3,443	10,258	1,566,220	1,839.4	465.1	923.5	637.2
1989	7,640	3,736	11,376	1,646,040	2,050.4	495.7	1,010.0	663.1
1990	9,119	4,960	14,079	1,820,130	2,303.2	647.4	1,211.5	731.8
1991	8,762	4,938	13,700	1,911,770	2,176.3	633.7	1,159.2	758.1
1992	9,456	5,148	14,604	1,932,270	2,312.3	650.8	1,217.0	757.5
1993	9,725	5,101	14,826	1,926,020	2,299.8	631.2	1,204.4	746.8
1994	9,102	4,434	13,536	1,857,670	1,726.7	612.0	1,081.5	713.6
1995	9,228	4,072	13,300	1,798,790	1,695.9	553.0	1,038.6	684.6
1996	8,915	3,834	12,749	1,682,280	1,609.0	512.6	979.2	634.1

Notes: Violent crimes include murder, forcible rape, robbery and aggravated assault; n/a not available; (1) Metropolitan Statistical Area - see Appendix A for areas included; (2) calculated by the editors using the following formula: (number of crimes in the MSA minus number of crimes in the city); (3) calculated by the editors using the following formula: ((number of crimes in the MSA minus number of crimes in the city) ÷ (population of the MSA minus population of the city)) x 100,000
Source: U.S. Department of Justice, FBI Uniform Crime Reports, 1977 - 1996

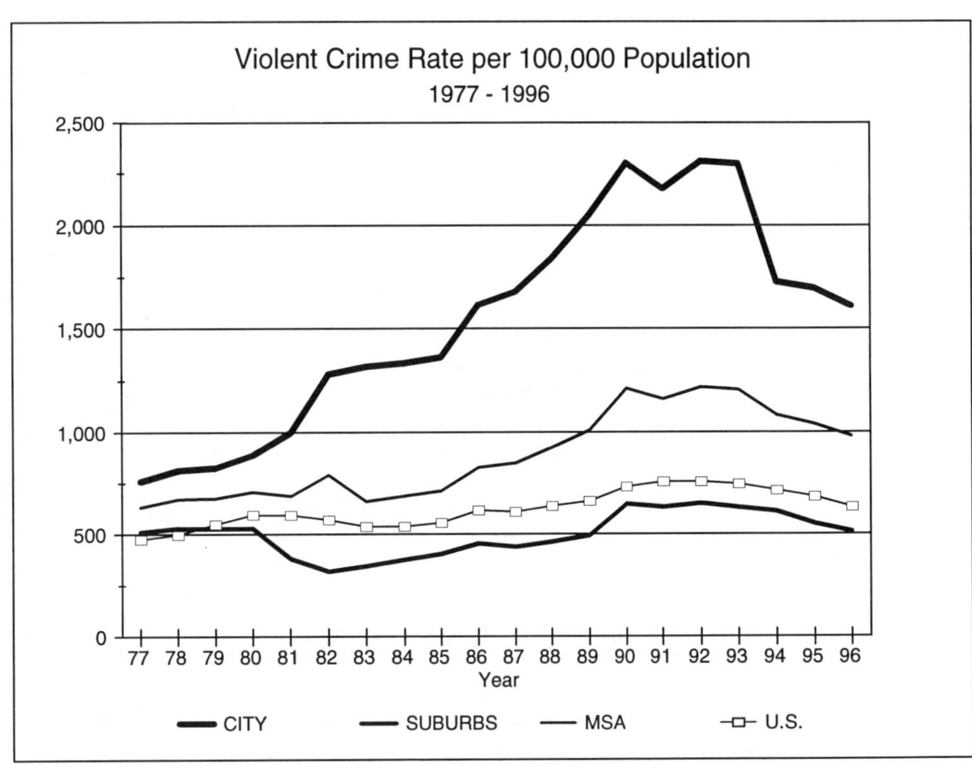

Note: Missing line segments indicate data not available.

Property Crimes and Property Crime Rates: 1977 - 1996

Year	Number				Rate per 100,000 population			
	City	Suburbs[2]	MSA[1]	U.S.	City	Suburbs[3]	MSA[1]	U.S.
1977	20,751	12,516	33,267	9,955,000	7,010.5	4,106.6	5,537.3	4,601.7
1978	20,684	11,509	32,193	10,123,400	6,917.7	3,792.1	5,343.3	4,642.5
1979	20,499	11,948	32,447	11,041,500	6,820.1	3,871.9	5,326.6	5,016.6
1980	23,449	13,776	37,225	12,063,700	7,544.9	4,287.7	5,889.3	5,353.3
1981	26,480	14,093	40,573	12,061,900	8,366.4	4,307.3	6,303.2	5,263.9
1982	28,887	15,910	44,797	11,652,000	9,023.8	4,807.7	6,880.7	5,032.5
1983	27,218	27,436	54,654	10,850,500	8,408.3	4,020.3	5,432.0	4,637.4
1984	28,336	27,541	55,877	10,608,500	8,535.1	3,958.2	5,436.6	4,492.1
1985	28,512	28,578	57,090	11,102,600	8,493.6	4,021.3	5,456.1	4,650.5
1986	29,894	28,914	58,808	11,722,700	8,798.4	4,021.2	5,554.1	4,862.6
1987	33,617	30,134	63,751	12,024,700	9,427.2	4,170.1	5,907.1	4,940.3
1988	37,164	32,563	69,727	12,356,900	10,031.0	4,398.6	6,277.2	5,027.1
1989	41,701	36,323	78,024	12,605,400	11,191.5	4,819.4	6,927.5	5,077.9
1990	40,743	37,616	78,359	12,655,500	10,290.4	4,909.7	6,742.9	5,088.5
1991	42,140	39,136	81,276	12,961,100	10,466.5	5,022.1	6,876.7	5,139.7
1992	42,033	36,163	78,196	12,505,900	10,278.2	4,571.6	6,516.4	4,902.7
1993	40,033	34,718	74,751	12,218,800	9,467.2	4,296.2	6,072.6	4,737.6
1994	41,955	30,701	72,656	12,131,900	7,959.3	4,237.6	5,805.0	4,660.0
1995	42,882	29,653	72,535	12,063,900	7,880.6	4,026.9	5,664.5	4,591.3
1996	44,603	31,717	76,320	11,791,300	8,050.1	4,240.7	5,861.8	4,444.8

Notes: Property crimes include burglary, larceny-theft and motor vehicle theft; n/a not available; (1) Metropolitan Statistical Area - see Appendix A for areas included; (2) calculated by the editors using the following formula: (number of crimes in the MSA minus number of crimes in the city); (3) calculated by the editors using the following formula: ((number of crimes in the MSA minus number of crimes in the city) ÷ (population of the MSA minus population of the city)) x 100,000
Source: U.S. Department of Justice, FBI Uniform Crime Reports, 1977 - 1996

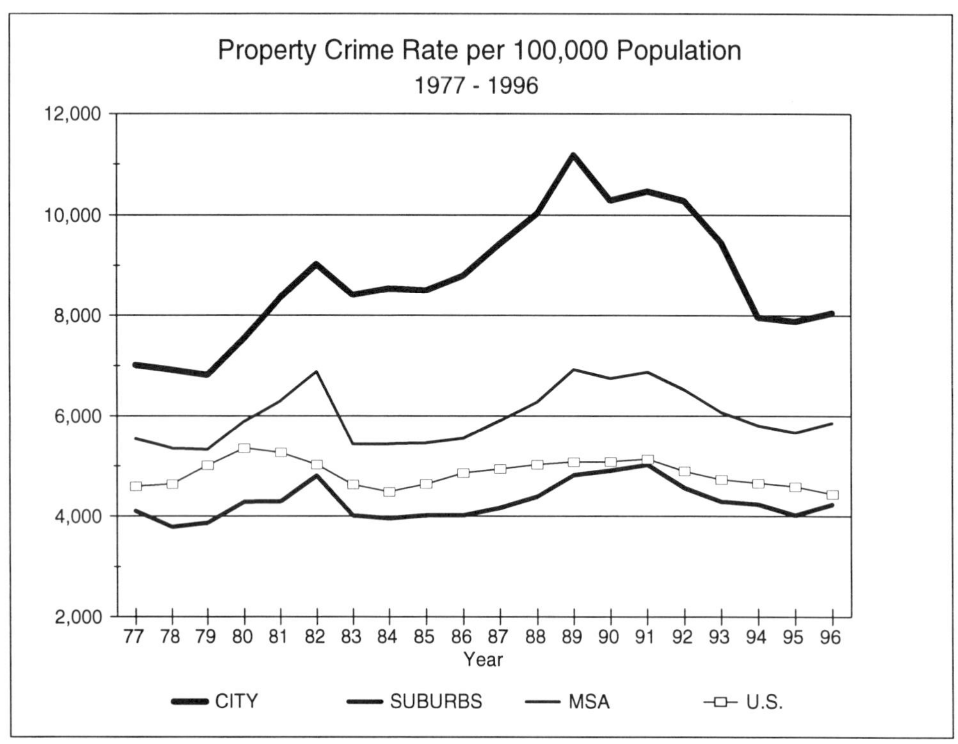

Note: Missing line segments indicate data not available.

Murders and Murder Rates: 1977 - 1996

Year	Number				Rate per 100,000 population			
	City	Suburbs[2]	MSA[1]	U.S.	City	Suburbs[3]	MSA[1]	U.S.
1977	47	24	71	19,120	15.9	7.9	11.8	8.8
1978	51	26	77	19,560	17.1	8.6	12.8	9.0
1979	50	34	84	21,460	16.6	11.0	13.8	9.7
1980	60	31	91	23,040	19.3	9.6	14.4	10.2
1981	51	27	78	22,520	16.1	8.3	12.1	9.8
1982	48	18	66	21,010	15.0	5.4	10.1	9.1
1983	44	50	94	19,310	13.6	7.3	9.3	8.3
1984	54	49	103	18,690	16.3	7.0	10.0	7.9
1985	56	39	95	18,980	16.7	5.5	9.1	7.9
1986	53	40	93	20,610	15.6	5.6	8.8	8.6
1987	52	51	103	20,100	14.6	7.1	9.5	8.3
1988	46	46	92	20,680	12.4	6.2	8.3	8.4
1989	73	63	136	21,500	19.6	8.4	12.1	8.7
1990	93	72	165	23,440	23.5	9.4	14.2	9.4
1991	114	64	178	24,700	28.3	8.2	15.1	9.8
1992	99	62	161	23,760	24.2	7.8	13.4	9.3
1993	122	82	204	24,530	28.9	10.1	16.6	9.5
1994	87	68	155	23,330	16.5	9.4	12.4	9.0
1995	89	58	147	21,610	16.4	7.9	11.5	8.2
1996	71	45	116	19,650	12.8	6.0	8.9	7.4

Notes: (1) Metropolitan Statistical Area - see Appendix A for areas included; (2) calculated by the editors using the following formula: (number of crimes in the MSA minus number of crimes in the city); (3) calculated by the editors using the following formula: ((number of crimes in the MSA minus number of crimes in the city) ÷ (population of the MSA minus population of the city)) x 100,000; n/a not avail.
Source: U.S. Department of Justice, FBI Uniform Crime Reports, 1977 - 1996

Forcible Rapes and Forcible Rape Rates: 1977 - 1996

Year	Number				Rate per 100,000 population			
	City	Suburbs[2]	MSA[1]	U.S.	City	Suburbs[3]	MSA[1]	U.S.
1977	119	48	167	63,500	40.2	15.7	27.8	29.4
1978	114	56	170	67,610	38.1	18.5	28.2	31.0
1979	115	51	166	76,390	38.3	16.5	27.3	34.7
1980	145	45	190	82,990	46.7	14.0	30.1	36.8
1981	198	66	264	82,500	62.6	20.2	41.0	36.0
1982	198	51	249	78,770	61.9	15.4	38.2	34.0
1983	258	116	374	78,920	79.7	17.0	37.2	33.7
1984	243	155	398	84,230	73.2	22.3	38.7	35.7
1985	226	175	401	88,670	67.3	24.6	38.3	37.1
1986	305	167	472	91,460	89.8	23.2	44.6	37.9
1987	308	182	490	91,110	86.4	25.2	45.4	37.4
1988	315	165	480	92,490	85.0	22.3	43.2	37.6
1989	325	170	495	94,500	87.2	22.6	43.9	38.1
1990	384	203	587	102,560	97.0	26.5	50.5	41.2
1991	409	207	616	106,590	101.6	26.6	52.1	42.3
1992	361	227	588	109,060	88.3	28.7	49.0	42.8
1993	356	219	575	106,010	84.2	27.1	46.7	41.1
1994	350	201	551	102,220	66.4	27.7	44.0	39.3
1995	366	180	546	97,470	67.3	24.4	42.6	37.1
1996	306	236	542	95,770	55.2	31.6	41.6	36.1

Notes: (1) Metropolitan Statistical Area - see Appendix A for areas included; (2) calculated by the editors using the following formula: (number of crimes in the MSA minus number of crimes in the city); (3) calculated by the editors using the following formula: ((number of crimes in the MSA minus number of crimes in the city) ÷ (population of the MSA minus population of the city)) x 100,000; n/a not avail.
Source: U.S. Department of Justice, FBI Uniform Crime Reports, 1977 - 1996

Robberies and Robbery Rates: 1977 - 1996

Year	Number				Rate per 100,000 population			
	City	Suburbs[2]	MSA[1]	U.S.	City	Suburbs[3]	MSA[1]	U.S.
1977	614	157	771	412,610	207.4	51.5	128.3	190.7
1978	709	131	840	426,930	237.1	43.2	139.4	195.8
1979	703	171	874	480,700	233.9	55.4	143.5	218.4
1980	686	245	931	565,840	220.7	76.3	147.3	251.1
1981	774	194	968	592,910	244.5	59.3	150.4	258.7
1982	990	208	1,198	553,130	309.3	62.9	184.0	238.9
1983	1,102	409	1,511	506,570	340.4	59.9	150.2	216.5
1984	1,144	438	1,582	485,010	344.6	62.9	153.9	205.4
1985	1,121	441	1,562	497,870	333.9	62.1	149.3	208.5
1986	1,454	569	2,023	542,780	427.9	79.1	191.1	225.1
1987	1,486	516	2,002	517,700	416.7	71.4	185.5	212.7
1988	1,933	631	2,564	542,970	521.7	85.2	230.8	220.9
1989	2,369	697	3,066	578,330	635.8	92.5	272.2	233.0
1990	3,208	832	4,040	639,270	810.2	108.6	347.6	257.0
1991	2,899	984	3,883	687,730	720.0	126.3	328.5	272.7
1992	3,058	989	4,047	672,480	747.8	125.0	337.3	263.6
1993	3,227	995	4,222	659,870	763.1	123.1	343.0	255.9
1994	2,713	828	3,541	618,950	514.7	114.3	282.9	237.7
1995	2,949	780	3,729	580,510	542.0	105.9	291.2	220.9
1996	2,594	848	3,442	537,050	468.2	113.4	264.4	202.4

Notes: (1) Metropolitan Statistical Area - see Appendix A for areas included; (2) calculated by the editors using the following formula: (number of crimes in the MSA minus number of crimes in the city); (3) calculated by the editors using the following formula: ((number of crimes in the MSA minus number of crimes in the city) ÷ (population of the MSA minus population of the city)) x 100,000; n/a not avail.
Source: U.S. Department of Justice, FBI Uniform Crime Reports, 1977 - 1996

Aggravated Assaults and Aggravated Assault Rates: 1977 - 1996

Year	Number				Rate per 100,000 population			
	City	Suburbs[2]	MSA[1]	U.S.	City	Suburbs[3]	MSA[1]	U.S.
1977	1,465	1,329	2,794	534,350	494.9	436.1	465.1	247.0
1978	1,561	1,399	2,960	571,460	522.1	461.0	491.3	262.1
1979	1,617	1,378	2,995	629,480	538.0	446.6	491.7	286.0
1980	1,868	1,388	3,256	672,650	601.0	432.0	515.1	298.5
1981	2,143	966	3,109	663,900	677.1	295.2	483.0	289.7
1982	2,864	778	3,642	669,480	894.7	235.1	559.4	289.2
1983	2,863	1,795	4,658	653,290	884.4	263.0	463.0	279.2
1984	2,990	1,985	4,975	685,350	900.6	285.3	484.0	290.2
1985	3,172	2,224	5,396	723,250	944.9	312.9	515.7	302.9
1986	3,675	2,501	6,176	834,320	1,081.6	347.8	583.3	346.1
1987	4,146	2,424	6,570	855,090	1,162.7	335.4	608.8	351.3
1988	4,521	2,601	7,122	910,090	1,220.3	351.3	641.2	370.2
1989	4,873	2,806	7,679	951,710	1,307.8	372.3	681.8	383.4
1990	5,434	3,853	9,287	1,054,860	1,372.5	502.9	799.2	424.1
1991	5,340	3,683	9,023	1,092,740	1,326.3	472.6	763.4	433.3
1992	5,938	3,870	9,808	1,126,970	1,452.0	489.2	817.3	441.8
1993	6,020	3,805	9,825	1,135,610	1,423.6	470.9	798.2	440.3
1994	5,952	3,337	9,289	1,113,180	1,129.2	460.6	742.2	427.6
1995	5,824	3,054	8,878	1,099,210	1,070.3	414.7	693.3	418.3
1996	5,944	2,705	8,649	1,029,810	1,072.8	361.7	664.3	388.2

Notes: (1) Metropolitan Statistical Area - see Appendix A for areas included; (2) calculated by the editors using the following formula: (number of crimes in the MSA minus number of crimes in the city); (3) calculated by the editors using the following formula: ((number of crimes in the MSA minus number of crimes in the city) ÷ (population of the MSA minus population of the city)) x 100,000; n/a not avail.
Source: U.S. Department of Justice, FBI Uniform Crime Reports, 1977 - 1996

Burglaries and Burglary Rates: 1977 - 1996

Year	Number				Rate per 100,000 population			
	City	Suburbs[2]	MSA[1]	U.S.	City	Suburbs[3]	MSA[1]	U.S.
1977	7,312	4,446	11,758	3,071,500	2,470.3	1,458.8	1,957.1	1,419.8
1978	7,009	4,002	11,011	3,128,300	2,344.1	1,318.6	1,827.6	1,434.6
1979	6,676	4,241	10,917	3,327,700	2,221.1	1,374.3	1,792.2	1,511.9
1980	8,245	4,996	13,241	3,795,200	2,652.9	1,555.0	2,094.8	1,684.1
1981	8,587	4,527	13,114	3,779,700	2,713.1	1,383.6	2,037.3	1,649.5
1982	8,805	5,018	13,823	3,447,100	2,750.5	1,516.3	2,123.2	1,488.8
1983	8,108	8,456	16,564	3,129,900	2,504.8	1,239.1	1,646.3	1,337.7
1984	8,664	8,925	17,589	2,984,400	2,609.7	1,282.7	1,711.3	1,263.7
1985	8,563	8,797	17,360	3,073,300	2,550.9	1,237.8	1,659.1	1,287.3
1986	9,598	9,289	18,887	3,241,400	2,824.9	1,291.8	1,783.8	1,344.6
1987	10,117	10,148	20,265	3,236,200	2,837.1	1,404.3	1,877.7	1,329.6
1988	10,605	10.883	21,488	3,218,100	2,862.4	1,470.1	1,934.5	1,309.2
1989	12,772	11,636	24,408	3,168,200	3,427.7	1,543.9	2,167.1	1,276.3
1990	10,891	11,899	22,790	3,073,900	2,750.7	1,553.1	1,961.1	1,235.9
1991	11,615	12,893	24,508	3,157,200	2,884.9	1,654.5	2,073.6	1,252.0
1992	12,565	11,663	24,228	2,979,900	3,072.5	1,474.4	2,019.0	1,168.2
1993	10,691	10,805	21,496	2,834,800	2,528.2	1,337.1	1,746.3	1,099.2
1994	10,326	8,705	19,031	2,712,800	1,958.9	1,201.5	1,520.5	1,042.0
1995	9,959	7,645	17,604	2,593,800	1,830.2	1,038.2	1,374.8	987.1
1996	10,227	7,811	18,038	2,501,500	1,845.8	1,044.4	1,385.4	943.0

Notes: (1) Metropolitan Statistical Area - see Appendix A for areas included; (2) calculated by the editors using the following formula: (number of crimes in the MSA minus number of crimes in the city); (3) calculated by the editors using the following formula: ((number of crimes in the MSA minus number of crimes in the city) ÷ (population of the MSA minus population of the city)) x 100,000; n/a not avail.
Source: U.S. Department of Justice, FBI Uniform Crime Reports, 1977 - 1996

Larceny-Thefts and Larceny-Theft Rates: 1977 - 1996

Year	Number				Rate per 100,000 population			
	City	Suburbs[2]	MSA[1]	U.S.	City	Suburbs[3]	MSA[1]	U.S.
1977	12,433	7,376	19,809	5,905,700	4,200.3	2,420.1	3,297.2	2,729.9
1978	12,429	6,771	19,200	5,991,000	4,156.9	2,231.0	3,186.7	2,747.4
1979	12,559	7,071	19,630	6,601,000	4,178.4	2,291.4	3,222.5	2,999.1
1980	13,760	8,132	21,892	7,136,900	4,427.4	2,531.1	3,463.5	3,167.0
1981	16,444	8,930	25,374	7,194,400	5,195.5	2,729.3	3,941.9	3,139.7
1982	18,762	10,302	29,064	7,142,500	5,860.9	3,113.0	4,464.2	3,084.8
1983	17,773	17,989	35,762	6,712,800	5,490.5	2,636.0	3,554.3	2,868.9
1984	18,297	17,439	35,736	6,591,900	5,511.3	2,506.3	3,477.0	2,791.3
1985	18,447	18,455	36,902	6,926,400	5,495.2	2,596.8	3,526.7	2,901.2
1986	18,637	18,165	36,802	7,257,200	5,485.2	2,526.3	3,475.8	3,010.3
1987	21,723	18,407	40,130	7,499,900	6,091.8	2,547.2	3,718.4	3,081.3
1988	24,236	19,881	44,117	7,705,900	6,541.6	2,685.5	3,971.6	3,134.9
1989	26,228	22,690	48,918	7,872,400	7,039.0	3,010.6	4,343.3	3,171.3
1990	27,153	23,734	50,887	7,945,700	6,858.0	3,097.8	4,378.9	3,194.8
1991	27,799	24,318	52,117	8,142,200	6,904.6	3,120.6	4,409.6	3,228.8
1992	27,014	22,777	49,791	7,915,200	6,605.7	2,879.4	4,149.3	3,103.0
1993	26,370	22,204	48,574	7,820,900	6,236.1	2,747.7	3,946.0	3,032.4
1994	28,469	20,430	48,899	7,879,800	5,400.8	2,819.9	3,906.9	3,026.7
1995	29,273	20,603	49,876	7,997,700	5,379.6	2,797.9	3,895.0	3,043.8
1996	30,199	22,225	52,424	7,894,600	5,450.4	2,971.6	4,026.4	2,975.9

Notes: (1) Metropolitan Statistical Area - see Appendix A for areas included; (2) calculated by the editors using the following formula: (number of crimes in the MSA minus number of crimes in the city); (3) calculated by the editors using the following formula: ((number of crimes in the MSA minus number of crimes in the city) ÷ (population of the MSA minus population of the city)) x 100,000; n/a not avail.
Source: U.S. Department of Justice, FBI Uniform Crime Reports, 1977 - 1996

Motor Vehicle Thefts and Motor Vehicle Theft Rates: 1977 - 1996

Year	Number				Rate per 100,000 population			
	City	Suburbs[2]	MSA[1]	U.S.	City	Suburbs[3]	MSA[1]	U.S.
1977	1,006	694	1,700	977,700	339.9	227.7	283.0	451.9
1978	1,246	736	1,982	1,004,100	416.7	242.5	329.0	460.5
1979	1,264	636	1,900	1,112,800	420.5	206.1	311.9	505.6
1980	1,444	648	2,092	1,131,700	464.6	201.7	331.0	502.2
1981	1,449	636	2,085	1,087,800	457.8	194.4	323.9	474.7
1982	1,320	590	1,910	1,062,400	412.3	178.3	293.4	458.8
1983	1,337	991	2,328	1,007,900	413.0	145.2	231.4	430.8
1984	1,375	1,177	2,552	1,032,200	414.2	169.2	248.3	437.1
1985	1,502	1,326	2,828	1,102,900	447.4	186.6	270.3	462.0
1986	1,659	1,460	3,119	1,224,100	488.3	203.0	294.6	507.8
1987	1,777	1,579	3,356	1,288,700	498.3	218.5	311.0	529.4
1988	2,323	1,799	4,122	1,432,900	627.0	243.0	371.1	582.9
1989	2,701	1,997	4,698	1,564,800	724.9	265.0	417.1	630.4
1990	2,699	1,983	4,682	1,635,900	681.7	258.8	402.9	657.8
1991	2,726	1,925	4,651	1,661,700	677.1	247.0	393.5	659.0
1992	2,454	1,723	4,177	1,610,800	600.1	217.8	348.1	631.5
1993	2,972	1,709	4,681	1,563,100	702.8	211.5	380.3	606.1
1994	3,160	1,566	4,726	1,539,300	599.5	216.2	377.6	591.3
1995	3,650	1,405	5,055	1,472,400	670.8	190.8	394.8	560.4
1996	4,177	1,681	5,858	1,395,200	753.9	224.8	449.9	525.9

Notes: (1) Metropolitan Statistical Area - see Appendix A for areas included; (2) calculated by the editors using the following formula: (number of crimes in the MSA minus number of crimes in the city); (3) calculated by the editors using the following formula: ((number of crimes in the MSA minus number of crimes in the city) ÷ (population of the MSA minus population of the city)) x 100,000; n/a not avail.
Source: U.S. Department of Justice, FBI Uniform Crime Reports, 1977 - 1996

HATE CRIMES

Criminal Incidents by Bias Motivation

Area	Race	Ethnicity	Religion	Sexual Orientation
Charlotte	n/a	n/a	n/a	n/a

Notes: Figures include both violent and property crimes. Law enforcement agencies must have submitted data for at least one quarter of calendar year 1995 to be included in this report, therefore figures shown may not represent complete 12-month totals; n/a not available
Source: U.S. Department of Justice, FBI Uniform Crime Reports, Hate Crime Statistics 1995

LAW ENFORCEMENT

Full-Time Law Enforcement Employees

Jurisdiction	Police Employees			Police Officers per 100,000 population
	Total	Officers	Civilians	
Charlotte	1,633	1,290	343	232.8

Notes: Data as of October 31, 1996
Source: U.S. Department of Justice, FBI Uniform Crime Reports, 1996

Number of Police Officers by Race

Race	Police Officers				Index of Representation[1]		
	1983		1992				
	Number	Pct.	Number	Pct.	1983	1992	% Chg.
Black	144	22.4	167	19.2	0.72	0.60	-16.7
Hispanic[2]	0	0.0	0	0.0	0.00	0.00	0.0

Notes: (1) The index of representation is calculated by dividing the percent of black/hispanic police officers by the percent of corresponding blacks/hispanics in the local population. An index approaching 1.0 indicates that a city is closer to achieving a representation of police officers equal to their proportion in the local population; (2) Hispanic officers can be of any race
Source: Bureau of Justice Statistics, Sourcebook of Criminal Justice Statistics, 1994

CORRECTIONS

Federal Correctional Facilities

Type	Year Opened	Security Level	Sex of Inmates	Rated Capacity	Population on 7/1/95	Number of Staff
None listed						

Notes: Data as of 1995
Source: Bureau of Justice Statistics, Sourcebook of Criminal Justice Statistics Online

City/County/Regional Correctional Facilities

Name	Year Opened	Year Renov.	Rated Capacity	1995 Pop.	Number of COs[1]	Number of Staff	ACA[2] Accred.
Mecklenburg Co Intake Ctr	1989	--	48	65	54	62	No
Mecklenburg Co Jail Annex	1991	--	618	516	112	115	No
Mecklenburg Co Jail North	1994	--	614	464	183	222	No
Mecklenburg Co Satellite Jail	1990	--	300	290	73	80	No

Notes: Data as of April 1996; (1) Correctional Officers; (2) American Correctional Assn. Accreditation
Source: American Correctional Association, 1996-1998 National Jail and Adult Detention Directory

Private Adult Correctional Facilities

Name	Date Opened	Rated Capacity	Present Pop.	Security Level	Facility Construct.	Expans. Plans	ACA[1] Accred.
None listed							

Notes: Data as of December 1996; (1) American Correctional Association Accreditation
Source: University of Florida, Center for Studies in Criminology and Law, Private Adult Correctional Facility Census, 10th Ed., March 15, 1997

Characteristics of Shock Incarceration Programs

Jurisdiction	Year Program Began	Number of Camps	Average Num. of Inmates	Number of Beds	Program Length	Voluntary/ Mandatory
North Carolina	1989	2	240	360	90 to 120 days	Voluntary

Note: Data as of July 1996;
Source: Sourcebook of Criminal Justice Statistics Online

DEATH PENALTY

Death Penalty Statistics

State	Prisoners Executed		Prisoners Under Sentence of Death					Avg. No. of Years on Death Row[4]
	1930-1995	1996[1]	Total[2]	White[3]	Black[3]	Hisp.	Women	
North Carolina	271	0	139	68	69	1	2	3.3

Notes: Data as of 12/31/95 unless otherwise noted; (1) Data as of 7/31/97; (2) Includes persons of other races; (3) Includes people of Hispanic origin; (4) Covers prisoners sentenced 1974 through 1995
Source: Bureau of Justice Statistics, Capital Punishment 1995 (released 12/96); Death Penalty Information Center Web Site, 9/30/97

Capital Offenses and Methods of Execution

Capital Offenses in North Carolina	Minimum Age for Imposition of Death Penalty	Mentally Retarded Excluded	Methods of Execution[1]
First-degree murder (N.C.G.S. 14-17).	17	No	Lethal injection; lethal gas

Notes: Data as of 12/31/95 unless otherwise noted; (1) Data as of 7/31/97
Source: Bureau of Justice Statistics, Capital Punishment 1995 (released 12/96); Death Penalty Information Center Web Site, 9/30/97

LAWS

Statutory Provisions Relating to the Purchase, Ownership and Use of Handguns

Jurisdiction	Instant Background Check	Federal Waiting Period Applies[1]	State Waiting Period (days)	License or Permit to Purchase	Regis-tration	Record of Sale Sent to Police	Concealed Carry Law
North Carolina	No	No	No	Yes[a]	No	Yes	Yes[b]

Note: Data as of 1996; (1) The Federal 5-day waiting period for handgun purchases applies to states that don't have instant background checks, waiting period requirements, or licensing procedures exempting them from the Federal requirement; (a) To purchase a handgun, a license or permit is required, which must be issued to qualified applicants within 30 days; (b) "Shall issue" permit system, liberally administered discretion by local authorities over permit issuance, or no permit required
Source: Sourcebook of Criminal Justice Statistics Online

Statutory Provisions Relating to Alcohol Use and Driving

Jurisdiction	Drinking Age	Blood Alcohol Concentration Levels as Evidence in State Courts[1]		Open Container Law[1]	Anti-Consumption Law[1]	Dram Shop Law[1]
		Illegal per se at 0.10%	Presumption at 0.10%			
North Carolina	21	(a)	No	Yes[b]	Yes[b,c]	Yes[d,e]

Note: Data as of January 1, 1997; (1) See Appendix C for an explanation of terms; (a) 0.08%; (b) Limited application; (c) Applies to drivers only; (d) State has a statute that places a monetary limit on the amount of damages that can be awarded in dram shop liability actions; (e) Applies specifically to the actions of intoxicated minors, but the law does not foreclose developing case law as to other types of dram shop action
Source: Sourcebook of Criminal Justice Statistics Online

Statutory Provisions Relating to Curfews

Jurisdiction	Year Enacted	Latest Revision	Age Group(s)	Curfew Provisions
Charlotte	1995	-	15 and under	11 pm to 6 am weekday nights midnight to 6 am weekend nights

Note: Data as of February 1996
Source: Sourcebook of Criminal Justice Statistics Online

Statutory Provisions Relating to Hate Crimes

Jurisdiction	Bias-Motivated Violence and Intimidation						Institutional Vandalism
	Civil Action	Criminal Penalty					
		Race/ Religion/ Ethnicity	Sexual Orientation	Mental/ Physical Disability	Gender	Age	
North Carolina	No	Yes	No	No	No	No	Yes

Source: Anti-Defamation League, 1997 Hate Crimes Laws

Chicago, Illinois

OVERVIEW

Between 1977 and 1996 the property crime rate increased 23.4%. Figures for the total and violent crime rates are not available.

Among violent crimes, the rates for: Murders increased 6.3%; Forcible Rapes (not available); Robberies increased 80.9%; and Aggravated Assaults increased 300.2%.

Among property crimes, the rates for: Burglaries increased 19.8%; Larceny-Thefts increased 26.1%; and Motor Vehicle Thefts increased 18.5%.

ANTI-CRIME PROGRAMS

Among their many programs:

- CAPS (Chicago Alternative Policing Strategy)—The police, the community and other government agencies and service providers work together to identify and solve problems of crime and disorder and to improve the quality of life.

  A group of independent evaluators concluded that as a result of CAPS (in 5 prototype districts) major crime problems have been reduced as have drug and gun problems and the perception of police service has improved. (Internet users can get up-to-date information on CAPS).

- JCPT (Joint Community-Police Training Project)—Provides classroom instruction on CAPS to community members.

- ICAM (Information Collection for Automated Mapping)—Police officers now have the aid of a computerized mapping program in analyzing and solving neighborhood crime problems.

- Court Advocacy—Each police district has a Court Advocacy Subcommittee that identifies and tracks cases of importance to the community in felony, misdemeanor, housing and other courts. Court advocates attend court to show community concern about crime and solidarity for victims.

- The CAPS Implementation Office and the Preventive Programs Section conduct numerous programs to increase the public's awareness of CAPS and to encourage community involvement in crime prevention. Seminars on a wide range of community safety topics are offered. *City of Chicago, Department of Police, 9/97*

CRIME RISK

Your Chances of Becoming a Victim[1]

Area	Any Crime	Violent Crime					Property Crime			
		Any	Murder	Forcible Rape[2]	Robbery	Aggrav. Assault	Any	Burglary	Larceny -Theft	Motor Vehicle Theft
City	n/a	n/a	1:3,491	n/a	1:103	1:74	1:14	1:68	1:23	1:81

Note: (1) Figures have been calculated by dividing the population of the city by the number of crimes reported to the FBI during 1996 and are expressed as odds (eg. 1:20 should be read as 1 in 20). (2) Figures have been calculated by dividing the female population of the city by the number of forcible rapes reported to the FBI during 1996. The female population of the city was estimated by calculating the ratio of females to males reported in the 1990 Census and applying that ratio to 1996 population estimate; n/a not available
Source: FBI Uniform Crime Reports 1996

CRIME STATISTICS

Total Crimes and Total Crime Rates: 1977 - 1996

Year	Number				Rate per 100,000 population			
	City	Suburbs[2]	MSA[1]	U.S.	City	Suburbs[3]	MSA[1]	U.S.
1977	203,839	189,323	393,162	10,984,500	6,654.9	4,913.6	5,684.8	5,077.6
1978	190,815	199,409	390,224	11,209,000	6,258.3	5,016.8	5,555.7	5,140.3
1979	186,728	209,261	395,989	12,249,500	6,100.6	5,283.1	5,639.5	5,565.5
1980	196,605	207,233	403,838	13,408,300	6,583.3	5,089.9	5,721.8	5,950.0
1981	173,316	207,813	381,129	13,423,800	5,752.8	5,059.6	5,353.0	5,858.2
1982	181,891	194,052	375,943	12,974,400	6,041.2	4,727.5	5,283.3	5,603.6
1983	241,603	134,784	376,387	12,108,600	7,996.9	4,473.8	6,237.8	5,175.0
1984	276,240	128,951	405,191	11,881,800	9,169.7	4,233.5	6,688.0	5,031.3
1985	277,260	129,913	407,173	12,431,400	9,245.6	4,216.1	6,696.7	5,207.1
1986	n/a	n/a	n/a	13,211,900	n/a	n/a	n/a	5,480.4
1987	n/a	n/a	n/a	13,508,700	n/a	n/a	n/a	5,550.0
1988	n/a	n/a	n/a	13,923,100	n/a	n/a	n/a	5,664.2
1989	n/a	n/a	n/a	14,251,400	n/a	n/a	n/a	5,741.0
1990	n/a	n/a	n/a	14,475,600	n/a	n/a	n/a	5,820.3
1991	n/a	n/a	n/a	14,872,900	n/a	n/a	n/a	5,897.8
1992	n/a	n/a	n/a	14,438,200	n/a	n/a	n/a	5,660.2
1993	n/a	n/a	n/a	14,144,800	n/a	n/a	n/a	5,484.4
1994	n/a	n/a	n/a	13,989,500	n/a	n/a	n/a	5,373.5
1995	n/a	n/a	n/a	13,862,700	n/a	n/a	n/a	5,275.9
1996	n/a	n/a	n/a	13,473,600	n/a	n/a	n/a	5,078.9

Notes: (1) Metropolitan Statistical Area - see Appendix A for areas included; (2) calculated by the editors using the following formula: (number of crimes in the MSA minus number of crimes in the city); (3) calculated by the editors using the following formula: ((number of crimes in the MSA minus number of crimes in the city) ÷ (population of the MSA minus population of the city)) x 100,000; n/a not avail.
Source: U.S. Department of Justice, FBI Uniform Crime Reports, 1977 - 1996

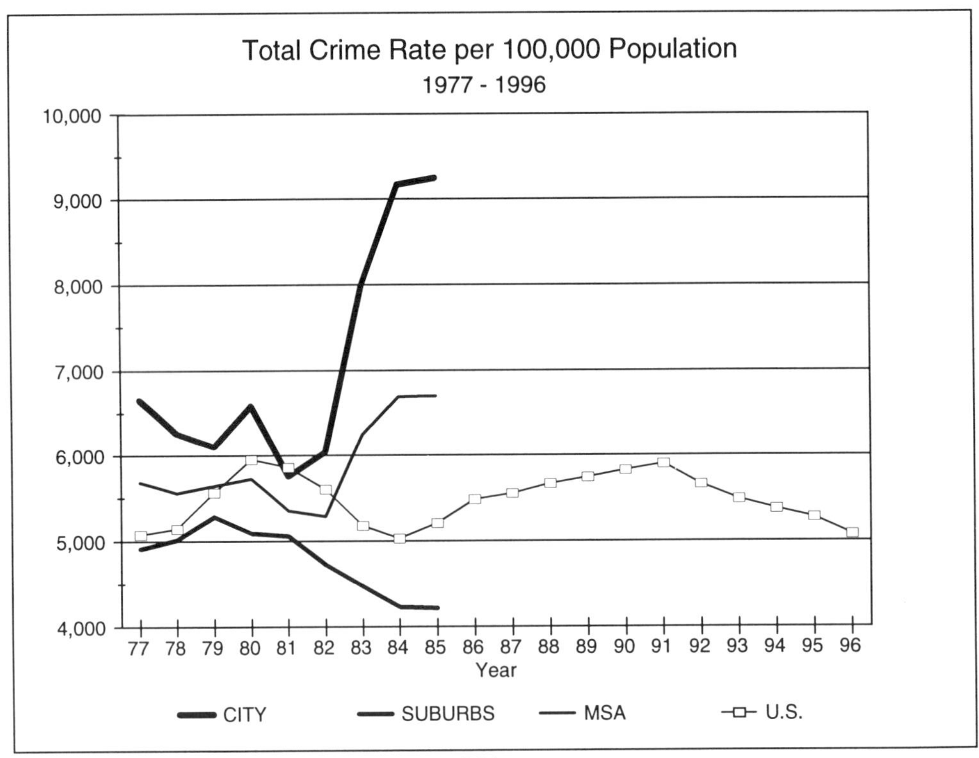

Note: Missing line segments indicate data not available.

Violent Crimes and Violent Crime Rates: 1977 - 1996

Year	Number				Rate per 100,000 population			
	City	Suburbs[2]	MSA[1]	U.S.	City	Suburbs[3]	MSA[1]	U.S.
1977	28,873	9,892	38,765	1,029,580	942.6	256.7	560.5	475.9
1978	27,686	11,063	38,749	1,085,550	908.0	278.3	551.7	497.8
1979	27,807	12,130	39,937	1,208,030	908.5	306.2	568.8	548.9
1980	28,658	12,629	41,287	1,344,520	959.6	310.2	585.0	596.6
1981	25,609	12,045	37,654	1,361,820	850.0	293.3	528.9	594.3
1982	26,404	11,789	38,193	1,322,390	877.0	287.2	536.7	571.1
1983	39,776	7,126	46,902	1,258,090	1,316.6	236.5	777.3	537.7
1984	59,957	7,477	67,434	1,273,280	1,990.3	245.5	1,113.0	539.2
1985	58,446	6,809	65,255	1,328,800	1,949.0	221.0	1,073.2	556.6
1986	n/a	n/a	n/a	1,489,170	n/a	n/a	n/a	617.7
1987	n/a	n/a	n/a	1,484,000	n/a	n/a	n/a	609.7
1988	n/a	n/a	n/a	1,566,220	n/a	n/a	n/a	637.2
1989	n/a	n/a	n/a	1,646,040	n/a	n/a	n/a	663.1
1990	n/a	n/a	n/a	1,820,130	n/a	n/a	n/a	731.8
1991	n/a	n/a	n/a	1,911,770	n/a	n/a	n/a	758.1
1992	n/a	n/a	n/a	1,932,270	n/a	n/a	n/a	757.5
1993	n/a	n/a	n/a	1,926,020	n/a	n/a	n/a	746.8
1994	n/a	n/a	n/a	1,857,670	n/a	n/a	n/a	713.6
1995	n/a	n/a	n/a	1,798,790	n/a	n/a	n/a	684.6
1996	n/a	n/a	n/a	1,682,280	n/a	n/a	n/a	634.1

Notes: Violent crimes include murder, forcible rape, robbery and aggravated assault; n/a not available; (1) Metropolitan Statistical Area - see Appendix A for areas included; (2) calculated by the editors using the following formula: (number of crimes in the MSA minus number of crimes in the city); (3) calculated by the editors using the following formula: ((number of crimes in the MSA minus number of crimes in the city) ÷ (population of the MSA minus population of the city)) x 100,000
Source: U.S. Department of Justice, FBI Uniform Crime Reports, 1977 - 1996

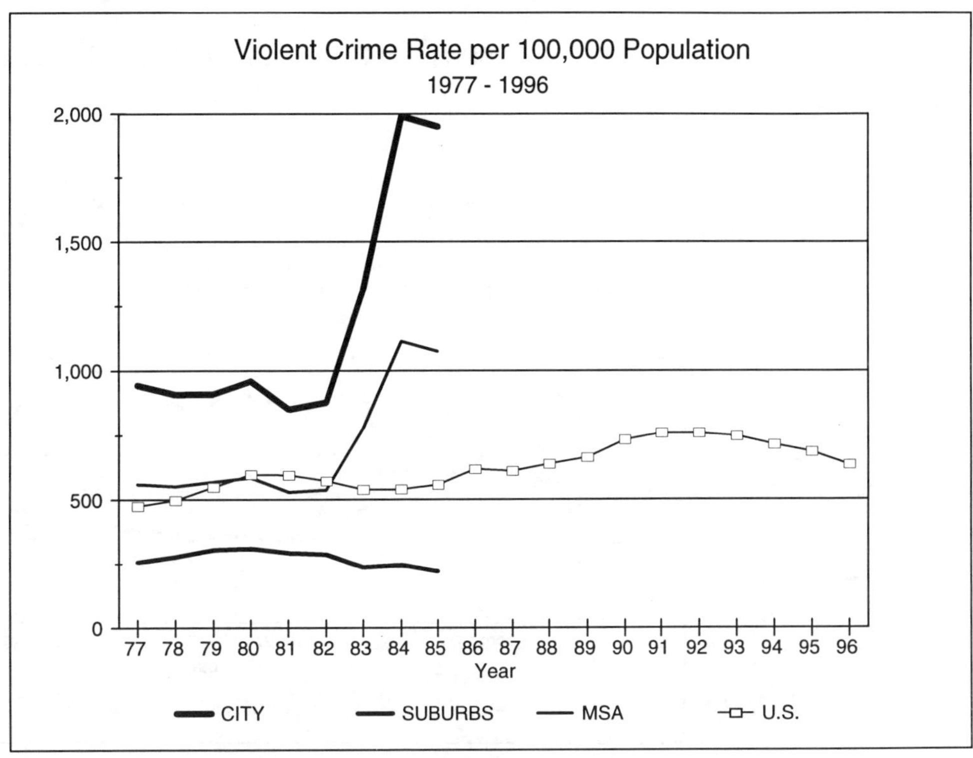

Note: Missing line segments indicate data not available.

Property Crimes and Property Crime Rates: 1977 - 1996

Year	Number				Rate per 100,000 population			
	City	Suburbs[2]	MSA[1]	U.S.	City	Suburbs[3]	MSA[1]	U.S.
1977	174,966	179,431	354,397	9,955,000	5,712.2	4,656.9	5,124.3	4,601.7
1978	163,129	188,346	351,475	10,123,400	5,350.2	4,738.5	5,004.0	4,642.5
1979	158,921	197,131	356,052	11,041,500	5,192.1	4,976.9	5,070.7	5,016.6
1980	167,947	194,604	362,551	12,063,700	5,623.7	4,779.7	5,136.8	5,353.3
1981	147,707	195,768	343,475	12,061,900	4,902.8	4,766.4	4,824.1	5,263.9
1982	155,487	182,263	337,750	11,652,000	5,164.2	4,440.3	4,746.6	5,032.5
1983	201,827	127,658	329,485	10,850,500	6,680.4	4,237.3	5,460.5	4,637.4
1984	216,283	121,474	337,757	10,608,500	7,179.5	3,988.0	5,574.9	4,492.1
1985	218,814	123,104	341,918	11,102,600	7,296.6	3,995.1	5,623.5	4,650.5
1986	226,536	124,792	351,328	11,722,700	7,543.4	4,046.0	5,771.3	4,862.6
1987	209,770	124,462	334,232	12,024,700	6,949.9	3,981.8	5,439.9	4,940.3
1988	225,656	127,725	353,381	12,356,900	7,536.7	4,090.4	5,777.3	5,027.1
1989	227,631	132,492	360,123	12,605,400	7,617.5	4,130.2	5,812.1	5,077.9
1990	228,829	136,811	365,640	12,655,500	8,220.2	4,221.4	6,069.1	5,088.5
1991	231,318	142,890	374,208	12,961,100	8,227.6	4,366.2	6,150.6	5,139.7
1992	213,731	190,265	403,996	12,505,900	7,544.6	4,040.8	5,357.0	4,902.7
1993	207,422	n/a	n/a	12,218,800	7,437.2	n/a	n/a	4,737.6
1994	205,001	n/a	n/a	12,131,900	7,314.9	n/a	n/a	4,660.0
1995	197,923	n/a	n/a	12,063,900	7,197.5	n/a	n/a	4,591.3
1996	194,058	n/a	n/a	11,791,300	7,046.1	n/a	n/a	4,444.8

Notes: Property crimes include burglary, larceny-theft and motor vehicle theft; n/a not available; (1) Metropolitan Statistical Area - see Appendix A for areas included; (2) calculated by the editors using the following formula: (number of crimes in the MSA minus number of crimes in the city); (3) calculated by the editors using the following formula: ((number of crimes in the MSA minus number of crimes in the city) ÷ (population of the MSA minus population of the city)) x 100,000
Source: U.S. Department of Justice, FBI Uniform Crime Reports, 1977 - 1996

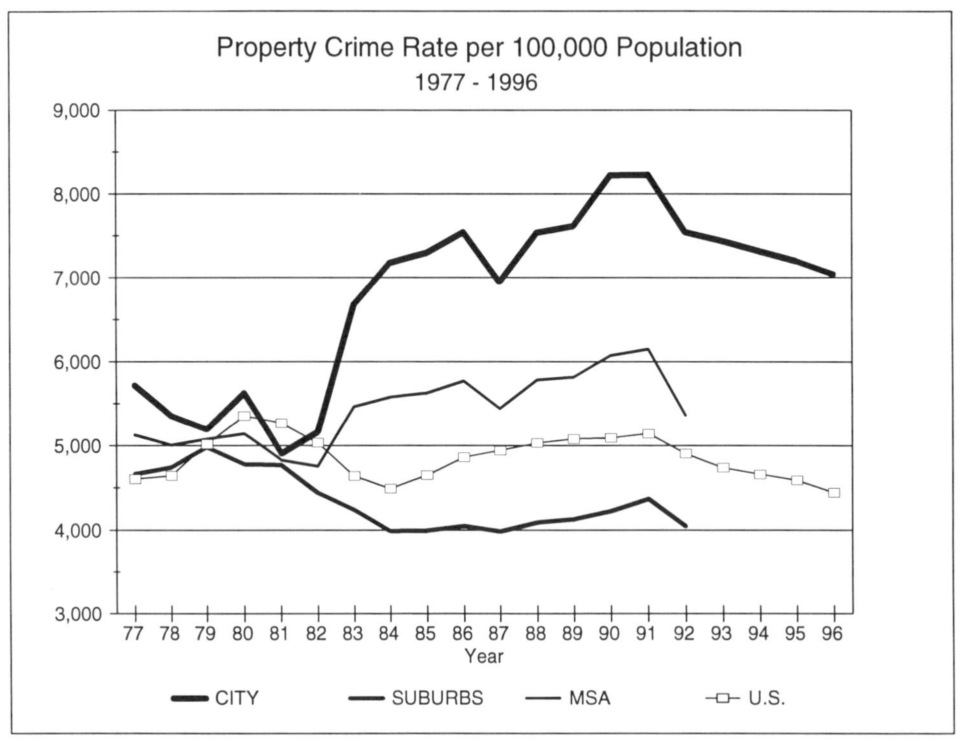

Note: Missing line segments indicate data not available.

Murders and Murder Rates: 1977 - 1996

Year	Number				Rate per 100,000 population			
	City	Suburbs[2]	MSA[1]	U.S.	City	Suburbs[3]	MSA[1]	U.S.
1977	823	127	950	19,120	26.9	3.3	13.7	8.8
1978	787	126	913	19,560	25.8	3.2	13.0	9.0
1979	856	145	1,001	21,460	28.0	3.7	14.3	9.7
1980	863	161	1,024	23,040	28.9	4.0	14.5	10.2
1981	877	135	1,012	22,520	29.1	3.3	14.2	9.8
1982	668	166	834	21,010	22.2	4.0	11.7	9.1
1983	729	108	837	19,310	24.1	3.6	13.9	8.3
1984	741	77	818	18,690	24.6	2.5	13.5	7.9
1985	666	67	733	18,980	22.2	2.2	12.1	7.9
1986	744	71	815	20,610	24.8	2.3	13.4	8.6
1987	691	66	757	20,100	22.9	2.1	12.3	8.3
1988	660	83	743	20,680	22.0	2.7	12.1	8.4
1989	742	70	812	21,500	24.8	2.2	13.1	8.7
1990	851	86	937	23,440	30.6	2.7	15.6	9.4
1991	925	102	1,027	24,700	32.9	3.1	16.9	9.8
1992	939	162	1,101	23,760	33.1	3.4	14.6	9.3
1993	845	n/a	n/a	24,530	30.3	n/a	n/a	9.5
1994	928	n/a	n/a	23,330	33.1	n/a	n/a	9.0
1995	824	n/a	n/a	21,610	30.0	n/a	n/a	8.2
1996	789	n/a	n/a	19,650	28.6	n/a	n/a	7.4

Notes: (1) Metropolitan Statistical Area - see Appendix A for areas included; (2) calculated by the editors using the following formula: (number of crimes in the MSA minus number of crimes in the city); (3) calculated by the editors using the following formula: ((number of crimes in the MSA minus number of crimes in the city) ÷ (population of the MSA minus population of the city)) x 100,000; n/a not avail.
Source: U.S. Department of Justice, FBI Uniform Crime Reports, 1977 - 1996

Forcible Rapes and Forcible Rape Rates: 1977 - 1996

Year	Number				Rate per 100,000 population			
	City	Suburbs[2]	MSA[1]	U.S.	City	Suburbs[3]	MSA[1]	U.S.
1977	1,227	477	1,704	63,500	40.1	12.4	24.6	29.4
1978	1,341	580	1,921	67,610	44.0	14.6	27.3	31.0
1979	1,655	733	2,388	76,390	54.1	18.5	34.0	34.7
1980	1,329	789	2,118	82,990	44.5	19.4	30.0	36.8
1981	1,255	623	1,878	82,500	41.7	15.2	26.4	36.0
1982	1,112	558	1,670	78,770	36.9	13.6	23.5	34.0
1983	2,246	345	2,591	78,920	74.3	11.5	42.9	33.7
1984	2,261	300	2,561	84,230	75.1	9.8	42.3	35.7
1985	1,792	383	2,175	88,670	59.8	12.4	35.8	37.1
1986	n/a	n/a	n/a	91,460	n/a	n/a	n/a	37.9
1987	n/a	n/a	n/a	91,110	n/a	n/a	n/a	37.4
1988	n/a	n/a	n/a	92,490	n/a	n/a	n/a	37.6
1989	n/a	n/a	n/a	94,500	n/a	n/a	n/a	38.1
1990	n/a	n/a	n/a	102,560	n/a	n/a	n/a	41.2
1991	n/a	n/a	n/a	106,590	n/a	n/a	n/a	42.3
1992	n/a	n/a	n/a	109,060	n/a	n/a	n/a	42.8
1993	n/a	n/a	n/a	106,010	n/a	n/a	n/a	41.1
1994	n/a	n/a	n/a	102,220	n/a	n/a	n/a	39.3
1995	n/a	n/a	n/a	97,470	n/a	n/a	n/a	37.1
1996	n/a	n/a	n/a	95,770	n/a	n/a	n/a	36.1

Notes: (1) Metropolitan Statistical Area - see Appendix A for areas included; (2) calculated by the editors using the following formula: (number of crimes in the MSA minus number of crimes in the city); (3) calculated by the editors using the following formula: ((number of crimes in the MSA minus number of crimes in the city) ÷ (population of the MSA minus population of the city)) x 100,000; n/a not avail.
Source: U.S. Department of Justice, FBI Uniform Crime Reports, 1977 - 1996

Robberies and Robbery Rates: 1977 - 1996

Year	Number				Rate per 100,000 population			
	City	Suburbs[2]	MSA[1]	U.S.	City	Suburbs[3]	MSA[1]	U.S.
1977	16,512	3,504	20,016	412,610	539.1	90.9	289.4	190.7
1978	15,233	4,047	19,280	426,930	499.6	101.8	274.5	195.8
1979	14,464	4,012	18,476	480,700	472.6	101.3	263.1	218.4
1980	16,261	4,467	20,728	565,840	544.5	109.7	293.7	251.1
1981	16,118	4,522	20,640	592,910	535.0	110.1	289.9	258.7
1982	16,307	4,004	20,311	553,130	541.6	97.5	285.4	238.9
1983	23,471	2,592	26,063	506,570	776.9	86.0	431.9	216.5
1984	28,535	2,654	31,189	485,010	947.2	87.1	514.8	205.4
1985	26,892	2,444	29,336	497,870	896.7	79.3	482.5	208.5
1986	30,918	2,460	33,378	542,780	1,029.5	79.8	548.3	225.1
1987	29,879	2,480	32,359	517,700	989.9	79.3	526.7	212.7
1988	28,975	2,690	31,665	542,970	967.7	86.1	517.7	220.9
1989	31,588	3,225	34,813	578,330	1,057.1	100.5	561.9	233.0
1990	37,156	3,352	40,508	639,270	1,334.8	103.4	672.4	257.0
1991	43,783	3,620	47,403	687,730	1,557.3	110.6	779.1	272.7
1992	38,448	5,097	43,545	672,480	1,357.2	108.2	577.4	263.6
1993	35,189	n/a	n/a	659,870	1,261.7	n/a	n/a	255.9
1994	33,925	n/a	n/a	618,950	1,210.5	n/a	n/a	237.7
1995	30,086	n/a	n/a	580,510	1,094.1	n/a	n/a	220.9
1996	26,860	n/a	n/a	537,050	975.3	n/a	n/a	202.4

Notes: (1) Metropolitan Statistical Area - see Appendix A for areas included; (2) calculated by the editors using the following formula: (number of crimes in the MSA minus number of crimes in the city); (3) calculated by the editors using the following formula: ((number of crimes in the MSA minus number of crimes in the city) ÷ (population of the MSA minus population of the city)) x 100,000; n/a not avail.
Source: U.S. Department of Justice, FBI Uniform Crime Reports, 1977 - 1996

Aggravated Assaults and Aggravated Assault Rates: 1977 - 1996

Year	Number				Rate per 100,000 population			
	City	Suburbs[2]	MSA[1]	U.S.	City	Suburbs[3]	MSA[1]	U.S.
1977	10,311	5,784	16,095	534,350	336.6	150.1	232.7	247.0
1978	10,325	6,310	16,635	571,460	338.6	158.7	236.8	262.1
1979	10,832	7,240	18,072	629,480	353.9	182.8	257.4	286.0
1980	10,205	7,212	17,417	672,650	341.7	177.1	246.8	298.5
1981	7,359	6,765	14,124	663,900	244.3	164.7	198.4	289.7
1982	8,317	7,061	15,378	669,480	276.2	172.0	216.1	289.2
1983	13,330	4,081	17,411	653,290	441.2	135.5	288.6	279.2
1984	28,420	4,446	32,866	685,350	943.4	146.0	542.5	290.2
1985	29,096	3,915	33,011	723,250	970.2	127.1	542.9	302.9
1986	33,529	4,184	37,713	834,320	1,116.5	135.7	619.5	346.1
1987	34,194	4,184	38,378	855,090	1,132.9	133.9	624.6	351.3
1988	35,988	3,783	39,771	910,090	1,202.0	121.2	650.2	370.2
1989	37,615	4,350	41,965	951,710	1,258.8	135.6	677.3	383.4
1990	41,114	4,953	46,067	1,054,860	1,476.9	152.8	764.7	424.1
1991	42,237	5,271	47,508	1,092,740	1,502.3	161.1	780.9	433.3
1992	41,080	8,218	49,298	1,126,970	1,450.1	174.5	653.7	441.8
1993	39,753	n/a	n/a	1,135,610	1,425.4	n/a	n/a	440.3
1994	40,380	n/a	n/a	1,113,180	1,440.9	n/a	n/a	427.6
1995	39,205	n/a	n/a	1,099,210	1,425.7	n/a	n/a	418.3
1996	37,097	n/a	n/a	1,029,810	1,347.0	n/a	n/a	388.2

Notes: (1) Metropolitan Statistical Area - see Appendix A for areas included; (2) calculated by the editors using the following formula: (number of crimes in the MSA minus number of crimes in the city); (3) calculated by the editors using the following formula: ((number of crimes in the MSA minus number of crimes in the city) ÷ (population of the MSA minus population of the city)) x 100,000; n/a not avail.
Source: U.S. Department of Justice, FBI Uniform Crime Reports, 1977 - 1996

Burglaries and Burglary Rates: 1977 - 1996

Year	Number				Rate per 100,000 population			
	City	Suburbs[2]	MSA[1]	U.S.	City	Suburbs[3]	MSA[1]	U.S.
1977	37,573	44,781	82,354	3,071,500	1,226.7	1,162.2	1,190.8	1,419.8
1978	34,165	47,433	81,598	3,128,300	1,120.5	1,193.3	1,161.7	1,434.6
1979	33,396	50,385	83,781	3,327,700	1,091.1	1,272.0	1,193.2	1,511.9
1980	34,288	53,322	87,610	3,795,200	1,148.1	1,309.7	1,241.3	1,684.1
1981	30,112	52,486	82,598	3,779,700	999.5	1,277.9	1,160.1	1,649.5
1982	32,249	47,270	79,519	3,447,100	1,071.1	1,151.6	1,117.5	1,488.8
1983	48,955	31,273	80,228	3,129,900	1,620.4	1,038.0	1,329.6	1,337.7
1984	55,240	27,054	82,294	2,984,400	1,833.7	888.2	1,358.3	1,263.7
1985	52,658	27,208	79,866	3,073,300	1,755.9	883.0	1,313.5	1,287.3
1986	56,274	26,491	82,765	3,241,400	1,873.9	858.9	1,359.6	1,344.6
1987	51,005	25,738	76,743	3,236,200	1,689.8	823.4	1,249.1	1,329.6
1988	52,060	24,944	77,004	3,218,100	1,738.8	798.8	1,258.9	1,309.2
1989	51,580	24,345	75,925	3,168,200	1,726.1	758.9	1,225.4	1,276.3
1990	50,203	24,141	74,344	3,073,900	1,803.4	744.9	1,234.0	1,235.9
1991	52,234	25,389	77,623	3,157,200	1,857.9	775.8	1,275.8	1,252.0
1992	49,046	36,102	85,148	2,979,900	1,731.3	766.7	1,129.1	1,168.2
1993	45,670	n/a	n/a	2,834,800	1,637.5	n/a	n/a	1,099.2
1994	43,821	n/a	n/a	2,712,800	1,563.6	n/a	n/a	1,042.0
1995	40,239	n/a	n/a	2,593,800	1,463.3	n/a	n/a	987.1
1996	40,475	n/a	n/a	2,501,500	1,469.6	n/a	n/a	943.0

Notes: (1) Metropolitan Statistical Area - see Appendix A for areas included; (2) calculated by the editors using the following formula: (number of crimes in the MSA minus number of crimes in the city); (3) calculated by the editors using the following formula: ((number of crimes in the MSA minus number of crimes in the city) ÷ (population of the MSA minus population of the city)) x 100,000; n/a not avail.
Source: U.S. Department of Justice, FBI Uniform Crime Reports, 1977 - 1996

Larceny-Thefts and Larceny-Theft Rates: 1977 - 1996

Year	Number				Rate per 100,000 population			
	City	Suburbs[2]	MSA[1]	U.S.	City	Suburbs[3]	MSA[1]	U.S.
1977	105,406	115,662	221,068	5,905,700	3,441.3	3,001.8	3,196.5	2,729.9
1978	99,036	122,491	221,527	5,991,000	3,248.1	3,081.7	3,153.9	2,747.4
1979	94,087	127,126	221,213	6,601,000	3,073.9	3,209.5	3,150.4	2,999.1
1980	102,873	123,435	226,308	7,136,900	3,444.7	3,031.7	3,206.5	3,167.0
1981	88,197	123,616	211,813	7,194,400	2,927.5	3,009.7	2,974.9	3,139.7
1982	92,388	117,573	209,961	7,142,500	3,068.5	2,864.3	2,950.7	3,084.8
1983	113,821	81,859	195,680	6,712,800	3,767.4	2,717.1	3,243.0	2,868.9
1984	117,408	79,395	196,803	6,591,900	3,897.3	2,606.6	3,248.4	2,791.3
1985	121,264	81,449	202,713	6,926,400	4,043.7	2,643.3	3,334.0	2,901.2
1986	121,751	83,868	205,619	7,257,200	4,054.2	2,719.1	3,377.7	3,010.3
1987	119,072	84,828	203,900	7,499,900	3,945.0	2,713.8	3,318.6	3,081.3
1988	128,584	87,869	216,453	7,705,900	4,294.6	2,814.0	3,538.7	3,134.9
1989	130,153	93,449	223,602	7,872,400	4,355.5	2,913.1	3,608.8	3,171.3
1990	130,000	98,347	228,347	7,945,700	4,670.0	3,034.6	3,790.3	3,194.8
1991	131,688	101,145	232,833	8,142,200	4,683.9	3,090.6	3,826.9	3,228.8
1992	119,697	135,531	255,228	7,915,200	4,225.2	2,878.4	3,384.3	3,103.0
1993	121,314	n/a	n/a	7,820,900	4,349.7	n/a	n/a	3,032.4
1994	121,164	n/a	n/a	7,879,800	4,323.4	n/a	n/a	3,026.7
1995	121,487	n/a	n/a	7,997,700	4,417.9	n/a	n/a	3,043.8
1996	119,492	n/a	n/a	7,894,600	4,338.7	n/a	n/a	2,975.9

Notes: (1) Metropolitan Statistical Area - see Appendix A for areas included; (2) calculated by the editors using the following formula: (number of crimes in the MSA minus number of crimes in the city); (3) calculated by the editors using the following formula: ((number of crimes in the MSA minus number of crimes in the city) ÷ (population of the MSA minus population of the city)) x 100,000; n/a not avail.
Source: U.S. Department of Justice, FBI Uniform Crime Reports, 1977 - 1996

Motor Vehicle Thefts and Motor Vehicle Theft Rates: 1977 - 1996

Year	Number				Rate per 100,000 population			
	City	Suburbs[2]	MSA[1]	U.S.	City	Suburbs[3]	MSA[1]	U.S.
1977	31,987	18,988	50,975	977,700	1,044.3	492.8	737.1	451.9
1978	29,928	18,422	48,350	1,004,100	981.6	463.5	688.4	460.5
1979	31,438	19,620	51,058	1,112,800	1,027.1	495.3	727.1	505.6
1980	30,786	17,847	48,633	1,131,700	1,030.9	438.3	689.1	502.2
1981	29,398	19,666	49,064	1,087,800	975.8	478.8	689.1	474.7
1982	30,850	17,420	48,270	1,062,400	1,024.6	424.4	678.4	458.8
1983	39,051	14,526	53,577	1,007,900	1,292.6	482.2	887.9	430.8
1984	43,635	15,025	58,660	1,032,200	1,448.5	493.3	968.2	437.1
1985	44,892	14,447	59,339	1,102,900	1,497.0	468.9	975.9	462.0
1986	48,511	14,433	62,944	1,224,100	1,615.4	467.9	1,034.0	507.8
1987	39,693	13,896	53,589	1,288,700	1,315.1	444.6	872.2	529.4
1988	45,012	14,912	59,924	1,432,900	1,503.4	477.6	979.7	582.9
1989	45,898	14,698	60,596	1,564,800	1,535.9	458.2	978.0	630.4
1990	48,626	14,323	62,949	1,635,900	1,746.8	442.0	1,044.9	657.8
1991	47,396	16,356	63,752	1,661,700	1,685.8	499.8	1,047.8	659.0
1992	44,988	18,632	63,620	1,610,800	1,588.1	395.7	843.6	631.5
1993	40,438	n/a	n/a	1,563,100	1,449.9	n/a	n/a	606.1
1994	40,016	n/a	n/a	1,539,300	1,427.9	n/a	n/a	591.3
1995	36,197	n/a	n/a	1,472,400	1,316.3	n/a	n/a	560.4
1996	34,091	n/a	n/a	1,395,200	1,237.8	n/a	n/a	525.9

Notes: (1) Metropolitan Statistical Area - see Appendix A for areas included; (2) calculated by the editors using the following formula: (number of crimes in the MSA minus number of crimes in the city); (3) calculated by the editors using the following formula: ((number of crimes in the MSA minus number of crimes in the city) ÷ (population of the MSA minus population of the city)) x 100,000; n/a not avail.
Source: U.S. Department of Justice, FBI Uniform Crime Reports, 1977 - 1996

HATE CRIMES

Criminal Incidents by Bias Motivation

Area	Race	Ethnicity	Religion	Sexual Orientation
Chicago	93	13	20	20

Notes: Figures include both violent and property crimes. Law enforcement agencies must have submitted data for at least one quarter of calendar year 1995 to be included in this report, therefore figures shown may not represent complete 12-month totals; n/a not available
Source: U.S. Department of Justice, FBI Uniform Crime Reports, Hate Crime Statistics 1995

ILLEGAL DRUGS

Drug Use by Adult Arrestees

Sex	Percent Testing Positive by Urinalysis (%)				
	Any Drug[1]	Cocaine	Marijuana	Opiates	Multiple Drugs
Male	82	52	47	20	35
Female	n/a	n/a	n/a	n/a	n/a

Notes: n/a not available; The catchment area is the entire city; (1) Includes cocaine, opiates, marijuana, methadone, phencyclidine (PCP), benzodiazepines, methaqualone, propoxyphene, barbiturates & amphetamines
Source: National Institute of Justice, 1996 Drug Use Forecasting, Annual Report on Adult and Juvenile Arrestees (released June 1997)

LAW ENFORCEMENT

Full-Time Law Enforcement Employees

Jurisdiction	Police Employees			Police Officers per 100,000 population
	Total	Officers	Civilians	
Chicago	15,687	13,032	2,655	473.2

Notes: Data as of October 31, 1996
Source: U.S. Department of Justice, FBI Uniform Crime Reports, 1996

Number of Police Officers by Race

Race	Police Officers 1983		Police Officers 1992		Index of Representation[1]		
	Number	Pct.	Number	Pct.	1983	1992	% Chg.
Black	2,508	20.1	3,063	24.9	0.51	0.64	25.5
Hispanic[2]	432	3.5	925	7.5	0.24	0.38	58.3

Notes: (1) The index of representation is calculated by dividing the percent of black/hispanic police officers by the percent of corresponding blacks/hispanics in the local population. An index approaching 1.0 indicates that a city is closer to achieving a representation of police officers equal to their proportion in the local population; (2) Hispanic officers can be of any race
Source: Bureau of Justice Statistics, Sourcebook of Criminal Justice Statistics, 1994

CORRECTIONS

Federal Correctional Facilities

Type	Year Opened	Security Level	Sex of Inmates	Rated Capacity	Population on 7/1/95	Number of Staff
Metropolitan Correctional/ Detention Center	1975	Admin.	Both	411	583	262

Notes: Data as of 1995
Source: Bureau of Justice Statistics, Sourcebook of Criminal Justice Statistics Online

City/County/Regional Correctional Facilities

Name	Year Opened	Year Renov.	Rated Capacity	1995 Pop.	Number of COs[1]	Number of Staff	ACA[2] Accred.
Cook County Dept of Corr	1929	1992	8,071	n/a	n/a	n/a	Yes

Notes: Data as of April 1996; (1) Correctional Officers; (2) American Correctional Assn. Accreditation
Source: American Correctional Association, 1996-1998 National Jail and Adult Detention Directory

Private Adult Correctional Facilities

Name	Date Opened	Rated Capacity	Present Pop.	Security Level	Facility Construct.	Expans. Plans	ACA[1] Accred.
None listed							

Notes: Data as of December 1996; (1) American Correctional Association Accreditation
Source: University of Florida, Center for Studies in Criminology and Law, Private Adult Correctional Facility Census, 10th Ed., March 15, 1997

Characteristics of Shock Incarceration Programs

Jurisdiction	Year Program Began	Number of Camps	Average Num. of Inmates	Number of Beds	Program Length	Voluntary/ Mandatory
Illinois	1990	3	641	644	120 days	Voluntary

Note: Data as of July 1996;
Source: Sourcebook of Criminal Justice Statistics Online

INMATES AND HIV/AIDS

HIV Testing Policies for Inmates

Jurisdiction	All Inmates at Some Time	All Convicted Inmates at Admission	Random Samples While in Custody	High-risk Groups	Upon Inmate Request	Upon Court Order	Upon Involvement in Incident
Cook Co.[1]	No	No	No	No	Yes	No	No

Notes: (1) All facilities reported following the same testing policy or authorities reported the policy to be jurisdiction-wide
Source: HIV in Prisons and Jails, 1993 (released August 1995)

Inmates Known to be Positive for HIV

Jurisdiction	Number of Jail Inmates in Facilities Providing Data	Type of HIV Infection/AIDS Cases: Total	Asymptomatic	Symptomatic	Confirmed AIDS	HIV/AIDS Cases as a Percent of Tot. Custody Pop.
Cook Co.	9,054	264	154	7	103	2.9

Source: HIV in Prisons and Jails, 1993 (released August, 1995)

DEATH PENALTY

Death Penalty Statistics

State	Prisoners Executed		Prisoners Under Sentence of Death					Avg. No. of Years on Death Row[4]
	1930-1995	1996[1]	Total[2]	White[3]	Black[3]	Hisp.	Women	
Illinois	97	1	154	56	98	7	5	7.1

Notes: Data as of 12/31/95 unless otherwise noted; (1) Data as of 7/31/97; (2) Includes persons of other races; (3) Includes people of Hispanic origin; (4) Covers prisoners sentenced 1974 through 1995
Source: Bureau of Justice Statistics, Capital Punishment 1995 (released 12/96); Death Penalty Information Center Web Site, 9/30/97

Capital Offenses and Methods of Execution

Capital Offenses in Illinois	Minimum Age for Imposition of Death Penalty	Mentally Retarded Excluded	Methods of Execution[1]
First-degree murder with 1 of 15 aggravating circumstances.	18	No	Lethal injection

Notes: Data as of 12/31/95 unless otherwise noted; (1) Data as of 7/31/97
Source: Bureau of Justice Statistics, Capital Punishment 1995 (released 12/96); Death Penalty Information Center Web Site, 9/30/97

LAWS

Statutory Provisions Relating to the Purchase, Ownership and Use of Handguns

Jurisdiction	Instant Background Check	Federal Waiting Period Applies[1]	State Waiting Period (days)	License or Permit to Purchase	Regis-tration	Record of Sale Sent to Police	Concealed Carry Law
Illinois	Yes	No	3	Yes[a]	(b)	Yes	Yes[c]

Note: Data as of 1996; (1) The Federal 5-day waiting period for handgun purchases applies to states that don't have instant background checks, waiting period requirements, or licensing procedures exempting them from the Federal requirement; (a) A Firearm Owner's Identifictaion Card (FOI) is required to possess or purchase a firearm, must be issued to qualified applicants within 30 days, and is valid for 5 years; (b) Chicago only. No handgun not already registered may be lawfully possessed; (c) No permit system exists and concealed carry is prohibited
Source: Sourcebook of Criminal Justice Statistics Online

Statutory Provisions Relating to Alcohol Use and Driving

Jurisdiction	Drinking Age	Blood Alcohol Concentration Levels as Evidence in State Courts[1]		Open Container Law[1]	Anti-Consump-tion Law[1]	Dram Shop Law[1]
		Illegal per se at 0.10%	Presumption at 0.10%			
Illinois	21	Yes	Yes	Yes	No	Yes[a]

Note: Data as of January 1, 1997; (1) See Appendix C for an explanation of terms; (a) Illinois has a statue that places a monetary limit on the amount of damages that can be awarded in dram shop liability actions
Source: Sourcebook of Criminal Justice Statistics Online

Statutory Provisions Relating to Curfews

Jurisdiction	Year Enacted	Latest Revision	Age Group(s)	Curfew Provisions
Chicago	1955	-	16 and under	10:30 pm to 6 am weekday nights 11:30 pm to 6 am weekend nights

Note: Data as of February 1996
Source: Sourcebook of Criminal Justice Statistics Online

Statutory Provisions Relating to Hate Crimes

Jurisdiction	Bias-Motivated Violence and Intimidation						Institutional Vandalism
		Criminal Penalty					
	Civil Action	Race/ Religion/ Ethnicity	Sexual Orientation	Mental/ Physical Disability	Gender	Age	
Illinois	Yes	Yes	Yes	Yes	Yes	No	Yes

Source: Anti-Defamation League, 1997 Hate Crimes Laws

Cincinnati, Ohio

OVERVIEW

The total crime rate for the city increased 2.3% between 1977 and 1996. During that same period, the violent crime rate increased 27.5% and the property crime rate decreased 1.0%.

Among violent crimes, the rates for: Murders decreased 50.3%; Forcible Rapes increased 21.1%; Robberies increased 22.1%; and Aggravated Assaults increased 38.7%.

Among property crimes, the rates for: Burglaries decreased 24.2%; Larceny-Thefts increased 10.2%; and Motor Vehicle Thefts increased 6.0%.

ANTI-CRIME PROGRAMS

Programs include:

- Community Oriented Policing—officers are assigned to neighborhoods to work with residents to solve crime and its problems
- Robbery Apprehension Program—hidden cameras and alarms are placed in selected businesses to alert the police to crimes in progress.
- Volunteer Surveillance Team—community volunteers conduct surveillance of areas recommended by the police..
- Safe Entry—police officers and firemen have access to secured buildings through a metal lock box.
- Citizen Police Academy—citizens attend special training classes from the Police Division, including some of the training provided to officers. The program seeks to bring the police and community together.
- Student Police Academy—students attend special training classes taught in cooperation with local schools and the Police Division. The program teaches youth how crime can affect them and seeks to bring youth and the police together.
- F.A.C.T. (Fight Against Crack Trafficking)—citizen volunteers, escorted by the police, march and sing rhyming chants in target areas to protest drug dealing in hopes of driving drug dealers out of the community.
- Blockwatch—neighbors report suspicious persons, autos and activities.
- Operation Identification—citizens are instructed in how to engrave and inventory their property which helps to identify and retrieve stolen property.
- Preventive Patrol Report—police officers who observe potential crime opportunities (open garage, items left in a vehicle, etc.) leave a notice for the owner.
  Cincinnati Police Division, Community Services Section, 7/97

CRIME RISK

Your Chances of Becoming a Victim[1]

Area	Any Crime	Violent Crime					Property Crime			
		Any	Murder	Forcible Rape[2]	Robbery	Aggrav. Assault	Any	Burglary	Larceny -Theft	Motor Vehicle Theft
City	1:13	1:92	1:11,264	1:611	1:203	1:200	1:15	1:63	1:22	1:198

Note: (1) Figures have been calculated by dividing the population of the city by the number of crimes reported to the FBI during 1996 and are expressed as odds (eg. 1:20 should be read as 1 in 20). (2) Figures have been calculated by dividing the female population of the city by the number of forcible rapes reported to the FBI during 1996. The female population of the city was estimated by calculating the ratio of females to males reported in the 1990 Census and applying that ratio to 1996 population estimate.
Source: FBI Uniform Crime Reports 1996

CRIME STATISTICS

Total Crimes and Total Crime Rates: 1977 - 1996

Year	Number				Rate per 100,000 population			
	City	Suburbs[2]	MSA[1]	U.S.	City	Suburbs[3]	MSA[1]	U.S.
1977	30,012	38,307	68,319	10,984,500	7,447.1	3,620.3	4,675.8	5,077.6
1978	30,296	38,549	68,845	11,209,000	7,593.0	3,941.1	4,999.2	5,140.3
1979	33,120	42,740	75,860	12,249,500	8,184.6	4,338.2	5,458.1	5,565.5
1980	32,985	47,271	80,256	13,408,300	8,609.7	4,695.2	5,774.2	5,950.0
1981	36,815	44,537	81,352	13,423,800	9,601.2	4,414.6	5,843.0	5,858.2
1982	33,684	42,310	75,994	12,974,400	8,772.4	4,187.9	5,450.4	5,603.6
1983	30,053	38,520	68,573	12,108,600	7,859.6	3,811.0	4,922.3	5,175.0
1984	29,171	36,968	66,139	11,881,800	7,700.9	3,590.7	4,696.2	5,031.3
1985	28,533	37,149	65,682	12,431,400	7,707.5	3,580.9	4,666.2	5,207.1
1986	27,699	40,585	68,284	13,211,900	7,476.5	3,908.9	4,847.1	5,480.4
1987	27,197	42,083	69,280	13,508,700	7,319.2	4,032.3	4,895.3	5,550.0
1988	27,550	31,026	58,576	13,923,100	7,292.5	2,899.8	4,046.0	5,664.2
1989	27,819	43,303	71,122	14,251,400	7,472.6	3,998.6	4,887.3	5,741.0
1990	27,507	43,276	70,783	14,475,600	7,556.0	3,974.3	4,871.7	5,820.3
1991	35,693	47,371	83,064	14,872,900	9,722.4	4,314.5	5,669.6	5,897.8
1992	32,682	47,478	80,160	14,438,200	8,840.0	4,017.1	5,166.2	5,660.2
1993	30,923	45,024	75,947	14,144,800	8,435.3	3,737.6	4,833.6	5,484.4
1994	29,403	45,827	75,230	13,989,500	8,012.7	3,790.4	4,773.5	5,373.5
1995	26,931	43,495	70,426	13,862,700	7,486.1	3,535.2	4,429.1	5,275.9
1996	27,455	n/a	n/a	13,473,600	7,616.7	n/a	n/a	5,078.9

Notes: (1) Metropolitan Statistical Area - see Appendix A for areas included; (2) calculated by the editors using the following formula: (number of crimes in the MSA minus number of crimes in the city); (3) calculated by the editors using the following formula: ((number of crimes in the MSA minus number of crimes in the city) ÷ (population of the MSA minus population of the city)) x 100,000; n/a not avail.
Source: U.S. Department of Justice, FBI Uniform Crime Reports, 1977 - 1996

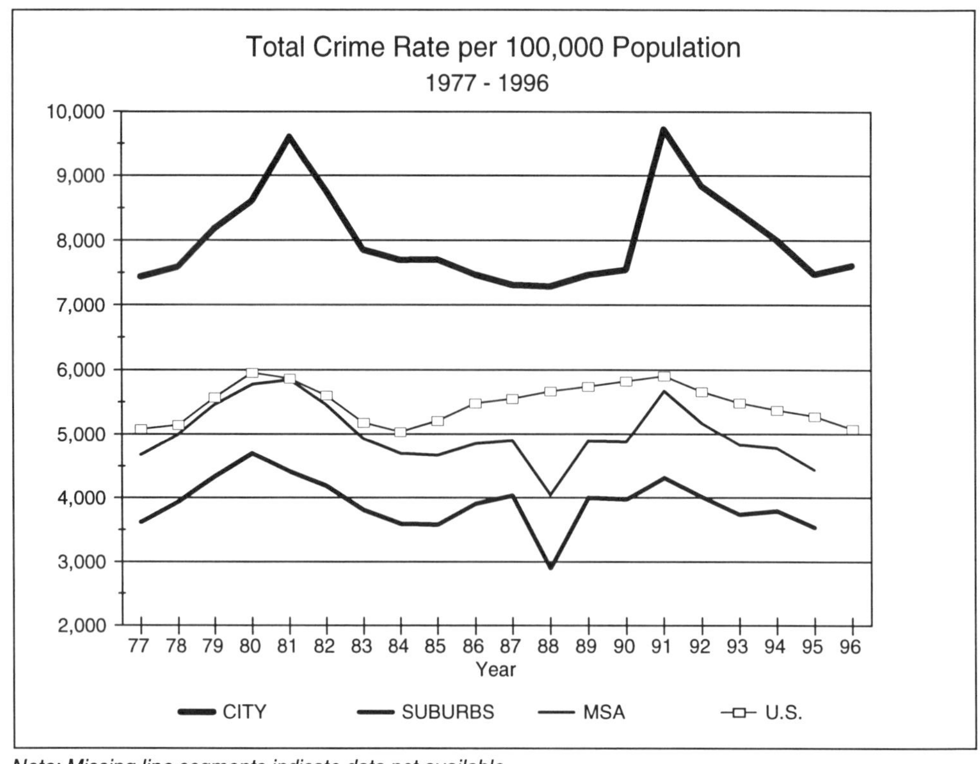

Note: Missing line segments indicate data not available.

Violent Crimes and Violent Crime Rates: 1977 - 1996

Year	Number				Rate per 100,000 population			
	City	Suburbs[2]	MSA[1]	U.S.	City	Suburbs[3]	MSA[1]	U.S.
1977	3,439	2,174	5,613	1,029,580	853.3	205.5	384.2	475.9
1978	3,303	2,384	5,687	1,085,550	827.8	243.7	413.0	497.8
1979	3,808	2,729	6,537	1,208,030	941.0	277.0	470.3	548.9
1980	3,930	3,314	7,244	1,344,520	1,025.8	329.2	521.2	596.6
1981	3,892	2,986	6,878	1,361,820	1,015.0	296.0	494.0	594.3
1982	3,764	2,943	6,707	1,322,390	980.3	291.3	481.0	571.1
1983	3,339	2,641	5,980	1,258,090	873.2	261.3	429.3	537.7
1984	3,447	2,364	5,811	1,273,280	910.0	229.6	412.6	539.2
1985	3,275	2,496	5,771	1,328,800	884.7	240.6	410.0	556.6
1986	3,340	2,481	5,821	1,489,170	901.5	239.0	413.2	617.7
1987	3,167	2,675	5,842	1,484,000	852.3	256.3	412.8	609.7
1988	3,199	1,670	4,869	1,566,220	846.8	156.1	336.3	637.2
1989	3,690	2,845	6,535	1,646,040	991.2	262.7	449.1	663.1
1990	4,476	3,056	7,532	1,820,130	1,229.5	280.7	518.4	731.8
1991	5,794	3,686	9,480	1,911,770	1,578.2	335.7	647.1	758.1
1992	5,793	4,258	10,051	1,932,270	1,566.9	360.3	647.8	757.5
1993	5,621	3,391	9,012	1,926,020	1,533.3	281.5	573.6	746.8
1994	4,855	3,836	8,691	1,857,670	1,323.1	317.3	551.5	713.6
1995	4,640	2,784	7,424	1,798,790	1,289.8	226.3	466.9	684.6
1996	3,921	n/a	n/a	1,682,280	1,087.8	n/a	n/a	634.1

Notes: Violent crimes include murder, forcible rape, robbery and aggravated assault; n/a not available; (1) Metropolitan Statistical Area - see Appendix A for areas included; (2) calculated by the editors using the following formula: (number of crimes in the MSA minus number of crimes in the city); (3) calculated by the editors using the following formula: ((number of crimes in the MSA minus number of crimes in the city) ÷ (population of the MSA minus population of the city)) x 100,000
Source: U.S. Department of Justice, FBI Uniform Crime Reports, 1977 - 1996

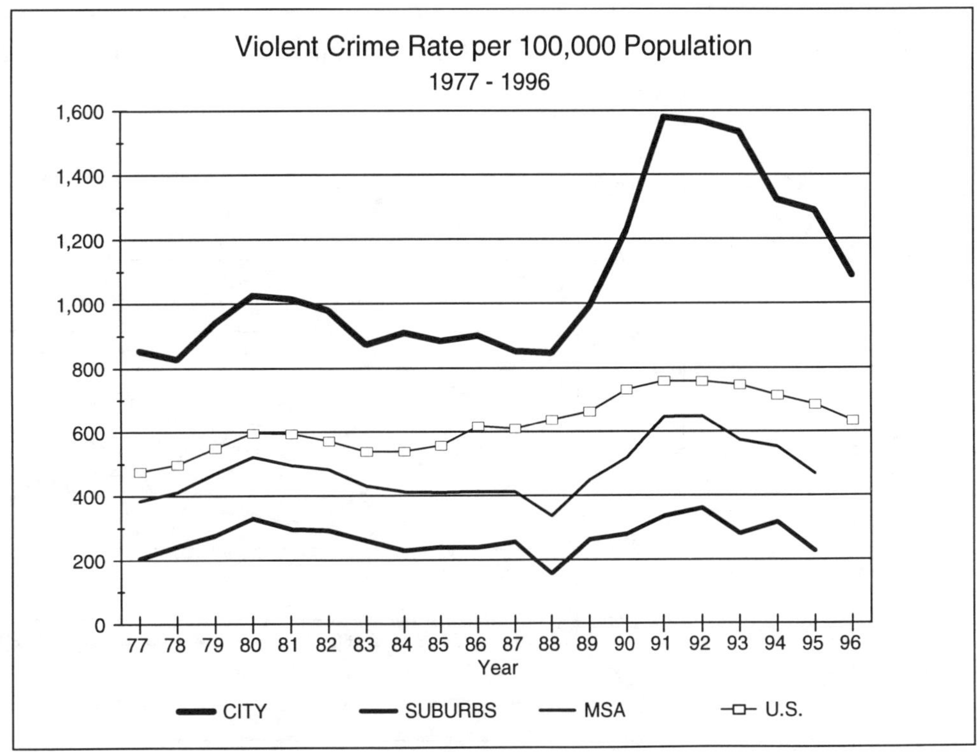

Note: Missing line segments indicate data not available.

Property Crimes and Property Crime Rates: 1977 - 1996

Year	Number				Rate per 100,000 population			
	City	Suburbs[2]	MSA[1]	U.S.	City	Suburbs[3]	MSA[1]	U.S.
1977	26,573	36,133	62,706	9,955,000	6,593.8	3,414.9	4,291.7	4,601.7
1978	26,993	36,165	63,158	10,123,400	6,765.2	3,697.4	4,586.2	4,642.5
1979	29,312	40,011	69,323	11,041,500	7,243.6	4,061.2	4,987.7	5,016.6
1980	29,055	43,957	73,012	12,063,700	7,583.9	4,366.0	5,253.0	5,353.3
1981	32,923	41,551	74,474	12,061,900	8,586.2	4,118.7	5,349.0	5,263.9
1982	29,920	39,367	69,287	11,652,000	7,792.2	3,896.6	4,969.4	5,032.5
1983	26,714	35,879	62,593	10,850,500	6,986.4	3,549.8	4,493.0	4,637.4
1984	25,724	34,604	60,328	10,608,500	6,790.9	3,361.1	4,283.6	4,492.1
1985	25,258	34,653	59,911	11,102,600	6,822.8	3,340.3	4,256.2	4,650.5
1986	24,359	38,104	62,463	11,722,700	6,574.9	3,669.9	4,433.9	4,862.6
1987	24,030	39,408	63,438	12,024,700	6,466.9	3,776.0	4,482.5	4,940.3
1988	24,351	29,356	53,707	12,356,900	6,445.8	2,743.7	3,709.7	5,027.1
1989	24,129	40,458	64,587	12,605,400	6,481.4	3,735.9	4,438.3	5,077.9
1990	23,031	40,220	63,251	12,655,500	6,326.5	3,693.6	4,353.3	5,088.5
1991	29,899	43,685	73,584	12,961,100	8,144.1	3,978.8	5,022.6	5,139.7
1992	26,889	43,220	70,109	12,505,900	7,273.1	3,656.8	4,518.4	4,902.7
1993	25,302	41,633	66,935	12,218,800	6,902.0	3,456.1	4,260.1	4,737.6
1994	24,548	41,991	66,539	12,131,900	6,689.7	3,473.1	4,222.1	4,660.0
1995	22,291	40,711	63,002	12,063,900	6,196.3	3,308.9	3,962.2	4,591.3
1996	23,534	n/a	n/a	11,791,300	6,528.9	n/a	n/a	4,444.8

Notes: Property crimes include burglary, larceny-theft and motor vehicle theft; n/a not available; (1) Metropolitan Statistical Area - see Appendix A for areas included; (2) calculated by the editors using the following formula: (number of crimes in the MSA minus number of crimes in the city); (3) calculated by the editors using the following formula: ((number of crimes in the MSA minus number of crimes in the city) ÷ (population of the MSA minus population of the city)) x 100,000
Source: U.S. Department of Justice, FBI Uniform Crime Reports, 1977 - 1996

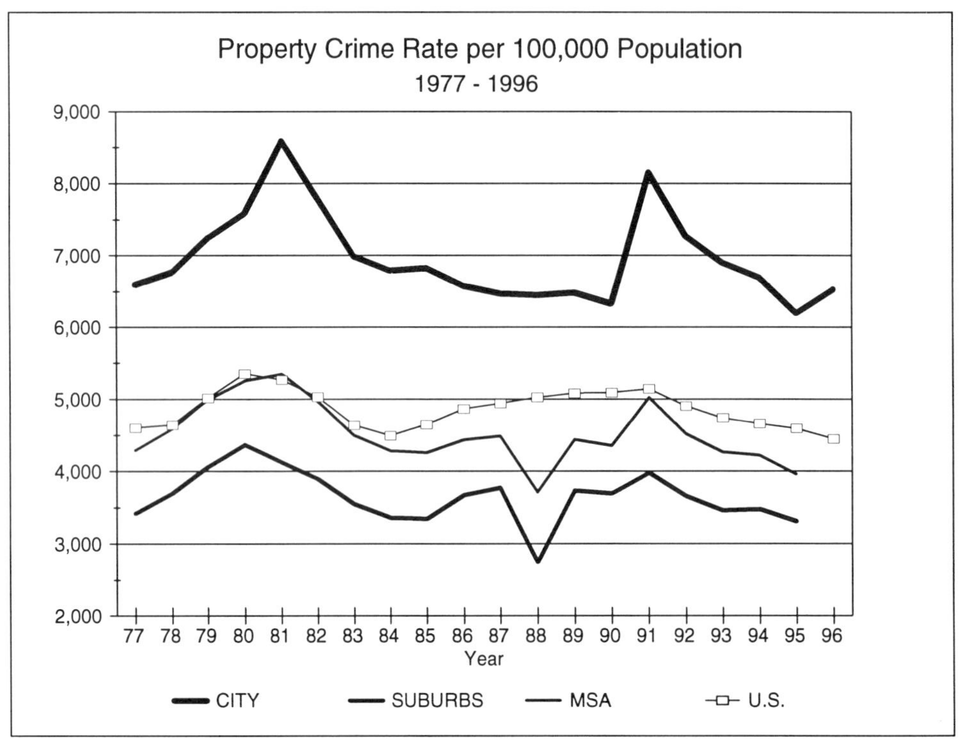

Note: Missing line segments indicate data not available.

Murders and Murder Rates: 1977 - 1996

Year	Number				Rate per 100,000 population			
	City	Suburbs[2]	MSA[1]	U.S.	City	Suburbs[3]	MSA[1]	U.S.
1977	72	37	109	19,120	17.9	3.5	7.5	8.8
1978	57	49	106	19,560	14.3	5.0	7.7	9.0
1979	50	43	93	21,460	12.4	4.4	6.7	9.7
1980	48	37	85	23,040	12.5	3.7	6.1	10.2
1981	43	33	76	22,520	11.2	3.3	5.5	9.8
1982	52	31	83	21,010	13.5	3.1	6.0	9.1
1983	27	20	47	19,310	7.1	2.0	3.4	8.3
1984	36	25	61	18,690	9.5	2.4	4.3	7.9
1985	45	29	74	18,980	12.2	2.8	5.3	7.9
1986	46	33	79	20,610	12.4	3.2	5.6	8.6
1987	69	27	96	20,100	18.6	2.6	6.8	8.3
1988	47	14	61	20,680	12.4	1.3	4.2	8.4
1989	45	36	81	21,500	12.1	3.3	5.6	8.7
1990	49	27	76	23,440	13.5	2.5	5.2	9.4
1991	54	17	71	24,700	14.7	1.5	4.8	9.8
1992	49	21	70	23,760	13.3	1.8	4.5	9.3
1993	39	20	59	24,530	10.6	1.7	3.8	9.5
1994	38	21	59	23,330	10.4	1.7	3.7	9.0
1995	50	19	69	21,610	13.9	1.5	4.3	8.2
1996	32	n/a	n/a	19,650	8.9	n/a	n/a	7.4

Notes: (1) Metropolitan Statistical Area - see Appendix A for areas included; (2) calculated by the editors using the following formula: (number of crimes in the MSA minus number of crimes in the city); (3) calculated by the editors using the following formula: ((number of crimes in the MSA minus number of crimes in the city) ÷ (population of the MSA minus population of the city)) x 100,000; n/a not avail.
Source: U.S. Department of Justice, FBI Uniform Crime Reports, 1977 - 1996

Forcible Rapes and Forcible Rape Rates: 1977 - 1996

Year	Number				Rate per 100,000 population			
	City	Suburbs[2]	MSA[1]	U.S.	City	Suburbs[3]	MSA[1]	U.S.
1977	291	164	455	63,500	72.2	15.5	31.1	29.4
1978	287	149	436	67,610	71.9	15.2	31.7	31.0
1979	282	203	485	76,390	69.7	20.6	34.9	34.7
1980	353	201	554	82,990	92.1	20.0	39.9	36.8
1981	289	153	442	82,500	75.4	15.2	31.7	36.0
1982	286	180	466	78,770	74.5	17.8	33.4	34.0
1983	308	176	484	78,920	80.5	17.4	34.7	33.7
1984	367	243	610	84,230	96.9	23.6	43.3	35.7
1985	360	249	609	88,670	97.2	24.0	43.3	37.1
1986	291	215	506	91,460	78.5	20.7	35.9	37.9
1987	344	272	616	91,110	92.6	26.1	43.5	37.4
1988	296	212	508	92,490	78.4	19.8	35.1	37.6
1989	351	280	631	94,500	94.3	25.9	43.4	38.1
1990	388	299	687	102,560	106.6	27.5	47.3	41.2
1991	478	384	862	106,590	130.2	35.0	58.8	42.3
1992	486	428	914	109,060	131.5	36.2	58.9	42.8
1993	449	391	840	106,010	122.5	32.5	53.5	41.1
1994	382	348	730	102,220	104.1	28.8	46.3	39.3
1995	408	320	728	97,470	113.4	26.0	45.8	37.1
1996	315	n/a	n/a	95,770	87.4	n/a	n/a	36.1

Notes: (1) Metropolitan Statistical Area - see Appendix A for areas included; (2) calculated by the editors using the following formula: (number of crimes in the MSA minus number of crimes in the city); (3) calculated by the editors using the following formula: ((number of crimes in the MSA minus number of crimes in the city) ÷ (population of the MSA minus population of the city)) x 100,000; n/a not avail.
Source: U.S. Department of Justice, FBI Uniform Crime Reports, 1977 - 1996

Robberies and Robbery Rates: 1977 - 1996

Year	Number				Rate per 100,000 population			
	City	Suburbs[2]	MSA[1]	U.S.	City	Suburbs[3]	MSA[1]	U.S.
1977	1,625	611	2,236	412,610	403.2	57.7	153.0	190.7
1978	1,300	656	1,956	426,930	325.8	67.1	142.0	195.8
1979	1,662	787	2,449	480,700	410.7	79.9	176.2	218.4
1980	1,686	959	2,645	565,840	440.1	95.3	190.3	251.1
1981	1,756	921	2,677	592,910	458.0	91.3	192.3	258.7
1982	1,590	734	2,324	553,130	414.1	72.7	166.7	238.9
1983	1,401	689	2,090	506,570	366.4	68.2	150.0	216.5
1984	1,332	588	1,920	485,010	351.6	57.1	136.3	205.4
1985	1,242	610	1,852	497,870	335.5	58.8	131.6	208.5
1986	1,216	580	1,796	542,780	328.2	55.9	127.5	225.1
1987	1,183	591	1,774	517,700	318.4	56.6	125.4	212.7
1988	1,211	384	1,595	542,970	320.6	35.9	110.2	220.9
1989	1,428	696	2,124	578,330	383.6	64.3	146.0	233.0
1990	1,613	616	2,229	639,270	443.1	56.6	153.4	257.0
1991	2,315	845	3,160	687,730	630.6	77.0	215.7	272.7
1992	2,294	891	3,185	672,480	620.5	75.4	205.3	263.6
1993	2,327	848	3,175	659,870	634.8	70.4	202.1	255.9
1994	2,131	834	2,965	618,950	580.7	69.0	188.1	237.7
1995	2,155	838	2,993	580,510	599.0	68.1	188.2	220.9
1996	1,774	n/a	n/a	537,050	492.2	n/a	n/a	202.4

Notes: (1) Metropolitan Statistical Area - see Appendix A for areas included; (2) calculated by the editors using the following formula: (number of crimes in the MSA minus number of crimes in the city); (3) calculated by the editors using the following formula: ((number of crimes in the MSA minus number of crimes in the city) ÷ (population of the MSA minus population of the city)) x 100,000; n/a not avail.
Source: U.S. Department of Justice, FBI Uniform Crime Reports, 1977 - 1996

Aggravated Assaults and Aggravated Assault Rates: 1977 - 1996

Year	Number				Rate per 100,000 population			
	City	Suburbs[2]	MSA[1]	U.S.	City	Suburbs[3]	MSA[1]	U.S.
1977	1,451	1,362	2,813	534,350	360.0	128.7	192.5	247.0
1978	1,659	1,530	3,189	571,460	415.8	156.4	231.6	262.1
1979	1,814	1,696	3,510	629,480	448.3	172.1	252.5	286.0
1980	1,843	2,117	3,960	672,650	481.1	210.3	284.9	298.5
1981	1,804	1,879	3,683	663,900	470.5	186.3	264.5	289.7
1982	1,836	1,998	3,834	669,480	478.2	197.8	275.0	289.2
1983	1,603	1,756	3,359	653,290	419.2	173.7	241.1	279.2
1984	1,712	1,508	3,220	685,350	452.0	146.5	228.6	290.2
1985	1,628	1,608	3,236	723,250	439.8	155.0	229.9	302.9
1986	1,787	1,653	3,440	834,320	482.3	159.2	244.2	346.1
1987	1,571	1,785	3,356	855,090	422.8	171.0	237.1	351.3
1988	1,645	1,060	2,705	910,090	435.4	99.1	186.8	370.2
1989	1,866	1,833	3,699	951,710	501.2	169.3	254.2	383.4
1990	2,426	2,114	4,540	1,054,860	666.4	194.1	312.5	424.1
1991	2,947	2,440	5,387	1,092,740	802.7	222.2	367.7	433.3
1992	2,964	2,918	5,882	1,126,970	801.7	246.9	379.1	441.8
1993	2,806	2,132	4,938	1,135,610	765.4	177.0	314.3	440.3
1994	2,304	2,633	4,937	1,113,180	627.9	217.8	313.3	427.6
1995	2,027	1,607	3,634	1,099,210	563.4	130.6	228.5	418.3
1996	1,800	n/a	n/a	1,029,810	499.4	n/a	n/a	388.2

Notes: (1) Metropolitan Statistical Area - see Appendix A for areas included; (2) calculated by the editors using the following formula: (number of crimes in the MSA minus number of crimes in the city); (3) calculated by the editors using the following formula: ((number of crimes in the MSA minus number of crimes in the city) ÷ (population of the MSA minus population of the city)) x 100,000; n/a not avail.
Source: U.S. Department of Justice, FBI Uniform Crime Reports, 1977 - 1996

Burglaries and Burglary Rates: 1977 - 1996

Year	Number				Rate per 100,000 population			
	City	Suburbs[2]	MSA[1]	U.S.	City	Suburbs[3]	MSA[1]	U.S.
1977	8,386	9,051	17,437	3,071,500	2,080.9	855.4	1,193.4	1,419.8
1978	8,551	9,139	17,690	3,128,300	2,143.1	934.3	1,284.6	1,434.6
1979	8,716	9,574	18,290	3,327,700	2,153.9	971.8	1,316.0	1,511.9
1980	8,857	11,188	20,045	3,795,200	2,311.8	1,111.2	1,442.2	1,684.1
1981	9,618	10,392	20,010	3,779,700	2,508.3	1,030.1	1,437.2	1,649.5
1982	8,669	9,179	17,848	3,447,100	2,257.7	908.5	1,280.1	1,488.8
1983	7,398	7,922	15,320	3,129,900	1,934.8	783.8	1,099.7	1,337.7
1984	7,255	7,412	14,667	2,984,400	1,915.3	719.9	1,041.4	1,263.7
1985	6,453	6,982	13,435	3,073,300	1,743.1	673.0	954.4	1,287.3
1986	6,034	7,310	13,344	3,241,400	1,628.7	704.1	947.2	1,344.6
1987	5,733	7,709	13,442	3,236,200	1,542.9	738.7	949.8	1,329.6
1988	5,856	4,891	10,747	3,218,100	1,550.1	457.1	742.3	1,309.2
1989	6,215	7,551	13,766	3,168,200	1,669.4	697.3	946.0	1,276.3
1990	5,896	7,265	13,161	3,073,900	1,619.6	667.2	905.8	1,235.9
1991	8,489	8,284	16,773	3,157,200	2,312.3	754.5	1,144.9	1,252.0
1992	7,076	8,591	15,667	2,979,900	1,913.9	726.9	1,009.7	1,168.2
1993	6,154	7,515	13,669	2,834,800	1,678.7	623.8	870.0	1,099.2
1994	6,020	7,095	13,115	2,712,800	1,640.5	586.8	832.2	1,042.0
1995	5,366	6,986	12,352	2,593,800	1,491.6	567.8	776.8	987.1
1996	5,687	n/a	n/a	2,501,500	1,577.7	n/a	n/a	943.0

Notes: (1) Metropolitan Statistical Area - see Appendix A for areas included; (2) calculated by the editors using the following formula: (number of crimes in the MSA minus number of crimes in the city); (3) calculated by the editors using the following formula: ((number of crimes in the MSA minus number of crimes in the city) ÷ (population of the MSA minus population of the city)) x 100,000; n/a not avail.
Source: U.S. Department of Justice, FBI Uniform Crime Reports, 1977 - 1996

Larceny-Thefts and Larceny-Theft Rates: 1977 - 1996

Year	Number				Rate per 100,000 population			
	City	Suburbs[2]	MSA[1]	U.S.	City	Suburbs[3]	MSA[1]	U.S.
1977	16,265	24,477	40,742	5,905,700	4,036.0	2,313.3	2,788.4	2,729.9
1978	16,531	24,336	40,867	5,991,000	4,143.1	2,488.0	2,967.6	2,747.4
1979	18,626	27,621	46,247	6,601,000	4,602.9	2,803.6	3,327.4	2,999.1
1980	18,474	29,983	48,457	7,136,900	4,822.1	2,978.1	3,486.3	3,167.0
1981	21,548	28,825	50,373	7,194,400	5,619.6	2,857.2	3,618.0	3,139.7
1982	19,883	27,901	47,784	7,142,500	5,178.2	2,761.7	3,427.2	3,084.8
1983	18,164	25,892	44,056	6,712,800	4,750.3	2,561.7	3,162.4	2,868.9
1984	17,366	25,219	42,585	6,591,900	4,584.5	2,449.5	3,023.8	2,791.3
1985	17,620	25,746	43,366	6,926,400	4,759.6	2,481.7	3,080.8	2,901.2
1986	17,169	28,668	45,837	7,257,200	4,634.2	2,761.1	3,253.7	3,010.3
1987	17,055	29,839	46,894	7,499,900	4,589.8	2,859.1	3,313.5	3,081.3
1988	17,020	23,029	40,049	7,705,900	4,505.2	2,152.3	2,766.3	3,134.9
1989	16,405	30,829	47,234	7,872,400	4,406.6	2,846.8	3,245.8	3,171.3
1990	15,458	30,712	46,170	7,945,700	4,246.2	2,820.5	3,177.7	3,194.8
1991	19,285	33,140	52,425	8,142,200	5,253.0	3,018.4	3,578.3	3,228.8
1992	17,695	32,345	50,040	7,915,200	4,786.2	2,736.7	3,225.0	3,103.0
1993	17,085	32,134	49,219	7,820,900	4,660.5	2,667.5	3,132.5	3,032.4
1994	16,796	32,778	49,574	7,879,800	4,577.2	2,711.1	3,145.6	3,026.7
1995	15,012	31,642	46,654	7,997,700	4,172.9	2,571.8	2,934.1	3,043.8
1996	16,025	n/a	n/a	7,894,600	4,445.7	n/a	n/a	2,975.9

Notes: (1) Metropolitan Statistical Area - see Appendix A for areas included; (2) calculated by the editors using the following formula: (number of crimes in the MSA minus number of crimes in the city); (3) calculated by the editors using the following formula: ((number of crimes in the MSA minus number of crimes in the city) ÷ (population of the MSA minus population of the city)) x 100,000; n/a not avail.
Source: U.S. Department of Justice, FBI Uniform Crime Reports, 1977 - 1996

Motor Vehicle Thefts and Motor Vehicle Theft Rates: 1977 - 1996

Year	Number				Rate per 100,000 population			
	City	Suburbs[2]	MSA[1]	U.S.	City	Suburbs[3]	MSA[1]	U.S.
1977	1,922	2,605	4,527	977,700	476.9	246.2	309.8	451.9
1978	1,911	2,690	4,601	1,004,100	478.9	275.0	334.1	460.5
1979	1,970	2,816	4,786	1,112,800	486.8	285.8	344.3	505.6
1980	1,724	2,786	4,510	1,131,700	450.0	276.7	324.5	502.2
1981	1,757	2,334	4,091	1,087,800	458.2	231.4	293.8	474.7
1982	1,368	2,287	3,655	1,062,400	356.3	226.4	262.1	458.8
1983	1,152	2,065	3,217	1,007,900	301.3	204.3	230.9	430.8
1984	1,103	1,973	3,076	1,032,200	291.2	191.6	218.4	437.1
1985	1,185	1,925	3,110	1,102,900	320.1	185.6	220.9	462.0
1986	1,156	2,126	3,282	1,224,100	312.0	204.8	233.0	507.8
1987	1,242	1,860	3,102	1,288,700	334.2	178.2	219.2	529.4
1988	1,475	1,436	2,911	1,432,900	390.4	134.2	201.1	582.9
1989	1,509	2,078	3,587	1,564,800	405.3	191.9	246.5	630.4
1990	1,677	2,243	3,920	1,635,900	460.7	206.0	269.8	657.8
1991	2,125	2,261	4,386	1,661,700	578.8	205.9	299.4	659.0
1992	2,118	2,284	4,402	1,610,800	572.9	193.2	283.7	631.5
1993	2,063	1,984	4,047	1,563,100	562.8	164.7	257.6	606.1
1994	1,732	2,118	3,850	1,539,300	472.0	175.2	244.3	591.3
1995	1,913	2,083	3,996	1,472,400	531.8	169.3	251.3	560.4
1996	1,822	n/a	n/a	1,395,200	505.5	n/a	n/a	525.9

Notes: (1) Metropolitan Statistical Area - see Appendix A for areas included; (2) calculated by the editors using the following formula: (number of crimes in the MSA minus number of crimes in the city); (3) calculated by the editors using the following formula: ((number of crimes in the MSA minus number of crimes in the city) ÷ (population of the MSA minus population of the city)) x 100,000; n/a not avail.
Source: U.S. Department of Justice, FBI Uniform Crime Reports, 1977 - 1996

HATE CRIMES

Criminal Incidents by Bias Motivation

Area	Race	Ethnicity	Religion	Sexual Orientation
Cincinnati	29	1	2	0

Notes: Figures include both violent and property crimes. Law enforcement agencies must have submitted data for at least one quarter of calendar year 1995 to be included in this report, therefore figures shown may not represent complete 12-month totals; n/a not available
Source: U.S. Department of Justice, FBI Uniform Crime Reports, Hate Crime Statistics 1995

LAW ENFORCEMENT

Full-Time Law Enforcement Employees

Jurisdiction	Police Employees			Police Officers per 100,000 population
	Total	Officers	Civilians	
Cincinnati	1,259	986	273	273.5

Notes: Data as of October 31, 1996
Source: U.S. Department of Justice, FBI Uniform Crime Reports, 1996

Number of Police Officers by Race

Race	Police Officers				Index of Representation[1]		
	1983		1992				
	Number	Pct.	Number	Pct.	1983	1992	% Chg.
Black	89	9.2	176	19.0	0.27	0.50	85.2
Hispanic[2]	1	0.1	1	0.1	0.13	0.14	7.7

Notes: (1) The index of representation is calculated by dividing the percent of black/hispanic police officers by the percent of corresponding blacks/hispanics in the local population. An index approaching 1.0 indicates that a city is closer to achieving a representation of police officers equal to their proportion in the local population; (2) Hispanic officers can be of any race
Source: Bureau of Justice Statistics, Sourcebook of Criminal Justice Statistics, 1994

CORRECTIONS

Federal Correctional Facilities

Type	Year Opened	Security Level	Sex of Inmates	Rated Capacity	Population on 7/1/95	Number of Staff
None listed						

Notes: Data as of 1995
Source: Bureau of Justice Statistics, Sourcebook of Criminal Justice Statistics Online

City/County/Regional Correctional Facilities

Name	Year Opened	Year Renov.	Rated Capacity	1995 Pop.	Number of COs[1]	Number of Staff	ACA[2] Accred.
Hamilton Co Justice Complex	1920	1992	822	n/a	n/a	n/a	No
Hamilton County-Queensgate Correctional Facility	1985	1993	1,240	1,724	n/a	n/a	No

Notes: Data as of April 1996; (1) Correctional Officers; (2) American Correctional Assn. Accreditation
Source: American Correctional Association, 1996-1998 National Jail and Adult Detention Directory

Private Adult Correctional Facilities

Name	Date Opened	Rated Capacity	Present Pop.	Security Level	Facility Construct.	Expans. Plans	ACA[1] Accred.
None listed							

Notes: Data as of December 1996; (1) American Correctional Association Accreditation
Source: University of Florida, Center for Studies in Criminology and Law, Private Adult Correctional Facility Census, 10th Ed., March 15, 1997

Characteristics of Shock Incarceration Programs

Jurisdiction	Year Program Began	Number of Camps	Average Num. of Inmates	Number of Beds	Program Length	Voluntary/ Mandatory
Ohio	1991 male; 1995 fem.	2	(a)	100 male; 40 female	(b)	Voluntary

Note: Data as of July 1996; (a) Phase I: 80 to 100 days; Phase II: 40 days; Phase III: 220 days; (b) Phase I: 90 days; Phase II: 30 days; Phase III: 6 months to one year
Source: Sourcebook of Criminal Justice Statistics Online

INMATES AND HIV/AIDS

HIV Testing Policies for Inmates

Jurisdiction	All Inmates at Some Time	All Convicted Inmates at Admission	Random Samples While in Custody	High-risk Groups	Upon Inmate Request	Upon Court Order	Upon Involvement in Incident
Hamilton Co.	No	No	No	No	No	No	Yes

Source: HIV in Prisons and Jails, 1993 (released August 1995)

Inmates Known to be Positive for HIV

Jurisdiction	Number of Jail Inmates in Facilities Providing Data	Type of HIV Infection/AIDS Cases				HIV/AIDS Cases as a Percent of Tot. Custody Pop.
		Total	Asymptomatic	Symptomatic	Confirmed AIDS	
Hamilton Co.[1]	1,849	n/a	n/a	n/a	n/a	n/a

Note: (1) Jurisdiction did not provide data on HIV/AIDS cases; n/a not available
Source: HIV in Prisons and Jails, 1993 (released August, 1995)

DEATH PENALTY

Death Penalty Statistics

State	Prisoners Executed		Prisoners Under Sentence of Death					Avg. No. of Years on Death Row[4]
	1930-1995	1996[1]	Total[2]	White[3]	Black[3]	Hisp.	Women	
Ohio	172	0	155	76	78	5	0	6.3

Notes: Data as of 12/31/95 unless otherwise noted; (1) Data as of 7/31/97; (2) Includes persons of other races; (3) Includes people of Hispanic origin; (4) Covers prisoners sentenced 1974 through 1995
Source: Bureau of Justice Statistics, Capital Punishment 1995 (released 12/96); Death Penalty Information Center Web Site, 9/30/97

Capital Offenses and Methods of Execution

Capital Offenses in Ohio	Minimum Age for Imposition of Death Penalty	Mentally Retarded Excluded	Methods of Execution[1]
Aggravated murder with 1 of 8 aggravating circumstances. (O.R.C. secs. 2929.01, 2903.01, and 2929.04).	18	No	Lethal injection; electrocution

Notes: Data as of 12/31/95 unless otherwise noted; (1) Data as of 7/31/97
Source: Bureau of Justice Statistics, Capital Punishment 1995 (released 12/96); Death Penalty Information Center Web Site, 9/30/97

LAWS

Statutory Provisions Relating to the Purchase, Ownership and Use of Handguns

Jurisdiction	Instant Background Check	Federal Waiting Period Applies[1]	State Waiting Period (days)	License or Permit to Purchase	Registration	Record of Sale Sent to Police	Concealed Carry Law
Ohio	No	Yes	(a)	(b)	(a)	(a)	Yes[c]

Note: Data as of 1996; (1) The Federal 5-day waiting period for handgun purchases applies to states that don't have instant background checks, waiting period requirements, or licensing procedures exempting them from the Federal requirement; (a) Local ordinance in certain cities or counties; (b) Some cities require a permit-to-purchase or firearm owner ID card; (c) No permit system exists and concealed carry is prohibited
Source: Sourcebook of Criminal Justice Statistics Online

Statutory Provisions Relating to Alcohol Use and Driving

Jurisdiction	Drinking Age	Blood Alcohol Concentration Levels as Evidence in State Courts[1]		Open Container Law[1]	Anti-Consumption Law[1]	Dram Shop Law[1]
		Illegal per se at 0.10%	Presumption at 0.10%			
Ohio	21	Yes	No	Yes	Yes	Yes

Note: Data as of January 1, 1997; (1) See Appendix C for an explanation of terms
Source: Sourcebook of Criminal Justice Statistics Online

Statutory Provisions Relating to Curfews

Jurisdiction	Year Enacted	Latest Revision	Age Group(s)	Curfew Provisions
Cincinnati	1994	-	16 and 17	Midnight to 5 am every night
			15 and under	10 pm to 5 am every night

Note: Data as of February 1996
Source: Sourcebook of Criminal Justice Statistics Online

Statutory Provisions Relating to Hate Crimes

Jurisdiction	Bias-Motivated Violence and Intimidation						Institutional Vandalism
	Civil Action	Criminal Penalty					
		Race/ Religion/ Ethnicity	Sexual Orientation	Mental/ Physical Disability	Gender	Age	
Ohio	Yes	Yes	No	No	No	No	Yes

Source: Anti-Defamation League, 1997 Hate Crimes Laws

Cleveland, Ohio

OVERVIEW

The total crime rate for the city decreased 16.5% between 1977 and 1996. During that same period, the violent crime rate decreased 0.6% and the property crime rate decreased 19.8%.

Among violent crimes, the rates for: Murders decreased 49.1%; Forcible Rapes increased 55.4%; Robberies decreased 22.9%; and Aggravated Assaults increased 57.7%.

Among property crimes, the rates for: Burglaries decreased 39.9%; Larceny-Thefts decreased 0.2%; and Motor Vehicle Thefts decreased 20.4%.

ANTI-CRIME PROGRAMS

In 1990 the Cleveland public school system and the Police Department formed an alliance to attack the gang problem. The School Board created a Youth Gang Unit within the school system which works closely with the Police Department's Youth/Gang Unit. Gang crimes have decreased. The public school experienced a 39% reduction in school-gang-related-incidents during the 1992-93 school year. *FBI Law Enforcement Bulletin*

The city also instituted a program which the National League of Cities (1993) considers among those which are innovative for combatting crime and violence:

- The Police District Committee Program was instituted to measure a community's satisfaction with police services. It also helps to inform citizens in crime prevention. The results have been an increased participation in Crime Watch Programs; improvement in police response time; a significant decline in crimes such as vandalism, break-ins and auto theft. *Exemplary Programs in Criminal Justice, National League of Cities, 1994*

CRIME RISK

Your Chances of Becoming a Victim[1]

Area	Any Crime	Violent Crime					Property Crime			
		Any	Murder	Forcible Rape[2]	Robbery	Aggrav. Assault	Any	Burglary	Larceny -Theft	Motor Vehicle Theft
City	1:13	1:65	1:4,816	1:410	1:122	1:176	1:17	1:64	1:37	1:57

Note: (1) Figures have been calculated by dividing the population of the city by the number of crimes reported to the FBI during 1996 and are expressed as odds (eg. 1:20 should be read as 1 in 20). (2) Figures have been calculated by dividing the female population of the city by the number of forcible rapes reported to the FBI during 1996. The female population of the city was estimated by calculating the ratio of females to males reported in the 1990 Census and applying that ratio to 1996 population estimate.
Source: FBI Uniform Crime Reports 1996

CRIME STATISTICS

Total Crimes and Total Crime Rates: 1977 - 1996

Year	Number				Rate per 100,000 population			
	City	Suburbs[2]	MSA[1]	U.S.	City	Suburbs[3]	MSA[1]	U.S.
1977	54,995	47,821	102,816	10,984,500	9,030.4	3,254.9	4,947.4	5,077.6
1978	50,952	45,378	96,330	11,209,000	8,563.4	3,361.2	4,952.6	5,140.3
1979	51,994	48,570	100,564	12,249,500	8,645.8	3,640.3	5,195.4	5,565.5
1980	57,602	49,192	106,794	13,408,300	10,058.7	3,719.0	5,634.4	5,950.0
1981	60,721	49,754	110,475	13,423,800	10,594.4	3,758.2	5,823.6	5,858.2
1982	54,925	46,629	101,554	12,974,400	9,569.7	3,517.3	5,345.9	5,603.6
1983	47,236	43,352	90,588	12,108,600	8,260.5	3,283.9	4,788.0	5,175.0
1984	47,761	38,436	86,197	11,881,800	8,575.7	2,923.9	4,605.8	5,031.3
1985	43,071	41,344	84,415	12,431,400	7,886.6	3,133.4	4,524.9	5,207.1
1986	44,235	43,968	88,203	13,211,900	8,093.6	3,329.8	4,724.4	5,480.4
1987	45,408	43,148	88,556	13,508,700	8,283.5	3,258.0	4,729.2	5,550.0
1988	44,831	42,575	87,406	13,923,100	8,233.2	3,220.6	4,683.0	5,664.2
1989	43,746	43,026	86,772	14,251,400	8,350.0	3,234.9	4,680.3	5,741.0
1990	46,085	42,479	88,564	14,475,600	9,114.6	3,204.7	4,836.6	5,820.3
1991	45,610	44,000	89,610	14,872,900	8,944.9	3,291.7	4,852.7	5,897.8
1992	42,536	54,542	97,078	14,438,200	8,283.8	3,155.5	4,330.1	5,660.2
1993	40,005	n/a	n/a	14,144,800	7,910.3	n/a	n/a	5,484.4
1994	37,745	n/a	n/a	13,989,500	7,456.1	n/a	n/a	5,373.5
1995	38,665	n/a	n/a	13,862,700	7,809.9	n/a	n/a	5,275.9
1996	37,409	n/a	n/a	13,473,600	7,541.4	n/a	n/a	5,078.9

Notes: (1) Metropolitan Statistical Area - see Appendix A for areas included; (2) calculated by the editors using the following formula: (number of crimes in the MSA minus number of crimes in the city); (3) calculated by the editors using the following formula: ((number of crimes in the MSA minus number of crimes in the city) ÷ (population of the MSA minus population of the city)) x 100,000; n/a not avail.
Source: U.S. Department of Justice, FBI Uniform Crime Reports, 1977 - 1996

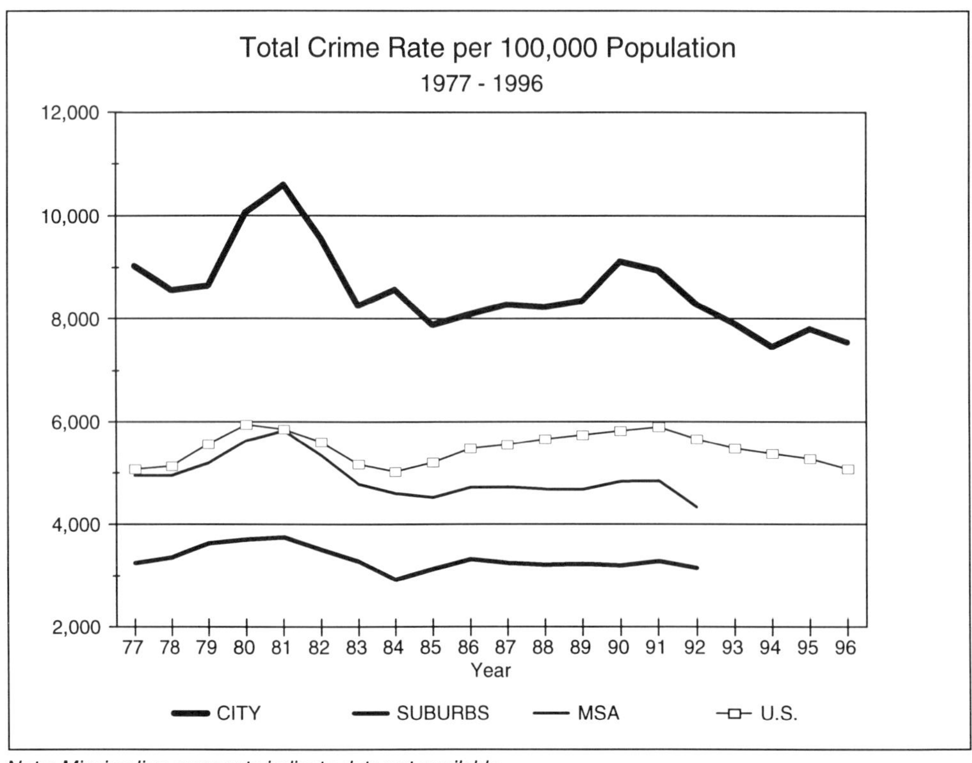

Note: Missing line segments indicate data not available.

Violent Crimes and Violent Crime Rates: 1977 - 1996

Year	Number				Rate per 100,000 population			
	City	Suburbs[2]	MSA[1]	U.S.	City	Suburbs[3]	MSA[1]	U.S.
1977	9,421	3,064	12,485	1,029,580	1,547.0	208.5	600.8	475.9
1978	9,697	3,032	12,729	1,085,550	1,629.7	224.6	654.4	497.8
1979	9,736	3,568	13,304	1,208,030	1,618.9	267.4	687.3	548.9
1980	11,466	3,585	15,051	1,344,520	2,002.2	271.0	794.1	596.6
1981	12,429	3,492	15,921	1,361,820	2,168.6	263.8	839.3	594.3
1982	9,386	3,344	12,730	1,322,390	1,635.4	252.2	670.1	571.1
1983	7,798	3,194	10,992	1,258,090	1,363.7	241.9	581.0	537.7
1984	7,332	2,318	9,650	1,273,280	1,316.5	176.3	515.6	539.2
1985	6,580	2,317	8,897	1,328,800	1,204.9	175.6	476.9	556.6
1986	7,115	2,488	9,603	1,489,170	1,301.8	188.4	514.4	617.7
1987	6,964	2,417	9,381	1,484,000	1,270.4	182.5	501.0	609.7
1988	7,333	2,484	9,817	1,566,220	1,346.7	187.9	526.0	637.2
1989	7,965	2,565	10,530	1,646,040	1,520.3	192.8	568.0	663.1
1990	9,190	2,665	11,855	1,820,130	1,817.6	201.1	647.4	731.8
1991	9,341	3,018	12,359	1,911,770	1,831.9	225.8	669.3	758.1
1992	8,532	3,829	12,361	1,932,270	1,661.6	221.5	551.4	757.5
1993	8,310	n/a	n/a	1,926,020	1,643.2	n/a	n/a	746.8
1994	7,744	n/a	n/a	1,857,670	1,529.7	n/a	n/a	713.6
1995	8,150	n/a	n/a	1,798,790	1,646.2	n/a	n/a	684.6
1996	7,631	n/a	n/a	1,682,280	1,538.4	n/a	n/a	634.1

Notes: Violent crimes include murder, forcible rape, robbery and aggravated assault; n/a not available; (1) Metropolitan Statistical Area - see Appendix A for areas included; (2) calculated by the editors using the following formula: (number of crimes in the MSA minus number of crimes in the city); (3) calculated by the editors using the following formula: ((number of crimes in the MSA minus number of crimes in the city) ÷ (population of the MSA minus population of the city)) x 100,000
Source: U.S. Department of Justice, FBI Uniform Crime Reports, 1977 - 1996

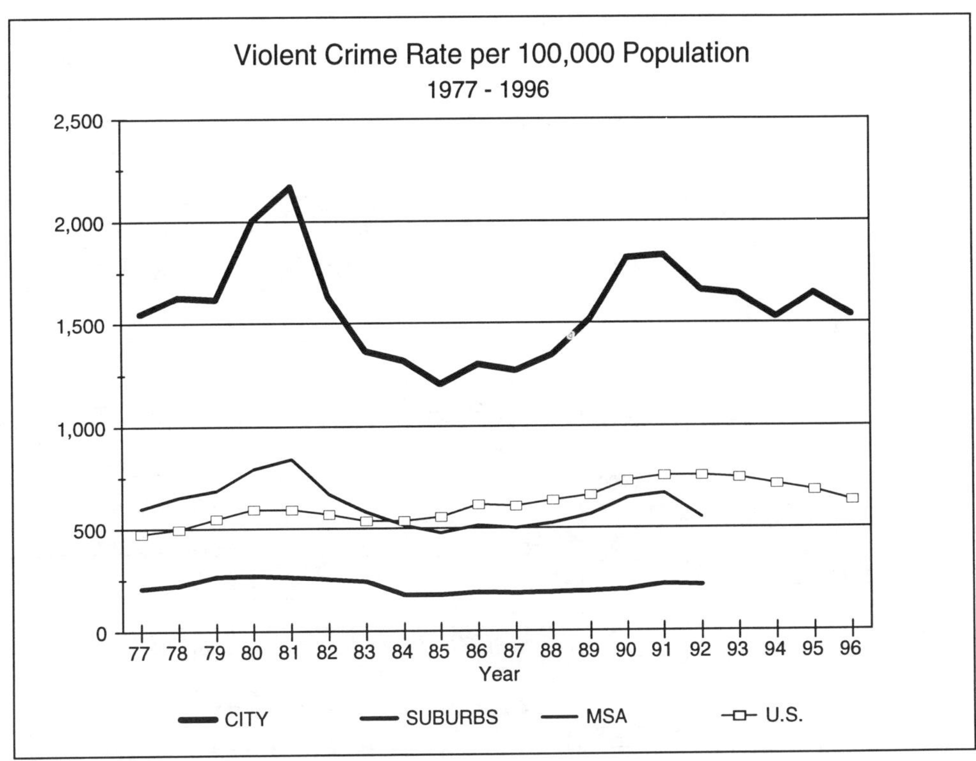

Note: Missing line segments indicate data not available.

Property Crimes and Property Crime Rates: 1977 - 1996

Year	Number				Rate per 100,000 population			
	City	Suburbs[2]	MSA[1]	U.S.	City	Suburbs[3]	MSA[1]	U.S.
1977	45,574	44,757	90,331	9,955,000	7,483.4	3,046.4	4,346.6	4,601.7
1978	41,255	42,346	83,601	10,123,400	6,933.6	3,136.6	4,298.1	4,642.5
1979	42,258	45,002	87,260	11,041,500	7,026.8	3,372.9	4,508.1	5,016.6
1980	46,136	45,607	91,743	12,063,700	8,056.5	3,447.9	4,840.3	5,353.3
1981	48,292	46,262	94,554	12,061,900	8,425.8	3,494.5	4,984.4	5,263.9
1982	45,539	43,285	88,824	11,652,000	7,934.4	3,265.0	4,675.8	5,032.5
1983	39,438	40,158	79,596	10,850,500	6,896.8	3,042.0	4,207.1	4,637.4
1984	40,429	36,118	76,547	10,608,500	7,259.2	2,747.5	4,090.2	4,492.1
1985	36,491	39,027	75,518	11,102,600	6,681.8	2,957.8	4,048.0	4,650.5
1986	37,120	41,480	78,600	11,722,700	6,791.8	3,141.4	4,210.0	4,862.6
1987	38,444	40,731	79,175	12,024,700	7,013.1	3,075.5	4,228.2	4,940.3
1988	37,498	40,091	77,589	12,356,900	6,886.5	3,032.7	4,157.0	5,027.1
1989	35,781	40,461	76,242	12,605,400	6,829.7	3,042.0	4,112.4	5,077.9
1990	36,895	39,814	76,709	12,655,500	7,297.0	3,003.7	4,189.2	5,088.5
1991	36,269	40,982	77,251	12,961,100	7,113.0	3,065.9	4,183.4	5,139.7
1992	34,004	50,713	84,717	12,505,900	6,622.2	2,934.0	3,778.7	4,902.7
1993	31,695	n/a	n/a	12,218,800	6,267.2	n/a	n/a	4,737.6
1994	30,001	n/a	n/a	12,131,900	5,926.4	n/a	n/a	4,660.0
1995	30,515	n/a	n/a	12,063,900	6,163.7	n/a	n/a	4,591.3
1996	29,778	n/a	n/a	11,791,300	6,003.0	n/a	n/a	4,444.8

Notes: Property crimes include burglary, larceny-theft and motor vehicle theft; n/a not available; (1) Metropolitan Statistical Area - see Appendix A for areas included; (2) calculated by the editors using the following formula: (number of crimes in the MSA minus number of crimes in the city); (3) calculated by the editors using the following formula: ((number of crimes in the MSA minus number of crimes in the city) ÷ (population of the MSA minus population of the city)) x 100,000
Source: U.S. Department of Justice, FBI Uniform Crime Reports, 1977 - 1996

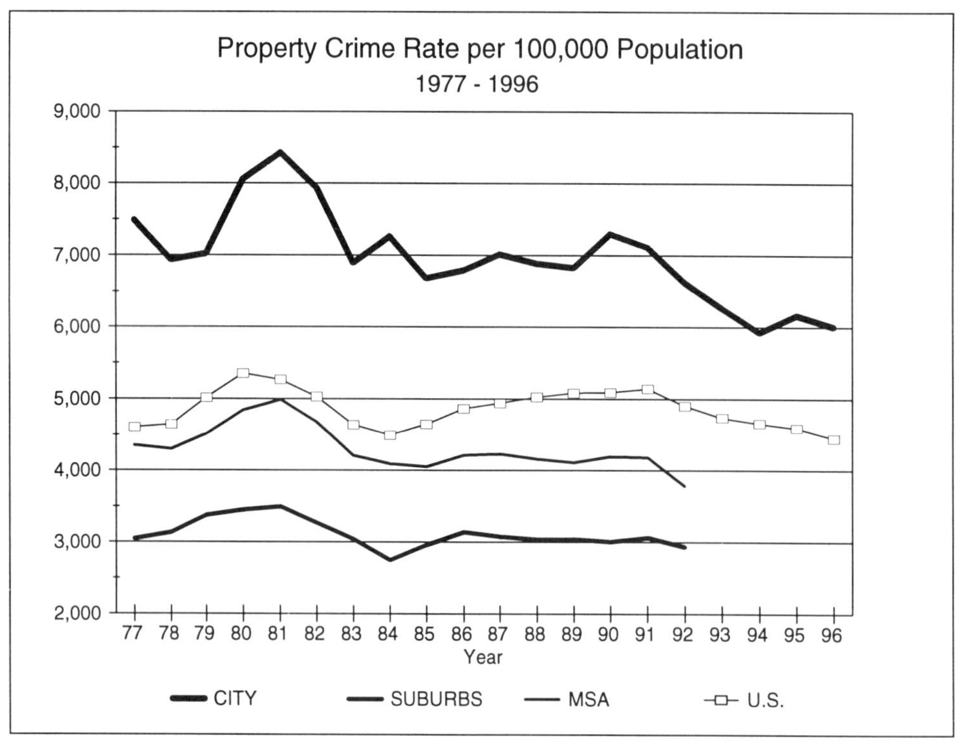

Note: Missing line segments indicate data not available.

Murders and Murder Rates: 1977 - 1996

Year	Number				Rate per 100,000 population			
	City	Suburbs[2]	MSA[1]	U.S.	City	Suburbs[3]	MSA[1]	U.S.
1977	249	47	296	19,120	40.9	3.2	14.2	8.8
1978	213	43	256	19,560	35.8	3.2	13.2	9.0
1979	274	50	324	21,460	45.6	3.7	16.7	9.7
1980	265	37	302	23,040	46.3	2.8	15.9	10.2
1981	233	31	264	22,520	40.7	2.3	13.9	9.8
1982	195	55	250	21,010	34.0	4.1	13.2	9.1
1983	148	35	183	19,310	25.9	2.7	9.7	8.3
1984	156	36	192	18,690	28.0	2.7	10.3	7.9
1985	131	37	168	18,980	24.0	2.8	9.0	7.9
1986	124	37	161	20,610	22.7	2.8	8.6	8.6
1987	145	28	173	20,100	26.5	2.1	9.2	8.3
1988	137	41	178	20,680	25.2	3.1	9.5	8.4
1989	144	36	180	21,500	27.5	2.7	9.7	8.7
1990	168	39	207	23,440	33.2	2.9	11.3	9.4
1991	175	44	219	24,700	34.3	3.3	11.9	9.8
1992	157	46	203	23,760	30.6	2.7	9.1	9.3
1993	167	n/a	n/a	24,530	33.0	n/a	n/a	9.5
1994	132	n/a	n/a	23,330	26.1	n/a	n/a	9.0
1995	129	n/a	n/a	21,610	26.1	n/a	n/a	8.2
1996	103	n/a	n/a	19,650	20.8	n/a	n/a	7.4

Notes: (1) Metropolitan Statistical Area - see Appendix A for areas included; (2) calculated by the editors using the following formula: (number of crimes in the MSA minus number of crimes in the city); (3) calculated by the editors using the following formula: ((number of crimes in the MSA minus number of crimes in the city) ÷ (population of the MSA minus population of the city)) x 100,000; n/a not avail.
Source: U.S. Department of Justice, FBI Uniform Crime Reports, 1977 - 1996

Forcible Rapes and Forcible Rape Rates: 1977 - 1996

Year	Number				Rate per 100,000 population			
	City	Suburbs[2]	MSA[1]	U.S.	City	Suburbs[3]	MSA[1]	U.S.
1977	508	170	678	63,500	83.4	11.6	32.6	29.4
1978	507	144	651	67,610	85.2	10.7	33.5	31.0
1979	612	197	809	76,390	101.8	14.8	41.8	34.7
1980	703	198	901	82,990	122.8	15.0	47.5	36.8
1981	621	178	799	82,500	108.3	13.4	42.1	36.0
1982	628	169	797	78,770	109.4	12.7	42.0	34.0
1983	716	225	941	78,920	125.2	17.0	49.7	33.7
1984	733	210	943	84,230	131.6	16.0	50.4	35.7
1985	745	231	976	88,670	136.4	17.5	52.3	37.1
1986	773	209	982	91,460	141.4	15.8	52.6	37.9
1987	750	200	950	91,110	136.8	15.1	50.7	37.4
1988	844	224	1,068	92,490	155.0	16.9	57.2	37.6
1989	837	248	1,085	94,500	159.8	18.6	58.5	38.1
1990	846	227	1,073	102,560	167.3	17.1	58.6	41.2
1991	913	267	1,180	106,590	179.1	20.0	63.9	42.3
1992	854	446	1,300	109,060	166.3	25.8	58.0	42.8
1993	834	n/a	n/a	106,010	164.9	n/a	n/a	41.1
1994	749	n/a	n/a	102,220	148.0	n/a	n/a	39.3
1995	689	n/a	n/a	97,470	139.2	n/a	n/a	37.1
1996	643	n/a	n/a	95,770	129.6	n/a	n/a	36.1

Notes: (1) Metropolitan Statistical Area - see Appendix A for areas included; (2) calculated by the editors using the following formula: (number of crimes in the MSA minus number of crimes in the city); (3) calculated by the editors using the following formula: ((number of crimes in the MSA minus number of crimes in the city) ÷ (population of the MSA minus population of the city)) x 100,000; n/a not avail.
Source: U.S. Department of Justice, FBI Uniform Crime Reports, 1977 - 1996

Robberies and Robbery Rates: 1977 - 1996

Year	Number				Rate per 100,000 population			
	City	Suburbs[2]	MSA[1]	U.S.	City	Suburbs[3]	MSA[1]	U.S.
1977	6,466	1,117	7,583	412,610	1,061.7	76.0	364.9	190.7
1978	6,354	1,090	7,444	426,930	1,067.9	80.7	382.7	195.8
1979	5,760	1,140	6,900	480,700	957.8	85.4	356.5	218.4
1980	6,802	1,216	8,018	565,840	1,187.8	91.9	423.0	251.1
1981	7,821	1,256	9,077	592,910	1,364.6	94.9	478.5	258.7
1982	5,296	1,032	6,328	553,130	922.7	77.8	333.1	238.9
1983	4,115	902	5,017	506,570	719.6	68.3	265.2	216.5
1984	4,090	733	4,823	485,010	734.4	55.8	257.7	205.4
1985	3,499	790	4,289	497,870	640.7	59.9	229.9	208.5
1986	3,698	846	4,544	542,780	676.6	64.1	243.4	225.1
1987	3,541	948	4,489	517,700	646.0	71.6	239.7	212.7
1988	3,795	921	4,716	542,970	697.0	69.7	252.7	220.9
1989	4,045	941	4,986	578,330	772.1	70.7	268.9	233.0
1990	4,917	1,062	5,979	639,270	972.5	80.1	326.5	257.0
1991	5,132	1,266	6,398	687,730	1,006.5	94.7	346.5	272.7
1992	4,423	1,459	5,882	672,480	861.4	84.4	262.4	263.6
1993	4,297	n/a	n/a	659,870	849.7	n/a	n/a	255.9
1994	3,924	n/a	n/a	618,950	775.1	n/a	n/a	237.7
1995	4,224	n/a	n/a	580,510	853.2	n/a	n/a	220.9
1996	4,062	n/a	n/a	537,050	818.9	n/a	n/a	202.4

Notes: (1) Metropolitan Statistical Area - see Appendix A for areas included; (2) calculated by the editors using the following formula: (number of crimes in the MSA minus number of crimes in the city); (3) calculated by the editors using the following formula: ((number of crimes in the MSA minus number of crimes in the city) ÷ (population of the MSA minus population of the city)) x 100,000; n/a not avail.
Source: U.S. Department of Justice, FBI Uniform Crime Reports, 1977 - 1996

Aggravated Assaults and Aggravated Assault Rates: 1977 - 1996

Year	Number				Rate per 100,000 population			
	City	Suburbs[2]	MSA[1]	U.S.	City	Suburbs[3]	MSA[1]	U.S.
1977	2,198	1,730	3,928	534,350	360.9	117.8	189.0	247.0
1978	2,623	1,755	4,378	571,460	440.8	130.0	225.1	262.1
1979	3,090	2,181	5,271	629,480	513.8	163.5	272.3	286.0
1980	3,696	2,134	5,830	672,650	645.4	161.3	307.6	298.5
1981	3,754	2,027	5,781	663,900	655.0	153.1	304.7	289.7
1982	3,267	2,088	5,355	669,480	569.2	157.5	281.9	289.2
1983	2,819	2,032	4,851	653,290	493.0	153.9	256.4	279.2
1984	2,353	1,339	3,692	685,350	422.5	101.9	197.3	290.2
1985	2,205	1,259	3,464	723,250	403.8	95.4	185.7	302.9
1986	2,520	1,396	3,916	834,320	461.1	105.7	209.7	346.1
1987	2,528	1,241	3,769	855,090	461.2	93.7	201.3	351.3
1988	2,557	1,298	3,855	910,090	469.6	98.2	206.5	370.2
1989	2,939	1,340	4,279	951,710	561.0	100.7	230.8	383.4
1990	3,259	1,337	4,596	1,054,860	644.6	100.9	251.0	424.1
1991	3,121	1,441	4,562	1,092,740	612.1	107.8	247.0	433.3
1992	3,098	1,878	4,976	1,126,970	603.3	108.7	222.0	441.8
1993	3,012	n/a	n/a	1,135,610	595.6	n/a	n/a	440.3
1994	2,939	n/a	n/a	1,113,180	580.6	n/a	n/a	427.6
1995	3,108	n/a	n/a	1,099,210	627.8	n/a	n/a	418.3
1996	2,823	n/a	n/a	1,029,810	569.1	n/a	n/a	388.2

Notes: (1) Metropolitan Statistical Area - see Appendix A for areas included; (2) calculated by the editors using the following formula: (number of crimes in the MSA minus number of crimes in the city); (3) calculated by the editors using the following formula: ((number of crimes in the MSA minus number of crimes in the city) ÷ (population of the MSA minus population of the city)) x 100,000; n/a not avail.
Source: U.S. Department of Justice, FBI Uniform Crime Reports, 1977 - 1996

Burglaries and Burglary Rates: 1977 - 1996

Year	Number				Rate per 100,000 population			
	City	Suburbs[2]	MSA[1]	U.S.	City	Suburbs[3]	MSA[1]	U.S.
1977	15,734	9,980	25,714	3,071,500	2,583.6	679.3	1,237.3	1,419.8
1978	14,234	9,647	23,881	3,128,300	2,392.3	714.6	1,227.8	1,434.6
1979	14,505	9,959	24,464	3,327,700	2,411.9	746.4	1,263.9	1,511.9
1980	17,850	11,238	29,088	3,795,200	3,117.0	849.6	1,534.7	1,684.1
1981	18,368	11,063	29,431	3,779,700	3,204.8	835.7	1,551.4	1,649.5
1982	16,760	10,181	26,941	3,447,100	2,920.1	768.0	1,418.2	1,488.8
1983	14,046	9,493	23,539	3,129,900	2,456.3	719.1	1,244.2	1,337.7
1984	12,904	8,185	21,089	2,984,400	2,317.0	622.6	1,126.9	1,263.7
1985	11,621	8,335	19,956	3,073,300	2,127.9	631.7	1,069.7	1,287.3
1986	11,928	8,555	20,483	3,241,400	2,182.4	647.9	1,097.1	1,344.6
1987	13,163	8,392	21,555	3,236,200	2,401.3	633.7	1,151.1	1,329.6
1988	12,052	7,671	19,723	3,218,100	2,213.3	580.3	1,056.7	1,309.2
1989	10,585	7,423	18,008	3,168,200	2,020.4	558.1	971.3	1,276.3
1990	10,198	7,066	17,264	3,073,900	2,016.9	533.1	942.8	1,235.9
1991	10,151	7,368	17,519	3,157,200	1,990.8	551.2	948.7	1,252.0
1992	9,000	10,232	19,232	2,979,900	1,752.7	592.0	857.8	1,168.2
1993	8,031	n/a	n/a	2,834,800	1,588.0	n/a	n/a	1,099.2
1994	8,007	n/a	n/a	2,712,800	1,581.7	n/a	n/a	1,042.0
1995	7,693	n/a	n/a	2,593,800	1,553.9	n/a	n/a	987.1
1996	7,708	n/a	n/a	2,501,500	1,553.9	n/a	n/a	943.0

Notes: (1) Metropolitan Statistical Area - see Appendix A for areas included; (2) calculated by the editors using the following formula: (number of crimes in the MSA minus number of crimes in the city); (3) calculated by the editors using the following formula: ((number of crimes in the MSA minus number of crimes in the city) ÷ (population of the MSA minus population of the city)) x 100,000; n/a not avail.
Source: U.S. Department of Justice, FBI Uniform Crime Reports, 1977 - 1996

Larceny-Thefts and Larceny-Theft Rates: 1977 - 1996

Year	Number				Rate per 100,000 population			
	City	Suburbs[2]	MSA[1]	U.S.	City	Suburbs[3]	MSA[1]	U.S.
1977	16,536	29,062	45,598	5,905,700	2,715.3	1,978.1	2,194.1	2,729.9
1978	14,364	27,023	41,387	5,991,000	2,414.1	2,001.6	2,127.8	2,747.4
1979	14,217	29,054	43,271	6,601,000	2,364.1	2,177.6	2,235.5	2,999.1
1980	14,100	28,387	42,487	7,136,900	2,462.2	2,146.1	2,241.6	3,167.0
1981	14,846	28,162	43,008	7,194,400	2,590.3	2,127.3	2,267.2	3,139.7
1982	15,650	26,527	42,177	7,142,500	2,726.7	2,001.0	2,220.2	3,084.8
1983	13,953	24,701	38,654	6,712,800	2,440.1	1,871.1	2,043.1	2,868.9
1984	13,607	22,739	36,346	6,591,900	2,443.2	1,729.8	1,942.1	2,791.3
1985	13,277	25,242	38,519	6,926,400	2,431.1	1,913.1	2,064.7	2,901.2
1986	13,453	27,055	40,508	7,257,200	2,461.5	2,048.9	2,169.7	3,010.3
1987	14,773	26,429	41,202	7,499,900	2,695.0	1,995.6	2,200.3	3,081.3
1988	15,471	26,830	42,301	7,705,900	2,841.2	2,029.6	2,266.4	3,134.9
1989	15,586	27,836	43,422	7,872,400	2,975.0	2,092.8	2,342.1	3,171.3
1990	15,289	27,019	42,308	7,945,700	3,023.8	2,038.4	2,310.5	3,194.8
1991	15,485	27,731	43,216	8,142,200	3,036.9	2,074.6	2,340.3	3,228.8
1992	14,240	33,906	48,146	7,915,200	2,773.2	1,961.6	2,147.5	3,103.0
1993	13,494	n/a	n/a	7,820,900	2,668.2	n/a	n/a	3,032.4
1994	12,931	n/a	n/a	7,879,800	2,554.4	n/a	n/a	3,026.7
1995	13,764	n/a	n/a	7,997,700	2,780.2	n/a	n/a	3,043.8
1996	13,441	n/a	n/a	7,894,600	2,709.6	n/a	n/a	2,975.9

Notes: (1) Metropolitan Statistical Area - see Appendix A for areas included; (2) calculated by the editors using the following formula: (number of crimes in the MSA minus number of crimes in the city); (3) calculated by the editors using the following formula: ((number of crimes in the MSA minus number of crimes in the city) ÷ (population of the MSA minus population of the city)) x 100,000; n/a not avail.
Source: U.S. Department of Justice, FBI Uniform Crime Reports, 1977 - 1996

Motor Vehicle Thefts and Motor Vehicle Theft Rates: 1977 - 1996

Year	Number				Rate per 100,000 population			
	City	Suburbs[2]	MSA[1]	U.S.	City	Suburbs[3]	MSA[1]	U.S.
1977	13,304	5,715	19,019	977,700	2,184.6	389.0	915.2	451.9
1978	12,657	5,676	18,333	1,004,100	2,127.2	420.4	942.5	460.5
1979	13,536	5,989	19,525	1,112,800	2,250.8	448.9	1,008.7	505.6
1980	14,186	5,982	20,168	1,131,700	2,477.2	452.2	1,064.1	502.2
1981	15,078	7,037	22,115	1,087,800	2,630.7	531.6	1,165.8	474.7
1982	13,129	6,577	19,706	1,062,400	2,287.5	496.1	1,037.3	458.8
1983	11,439	5,964	17,403	1,007,900	2,000.4	451.8	919.8	430.8
1984	13,918	5,194	19,112	1,032,200	2,499.1	395.1	1,021.2	437.1
1985	11,593	5,450	17,043	1,102,900	2,122.8	413.1	913.6	462.0
1986	11,739	5,870	17,609	1,224,100	2,147.9	444.5	943.2	507.8
1987	10,508	5,910	16,418	1,288,700	1,916.9	446.2	876.8	529.4
1988	9,975	5,590	15,565	1,432,900	1,831.9	422.9	833.9	582.9
1989	9,610	5,202	14,812	1,564,800	1,834.3	391.1	798.9	630.4
1990	11,408	5,729	17,137	1,635,900	2,256.3	432.2	935.9	657.8
1991	10,633	5,883	16,516	1,661,700	2,085.3	440.1	894.4	659.0
1992	10,764	6,575	17,339	1,610,800	2,096.3	380.4	773.4	631.5
1993	10,170	n/a	n/a	1,563,100	2,011.0	n/a	n/a	606.1
1994	9,063	n/a	n/a	1,539,300	1,790.3	n/a	n/a	591.3
1995	9,058	n/a	n/a	1,472,400	1,829.6	n/a	n/a	560.4
1996	8,629	n/a	n/a	1,395,200	1,739.5	n/a	n/a	525.9

Notes: (1) Metropolitan Statistical Area - see Appendix A for areas included; (2) calculated by the editors using the following formula: (number of crimes in the MSA minus number of crimes in the city); (3) calculated by the editors using the following formula: ((number of crimes in the MSA minus number of crimes in the city) ÷ (population of the MSA minus population of the city)) x 100,000; n/a not avail.
Source: U.S. Department of Justice, FBI Uniform Crime Reports, 1977 - 1996

HATE CRIMES

Criminal Incidents by Bias Motivation

Area	Race	Ethnicity	Religion	Sexual Orientation
Cleveland	6	0	0	0

Notes: Figures include both violent and property crimes. Law enforcement agencies must have submitted data for at least one quarter of calendar year 1995 to be included in this report, therefore figures shown may not represent complete 12-month totals; n/a not available
Source: U.S. Department of Justice, FBI Uniform Crime Reports, Hate Crime Statistics 1995

ILLEGAL DRUGS

Drug Use by Adult Arrestees

Sex	Percent Testing Positive by Urinalysis (%)				
	Any Drug[1]	Cocaine	Marijuana	Opiates	Multiple Drugs
Male	67	41	37	3	18
Female	70	52	22	6	13

Notes: The catchment area is the entire city; (1) Includes cocaine, opiates, marijuana, methadone, phencyclidine (PCP), benzodiazepines, methaqualone, propoxyphene, barbiturates & amphetamines
Source: National Institute of Justice, 1996 Drug Use Forecasting, Annual Report on Adult and Juvenile Arrestees (released June 1997)

LAW ENFORCEMENT

Full-Time Law Enforcement Employees

Jurisdiction	Police Employees			Police Officers per 100,000 population
	Total	Officers	Civilians	
Cleveland	2,359	1,785	574	359.8

Notes: Data as of October 31, 1996
Source: U.S. Department of Justice, FBI Uniform Crime Reports, 1996

Number of Police Officers by Race

Race	Police Officers				Index of Representation[1]		
	1983		1992				
	Number	Pct.	Number	Pct.	1983	1992	% Chg.
Black	238	11.4	439	26.3	0.26	0.56	115.4
Hispanic[2]	6	0.3	66	4.0	0.06	0.85	1,316.7

Notes: (1) The index of representation is calculated by dividing the percent of black/hispanic police officers by the percent of corresponding blacks/hispanics in the local population. An index approaching 1.0 indicates that a city is closer to achieving a representation of police officers equal to their proportion in the local population; (2) Hispanic officers can be of any race
Source: Bureau of Justice Statistics, Sourcebook of Criminal Justice Statistics, 1994

CORRECTIONS

Federal Correctional Facilities

Type	Year Opened	Security Level	Sex of Inmates	Rated Capacity	Population on 7/1/95	Number of Staff
None listed						

Notes: Data as of 1995
Source: Bureau of Justice Statistics, Sourcebook of Criminal Justice Statistics Online

City/County/Regional Correctional Facilities

Name	Year Opened	Year Renov.	Rated Capacity	1995 Pop.	Number of COs[1]	Number of Staff	ACA[2] Accred.
Cuyahoga County Jail	1977	--	770	n/a	n/a	n/a	No

Notes: Data as of April 1996; (1) Correctional Officers; (2) American Correctional Assn. Accreditation
Source: American Correctional Association, 1996-1998 National Jail and Adult Detention Directory

Private Adult Correctional Facilities

Name	Date Opened	Rated Capacity	Present Pop.	Security Level	Facility Construct.	Expans. Plans	ACA[1] Accred.
None listed							

Notes: Data as of December 1996; (1) American Correctional Association Accreditation
Source: University of Florida, Center for Studies in Criminology and Law, Private Adult Correctional Facility Census, 10th Ed., March 15, 1997

Characteristics of Shock Incarceration Programs

Jurisdiction	Year Program Began	Number of Camps	Average Num. of Inmates	Number of Beds	Program Length	Voluntary/ Mandatory
Ohio	1991 male; 1995 fem.	2	(a)	100 male; 40 female	(b)	Voluntary

Note: Data as of July 1996; (a) Phase I: 80 to 100 days; Phase II: 40 days; Phase III: 220 days; (b) Phase I: 90 days; Phase II: 30 days; Phase III: 6 months to one year
Source: Sourcebook of Criminal Justice Statistics Online

DEATH PENALTY

Death Penalty Statistics

State	Prisoners Executed		Prisoners Under Sentence of Death					Avg. No. of Years on Death Row[4]
	1930-1995	1996[1]	Total[2]	White[3]	Black[3]	Hisp.	Women	
Ohio	172	0	155	76	78	5	0	6.3

Notes: Data as of 12/31/95 unless otherwise noted; (1) Data as of 7/31/97; (2) Includes persons of other races; (3) Includes people of Hispanic origin; (4) Covers prisoners sentenced 1974 through 1995
Source: Bureau of Justice Statistics, Capital Punishment 1995 (released 12/96); Death Penalty Information Center Web Site, 9/30/97

Capital Offenses and Methods of Execution

Capital Offenses in Ohio	Minimum Age for Imposition of Death Penalty	Mentally Retarded Excluded	Methods of Execution[1]
Aggravated murder with 1 of 8 aggravating circumstances. (O.R.C. secs. 2929.01, 2903.01, and 2929.04).	18	No	Lethal injection; electrocution

Notes: Data as of 12/31/95 unless otherwise noted; (1) Data as of 7/31/97
Source: Bureau of Justice Statistics, Capital Punishment 1995 (released 12/96); Death Penalty Information Center Web Site, 9/30/97

LAWS

Statutory Provisions Relating to the Purchase, Ownership and Use of Handguns

Jurisdiction	Instant Background Check	Federal Waiting Period Applies[1]	State Waiting Period (days)	License or Permit to Purchase	Registration	Record of Sale Sent to Police	Concealed Carry Law
Ohio	No	Yes	(a)	(b)	(a)	(a)	Yes[c]

Note: Data as of 1996; (1) The Federal 5-day waiting period for handgun purchases applies to states that don't have instant background checks, waiting period requirements, or licensing procedures exempting them from the Federal requirement; (a) Local ordinance in certain cities or counties; (b) Some cities require a permit-to-purchase or firearm owner ID card; (c) No permit system exists and concealed carry is prohibited
Source: Sourcebook of Criminal Justice Statistics Online

Statutory Provisions Relating to Alcohol Use and Driving

Jurisdiction	Drinking Age	Blood Alcohol Concentration Levels as Evidence in State Courts[1]		Open Container Law[1]	Anti-Consumption Law[1]	Dram Shop Law[1]
		Illegal per se at 0.10%	Presumption at 0.10%			
Ohio	21	Yes	No	Yes	Yes	Yes

Note: Data as of January 1, 1997; (1) See Appendix C for an explanation of terms
Source: Sourcebook of Criminal Justice Statistics Online

Statutory Provisions Relating to Curfews

Jurisdiction	Year Enacted	Latest Revision	Age Group(s)	Curfew Provisions
Cleveland	1976	1993	17 year olds	Midnight to 5 am every night 9 am to 2 pm school days
			13 through 16	11 pm to 5 am every night 9 am to 2 pm school days
			12 and under	Darkness till dawn every night 9 am to 2 pm school days

Note: Data as of February 1996
Source: Sourcebook of Criminal Justice Statistics Online

Statutory Provisions Relating to Hate Crimes

Jurisdiction	Bias-Motivated Violence and Intimidation						Institutional Vandalism
	Civil Action	Criminal Penalty					
		Race/ Religion/ Ethnicity	Sexual Orientation	Mental/ Physical Disability	Gender	Age	
Ohio	Yes	Yes	No	No	No	No	Yes

Source: Anti-Defamation League, 1997 Hate Crimes Laws

Colorado Springs, Colorado

OVERVIEW

The total crime rate for the city decreased 17.8% between 1977 and 1996. During that same period, the violent crime rate increased 3.7% and the property crime rate decreased 19.2%.

Among violent crimes, the rates for: Murders decreased 44.6%; Forcible Rapes increased 18.1%; Robberies decreased 29.1%; and Aggravated Assaults increased 31.9%.

Among property crimes, the rates for: Burglaries decreased 54.2%; Larceny-Thefts decreased 3.4%; and Motor Vehicle Thefts decreased 6.5%.

ANTI-CRIME PROGRAMS

Information not available at time of publication.

CRIME RISK

Your Chances of Becoming a Victim[1]

Area	Any Crime	Violent Crime					Property Crime			
		Any	Murder	Forcible Rape[2]	Robbery	Aggrav. Assault	Any	Burglary	Larceny -Theft	Motor Vehicle Theft
City	1:16	1:208	1:27,585	1:710	1:731	1:371	1:17	1:100	1:23	1:241

Note: (1) Figures have been calculated by dividing the population of the city by the number of crimes reported to the FBI during 1996 and are expressed as odds (eg. 1:20 should be read as 1 in 20). (2) Figures have been calculated by dividing the female population of the city by the number of forcible rapes reported to the FBI during 1996. The female population of the city was estimated by calculating the ratio of females to males reported in the 1990 Census and applying that ratio to 1996 population estimate.
Source: FBI Uniform Crime Reports 1996

CRIME STATISTICS

Total Crimes and Total Crime Rates: 1977 - 1996

Year	Number				Rate per 100,000 population			
	City	Suburbs[2]	MSA[1]	U.S.	City	Suburbs[3]	MSA[1]	U.S.
1977	13,882	4,291	18,173	10,984,500	7,544.6	4,243.3	6,373.7	5,077.6
1978	13,259	4,402	17,661	11,209,000	6,254.2	5,259.9	5,972.8	5,140.3
1979	14,871	3,518	18,389	12,249,500	7,673.8	3,233.8	6,077.5	5,565.5
1980	16,910	3,973	20,883	13,408,300	8,169.9	3,592.1	6,575.6	5,950.0
1981	18,836	3,716	22,552	13,423,800	8,840.6	3,263.8	6,898.4	5,858.2
1982	18,454	3,539	21,993	12,974,400	8,428.1	3,024.6	6,546.2	5,603.6
1983	18,097	3,114	21,211	12,108,600	8,017.6	2,783.5	6,283.1	5,175.0
1984	17,917	3,123	21,040	11,881,800	7,458.4	3,030.4	6,129.1	5,031.3
1985	21,835	3,643	25,478	12,431,400	8,668.6	3,534.9	7,178.0	5,207.1
1986	22,833	3,910	26,743	13,211,900	8,967.2	3,754.4	7,454.0	5,480.4
1987	22,826	3,903	26,729	13,508,700	8,297.2	3,590.4	6,964.1	5,550.0
1988	22,174	3,642	25,816	13,923,100	7,949.3	3,304.2	6,633.7	5,664.2
1989	21,553	3,582	25,135	14,251,400	7,549.7	3,246.7	6,350.3	5,741.0
1990	21,017	3,630	24,647	14,475,600	7,475.6	3,132.7	6,208.1	5,820.3
1991	21,444	3,799	25,243	14,872,900	7,441.0	3,198.5	6,202.8	5,897.8
1992	20,194	3,379	23,573	14,438,200	6,819.4	2,768.7	5,637.2	5,660.2
1993	19,608	3,985	23,593	14,144,800	6,440.7	3,088.6	5,442.9	5,484.4
1994	20,811	3,792	24,603	13,989,500	6,667.6	2,866.7	5,536.2	5,373.5
1995	21,949	3,851	25,800	13,862,700	6,765.2	2,764.1	5,563.2	5,275.9
1996	20,523	3,681	24,204	13,473,600	6,199.9	2,589.6	5,115.3	5,078.9

Notes: (1) Metropolitan Statistical Area - see Appendix A for areas included; (2) calculated by the editors using the following formula: (number of crimes in the MSA minus number of crimes in the city); (3) calculated by the editors using the following formula: ((number of crimes in the MSA minus number of crimes in the city) ÷ (population of the MSA minus population of the city)) x 100,000; n/a not avail.
Source: U.S. Department of Justice, FBI Uniform Crime Reports, 1977 - 1996

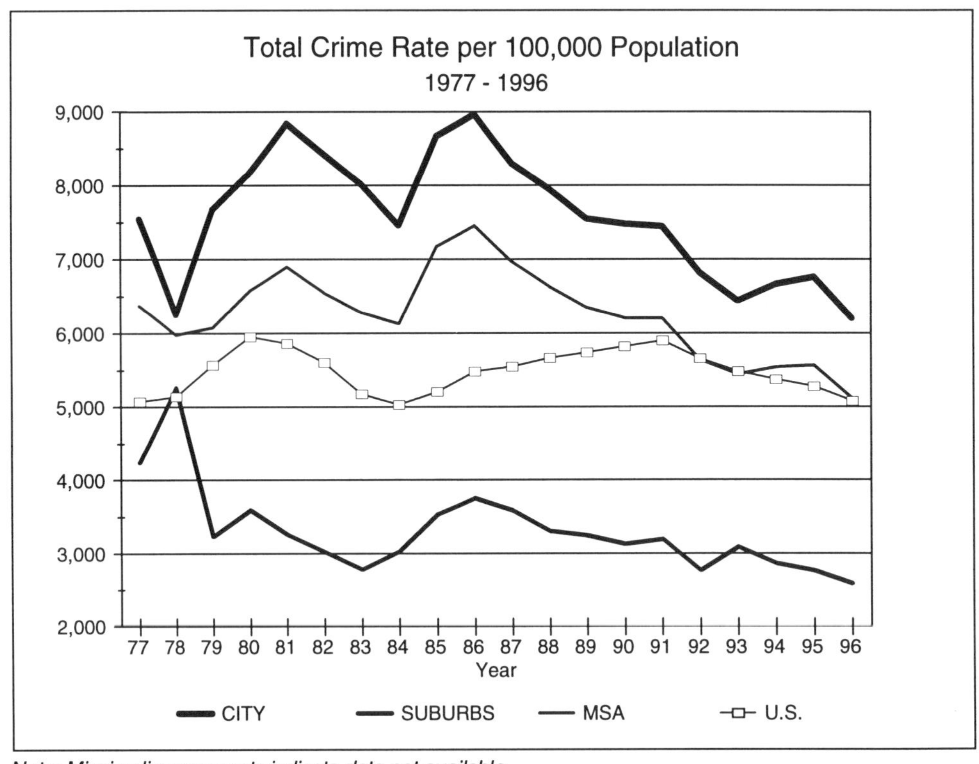

Note: Missing line segments indicate data not available.

Violent Crimes and Violent Crime Rates: 1977 - 1996

Year	Number				Rate per 100,000 population			
	City	Suburbs[2]	MSA[1]	U.S.	City	Suburbs[3]	MSA[1]	U.S.
1977	855	320	1,175	1,029,580	464.7	316.4	412.1	475.9
1978	956	401	1,357	1,085,550	450.9	479.1	458.9	497.8
1979	1,092	289	1,381	1,208,030	563.5	265.7	456.4	548.9
1980	1,182	251	1,433	1,344,520	571.1	226.9	451.2	596.6
1981	1,463	301	1,764	1,361,820	686.7	264.4	539.6	594.3
1982	1,340	235	1,575	1,322,390	612.0	200.8	468.8	571.1
1983	1,267	188	1,455	1,258,090	561.3	168.0	431.0	537.7
1984	1,189	195	1,384	1,273,280	494.9	189.2	403.2	539.2
1985	1,169	196	1,365	1,328,800	464.1	190.2	384.6	556.6
1986	1,555	235	1,790	1,489,170	610.7	225.6	498.9	617.7
1987	1,390	275	1,665	1,484,000	505.3	253.0	433.8	609.7
1988	1,293	249	1,542	1,566,220	463.5	225.9	396.2	637.2
1989	1,345	269	1,614	1,646,040	471.1	243.8	407.8	663.1
1990	1,184	326	1,510	1,820,130	421.1	281.3	380.3	731.8
1991	1,385	334	1,719	1,911,770	480.6	281.2	422.4	758.1
1992	1,542	321	1,863	1,932,270	520.7	263.0	445.5	757.5
1993	1,555	408	1,963	1,926,020	510.8	316.2	452.9	746.8
1994	1,503	381	1,884	1,857,670	481.5	288.0	423.9	713.6
1995	1,566	365	1,931	1,798,790	482.7	262.0	416.4	684.6
1996	1,595	353	1,948	1,682,280	481.8	248.3	411.7	634.1

Notes: Violent crimes include murder, forcible rape, robbery and aggravated assault; n/a not available; (1) Metropolitan Statistical Area - see Appendix A for areas included; (2) calculated by the editors using the following formula: (number of crimes in the MSA minus number of crimes in the city); (3) calculated by the editors using the following formula: ((number of crimes in the MSA minus number of crimes in the city) ÷ (population of the MSA minus population of the city)) x 100,000
Source: U.S. Department of Justice, FBI Uniform Crime Reports, 1977 - 1996

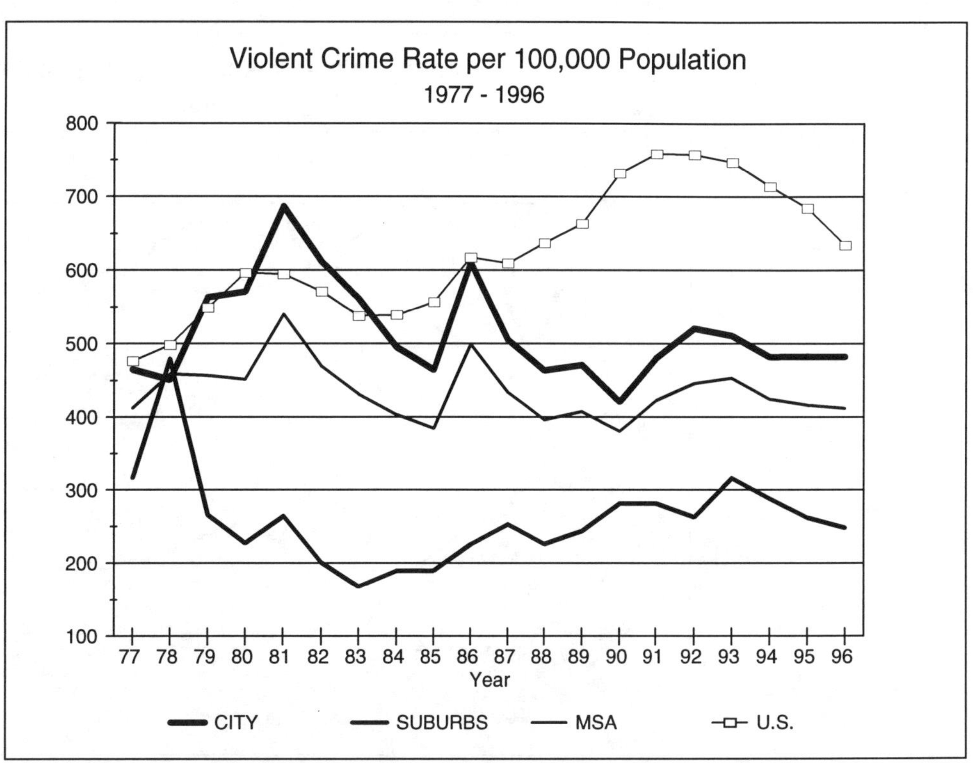

Note: Missing line segments indicate data not available.

Property Crimes and Property Crime Rates: 1977 - 1996

Year	Number				Rate per 100,000 population			
	City	Suburbs[2]	MSA[1]	U.S.	City	Suburbs[3]	MSA[1]	U.S.
1977	13,027	3,971	16,998	9,955,000	7,079.9	3,926.9	5,961.6	4,601.7
1978	12,303	4,001	16,304	10,123,400	5,803.3	4,780.7	5,513.9	4,642.5
1979	13,779	3,229	17,008	11,041,500	7,110.3	2,968.2	5,621.0	5,016.6
1980	15,728	3,722	19,450	12,063,700	7,598.8	3,365.1	6,124.4	5,353.3
1981	17,373	3,415	20,788	12,061,900	8,154.0	2,999.4	6,358.8	5,263.9
1982	17,114	3,304	20,418	11,652,000	7,816.1	2,823.8	6,077.4	5,032.5
1983	16,830	2,926	19,756	10,850,500	7,456.2	2,615.5	5,852.1	4,637.4
1984	16,728	2,928	19,656	10,608,500	6,963.4	2,841.2	5,725.9	4,492.1
1985	20,666	3,447	24,113	11,102,600	8,204.5	3,344.7	6,793.5	4,650.5
1986	21,278	3,675	24,953	11,722,700	8,356.5	3,528.7	6,955.1	4,862.6
1987	21,436	3,628	25,064	12,024,700	7,791.9	3,337.4	6,530.3	4,940.3
1988	20,881	3,393	24,274	12,356,900	7,485.7	3,078.3	6,237.4	5,027.1
1989	20,208	3,313	23,521	12,605,400	7,078.6	3,002.9	5,942.5	5,077.9
1990	19,833	3,304	23,137	12,655,500	7,054.5	2,851.4	5,827.8	5,088.5
1991	20,059	3,465	23,524	12,961,100	6,960.4	2,917.3	5,780.4	5,139.7
1992	18,652	3,058	21,710	12,505,900	6,298.7	2,505.7	5,191.7	4,902.7
1993	18,053	3,577	21,630	12,218,800	5,929.9	2,772.4	4,990.1	4,737.6
1994	19,308	3,411	22,719	12,131,900	6,186.0	2,578.7	5,112.3	4,660.0
1995	20,383	3,486	23,869	12,063,900	6,282.5	2,502.1	5,146.8	4,591.3
1996	18,928	3,328	22,256	11,791,300	5,718.1	2,341.3	4,703.6	4,444.8

Notes: Property crimes include burglary, larceny-theft and motor vehicle theft; n/a not available; (1) Metropolitan Statistical Area - see Appendix A for areas included; (2) calculated by the editors using the following formula: (number of crimes in the MSA minus number of crimes in the city); (3) calculated by the editors using the following formula: ((number of crimes in the MSA minus number of crimes in the city) ÷ (population of the MSA minus population of the city)) x 100,000
Source: U.S. Department of Justice, FBI Uniform Crime Reports, 1977 - 1996

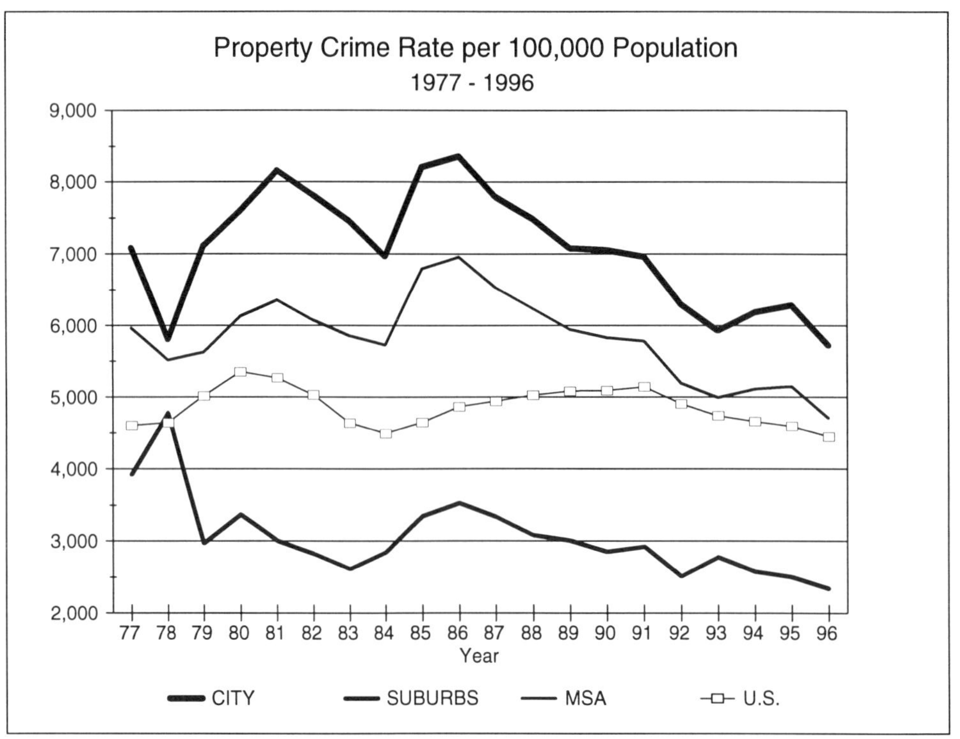

Note: Missing line segments indicate data not available.

Murders and Murder Rates: 1977 - 1996

Year	Number				Rate per 100,000 population			
	City	Suburbs[2]	MSA[1]	U.S.	City	Suburbs[3]	MSA[1]	U.S.
1977	12	4	16	19,120	6.5	4.0	5.6	8.8
1978	10	3	13	19,560	4.7	3.6	4.4	9.0
1979	10	2	12	21,460	5.2	1.8	4.0	9.7
1980	14	6	20	23,040	6.8	5.4	6.3	10.2
1981	18	4	22	22,520	8.4	3.5	6.7	9.8
1982	7	8	15	21,010	3.2	6.8	4.5	9.1
1983	14	5	19	19,310	6.2	4.5	5.6	8.3
1984	12	3	15	18,690	5.0	2.9	4.4	7.9
1985	13	5	18	18,980	5.2	4.9	5.1	7.9
1986	23	2	25	20,610	9.0	1.9	7.0	8.6
1987	15	6	21	20,100	5.5	5.5	5.5	8.3
1988	10	9	19	20,680	3.6	8.2	4.9	8.4
1989	9	5	14	21,500	3.2	4.5	3.5	8.7
1990	9	1	10	23,440	3.2	0.9	2.5	9.4
1991	25	4	29	24,700	8.7	3.4	7.1	9.8
1992	17	4	21	23,760	5.7	3.3	5.0	9.3
1993	19	5	24	24,530	6.2	3.9	5.5	9.5
1994	14	5	19	23,330	4.5	3.8	4.3	9.0
1995	18	6	24	21,610	5.5	4.3	5.2	8.2
1996	12	8	20	19,650	3.6	5.6	4.2	7.4

Notes: (1) Metropolitan Statistical Area - see Appendix A for areas included; (2) calculated by the editors using the following formula: (number of crimes in the MSA minus number of crimes in the city); (3) calculated by the editors using the following formula: ((number of crimes in the MSA minus number of crimes in the city) ÷ (population of the MSA minus population of the city)) x 100,000; n/a not avail.
Source: U.S. Department of Justice, FBI Uniform Crime Reports, 1977 - 1996

Forcible Rapes and Forcible Rape Rates: 1977 - 1996

Year	Number				Rate per 100,000 population			
	City	Suburbs[2]	MSA[1]	U.S.	City	Suburbs[3]	MSA[1]	U.S.
1977	112	48	160	63,500	60.9	47.5	56.1	29.4
1978	133	87	220	67,610	62.7	104.0	74.4	31.0
1979	137	56	193	76,390	70.7	51.5	63.8	34.7
1980	151	39	190	82,990	73.0	35.3	59.8	36.8
1981	158	34	192	82,500	74.2	29.9	58.7	36.0
1982	172	31	203	78,770	78.6	26.5	60.4	34.0
1983	151	44	195	78,920	66.9	39.3	57.8	33.7
1984	169	49	218	84,230	70.4	47.5	63.5	35.7
1985	182	52	234	88,670	72.3	50.5	65.9	37.1
1986	180	67	247	91,460	70.7	64.3	68.8	37.9
1987	167	39	206	91,110	60.7	35.9	53.7	37.4
1988	189	19	208	92,490	67.8	17.2	53.4	37.6
1989	190	26	216	94,500	66.6	23.6	54.6	38.1
1990	201	39	240	102,560	71.5	33.7	60.5	41.2
1991	231	18	249	106,590	80.2	15.2	61.2	42.3
1992	226	27	253	109,060	76.3	22.1	60.5	42.8
1993	265	23	288	106,010	87.0	17.8	66.4	41.1
1994	228	21	249	102,220	73.0	15.9	56.0	39.3
1995	207	22	229	97,470	63.8	15.8	49.4	37.1
1996	238	26	264	95,770	71.9	18.3	55.8	36.1

Notes: (1) Metropolitan Statistical Area - see Appendix A for areas included; (2) calculated by the editors using the following formula: (number of crimes in the MSA minus number of crimes in the city); (3) calculated by the editors using the following formula: ((number of crimes in the MSA minus number of crimes in the city) ÷ (population of the MSA minus population of the city)) x 100,000; n/a not avail.
Source: U.S. Department of Justice, FBI Uniform Crime Reports, 1977 - 1996

Robberies and Robbery Rates: 1977 - 1996

Year	Number				Rate per 100,000 population			
	City	Suburbs[2]	MSA[1]	U.S.	City	Suburbs[3]	MSA[1]	U.S.
1977	355	98	453	412,610	192.9	96.9	158.9	190.7
1978	319	68	387	426,930	150.5	81.3	130.9	195.8
1979	368	37	405	480,700	189.9	34.0	133.9	218.4
1980	405	51	456	565,840	195.7	46.1	143.6	251.1
1981	557	49	606	592,910	261.4	43.0	185.4	258.7
1982	453	42	495	553,130	206.9	35.9	147.3	238.9
1983	446	36	482	506,570	197.6	32.2	142.8	216.5
1984	390	28	418	485,010	162.3	27.2	121.8	205.4
1985	371	33	404	497,870	147.3	32.0	113.8	208.5
1986	596	52	648	542,780	234.1	49.9	180.6	225.1
1987	510	43	553	517,700	185.4	39.6	144.1	212.7
1988	337	25	362	542,970	120.8	22.7	93.0	220.9
1989	348	24	372	578,330	121.9	21.8	94.0	233.0
1990	258	26	284	639,270	91.8	22.4	71.5	257.0
1991	387	29	416	687,730	134.3	24.4	102.2	272.7
1992	448	25	473	672,480	151.3	20.5	113.1	263.6
1993	389	36	425	659,870	127.8	27.9	98.0	255.9
1994	401	27	428	618,950	128.5	20.4	96.3	237.7
1995	416	31	447	580,510	128.2	22.3	96.4	220.9
1996	453	27	480	537,050	136.8	19.0	101.4	202.4

Notes: (1) Metropolitan Statistical Area - see Appendix A for areas included; (2) calculated by the editors using the following formula: (number of crimes in the MSA minus number of crimes in the city); (3) calculated by the editors using the following formula: ((number of crimes in the MSA minus number of crimes in the city) ÷ (population of the MSA minus population of the city)) x 100,000; n/a not avail.
Source: U.S. Department of Justice, FBI Uniform Crime Reports, 1977 - 1996

Aggravated Assaults and Aggravated Assault Rates: 1977 - 1996

Year	Number				Rate per 100,000 population			
	City	Suburbs[2]	MSA[1]	U.S.	City	Suburbs[3]	MSA[1]	U.S.
1977	376	170	546	534,350	204.3	168.1	191.5	247.0
1978	494	243	737	571,460	233.0	290.4	249.2	262.1
1979	577	194	771	629,480	297.7	178.3	254.8	286.0
1980	612	155	767	672,650	295.7	140.1	241.5	298.5
1981	730	214	944	663,900	342.6	188.0	288.8	289.7
1982	708	154	862	669,480	323.3	131.6	256.6	289.2
1983	656	103	759	653,290	290.6	92.1	224.8	279.2
1984	618	115	733	685,350	257.3	111.6	213.5	290.2
1985	603	106	709	723,250	239.4	102.9	199.7	302.9
1986	756	114	870	834,320	296.9	109.5	242.5	346.1
1987	698	187	885	855,090	253.7	172.0	230.6	351.3
1988	757	196	953	910,090	271.4	177.8	244.9	370.2
1989	798	214	1,012	951,710	279.5	194.0	255.7	383.4
1990	716	260	976	1,054,860	254.7	224.4	245.8	424.1
1991	742	283	1,025	1,092,740	257.5	238.3	251.9	433.3
1992	851	265	1,116	1,126,970	287.4	217.1	266.9	441.8
1993	882	344	1,226	1,135,610	289.7	266.6	282.8	440.3
1994	860	328	1,188	1,113,180	275.5	248.0	267.3	427.6
1995	925	306	1,231	1,099,210	285.1	219.6	265.4	418.3
1996	892	292	1,184	1,029,810	269.5	205.4	250.2	388.2

Notes: (1) Metropolitan Statistical Area - see Appendix A for areas included; (2) calculated by the editors using the following formula: (number of crimes in the MSA minus number of crimes in the city); (3) calculated by the editors using the following formula: ((number of crimes in the MSA minus number of crimes in the city) ÷ (population of the MSA minus population of the city)) x 100,000; n/a not avail.
Source: U.S. Department of Justice, FBI Uniform Crime Reports, 1977 - 1996

Burglaries and Burglary Rates: 1977 - 1996

Year	Number				Rate per 100,000 population			
	City	Suburbs[2]	MSA[1]	U.S.	City	Suburbs[3]	MSA[1]	U.S.
1977	4,014	1,321	5,335	3,071,500	2,181.5	1,306.3	1,871.1	1,419.8
1978	3,849	1,420	5,269	3,128,300	1,815.6	1,696.7	1,781.9	1,434.6
1979	4,045	1,074	5,119	3,327,700	2,087.3	987.2	1,691.8	1,511.9
1980	5,067	1,366	6,433	3,795,200	2,448.1	1,235.0	2,025.6	1,684.1
1981	5,634	1,288	6,922	3,779,700	2,644.3	1,131.3	2,117.4	1,649.5
1982	4,938	1,130	6,068	3,447,100	2,255.2	965.8	1,806.1	1,488.8
1983	4,339	935	5,274	3,129,900	1,922.3	835.8	1,562.3	1,337.7
1984	4,426	854	5,280	2,984,400	1,842.4	828.7	1,538.1	1,263.7
1985	6,080	1,012	7,092	3,073,300	2,413.8	982.0	1,998.1	1,287.3
1986	6,361	1,172	7,533	3,241,400	2,498.1	1,125.4	2,099.7	1,344.6
1987	5,925	1,119	7,044	3,236,200	2,153.7	1,029.4	1,835.3	1,329.6
1988	5,010	1,171	6,181	3,218,100	1,796.1	1,062.4	1,588.3	1,309.2
1989	4,300	966	5,266	3,168,200	1,506.2	875.6	1,330.4	1,276.3
1990	4,064	941	5,005	3,073,900	1,445.5	812.1	1,260.7	1,235.9
1991	3,865	1,038	4,903	3,157,200	1,341.1	873.9	1,204.8	1,252.0
1992	3,783	829	4,612	2,979,900	1,277.5	679.3	1,102.9	1,168.2
1993	3,645	852	4,497	2,834,800	1,197.3	660.3	1,037.5	1,099.2
1994	3,033	824	3,857	2,712,800	971.7	622.9	867.9	1,042.0
1995	3,446	798	4,244	2,593,800	1,062.1	572.8	915.1	987.1
1996	3,304	889	4,193	2,501,500	998.1	625.4	886.2	943.0

Notes: (1) Metropolitan Statistical Area - see Appendix A for areas included; (2) calculated by the editors using the following formula: (number of crimes in the MSA minus number of crimes in the city); (3) calculated by the editors using the following formula: ((number of crimes in the MSA minus number of crimes in the city) ÷ (population of the MSA minus population of the city)) x 100,000; n/a not avail.
Source: U.S. Department of Justice, FBI Uniform Crime Reports, 1977 - 1996

Larceny-Thefts and Larceny-Theft Rates: 1977 - 1996

Year	Number				Rate per 100,000 population			
	City	Suburbs[2]	MSA[1]	U.S.	City	Suburbs[3]	MSA[1]	U.S.
1977	8,195	2,419	10,614	5,905,700	4,453.8	2,392.1	3,722.6	2,729.9
1978	7,682	2,350	10,032	5,991,000	3,623.6	2,808.0	3,392.7	2,747.4
1979	8,790	2,027	10,817	6,601,000	4,535.9	1,863.3	3,575.0	2,999.1
1980	9,713	2,177	11,890	7,136,900	4,692.7	1,968.3	3,743.9	3,167.0
1981	10,851	1,996	12,847	7,194,400	5,092.9	1,753.1	3,929.7	3,139.7
1982	11,224	2,034	13,258	7,142,500	5,126.1	1,738.4	3,946.2	3,084.8
1983	11,550	1,870	13,420	6,712,800	5,117.0	1,671.6	3,975.2	2,868.9
1984	11,378	1,947	13,325	6,591,900	4,736.4	1,889.3	3,881.6	2,791.3
1985	13,507	2,247	15,754	6,926,400	5,362.3	2,180.3	4,438.4	2,901.2
1986	13,749	2,299	16,048	7,257,200	5,399.6	2,207.5	4,473.0	3,010.3
1987	13,878	2,301	16,179	7,499,900	5,044.6	2,116.7	4,215.3	3,081.3
1988	14,222	2,010	16,232	7,705,900	5,098.5	1,823.6	4,171.0	3,134.9
1989	14,298	2,126	16,424	7,872,400	5,008.4	1,927.0	4,149.5	3,171.3
1990	14,614	2,202	16,816	7,945,700	5,198.1	1,900.3	4,235.6	3,194.8
1991	15,000	2,256	17,256	8,142,200	5,204.9	1,899.4	4,240.2	3,228.8
1992	13,791	2,094	15,885	7,915,200	4,657.2	1,715.8	3,798.7	3,103.0
1993	13,391	2,555	15,946	7,820,900	4,398.6	1,980.3	3,678.8	3,032.4
1994	15,185	2,412	17,597	7,879,800	4,865.1	1,823.4	3,959.7	3,026.7
1995	15,549	2,446	17,995	7,997,700	4,792.6	1,755.6	3,880.2	3,043.8
1996	14,248	2,195	16,443	7,894,600	4,304.3	1,544.2	3,475.1	2,975.9

Notes: (1) Metropolitan Statistical Area - see Appendix A for areas included; (2) calculated by the editors using the following formula: (number of crimes in the MSA minus number of crimes in the city); (3) calculated by the editors using the following formula: ((number of crimes in the MSA minus number of crimes in the city) ÷ (population of the MSA minus population of the city)) x 100,000; n/a not avail.
Source: U.S. Department of Justice, FBI Uniform Crime Reports, 1977 - 1996

Motor Vehicle Thefts and Motor Vehicle Theft Rates: 1977 - 1996

Year	Number				Rate per 100,000 population			
	City	Suburbs[2]	MSA[1]	U.S.	City	Suburbs[3]	MSA[1]	U.S.
1977	818	231	1,049	977,700	444.6	228.4	367.9	451.9
1978	772	231	1,003	1,004,100	364.2	276.0	339.2	460.5
1979	944	128	1,072	1,112,800	487.1	117.7	354.3	505.6
1980	948	179	1,127	1,131,700	458.0	161.8	354.9	502.2
1981	888	131	1,019	1,087,800	416.8	115.1	311.7	474.7
1982	952	140	1,092	1,062,400	434.8	119.7	325.0	458.8
1983	941	121	1,062	1,007,900	416.9	108.2	314.6	430.8
1984	924	127	1,051	1,032,200	384.6	123.2	306.2	437.1
1985	1,079	188	1,267	1,102,900	428.4	182.4	357.0	462.0
1986	1,168	204	1,372	1,224,100	458.7	195.9	382.4	507.8
1987	1,633	208	1,841	1,288,700	593.6	191.3	479.7	529.4
1988	1,649	212	1,861	1,432,900	591.2	192.3	478.2	582.9
1989	1,610	221	1,831	1,564,800	564.0	200.3	462.6	630.4
1990	1,155	161	1,316	1,635,900	410.8	138.9	331.5	657.8
1991	1,194	171	1,365	1,661,700	414.3	144.0	335.4	659.0
1992	1,078	135	1,213	1,610,800	364.0	110.6	290.1	631.5
1993	1,017	170	1,187	1,563,100	334.1	131.8	273.8	606.1
1994	1,090	175	1,265	1,539,300	349.2	132.3	284.7	591.3
1995	1,388	242	1,630	1,472,400	427.8	173.7	351.5	560.4
1996	1,376	244	1,620	1,395,200	415.7	171.7	342.4	525.9

Notes: (1) Metropolitan Statistical Area - see Appendix A for areas included; (2) calculated by the editors using the following formula: (number of crimes in the MSA minus number of crimes in the city); (3) calculated by the editors using the following formula: ((number of crimes in the MSA minus number of crimes in the city) ÷ (population of the MSA minus population of the city)) x 100,000; n/a not avail.
Source: U.S. Department of Justice, FBI Uniform Crime Reports, 1977 - 1996

HATE CRIMES

Criminal Incidents by Bias Motivation

Area	Race	Ethnicity	Religion	Sexual Orientation
Colorado Springs	9	3	0	2

Notes: Figures include both violent and property crimes. Law enforcement agencies must have submitted data for at least one quarter of calendar year 1995 to be included in this report, therefore figures shown may not represent complete 12-month totals; n/a not available
Source: U.S. Department of Justice, FBI Uniform Crime Reports, Hate Crime Statistics 1995

LAW ENFORCEMENT

Full-Time Law Enforcement Employees

Jurisdiction	Police Employees			Police Officers per 100,000 population
	Total	Officers	Civilians	
Colorado Springs	720	498	222	150.4

Notes: Data as of October 31, 1996
Source: U.S. Department of Justice, FBI Uniform Crime Reports, 1996

CORRECTIONS

Federal Correctional Facilities

Type	Year Opened	Security Level	Sex of Inmates	Rated Capacity	Population on 7/1/95	Number of Staff
None listed						

Notes: Data as of 1995
Source: Bureau of Justice Statistics, Sourcebook of Criminal Justice Statistics Online

City/County/Regional Correctional Facilities

Name	Year Opened	Year Renov.	Rated Capacity	1995 Pop.	Number of COs[1]	Number of Staff	ACA[2] Accred.
El Paso County Criminal Justice Ctr	1988	--	408	n/a	n/a	n/a	No

Notes: Data as of April 1996; (1) Correctional Officers; (2) American Correctional Assn. Accreditation
Source: American Correctional Association, 1996-1998 National Jail and Adult Detention Directory

Private Adult Correctional Facilities

Name	Date Opened	Rated Capacity	Present Pop.	Security Level	Facility Construct.	Expans. Plans	ACA[1] Accred.
None listed							

Notes: Data as of December 1996; (1) American Correctional Association Accreditation
Source: University of Florida, Center for Studies in Criminology and Law, Private Adult Correctional Facility Census, 10th Ed., March 15, 1997

Characteristics of Shock Incarceration Programs

Jurisdiction	Year Program Began	Number of Camps	Average Num. of Inmates	Number of Beds	Program Length	Voluntary/ Mandatory
Colorado	1991	1	110	100	90 to 120 days	Voluntary

Note: Data as of July 1996;
Source: Sourcebook of Criminal Justice Statistics Online

DEATH PENALTY

Death Penalty Statistics

State	Prisoners Executed		Prisoners Under Sentence of Death					Avg. No. of Years on Death Row[4]
	1930-1995	1996[1]	Total[2]	White[3]	Black[3]	Hisp.	Women	
Colorado	47	0	4	3	1	1	0	n/c

Notes: Data as of 12/31/95 unless otherwise noted; n/c not calculated on fewer than 10 inmates; (1) Data as of 7/31/97; (2) Includes persons of other races; (3) Includes people of Hispanic origin; (4) Covers prisoners sentenced 1974 through 1995
Source: Bureau of Justice Statistics, Capital Punishment 1995 (released 12/96); Death Penalty Information Center Web Site, 9/30/97

Capital Offenses and Methods of Execution

Capital Offenses in Colorado	Minimum Age for Imposition of Death Penalty	Mentally Retarded Excluded	Methods of Execution[1]
First-degree murder with at least 1 of 13 aggravating factors; treason.	18	Yes	Lethal injection

Notes: Data as of 12/31/95 unless otherwise noted; (1) Data as of 7/31/97
Source: Bureau of Justice Statistics, Capital Punishment 1995 (released 12/96); Death Penalty Information Center Web Site, 9/30/97

LAWS

Statutory Provisions Relating to the Purchase, Ownership and Use of Handguns

Jurisdiction	Instant Background Check	Federal Waiting Period Applies[1]	State Waiting Period (days)	License or Permit to Purchase	Regis-tration	Record of Sale Sent to Police	Concealed Carry Law
Colorado	Yes	No	No	No	No	No	Yes[a]

Note: Data as of 1996; (1) The Federal 5-day waiting period for handgun purchases applies to states that don't have instant background checks, waiting period requirements, or licensing procedures exempting them from the Federal requirement; (a) Restrictively administered discretion by local authorities over permit issuance, or permits are unavailable and carrying is prohibited in most circumstances
Source: Sourcebook of Criminal Justice Statistics Online

Statutory Provisions Relating to Alcohol Use and Driving

Jurisdiction	Drinking Age	Blood Alcohol Concentration Levels as Evidence in State Courts[1]		Open Container Law[1]	Anti-Consump-tion Law[1]	Dram Shop Law[1]
		Illegal per se at 0.10%	Presumption at 0.10%			
Colorado	21	Yes	(a)	No	Yes	Yes

Note: Data as of January 1, 1997; (1) See Appendix C for an explanation of terms; (a) Presumption of driving while impaired at 0.05%; presumption of driving while under the influence at 0.10%
Source: Sourcebook of Criminal Justice Statistics Online

Statutory Provisions Relating to Curfews

Jurisdiction	Year Enacted	Latest Revision	Age Group(s)	Curfew Provisions
Colorado Springs	1992	-	17 and under	10 pm to 6 am weekday nights midnight to 6 am weekend nights

Note: Data as of February 1996
Source: Sourcebook of Criminal Justice Statistics Online

Statutory Provisions Relating to Hate Crimes

Jurisdiction	Bias-Motivated Violence and Intimidation						Institutional Vandalism
		Criminal Penalty					
	Civil Action	Race/ Religion/ Ethnicity	Sexual Orientation	Mental/ Physical Disability	Gender	Age	
Colorado	Yes	Yes	No	No	No	No	Yes

Source: Anti-Defamation League, 1997 Hate Crimes Laws

Columbus, Ohio

OVERVIEW

The total crime rate for the city increased 17.4% between 1977 and 1996. During that same period, the violent crime rate increased 59.5% and the property crime rate increased 14.0%.

Among violent crimes, the rates for: Murders increased 6.9%; Forcible Rapes increased 43.4%; Robberies increased 57.4%; and Aggravated Assaults increased 71.2%.

Among property crimes, the rates for: Burglaries decreased 14.7%; Larceny-Thefts increased 20.3%; and Motor Vehicle Thefts increased 72.3%.

ANTI-CRIME PROGRAMS

The Community Liaison Section under the Strategic Response Bureau of the Division of Police works directly with neighborhood groups, associations, organizations, and individuals to solve community problems. Programs which have been supported: Neighborhood Watch, Crime Prevention Through Environmental Design, Eddie Eagle Gun Safety for Adults and/or Children, "Stranger Danger", the Ameritech Safe & Smart program, Cellular Blockwatch/Patrol, etc. *Community Liaison Section, Division of Police, 5/97*

CRIME RISK

Your Chances of Becoming a Victim[1]

Area	Any Crime	Violent Crime					Property Crime			
		Any	Murder	Forcible Rape[2]	Robbery	Aggrav. Assault	Any	Burglary	Larceny -Theft	Motor Vehicle Theft
City	1:10	1:103	1:7,194	1:581	1:193	1:286	1:12	1:49	1:19	1:84

Note: (1) Figures have been calculated by dividing the population of the city by the number of crimes reported to the FBI during 1996 and are expressed as odds (eg. 1:20 should be read as 1 in 20).
(2) Figures have been calculated by dividing the female population of the city by the number of forcible rapes reported to the FBI during 1996. The female population of the city was estimated by calculating the ratio of females to males reported in the 1990 Census and applying that ratio to 1996 population estimate.
Source: FBI Uniform Crime Reports 1996

CRIME STATISTICS

Total Crimes and Total Crime Rates: 1977 - 1996

Year	Number				Rate per 100,000 population			
	City	Suburbs[2]	MSA[1]	U.S.	City	Suburbs[3]	MSA[1]	U.S.
1977	43,229	19,374	62,603	10,984,500	8,125.8	3,941.6	6,116.4	5,077.6
1978	44,840	20,568	65,408	11,209,000	8,557.3	3,539.0	5,918.3	5,140.3
1979	50,605	24,437	75,042	12,249,500	9,475.7	4,410.6	6,896.6	5,565.5
1980	55,362	26,760	82,122	13,408,300	9,843.6	5,082.3	7,541.4	5,950.0
1981	55,293	25,650	80,943	13,423,800	9,823.0	4,867.3	7,426.8	5,858.2
1982	49,286	23,118	72,404	12,974,400	8,743.6	4,380.7	6,634.1	5,603.6
1983	43,619	24,501	68,120	12,108,600	7,770.7	3,631.6	5,511.4	5,175.0
1984	45,613	25,547	71,160	11,881,800	8,021.9	3,682.8	5,637.4	5,031.3
1985	43,374	25,561	68,935	12,431,400	7,667.6	3,588.3	5,393.9	5,207.1
1986	46,552	28,115	74,667	13,211,900	8,223.1	3,943.7	5,837.8	5,480.4
1987	51,941	29,277	81,218	13,508,700	9,147.8	4,094.6	6,331.2	5,550.0
1988	56,769	32,213	88,982	13,923,100	9,647.6	4,338.3	6,685.6	5,664.2
1989	59,491	31,115	90,606	14,251,400	10,394.3	3,997.3	6,707.9	5,741.0
1990	62,703	31,415	94,118	14,475,600	9,907.1	4,219.6	6,832.9	5,820.3
1991	64,778	32,258	97,036	14,872,900	10,144.8	4,296.5	6,984.4	5,897.8
1992	58,221	29,697	87,918	14,438,200	9,054.2	4,111.7	6,439.6	5,660.2
1993	56,322	27,940	84,262	14,144,800	8,706.0	3,703.4	6,012.8	5,484.4
1994	56,343	27,498	83,841	13,989,500	8,696.8	3,641.3	5,975.7	5,373.5
1995	58,715	29,303	88,018	13,862,700	9,192.5	3,713.8	6,164.8	5,275.9
1996	61,083	29,526	90,609	13,473,600	9,539.8	3,734.8	6,332.5	5,078.9

Notes: (1) Metropolitan Statistical Area - see Appendix A for areas included; (2) calculated by the editors using the following formula: (number of crimes in the MSA minus number of crimes in the city); (3) calculated by the editors using the following formula: ((number of crimes in the MSA minus number of crimes in the city) ÷ (population of the MSA minus population of the city)) x 100,000; n/a not avail.
Source: U.S. Department of Justice, FBI Uniform Crime Reports, 1977 - 1996

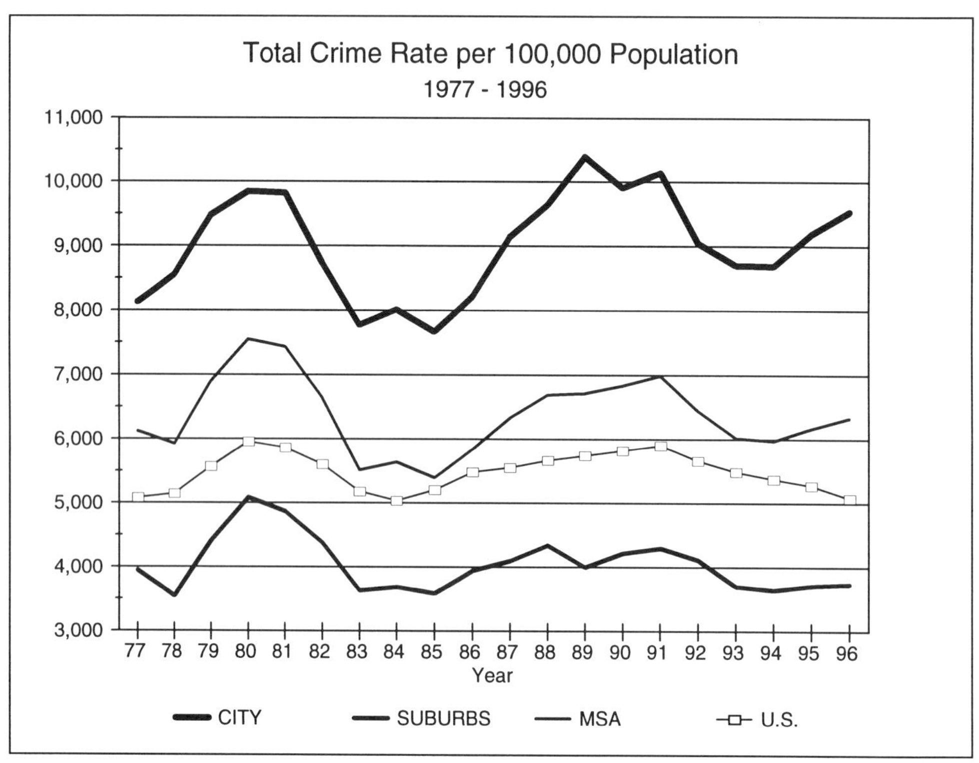

Note: Missing line segments indicate data not available.

Violent Crimes and Violent Crime Rates: 1977 - 1996

Year	Number				Rate per 100,000 population			
	City	Suburbs[2]	MSA[1]	U.S.	City	Suburbs[3]	MSA[1]	U.S.
1977	3,238	995	4,233	1,029,580	608.6	202.4	413.6	475.9
1978	3,354	1,042	4,396	1,085,550	640.1	179.3	397.8	497.8
1979	4,242	1,341	5,583	1,208,030	794.3	242.0	513.1	548.9
1980	5,130	1,691	6,821	1,344,520	912.1	321.2	626.4	596.6
1981	5,263	1,755	7,018	1,361,820	935.0	333.0	643.9	594.3
1982	4,337	1,728	6,065	1,322,390	769.4	327.4	555.7	571.1
1983	4,197	1,631	5,828	1,258,090	747.7	241.8	471.5	537.7
1984	4,352	1,778	6,130	1,273,280	765.4	256.3	485.6	539.2
1985	4,392	2,070	6,462	1,328,800	776.4	290.6	505.6	556.6
1986	5,148	2,260	7,408	1,489,170	909.4	317.0	579.2	617.7
1987	5,381	2,211	7,592	1,484,000	947.7	309.2	591.8	609.7
1988	5,802	2,504	8,306	1,566,220	986.0	337.2	624.1	637.2
1989	5,986	2,669	8,655	1,646,040	1,045.9	342.9	640.8	663.1
1990	7,022	1,896	8,918	1,820,130	1,109.5	254.7	647.4	731.8
1991	7,221	2,793	10,014	1,911,770	1,130.9	372.0	720.8	758.1
1992	7,029	2,481	9,510	1,932,270	1,093.1	343.5	696.6	757.5
1993	7,146	2,415	9,561	1,926,020	1,104.6	320.1	682.3	746.8
1994	6,761	2,348	9,109	1,857,670	1,043.6	310.9	649.2	713.6
1995	6,624	2,963	9,587	1,798,790	1,037.1	375.5	671.5	684.6
1996	6,216	2,077	8,293	1,682,280	970.8	262.7	579.6	634.1

Notes: Violent crimes include murder, forcible rape, robbery and aggravated assault; n/a not available; (1) Metropolitan Statistical Area - see Appendix A for areas included; (2) calculated by the editors using the following formula: (number of crimes in the MSA minus number of crimes in the city); (3) calculated by the editors using the following formula: ((number of crimes in the MSA minus number of crimes in the city) ÷ (population of the MSA minus population of the city)) x 100,000
Source: U.S. Department of Justice, FBI Uniform Crime Reports, 1977 - 1996

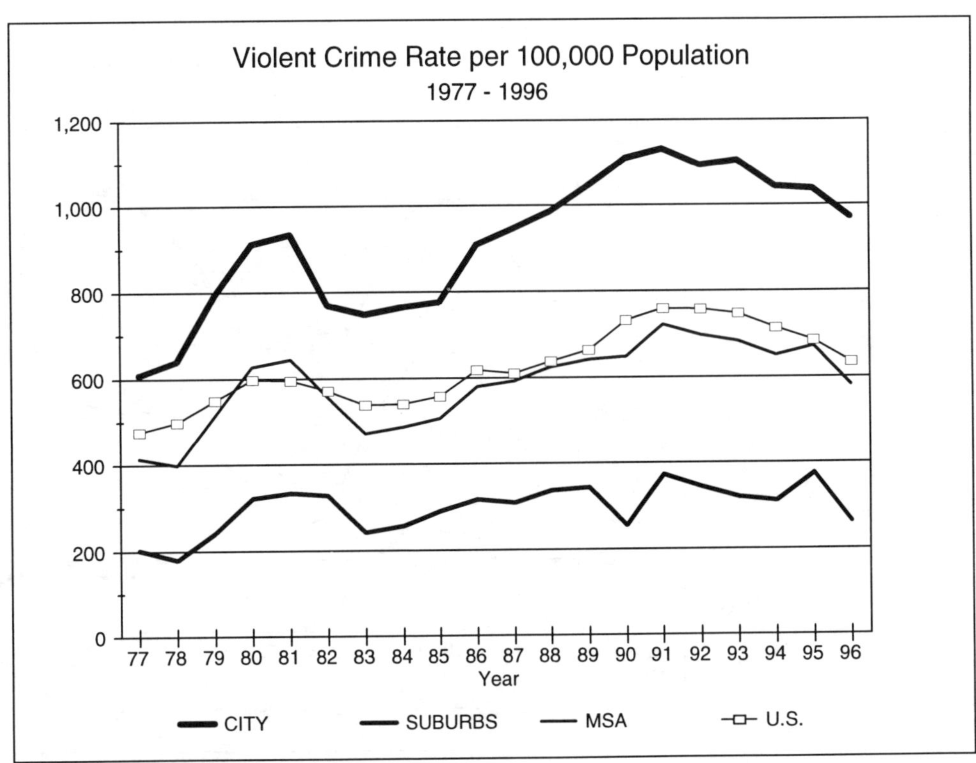

Note: Missing line segments indicate data not available.

Property Crimes and Property Crime Rates: 1977 - 1996

Year	Number				Rate per 100,000 population			
	City	Suburbs[2]	MSA[1]	U.S.	City	Suburbs[3]	MSA[1]	U.S.
1977	39,991	18,379	58,370	9,955,000	7,517.1	3,739.2	5,702.9	4,601.7
1978	41,486	19,526	61,012	10,123,400	7,917.2	3,359.7	5,520.6	4,642.5
1979	46,363	23,096	69,459	11,041,500	8,681.4	4,168.6	6,383.5	5,016.6
1980	50,232	25,069	75,301	12,063,700	8,931.5	4,761.1	6,915.0	5,353.3
1981	50,030	23,895	73,925	12,061,900	8,888.0	4,534.3	6,782.8	5,263.9
1982	44,949	21,390	66,339	11,652,000	7,974.2	4,053.3	6,078.4	5,032.5
1983	39,422	22,870	62,292	10,850,500	7,023.0	3,389.9	5,039.9	4,637.4
1984	41,261	23,769	65,030	10,608,500	7,256.5	3,426.5	5,151.8	4,492.1
1985	38,982	23,491	62,473	11,102,600	6,891.2	3,297.7	4,888.2	4,650.5
1986	41,404	25,855	67,259	11,722,700	7,313.7	3,626.7	5,258.6	4,862.6
1987	46,560	27,066	73,626	12,024,700	8,200.1	3,785.3	5,739.4	4,940.3
1988	50,967	29,709	80,676	12,356,900	8,661.6	4,001.1	6,061.5	5,027.1
1989	53,505	28,446	81,951	12,605,400	9,348.4	3,654.4	6,067.1	5,077.9
1990	55,681	29,519	85,200	12,655,500	8,797.6	3,964.9	6,185.5	5,088.5
1991	57,557	29,465	87,022	12,961,100	9,013.9	3,924.5	6,263.6	5,139.7
1992	51,192	27,216	78,408	12,505,900	7,961.1	3,768.2	5,743.0	4,902.7
1993	49,176	25,525	74,701	12,218,800	7,601.4	3,383.3	5,330.5	4,737.6
1994	49,582	25,150	74,732	12,131,900	7,653.2	3,330.3	5,326.4	4,660.0
1995	52,091	26,340	78,431	12,063,900	8,155.4	3,338.3	5,493.3	4,591.3
1996	54,867	27,449	82,316	11,791,300	8,569.0	3,472.1	5,752.9	4,444.8

Notes: Property crimes include burglary, larceny-theft and motor vehicle theft; n/a not available; (1) Metropolitan Statistical Area - see Appendix A for areas included; (2) calculated by the editors using the following formula: (number of crimes in the MSA minus number of crimes in the city); (3) calculated by the editors using the following formula: ((number of crimes in the MSA minus number of crimes in the city) ÷ (population of the MSA minus population of the city)) x 100,000
Source: U.S. Department of Justice, FBI Uniform Crime Reports, 1977 - 1996

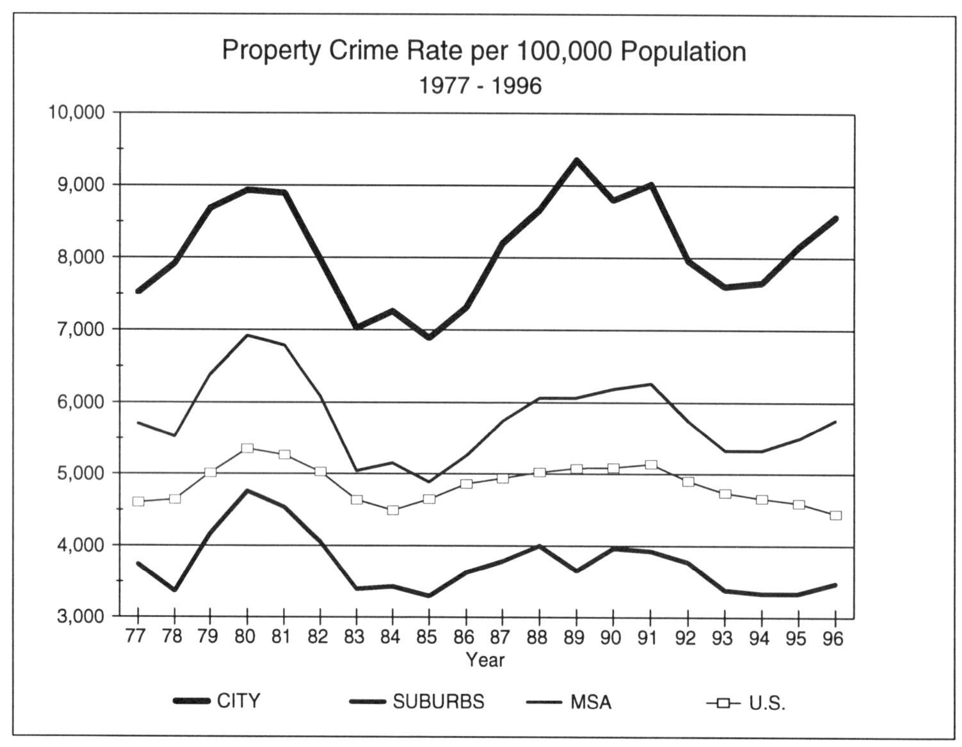

Note: Missing line segments indicate data not available.

Murders and Murder Rates: 1977 - 1996

Year	Number				Rate per 100,000 population			
	City	Suburbs[2]	MSA[1]	U.S.	City	Suburbs[3]	MSA[1]	U.S.
1977	69	5	74	19,120	13.0	1.0	7.2	8.8
1978	68	17	85	19,560	13.0	2.9	7.7	9.0
1979	69	22	91	21,460	12.9	4.0	8.4	9.7
1980	87	21	108	23,040	15.5	4.0	9.9	10.2
1981	91	20	111	22,520	16.2	3.8	10.2	9.8
1982	92	8	100	21,010	16.3	1.5	9.2	9.1
1983	74	18	92	19,310	13.2	2.7	7.4	8.3
1984	62	14	76	18,690	10.9	2.0	6.0	7.9
1985	72	10	82	18,980	12.7	1.4	6.4	7.9
1986	78	24	102	20,610	13.8	3.4	8.0	8.6
1987	85	18	103	20,100	15.0	2.5	8.0	8.3
1988	69	13	82	20,680	11.7	1.8	6.2	8.4
1989	90	21	111	21,500	15.7	2.7	8.2	8.7
1990	89	21	110	23,440	14.1	2.8	8.0	9.4
1991	138	11	149	24,700	21.6	1.5	10.7	9.8
1992	113	17	130	23,760	17.6	2.4	9.5	9.3
1993	105	12	117	24,530	16.2	1.6	8.3	9.5
1994	100	13	113	23,330	15.4	1.7	8.1	9.0
1995	77	16	93	21,610	12.1	2.0	6.5	8.2
1996	89	16	105	19,650	13.9	2.0	7.3	7.4

Notes: (1) Metropolitan Statistical Area - see Appendix A for areas included; (2) calculated by the editors using the following formula: (number of crimes in the MSA minus number of crimes in the city); (3) calculated by the editors using the following formula: ((number of crimes in the MSA minus number of crimes in the city) ÷ (population of the MSA minus population of the city)) x 100,000; n/a not avail.
Source: U.S. Department of Justice, FBI Uniform Crime Reports, 1977 - 1996

Forcible Rapes and Forcible Rape Rates: 1977 - 1996

Year	Number				Rate per 100,000 population			
	City	Suburbs[2]	MSA[1]	U.S.	City	Suburbs[3]	MSA[1]	U.S.
1977	331	72	403	63,500	62.2	14.6	39.4	29.4
1978	309	92	401	67,610	59.0	15.8	36.3	31.0
1979	423	107	530	76,390	79.2	19.3	48.7	34.7
1980	460	134	594	82,990	81.8	25.4	54.5	36.8
1981	396	138	534	82,500	70.4	26.2	49.0	36.0
1982	332	123	455	78,770	58.9	23.3	41.7	34.0
1983	324	129	453	78,920	57.7	19.1	36.7	33.7
1984	394	156	550	84,230	69.3	22.5	43.6	35.7
1985	406	159	565	88,670	71.8	22.3	44.2	37.1
1986	550	200	750	91,460	97.2	28.1	58.6	37.9
1987	534	205	739	91,110	94.0	28.7	57.6	37.4
1988	594	236	830	92,490	100.9	31.8	62.4	37.6
1989	543	218	761	94,500	94.9	28.0	56.3	38.1
1990	647	188	835	102,560	102.2	25.3	60.6	41.2
1991	650	280	930	106,590	101.8	37.3	66.9	42.3
1992	684	286	970	109,060	106.4	39.6	71.0	42.8
1993	658	229	887	106,010	101.7	30.4	63.3	41.1
1994	679	235	914	102,220	104.8	31.1	65.1	39.3
1995	636	248	884	97,470	99.6	31.4	61.9	37.1
1996	571	229	800	95,770	89.2	29.0	55.9	36.1

Notes: (1) Metropolitan Statistical Area - see Appendix A for areas included; (2) calculated by the editors using the following formula: (number of crimes in the MSA minus number of crimes in the city); (3) calculated by the editors using the following formula: ((number of crimes in the MSA minus number of crimes in the city) ÷ (population of the MSA minus population of the city)) x 100,000; n/a not avail.
Source: U.S. Department of Justice, FBI Uniform Crime Reports, 1977 - 1996

Robberies and Robbery Rates: 1977 - 1996

Year	Number				Rate per 100,000 population			
	City	Suburbs[2]	MSA[1]	U.S.	City	Suburbs[3]	MSA[1]	U.S.
1977	1,752	331	2,083	412,610	329.3	67.3	203.5	190.7
1978	1,923	385	2,308	426,930	367.0	66.2	208.8	195.8
1979	2,445	537	2,982	480,700	457.8	96.9	274.1	218.4
1980	3,224	720	3,944	565,840	573.2	136.7	362.2	251.1
1981	3,356	671	4,027	592,910	596.2	127.3	369.5	258.7
1982	2,507	450	2,957	553,130	444.8	85.3	270.9	238.9
1983	2,407	499	2,906	506,570	428.8	74.0	235.1	216.5
1984	2,298	457	2,755	485,010	404.1	65.9	218.3	205.4
1985	2,144	442	2,586	497,870	379.0	62.0	202.3	208.5
1986	2,255	484	2,739	542,780	398.3	67.9	214.1	225.1
1987	2,864	534	3,398	517,700	504.4	74.7	264.9	212.7
1988	3,028	698	3,726	542,970	514.6	94.0	280.0	220.9
1989	3,127	659	3,786	578,330	546.4	84.7	280.3	233.0
1990	3,541	672	4,213	639,270	559.5	90.3	305.9	257.0
1991	3,747	765	4,512	687,730	586.8	101.9	324.8	272.7
1992	3,585	706	4,291	672,480	557.5	97.7	314.3	263.6
1993	3,887	571	4,458	659,870	600.8	75.7	318.1	255.9
1994	3,599	587	4,186	618,950	555.5	77.7	298.4	237.7
1995	3,329	636	3,965	580,510	521.2	80.6	277.7	220.9
1996	3,318	595	3,913	537,050	518.2	75.3	273.5	202.4

Notes: (1) Metropolitan Statistical Area - see Appendix A for areas included; (2) calculated by the editors using the following formula: (number of crimes in the MSA minus number of crimes in the city); (3) calculated by the editors using the following formula: ((number of crimes in the MSA minus number of crimes in the city) ÷ (population of the MSA minus population of the city)) x 100,000; n/a not avail.
Source: U.S. Department of Justice, FBI Uniform Crime Reports, 1977 - 1996

Aggravated Assaults and Aggravated Assault Rates: 1977 - 1996

Year	Number				Rate per 100,000 population			
	City	Suburbs[2]	MSA[1]	U.S.	City	Suburbs[3]	MSA[1]	U.S.
1977	1,086	587	1,673	534,350	204.1	119.4	163.5	247.0
1978	1,054	548	1,602	571,460	201.1	94.3	145.0	262.1
1979	1,305	675	1,980	629,480	244.4	121.8	182.0	286.0
1980	1,359	816	2,175	672,650	241.6	155.0	199.7	298.5
1981	1,420	926	2,346	663,900	252.3	175.7	215.3	289.7
1982	1,406	1,147	2,553	669,480	249.4	217.4	233.9	289.2
1983	1,392	985	2,377	653,290	248.0	146.0	192.3	279.2
1984	1,598	1,151	2,749	685,350	281.0	165.9	217.8	290.2
1985	1,770	1,459	3,229	723,250	312.9	204.8	252.7	302.9
1986	2,265	1,552	3,817	834,320	400.1	217.7	298.4	346.1
1987	1,898	1,454	3,352	855,090	334.3	203.4	261.3	351.3
1988	2,111	1,557	3,668	910,090	358.8	209.7	275.6	370.2
1989	2,226	1,771	3,997	951,710	388.9	227.5	295.9	383.4
1990	2,745	1,015	3,760	1,054,860	433.7	136.3	273.0	424.1
1991	2,686	1,737	4,423	1,092,740	420.7	231.4	318.4	433.3
1992	2,647	1,472	4,119	1,126,970	411.6	203.8	301.7	441.8
1993	2,496	1,603	4,099	1,135,610	385.8	212.5	292.5	440.3
1994	2,383	1,513	3,896	1,113,180	367.8	200.4	277.7	427.6
1995	2,582	2,063	4,645	1,099,210	404.2	261.5	325.3	418.3
1996	2,238	1,237	3,475	1,029,810	349.5	156.5	242.9	388.2

Notes: (1) Metropolitan Statistical Area - see Appendix A for areas included; (2) calculated by the editors using the following formula: (number of crimes in the MSA minus number of crimes in the city); (3) calculated by the editors using the following formula: ((number of crimes in the MSA minus number of crimes in the city) ÷ (population of the MSA minus population of the city)) x 100,000; n/a not avail.
Source: U.S. Department of Justice, FBI Uniform Crime Reports, 1977 - 1996

Burglaries and Burglary Rates: 1977 - 1996

Year	Number				Rate per 100,000 population			
	City	Suburbs[2]	MSA[1]	U.S.	City	Suburbs[3]	MSA[1]	U.S.
1977	12,681	4,508	17,189	3,071,500	2,383.6	917.2	1,679.4	1,419.8
1978	13,869	4,586	18,455	3,128,300	2,646.8	789.1	1,669.9	1,434.6
1979	15,015	5,544	20,559	3,327,700	2,811.5	1,000.6	1,889.4	1,511.9
1980	17,100	6,333	23,433	3,795,200	3,040.5	1,202.8	2,151.9	1,684.1
1981	17,518	6,184	23,702	3,779,700	3,112.1	1,173.5	2,174.7	1,649.5
1982	14,918	5,390	20,308	3,447,100	2,646.5	1,021.4	1,860.7	1,488.8
1983	12,918	5,844	18,762	3,129,900	2,301.3	866.2	1,518.0	1,337.7
1984	12,943	5,785	18,728	2,984,400	2,276.3	834.0	1,483.7	1,263.7
1985	11,101	5,334	16,435	3,073,300	1,962.4	748.8	1,286.0	1,287.3
1986	12,121	5,760	17,881	3,241,400	2,141.1	808.0	1,398.0	1,344.6
1987	14,218	5,995	20,213	3,236,200	2,504.1	838.4	1,575.7	1,329.6
1988	15,483	6,224	21,707	3,218,100	2,631.2	838.2	1,630.9	1,309.2
1989	14,982	6,245	21,227	3,168,200	2,617.7	802.3	1,571.5	1,276.3
1990	14,828	6,001	20,829	3,073,900	2,342.8	806.0	1,512.2	1,235.9
1991	16,398	6,075	22,473	3,157,200	2,568.1	809.1	1,617.5	1,252.0
1992	15,020	5,345	20,365	2,979,900	2,335.8	740.0	1,491.6	1,168.2
1993	13,055	5,072	18,127	2,834,800	2,018.0	672.3	1,293.5	1,099.2
1994	13,086	4,614	17,700	2,712,800	2,019.9	611.0	1,261.5	1,042.0
1995	13,146	5,030	18,176	2,593,800	2,058.1	637.5	1,273.0	987.1
1996	13,013	5,508	18,521	2,501,500	2,032.3	696.7	1,294.4	943.0

Notes: (1) Metropolitan Statistical Area - see Appendix A for areas included; (2) calculated by the editors using the following formula: (number of crimes in the MSA minus number of crimes in the city); (3) calculated by the editors using the following formula: ((number of crimes in the MSA minus number of crimes in the city) ÷ (population of the MSA minus population of the city)) x 100,000; n/a not avail.
Source: U.S. Department of Justice, FBI Uniform Crime Reports, 1977 - 1996

Larceny-Thefts and Larceny-Theft Rates: 1977 - 1996

Year	Number				Rate per 100,000 population			
	City	Suburbs[2]	MSA[1]	U.S.	City	Suburbs[3]	MSA[1]	U.S.
1977	23,641	12,846	36,487	5,905,700	4,443.8	2,613.5	3,564.8	2,729.9
1978	23,946	13,842	37,788	5,991,000	4,569.8	2,381.7	3,419.2	2,747.4
1979	27,538	16,233	43,771	6,601,000	5,156.4	2,929.9	4,022.7	2,999.1
1980	29,809	17,479	47,288	7,136,900	5,300.2	3,319.6	4,342.5	3,167.0
1981	29,613	16,766	46,379	7,194,400	5,260.8	3,181.5	4,255.4	3,139.7
1982	27,432	15,137	42,569	7,142,500	4,866.6	2,868.4	3,900.4	3,084.8
1983	24,014	16,015	40,029	6,712,800	4,278.1	2,373.8	3,238.6	2,868.9
1984	25,653	16,847	42,500	6,591,900	4,511.5	2,428.7	3,366.9	2,791.3
1985	25,087	16,880	41,967	6,926,400	4,434.8	2,369.6	3,283.7	2,901.2
1986	26,491	18,680	45,171	7,257,200	4,679.4	2,620.3	3,531.7	3,010.3
1987	28,786	19,577	48,363	7,499,900	5,069.7	2,738.0	3,770.0	3,081.3
1988	29,742	21,858	51,600	7,705,900	5,054.5	2,943.8	3,876.9	3,134.9
1989	31,541	20,464	52,005	7,872,400	5,510.9	2,629.0	3,850.1	3,171.3
1990	32,387	21,554	53,941	7,945,700	5,117.2	2,895.1	3,916.1	3,194.8
1991	32,983	21,460	54,443	8,142,200	5,165.4	2,858.3	3,918.7	3,228.8
1992	29,210	20,110	49,320	7,915,200	4,542.6	2,784.4	3,612.4	3,103.0
1993	29,051	18,945	47,996	7,820,900	4,490.6	2,511.1	3,424.9	3,032.4
1994	29,776	18,881	48,657	7,879,800	4,596.1	2,500.2	3,468.0	3,026.7
1995	31,905	19,565	51,470	7,997,700	4,995.1	2,479.6	3,605.0	3,043.8
1996	34,244	20,187	54,431	7,894,600	5,348.1	2,553.5	3,804.1	2,975.9

Notes: (1) Metropolitan Statistical Area - see Appendix A for areas included; (2) calculated by the editors using the following formula: (number of crimes in the MSA minus number of crimes in the city); (3) calculated by the editors using the following formula: ((number of crimes in the MSA minus number of crimes in the city) ÷ (population of the MSA minus population of the city)) x 100,000; n/a not avail.
Source: U.S. Department of Justice, FBI Uniform Crime Reports, 1977 - 1996

Motor Vehicle Thefts and Motor Vehicle Theft Rates: 1977 - 1996

Year	Number				Rate per 100,000 population			
	City	Suburbs[2]	MSA[1]	U.S.	City	Suburbs[3]	MSA[1]	U.S.
1977	3,669	1,025	4,694	977,700	689.7	208.5	458.6	451.9
1978	3,671	1,098	4,769	1,004,100	700.6	188.9	431.5	460.5
1979	3,810	1,319	5,129	1,112,800	713.4	238.1	471.4	505.6
1980	3,323	1,257	4,580	1,131,700	590.8	238.7	420.6	502.2
1981	2,899	945	3,844	1,087,800	515.0	179.3	352.7	474.7
1982	2,599	863	3,462	1,062,400	461.1	163.5	317.2	458.8
1983	2,490	1,011	3,501	1,007,900	443.6	149.9	283.3	430.8
1984	2,665	1,137	3,802	1,032,200	468.7	163.9	301.2	437.1
1985	2,794	1,277	4,071	1,102,900	493.9	179.3	318.5	462.0
1986	2,792	1,415	4,207	1,224,100	493.2	198.5	328.9	507.8
1987	3,556	1,494	5,050	1,288,700	626.3	208.9	393.7	529.4
1988	5,742	1,627	7,369	1,432,900	975.8	219.1	553.7	582.9
1989	6,982	1,737	8,719	1,564,800	1,219.9	223.2	645.5	630.4
1990	8,466	1,964	10,430	1,635,900	1,337.6	263.8	757.2	657.8
1991	8,176	1,930	10,106	1,661,700	1,280.4	257.1	727.4	659.0
1992	6,962	1,761	8,723	1,610,800	1,082.7	243.8	638.9	631.5
1993	7,070	1,508	8,578	1,563,100	1,092.8	199.9	612.1	606.1
1994	6,720	1,655	8,375	1,539,300	1,037.3	219.2	596.9	591.3
1995	7,040	1,745	8,785	1,472,400	1,102.2	221.2	615.3	560.4
1996	7,610	1,754	9,364	1,395,200	1,188.5	221.9	654.4	525.9

Notes: (1) Metropolitan Statistical Area - see Appendix A for areas included; (2) calculated by the editors using the following formula: (number of crimes in the MSA minus number of crimes in the city); (3) calculated by the editors using the following formula: ((number of crimes in the MSA minus number of crimes in the city) ÷ (population of the MSA minus population of the city)) x 100,000; n/a not avail.
Source: U.S. Department of Justice, FBI Uniform Crime Reports, 1977 - 1996

HATE CRIMES

Criminal Incidents by Bias Motivation

Area	Race	Ethnicity	Religion	Sexual Orientation
Columbus	94	0	2	16

Notes: Figures include both violent and property crimes. Law enforcement agencies must have submitted data for at least one quarter of calendar year 1995 to be included in this report, therefore figures shown may not represent complete 12-month totals; n/a not available
Source: U.S. Department of Justice, FBI Uniform Crime Reports, Hate Crime Statistics 1995

LAW ENFORCEMENT

Full-Time Law Enforcement Employees

Jurisdiction	Police Employees			Police Officers per 100,000 population
	Total	Officers	Civilians	
Columbus	2,029	1,641	388	256.3

Notes: Data as of October 31, 1996
Source: U.S. Department of Justice, FBI Uniform Crime Reports, 1996

Number of Police Officers by Race

Race	Police Officers				Index of Representation[1]		
	1983		1992				
	Number	Pct.	Number	Pct.	1983	1992	% Chg.
Black	133	11.1	256	17.7	0.50	0.78	56.0
Hispanic[2]	0	0.0	1	0.1	0.00	0.05	-

Notes: (1) The index of representation is calculated by dividing the percent of black/hispanic police officers by the percent of corresponding blacks/hispanics in the local population. An index approaching 1.0 indicates that a city is closer to achieving a representation of police officers equal to their proportion in the local population; (2) Hispanic officers can be of any race
Source: Bureau of Justice Statistics, Sourcebook of Criminal Justice Statistics, 1994

CORRECTIONS

Federal Correctional Facilities

Type	Year Opened	Security Level	Sex of Inmates	Rated Capacity	Population on 7/1/95	Number of Staff
None listed						

Notes: Data as of 1995
Source: Bureau of Justice Statistics, Sourcebook of Criminal Justice Statistics Online

City/County/Regional Correctional Facilities

Name	Year Opened	Year Renov.	Rated Capacity	1995 Pop.	Number of COs[1]	Number of Staff	ACA[2] Accred.
Franklin Co Corrections Ctr	1986	1991	1,209	1,610	372	407	No
Franklin Co Work Release	1964	1989	128	108	n/a	28	No

Notes: Data as of April 1996; (1) Correctional Officers; (2) American Correctional Assn. Accreditation
Source: American Correctional Association, 1996-1998 National Jail and Adult Detention Directory

Private Adult Correctional Facilities

Name	Date Opened	Rated Capacity	Present Pop.	Security Level	Facility Construct.	Expans. Plans	ACA[1] Accred.
None listed							

Notes: Data as of December 1996; (1) American Correctional Association Accreditation
Source: University of Florida, Center for Studies in Criminology and Law, Private Adult Correctional Facility Census, 10th Ed., March 15, 1997

Characteristics of Shock Incarceration Programs

Jurisdiction	Year Program Began	Number of Camps	Average Num. of Inmates	Number of Beds	Program Length	Voluntary/ Mandatory
Ohio	1991 male; 1995 fem.	2	(a)	100 male; 40 female	(b)	Voluntary

Note: Data as of July 1996; (a) Phase I: 80 to 100 days; Phase II: 40 days; Phase III: 220 days; (b) Phase I: 90 days; Phase II: 30 days; Phase III: 6 months to one year
Source: Sourcebook of Criminal Justice Statistics Online

INMATES AND HIV/AIDS

HIV Testing Policies for Inmates

Jurisdiction	All Inmates at Some Time	All Convicted Inmates at Admission	Random Samples While in Custody	High-risk Groups	Upon Inmate Request	Upon Court Order	Upon Involvement in Incident
Franklin Co.	No	No	No	No	Yes	Yes	No

Source: HIV in Prisons and Jails, 1993 (released August 1995)

Inmates Known to be Positive for HIV

Jurisdiction	Number of Jail Inmates in Facilities Providing Data	Type of HIV Infection/AIDS Cases				HIV/AIDS Cases as a Percent of Tot. Custody Pop.
		Total	Asymptomatic	Symptomatic	Confirmed AIDS	
Franklin Co.[1]	1,523	n/a	n/a	n/a	n/a	n/a

Note: (1) Jurisdiction did not provide data on HIV/AIDS cases; n/a not available
Source: HIV in Prisons and Jails, 1993 (released August, 1995)

DEATH PENALTY

Death Penalty Statistics

State	Prisoners Executed		Prisoners Under Sentence of Death					Avg. No. of Years on Death Row[4]
	1930-1995	1996[1]	Total[2]	White[3]	Black[3]	Hisp.	Women	
Ohio	172	0	155	76	78	5	0	6.3

Notes: Data as of 12/31/95 unless otherwise noted; (1) Data as of 7/31/97; (2) Includes persons of other races; (3) Includes people of Hispanic origin; (4) Covers prisoners sentenced 1974 through 1995
Source: Bureau of Justice Statistics, Capital Punishment 1995 (released 12/96); Death Penalty Information Center Web Site, 9/30/97

Capital Offenses and Methods of Execution

Capital Offenses in Ohio	Minimum Age for Imposition of Death Penalty	Mentally Retarded Excluded	Methods of Execution[1]
Aggravated murder with 1 of 8 aggravating circumstances. (O.R.C. secs. 2929.01, 2903.01, and 2929.04).	18	No	Lethal injection; electrocution

Notes: Data as of 12/31/95 unless otherwise noted; (1) Data as of 7/31/97
Source: Bureau of Justice Statistics, Capital Punishment 1995 (released 12/96); Death Penalty Information Center Web Site, 9/30/97

LAWS

Statutory Provisions Relating to the Purchase, Ownership and Use of Handguns

Jurisdiction	Instant Background Check	Federal Waiting Period Applies[1]	State Waiting Period (days)	License or Permit to Purchase	Regis-tration	Record of Sale Sent to Police	Concealed Carry Law
Ohio	No	Yes	(a)	(b)	(a)	(a)	Yes[c]

Note: Data as of 1996; (1) The Federal 5-day waiting period for handgun purchases applies to states that don't have instant background checks, waiting period requirements, or licensing procedures exempting them from the Federal requirement; (a) Local ordinance in certain cities or counties; (b) Some cities require a permit-to-purchase or firearm owner ID card; (c) No permit system exists and concealed carry is prohibited
Source: Sourcebook of Criminal Justice Statistics Online

Statutory Provisions Relating to Alcohol Use and Driving

Jurisdiction	Drinking Age	Blood Alcohol Concentration Levels as Evidence in State Courts[1]		Open Container Law[1]	Anti-Consump-tion Law[1]	Dram Shop Law[1]
		Illegal per se at 0.10%	Presumption at 0.10%			
Ohio	21	Yes	No	Yes	Yes	Yes

Note: Data as of January 1, 1997; (1) See Appendix C for an explanation of terms
Source: Sourcebook of Criminal Justice Statistics Online

Statutory Provisions Relating to Curfews

Jurisdiction	Year Enacted	Latest Revision	Age Group(s)	Curfew Provisions
Columbus	1979	-	13 through 17	Midnight to 4:30 am every night
			12 and under	1 hr after sunset to sunrise every night

Note: Data as of February 1996
Source: Sourcebook of Criminal Justice Statistics Online

Statutory Provisions Relating to Hate Crimes

Jurisdiction	Bias-Motivated Violence and Intimidation						Institutional Vandalism
	Civil Action	Criminal Penalty					
		Race/ Religion/ Ethnicity	Sexual Orientation	Mental/ Physical Disability	Gender	Age	
Ohio	Yes	Yes	No	No	No	No	Yes

Source: Anti-Defamation League, 1997 Hate Crimes Laws

Dallas, Texas

OVERVIEW

The total crime rate for the city decreased 6.8% between 1977 and 1996. During that same period, the violent crime rate increased 45.8% and the property crime rate decreased 12.9%.

Among violent crimes, the rates for: Murders decreased 22.6%; Forcible Rapes decreased 7.4%; Robberies increased 34.1%; and Aggravated Assaults increased 66.6%.

Among property crimes, the rates for: Burglaries decreased 41.4%; Larceny-Thefts decreased 16.5%; and Motor Vehicle Thefts increased 139.6%.

ANTI-CRIME PROGRAMS

Among the city's numerous programs:

- Neighborhood Assistance Centers—operates 14 throughout the city, staffed with police officers and civilian personnel whose purpose is to develop programs and to offer services that best meet the needs of that particular community.
- Narcotics Enforcement & Street Narcotic Squads—street squads target street level drug dealers who are responsible for the majority of narcotics arrests.
- Better Kids, Better Dallas (BKBD)—offers incentives for academic performance in elementary schools, provides community scholarships, broadens youth programs and supports crime watch programs and guns, alcohol and drug-reduction programs.
- First Offender Program—designed to counsel juveniles who have a first brush with the law. The program works with offenders and parents.
- Teens, Crime and the Community—engages teens as crime prevention resources in their schools and communities.
- Support, Abatement, Forfeiture Enforcement Team (S.A.F.E.T.)—designed to locate and force property owners to upgrade dilapidated structures which serve as havens for drug dealing and other types of criminal activity.
- Citizens Police Academy—established in 1993, the citizens in the program learn about the Police Department and how it functions in a 12-week "course".
- HEAT (Help End Auto Theft)—vehicles with stickers can be stopped and checked by law officers.
- Mobile Storefronts—these are moved to areas which are experiencing crime problems and stay there until problems are eliminated.
- Gang Task Force—combats gang-related violence.
  City of Dallas, Police Department, 7/97

CRIME RISK

Your Chances of Becoming a Victim[1]

Area	Any Crime	Violent Crime					Property Crime			
		Any	Murder	Forcible Rape[2]	Robbery	Aggrav. Assault	Any	Burglary	Larceny -Theft	Motor Vehicle Theft
City	1:11	1:65	1:4,887	1:727	1:173	1:115	1:13	1:59	1:22	1:62

Note: (1) Figures have been calculated by dividing the population of the city by the number of crimes reported to the FBI during 1996 and are expressed as odds (eg. 1:20 should be read as 1 in 20).
(2) Figures have been calculated by dividing the female population of the city by the number of forcible rapes reported to the FBI during 1996. The female population of the city was estimated by calculating the ratio of females to males reported in the 1990 Census and applying that ratio to 1996 population estimate.
Source: FBI Uniform Crime Reports 1996

CRIME STATISTICS

Total Crimes and Total Crime Rates: 1977 - 1996

Year	Number				Rate per 100,000 population			
	City	Suburbs[2]	MSA[1]	U.S.	City	Suburbs[3]	MSA[1]	U.S.
1977	85,806	107,319	193,125	10,984,500	10,154.6	5,935.9	7,279.6	5,077.6
1978	86,569	109,414	195,983	11,209,000	10,220.7	5,860.8	7,221.5	5,140.3
1979	93,761	123,853	217,614	12,249,500	10,627.8	6,477.3	7,787.7	5,565.5
1980	106,010	139,152	245,162	13,408,300	11,777.5	6,741.5	8,270.7	5,950.0
1981	111,582	141,383	252,965	13,423,800	11,905.0	6,577.9	8,195.5	5,858.2
1982	115,864	141,375	257,239	12,974,400	11,937.1	6,351.5	8,047.6	5,603.6
1983	107,808	54,841	162,649	12,108,600	10,793.5	4,804.8	7,599.7	5,175.0
1984	113,446	62,505	175,951	11,881,800	11,485.9	5,455.1	8,247.0	5,031.3
1985	129,496	76,315	205,811	12,431,400	12,982.5	6,338.8	9,349.1	5,207.1
1986	153,926	89,395	243,321	13,211,900	15,142.9	7,307.4	10,863.4	5,480.4
1987	164,452	97,583	262,035	13,508,700	16,283.2	7,261.9	11,132.8	5,550.0
1988	170,402	97,314	267,716	13,923,100	16,741.9	7,081.7	11,192.2	5,664.2
1989	166,451	96,534	262,985	14,251,400	16,706.6	6,854.1	10,936.2	5,741.0
1990	156,267	97,094	253,361	14,475,600	15,520.0	6,678.9	10,296.6	5,820.3
1991	154,929	97,368	252,297	14,872,900	15,065.6	6,558.0	10,039.3	5,897.8
1992	130,082	96,869	226,951	14,438,200	12,429.5	5,911.4	8,451.7	5,660.2
1993	110,799	89,778	200,577	14,144,800	10,627.0	5,255.0	7,290.9	5,484.4
1994	100,707	88,223	188,930	13,989,500	9,476.7	5,066.6	6,738.0	5,373.5
1995	98,624	88,624	187,248	13,862,700	9,464.1	4,903.6	6,571.5	5,275.9
1996	100,401	84,470	184,871	13,473,600	9,466.6	4,564.3	6,350.2	5,078.9

Notes: (1) Metropolitan Statistical Area - see Appendix A for areas included; (2) calculated by the editors using the following formula: (number of crimes in the MSA minus number of crimes in the city); (3) calculated by the editors using the following formula: ((number of crimes in the MSA minus number of crimes in the city) ÷ (population of the MSA minus population of the city)) x 100,000; n/a not avail.
Source: U.S. Department of Justice, FBI Uniform Crime Reports, 1977 - 1996

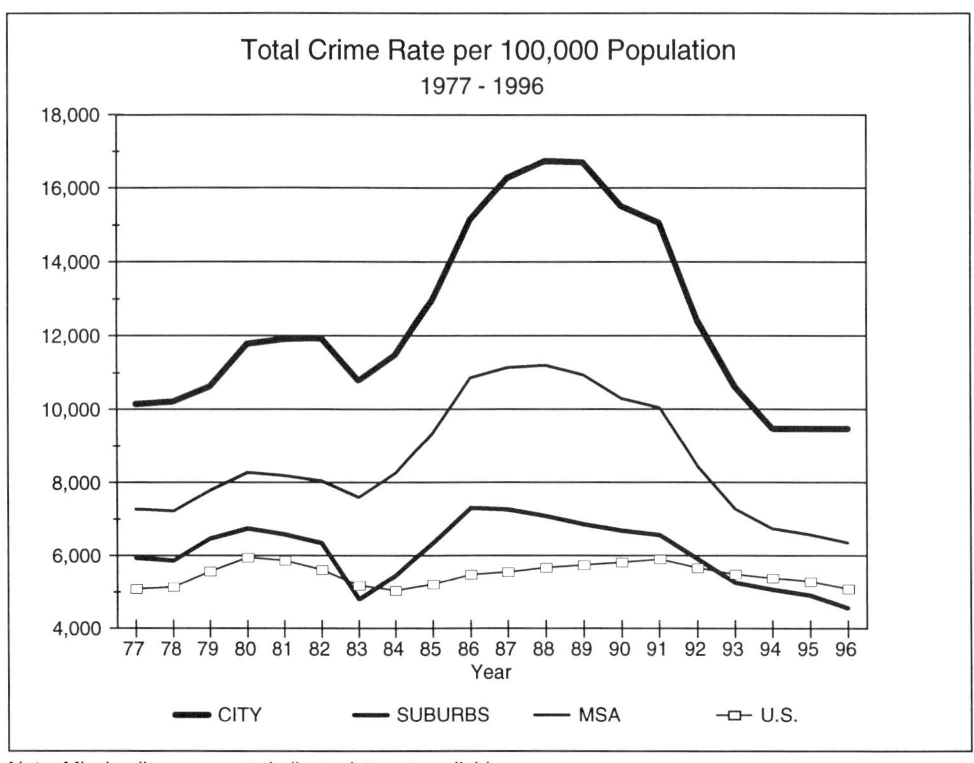

Note: Missing line segments indicate data not available.

Violent Crimes and Violent Crime Rates: 1977 - 1996

Year	Number				Rate per 100,000 population			
	City	Suburbs[2]	MSA[1]	U.S.	City	Suburbs[3]	MSA[1]	U.S.
1977	8,899	6,080	14,979	1,029,580	1,053.1	336.3	564.6	475.9
1978	9,884	6,562	16,446	1,085,550	1,166.9	351.5	606.0	497.8
1979	11,453	7,937	19,390	1,208,030	1,298.2	415.1	693.9	548.9
1980	12,681	9,607	22,288	1,344,520	1,408.8	465.4	751.9	596.6
1981	12,749	9,785	22,534	1,361,820	1,360.2	455.3	730.0	594.3
1982	13,053	9,897	22,950	1,322,390	1,344.8	444.6	718.0	571.1
1983	11,478	2,908	14,386	1,258,090	1,149.1	254.8	672.2	537.7
1984	12,110	3,361	15,471	1,273,280	1,226.1	293.3	725.1	539.2
1985	14,364	4,186	18,550	1,328,800	1,440.0	347.7	842.6	556.6
1986	19,275	4,625	23,900	1,489,170	1,896.2	378.1	1,067.0	617.7
1987	20,086	4,598	24,684	1,484,000	1,988.8	342.2	1,048.7	609.7
1988	21,135	5,022	26,157	1,566,220	2,076.5	365.5	1,093.5	637.2
1989	21,228	5,335	26,563	1,646,040	2,130.6	378.8	1,104.6	663.1
1990	24,550	6,550	31,100	1,820,130	2,438.2	450.6	1,263.9	731.8
1991	26,411	7,104	33,515	1,911,770	2,568.3	478.5	1,333.6	758.1
1992	21,682	8,515	30,197	1,932,270	2,071.7	519.6	1,124.5	757.5
1993	18,176	7,859	26,035	1,926,020	1,743.3	460.0	946.4	746.8
1994	16,886	7,447	24,333	1,857,670	1,589.0	427.7	867.8	713.6
1995	15,969	7,374	23,343	1,798,790	1,532.4	408.0	819.2	684.6
1996	16,280	6,555	22,835	1,682,280	1,535.0	354.2	784.4	634.1

Notes: Violent crimes include murder, forcible rape, robbery and aggravated assault; n/a not available; (1) Metropolitan Statistical Area - see Appendix A for areas included; (2) calculated by the editors using the following formula: (number of crimes in the MSA minus number of crimes in the city); (3) calculated by the editors using the following formula: ((number of crimes in the MSA minus number of crimes in the city) ÷ (population of the MSA minus population of the city)) x 100,000
Source: U.S. Department of Justice, FBI Uniform Crime Reports, 1977 - 1996

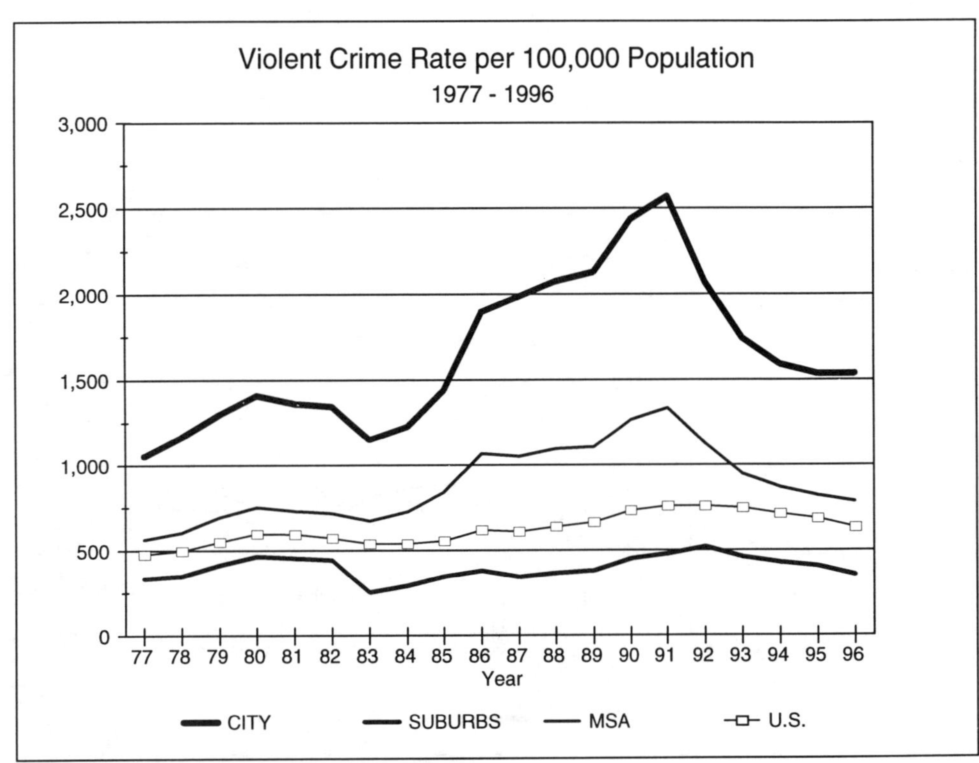

Note: Missing line segments indicate data not available.

Property Crimes and Property Crime Rates: 1977 - 1996

Year	Number				Rate per 100,000 population			
	City	Suburbs[2]	MSA[1]	U.S.	City	Suburbs[3]	MSA[1]	U.S.
1977	76,907	101,239	178,146	9,955,000	9,101.4	5,599.6	6,715.0	4,601.7
1978	76,685	102,852	179,537	10,123,400	9,053.7	5,509.3	6,615.5	4,642.5
1979	82,308	115,916	198,224	11,041,500	9,329.6	6,062.2	7,093.8	5,016.6
1980	93,329	129,545	222,874	12,063,700	10,368.7	6,276.0	7,518.8	5,353.3
1981	98,833	131,598	230,431	12,061,900	10,544.7	6,122.6	7,465.4	5,263.9
1982	102,811	131,478	234,289	11,652,000	10,592.3	5,906.9	7,329.6	5,032.5
1983	96,330	51,933	148,263	10,850,500	9,644.3	4,550.0	6,927.5	4,637.4
1984	101,336	59,144	160,480	10,608,500	10,259.8	5,161.8	7,521.9	4,492.1
1985	115,132	72,129	187,261	11,102,600	11,542.4	5,991.1	8,506.4	4,650.5
1986	134,651	84,770	219,421	11,722,700	13,246.7	6,929.4	9,796.3	4,862.6
1987	144,366	92,985	237,351	12,024,700	14,294.4	6,919.7	10,084.1	4,940.3
1988	149,267	92,292	241,559	12,356,900	14,665.4	6,716.3	10,098.7	5,027.1
1989	145,223	91,199	236,422	12,605,400	14,575.9	6,475.3	9,831.6	5,077.9
1990	131,717	90,544	222,261	12,655,500	13,081.7	6,228.3	9,032.7	5,088.5
1991	128,518	90,264	218,782	12,961,100	12,497.4	6,079.5	8,705.7	5,139.7
1992	108,400	88,354	196,754	12,505,900	10,357.7	5,391.7	7,327.2	4,902.7
1993	92,623	81,919	174,542	12,218,800	8,883.7	4,794.9	6,344.5	4,737.6
1994	83,821	80,776	164,597	12,131,900	7,887.7	4,638.9	5,870.2	4,660.0
1995	82,655	81,250	163,905	12,063,900	7,931.7	4,495.6	5,752.3	4,591.3
1996	84,121	77,915	162,036	11,791,300	7,931.6	4,210.1	5,565.8	4,444.8

Notes: Property crimes include burglary, larceny-theft and motor vehicle theft; n/a not available; (1) Metropolitan Statistical Area - see Appendix A for areas included; (2) calculated by the editors using the following formula: (number of crimes in the MSA minus number of crimes in the city); (3) calculated by the editors using the following formula: ((number of crimes in the MSA minus number of crimes in the city) ÷ (population of the MSA minus population of the city)) x 100,000
Source: U.S. Department of Justice, FBI Uniform Crime Reports, 1977 - 1996

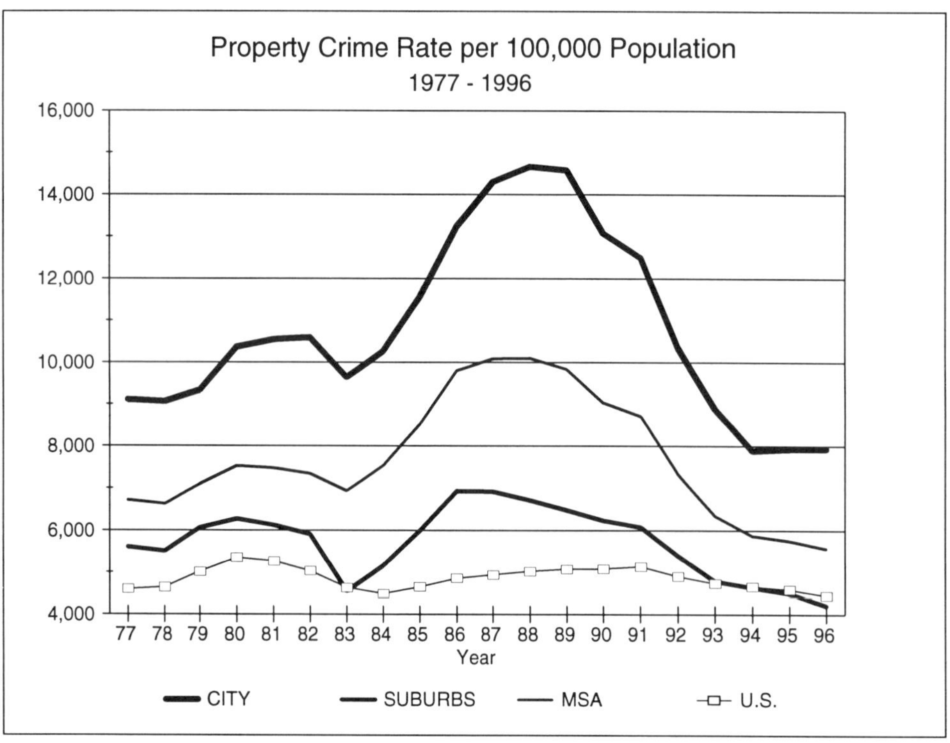

Note: Missing line segments indicate data not available.

Murders and Murder Rates: 1977 - 1996

Year	Number				Rate per 100,000 population			
	City	Suburbs[2]	MSA[1]	U.S.	City	Suburbs[3]	MSA[1]	U.S.
1977	224	179	403	19,120	26.5	9.9	15.2	8.8
1978	230	185	415	19,560	27.2	9.9	15.3	9.0
1979	307	203	510	21,460	34.8	10.6	18.3	9.7
1980	319	218	537	23,040	35.4	10.6	18.1	10.2
1981	298	209	507	22,520	31.8	9.7	16.4	9.8
1982	306	203	509	21,010	31.5	9.1	15.9	9.1
1983	268	67	335	19,310	26.8	5.9	15.7	8.3
1984	294	88	382	18,690	29.8	7.7	17.9	7.9
1985	301	77	378	18,980	30.2	6.4	17.2	7.9
1986	347	99	446	20,610	34.1	8.1	19.9	8.6
1987	323	71	394	20,100	32.0	5.3	16.7	8.3
1988	366	71	437	20,680	36.0	5.2	18.3	8.4
1989	351	66	417	21,500	35.2	4.7	17.3	8.7
1990	447	79	526	23,440	44.4	5.4	21.4	9.4
1991	500	100	600	24,700	48.6	6.7	23.9	9.8
1992	387	83	470	23,760	37.0	5.1	17.5	9.3
1993	317	86	403	24,530	30.4	5.0	14.6	9.5
1994	295	78	373	23,330	27.8	4.5	13.3	9.0
1995	276	64	340	21,610	26.5	3.5	11.9	8.2
1996	217	68	285	19,650	20.5	3.7	9.8	7.4

Notes: (1) Metropolitan Statistical Area - see Appendix A for areas included; (2) calculated by the editors using the following formula: (number of crimes in the MSA minus number of crimes in the city); (3) calculated by the editors using the following formula: ((number of crimes in the MSA minus number of crimes in the city) ÷ (population of the MSA minus population of the city)) x 100,000; n/a not avail.
Source: U.S. Department of Justice, FBI Uniform Crime Reports, 1977 - 1996

Forcible Rapes and Forcible Rape Rates: 1977 - 1996

Year	Number				Rate per 100,000 population			
	City	Suburbs[2]	MSA[1]	U.S.	City	Suburbs[3]	MSA[1]	U.S.
1977	637	478	1,115	63,500	75.4	26.4	42.0	29.4
1978	822	568	1,390	67,610	97.0	30.4	51.2	31.0
1979	983	699	1,682	76,390	111.4	36.6	60.2	34.7
1980	1,121	742	1,863	82,990	124.5	35.9	62.8	36.8
1981	1,121	887	2,008	82,500	119.6	41.3	65.1	36.0
1982	1,105	920	2,025	78,770	113.8	41.3	63.4	34.0
1983	891	220	1,111	78,920	89.2	19.3	51.9	33.7
1984	1,022	321	1,343	84,230	103.5	28.0	62.9	35.7
1985	1,149	404	1,553	88,670	115.2	33.6	70.5	37.1
1986	1,255	420	1,675	91,460	123.5	34.3	74.8	37.9
1987	1,260	467	1,727	91,110	124.8	34.8	73.4	37.4
1988	1,306	425	1,731	92,490	128.3	30.9	72.4	37.6
1989	1,185	526	1,711	94,500	118.9	37.3	71.2	38.1
1990	1,344	536	1,880	102,560	133.5	36.9	76.4	41.2
1991	1,208	587	1,795	106,590	117.5	39.5	71.4	42.3
1992	1,096	625	1,721	109,060	104.7	38.1	64.1	42.8
1993	1,000	623	1,623	106,010	95.9	36.5	59.0	41.1
1994	957	533	1,490	102,220	90.1	30.6	53.1	39.3
1995	852	570	1,422	97,470	81.8	31.5	49.9	37.1
1996	740	540	1,280	95,770	69.8	29.2	44.0	36.1

Notes: (1) Metropolitan Statistical Area - see Appendix A for areas included; (2) calculated by the editors using the following formula: (number of crimes in the MSA minus number of crimes in the city); (3) calculated by the editors using the following formula: ((number of crimes in the MSA minus number of crimes in the city) ÷ (population of the MSA minus population of the city)) x 100,000; n/a not avail.
Source: U.S. Department of Justice, FBI Uniform Crime Reports, 1977 - 1996

Robberies and Robbery Rates: 1977 - 1996

Year	Number				Rate per 100,000 population			
	City	Suburbs[2]	MSA[1]	U.S.	City	Suburbs[3]	MSA[1]	U.S.
1977	3,637	1,886	5,523	412,610	430.4	104.3	208.2	190.7
1978	3,835	2,173	6,008	426,930	452.8	116.4	221.4	195.8
1979	4,456	2,873	7,329	480,700	505.1	150.3	262.3	218.4
1980	4,983	3,595	8,578	565,840	553.6	174.2	289.4	251.1
1981	5,402	3,686	9,088	592,910	576.4	171.5	294.4	258.7
1982	5,695	3,598	9,293	553,130	586.7	161.6	290.7	238.9
1983	4,914	748	5,662	506,570	492.0	65.5	264.6	216.5
1984	4,841	765	5,606	485,010	490.1	66.8	262.8	205.4
1985	6,051	1,019	7,070	497,870	606.6	84.6	321.2	208.5
1986	9,289	1,430	10,719	542,780	913.8	116.9	478.6	225.1
1987	9,091	1,457	10,548	517,700	900.1	108.4	448.1	212.7
1988	9,647	1,505	11,152	542,970	947.8	109.5	466.2	220.9
1989	9,442	1,448	10,890	578,330	947.7	102.8	452.9	233.0
1990	10,565	1,465	12,030	639,270	1,049.3	100.8	488.9	257.0
1991	11,254	1,763	13,017	687,730	1,094.4	118.7	518.0	272.7
1992	9,532	1,819	11,351	672,480	910.8	111.0	422.7	263.6
1993	7,420	1,559	8,979	659,870	711.7	91.3	326.4	255.9
1994	7,077	1,547	8,624	618,950	666.0	88.8	307.6	237.7
1995	5,899	1,477	7,376	580,510	566.1	81.7	258.9	220.9
1996	6,122	1,337	7,459	537,050	577.2	72.2	256.2	202.4

Notes: (1) Metropolitan Statistical Area - see Appendix A for areas included; (2) calculated by the editors using the following formula: (number of crimes in the MSA minus number of crimes in the city); (3) calculated by the editors using the following formula: ((number of crimes in the MSA minus number of crimes in the city) ÷ (population of the MSA minus population of the city)) x 100,000; n/a not avail.
Source: U.S. Department of Justice, FBI Uniform Crime Reports, 1977 - 1996

Aggravated Assaults and Aggravated Assault Rates: 1977 - 1996

Year	Number				Rate per 100,000 population			
	City	Suburbs[2]	MSA[1]	U.S.	City	Suburbs[3]	MSA[1]	U.S.
1977	4,401	3,537	7,938	534,350	520.8	195.6	299.2	247.0
1978	4,997	3,636	8,633	571,460	590.0	194.8	318.1	262.1
1979	5,707	4,162	9,869	629,480	646.9	217.7	353.2	286.0
1980	6,258	5,052	11,310	672,650	695.3	244.8	381.5	298.5
1981	5,928	5,003	10,931	663,900	632.5	232.8	354.1	289.7
1982	5,947	5,176	11,123	669,480	612.7	232.5	348.0	289.2
1983	5,405	1,873	7,278	653,290	541.1	164.1	340.1	279.2
1984	5,953	2,187	8,140	685,350	602.7	190.9	381.5	290.2
1985	6,863	2,686	9,549	723,250	688.0	223.1	433.8	302.9
1986	8,384	2,676	11,060	834,320	824.8	218.7	493.8	346.1
1987	9,412	2,603	12,015	855,090	931.9	193.7	510.5	351.3
1988	9,816	3,021	12,837	910,090	964.4	219.8	536.7	370.2
1989	10,250	3,295	13,545	951,710	1,028.8	234.0	563.3	383.4
1990	12,194	4,470	16,664	1,054,860	1,211.1	307.5	677.2	424.1
1991	13,449	4,654	18,103	1,092,740	1,307.8	313.5	720.3	433.3
1992	10,667	5,988	16,655	1,126,970	1,019.2	365.4	620.2	441.8
1993	9,439	5,591	15,030	1,135,610	905.3	327.3	546.3	440.3
1994	8,557	5,289	13,846	1,113,180	805.2	303.7	493.8	427.6
1995	8,942	5,263	14,205	1,099,210	858.1	291.2	498.5	418.3
1996	9,201	4,610	13,811	1,029,810	867.5	249.1	474.4	388.2

Notes: (1) Metropolitan Statistical Area - see Appendix A for areas included; (2) calculated by the editors using the following formula: (number of crimes in the MSA minus number of crimes in the city); (3) calculated by the editors using the following formula: ((number of crimes in the MSA minus number of crimes in the city) ÷ (population of the MSA minus population of the city)) x 100,000; n/a not avail.
Source: U.S. Department of Justice, FBI Uniform Crime Reports, 1977 - 1996

Burglaries and Burglary Rates: 1977 - 1996

Year	Number				Rate per 100,000 population			
	City	Suburbs[2]	MSA[1]	U.S.	City	Suburbs[3]	MSA[1]	U.S.
1977	24,418	30,883	55,301	3,071,500	2,889.7	1,708.2	2,084.5	1,419.8
1978	24,163	30,688	54,851	3,128,300	2,852.8	1,643.8	2,021.1	1,434.6
1979	26,442	36,294	62,736	3,327,700	2,997.2	1,898.1	2,245.1	1,511.9
1980	30,133	39,102	69,235	3,795,200	3,347.7	1,894.4	2,335.7	1,684.1
1981	34,159	39,577	73,736	3,779,700	3,644.5	1,841.3	2,388.9	1,649.5
1982	33,320	37,909	71,229	3,447,100	3,432.8	1,703.1	2,228.4	1,488.8
1983	29,576	13,385	42,961	3,129,900	2,961.1	1,172.7	2,007.3	1,337.7
1984	29,956	15,268	45,224	2,984,400	3,032.9	1,332.5	2,119.7	1,263.7
1985	31,460	18,988	50,448	3,073,300	3,154.0	1,577.2	2,291.6	1,287.3
1986	37,703	24,067	61,770	3,241,400	3,709.1	1,967.3	2,757.8	1,344.6
1987	39,237	25,839	65,076	3,236,200	3,885.1	1,922.9	2,764.8	1,329.6
1988	42,543	25,388	67,931	3,218,100	4,179.8	1,847.5	2,840.0	1,309.2
1989	38,652	24,162	62,814	3,168,200	3,879.5	1,715.6	2,612.1	1,276.3
1990	32,975	21,704	54,679	3,073,900	3,275.0	1,493.0	2,222.2	1,235.9
1991	31,513	21,678	53,191	3,157,200	3,064.4	1,460.1	2,116.6	1,252.0
1992	24,806	20,467	45,273	2,979,900	2,370.2	1,249.0	1,686.0	1,168.2
1993	20,975	17,973	38,948	2,834,800	2,011.8	1,052.0	1,415.7	1,099.2
1994	17,860	17,064	34,924	2,712,800	1,680.7	980.0	1,245.5	1,042.0
1995	16,705	16,303	33,008	2,593,800	1,603.0	902.1	1,158.4	987.1
1996	17,960	15,154	33,114	2,501,500	1,693.4	818.8	1,137.4	943.0

Notes: (1) Metropolitan Statistical Area - see Appendix A for areas included; (2) calculated by the editors using the following formula: (number of crimes in the MSA minus number of crimes in the city); (3) calculated by the editors using the following formula: ((number of crimes in the MSA minus number of crimes in the city) ÷ (population of the MSA minus population of the city)) x 100,000; n/a not avail.
Source: U.S. Department of Justice, FBI Uniform Crime Reports, 1977 - 1996

Larceny-Thefts and Larceny-Theft Rates: 1977 - 1996

Year	Number				Rate per 100,000 population			
	City	Suburbs[2]	MSA[1]	U.S.	City	Suburbs[3]	MSA[1]	U.S.
1977	46,788	63,760	110,548	5,905,700	5,537.0	3,526.6	4,167.0	2,729.9
1978	46,560	64,873	111,433	5,991,000	5,497.0	3,475.0	4,106.1	2,747.4
1979	48,019	70,974	118,993	6,601,000	5,442.9	3,711.8	4,258.4	2,999.1
1980	55,372	81,001	136,373	7,136,900	6,151.7	3,924.2	4,600.6	3,167.0
1981	57,112	82,220	139,332	7,194,400	6,093.4	3,825.3	4,514.0	3,139.7
1982	62,276	83,858	146,134	7,142,500	6,416.1	3,767.5	4,571.7	3,084.8
1983	59,593	35,418	95,011	6,712,800	5,966.3	3,103.1	4,439.3	2,868.9
1984	63,096	39,945	103,041	6,591,900	6,388.2	3,486.2	4,829.7	2,791.3
1985	73,401	48,193	121,594	6,926,400	7,358.7	4,003.0	5,523.5	2,901.2
1986	80,734	53,926	134,660	7,257,200	7,942.4	4,408.1	6,012.1	3,010.3
1987	85,255	59,541	144,796	7,499,900	8,441.5	4,430.9	6,151.8	3,081.3
1988	82,366	59,273	141,639	7,705,900	8,092.4	4,313.4	5,921.4	3,134.9
1989	79,272	58,633	137,905	7,872,400	7,956.5	4,163.1	5,734.7	3,171.3
1990	74,229	60,474	134,703	7,945,700	7,372.2	4,159.9	5,474.4	3,194.8
1991	71,920	60,308	132,228	8,142,200	6,993.6	4,061.9	5,261.6	3,228.8
1992	63,079	60,017	123,096	7,915,200	6,027.3	3,662.5	4,584.1	3,103.0
1993	54,183	57,272	111,455	7,820,900	5,196.8	3,352.3	4,051.3	3,032.4
1994	48,268	57,079	105,347	7,879,800	4,542.1	3,278.0	3,757.1	3,026.7
1995	49,068	58,224	107,292	7,997,700	4,708.6	3,221.6	3,765.4	3,043.8
1996	49,018	56,858	105,876	7,894,600	4,621.8	3,072.3	3,636.8	2,975.9

Notes: (1) Metropolitan Statistical Area - see Appendix A for areas included; (2) calculated by the editors using the following formula: (number of crimes in the MSA minus number of crimes in the city); (3) calculated by the editors using the following formula: ((number of crimes in the MSA minus number of crimes in the city) ÷ (population of the MSA minus population of the city)) x 100,000; n/a not avail.
Source: U.S. Department of Justice, FBI Uniform Crime Reports, 1977 - 1996

Motor Vehicle Thefts and Motor Vehicle Theft Rates: 1977 - 1996

Year	Number				Rate per 100,000 population			
	City	Suburbs[2]	MSA[1]	U.S.	City	Suburbs[3]	MSA[1]	U.S.
1977	5,701	6,596	12,297	977,700	674.7	364.8	463.5	451.9
1978	5,962	7,291	13,253	1,004,100	703.9	390.5	488.3	460.5
1979	7,847	8,648	16,495	1,112,800	889.5	452.3	590.3	505.6
1980	7,824	9,442	17,266	1,131,700	869.2	457.4	582.5	502.2
1981	7,562	9,801	17,363	1,087,800	806.8	456.0	562.5	474.7
1982	7,215	9,711	16,926	1,062,400	743.3	436.3	529.5	458.8
1983	7,161	3,130	10,291	1,007,900	716.9	274.2	480.8	430.8
1984	8,284	3,931	12,215	1,032,200	838.7	343.1	572.5	437.1
1985	10,271	4,948	15,219	1,102,900	1,029.7	411.0	691.3	462.0
1986	16,214	6,777	22,991	1,224,100	1,595.1	554.0	1,026.5	507.8
1987	19,874	7,605	27,479	1,288,700	1,967.8	565.9	1,167.5	529.4
1988	24,358	7,631	31,989	1,432,900	2,393.2	555.3	1,337.3	582.9
1989	27,299	8,404	35,703	1,564,800	2,740.0	596.7	1,484.7	630.4
1990	24,513	8,366	32,879	1,635,900	2,434.6	575.5	1,336.2	657.8
1991	25,085	8,278	33,363	1,661,700	2,439.3	557.5	1,327.6	659.0
1992	20,515	7,870	28,385	1,610,800	1,960.2	480.3	1,057.1	631.5
1993	17,465	6,674	24,139	1,563,100	1,675.1	390.6	877.4	606.1
1994	17,693	6,633	24,326	1,539,300	1,664.9	380.9	867.6	591.3
1995	16,882	6,723	23,605	1,472,400	1,620.0	372.0	828.4	560.4
1996	17,143	5,903	23,046	1,395,200	1,616.4	319.0	791.6	525.9

Notes: (1) Metropolitan Statistical Area - see Appendix A for areas included; (2) calculated by the editors using the following formula: (number of crimes in the MSA minus number of crimes in the city); (3) calculated by the editors using the following formula: ((number of crimes in the MSA minus number of crimes in the city) ÷ (population of the MSA minus population of the city)) x 100,000; n/a not avail.
Source: U.S. Department of Justice, FBI Uniform Crime Reports, 1977 - 1996

HATE CRIMES

Criminal Incidents by Bias Motivation

Area	Race	Ethnicity	Religion	Sexual Orientation
Dallas	27	2	1	10

Notes: Figures include both violent and property crimes. Law enforcement agencies must have submitted data for at least one quarter of calendar year 1995 to be included in this report, therefore figures shown may not represent complete 12-month totals; n/a not available
Source: U.S. Department of Justice, FBI Uniform Crime Reports, Hate Crime Statistics 1995

ILLEGAL DRUGS

Drug Use by Adult Arrestees

Sex	Percent Testing Positive by Urinalysis (%)				
	Any Drug[1]	Cocaine	Marijuana	Opiates	Multiple Drugs
Male	63	32	44	5	20
Female	58	36	27	10	21

Notes: The catchment area is the entire county; (1) Includes cocaine, opiates, marijuana, methadone, phencyclidine (PCP), benzodiazepines, methaqualone, propoxyphene, barbiturates & amphetamines
Source: National Institute of Justice, 1996 Drug Use Forecasting, Annual Report on Adult and Juvenile Arrestees (released June 1997)

LAW ENFORCEMENT

Full-Time Law Enforcement Employees

Jurisdiction	Police Employees			Police Officers per 100,000 population
	Total	Officers	Civilians	
Dallas	3,553	2,822	731	266.1

Notes: Data as of October 31, 1996
Source: U.S. Department of Justice, FBI Uniform Crime Reports, 1996

Number of Police Officers by Race

Race	Police Officers 1983		Police Officers 1992		Index of Representation[1]		
	Number	Pct.	Number	Pct.	1983	1992	% Chg.
Black	169	8.2	546	19.0	0.28	0.64	128.6
Hispanic[2]	96	4.7	234	8.1	0.37	0.39	5.4

Notes: (1) The index of representation is calculated by dividing the percent of black/hispanic police officers by the percent of corresponding blacks/hispanics in the local population. An index approaching 1.0 indicates that a city is closer to achieving a representation of police officers equal to their proportion in the local population; (2) Hispanic officers can be of any race
Source: Bureau of Justice Statistics, Sourcebook of Criminal Justice Statistics, 1994

CORRECTIONS

Federal Correctional Facilities

Type	Year Opened	Security Level	Sex of Inmates	Rated Capacity	Population on 7/1/95	Number of Staff
None listed						

Notes: Data as of 1995
Source: Bureau of Justice Statistics, Sourcebook of Criminal Justice Statistics Online

City/County/Regional Correctional Facilities

Name	Year Opened	Year Renov.	Rated Capacity	1995 Pop.	Number of COs[1]	Number of Staff	ACA[2] Accred.
Dallas Co Decker Det Ctr	1962	--	1,272	n/a	n/a	n/a	No
Dallas Co Govt Ctr Jail	1967	--	1,001	n/a	n/a	n/a	No
Dallas Co Old County Jail	1914	1988	560	n/a	n/a	n/a	No
Dallas Co-Lew St Just Ctr	1983	1988	918	n/a	n/a	n/a	No

Notes: Data as of April 1996; (1) Correctional Officers; (2) American Correctional Assn. Accreditation
Source: American Correctional Association, 1996-1998 National Jail and Adult Detention Directory

Private Adult Correctional Facilities

Name	Date Opened	Rated Capacity	Present Pop.	Security Level	Facility Construct.	Expans. Plans	ACA[1] Accred.
Jesse R. Dawson State Jail	1/98	2,000	n/a	Min/Med	New	None	Will be sought

Notes: Data as of December 1996; (1) American Correctional Association Accreditation
Source: University of Florida, Center for Studies in Criminology and Law, Private Adult Correctional Facility Census, 10th Ed., March 15, 1997

Characteristics of Shock Incarceration Programs

Jurisdiction	Year Program Began	Number of Camps	Average Num. of Inmates	Number of Beds	Program Length	Voluntary/ Mandatory
Texas	1989	2	250	500 male; 20 female	75 to 90 days	Mandatory

Note: Data as of July 1996;
Source: Sourcebook of Criminal Justice Statistics Online

INMATES AND HIV/AIDS

HIV Testing Policies for Inmates

Jurisdiction	All Inmates at Some Time	All Convicted Inmates at Admission	Random Samples While in Custody	High-risk Groups	Upon Inmate Request	Upon Court Order	Upon Involvement in Incident
Dallas Co.	No	No	No	No	Yes	No	No

Source: HIV in Prisons and Jails, 1993 (released August 1995)

Inmates Known to be Positive for HIV

Jurisdiction	Number of Jail Inmates in Facilities Providing Data	Type of HIV Infection/AIDS Cases				HIV/AIDS Cases as a Percent of Tot. Custody Pop.
		Total	Asymptomatic	Symptomatic	Confirmed AIDS	
Dallas Co.	7,592	165	55	29	81	2.2

Source: HIV in Prisons and Jails, 1993 (released August, 1995)

DEATH PENALTY

Death Penalty Statistics

State	Prisoners Executed		Prisoners Under Sentence of Death					Avg. No. of Years on Death Row[4]
	1930-1995	1996[1]	Total[2]	White[3]	Black[3]	Hisp.	Women	
Texas	401	3	404	241	158	68	6	6.5

Notes: Data as of 12/31/95 unless otherwise noted; (1) Data as of 7/31/97; (2) Includes persons of other races; (3) Includes people of Hispanic origin; (4) Covers prisoners sentenced 1974 through 1995
Source: Bureau of Justice Statistics, Capital Punishment 1995 (released 12/96); Death Penalty Information Center Web Site, 9/30/97

Capital Offenses and Methods of Execution

Capital Offenses in Texas	Minimum Age for Imposition of Death Penalty	Mentally Retarded Excluded	Methods of Execution[1]
Criminal homicide with 1 of 8 aggravating circumstances.	17	No	Lethal injection

Notes: Data as of 12/31/95 unless otherwise noted; (1) Data as of 7/31/97
Source: Bureau of Justice Statistics, Capital Punishment 1995 (released 12/96); Death Penalty Information Center Web Site, 9/30/97

LAWS

Statutory Provisions Relating to the Purchase, Ownership and Use of Handguns

Jurisdiction	Instant Background Check	Federal Waiting Period Applies[1]	State Waiting Period (days)	License or Permit to Purchase	Regis-tration	Record of Sale Sent to Police	Concealed Carry Law
Texas	No	Yes[a]	No	No	No	No	Yes[b]

Note: Data as of 1996; (1) The Federal 5-day waiting period for handgun purchases applies to states that don't have instant background checks, waiting period requirements, or licensing procedures exempting them from the Federal requirement; (a) The Federal waiting period does not apply to a person holding a valid permit or license to carry a firearm, issued within 5 years of proposed purchase; (b) "Shall issue" permit system, liberally administered discretion by local authorities over permit issuance, or no permit required
Source: Sourcebook of Criminal Justice Statistics Online

Statutory Provisions Relating to Alcohol Use and Driving

Jurisdiction	Drinking Age	Blood Alcohol Concentration Levels as Evidence in State Courts[1]		Open Container Law[1]	Anti-Consump-tion Law[1]	Dram Shop Law[1]
		Illegal per se at 0.10%	Presumption at 0.10%			
Texas	21	Yes	No	No	Yes[a]	Yes[b]

Note: Data as of January 1, 1997; (1) See Appendix C for an explanation of terms; (a) Applies to drivers only; (b) Statutory law has limited dram shop actions
Source: Sourcebook of Criminal Justice Statistics Online

Statutory Provisions Relating to Curfews

Jurisdiction	Year Enacted	Latest Revision	Age Group(s)	Curfew Provisions
Dallas	1991	-	16 and under	11 pm to 6 am weekday nights midnight to 6 am weekend nights

Note: Data as of February 1996
Source: Sourcebook of Criminal Justice Statistics Online

Statutory Provisions Relating to Hate Crimes

Jurisdiction	Bias-Motivated Violence and Intimidation						Institutional Vandalism
		Criminal Penalty					
	Civil Action	Race/ Religion/ Ethnicity	Sexual Orientation	Mental/ Physical Disability	Gender	Age	
Texas	No	No	No	No	No	No	Yes

Source: Anti-Defamation League, 1997 Hate Crimes Laws

Denver, Colorado

OVERVIEW

The total crime rate for the city decreased 41.5% between 1977 and 1996. During that same period, the violent crime rate decreased 29.9% and the property crime rate decreased 42.6%.

Among violent crimes, the rates for: Murders decreased 19.5%; Forcible Rapes decreased 29.4%; Robberies decreased 50.9%; and Aggravated Assaults decreased 4.4%.

Among property crimes, the rates for: Burglaries decreased 59.5%; Larceny-Thefts decreased 37.5%; and Motor Vehicle Thefts decreased 13.3%.

ANTI-CRIME PROGRAMS

In March of 1994 the Safe City Office was established. As a result of Safe City recommendations a new juvenile curfew program, SafeNite was instituted. It is unlawful for youth under the age of 18 to be in a public place from 11:00 P.M. to 5:00 A.M on Sunday through Thursday and Midnight to 5:00 A.M. on Friday and Saturday nights.

A summer youth employment program was also begun which enabled the city to hire over 1,000 students to receive paid on the job training in city agencies. The program has been expanded to include private sector employers as well.

The Safe City Youth Summit is an annual event, planned and organized by youth. The youth present and discuss their recommendations in a full day of workshops on anti-violence issues. *Director, Safe City Coordinator, 7/97*

CRIME RISK

Your Chances of Becoming a Victim[1]

Area	Any Crime	Violent Crime					Property Crime			
		Any	Murder	Forcible Rape[2]	Robbery	Aggrav. Assault	Any	Burglary	Larceny -Theft	Motor Vehicle Theft
City	1:15	1:135	1:8,066	1:739	1:389	1:248	1:17	1:66	1:30	1:95

Note: (1) Figures have been calculated by dividing the population of the city by the number of crimes reported to the FBI during 1996 and are expressed as odds (eg. 1:20 should be read as 1 in 20).
(2) Figures have been calculated by dividing the female population of the city by the number of forcible rapes reported to the FBI during 1996. The female population of the city was estimated by calculating the ratio of females to males reported in the 1990 Census and applying that ratio to 1996 population estimate.
Source: FBI Uniform Crime Reports 1996

CRIME STATISTICS

Total Crimes and Total Crime Rates: 1977 - 1996

Year	Number				Rate per 100,000 population			
	City	Suburbs[2]	MSA[1]	U.S.	City	Suburbs[3]	MSA[1]	U.S.
1977	53,937	62,924	116,861	10,984,500	11,355.2	6,256.4	7,892.0	5,077.6
1978	50,993	68,147	119,140	11,209,000	10,735.4	6,662.5	7,954.1	5,140.3
1979	51,990	73,648	125,638	12,249,500	10,688.6	6,847.4	8,043.5	5,565.5
1980	58,782	76,094	134,876	13,408,300	12,013.0	6,766.2	8,356.9	5,950.0
1981	60,417	78,591	139,008	13,423,800	11,994.8	6,788.7	8,367.1	5,858.2
1982	58,972	76,951	135,923	12,974,400	11,392.5	6,468.0	7,961.0	5,603.6
1983	55,339	62,100	117,439	12,108,600	10,368.3	6,089.0	7,559.1	5,175.0
1984	51,914	67,028	118,942	11,881,800	9,904.0	6,371.0	7,545.9	5,031.3
1985	53,234	76,484	129,718	12,431,400	10,376.0	6,978.2	8,061.6	5,207.1
1986	55,671	77,626	133,297	13,211,900	10,734.3	7,005.9	8,194.6	5,480.4
1987	46,184	72,805	118,989	13,508,700	9,064.1	6,397.0	7,221.7	5,550.0
1988	41,501	69,606	111,107	13,923,100	8,291.0	6,100.7	6,768.6	5,664.2
1989	37,650	70,497	108,147	14,251,400	7,612.4	6,153.1	6,593.1	5,741.0
1990	36,269	70,766	107,035	14,475,600	7,756.2	6,164.3	6,625.0	5,820.3
1991	36,558	73,097	109,655	14,872,900	7,624.7	6,211.7	6,620.7	5,897.8
1992	40,176	72,717	112,893	14,438,200	8,154.7	6,013.8	6,633.6	5,660.2
1993	39,796	67,263	107,059	14,144,800	7,984.7	5,341.2	6,090.8	5,484.4
1994	35,434	65,500	100,934	13,989,500	6,933.1	5,073.3	5,600.7	5,373.5
1995	34,769	67,694	102,463	13,862,700	6,873.5	5,102.4	5,591.3	5,275.9
1996	34,314	66,954	101,268	13,473,600	6,647.1	4,946.4	5,415.9	5,078.9

Notes: (1) Metropolitan Statistical Area - see Appendix A for areas included; (2) calculated by the editors using the following formula: (number of crimes in the MSA minus number of crimes in the city); (3) calculated by the editors using the following formula: ((number of crimes in the MSA minus number of crimes in the city) ÷ (population of the MSA minus population of the city)) x 100,000; n/a not avail.
Source: U.S. Department of Justice, FBI Uniform Crime Reports, 1977 - 1996

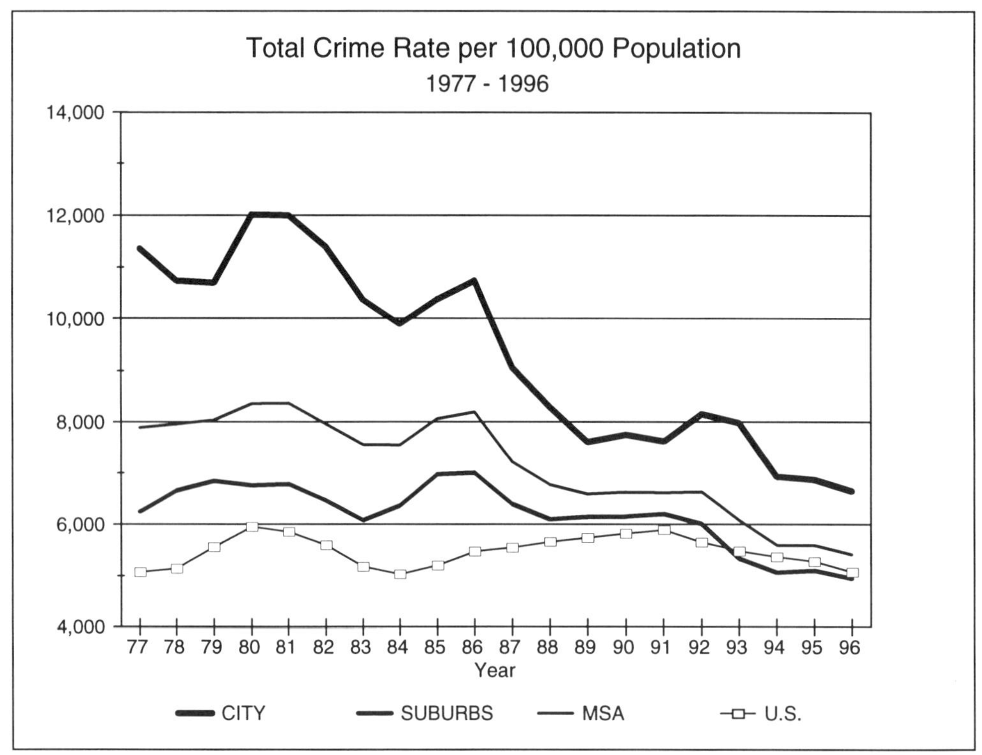

Note: Missing line segments indicate data not available.

Violent Crimes and Violent Crime Rates: 1977 - 1996

Year	Number				Rate per 100,000 population			
	City	Suburbs[2]	MSA[1]	U.S.	City	Suburbs[3]	MSA[1]	U.S.
1977	5,032	4,596	9,628	1,029,580	1,059.4	457.0	650.2	475.9
1978	4,877	4,024	8,901	1,085,550	1,026.7	393.4	594.3	497.8
1979	5,118	4,399	9,517	1,208,030	1,052.2	409.0	609.3	548.9
1980	5,520	4,814	10,334	1,344,520	1,128.1	428.1	640.3	596.6
1981	5,085	5,329	10,414	1,361,820	1,009.5	460.3	626.8	594.3
1982	4,935	5,241	10,176	1,322,390	953.4	440.5	596.0	571.1
1983	4,379	4,634	9,013	1,258,090	820.4	454.4	580.1	537.7
1984	4,100	4,813	8,913	1,273,280	782.2	457.5	565.5	539.2
1985	4,252	5,347	9,599	1,328,800	828.8	487.8	596.5	556.6
1986	4,650	6,077	10,727	1,489,170	896.6	548.5	659.5	617.7
1987	3,841	5,656	9,497	1,484,000	753.8	497.0	576.4	609.7
1988	3,634	5,570	9,204	1,566,220	726.0	488.2	560.7	637.2
1989	3,572	5,797	9,369	1,646,040	722.2	506.0	571.2	663.1
1990	4,205	6,504	10,709	1,820,130	899.3	566.5	662.8	731.8
1991	5,034	7,058	12,092	1,911,770	1,049.9	599.8	730.1	758.1
1992	5,303	7,524	12,827	1,932,270	1,076.4	622.3	753.7	757.5
1993	5,252	7,610	12,862	1,926,020	1,053.8	604.3	731.7	746.8
1994	4,706	7,018	11,724	1,857,670	920.8	543.6	650.5	713.6
1995	4,357	5,052	9,409	1,798,790	861.3	380.8	513.4	684.6
1996	3,832	4,777	8,609	1,682,280	742.3	352.9	460.4	634.1

Notes: Violent crimes include murder, forcible rape, robbery and aggravated assault; n/a not available; (1) Metropolitan Statistical Area - see Appendix A for areas included; (2) calculated by the editors using the following formula: (number of crimes in the MSA minus number of crimes in the city); (3) calculated by the editors using the following formula: ((number of crimes in the MSA minus number of crimes in the city) ÷ (population of the MSA minus population of the city)) x 100,000
Source: U.S. Department of Justice, FBI Uniform Crime Reports, 1977 - 1996

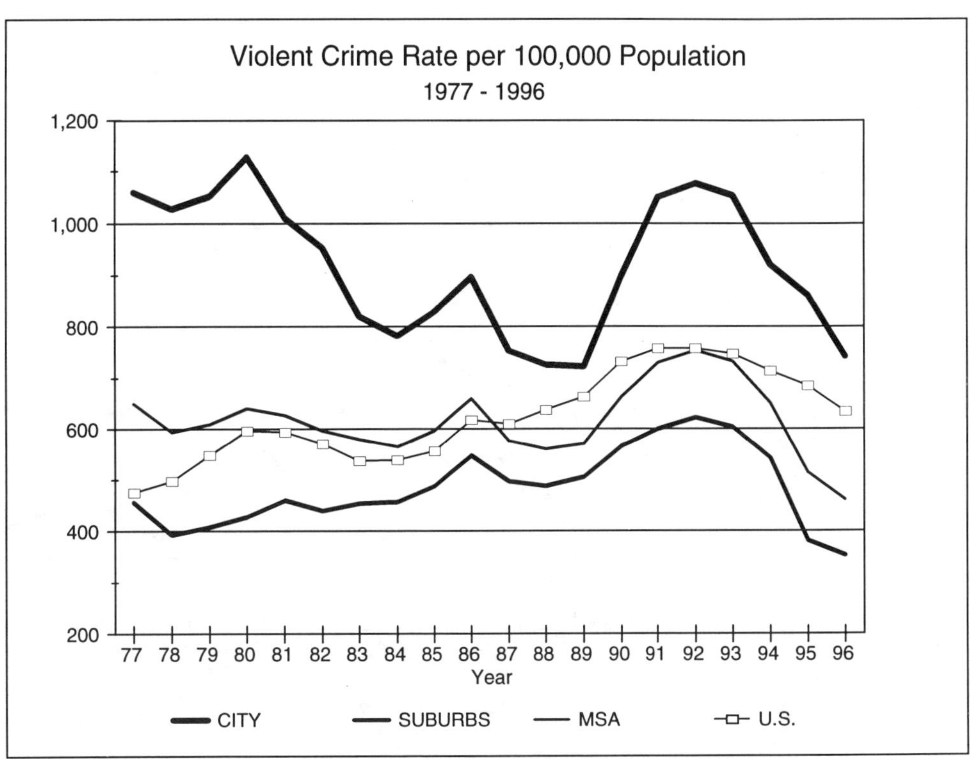

Note: Missing line segments indicate data not available.

Property Crimes and Property Crime Rates: 1977 - 1996

Year	Number				Rate per 100,000 population			
	City	Suburbs[2]	MSA[1]	U.S.	City	Suburbs[3]	MSA[1]	U.S.
1977	48,905	58,328	107,233	9,955,000	10,295.8	5,799.4	7,241.8	4,601.7
1978	46,116	64,123	110,239	10,123,400	9,708.6	6,269.1	7,359.8	4,642.5
1979	46,872	69,249	116,121	11,041,500	9,636.4	6,438.4	7,434.3	5,016.6
1980	53,262	71,280	124,542	12,063,700	10,884.9	6,338.1	7,716.6	5,353.3
1981	55,332	73,262	128,594	12,061,900	10,985.2	6,328.4	7,740.2	5,263.9
1982	54,037	71,710	125,747	11,652,000	10,439.1	6,027.5	7,365.0	5,032.5
1983	50,960	57,466	108,426	10,850,500	9,547.9	5,634.6	6,979.0	4,637.4
1984	47,814	62,215	110,029	10,608,500	9,121.8	5,913.5	6,980.4	4,492.1
1985	48,982	71,137	120,119	11,102,600	9,547.3	6,490.3	7,465.0	4,650.5
1986	51,021	71,549	122,570	11,722,700	9,837.7	6,457.4	7,535.2	4,862.6
1987	42,343	67,149	109,492	12,024,700	8,310.2	5,900.0	6,645.3	4,940.3
1988	37,867	64,036	101,903	12,356,900	7,565.0	5,612.5	6,207.9	5,027.1
1989	34,078	64,700	98,778	12,605,400	6,890.2	5,647.2	6,022.0	5,077.9
1990	32,064	64,262	96,326	12,655,500	6,857.0	5,597.7	5,962.2	5,088.5
1991	31,524	66,039	97,563	12,961,100	6,574.8	5,611.9	5,890.7	5,139.7
1992	34,873	65,193	100,066	12,505,900	7,078.3	5,391.6	5,879.9	4,902.7
1993	34,544	59,653	94,197	12,218,800	6,931.0	4,736.9	5,359.0	4,737.6
1994	30,728	58,482	89,210	12,131,900	6,012.3	4,529.7	4,950.1	4,660.0
1995	30,412	62,642	93,054	12,063,900	6,012.1	4,721.6	5,077.9	4,591.3
1996	30,482	62,177	92,659	11,791,300	5,904.8	4,593.5	4,955.5	4,444.8

Notes: Property crimes include burglary, larceny-theft and motor vehicle theft; n/a not available; (1) Metropolitan Statistical Area - see Appendix A for areas included; (2) calculated by the editors using the following formula: (number of crimes in the MSA minus number of crimes in the city); (3) calculated by the editors using the following formula: ((number of crimes in the MSA minus number of crimes in the city) ÷ (population of the MSA minus population of the city)) x 100,000
Source: U.S. Department of Justice, FBI Uniform Crime Reports, 1977 - 1996

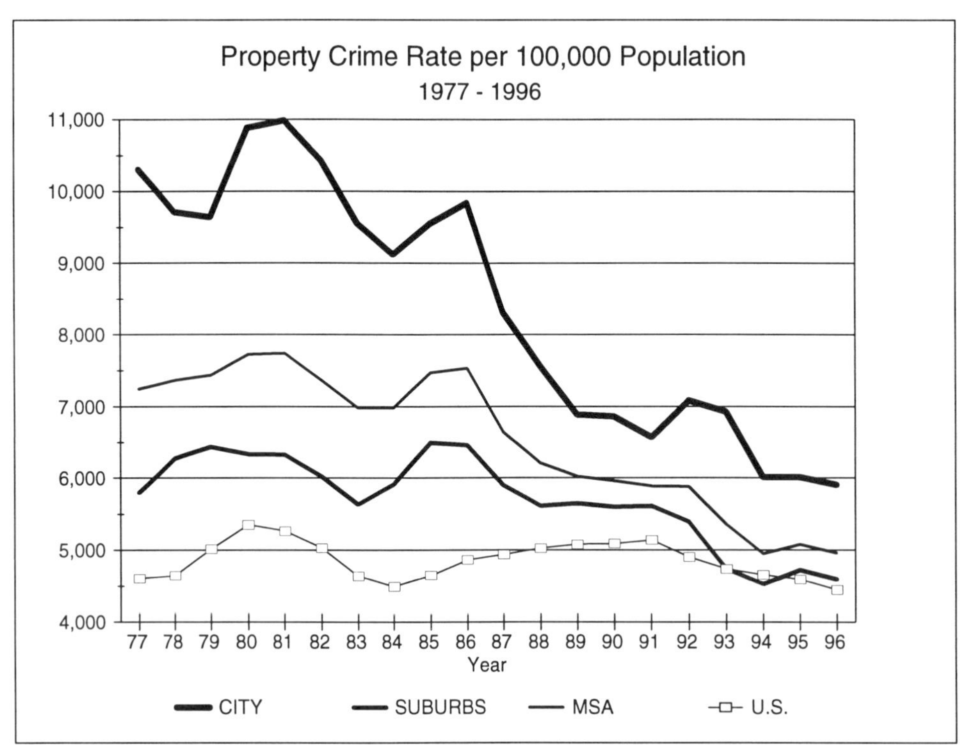

Note: Missing line segments indicate data not available.

Murders and Murder Rates: 1977 - 1996

Year	Number				Rate per 100,000 population			
	City	Suburbs[2]	MSA[1]	U.S.	City	Suburbs[3]	MSA[1]	U.S.
1977	73	31	104	19,120	15.4	3.1	7.0	8.8
1978	97	45	142	19,560	20.4	4.4	9.5	9.0
1979	66	42	108	21,460	13.6	3.9	6.9	9.7
1980	99	52	151	23,040	20.2	4.6	9.4	10.2
1981	100	70	170	22,520	19.9	6.0	10.2	9.8
1982	68	53	121	21,010	13.1	4.5	7.1	9.1
1983	78	52	130	19,310	14.6	5.1	8.4	8.3
1984	82	38	120	18,690	15.6	3.6	7.6	7.9
1985	72	34	106	18,980	14.0	3.1	6.6	7.9
1986	91	47	138	20,610	17.5	4.2	8.5	8.6
1987	79	48	127	20,100	15.5	4.2	7.7	8.3
1988	69	49	118	20,680	13.8	4.3	7.2	8.4
1989	55	29	84	21,500	11.1	2.5	5.1	8.7
1990	67	26	93	23,440	14.3	2.3	5.8	9.4
1991	88	33	121	24,700	18.4	2.8	7.3	9.8
1992	95	45	140	23,760	19.3	3.7	8.2	9.3
1993	74	58	132	24,530	14.8	4.6	7.5	9.5
1994	81	41	122	23,330	15.8	3.2	6.8	9.0
1995	81	45	126	21,610	16.0	3.4	6.9	8.2
1996	64	42	106	19,650	12.4	3.1	5.7	7.4

Notes: (1) Metropolitan Statistical Area - see Appendix A for areas included; (2) calculated by the editors using the following formula: (number of crimes in the MSA minus number of crimes in the city); (3) calculated by the editors using the following formula: ((number of crimes in the MSA minus number of crimes in the city) ÷ (population of the MSA minus population of the city)) x 100,000; n/a not avail.
Source: U.S. Department of Justice, FBI Uniform Crime Reports, 1977 - 1996

Forcible Rapes and Forcible Rape Rates: 1977 - 1996

Year	Number				Rate per 100,000 population			
	City	Suburbs[2]	MSA[1]	U.S.	City	Suburbs[3]	MSA[1]	U.S.
1977	466	271	737	63,500	98.1	26.9	49.8	29.4
1978	577	308	885	67,610	121.5	30.1	59.1	31.0
1979	626	340	966	76,390	128.7	31.6	61.8	34.7
1980	704	344	1,048	82,990	143.9	30.6	64.9	36.8
1981	471	365	836	82,500	93.5	31.5	50.3	36.0
1982	516	354	870	78,770	99.7	29.8	51.0	34.0
1983	430	315	745	78,920	80.6	30.9	48.0	33.7
1984	427	307	734	84,230	81.5	29.2	46.6	35.7
1985	418	334	752	88,670	81.5	30.5	46.7	37.1
1986	424	336	760	91,460	81.8	30.3	46.7	37.9
1987	401	350	751	91,110	78.7	30.8	45.6	37.4
1988	370	334	704	92,490	73.9	29.3	42.9	37.6
1989	325	340	665	94,500	65.7	29.7	40.5	38.1
1990	375	438	813	102,560	80.2	38.2	50.3	41.2
1991	427	470	897	106,590	89.1	39.9	54.2	42.3
1992	437	446	883	109,060	88.7	36.9	51.9	42.8
1993	393	407	800	106,010	78.9	32.3	45.5	41.1
1994	366	427	793	102,220	71.6	33.1	44.0	39.3
1995	320	407	727	97,470	63.3	30.7	39.7	37.1
1996	358	514	872	95,770	69.3	38.0	46.6	36.1

Notes: (1) Metropolitan Statistical Area - see Appendix A for areas included; (2) calculated by the editors using the following formula: (number of crimes in the MSA minus number of crimes in the city); (3) calculated by the editors using the following formula: ((number of crimes in the MSA minus number of crimes in the city) ÷ (population of the MSA minus population of the city)) x 100,000; n/a not avail.
Source: U.S. Department of Justice, FBI Uniform Crime Reports, 1977 - 1996

Robberies and Robbery Rates: 1977 - 1996

Year	Number				Rate per 100,000 population			
	City	Suburbs[2]	MSA[1]	U.S.	City	Suburbs[3]	MSA[1]	U.S.
1977	2,488	1,196	3,684	412,610	523.8	118.9	248.8	190.7
1978	2,362	1,146	3,508	426,930	497.3	112.0	234.2	195.8
1979	2,257	1,327	3,584	480,700	464.0	123.4	229.5	218.4
1980	2,366	1,342	3,708	565,840	483.5	119.3	229.7	251.1
1981	2,403	1,298	3,701	592,910	477.1	112.1	222.8	258.7
1982	2,386	1,239	3,625	553,130	460.9	104.1	212.3	238.9
1983	1,924	1,031	2,955	506,570	360.5	101.1	190.2	216.5
1984	1,681	1,074	2,755	485,010	320.7	102.1	174.8	205.4
1985	1,917	1,222	3,139	497,870	373.6	111.5	195.1	208.5
1986	2,099	1,428	3,527	542,780	404.7	128.9	216.8	225.1
1987	1,612	1,308	2,920	517,700	316.4	114.9	177.2	212.7
1988	1,393	1,070	2,463	542,970	278.3	93.8	150.0	220.9
1989	1,267	942	2,209	578,330	256.2	82.2	134.7	233.0
1990	1,312	993	2,305	639,270	280.6	86.5	142.7	257.0
1991	1,635	1,114	2,749	687,730	341.0	94.7	166.0	272.7
1992	1,804	1,371	3,175	672,480	366.2	113.4	186.6	263.6
1993	1,863	1,415	3,278	659,870	373.8	112.4	186.5	255.9
1994	1,714	1,224	2,938	618,950	335.4	94.8	163.0	237.7
1995	1,413	1,182	2,595	580,510	279.3	89.1	141.6	220.9
1996	1,327	1,322	2,649	537,050	257.1	97.7	141.7	202.4

Notes: (1) Metropolitan Statistical Area - see Appendix A for areas included; (2) calculated by the editors using the following formula: (number of crimes in the MSA minus number of crimes in the city); (3) calculated by the editors using the following formula: ((number of crimes in the MSA minus number of crimes in the city) ÷ (population of the MSA minus population of the city)) x 100,000; n/a not avail.
Source: U.S. Department of Justice, FBI Uniform Crime Reports, 1977 - 1996

Aggravated Assaults and Aggravated Assault Rates: 1977 - 1996

Year	Number				Rate per 100,000 population			
	City	Suburbs[2]	MSA[1]	U.S.	City	Suburbs[3]	MSA[1]	U.S.
1977	2,005	3,098	5,103	534,350	422.1	308.0	344.6	247.0
1978	1,841	2,525	4,366	571,460	387.6	246.9	291.5	262.1
1979	2,169	2,690	4,859	629,480	445.9	250.1	311.1	286.0
1980	2,351	3,076	5,427	672,650	480.5	273.5	336.3	298.5
1981	2,111	3,596	5,707	663,900	419.1	310.6	343.5	289.7
1982	1,965	3,595	5,560	669,480	379.6	302.2	325.7	289.2
1983	1,947	3,236	5,183	653,290	364.8	317.3	333.6	279.2
1984	1,910	3,394	5,304	685,350	364.4	322.6	336.5	290.2
1985	1,845	3,757	5,602	723,250	359.6	342.8	348.1	302.9
1986	2,036	4,266	6,302	834,320	392.6	385.0	387.4	346.1
1987	1,749	3,950	5,699	855,090	343.3	347.1	345.9	351.3
1988	1,802	4,117	5,919	910,090	360.0	360.8	360.6	370.2
1989	1,925	4,486	6,411	951,710	389.2	391.5	390.8	383.4
1990	2,451	5,047	7,498	1,054,860	524.2	439.6	464.1	424.1
1991	2,884	5,441	8,325	1,092,740	601.5	462.4	502.6	433.3
1992	2,967	5,662	8,629	1,126,970	602.2	468.3	507.0	441.8
1993	2,922	5,730	8,652	1,135,610	586.3	455.0	492.2	440.3
1994	2,545	5,326	7,871	1,113,180	498.0	412.5	436.8	427.6
1995	2,543	3,418	5,961	1,099,210	502.7	257.6	325.3	418.3
1996	2,083	2,899	4,982	1,029,810	403.5	214.2	266.4	388.2

Notes: (1) Metropolitan Statistical Area - see Appendix A for areas included; (2) calculated by the editors using the following formula: (number of crimes in the MSA minus number of crimes in the city); (3) calculated by the editors using the following formula: ((number of crimes in the MSA minus number of crimes in the city) ÷ (population of the MSA minus population of the city)) x 100,000; n/a not avail.
Source: U.S. Department of Justice, FBI Uniform Crime Reports, 1977 - 1996

Burglaries and Burglary Rates: 1977 - 1996

Year	Number				Rate per 100,000 population			
	City	Suburbs[2]	MSA[1]	U.S.	City	Suburbs[3]	MSA[1]	U.S.
1977	17,708	17,213	34,921	3,071,500	3,728.0	1,711.5	2,358.3	1,419.8
1978	17,108	16,988	34,096	3,128,300	3,601.7	1,660.9	2,276.3	1,434.6
1979	16,031	17,666	33,697	3,327,700	3,295.8	1,642.5	2,157.3	1,511.9
1980	19,799	19,608	39,407	3,795,200	4,046.2	1,743.5	2,441.7	1,684.1
1981	20,181	20,225	40,406	3,779,700	4,006.6	1,747.0	2,432.1	1,649.5
1982	16,213	17,969	34,182	3,447,100	3,132.1	1,510.4	2,002.0	1,488.8
1983	14,053	13,891	27,944	3,129,900	2,633.0	1,362.0	1,798.7	1,337.7
1984	15,035	15,566	30,601	2,984,400	2,868.3	1,479.5	1,941.4	1,263.7
1985	16,459	18,782	35,241	3,073,300	3,208.1	1,713.6	2,190.1	1,287.3
1986	17,182	19,034	36,216	3,241,400	3,313.0	1,717.9	2,226.4	1,344.6
1987	13,704	16,376	30,080	3,236,200	2,689.5	1,438.9	1,825.6	1,329.6
1988	11,545	14,814	26,359	3,218,100	2,306.4	1,298.4	1,605.8	1,309.2
1989	10,280	13,635	23,915	3,168,200	2,078.5	1,190.1	1,458.0	1,276.3
1990	9,339	13,164	22,503	3,073,900	1,997.2	1,146.7	1,392.8	1,235.9
1991	9,180	12,948	22,128	3,157,200	1,914.6	1,100.3	1,336.0	1,252.0
1992	8,897	12,614	21,511	2,979,900	1,805.9	1,043.2	1,264.0	1,168.2
1993	9,128	11,160	20,288	2,834,800	1,831.5	886.2	1,154.2	1,099.2
1994	7,759	10,517	18,276	2,712,800	1,518.1	814.6	1,014.1	1,042.0
1995	7,410	10,676	18,086	2,593,800	1,464.9	804.7	986.9	987.1
1996	7,788	10,829	18,617	2,501,500	1,508.6	800.0	995.7	943.0

Notes: (1) Metropolitan Statistical Area - see Appendix A for areas included; (2) calculated by the editors using the following formula: (number of crimes in the MSA minus number of crimes in the city); (3) calculated by the editors using the following formula: ((number of crimes in the MSA minus number of crimes in the city) ÷ (population of the MSA minus population of the city)) x 100,000; n/a not avail.
Source: U.S. Department of Justice, FBI Uniform Crime Reports, 1977 - 1996

Larceny-Thefts and Larceny-Theft Rates: 1977 - 1996

Year	Number				Rate per 100,000 population			
	City	Suburbs[2]	MSA[1]	U.S.	City	Suburbs[3]	MSA[1]	U.S.
1977	25,438	37,701	63,139	5,905,700	5,355.4	3,748.5	4,264.0	2,729.9
1978	23,376	42,999	66,375	5,991,000	4,921.3	4,203.9	4,431.4	2,747.4
1979	25,540	47,265	72,805	6,601,000	5,250.7	4,394.4	4,661.1	2,999.1
1980	28,206	47,702	75,908	7,136,900	5,764.3	4,241.6	4,703.3	3,167.0
1981	30,467	49,056	79,523	7,194,400	6,048.7	4,237.5	4,786.6	3,139.7
1982	33,140	49,836	82,976	7,142,500	6,402.2	4,188.9	4,859.9	3,084.8
1983	32,069	40,487	72,556	6,712,800	6,008.4	3,969.8	4,670.2	2,868.9
1984	27,757	42,769	70,526	6,591,900	5,295.4	4,065.2	4,474.3	2,791.3
1985	27,480	47,618	75,098	6,926,400	5,356.2	4,344.5	4,667.1	2,901.2
1986	27,238	47,479	74,717	7,257,200	5,252.0	4,285.1	4,593.3	3,010.3
1987	23,174	46,310	69,484	7,499,900	4,548.1	4,069.0	4,217.2	3,081.3
1988	21,344	44,814	66,158	7,705,900	4,264.1	3,927.8	4,030.3	3,134.9
1989	18,172	46,333	64,505	7,872,400	3,674.2	4,044.1	3,932.5	3,171.3
1990	16,792	46,910	63,702	7,945,700	3,591.0	4,086.2	3,942.9	3,194.8
1991	16,530	48,693	65,223	8,142,200	3,447.6	4,137.9	3,938.0	3,228.8
1992	17,892	47,116	65,008	7,915,200	3,631.6	3,896.6	3,819.9	3,103.0
1993	17,858	43,754	61,612	7,820,900	3,583.1	3,474.4	3,505.2	3,032.4
1994	16,723	43,763	60,486	7,879,800	3,272.1	3,389.6	3,356.3	3,026.7
1995	17,761	47,515	65,276	7,997,700	3,511.2	3,581.4	3,562.0	3,043.8
1996	17,269	46,367	63,636	7,894,600	3,345.3	3,425.5	3,403.3	2,975.9

Notes: (1) Metropolitan Statistical Area - see Appendix A for areas included; (2) calculated by the editors using the following formula: (number of crimes in the MSA minus number of crimes in the city); (3) calculated by the editors using the following formula: ((number of crimes in the MSA minus number of crimes in the city) ÷ (population of the MSA minus population of the city)) x 100,000; n/a not avail.
Source: U.S. Department of Justice, FBI Uniform Crime Reports, 1977 - 1996

Motor Vehicle Thefts and Motor Vehicle Theft Rates: 1977 - 1996

Year	Number				Rate per 100,000 population			
	City	Suburbs[2]	MSA[1]	U.S.	City	Suburbs[3]	MSA[1]	U.S.
1977	5,759	3,414	9,173	977,700	1,212.4	339.4	619.5	451.9
1978	5,632	4,136	9,768	1,004,100	1,185.7	404.4	652.1	460.5
1979	5,301	4,318	9,619	1,112,800	1,089.8	401.5	615.8	505.6
1980	5,257	3,970	9,227	1,131,700	1,074.4	353.0	571.7	502.2
1981	4,684	3,981	8,665	1,087,800	929.9	343.9	521.6	474.7
1982	4,684	3,905	8,589	1,062,400	904.9	328.2	503.1	458.8
1983	4,838	3,088	7,926	1,007,900	906.4	302.8	510.2	430.8
1984	5,022	3,880	8,902	1,032,200	958.1	368.8	564.8	437.1
1985	5,043	4,737	9,780	1,102,900	982.9	432.2	607.8	462.0
1986	6,601	5,036	11,637	1,224,100	1,272.8	454.5	715.4	507.8
1987	5,465	4,463	9,928	1,288,700	1,072.6	392.1	602.6	529.4
1988	4,978	4,408	9,386	1,432,900	994.5	386.3	571.8	582.9
1989	5,626	4,732	10,358	1,564,800	1,137.5	413.0	631.5	630.4
1990	5,933	4,188	10,121	1,635,900	1,268.8	364.8	626.4	657.8
1991	5,814	4,398	10,212	1,661,700	1,212.6	373.7	616.6	659.0
1992	8,084	5,463	13,547	1,610,800	1,640.8	451.8	796.0	631.5
1993	7,558	4,739	12,297	1,563,100	1,516.4	376.3	699.6	606.1
1994	6,246	4,202	10,448	1,539,300	1,222.1	325.5	579.7	591.3
1995	5,241	4,451	9,692	1,472,400	1,036.1	335.5	528.9	560.4
1996	5,425	4,981	10,406	1,395,200	1,050.9	368.0	556.5	525.9

Notes: (1) Metropolitan Statistical Area - see Appendix A for areas included; (2) calculated by the editors using the following formula: (number of crimes in the MSA minus number of crimes in the city); (3) calculated by the editors using the following formula: ((number of crimes in the MSA minus number of crimes in the city) ÷ (population of the MSA minus population of the city)) x 100,000; n/a not avail.
Source: U.S. Department of Justice, FBI Uniform Crime Reports, 1977 - 1996

HATE CRIMES

Criminal Incidents by Bias Motivation

Area	Race	Ethnicity	Religion	Sexual Orientation
Denver	5	5	4	5

Notes: Figures include both violent and property crimes. Law enforcement agencies must have submitted data for at least one quarter of calendar year 1995 to be included in this report, therefore figures shown may not represent complete 12-month totals; n/a not available
Source: U.S. Department of Justice, FBI Uniform Crime Reports, Hate Crime Statistics 1995

ILLEGAL DRUGS

Drug Use by Adult Arrestees

Sex	Percent Testing Positive by Urinalysis (%)				
	Any Drug[1]	Cocaine	Marijuana	Opiates	Multiple Drugs
Male	71	44	42	5	24
Female	69	53	27	5	17

Notes: The catchment area is the entire city; (1) Includes cocaine, opiates, marijuana, methadone, phencyclidine (PCP), benzodiazepines, methaqualone, propoxyphene, barbiturates & amphetamines
Source: National Institute of Justice, 1996 Drug Use Forecasting, Annual Report on Adult and Juvenile Arrestees (released June 1997)

LAW ENFORCEMENT

Full-Time Law Enforcement Employees

Jurisdiction	Police Employees			Police Officers per 100,000 population
	Total	Officers	Civilians	
Denver	1,600	1,408	192	272.7

Notes: Data as of October 31, 1996
Source: U.S. Department of Justice, FBI Uniform Crime Reports, 1996

Number of Police Officers by Race

Race	Police Officers 1983 Number	1983 Pct.	1992 Number	1992 Pct.	Index of Representation[1] 1983	1992	% Chg.
Black	82	5.9	130	9.6	0.49	0.72	46.9
Hispanic[2]	180	13.1	122	9.1	0.69	0.40	-42.0

Notes: (1) The index of representation is calculated by dividing the percent of black/hispanic police officers by the percent of corresponding blacks/hispanics in the local population. An index approaching 1.0 indicates that a city is closer to achieving a representation of police officers equal to their proportion in the local population; (2) Hispanic officers can be of any race
Source: Bureau of Justice Statistics, Sourcebook of Criminal Justice Statistics, 1994

CORRECTIONS

Federal Correctional Facilities

Type	Year Opened	Security Level	Sex of Inmates	Rated Capacity	Population on 7/1/95	Number of Staff
None listed						

Notes: Data as of 1995
Source: Bureau of Justice Statistics, Sourcebook of Criminal Justice Statistics Online

City/County/Regional Correctional Facilities

Name	Year Opened	Year Renov.	Rated Capacity	1995 Pop.	Number of COs[1]	Number of Staff	ACA[2] Accred.
Denver County Jail	1955	1995	1,352	1,816	619	785	Yes
Denver Pre-Arraignment Detention Facility	1978	--	158	n/a	n/a	n/a	Yes

Notes: Data as of April 1996; (1) Correctional Officers; (2) American Correctional Assn. Accreditation
Source: American Correctional Association, 1996-1998 National Jail and Adult Detention Directory

Private Adult Correctional Facilities

Name	Date Opened	Rated Capacity	Present Pop.	Security Level	Facility Construct.	Expans. Plans	ACA[1] Accred.
None listed							

Notes: Data as of December 1996; (1) American Correctional Association Accreditation
Source: University of Florida, Center for Studies in Criminology and Law, Private Adult Correctional Facility Census, 10th Ed., March 15, 1997

Characteristics of Shock Incarceration Programs

Jurisdiction	Year Program Began	Number of Camps	Average Num. of Inmates	Number of Beds	Program Length	Voluntary/ Mandatory
Colorado	1991	1	110	100	90 to 120 days	Voluntary

Note: Data as of July 1996;
Source: Sourcebook of Criminal Justice Statistics Online

INMATES AND HIV/AIDS

HIV Testing Policies for Inmates

Jurisdiction	All Inmates at Some Time	All Convicted Inmates at Admission	Random Samples While in Custody	High-risk Groups	Upon Inmate Request	Upon Court Order	Upon Involvement in Incident
Denver Co.[1,2]	No	No	No	No	Yes	Yes	No

Notes: (1) Includes inmates held by the city of Denver; (2) All facilities reported following the same testing policy or authorities reported the policy to be jurisdiction-wide
Source: HIV in Prisons and Jails, 1993 (released August 1995)

Inmates Known to be Positive for HIV

Jurisdiction	Number of Jail Inmates in Facilities Providing Data	Type of HIV Infection/AIDS Cases: Total	Asymptomatic	Symptomatic	Confirmed AIDS	HIV/AIDS Cases as a Percent of Tot. Custody Pop.
Denver Co.[1]	260	5	5	0	0	1.9

Note: (1) Some but not all facilities reported data on HIV/AIDS cases. Excludes inmates in facilities that did not report data.
Source: HIV in Prisons and Jails, 1993 (released August, 1995)

DEATH PENALTY

Death Penalty Statistics

State	Prisoners Executed		Prisoners Under Sentence of Death					Avg. No. of Years on Death Row[4]
	1930-1995	1996[1]	Total[2]	White[3]	Black[3]	Hisp.	Women	
Colorado	47	0	4	3	1	1	0	n/c

Notes: Data as of 12/31/95 unless otherwise noted; n/c not calculated on fewer than 10 inmates; (1) Data as of 7/31/97; (2) Includes persons of other races; (3) Includes people of Hispanic origin; (4) Covers prisoners sentenced 1974 through 1995
Source: Bureau of Justice Statistics, Capital Punishment 1995 (released 12/96); Death Penalty Information Center Web Site, 9/30/97

Capital Offenses and Methods of Execution

Capital Offenses in Colorado	Minimum Age for Imposition of Death Penalty	Mentally Retarded Excluded	Methods of Execution[1]
First-degree murder with at least 1 of 13 aggravating factors; treason.	18	Yes	Lethal injection

Notes: Data as of 12/31/95 unless otherwise noted; (1) Data as of 7/31/97
Source: Bureau of Justice Statistics, Capital Punishment 1995 (released 12/96); Death Penalty Information Center Web Site, 9/30/97

LAWS

Statutory Provisions Relating to the Purchase, Ownership and Use of Handguns

Jurisdiction	Instant Background Check	Federal Waiting Period Applies[1]	State Waiting Period (days)	License or Permit to Purchase	Regis-tration	Record of Sale Sent to Police	Concealed Carry Law
Colorado	Yes	No	No	No	No	No	Yes[a]

Note: Data as of 1996; (1) The Federal 5-day waiting period for handgun purchases applies to states that don't have instant background checks, waiting period requirements, or licensing procedures exempting them from the Federal requirement; (a) Restrictively administered discretion by local authorities over permit issuance, or permits are unavailable and carrying is prohibited in most circumstances
Source: Sourcebook of Criminal Justice Statistics Online

Statutory Provisions Relating to Alcohol Use and Driving

Jurisdiction	Drinking Age	Blood Alcohol Concentration Levels as Evidence in State Courts[1]		Open Container Law[1]	Anti-Consump-tion Law[1]	Dram Shop Law[1]
		Illegal per se at 0.10%	Presumption at 0.10%			
Colorado	21	Yes	(a)	No	Yes	Yes

Note: Data as of January 1, 1997; (1) See Appendix C for an explanation of terms; (a) Presumption of driving while impaired at 0.05%; presumption of driving while under the influence at 0.10%
Source: Sourcebook of Criminal Justice Statistics Online

Statutory Provisions Relating to Curfews

Jurisdiction	Year Enacted	Latest Revision	Age Group(s)	Curfew Provisions
Denver	1973	1994	17 and under	11 pm to 5 am weekday nights midnight to 5 am weekend nights

Note: Data as of February 1996
Source: Sourcebook of Criminal Justice Statistics Online

Statutory Provisions Relating to Hate Crimes

Jurisdiction	Bias-Motivated Violence and Intimidation						Institutional Vandalism
	Civil Action	Criminal Penalty					
		Race/ Religion/ Ethnicity	Sexual Orientation	Mental/ Physical Disability	Gender	Age	
Colorado	Yes	Yes	No	No	No	No	Yes

Source: Anti-Defamation League, 1997 Hate Crimes Laws

Detroit, Michigan

OVERVIEW

The total crime rate for the city increased 25.0% between 1977 and 1996. During that same period, the violent crime rate increased 24.3% and the property crime rate increased 25.2%.

Among violent crimes, the rates for: Murders increased 14.8%; Forcible Rapes increased 12.7%; Robberies decreased 22.7%; and Aggravated Assaults increased 142.0%.

Among property crimes, the rates for: Burglaries decreased 22.6%; Larceny-Thefts increased 26.4%; and Motor Vehicle Thefts increased 100.7%.

ANTI-CRIME PROGRAMS

Information not available at time of publication.

CRIME RISK

Your Chances of Becoming a Victim[1]

Area	Any Crime	Violent Crime					Property Crime			
		Any	Murder	Forcible Rape[2]	Robbery	Aggrav. Assault	Any	Burglary	Larceny -Theft	Motor Vehicle Theft
City	1:8	1:43	1:2,342	1:481	1:105	1:82	1:10	1:47	1:24	1:29

Note: (1) Figures have been calculated by dividing the population of the city by the number of crimes reported to the FBI during 1996 and are expressed as odds (eg. 1:20 should be read as 1 in 20).
(2) Figures have been calculated by dividing the female population of the city by the number of forcible rapes reported to the FBI during 1996. The female population of the city was estimated by calculating the ratio of females to males reported in the 1990 Census and applying that ratio to 1996 population estimate.
Source: FBI Uniform Crime Reports 1996

CRIME STATISTICS

Total Crimes and Total Crime Rates: 1977 - 1996

Year	Number				Rate per 100,000 population			
	City	Suburbs[2]	MSA[1]	U.S.	City	Suburbs[3]	MSA[1]	U.S.
1977	123,748	170,718	294,466	10,984,500	9,592.9	5,467.7	6,673.8	5,077.6
1978	110,511	167,434	277,945	11,209,000	8,784.7	5,316.8	6,306.6	5,140.3
1979	110,725	187,118	297,843	12,249,500	8,795.2	5,966.2	6,776.5	5,565.5
1980	127,420	201,635	329,055	13,408,300	10,642.1	6,416.5	7,582.3	5,950.0
1981	143,107	200,168	343,275	13,423,800	11,987.5	6,388.6	7,933.3	5,858.2
1982	152,962	197,252	350,214	12,974,400	12,942.4	6,359.1	8,175.4	5,603.6
1983	151,832	192,135	343,967	12,108,600	12,900.3	5,962.7	7,818.8	5,175.0
1984	161,586	186,456	348,042	11,881,800	14,253.6	5,793.4	7,997.2	5,031.3
1985	149,954	186,535	336,489	12,431,400	13,749.9	5,768.1	7,781.0	5,207.1
1986	140,415	194,860	335,275	13,211,900	12,800.5	5,990.6	7,708.0	5,480.4
1987	138,411	197,149	335,560	13,508,700	12,680.5	6,015.2	7,680.4	5,550.0
1988	131,334	183,646	314,980	13,923,100	12,085.4	5,523.5	7,139.9	5,664.2
1989	125,687	179,150	304,837	14,251,400	12,090.0	5,378.7	6,975.1	5,741.0
1990	125,325	179,336	304,661	14,475,600	12,192.3	5,342.8	6,948.6	5,820.3
1991	127,080	184,743	311,823	14,872,900	12,263.5	5,461.3	7,056.4	5,897.8
1992	117,246	163,930	281,176	14,438,200	11,229.1	4,982.3	6,487.1	5,660.2
1993	n/a	n/a	n/a	14,144,800	n/a	n/a	n/a	5,484.4
1994	121,827	154,733	276,560	13,989,500	11,917.2	4,665.2	6,373.8	5,373.5
1995	119,065	147,135	266,200	13,862,700	11,938.8	4,410.8	6,143.4	5,275.9
1996	120,188	144,596	264,784	13,473,600	11,991.2	4,314.4	6,081.7	5,078.9

Notes: (1) Metropolitan Statistical Area - see Appendix A for areas included; (2) calculated by the editors using the following formula: (number of crimes in the MSA minus number of crimes in the city); (3) calculated by the editors using the following formula: ((number of crimes in the MSA minus number of crimes in the city) ÷ (population of the MSA minus population of the city)) x 100,000; n/a not avail.
Source: U.S. Department of Justice, FBI Uniform Crime Reports, 1977 - 1996

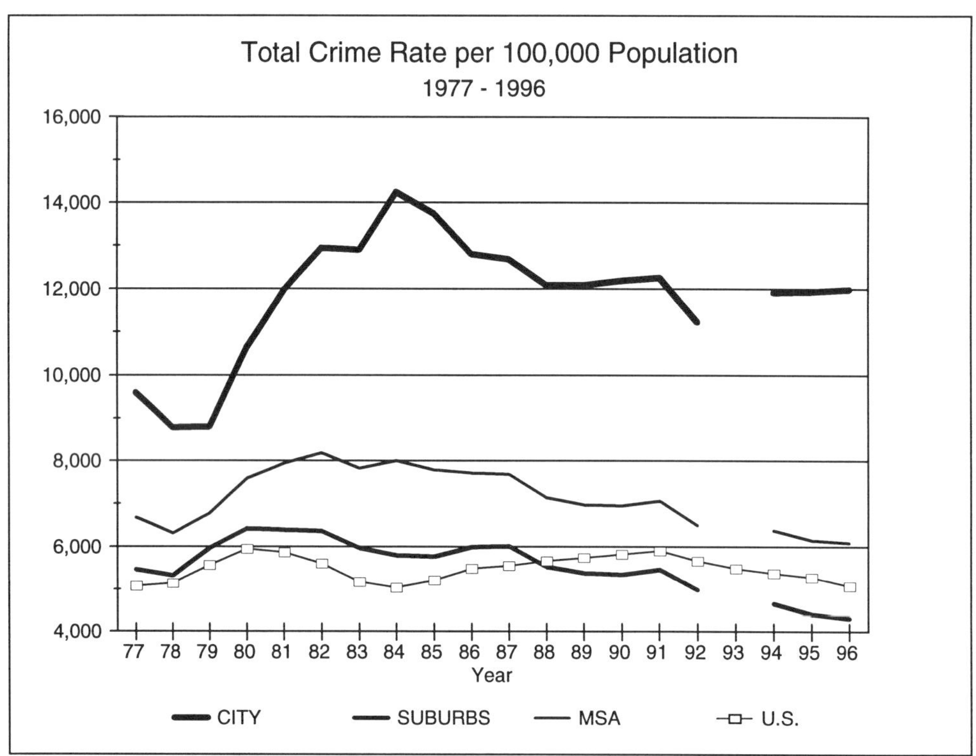

Note: Missing line segments indicate data not available.

Violent Crimes and Violent Crime Rates: 1977 - 1996

Year	Number				Rate per 100,000 population			
	City	Suburbs[2]	MSA[1]	U.S.	City	Suburbs[3]	MSA[1]	U.S.
1977	24,071	12,359	36,430	1,029,580	1,866.0	395.8	825.6	475.9
1978	21,602	12,794	34,396	1,085,550	1,717.2	406.3	780.5	497.8
1979	21,021	13,541	34,562	1,208,030	1,669.8	431.8	786.4	548.9
1980	23,288	14,015	37,303	1,344,520	1,945.0	446.0	859.6	596.6
1981	23,176	13,524	36,700	1,361,820	1,941.4	431.6	848.2	594.3
1982	23,746	14,402	38,148	1,322,390	2,009.2	464.3	890.5	571.1
1983	25,527	16,791	42,318	1,258,090	2,168.9	521.1	961.9	537.7
1984	26,567	15,384	41,951	1,273,280	2,343.5	478.0	963.9	539.2
1985	25,904	16,054	41,958	1,328,800	2,375.2	496.4	970.2	556.6
1986	27,277	18,008	45,285	1,489,170	2,486.6	553.6	1,041.1	617.7
1987	27,778	16,953	44,731	1,484,000	2,544.9	517.2	1,023.8	609.7
1988	25,805	15,890	41,695	1,566,220	2,374.6	477.9	945.1	637.2
1989	24,956	13,992	38,948	1,646,040	2,400.5	420.1	891.2	663.1
1990	27,747	15,678	43,425	1,820,130	2,699.4	467.1	990.4	731.8
1991	28,262	15,980	44,242	1,911,770	2,727.3	472.4	1,001.2	758.1
1992	26,447	16,066	42,513	1,932,270	2,532.9	488.3	980.8	757.5
1993	n/a	n/a	n/a	1,926,020	n/a	n/a	n/a	746.8
1994	27,471	15,375	42,846	1,857,670	2,687.2	463.6	987.5	713.6
1995	24,011	14,157	38,168	1,798,790	2,407.6	424.4	880.8	684.6
1996	23,239	12,848	36,087	1,682,280	2,318.6	383.4	828.9	634.1

Notes: Violent crimes include murder, forcible rape, robbery and aggravated assault; n/a not available; (1) Metropolitan Statistical Area - see Appendix A for areas included; (2) calculated by the editors using the following formula: (number of crimes in the MSA minus number of crimes in the city); (3) calculated by the editors using the following formula: ((number of crimes in the MSA minus number of crimes in the city) ÷ (population of the MSA minus population of the city)) x 100,000
Source: U.S. Department of Justice, FBI Uniform Crime Reports, 1977 - 1996

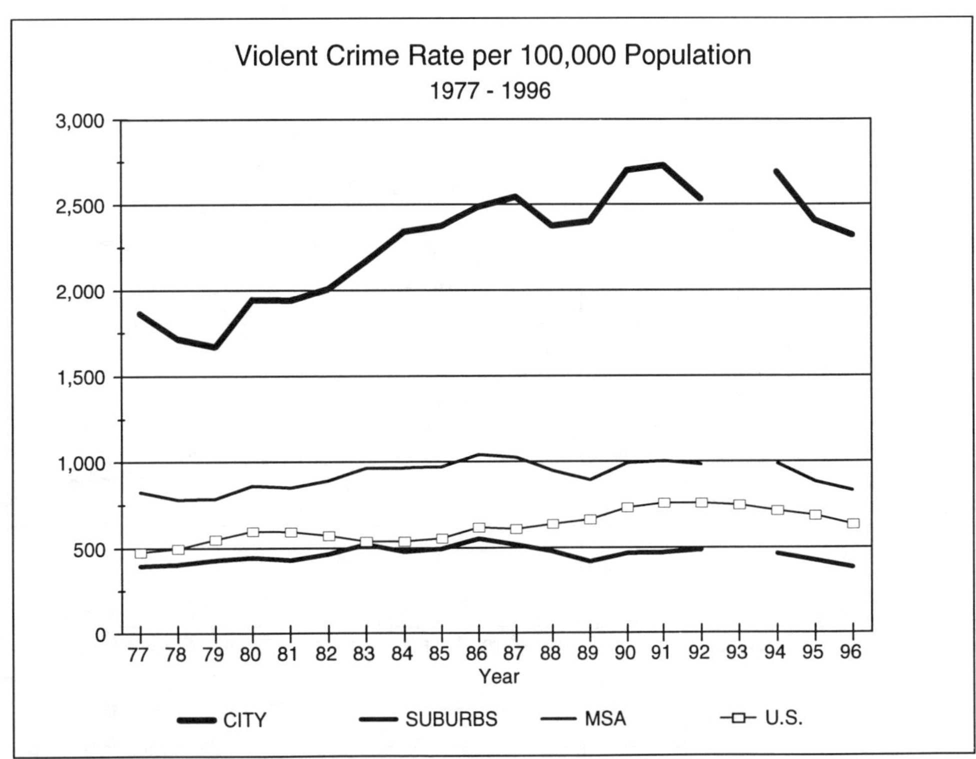

Note: Missing line segments indicate data not available.

Property Crimes and Property Crime Rates: 1977 - 1996

Year	Number				Rate per 100,000 population			
	City	Suburbs[2]	MSA[1]	U.S.	City	Suburbs[3]	MSA[1]	U.S.
1977	99,677	158,359	258,036	9,955,000	7,726.9	5,071.9	5,848.1	4,601.7
1978	88,909	154,640	243,549	10,123,400	7,067.5	4,910.5	5,526.2	4,642.5
1979	89,704	173,577	263,281	11,041,500	7,125.4	5,534.4	5,990.2	5,016.6
1980	104,132	187,620	291,752	12,063,700	8,697.1	5,970.5	6,722.8	5,353.3
1981	119,931	186,644	306,575	12,061,900	10,046.1	5,957.0	7,085.1	5,263.9
1982	129,216	182,850	312,066	11,652,000	10,933.2	5,894.8	7,284.9	5,032.5
1983	126,305	175,344	301,649	10,850,500	10,731.4	5,441.6	6,856.8	4,637.4
1984	135,019	171,072	306,091	10,608,500	11,910.1	5,315.4	7,033.2	4,492.1
1985	124,050	170,481	294,531	11,102,600	11,374.7	5,271.6	6,810.7	4,650.5
1986	113,138	176,852	289,990	11,722,700	10,313.9	5,437.0	6,666.9	4,862.6
1987	110,633	180,196	290,829	12,024,700	10,135.7	5,497.9	6,656.6	4,940.3
1988	105,529	167,756	273,285	12,356,900	9,710.8	5,045.5	6,194.8	5,027.1
1989	100,731	165,158	265,889	12,605,400	9,689.4	4,958.6	6,083.9	5,077.9
1990	97,578	163,658	261,236	12,655,500	9,492.9	4,875.7	5,958.2	5,088.5
1991	98,818	168,763	267,581	12,961,100	9,536.2	4,988.9	6,055.2	5,139.7
1992	90,799	147,864	238,663	12,505,900	8,696.2	4,494.0	5,506.3	4,902.7
1993	93,971	140,252	234,223	12,218,800	9,212.3	4,236.6	5,408.6	4,737.6
1994	94,356	139,358	233,714	12,131,900	9,229.9	4,201.7	5,386.3	4,660.0
1995	95,054	132,978	228,032	12,063,900	9,531.2	3,986.4	5,262.6	4,591.3
1996	96,949	131,748	228,697	11,791,300	9,672.7	3,931.1	5,252.9	4,444.8

Notes: Property crimes include burglary, larceny-theft and motor vehicle theft; n/a not available; (1) Metropolitan Statistical Area - see Appendix A for areas included; (2) calculated by the editors using the following formula: (number of crimes in the MSA minus number of crimes in the city); (3) calculated by the editors using the following formula: ((number of crimes in the MSA minus number of crimes in the city) ÷ (population of the MSA minus population of the city)) x 100,000
Source: U.S. Department of Justice, FBI Uniform Crime Reports, 1977 - 1996

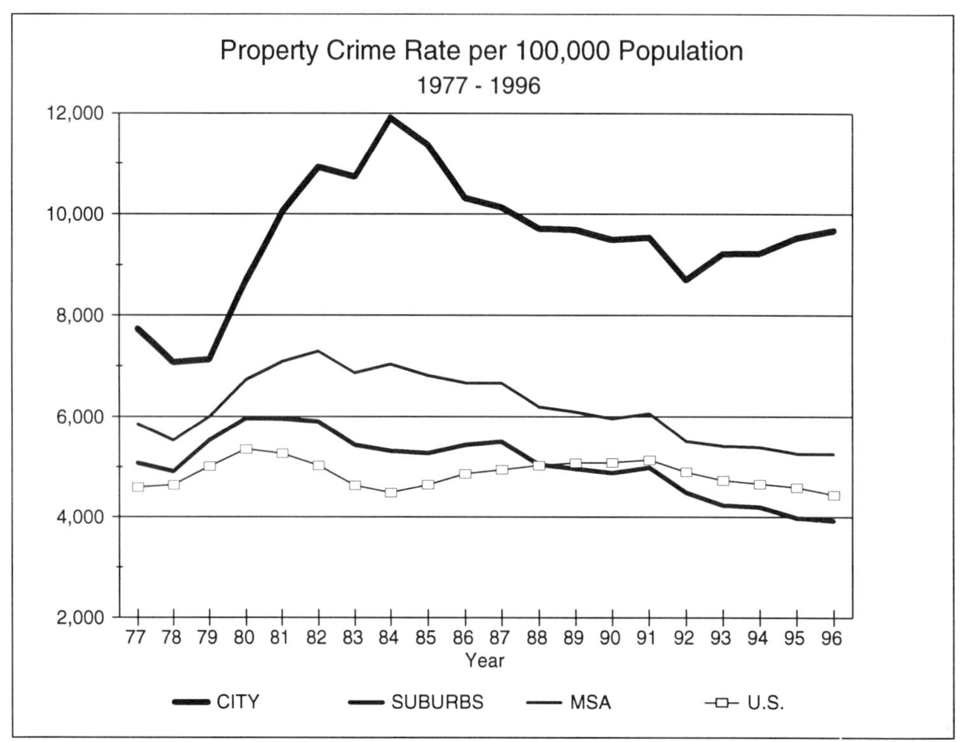

Note: Missing line segments indicate data not available.

Murders and Murder Rates: 1977 - 1996

Year	Number				Rate per 100,000 population			
	City	Suburbs[2]	MSA[1]	U.S.	City	Suburbs[3]	MSA[1]	U.S.
1977	480	141	621	19,120	37.2	4.5	14.1	8.8
1978	498	173	671	19,560	39.6	5.5	15.2	9.0
1979	452	153	605	21,460	35.9	4.9	13.8	9.7
1980	547	151	698	23,040	45.7	4.8	16.1	10.2
1981	502	133	635	22,520	42.1	4.2	14.7	9.8
1982	513	101	614	21,010	43.4	3.3	14.3	9.1
1983	580	146	726	19,310	49.3	4.5	16.5	8.3
1984	514	134	648	18,690	45.3	4.2	14.9	7.9
1985	635	158	793	18,980	58.2	4.9	18.3	7.9
1986	648	138	786	20,610	59.1	4.2	18.1	8.6
1987	686	196	882	20,100	62.8	6.0	20.2	8.3
1988	629	139	768	20,680	57.9	4.2	17.4	8.4
1989	624	140	764	21,500	60.0	4.2	17.5	8.7
1990	582	131	713	23,440	56.6	3.9	16.3	9.4
1991	615	129	744	24,700	59.3	3.8	16.8	9.8
1992	595	119	714	23,760	57.0	3.6	16.5	9.3
1993	579	107	686	24,530	56.8	3.2	15.8	9.5
1994	541	126	667	23,330	52.9	3.8	15.4	9.0
1995	475	89	564	21,610	47.6	2.7	13.0	8.2
1996	428	89	517	19,650	42.7	2.7	11.9	7.4

Notes: (1) Metropolitan Statistical Area - see Appendix A for areas included; (2) calculated by the editors using the following formula: (number of crimes in the MSA minus number of crimes in the city); (3) calculated by the editors using the following formula: ((number of crimes in the MSA minus number of crimes in the city) ÷ (population of the MSA minus population of the city)) x 100,000; n/a not avail.
Source: U.S. Department of Justice, FBI Uniform Crime Reports, 1977 - 1996

Forcible Rapes and Forcible Rape Rates: 1977 - 1996

Year	Number				Rate per 100,000 population			
	City	Suburbs[2]	MSA[1]	U.S.	City	Suburbs[3]	MSA[1]	U.S.
1977	1,277	818	2,095	63,500	99.0	26.2	47.5	29.4
1978	1,288	839	2,127	67,610	102.4	26.6	48.3	31.0
1979	1,369	912	2,281	76,390	108.7	29.1	51.9	34.7
1980	1,313	1,024	2,337	82,990	109.7	32.6	53.9	36.8
1981	1,229	966	2,195	82,500	102.9	30.8	50.7	36.0
1982	1,167	966	2,133	78,770	98.7	31.1	49.8	34.0
1983	1,514	1,277	2,791	78,920	128.6	39.6	63.4	33.7
1984	1,519	1,268	2,787	84,230	134.0	39.4	64.0	35.7
1985	1,575	1,367	2,942	88,670	144.4	42.3	68.0	37.1
1986	1,351	1,447	2,798	91,460	123.2	44.5	64.3	37.9
1987	1,417	1,341	2,758	91,110	129.8	40.9	63.1	37.4
1988	1,447	1,313	2,760	92,490	133.2	39.5	62.6	37.6
1989	1,424	1,362	2,786	94,500	137.0	40.9	63.7	38.1
1990	1,657	1,442	3,099	102,560	161.2	43.0	70.7	41.2
1991	1,427	1,660	3,087	106,590	137.7	49.1	69.9	42.3
1992	1,225	1,663	2,888	109,060	117.3	50.5	66.6	42.8
1993	n/a	n/a	n/a	106,010	n/a	n/a	n/a	41.1
1994	1,116	1,345	2,461	102,220	109.2	40.6	56.7	39.3
1995	1,104	1,225	2,329	97,470	110.7	36.7	53.7	37.1
1996	1,119	1,119	2,238	95,770	111.6	33.4	51.4	36.1

Notes: (1) Metropolitan Statistical Area - see Appendix A for areas included; (2) calculated by the editors using the following formula: (number of crimes in the MSA minus number of crimes in the city); (3) calculated by the editors using the following formula: ((number of crimes in the MSA minus number of crimes in the city) ÷ (population of the MSA minus population of the city)) x 100,000; n/a not avail.
Source: U.S. Department of Justice, FBI Uniform Crime Reports, 1977 - 1996

Robberies and Robbery Rates: 1977 - 1996

Year	Number				Rate per 100,000 population			
	City	Suburbs[2]	MSA[1]	U.S.	City	Suburbs[3]	MSA[1]	U.S.
1977	15,832	4,215	20,047	412,610	1,227.3	135.0	454.3	190.7
1978	12,283	3,968	16,251	426,930	976.4	126.0	368.7	195.8
1979	11,413	4,036	15,449	480,700	906.6	128.7	351.5	218.4
1980	13,429	4,309	17,738	565,840	1,121.6	137.1	408.7	251.1
1981	14,797	4,203	19,000	592,910	1,239.5	134.1	439.1	258.7
1982	16,037	4,335	20,372	553,130	1,356.9	139.8	475.6	238.9
1983	16,922	4,657	21,579	506,570	1,437.8	144.5	490.5	216.5
1984	18,352	5,021	23,373	485,010	1,618.8	156.0	537.1	205.4
1985	16,769	4,957	21,726	497,870	1,537.6	153.3	502.4	208.5
1986	16,421	5,729	22,150	542,780	1,497.0	176.1	509.2	225.1
1987	15,093	5,283	20,376	517,700	1,382.7	161.2	466.4	212.7
1988	12,978	4,332	17,310	542,970	1,194.2	130.3	392.4	220.9
1989	11,902	3,674	15,576	578,330	1,144.9	110.3	356.4	233.0
1990	13,010	3,704	16,714	639,270	1,265.7	110.3	381.2	257.0
1991	13,569	3,794	17,363	687,730	1,309.4	112.2	392.9	272.7
1992	12,194	3,675	15,869	672,480	1,167.9	111.7	366.1	263.6
1993	13,591	3,741	17,332	659,870	1,332.4	113.0	400.2	255.9
1994	12,772	3,102	15,874	618,950	1,249.4	93.5	365.8	237.7
1995	10,076	2,755	12,831	580,510	1,010.3	82.6	296.1	220.9
1996	9,504	2,686	12,190	537,050	948.2	80.1	280.0	202.4

Notes: (1) Metropolitan Statistical Area - see Appendix A for areas included; (2) calculated by the editors using the following formula: (number of crimes in the MSA minus number of crimes in the city); (3) calculated by the editors using the following formula: ((number of crimes in the MSA minus number of crimes in the city) ÷ (population of the MSA minus population of the city)) x 100,000; n/a not avail.
Source: U.S. Department of Justice, FBI Uniform Crime Reports, 1977 - 1996

Aggravated Assaults and Aggravated Assault Rates: 1977 - 1996

Year	Number				Rate per 100,000 population			
	City	Suburbs[2]	MSA[1]	U.S.	City	Suburbs[3]	MSA[1]	U.S.
1977	6,482	7,185	13,667	534,350	502.5	230.1	309.7	247.0
1978	7,533	7,814	15,347	571,460	598.8	248.1	348.2	262.1
1979	7,787	8,440	16,227	629,480	618.5	269.1	369.2	286.0
1980	7,999	8,531	16,530	672,650	668.1	271.5	380.9	298.5
1981	6,648	8,222	14,870	663,900	556.9	262.4	343.7	289.7
1982	6,029	9,000	15,029	669,480	510.1	290.1	350.8	289.2
1983	6,511	10,711	17,222	653,290	553.2	332.4	391.5	279.2
1984	6,182	8,961	15,143	685,350	545.3	278.4	348.0	290.2
1985	6,925	9,572	16,497	723,250	635.0	296.0	381.5	302.9
1986	8,857	10,694	19,551	834,320	807.4	328.8	449.5	346.1
1987	10,582	10,133	20,715	855,090	969.5	309.2	474.1	351.3
1988	10,751	10,106	20,857	910,090	989.3	304.0	472.8	370.2
1989	11,006	8,816	19,822	951,710	1,058.7	264.7	453.6	383.4
1990	12,498	10,401	22,899	1,054,860	1,215.9	309.9	522.3	424.1
1991	12,651	10,397	23,048	1,092,740	1,220.8	307.3	521.6	433.3
1992	12,433	10,609	23,042	1,126,970	1,190.8	322.4	531.6	441.8
1993	12,999	11,447	24,446	1,135,610	1,274.3	345.8	564.5	440.3
1994	13,042	10,802	23,844	1,113,180	1,275.8	325.7	549.5	427.6
1995	12,356	10,088	22,444	1,099,210	1,238.9	302.4	518.0	418.3
1996	12,188	8,954	21,142	1,029,810	1,216.0	267.2	485.6	388.2

Notes: (1) Metropolitan Statistical Area - see Appendix A for areas included; (2) calculated by the editors using the following formula: (number of crimes in the MSA minus number of crimes in the city); (3) calculated by the editors using the following formula: ((number of crimes in the MSA minus number of crimes in the city) ÷ (population of the MSA minus population of the city)) x 100,000; n/a not avail.
Source: U.S. Department of Justice, FBI Uniform Crime Reports, 1977 - 1996

Burglaries and Burglary Rates: 1977 - 1996

Year	Number				Rate per 100,000 population			
	City	Suburbs[2]	MSA[1]	U.S.	City	Suburbs[3]	MSA[1]	U.S.
1977	35,742	37,559	73,301	3,071,500	2,770.7	1,202.9	1,661.3	1,419.8
1978	32,575	36,593	69,168	3,128,300	2,589.4	1,162.0	1,569.4	1,434.6
1979	32,701	38,655	71,356	3,327,700	2,597.5	1,232.5	1,623.5	1,511.9
1980	40,848	45,141	85,989	3,795,200	3,411.6	1,436.5	1,981.4	1,684.1
1981	46,224	48,667	94,891	3,779,700	3,872.0	1,553.3	2,193.0	1,649.5
1982	49,635	46,746	96,381	3,447,100	4,199.7	1,507.0	2,249.9	1,488.8
1983	45,593	44,811	90,404	3,129,900	3,873.8	1,390.7	2,055.0	1,337.7
1984	44,360	42,899	87,259	2,984,400	3,913.0	1,332.9	2,005.0	1,263.7
1985	40,385	39,045	79,430	3,073,300	3,703.1	1,207.4	1,836.7	1,287.3
1986	38,975	38,832	77,807	3,241,400	3,553.0	1,193.8	1,788.8	1,344.6
1987	36,900	37,290	74,190	3,236,200	3,380.6	1,137.7	1,698.1	1,329.6
1988	32,147	33,669	65,816	3,218,100	2,958.2	1,012.7	1,491.9	1,309.2
1989	29,031	30,401	59,432	3,168,200	2,792.5	912.7	1,359.9	1,276.3
1990	26,063	27,334	53,397	3,073,900	2,535.6	814.3	1,217.9	1,235.9
1991	26,059	28,413	54,472	3,157,200	2,514.8	839.9	1,232.7	1,252.0
1992	22,048	24,136	46,184	2,979,900	2,111.6	733.6	1,065.5	1,168.2
1993	23,092	22,649	45,741	2,834,800	2,263.8	684.2	1,056.2	1,099.2
1994	22,156	22,201	44,357	2,712,800	2,167.3	669.4	1,022.3	1,042.0
1995	22,366	20,192	42,558	2,593,800	2,242.7	605.3	982.2	987.1
1996	21,491	20,168	41,659	2,501,500	2,144.2	601.8	956.9	943.0

Notes: (1) Metropolitan Statistical Area - see Appendix A for areas included; (2) calculated by the editors using the following formula: (number of crimes in the MSA minus number of crimes in the city); (3) calculated by the editors using the following formula: ((number of crimes in the MSA minus number of crimes in the city) ÷ (population of the MSA minus population of the city)) x 100,000; n/a not avail.
Source: U.S. Department of Justice, FBI Uniform Crime Reports, 1977 - 1996

Larceny-Thefts and Larceny-Theft Rates: 1977 - 1996

Year	Number				Rate per 100,000 population			
	City	Suburbs[2]	MSA[1]	U.S.	City	Suburbs[3]	MSA[1]	U.S.
1977	41,959	103,501	145,460	5,905,700	3,252.6	3,314.9	3,296.7	2,729.9
1978	36,840	100,760	137,600	5,991,000	2,928.5	3,199.6	3,122.2	2,747.4
1979	35,501	114,534	150,035	6,601,000	2,819.9	3,651.9	3,413.6	2,999.1
1980	41,066	122,718	163,784	7,136,900	3,429.8	3,905.2	3,774.0	3,167.0
1981	46,186	117,769	163,955	7,194,400	3,868.8	3,758.7	3,789.1	3,139.7
1982	48,001	114,451	162,452	7,142,500	4,061.5	3,689.7	3,792.3	3,084.8
1983	45,424	107,568	152,992	6,712,800	3,859.4	3,338.2	3,477.7	2,868.9
1984	48,154	102,113	150,267	6,591,900	4,247.7	3,172.8	3,452.8	2,791.3
1985	46,014	105,104	151,118	6,926,400	4,219.2	3,250.0	3,494.5	2,901.2
1986	42,250	109,730	151,980	7,257,200	3,851.6	3,373.5	3,494.0	3,010.3
1987	43,914	116,377	160,291	7,499,900	4,023.2	3,550.8	3,668.8	3,081.3
1988	43,259	109,153	152,412	7,705,900	3,980.7	3,283.0	3,454.8	3,134.9
1989	43,577	110,913	154,490	7,872,400	4,191.7	3,330.0	3,535.0	3,171.3
1990	41,139	114,982	156,121	7,945,700	4,002.2	3,425.5	3,560.7	3,194.8
1991	44,019	119,650	163,669	8,142,200	4,247.9	3,537.0	3,703.7	3,228.8
1992	41,407	105,834	147,241	7,915,200	3,965.7	3,216.6	3,397.0	3,103.0
1993	42,818	100,543	143,361	7,820,900	4,197.6	3,037.1	3,310.4	3,032.4
1994	42,631	99,164	141,795	7,879,800	4,170.2	2,989.8	3,267.9	3,026.7
1995	43,415	94,925	138,340	7,997,700	4,353.3	2,845.6	3,192.6	3,043.8
1996	41,193	93,704	134,897	7,894,600	4,109.9	2,795.9	3,098.4	2,975.9

Notes: (1) Metropolitan Statistical Area - see Appendix A for areas included; (2) calculated by the editors using the following formula: (number of crimes in the MSA minus number of crimes in the city); (3) calculated by the editors using the following formula: ((number of crimes in the MSA minus number of crimes in the city) ÷ (population of the MSA minus population of the city)) x 100,000; n/a not avail.
Source: U.S. Department of Justice, FBI Uniform Crime Reports, 1977 - 1996

Motor Vehicle Thefts and Motor Vehicle Theft Rates: 1977 - 1996

Year	Number				Rate per 100,000 population			
	City	Suburbs[2]	MSA[1]	U.S.	City	Suburbs[3]	MSA[1]	U.S.
1977	21,976	17,299	39,275	977,700	1,703.6	554.0	890.1	451.9
1978	19,494	17,287	36,781	1,004,100	1,549.6	548.9	834.6	460.5
1979	21,502	20,388	41,890	1,112,800	1,708.0	650.1	953.1	505.6
1980	22,218	19,761	41,979	1,131,700	1,855.6	628.8	967.3	502.2
1981	27,521	20,208	47,729	1,087,800	2,305.3	645.0	1,103.0	474.7
1982	31,580	21,653	53,233	1,062,400	2,672.0	698.1	1,242.7	458.8
1983	35,288	22,965	58,253	1,007,900	2,998.2	712.7	1,324.2	430.8
1984	42,505	26,060	68,565	1,032,200	3,749.4	809.7	1,575.5	437.1
1985	37,651	26,332	63,983	1,102,900	3,452.4	814.2	1,479.5	462.0
1986	31,913	28,290	60,203	1,224,100	2,909.3	869.7	1,384.1	507.8
1987	29,819	26,529	56,348	1,288,700	2,731.9	809.4	1,289.7	529.4
1988	30,123	24,934	55,057	1,432,900	2,771.9	749.9	1,248.0	582.9
1989	28,123	23,844	51,967	1,564,800	2,705.2	715.9	1,189.1	630.4
1990	30,376	21,342	51,718	1,635,900	2,955.1	635.8	1,179.6	657.8
1991	28,740	20,700	49,440	1,661,700	2,773.5	611.9	1,118.8	659.0
1992	27,344	17,894	45,238	1,610,800	2,618.8	543.8	1,043.7	631.5
1993	28,061	17,060	45,121	1,563,100	2,750.9	515.3	1,041.9	606.1
1994	29,569	17,993	47,562	1,539,300	2,892.4	542.5	1,096.1	591.3
1995	29,273	17,861	47,134	1,472,400	2,935.2	535.4	1,087.8	560.4
1996	34,265	17,876	52,141	1,395,200	3,418.6	533.4	1,197.6	525.9

Notes: (1) Metropolitan Statistical Area - see Appendix A for areas included; (2) calculated by the editors using the following formula: (number of crimes in the MSA minus number of crimes in the city); (3) calculated by the editors using the following formula: ((number of crimes in the MSA minus number of crimes in the city) ÷ (population of the MSA minus population of the city)) x 100,000; n/a not avail.
Source: U.S. Department of Justice, FBI Uniform Crime Reports, 1977 - 1996

HATE CRIMES

Criminal Incidents by Bias Motivation

Area	Race	Ethnicity	Religion	Sexual Orientation
Detroit	8	1	0	0

Notes: Figures include both violent and property crimes. Law enforcement agencies must have submitted data for at least one quarter of calendar year 1995 to be included in this report, therefore figures shown may not represent complete 12-month totals; n/a not available
Source: U.S. Department of Justice, FBI Uniform Crime Reports, Hate Crime Statistics 1995

ILLEGAL DRUGS

Drug Use by Adult Arrestees

Sex	Percent Testing Positive by Urinalysis (%)				
	Any Drug[1]	Cocaine	Marijuana	Opiates	Multiple Drugs
Male	66	27	46	7	15
Female	69	53	19	18	21

Notes: The catchment area is the entire city; (1) Includes cocaine, opiates, marijuana, methadone, phencyclidine (PCP), benzodiazepines, methaqualone, propoxyphene, barbiturates & amphetamines
Source: National Institute of Justice, 1996 Drug Use Forecasting, Annual Report on Adult and Juvenile Arrestees (released June 1997)

LAW ENFORCEMENT

Full-Time Law Enforcement Employees

Jurisdiction	Police Employees			Police Officers per 100,000 population
	Total	Officers	Civilians	
Detroit	4,453	3,917	536	390.8

Notes: Data as of October 31, 1996
Source: U.S. Department of Justice, FBI Uniform Crime Reports, 1996

Number of Police Officers by Race

Race	Police Officers 1983		Police Officers 1992		Index of Representation[1]		
	Number	Pct.	Number	Pct.	1983	1992	% Chg.
Black	1,238	30.7	2,556	53.4	0.49	0.70	42.9
Hispanic[2]	32	0.8	62	1.3	0.29	0.43	48.3

Notes: (1) The index of representation is calculated by dividing the percent of black/hispanic police officers by the percent of corresponding blacks/hispanics in the local population. An index approaching 1.0 indicates that a city is closer to achieving a representation of police officers equal to their proportion in the local population; (2) Hispanic officers can be of any race
Source: Bureau of Justice Statistics, Sourcebook of Criminal Justice Statistics, 1994

CORRECTIONS

Federal Correctional Facilities

Type	Year Opened	Security Level	Sex of Inmates	Rated Capacity	Population on 7/1/95	Number of Staff
None listed						

Notes: Data as of 1995
Source: Bureau of Justice Statistics, Sourcebook of Criminal Justice Statistics Online

City/County/Regional Correctional Facilities

Name	Year Opened	Year Renov.	Rated Capacity	1995 Pop.	Number of COs[1]	Number of Staff	ACA[2] Accred.
Wayne Co Jail-Div I/II/III	1930	--	2,585	n/a	1,168	1,526	No

Notes: Data as of April 1996; (1) Correctional Officers; (2) American Correctional Assn. Accreditation
Source: American Correctional Association, 1996-1998 National Jail and Adult Detention Directory

Private Adult Correctional Facilities

Name	Date Opened	Rated Capacity	Present Pop.	Security Level	Facility Construct.	Expans. Plans	ACA[1] Accred.
None listed							

Notes: Data as of December 1996; (1) American Correctional Association Accreditation
Source: University of Florida, Center for Studies in Criminology and Law, Private Adult Correctional Facility Census, 10th Ed., March 15, 1997

Characteristics of Shock Incarceration Programs

Jurisdiction	Year Program Began	Number of Camps	Average Num. of Inmates	Number of Beds	Program Length	Voluntary/ Mandatory
Michigan	1988	1	319	360	90 days	Voluntary

Note: Data as of July 1996;
Source: Sourcebook of Criminal Justice Statistics Online

INMATES AND HIV/AIDS

HIV Testing Policies for Inmates

Jurisdiction	All Inmates at Some Time	All Convicted Inmates at Admission	Random Samples While in Custody	High-risk Groups	Upon Inmate Request	Upon Court Order	Upon Involve-ment in Incident
Wayne Co.	No	No	No	No	No	Yes	No

Source: HIV in Prisons and Jails, 1993 (released August 1995)

Inmates Known to be Positive for HIV

Jurisdiction	Number of Jail Inmates in Facilities Providing Data	Type of HIV Infection/AIDS Cases: Total	Asymp-tomatic	Symp-tomatic	Confirmed AIDS	HIV/AIDS Cases as a Percent of Tot. Custody Pop.
Wayne Co.[1]	2,280	n/a	n/a	n/a	n/a	n/a

Note: (1) Jurisdiction did not provide data on HIV/AIDS cases; n/a not available
Source: HIV in Prisons and Jails, 1993 (released August, 1995)

DEATH PENALTY

Michigan did not have the death penalty as of July 31, 1997.
Source: Death Penalty Information Center Web Site, 9/30/97

LAWS

Statutory Provisions Relating to the Purchase, Ownership and Use of Handguns

Jurisdiction	Instant Background Check	Federal Waiting Period Applies[1]	State Waiting Period (days)	License or Permit to Purchase	Registration	Record of Sale Sent to Police	Concealed Carry Law
Michigan	No	No	No	Yes[a]	Yes	Yes	Yes[b]

Note: Data as of 1996; (1) The Federal 5-day waiting period for handgun purchases applies to states that don't have instant background checks, waiting period requirements, or licensing procedures exempting them from the Federal requirement; (a) A handgun purchaser must obtain a license to purchase from local law enforcement, and within 10 days present to such official the license and handgun purchased to obtain a certificate of inspection; (b) Restrictively administered discretion by local authorities over permit issuance, or permits are unavailable and carrying is prohibited in most circumstances
Source: Sourcebook of Criminal Justice Statistics Online

Statutory Provisions Relating to Alcohol Use and Driving

Jurisdiction	Drinking Age	Blood Alcohol Concentration Levels as Evidence in State Courts[1]		Open Container Law[1]	Anti-Consumption Law[1]	Dram Shop Law[1]
		Illegal per se at 0.10%	Presumption at 0.10%			
Michigan	21	Yes	(a)	Yes	Yes	Yes

Note: Data as of January 1, 1997; (1) See Appendix C for an explanation of terms; (a) Presumption of driving while impaired at 0.07%; presumption of driving under the influence at 0.10%
Source: Sourcebook of Criminal Justice Statistics Online

Statutory Provisions Relating to Curfews

Jurisdiction	Year Enacted	Latest Revision	Age Group(s)	Curfew Provisions
Detroit	1925	1987	16 and 17	9pm-6am non-daylight saving time nights 10pm-6am daylight saving time nights
			15 and under	8 pm to 6 am every night

Note: Data as of February 1996
Source: Sourcebook of Criminal Justice Statistics Online

Statutory Provisions Relating to Hate Crimes

Jurisdiction	Bias-Motivated Violence and Intimidation						Institutional Vandalism
	Civil Action	Criminal Penalty					
		Race/ Religion/ Ethnicity	Sexual Orientation	Mental/ Physical Disability	Gender	Age	
Michigan	Yes	Yes	No	No	Yes	No	No

Source: Anti-Defamation League, 1997 Hate Crimes Laws

Durham, North Carolina

OVERVIEW

The total crime rate for the city increased 50.1% between 1977 and 1996. During that same period, the violent crime rate increased 92.3% and the property crime rate increased 46.5%.

Among violent crimes, the rates for: Murders increased 137.9%; Forcible Rapes decreased 7.1%; Robberies increased 199.1%; and Aggravated Assaults increased 50.8%.

Among property crimes, the rates for: Burglaries increased 41.3%; Larceny-Thefts increased 38.7%; and Motor Vehicle Thefts increased 166.4%.

ANTI-CRIME PROGRAMS

Anti-crime programs which have been designed for teens include:

- Teen Watch—Offspring of Neighborhood Watch where teen residents look out for potential problems and report them to the police.
- Summer Youth Academy—One week camping experience designed to address critical issues and concerns facing youth.

Other programs:

- Partners Against Crime Initiative in which efforts are made by all components of a community to bring a comprehensive approach to the community's crime problems. It seeks to "mind the social and economic fabric of the community through a range of programs designed to promote entrepreneurship and local economic development, to stabilize families, to promote job preparedness through skills enhancement, and to discourage area youth from engaging in dysfunctional or antisocial behavior." *Durham Police Department, 9/97*

CRIME RISK

Your Chances of Becoming a Victim[1]

Area	Any Crime	Violent Crime					Property Crime			
		Any	Murder	Forcible Rape[2]	Robbery	Aggrav. Assault	Any	Burglary	Larceny -Theft	Motor Vehicle Theft
City	1:9	1:88	1:3,624	1:949	1:183	1:197	1:10	1:35	1:16	1:98

Note: (1) Figures have been calculated by dividing the population of the city by the number of crimes reported to the FBI during 1996 and are expressed as odds (eg. 1:20 should be read as 1 in 20). (2) Figures have been calculated by dividing the female population of the city by the number of forcible rapes reported to the FBI during 1996. The female population of the city was estimated by calculating the ratio of females to males reported in the 1990 Census and applying that ratio to 1996 population estimate.
Source: FBI Uniform Crime Reports 1996

CRIME STATISTICS

Total Crimes and Total Crime Rates: 1977 - 1996

Year	Number				Rate per 100,000 population			
	City	Suburbs[2]	MSA[1]	U.S.	City	Suburbs[3]	MSA[1]	U.S.
1977	7,828	16,441	24,269	10,984,500	7,549.7	4,315.7	5,007.6	5,077.6
1978	8,178	16,365	24,543	11,209,000	7,863.5	4,224.6	4,994.8	5,140.3
1979	10,392	20,286	30,678	12,249,500	9,859.7	5,186.8	6,178.8	5,565.5
1980	10,532	22,793	33,325	13,408,300	10,561.0	5,145.7	6,140.8	5,950.0
1981	10,746	24,404	35,150	13,423,800	10,581.2	5,639.2	6,578.5	5,858.2
1982	11,224	23,092	34,316	12,974,400	10,927.1	5,275.7	6,349.9	5,603.6
1983	10,199	22,211	32,410	12,108,600	9,826.4	4,692.8	5,616.1	5,175.0
1984	9,940	21,633	31,573	11,881,800	9,580.9	4,418.6	5,321.2	5,031.3
1985	9,781	22,405	32,186	12,431,400	9,450.9	4,356.0	5,209.4	5,207.1
1986	9,826	25,231	35,057	13,211,900	9,380.4	4,846.7	5,606.2	5,480.4
1987	10,528	27,570	38,098	13,508,700	9,127.5	5,074.8	5,784.5	5,550.0
1988	10,737	26,987	37,724	13,923,100	9,121.3	4,827.3	5,574.2	5,664.2
1989	11,424	29,448	40,872	14,251,400	9,770.7	5,123.3	5,908.8	5,741.0
1990	12,657	29,525	42,182	14,475,600	9,265.0	4,934.7	5,739.6	5,820.3
1991	14,181	35,082	49,263	14,872,900	10,213.6	5,769.3	6,595.4	5,897.8
1992	15,210	42,858	58,068	14,438,200	10,785.1	5,779.4	6,579.2	5,660.2
1993	14,980	40,607	55,587	14,144,800	10,462.9	5,206.4	6,021.7	5,484.4
1994	15,550	42,700	58,250	13,989,500	10,669.0	5,378.1	6,198.7	5,373.5
1995	15,866	43,299	59,165	13,862,700	10,869.0	5,181.9	6,027.6	5,275.9
1996	16,838	43,866	60,704	13,473,600	11,333.3	5,158.1	6,076.4	5,078.9

Notes: (1) Metropolitan Statistical Area - see Appendix A for areas included; (2) calculated by the editors using the following formula: (number of crimes in the MSA minus number of crimes in the city); (3) calculated by the editors using the following formula: ((number of crimes in the MSA minus number of crimes in the city) ÷ (population of the MSA minus population of the city)) x 100,000; n/a not avail.
Source: U.S. Department of Justice, FBI Uniform Crime Reports, 1977 - 1996

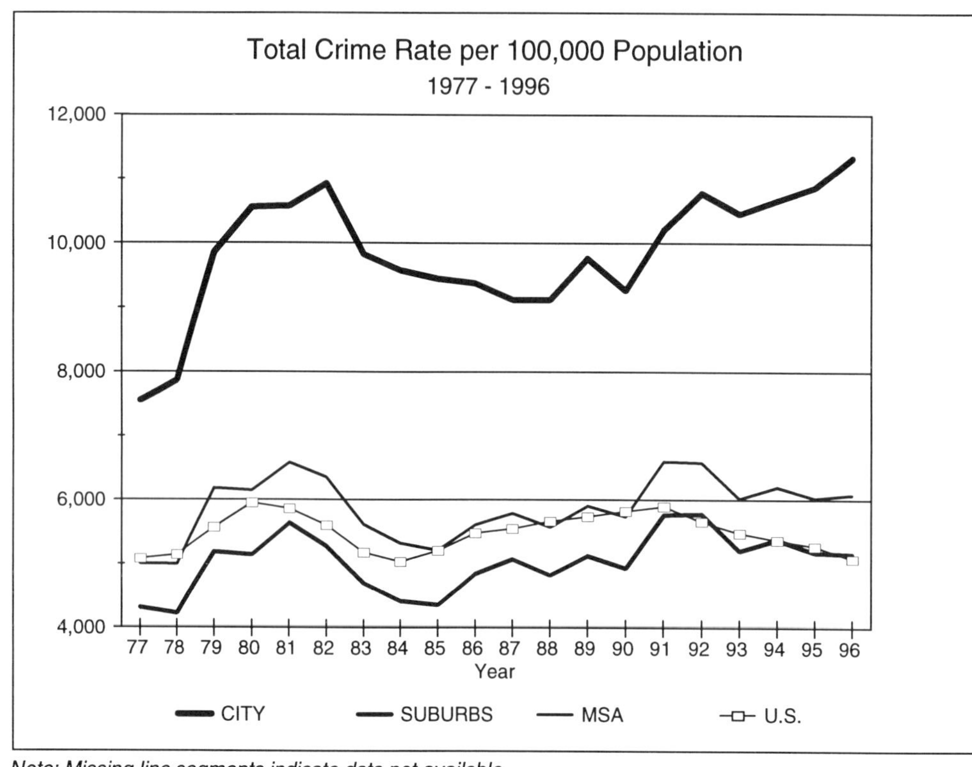

Note: Missing line segments indicate data not available.

Violent Crimes and Violent Crime Rates: 1977 - 1996

Year	Number				Rate per 100,000 population			
	City	Suburbs[2]	MSA[1]	U.S.	City	Suburbs[3]	MSA[1]	U.S.
1977	613	1,066	1,679	1,029,580	591.2	279.8	346.4	475.9
1978	640	1,125	1,765	1,085,550	615.4	290.4	359.2	497.8
1979	742	1,430	2,172	1,208,030	704.0	365.6	437.5	548.9
1980	640	1,529	2,169	1,344,520	641.8	345.2	399.7	596.6
1981	612	1,470	2,082	1,361,820	602.6	339.7	389.7	594.3
1982	886	1,380	2,266	1,322,390	862.6	315.3	419.3	571.1
1983	600	1,743	2,343	1,258,090	578.1	368.3	406.0	537.7
1984	607	1,666	2,273	1,273,280	585.1	340.3	383.1	539.2
1985	678	1,723	2,401	1,328,800	655.1	335.0	388.6	556.6
1986	636	2,023	2,659	1,489,170	607.2	388.6	425.2	617.7
1987	711	2,006	2,717	1,484,000	616.4	369.2	412.5	609.7
1988	701	2,077	2,778	1,566,220	595.5	371.5	410.5	637.2
1989	798	2,235	3,033	1,646,040	682.5	388.8	438.5	663.1
1990	1,013	2,304	3,317	1,820,130	741.5	385.1	451.3	731.8
1991	1,614	3,160	4,774	1,911,770	1,162.5	519.7	639.2	758.1
1992	1,791	4,360	6,151	1,932,270	1,270.0	587.9	696.9	757.5
1993	1,707	4,115	5,822	1,926,020	1,192.3	527.6	630.7	746.8
1994	1,729	4,235	5,964	1,857,670	1,186.3	533.4	634.7	713.6
1995	1,835	4,054	5,889	1,798,790	1,257.1	485.2	600.0	684.6
1996	1,689	4,014	5,703	1,682,280	1,136.8	472.0	570.9	634.1

Notes: Violent crimes include murder, forcible rape, robbery and aggravated assault; n/a not available; (1) Metropolitan Statistical Area - see Appendix A for areas included; (2) calculated by the editors using the following formula: (number of crimes in the MSA minus number of crimes in the city); (3) calculated by the editors using the following formula: ((number of crimes in the MSA minus number of crimes in the city) ÷ (population of the MSA minus population of the city)) x 100,000
Source: U.S. Department of Justice, FBI Uniform Crime Reports, 1977 - 1996

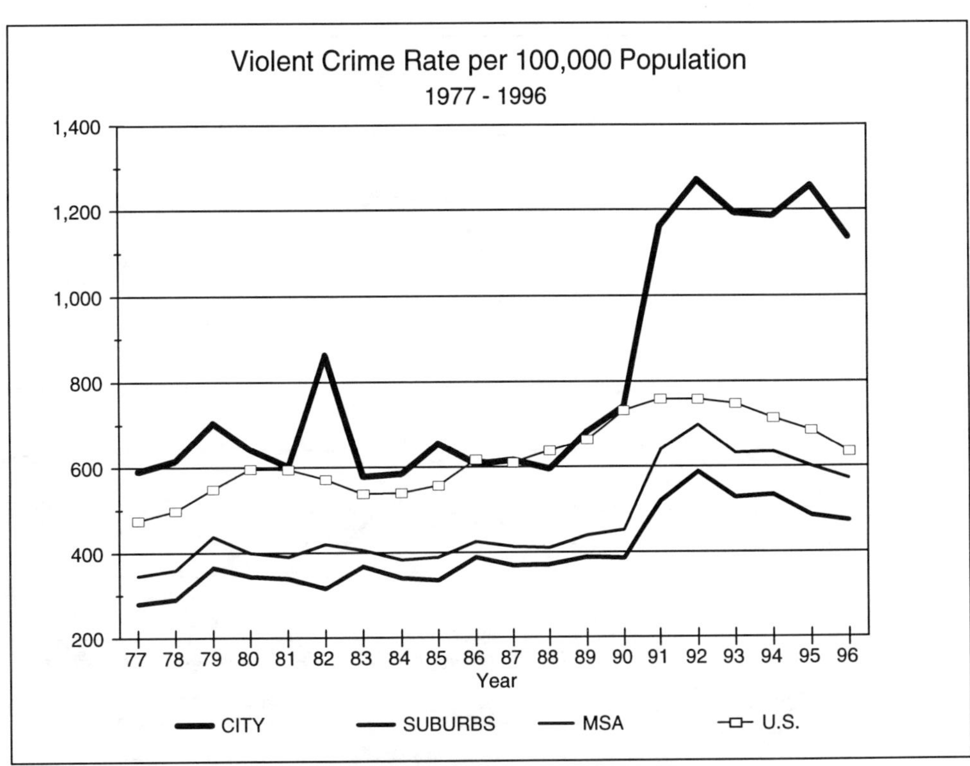

Note: Missing line segments indicate data not available.

Property Crimes and Property Crime Rates: 1977 - 1996

Year	Number				Rate per 100,000 population			
	City	Suburbs[2]	MSA[1]	U.S.	City	Suburbs[3]	MSA[1]	U.S.
1977	7,215	15,375	22,590	9,955,000	6,958.5	4,035.9	4,661.2	4,601.7
1978	7,538	15,240	22,778	10,123,400	7,248.1	3,934.2	4,635.6	4,642.5
1979	9,650	18,856	28,506	11,041,500	9,155.7	4,821.2	5,741.3	5,016.6
1980	9,892	21,264	31,156	12,063,700	9,919.3	4,800.5	5,741.1	5,353.3
1981	10,134	22,934	33,068	12,061,900	9,978.6	5,299.5	6,188.8	5,263.9
1982	10,338	21,712	32,050	11,652,000	10,064.5	4,960.4	5,930.6	5,032.5
1983	9,599	20,468	30,067	10,850,500	9,248.3	4,324.5	5,210.1	4,637.4
1984	9,333	19,967	29,300	10,608,500	8,995.8	4,078.3	4,938.1	4,492.1
1985	9,103	20,682	29,785	11,102,600	8,795.8	4,021.0	4,820.8	4,650.5
1986	9,190	23,208	32,398	11,722,700	8,773.3	4,458.1	5,181.0	4,862.6
1987	9,817	25,564	35,381	12,024,700	8,511.1	4,705.5	5,372.0	4,940.3
1988	10,036	24,910	34,946	12,356,900	8,525.8	4,455.8	5,163.7	5,027.1
1989	10,626	27,213	37,839	12,605,400	9,088.2	4,734.4	5,470.4	5,077.9
1990	11,644	27,221	38,865	12,655,500	8,523.5	4,549.6	5,288.3	5,088.5
1991	12,567	31,922	44,489	12,961,100	9,051.2	5,249.6	5,956.3	5,139.7
1992	13,419	38,498	51,917	12,505,900	9,515.1	5,191.4	5,882.3	4,902.7
1993	13,273	36,492	49,765	12,218,800	9,270.7	4,678.8	5,391.0	4,737.6
1994	13,821	38,465	52,286	12,131,900	9,482.7	4,844.7	5,564.1	4,660.0
1995	14,031	39,245	53,276	12,063,900	9,611.9	4,696.7	5,427.7	4,591.3
1996	15,149	39,852	55,001	11,791,300	10,196.5	4,686.1	5,505.6	4,444.8

Notes: Property crimes include burglary, larceny-theft and motor vehicle theft; n/a not available; (1) Metropolitan Statistical Area - see Appendix A for areas included; (2) calculated by the editors using the following formula: (number of crimes in the MSA minus number of crimes in the city); (3) calculated by the editors using the following formula: ((number of crimes in the MSA minus number of crimes in the city) ÷ (population of the MSA minus population of the city)) x 100,000
Source: U.S. Department of Justice, FBI Uniform Crime Reports, 1977 - 1996

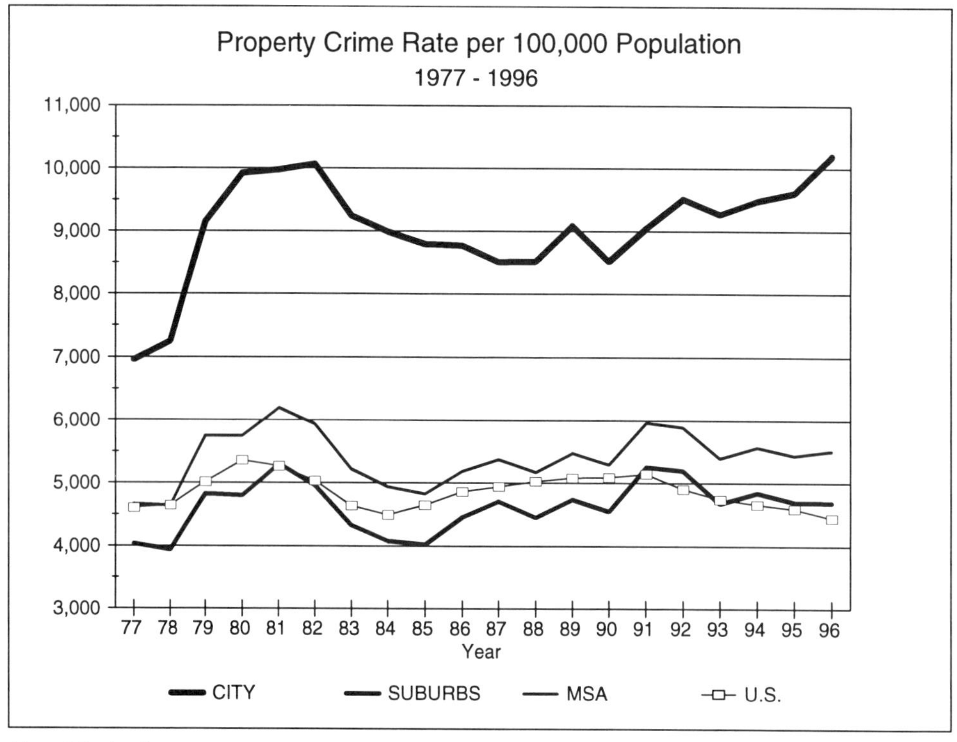

Note: Missing line segments indicate data not available.

Murders and Murder Rates: 1977 - 1996

Year	Number				Rate per 100,000 population			
	City	Suburbs[2]	MSA[1]	U.S.	City	Suburbs[3]	MSA[1]	U.S.
1977	12	26	38	19,120	11.6	6.8	7.8	8.8
1978	16	31	47	19,560	15.4	8.0	9.6	9.0
1979	17	30	47	21,460	16.1	7.7	9.5	9.7
1980	12	38	50	23,040	12.0	8.6	9.2	10.2
1981	13	23	36	22,520	12.8	5.3	6.7	9.8
1982	20	39	59	21,010	19.5	8.9	10.9	9.1
1983	13	37	50	19,310	12.5	7.8	8.7	8.3
1984	14	27	41	18,690	13.5	5.5	6.9	7.9
1985	19	50	69	18,980	18.4	9.7	11.2	7.9
1986	20	43	63	20,610	19.1	8.3	10.1	8.6
1987	14	38	52	20,100	12.1	7.0	7.9	8.3
1988	16	31	47	20,680	13.6	5.5	6.9	8.4
1989	11	35	46	21,500	9.4	6.1	6.7	8.7
1990	23	46	69	23,440	16.8	7.7	9.4	9.4
1991	30	47	77	24,700	21.6	7.7	10.3	9.8
1992	31	49	80	23,760	22.0	6.6	9.1	9.3
1993	26	60	86	24,530	18.2	7.7	9.3	9.5
1994	35	64	99	23,330	24.0	8.1	10.5	9.0
1995	24	64	88	21,610	16.4	7.7	9.0	8.2
1996	41	58	99	19,650	27.6	6.8	9.9	7.4

Notes: (1) Metropolitan Statistical Area - see Appendix A for areas included; (2) calculated by the editors using the following formula: (number of crimes in the MSA minus number of crimes in the city); (3) calculated by the editors using the following formula: ((number of crimes in the MSA minus number of crimes in the city) ÷ (population of the MSA minus population of the city)) x 100,000; n/a not avail.
Source: U.S. Department of Justice, FBI Uniform Crime Reports, 1977 - 1996

Forcible Rapes and Forcible Rape Rates: 1977 - 1996

Year	Number				Rate per 100,000 population			
	City	Suburbs[2]	MSA[1]	U.S.	City	Suburbs[3]	MSA[1]	U.S.
1977	63	76	139	63,500	60.8	19.9	28.7	29.4
1978	57	102	159	67,610	54.8	26.3	32.4	31.0
1979	72	95	167	76,390	68.3	24.3	33.6	34.7
1980	66	141	207	82,990	66.2	31.8	38.1	36.8
1981	65	133	198	82,500	64.0	30.7	37.1	36.0
1982	62	115	177	78,770	60.4	26.3	32.8	34.0
1983	57	118	175	78,920	54.9	24.9	30.3	33.7
1984	79	111	190	84,230	76.1	22.7	32.0	35.7
1985	60	121	181	88,670	58.0	23.5	29.3	37.1
1986	48	150	198	91,460	45.8	28.8	31.7	37.9
1987	70	136	206	91,110	60.7	25.0	31.3	37.4
1988	77	153	230	92,490	65.4	27.4	34.0	37.6
1989	72	164	236	94,500	61.6	28.5	34.1	38.1
1990	79	180	259	102,560	57.8	30.1	35.2	41.2
1991	98	195	293	106,590	70.6	32.1	39.2	42.3
1992	111	283	394	109,060	78.7	38.2	44.6	42.8
1993	109	208	317	106,010	76.1	26.7	34.3	41.1
1994	78	206	284	102,220	53.5	25.9	30.2	39.3
1995	82	215	297	97,470	56.2	25.7	30.3	37.1
1996	84	188	272	95,770	56.5	22.1	27.2	36.1

Notes: (1) Metropolitan Statistical Area - see Appendix A for areas included; (2) calculated by the editors using the following formula: (number of crimes in the MSA minus number of crimes in the city); (3) calculated by the editors using the following formula: ((number of crimes in the MSA minus number of crimes in the city) ÷ (population of the MSA minus population of the city)) x 100,000; n/a not avail.
Source: U.S. Department of Justice, FBI Uniform Crime Reports, 1977 - 1996

Robberies and Robbery Rates: 1977 - 1996

Year	Number				Rate per 100,000 population			
	City	Suburbs[2]	MSA[1]	U.S.	City	Suburbs[3]	MSA[1]	U.S.
1977	189	223	412	412,610	182.3	58.5	85.0	190.7
1978	184	241	425	426,930	176.9	62.2	86.5	195.8
1979	255	312	567	480,700	241.9	79.8	114.2	218.4
1980	270	372	642	565,840	270.7	84.0	118.3	251.1
1981	245	417	662	592,910	241.2	96.4	123.9	258.7
1982	322	411	733	553,130	313.5	93.9	135.6	238.9
1983	271	448	719	506,570	261.1	94.7	124.6	216.5
1984	244	403	647	485,010	235.2	82.3	109.0	205.4
1985	275	405	680	497,870	265.7	78.7	110.1	208.5
1986	281	475	756	542,780	268.3	91.2	120.9	225.1
1987	307	564	871	517,700	266.2	103.8	132.2	212.7
1988	316	479	795	542,970	268.4	85.7	117.5	220.9
1989	328	535	863	578,330	280.5	93.1	124.8	233.0
1990	431	570	1,001	639,270	315.5	95.3	136.2	257.0
1991	771	954	1,725	687,730	555.3	156.9	230.9	272.7
1992	828	1,364	2,192	672,480	587.1	183.9	248.4	263.6
1993	848	1,289	2,137	659,870	592.3	165.3	231.5	255.9
1994	848	1,339	2,187	618,950	581.8	168.6	232.7	237.7
1995	904	1,141	2,045	580,510	619.3	136.6	208.3	220.9
1996	810	1,200	2,010	537,050	545.2	141.1	201.2	202.4

Notes: (1) Metropolitan Statistical Area - see Appendix A for areas included; (2) calculated by the editors using the following formula: (number of crimes in the MSA minus number of crimes in the city); (3) calculated by the editors using the following formula: ((number of crimes in the MSA minus number of crimes in the city) ÷ (population of the MSA minus population of the city)) x 100,000; n/a not avail.
Source: U.S. Department of Justice, FBI Uniform Crime Reports, 1977 - 1996

Aggravated Assaults and Aggravated Assault Rates: 1977 - 1996

Year	Number				Rate per 100,000 population			
	City	Suburbs[2]	MSA[1]	U.S.	City	Suburbs[3]	MSA[1]	U.S.
1977	349	741	1,090	534,350	336.6	194.5	224.9	247.0
1978	383	751	1,134	571,460	368.3	193.9	230.8	262.1
1979	398	993	1,391	629,480	377.6	253.9	280.2	286.0
1980	292	978	1,270	672,650	292.8	220.8	234.0	298.5
1981	289	897	1,186	663,900	284.6	207.3	222.0	289.7
1982	482	815	1,297	669,480	469.3	186.2	240.0	289.2
1983	259	1,140	1,399	653,290	249.5	240.9	242.4	279.2
1984	270	1,125	1,395	685,350	260.2	229.8	235.1	290.2
1985	324	1,147	1,471	723,250	313.1	223.0	238.1	302.9
1986	287	1,355	1,642	834,320	274.0	260.3	262.6	346.1
1987	320	1,268	1,588	855,090	277.4	233.4	241.1	351.3
1988	292	1,414	1,706	910,090	248.1	252.9	252.1	370.2
1989	387	1,501	1,888	951,710	331.0	261.1	272.9	383.4
1990	480	1,508	1,988	1,054,860	351.4	252.0	270.5	424.1
1991	715	1,964	2,679	1,092,740	515.0	323.0	358.7	433.3
1992	821	2,664	3,485	1,126,970	582.2	359.2	394.9	441.8
1993	724	2,558	3,282	1,135,610	505.7	328.0	355.5	440.3
1994	768	2,626	3,394	1,113,180	526.9	330.7	361.2	427.6
1995	825	2,634	3,459	1,099,210	565.2	315.2	352.4	418.3
1996	754	2,568	3,322	1,029,810	507.5	302.0	332.5	388.2

Notes: (1) Metropolitan Statistical Area - see Appendix A for areas included; (2) calculated by the editors using the following formula: (number of crimes in the MSA minus number of crimes in the city); (3) calculated by the editors using the following formula: ((number of crimes in the MSA minus number of crimes in the city) ÷ (population of the MSA minus population of the city)) x 100,000; n/a not avail.
Source: U.S. Department of Justice, FBI Uniform Crime Reports, 1977 - 1996

Burglaries and Burglary Rates: 1977 - 1996

Year	Number				Rate per 100,000 population			
	City	Suburbs[2]	MSA[1]	U.S.	City	Suburbs[3]	MSA[1]	U.S.
1977	2,087	4,731	6,818	3,071,500	2,012.8	1,241.9	1,406.8	1,419.8
1978	2,084	4,683	6,767	3,128,300	2,003.8	1,208.9	1,377.2	1,434.6
1979	2,773	5,285	8,058	3,327,700	2,631.0	1,351.3	1,622.9	1,511.9
1980	2,857	6,281	9,138	3,795,200	2,864.9	1,418.0	1,683.9	1,684.1
1981	2,764	6,289	9,053	3,779,700	2,721.6	1,453.2	1,694.3	1,649.5
1982	2,730	6,191	8,921	3,447,100	2,657.8	1,414.4	1,650.7	1,488.8
1983	2,597	6,102	8,699	3,129,900	2,502.1	1,289.2	1,507.4	1,337.7
1984	2,597	5,506	8,103	2,984,400	2,503.2	1,124.6	1,365.7	1,263.7
1985	2,690	5,665	8,355	3,073,300	2,599.2	1,101.4	1,352.3	1,287.3
1986	2,690	6,019	8,709	3,241,400	2,568.0	1,156.2	1,392.7	1,344.6
1987	2,973	7,915	10,888	3,236,200	2,577.5	1,456.9	1,653.2	1,329.6
1988	3,350	6,860	10,210	3,218,100	2,845.9	1,227.1	1,508.7	1,309.2
1989	3,641	7,124	10,765	3,168,200	3,114.1	1,239.4	1,556.3	1,276.3
1990	3,881	7,153	11,034	3,073,900	2,840.9	1,195.5	1,501.4	1,235.9
1991	5,007	9,325	14,332	3,157,200	3,606.2	1,533.5	1,918.8	1,252.0
1992	5,124	11,682	16,806	2,979,900	3,633.3	1,575.3	1,904.2	1,168.2
1993	4,851	9,414	14,265	2,834,800	3,388.2	1,207.0	1,545.3	1,099.2
1994	4,729	9,794	14,523	2,712,800	3,244.6	1,233.6	1,545.5	1,042.0
1995	4,522	9,558	14,080	2,593,800	3,097.8	1,143.9	1,434.4	987.1
1996	4,226	8,859	13,085	2,501,500	2,844.4	1,041.7	1,309.8	943.0

Notes: (1) Metropolitan Statistical Area - see Appendix A for areas included; (2) calculated by the editors using the following formula: (number of crimes in the MSA minus number of crimes in the city); (3) calculated by the editors using the following formula: ((number of crimes in the MSA minus number of crimes in the city) ÷ (population of the MSA minus population of the city)) x 100,000; n/a not avail.
Source: U.S. Department of Justice, FBI Uniform Crime Reports, 1977 - 1996

Larceny-Thefts and Larceny-Theft Rates: 1977 - 1996

Year	Number				Rate per 100,000 population			
	City	Suburbs[2]	MSA[1]	U.S.	City	Suburbs[3]	MSA[1]	U.S.
1977	4,729	9,653	14,382	5,905,700	4,560.9	2,533.9	2,967.5	2,729.9
1978	5,063	9,672	14,735	5,991,000	4,868.3	2,496.8	2,998.7	2,747.4
1979	6,348	12,491	18,839	6,601,000	6,022.8	3,193.8	3,794.3	2,999.1
1980	6,554	13,982	20,536	7,136,900	6,572.1	3,156.5	3,784.2	3,167.0
1981	6,988	15,706	22,694	7,194,400	6,880.9	3,629.3	4,247.3	3,139.7
1982	7,195	14,618	21,813	7,142,500	7,004.7	3,339.7	4,036.3	3,084.8
1983	6,623	13,460	20,083	6,712,800	6,381.0	2,843.8	3,480.0	2,868.9
1984	6,424	13,273	19,697	6,591,900	6,191.9	2,711.0	3,319.7	2,791.3
1985	5,991	13,690	19,681	6,926,400	5,788.8	2,661.6	3,185.4	2,901.2
1986	6,049	15,751	21,800	7,257,200	5,774.7	3,025.7	3,486.2	3,010.3
1987	6,312	16,319	22,631	7,499,900	5,472.3	3,003.8	3,436.1	3,081.3
1988	6,084	16,648	22,732	7,705,900	5,168.5	2,977.9	3,358.9	3,134.9
1989	6,335	18,366	24,701	7,872,400	5,418.2	3,195.3	3,571.0	3,171.3
1990	7,062	18,462	25,524	7,945,700	5,169.4	3,085.7	3,473.0	3,194.8
1991	6,802	20,803	27,605	8,142,200	4,899.0	3,421.1	3,695.8	3,228.8
1992	7,397	24,740	32,137	7,915,200	5,245.1	3,336.2	3,641.2	3,103.0
1993	7,471	25,117	32,588	7,820,900	5,218.2	3,220.4	3,530.2	3,032.4
1994	7,918	26,473	34,391	7,879,800	5,432.6	3,334.3	3,659.7	3,026.7
1995	8,376	27,188	35,564	7,997,700	5,738.0	3,253.8	3,623.2	3,043.8
1996	9,400	28,160	37,560	7,894,600	6,326.9	3,311.2	3,759.7	2,975.9

Notes: (1) Metropolitan Statistical Area - see Appendix A for areas included; (2) calculated by the editors using the following formula: (number of crimes in the MSA minus number of crimes in the city); (3) calculated by the editors using the following formula: ((number of crimes in the MSA minus number of crimes in the city) ÷ (population of the MSA minus population of the city)) x 100,000; n/a not avail.
Source: U.S. Department of Justice, FBI Uniform Crime Reports, 1977 - 1996

Motor Vehicle Thefts and Motor Vehicle Theft Rates: 1977 - 1996

Year	Number				Rate per 100,000 population			
	City	Suburbs[2]	MSA[1]	U.S.	City	Suburbs[3]	MSA[1]	U.S.
1977	399	991	1,390	977,700	384.8	260.1	286.8	451.9
1978	391	885	1,276	1,004,100	376.0	228.5	259.7	460.5
1979	529	1,080	1,609	1,112,800	501.9	276.1	324.1	505.6
1980	481	1,001	1,482	1,131,700	482.3	226.0	273.1	502.2
1981	382	939	1,321	1,087,800	376.1	217.0	247.2	474.7
1982	413	903	1,316	1,062,400	402.1	206.3	243.5	458.8
1983	379	906	1,285	1,007,900	365.2	191.4	222.7	430.8
1984	312	1,188	1,500	1,032,200	300.7	242.7	252.8	437.1
1985	422	1,327	1,749	1,102,900	407.8	258.0	283.1	462.0
1986	451	1,438	1,889	1,224,100	430.5	276.2	302.1	507.8
1987	532	1,330	1,862	1,288,700	461.2	244.8	282.7	529.4
1988	602	1,402	2,004	1,432,900	511.4	250.8	296.1	582.9
1989	650	1,723	2,373	1,564,800	555.9	299.8	343.1	630.4
1990	701	1,606	2,307	1,635,900	513.1	268.4	313.9	657.8
1991	758	1,794	2,552	1,661,700	545.9	295.0	341.7	659.0
1992	898	2,076	2,974	1,610,800	636.8	279.9	337.0	631.5
1993	951	1,961	2,912	1,563,100	664.2	251.4	315.5	606.1
1994	1,174	2,198	3,372	1,539,300	805.5	276.8	358.8	591.3
1995	1,133	2,499	3,632	1,472,400	776.2	299.1	370.0	560.4
1996	1,523	2,833	4,356	1,395,200	1,025.1	333.1	436.0	525.9

Notes: (1) Metropolitan Statistical Area - see Appendix A for areas included; (2) calculated by the editors using the following formula: (number of crimes in the MSA minus number of crimes in the city); (3) calculated by the editors using the following formula: ((number of crimes in the MSA minus number of crimes in the city) ÷ (population of the MSA minus population of the city)) x 100,000; n/a not avail.
Source: U.S. Department of Justice, FBI Uniform Crime Reports, 1977 - 1996

HATE CRIMES

Criminal Incidents by Bias Motivation

Area	Race	Ethnicity	Religion	Sexual Orientation
Durham	2	0	0	0

Notes: Figures include both violent and property crimes. Law enforcement agencies must have submitted data for at least one quarter of calendar year 1995 to be included in this report, therefore figures shown may not represent complete 12-month totals; n/a not available
Source: U.S. Department of Justice, FBI Uniform Crime Reports, Hate Crime Statistics 1995

LAW ENFORCEMENT

Full-Time Law Enforcement Employees

Jurisdiction	Police Employees			Police Officers per 100,000 population
	Total	Officers	Civilians	
Durham	413	354	59	238.3

Notes: Data as of October 31, 1996
Source: U.S. Department of Justice, FBI Uniform Crime Reports, 1996

CORRECTIONS

Federal Correctional Facilities

Type	Year Opened	Security Level	Sex of Inmates	Rated Capacity	Population on 7/1/95	Number of Staff
None listed						

Notes: Data as of 1995
Source: Bureau of Justice Statistics, Sourcebook of Criminal Justice Statistics Online

City/County/Regional Correctional Facilities

Name	Year Opened	Year Renov.	Rated Capacity	1995 Pop.	Number of COs[1]	Number of Staff	ACA[2] Accred.
Durham County Jail	1995	--	576	307	206	232	No

Notes: Data as of April 1996; (1) Correctional Officers; (2) American Correctional Assn. Accreditation
Source: American Correctional Association, 1996-1998 National Jail and Adult Detention Directory

Private Adult Correctional Facilities

Name	Date Opened	Rated Capacity	Present Pop.	Security Level	Facility Construct.	Expans. Plans	ACA[1] Accred.
None listed							

Notes: Data as of December 1996; (1) American Correctional Association Accreditation
Source: University of Florida, Center for Studies in Criminology and Law, Private Adult Correctional Facility Census, 10th Ed., March 15, 1997

Characteristics of Shock Incarceration Programs

Jurisdiction	Year Program Began	Number of Camps	Average Num. of Inmates	Number of Beds	Program Length	Voluntary/ Mandatory
North Carolina	1989	2	240	360	90 to 120 days	Voluntary

Note: Data as of July 1996;
Source: Sourcebook of Criminal Justice Statistics Online

DEATH PENALTY

Death Penalty Statistics

State	Prisoners Executed		Prisoners Under Sentence of Death					Avg. No. of Years on Death Row[4]
	1930-1995	1996[1]	Total[2]	White[3]	Black[3]	Hisp.	Women	
North Carolina	271	0	139	68	69	1	2	3.3

Notes: Data as of 12/31/95 unless otherwise noted; (1) Data as of 7/31/97; (2) Includes persons of other races; (3) Includes people of Hispanic origin; (4) Covers prisoners sentenced 1974 through 1995
Source: Bureau of Justice Statistics, Capital Punishment 1995 (released 12/96); Death Penalty Information Center Web Site, 9/30/97

Capital Offenses and Methods of Execution

Capital Offenses in North Carolina	Minimum Age for Imposition of Death Penalty	Mentally Retarded Excluded	Methods of Execution[1]
First-degree murder (N.C.G.S. 14-17).	17	No	Lethal injection; lethal gas

Notes: Data as of 12/31/95 unless otherwise noted; (1) Data as of 7/31/97
Source: Bureau of Justice Statistics, Capital Punishment 1995 (released 12/96); Death Penalty Information Center Web Site, 9/30/97

LAWS

Statutory Provisions Relating to the Purchase, Ownership and Use of Handguns

Jurisdiction	Instant Background Check	Federal Waiting Period Applies[1]	State Waiting Period (days)	License or Permit to Purchase	Regis-tration	Record of Sale Sent to Police	Concealed Carry Law
North Carolina	No	No	No	Yes[a]	No	Yes	Yes[b]

Note: Data as of 1996; (1) The Federal 5-day waiting period for handgun purchases applies to states that don't have instant background checks, waiting period requirements, or licensing procedures exempting them from the Federal requirement; (a) To purchase a handgun, a license or permit is required, which must be issued to qualified applicants within 30 days; (b) "Shall issue" permit system, liberally administered discretion by local authorities over permit issuance, or no permit required
Source: Sourcebook of Criminal Justice Statistics Online

Statutory Provisions Relating to Alcohol Use and Driving

Jurisdiction	Drinking Age	Blood Alcohol Concentration Levels as Evidence in State Courts[1]		Open Container Law[1]	Anti-Consump-tion Law[1]	Dram Shop Law[1]
		Illegal per se at 0.10%	Presumption at 0.10%			
North Carolina	21	(a)	No	Yes[b]	Yes[b,c]	Yes[d,e]

Note: Data as of January 1, 1997; (1) See Appendix C for an explanation of terms; (a) 0.08%; (b) Limited application; (c) Applies to drivers only; (d) State has a statute that places a monetary limit on the amount of damages that can be awarded in dram shop liability actions; (e) Applies specifically to the actions of intoxicated minors, but the law does not foreclose developing case law as to other types of dram shop action
Source: Sourcebook of Criminal Justice Statistics Online

Statutory Provisions Relating to Hate Crimes

Jurisdiction	Bias-Motivated Violence and Intimidation						Institutional Vandalism
		Criminal Penalty					
	Civil Action	Race/ Religion/ Ethnicity	Sexual Orientation	Mental/ Physical Disability	Gender	Age	
North Carolina	No	Yes	No	No	No	No	Yes

Source: Anti-Defamation League, 1997 Hate Crimes Laws

Eugene, Oregon

OVERVIEW

The total crime rate for the city increased 18.0% between 1977 and 1996. During that same period, the violent crime rate increased 33.7% and the property crime rate increased 17.1%.

Among violent crimes, the rates for: Murders decreased 48.4%; Forcible Rapes decreased 10.1%; Robberies increased 102.2%; and Aggravated Assaults increased 15.8%.

Among property crimes, the rates for: Burglaries decreased 22.1%; Larceny-Thefts increased 29.5%; and Motor Vehicle Thefts increased 40.6%.

ANTI-CRIME PROGRAMS

Information not available at time of publication.

CRIME RISK

Your Chances of Becoming a Victim[1]

Area	Any Crime	Violent Crime					Property Crime			
		Any	Murder	Forcible Rape[2]	Robbery	Aggrav. Assault	Any	Burglary	Larceny -Theft	Motor Vehicle Theft
City	1:10	1:166	1:61,319	1:1,274	1:453	1:295	1:11	1:64	1:14	1:161

Note: (1) Figures have been calculated by dividing the population of the city by the number of crimes reported to the FBI during 1996 and are expressed as odds (eg. 1:20 should be read as 1 in 20). (2) Figures have been calculated by dividing the female population of the city by the number of forcible rapes reported to the FBI during 1996. The female population of the city was estimated by calculating the ratio of females to males reported in the 1990 Census and applying that ratio to 1996 population estimate.
Source: FBI Uniform Crime Reports 1996

CRIME STATISTICS

Total Crimes and Total Crime Rates: 1977 - 1996

Year	Number				Rate per 100,000 population			
	City	Suburbs[2]	MSA[1]	U.S.	City	Suburbs[3]	MSA[1]	U.S.
1977	8,163	7,433	15,596	10,984,500	8,417.2	4,926.4	6,292.2	5,077.6
1978	8,864	7,957	16,821	11,209,000	8,904.6	4,979.8	6,486.4	5,140.3
1979	9,727	9,006	18,733	12,249,500	9,250.7	5,583.3	7,030.5	5,565.5
1980	10,813	9,628	20,441	13,408,300	10,330.4	5,784.0	7,539.2	5,950.0
1981	10,645	9,634	20,279	13,423,800	10,029.5	5,707.8	7,376.2	5,858.2
1982	9,513	8,381	17,894	12,974,400	8,956.2	4,961.7	6,503.8	5,603.6
1983	8,700	6,956	15,656	12,108,600	8,150.8	4,098.1	5,662.7	5,175.0
1984	8,740	7,517	16,257	11,881,800	8,425.4	4,451.7	5,963.9	5,031.3
1985	8,592	8,084	16,676	12,431,400	8,417.2	4,882.6	6,230.6	5,207.1
1986	8,649	7,748	16,397	13,211,900	8,437.9	4,660.3	6,101.1	5,480.4
1987	10,419	7,916	18,335	13,508,700	9,789.5	4,968.7	6,899.4	5,550.0
1988	8,892	7,715	16,607	13,923,100	8,334.9	4,831.0	6,234.3	5,664.2
1989	9,712	7,088	16,800	14,251,400	8,819.5	4,290.5	6,101.9	5,741.0
1990	9,026	6,372	15,398	14,475,600	8,011.1	3,742.9	5,442.7	5,820.3
1991	9,052	7,043	16,095	14,872,900	7,815.1	4,024.3	5,534.0	5,897.8
1992	9,399	6,689	16,088	14,438,200	7,964.8	3,751.6	5,429.5	5,660.2
1993	8,697	7,549	16,246	14,144,800	7,346.1	4,230.8	5,473.4	5,484.4
1994	10,457	9,595	20,052	13,989,500	8,678.2	5,283.5	6,637.5	5,373.5
1995	11,876	10,137	22,013	13,862,700	9,878.1	5,506.3	7,233.4	5,275.9
1996	12,181	9,232	21,413	13,473,600	9,932.6	4,916.3	6,898.0	5,078.9

Notes: (1) Metropolitan Statistical Area - see Appendix A for areas included; (2) calculated by the editors using the following formula: (number of crimes in the MSA minus number of crimes in the city); (3) calculated by the editors using the following formula: ((number of crimes in the MSA minus number of crimes in the city) ÷ (population of the MSA minus population of the city)) x 100,000; n/a not avail.
Source: U.S. Department of Justice, FBI Uniform Crime Reports, 1977 - 1996

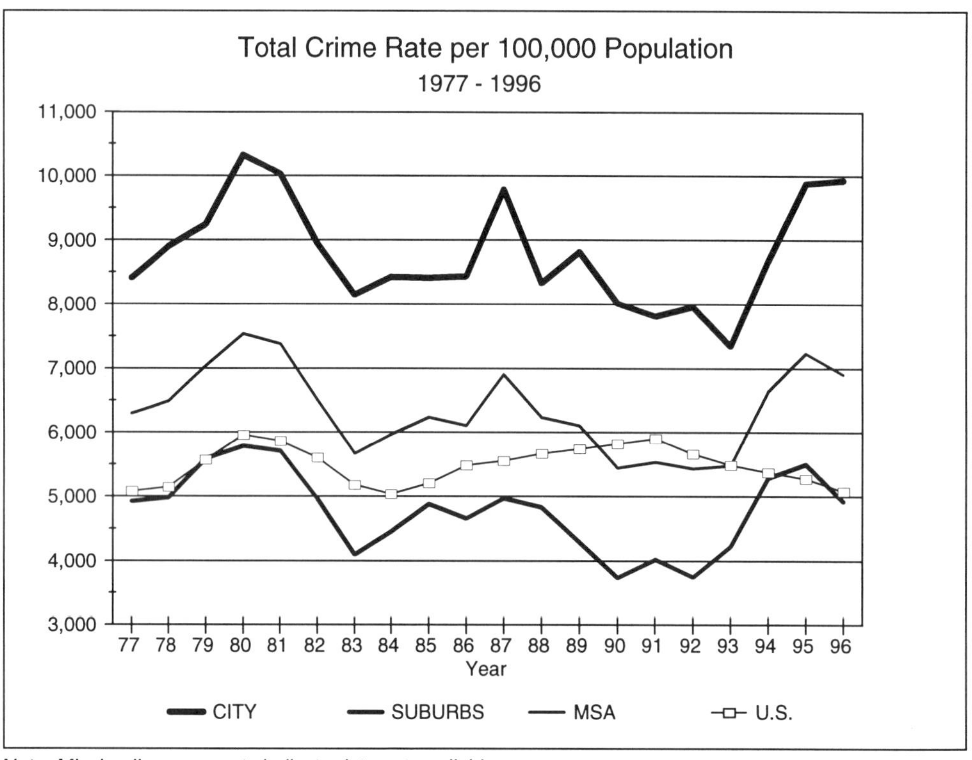

Note: Missing line segments indicate data not available.

Violent Crimes and Violent Crime Rates: 1977 - 1996

Year	Number				Rate per 100,000 population			
	City	Suburbs[2]	MSA[1]	U.S.	City	Suburbs[3]	MSA[1]	U.S.
1977	437	314	751	1,029,580	450.6	208.1	303.0	475.9
1978	487	340	827	1,085,550	489.2	212.8	318.9	497.8
1979	523	309	832	1,208,030	497.4	191.6	312.3	548.9
1980	634	317	951	1,344,520	605.7	190.4	350.8	596.6
1981	428	344	772	1,361,820	403.3	203.8	280.8	594.3
1982	340	345	685	1,322,390	320.1	204.2	249.0	571.1
1983	374	329	703	1,258,090	350.4	193.8	254.3	537.7
1984	408	382	790	1,273,280	393.3	226.2	289.8	539.2
1985	377	411	788	1,328,800	369.3	248.2	294.4	556.6
1986	332	341	673	1,489,170	323.9	205.1	250.4	617.7
1987	378	426	804	1,484,000	355.2	267.4	302.5	609.7
1988	361	521	882	1,566,220	338.4	326.2	331.1	637.2
1989	403	399	802	1,646,040	366.0	241.5	291.3	663.1
1990	463	449	912	1,820,130	410.9	263.7	322.4	731.8
1991	379	489	868	1,911,770	327.2	279.4	298.4	758.1
1992	487	478	965	1,932,270	412.7	268.1	325.7	757.5
1993	470	475	945	1,926,020	397.0	266.2	318.4	746.8
1994	536	440	976	1,857,670	444.8	242.3	323.1	713.6
1995	726	503	1,229	1,798,790	603.9	273.2	403.8	684.6
1996	739	542	1,281	1,682,280	602.6	288.6	412.7	634.1

Notes: Violent crimes include murder, forcible rape, robbery and aggravated assault; n/a not available; (1) Metropolitan Statistical Area - see Appendix A for areas included; (2) calculated by the editors using the following formula: (number of crimes in the MSA minus number of crimes in the city); (3) calculated by the editors using the following formula: ((number of crimes in the MSA minus number of crimes in the city) ÷ (population of the MSA minus population of the city)) x 100,000
Source: U.S. Department of Justice, FBI Uniform Crime Reports, 1977 - 1996

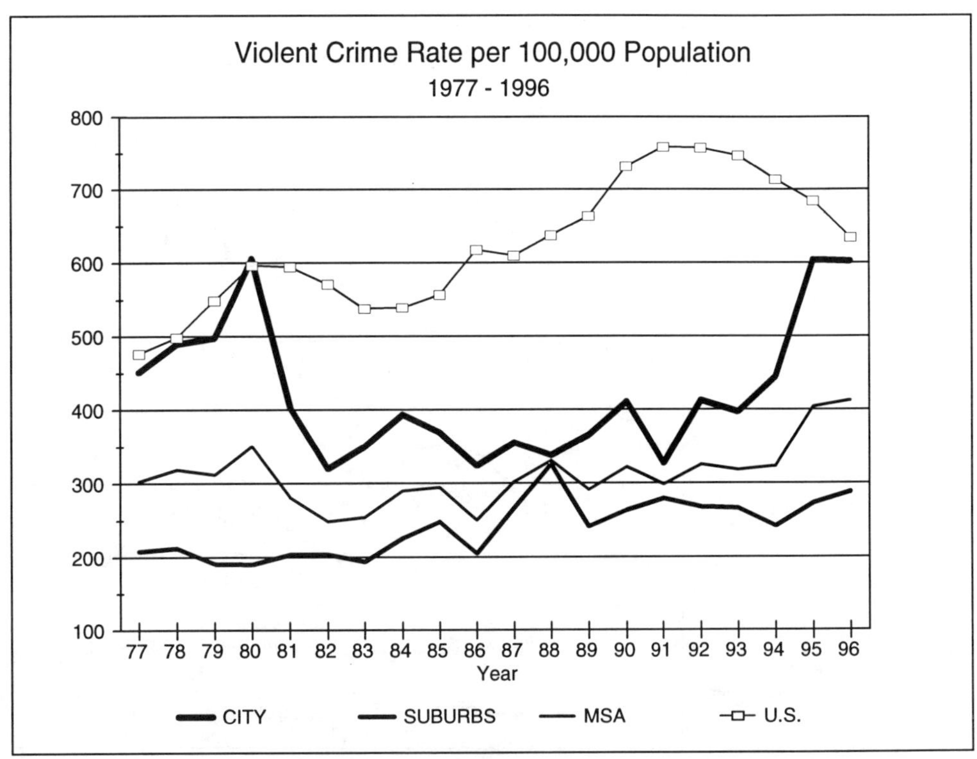

Note: Missing line segments indicate data not available.

Property Crimes and Property Crime Rates: 1977 - 1996

Year	Number				Rate per 100,000 population			
	City	Suburbs[2]	MSA[1]	U.S.	City	Suburbs[3]	MSA[1]	U.S.
1977	7,726	7,119	14,845	9,955,000	7,966.6	4,718.3	5,989.2	4,601.7
1978	8,377	7,617	15,994	10,123,400	8,415.4	4,767.0	6,167.5	4,642.5
1979	9,204	8,697	17,901	11,041,500	8,753.3	5,391.7	6,718.3	5,016.6
1980	10,179	9,311	19,490	12,063,700	9,724.7	5,593.6	7,188.4	5,353.3
1981	10,217	9,290	19,507	12,061,900	9,626.2	5,503.9	7,095.4	5,263.9
1982	9,173	8,036	17,209	11,652,000	8,636.1	4,757.5	6,254.8	5,032.5
1983	8,326	6,627	14,953	10,850,500	7,800.4	3,904.3	5,408.4	4,637.4
1984	8,332	7,135	15,467	10,608,500	8,032.1	4,225.5	5,674.1	4,492.1
1985	8,215	7,673	15,888	11,102,600	8,047.8	4,634.3	5,936.2	4,650.5
1986	8,317	7,407	15,724	11,722,700	8,114.0	4,455.2	5,850.7	4,862.6
1987	10,041	7,490	17,531	12,024,700	9,434.4	4,701.3	6,596.9	4,940.3
1988	8,531	7,194	15,725	12,356,900	7,996.5	4,504.8	5,903.2	5,027.1
1989	9,309	6,689	15,998	12,605,400	8,453.6	4,048.9	5,810.6	5,077.9
1990	8,563	5,923	14,486	12,655,500	7,600.1	3,479.1	5,120.3	5,088.5
1991	8,673	6,554	15,227	12,961,100	7,487.9	3,744.9	5,235.6	5,139.7
1992	8,912	6,211	15,123	12,505,900	7,552.2	3,483.5	5,103.9	4,902.7
1993	8,227	7,074	15,301	12,218,800	6,949.1	3,964.6	5,155.0	4,737.6
1994	9,921	9,155	19,076	12,131,900	8,233.3	5,041.2	6,314.4	4,660.0
1995	11,150	9,634	20,784	12,063,900	9,274.2	5,233.1	6,829.6	4,591.3
1996	11,442	8,690	20,132	11,791,300	9,330.0	4,627.6	6,485.4	4,444.8

Notes: Property crimes include burglary, larceny-theft and motor vehicle theft; n/a not available; (1) Metropolitan Statistical Area - see Appendix A for areas included; (2) calculated by the editors using the following formula: (number of crimes in the MSA minus number of crimes in the city); (3) calculated by the editors using the following formula: ((number of crimes in the MSA minus number of crimes in the city) ÷ (population of the MSA minus population of the city)) x 100,000
Source: U.S. Department of Justice, FBI Uniform Crime Reports, 1977 - 1996

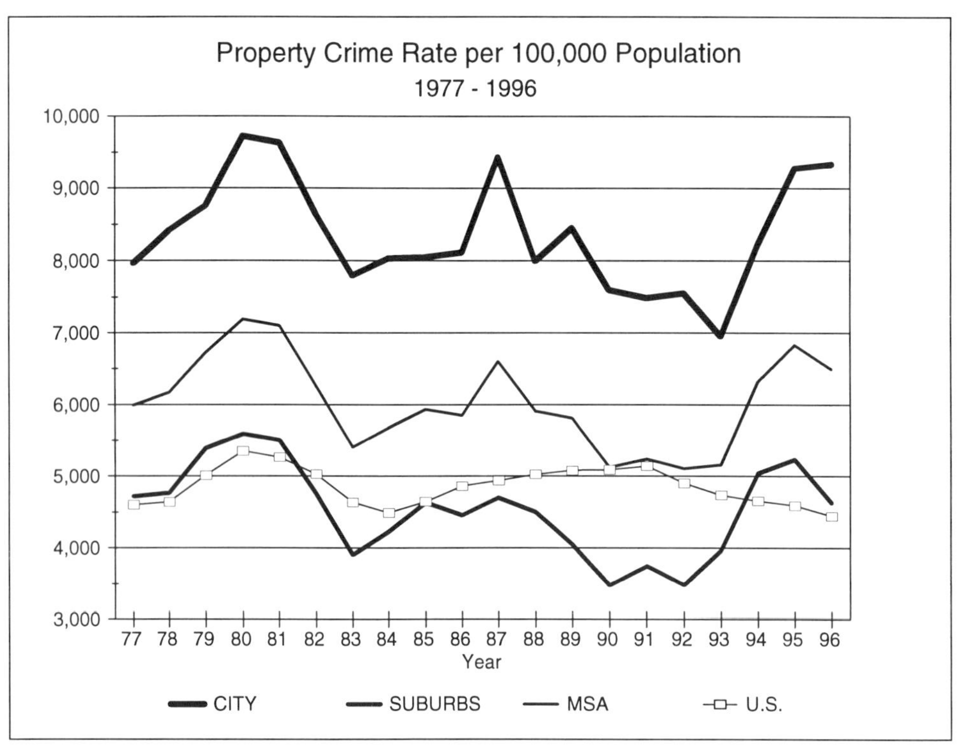

Note: Missing line segments indicate data not available.

Murders and Murder Rates: 1977 - 1996

Year	Number				Rate per 100,000 population			
	City	Suburbs[2]	MSA[1]	U.S.	City	Suburbs[3]	MSA[1]	U.S.
1977	3	4	7	19,120	3.1	2.7	2.8	8.8
1978	6	5	11	19,560	6.0	3.1	4.2	9.0
1979	1	7	8	21,460	1.0	4.3	3.0	9.7
1980	2	4	6	23,040	1.9	2.4	2.2	10.2
1981	1	4	5	22,520	0.9	2.4	1.8	9.8
1982	6	8	14	21,010	5.6	4.7	5.1	9.1
1983	2	4	6	19,310	1.9	2.4	2.2	8.3
1984	4	7	11	18,690	3.9	4.1	4.0	7.9
1985	1	7	8	18,980	1.0	4.2	3.0	7.9
1986	8	8	16	20,610	7.8	4.8	6.0	8.6
1987	3	5	8	20,100	2.8	3.1	3.0	8.3
1988	1	11	12	20,680	0.9	6.9	4.5	8.4
1989	3	8	11	21,500	2.7	4.8	4.0	8.7
1990	1	4	5	23,440	0.9	2.3	1.8	9.4
1991	0	4	4	24,700	0.0	2.3	1.4	9.8
1992	2	9	11	23,760	1.7	5.0	3.7	9.3
1993	3	3	6	24,530	2.5	1.7	2.0	9.5
1994	2	3	5	23,330	1.7	1.7	1.7	9.0
1995	3	9	12	21,610	2.5	4.9	3.9	8.2
1996	2	9	11	19,650	1.6	4.8	3.5	7.4

Notes: (1) Metropolitan Statistical Area - see Appendix A for areas included; (2) calculated by the editors using the following formula: (number of crimes in the MSA minus number of crimes in the city); (3) calculated by the editors using the following formula: ((number of crimes in the MSA minus number of crimes in the city) ÷ (population of the MSA minus population of the city)) x 100,000; n/a not avail.
Source: U.S. Department of Justice, FBI Uniform Crime Reports, 1977 - 1996

Forcible Rapes and Forcible Rape Rates: 1977 - 1996

Year	Number				Rate per 100,000 population			
	City	Suburbs[2]	MSA[1]	U.S.	City	Suburbs[3]	MSA[1]	U.S.
1977	44	50	94	63,500	45.4	33.1	37.9	29.4
1978	71	55	126	67,610	71.3	34.4	48.6	31.0
1979	58	53	111	76,390	55.2	32.9	41.7	34.7
1980	42	68	110	82,990	40.1	40.9	40.6	36.8
1981	50	67	117	82,500	47.1	39.7	42.6	36.0
1982	22	76	98	78,770	20.7	45.0	35.6	34.0
1983	43	54	97	78,920	40.3	31.8	35.1	33.7
1984	59	86	145	84,230	56.9	50.9	53.2	35.7
1985	41	67	108	88,670	40.2	40.5	40.4	37.1
1986	29	44	73	91,460	28.3	26.5	27.2	37.9
1987	48	62	110	91,110	45.1	38.9	41.4	37.4
1988	44	78	122	92,490	41.2	48.8	45.8	37.6
1989	48	62	110	94,500	43.6	37.5	40.0	38.1
1990	76	64	140	102,560	67.5	37.6	49.5	41.2
1991	59	81	140	106,590	50.9	46.3	48.1	42.3
1992	57	66	123	109,060	48.3	37.0	41.5	42.8
1993	64	70	134	106,010	54.1	39.2	45.1	41.1
1994	51	87	138	102,220	42.3	47.9	45.7	39.3
1995	41	84	125	97,470	34.1	45.6	41.1	37.1
1996	50	75	125	95,770	40.8	39.9	40.3	36.1

Notes: (1) Metropolitan Statistical Area - see Appendix A for areas included; (2) calculated by the editors using the following formula: (number of crimes in the MSA minus number of crimes in the city); (3) calculated by the editors using the following formula: ((number of crimes in the MSA minus number of crimes in the city) ÷ (population of the MSA minus population of the city)) x 100,000; n/a not avail.
Source: U.S. Department of Justice, FBI Uniform Crime Reports, 1977 - 1996

Robberies and Robbery Rates: 1977 - 1996

Year	Number				Rate per 100,000 population			
	City	Suburbs[2]	MSA[1]	U.S.	City	Suburbs[3]	MSA[1]	U.S.
1977	106	70	176	412,610	109.3	46.4	71.0	190.7
1978	164	99	263	426,930	164.8	62.0	101.4	195.8
1979	207	96	303	480,700	196.9	59.5	113.7	218.4
1980	207	120	327	565,840	197.8	72.1	120.6	251.1
1981	167	96	263	592,910	157.3	56.9	95.7	258.7
1982	149	107	256	553,130	140.3	63.3	93.0	238.9
1983	161	87	248	506,570	150.8	51.3	89.7	216.5
1984	144	84	228	485,010	138.8	49.7	83.6	205.4
1985	122	77	199	497,870	119.5	46.5	74.4	208.5
1986	142	94	236	542,780	138.5	56.5	87.8	225.1
1987	161	89	250	517,700	151.3	55.9	94.1	212.7
1988	166	79	245	542,970	155.6	49.5	92.0	220.9
1989	168	63	231	578,330	152.6	38.1	83.9	233.0
1990	197	88	285	639,270	174.8	51.7	100.7	257.0
1991	186	82	268	687,730	160.6	46.9	92.1	272.7
1992	228	88	316	672,480	193.2	49.4	106.6	263.6
1993	166	87	253	659,870	140.2	48.8	85.2	255.9
1994	213	118	331	618,950	176.8	65.0	109.6	237.7
1995	273	140	413	580,510	227.1	76.0	135.7	220.9
1996	271	140	411	537,050	221.0	74.6	132.4	202.4

Notes: (1) Metropolitan Statistical Area - see Appendix A for areas included; (2) calculated by the editors using the following formula: (number of crimes in the MSA minus number of crimes in the city); (3) calculated by the editors using the following formula: ((number of crimes in the MSA minus number of crimes in the city) ÷ (population of the MSA minus population of the city)) x 100,000; n/a not avail.
Source: U.S. Department of Justice, FBI Uniform Crime Reports, 1977 - 1996

Aggravated Assaults and Aggravated Assault Rates: 1977 - 1996

Year	Number				Rate per 100,000 population			
	City	Suburbs[2]	MSA[1]	U.S.	City	Suburbs[3]	MSA[1]	U.S.
1977	284	190	474	534,350	292.8	125.9	191.2	247.0
1978	246	181	427	571,460	247.1	113.3	164.7	262.1
1979	257	153	410	629,480	244.4	94.9	153.9	286.0
1980	383	125	508	672,650	365.9	75.1	187.4	298.5
1981	210	177	387	663,900	197.9	104.9	140.8	289.7
1982	163	154	317	669,480	153.5	91.2	115.2	289.2
1983	168	184	352	653,290	157.4	108.4	127.3	279.2
1984	201	205	406	685,350	193.8	121.4	148.9	290.2
1985	213	260	473	723,250	208.7	157.0	176.7	302.9
1986	153	195	348	834,320	149.3	117.3	129.5	346.1
1987	166	270	436	855,090	156.0	169.5	164.1	351.3
1988	150	353	503	910,090	140.6	221.0	188.8	370.2
1989	184	266	450	951,710	167.1	161.0	163.4	383.4
1990	189	293	482	1,054,860	167.7	172.1	170.4	424.1
1991	134	322	456	1,092,740	115.7	184.0	156.8	433.3
1992	200	315	515	1,126,970	169.5	176.7	173.8	441.8
1993	237	315	552	1,135,610	200.2	176.5	186.0	440.3
1994	270	232	502	1,113,180	224.1	127.8	166.2	427.6
1995	409	270	679	1,099,210	340.2	146.7	223.1	418.3
1996	416	318	734	1,029,810	339.2	169.3	236.5	388.2

Notes: (1) Metropolitan Statistical Area - see Appendix A for areas included; (2) calculated by the editors using the following formula: (number of crimes in the MSA minus number of crimes in the city); (3) calculated by the editors using the following formula: ((number of crimes in the MSA minus number of crimes in the city) ÷ (population of the MSA minus population of the city)) x 100,000; n/a not avail.
Source: U.S. Department of Justice, FBI Uniform Crime Reports, 1977 - 1996

Burglaries and Burglary Rates: 1977 - 1996

Year	Number				Rate per 100,000 population			
	City	Suburbs[2]	MSA[1]	U.S.	City	Suburbs[3]	MSA[1]	U.S.
1977	1,943	2,007	3,950	3,071,500	2,003.5	1,330.2	1,593.6	1,419.8
1978	2,145	2,388	4,533	3,128,300	2,154.8	1,494.5	1,748.0	1,434.6
1979	2,210	2,754	4,964	3,327,700	2,101.8	1,707.3	1,863.0	1,511.9
1980	2,304	2,868	5,172	3,795,200	2,201.2	1,723.0	1,907.6	1,684.1
1981	2,470	2,935	5,405	3,779,700	2,327.2	1,738.9	1,966.0	1,649.5
1982	1,910	2,498	4,408	3,447,100	1,798.2	1,478.9	1,602.1	1,488.8
1983	1,813	2,086	3,899	3,129,900	1,698.6	1,229.0	1,410.2	1,337.7
1984	1,954	2,328	4,282	2,984,400	1,883.7	1,378.7	1,570.9	1,263.7
1985	2,076	2,459	4,535	3,073,300	2,033.8	1,485.2	1,694.4	1,287.3
1986	2,185	2,561	4,746	3,241,400	2,131.7	1,540.4	1,765.9	1,344.6
1987	2,459	2,479	4,938	3,236,200	2,310.4	1,556.0	1,858.2	1,329.6
1988	1,916	2,236	4,152	3,218,100	1,796.0	1,400.2	1,558.7	1,309.2
1989	1,582	1,882	3,464	3,168,200	1,436.6	1,139.2	1,258.2	1,276.3
1990	1,530	1,459	2,989	3,073,900	1,358.0	857.0	1,056.5	1,235.9
1991	1,629	1,671	3,300	3,157,200	1,406.4	954.8	1,134.7	1,252.0
1992	1,799	1,403	3,202	2,979,900	1,524.5	786.9	1,080.6	1,168.2
1993	1,381	1,635	3,016	2,834,800	1,166.5	916.3	1,016.1	1,099.2
1994	1,869	2,244	4,113	2,712,800	1,551.1	1,235.7	1,361.5	1,042.0
1995	2,036	2,198	4,234	2,593,800	1,693.5	1,193.9	1,391.3	987.1
1996	1,914	1,999	3,913	2,501,500	1,560.7	1,064.5	1,260.5	943.0

Notes: (1) Metropolitan Statistical Area - see Appendix A for areas included; (2) calculated by the editors using the following formula: (number of crimes in the MSA minus number of crimes in the city); (3) calculated by the editors using the following formula: ((number of crimes in the MSA minus number of crimes in the city) ÷ (population of the MSA minus population of the city)) x 100,000; n/a not avail.
Source: U.S. Department of Justice, FBI Uniform Crime Reports, 1977 - 1996

Larceny-Thefts and Larceny-Theft Rates: 1977 - 1996

Year	Number				Rate per 100,000 population			
	City	Suburbs[2]	MSA[1]	U.S.	City	Suburbs[3]	MSA[1]	U.S.
1977	5,354	4,722	10,076	5,905,700	5,520.7	3,129.6	4,065.2	2,729.9
1978	5,736	4,743	10,479	5,991,000	5,762.3	2,968.4	4,040.8	2,747.4
1979	6,554	5,452	12,006	6,601,000	6,233.1	3,380.0	4,505.9	2,999.1
1980	7,478	5,931	13,409	7,136,900	7,144.2	3,563.1	4,945.6	3,167.0
1981	7,373	5,930	13,303	7,194,400	6,946.7	3,513.3	4,838.8	3,139.7
1982	6,933	5,239	12,172	7,142,500	6,527.2	3,101.6	4,424.1	3,084.8
1983	6,195	4,232	10,427	6,712,800	5,803.9	2,493.3	3,771.4	2,868.9
1984	6,076	4,504	10,580	6,591,900	5,857.3	2,667.3	3,881.3	2,791.3
1985	5,749	4,800	10,549	6,926,400	5,632.0	2,899.1	3,941.4	2,901.2
1986	5,720	4,452	10,172	7,257,200	5,580.4	2,677.8	3,784.8	3,010.3
1987	7,035	4,539	11,574	7,499,900	6,610.0	2,849.1	4,355.3	3,081.3
1988	6,175	4,502	10,677	7,705,900	5,788.1	2,819.1	4,008.2	3,134.9
1989	7,297	4,392	11,689	7,872,400	6,626.5	2,658.5	4,245.6	3,171.3
1990	6,624	4,097	10,721	7,945,700	5,879.2	2,406.6	3,789.5	3,194.8
1991	6,630	4,449	11,079	8,142,200	5,724.1	2,542.1	3,809.4	3,228.8
1992	6,697	4,431	11,128	7,915,200	5,675.1	2,485.2	3,755.6	3,103.0
1993	6,471	5,067	11,538	7,820,900	5,465.8	2,839.8	3,887.2	3,032.4
1994	7,382	6,196	13,578	7,879,800	6,126.2	3,411.8	4,494.5	3,026.7
1995	8,444	6,649	15,093	7,997,700	7,023.4	3,611.7	4,959.5	3,043.8
1996	8,765	5,961	14,726	7,894,600	7,147.1	3,174.4	4,743.9	2,975.9

Notes: (1) Metropolitan Statistical Area - see Appendix A for areas included; (2) calculated by the editors using the following formula: (number of crimes in the MSA minus number of crimes in the city); (3) calculated by the editors using the following formula: ((number of crimes in the MSA minus number of crimes in the city) ÷ (population of the MSA minus population of the city)) x 100,000; n/a not avail.
Source: U.S. Department of Justice, FBI Uniform Crime Reports, 1977 - 1996

Motor Vehicle Thefts and Motor Vehicle Theft Rates: 1977 - 1996

Year	Number				Rate per 100,000 population			
	City	Suburbs[2]	MSA[1]	U.S.	City	Suburbs[3]	MSA[1]	U.S.
1977	429	390	819	977,700	442.4	258.5	330.4	451.9
1978	496	486	982	1,004,100	498.3	304.2	378.7	460.5
1979	440	491	931	1,112,800	418.5	304.4	349.4	505.6
1980	397	512	909	1,131,700	379.3	307.6	335.3	502.2
1981	374	425	799	1,087,800	352.4	251.8	290.6	474.7
1982	330	299	629	1,062,400	310.7	177.0	228.6	458.8
1983	318	309	627	1,007,900	297.9	182.0	226.8	430.8
1984	302	303	605	1,032,200	291.1	179.4	221.9	437.1
1985	390	414	804	1,102,900	382.1	250.0	300.4	462.0
1986	412	394	806	1,224,100	401.9	237.0	299.9	507.8
1987	547	472	1,019	1,288,700	514.0	296.3	383.4	529.4
1988	440	456	896	1,432,900	412.4	285.5	336.4	582.9
1989	430	415	845	1,564,800	390.5	251.2	306.9	630.4
1990	409	367	776	1,635,900	363.0	215.6	274.3	657.8
1991	414	434	848	1,661,700	357.4	248.0	291.6	659.0
1992	416	377	793	1,610,800	352.5	211.4	267.6	631.5
1993	375	372	747	1,563,100	316.7	208.5	251.7	606.1
1994	670	715	1,385	1,539,300	556.0	393.7	458.5	591.3
1995	670	787	1,457	1,472,400	557.3	427.5	478.8	560.4
1996	763	730	1,493	1,395,200	622.2	388.7	481.0	525.9

Notes: (1) Metropolitan Statistical Area - see Appendix A for areas included; (2) calculated by the editors using the following formula: (number of crimes in the MSA minus number of crimes in the city); (3) calculated by the editors using the following formula: ((number of crimes in the MSA minus number of crimes in the city) ÷ (population of the MSA minus population of the city)) x 100,000; n/a not avail.
Source: U.S. Department of Justice, FBI Uniform Crime Reports, 1977 - 1996

HATE CRIMES

Criminal Incidents by Bias Motivation

Area	Race	Ethnicity	Religion	Sexual Orientation
Eugene	10	3	1	4

Notes: Figures include both violent and property crimes. Law enforcement agencies must have submitted data for at least one quarter of calendar year 1995 to be included in this report, therefore figures shown may not represent complete 12-month totals; n/a not available
Source: U.S. Department of Justice, FBI Uniform Crime Reports, Hate Crime Statistics 1995

LAW ENFORCEMENT

Full-Time Law Enforcement Employees

Jurisdiction	Police Employees			Police Officers per 100,000 population
	Total	Officers	Civilians	
Eugene	328	165	163	134.5

Notes: Data as of October 31, 1996
Source: U.S. Department of Justice, FBI Uniform Crime Reports, 1996

CORRECTIONS

Federal Correctional Facilities

Type	Year Opened	Security Level	Sex of Inmates	Rated Capacity	Population on 7/1/95	Number of Staff
None listed						

Notes: Data as of 1995
Source: Bureau of Justice Statistics, Sourcebook of Criminal Justice Statistics Online

City/County/Regional Correctional Facilities

Name	Year Opened	Year Renov.	Rated Capacity	1995 Pop.	Number of COs[1]	Number of Staff	ACA[2] Accred.
None listed							

Notes: Data as of April 1996; (1) Correctional Officers; (2) American Correctional Assn. Accreditation
Source: American Correctional Association, 1996-1998 National Jail and Adult Detention Directory

Private Adult Correctional Facilities

Name	Date Opened	Rated Capacity	Present Pop.	Security Level	Facility Construct.	Expans. Plans	ACA[1] Accred.
None listed							

Notes: Data as of December 1996; (1) American Correctional Association Accreditation
Source: University of Florida, Center for Studies in Criminology and Law, Private Adult Correctional Facility Census, 10th Ed., March 15, 1997

Characteristics of Shock Incarceration Programs

Jurisdiction	Year Program Began	Number of Camps	Average Num. of Inmates	Number of Beds	Program Length	Voluntary/ Mandatory
Oregon did not have a shock incarceration program as of July 1996						

Source: Sourcebook of Criminal Justice Statistics Online

DEATH PENALTY

Death Penalty Statistics

State	Prisoners Executed		Prisoners Under Sentence of Death					Avg. No. of Years on Death Row[4]
	1930-1995	1996[1]	Total[2]	White[3]	Black[3]	Hisp.	Women	
Oregon	19	1	20	18	1	1	0	2.5

Notes: Data as of 12/31/95 unless otherwise noted; (1) Data as of 7/31/97; (2) Includes persons of other races; (3) Includes people of Hispanic origin; (4) Covers prisoners sentenced 1974 through 1995
Source: Bureau of Justice Statistics, Capital Punishment 1995 (released 12/96); Death Penalty Information Center Web Site, 9/30/97

Capital Offenses and Methods of Execution

Capital Offenses in Oregon	Minimum Age for Imposition of Death Penalty	Mentally Retarded Excluded	Methods of Execution[1]
Aggravated murder (ORS 163.095).	18	No	Lethal injection

Notes: Data as of 12/31/95 unless otherwise noted; (1) Data as of 7/31/97
Source: Bureau of Justice Statistics, Capital Punishment 1995 (released 12/96); Death Penalty Information Center Web Site, 9/30/97

LAWS

Statutory Provisions Relating to the Purchase, Ownership and Use of Handguns

Jurisdiction	Instant Background Check	Federal Waiting Period Applies[1]	State Waiting Period (days)	License or Permit to Purchase	Regis-tration	Record of Sale Sent to Police	Concealed Carry Law
Oregon	Yes	No	No	No	No	Yes	Yes[a]

Note: Data as of 1996; (1) The Federal 5-day waiting period for handgun purchases applies to states that don't have instant background checks, waiting period requirements, or licensing procedures exempting them from the Federal requirement; (a) "Shall issue" permit system, liberally administered discretion by local authorities over permit issuance, or no permit required
Source: Sourcebook of Criminal Justice Statistics Online

Statutory Provisions Relating to Alcohol Use and Driving

Jurisdiction	Drinking Age	Blood Alcohol Concentration Levels as Evidence in State Courts[1]		Open Container Law[1]	Anti-Consump-tion Law[1]	Dram Shop Law[1]
		Illegal per se at 0.10%	Presumption at 0.10%			
Oregon	21	(a)	(b)	Yes	Yes	Yes

Note: Data as of January 1, 1997; (1) See Appendix C for an explanation of terms; (a) 0.08%; (b) Not less than 0.08% constitutes being under the influence of intoxicating liquor
Source: Sourcebook of Criminal Justice Statistics Online

Statutory Provisions Relating to Curfews

Jurisdiction	Year Enacted	Latest Revision	Age Group(s)	Curfew Provisions
Eugene	1971	-	17 and under	Midnight to 4 am every night

Note: Data as of February 1996
Source: Sourcebook of Criminal Justice Statistics Online

Statutory Provisions Relating to Hate Crimes

Jurisdiction	Bias-Motivated Violence and Intimidation						Institutional Vandalism
	Civil Action	Criminal Penalty					
		Race/ Religion/ Ethnicity	Sexual Orientation	Mental/ Physical Disability	Gender	Age	
Oregon	Yes	Yes	Yes	No	No	No	Yes

Source: Anti-Defamation League, 1997 Hate Crimes Laws

Flint, Michigan

OVERVIEW

The total crime rate for the city decreased 6.6% between 1977 and 1996. During that same period, the violent crime rate increased 37.0% and the property crime rate decreased 13.8%.

Among violent crimes, the rates for: Murders increased 7.1%; Forcible Rapes increased 19.5%; Robberies increased 38.8%; and Aggravated Assaults increased 38.6%.

Among property crimes, the rates for: Burglaries decreased 9.7%; Larceny-Thefts decreased 31.7%; and Motor Vehicle Thefts increased 148.5%.

ANTI-CRIME PROGRAMS

Information not available at time of publication.

CRIME RISK

Your Chances of Becoming a Victim[1]

Area	Any Crime	Violent Crime					Property Crime			
		Any	Murder	Forcible Rape[2]	Robbery	Aggrav. Assault	Any	Burglary	Larceny -Theft	Motor Vehicle Theft
City	1:9	1:42	1:3,490	1:408	1:149	1:64	1:11	1:34	1:22	1:62

Note: (1) Figures have been calculated by dividing the population of the city by the number of crimes reported to the FBI during 1996 and are expressed as odds (eg. 1:20 should be read as 1 in 20). (2) Figures have been calculated by dividing the female population of the city by the number of forcible rapes reported to the FBI during 1996. The female population of the city was estimated by calculating the ratio of females to males reported in the 1990 Census and applying that ratio to 1996 population estimate.
Source: FBI Uniform Crime Reports 1996

CRIME STATISTICS

Total Crimes and Total Crime Rates: 1977 - 1996

Year	Number				Rate per 100,000 population			
	City	Suburbs[2]	MSA[1]	U.S.	City	Suburbs[3]	MSA[1]	U.S.
1977	20,199	15,002	35,201	10,984,500	12,316.5	4,188.0	6,740.7	5,077.6
1978	19,167	14,687	33,854	11,209,000	11,758.9	4,248.7	6,655.3	5,140.3
1979	20,147	18,228	38,375	12,249,500	12,284.5	5,086.5	7,346.5	5,565.5
1980	21,201	19,906	41,107	13,408,300	13,285.8	5,499.4	7,881.8	5,950.0
1981	23,649	20,171	43,820	13,423,800	14,863.6	5,589.1	8,426.8	5,858.2
1982	22,509	17,943	40,452	12,974,400	14,290.0	5,021.9	7,857.7	5,603.6
1983	21,844	12,293	34,137	12,108,600	13,929.0	4,303.8	7,715.3	5,175.0
1984	22,323	13,164	35,487	11,881,800	14,558.5	4,624.8	8,102.6	5,031.3
1985	22,354	13,374	35,728	12,431,400	14,979.9	4,685.8	8,220.1	5,207.1
1986	23,582	13,853	37,435	13,211,900	15,711.1	4,824.6	8,561.8	5,480.4
1987	22,697	14,514	37,211	13,508,700	15,513.9	4,993.9	8,516.4	5,550.0
1988	21,239	14,194	35,433	13,923,100	14,424.1	4,852.5	8,057.4	5,664.2
1989	19,680	14,870	34,550	14,251,400	13,846.6	5,127.3	7,994.9	5,741.0
1990	18,963	14,633	33,596	14,475,600	13,471.8	5,052.6	7,806.2	5,820.3
1991	18,888	14,656	33,544	14,872,900	13,314.4	5,021.4	7,733.9	5,897.8
1992	18,738	13,663	32,401	14,438,200	13,112.1	4,647.5	7,416.2	5,660.2
1993	n/a	n/a	n/a	14,144,800	n/a	n/a	n/a	5,484.4
1994	18,412	14,554	32,966	13,989,500	13,130.3	4,916.4	7,556.6	5,373.5
1995	17,338	13,439	30,777	13,862,700	12,479.3	4,529.4	7,064.8	5,275.9
1996	16,054	12,343	28,397	13,473,600	11,501.0	4,140.7	6,488.1	5,078.9

Notes: (1) Metropolitan Statistical Area - see Appendix A for areas included; (2) calculated by the editors using the following formula: (number of crimes in the MSA minus number of crimes in the city); (3) calculated by the editors using the following formula: ((number of crimes in the MSA minus number of crimes in the city) ÷ (population of the MSA minus population of the city)) x 100,000; n/a not avail.
Source: U.S. Department of Justice, FBI Uniform Crime Reports, 1977 - 1996

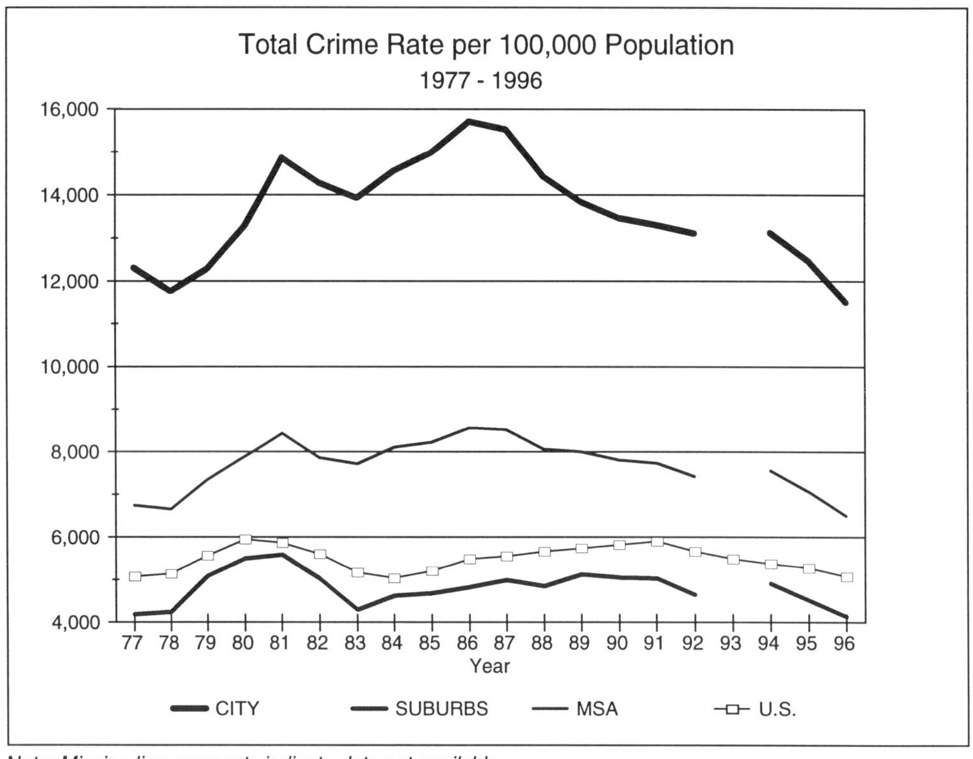

Note: Missing line segments indicate data not available.

Violent Crimes and Violent Crime Rates: 1977 - 1996

Year	Number				Rate per 100,000 population			
	City	Suburbs[2]	MSA[1]	U.S.	City	Suburbs[3]	MSA[1]	U.S.
1977	2,852	1,158	4,010	1,029,580	1,739.0	323.3	767.9	475.9
1978	3,063	1,004	4,067	1,085,550	1,879.1	290.4	799.5	497.8
1979	3,294	1,242	4,536	1,208,030	2,008.5	346.6	868.4	548.9
1980	3,074	1,277	4,351	1,344,520	1,926.4	352.8	834.3	596.6
1981	3,377	1,278	4,655	1,361,820	2,122.5	354.1	895.2	594.3
1982	3,125	1,183	4,308	1,322,390	1,983.9	331.1	836.8	571.1
1983	3,278	985	4,263	1,258,090	2,090.2	344.8	963.5	537.7
1984	3,593	1,182	4,775	1,273,280	2,343.3	415.3	1,090.3	539.2
1985	4,348	1,086	5,434	1,328,800	2,913.7	380.5	1,250.2	556.6
1986	5,195	1,321	6,516	1,489,170	3,461.1	460.1	1,490.3	617.7
1987	4,563	1,364	5,927	1,484,000	3,118.9	469.3	1,356.5	609.7
1988	4,024	1,351	5,375	1,566,220	2,732.8	461.9	1,222.3	637.2
1989	3,396	1,371	4,767	1,646,040	2,389.4	472.7	1,103.1	663.1
1990	3,533	1,415	4,948	1,820,130	2,509.9	488.6	1,149.7	731.8
1991	3,363	1,377	4,740	1,911,770	2,370.6	471.8	1,092.8	758.1
1992	3,755	1,240	4,995	1,932,270	2,627.6	421.8	1,143.3	757.5
1993	n/a	n/a	n/a	1,926,020	n/a	n/a	n/a	746.8
1994	3,999	1,381	5,380	1,857,670	2,851.8	466.5	1,233.2	713.6
1995	3,892	1,226	5,118	1,798,790	2,801.3	413.2	1,174.8	684.6
1996	3,325	1,040	4,365	1,682,280	2,382.0	348.9	997.3	634.1

Notes: Violent crimes include murder, forcible rape, robbery and aggravated assault; n/a not available; (1) Metropolitan Statistical Area - see Appendix A for areas included; (2) calculated by the editors using the following formula: (number of crimes in the MSA minus number of crimes in the city); (3) calculated by the editors using the following formula: ((number of crimes in the MSA minus number of crimes in the city) ÷ (population of the MSA minus population of the city)) x 100,000
Source: U.S. Department of Justice, FBI Uniform Crime Reports, 1977 - 1996

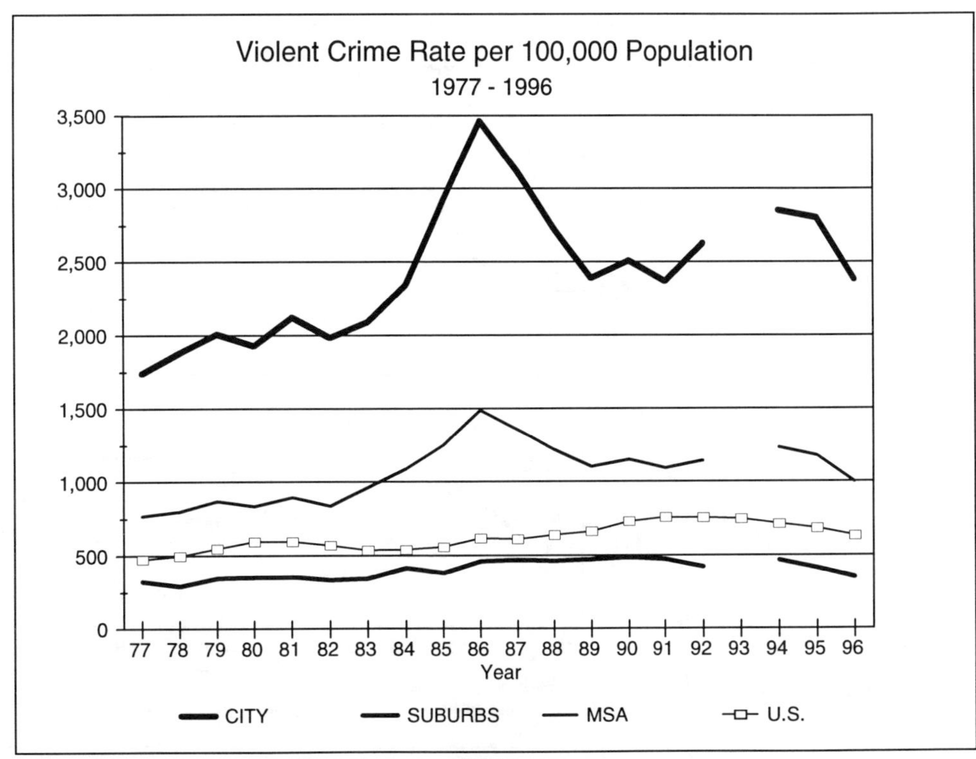

Note: Missing line segments indicate data not available.

Property Crimes and Property Crime Rates: 1977 - 1996

Year	Number				Rate per 100,000 population			
	City	Suburbs[2]	MSA[1]	U.S.	City	Suburbs[3]	MSA[1]	U.S.
1977	17,347	13,844	31,191	9,955,000	10,577.4	3,864.7	5,972.8	4,601.7
1978	16,104	13,683	29,787	10,123,400	9,879.8	3,958.3	5,855.7	4,642.5
1979	16,853	16,986	33,839	11,041,500	10,276.0	4,740.0	6,478.1	5,016.6
1980	18,127	18,629	36,756	12,063,700	11,359.5	5,146.6	7,047.6	5,353.3
1981	20,272	18,893	39,165	12,061,900	12,741.1	5,235.0	7,531.6	5,263.9
1982	19,384	16,760	36,144	11,652,000	12,306.1	4,690.8	7,020.9	5,032.5
1983	18,566	11,308	29,874	10,850,500	11,838.7	3,958.9	6,751.9	4,637.4
1984	18,730	11,982	30,712	10,608,500	12,215.2	4,209.6	7,012.3	4,492.1
1985	18,006	12,288	30,294	11,102,600	12,066.2	4,305.3	6,969.9	4,650.5
1986	18,387	12,532	30,919	11,722,700	12,250.0	4,364.5	7,071.5	4,862.6
1987	18,134	13,150	31,284	12,024,700	12,395.0	4,524.6	7,159.9	4,940.3
1988	17,215	12,843	30,058	12,356,900	11,691.2	4,390.6	6,835.1	5,027.1
1989	16,284	13,499	29,783	12,605,400	11,457.2	4,654.5	6,891.9	5,077.9
1990	15,430	13,218	28,648	12,655,500	10,961.8	4,564.0	6,656.5	5,088.5
1991	15,525	13,279	28,804	12,961,100	10,943.8	4,549.7	6,641.0	5,139.7
1992	14,983	12,423	27,406	12,505,900	10,484.5	4,225.7	6,272.9	4,902.7
1993	14,032	12,076	26,108	12,218,800	10,025.7	4,087.0	5,995.8	4,737.6
1994	14,413	13,173	27,586	12,131,900	10,278.5	4,449.9	6,323.4	4,660.0
1995	13,446	12,213	25,659	12,063,900	9,678.0	4,116.2	5,890.0	4,591.3
1996	12,729	11,303	24,032	11,791,300	9,119.0	3,791.8	5,490.8	4,444.8

Notes: Property crimes include burglary, larceny-theft and motor vehicle theft; n/a not available; (1) Metropolitan Statistical Area - see Appendix A for areas included; (2) calculated by the editors using the following formula: (number of crimes in the MSA minus number of crimes in the city); (3) calculated by the editors using the following formula: ((number of crimes in the MSA minus number of crimes in the city) ÷ (population of the MSA minus population of the city)) x 100,000
Source: U.S. Department of Justice, FBI Uniform Crime Reports, 1977 - 1996

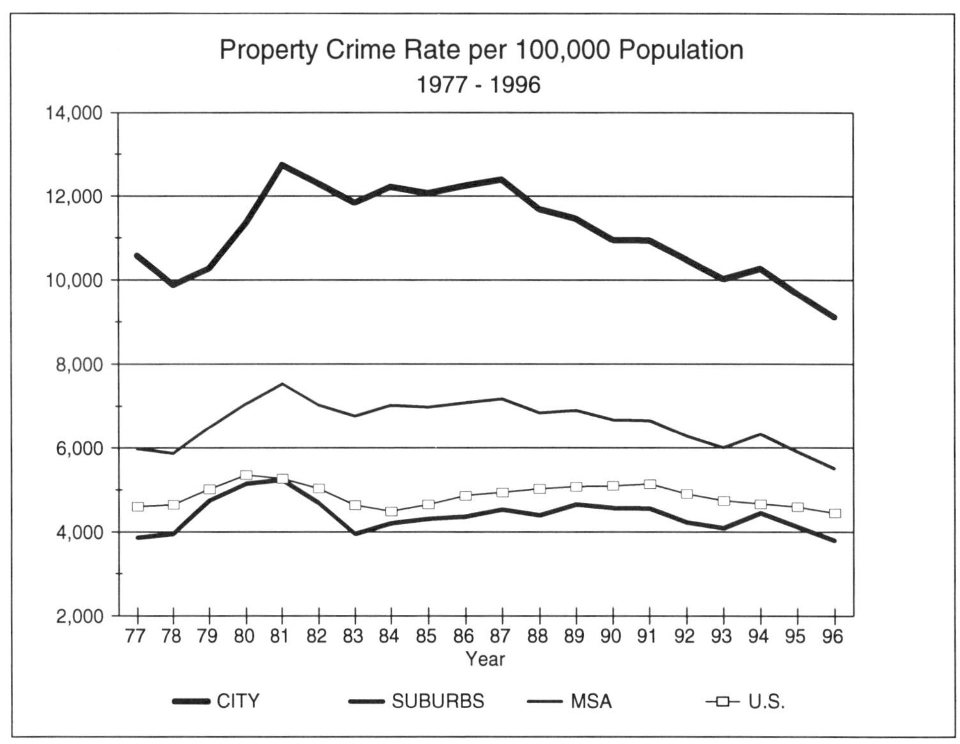

Note: Missing line segments indicate data not available.

Murders and Murder Rates: 1977 - 1996

Year	Number				Rate per 100,000 population			
	City	Suburbs[2]	MSA[1]	U.S.	City	Suburbs[3]	MSA[1]	U.S.
1977	44	8	52	19,120	26.8	2.2	10.0	8.8
1978	37	14	51	19,560	22.7	4.0	10.0	9.0
1979	36	12	48	21,460	22.0	3.3	9.2	9.7
1980	34	13	47	23,040	21.3	3.6	9.0	10.2
1981	34	7	41	22,520	21.4	1.9	7.9	9.8
1982	33	9	42	21,010	21.0	2.5	8.2	9.1
1983	32	9	41	19,310	20.4	3.2	9.3	8.3
1984	46	12	58	18,690	30.0	4.2	13.2	7.9
1985	47	11	58	18,980	31.5	3.9	13.3	7.9
1986	61	11	72	20,610	40.6	3.8	16.5	8.6
1987	52	12	64	20,100	35.5	4.1	14.6	8.3
1988	44	12	56	20,680	29.9	4.1	12.7	8.4
1989	59	5	64	21,500	41.5	1.7	14.8	8.7
1990	55	18	73	23,440	39.1	6.2	17.0	9.4
1991	52	9	61	24,700	36.7	3.1	14.1	9.8
1992	52	5	57	23,760	36.4	1.7	13.0	9.3
1993	48	6	54	24,530	34.3	2.0	12.4	9.5
1994	58	12	70	23,330	41.4	4.1	16.0	9.0
1995	41	11	52	21,610	29.5	3.7	11.9	8.2
1996	40	10	50	19,650	28.7	3.4	11.4	7.4

Notes: (1) Metropolitan Statistical Area - see Appendix A for areas included; (2) calculated by the editors using the following formula: (number of crimes in the MSA minus number of crimes in the city); (3) calculated by the editors using the following formula: ((number of crimes in the MSA minus number of crimes in the city) ÷ (population of the MSA minus population of the city)) x 100,000; n/a not avail.
Source: U.S. Department of Justice, FBI Uniform Crime Reports, 1977 - 1996

Forcible Rapes and Forcible Rape Rates: 1977 - 1996

Year	Number				Rate per 100,000 population			
	City	Suburbs[2]	MSA[1]	U.S.	City	Suburbs[3]	MSA[1]	U.S.
1977	179	55	234	63,500	109.1	15.4	44.8	29.4
1978	126	69	195	67,610	77.3	20.0	38.3	31.0
1979	170	109	279	76,390	103.7	30.4	53.4	34.7
1980	159	138	297	82,990	99.6	38.1	56.9	36.8
1981	178	135	313	82,500	111.9	37.4	60.2	36.0
1982	166	109	275	78,770	105.4	30.5	53.4	34.0
1983	199	112	311	78,920	126.9	39.2	70.3	33.7
1984	249	103	352	84,230	162.4	36.2	80.4	35.7
1985	285	84	369	88,670	191.0	29.4	84.9	37.1
1986	276	98	374	91,460	183.9	34.1	85.5	37.9
1987	276	136	412	91,110	188.7	46.8	94.3	37.4
1988	275	124	399	92,490	186.8	42.4	90.7	37.6
1989	201	152	353	94,500	141.4	52.4	81.7	38.1
1990	161	146	307	102,560	114.4	50.4	71.3	41.2
1991	151	181	332	106,590	106.4	62.0	76.5	42.3
1992	238	171	409	109,060	166.5	58.2	93.6	42.8
1993	n/a	n/a	n/a	106,010	n/a	n/a	n/a	41.1
1994	202	141	343	102,220	144.1	47.6	78.6	39.3
1995	206	152	358	97,470	148.3	51.2	82.2	37.1
1996	182	104	286	95,770	130.4	34.9	65.3	36.1

Notes: (1) Metropolitan Statistical Area - see Appendix A for areas included; (2) calculated by the editors using the following formula: (number of crimes in the MSA minus number of crimes in the city); (3) calculated by the editors using the following formula: ((number of crimes in the MSA minus number of crimes in the city) ÷ (population of the MSA minus population of the city)) x 100,000; n/a not avail.
Source: U.S. Department of Justice, FBI Uniform Crime Reports, 1977 - 1996

Robberies and Robbery Rates: 1977 - 1996

Year	Number				Rate per 100,000 population			
	City	Suburbs[2]	MSA[1]	U.S.	City	Suburbs[3]	MSA[1]	U.S.
1977	793	191	984	412,610	483.5	53.3	188.4	190.7
1978	684	232	916	426,930	419.6	67.1	180.1	195.8
1979	727	234	961	480,700	443.3	65.3	184.0	218.4
1980	729	304	1,033	565,840	456.8	84.0	198.1	251.1
1981	891	295	1,186	592,910	560.0	81.7	228.1	258.7
1982	787	290	1,077	553,130	499.6	81.2	209.2	238.9
1983	778	227	1,005	506,570	496.1	79.5	227.1	216.5
1984	882	255	1,137	485,010	575.2	89.6	259.6	205.4
1985	1,161	321	1,482	497,870	778.0	112.5	341.0	208.5
1986	1,528	357	1,885	542,780	1,018.0	124.3	431.1	225.1
1987	1,379	329	1,708	517,700	942.6	113.2	390.9	212.7
1988	1,177	353	1,530	542,970	799.3	120.7	347.9	220.9
1989	1,051	349	1,400	578,330	739.5	120.3	324.0	233.0
1990	925	288	1,213	639,270	657.1	99.4	281.8	257.0
1991	915	281	1,196	687,730	645.0	96.3	275.7	272.7
1992	955	246	1,201	672,480	668.3	83.7	274.9	263.6
1993	1,039	245	1,284	659,870	742.4	82.9	294.9	255.9
1994	1,169	403	1,572	618,950	833.7	136.1	360.3	237.7
1995	1,030	258	1,288	580,510	741.4	87.0	295.7	220.9
1996	937	232	1,169	537,050	671.3	77.8	267.1	202.4

Notes: (1) Metropolitan Statistical Area - see Appendix A for areas included; (2) calculated by the editors using the following formula: (number of crimes in the MSA minus number of crimes in the city); (3) calculated by the editors using the following formula: ((number of crimes in the MSA minus number of crimes in the city) ÷ (population of the MSA minus population of the city)) x 100,000; n/a not avail.
Source: U.S. Department of Justice, FBI Uniform Crime Reports, 1977 - 1996

Aggravated Assaults and Aggravated Assault Rates: 1977 - 1996

Year	Number				Rate per 100,000 population			
	City	Suburbs[2]	MSA[1]	U.S.	City	Suburbs[3]	MSA[1]	U.S.
1977	1,836	904	2,740	534,350	1,119.5	252.4	524.7	247.0
1978	2,216	689	2,905	571,460	1,359.5	199.3	571.1	262.1
1979	2,361	887	3,248	629,480	1,439.6	247.5	621.8	286.0
1980	2,152	822	2,974	672,650	1,348.6	227.1	570.2	298.5
1981	2,274	841	3,115	663,900	1,429.2	233.0	599.0	289.7
1982	2,139	775	2,914	669,480	1,358.0	216.9	566.0	289.2
1983	2,269	637	2,906	653,290	1,446.8	223.0	656.8	279.2
1984	2,416	812	3,228	685,350	1,575.7	285.3	737.0	290.2
1985	2,855	670	3,525	723,250	1,913.2	234.7	811.0	302.9
1986	3,330	855	4,185	834,320	2,218.6	297.8	957.2	346.1
1987	2,856	887	3,743	855,090	1,952.1	305.2	856.7	351.3
1988	2,528	862	3,390	910,090	1,716.8	294.7	770.9	370.2
1989	2,085	865	2,950	951,710	1,467.0	298.3	682.6	383.4
1990	2,392	963	3,355	1,054,860	1,699.3	332.5	779.5	424.1
1991	2,245	906	3,151	1,092,740	1,582.5	310.4	726.5	433.3
1992	2,510	818	3,328	1,126,970	1,756.4	278.2	761.7	441.8
1993	2,507	808	3,315	1,135,610	1,791.2	273.5	761.3	440.3
1994	2,570	825	3,395	1,113,180	1,832.8	278.7	778.2	427.6
1995	2,615	805	3,420	1,099,210	1,882.2	271.3	785.1	418.3
1996	2,166	694	2,860	1,029,810	1,551.7	232.8	653.5	388.2

Notes: (1) Metropolitan Statistical Area - see Appendix A for areas included; (2) calculated by the editors using the following formula: (number of crimes in the MSA minus number of crimes in the city); (3) calculated by the editors using the following formula: ((number of crimes in the MSA minus number of crimes in the city) ÷ (population of the MSA minus population of the city)) x 100,000; n/a not avail.
Source: U.S. Department of Justice, FBI Uniform Crime Reports, 1977 - 1996

Burglaries and Burglary Rates: 1977 - 1996

Year	Number				Rate per 100,000 population			
	City	Suburbs[2]	MSA[1]	U.S.	City	Suburbs[3]	MSA[1]	U.S.
1977	5,385	3,714	9,099	3,071,500	3,283.5	1,036.8	1,742.4	1,419.8
1978	4,765	3,548	8,313	3,128,300	2,923.3	1,026.4	1,634.2	1,434.6
1979	4,807	4,018	8,825	3,327,700	2,931.0	1,121.2	1,689.4	1,511.9
1980	6,052	5,057	11,109	3,795,200	3,792.6	1,397.1	2,130.0	1,684.1
1981	7,433	5,792	13,225	3,779,700	4,671.7	1,604.9	2,543.2	1,649.5
1982	7,045	4,852	11,897	3,447,100	4,472.6	1,358.0	2,311.0	1,488.8
1983	7,031	2,939	9,970	3,129,900	4,483.4	1,028.9	2,253.3	1,337.7
1984	6,813	3,155	9,968	2,984,400	4,443.3	1,108.4	2,275.9	1,263.7
1985	6,344	3,028	9,372	3,073,300	4,251.2	1,060.9	2,156.3	1,287.3
1986	6,357	3,011	9,368	3,241,400	4,235.2	1,048.6	2,142.6	1,344.6
1987	6,586	3,027	9,613	3,236,200	4,501.7	1,041.5	2,200.1	1,329.6
1988	6,046	2,757	8,803	3,218,100	4,106.0	942.5	2,001.8	1,309.2
1989	5,589	3,070	8,659	3,168,200	3,932.3	1,058.6	2,003.7	1,276.3
1990	5,033	2,815	7,848	3,073,900	3,575.6	972.0	1,823.5	1,235.9
1991	5,071	3,098	8,169	3,157,200	3,574.6	1,061.4	1,883.4	1,252.0
1992	4,388	2,619	7,007	2,979,900	3,070.5	890.8	1,603.8	1,168.2
1993	4,024	2,261	6,285	2,834,800	2,875.1	765.2	1,443.4	1,099.2
1994	4,235	2,502	6,737	2,712,800	3,020.1	845.2	1,544.3	1,042.0
1995	4,137	2,368	6,505	2,593,800	2,977.7	798.1	1,493.2	987.1
1996	4,141	2,290	6,431	2,501,500	2,966.6	768.2	1,469.4	943.0

Notes: (1) Metropolitan Statistical Area - see Appendix A for areas included; (2) calculated by the editors using the following formula: (number of crimes in the MSA minus number of crimes in the city); (3) calculated by the editors using the following formula: ((number of crimes in the MSA minus number of crimes in the city) ÷ (population of the MSA minus population of the city)) x 100,000; n/a not avail.
Source: U.S. Department of Justice, FBI Uniform Crime Reports, 1977 - 1996

Larceny-Thefts and Larceny-Theft Rates: 1977 - 1996

Year	Number				Rate per 100,000 population			
	City	Suburbs[2]	MSA[1]	U.S.	City	Suburbs[3]	MSA[1]	U.S.
1977	10,899	9,290	20,189	5,905,700	6,645.7	2,593.4	3,866.0	2,729.9
1978	10,066	9,436	19,502	5,991,000	6,175.5	2,729.7	3,833.8	2,747.4
1979	10,912	11,875	22,787	6,601,000	6,653.5	3,313.7	4,362.3	2,999.1
1980	11,089	12,572	23,661	7,136,900	6,949.0	3,473.3	4,536.7	3,167.0
1981	11,891	12,257	24,148	7,194,400	7,473.6	3,396.2	4,643.8	3,139.7
1982	11,439	11,152	22,591	7,142,500	7,262.1	3,121.3	4,388.2	3,084.8
1983	10,616	7,809	18,425	6,712,800	6,769.4	2,733.9	4,164.3	2,868.9
1984	10,397	8,075	18,472	6,591,900	6,780.7	2,836.9	4,217.6	2,791.3
1985	9,747	8,270	18,017	6,926,400	6,531.7	2,897.5	4,145.3	2,901.2
1986	9,800	8,460	18,260	7,257,200	6,529.1	2,946.3	4,176.3	3,010.3
1987	9,709	9,001	18,710	7,499,900	6,636.3	3,097.0	4,282.1	3,081.3
1988	8,783	8,949	17,732	7,705,900	5,964.8	3,059.4	4,032.2	3,134.9
1989	8,044	9,037	17,081	7,872,400	5,659.6	3,116.0	3,952.6	3,171.3
1990	8,158	9,059	17,217	7,945,700	5,795.6	3,127.9	4,000.4	3,194.8
1991	8,304	9,167	17,471	8,142,200	5,853.6	3,140.8	4,028.1	3,228.8
1992	8,186	8,583	16,769	7,915,200	5,728.2	2,919.5	3,838.2	3,103.0
1993	7,701	8,797	16,498	7,820,900	5,502.3	2,977.2	3,788.8	3,032.4
1994	7,587	9,270	16,857	7,879,800	5,410.6	3,131.4	3,864.0	3,026.7
1995	7,346	8,639	15,985	7,997,700	5,287.4	2,911.6	3,669.3	3,043.8
1996	6,340	7,911	14,251	7,894,600	4,541.9	2,653.9	3,256.1	2,975.9

Notes: (1) Metropolitan Statistical Area - see Appendix A for areas included; (2) calculated by the editors using the following formula: (number of crimes in the MSA minus number of crimes in the city); (3) calculated by the editors using the following formula: ((number of crimes in the MSA minus number of crimes in the city) ÷ (population of the MSA minus population of the city)) x 100,000; n/a not avail.
Source: U.S. Department of Justice, FBI Uniform Crime Reports, 1977 - 1996

Motor Vehicle Thefts and Motor Vehicle Theft Rates: 1977 - 1996

Year	Number				Rate per 100,000 population			
	City	Suburbs[2]	MSA[1]	U.S.	City	Suburbs[3]	MSA[1]	U.S.
1977	1,063	840	1,903	977,700	648.2	234.5	364.4	451.9
1978	1,273	699	1,972	1,004,100	781.0	202.2	387.7	460.5
1979	1,134	1,093	2,227	1,112,800	691.5	305.0	426.3	505.6
1980	986	1,000	1,986	1,131,700	617.9	276.3	380.8	502.2
1981	948	844	1,792	1,087,800	595.8	233.9	344.6	474.7
1982	900	756	1,656	1,062,400	571.4	211.6	321.7	458.8
1983	919	560	1,479	1,007,900	586.0	196.1	334.3	430.8
1984	1,520	752	2,272	1,032,200	991.3	264.2	518.8	437.1
1985	1,915	990	2,905	1,102,900	1,283.3	346.9	668.4	462.0
1986	2,230	1,061	3,291	1,224,100	1,485.7	369.5	752.7	507.8
1987	1,839	1,122	2,961	1,288,700	1,257.0	386.1	677.7	529.4
1988	2,386	1,137	3,523	1,432,900	1,620.4	388.7	801.1	582.9
1989	2,651	1,392	4,043	1,564,800	1,865.2	480.0	935.6	630.4
1990	2,239	1,344	3,583	1,635,900	1,590.6	464.1	832.5	657.8
1991	2,150	1,014	3,164	1,661,700	1,515.6	347.4	729.5	659.0
1992	2,409	1,221	3,630	1,610,800	1,685.7	415.3	830.9	631.5
1993	2,307	1,018	3,325	1,563,100	1,648.3	344.5	763.6	606.1
1994	2,591	1,401	3,992	1,539,300	1,847.7	473.3	915.1	591.3
1995	1,963	1,206	3,169	1,472,400	1,412.9	406.5	727.4	560.4
1996	2,248	1,102	3,350	1,395,200	1,610.5	369.7	765.4	525.9

Notes: (1) Metropolitan Statistical Area - see Appendix A for areas included; (2) calculated by the editors using the following formula: (number of crimes in the MSA minus number of crimes in the city); (3) calculated by the editors using the following formula: ((number of crimes in the MSA minus number of crimes in the city) ÷ (population of the MSA minus population of the city)) x 100,000; n/a not avail.
Source: U.S. Department of Justice, FBI Uniform Crime Reports, 1977 - 1996

HATE CRIMES

Criminal Incidents by Bias Motivation

Area	Race	Ethnicity	Religion	Sexual Orientation
Flint	0	1	0	0

Notes: Figures include both violent and property crimes. Law enforcement agencies must have submitted data for at least one quarter of calendar year 1995 to be included in this report, therefore figures shown may not represent complete 12-month totals; n/a not available
Source: U.S. Department of Justice, FBI Uniform Crime Reports, Hate Crime Statistics 1995

LAW ENFORCEMENT

Full-Time Law Enforcement Employees

Jurisdiction	Police Employees			Police Officers per 100,000 population
	Total	Officers	Civilians	
Flint	350	306	44	219.2

Notes: Data as of October 31, 1996
Source: U.S. Department of Justice, FBI Uniform Crime Reports, 1996

CORRECTIONS

Federal Correctional Facilities

Type	Year Opened	Security Level	Sex of Inmates	Rated Capacity	Population on 7/1/95	Number of Staff
None listed						

Notes: Data as of 1995
Source: Bureau of Justice Statistics, Sourcebook of Criminal Justice Statistics Online

City/County/Regional Correctional Facilities

Name	Year Opened	Year Renov.	Rated Capacity	1995 Pop.	Number of COs[1]	Number of Staff	ACA[2] Accred.
Genesee Co Jail	1988	--	356	n/a	n/a	n/a	No

Notes: Data as of April 1996; (1) Correctional Officers; (2) American Correctional Assn. Accreditation
Source: American Correctional Association, 1996-1998 National Jail and Adult Detention Directory

Private Adult Correctional Facilities

Name	Date Opened	Rated Capacity	Present Pop.	Security Level	Facility Construct.	Expans. Plans	ACA[1] Accred.
None listed							

Notes: Data as of December 1996; (1) American Correctional Association Accreditation
Source: University of Florida, Center for Studies in Criminology and Law, Private Adult Correctional Facility Census, 10th Ed., March 15, 1997

Characteristics of Shock Incarceration Programs

Jurisdiction	Year Program Began	Number of Camps	Average Num. of Inmates	Number of Beds	Program Length	Voluntary/ Mandatory
Michigan	1988	1	319	360	90 days	Voluntary

Note: Data as of July 1996;
Source: Sourcebook of Criminal Justice Statistics Online

DEATH PENALTY

Michigan did not have the death penalty as of July 31, 1997.
Source: Death Penalty Information Center Web Site, 9/30/97

LAWS

Statutory Provisions Relating to the Purchase, Ownership and Use of Handguns

Jurisdiction	Instant Background Check	Federal Waiting Period Applies[1]	State Waiting Period (days)	License or Permit to Purchase	Regis- tration	Record of Sale Sent to Police	Concealed Carry Law
Michigan	No	No	No	Yes[a]	Yes	Yes	Yes[b]

Note: Data as of 1996; (1) The Federal 5-day waiting period for handgun purchases applies to states that don't have instant background checks, waiting period requirements, or licensing procedures exempting them from the Federal requirement; (a) A handgun purchaser must obtain a license to purchase from local law enforcement, and within 10 days present to such official the license and handgun purchased to obtain a certificate of inspection; (b) Restrictively administered discretion by local authorities over permit issuance, or permits are unavailable and carrying is prohibited in most circumstances
Source: Sourcebook of Criminal Justice Statistics Online

Statutory Provisions Relating to Alcohol Use and Driving

Jurisdiction	Drinking Age	Blood Alcohol Concentration Levels as Evidence in State Courts[1]		Open Container Law[1]	Anti-Consump- tion Law[1]	Dram Shop Law[1]
		Illegal per se at 0.10%	Presumption at 0.10%			
Michigan	21	Yes	(a)	Yes	Yes	Yes

Note: Data as of January 1, 1997; (1) See Appendix C for an explanation of terms; (a) Presumption of driving while impaired at 0.07%; presumption of driving under the influence at 0.10%
Source: Sourcebook of Criminal Justice Statistics Online

Statutory Provisions Relating to Curfews

Jurisdiction	Year Enacted	Latest Revision	Age Group(s)	Curfew Provisions
Flint	1989	1994	16 and 17	Midnight to 6 am every night
			13 through 15	11 pm to 6 am every night
			12 and under	10 pm to 6 am every night

Note: Data as of February 1996
Source: Sourcebook of Criminal Justice Statistics Online

Statutory Provisions Relating to Hate Crimes

Jurisdiction	Bias-Motivated Violence and Intimidation						Institutional Vandalism
		Criminal Penalty					
	Civil Action	Race/ Religion/ Ethnicity	Sexual Orientation	Mental/ Physical Disability	Gender	Age	
Michigan	Yes	Yes	No	No	Yes	No	No

Source: Anti-Defamation League, 1997 Hate Crimes Laws

Fort Lauderdale, Florida

OVERVIEW

The total crime rate for the city increased 49.6% between 1977 and 1996. During that same period, the violent crime rate increased 234.8% and the property crime rate increased 40.8%.

Among violent crimes, the rates for: Murders increased 27.8%; Forcible Rapes increased 77.3%; Robberies increased 172.9%; and Aggravated Assaults increased 394.4%.

Among property crimes, the rates for: Burglaries decreased 7.1%; Larceny-Thefts increased 47.9%; and Motor Vehicle Thefts increased 226.3%.

ANTI-CRIME PROGRAMS

Some of the community-oriented programs include Civilian Police Academy; Citizens on Patrol; Neighborhood Crime Walks where residents walk with beat officers throughout neighborhoods to demonstrate unity and presence; Community Policing Initiative where 9 officers are assigned to specific areas as identified by a Citizen's Steering Committee.

The Bicycle Patrols Program is a business-oriented project in which bicycle patrol officers liaison regularly with business owners and operators, and frequently attend business association meetings to help address specific concerns.

Several programs target juvenile crimes:

- Project J.A.M. (Juvenile Alternative Motivation) which establishes sports programs for disadvantaged youth.
- Parents Against Gangs provides gang awareness for concerned parents.
- Police Referral Outreach Program—Police Officers refer troubled teens to intervention programs.

Other programs include:

- T.A.G. (Threat Abatement Group)—Detectives assigned to proactive, early intervention in domestic abuse, stalking, and workplace violence cases.
- C.A.T. (Combat Auto Theft)—Residents have identifiable stickers attached to the rear of their cars allowing officers to stop them after dark to make sure the driver is the owner of the vehicle. *Ft. Lauderdale Police Department, 9/97*

The city instituted a program which the National League of Cities (1993) considers among those which are innovative for combatting crime and violence:

- Neighborhood Patrol Phone Project-Through a special phone number the project provides citizens with direct access to a police officer working in their area. Police feel it has enhanced their productivity and communication between police and citizenry. *Exemplary Programs in Criminal Justice, National League of Cities, 1994*

CRIME RISK

Your Chances of Becoming a Victim[1]

Area	Any Crime	Violent Crime					Property Crime			
		Any	Murder	Forcible Rape[2]	Robbery	Aggrav. Assault	Any	Burglary	Larceny -Theft	Motor Vehicle Theft
City	1:7	1:65	1:4,943	1:871	1:142	1:133	1:7	1:35	1:11	1:55

Note: (1) Figures have been calculated by dividing the population of the city by the number of crimes reported to the FBI during 1996 and are expressed as odds (eg. 1:20 should be read as 1 in 20). (2) Figures have been calculated by dividing the female population of the city by the number of forcible rapes reported to the FBI during 1996. The female population of the city was estimated by calculating the ratio of females to males reported in the 1990 Census and applying that ratio to 1996 population estimate.
Source: FBI Uniform Crime Reports 1996

CRIME STATISTICS

Total Crimes and Total Crime Rates: 1977 - 1996

Year	Number				Rate per 100,000 population			
	City	Suburbs[2]	MSA[1]	U.S.	City	Suburbs[3]	MSA[1]	U.S.
1977	15,408	52,701	68,109	10,984,500	10,136.8	7,288.5	7,783.2	5,077.6
1978	16,726	53,838	70,564	11,209,000	11,225.5	7,256.8	7,920.6	5,140.3
1979	19,309	60,746	80,055	12,249,500	12,178.6	8,060.8	8,776.5	5,565.5
1980	20,955	72,392	93,347	13,408,300	13,604.1	8,569.0	9,345.4	5,950.0
1981	22,022	73,222	95,244	13,423,800	13,454.5	8,156.6	8,973.6	5,858.2
1982	21,823	66,506	88,329	12,974,400	13,013.0	7,230.7	8,122.4	5,603.6
1983	19,288	56,758	76,046	12,108,600	11,217.1	6,018.4	6,820.1	5,175.0
1984	20,864	55,821	76,685	11,881,800	12,962.7	5,800.2	6,826.4	5,031.3
1985	21,844	67,416	89,260	12,431,400	14,074.4	6,900.3	7,883.8	5,207.1
1986	22,010	72,769	94,779	13,211,900	13,806.3	7,251.0	8,149.6	5,480.4
1987	22,012	78,123	100,135	13,508,700	14,382.1	7,633.6	8,511.5	5,550.0
1988	n/a	n/a	n/a	13,923,100	n/a	n/a	n/a	5,664.2
1989	25,789	82,368	108,157	14,251,400	17,241.5	7,699.8	8,870.3	5,741.0
1990	25,566	85,508	111,074	14,475,600	17,115.1	7,730.5	8,847.1	5,820.3
1991	24,334	85,363	109,697	14,872,900	15,874.3	7,520.4	8,514.3	5,897.8
1992	25,044	86,551	111,595	14,438,200	16,082.0	7,505.8	8,526.2	5,660.2
1993	25,775	91,775	117,550	14,144,800	17,105.4	7,847.4	8,904.1	5,484.4
1994	27,775	97,938	125,713	13,989,500	18,070.8	8,168.0	9,293.2	5,373.5
1995	25,036	89,186	114,222	13,862,700	15,143.2	7,199.6	8,134.9	5,275.9
1996	25,487	n/a	n/a	13,473,600	15,165.5	n/a	n/a	5,078.9

Notes: (1) Metropolitan Statistical Area - see Appendix A for areas included; (2) calculated by the editors using the following formula: (number of crimes in the MSA minus number of crimes in the city); (3) calculated by the editors using the following formula: ((number of crimes in the MSA minus number of crimes in the city) ÷ (population of the MSA minus population of the city)) x 100,000; n/a not avail.
Source: U.S. Department of Justice, FBI Uniform Crime Reports, 1977 - 1996

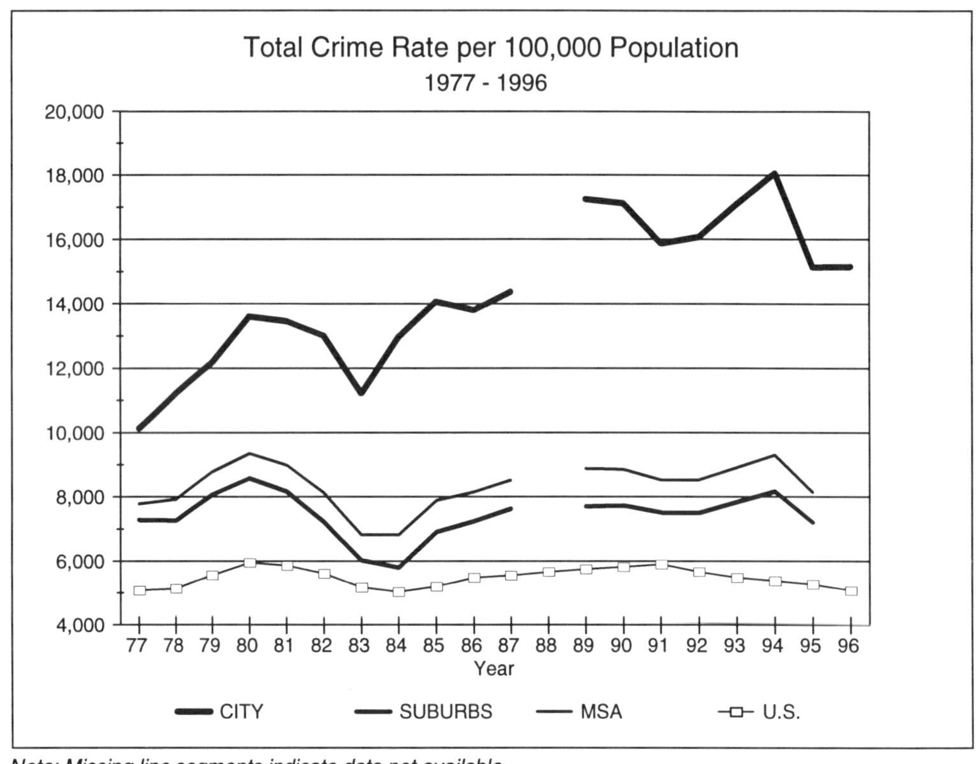

Note: Missing line segments indicate data not available.

Violent Crimes and Violent Crime Rates: 1977 - 1996

Year	Number				Rate per 100,000 population			
	City	Suburbs[2]	MSA[1]	U.S.	City	Suburbs[3]	MSA[1]	U.S.
1977	698	3,886	4,584	1,029,580	459.2	537.4	523.8	475.9
1978	921	4,558	5,479	1,085,550	618.1	614.4	615.0	497.8
1979	1,315	5,363	6,678	1,208,030	829.4	711.6	732.1	548.9
1980	1,891	8,008	9,899	1,344,520	1,227.6	947.9	991.0	596.6
1981	2,051	8,071	10,122	1,361,820	1,253.1	899.1	953.7	594.3
1982	1,970	6,778	8,748	1,322,390	1,174.7	736.9	804.4	571.1
1983	1,605	5,678	7,283	1,258,090	933.4	602.1	653.2	537.7
1984	1,913	5,921	7,834	1,273,280	1,188.5	615.2	697.4	539.2
1985	2,233	7,363	9,596	1,328,800	1,438.8	753.6	847.6	556.6
1986	2,032	8,107	10,139	1,489,170	1,274.6	807.8	871.8	617.7
1987	1,889	8,614	10,503	1,484,000	1,234.2	841.7	892.8	609.7
1988	n/a	n/a	n/a	1,566,220	n/a	n/a	n/a	637.2
1989	2,552	9,396	11,948	1,646,040	1,706.2	878.3	979.9	663.1
1990	2,427	10,344	12,771	1,820,130	1,624.7	935.2	1,017.2	731.8
1991	2,178	9,526	11,704	1,911,770	1,420.8	839.2	908.4	758.1
1992	2,282	10,530	12,812	1,932,270	1,465.4	913.2	978.9	757.5
1993	2,350	10,923	13,273	1,926,020	1,559.6	934.0	1,005.4	746.8
1994	2,440	10,615	13,055	1,857,670	1,587.5	885.3	965.1	713.6
1995	2,293	9,612	11,905	1,798,790	1,386.9	775.9	847.9	684.6
1996	2,584	n/a	n/a	1,682,280	1,537.6	n/a	n/a	634.1

Notes: Violent crimes include murder, forcible rape, robbery and aggravated assault; n/a not available; (1) Metropolitan Statistical Area - see Appendix A for areas included; (2) calculated by the editors using the following formula: (number of crimes in the MSA minus number of crimes in the city); (3) calculated by the editors using the following formula: ((number of crimes in the MSA minus number of crimes in the city) ÷ (population of the MSA minus population of the city)) x 100,000
Source: U.S. Department of Justice, FBI Uniform Crime Reports, 1977 - 1996

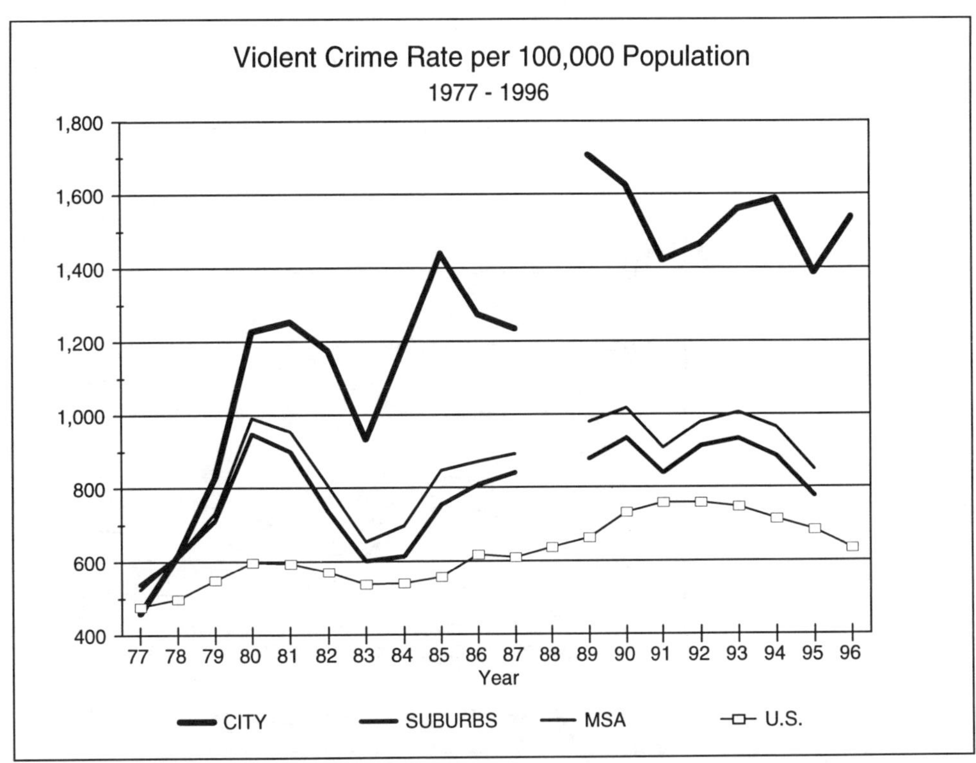

Note: Missing line segments indicate data not available.

Property Crimes and Property Crime Rates: 1977 - 1996

Year	Number				Rate per 100,000 population			
	City	Suburbs[2]	MSA[1]	U.S.	City	Suburbs[3]	MSA[1]	U.S.
1977	14,710	48,815	63,525	9,955,000	9,677.6	6,751.1	7,259.4	4,601.7
1978	15,805	49,280	65,085	10,123,400	10,607.4	6,642.4	7,305.6	4,642.5
1979	17,994	55,383	73,377	11,041,500	11,349.2	7,349.1	8,044.4	5,016.6
1980	19,064	64,384	83,448	12,063,700	12,376.4	7,621.1	8,354.4	5,353.3
1981	19,971	65,151	85,122	12,061,900	12,201.5	7,257.5	8,020.0	5,263.9
1982	19,853	59,728	79,581	11,652,000	11,838.3	6,493.7	7,317.9	5,032.5
1983	17,683	51,080	68,763	10,850,500	10,283.7	5,416.3	6,166.9	4,637.4
1984	18,951	49,900	68,851	10,608,500	11,774.2	5,185.0	6,129.1	4,492.1
1985	19,611	60,053	79,664	11,102,600	12,635.6	6,146.7	7,036.2	4,650.5
1986	19,978	64,662	84,640	11,722,700	12,531.7	6,443.2	7,277.8	4,862.6
1987	20,123	69,509	89,632	12,024,700	13,147.9	6,791.9	7,618.8	4,940.3
1988	n/a	n/a	n/a	12,356,900	n/a	n/a	n/a	5,027.1
1989	23,237	72,972	96,209	12,605,400	15,535.4	6,821.4	7,890.4	5,077.9
1990	23,139	75,164	98,303	12,655,500	15,490.3	6,795.3	7,829.9	5,088.5
1991	22,156	75,837	97,993	12,961,100	14,453.5	6,681.2	7,605.9	5,139.7
1992	22,762	76,021	98,783	12,505,900	14,616.6	6,592.7	7,547.4	4,902.7
1993	23,425	80,852	104,277	12,218,800	15,545.9	6,913.4	7,898.7	4,737.6
1994	25,335	87,323	112,658	12,131,900	16,483.3	7,282.7	8,328.1	4,660.0
1995	22,743	79,574	102,317	12,063,900	13,756.3	6,423.7	7,287.0	4,591.3
1996	22,903	n/a	n/a	11,791,300	13,628.0	n/a	n/a	4,444.8

Notes: Property crimes include burglary, larceny-theft and motor vehicle theft; n/a not available; (1) Metropolitan Statistical Area - see Appendix A for areas included; (2) calculated by the editors using the following formula: (number of crimes in the MSA minus number of crimes in the city); (3) calculated by the editors using the following formula: ((number of crimes in the MSA minus number of crimes in the city) ÷ (population of the MSA minus population of the city)) x 100,000
Source: U.S. Department of Justice, FBI Uniform Crime Reports, 1977 - 1996

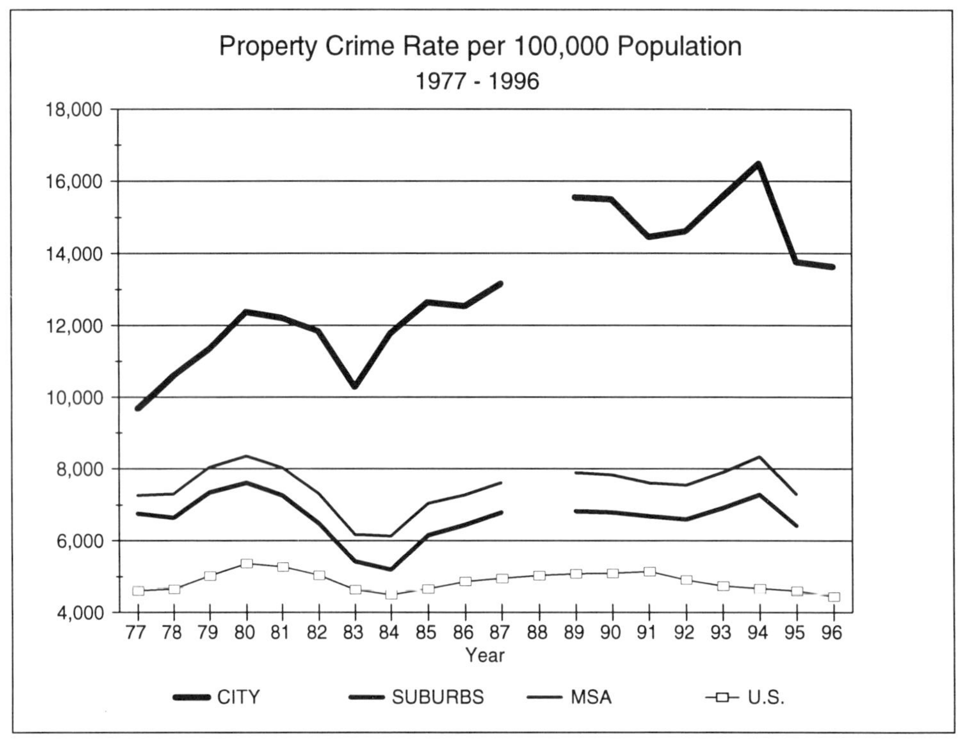

Note: Missing line segments indicate data not available.

Murders and Murder Rates: 1977 - 1996

Year	Number				Rate per 100,000 population			
	City	Suburbs[2]	MSA[1]	U.S.	City	Suburbs[3]	MSA[1]	U.S.
1977	24	56	80	19,120	15.8	7.7	9.1	8.8
1978	26	70	96	19,560	17.4	9.4	10.8	9.0
1979	43	86	129	21,460	27.1	11.4	14.1	9.7
1980	44	130	174	23,040	28.6	15.4	17.4	10.2
1981	49	122	171	22,520	29.9	13.6	16.1	9.8
1982	50	99	149	21,010	29.8	10.8	13.7	9.1
1983	43	82	125	19,310	25.0	8.7	11.2	8.3
1984	39	78	117	18,690	24.2	8.1	10.4	7.9
1985	43	89	132	18,980	27.7	9.1	11.7	7.9
1986	39	90	129	20,610	24.5	9.0	11.1	8.6
1987	53	81	134	20,100	34.6	7.9	11.4	8.3
1988	n/a	n/a	n/a	20,680	n/a	n/a	n/a	8.4
1989	30	85	115	21,500	20.1	7.9	9.4	8.7
1990	31	89	120	23,440	20.8	8.0	9.6	9.4
1991	27	70	97	24,700	17.6	6.2	7.5	9.8
1992	12	73	85	23,760	7.7	6.3	6.5	9.3
1993	31	73	104	24,530	20.6	6.2	7.9	9.5
1994	33	70	103	23,330	21.5	5.8	7.6	9.0
1995	27	55	82	21,610	16.3	4.4	5.8	8.2
1996	34	n/a	n/a	19,650	20.2	n/a	n/a	7.4

Notes: (1) Metropolitan Statistical Area - see Appendix A for areas included; (2) calculated by the editors using the following formula: (number of crimes in the MSA minus number of crimes in the city); (3) calculated by the editors using the following formula: ((number of crimes in the MSA minus number of crimes in the city) ÷ (population of the MSA minus population of the city)) x 100,000; n/a not avail.
Source: U.S. Department of Justice, FBI Uniform Crime Reports, 1977 - 1996

Forcible Rapes and Forcible Rape Rates: 1977 - 1996

Year	Number				Rate per 100,000 population			
	City	Suburbs[2]	MSA[1]	U.S.	City	Suburbs[3]	MSA[1]	U.S.
1977	49	236	285	63,500	32.2	32.6	32.6	29.4
1978	79	307	386	67,610	53.0	41.4	43.3	31.0
1979	78	375	453	76,390	49.2	49.8	49.7	34.7
1980	94	445	539	82,990	61.0	52.7	54.0	36.8
1981	94	451	545	82,500	57.4	50.2	51.3	36.0
1982	111	389	500	78,770	66.2	42.3	46.0	34.0
1983	107	345	452	78,920	62.2	36.6	40.5	33.7
1984	122	383	505	84,230	75.8	39.8	45.0	35.7
1985	108	433	541	88,670	69.6	44.3	47.8	37.1
1986	95	432	527	91,460	59.6	43.0	45.3	37.9
1987	101	409	510	91,110	66.0	40.0	43.4	37.4
1988	n/a	n/a	n/a	92,490	n/a	n/a	n/a	37.6
1989	72	348	420	94,500	48.1	32.5	34.4	38.1
1990	114	379	493	102,560	76.3	34.3	39.3	41.2
1991	104	356	460	106,590	67.8	31.4	35.7	42.3
1992	70	442	512	109,060	45.0	38.3	39.1	42.8
1993	76	457	533	106,010	50.4	39.1	40.4	41.1
1994	94	443	537	102,220	61.2	36.9	39.7	39.3
1995	102	433	535	97,470	61.7	35.0	38.1	37.1
1996	96	n/a	n/a	95,770	57.1	n/a	n/a	36.1

Notes: (1) Metropolitan Statistical Area - see Appendix A for areas included; (2) calculated by the editors using the following formula: (number of crimes in the MSA minus number of crimes in the city); (3) calculated by the editors using the following formula: ((number of crimes in the MSA minus number of crimes in the city) ÷ (population of the MSA minus population of the city)) x 100,000; n/a not avail.
Source: U.S. Department of Justice, FBI Uniform Crime Reports, 1977 - 1996

Robberies and Robbery Rates: 1977 - 1996

Year	Number				Rate per 100,000 population			
	City	Suburbs[2]	MSA[1]	U.S.	City	Suburbs[3]	MSA[1]	U.S.
1977	393	1,242	1,635	412,610	258.6	171.8	186.8	190.7
1978	491	1,433	1,924	426,930	329.5	193.2	216.0	195.8
1979	812	2,126	2,938	480,700	512.1	282.1	322.1	218.4
1980	1,285	3,425	4,710	565,840	834.2	405.4	471.5	251.1
1981	1,347	3,371	4,718	592,910	823.0	375.5	444.5	258.7
1982	1,286	2,718	4,004	553,130	766.8	295.5	368.2	238.9
1983	896	2,009	2,905	506,570	521.1	213.0	260.5	216.5
1984	1,116	2,142	3,258	485,010	693.4	222.6	290.0	205.4
1985	1,369	3,056	4,425	497,870	882.1	312.8	390.8	208.5
1986	1,271	3,465	4,736	542,780	797.3	345.3	407.2	225.1
1987	1,198	3,545	4,743	517,700	782.7	346.4	403.2	212.7
1988	n/a	n/a	n/a	542,970	n/a	n/a	n/a	220.9
1989	1,474	3,738	5,212	578,330	985.5	349.4	427.5	233.0
1990	1,306	3,858	5,164	639,270	874.3	348.8	411.3	257.0
1991	1,146	3,330	4,476	687,730	747.6	293.4	347.4	272.7
1992	1,309	3,276	4,585	672,480	840.6	284.1	350.3	263.6
1993	1,270	3,569	4,839	659,870	842.8	305.2	366.5	255.9
1994	1,274	3,217	4,491	618,950	828.9	268.3	332.0	237.7
1995	1,113	3,130	4,243	580,510	673.2	252.7	302.2	220.9
1996	1,186	n/a	n/a	537,050	705.7	n/a	n/a	202.4

Notes: (1) Metropolitan Statistical Area - see Appendix A for areas included; (2) calculated by the editors using the following formula: (number of crimes in the MSA minus number of crimes in the city); (3) calculated by the editors using the following formula: ((number of crimes in the MSA minus number of crimes in the city) ÷ (population of the MSA minus population of the city)) x 100,000; n/a not avail.
Source: U.S. Department of Justice, FBI Uniform Crime Reports, 1977 - 1996

Aggravated Assaults and Aggravated Assault Rates: 1977 - 1996

Year	Number				Rate per 100,000 population			
	City	Suburbs[2]	MSA[1]	U.S.	City	Suburbs[3]	MSA[1]	U.S.
1977	232	2,352	2,584	534,350	152.6	325.3	295.3	247.0
1978	325	2,748	3,073	571,460	218.1	370.4	344.9	262.1
1979	382	2,776	3,158	629,480	240.9	368.4	346.2	286.0
1980	468	4,008	4,476	672,650	303.8	474.4	448.1	298.5
1981	561	4,127	4,688	663,900	342.7	459.7	441.7	289.7
1982	523	3,572	4,095	669,480	311.9	388.4	376.6	289.2
1983	559	3,242	3,801	653,290	325.1	343.8	340.9	279.2
1984	636	3,318	3,954	685,350	395.1	344.8	352.0	290.2
1985	713	3,785	4,498	723,250	459.4	387.4	397.3	302.9
1986	627	4,120	4,747	834,320	393.3	410.5	408.2	346.1
1987	537	4,579	5,116	855,090	350.9	447.4	434.9	351.3
1988	n/a	n/a	n/a	910,090	n/a	n/a	n/a	370.2
1989	976	5,225	6,201	951,710	652.5	488.4	508.6	383.4
1990	976	6,018	6,994	1,054,860	653.4	544.1	557.1	424.1
1991	901	5,770	6,671	1,092,740	587.8	508.3	517.8	433.3
1992	891	6,739	7,630	1,126,970	572.2	584.4	583.0	441.8
1993	973	6,824	7,797	1,135,610	645.7	583.5	590.6	440.3
1994	1,039	6,885	7,924	1,113,180	676.0	574.2	585.8	427.6
1995	1,051	5,994	7,045	1,099,210	635.7	483.9	501.7	418.3
1996	1,268	n/a	n/a	1,029,810	754.5	n/a	n/a	388.2

Notes: (1) Metropolitan Statistical Area - see Appendix A for areas included; (2) calculated by the editors using the following formula: (number of crimes in the MSA minus number of crimes in the city); (3) calculated by the editors using the following formula: ((number of crimes in the MSA minus number of crimes in the city) ÷ (population of the MSA minus population of the city)) x 100,000; n/a not avail.
Source: U.S. Department of Justice, FBI Uniform Crime Reports, 1977 - 1996

Burglaries and Burglary Rates: 1977 - 1996

Year	Number				Rate per 100,000 population			
	City	Suburbs[2]	MSA[1]	U.S.	City	Suburbs[3]	MSA[1]	U.S.
1977	4,620	12,819	17,439	3,071,500	3,039.5	1,772.9	1,992.9	1,419.8
1978	4,972	13,532	18,504	3,128,300	3,336.9	1,824.0	2,077.0	1,434.6
1979	5,925	15,225	21,150	3,327,700	3,737.0	2,020.3	2,318.7	1,511.9
1980	7,117	21,139	28,256	3,795,200	4,620.4	2,502.2	2,828.9	1,684.1
1981	7,823	21,302	29,125	3,779,700	4,779.5	2,373.0	2,744.1	1,649.5
1982	7,070	16,747	23,817	3,447,100	4,215.8	1,820.8	2,190.1	1,488.8
1983	6,050	14,103	20,153	3,129,900	3,518.4	1,495.4	1,807.4	1,337.7
1984	6,450	13,669	20,119	2,984,400	4,007.4	1,420.3	1,791.0	1,263.7
1985	6,430	16,902	23,332	3,073,300	4,142.9	1,730.0	2,060.8	1,287.3
1986	6,734	18,267	25,001	3,241,400	4,224.1	1,820.2	2,149.7	1,344.6
1987	6,162	18,554	24,716	3,236,200	4,026.1	1,813.0	2,100.9	1,329.6
1988	n/a	n/a	n/a	3,218,100	n/a	n/a	n/a	1,309.2
1989	6,882	18,596	25,478	3,168,200	4,601.0	1,738.4	2,089.5	1,276.3
1990	6,305	18,895	25,200	3,073,900	4,220.9	1,708.2	2,007.2	1,235.9
1991	6,208	17,482	23,690	3,157,200	4,049.8	1,540.1	1,838.7	1,252.0
1992	6,305	17,417	23,722	2,979,900	4,048.8	1,510.4	1,812.4	1,168.2
1993	5,822	17,698	23,520	2,834,800	3,863.7	1,513.3	1,781.6	1,099.2
1994	5,405	17,567	22,972	2,712,800	3,516.6	1,465.1	1,698.2	1,042.0
1995	4,876	15,913	20,789	2,593,800	2,949.3	1,284.6	1,480.6	987.1
1996	4,744	n/a	n/a	2,501,500	2,822.8	n/a	n/a	943.0

Notes: (1) Metropolitan Statistical Area - see Appendix A for areas included; (2) calculated by the editors using the following formula: (number of crimes in the MSA minus number of crimes in the city); (3) calculated by the editors using the following formula: ((number of crimes in the MSA minus number of crimes in the city) ÷ (population of the MSA minus population of the city)) x 100,000; n/a not avail.
Source: U.S. Department of Justice, FBI Uniform Crime Reports, 1977 - 1996

Larceny-Thefts and Larceny-Theft Rates: 1977 - 1996

Year	Number				Rate per 100,000 population			
	City	Suburbs[2]	MSA[1]	U.S.	City	Suburbs[3]	MSA[1]	U.S.
1977	9,249	32,541	41,790	5,905,700	6,084.9	4,500.4	4,775.6	2,729.9
1978	9,871	32,100	41,971	5,991,000	6,624.8	4,326.8	4,711.1	2,747.4
1979	10,785	36,190	46,975	6,601,000	6,802.4	4,802.3	5,149.9	2,999.1
1980	10,288	38,331	48,619	7,136,900	6,679.0	4,537.2	4,867.5	3,167.0
1981	10,398	38,777	49,175	7,194,400	6,352.8	4,319.6	4,633.1	3,139.7
1982	10,953	38,136	49,089	7,142,500	6,531.2	4,146.2	4,514.0	3,084.8
1983	9,988	32,981	42,969	6,712,800	5,808.6	3,497.2	3,853.6	2,868.9
1984	10,725	32,291	43,016	6,591,900	6,663.4	3,355.3	3,829.3	2,791.3
1985	11,157	37,996	49,153	6,926,400	7,188.6	3,889.1	4,341.4	2,901.2
1986	11,156	40,775	51,931	7,257,200	6,997.9	4,063.0	4,465.3	3,010.3
1987	11,466	43,952	55,418	7,499,900	7,491.6	4,294.7	4,710.6	3,081.3
1988	n/a	n/a	n/a	7,705,900	n/a	n/a	n/a	3,134.9
1989	13,803	45,738	59,541	7,872,400	9,228.1	4,275.6	4,883.1	3,171.3
1990	14,409	47,545	61,954	7,945,700	9,646.1	4,298.4	4,934.7	3,194.8
1991	13,765	49,993	63,758	8,142,200	8,979.6	4,404.3	4,948.7	3,228.8
1992	13,621	49,921	63,542	7,915,200	8,746.7	4,329.2	4,854.8	3,103.0
1993	14,477	52,959	67,436	7,820,900	9,607.6	4,528.4	5,108.1	3,032.4
1994	16,382	56,654	73,036	7,879,800	10,658.4	4,724.9	5,399.1	3,026.7
1995	14,836	52,973	67,809	7,997,700	8,973.7	4,276.3	4,829.4	3,043.8
1996	15,125	n/a	n/a	7,894,600	8,999.8	n/a	n/a	2,975.9

Notes: (1) Metropolitan Statistical Area - see Appendix A for areas included; (2) calculated by the editors using the following formula: (number of crimes in the MSA minus number of crimes in the city); (3) calculated by the editors using the following formula: ((number of crimes in the MSA minus number of crimes in the city) ÷ (population of the MSA minus population of the city)) x 100,000; n/a not avail.
Source: U.S. Department of Justice, FBI Uniform Crime Reports, 1977 - 1996

Motor Vehicle Thefts and Motor Vehicle Theft Rates: 1977 - 1996

Year	Number				Rate per 100,000 population			
	City	Suburbs[2]	MSA[1]	U.S.	City	Suburbs[3]	MSA[1]	U.S.
1977	841	3,455	4,296	977,700	553.3	477.8	490.9	451.9
1978	962	3,648	4,610	1,004,100	645.6	491.7	517.5	460.5
1979	1,284	3,968	5,252	1,112,800	809.8	526.5	575.8	505.6
1980	1,659	4,914	6,573	1,131,700	1,077.0	581.7	658.1	502.2
1981	1,750	5,072	6,822	1,087,800	1,069.2	565.0	642.7	474.7
1982	1,830	4,845	6,675	1,062,400	1,091.2	526.8	613.8	458.8
1983	1,645	3,996	5,641	1,007,900	956.7	423.7	505.9	430.8
1984	1,776	3,940	5,716	1,032,200	1,103.4	409.4	508.8	437.1
1985	2,024	5,155	7,179	1,102,900	1,304.1	527.6	634.1	462.0
1986	2,088	5,620	7,708	1,224,100	1,309.7	560.0	662.8	507.8
1987	2,495	7,003	9,498	1,288,700	1,630.2	684.3	807.3	529.4
1988	n/a	n/a	n/a	1,432,900	n/a	n/a	n/a	582.9
1989	2,552	8,638	11,190	1,564,800	1,706.2	807.5	917.7	630.4
1990	2,425	8,724	11,149	1,635,900	1,623.4	788.7	888.0	657.8
1991	2,183	8,362	10,545	1,661,700	1,424.1	736.7	818.5	659.0
1992	2,836	8,683	11,519	1,610,800	1,821.1	753.0	880.1	631.5
1993	3,126	10,195	13,321	1,563,100	2,074.6	871.7	1,009.0	606.1
1994	3,548	13,102	16,650	1,539,300	2,308.4	1,092.7	1,230.8	591.3
1995	3,031	10,688	13,719	1,472,400	1,833.3	862.8	977.1	560.4
1996	3,034	n/a	n/a	1,395,200	1,805.3	n/a	n/a	525.9

Notes: (1) Metropolitan Statistical Area - see Appendix A for areas included; (2) calculated by the editors using the following formula: (number of crimes in the MSA minus number of crimes in the city); (3) calculated by the editors using the following formula: ((number of crimes in the MSA minus number of crimes in the city) ÷ (population of the MSA minus population of the city)) x 100,000; n/a not avail.
Source: U.S. Department of Justice, FBI Uniform Crime Reports, 1977 - 1996

HATE CRIMES

Criminal Incidents by Bias Motivation

Area	Race	Ethnicity	Religion	Sexual Orientation
Fort Lauderdale	1	0	0	0

Notes: Figures include both violent and property crimes. Law enforcement agencies must have submitted data for at least one quarter of calendar year 1995 to be included in this report, therefore figures shown may not represent complete 12-month totals; n/a not available
Source: U.S. Department of Justice, FBI Uniform Crime Reports, Hate Crime Statistics 1995

ILLEGAL DRUGS

Drug Use by Adult Arrestees

Sex	Percent Testing Positive by Urinalysis (%)				
	Any Drug[1]	Cocaine	Marijuana	Opiates	Multiple Drugs
Male	67	44	38	2	19
Female	66	52	24	3	19

Notes: The catchment area is the entire county; (1) Includes cocaine, opiates, marijuana, methadone, phencyclidine (PCP), benzodiazepines, methaqualone, propoxyphene, barbiturates & amphetamines
Source: National Institute of Justice, 1996 Drug Use Forecasting, Annual Report on Adult and Juvenile Arrestees (released June 1997)

LAW ENFORCEMENT

Full-Time Law Enforcement Employees

Jurisdiction	Police Employees			Police Officers per 100,000 population
	Total	Officers	Civilians	
Fort Lauderdale	709	444	265	264.2

Notes: Data as of October 31, 1996
Source: U.S. Department of Justice, FBI Uniform Crime Reports, 1996

CORRECTIONS

Federal Correctional Facilities

Type	Year Opened	Security Level	Sex of Inmates	Rated Capacity	Population on 7/1/95	Number of Staff
None listed						

Notes: Data as of 1995
Source: Bureau of Justice Statistics, Sourcebook of Criminal Justice Statistics Online

City/County/Regional Correctional Facilities

Name	Year Opened	Year Renov.	Rated Capacity	1995 Pop.	Number of COs[1]	Number of Staff	ACA[2] Accred.
Broward County Department of Correction & Rehabilitation	1954	1989	3,656	3,155	998	1,294	Yes

Notes: Data as of April 1996; (1) Correctional Officers; (2) American Correctional Assn. Accreditation
Source: American Correctional Association, 1996-1998 National Jail and Adult Detention Directory

Private Adult Correctional Facilities

Name	Date Opened	Rated Capacity	Present Pop.	Security Level	Facility Construct.	Expans. Plans	ACA[1] Accred.
None listed							

Notes: Data as of December 1996; (1) American Correctional Association Accreditation
Source: University of Florida, Center for Studies in Criminology and Law, Private Adult Correctional Facility Census, 10th Ed., March 15, 1997

Characteristics of Shock Incarceration Programs

Jurisdiction	Year Program Began	Number of Camps	Average Num. of Inmates	Number of Beds	Program Length	Voluntary/ Mandatory
Florida	1987	1	94	112	120 days min.	n/a

Note: Data as of July 1996;
Source: Sourcebook of Criminal Justice Statistics Online

INMATES AND HIV/AIDS

HIV Testing Policies for Inmates

Jurisdiction	All Inmates at Some Time	All Convicted Inmates at Admission	Random Samples While in Custody	High-risk Groups	Upon Inmate Request	Upon Court Order	Upon Involvement in Incident
Broward Co.[1]	No	No	No	No	Yes	Yes	Yes

Notes: (1) All facilities reported following the same testing policy or authorities reported the policy to be jurisdiction-wide
Source: HIV in Prisons and Jails, 1993 (released August 1995)

Inmates Known to be Positive for HIV

Jurisdiction	Number of Jail Inmates in Facilities Providing Data	Type of HIV Infection/AIDS Cases				HIV/AIDS Cases as a Percent of Tot. Custody Pop.
		Total	Asymptomatic	Symptomatic	Confirmed AIDS	
Broward Co.	2,921	94	44	5	45	3.2

Source: HIV in Prisons and Jails, 1993 (released August, 1995)

DEATH PENALTY

Death Penalty Statistics

State	Prisoners Executed		Prisoners Under Sentence of Death					Avg. No. of Years on Death Row[4]
	1930-1995	1996[1]	Total[2]	White[3]	Black[3]	Hisp.	Women	
Florida	206	2	362	228	134	35	6	6.9

Notes: Data as of 12/31/95 unless otherwise noted; (1) Data as of 7/31/97; (2) Includes persons of other races; (3) Includes people of Hispanic origin; (4) Covers prisoners sentenced 1974 through 1995
Source: Bureau of Justice Statistics, Capital Punishment 1995 (released 12/96); Death Penalty Information Center Web Site, 9/30/97

Capital Offenses and Methods of Execution

Capital Offenses in Florida	Minimum Age for Imposition of Death Penalty	Mentally Retarded Excluded	Methods of Execution[1]
First-degree murder; felony murder; capital drug-trafficking.	16	No	Electrocution

Notes: Data as of 12/31/95 unless otherwise noted; (1) Data as of 7/31/97
Source: Bureau of Justice Statistics, Capital Punishment 1995 (released 12/96); Death Penalty Information Center Web Site, 9/30/97

LAWS

Statutory Provisions Relating to the Purchase, Ownership and Use of Handguns

Jurisdiction	Instant Background Check	Federal Waiting Period Applies[1]	State Waiting Period (days)	License or Permit to Purchase	Registration	Record of Sale Sent to Police	Concealed Carry Law
Florida	Yes[a]	No	3[b,c]	No	No	No	Yes[d]

Note: Data as of 1996; (1) The Federal 5-day waiting period for handgun purchases applies to states that don't have instant background checks, waiting period requirements, or licensing procedures exempting them from the Federal requirement; (a) Concealed firearm carry permit holders are exempt from Instant Check; (b) The State waiting period does not apply to a person holding a valid permit or license to carry a firearm; (c) Purchases from licensed dealers only; (d) "Shall issue" permit system, liberally administered discretion by local authorities over permit issuance, or no permit required
Source: Sourcebook of Criminal Justice Statistics Online

Statutory Provisions Relating to Alcohol Use and Driving

Jurisdiction	Drinking Age	Blood Alcohol Concentration Levels as Evidence in State Courts[1]		Open Container Law[1]	Anti-Consumption Law[1]	Dram Shop Law[1]
		Illegal per se at 0.10%	Presumption at 0.10%			
Florida	21	(a)	(a,b)	Yes	No	Yes[c]

Note: Data as of January 1, 1997; (1) See Appendix C for an explanation of terms; (a) 0.08%; (b) Constitutes prima facie evidence; (c) Applies only to the actions of intoxicated minors or persons known to be habitually addicted to alcohol
Source: Sourcebook of Criminal Justice Statistics Online

Statutory Provisions Relating to Hate Crimes

Jurisdiction	Bias-Motivated Violence and Intimidation						Institutional Vandalism
	Civil Action	Criminal Penalty					
		Race/ Religion/ Ethnicity	Sexual Orientation	Mental/ Physical Disability	Gender	Age	
Florida	Yes	Yes	Yes	No	No	No	Yes

Source: Anti-Defamation League, 1997 Hate Crimes Laws

Fort Wayne, Indiana

OVERVIEW

The total crime rate for the city increased 9.2% between 1977 and 1996. During that same period, the violent crime rate increased 114.5% and the property crime rate increased 4.9%.

Among violent crimes, the rates for: Murders increased 6.1%; Forcible Rapes increased 82.1%; Robberies increased 103.2%; and Aggravated Assaults increased 150.7%.

Among property crimes, the rates for: Burglaries decreased 29.5%; Larceny-Thefts increased 6.6%; and Motor Vehicle Thefts increased 112.5%.

ANTI-CRIME PROGRAMS

Information not available at time of publication.

CRIME RISK

Your Chances of Becoming a Victim[1]

Area	Any Crime	Violent Crime					Property Crime			
		Any	Murder	Forcible Rape[2]	Robbery	Aggrav. Assault	Any	Burglary	Larceny -Theft	Motor Vehicle Theft
City	1:13	1:174	1:14,323	1:805	1:373	1:427	1:14	1:97	1:20	1:119

Note: (1) Figures have been calculated by dividing the population of the city by the number of crimes reported to the FBI during 1996 and are expressed as odds (eg. 1:20 should be read as 1 in 20).
(2) Figures have been calculated by dividing the female population of the city by the number of forcible rapes reported to the FBI during 1996. The female population of the city was estimated by calculating the ratio of females to males reported in the 1990 Census and applying that ratio to 1996 population estimate.
Source: FBI Uniform Crime Reports 1996

CRIME STATISTICS

Total Crimes and Total Crime Rates: 1977 - 1996

Year	Number				Rate per 100,000 population			
	City	Suburbs[2]	MSA[1]	U.S.	City	Suburbs[3]	MSA[1]	U.S.
1977	12,505	4,024	16,529	10,984,500	6,870.9	1,946.3	4,251.8	5,077.6
1978	12,686	4,076	16,762	11,209,000	7,008.8	2,136.5	4,508.6	5,140.3
1979	13,611	4,375	17,986	12,249,500	7,400.8	2,260.2	4,764.8	5,565.5
1980	15,101	4,507	19,608	13,408,300	8,829.0	2,152.3	5,154.0	5,950.0
1981	13,112	4,138	17,250	13,423,800	7,659.2	1,974.3	4,530.2	5,858.2
1982	13,351	3,937	17,288	12,974,400	7,791.7	1,876.7	4,536.0	5,603.6
1983	13,613	3,620	17,233	12,108,600	7,933.0	1,996.6	4,883.2	5,175.0
1984	12,549	3,155	15,704	11,881,800	7,471.6	1,726.0	4,477.3	5,031.3
1985	12,226	3,384	15,610	12,431,400	7,390.5	1,849.2	4,480.2	5,207.1
1986	13,022	3,818	16,840	13,211,900	7,863.6	2,084.2	4,828.1	5,480.4
1987	n/a	n/a	n/a	13,508,700	n/a	n/a	n/a	5,550.0
1988	16,620	4,368	20,988	13,923,100	9,325.9	2,310.5	5,714.7	5,664.2
1989	16,416	5,039	21,455	14,251,400	9,070.9	2,670.3	5,803.7	5,741.0
1990	16,055	4,625	20,680	14,475,600	9,276.5	2,424.8	5,684.3	5,820.3
1991	17,104	5,176	22,280	14,872,900	9,766.6	2,681.9	6,052.2	5,897.8
1992	15,841	6,538	22,379	14,438,200	8,992.9	2,255.9	4,802.7	5,660.2
1993	14,857	6,351	21,208	14,144,800	8,470.1	2,172.4	4,534.0	5,484.4
1994	12,914	7,209	20,123	13,989,500	7,312.4	2,449.3	4,273.0	5,373.5
1995	12,765	7,111	19,876	13,862,700	6,900.6	2,467.1	4,200.2	5,275.9
1996	13,966	7,147	21,113	13,473,600	7,500.7	2,463.5	4,432.6	5,078.9

Notes: (1) Metropolitan Statistical Area - see Appendix A for areas included; (2) calculated by the editors using the following formula: (number of crimes in the MSA minus number of crimes in the city); (3) calculated by the editors using the following formula: ((number of crimes in the MSA minus number of crimes in the city) ÷ (population of the MSA minus population of the city)) x 100,000; n/a not avail.
Source: U.S. Department of Justice, FBI Uniform Crime Reports, 1977 - 1996

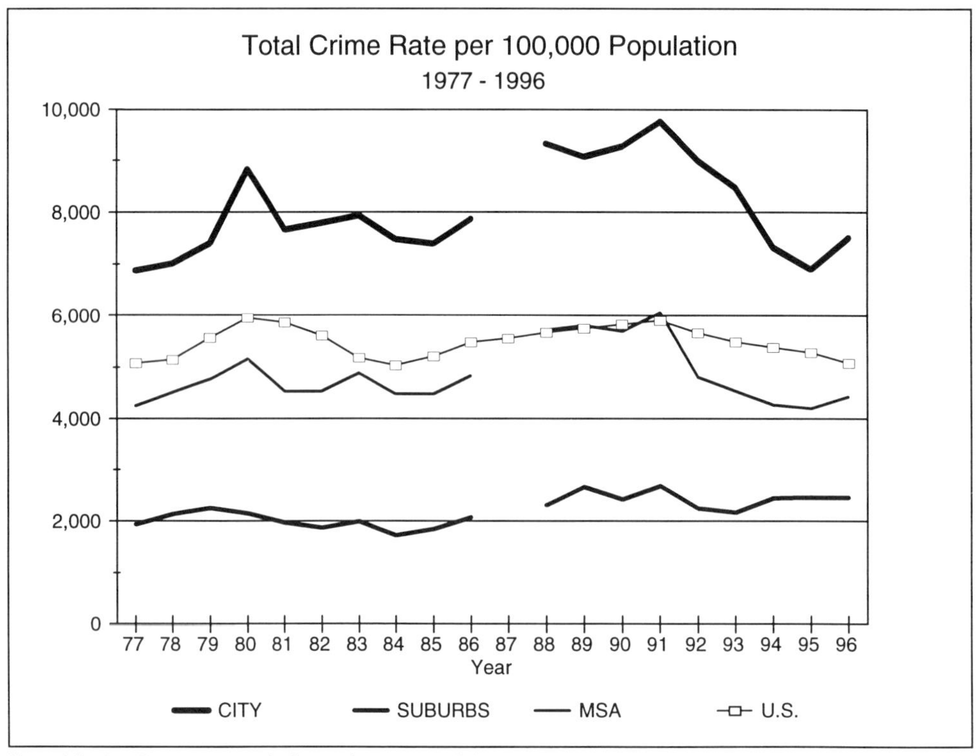

Note: Missing line segments indicate data not available.

Violent Crimes and Violent Crime Rates: 1977 - 1996

Year	Number				Rate per 100,000 population			
	City	Suburbs[2]	MSA[1]	U.S.	City	Suburbs[3]	MSA[1]	U.S.
1977	487	247	734	1,029,580	267.6	119.5	188.8	475.9
1978	414	187	601	1,085,550	228.7	98.0	161.7	497.8
1979	649	240	889	1,208,030	352.9	124.0	235.5	548.9
1980	1,017	196	1,213	1,344,520	594.6	93.6	318.8	596.6
1981	821	190	1,011	1,361,820	479.6	90.7	265.5	594.3
1982	775	211	986	1,322,390	452.3	100.6	258.7	571.1
1983	660	150	810	1,258,090	384.6	82.7	229.5	537.7
1984	707	144	851	1,273,280	420.9	78.8	242.6	539.2
1985	808	171	979	1,328,800	488.4	93.4	281.0	556.6
1986	747	220	967	1,489,170	451.1	120.1	277.2	617.7
1987	n/a	n/a	n/a	1,484,000	n/a	n/a	n/a	609.7
1988	1,086	213	1,299	1,566,220	609.4	112.7	353.7	637.2
1989	1,064	292	1,356	1,646,040	587.9	154.7	366.8	663.1
1990	1,326	223	1,549	1,820,130	766.2	116.9	425.8	731.8
1991	1,098	268	1,366	1,911,770	627.0	138.9	371.1	758.1
1992	977	494	1,471	1,932,270	554.6	170.5	315.7	757.5
1993	1,027	569	1,596	1,926,020	585.5	194.6	341.2	746.8
1994	982	635	1,617	1,857,670	556.0	215.7	343.4	713.6
1995	931	621	1,552	1,798,790	503.3	215.4	328.0	684.6
1996	1,069	604	1,673	1,682,280	574.1	208.2	351.2	634.1

Notes: Violent crimes include murder, forcible rape, robbery and aggravated assault; n/a not available; (1) Metropolitan Statistical Area - see Appendix A for areas included; (2) calculated by the editors using the following formula: (number of crimes in the MSA minus number of crimes in the city); (3) calculated by the editors using the following formula: ((number of crimes in the MSA minus number of crimes in the city) ÷ (population of the MSA minus population of the city)) x 100,000
Source: U.S. Department of Justice, FBI Uniform Crime Reports, 1977 - 1996

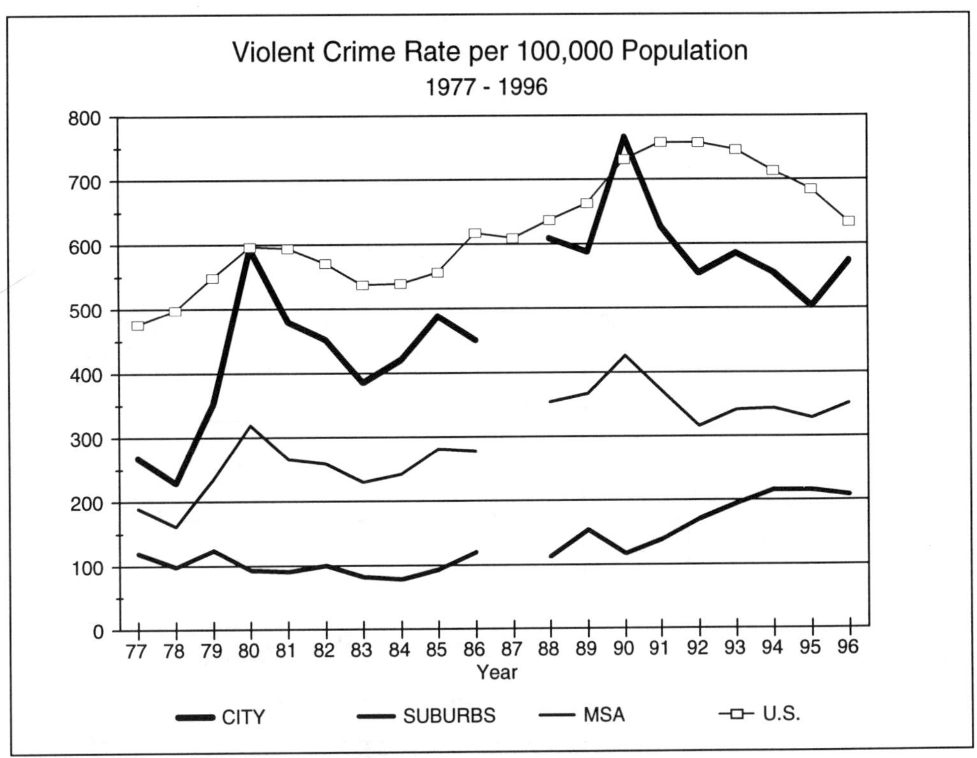

Note: Missing line segments indicate data not available.

Property Crimes and Property Crime Rates: 1977 - 1996

Year	Number				Rate per 100,000 population			
	City	Suburbs[2]	MSA[1]	U.S.	City	Suburbs[3]	MSA[1]	U.S.
1977	12,018	3,777	15,795	9,955,000	6,603.3	1,826.8	4,063.0	4,601.7
1978	12,272	3,889	16,161	10,123,400	6,780.1	2,038.5	4,347.0	4,642.5
1979	12,962	4,135	17,097	11,041,500	7,047.9	2,136.3	4,529.3	5,016.6
1980	14,084	4,311	18,395	12,063,700	8,234.4	2,058.7	4,835.2	5,353.3
1981	12,291	3,948	16,239	12,061,900	7,179.7	1,883.7	4,264.7	5,263.9
1982	12,576	3,726	16,302	11,652,000	7,339.4	1,776.2	4,277.3	5,032.5
1983	12,953	3,470	16,423	10,850,500	7,548.4	1,913.9	4,653.7	4,637.4
1984	11,842	3,011	14,853	10,608,500	7,050.7	1,647.2	4,234.7	4,492.1
1985	11,418	3,213	14,631	11,102,600	6,902.1	1,755.8	4,199.2	4,650.5
1986	12,275	3,598	15,873	11,722,700	7,412.5	1,964.1	4,550.9	4,862.6
1987	n/a	n/a	n/a	12,024,700	n/a	n/a	n/a	4,940.3
1988	15,534	4,155	19,689	12,356,900	8,716.5	2,197.8	5,361.0	5,027.1
1989	15,352	4,747	20,099	12,605,400	8,482.9	2,515.6	5,436.9	5,077.9
1990	14,729	4,402	19,131	12,655,500	8,510.3	2,307.9	5,258.5	5,088.5
1991	16,006	4,908	20,914	12,961,100	9,139.6	2,543.0	5,681.2	5,139.7
1992	14,864	6,044	20,908	12,505,900	8,438.2	2,085.5	4,487.0	4,902.7
1993	13,830	5,782	19,612	12,218,800	7,884.6	1,977.8	4,192.8	4,737.6
1994	11,932	6,574	18,506	12,131,900	6,756.4	2,233.5	3,929.6	4,660.0
1995	11,834	6,490	18,324	12,063,900	6,397.3	2,251.6	3,872.2	4,591.3
1996	12,897	6,543	19,440	11,791,300	6,926.6	2,255.3	4,081.4	4,444.8

Notes: Property crimes include burglary, larceny-theft and motor vehicle theft; n/a not available; (1) Metropolitan Statistical Area - see Appendix A for areas included; (2) calculated by the editors using the following formula: (number of crimes in the MSA minus number of crimes in the city); (3) calculated by the editors using the following formula: ((number of crimes in the MSA minus number of crimes in the city) ÷ (population of the MSA minus population of the city)) x 100,000
Source: U.S. Department of Justice, FBI Uniform Crime Reports, 1977 - 1996

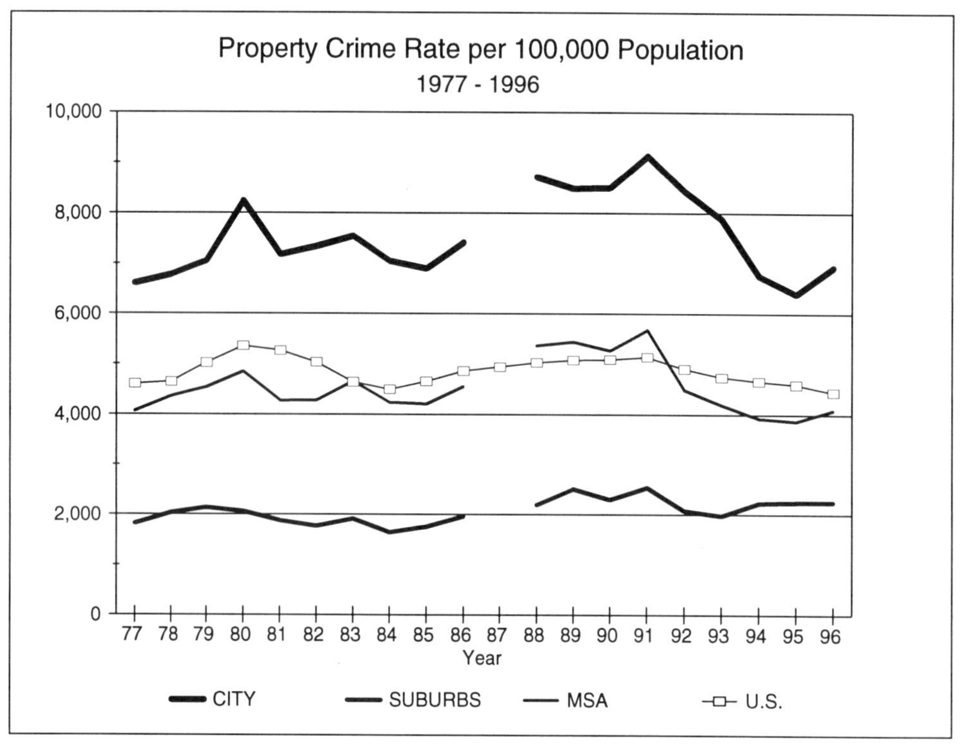

Note: Missing line segments indicate data not available.

Murders and Murder Rates: 1977 - 1996

Year	Number				Rate per 100,000 population			
	City	Suburbs[2]	MSA[1]	U.S.	City	Suburbs[3]	MSA[1]	U.S.
1977	12	6	18	19,120	6.6	2.9	4.6	8.8
1978	15	2	17	19,560	8.3	1.0	4.6	9.0
1979	8	5	13	21,460	4.3	2.6	3.4	9.7
1980	13	4	17	23,040	7.6	1.9	4.5	10.2
1981	18	7	25	22,520	10.5	3.3	6.6	9.8
1982	21	4	25	21,010	12.3	1.9	6.6	9.1
1983	15	2	17	19,310	8.7	1.1	4.8	8.3
1984	3	5	8	18,690	1.8	2.7	2.3	7.9
1985	21	5	26	18,980	12.7	2.7	7.5	7.9
1986	16	4	20	20,610	9.7	2.2	5.7	8.6
1987	n/a	n/a	n/a	20,100	n/a	n/a	n/a	8.3
1988	11	4	15	20,680	6.2	2.1	4.1	8.4
1989	14	9	23	21,500	7.7	4.8	6.2	8.7
1990	17	4	21	23,440	9.8	2.1	5.8	9.4
1991	23	3	26	24,700	13.1	1.6	7.1	9.8
1992	18	10	28	23,760	10.2	3.5	6.0	9.3
1993	28	13	41	24,530	16.0	4.4	8.8	9.5
1994	38	11	49	23,330	21.5	3.7	10.4	9.0
1995	23	9	32	21,610	12.4	3.1	6.8	8.2
1996	13	3	16	19,650	7.0	1.0	3.4	7.4

Notes: (1) Metropolitan Statistical Area - see Appendix A for areas included; (2) calculated by the editors using the following formula: (number of crimes in the MSA minus number of crimes in the city); (3) calculated by the editors using the following formula: ((number of crimes in the MSA minus number of crimes in the city) ÷ (population of the MSA minus population of the city)) x 100,000; n/a not avail.
Source: U.S. Department of Justice, FBI Uniform Crime Reports, 1977 - 1996

Forcible Rapes and Forcible Rape Rates: 1977 - 1996

Year	Number				Rate per 100,000 population			
	City	Suburbs[2]	MSA[1]	U.S.	City	Suburbs[3]	MSA[1]	U.S.
1977	65	19	84	63,500	35.7	9.2	21.6	29.4
1978	59	26	85	67,610	32.6	13.6	22.9	31.0
1979	77	30	107	76,390	41.9	15.5	28.3	34.7
1980	83	26	109	82,990	48.5	12.4	28.7	36.8
1981	85	16	101	82,500	49.7	7.6	26.5	36.0
1982	79	18	97	78,770	46.1	8.6	25.5	34.0
1983	91	15	106	78,920	53.0	8.3	30.0	33.7
1984	90	15	105	84,230	53.6	8.2	29.9	35.7
1985	83	11	94	88,670	50.2	6.0	27.0	37.1
1986	78	17	95	91,460	47.1	9.3	27.2	37.9
1987	n/a	n/a	n/a	91,110	n/a	n/a	n/a	37.4
1988	79	23	102	92,490	44.3	12.2	27.8	37.6
1989	97	27	124	94,500	53.6	14.3	33.5	38.1
1990	95	27	122	102,560	54.9	14.2	33.5	41.2
1991	114	30	144	106,590	65.1	15.5	39.1	42.3
1992	126	44	170	109,060	71.5	15.2	36.5	42.8
1993	130	36	166	106,010	74.1	12.3	35.5	41.1
1994	100	45	145	102,220	56.6	15.3	30.8	39.3
1995	84	36	120	97,470	45.4	12.5	25.4	37.1
1996	121	50	171	95,770	65.0	17.2	35.9	36.1

Notes: (1) Metropolitan Statistical Area - see Appendix A for areas included; (2) calculated by the editors using the following formula: (number of crimes in the MSA minus number of crimes in the city); (3) calculated by the editors using the following formula: ((number of crimes in the MSA minus number of crimes in the city) ÷ (population of the MSA minus population of the city)) x 100,000; n/a not avail.
Source: U.S. Department of Justice, FBI Uniform Crime Reports, 1977 - 1996

Robberies and Robbery Rates: 1977 - 1996

Year	Number				Rate per 100,000 population			
	City	Suburbs[2]	MSA[1]	U.S.	City	Suburbs[3]	MSA[1]	U.S.
1977	240	21	261	412,610	131.9	10.2	67.1	190.7
1978	213	21	234	426,930	117.7	11.0	62.9	195.8
1979	353	38	391	480,700	191.9	19.6	103.6	218.4
1980	583	55	638	565,840	340.9	26.3	167.7	251.1
1981	384	44	428	592,910	224.3	21.0	112.4	258.7
1982	387	33	420	553,130	225.9	15.7	110.2	238.9
1983	340	29	369	506,570	198.1	16.0	104.6	216.5
1984	270	37	307	485,010	160.8	20.2	87.5	205.4
1985	303	34	337	497,870	183.2	18.6	96.7	208.5
1986	355	35	390	542,780	214.4	19.1	111.8	225.1
1987	n/a	n/a	n/a	517,700	n/a	n/a	n/a	212.7
1988	597	45	642	542,970	335.0	23.8	174.8	220.9
1989	545	85	630	578,330	301.1	45.0	170.4	233.0
1990	475	58	533	639,270	274.5	30.4	146.5	257.0
1991	573	65	638	687,730	327.2	33.7	173.3	272.7
1992	533	51	584	672,480	302.6	17.6	125.3	263.6
1993	552	57	609	659,870	314.7	19.5	130.2	255.9
1994	577	79	656	618,950	326.7	26.8	139.3	237.7
1995	594	92	686	580,510	321.1	31.9	145.0	220.9
1996	499	67	566	537,050	268.0	23.1	118.8	202.4

Notes: (1) Metropolitan Statistical Area - see Appendix A for areas included; (2) calculated by the editors using the following formula: (number of crimes in the MSA minus number of crimes in the city); (3) calculated by the editors using the following formula: ((number of crimes in the MSA minus number of crimes in the city) ÷ (population of the MSA minus population of the city)) x 100,000; n/a not avail.
Source: U.S. Department of Justice, FBI Uniform Crime Reports, 1977 - 1996

Aggravated Assaults and Aggravated Assault Rates: 1977 - 1996

Year	Number				Rate per 100,000 population			
	City	Suburbs[2]	MSA[1]	U.S.	City	Suburbs[3]	MSA[1]	U.S.
1977	170	201	371	534,350	93.4	97.2	95.4	247.0
1978	127	138	265	571,460	70.2	72.3	71.3	262.1
1979	211	167	378	629,480	114.7	86.3	100.1	286.0
1980	338	111	449	672,650	197.6	53.0	118.0	298.5
1981	334	123	457	663,900	195.1	58.7	120.0	289.7
1982	288	156	444	669,480	168.1	74.4	116.5	289.2
1983	214	104	318	653,290	124.7	57.4	90.1	279.2
1984	344	87	431	685,350	204.8	47.6	122.9	290.2
1985	401	121	522	723,250	242.4	66.1	149.8	302.9
1986	298	164	462	834,320	180.0	89.5	132.5	346.1
1987	n/a	n/a	n/a	855,090	n/a	n/a	n/a	351.3
1988	399	141	540	910,090	223.9	74.6	147.0	370.2
1989	408	171	579	951,710	225.4	90.6	156.6	383.4
1990	739	134	873	1,054,860	427.0	70.3	240.0	424.1
1991	388	170	558	1,092,740	221.6	88.1	151.6	433.3
1992	300	389	689	1,126,970	170.3	134.2	147.9	441.8
1993	317	463	780	1,135,610	180.7	158.4	166.8	440.3
1994	267	500	767	1,113,180	151.2	169.9	162.9	427.6
1995	230	484	714	1,099,210	124.3	167.9	150.9	418.3
1996	436	484	920	1,029,810	234.2	166.8	193.2	388.2

Notes: (1) Metropolitan Statistical Area - see Appendix A for areas included; (2) calculated by the editors using the following formula: (number of crimes in the MSA minus number of crimes in the city); (3) calculated by the editors using the following formula: ((number of crimes in the MSA minus number of crimes in the city) ÷ (population of the MSA minus population of the city)) x 100,000; n/a not avail.
Source: U.S. Department of Justice, FBI Uniform Crime Reports, 1977 - 1996

Burglaries and Burglary Rates: 1977 - 1996

Year	Number				Rate per 100,000 population			
	City	Suburbs[2]	MSA[1]	U.S.	City	Suburbs[3]	MSA[1]	U.S.
1977	2,670	1,132	3,802	3,071,500	1,467.0	547.5	978.0	1,419.8
1978	2,361	1,216	3,577	3,128,300	1,304.4	637.4	962.1	1,434.6
1979	2,493	1,191	3,684	3,327,700	1,355.5	615.3	976.0	1,511.9
1980	3,419	1,379	4,798	3,795,200	1,999.0	658.5	1,261.2	1,684.1
1981	2,384	1,170	3,554	3,779,700	1,392.6	558.2	933.3	1,649.5
1982	2,038	978	3,016	3,447,100	1,189.4	466.2	791.3	1,488.8
1983	2,189	1,021	3,210	3,129,900	1,275.6	563.1	909.6	1,337.7
1984	1,822	891	2,713	2,984,400	1,084.8	487.4	773.5	1,263.7
1985	1,826	948	2,774	3,073,300	1,103.8	518.0	796.2	1,287.3
1986	1,864	904	2,768	3,241,400	1,125.6	493.5	793.6	1,344.6
1987	n/a	n/a	n/a	3,236,200	n/a	n/a	n/a	1,329.6
1988	3,527	1,337	4,864	3,218,100	1,979.1	707.2	1,324.4	1,309.2
1989	3,107	1,278	4,385	3,168,200	1,716.8	677.2	1,186.2	1,276.3
1990	2,449	1,115	3,564	3,073,900	1,415.0	584.6	979.6	1,235.9
1991	2,726	1,295	4,021	3,157,200	1,556.6	671.0	1,092.3	1,252.0
1992	2,392	1,217	3,609	2,979,900	1,357.9	419.9	774.5	1,168.2
1993	2,028	1,182	3,210	2,834,800	1,156.2	404.3	686.3	1,099.2
1994	1,778	1,224	3,002	2,712,800	1,006.8	415.9	637.5	1,042.0
1995	1,800	1,194	2,994	2,593,800	973.1	414.2	632.7	987.1
1996	1,927	1,273	3,200	2,501,500	1,034.9	438.8	671.8	943.0

Notes: (1) Metropolitan Statistical Area - see Appendix A for areas included; (2) calculated by the editors using the following formula: (number of crimes in the MSA minus number of crimes in the city); (3) calculated by the editors using the following formula: ((number of crimes in the MSA minus number of crimes in the city) ÷ (population of the MSA minus population of the city)) x 100,000; n/a not avail.
Source: U.S. Department of Justice, FBI Uniform Crime Reports, 1977 - 1996

Larceny-Thefts and Larceny-Theft Rates: 1977 - 1996

Year	Number				Rate per 100,000 population			
	City	Suburbs[2]	MSA[1]	U.S.	City	Suburbs[3]	MSA[1]	U.S.
1977	8,629	2,437	11,066	5,905,700	4,741.2	1,178.7	2,846.5	2,729.9
1978	9,100	2,335	11,435	5,991,000	5,027.6	1,223.9	3,075.8	2,747.4
1979	9,559	2,540	12,099	6,601,000	5,197.6	1,312.2	3,205.2	2,999.1
1980	9,860	2,553	12,413	7,136,900	5,764.8	1,219.2	3,262.8	3,167.0
1981	9,387	2,437	11,824	7,194,400	5,483.3	1,162.8	3,105.2	3,139.7
1982	9,906	2,499	12,405	7,142,500	5,781.2	1,191.3	3,254.8	3,084.8
1983	10,134	2,199	12,333	6,712,800	5,905.6	1,212.9	3,494.7	2,868.9
1984	9,376	1,841	11,217	6,591,900	5,582.4	1,007.2	3,198.0	2,791.3
1985	8,954	1,999	10,953	6,926,400	5,412.6	1,092.4	3,143.6	2,901.2
1986	9,719	2,389	12,108	7,257,200	5,869.0	1,304.1	3,471.4	3,010.3
1987	n/a	n/a	n/a	7,499,900	n/a	n/a	n/a	3,081.3
1988	11,053	2,528	13,581	7,705,900	6,202.1	1,337.2	3,697.9	3,134.9
1989	11,057	3,088	14,145	7,872,400	6,109.7	1,636.4	3,826.3	3,171.3
1990	10,951	2,948	13,899	7,945,700	6,327.4	1,545.6	3,820.4	3,194.8
1991	11,354	3,191	14,545	8,142,200	6,483.3	1,653.4	3,951.1	3,228.8
1992	10,740	4,382	15,122	7,915,200	6,097.0	1,512.0	3,245.3	3,103.0
1993	10,016	4,082	14,098	7,820,900	5,710.2	1,396.3	3,014.0	3,032.4
1994	8,477	4,775	13,252	7,879,800	4,800.0	1,622.3	2,814.0	3,026.7
1995	8,081	4,662	12,743	7,997,700	4,368.5	1,617.4	2,692.8	3,043.8
1996	9,407	4,734	14,141	7,894,600	5,052.2	1,631.8	2,968.9	2,975.9

Notes: (1) Metropolitan Statistical Area - see Appendix A for areas included; (2) calculated by the editors using the following formula: (number of crimes in the MSA minus number of crimes in the city); (3) calculated by the editors using the following formula: ((number of crimes in the MSA minus number of crimes in the city) ÷ (population of the MSA minus population of the city)) x 100,000; n/a not avail.
Source: U.S. Department of Justice, FBI Uniform Crime Reports, 1977 - 1996

Motor Vehicle Thefts and Motor Vehicle Theft Rates: 1977 - 1996

Year	Number				Rate per 100,000 population			
	City	Suburbs[2]	MSA[1]	U.S.	City	Suburbs[3]	MSA[1]	U.S.
1977	719	208	927	977,700	395.1	100.6	238.5	451.9
1978	811	338	1,149	1,004,100	448.1	177.2	309.1	460.5
1979	910	404	1,314	1,112,800	494.8	208.7	348.1	505.6
1980	805	379	1,184	1,131,700	470.7	181.0	311.2	502.2
1981	520	341	861	1,087,800	303.8	162.7	226.1	474.7
1982	632	249	881	1,062,400	368.8	118.7	231.2	458.8
1983	630	250	880	1,007,900	367.1	137.9	249.4	430.8
1984	644	279	923	1,032,200	383.4	152.6	263.2	437.1
1985	638	266	904	1,102,900	385.7	145.4	259.5	462.0
1986	692	305	997	1,224,100	417.9	166.5	285.8	507.8
1987	n/a	n/a	n/a	1,288,700	n/a	n/a	n/a	529.4
1988	954	290	1,244	1,432,900	535.3	153.4	338.7	582.9
1989	1,188	381	1,569	1,564,800	656.4	201.9	424.4	630.4
1990	1,329	339	1,668	1,635,900	767.9	177.7	458.5	657.8
1991	1,926	422	2,348	1,661,700	1,099.8	218.7	637.8	659.0
1992	1,732	445	2,177	1,610,800	983.2	153.5	467.2	631.5
1993	1,786	518	2,304	1,563,100	1,018.2	177.2	492.6	606.1
1994	1,677	575	2,252	1,539,300	949.6	195.4	478.2	591.3
1995	1,953	634	2,587	1,472,400	1,055.8	220.0	546.7	560.4
1996	1,563	536	2,099	1,395,200	839.4	184.8	440.7	525.9

Notes: (1) Metropolitan Statistical Area - see Appendix A for areas included; (2) calculated by the editors using the following formula: (number of crimes in the MSA minus number of crimes in the city); (3) calculated by the editors using the following formula: ((number of crimes in the MSA minus number of crimes in the city) ÷ (population of the MSA minus population of the city)) x 100,000; n/a not avail.
Source: U.S. Department of Justice, FBI Uniform Crime Reports, 1977 - 1996

HATE CRIMES

Criminal Incidents by Bias Motivation

Area	Race	Ethnicity	Religion	Sexual Orientation
Fort Wayne	n/a	n/a	n/a	n/a

Notes: Figures include both violent and property crimes. Law enforcement agencies must have submitted data for at least one quarter of calendar year 1995 to be included in this report, therefore figures shown may not represent complete 12-month totals; n/a not available
Source: U.S. Department of Justice, FBI Uniform Crime Reports, Hate Crime Statistics 1995

LAW ENFORCEMENT

Full-Time Law Enforcement Employees

Jurisdiction	Police Employees			Police Officers per 100,000 population
	Total	Officers	Civilians	
Fort Wayne	467	383	84	205.7

Notes: Data as of October 31, 1996
Source: U.S. Department of Justice, FBI Uniform Crime Reports, 1996

CORRECTIONS

Federal Correctional Facilities

Type	Year Opened	Security Level	Sex of Inmates	Rated Capacity	Population on 7/1/95	Number of Staff
None listed						

Notes: Data as of 1995
Source: Bureau of Justice Statistics, Sourcebook of Criminal Justice Statistics Online

City/County/Regional Correctional Facilities

Name	Year Opened	Year Renov.	Rated Capacity	1995 Pop.	Number of COs[1]	Number of Staff	ACA[2] Accred.
Allen County Jail	1981	1994	382	604	82	94	No

Notes: Data as of April 1996; (1) Correctional Officers; (2) American Correctional Assn. Accreditation
Source: American Correctional Association, 1996-1998 National Jail and Adult Detention Directory

Private Adult Correctional Facilities

Name	Date Opened	Rated Capacity	Present Pop.	Security Level	Facility Construct.	Expans. Plans	ACA[1] Accred.
None listed							

Notes: Data as of December 1996; (1) American Correctional Association Accreditation
Source: University of Florida, Center for Studies in Criminology and Law, Private Adult Correctional Facility Census, 10th Ed., March 15, 1997

Characteristics of Shock Incarceration Programs

Jurisdiction	Year Program Began	Number of Camps	Average Num. of Inmates	Number of Beds	Program Length	Voluntary/ Mandatory
Indiana did not have a shock incarceration program as of July 1996						

Source: Sourcebook of Criminal Justice Statistics Online

DEATH PENALTY

Death Penalty Statistics

State	Prisoners Executed		Prisoners Under Sentence of Death					Avg. No. of Years on Death Row[4]
	1930-1995	1996[1]	Total[2]	White[3]	Black[3]	Hisp.	Women	
Indiana	44	1	46	31	15	2	0	8.4

Notes: Data as of 12/31/95 unless otherwise noted; (1) Data as of 7/31/97; (2) Includes persons of other races; (3) Includes people of Hispanic origin; (4) Covers prisoners sentenced 1974 through 1995
Source: Bureau of Justice Statistics, Capital Punishment 1995 (released 12/96); Death Penalty Information Center Web Site, 9/30/97

Capital Offenses and Methods of Execution

Capital Offenses in Indiana	Minimum Age for Imposition of Death Penalty	Mentally Retarded Excluded	Methods of Execution[1]
Murder with 14 aggravating circum-stances.	16	Yes	Lethal injection

Notes: Data as of 12/31/95 unless otherwise noted; (1) Data as of 7/31/97
Source: Bureau of Justice Statistics, Capital Punishment 1995 (released 12/96); Death Penalty Information Center Web Site, 9/30/97

LAWS

Statutory Provisions Relating to the Purchase, Ownership and Use of Handguns

Jurisdiction	Instant Background Check	Federal Waiting Period Applies[1]	State Waiting Period (days)	License or Permit to Purchase	Regis-tration	Record of Sale Sent to Police	Concealed Carry Law
Indiana	No	No	7[a]	No	No	Yes	Yes[b]

Note: Data as of 1996; (1) The Federal 5-day waiting period for handgun purchases applies to states that don't have instant background checks, waiting period requirements, or licensing procedures exempting them from the Federal requirement; (a) The State waiting period does not apply to a person holding an unlimited carry permit; (b) "Shall issue" permit system, liberally administered discretion by local authorities over permit issuance, or no permit required
Source: Sourcebook of Criminal Justice Statistics Online

Statutory Provisions Relating to Alcohol Use and Driving

Jurisdiction	Drinking Age	Blood Alcohol Concentration Levels as Evidence in State Courts[1]		Open Container Law[1]	Anti-Consump-tion Law[1]	Dram Shop Law[1]
		Illegal per se at 0.10%	Presumption at 0.10%			
Indiana	21	Yes	Yes[a]	Yes[b]	Yes[c]	Yes

Note: Data as of January 1, 1997; (1) See Appendix C for an explanation of terms; (a) Has both prima facie and presumptive evidence laws with blood alcohol concentration levels at 0.10%; (b) Provided the driver has an alcohol concentration of 0.04% or more; (c) Applies to drivers only
Source: Sourcebook of Criminal Justice Statistics Online

Statutory Provisions Relating to Curfews

Jurisdiction	Year Enacted	Latest Revision	Age Group(s)	Curfew Provisions
Fort Wayne	1992	-	15 through 17	11 pm to 5 am weekday nights 1 am to 5 am weekend nights
			14 and under	11 pm to 5 am every night

Note: Data as of February 1996
Source: Sourcebook of Criminal Justice Statistics Online

Statutory Provisions Relating to Hate Crimes

Jurisdiction	Bias-Motivated Violence and Intimidation						Institutional Vandalism
	Civil Action	Criminal Penalty					
		Race/ Religion/ Ethnicity	Sexual Orientation	Mental/ Physical Disability	Gender	Age	
Indiana	No	No	No	No	No	No	Yes

Source: Anti-Defamation League, 1997 Hate Crimes Laws

Fort Worth, Texas

OVERVIEW

The total crime rate for the city decreased 17.1% between 1977 and 1996. During that same period, the violent crime rate increased 52.3% and the property crime rate decreased 22.3%.

Among violent crimes, the rates for: Murders decreased 47.7%; Forcible Rapes increased 20.0%; Robberies increased 17.0%; and Aggravated Assaults increased 103.2%.

Among property crimes, the rates for: Burglaries decreased 50.2%; Larceny-Thefts decreased 11.8%; and Motor Vehicle Thefts increased 32.7%.

ANTI-CRIME PROGRAMS

Some of the city's programs include:

- Code Blue—instituted Citizens on Patrol who are trained to use police portable radios.
- D.A.R.E. (Drug Abuse Resistance Education)—an educational program to deter drug abuse taught by officers to children in schools.
- Weed & Seed—"weeds" defines an area through intensive law enforcement efforts that remove habitual criminals and then "seeds" the area with services and economic opportunities.
- COPS grants—includes grants to hire 20 community oriented police officers, to add technical equipment, to employ personnel to staff information desks, to combat domestic violence, and to aid in reducing motor vehicle thefts.
- Comin' Up—gang intervention program which hires gang members to fight gang problems.
- Fort Worth Crime Control & Prevention District—raised the sales tax by a cent to pay for a wide variety of programs.
- H.E.A.T. (Help End Auto Theft)—stickers are affixed to autos so that police may stop them to see if they are driven by the owner. *Fort Worth Police Department, 6/97*

CRIME RISK

Your Chances of Becoming a Victim[1]

Area	Any Crime	Violent Crime					Property Crime			
		Any	Murder	Forcible Rape[2]	Robbery	Aggrav. Assault	Any	Burglary	Larceny -Theft	Motor Vehicle Theft
City	1:12	1:94	1:6,916	1:751	1:278	1:162	1:14	1:59	1:22	1:104

Note: (1) Figures have been calculated by dividing the population of the city by the number of crimes reported to the FBI during 1996 and are expressed as odds (eg. 1:20 should be read as 1 in 20). (2) Figures have been calculated by dividing the female population of the city by the number of forcible rapes reported to the FBI during 1996. The female population of the city was estimated by calculating the ratio of females to males reported in the 1990 Census and applying that ratio to 1996 population estimate.
Source: FBI Uniform Crime Reports 1996

CRIME STATISTICS

Total Crimes and Total Crime Rates: 1977 - 1996

Year	Number				Rate per 100,000 population			
	City	Suburbs[2]	MSA[1]	U.S.	City	Suburbs[3]	MSA[1]	U.S.
1977	36,743	156,382	193,125	10,984,500	9,984.5	6,844.0	7,279.6	5,077.6
1978	36,008	159,975	195,983	11,209,000	9,811.4	6,816.5	7,221.5	5,140.3
1979	42,690	174,924	217,614	12,249,500	11,100.4	7,259.0	7,787.7	5,565.5
1980	48,492	196,670	245,162	13,408,300	12,671.7	7,618.3	8,270.7	5,950.0
1981	47,153	205,812	252,965	13,423,800	11,833.2	7,656.3	8,195.5	5,858.2
1982	47,128	210,111	257,239	12,974,400	11,420.5	7,547.6	8,047.6	5,603.6
1983	45,858	39,146	85,004	12,108,600	10,799.0	5,472.4	7,456.6	5,175.0
1984	50,111	44,931	95,042	11,881,800	11,929.8	6,044.4	8,169.3	5,031.3
1985	58,858	54,901	113,759	12,431,400	13,866.9	6,764.3	9,203.3	5,207.1
1986	72,015	61,284	133,299	13,211,900	16,649.3	7,383.4	10,557.8	5,480.4
1987	77,563	64,489	142,052	13,508,700	17,941.7	7,161.4	10,658.1	5,550.0
1988	74,262	64,028	138,290	13,923,100	17,155.0	7,065.1	10,326.7	5,664.2
1989	67,538	65,267	132,805	14,251,400	15,676.2	6,815.0	9,564.5	5,741.0
1990	67,040	65,962	133,002	14,475,600	14,977.0	6,799.2	9,381.2	5,820.3
1991	77,595	69,280	146,875	14,872,900	16,972.9	6,992.2	10,143.4	5,897.8
1992	65,764	61,924	127,688	14,438,200	14,134.8	5,963.1	8,491.5	5,660.2
1993	49,801	56,084	105,885	14,144,800	10,747.5	5,214.9	6,880.9	5,484.4
1994	43,400	54,069	97,469	13,989,500	9,189.3	4,932.7	6,214.5	5,373.5
1995	39,667	53,860	93,527	13,862,700	8,617.2	4,778.9	5,892.0	5,275.9
1996	38,902	56,184	95,086	13,473,600	8,272.6	4,881.7	5,865.3	5,078.9

Notes: (1) Metropolitan Statistical Area - see Appendix A for areas included; (2) calculated by the editors using the following formula: (number of crimes in the MSA minus number of crimes in the city); (3) calculated by the editors using the following formula: ((number of crimes in the MSA minus number of crimes in the city) ÷ (population of the MSA minus population of the city)) x 100,000; n/a not avail.
Source: U.S. Department of Justice, FBI Uniform Crime Reports, 1977 - 1996

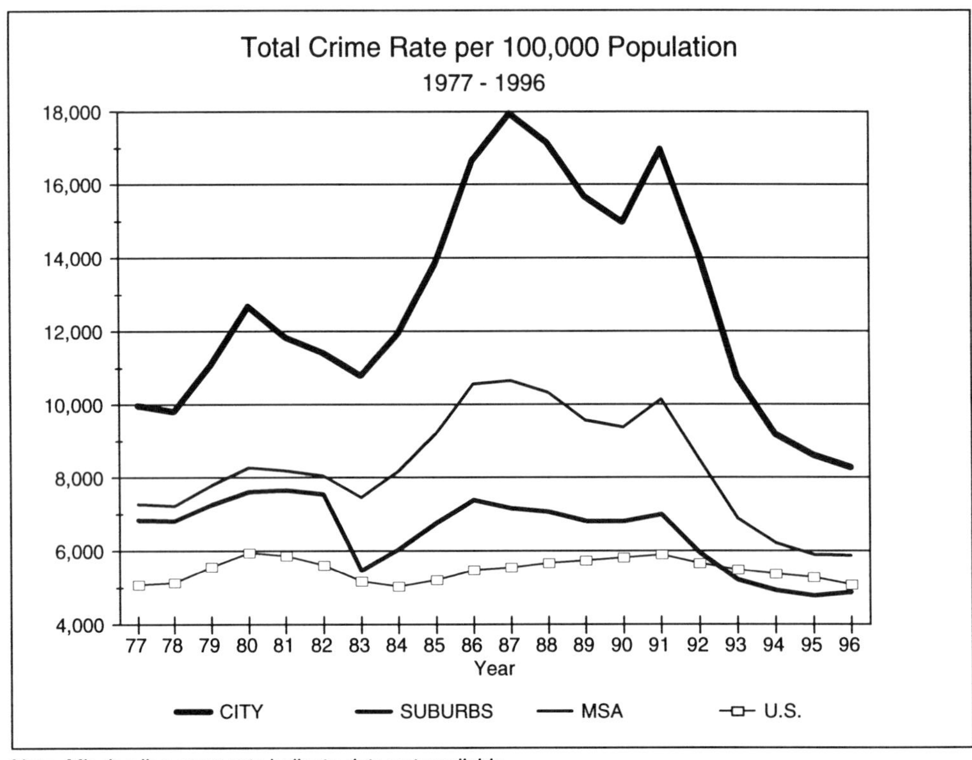

Note: Missing line segments indicate data not available.

Violent Crimes and Violent Crime Rates: 1977 - 1996

Year	Number				Rate per 100,000 population			
	City	Suburbs[2]	MSA[1]	U.S.	City	Suburbs[3]	MSA[1]	U.S.
1977	2,561	12,418	14,979	1,029,580	695.9	543.5	564.6	475.9
1978	2,670	13,776	16,446	1,085,550	727.5	587.0	606.0	497.8
1979	3,799	15,591	19,390	1,208,030	987.8	647.0	693.9	548.9
1980	4,693	17,595	22,288	1,344,520	1,226.4	681.6	751.9	596.6
1981	4,946	17,588	22,534	1,361,820	1,241.2	654.3	730.0	594.3
1982	4,901	18,049	22,950	1,322,390	1,187.7	648.4	718.0	571.1
1983	5,104	2,009	7,113	1,258,090	1,201.9	280.8	624.0	537.7
1984	5,452	2,367	7,819	1,273,280	1,297.9	318.4	672.1	539.2
1985	6,352	3,043	9,395	1,328,800	1,496.5	374.9	760.1	556.6
1986	7,870	3,823	11,693	1,489,170	1,819.5	460.6	926.1	617.7
1987	7,691	3,763	11,454	1,484,000	1,779.1	417.9	859.4	609.7
1988	7,326	3,705	11,031	1,566,220	1,692.4	408.8	823.7	637.2
1989	6,668	4,014	10,682	1,646,040	1,547.7	419.1	769.3	663.1
1990	7,826	4,715	12,541	1,820,130	1,748.4	486.0	884.6	731.8
1991	8,914	5,454	14,368	1,911,770	1,949.8	550.5	992.3	758.1
1992	9,392	5,641	15,033	1,932,270	2,018.6	543.2	999.7	757.5
1993	6,979	5,710	12,689	1,926,020	1,506.1	530.9	824.6	746.8
1994	6,035	5,722	11,757	1,857,670	1,277.8	522.0	749.6	713.6
1995	5,344	5,526	10,870	1,798,790	1,160.9	490.3	684.8	684.6
1996	4,984	5,746	10,730	1,682,280	1,059.9	499.3	661.9	634.1

Notes: Violent crimes include murder, forcible rape, robbery and aggravated assault; n/a not available; (1) Metropolitan Statistical Area - see Appendix A for areas included; (2) calculated by the editors using the following formula: (number of crimes in the MSA minus number of crimes in the city); (3) calculated by the editors using the following formula: ((number of crimes in the MSA minus number of crimes in the city) ÷ (population of the MSA minus population of the city)) x 100,000
Source: U.S. Department of Justice, FBI Uniform Crime Reports, 1977 - 1996

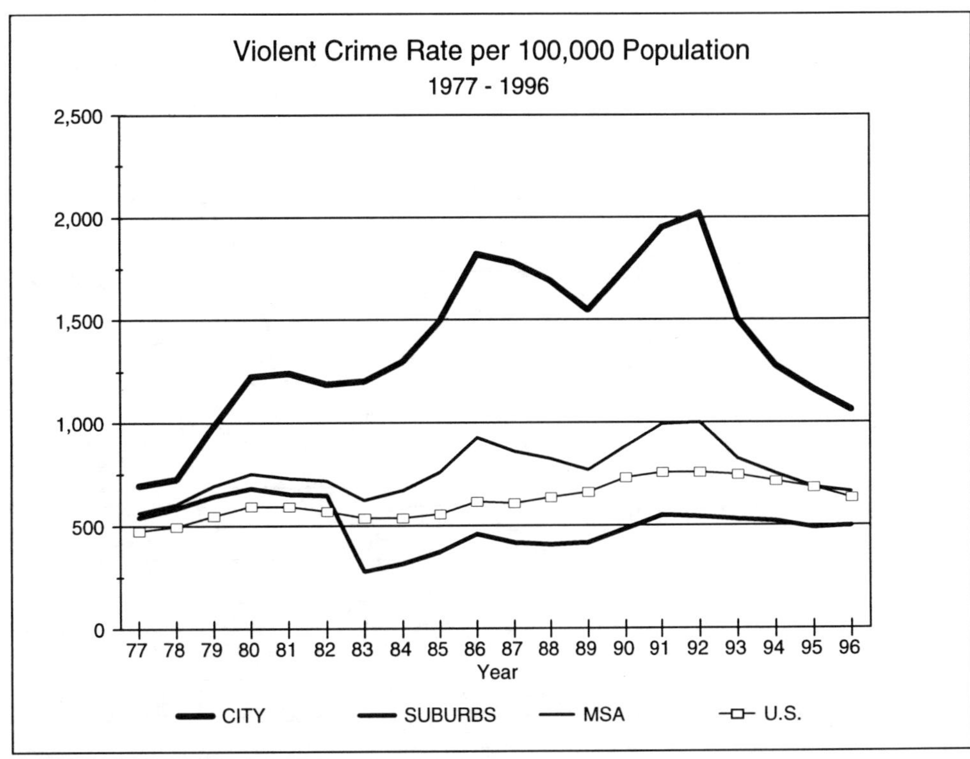

Note: Missing line segments indicate data not available.

Property Crimes and Property Crime Rates: 1977 - 1996

Year	Number				Rate per 100,000 population			
	City	Suburbs[2]	MSA[1]	U.S.	City	Suburbs[3]	MSA[1]	U.S.
1977	34,182	143,964	178,146	9,955,000	9,288.6	6,300.5	6,715.0	4,601.7
1978	33,338	146,199	179,537	10,123,400	9,083.9	6,229.5	6,615.5	4,642.5
1979	38,891	159,333	198,224	11,041,500	10,112.5	6,612.0	7,093.8	5,016.6
1980	43,799	179,075	222,874	12,063,700	11,445.4	6,936.7	7,518.8	5,353.3
1981	42,207	188,224	230,431	12,061,900	10,591.9	7,002.0	7,465.4	5,263.9
1982	42,227	192,062	234,289	11,652,000	10,232.9	6,899.3	7,329.6	5,032.5
1983	40,754	37,137	77,891	10,850,500	9,597.1	5,191.5	6,832.6	4,637.4
1984	44,659	42,564	87,223	10,608,500	10,631.8	5,725.9	7,497.2	4,492.1
1985	52,506	51,858	104,364	11,102,600	12,370.4	6,389.4	8,443.2	4,650.5
1986	64,145	57,461	121,606	11,722,700	14,829.8	6,922.8	9,631.6	4,862.6
1987	69,872	60,726	130,598	12,024,700	16,162.7	6,743.5	9,798.7	4,940.3
1988	66,936	60,323	127,259	12,356,900	15,462.6	6,656.3	9,503.0	5,027.1
1989	60,870	61,253	122,123	12,605,400	14,128.5	6,395.9	8,795.1	5,077.9
1990	59,214	61,247	120,461	12,655,500	13,228.7	6,313.2	8,496.6	5,088.5
1991	68,681	63,826	132,507	12,961,100	15,023.0	6,441.7	9,151.1	5,139.7
1992	56,372	56,283	112,655	12,505,900	12,116.2	5,419.9	7,491.8	4,902.7
1993	42,822	50,374	93,196	12,218,800	9,241.4	4,684.0	6,056.3	4,737.6
1994	37,365	48,347	85,712	12,131,900	7,911.5	4,410.7	5,464.9	4,660.0
1995	34,323	48,334	82,657	12,063,900	7,456.3	4,288.6	5,207.2	4,591.3
1996	33,918	50,438	84,356	11,791,300	7,212.7	4,382.5	5,203.4	4,444.8

Notes: Property crimes include burglary, larceny-theft and motor vehicle theft; n/a not available; (1) Metropolitan Statistical Area - see Appendix A for areas included; (2) calculated by the editors using the following formula: (number of crimes in the MSA minus number of crimes in the city); (3) calculated by the editors using the following formula: ((number of crimes in the MSA minus number of crimes in the city) ÷ (population of the MSA minus population of the city)) x 100,000
Source: U.S. Department of Justice, FBI Uniform Crime Reports, 1977 - 1996

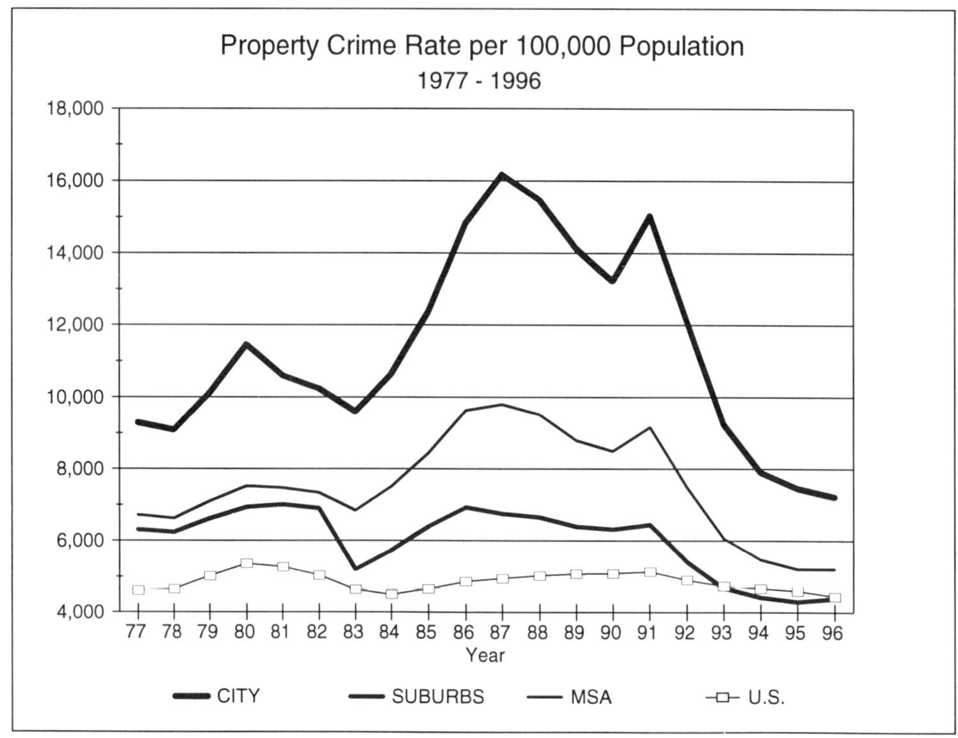

Note: Missing line segments indicate data not available.

Murders and Murder Rates: 1977 - 1996

Year	Number				Rate per 100,000 population			
	City	Suburbs[2]	MSA[1]	U.S.	City	Suburbs[3]	MSA[1]	U.S.
1977	102	301	403	19,120	27.7	13.2	15.2	8.8
1978	86	329	415	19,560	23.4	14.0	15.3	9.0
1979	99	411	510	21,460	25.7	17.1	18.3	9.7
1980	106	431	537	23,040	27.7	16.7	18.1	10.2
1981	113	394	507	22,520	28.4	14.7	16.4	9.8
1982	103	406	509	21,010	25.0	14.6	15.9	9.1
1983	112	54	166	19,310	26.4	7.5	14.6	8.3
1984	119	53	172	18,690	28.3	7.1	14.8	7.9
1985	128	59	187	18,980	30.2	7.3	15.1	7.9
1986	200	67	267	20,610	46.2	8.1	21.1	8.6
1987	135	54	189	20,100	31.2	6.0	14.2	8.3
1988	97	48	145	20,680	22.4	5.3	10.8	8.4
1989	113	46	159	21,500	26.2	4.8	11.5	8.7
1990	130	37	167	23,440	29.0	3.8	11.8	9.4
1991	195	63	258	24,700	42.7	6.4	17.8	9.8
1992	153	44	197	23,760	32.9	4.2	13.1	9.3
1993	133	47	180	24,530	28.7	4.4	11.7	9.5
1994	132	54	186	23,330	27.9	4.9	11.9	9.0
1995	108	40	148	21,610	23.5	3.5	9.3	8.2
1996	68	40	108	19,650	14.5	3.5	6.7	7.4

Notes: (1) Metropolitan Statistical Area - see Appendix A for areas included; (2) calculated by the editors using the following formula: (number of crimes in the MSA minus number of crimes in the city); (3) calculated by the editors using the following formula: ((number of crimes in the MSA minus number of crimes in the city) ÷ (population of the MSA minus population of the city)) x 100,000; n/a not avail.
Source: U.S. Department of Justice, FBI Uniform Crime Reports, 1977 - 1996

Forcible Rapes and Forcible Rape Rates: 1977 - 1996

Year	Number				Rate per 100,000 population			
	City	Suburbs[2]	MSA[1]	U.S.	City	Suburbs[3]	MSA[1]	U.S.
1977	208	907	1,115	63,500	56.5	39.7	42.0	29.4
1978	265	1,125	1,390	67,610	72.2	47.9	51.2	31.0
1979	345	1,337	1,682	76,390	89.7	55.5	60.2	34.7
1980	338	1,525	1,863	82,990	88.3	59.1	62.8	36.8
1981	435	1,573	2,008	82,500	109.2	58.5	65.1	36.0
1982	470	1,555	2,025	78,770	113.9	55.9	63.4	34.0
1983	454	190	644	78,920	106.9	26.6	56.5	33.7
1984	467	259	726	84,230	111.2	34.8	62.4	35.7
1985	483	273	756	88,670	113.8	33.6	61.2	37.1
1986	559	297	856	91,460	129.2	35.8	67.8	37.9
1987	476	269	745	91,110	110.1	29.9	55.9	37.4
1988	489	338	827	92,490	113.0	37.3	61.8	37.6
1989	454	335	789	94,500	105.4	35.0	56.8	38.1
1990	432	397	829	102,560	96.5	40.9	58.5	41.2
1991	442	483	925	106,590	96.7	48.7	63.9	42.3
1992	525	491	1,016	109,060	112.8	47.3	67.6	42.8
1993	507	480	987	106,010	109.4	44.6	64.1	41.1
1994	413	494	907	102,220	87.4	45.1	57.8	39.3
1995	332	435	767	97,470	72.1	38.6	48.3	37.1
1996	319	466	785	95,770	67.8	40.5	48.4	36.1

Notes: (1) Metropolitan Statistical Area - see Appendix A for areas included; (2) calculated by the editors using the following formula: (number of crimes in the MSA minus number of crimes in the city); (3) calculated by the editors using the following formula: ((number of crimes in the MSA minus number of crimes in the city) ÷ (population of the MSA minus population of the city)) x 100,000; n/a not avail.
Source: U.S. Department of Justice, FBI Uniform Crime Reports, 1977 - 1996

Robberies and Robbery Rates: 1977 - 1996

Year	Number				Rate per 100,000 population			
	City	Suburbs[2]	MSA[1]	U.S.	City	Suburbs[3]	MSA[1]	U.S.
1977	1,132	4,391	5,523	412,610	307.6	192.2	208.2	190.7
1978	1,218	4,790	6,008	426,930	331.9	204.1	221.4	195.8
1979	1,783	5,546	7,329	480,700	463.6	230.1	262.3	218.4
1980	2,286	6,292	8,578	565,840	597.4	243.7	289.4	251.1
1981	2,312	6,776	9,088	592,910	580.2	252.1	294.4	258.7
1982	2,233	7,060	9,293	553,130	541.1	253.6	290.7	238.9
1983	2,020	583	2,603	506,570	475.7	81.5	228.3	216.5
1984	2,080	633	2,713	485,010	495.2	85.2	233.2	205.4
1985	2,620	882	3,502	497,870	617.3	108.7	283.3	208.5
1986	3,373	1,286	4,659	542,780	779.8	154.9	369.0	225.1
1987	3,270	1,241	4,511	517,700	756.4	137.8	338.5	212.7
1988	3,115	1,272	4,387	542,970	719.6	140.4	327.6	220.9
1989	2,525	1,131	3,656	578,330	586.1	118.1	263.3	233.0
1990	2,801	1,207	4,008	639,270	625.8	124.4	282.7	257.0
1991	3,426	1,460	4,886	687,730	749.4	147.4	337.4	272.7
1992	3,488	1,415	4,903	672,480	749.7	136.3	326.1	263.6
1993	2,750	1,312	4,062	659,870	593.5	122.0	264.0	255.9
1994	2,379	1,248	3,627	618,950	503.7	113.9	231.3	237.7
1995	1,965	1,040	3,005	580,510	426.9	92.3	189.3	220.9
1996	1,692	1,109	2,801	537,050	359.8	96.4	172.8	202.4

Notes: (1) Metropolitan Statistical Area - see Appendix A for areas included; (2) calculated by the editors using the following formula: (number of crimes in the MSA minus number of crimes in the city); (3) calculated by the editors using the following formula: ((number of crimes in the MSA minus number of crimes in the city) ÷ (population of the MSA minus population of the city)) x 100,000; n/a not avail.
Source: U.S. Department of Justice, FBI Uniform Crime Reports, 1977 - 1996

Aggravated Assaults and Aggravated Assault Rates: 1977 - 1996

Year	Number				Rate per 100,000 population			
	City	Suburbs[2]	MSA[1]	U.S.	City	Suburbs[3]	MSA[1]	U.S.
1977	1,119	6,819	7,938	534,350	304.1	298.4	299.2	247.0
1978	1,101	7,532	8,633	571,460	300.0	320.9	318.1	262.1
1979	1,572	8,297	9,869	629,480	408.8	344.3	353.2	286.0
1980	1,963	9,347	11,310	672,650	513.0	362.1	381.5	298.5
1981	2,086	8,845	10,931	663,900	523.5	329.0	354.1	289.7
1982	2,095	9,028	11,123	669,480	507.7	324.3	348.0	289.2
1983	2,518	1,182	3,700	653,290	593.0	165.2	324.6	279.2
1984	2,786	1,422	4,208	685,350	663.3	191.3	361.7	290.2
1985	3,121	1,829	4,950	723,250	735.3	225.4	400.5	302.9
1986	3,738	2,173	5,911	834,320	864.2	261.8	468.2	346.1
1987	3,810	2,199	6,009	855,090	881.3	244.2	450.9	351.3
1988	3,625	2,047	5,672	910,090	837.4	225.9	423.6	370.2
1989	3,576	2,502	6,078	951,710	830.0	261.3	437.7	383.4
1990	4,463	3,074	7,537	1,054,860	997.1	316.9	531.6	424.1
1991	4,851	3,448	8,299	1,092,740	1,061.1	348.0	573.1	433.3
1992	5,226	3,691	8,917	1,126,970	1,123.2	355.4	593.0	441.8
1993	3,589	3,871	7,460	1,135,610	774.5	359.9	484.8	440.3
1994	3,111	3,926	7,037	1,113,180	658.7	358.2	448.7	427.6
1995	2,939	4,011	6,950	1,099,210	638.5	355.9	437.8	418.3
1996	2,905	4,131	7,036	1,029,810	617.8	358.9	434.0	388.2

Notes: (1) Metropolitan Statistical Area - see Appendix A for areas included; (2) calculated by the editors using the following formula: (number of crimes in the MSA minus number of crimes in the city); (3) calculated by the editors using the following formula: ((number of crimes in the MSA minus number of crimes in the city) ÷ (population of the MSA minus population of the city)) x 100,000; n/a not avail.
Source: U.S. Department of Justice, FBI Uniform Crime Reports, 1977 - 1996

Burglaries and Burglary Rates: 1977 - 1996

Year	Number				Rate per 100,000 population			
	City	Suburbs[2]	MSA[1]	U.S.	City	Suburbs[3]	MSA[1]	U.S.
1977	12,448	42,853	55,301	3,071,500	3,382.6	1,875.4	2,084.5	1,419.8
1978	11,006	43,845	54,851	3,128,300	2,998.9	1,868.2	2,021.1	1,434.6
1979	15,033	47,703	62,736	3,327,700	3,908.9	1,979.6	2,245.1	1,511.9
1980	15,001	54,234	69,235	3,795,200	3,920.0	2,100.8	2,335.7	1,684.1
1981	14,276	59,460	73,736	3,779,700	3,582.6	2,211.9	2,388.9	1,649.5
1982	13,426	57,803	71,229	3,447,100	3,253.5	2,076.4	2,228.4	1,488.8
1983	12,782	9,891	22,673	3,129,900	3,010.0	1,382.7	1,988.9	1,337.7
1984	13,872	10,788	24,660	2,984,400	3,302.5	1,451.3	2,119.6	1,263.7
1985	15,873	12,404	28,277	3,073,300	3,739.7	1,528.3	2,287.6	1,287.3
1986	19,257	15,110	34,367	3,241,400	4,452.1	1,820.4	2,722.0	1,344.6
1987	20,567	15,655	36,222	3,236,200	4,757.5	1,738.5	2,717.7	1,329.6
1988	19,106	15,243	34,349	3,218,100	4,413.6	1,682.0	2,565.0	1,309.2
1989	17,216	15,580	32,796	3,168,200	3,996.0	1,626.8	2,361.9	1,276.3
1990	15,298	14,276	29,574	3,073,900	3,417.6	1,471.5	2,086.0	1,235.9
1991	16,878	14,407	31,285	3,157,200	3,691.8	1,454.0	2,160.6	1,252.0
1992	14,304	12,219	26,523	2,979,900	3,074.4	1,176.7	1,763.8	1,168.2
1993	10,505	10,864	21,369	2,834,800	2,267.1	1,010.2	1,388.7	1,099.2
1994	8,295	9,464	17,759	2,712,800	1,756.3	863.4	1,132.3	1,042.0
1995	7,334	9,235	16,569	2,593,800	1,593.2	819.4	1,043.8	987.1
1996	7,917	9,816	17,733	2,501,500	1,683.6	852.9	1,093.8	943.0

Notes: (1) Metropolitan Statistical Area - see Appendix A for areas included; (2) calculated by the editors using the following formula: (number of crimes in the MSA minus number of crimes in the city); (3) calculated by the editors using the following formula: ((number of crimes in the MSA minus number of crimes in the city) ÷ (population of the MSA minus population of the city)) x 100,000; n/a not avail.
Source: U.S. Department of Justice, FBI Uniform Crime Reports, 1977 - 1996

Larceny-Thefts and Larceny-Theft Rates: 1977 - 1996

Year	Number				Rate per 100,000 population			
	City	Suburbs[2]	MSA[1]	U.S.	City	Suburbs[3]	MSA[1]	U.S.
1977	19,068	91,480	110,548	5,905,700	5,181.5	4,003.6	4,167.0	2,729.9
1978	19,521	91,912	111,433	5,991,000	5,319.1	3,916.4	4,106.1	2,747.4
1979	20,727	98,266	118,993	6,601,000	5,389.5	4,077.8	4,258.4	2,999.1
1980	25,398	110,975	136,373	7,136,900	6,636.9	4,298.8	4,600.6	3,167.0
1981	24,123	115,209	139,332	7,194,400	6,053.7	4,285.8	4,514.0	3,139.7
1982	25,063	121,071	146,134	7,142,500	6,073.5	4,349.1	4,571.7	3,084.8
1983	24,456	24,239	48,695	6,712,800	5,759.1	3,388.5	4,271.5	2,868.9
1984	26,629	27,988	54,617	6,591,900	6,339.5	3,765.1	4,694.6	2,791.3
1985	30,877	34,501	65,378	6,926,400	7,274.6	4,250.9	5,289.2	2,901.2
1986	35,334	36,334	71,668	7,257,200	8,168.9	4,377.4	5,676.4	3,010.3
1987	38,492	38,588	77,080	7,499,900	8,903.9	4,285.1	5,783.3	3,081.3
1988	38,473	38,534	77,007	7,705,900	8,887.5	4,252.0	5,750.4	3,134.9
1989	34,680	38,925	73,605	7,872,400	8,049.6	4,064.4	5,300.9	3,171.3
1990	34,710	40,069	74,779	7,945,700	7,754.4	4,130.2	5,274.5	3,194.8
1991	38,333	41,861	80,194	8,142,200	8,384.8	4,224.9	5,538.3	3,228.8
1992	32,128	37,709	69,837	7,915,200	6,905.4	3,631.3	4,644.3	3,103.0
1993	26,310	34,220	60,530	7,820,900	5,677.9	3,181.9	3,933.5	3,032.4
1994	23,712	33,659	57,371	7,879,800	5,020.7	3,070.7	3,657.9	3,026.7
1995	22,128	33,989	56,117	7,997,700	4,807.1	3,015.8	3,535.3	3,043.8
1996	21,481	35,836	57,317	7,894,600	4,568.0	3,113.7	3,535.6	2,975.9

Notes: (1) Metropolitan Statistical Area - see Appendix A for areas included; (2) calculated by the editors using the following formula: (number of crimes in the MSA minus number of crimes in the city); (3) calculated by the editors using the following formula: ((number of crimes in the MSA minus number of crimes in the city) ÷ (population of the MSA minus population of the city)) x 100,000; n/a not avail.
Source: U.S. Department of Justice, FBI Uniform Crime Reports, 1977 - 1996

Motor Vehicle Thefts and Motor Vehicle Theft Rates: 1977 - 1996

Year	Number				Rate per 100,000 population			
	City	Suburbs[2]	MSA[1]	U.S.	City	Suburbs[3]	MSA[1]	U.S.
1977	2,666	9,631	12,297	977,700	724.5	421.5	463.5	451.9
1978	2,811	10,442	13,253	1,004,100	765.9	444.9	488.3	460.5
1979	3,131	13,364	16,495	1,112,800	814.1	554.6	590.3	505.6
1980	3,400	13,866	17,266	1,131,700	888.5	537.1	582.5	502.2
1981	3,808	13,555	17,363	1,087,800	955.6	504.2	562.5	474.7
1982	3,738	13,188	16,926	1,062,400	905.8	473.7	529.5	458.8
1983	3,516	3,007	6,523	1,007,900	828.0	420.4	572.2	430.8
1984	4,158	3,788	7,946	1,032,200	989.9	509.6	683.0	437.1
1985	5,756	4,953	10,709	1,102,900	1,356.1	610.3	866.4	462.0
1986	9,554	6,017	15,571	1,224,100	2,208.8	724.9	1,233.3	507.8
1987	10,813	6,483	17,296	1,288,700	2,501.2	719.9	1,297.7	529.4
1988	9,357	6,546	15,903	1,432,900	2,161.5	722.3	1,187.5	582.9
1989	8,974	6,748	15,722	1,564,800	2,083.0	704.6	1,132.3	630.4
1990	9,206	6,902	16,108	1,635,900	2,056.7	711.4	1,136.2	657.8
1991	13,470	7,558	21,028	1,661,700	2,946.4	762.8	1,452.2	659.0
1992	9,940	6,355	16,295	1,610,800	2,136.4	612.0	1,083.6	631.5
1993	6,007	5,290	11,297	1,563,100	1,296.4	491.9	734.1	606.1
1994	5,358	5,224	10,582	1,539,300	1,134.5	476.6	674.7	591.3
1995	4,861	5,110	9,971	1,472,400	1,056.0	453.4	628.2	560.4
1996	4,520	4,786	9,306	1,395,200	961.2	415.8	574.0	525.9

Notes: (1) Metropolitan Statistical Area - see Appendix A for areas included; (2) calculated by the editors using the following formula: (number of crimes in the MSA minus number of crimes in the city); (3) calculated by the editors using the following formula: ((number of crimes in the MSA minus number of crimes in the city) ÷ (population of the MSA minus population of the city)) x 100,000; n/a not avail.
Source: U.S. Department of Justice, FBI Uniform Crime Reports, 1977 - 1996

HATE CRIMES

Criminal Incidents by Bias Motivation

Area	Race	Ethnicity	Religion	Sexual Orientation
Fort Worth	23	3	6	4

Notes: Figures include both violent and property crimes. Law enforcement agencies must have submitted data for at least one quarter of calendar year 1995 to be included in this report, therefore figures shown may not represent complete 12-month totals; n/a not available
Source: U.S. Department of Justice, FBI Uniform Crime Reports, Hate Crime Statistics 1995

LAW ENFORCEMENT

Full-Time Law Enforcement Employees

Jurisdiction	Police Employees			Police Officers per 100,000 population
	Total	Officers	Civilians	
Fort Worth	1,479	1,166	313	248.0

Notes: Data as of October 31, 1996
Source: U.S. Department of Justice, FBI Uniform Crime Reports, 1996

Number of Police Officers by Race

Race	Police Officers 1983		Police Officers 1992		Index of Representation[1]		
	Number	Pct.	Number	Pct.	1983	1992	% Chg.
Black	43	5.6	112	11.6	0.25	0.52	108.0
Hispanic[2]	51	6.7	85	8.8	0.52	0.45	-13.5

Notes: (1) The index of representation is calculated by dividing the percent of black/hispanic police officers by the percent of corresponding blacks/hispanics in the local population. An index approaching 1.0 indicates that a city is closer to achieving a representation of police officers equal to their proportion in the local population; (2) Hispanic officers can be of any race
Source: Bureau of Justice Statistics, Sourcebook of Criminal Justice Statistics, 1994

CORRECTIONS

Federal Correctional Facilities

Type	Year Opened	Security Level	Sex of Inmates	Rated Capacity	Population on 7/1/95	Number of Staff
Federal Medical Center	1971	Admin.	Male	1,132	1,377	435

Notes: Data as of 1995
Source: Bureau of Justice Statistics, Sourcebook of Criminal Justice Statistics Online

City/County/Regional Correctional Facilities

Name	Year Opened	Year Renov.	Rated Capacity	1995 Pop.	Number of COs[1]	Number of Staff	ACA[2] Accred.
Tarrant Co Belknap Facil.	1961	1987	1,246	n/a	n/a	n/a	No
Tarrant Co Corr Ctr	1992	1994	2,088	2,694	n/a	n/a	No
Tarrant Co Greenbay Facil.	1988	--	480	n/a	n/a	n/a	No

Notes: Data as of April 1996; (1) Correctional Officers; (2) American Correctional Assn. Accreditation
Source: American Correctional Association, 1996-1998 National Jail and Adult Detention Directory

Private Adult Correctional Facilities

Name	Date Opened	Rated Capacity	Present Pop.	Security Level	Facility Construct.	Expans. Plans	ACA[1] Accred.
N. Texas Intermediate Sanction Facility	8/91	400	384	Min.	Renov.	None	No
Tarrant Co Community Correction Facility	2/92	320	312	Min.	New	Yes; 80 beds	Yes; 8/93

Notes: Data as of December 1996; (1) American Correctional Association Accreditation
Source: University of Florida, Center for Studies in Criminology and Law, Private Adult Correctional Facility Census, 10th Ed., March 15, 1997

Characteristics of Shock Incarceration Programs

Jurisdiction	Year Program Began	Number of Camps	Average Num. of Inmates	Number of Beds	Program Length	Voluntary/ Mandatory
Texas	1989	2	250	500 male; 20 female	75 to 90 days	Mandatory

Note: Data as of July 1996;
Source: Sourcebook of Criminal Justice Statistics Online

INMATES AND HIV/AIDS

HIV Testing Policies for Inmates

Jurisdiction	All Inmates at Some Time	All Convicted Inmates at Admission	Random Samples While in Custody	High-risk Groups	Upon Inmate Request	Upon Court Order	Upon Involvement in Incident
Tarrant Co.	No	No	No	No	Yes	Yes	No

Source: HIV in Prisons and Jails, 1993 (released August 1995)

Inmates Known to be Positive for HIV

Jurisdiction	Number of Jail Inmates in Facilities Providing Data	Type of HIV Infection/AIDS Cases				HIV/AIDS Cases as a Percent of Tot. Custody Pop.
		Total	Asymptomatic	Symptomatic	Confirmed AIDS	
Tarrant Co.[1]	4,408	n/a	n/a	n/a	n/a	n/a

Note: (1) Jurisdiction did not provide data on HIV/AIDS cases; n/a not available
Source: HIV in Prisons and Jails, 1993 (released August, 1995)

DEATH PENALTY

Death Penalty Statistics

State	Prisoners Executed		Prisoners Under Sentence of Death					Avg. No. of Years on Death Row[4]
	1930-1995	1996[1]	Total[2]	White[3]	Black[3]	Hisp.	Women	
Texas	401	3	404	241	158	68	6	6.5

Notes: Data as of 12/31/95 unless otherwise noted; (1) Data as of 7/31/97; (2) Includes persons of other races; (3) Includes people of Hispanic origin; (4) Covers prisoners sentenced 1974 through 1995
Source: Bureau of Justice Statistics, Capital Punishment 1995 (released 12/96); Death Penalty Information Center Web Site, 9/30/97

Capital Offenses and Methods of Execution

Capital Offenses in Texas	Minimum Age for Imposition of Death Penalty	Mentally Retarded Excluded	Methods of Execution[1]
Criminal homicide with 1 of 8 aggravating circumstances.	17	No	Lethal injection

Notes: Data as of 12/31/95 unless otherwise noted; (1) Data as of 7/31/97
Source: Bureau of Justice Statistics, Capital Punishment 1995 (released 12/96); Death Penalty Information Center Web Site, 9/30/97

LAWS

Statutory Provisions Relating to the Purchase, Ownership and Use of Handguns

Jurisdiction	Instant Background Check	Federal Waiting Period Applies[1]	State Waiting Period (days)	License or Permit to Purchase	Regis-tration	Record of Sale Sent to Police	Concealed Carry Law
Texas	No	Yes[a]	No	No	No	No	Yes[b]

Note: Data as of 1996; (1) The Federal 5-day waiting period for handgun purchases applies to states that don't have instant background checks, waiting period requirements, or licensing procedures exempting them from the Federal requirement; (a) The Federal waiting period does not apply to a person holding a valid permit or license to carry a firearm, issued within 5 years of proposed purchase; (b) "Shall issue" permit system, liberally administered discretion by local authorities over permit issuance, or no permit required
Source: Sourcebook of Criminal Justice Statistics Online

Statutory Provisions Relating to Alcohol Use and Driving

Jurisdiction	Drinking Age	Blood Alcohol Concentration Levels as Evidence in State Courts[1]		Open Container Law[1]	Anti-Consump-tion Law[1]	Dram Shop Law[1]
		Illegal per se at 0.10%	Presumption at 0.10%			
Texas	21	Yes	No	No	Yes[a]	Yes[b]

Note: Data as of January 1, 1997; (1) See Appendix C for an explanation of terms; (a) Applies to drivers only; (b) Statutory law has limited dram shop actions
Source: Sourcebook of Criminal Justice Statistics Online

Statutory Provisions Relating to Curfews

Jurisdiction	Year Enacted	Latest Revision	Age Group(s)	Curfew Provisions
Fort Worth	1994	-	16 and under	11 pm to 6 am weekday nights midnight to 6 am weekend nights

Note: Data as of February 1996
Source: Sourcebook of Criminal Justice Statistics Online

Statutory Provisions Relating to Hate Crimes

Jurisdiction	Bias-Motivated Violence and Intimidation						Institutional Vandalism
	Civil Action	Criminal Penalty					
		Race/ Religion/ Ethnicity	Sexual Orientation	Mental/ Physical Disability	Gender	Age	
Texas	No	No	No	No	No	No	Yes

Source: Anti-Defamation League, 1997 Hate Crimes Laws

Grand Rapids, Michigan

OVERVIEW

The total crime rate for the city increased 1.7% between 1977 and 1996. During that same period, the violent crime rate increased 92.4% and the property crime rate decreased 7.1%.

Among violent crimes, the rates for: Murders increased 36.8%; Forcible Rapes increased 2.1%; Robberies increased 69.0%; and Aggravated Assaults increased 117.6%.

Among property crimes, the rates for: Burglaries decreased 28.6%; Larceny-Thefts decreased 2.1%; and Motor Vehicle Thefts increased 75.8%.

ANTI-CRIME PROGRAMS

The police believe the job of combatting crime cannot be accomplished without the social, health, municipal, mental health, educational services, and existing neighborhood organizations collaboratively working together. They have identified problem neighborhoods and assigned special Neighborhood Patrol and Vice Units to these areas and created Neighborhood Service Boards which manage service programs. They have also created Neighborhood Service Centers, staffed by youth violators, through which programs such as job skill training; health services, drug, alcohol abuse referral; family counseling; parenting classes; trash, garbage, abandoned vehicles education, etc., are provided. The results have shown violent crime activity reduced by 48%. *Grand Rapids Police Department, 9/97*

CRIME RISK

Your Chances of Becoming a Victim[1]

Area	Any Crime	Violent Crime					Property Crime			
		Any	Murder	Forcible Rape[2]	Robbery	Aggrav. Assault	Any	Burglary	Larceny -Theft	Motor Vehicle Theft
City	1:13	1:79	1:9,618	1:1,001	1:285	1:117	1:16	1:63	1:24	1:179

Note: (1) Figures have been calculated by dividing the population of the city by the number of crimes reported to the FBI during 1996 and are expressed as odds (eg. 1:20 should be read as 1 in 20).
(2) Figures have been calculated by dividing the female population of the city by the number of forcible rapes reported to the FBI during 1996. The female population of the city was estimated by calculating the ratio of females to males reported in the 1990 Census and applying that ratio to 1996 population estimate.
Source: FBI Uniform Crime Reports 1996

CRIME STATISTICS

Total Crimes and Total Crime Rates: 1977 - 1996

Year	Number				Rate per 100,000 population			
	City	Suburbs[2]	MSA[1]	U.S.	City	Suburbs[3]	MSA[1]	U.S.
1977	13,807	12,838	26,645	10,984,500	7,463.2	3,370.3	4,708.3	5,077.6
1978	12,544	13,026	25,570	11,209,000	6,817.4	3,312.8	4,430.0	5,140.3
1979	14,624	14,943	29,567	12,249,500	7,887.1	3,692.9	5,010.9	5,565.5
1980	16,185	16,876	33,061	13,408,300	8,912.3	3,980.0	5,459.0	5,950.0
1981	17,049	17,036	34,085	13,423,800	9,415.8	4,029.6	5,644.7	5,858.2
1982	18,051	15,048	33,099	12,974,400	10,069.8	3,595.3	5,536.8	5,603.6
1983	16,917	14,280	31,197	12,108,600	9,478.9	3,427.0	5,241.7	5,175.0
1984	16,133	14,050	30,183	11,881,800	8,866.2	3,257.8	4,922.0	5,031.3
1985	15,870	15,349	31,219	12,431,400	8,659.4	3,421.6	4,940.8	5,207.1
1986	16,419	16,532	32,951	13,211,900	8,906.9	3,662.2	5,182.9	5,480.4
1987	17,335	16,822	34,157	13,508,700	9,248.2	3,583.5	5,200.0	5,550.0
1988	15,637	18,185	33,822	13,923,100	8,215.2	3,797.8	5,054.3	5,664.2
1989	15,736	18,129	33,865	14,251,400	8,458.6	3,724.5	5,033.5	5,741.0
1990	16,400	19,190	35,590	14,475,600	8,671.5	3,804.2	5,131.5	5,820.3
1991	17,494	20,529	38,023	14,872,900	9,178.2	4,038.2	5,439.8	5,897.8
1992	17,015	33,838	50,853	14,438,200	8,861.6	4,451.5	5,340.8	5,660.2
1993	n/a	n/a	n/a	14,144,800	n/a	n/a	n/a	5,484.4
1994	15,336	32,969	48,305	13,989,500	7,967.3	4,236.8	4,976.6	5,373.5
1995	14,556	n/a	n/a	13,862,700	7,602.8	n/a	n/a	5,275.9
1996	14,600	31,197	45,797	13,473,600	7,590.0	3,886.2	4,602.2	5,078.9

Notes: (1) Metropolitan Statistical Area - see Appendix A for areas included; (2) calculated by the editors using the following formula: (number of crimes in the MSA minus number of crimes in the city); (3) calculated by the editors using the following formula: ((number of crimes in the MSA minus number of crimes in the city) ÷ (population of the MSA minus population of the city)) x 100,000; n/a not avail.
Source: U.S. Department of Justice, FBI Uniform Crime Reports, 1977 - 1996

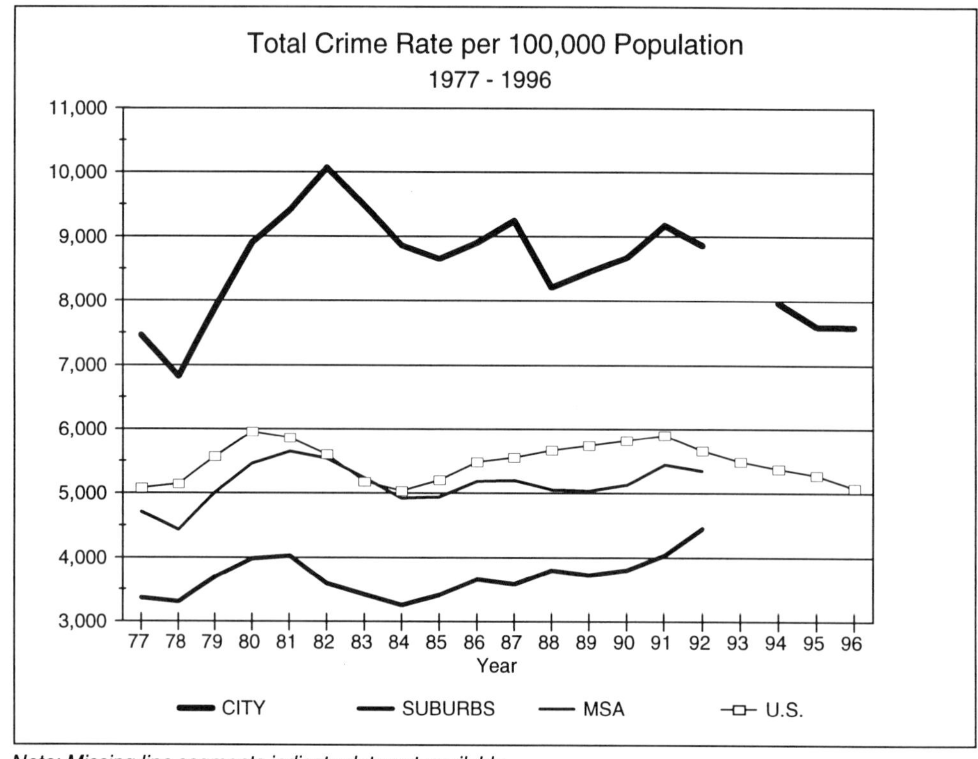

Note: Missing line segments indicate data not available.

Violent Crimes and Violent Crime Rates: 1977 - 1996

Year	Number				Rate per 100,000 population			
	City	Suburbs[2]	MSA[1]	U.S.	City	Suburbs[3]	MSA[1]	U.S.
1977	1,221	509	1,730	1,029,580	660.0	133.6	305.7	475.9
1978	1,274	578	1,852	1,085,550	692.4	147.0	320.9	497.8
1979	1,603	625	2,228	1,208,030	864.5	154.5	377.6	548.9
1980	1,787	702	2,489	1,344,520	984.0	165.6	411.0	596.6
1981	1,876	666	2,542	1,361,820	1,036.1	157.5	421.0	594.3
1982	2,016	630	2,646	1,322,390	1,124.6	150.5	442.6	571.1
1983	1,994	615	2,609	1,258,090	1,117.3	147.6	438.4	537.7
1984	2,028	723	2,751	1,273,280	1,114.5	167.6	448.6	539.2
1985	2,214	724	2,938	1,328,800	1,208.1	161.4	465.0	556.6
1986	2,142	734	2,876	1,489,170	1,162.0	162.6	452.4	617.7
1987	2,251	810	3,061	1,484,000	1,200.9	172.5	466.0	609.7
1988	2,317	900	3,217	1,566,220	1,217.3	188.0	480.7	637.2
1989	2,309	1,011	3,320	1,646,040	1,241.2	207.7	493.5	663.1
1990	3,025	1,131	4,156	1,820,130	1,599.5	224.2	599.2	731.8
1991	3,278	1,236	4,514	1,911,770	1,719.8	243.1	645.8	758.1
1992	3,040	2,624	5,664	1,932,270	1,583.3	345.2	594.9	757.5
1993	n/a	n/a	n/a	1,926,020	n/a	n/a	n/a	746.8
1994	2,847	3,329	6,176	1,857,670	1,479.1	427.8	636.3	713.6
1995	2,464	n/a	n/a	1,798,790	1,287.0	n/a	n/a	684.6
1996	2,443	2,432	4,875	1,682,280	1,270.0	303.0	489.9	634.1

Notes: Violent crimes include murder, forcible rape, robbery and aggravated assault; n/a not available; (1) Metropolitan Statistical Area - see Appendix A for areas included; (2) calculated by the editors using the following formula: (number of crimes in the MSA minus number of crimes in the city); (3) calculated by the editors using the following formula: ((number of crimes in the MSA minus number of crimes in the city) ÷ (population of the MSA minus population of the city)) x 100,000
Source: U.S. Department of Justice, FBI Uniform Crime Reports, 1977 - 1996

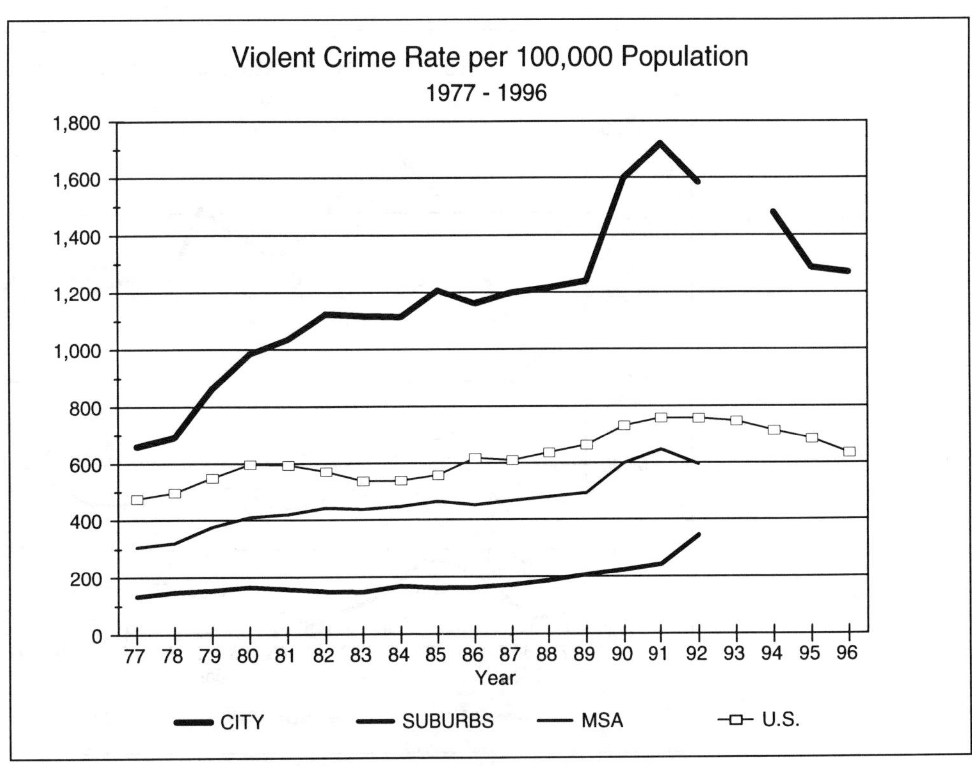

Note: Missing line segments indicate data not available.

Property Crimes and Property Crime Rates: 1977 - 1996

Year	Number				Rate per 100,000 population			
	City	Suburbs[2]	MSA[1]	U.S.	City	Suburbs[3]	MSA[1]	U.S.
1977	12,586	12,329	24,915	9,955,000	6,803.2	3,236.7	4,402.6	4,601.7
1978	11,270	12,448	23,718	10,123,400	6,125.0	3,165.8	4,109.2	4,642.5
1979	13,021	14,318	27,339	11,041,500	7,022.6	3,538.5	4,633.3	5,016.6
1980	14,398	16,174	30,572	12,063,700	7,928.3	3,814.5	5,048.0	5,353.3
1981	15,173	16,370	31,543	12,061,900	8,379.7	3,872.1	5,223.7	5,263.9
1982	16,035	14,418	30,453	11,652,000	8,945.2	3,444.8	5,094.2	5,032.5
1983	14,923	13,665	28,588	10,850,500	8,361.6	3,279.4	4,803.4	4,637.4
1984	14,105	13,327	27,432	10,608,500	7,751.7	3,090.2	4,473.4	4,492.1
1985	13,656	14,625	28,281	11,102,600	7,451.3	3,260.2	4,475.8	4,650.5
1986	14,277	15,798	30,075	11,722,700	7,744.9	3,499.6	4,730.6	4,862.6
1987	15,084	16,012	31,096	12,024,700	8,047.3	3,410.9	4,734.0	4,940.3
1988	13,320	17,285	30,605	12,356,900	6,997.9	3,609.8	4,573.5	5,027.1
1989	13,427	17,118	30,545	12,605,400	7,217.4	3,516.8	4,540.1	5,077.9
1990	13,375	18,059	31,434	12,655,500	7,072.0	3,580.0	4,532.2	5,088.5
1991	14,216	19,293	33,509	12,961,100	7,458.4	3,795.0	4,794.0	5,139.7
1992	13,975	31,214	45,189	12,505,900	7,278.3	4,106.3	4,746.0	4,902.7
1993	13,063	29,774	42,837	12,218,800	6,799.4	3,833.4	4,421.5	4,737.6
1994	12,489	29,640	42,129	12,131,900	6,488.3	3,809.0	4,340.3	4,660.0
1995	12,092	n/a	n/a	12,063,900	6,315.8	n/a	n/a	4,591.3
1996	12,157	28,765	40,922	11,791,300	6,320.0	3,583.3	4,112.3	4,444.8

Notes: Property crimes include burglary, larceny-theft and motor vehicle theft; n/a not available; (1) Metropolitan Statistical Area - see Appendix A for areas included; (2) calculated by the editors using the following formula: (number of crimes in the MSA minus number of crimes in the city); (3) calculated by the editors using the following formula: ((number of crimes in the MSA minus number of crimes in the city) ÷ (population of the MSA minus population of the city)) x 100,000
Source: U.S. Department of Justice, FBI Uniform Crime Reports, 1977 - 1996

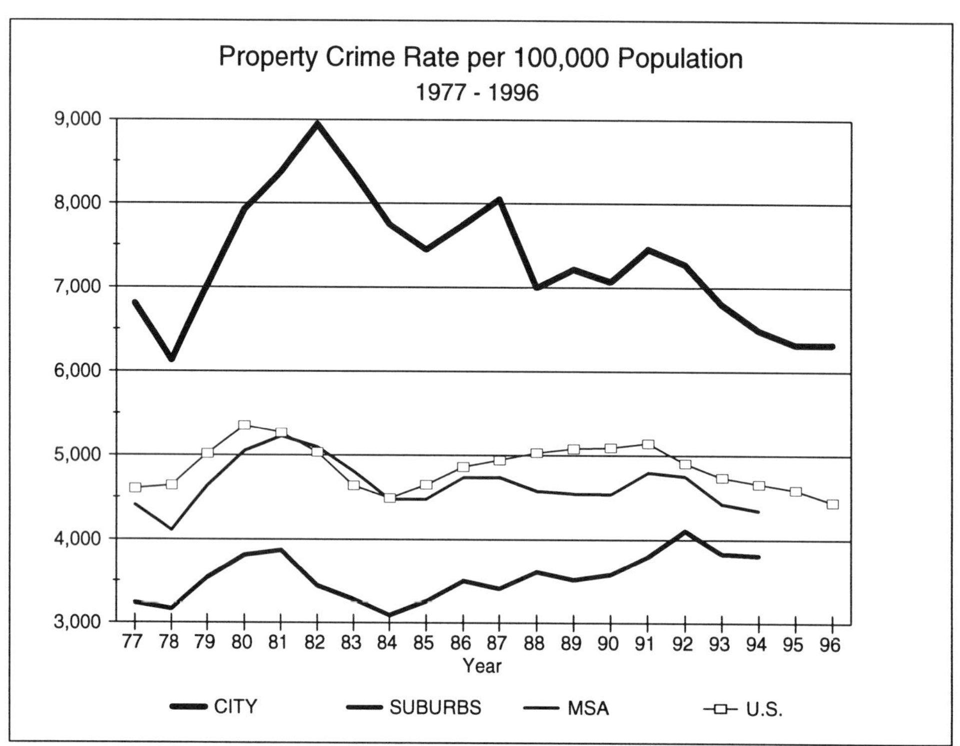

Note: Missing line segments indicate data not available.

Murders and Murder Rates: 1977 - 1996

Year	Number				Rate per 100,000 population			
	City	Suburbs[2]	MSA[1]	U.S.	City	Suburbs[3]	MSA[1]	U.S.
1977	14	6	20	19,120	7.6	1.6	3.5	8.8
1978	12	6	18	19,560	6.5	1.5	3.1	9.0
1979	14	5	19	21,460	7.6	1.2	3.2	9.7
1980	28	7	35	23,040	15.4	1.7	5.8	10.2
1981	24	3	27	22,520	13.3	0.7	4.5	9.8
1982	22	12	34	21,010	12.3	2.9	5.7	9.1
1983	20	5	25	19,310	11.2	1.2	4.2	8.3
1984	19	11	30	18,690	10.4	2.6	4.9	7.9
1985	19	1	20	18,980	10.4	0.2	3.2	7.9
1986	21	9	30	20,610	11.4	2.0	4.7	8.6
1987	15	8	23	20,100	8.0	1.7	3.5	8.3
1988	24	5	29	20,680	12.6	1.0	4.3	8.4
1989	13	8	21	21,500	7.0	1.6	3.1	8.7
1990	18	4	22	23,440	9.5	0.8	3.2	9.4
1991	22	10	32	24,700	11.5	2.0	4.6	9.8
1992	13	23	36	23,760	6.8	3.0	3.8	9.3
1993	33	19	52	24,530	17.2	2.4	5.4	9.5
1994	23	23	46	23,330	11.9	3.0	4.7	9.0
1995	24	n/a	n/a	21,610	12.5	n/a	n/a	8.2
1996	20	18	38	19,650	10.4	2.2	3.8	7.4

Notes: (1) Metropolitan Statistical Area - see Appendix A for areas included; (2) calculated by the editors using the following formula: (number of crimes in the MSA minus number of crimes in the city); (3) calculated by the editors using the following formula: ((number of crimes in the MSA minus number of crimes in the city) ÷ (population of the MSA minus population of the city)) x 100,000; n/a not avail.
Source: U.S. Department of Justice, FBI Uniform Crime Reports, 1977 - 1996

Forcible Rapes and Forcible Rape Rates: 1977 - 1996

Year	Number				Rate per 100,000 population			
	City	Suburbs[2]	MSA[1]	U.S.	City	Suburbs[3]	MSA[1]	U.S.
1977	95	86	181	63,500	51.4	22.6	32.0	29.4
1978	121	96	217	67,610	65.8	24.4	37.6	31.0
1979	157	96	253	76,390	84.7	23.7	42.9	34.7
1980	188	110	298	82,990	103.5	25.9	49.2	36.8
1981	190	130	320	82,500	104.9	30.7	53.0	36.0
1982	173	101	274	78,770	96.5	24.1	45.8	34.0
1983	198	110	308	78,920	110.9	26.4	51.8	33.7
1984	193	171	364	84,230	106.1	39.7	59.4	35.7
1985	219	167	386	88,670	119.5	37.2	61.1	37.1
1986	220	143	363	91,460	119.3	31.7	57.1	37.9
1987	268	184	452	91,110	143.0	39.2	68.8	37.4
1988	307	168	475	92,490	161.3	35.1	71.0	37.6
1989	297	223	520	94,500	159.6	45.8	77.3	38.1
1990	378	273	651	102,560	199.9	54.1	93.9	41.2
1991	370	275	645	106,590	194.1	54.1	92.3	42.3
1992	413	500	913	109,060	215.1	65.8	95.9	42.8
1993	n/a	n/a	n/a	106,010	n/a	n/a	n/a	41.1
1994	113	504	617	102,220	58.7	64.8	63.6	39.3
1995	109	n/a	n/a	97,470	56.9	n/a	n/a	37.1
1996	101	344	445	95,770	52.5	42.9	44.7	36.1

Notes: (1) Metropolitan Statistical Area - see Appendix A for areas included; (2) calculated by the editors using the following formula: (number of crimes in the MSA minus number of crimes in the city); (3) calculated by the editors using the following formula: ((number of crimes in the MSA minus number of crimes in the city) ÷ (population of the MSA minus population of the city)) x 100,000; n/a not avail.
Source: U.S. Department of Justice, FBI Uniform Crime Reports, 1977 - 1996

Robberies and Robbery Rates: 1977 - 1996

Year	Number				Rate per 100,000 population			
	City	Suburbs[2]	MSA[1]	U.S.	City	Suburbs[3]	MSA[1]	U.S.
1977	384	109	493	412,610	207.6	28.6	87.1	190.7
1978	398	115	513	426,930	216.3	29.2	88.9	195.8
1979	565	121	686	480,700	304.7	29.9	116.3	218.4
1980	529	147	676	565,840	291.3	34.7	111.6	251.1
1981	562	144	706	592,910	310.4	34.1	116.9	258.7
1982	631	121	752	553,130	352.0	28.9	125.8	238.9
1983	598	148	746	506,570	335.1	35.5	125.3	216.5
1984	561	95	656	485,010	308.3	22.0	107.0	205.4
1985	673	143	816	497,870	367.2	31.9	129.1	208.5
1986	455	103	558	542,780	246.8	22.8	87.8	225.1
1987	504	99	603	517,700	268.9	21.1	91.8	212.7
1988	498	142	640	542,970	261.6	29.7	95.6	220.9
1989	590	174	764	578,330	317.1	35.7	113.6	233.0
1990	681	174	855	639,270	360.1	34.5	123.3	257.0
1991	771	201	972	687,730	404.5	39.5	139.1	272.7
1992	756	383	1,139	672,480	393.7	50.4	119.6	263.6
1993	829	464	1,293	659,870	431.5	59.7	133.5	255.9
1994	888	549	1,437	618,950	461.3	70.6	148.0	237.7
1995	662	n/a	n/a	580,510	345.8	n/a	n/a	220.9
1996	675	375	1,050	537,050	350.9	46.7	105.5	202.4

Notes: (1) Metropolitan Statistical Area - see Appendix A for areas included; (2) calculated by the editors using the following formula: (number of crimes in the MSA minus number of crimes in the city); (3) calculated by the editors using the following formula: ((number of crimes in the MSA minus number of crimes in the city) ÷ (population of the MSA minus population of the city)) x 100,000; n/a not avail.
Source: U.S. Department of Justice, FBI Uniform Crime Reports, 1977 - 1996

Aggravated Assaults and Aggravated Assault Rates: 1977 - 1996

Year	Number				Rate per 100,000 population			
	City	Suburbs[2]	MSA[1]	U.S.	City	Suburbs[3]	MSA[1]	U.S.
1977	728	308	1,036	534,350	393.5	80.9	183.1	247.0
1978	743	361	1,104	571,460	403.8	91.8	191.3	262.1
1979	867	403	1,270	629,480	467.6	99.6	215.2	286.0
1980	1,042	438	1,480	672,650	573.8	103.3	244.4	298.5
1981	1,100	389	1,489	663,900	607.5	92.0	246.6	289.7
1982	1,190	396	1,586	669,480	663.8	94.6	265.3	289.2
1983	1,178	352	1,530	653,290	660.1	84.5	257.1	279.2
1984	1,255	446	1,701	685,350	689.7	103.4	277.4	290.2
1985	1,303	413	1,716	723,250	711.0	92.1	271.6	302.9
1986	1,446	479	1,925	834,320	784.4	106.1	302.8	346.1
1987	1,464	519	1,983	855,090	781.0	110.6	301.9	351.3
1988	1,488	585	2,073	910,090	781.7	122.2	309.8	370.2
1989	1,409	606	2,015	951,710	757.4	124.5	299.5	383.4
1990	1,948	680	2,628	1,054,860	1,030.0	134.8	378.9	424.1
1991	2,115	750	2,865	1,092,740	1,109.6	147.5	409.9	433.3
1992	1,858	1,718	3,576	1,126,970	967.7	226.0	375.6	441.8
1993	1,793	1,948	3,741	1,135,610	933.3	250.8	386.1	440.3
1994	1,823	2,253	4,076	1,113,180	947.1	289.5	419.9	427.6
1995	1,669	n/a	n/a	1,099,210	871.7	n/a	n/a	418.3
1996	1,647	1,695	3,342	1,029,810	856.2	211.1	335.8	388.2

Notes: (1) Metropolitan Statistical Area - see Appendix A for areas included; (2) calculated by the editors using the following formula: (number of crimes in the MSA minus number of crimes in the city); (3) calculated by the editors using the following formula: ((number of crimes in the MSA minus number of crimes in the city) ÷ (population of the MSA minus population of the city)) x 100,000; n/a not avail.
Source: U.S. Department of Justice, FBI Uniform Crime Reports, 1977 - 1996

Burglaries and Burglary Rates: 1977 - 1996

Year	Number				Rate per 100,000 population			
	City	Suburbs[2]	MSA[1]	U.S.	City	Suburbs[3]	MSA[1]	U.S.
1977	4,086	3,104	7,190	3,071,500	2,208.6	814.9	1,270.5	1,419.8
1978	3,586	3,221	6,807	3,128,300	1,948.9	819.2	1,179.3	1,434.6
1979	4,221	3,117	7,338	3,327,700	2,276.5	770.3	1,243.6	1,511.9
1980	4,437	3,596	8,033	3,795,200	2,443.3	848.1	1,326.4	1,684.1
1981	4,660	3,814	8,474	3,779,700	2,573.6	902.1	1,403.3	1,649.5
1982	4,717	3,119	7,836	3,447,100	2,631.4	745.2	1,310.8	1,488.8
1983	4,482	3,114	7,596	3,129,900	2,511.3	747.3	1,276.3	1,337.7
1984	4,206	2,690	6,896	2,984,400	2,311.5	623.7	1,124.5	1,263.7
1985	3,576	2,840	6,416	3,073,300	1,951.2	633.1	1,015.4	1,287.3
1986	3,508	2,983	6,491	3,241,400	1,903.0	660.8	1,021.0	1,344.6
1987	3,984	2,932	6,916	3,236,200	2,125.5	624.6	1,052.9	1,329.6
1988	3,728	3,310	7,038	3,218,100	1,958.6	691.3	1,051.7	1,309.2
1989	3,697	2,913	6,610	3,168,200	1,987.2	598.5	982.5	1,276.3
1990	3,743	3,149	6,892	3,073,900	1,979.1	624.3	993.7	1,235.9
1991	4,270	3,521	7,791	3,157,200	2,240.2	692.6	1,114.6	1,252.0
1992	3,777	7,054	10,831	2,979,900	1,967.1	928.0	1,137.5	1,168.2
1993	3,161	6,168	9,329	2,834,800	1,645.3	794.1	962.9	1,099.2
1994	3,172	6,200	9,372	2,712,800	1,647.9	796.7	965.5	1,042.0
1995	3,113	n/a	n/a	2,593,800	1,626.0	n/a	n/a	987.1
1996	3,033	5,612	8,645	2,501,500	1,576.7	699.1	868.7	943.0

Notes: (1) Metropolitan Statistical Area - see Appendix A for areas included; (2) calculated by the editors using the following formula: (number of crimes in the MSA minus number of crimes in the city); (3) calculated by the editors using the following formula: ((number of crimes in the MSA minus number of crimes in the city) ÷ (population of the MSA minus population of the city)) x 100,000; n/a not avail.
Source: U.S. Department of Justice, FBI Uniform Crime Reports, 1977 - 1996

Larceny-Thefts and Larceny-Theft Rates: 1977 - 1996

Year	Number				Rate per 100,000 population			
	City	Suburbs[2]	MSA[1]	U.S.	City	Suburbs[3]	MSA[1]	U.S.
1977	7,913	8,750	16,663	5,905,700	4,277.3	2,297.1	2,944.4	2,729.9
1978	7,049	8,575	15,624	5,991,000	3,831.0	2,180.8	2,706.9	2,747.4
1979	8,047	10,509	18,556	6,601,000	4,340.0	2,597.1	3,144.8	2,999.1
1980	9,275	11,932	21,207	7,136,900	5,107.3	2,814.0	3,501.7	3,167.0
1981	9,905	11,935	21,840	7,194,400	5,470.3	2,823.0	3,616.8	3,139.7
1982	10,733	10,719	21,452	7,142,500	5,987.5	2,561.0	3,588.5	3,084.8
1983	9,804	10,056	19,860	6,712,800	5,493.4	2,413.3	3,336.9	2,868.9
1984	9,251	10,104	19,355	6,591,900	5,084.1	2,342.8	3,156.2	2,791.3
1985	9,318	11,119	20,437	6,926,400	5,084.3	2,478.6	3,234.4	2,901.2
1986	9,572	12,039	21,611	7,257,200	5,192.6	2,666.9	3,399.2	3,010.3
1987	9,970	12,211	22,181	7,499,900	5,319.0	2,601.2	3,376.8	3,081.3
1988	8,347	13,008	21,355	7,705,900	4,385.2	2,716.6	3,191.2	3,134.9
1989	8,126	13,285	21,411	7,872,400	4,368.0	2,729.3	3,182.4	3,171.3
1990	8,138	13,991	22,129	7,945,700	4,303.0	2,773.6	3,190.6	3,194.8
1991	8,675	14,859	23,534	8,142,200	4,551.3	2,922.8	3,366.9	3,228.8
1992	9,090	22,593	31,683	7,915,200	4,734.2	2,972.2	3,327.5	3,103.0
1993	8,827	22,041	30,868	7,820,900	4,594.5	2,837.8	3,186.1	3,032.4
1994	8,241	21,772	30,013	7,879,800	4,281.4	2,797.9	3,092.1	3,026.7
1995	8,089	n/a	n/a	7,997,700	4,225.0	n/a	n/a	3,043.8
1996	8,051	21,338	29,389	7,894,600	4,185.4	2,658.1	2,953.3	2,975.9

Notes: (1) Metropolitan Statistical Area - see Appendix A for areas included; (2) calculated by the editors using the following formula: (number of crimes in the MSA minus number of crimes in the city); (3) calculated by the editors using the following formula: ((number of crimes in the MSA minus number of crimes in the city) ÷ (population of the MSA minus population of the city)) x 100,000; n/a not avail.
Source: U.S. Department of Justice, FBI Uniform Crime Reports, 1977 - 1996

Motor Vehicle Thefts and Motor Vehicle Theft Rates: 1977 - 1996

Year	Number				Rate per 100,000 population			
	City	Suburbs[2]	MSA[1]	U.S.	City	Suburbs[3]	MSA[1]	U.S.
1977	587	475	1,062	977,700	317.3	124.7	187.7	451.9
1978	635	652	1,287	1,004,100	345.1	165.8	223.0	460.5
1979	753	692	1,445	1,112,800	406.1	171.0	244.9	505.6
1980	686	646	1,332	1,131,700	377.7	152.4	219.9	502.2
1981	608	621	1,229	1,087,800	335.8	146.9	203.5	474.7
1982	585	580	1,165	1,062,400	326.3	138.6	194.9	458.8
1983	637	495	1,132	1,007,900	356.9	118.8	190.2	430.8
1984	648	533	1,181	1,032,200	356.1	123.6	192.6	437.1
1985	762	666	1,428	1,102,900	415.8	148.5	226.0	462.0
1986	1,197	776	1,973	1,224,100	649.3	171.9	310.3	507.8
1987	1,130	869	1,999	1,288,700	602.9	185.1	304.3	529.4
1988	1,245	967	2,212	1,432,900	654.1	201.9	330.6	582.9
1989	1,604	920	2,524	1,564,800	862.2	189.0	375.2	630.4
1990	1,494	919	2,413	1,635,900	789.9	182.2	347.9	657.8
1991	1,271	913	2,184	1,661,700	666.8	179.6	312.5	659.0
1992	1,108	1,567	2,675	1,610,800	577.1	206.1	280.9	631.5
1993	1,075	1,565	2,640	1,563,100	559.5	201.5	272.5	606.1
1994	1,076	1,668	2,744	1,539,300	559.0	214.4	282.7	591.3
1995	890	n/a	n/a	1,472,400	464.9	n/a	n/a	560.4
1996	1,073	1,815	2,888	1,395,200	557.8	226.1	290.2	525.9

Notes: (1) Metropolitan Statistical Area - see Appendix A for areas included; (2) calculated by the editors using the following formula: (number of crimes in the MSA minus number of crimes in the city); (3) calculated by the editors using the following formula: ((number of crimes in the MSA minus number of crimes in the city) ÷ (population of the MSA minus population of the city)) x 100,000; n/a not avail.
Source: U.S. Department of Justice, FBI Uniform Crime Reports, 1977 - 1996

HATE CRIMES

Criminal Incidents by Bias Motivation

Area	Race	Ethnicity	Religion	Sexual Orientation
Grand Rapids	9	0	0	2

Notes: Figures include both violent and property crimes. Law enforcement agencies must have submitted data for at least one quarter of calendar year 1995 to be included in this report, therefore figures shown may not represent complete 12-month totals; n/a not available
Source: U.S. Department of Justice, FBI Uniform Crime Reports, Hate Crime Statistics 1995

LAW ENFORCEMENT

Full-Time Law Enforcement Employees

Jurisdiction	Police Employees			Police Officers per 100,000 population
	Total	Officers	Civilians	
Grand Rapids	448	374	74	194.4

Notes: Data as of October 31, 1996
Source: U.S. Department of Justice, FBI Uniform Crime Reports, 1996

CORRECTIONS

Federal Correctional Facilities

Type	Year Opened	Security Level	Sex of Inmates	Rated Capacity	Population on 7/1/95	Number of Staff
None listed						

Notes: Data as of 1995
Source: Bureau of Justice Statistics, Sourcebook of Criminal Justice Statistics Online

City/County/Regional Correctional Facilities

Name	Year Opened	Year Renov.	Rated Capacity	1995 Pop.	Number of COs[1]	Number of Staff	ACA[2] Accred.
Kent Co Corr Facility	1958	1992	994	1,033	206	299	No
Kent Co Salvation Army Annex/Work Release	1982	1993	102	91	9	9	No

Notes: Data as of April 1996; (1) Correctional Officers; (2) American Correctional Assn. Accreditation
Source: American Correctional Association, 1996-1998 National Jail and Adult Detention Directory

Private Adult Correctional Facilities

Name	Date Opened	Rated Capacity	Present Pop.	Security Level	Facility Construct.	Expans. Plans	ACA[1] Accred.
None listed							

Notes: Data as of December 1996; (1) American Correctional Association Accreditation
Source: University of Florida, Center for Studies in Criminology and Law, Private Adult Correctional Facility Census, 10th Ed., March 15, 1997

Characteristics of Shock Incarceration Programs

Jurisdiction	Year Program Began	Number of Camps	Average Num. of Inmates	Number of Beds	Program Length	Voluntary/ Mandatory
Michigan	1988	1	319	360	90 days	Voluntary

Note: Data as of July 1996;
Source: Sourcebook of Criminal Justice Statistics Online

DEATH PENALTY

Michigan did not have the death penalty as of July 31, 1997.
Source: Death Penalty Information Center Web Site, 9/30/97

LAWS

Statutory Provisions Relating to the Purchase, Ownership and Use of Handguns

Jurisdiction	Instant Background Check	Federal Waiting Period Applies[1]	State Waiting Period (days)	License or Permit to Purchase	Regis-tration	Record of Sale Sent to Police	Concealed Carry Law
Michigan	No	No	No	Yes[a]	Yes	Yes	Yes[b]

Note: Data as of 1996; (1) The Federal 5-day waiting period for handgun purchases applies to states that don't have instant background checks, waiting period requirements, or licensing procedures exempting them from the Federal requirement; (a) A handgun purchaser must obtain a license to purchase from local law enforcement, and within 10 days present to such official the license and handgun purchased to obtain a certificate of inspection; (b) Restrictively administered discretion by local authorities over permit issuance, or permits are unavailable and carrying is prohibited in most circumstances
Source: Sourcebook of Criminal Justice Statistics Online

Statutory Provisions Relating to Alcohol Use and Driving

Jurisdiction	Drinking Age	Blood Alcohol Concentration Levels as Evidence in State Courts[1]		Open Container Law[1]	Anti-Consump-tion Law[1]	Dram Shop Law[1]
		Illegal per se at 0.10%	Presumption at 0.10%			
Michigan	21	Yes	(a)	Yes	Yes	Yes

Note: Data as of January 1, 1997; (1) See Appendix C for an explanation of terms; (a) Presumption of driving while impaired at 0.07%; presumption of driving under the influence at 0.10%
Source: Sourcebook of Criminal Justice Statistics Online

Statutory Provisions Relating to Curfews

Jurisdiction	Year Enacted	Latest Revision	Age Group(s)	Curfew Provisions
Grand Rapids	1967	1970	16 and 17	Midnight to 6 am every night
			13 through 15	11 pm to 6 am every night
			12 and under	10 pm to 6 am every night

Note: Data as of February 1996
Source: Sourcebook of Criminal Justice Statistics Online

Statutory Provisions Relating to Hate Crimes

Jurisdiction	Bias-Motivated Violence and Intimidation						Institutional Vandalism
	Civil Action	Criminal Penalty					
		Race/ Religion/ Ethnicity	Sexual Orientation	Mental/ Physical Disability	Gender	Age	
Michigan	Yes	Yes	No	No	Yes	No	No

Source: Anti-Defamation League, 1997 Hate Crimes Laws

Greensboro, North Carolina

OVERVIEW

The total crime rate for the city increased 32.1% between 1977 and 1996. During that same period, the violent crime rate increased 61.8% and the property crime rate increased 28.9%.

Among violent crimes, the rates for: Murders decreased 17.5%; Forcible Rapes increased 98.3%; Robberies increased 265.1%; and Aggravated Assaults increased 19.3%.

Among property crimes, the rates for: Burglaries increased 12.9%; Larceny-Thefts increased 29.8%; and Motor Vehicle Thefts increased 105.0%.

ANTI-CRIME PROGRAMS

Not available at time of publication.

CRIME RISK

Your Chances of Becoming a Victim[1]

Area	Any Crime	Violent Crime					Property Crime			
		Any	Murder	Forcible Rape[2]	Robbery	Aggrav. Assault	Any	Burglary	Larceny -Theft	Motor Vehicle Theft
City	1:12	1:105	1:8,834	1:1,145	1:286	1:185	1:14	1:63	1:20	1:194

Note: (1) Figures have been calculated by dividing the population of the city by the number of crimes reported to the FBI during 1996 and are expressed as odds (eg. 1:20 should be read as 1 in 20).
(2) Figures have been calculated by dividing the female population of the city by the number of forcible rapes reported to the FBI during 1996. The female population of the city was estimated by calculating the ratio of females to males reported in the 1990 Census and applying that ratio to 1996 population estimate.
Source: FBI Uniform Crime Reports 1996

CRIME STATISTICS

Total Crimes and Total Crime Rates: 1977 - 1996

Year	Number				Rate per 100,000 population			
	City	Suburbs[2]	MSA[1]	U.S.	City	Suburbs[3]	MSA[1]	U.S.
1977	9,834	25,107	34,941	10,984,500	6,108.1	4,068.8	4,490.8	5,077.6
1978	9,742	26,318	36,060	11,209,000	5,976.7	4,249.1	4,609.0	5,140.3
1979	10,301	29,727	40,028	12,249,500	6,311.3	4,785.3	5,102.9	5,565.5
1980	12,462	32,266	44,728	13,408,300	8,046.0	4,820.9	5,427.0	5,950.0
1981	12,014	31,170	43,184	13,423,800	7,616.9	4,573.2	5,145.2	5,858.2
1982	11,160	30,908	42,068	12,974,400	6,995.5	4,483.5	4,955.6	5,603.6
1983	9,782	29,181	38,963	12,108,600	6,068.2	4,041.6	4,411.5	5,175.0
1984	8,812	26,909	35,721	11,881,800	5,465.4	3,687.5	4,009.2	5,031.3
1985	9,989	26,060	36,049	12,431,400	6,179.4	3,528.6	4,004.6	5,207.1
1986	11,138	29,797	40,935	13,211,900	6,807.5	3,985.7	4,492.3	5,480.4
1987	11,725	32,033	43,758	13,508,700	6,553.2	4,367.7	4,796.3	5,550.0
1988	13,140	32,600	45,740	13,923,100	7,188.1	4,342.8	4,900.0	5,664.2
1989	14,764	37,938	52,702	14,251,400	8,009.9	5,032.9	5,617.9	5,741.0
1990	14,332	40,416	54,748	14,475,600	7,809.5	5,320.1	5,804.5	5,820.3
1991	16,769	44,959	61,728	14,872,900	8,990.4	5,823.0	6,439.3	5,897.8
1992	15,593	50,613	66,206	14,438,200	8,230.5	5,652.9	6,103.0	5,660.2
1993	15,303	51,665	66,968	14,144,800	7,931.0	5,720.3	6,109.4	5,484.4
1994	16,998	53,168	70,166	13,989,500	8,653.7	5,782.7	6,288.1	5,373.5
1995	18,044	54,494	72,538	13,862,700	9,038.5	5,874.8	6,435.1	5,275.9
1996	16,393	54,249	70,642	13,473,600	8,068.0	5,746.3	6,157.5	5,078.9

Notes: (1) Metropolitan Statistical Area - see Appendix A for areas included; (2) calculated by the editors using the following formula: (number of crimes in the MSA minus number of crimes in the city); (3) calculated by the editors using the following formula: ((number of crimes in the MSA minus number of crimes in the city) ÷ (population of the MSA minus population of the city)) x 100,000; n/a not avail.
Source: U.S. Department of Justice, FBI Uniform Crime Reports, 1977 - 1996

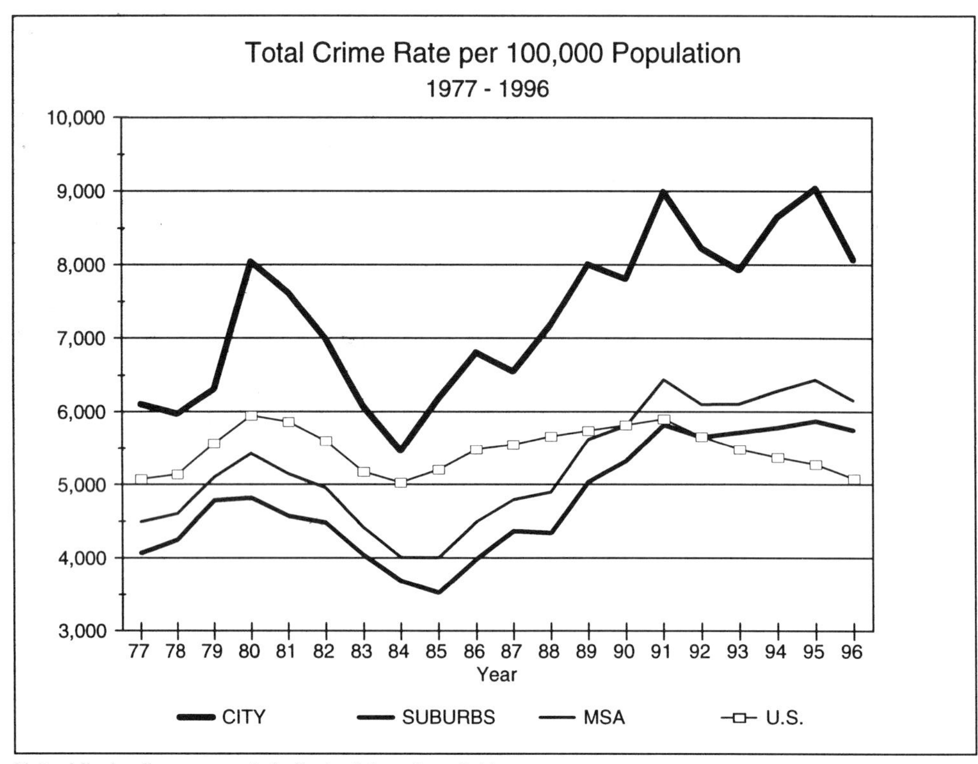

Note: Missing line segments indicate data not available.

Violent Crimes and Violent Crime Rates: 1977 - 1996

Year	Number				Rate per 100,000 population			
	City	Suburbs[2]	MSA[1]	U.S.	City	Suburbs[3]	MSA[1]	U.S.
1977	944	2,403	3,347	1,029,580	586.3	389.4	430.2	475.9
1978	993	2,493	3,486	1,085,550	609.2	402.5	445.6	497.8
1979	997	2,542	3,539	1,208,030	610.9	409.2	451.2	548.9
1980	1,152	2,995	4,147	1,344,520	743.8	447.5	503.2	596.6
1981	1,030	3,380	4,410	1,361,820	653.0	495.9	525.4	594.3
1982	1,121	3,528	4,649	1,322,390	702.7	511.8	547.6	571.1
1983	947	3,396	4,343	1,258,090	587.5	470.3	491.7	537.7
1984	897	3,165	4,062	1,273,280	556.3	433.7	455.9	539.2
1985	1,004	3,397	4,401	1,328,800	621.1	460.0	488.9	556.6
1986	1,199	4,284	5,483	1,489,170	732.8	573.0	601.7	617.7
1987	1,080	4,190	5,270	1,484,000	603.6	571.3	577.6	609.7
1988	1,286	3,648	4,934	1,566,220	703.5	486.0	528.6	637.2
1989	1,716	3,966	5,682	1,646,040	931.0	526.1	605.7	663.1
1990	1,620	4,471	6,091	1,820,130	882.7	588.5	645.8	731.8
1991	1,799	5,227	7,026	1,911,770	964.5	677.0	732.9	758.1
1992	1,626	5,859	7,485	1,932,270	858.3	654.4	690.0	757.5
1993	1,720	5,995	7,715	1,926,020	891.4	663.8	703.8	746.8
1994	2,007	6,048	8,055	1,857,670	1,021.8	657.8	721.9	713.6
1995	2,098	5,819	7,917	1,798,790	1,050.9	627.3	702.3	684.6
1996	1,927	5,635	7,562	1,682,280	948.4	596.9	659.1	634.1

Notes: Violent crimes include murder, forcible rape, robbery and aggravated assault; n/a not available; (1) Metropolitan Statistical Area - see Appendix A for areas included; (2) calculated by the editors using the following formula: (number of crimes in the MSA minus number of crimes in the city); (3) calculated by the editors using the following formula: ((number of crimes in the MSA minus number of crimes in the city) ÷ (population of the MSA minus population of the city)) x 100,000
Source: U.S. Department of Justice, FBI Uniform Crime Reports, 1977 - 1996

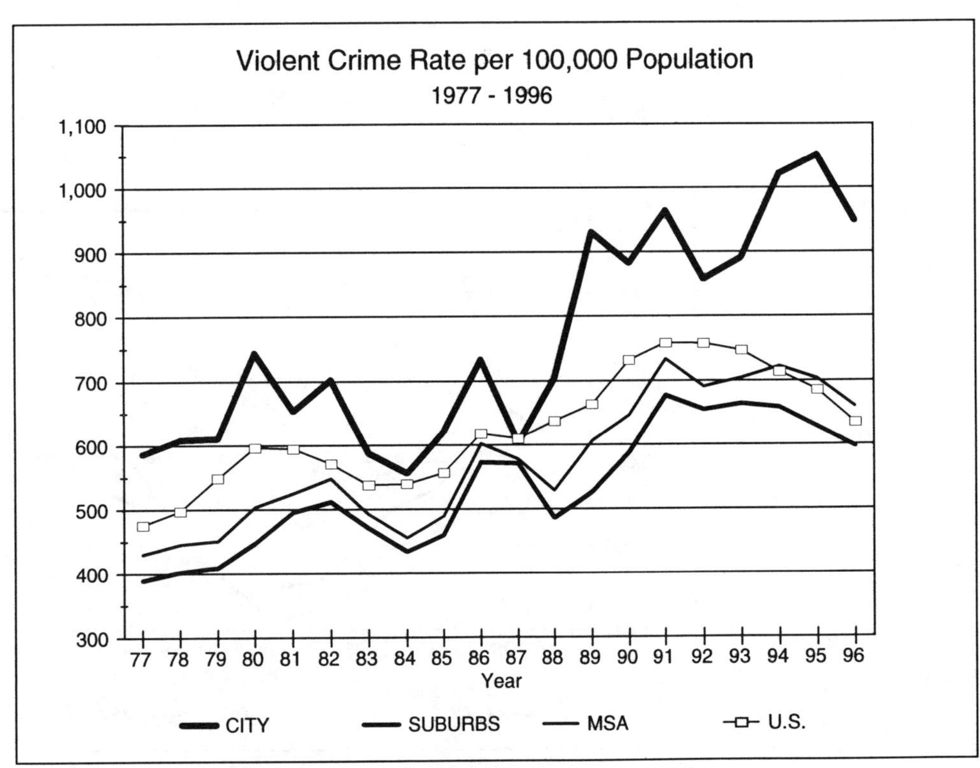

Note: Missing line segments indicate data not available.

Property Crimes and Property Crime Rates: 1977 - 1996

Year	Number				Rate per 100,000 population			
	City	Suburbs[2]	MSA[1]	U.S.	City	Suburbs[3]	MSA[1]	U.S.
1977	8,890	22,704	31,594	9,955,000	5,521.7	3,679.4	4,060.6	4,601.7
1978	8,749	23,825	32,574	10,123,400	5,367.5	3,846.6	4,163.5	4,642.5
1979	9,304	27,185	36,489	11,041,500	5,700.5	4,376.1	4,651.7	5,016.6
1980	11,310	29,271	40,581	12,063,700	7,302.2	4,373.4	4,923.8	5,353.3
1981	10,984	27,790	38,774	12,061,900	6,963.8	4,077.3	4,619.7	5,263.9
1982	10,039	27,380	37,419	11,652,000	6,292.8	3,971.7	4,407.9	5,032.5
1983	8,835	25,785	34,620	10,850,500	5,480.8	3,571.2	3,919.8	4,637.4
1984	7,915	23,744	31,659	10,608,500	4,909.1	3,253.8	3,553.3	4,492.1
1985	8,985	22,663	31,648	11,102,600	5,558.3	3,068.6	3,515.7	4,650.5
1986	9,939	25,513	35,452	11,722,700	6,074.7	3,412.6	3,890.6	4,862.6
1987	10,645	27,843	38,488	12,024,700	5,949.6	3,796.4	4,218.6	4,940.3
1988	11,854	28,952	40,806	12,356,900	6,484.6	3,856.8	4,371.4	5,027.1
1989	13,048	33,972	47,020	12,605,400	7,079.0	4,506.8	5,012.2	5,077.9
1990	12,712	35,945	48,657	12,655,500	6,926.7	4,731.6	5,158.7	5,088.5
1991	14,970	39,732	54,702	12,961,100	8,025.9	5,146.0	5,706.4	5,139.7
1992	13,967	44,754	58,721	12,505,900	7,372.2	4,998.5	5,413.1	4,902.7
1993	13,583	45,670	59,253	12,218,800	7,039.6	5,056.5	5,405.6	4,737.6
1994	14,991	47,120	62,111	12,131,900	7,632.0	5,124.9	5,566.2	4,660.0
1995	15,946	48,675	64,621	12,063,900	7,987.6	5,247.5	5,732.8	4,591.3
1996	14,466	48,614	63,080	11,791,300	7,119.6	5,149.4	5,498.4	4,444.8

Notes: Property crimes include burglary, larceny-theft and motor vehicle theft; n/a not available; (1) Metropolitan Statistical Area - see Appendix A for areas included; (2) calculated by the editors using the following formula: (number of crimes in the MSA minus number of crimes in the city); (3) calculated by the editors using the following formula: ((number of crimes in the MSA minus number of crimes in the city) ÷ (population of the MSA minus population of the city)) x 100,000
Source: U.S. Department of Justice, FBI Uniform Crime Reports, 1977 - 1996

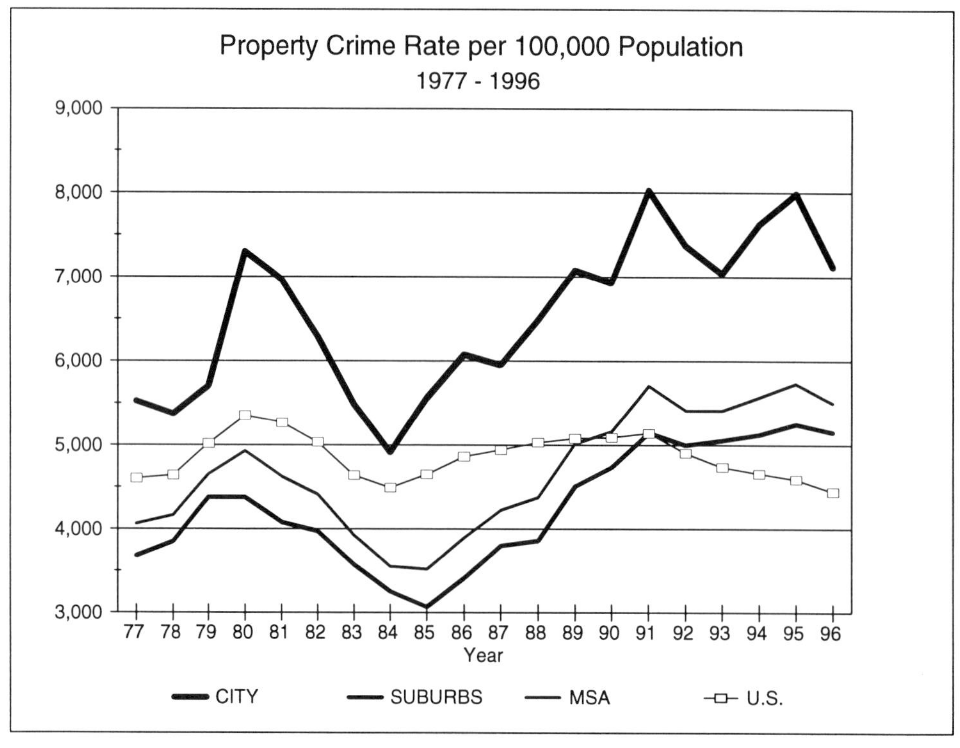

Note: Missing line segments indicate data not available.

Murders and Murder Rates: 1977 - 1996

Year	Number				Rate per 100,000 population			
	City	Suburbs[2]	MSA[1]	U.S.	City	Suburbs[3]	MSA[1]	U.S.
1977	22	74	96	19,120	13.7	12.0	12.3	8.8
1978	14	60	74	19,560	8.6	9.7	9.5	9.0
1979	22	55	77	21,460	13.5	8.9	9.8	9.7
1980	22	46	68	23,040	14.2	6.9	8.3	10.2
1981	11	50	61	22,520	7.0	7.3	7.3	9.8
1982	15	47	62	21,010	9.4	6.8	7.3	9.1
1983	11	51	62	19,310	6.8	7.1	7.0	8.3
1984	8	51	59	18,690	5.0	7.0	6.6	7.9
1985	13	51	64	18,980	8.0	6.9	7.1	7.9
1986	18	60	78	20,610	11.0	8.0	8.6	8.6
1987	18	62	80	20,100	10.1	8.5	8.8	8.3
1988	16	48	64	20,680	8.8	6.4	6.9	8.4
1989	24	61	85	21,500	13.0	8.1	9.1	8.7
1990	20	53	73	23,440	10.9	7.0	7.7	9.4
1991	35	60	95	24,700	18.8	7.8	9.9	9.8
1992	23	87	110	23,760	12.1	9.7	10.1	9.3
1993	27	89	116	24,530	14.0	9.9	10.6	9.5
1994	21	104	125	23,330	10.7	11.3	11.2	9.0
1995	36	63	99	21,610	18.0	6.8	8.8	8.2
1996	23	63	86	19,650	11.3	6.7	7.5	7.4

Notes: (1) Metropolitan Statistical Area - see Appendix A for areas included; (2) calculated by the editors using the following formula: (number of crimes in the MSA minus number of crimes in the city); (3) calculated by the editors using the following formula: ((number of crimes in the MSA minus number of crimes in the city) ÷ (population of the MSA minus population of the city)) x 100,000; n/a not avail.
Source: U.S. Department of Justice, FBI Uniform Crime Reports, 1977 - 1996

Forcible Rapes and Forcible Rape Rates: 1977 - 1996

Year	Number				Rate per 100,000 population			
	City	Suburbs[2]	MSA[1]	U.S.	City	Suburbs[3]	MSA[1]	U.S.
1977	38	117	155	63,500	23.6	19.0	19.9	29.4
1978	42	127	169	67,610	25.8	20.5	21.6	31.0
1979	39	137	176	76,390	23.9	22.1	22.4	34.7
1980	47	133	180	82,990	30.3	19.9	21.8	36.8
1981	53	165	218	82,500	33.6	24.2	26.0	36.0
1982	75	145	220	78,770	47.0	21.0	25.9	34.0
1983	43	143	186	78,920	26.7	19.8	21.1	33.7
1984	56	132	188	84,230	34.7	18.1	21.1	35.7
1985	54	164	218	88,670	33.4	22.2	24.2	37.1
1986	66	188	254	91,460	40.3	25.1	27.9	37.9
1987	81	188	269	91,110	45.3	25.6	29.5	37.4
1988	93	232	325	92,490	50.9	30.9	34.8	37.6
1989	96	235	331	94,500	52.1	31.2	35.3	38.1
1990	114	305	419	102,560	62.1	40.1	44.4	41.2
1991	114	255	369	106,590	61.1	33.0	38.5	42.3
1992	106	341	447	109,060	56.0	38.1	41.2	42.8
1993	105	333	438	106,010	54.4	36.9	40.0	41.1
1994	89	303	392	102,220	45.3	33.0	35.1	39.3
1995	88	273	361	97,470	44.1	29.4	32.0	37.1
1996	95	320	415	95,770	46.8	33.9	36.2	36.1

Notes: (1) Metropolitan Statistical Area - see Appendix A for areas included; (2) calculated by the editors using the following formula: (number of crimes in the MSA minus number of crimes in the city); (3) calculated by the editors using the following formula: ((number of crimes in the MSA minus number of crimes in the city) ÷ (population of the MSA minus population of the city)) x 100,000; n/a not avail.
Source: U.S. Department of Justice, FBI Uniform Crime Reports, 1977 - 1996

Robberies and Robbery Rates: 1977 - 1996

Year	Number				Rate per 100,000 population			
	City	Suburbs[2]	MSA[1]	U.S.	City	Suburbs[3]	MSA[1]	U.S.
1977	154	411	565	412,610	95.7	66.6	72.6	190.7
1978	190	495	685	426,930	116.6	79.9	87.6	195.8
1979	196	579	775	480,700	120.1	93.2	98.8	218.4
1980	295	557	852	565,840	190.5	83.2	103.4	251.1
1981	302	588	890	592,910	191.5	86.3	106.0	258.7
1982	236	695	931	553,130	147.9	100.8	109.7	238.9
1983	227	528	755	506,570	140.8	73.1	85.5	216.5
1984	180	497	677	485,010	111.6	68.1	76.0	205.4
1985	234	483	717	497,870	144.8	65.4	79.6	208.5
1986	300	622	922	542,780	183.4	83.2	101.2	225.1
1987	310	611	921	517,700	173.3	83.3	101.0	212.7
1988	352	737	1,089	542,970	192.6	98.2	116.7	220.9
1989	633	1,070	1,703	578,330	343.4	141.9	181.5	233.0
1990	488	1,106	1,594	639,270	265.9	145.6	169.0	257.0
1991	594	1,477	2,071	687,730	318.5	191.3	216.0	272.7
1992	687	1,676	2,363	672,480	362.6	187.2	217.8	263.6
1993	791	1,748	2,539	659,870	409.9	193.5	231.6	255.9
1994	767	1,739	2,506	618,950	390.5	189.1	224.6	237.7
1995	785	1,683	2,468	580,510	393.2	181.4	218.9	220.9
1996	710	1,612	2,322	537,050	349.4	170.8	202.4	202.4

Notes: (1) Metropolitan Statistical Area - see Appendix A for areas included; (2) calculated by the editors using the following formula: (number of crimes in the MSA minus number of crimes in the city); (3) calculated by the editors using the following formula: ((number of crimes in the MSA minus number of crimes in the city) ÷ (population of the MSA minus population of the city)) x 100,000; n/a not avail.
Source: U.S. Department of Justice, FBI Uniform Crime Reports, 1977 - 1996

Aggravated Assaults and Aggravated Assault Rates: 1977 - 1996

Year	Number				Rate per 100,000 population			
	City	Suburbs[2]	MSA[1]	U.S.	City	Suburbs[3]	MSA[1]	U.S.
1977	730	1,801	2,531	534,350	453.4	291.9	325.3	247.0
1978	747	1,811	2,558	571,460	458.3	292.4	327.0	262.1
1979	740	1,771	2,511	629,480	453.4	285.1	320.1	286.0
1980	788	2,259	3,047	672,650	508.8	337.5	369.7	298.5
1981	664	2,577	3,241	663,900	421.0	378.1	386.1	289.7
1982	795	2,641	3,436	669,480	498.3	383.1	404.8	289.2
1983	666	2,674	3,340	653,290	413.2	370.4	378.2	279.2
1984	653	2,485	3,138	685,350	405.0	340.5	352.2	290.2
1985	703	2,699	3,402	723,250	434.9	365.5	377.9	302.9
1986	815	3,414	4,229	834,320	498.1	456.7	464.1	346.1
1987	671	3,329	4,000	855,090	375.0	453.9	438.4	351.3
1988	825	2,631	3,456	910,090	451.3	350.5	370.2	370.2
1989	963	2,600	3,563	951,710	522.5	344.9	379.8	383.4
1990	998	3,007	4,005	1,054,860	543.8	395.8	424.6	424.1
1991	1,056	3,435	4,491	1,092,740	566.2	444.9	468.5	433.3
1992	810	3,755	4,565	1,126,970	427.5	419.4	420.8	441.8
1993	797	3,825	4,622	1,135,610	413.1	423.5	421.7	440.3
1994	1,130	3,902	5,032	1,113,180	575.3	424.4	451.0	427.6
1995	1,189	3,800	4,989	1,099,210	595.6	409.7	442.6	418.3
1996	1,099	3,640	4,739	1,029,810	540.9	385.6	413.1	388.2

Notes: (1) Metropolitan Statistical Area - see Appendix A for areas included; (2) calculated by the editors using the following formula: (number of crimes in the MSA minus number of crimes in the city); (3) calculated by the editors using the following formula: ((number of crimes in the MSA minus number of crimes in the city) ÷ (population of the MSA minus population of the city)) x 100,000; n/a not avail.
Source: U.S. Department of Justice, FBI Uniform Crime Reports, 1977 - 1996

Burglaries and Burglary Rates: 1977 - 1996

Year	Number				Rate per 100,000 population			
	City	Suburbs[2]	MSA[1]	U.S.	City	Suburbs[3]	MSA[1]	U.S.
1977	2,265	7,660	9,925	3,071,500	1,406.8	1,241.4	1,275.6	1,419.8
1978	2,303	7,970	10,273	3,128,300	1,412.9	1,286.8	1,313.0	1,434.6
1979	2,432	8,653	11,085	3,327,700	1,490.1	1,392.9	1,413.1	1,511.9
1980	3,082	9,804	12,886	3,795,200	1,989.9	1,464.8	1,563.5	1,684.1
1981	2,952	9,746	12,698	3,779,700	1,871.6	1,429.9	1,512.9	1,649.5
1982	2,509	9,214	11,723	3,447,100	1,572.7	1,336.6	1,381.0	1,488.8
1983	2,205	8,087	10,292	3,129,900	1,367.9	1,120.1	1,165.3	1,337.7
1984	1,796	7,102	8,898	2,984,400	1,113.9	973.2	998.7	1,263.7
1985	2,204	7,211	9,415	3,073,300	1,363.4	976.4	1,045.9	1,287.3
1986	2,421	8,498	10,919	3,241,400	1,479.7	1,136.7	1,198.3	1,344.6
1987	2,534	9,084	11,618	3,236,200	1,416.3	1,238.6	1,273.4	1,329.6
1988	2,861	9,448	12,309	3,218,100	1,565.1	1,258.6	1,318.6	1,309.2
1989	3,125	11,056	14,181	3,168,200	1,695.4	1,466.7	1,511.6	1,276.3
1990	2,767	12,400	15,167	3,073,900	1,507.7	1,632.3	1,608.0	1,235.9
1991	3,379	14,114	17,493	3,157,200	1,811.6	1,828.0	1,824.8	1,252.0
1992	3,342	14,905	18,247	2,979,900	1,764.0	1,664.7	1,682.1	1,168.2
1993	3,177	14,706	17,883	2,834,800	1,646.5	1,628.2	1,631.5	1,099.2
1994	3,245	14,652	17,897	2,712,800	1,652.0	1,593.6	1,603.9	1,042.0
1995	3,671	14,256	17,927	2,593,800	1,838.9	1,536.9	1,590.4	987.1
1996	3,228	12,511	15,739	2,501,500	1,588.7	1,325.2	1,371.9	943.0

Notes: (1) Metropolitan Statistical Area - see Appendix A for areas included; (2) calculated by the editors using the following formula: (number of crimes in the MSA minus number of crimes in the city); (3) calculated by the editors using the following formula: ((number of crimes in the MSA minus number of crimes in the city) ÷ (population of the MSA minus population of the city)) x 100,000; n/a not avail.
Source: U.S. Department of Justice, FBI Uniform Crime Reports, 1977 - 1996

Larceny-Thefts and Larceny-Theft Rates: 1977 - 1996

Year	Number				Rate per 100,000 population			
	City	Suburbs[2]	MSA[1]	U.S.	City	Suburbs[3]	MSA[1]	U.S.
1977	6,220	13,757	19,977	5,905,700	3,863.4	2,229.4	2,567.5	2,729.9
1978	6,055	14,453	20,508	5,991,000	3,714.7	2,333.5	2,621.2	2,747.4
1979	6,387	16,879	23,266	6,601,000	3,913.3	2,717.1	2,966.0	2,999.1
1980	7,711	17,787	25,498	7,136,900	4,978.6	2,657.6	3,093.8	3,167.0
1981	7,557	16,507	24,064	7,194,400	4,791.1	2,421.9	2,867.1	3,139.7
1982	7,130	16,700	23,830	7,142,500	4,469.4	2,422.5	2,807.2	3,084.8
1983	6,255	16,454	22,709	6,712,800	3,880.3	2,278.9	2,571.2	2,868.9
1984	5,805	15,442	21,247	6,591,900	3,600.4	2,116.1	2,384.7	2,791.3
1985	6,398	14,148	20,546	6,926,400	3,957.9	1,915.7	2,282.4	2,901.2
1986	7,131	15,478	22,609	7,257,200	4,358.4	2,070.3	2,481.2	3,010.3
1987	7,655	17,198	24,853	7,499,900	4,278.4	2,344.9	2,724.1	3,081.3
1988	8,391	17,705	26,096	7,705,900	4,590.2	2,358.6	2,795.6	3,134.9
1989	9,217	20,750	29,967	7,872,400	5,000.5	2,752.7	3,194.4	3,171.3
1990	9,161	21,483	30,644	7,945,700	4,991.8	2,827.9	3,248.9	3,194.8
1991	10,768	23,411	34,179	8,142,200	5,773.1	3,032.2	3,565.5	3,228.8
1992	9,957	27,461	37,418	7,915,200	5,255.6	3,067.1	3,449.3	3,103.0
1993	9,657	28,297	37,954	7,820,900	5,004.9	3,133.0	3,462.5	3,032.4
1994	10,787	29,655	40,442	7,879,800	5,491.7	3,225.4	3,624.3	3,026.7
1995	11,067	31,591	42,658	7,997,700	5,543.6	3,405.7	3,784.4	3,043.8
1996	10,190	32,513	42,703	7,894,600	5,015.1	3,443.9	3,722.2	2,975.9

Notes: (1) Metropolitan Statistical Area - see Appendix A for areas included; (2) calculated by the editors using the following formula: (number of crimes in the MSA minus number of crimes in the city); (3) calculated by the editors using the following formula: ((number of crimes in the MSA minus number of crimes in the city) ÷ (population of the MSA minus population of the city)) x 100,000; n/a not avail.
Source: U.S. Department of Justice, FBI Uniform Crime Reports, 1977 - 1996

Motor Vehicle Thefts and Motor Vehicle Theft Rates: 1977 - 1996

Year	Number				Rate per 100,000 population			
	City	Suburbs[2]	MSA[1]	U.S.	City	Suburbs[3]	MSA[1]	U.S.
1977	405	1,287	1,692	977,700	251.6	208.6	217.5	451.9
1978	391	1,402	1,793	1,004,100	239.9	226.4	229.2	460.5
1979	485	1,653	2,138	1,112,800	297.2	266.1	272.6	505.6
1980	517	1,680	2,197	1,131,700	333.8	251.0	266.6	502.2
1981	475	1,537	2,012	1,087,800	301.1	225.5	239.7	474.7
1982	400	1,466	1,866	1,062,400	250.7	212.7	219.8	458.8
1983	375	1,244	1,619	1,007,900	232.6	172.3	183.3	430.8
1984	314	1,200	1,514	1,032,200	194.8	164.4	169.9	437.1
1985	383	1,304	1,687	1,102,900	236.9	176.6	187.4	462.0
1986	387	1,537	1,924	1,224,100	236.5	205.6	211.1	507.8
1987	456	1,561	2,017	1,288,700	254.9	212.8	221.1	529.4
1988	602	1,799	2,401	1,432,900	329.3	239.7	257.2	582.9
1989	706	2,166	2,872	1,564,800	383.0	287.3	306.1	630.4
1990	784	2,062	2,846	1,635,900	427.2	271.4	301.7	657.8
1991	823	2,207	3,030	1,661,700	441.2	285.8	316.1	659.0
1992	668	2,388	3,056	1,610,800	352.6	266.7	281.7	631.5
1993	749	2,667	3,416	1,563,100	388.2	295.3	311.6	606.1
1994	959	2,813	3,772	1,539,300	488.2	306.0	338.0	591.3
1995	1,208	2,828	4,036	1,472,400	605.1	304.9	358.0	560.4
1996	1,048	3,590	4,638	1,395,200	515.8	380.3	404.3	525.9

Notes: (1) Metropolitan Statistical Area - see Appendix A for areas included; (2) calculated by the editors using the following formula: (number of crimes in the MSA minus number of crimes in the city); (3) calculated by the editors using the following formula: ((number of crimes in the MSA minus number of crimes in the city) ÷ (population of the MSA minus population of the city)) x 100,000; n/a not avail.
Source: U.S. Department of Justice, FBI Uniform Crime Reports, 1977 - 1996

HATE CRIMES

Criminal Incidents by Bias Motivation

Area	Race	Ethnicity	Religion	Sexual Orientation
Greensboro	1	0	0	1

Notes: Figures include both violent and property crimes. Law enforcement agencies must have submitted data for at least one quarter of calendar year 1995 to be included in this report, therefore figures shown may not represent complete 12-month totals; n/a not available
Source: U.S. Department of Justice, FBI Uniform Crime Reports, Hate Crime Statistics 1995

LAW ENFORCEMENT

Full-Time Law Enforcement Employees

Jurisdiction	Police Employees			Police Officers per 100,000 population
	Total	Officers	Civilians	
Greensboro	582	457	125	224.9

Notes: Data as of October 31, 1996
Source: U.S. Department of Justice, FBI Uniform Crime Reports, 1996

CORRECTIONS

Federal Correctional Facilities

Type	Year Opened	Security Level	Sex of Inmates	Rated Capacity	Population on 7/1/95	Number of Staff
None listed						

Notes: Data as of 1995
Source: Bureau of Justice Statistics, Sourcebook of Criminal Justice Statistics Online

City/County/Regional Correctional Facilities

Name	Year Opened	Year Renov.	Rated Capacity	1995 Pop.	Number of COs[1]	Number of Staff	ACA[2] Accred.
Guilford County Jail	1975	--	288	n/a	n/a	n/a	No

Notes: Data as of April 1996; (1) Correctional Officers; (2) American Correctional Assn. Accreditation
Source: American Correctional Association, 1996-1998 National Jail and Adult Detention Directory

Private Adult Correctional Facilities

Name	Date Opened	Rated Capacity	Present Pop.	Security Level	Facility Construct.	Expans. Plans	ACA[1] Accred.
None listed							

Notes: Data as of December 1996; (1) American Correctional Association Accreditation
Source: University of Florida, Center for Studies in Criminology and Law, Private Adult Correctional Facility Census, 10th Ed., March 15, 1997

Characteristics of Shock Incarceration Programs

Jurisdiction	Year Program Began	Number of Camps	Average Num. of Inmates	Number of Beds	Program Length	Voluntary/ Mandatory
North Carolina	1989	2	240	360	90 to 120 days	Voluntary

Note: Data as of July 1996;
Source: Sourcebook of Criminal Justice Statistics Online

DEATH PENALTY

Death Penalty Statistics

State	Prisoners Executed		Prisoners Under Sentence of Death					Avg. No. of Years on Death Row[4]
	1930-1995	1996[1]	Total[2]	White[3]	Black[3]	Hisp.	Women	
North Carolina	271	0	139	68	69	1	2	3.3

Notes: Data as of 12/31/95 unless otherwise noted; (1) Data as of 7/31/97; (2) Includes persons of other races; (3) Includes people of Hispanic origin; (4) Covers prisoners sentenced 1974 through 1995
Source: Bureau of Justice Statistics, Capital Punishment 1995 (released 12/96); Death Penalty Information Center Web Site, 9/30/97

Capital Offenses and Methods of Execution

Capital Offenses in North Carolina	Minimum Age for Imposition of Death Penalty	Mentally Retarded Excluded	Methods of Execution[1]
First-degree murder (N.C.G.S. 14-17).	17	No	Lethal injection; lethal gas

Notes: Data as of 12/31/95 unless otherwise noted; (1) Data as of 7/31/97
Source: Bureau of Justice Statistics, Capital Punishment 1995 (released 12/96); Death Penalty Information Center Web Site, 9/30/97

LAWS

Statutory Provisions Relating to the Purchase, Ownership and Use of Handguns

Jurisdiction	Instant Background Check	Federal Waiting Period Applies[1]	State Waiting Period (days)	License or Permit to Purchase	Regis-tration	Record of Sale Sent to Police	Concealed Carry Law
North Carolina	No	No	No	Yes[a]	No	Yes	Yes[b]

Note: Data as of 1996; (1) The Federal 5-day waiting period for handgun purchases applies to states that don't have instant background checks, waiting period requirements, or licensing procedures exempting them from the Federal requirement; (a) To purchase a handgun, a license or permit is required, which must be issued to qualified applicants within 30 days; (b) "Shall issue" permit system, liberally administered discretion by local authorities over permit issuance, or no permit required
Source: Sourcebook of Criminal Justice Statistics Online

Statutory Provisions Relating to Alcohol Use and Driving

Jurisdiction	Drinking Age	Blood Alcohol Concentration Levels as Evidence in State Courts[1]		Open Container Law[1]	Anti-Consump-tion Law[1]	Dram Shop Law[1]
		Illegal per se at 0.10%	Presumption at 0.10%			
North Carolina	21	(a)	No	Yes[b]	Yes[b,c]	Yes[d,e]

Note: Data as of January 1, 1997; (1) See Appendix C for an explanation of terms; (a) 0.08%; (b) Limited application; (c) Applies to drivers only; (d) State has a statute that places a monetary limit on the amount of damages that can be awarded in dram shop liability actions; (e) Applies specifically to the actions of intoxicated minors, but the law does not foreclose developing case law as to other types of dram shop action
Source: Sourcebook of Criminal Justice Statistics Online

Statutory Provisions Relating to Hate Crimes

Jurisdiction	Bias-Motivated Violence and Intimidation						Institutional Vandalism
	Civil Action	Criminal Penalty					
		Race/ Religion/ Ethnicity	Sexual Orientation	Mental/ Physical Disability	Gender	Age	
North Carolina	No	Yes	No	No	No	No	Yes

Source: Anti-Defamation League, 1997 Hate Crimes Laws

Honolulu, Hawaii

OVERVIEW

The total crime rate for the metro area increased 5.1% between 1977 and 1996. During that same period, the violent crime rate increased 36.1% and the property crime rate increased 4.0%.

Among violent crimes, the rates for: Murders decreased 51.6%; Forcible Rapes increased 3.7%; Robberies increased 8.1%; and Aggravated Assaults increased 148.6%.

Among property crimes, the rates for: Burglaries decreased 44.2%; Larceny-Thefts increased 21.8%; and Motor Vehicle Thefts increased 39.8%.

ANTI-CRIME PROGRAMS

Programs include:

- Criminal Investigation Assessment—seeks to enhance crime solving through profiling, which can characterize offenders and help detectives narrow the scope of their investigations.
- Pu'uhonua ("a place of peace and safety")—includes services for victims of abuse.
- Gang Intervention Unit—gathers and disseminates gang-related information and planning action in response to criminal activity.
- CrimeStoppers—encourages the public to provide tips on crimes to the police.
- PAGE (Positive Alternative Gang Education)—sends officers into schools to teach about alternatives to involvement with gangs.
  Police Department, 6/97

CRIME RISK

Your Chances of Becoming a Victim[1]

Area	Any Crime	Violent Crime						Property Crime			
		Any	Murder	Forcible Rape[2]	Robbery	Aggrav. Assault		Any	Burglary	Larceny -Theft	Motor Vehicle Theft
MSA	1:15	1:320	1:32,520	1:1,937	1:618	1:815		1:15	1:97	1:21	1:138

Note: (1) Figures have been calculated by dividing the population of the MSA by the number of crimes reported to the FBI during 1996 and are expressed as odds (eg. 1:20 should be read as 1 in 20).
(2) Figures have been calculated by dividing the female population of the MSA by the number of forcible rapes reported to the FBI during 1996. The female population of the MSA was estimated by calculating the ratio of females to males reported in the 1990 Census and applying that ratio to 1996 population estimate.
Source: FBI Uniform Crime Reports 1996

CRIME STATISTICS

Total Crimes and Total Crime Rates: 1977 - 1996

Year	Number				Rate per 100,000 population			
	City	Suburbs[2]	MSA[1]	U.S.	City	Suburbs[3]	MSA[1]	U.S.
1977	n/a	n/a	46,984	10,984,500	n/a	n/a	6,507.6	5,077.6
1978	n/a	n/a	51,892	11,209,000	n/a	n/a	7,155.0	5,140.3
1979	n/a	n/a	52,926	12,249,500	n/a	n/a	7,207.0	5,565.5
1980	n/a	n/a	57,718	13,408,300	n/a	n/a	7,574.3	5,950.0
1981	n/a	n/a	49,548	13,423,800	n/a	n/a	6,407.1	5,858.2
1982	n/a	n/a	50,600	12,974,400	n/a	n/a	6,444.4	5,603.6
1983	n/a	n/a	46,228	12,108,600	n/a	n/a	5,720.6	5,175.0
1984	n/a	n/a	44,560	11,881,800	n/a	n/a	5,496.0	5,031.3
1985	n/a	n/a	42,048	12,431,400	n/a	n/a	5,146.1	5,207.1
1986	n/a	n/a	46,455	13,211,900	n/a	n/a	5,642.5	5,480.4
1987	n/a	n/a	48,949	13,508,700	n/a	n/a	5,879.0	5,550.0
1988	n/a	n/a	49,469	13,923,100	n/a	n/a	5,898.6	5,664.2
1989	n/a	n/a	52,909	14,251,400	n/a	n/a	6,232.2	5,741.0
1990	n/a	n/a	51,028	14,475,600	n/a	n/a	6,102.1	5,820.3
1991	n/a	n/a	51,032	14,872,900	n/a	n/a	5,958.7	5,897.8
1992	n/a	n/a	53,558	14,438,200	n/a	n/a	6,118.8	5,660.2
1993	n/a	n/a	56,405	14,144,800	n/a	n/a	6,442.9	5,484.4
1994	n/a	n/a	60,825	13,989,500	n/a	n/a	6,906.5	5,373.5
1995	n/a	n/a	67,145	13,862,700	n/a	n/a	7,627.8	5,275.9
1996	n/a	n/a	60,059	13,473,600	n/a	n/a	6,840.1	5,078.9

Notes: (1) Metropolitan Statistical Area - see Appendix A for areas included; (2) calculated by the editors using the following formula: (number of crimes in the MSA minus number of crimes in the city); (3) calculated by the editors using the following formula: ((number of crimes in the MSA minus number of crimes in the city) ÷ (population of the MSA minus population of the city)) x 100,000; n/a not avail.
Source: U.S. Department of Justice, FBI Uniform Crime Reports, 1977 - 1996

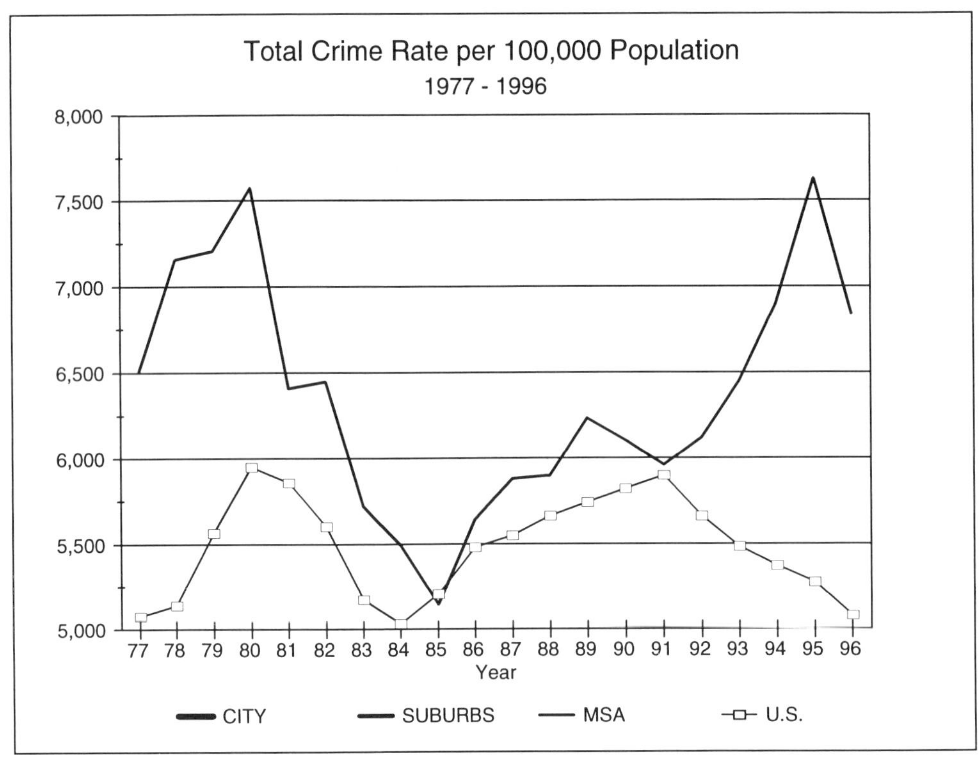

Note: Missing line segments indicate data not available.

Violent Crimes and Violent Crime Rates: 1977 - 1996

Year	Number				Rate per 100,000 population			
	City	Suburbs[2]	MSA[1]	U.S.	City	Suburbs[3]	MSA[1]	U.S.
1977	n/a	n/a	1,660	1,029,580	n/a	n/a	229.9	475.9
1978	n/a	n/a	2,044	1,085,550	n/a	n/a	281.8	497.8
1979	n/a	n/a	2,196	1,208,030	n/a	n/a	299.0	548.9
1980	n/a	n/a	2,456	1,344,520	n/a	n/a	322.3	596.6
1981	n/a	n/a	1,965	1,361,820	n/a	n/a	254.1	594.3
1982	n/a	n/a	2,151	1,322,390	n/a	n/a	273.9	571.1
1983	n/a	n/a	2,136	1,258,090	n/a	n/a	264.3	537.7
1984	n/a	n/a	1,950	1,273,280	n/a	n/a	240.5	539.2
1985	n/a	n/a	1,801	1,328,800	n/a	n/a	220.4	556.6
1986	n/a	n/a	2,076	1,489,170	n/a	n/a	252.2	617.7
1987	n/a	n/a	2,258	1,484,000	n/a	n/a	271.2	609.7
1988	n/a	n/a	2,186	1,566,220	n/a	n/a	260.7	637.2
1989	n/a	n/a	2,297	1,646,040	n/a	n/a	270.6	663.1
1990	n/a	n/a	2,412	1,820,130	n/a	n/a	288.4	731.8
1991	n/a	n/a	2,058	1,911,770	n/a	n/a	240.3	758.1
1992	n/a	n/a	2,382	1,932,270	n/a	n/a	272.1	757.5
1993	n/a	n/a	2,501	1,926,020	n/a	n/a	285.7	746.8
1994	n/a	n/a	2,528	1,857,670	n/a	n/a	287.0	713.6
1995	n/a	n/a	2,882	1,798,790	n/a	n/a	327.4	684.6
1996	n/a	n/a	2,748	1,682,280	n/a	n/a	313.0	634.1

Notes: Violent crimes include murder, forcible rape, robbery and aggravated assault; n/a not available; (1) Metropolitan Statistical Area - see Appendix A for areas included; (2) calculated by the editors using the following formula: (number of crimes in the MSA minus number of crimes in the city); (3) calculated by the editors using the following formula: ((number of crimes in the MSA minus number of crimes in the city) ÷ (population of the MSA minus population of the city)) x 100,000
Source: U.S. Department of Justice, FBI Uniform Crime Reports, 1977 - 1996

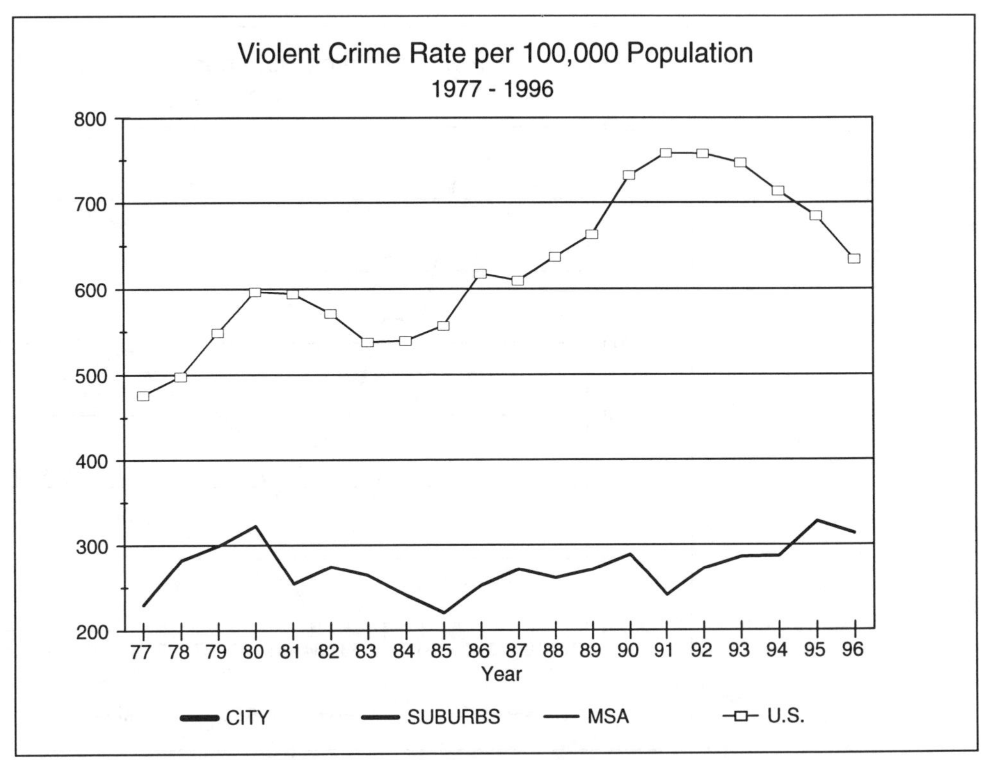

Note: Missing line segments indicate data not available.

Property Crimes and Property Crime Rates: 1977 - 1996

Year	Number				Rate per 100,000 population			
	City	Suburbs[2]	MSA[1]	U.S.	City	Suburbs[3]	MSA[1]	U.S.
1977	n/a	n/a	45,324	9,955,000	n/a	n/a	6,277.7	4,601.7
1978	n/a	n/a	49,848	10,123,400	n/a	n/a	6,873.1	4,642.5
1979	n/a	n/a	50,730	11,041,500	n/a	n/a	6,908.0	5,016.6
1980	n/a	n/a	55,262	12,063,700	n/a	n/a	7,252.0	5,353.3
1981	n/a	n/a	47,583	12,061,900	n/a	n/a	6,153.0	5,263.9
1982	n/a	n/a	48,449	11,652,000	n/a	n/a	6,170.4	5,032.5
1983	n/a	n/a	44,092	10,850,500	n/a	n/a	5,456.3	4,637.4
1984	n/a	n/a	42,610	10,608,500	n/a	n/a	5,255.5	4,492.1
1985	n/a	n/a	40,247	11,102,600	n/a	n/a	4,925.7	4,650.5
1986	n/a	n/a	44,379	11,722,700	n/a	n/a	5,390.3	4,862.6
1987	n/a	n/a	46,691	12,024,700	n/a	n/a	5,607.8	4,940.3
1988	n/a	n/a	47,283	12,356,900	n/a	n/a	5,637.9	5,027.1
1989	n/a	n/a	50,612	12,605,400	n/a	n/a	5,961.7	5,077.9
1990	n/a	n/a	48,616	12,655,500	n/a	n/a	5,813.7	5,088.5
1991	n/a	n/a	48,974	12,961,100	n/a	n/a	5,718.4	5,139.7
1992	n/a	n/a	51,176	12,505,900	n/a	n/a	5,846.7	4,902.7
1993	n/a	n/a	53,904	12,218,800	n/a	n/a	6,157.3	4,737.6
1994	n/a	n/a	58,297	12,131,900	n/a	n/a	6,619.5	4,660.0
1995	n/a	n/a	64,263	12,063,900	n/a	n/a	7,300.4	4,591.3
1996	n/a	n/a	57,311	11,791,300	n/a	n/a	6,527.1	4,444.8

Notes: Property crimes include burglary, larceny-theft and motor vehicle theft; n/a not available;
(1) Metropolitan Statistical Area - see Appendix A for areas included; (2) calculated by the editors using the following formula: (number of crimes in the MSA minus number of crimes in the city);
(3) calculated by the editors using the following formula: ((number of crimes in the MSA minus number of crimes in the city) ÷ (population of the MSA minus population of the city)) x 100,000
Source: U.S. Department of Justice, FBI Uniform Crime Reports, 1977 - 1996

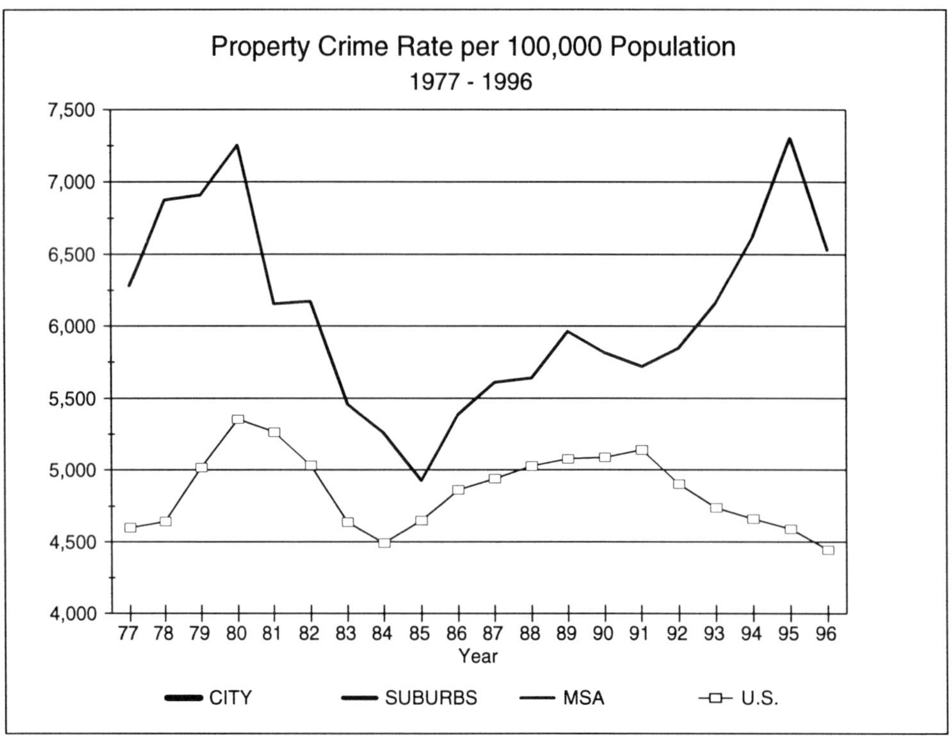

Note: Missing line segments indicate data not available.

Murders and Murder Rates: 1977 - 1996

Year	Number				Rate per 100,000 population			
	City	Suburbs[2]	MSA[1]	U.S.	City	Suburbs[3]	MSA[1]	U.S.
1977	n/a	n/a	46	19,120	n/a	n/a	6.4	8.8
1978	n/a	n/a	38	19,560	n/a	n/a	5.2	9.0
1979	n/a	n/a	48	21,460	n/a	n/a	6.5	9.7
1980	n/a	n/a	65	23,040	n/a	n/a	8.5	10.2
1981	n/a	n/a	40	22,520	n/a	n/a	5.2	9.8
1982	n/a	n/a	25	21,010	n/a	n/a	3.2	9.1
1983	n/a	n/a	45	19,310	n/a	n/a	5.6	8.3
1984	n/a	n/a	25	18,690	n/a	n/a	3.1	7.9
1985	n/a	n/a	36	18,980	n/a	n/a	4.4	7.9
1986	n/a	n/a	46	20,610	n/a	n/a	5.6	8.6
1987	n/a	n/a	36	20,100	n/a	n/a	4.3	8.3
1988	n/a	n/a	28	20,680	n/a	n/a	3.3	8.4
1989	n/a	n/a	43	21,500	n/a	n/a	5.1	8.7
1990	n/a	n/a	34	23,440	n/a	n/a	4.1	9.4
1991	n/a	n/a	29	24,700	n/a	n/a	3.4	9.8
1992	n/a	n/a	31	23,760	n/a	n/a	3.5	9.3
1993	n/a	n/a	31	24,530	n/a	n/a	3.5	9.5
1994	n/a	n/a	35	23,330	n/a	n/a	4.0	9.0
1995	n/a	n/a	38	21,610	n/a	n/a	4.3	8.2
1996	n/a	n/a	27	19,650	n/a	n/a	3.1	7.4

Notes: (1) Metropolitan Statistical Area - see Appendix A for areas included; (2) calculated by the editors using the following formula: (number of crimes in the MSA minus number of crimes in the city); (3) calculated by the editors using the following formula: ((number of crimes in the MSA minus number of crimes in the city) ÷ (population of the MSA minus population of the city)) x 100,000; n/a not avail.
Source: U.S. Department of Justice, FBI Uniform Crime Reports, 1977 - 1996

Forcible Rapes and Forcible Rape Rates: 1977 - 1996

Year	Number				Rate per 100,000 population			
	City	Suburbs[2]	MSA[1]	U.S.	City	Suburbs[3]	MSA[1]	U.S.
1977	n/a	n/a	176	63,500	n/a	n/a	24.4	29.4
1978	n/a	n/a	187	67,610	n/a	n/a	25.8	31.0
1979	n/a	n/a	223	76,390	n/a	n/a	30.4	34.7
1980	n/a	n/a	264	82,990	n/a	n/a	34.6	36.8
1981	n/a	n/a	265	82,500	n/a	n/a	34.3	36.0
1982	n/a	n/a	269	78,770	n/a	n/a	34.3	34.0
1983	n/a	n/a	249	78,920	n/a	n/a	30.8	33.7
1984	n/a	n/a	255	84,230	n/a	n/a	31.5	35.7
1985	n/a	n/a	248	88,670	n/a	n/a	30.4	37.1
1986	n/a	n/a	241	91,460	n/a	n/a	29.3	37.9
1987	n/a	n/a	322	91,110	n/a	n/a	38.7	37.4
1988	n/a	n/a	283	92,490	n/a	n/a	33.7	37.6
1989	n/a	n/a	412	94,500	n/a	n/a	48.5	38.1
1990	n/a	n/a	278	102,560	n/a	n/a	33.2	41.2
1991	n/a	n/a	275	106,590	n/a	n/a	32.1	42.3
1992	n/a	n/a	326	109,060	n/a	n/a	37.2	42.8
1993	n/a	n/a	286	106,010	n/a	n/a	32.7	41.1
1994	n/a	n/a	266	102,220	n/a	n/a	30.2	39.3
1995	n/a	n/a	217	97,470	n/a	n/a	24.7	37.1
1996	n/a	n/a	222	95,770	n/a	n/a	25.3	36.1

Notes: (1) Metropolitan Statistical Area - see Appendix A for areas included; (2) calculated by the editors using the following formula: (number of crimes in the MSA minus number of crimes in the city); (3) calculated by the editors using the following formula: ((number of crimes in the MSA minus number of crimes in the city) ÷ (population of the MSA minus population of the city)) x 100,000; n/a not avail.
Source: U.S. Department of Justice, FBI Uniform Crime Reports, 1977 - 1996

Robberies and Robbery Rates: 1977 - 1996

Year	Number				Rate per 100,000 population			
	City	Suburbs[2]	MSA[1]	U.S.	City	Suburbs[3]	MSA[1]	U.S.
1977	n/a	n/a	1,081	412,610	n/a	n/a	149.7	190.7
1978	n/a	n/a	1,473	426,930	n/a	n/a	203.1	195.8
1979	n/a	n/a	1,568	480,700	n/a	n/a	213.5	218.4
1980	n/a	n/a	1,729	565,840	n/a	n/a	226.9	251.1
1981	n/a	n/a	1,320	592,910	n/a	n/a	170.7	258.7
1982	n/a	n/a	1,457	553,130	n/a	n/a	185.6	238.9
1983	n/a	n/a	1,243	506,570	n/a	n/a	153.8	216.5
1984	n/a	n/a	1,117	485,010	n/a	n/a	137.8	205.4
1985	n/a	n/a	965	497,870	n/a	n/a	118.1	208.5
1986	n/a	n/a	1,052	542,780	n/a	n/a	127.8	225.1
1987	n/a	n/a	985	517,700	n/a	n/a	118.3	212.7
1988	n/a	n/a	833	542,970	n/a	n/a	99.3	220.9
1989	n/a	n/a	815	578,330	n/a	n/a	96.0	233.0
1990	n/a	n/a	889	639,270	n/a	n/a	106.3	257.0
1991	n/a	n/a	860	687,730	n/a	n/a	100.4	272.7
1992	n/a	n/a	1,013	672,480	n/a	n/a	115.7	263.6
1993	n/a	n/a	1,085	659,870	n/a	n/a	123.9	255.9
1994	n/a	n/a	1,058	618,950	n/a	n/a	120.1	237.7
1995	n/a	n/a	1,371	580,510	n/a	n/a	155.7	220.9
1996	n/a	n/a	1,421	537,050	n/a	n/a	161.8	202.4

Notes: (1) Metropolitan Statistical Area - see Appendix A for areas included; (2) calculated by the editors using the following formula: (number of crimes in the MSA minus number of crimes in the city); (3) calculated by the editors using the following formula: ((number of crimes in the MSA minus number of crimes in the city) ÷ (population of the MSA minus population of the city)) x 100,000; n/a not avail.
Source: U.S. Department of Justice, FBI Uniform Crime Reports, 1977 - 1996

Aggravated Assaults and Aggravated Assault Rates: 1977 - 1996

Year	Number				Rate per 100,000 population			
	City	Suburbs[2]	MSA[1]	U.S.	City	Suburbs[3]	MSA[1]	U.S.
1977	n/a	n/a	357	534,350	n/a	n/a	49.4	247.0
1978	n/a	n/a	346	571,460	n/a	n/a	47.7	262.1
1979	n/a	n/a	357	629,480	n/a	n/a	48.6	286.0
1980	n/a	n/a	398	672,650	n/a	n/a	52.2	298.5
1981	n/a	n/a	340	663,900	n/a	n/a	44.0	289.7
1982	n/a	n/a	400	669,480	n/a	n/a	50.9	289.2
1983	n/a	n/a	599	653,290	n/a	n/a	74.1	279.2
1984	n/a	n/a	553	685,350	n/a	n/a	68.2	290.2
1985	n/a	n/a	552	723,250	n/a	n/a	67.6	302.9
1986	n/a	n/a	737	834,320	n/a	n/a	89.5	346.1
1987	n/a	n/a	915	855,090	n/a	n/a	109.9	351.3
1988	n/a	n/a	1,042	910,090	n/a	n/a	124.2	370.2
1989	n/a	n/a	1,027	951,710	n/a	n/a	121.0	383.4
1990	n/a	n/a	1,211	1,054,860	n/a	n/a	144.8	424.1
1991	n/a	n/a	894	1,092,740	n/a	n/a	104.4	433.3
1992	n/a	n/a	1,012	1,126,970	n/a	n/a	115.6	441.8
1993	n/a	n/a	1,099	1,135,610	n/a	n/a	125.5	440.3
1994	n/a	n/a	1,169	1,113,180	n/a	n/a	132.7	427.6
1995	n/a	n/a	1,256	1,099,210	n/a	n/a	142.7	418.3
1996	n/a	n/a	1,078	1,029,810	n/a	n/a	122.8	388.2

Notes: (1) Metropolitan Statistical Area - see Appendix A for areas included; (2) calculated by the editors using the following formula: (number of crimes in the MSA minus number of crimes in the city); (3) calculated by the editors using the following formula: ((number of crimes in the MSA minus number of crimes in the city) ÷ (population of the MSA minus population of the city)) x 100,000; n/a not avail.
Source: U.S. Department of Justice, FBI Uniform Crime Reports, 1977 - 1996

Burglaries and Burglary Rates: 1977 - 1996

Year	Number				Rate per 100,000 population			
	City	Suburbs[2]	MSA[1]	U.S.	City	Suburbs[3]	MSA[1]	U.S.
1977	n/a	n/a	13,291	3,071,500	n/a	n/a	1,840.9	1,419.8
1978	n/a	n/a	13,878	3,128,300	n/a	n/a	1,913.5	1,434.6
1979	n/a	n/a	12,803	3,327,700	n/a	n/a	1,743.4	1,511.9
1980	n/a	n/a	13,848	3,795,200	n/a	n/a	1,817.3	1,684.1
1981	n/a	n/a	12,576	3,779,700	n/a	n/a	1,626.2	1,649.5
1982	n/a	n/a	12,381	3,447,100	n/a	n/a	1,576.8	1,488.8
1983	n/a	n/a	10,044	3,129,900	n/a	n/a	1,242.9	1,337.7
1984	n/a	n/a	9,320	2,984,400	n/a	n/a	1,149.5	1,263.7
1985	n/a	n/a	8,989	3,073,300	n/a	n/a	1,100.1	1,287.3
1986	n/a	n/a	10,675	3,241,400	n/a	n/a	1,296.6	1,344.6
1987	n/a	n/a	9,136	3,236,200	n/a	n/a	1,097.3	1,329.6
1988	n/a	n/a	9,811	3,218,100	n/a	n/a	1,169.8	1,309.2
1989	n/a	n/a	10,685	3,168,200	n/a	n/a	1,258.6	1,276.3
1990	n/a	n/a	9,785	3,073,900	n/a	n/a	1,170.1	1,235.9
1991	n/a	n/a	9,905	3,157,200	n/a	n/a	1,156.5	1,252.0
1992	n/a	n/a	9,106	2,979,900	n/a	n/a	1,040.3	1,168.2
1993	n/a	n/a	9,296	2,834,800	n/a	n/a	1,061.8	1,099.2
1994	n/a	n/a	10,018	2,712,800	n/a	n/a	1,137.5	1,042.0
1995	n/a	n/a	10,127	2,593,800	n/a	n/a	1,150.4	987.1
1996	n/a	n/a	9,026	2,501,500	n/a	n/a	1,028.0	943.0

Notes: (1) Metropolitan Statistical Area - see Appendix A for areas included; (2) calculated by the editors using the following formula: (number of crimes in the MSA minus number of crimes in the city); (3) calculated by the editors using the following formula: ((number of crimes in the MSA minus number of crimes in the city) ÷ (population of the MSA minus population of the city)) x 100,000; n/a not avail.
Source: U.S. Department of Justice, FBI Uniform Crime Reports, 1977 - 1996

Larceny-Thefts and Larceny-Theft Rates: 1977 - 1996

Year	Number				Rate per 100,000 population			
	City	Suburbs[2]	MSA[1]	U.S.	City	Suburbs[3]	MSA[1]	U.S.
1977	n/a	n/a	28,286	5,905,700	n/a	n/a	3,917.8	2,729.9
1978	n/a	n/a	31,567	5,991,000	n/a	n/a	4,352.5	2,747.4
1979	n/a	n/a	32,166	6,601,000	n/a	n/a	4,380.1	2,999.1
1980	n/a	n/a	36,189	7,136,900	n/a	n/a	4,749.1	3,167.0
1981	n/a	n/a	31,362	7,194,400	n/a	n/a	4,055.4	3,139.7
1982	n/a	n/a	32,416	7,142,500	n/a	n/a	4,128.5	3,084.8
1983	n/a	n/a	30,195	6,712,800	n/a	n/a	3,736.6	2,868.9
1984	n/a	n/a	30,191	6,591,900	n/a	n/a	3,723.7	2,791.3
1985	n/a	n/a	28,837	6,926,400	n/a	n/a	3,529.3	2,901.2
1986	n/a	n/a	30,846	7,257,200	n/a	n/a	3,746.6	3,010.3
1987	n/a	n/a	34,239	7,499,900	n/a	n/a	4,112.2	3,081.3
1988	n/a	n/a	34,227	7,705,900	n/a	n/a	4,081.2	3,134.9
1989	n/a	n/a	36,325	7,872,400	n/a	n/a	4,278.8	3,171.3
1990	n/a	n/a	35,514	7,945,700	n/a	n/a	4,246.9	3,194.8
1991	n/a	n/a	36,019	8,142,200	n/a	n/a	4,205.7	3,228.8
1992	n/a	n/a	38,563	7,915,200	n/a	n/a	4,405.7	3,103.0
1993	n/a	n/a	40,148	7,820,900	n/a	n/a	4,586.0	3,032.4
1994	n/a	n/a	42,552	7,879,800	n/a	n/a	4,831.7	3,026.7
1995	n/a	n/a	46,696	7,997,700	n/a	n/a	5,304.8	3,043.8
1996	n/a	n/a	41,915	7,894,600	n/a	n/a	4,773.7	2,975.9

Notes: (1) Metropolitan Statistical Area - see Appendix A for areas included; (2) calculated by the editors using the following formula: (number of crimes in the MSA minus number of crimes in the city); (3) calculated by the editors using the following formula: ((number of crimes in the MSA minus number of crimes in the city) ÷ (population of the MSA minus population of the city)) x 100,000; n/a not avail.
Source: U.S. Department of Justice, FBI Uniform Crime Reports, 1977 - 1996

Motor Vehicle Thefts and Motor Vehicle Theft Rates: 1977 - 1996

Year	Number				Rate per 100,000 population			
	City	Suburbs[2]	MSA[1]	U.S.	City	Suburbs[3]	MSA[1]	U.S.
1977	n/a	n/a	3,747	977,700	n/a	n/a	519.0	451.9
1978	n/a	n/a	4,403	1,004,100	n/a	n/a	607.1	460.5
1979	n/a	n/a	5,761	1,112,800	n/a	n/a	784.5	505.6
1980	n/a	n/a	5,225	1,131,700	n/a	n/a	685.7	502.2
1981	n/a	n/a	3,645	1,087,800	n/a	n/a	471.3	474.7
1982	n/a	n/a	3,652	1,062,400	n/a	n/a	465.1	458.8
1983	n/a	n/a	3,853	1,007,900	n/a	n/a	476.8	430.8
1984	n/a	n/a	3,099	1,032,200	n/a	n/a	382.2	437.1
1985	n/a	n/a	2,421	1,102,900	n/a	n/a	296.3	462.0
1986	n/a	n/a	2,858	1,224,100	n/a	n/a	347.1	507.8
1987	n/a	n/a	3,316	1,288,700	n/a	n/a	398.3	529.4
1988	n/a	n/a	3,245	1,432,900	n/a	n/a	386.9	582.9
1989	n/a	n/a	3,602	1,564,800	n/a	n/a	424.3	630.4
1990	n/a	n/a	3,317	1,635,900	n/a	n/a	396.7	657.8
1991	n/a	n/a	3,050	1,661,700	n/a	n/a	356.1	659.0
1992	n/a	n/a	3,507	1,610,800	n/a	n/a	400.7	631.5
1993	n/a	n/a	4,460	1,563,100	n/a	n/a	509.4	606.1
1994	n/a	n/a	5,727	1,539,300	n/a	n/a	650.3	591.3
1995	n/a	n/a	7,440	1,472,400	n/a	n/a	845.2	560.4
1996	n/a	n/a	6,370	1,395,200	n/a	n/a	725.5	525.9

Notes: (1) Metropolitan Statistical Area - see Appendix A for areas included; (2) calculated by the editors using the following formula: (number of crimes in the MSA minus number of crimes in the city); (3) calculated by the editors using the following formula: ((number of crimes in the MSA minus number of crimes in the city) ÷ (population of the MSA minus population of the city)) x 100,000; n/a not avail.
Source: U.S. Department of Justice, FBI Uniform Crime Reports, 1977 - 1996

HATE CRIMES

Criminal Incidents by Bias Motivation

Area	Race	Ethnicity	Religion	Sexual Orientation
Honolulu	n/a	n/a	n/a	n/a

Notes: Figures include both violent and property crimes. Law enforcement agencies must have submitted data for at least one quarter of calendar year 1995 to be included in this report, therefore figures shown may not represent complete 12-month totals; n/a not available
Source: U.S. Department of Justice, FBI Uniform Crime Reports, Hate Crime Statistics 1995

LAW ENFORCEMENT

Full-Time Law Enforcement Employees

Jurisdiction	Police Employees			Police Officers per 100,000 population
	Total	Officers	Civilians	
Honolulu	2,251	1,815	436	206.7

Notes: Data as of October 31, 1996
Source: U.S. Department of Justice, FBI Uniform Crime Reports, 1996

Number of Police Officers by Race

Race	Police Officers				Index of Representation[1]		
	1983		1992				
	Number	Pct.	Number	Pct.	1983	1992	% Chg.
Black	11	0.7	28	1.5	0.58	1.07	84.5
Hispanic[2]	4	0.3	30	1.6	0.04	0.35	775.0

Notes: (1) The index of representation is calculated by dividing the percent of black/hispanic police officers by the percent of corresponding blacks/hispanics in the local population. An index approaching 1.0 indicates that a city is closer to achieving a representation of police officers equal to their proportion in the local population; (2) Hispanic officers can be of any race
Source: Bureau of Justice Statistics, Sourcebook of Criminal Justice Statistics, 1994

CORRECTIONS

Federal Correctional Facilities

Type	Year Opened	Security Level	Sex of Inmates	Rated Capacity	Population on 7/1/95	Number of Staff
None listed						

Notes: Data as of 1995
Source: Bureau of Justice Statistics, Sourcebook of Criminal Justice Statistics Online

City/County/Regional Correctional Facilities

Name	Year Opened	Year Renov.	Rated Capacity	1995 Pop.	Number of COs[1]	Number of Staff	ACA[2] Accred.
Oahu Community Corr Ctr	1918	--	803	814	n/a	n/a	No

Notes: Data as of April 1996; (1) Correctional Officers; (2) American Correctional Assn. Accreditation
Source: American Correctional Association, 1996-1998 National Jail and Adult Detention Directory

Private Adult Correctional Facilities

Name	Date Opened	Rated Capacity	Present Pop.	Security Level	Facility Construct.	Expans. Plans	ACA[1] Accred.
None listed							

Notes: Data as of December 1996; (1) American Correctional Association Accreditation
Source: University of Florida, Center for Studies in Criminology and Law, Private Adult Correctional Facility Census, 10th Ed., March 15, 1997

Characteristics of Shock Incarceration Programs

Jurisdiction	Year Program Began	Number of Camps	Average Num. of Inmates	Number of Beds	Program Length	Voluntary/ Mandatory
Hawaii did not have a shock incarceration program as of July 1996						

Source: Sourcebook of Criminal Justice Statistics Online

DEATH PENALTY

Hawaii did not have the death penalty as of July 31, 1997.
Source: Death Penalty Information Center Web Site, 9/30/97

LAWS

Statutory Provisions Relating to the Purchase, Ownership and Use of Handguns

Jurisdiction	Instant Background Check	Federal Waiting Period Applies[1]	State Waiting Period (days)	License or Permit to Purchase	Regis-tration	Record of Sale Sent to Police	Concealed Carry Law
Hawaii	No	No	No	Yes[a]	Yes[b]	Yes	Yes[c]

Note: Data as of 1996; (1) The Federal 5-day waiting period for handgun purchases applies to states that don't have instant background checks, waiting period requirements, or licensing procedures exempting them from the Federal requirement; (a) Purchase permits, required for all firearms, may not be issued until 14 days after application. A handgun purchase permit is valid for 10 days, for one handgun; (b) Every person arriving in Hawaii is required to register any firearm(s) brought into the State within 3 days of arrival of the person or firearm(s), whichever occurs later. Handguns purchased from licensed dealers must be registered within 5 days; (c) Restrictively administered discretion by local authorities over permit issuance, or permits are unavailable and carrying is prohibited in most circumstances
Source: Sourcebook of Criminal Justice Statistics Online

Statutory Provisions Relating to Alcohol Use and Driving

Jurisdiction	Drinking Age	Blood Alcohol Concentration Levels as Evidence in State Courts[1]		Open Container Law[1]	Anti-Consump-tion Law[1]	Dram Shop Law[1]
		Illegal per se at 0.10%	Presumption at 0.10%			
Hawaii	21	(a)	(a,b)	Yes	Yes	(c)

Note: Data as of January 1, 1997; (1) See Appendix C for an explanation of terms; (a) 0.08%; (b) Competent evidence of driving while intoxicated; (c) Adopted via case law decisions
Source: Sourcebook of Criminal Justice Statistics Online

Statutory Provisions Relating to Curfews

Jurisdiction	Year Enacted	Latest Revision	Age Group(s)	Curfew Provisions
Honolulu	1896	1980	15 and under	10 pm to 4 am every night

Note: Data as of February 1996
Source: Sourcebook of Criminal Justice Statistics Online

Statutory Provisions Relating to Hate Crimes

Jurisdiction	Bias-Motivated Violence and Intimidation							Institutional Vandalism
	Civil Action	Criminal Penalty						
		Race/ Religion/ Ethnicity	Sexual Orientation	Mental/ Physical Disability	Gender	Age		
Hawaii	No	No	No	No	No	No		Yes

Source: Anti-Defamation League, 1997 Hate Crimes Laws

Houston, Texas

OVERVIEW

The total crime rate for the city increased 1.2% between 1977 and 1996. During that same period, the violent crime rate increased 111.8% and the property crime rate decreased 8.3%.

Among violent crimes, the rates for: Murders decreased 39.3%; Forcible Rapes decreased 9.0%; Robberies increased 18.0%; and Aggravated Assaults increased 526.2%.

Among property crimes, the rates for: Burglaries decreased 33.3%; Larceny-Thefts decreased 6.1%; and Motor Vehicle Thefts increased 43.1%.

ANTI-CRIME PROGRAMS

The city instituted two programs which the National League of Cities (1993) considers among those which are innovative for combatting crime and violence:

- 655 Program—in which tax money was redirected from street repair funds to the Police Department to hire 655 additional officers. Crime has decreased and response time has increased as a result.
- Parolee Analysis/Apprehension Program—parole violators were identified and tracked. A 10-day "Sweep Week" was instituted and netted a large number of violators including more than 60% who had been designated as violent offenders. The program has been useful in combatting the Harris County area's reputation as a "free zone" for parolees.
Exemplary Programs in Criminal Justice, National League of Cities, 1994

CRIME RISK

Your Chances of Becoming a Victim[1]

Area	Any Crime	Violent Crime					Property Crime			
		Any	Murder	Forcible Rape[2]	Robbery	Aggrav. Assault	Any	Burglary	Larceny -Theft	Motor Vehicle Theft
City	1:13	1:79	1:6,790	1:892	1:214	1:137	1:16	1:70	1:27	1:79

Note: (1) Figures have been calculated by dividing the population of the city by the number of crimes reported to the FBI during 1996 and are expressed as odds (eg. 1:20 should be read as 1 in 20). (2) Figures have been calculated by dividing the female population of the city by the number of forcible rapes reported to the FBI during 1996. The female population of the city was estimated by calculating the ratio of females to males reported in the 1990 Census and applying that ratio to 1996 population estimate.
Source: FBI Uniform Crime Reports 1996

CRIME STATISTICS

Total Crimes and Total Crime Rates: 1977 - 1996

Year	Number				Rate per 100,000 population			
	City	Suburbs[2]	MSA[1]	U.S.	City	Suburbs[3]	MSA[1]	U.S.
1977	117,288	45,688	162,976	10,984,500	7,542.6	3,975.7	6,026.8	5,077.6
1978	132,000	46,793	178,793	11,209,000	8,391.6	5,165.4	7,212.6	5,140.3
1979	141,748	51,390	193,138	12,249,500	8,751.8	4,895.2	7,235.1	5,565.5
1980	143,926	55,567	199,493	13,408,300	8,886.3	4,370.2	6,900.1	5,950.0
1981	n/a	n/a	n/a	13,423,800	n/a	n/a	n/a	5,858.2
1982	166,063	71,278	237,341	12,974,400	9,887.0	4,956.6	7,612.8	5,603.6
1983	151,566	62,963	214,529	12,108,600	8,767.2	4,865.0	7,096.6	5,175.0
1984	149,199	69,611	218,810	11,881,800	8,262.3	4,953.2	6,814.0	5,031.3
1985	155,910	74,304	230,214	12,431,400	8,927.6	4,976.2	7,106.3	5,207.1
1986	168,150	81,165	249,315	13,211,900	9,448.3	5,333.7	7,551.8	5,480.4
1987	163,428	85,211	248,639	13,508,700	9,392.4	5,634.8	7,645.2	5,550.0
1988	177,912	89,896	267,808	13,923,100	10,311.2	5,986.3	8,298.7	5,664.2
1989	185,334	92,169	277,503	14,251,400	10,816.1	5,897.8	8,470.1	5,741.0
1990	184,869	95,623	280,492	14,475,600	11,337.8	5,721.2	8,494.8	5,820.3
1991	180,308	95,878	276,186	14,872,900	10,824.4	5,616.7	8,188.7	5,897.8
1992	148,284	91,667	239,951	14,438,200	8,747.1	5,213.0	6,947.7	5,660.2
1993	n/a	n/a	n/a	14,144,800	n/a	n/a	n/a	5,484.4
1994	128,079	79,087	207,166	13,989,500	7,285.4	4,135.2	5,644.0	5,373.5
1995	131,602	78,062	209,664	13,862,700	7,588.0	3,928.3	5,633.8	5,275.9
1996	135,329	83,715	219,044	13,473,600	7,636.5	4,123.8	5,761.0	5,078.9

Notes: (1) Metropolitan Statistical Area - see Appendix A for areas included; (2) calculated by the editors using the following formula: (number of crimes in the MSA minus number of crimes in the city); (3) calculated by the editors using the following formula: ((number of crimes in the MSA minus number of crimes in the city) ÷ (population of the MSA minus population of the city)) x 100,000; n/a not avail.
Source: U.S. Department of Justice, FBI Uniform Crime Reports, 1977 - 1996

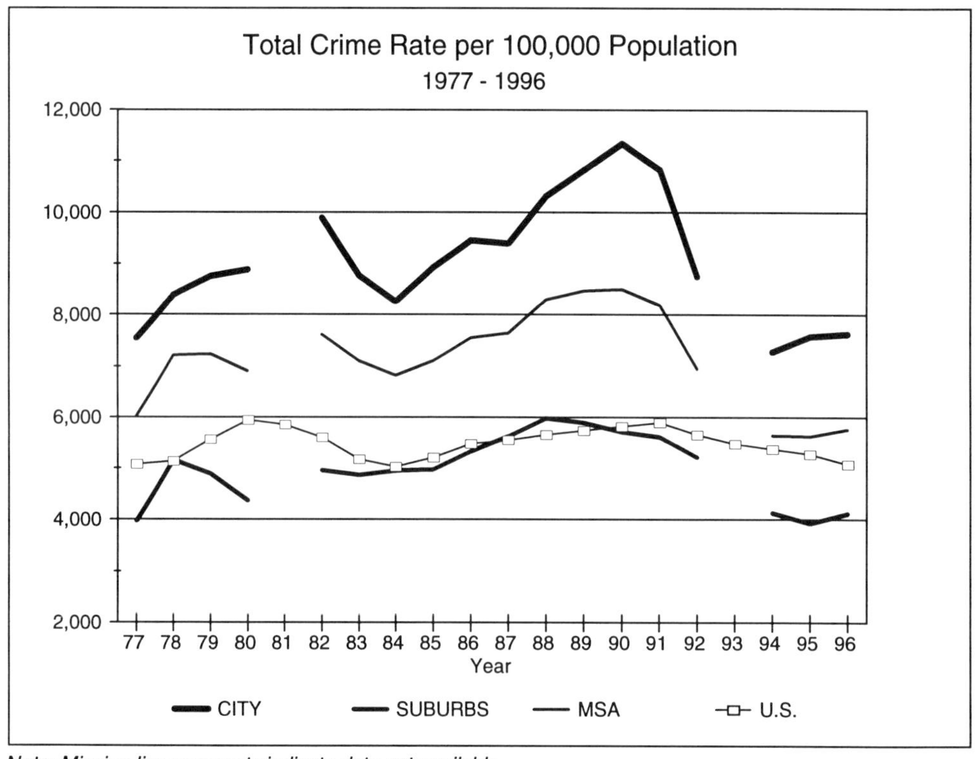

Note: Missing line segments indicate data not available.

Violent Crimes and Violent Crime Rates: 1977 - 1996

Year	Number				Rate per 100,000 population			
	City	Suburbs[2]	MSA[1]	U.S.	City	Suburbs[3]	MSA[1]	U.S.
1977	9,304	3,377	12,681	1,029,580	598.3	293.9	468.9	475.9
1978	10,852	3,288	14,140	1,085,550	689.9	363.0	570.4	497.8
1979	14,216	3,763	17,979	1,208,030	877.7	358.4	673.5	548.9
1980	15,787	4,995	20,782	1,344,520	974.7	392.8	718.8	596.6
1981	n/a	n/a	n/a	1,361,820	n/a	n/a	n/a	594.3
1982	17,801	5,990	23,791	1,322,390	1,059.8	416.5	763.1	571.1
1983	15,919	5,004	20,923	1,258,090	920.8	386.6	692.1	537.7
1984	15,155	4,984	20,139	1,273,280	839.2	354.6	627.2	539.2
1985	16,461	5,413	21,874	1,328,800	942.6	362.5	675.2	556.6
1986	20,576	6,029	26,605	1,489,170	1,156.2	396.2	805.9	617.7
1987	18,971	5,891	24,862	1,484,000	1,090.3	389.6	764.5	609.7
1988	19,817	6,444	26,261	1,566,220	1,148.5	429.1	813.8	637.2
1989	19,528	6,716	26,244	1,646,040	1,139.7	429.8	801.0	663.1
1990	22,637	8,415	31,052	1,820,130	1,388.3	503.5	940.4	731.8
1991	26,651	9,661	36,312	1,911,770	1,599.9	566.0	1,076.6	758.1
1992	24,837	10,115	34,952	1,932,270	1,465.1	575.2	1,012.0	757.5
1993	n/a	n/a	n/a	1,926,020	n/a	n/a	n/a	746.8
1994	22,986	9,232	32,218	1,857,670	1,307.5	482.7	877.7	713.6
1995	22,260	9,601	31,861	1,798,790	1,283.5	483.1	856.1	684.6
1996	22,456	10,203	32,659	1,682,280	1,267.2	502.6	859.0	634.1

Notes: Violent crimes include murder, forcible rape, robbery and aggravated assault; n/a not available; (1) Metropolitan Statistical Area - see Appendix A for areas included; (2) calculated by the editors using the following formula: (number of crimes in the MSA minus number of crimes in the city); (3) calculated by the editors using the following formula: ((number of crimes in the MSA minus number of crimes in the city) ÷ (population of the MSA minus population of the city)) x 100,000
Source: U.S. Department of Justice, FBI Uniform Crime Reports, 1977 - 1996

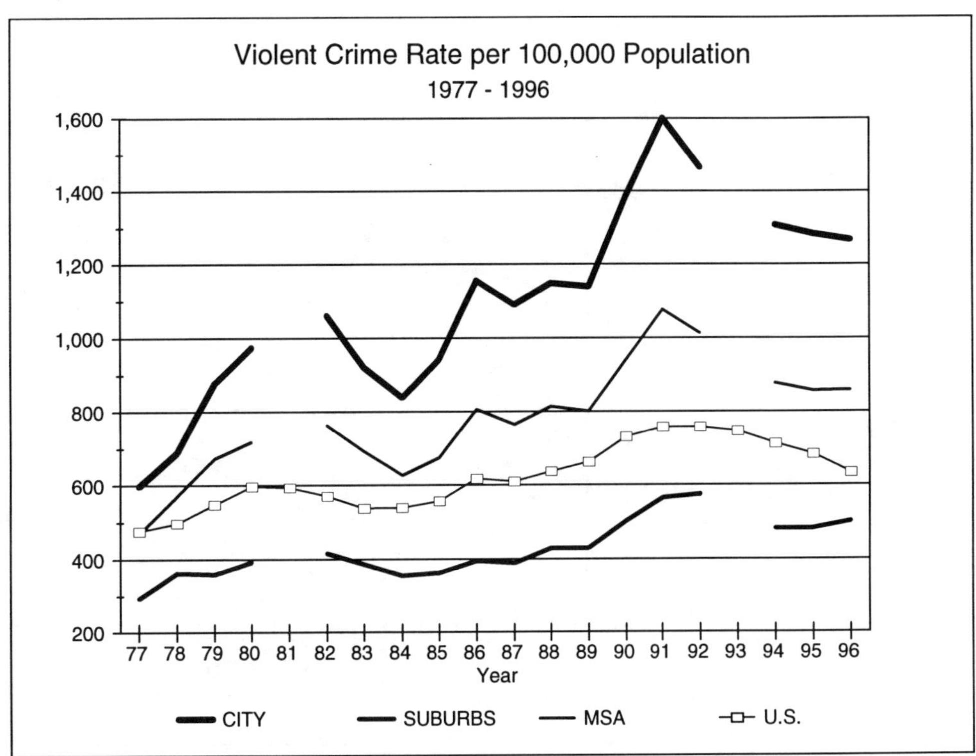

Note: Missing line segments indicate data not available.

Property Crimes and Property Crime Rates: 1977 - 1996

Year	Number				Rate per 100,000 population			
	City	Suburbs[2]	MSA[1]	U.S.	City	Suburbs[3]	MSA[1]	U.S.
1977	107,984	42,311	150,295	9,955,000	6,944.3	3,681.8	5,557.9	4,601.7
1978	121,148	43,505	164,653	10,123,400	7,701.7	4,802.4	6,642.2	4,642.5
1979	127,532	47,627	175,159	11,041,500	7,874.1	4,536.8	6,561.6	5,016.6
1980	128,139	50,572	178,711	12,063,700	7,911.6	3,977.3	6,181.3	5,353.3
1981	n/a	n/a	n/a	12,061,900	n/a	n/a	n/a	5,263.9
1982	148,262	65,288	213,550	11,652,000	8,827.2	4,540.0	6,849.7	5,032.5
1983	135,647	57,959	193,606	10,850,500	7,846.4	4,478.3	6,404.4	4,637.4
1984	134,044	64,627	198,671	10,608,500	7,423.0	4,598.5	6,186.9	4,492.1
1985	139,449	68,891	208,340	11,102,600	7,985.1	4,613.7	6,431.1	4,650.5
1986	147,574	75,136	222,710	11,722,700	8,292.2	4,937.5	6,745.9	4,862.6
1987	144,457	79,320	223,777	12,024,700	8,302.1	5,245.3	6,880.7	4,940.3
1988	158,095	83,452	241,547	12,356,900	9,162.7	5,557.2	7,484.9	5,027.1
1989	165,806	85,453	251,259	12,605,400	9,676.5	5,468.1	7,669.1	5,077.9
1990	162,232	87,208	249,440	12,655,500	9,949.5	5,217.7	7,554.4	5,088.5
1991	153,657	86,217	239,874	12,961,100	9,224.5	5,050.7	7,112.0	5,139.7
1992	123,447	81,552	204,999	12,505,900	7,282.0	4,637.8	5,935.7	4,902.7
1993	116,110	76,063	192,173	12,218,800	6,733.6	4,053.6	5,337.0	4,737.6
1994	105,093	69,855	174,948	12,131,900	5,977.9	3,652.5	4,766.3	4,660.0
1995	109,342	68,461	177,803	12,063,900	6,304.5	3,445.1	4,777.7	4,591.3
1996	112,873	73,512	186,385	11,791,300	6,369.3	3,621.2	4,902.1	4,444.8

Notes: Property crimes include burglary, larceny-theft and motor vehicle theft; n/a not available; (1) Metropolitan Statistical Area - see Appendix A for areas included; (2) calculated by the editors using the following formula: (number of crimes in the MSA minus number of crimes in the city); (3) calculated by the editors using the following formula: ((number of crimes in the MSA minus number of crimes in the city) ÷ (population of the MSA minus population of the city)) x 100,000
Source: U.S. Department of Justice, FBI Uniform Crime Reports, 1977 - 1996

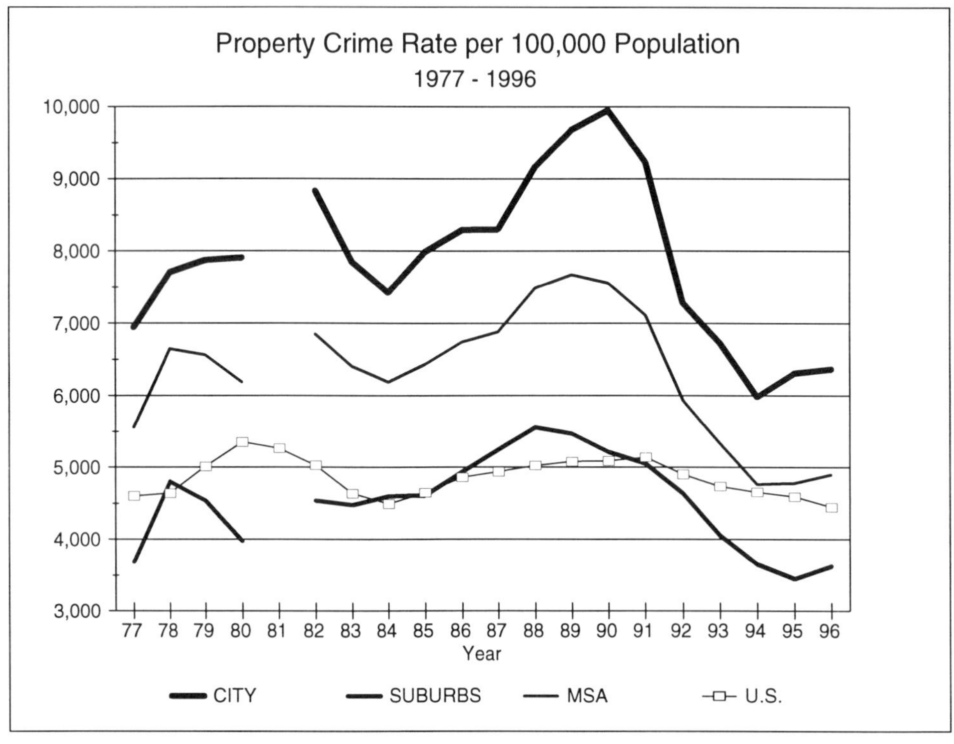

Note: Missing line segments indicate data not available.

Murders and Murder Rates: 1977 - 1996

Year	Number				Rate per 100,000 population			
	City	Suburbs[2]	MSA[1]	U.S.	City	Suburbs[3]	MSA[1]	U.S.
1977	376	112	488	19,120	24.2	9.7	18.0	8.8
1978	484	98	582	19,560	30.8	10.8	23.5	9.0
1979	654	147	801	21,460	40.4	14.0	30.0	9.7
1980	633	166	799	23,040	39.1	13.1	27.6	10.2
1981	n/a	n/a	n/a	22,520	n/a	n/a	n/a	9.8
1982	678	201	879	21,010	40.4	14.0	28.2	9.1
1983	561	158	719	19,310	32.5	12.2	23.8	8.3
1984	473	136	609	18,690	26.2	9.7	19.0	7.9
1985	457	135	592	18,980	26.2	9.0	18.3	7.9
1986	408	117	525	20,610	22.9	7.7	15.9	8.6
1987	323	127	450	20,100	18.6	8.4	13.8	8.3
1988	440	124	564	20,680	25.5	8.3	17.5	8.4
1989	459	110	569	21,500	26.8	7.0	17.4	8.7
1990	568	129	697	23,440	34.8	7.7	21.1	9.4
1991	608	164	772	24,700	36.5	9.6	22.9	9.8
1992	465	142	607	23,760	27.4	8.1	17.6	9.3
1993	446	125	571	24,530	25.9	6.7	15.9	9.5
1994	375	128	503	23,330	21.3	6.7	13.7	9.0
1995	316	130	446	21,610	18.2	6.5	12.0	8.2
1996	261	112	373	19,650	14.7	5.5	9.8	7.4

Notes: (1) Metropolitan Statistical Area - see Appendix A for areas included; (2) calculated by the editors using the following formula: (number of crimes in the MSA minus number of crimes in the city); (3) calculated by the editors using the following formula: ((number of crimes in the MSA minus number of crimes in the city) ÷ (population of the MSA minus population of the city)) x 100,000; n/a not avail.
Source: U.S. Department of Justice, FBI Uniform Crime Reports, 1977 - 1996

Forcible Rapes and Forcible Rape Rates: 1977 - 1996

Year	Number				Rate per 100,000 population			
	City	Suburbs[2]	MSA[1]	U.S.	City	Suburbs[3]	MSA[1]	U.S.
1977	965	276	1,241	63,500	62.1	24.0	45.9	29.4
1978	1,098	335	1,433	67,610	69.8	37.0	57.8	31.0
1979	1,481	342	1,823	76,390	91.4	32.6	68.3	34.7
1980	1,439	465	1,904	82,990	88.8	36.6	65.9	36.8
1981	n/a	n/a	n/a	82,500	n/a	n/a	n/a	36.0
1982	1,270	498	1,768	78,770	75.6	34.6	56.7	34.0
1983	1,179	431	1,610	78,920	68.2	33.3	53.3	33.7
1984	1,269	553	1,822	84,230	70.3	39.3	56.7	35.7
1985	1,711	459	2,170	88,670	98.0	30.7	67.0	37.1
1986	1,524	499	2,023	91,460	85.6	32.8	61.3	37.9
1987	1,172	480	1,652	91,110	67.4	31.7	50.8	37.4
1988	1,206	466	1,672	92,490	69.9	31.0	51.8	37.6
1989	1,152	424	1,576	94,500	67.2	27.1	48.1	38.1
1990	1,335	513	1,848	102,560	81.9	30.7	56.0	41.2
1991	1,213	673	1,886	106,590	72.8	39.4	55.9	42.3
1992	1,169	822	1,991	109,060	69.0	46.7	57.6	42.8
1993	1,109	1,346	2,455	106,010	64.3	71.7	68.2	41.1
1994	931	1,023	1,954	102,220	53.0	53.5	53.2	39.3
1995	837	725	1,562	97,470	48.3	36.5	42.0	37.1
1996	1,002	706	1,708	95,770	56.5	34.8	44.9	36.1

Notes: (1) Metropolitan Statistical Area - see Appendix A for areas included; (2) calculated by the editors using the following formula: (number of crimes in the MSA minus number of crimes in the city); (3) calculated by the editors using the following formula: ((number of crimes in the MSA minus number of crimes in the city) ÷ (population of the MSA minus population of the city)) x 100,000; n/a not avail.
Source: U.S. Department of Justice, FBI Uniform Crime Reports, 1977 - 1996

Robberies and Robbery Rates: 1977 - 1996

Year	Number				Rate per 100,000 population			
	City	Suburbs[2]	MSA[1]	U.S.	City	Suburbs[3]	MSA[1]	U.S.
1977	6,153	1,105	7,258	412,610	395.7	96.2	268.4	190.7
1978	7,352	991	8,343	426,930	467.4	109.4	336.6	195.8
1979	9,311	1,217	10,528	480,700	574.9	115.9	394.4	218.4
1980	10,864	1,479	12,343	565,840	670.8	116.3	426.9	251.1
1981	n/a	n/a	n/a	592,910	n/a	n/a	n/a	258.7
1982	12,392	2,021	14,413	553,130	737.8	140.5	462.3	238.9
1983	10,270	1,642	11,912	506,570	594.1	126.9	394.0	216.5
1984	9,157	1,642	10,799	485,010	507.1	116.8	336.3	205.4
1985	9,589	1,814	11,403	497,870	549.1	121.5	352.0	208.5
1986	10,926	2,012	12,938	542,780	613.9	132.2	391.9	225.1
1987	9,692	1,805	11,497	517,700	557.0	119.4	353.5	212.7
1988	10,049	2,078	12,127	542,970	582.4	138.4	375.8	220.9
1989	9,820	1,988	11,808	578,330	573.1	127.2	360.4	233.0
1990	12,921	2,602	15,523	639,270	792.4	155.7	470.1	257.0
1991	13,883	3,022	16,905	687,730	833.4	177.0	501.2	272.7
1992	11,130	2,666	13,796	672,480	656.5	151.6	399.5	263.6
1993	n/a	n/a	n/a	659,870	n/a	n/a	n/a	255.9
1994	9,981	2,175	12,156	618,950	567.7	113.7	331.2	237.7
1995	9,222	2,241	11,463	580,510	531.7	112.8	308.0	220.9
1996	8,276	2,233	10,509	537,050	467.0	110.0	276.4	202.4

Notes: (1) Metropolitan Statistical Area - see Appendix A for areas included; (2) calculated by the editors using the following formula: (number of crimes in the MSA minus number of crimes in the city); (3) calculated by the editors using the following formula: ((number of crimes in the MSA minus number of crimes in the city) ÷ (population of the MSA minus population of the city)) x 100,000; n/a not avail.
Source: U.S. Department of Justice, FBI Uniform Crime Reports, 1977 - 1996

Aggravated Assaults and Aggravated Assault Rates: 1977 - 1996

Year	Number				Rate per 100,000 population			
	City	Suburbs[2]	MSA[1]	U.S.	City	Suburbs[3]	MSA[1]	U.S.
1977	1,810	1,884	3,694	534,350	116.4	163.9	136.6	247.0
1978	1,918	1,864	3,782	571,460	121.9	205.8	152.6	262.1
1979	2,770	2,057	4,827	629,480	171.0	195.9	180.8	286.0
1980	2,851	2,885	5,736	672,650	176.0	226.9	198.4	298.5
1981	n/a	n/a	n/a	663,900	n/a	n/a	n/a	289.7
1982	3,461	3,270	6,731	669,480	206.1	227.4	215.9	289.2
1983	3,909	2,773	6,682	653,290	226.1	214.3	221.0	279.2
1984	4,256	2,653	6,909	685,350	235.7	188.8	215.2	290.2
1985	4,704	3,005	7,709	723,250	269.4	201.2	238.0	302.9
1986	7,718	3,401	11,119	834,320	433.7	223.5	336.8	346.1
1987	7,784	3,479	11,263	855,090	447.4	230.1	346.3	351.3
1988	8,122	3,776	11,898	910,090	470.7	251.4	368.7	370.2
1989	8,097	4,194	12,291	951,710	472.5	268.4	375.2	383.4
1990	7,813	5,171	12,984	1,054,860	479.2	309.4	393.2	424.1
1991	10,947	5,802	16,749	1,092,740	657.2	339.9	496.6	433.3
1992	12,073	6,485	18,558	1,126,970	712.2	368.8	537.3	441.8
1993	n/a	n/a	n/a	1,135,610	n/a	n/a	n/a	440.3
1994	11,699	5,906	17,605	1,113,180	665.5	308.8	479.6	427.6
1995	11,885	6,505	18,390	1,099,210	685.3	327.3	494.2	418.3
1996	12,917	7,152	20,069	1,029,810	728.9	352.3	527.8	388.2

Notes: (1) Metropolitan Statistical Area - see Appendix A for areas included; (2) calculated by the editors using the following formula: (number of crimes in the MSA minus number of crimes in the city); (3) calculated by the editors using the following formula: ((number of crimes in the MSA minus number of crimes in the city) ÷ (population of the MSA minus population of the city)) x 100,000; n/a not avail.
Source: U.S. Department of Justice, FBI Uniform Crime Reports, 1977 - 1996

Burglaries and Burglary Rates: 1977 - 1996

Year	Number				Rate per 100,000 population			
	City	Suburbs[2]	MSA[1]	U.S.	City	Suburbs[3]	MSA[1]	U.S.
1977	33,419	13,547	46,966	3,071,500	2,149.1	1,178.8	1,736.8	1,419.8
1978	37,894	13,469	51,363	3,128,300	2,409.0	1,486.8	2,072.0	1,434.6
1979	48,952	16,450	65,402	3,327,700	3,022.4	1,567.0	2,450.0	1,511.9
1980	49,280	17,779	67,059	3,795,200	3,042.6	1,398.3	2,319.5	1,684.1
1981	n/a	n/a	n/a	3,779,700	n/a	n/a	n/a	1,649.5
1982	53,305	23,556	76,861	3,447,100	3,173.7	1,638.1	2,465.3	1,488.8
1983	41,613	19,129	60,742	3,129,900	2,407.1	1,478.0	2,009.3	1,337.7
1984	38,201	20,520	58,721	2,984,400	2,115.5	1,460.1	1,828.7	1,263.7
1985	40,207	21,486	61,693	3,073,300	2,302.3	1,438.9	1,904.4	1,287.3
1986	44,530	25,293	69,823	3,241,400	2,502.1	1,662.1	2,114.9	1,344.6
1987	44,601	25,873	70,474	3,236,200	2,563.3	1,710.9	2,166.9	1,329.6
1988	50,178	27,621	77,799	3,218,100	2,908.2	1,839.3	2,410.8	1,309.2
1989	47,043	25,176	72,219	3,168,200	2,745.4	1,611.0	2,204.3	1,276.3
1990	42,986	24,323	67,309	3,073,900	2,636.3	1,455.3	2,038.5	1,235.9
1991	39,726	23,967	63,693	3,157,200	2,384.9	1,404.0	1,888.4	1,252.0
1992	30,207	20,916	51,123	2,979,900	1,781.9	1,189.5	1,480.2	1,168.2
1993	27,022	18,353	45,375	2,834,800	1,567.1	978.1	1,260.1	1,099.2
1994	25,518	18,045	43,563	2,712,800	1,451.5	943.5	1,186.8	1,042.0
1995	24,830	17,131	41,961	2,593,800	1,431.7	862.1	1,127.5	987.1
1996	25,402	17,934	43,336	2,501,500	1,433.4	883.4	1,139.8	943.0

Notes: (1) Metropolitan Statistical Area - see Appendix A for areas included; (2) calculated by the editors using the following formula: (number of crimes in the MSA minus number of crimes in the city); (3) calculated by the editors using the following formula: ((number of crimes in the MSA minus number of crimes in the city) ÷ (population of the MSA minus population of the city)) x 100,000; n/a not avail.
Source: U.S. Department of Justice, FBI Uniform Crime Reports, 1977 - 1996

Larceny-Thefts and Larceny-Theft Rates: 1977 - 1996

Year	Number				Rate per 100,000 population			
	City	Suburbs[2]	MSA[1]	U.S.	City	Suburbs[3]	MSA[1]	U.S.
1977	60,839	23,887	84,726	5,905,700	3,912.5	2,078.6	3,133.1	2,729.9
1978	65,834	24,771	90,605	5,991,000	4,185.3	2,734.4	3,655.0	2,747.4
1979	54,008	25,197	79,205	6,601,000	3,334.6	2,400.2	2,967.1	2,999.1
1980	50,719	25,971	76,690	7,136,900	3,131.5	2,042.5	2,652.6	3,167.0
1981	n/a	n/a	n/a	7,194,400	n/a	n/a	n/a	3,139.7
1982	61,747	33,225	94,972	7,142,500	3,676.3	2,310.4	3,046.3	3,084.8
1983	63,235	31,126	94,361	6,712,800	3,657.8	2,405.0	3,121.4	2,868.9
1984	67,038	35,802	102,840	6,591,900	3,712.4	2,547.5	3,202.6	2,791.3
1985	67,496	38,503	105,999	6,926,400	3,864.9	2,578.6	3,272.0	2,901.2
1986	68,856	39,459	108,315	7,257,200	3,869.0	2,593.0	3,280.9	3,010.3
1987	71,206	43,785	114,991	7,499,900	4,092.3	2,895.4	3,535.8	3,081.3
1988	77,492	44,387	121,879	7,705,900	4,491.2	2,955.8	3,776.7	3,134.9
1989	81,758	46,716	128,474	7,872,400	4,771.4	2,989.3	3,921.4	3,171.3
1990	78,393	47,799	126,192	7,945,700	4,807.8	2,859.8	3,821.8	3,194.8
1991	73,769	46,295	120,064	8,142,200	4,428.6	2,712.0	3,559.8	3,228.8
1992	62,302	45,617	107,919	7,915,200	3,675.1	2,594.2	3,124.8	3,103.0
1993	61,569	44,693	106,262	7,820,900	3,570.6	2,381.8	2,951.1	3,032.4
1994	56,945	40,958	97,903	7,879,800	3,239.2	2,141.6	2,667.3	3,026.7
1995	61,976	41,783	103,759	7,997,700	3,573.5	2,102.6	2,788.1	3,043.8
1996	65,080	46,823	111,903	7,894,600	3,672.4	2,306.5	2,943.1	2,975.9

Notes: (1) Metropolitan Statistical Area - see Appendix A for areas included; (2) calculated by the editors using the following formula: (number of crimes in the MSA minus number of crimes in the city); (3) calculated by the editors using the following formula: ((number of crimes in the MSA minus number of crimes in the city) ÷ (population of the MSA minus population of the city)) x 100,000; n/a not avail.
Source: U.S. Department of Justice, FBI Uniform Crime Reports, 1977 - 1996

Motor Vehicle Thefts and Motor Vehicle Theft Rates: 1977 - 1996

Year	Number				Rate per 100,000 population			
	City	Suburbs[2]	MSA[1]	U.S.	City	Suburbs[3]	MSA[1]	U.S.
1977	13,726	4,877	18,603	977,700	882.7	424.4	687.9	451.9
1978	17,420	5,265	22,685	1,004,100	1,107.4	581.2	915.1	460.5
1979	24,572	5,980	30,552	1,112,800	1,517.1	569.6	1,144.5	505.6
1980	28,140	6,822	34,962	1,131,700	1,737.4	536.5	1,209.3	502.2
1981	n/a	n/a	n/a	1,087,800	n/a	n/a	n/a	474.7
1982	33,210	8,507	41,717	1,062,400	1,977.2	591.6	1,338.1	458.8
1983	30,799	7,704	38,503	1,007,900	1,781.5	595.3	1,273.7	430.8
1984	28,805	8,305	37,110	1,032,200	1,595.2	590.9	1,155.7	437.1
1985	31,746	8,902	40,648	1,102,900	1,817.8	596.2	1,254.7	462.0
1986	34,188	10,384	44,572	1,224,100	1,921.0	682.4	1,350.1	507.8
1987	28,650	9,662	38,312	1,288,700	1,646.6	638.9	1,178.0	529.4
1988	30,425	11,444	41,869	1,432,900	1,763.3	762.1	1,297.4	582.9
1989	37,005	13,561	50,566	1,564,800	2,159.6	867.8	1,543.4	630.4
1990	40,853	15,086	55,939	1,635,900	2,505.5	902.6	1,694.1	657.8
1991	40,162	15,955	56,117	1,661,700	2,411.0	934.7	1,663.8	659.0
1992	30,938	15,019	45,957	1,610,800	1,825.0	854.1	1,330.7	631.5
1993	27,519	13,017	40,536	1,563,100	1,595.9	693.7	1,125.8	606.1
1994	22,630	10,852	33,482	1,539,300	1,287.2	567.4	912.2	591.3
1995	22,536	9,547	32,083	1,472,400	1,299.4	480.4	862.1	560.4
1996	22,391	8,755	31,146	1,395,200	1,263.5	431.3	819.2	525.9

Notes: (1) Metropolitan Statistical Area - see Appendix A for areas included; (2) calculated by the editors using the following formula: (number of crimes in the MSA minus number of crimes in the city); (3) calculated by the editors using the following formula: ((number of crimes in the MSA minus number of crimes in the city) ÷ (population of the MSA minus population of the city)) x 100,000; n/a not avail.
Source: U.S. Department of Justice, FBI Uniform Crime Reports, 1977 - 1996

HATE CRIMES

Criminal Incidents by Bias Motivation

Area	Race	Ethnicity	Religion	Sexual Orientation
Houston	18	2	6	13

Notes: Figures include both violent and property crimes. Law enforcement agencies must have submitted data for at least one quarter of calendar year 1995 to be included in this report, therefore figures shown may not represent complete 12-month totals; n/a not available
Source: U.S. Department of Justice, FBI Uniform Crime Reports, Hate Crime Statistics 1995

ILLEGAL DRUGS

Drug Use by Adult Arrestees

Sex	Percent Testing Positive by Urinalysis (%)				
	Any Drug[1]	Cocaine	Marijuana	Opiates	Multiple Drugs
Male	64	39	33	8	29
Female	54	34	26	4	16

Notes: The catchment area is the entire city; (1) Includes cocaine, opiates, marijuana, methadone, phencyclidine (PCP), benzodiazepines, methaqualone, propoxyphene, barbiturates & amphetamines
Source: National Institute of Justice, 1996 Drug Use Forecasting, Annual Report on Adult and Juvenile Arrestees (released June 1997)

LAW ENFORCEMENT

Full-Time Law Enforcement Employees

Jurisdiction	Police Employees			Police Officers per 100,000 population
	Total	Officers	Civilians	
Houston	7,335	5,252	2,083	296.4

Notes: Data as of October 31, 1996
Source: U.S. Department of Justice, FBI Uniform Crime Reports, 1996

Number of Police Officers by Race

Race	Police Officers 1983		Police Officers 1992		Index of Representation[1]		
	Number	Pct.	Number	Pct.	1983	1992	% Chg.
Black	355	9.8	595	14.7	0.35	0.52	48.6
Hispanic[2]	314	8.7	506	12.5	0.49	0.44	-10.2

Notes: (1) The index of representation is calculated by dividing the percent of black/hispanic police officers by the percent of corresponding blacks/hispanics in the local population. An index approaching 1.0 indicates that a city is closer to achieving a representation of police officers equal to their proportion in the local population; (2) Hispanic officers can be of any race
Source: Bureau of Justice Statistics, Sourcebook of Criminal Justice Statistics, 1994

CORRECTIONS

Federal Correctional Facilities

Type	Year Opened	Security Level	Sex of Inmates	Rated Capacity	Population on 7/1/95	Number of Staff
None listed						

Notes: Data as of 1995
Source: Bureau of Justice Statistics, Sourcebook of Criminal Justice Statistics Online

City/County/Regional Correctional Facilities

Name	Year Opened	Year Renov.	Rated Capacity	1995 Pop.	Number of COs[1]	Number of Staff	ACA[2] Accred.
Harris County Downtown Central Jail	1982	1990	8,700	8,201	n/a	2,235	No

Notes: Data as of April 1996; (1) Correctional Officers; (2) American Correctional Assn. Accreditation
Source: American Correctional Association, 1996-1998 National Jail and Adult Detention Directory

Private Adult Correctional Facilities

Name	Date Opened	Rated Capacity	Present Pop.	Security Level	Facility Construct.	Expans. Plans	ACA[1] Accred.
Houston Processing Ctr	5/84	411	382	Min.	New	None	Yes-1/86
S. Texas Intermediate Sanction Facility	12/93	400	400	Min.	Renov.	None	In prog.

Notes: Data as of December 1996; (1) American Correctional Association Accreditation
Source: University of Florida, Center for Studies in Criminology and Law, Private Adult Correctional Facility Census, 10th Ed., March 15, 1997

Characteristics of Shock Incarceration Programs

Jurisdiction	Year Program Began	Number of Camps	Average Num. of Inmates	Number of Beds	Program Length	Voluntary/ Mandatory
Texas	1989	2	250	500 male; 20 female	75 to 90 days	Mandatory

Note: Data as of July 1996;
Source: Sourcebook of Criminal Justice Statistics Online

INMATES AND HIV/AIDS

HIV Testing Policies for Inmates

Jurisdiction	All Inmates at Some Time	All Convicted Inmates at Admission	Random Samples While in Custody	High-risk Groups	Upon Inmate Request	Upon Court Order	Upon Involvement in Incident
Harris Co.[1]	No	No	No	No	Yes	Yes	No

Notes: (1) All facilities reported following the same testing policy or authorities reported the policy to be jurisdiction-wide
Source: HIV in Prisons and Jails, 1993 (released August 1995)

Inmates Known to be Positive for HIV

Jurisdiction	Number of Jail Inmates in Facilities Providing Data	Type of HIV Infection/AIDS Cases: Total	Asymptomatic	Symptomatic	Confirmed AIDS	HIV/AIDS Cases as a Percent of Tot. Custody Pop.
Harris Co.	9,472	181	40	103	38	1.9

Source: HIV in Prisons and Jails, 1993 (released August, 1995)

DEATH PENALTY

Death Penalty Statistics

State	Prisoners Executed		Prisoners Under Sentence of Death					Avg. No. of Years on Death Row[4]
	1930-1995	1996[1]	Total[2]	White[3]	Black[3]	Hisp.	Women	
Texas	401	3	404	241	158	68	6	6.5

Notes: Data as of 12/31/95 unless otherwise noted; (1) Data as of 7/31/97; (2) Includes persons of other races; (3) Includes people of Hispanic origin; (4) Covers prisoners sentenced 1974 through 1995
Source: Bureau of Justice Statistics, Capital Punishment 1995 (released 12/96); Death Penalty Information Center Web Site, 9/30/97

Capital Offenses and Methods of Execution

Capital Offenses in Texas	Minimum Age for Imposition of Death Penalty	Mentally Retarded Excluded	Methods of Execution[1]
Criminal homicide with 1 of 8 aggravating circumstances.	17	No	Lethal injection

Notes: Data as of 12/31/95 unless otherwise noted; (1) Data as of 7/31/97
Source: Bureau of Justice Statistics, Capital Punishment 1995 (released 12/96); Death Penalty Information Center Web Site, 9/30/97

LAWS

Statutory Provisions Relating to the Purchase, Ownership and Use of Handguns

Jurisdiction	Instant Background Check	Federal Waiting Period Applies[1]	State Waiting Period (days)	License or Permit to Purchase	Regis-tration	Record of Sale Sent to Police	Concealed Carry Law
Texas	No	Yes[a]	No	No	No	No	Yes[b]

Note: Data as of 1996; (1) The Federal 5-day waiting period for handgun purchases applies to states that don't have instant background checks, waiting period requirements, or licensing procedures exempting them from the Federal requirement; (a) The Federal waiting period does not apply to a person holding a valid permit or license to carry a firearm, issued within 5 years of proposed purchase; (b) "Shall issue" permit system, liberally administered discretion by local authorities over permit issuance, or no permit required
Source: Sourcebook of Criminal Justice Statistics Online

Statutory Provisions Relating to Alcohol Use and Driving

Jurisdiction	Drinking Age	Blood Alcohol Concentration Levels as Evidence in State Courts[1]		Open Container Law[1]	Anti-Consump-tion Law[1]	Dram Shop Law[1]
		Illegal per se at 0.10%	Presumption at 0.10%			
Texas	21	Yes	No	No	Yes[a]	Yes[b]

Note: Data as of January 1, 1997; (1) See Appendix C for an explanation of terms; (a) Applies to drivers only; (b) Statutory law has limited dram shop actions
Source: Sourcebook of Criminal Justice Statistics Online

Statutory Provisions Relating to Curfews

Jurisdiction	Year Enacted	Latest Revision	Age Group(s)	Curfew Provisions
Houston	1992	-	17 and under	Midnight to 6 am every night 9 am to 2:30 pm school days

Note: Data as of February 1996
Source: Sourcebook of Criminal Justice Statistics Online

Statutory Provisions Relating to Hate Crimes

Jurisdiction	Bias-Motivated Violence and Intimidation						Institutional Vandalism
		Criminal Penalty					
	Civil Action	Race/ Religion/ Ethnicity	Sexual Orientation	Mental/ Physical Disability	Gender	Age	
Texas	No	No	No	No	No	No	Yes

Source: Anti-Defamation League, 1997 Hate Crimes Laws

Indianapolis, Indiana

OVERVIEW

The total crime rate for the city increased 0.3% between 1977 and 1996. During that same period, the violent crime rate increased 77.7% and the property crime rate decreased 9.3%.

Among violent crimes, the rates for: Murders increased 30.1%; Forcible Rapes increased 11.0%; Robberies increased 10.2%; and Aggravated Assaults increased 218.2%.

Among property crimes, the rates for: Burglaries decreased 18.4%; Larceny-Thefts decreased 15.4%; and Motor Vehicle Thefts increased 40.8%.

ANTI-CRIME PROGRAMS

The city has instituted several programs which include:

- Community Policing—instead of merely making a report and leaving, police now try to find a long-term solution to the problem.
- Take-Home Cars—a police officer can take home a police car and use it for shopping, movies, etc. which increases police visibility, puts police cars in neighborhoods and business parking lots, and increases officer morale (and efficiency). The cars are also equipped with computer terminals which provides officers with instant access to records/wanted check, and driver's license and vehicle information.
- Bicycle Patrols—off-duty police officers are hired to patrol the Downtown area on bicycles. This is paid for by the business community in the Downtown district.
Police Department, 6/97

CRIME RISK

Your Chances of Becoming a Victim[1]

Area	Any Crime	Violent Crime					Property Crime			
		Any	Murder	Forcible Rape[2]	Robbery	Aggrav. Assault	Any	Burglary	Larceny -Theft	Motor Vehicle Theft
City	1:21	1:105	1:6,820	1:963	1:299	1:182	1:25	1:100	1:46	1:133

Note: (1) Figures have been calculated by dividing the population of the city by the number of crimes reported to the FBI during 1996 and are expressed as odds (eg. 1:20 should be read as 1 in 20). (2) Figures have been calculated by dividing the female population of the city by the number of forcible rapes reported to the FBI during 1996. The female population of the city was estimated by calculating the ratio of females to males reported in the 1990 Census and applying that ratio to 1996 population estimate.
Source: FBI Uniform Crime Reports 1996

CRIME STATISTICS

Total Crimes and Total Crime Rates: 1977 - 1996

Year	Number				Rate per 100,000 population			
	City	Suburbs[2]	MSA[1]	U.S.	City	Suburbs[3]	MSA[1]	U.S.
1977	34,274	27,107	61,381	10,984,500	4,861.6	6,237.1	5,386.2	5,077.6
1978	34,837	29,173	64,010	11,209,000	4,948.4	6,608.2	5,588.1	5,140.3
1979	35,105	29,216	64,321	12,249,500	6,831.4	4,506.8	5,534.7	5,565.5
1980	37,220	32,607	69,827	13,408,300	5,326.6	7,038.8	6,009.2	5,950.0
1981	33,898	28,580	62,478	13,423,800	7,340.1	4,075.7	5,372.0	5,858.2
1982	34,736	30,215	64,951	12,974,400	7,507.9	4,307.5	5,579.5	5,603.6
1983	31,302	28,621	59,923	12,108,600	6,754.1	4,074.4	5,139.6	5,175.0
1984	29,103	28,805	57,908	11,881,800	6,170.8	4,039.6	4,888.1	5,031.3
1985	29,651	29,405	59,056	12,431,400	6,286.6	4,062.6	4,940.0	5,207.1
1986	29,726	27,787	57,513	13,211,900	6,316.7	3,828.3	4,807.1	5,480.4
1987	30,358	32,130	62,488	13,508,700	6,341.9	4,338.9	5,125.3	5,550.0
1988	29,684	33,168	62,852	13,923,100	6,143.4	4,388.8	5,073.1	5,664.2
1989	31,498	36,400	67,898	14,251,400	6,507.1	4,780.3	5,451.4	5,741.0
1990	32,635	39,484	72,119	14,475,600	6,749.1	5,149.6	5,768.2	5,820.3
1991	36,005	40,637	76,642	14,872,900	7,357.1	5,237.8	6,057.6	5,897.8
1992	35,858	48,600	84,458	14,438,200	7,259.8	5,302.4	5,987.8	5,660.2
1993	n/a	n/a	n/a	14,144,800	n/a	n/a	n/a	5,484.4
1994[a]	35,660	n/a	n/a	13,989,500	4,620.4	n/a	n/a	5,373.5
1995	36,469	n/a	n/a	13,862,700	4,719.1	n/a	n/a	5,275.9
1996	37,917	42,267	80,184	13,473,600	4,877.0	5,974.8	5,400.0	5,078.9

Notes: (1) Metropolitan Statistical Area - see Appendix A for areas included; (2) calculated by the editors using the following formula: (number of crimes in the MSA minus number of crimes in the city); (3) calculated by the editors using the following formula: ((number of crimes in the MSA minus number of crimes in the city) ÷ (population of the MSA minus population of the city)) x 100,000; n/a not avail.; (a) Indianapolis merged with Marion County to create a unified city-county government
Source: U.S. Department of Justice, FBI Uniform Crime Reports, 1977 - 1996

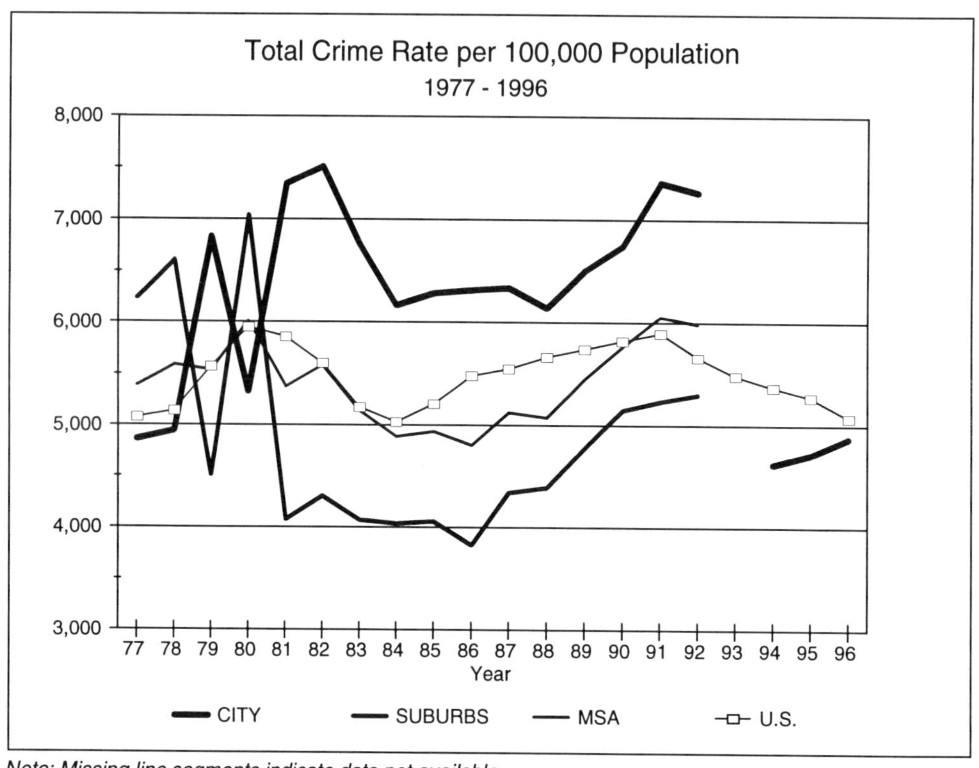

Note: Missing line segments indicate data not available.

Violent Crimes and Violent Crime Rates: 1977 - 1996

Year	Number				Rate per 100,000 population			
	City	Suburbs[2]	MSA[1]	U.S.	City	Suburbs[3]	MSA[1]	U.S.
1977	3,785	1,529	5,314	1,029,580	536.9	351.8	466.3	475.9
1978	3,733	1,578	5,311	1,085,550	530.3	357.4	463.7	497.8
1979	4,178	1,454	5,632	1,208,030	813.0	224.3	484.6	548.9
1980	4,453	1,566	6,019	1,344,520	637.3	338.0	518.0	596.6
1981	4,539	1,468	6,007	1,361,820	982.9	209.3	516.5	594.3
1982	4,341	1,380	5,721	1,322,390	938.3	196.7	491.4	571.1
1983	4,139	1,421	5,560	1,258,090	893.1	202.3	476.9	537.7
1984	4,366	1,786	6,152	1,273,280	925.7	250.5	519.3	539.2
1985	4,622	1,662	6,284	1,328,800	980.0	229.6	525.7	556.6
1986	4,307	1,325	5,632	1,489,170	915.2	182.5	470.7	617.7
1987	4,543	1,643	6,186	1,484,000	949.0	221.9	507.4	609.7
1988	5,635	1,853	7,488	1,566,220	1,166.2	245.2	604.4	637.2
1989	5,859	1,692	7,551	1,646,040	1,210.4	222.2	606.3	663.1
1990	6,224	2,042	8,266	1,820,130	1,287.1	266.3	661.1	731.8
1991	7,072	2,201	9,273	1,911,770	1,445.1	283.7	732.9	758.1
1992	6,814	3,106	9,920	1,932,270	1,379.6	338.9	703.3	757.5
1993	n/a	n/a	n/a	1,926,020	n/a	n/a	n/a	746.8
1994[a]	6,467	n/a	n/a	1,857,670	837.9	n/a	n/a	713.6
1995	6,715	n/a	n/a	1,798,790	868.9	n/a	n/a	684.6
1996	7,418	3,369	10,787	1,682,280	954.1	476.2	726.5	634.1

Notes: Violent crimes include murder, forcible rape, robbery and aggravated assault; n/a not available; (1) Metropolitan Statistical Area - see Appendix A for areas included; (2) calculated by the editors using the following formula: (number of crimes in the MSA minus number of crimes in the city); (3) calculated by the editors using the following formula: ((number of crimes in the MSA minus number of crimes in the city) ÷ (population of the MSA minus population of the city)) x 100,000; (a) Indianapolis merged with Marion County to create a unified city-county government
Source: U.S. Department of Justice, FBI Uniform Crime Reports, 1977 - 1996

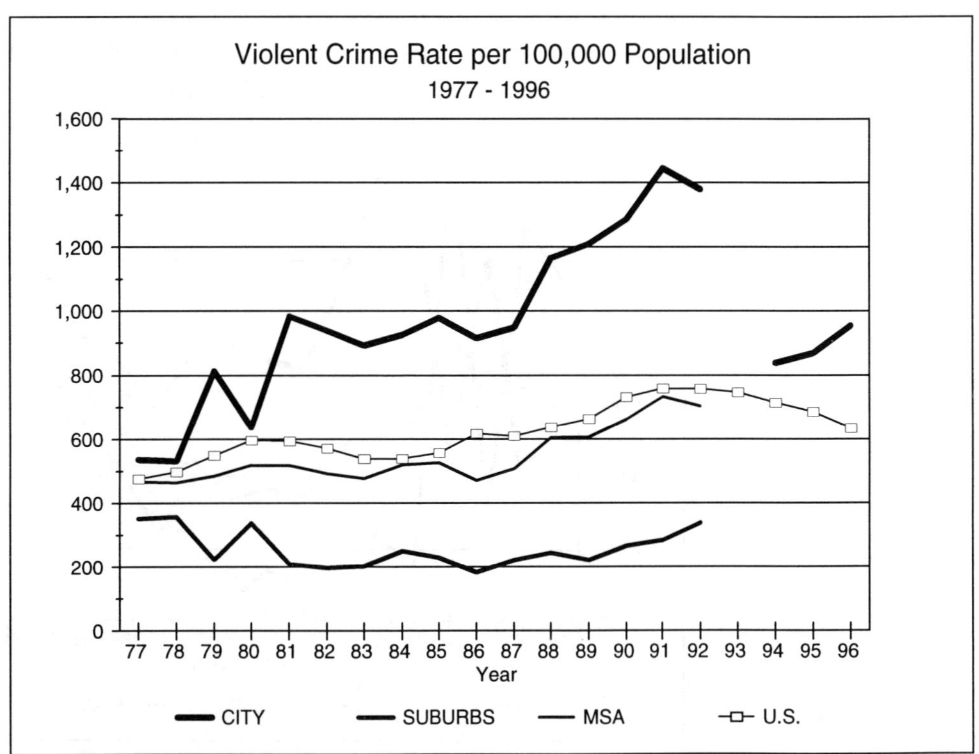

Note: Missing line segments indicate data not available.

Property Crimes and Property Crime Rates: 1977 - 1996

Year	Number				Rate per 100,000 population			
	City	Suburbs[2]	MSA[1]	U.S.	City	Suburbs[3]	MSA[1]	U.S.
1977	30,489	25,578	56,067	9,955,000	4,324.7	5,885.3	4,919.8	4,601.7
1978	31,104	27,595	58,699	10,123,400	4,418.2	6,250.8	5,124.5	4,642.5
1979	30,927	27,762	58,689	11,041,500	6,018.4	4,282.5	5,050.1	5,016.6
1980	32,767	31,041	63,808	12,063,700	4,689.4	6,700.7	5,491.2	5,353.3
1981	29,359	27,112	56,471	12,061,900	6,357.2	3,866.4	4,855.5	5,263.9
1982	30,395	28,835	59,230	11,652,000	6,569.7	4,110.8	5,088.0	5,032.5
1983	27,163	27,200	54,363	10,850,500	5,861.0	3,872.1	4,662.7	4,637.4
1984	24,737	27,019	51,756	10,608,500	5,245.1	3,789.2	4,368.8	4,492.1
1985	25,029	27,743	52,772	11,102,600	5,306.6	3,832.9	4,414.4	4,650.5
1986	25,419	26,462	51,881	11,722,700	5,401.5	3,645.8	4,336.3	4,862.6
1987	25,815	30,487	56,302	12,024,700	5,392.8	4,117.0	4,617.9	4,940.3
1988	24,049	31,315	55,364	12,356,900	4,977.2	4,143.6	4,468.7	5,027.1
1989	25,639	34,708	60,347	12,605,400	5,296.7	4,558.1	4,845.1	5,077.9
1990	26,411	37,442	63,853	12,655,500	5,461.9	4,883.2	5,107.0	5,088.5
1991	28,933	38,436	67,369	12,961,100	5,912.0	4,954.1	5,324.6	5,139.7
1992	29,044	45,494	74,538	12,505,900	5,880.2	4,963.5	5,284.5	4,902.7
1993	n/a	n/a	n/a	12,218,800	n/a	n/a	n/a	4,737.6
1994[a]	29,193	n/a	n/a	12,131,900	3,782.5	n/a	n/a	4,660.0
1995	29,754	n/a	n/a	12,063,900	3,850.2	n/a	n/a	4,591.3
1996	30,499	38,898	69,397	11,791,300	3,922.9	5,498.6	4,673.6	4,444.8

Notes: Property crimes include burglary, larceny-theft and motor vehicle theft; n/a not available; (1) Metropolitan Statistical Area - see Appendix A for areas included; (2) calculated by the editors using the following formula: (number of crimes in the MSA minus number of crimes in the city); (3) calculated by the editors using the following formula: ((number of crimes in the MSA minus number of crimes in the city) ÷ (population of the MSA minus population of the city)) x 100,000; (a) Indianapolis merged with Marion County to create a unified city-county government
Source: U.S. Department of Justice, FBI Uniform Crime Reports, 1977 - 1996

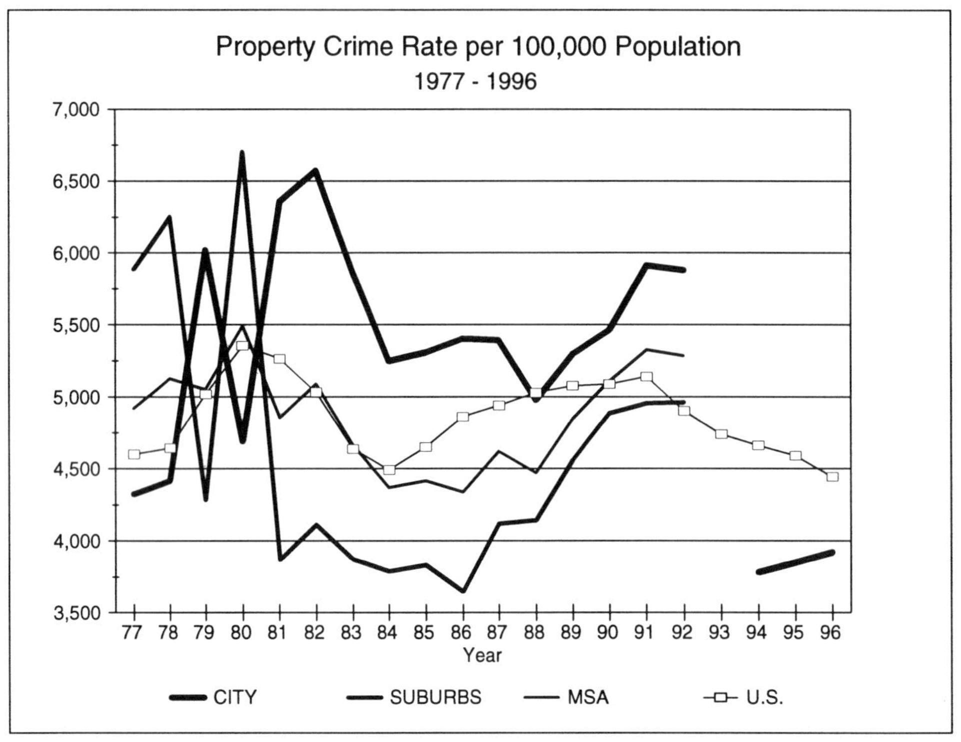

Note: Missing line segments indicate data not available.

Murders and Murder Rates: 1977 - 1996

Year	Number				Rate per 100,000 population			
	City	Suburbs[2]	MSA[1]	U.S.	City	Suburbs[3]	MSA[1]	U.S.
1977	80	22	102	19,120	11.3	5.1	9.0	8.8
1978	76	24	100	19,560	10.8	5.4	8.7	9.0
1979	92	34	126	21,460	17.9	5.2	10.8	9.7
1980	107	31	138	23,040	15.3	6.7	11.9	10.2
1981	65	23	88	22,520	14.1	3.3	7.6	9.8
1982	69	24	93	21,010	14.9	3.4	8.0	9.1
1983	56	9	65	19,310	12.1	1.3	5.6	8.3
1984	49	19	68	18,690	10.4	2.7	5.7	7.9
1985	59	26	85	18,980	12.5	3.6	7.1	7.9
1986	63	21	84	20,610	13.4	2.9	7.0	8.6
1987	57	23	80	20,100	11.9	3.1	6.6	8.3
1988	79	29	108	20,680	16.3	3.8	8.7	8.4
1989	41	39	80	21,500	8.5	5.1	6.4	8.7
1990	58	29	87	23,440	12.0	3.8	7.0	9.4
1991	95	27	122	24,700	19.4	3.5	9.6	9.8
1992	88	32	120	23,760	17.8	3.5	8.5	9.3
1993	n/a	n/a	n/a	24,530	n/a	n/a	n/a	9.5
1994[a]	108	n/a	n/a	23,330	14.0	n/a	n/a	9.0
1995	99	n/a	n/a	21,610	12.8	n/a	n/a	8.2
1996	114	34	148	19,650	14.7	4.8	10.0	7.4

Notes: (1) Metropolitan Statistical Area - see Appendix A for areas included; (2) calculated by the editors using the following formula: (number of crimes in the MSA minus number of crimes in the city); (3) calculated by the editors using the following formula: ((number of crimes in the MSA minus number of crimes in the city) ÷ (population of the MSA minus population of the city)) x 100,000; n/a not avail.; (a) Indianapolis merged with Marion County to create a unified city-county government
Source: U.S. Department of Justice, FBI Uniform Crime Reports, 1977 - 1996

Forcible Rapes and Forcible Rape Rates: 1977 - 1996

Year	Number				Rate per 100,000 population			
	City	Suburbs[2]	MSA[1]	U.S.	City	Suburbs[3]	MSA[1]	U.S.
1977	346	155	501	63,500	49.1	35.7	44.0	29.4
1978	341	139	480	67,610	48.4	31.5	41.9	31.0
1979	439	177	616	76,390	85.4	27.3	53.0	34.7
1980	410	171	581	82,990	58.7	36.9	50.0	36.8
1981	400	157	557	82,500	86.6	22.4	47.9	36.0
1982	387	155	542	78,770	83.6	22.1	46.6	34.0
1983	376	126	502	78,920	81.1	17.9	43.1	33.7
1984	324	114	438	84,230	68.7	16.0	37.0	35.7
1985	346	129	475	88,670	73.4	17.8	39.7	37.1
1986	438	132	570	91,460	93.1	18.2	47.6	37.9
1987	432	175	607	91,110	90.2	23.6	49.8	37.4
1988	422	236	658	92,490	87.3	31.2	53.1	37.6
1989	483	216	699	94,500	99.8	28.4	56.1	38.1
1990	541	294	835	102,560	111.9	38.3	66.8	41.2
1991	561	274	835	106,590	114.6	35.3	66.0	42.3
1992	541	373	914	109,060	109.5	40.7	64.8	42.8
1993	n/a	n/a	n/a	106,010	n/a	n/a	n/a	41.1
1994[a]	483	n/a	n/a	102,220	62.6	n/a	n/a	39.3
1995	457	n/a	n/a	97,470	59.1	n/a	n/a	37.1
1996	424	292	716	95,770	54.5	41.3	48.2	36.1

Notes: (1) Metropolitan Statistical Area - see Appendix A for areas included; (2) calculated by the editors using the following formula: (number of crimes in the MSA minus number of crimes in the city); (3) calculated by the editors using the following formula: ((number of crimes in the MSA minus number of crimes in the city) ÷ (population of the MSA minus population of the city)) x 100,000; n/a not avail.; (a) Indianapolis merged with Marion County to create a unified city-county government
Source: U.S. Department of Justice, FBI Uniform Crime Reports, 1977 - 1996

Robberies and Robbery Rates: 1977 - 1996

Year	Number				Rate per 100,000 population			
	City	Suburbs[2]	MSA[1]	U.S.	City	Suburbs[3]	MSA[1]	U.S.
1977	2,139	608	2,747	412,610	303.4	139.9	241.0	190.7
1978	1,963	592	2,555	426,930	278.8	134.1	223.1	195.8
1979	2,053	534	2,587	480,700	399.5	82.4	222.6	218.4
1980	2,193	656	2,849	565,840	313.8	141.6	245.2	251.1
1981	2,194	608	2,802	592,910	475.1	86.7	240.9	258.7
1982	1,993	523	2,516	553,130	430.8	74.6	216.1	238.9
1983	1,821	485	2,306	506,570	392.9	69.0	197.8	216.5
1984	1,842	575	2,417	485,010	390.6	80.6	204.0	205.4
1985	1,795	460	2,255	497,870	380.6	63.6	188.6	208.5
1986	1,571	458	2,029	542,780	333.8	63.1	169.6	225.1
1987	1,334	491	1,825	517,700	278.7	66.3	149.7	212.7
1988	1,464	447	1,911	542,970	303.0	59.1	154.2	220.9
1989	1,806	613	2,419	578,330	373.1	80.5	194.2	233.0
1990	1,642	515	2,157	639,270	339.6	67.2	172.5	257.0
1991	2,001	586	2,587	687,730	408.9	75.5	204.5	272.7
1992	2,157	903	3,060	672,480	436.7	98.5	216.9	263.6
1993	n/a	n/a	n/a	659,870	n/a	n/a	n/a	255.9
1994[a]	2,454	n/a	n/a	618,950	318.0	n/a	n/a	237.7
1995	2,523	n/a	n/a	580,510	326.5	n/a	n/a	220.9
1996	2,600	887	3,487	537,050	334.4	125.4	234.8	202.4

Notes: (1) Metropolitan Statistical Area - see Appendix A for areas included; (2) calculated by the editors using the following formula: (number of crimes in the MSA minus number of crimes in the city); (3) calculated by the editors using the following formula: ((number of crimes in the MSA minus number of crimes in the city) ÷ (population of the MSA minus population of the city)) x 100,000; n/a not avail.; (a) Indianapolis merged with Marion County to create a unified city-county government
Source: U.S. Department of Justice, FBI Uniform Crime Reports, 1977 - 1996

Aggravated Assaults and Aggravated Assault Rates: 1977 - 1996

Year	Number				Rate per 100,000 population			
	City	Suburbs[2]	MSA[1]	U.S.	City	Suburbs[3]	MSA[1]	U.S.
1977	1,220	744	1,964	534,350	173.0	171.2	172.3	247.0
1978	1,353	823	2,176	571,460	192.2	186.4	190.0	262.1
1979	1,594	709	2,303	629,480	310.2	109.4	198.2	286.0
1980	1,743	708	2,451	672,650	249.4	152.8	210.9	298.5
1981	1,880	680	2,560	663,900	407.1	97.0	220.1	289.7
1982	1,892	678	2,570	669,480	408.9	96.7	220.8	289.2
1983	1,886	801	2,687	653,290	406.9	114.0	230.5	279.2
1984	2,151	1,078	3,229	685,350	456.1	151.2	272.6	290.2
1985	2,422	1,047	3,469	723,250	513.5	144.7	290.2	302.9
1986	2,235	714	2,949	834,320	474.9	98.4	246.5	346.1
1987	2,720	954	3,674	855,090	568.2	128.8	301.3	351.3
1988	3,670	1,141	4,811	910,090	759.5	151.0	388.3	370.2
1989	3,529	824	4,353	951,710	729.0	108.2	349.5	383.4
1990	3,983	1,204	5,187	1,054,860	823.7	157.0	414.9	424.1
1991	4,415	1,314	5,729	1,092,740	902.1	169.4	452.8	433.3
1992	4,028	1,798	5,826	1,126,970	815.5	196.2	413.0	441.8
1993	n/a	n/a	n/a	1,135,610	n/a	n/a	n/a	440.3
1994[a]	3,422	n/a	n/a	1,113,180	443.4	n/a	n/a	427.6
1995	3,636	n/a	n/a	1,099,210	470.5	n/a	n/a	418.3
1996	4,280	2,156	6,436	1,029,810	550.5	304.8	433.4	388.2

Notes: (1) Metropolitan Statistical Area - see Appendix A for areas included; (2) calculated by the editors using the following formula: (number of crimes in the MSA minus number of crimes in the city); (3) calculated by the editors using the following formula: ((number of crimes in the MSA minus number of crimes in the city) ÷ (population of the MSA minus population of the city)) x 100,000; n/a not avail.; (a) Indianapolis merged with Marion County to create a unified city-county government
Source: U.S. Department of Justice, FBI Uniform Crime Reports, 1977 - 1996

Burglaries and Burglary Rates: 1977 - 1996

Year	Number				Rate per 100,000 population			
	City	Suburbs[2]	MSA[1]	U.S.	City	Suburbs[3]	MSA[1]	U.S.
1977	8,665	6,578	15,243	3,071,500	1,229.1	1,513.5	1,337.6	1,419.8
1978	8,738	7,319	16,057	3,128,300	1,241.2	1,657.9	1,401.8	1,434.6
1979	8,549	7,102	15,651	3,327,700	1,663.6	1,095.5	1,346.7	1,511.9
1980	10,074	7,809	17,883	3,795,200	1,441.7	1,685.7	1,539.0	1,684.1
1981	9,985	6,483	16,468	3,779,700	2,162.1	924.5	1,415.9	1,649.5
1982	9,996	6,865	16,861	3,447,100	2,160.6	978.7	1,448.4	1,488.8
1983	9,235	6,277	15,512	3,129,900	1,992.6	893.6	1,330.5	1,337.7
1984	8,163	6,573	14,736	2,984,400	1,730.8	921.8	1,243.9	1,263.7
1985	8,209	6,690	14,899	3,073,300	1,740.5	924.3	1,246.3	1,287.3
1986	8,247	6,306	14,553	3,241,400	1,752.5	868.8	1,216.4	1,344.6
1987	8,744	6,894	15,638	3,236,200	1,826.6	931.0	1,282.6	1,329.6
1988	7,714	7,464	15,178	3,218,100	1,596.5	987.6	1,225.1	1,309.2
1989	8,520	7,913	16,433	3,168,200	1,760.1	1,039.2	1,319.4	1,276.3
1990	7,878	7,601	15,479	3,073,900	1,629.2	991.3	1,238.0	1,235.9
1991	8,732	8,123	16,855	3,157,200	1,784.3	1,047.0	1,332.2	1,252.0
1992	8,102	9,622	17,724	2,979,900	1,640.3	1,049.8	1,256.6	1,168.2
1993	n/a	n/a	n/a	2,834,800	n/a	n/a	n/a	1,099.2
1994[a]	8,151	n/a	n/a	2,712,800	1,056.1	n/a	n/a	1,042.0
1995	7,797	n/a	n/a	2,593,800	1,008.9	n/a	n/a	987.1
1996	7,797	6,796	14,593	2,501,500	1,002.9	960.7	982.8	943.0

Notes: (1) Metropolitan Statistical Area - see Appendix A for areas included; (2) calculated by the editors using the following formula: (number of crimes in the MSA minus number of crimes in the city); (3) calculated by the editors using the following formula: ((number of crimes in the MSA minus number of crimes in the city) ÷ (population of the MSA minus population of the city)) x 100,000; n/a not avail.; (a) Indianapolis merged with Marion County to create a unified city-county government
Source: U.S. Department of Justice, FBI Uniform Crime Reports, 1977 - 1996

Larceny-Thefts and Larceny-Theft Rates: 1977 - 1996

Year	Number				Rate per 100,000 population			
	City	Suburbs[2]	MSA[1]	U.S.	City	Suburbs[3]	MSA[1]	U.S.
1977	18,051	16,495	34,546	5,905,700	2,560.4	3,795.4	3,031.4	2,729.9
1978	18,692	17,157	35,849	5,991,000	2,655.1	3,886.4	3,129.6	2,747.4
1979	18,927	17,429	36,356	6,601,000	3,683.2	2,688.6	3,128.4	2,999.1
1980	18,906	19,978	38,884	7,136,900	2,705.7	4,312.6	3,346.3	3,167.0
1981	16,782	18,371	35,153	7,194,400	3,633.9	2,619.9	3,022.5	3,139.7
1982	17,497	19,487	36,984	7,142,500	3,781.9	2,778.1	3,177.0	3,084.8
1983	15,123	18,460	33,583	6,712,800	3,263.1	2,627.9	2,880.4	2,868.9
1984	13,552	17,643	31,195	6,591,900	2,873.5	2,474.3	2,633.2	2,791.3
1985	13,927	18,469	32,396	6,926,400	2,952.8	2,551.7	2,709.9	2,901.2
1986	13,815	17,711	31,526	7,257,200	2,935.7	2,440.1	2,635.0	3,010.3
1987	13,336	20,723	34,059	7,499,900	2,785.9	2,798.5	2,793.6	3,081.3
1988	12,758	21,198	33,956	7,705,900	2,640.4	2,804.9	2,740.8	3,134.9
1989	13,122	23,751	36,873	7,872,400	2,710.8	3,119.1	2,960.5	3,171.3
1990	13,697	26,611	40,308	7,945,700	2,832.6	3,470.6	3,223.9	3,194.8
1991	14,970	27,026	41,996	8,142,200	3,058.9	3,483.5	3,319.2	3,228.8
1992	15,730	32,100	47,830	7,915,200	3,184.7	3,502.2	3,391.0	3,103.0
1993	n/a	n/a	n/a	7,820,900	n/a	n/a	n/a	3,032.4
1994[a]	15,041	n/a	n/a	7,879,800	1,948.8	n/a	n/a	3,026.7
1995	15,941	n/a	n/a	7,997,700	2,062.8	n/a	n/a	3,043.8
1996	16,842	28,346	45,188	7,894,600	2,166.3	4,007.0	3,043.2	2,975.9

Notes: (1) Metropolitan Statistical Area - see Appendix A for areas included; (2) calculated by the editors using the following formula: (number of crimes in the MSA minus number of crimes in the city); (3) calculated by the editors using the following formula: ((number of crimes in the MSA minus number of crimes in the city) ÷ (population of the MSA minus population of the city)) x 100,000; n/a not avail.; (a) Indianapolis merged with Marion County to create a unified city-county government
Source: U.S. Department of Justice, FBI Uniform Crime Reports, 1977 - 1996

Motor Vehicle Thefts and Motor Vehicle Theft Rates: 1977 - 1996

Year	Number				Rate per 100,000 population			
	City	Suburbs[2]	MSA[1]	U.S.	City	Suburbs[3]	MSA[1]	U.S.
1977	3,773	2,505	6,278	977,700	535.2	576.4	550.9	451.9
1978	3,674	3,119	6,793	1,004,100	521.9	706.5	593.0	460.5
1979	3,451	3,231	6,682	1,112,800	671.6	498.4	575.0	505.6
1980	3,787	3,254	7,041	1,131,700	542.0	702.4	605.9	502.2
1981	2,592	2,258	4,850	1,087,800	561.3	322.0	417.0	474.7
1982	2,902	2,483	5,385	1,062,400	627.2	354.0	462.6	458.8
1983	2,805	2,463	5,268	1,007,900	605.2	350.6	451.8	430.8
1984	3,022	2,803	5,825	1,032,200	640.8	393.1	491.7	437.1
1985	2,893	2,584	5,477	1,102,900	613.4	357.0	458.1	462.0
1986	3,357	2,445	5,802	1,224,100	713.4	336.9	484.9	507.8
1987	3,735	2,870	6,605	1,288,700	780.2	387.6	541.7	529.4
1988	3,577	2,653	6,230	1,432,900	740.3	351.0	502.9	582.9
1989	3,997	3,044	7,041	1,564,800	825.7	399.8	565.3	630.4
1990	4,836	3,230	8,066	1,635,900	1,000.1	421.3	645.1	657.8
1991	5,231	3,287	8,518	1,661,700	1,068.9	423.7	673.2	659.0
1992	5,212	3,772	8,984	1,610,800	1,055.2	411.5	636.9	631.5
1993	n/a	n/a	n/a	1,563,100	n/a	n/a	n/a	606.1
1994[a]	6,001	n/a	n/a	1,539,300	777.5	n/a	n/a	591.3
1995	6,016	n/a	n/a	1,472,400	778.5	n/a	n/a	560.4
1996	5,860	3,756	9,616	1,395,200	753.7	530.9	647.6	525.9

Notes: (1) Metropolitan Statistical Area - see Appendix A for areas included; (2) calculated by the editors using the following formula: (number of crimes in the MSA minus number of crimes in the city); (3) calculated by the editors using the following formula: ((number of crimes in the MSA minus number of crimes in the city) ÷ (population of the MSA minus population of the city)) x 100,000; n/a not avail.; (a) Indianapolis merged with Marion County to create a unified city-county government
Source: U.S. Department of Justice, FBI Uniform Crime Reports, 1977 - 1996

HATE CRIMES

Criminal Incidents by Bias Motivation

Area	Race	Ethnicity	Religion	Sexual Orientation
Indianapolis	n/a	n/a	n/a	n/a

Notes: Figures include both violent and property crimes. Law enforcement agencies must have submitted data for at least one quarter of calendar year 1995 to be included in this report, therefore figures shown may not represent complete 12-month totals; n/a not available
Source: U.S. Department of Justice, FBI Uniform Crime Reports, Hate Crime Statistics 1995

ILLEGAL DRUGS

Drug Use by Adult Arrestees

Sex	Percent Testing Positive by Urinalysis (%)				
	Any Drug[1]	Cocaine	Marijuana	Opiates	Multiple Drugs
Male	74	42	51	3	24
Female	72	52	31	3	23

Notes: The catchment area is the entire county; (1) Includes cocaine, opiates, marijuana, methadone, phencyclidine (PCP), benzodiazepines, methaqualone, propoxyphene, barbiturates & amphetamines
Source: National Institute of Justice, 1996 Drug Use Forecasting, Annual Report on Adult and Juvenile Arrestees (released June 1997)

LAW ENFORCEMENT

Full-Time Law Enforcement Employees

Jurisdiction	Police Employees			Police Officers per 100,000 population
	Total	Officers	Civilians	
Indianapolis	1,275	1,013	262	130.3

Notes: Data as of October 31, 1996
Source: U.S. Department of Justice, FBI Uniform Crime Reports, 1996

Number of Police Officers by Race

Race	Police Officers 1983		1992		Index of Representation[1]		
	Number	Pct.	Number	Pct.	1983	1992	% Chg.
Black	123	13.1	174	17.8	0.60	0.78	30.0
Hispanic[2]	1	0.1	0	0.0	0.11	0.00	-100.0

Notes: (1) The index of representation is calculated by dividing the percent of black/hispanic police officers by the percent of corresponding blacks/hispanics in the local population. An index approaching 1.0 indicates that a city is closer to achieving a representation of police officers equal to their proportion in the local population; (2) Hispanic officers can be of any race
Source: Bureau of Justice Statistics, Sourcebook of Criminal Justice Statistics, 1994

CORRECTIONS

Federal Correctional Facilities

Type	Year Opened	Security Level	Sex of Inmates	Rated Capacity	Population on 7/1/95	Number of Staff
None listed						

Notes: Data as of 1995
Source: Bureau of Justice Statistics, Sourcebook of Criminal Justice Statistics Online

City/County/Regional Correctional Facilities

Name	Year Opened	Year Renov.	Rated Capacity	1995 Pop.	Number of COs[1]	Number of Staff	ACA[2] Accred.
Marion Co Comm Corr Ctr	1990	--	279	235	22	n/a	No
Marion Co Jail	1965	1985	1,148	n/a	n/a	n/a	No

Notes: Data as of April 1996; (1) Correctional Officers; (2) American Correctional Assn. Accreditation
Source: American Correctional Association, 1996-1998 National Jail and Adult Detention Directory

Private Adult Correctional Facilities

Name	Date Opened	Rated Capacity	Present Pop.	Security Level	Facility Construct.	Expans. Plans	ACA[1] Accred.
Marion Co Jail Annex	1/98	670	n/a	Med.	New	None	Will be sought

Notes: Data as of December 1996; (1) American Correctional Association Accreditation
Source: University of Florida, Center for Studies in Criminology and Law, Private Adult Correctional Facility Census, 10th Ed., March 15, 1997

Characteristics of Shock Incarceration Programs

Jurisdiction	Year Program Began	Number of Camps	Average Num. of Inmates	Number of Beds	Program Length	Voluntary/ Mandatory
Indiana did not have a shock incarceration program as of July 1996						

Source: Sourcebook of Criminal Justice Statistics Online

DEATH PENALTY

Death Penalty Statistics

State	Prisoners Executed 1930-1995	1996[1]	Prisoners Under Sentence of Death Total[2]	White[3]	Black[3]	Hisp.	Women	Avg. No. of Years on Death Row[4]
Indiana	44	1	46	31	15	2	0	8.4

Notes: Data as of 12/31/95 unless otherwise noted; (1) Data as of 7/31/97; (2) Includes persons of other races; (3) Includes people of Hispanic origin; (4) Covers prisoners sentenced 1974 through 1995
Source: Bureau of Justice Statistics, Capital Punishment 1995 (released 12/96); Death Penalty Information Center Web Site, 9/30/97

Capital Offenses and Methods of Execution

Capital Offenses in Indiana	Minimum Age for Imposition of Death Penalty	Mentally Retarded Excluded	Methods of Execution[1]
Murder with 14 aggravating circum-stances.	16	Yes	Lethal injection

Notes: Data as of 12/31/95 unless otherwise noted; (1) Data as of 7/31/97
Source: Bureau of Justice Statistics, Capital Punishment 1995 (released 12/96); Death Penalty Information Center Web Site, 9/30/97

LAWS

Statutory Provisions Relating to the Purchase, Ownership and Use of Handguns

Jurisdiction	Instant Background Check	Federal Waiting Period Applies[1]	State Waiting Period (days)	License or Permit to Purchase	Registration	Record of Sale Sent to Police	Concealed Carry Law
Indiana	No	No	7[a]	No	No	Yes	Yes[b]

Note: Data as of 1996; (1) The Federal 5-day waiting period for handgun purchases applies to states that don't have instant background checks, waiting period requirements, or licensing procedures exempting them from the Federal requirement; (a) The State waiting period does not apply to a person holding an unlimited carry permit; (b) "Shall issue" permit system, liberally administered discretion by local authorities over permit issuance, or no permit required
Source: Sourcebook of Criminal Justice Statistics Online

Statutory Provisions Relating to Alcohol Use and Driving

Jurisdiction	Drinking Age	Blood Alcohol Concentration Levels as Evidence in State Courts[1]		Open Container Law[1]	Anti-Consumption Law[1]	Dram Shop Law[1]
		Illegal per se at 0.10%	Presumption at 0.10%			
Indiana	21	Yes	Yes[a]	Yes[b]	Yes[c]	Yes

Note: Data as of January 1, 1997; (1) See Appendix C for an explanation of terms; (a) Has both prima facie and presumptive evidence laws with blood alcohol concentration levels at 0.10%; (b) Provided the driver has an alcohol concentration of 0.04% or more; (c) Applies to drivers only
Source: Sourcebook of Criminal Justice Statistics Online

Statutory Provisions Relating to Curfews

Jurisdiction	Year Enacted	Latest Revision	Age Group(s)	Curfew Provisions
Indianapolis	1971	-	16 and 17	11 pm to 6 am weekday nights 1 am to 6 am weekend nights
			15 and under	11 pm to 6 am every night

Note: Data as of February 1996
Source: Sourcebook of Criminal Justice Statistics Online

Statutory Provisions Relating to Hate Crimes

Jurisdiction	Bias-Motivated Violence and Intimidation						Institutional Vandalism
	Civil Action	Criminal Penalty					
		Race/ Religion/ Ethnicity	Sexual Orientation	Mental/ Physical Disability	Gender	Age	
Indiana	No	No	No	No	No	No	Yes

Source: Anti-Defamation League, 1997 Hate Crimes Laws

Jacksonville, Florida

OVERVIEW

The total crime rate for the city increased 26.5% between 1977 and 1996. During that same period, the violent crime rate increased 79.1% and the property crime rate increased 19.6%.

Among violent crimes, the rates for: Murders decreased 15.8%; Forcible Rapes increased 74.2%; Robberies increased 45.6%; and Aggravated Assaults increased 103.8%.

Among property crimes, the rates for: Burglaries increased 1.1%; Larceny-Thefts increased 20.7%; and Motor Vehicle Thefts increased 114.6%.

ANTI-CRIME PROGRAMS

Under a program put together by the State Attorney's Office in Jacksonville, the juvenile justice system intervenes early when juveniles are arrested for violent crimes and instead of sending those convicted to Florida's juvenile prisons they are kept in Jacksonville, at the newly built Duval County Jail. Housed on one floor separate from adult inmates, the youthful offenders participate in a school program along with drug and sex education courses and counseling for returning to society. For those who complete their sentences without bad conduct reports, criminal convictions are withheld, enabling them to tell prospective employers they have never committed a crime. *New York Times, 10/4/97*

CRIME RISK

Your Chances of Becoming a Victim[1]

Area	Any Crime	Violent Crime					Property Crime			
		Any	Murder	Forcible Rape[2]	Robbery	Aggrav. Assault	Any	Burglary	Larceny -Theft	Motor Vehicle Theft
City	1:12	1:71	1:8,122	1:519	1:247	1:111	1:14	1:52	1:22	1:145

Note: (1) Figures have been calculated by dividing the population of the city by the number of crimes reported to the FBI during 1996 and are expressed as odds (eg. 1:20 should be read as 1 in 20). (2) Figures have been calculated by dividing the female population of the city by the number of forcible rapes reported to the FBI during 1996. The female population of the city was estimated by calculating the ratio of females to males reported in the 1990 Census and applying that ratio to 1996 population estimate.
Source: FBI Uniform Crime Reports 1996

CRIME STATISTICS

Total Crimes and Total Crime Rates: 1977 - 1996

Year	Number				Rate per 100,000 population			
	City	Suburbs[2]	MSA[1]	U.S.	City	Suburbs[3]	MSA[1]	U.S.
1977	35,999	7,011	43,010	10,984,500	6,818.0	4,371.1	6,247.9	5,077.6
1978	36,274	8,563	44,837	11,209,000	6,844.2	5,428.0	6,519.3	5,140.3
1979	39,349	9,399	48,748	12,249,500	7,201.3	5,249.7	6,719.6	5,565.5
1980	42,890	9,662	52,552	13,408,300	7,901.7	4,992.0	7,136.9	5,950.0
1981	45,070	10,193	55,263	13,423,800	7,836.1	4,917.5	7,062.9	5,858.2
1982	45,155	10,974	56,129	12,974,400	7,641.0	5,207.8	7,001.4	5,603.6
1983	42,330	10,014	52,344	12,108,600	6,985.9	5,032.1	6,502.9	5,175.0
1984	42,659	10,766	53,425	11,881,800	7,324.4	5,149.1	6,749.8	5,031.3
1985	48,924	12,211	61,135	12,431,400	8,140.3	5,485.9	7,422.9	5,207.1
1986	59,410	15,184	74,594	13,211,900	9,634.0	6,621.2	8,817.3	5,480.4
1987	74,227	16,339	90,566	13,508,700	11,784.2	6,582.0	10,313.6	5,550.0
1988	n/a	n/a	n/a	13,923,100	n/a	n/a	n/a	5,664.2
1989	67,651	14,034	81,685	14,251,400	10,332.5	5,240.1	8,854.2	5,741.0
1990	66,618	16,317	82,935	14,475,600	10,463.3	6,042.3	9,146.6	5,820.3
1991	69,217	16,378	85,595	14,872,900	10,591.5	5,910.1	9,197.5	5,897.8
1992	69,777	16,909	86,686	14,438,200	10,510.2	6,006.5	9,169.1	5,660.2
1993	67,513	15,579	83,092	14,144,800	10,041.9	5,297.2	8,598.0	5,484.4
1994	65,997	14,041	80,038	13,989,500	9,623.7	4,680.6	8,119.4	5,373.5
1995	61,129	13,621	74,750	13,862,700	9,000.8	4,395.4	7,557.8	5,275.9
1996	59,534	n/a	n/a	13,473,600	8,623.5	n/a	n/a	5,078.9

Notes: (1) Metropolitan Statistical Area - see Appendix A for areas included; (2) calculated by the editors using the following formula: (number of crimes in the MSA minus number of crimes in the city); (3) calculated by the editors using the following formula: ((number of crimes in the MSA minus number of crimes in the city) ÷ (population of the MSA minus population of the city)) x 100,000; n/a not avail.
Source: U.S. Department of Justice, FBI Uniform Crime Reports, 1977 - 1996

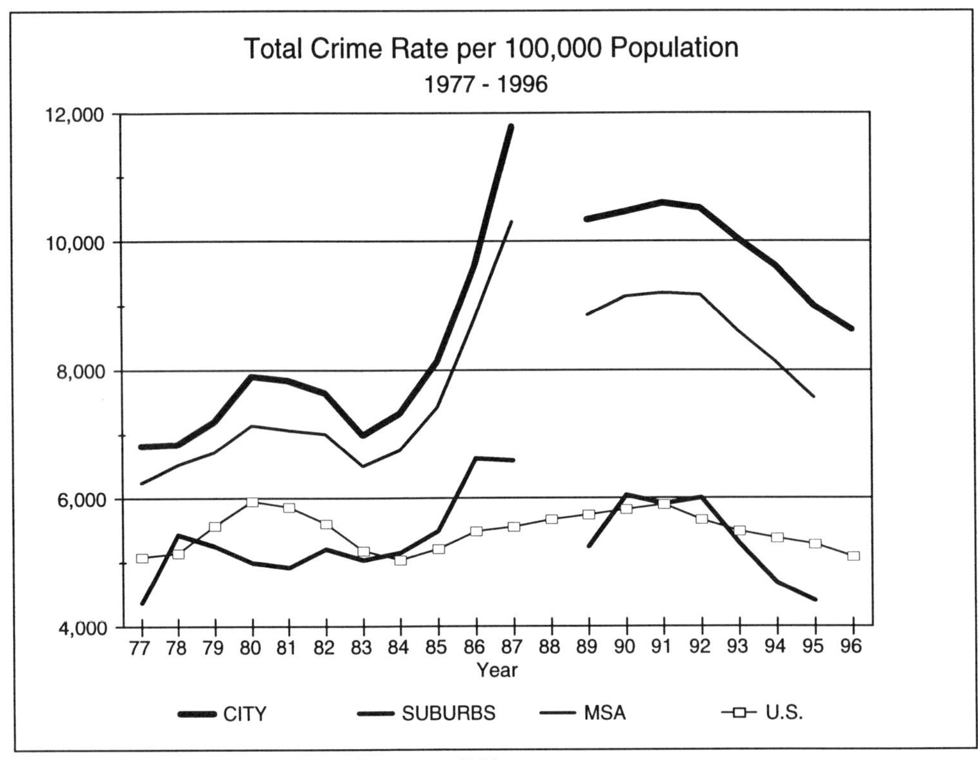

Note: Missing line segments indicate data not available.

Violent Crimes and Violent Crime Rates: 1977 - 1996

Year	Number				Rate per 100,000 population			
	City	Suburbs[2]	MSA[1]	U.S.	City	Suburbs[3]	MSA[1]	U.S.
1977	4,171	699	4,870	1,029,580	790.0	435.8	707.4	475.9
1978	4,368	795	5,163	1,085,550	824.2	503.9	750.7	497.8
1979	4,903	900	5,803	1,208,030	897.3	502.7	799.9	548.9
1980	4,848	1,000	5,848	1,344,520	893.2	516.7	794.2	596.6
1981	5,634	908	6,542	1,361,820	979.6	438.1	836.1	594.3
1982	5,643	1,099	6,742	1,322,390	954.9	521.5	841.0	571.1
1983	5,670	923	6,593	1,258,090	935.7	463.8	819.1	537.7
1984	6,228	1,161	7,389	1,273,280	1,069.3	555.3	933.5	539.2
1985	7,301	1,477	8,778	1,328,800	1,214.8	663.6	1,065.8	556.6
1986	8,003	1,899	9,902	1,489,170	1,297.8	828.1	1,170.5	617.7
1987	9,577	1,664	11,241	1,484,000	1,520.4	670.3	1,280.1	609.7
1988	n/a	n/a	n/a	1,566,220	n/a	n/a	n/a	637.2
1989	9,449	1,376	10,825	1,646,040	1,443.2	513.8	1,173.4	663.1
1990	11,654	2,030	13,684	1,820,130	1,830.4	751.7	1,509.2	731.8
1991	11,505	1,963	13,468	1,911,770	1,760.5	708.4	1,447.2	758.1
1992	11,548	2,071	13,619	1,932,270	1,739.4	735.7	1,440.5	757.5
1993	11,417	2,305	13,722	1,926,020	1,698.2	783.7	1,419.9	746.8
1994	10,423	1,954	12,377	1,857,670	1,519.9	651.4	1,255.6	713.6
1995	9,596	1,962	11,558	1,798,790	1,412.9	633.1	1,168.6	684.6
1996	9,765	n/a	n/a	1,682,280	1,414.5	n/a	n/a	634.1

Notes: Violent crimes include murder, forcible rape, robbery and aggravated assault; n/a not available; (1) Metropolitan Statistical Area - see Appendix A for areas included; (2) calculated by the editors using the following formula: (number of crimes in the MSA minus number of crimes in the city); (3) calculated by the editors using the following formula: ((number of crimes in the MSA minus number of crimes in the city) ÷ (population of the MSA minus population of the city)) x 100,000
Source: U.S. Department of Justice, FBI Uniform Crime Reports, 1977 - 1996

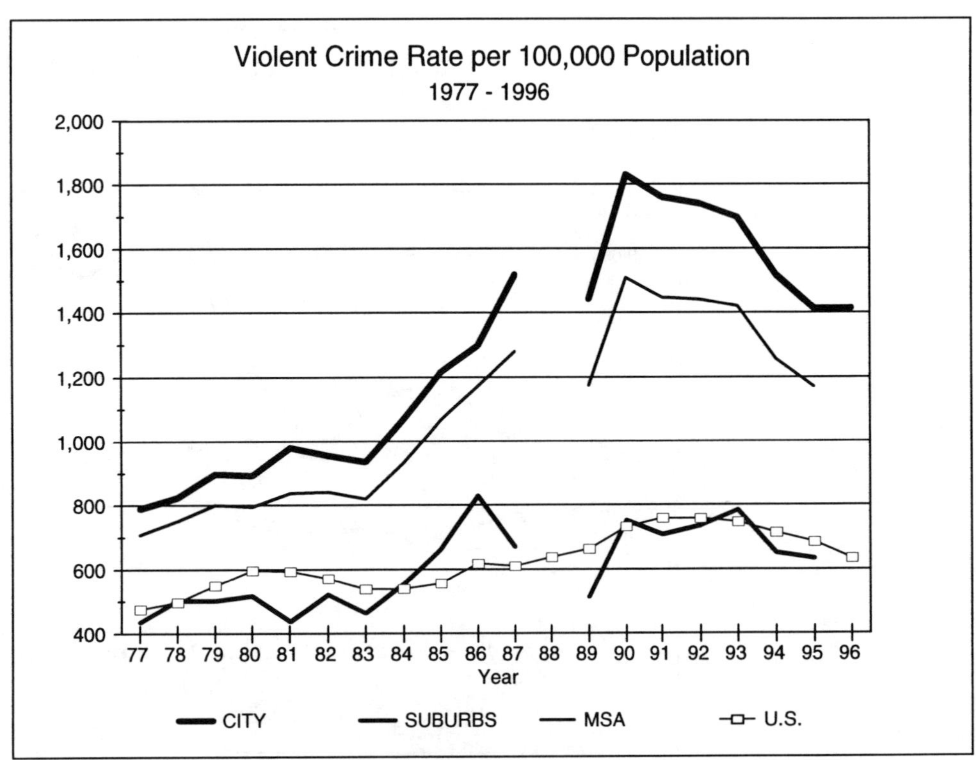

Note: Missing line segments indicate data not available.

Property Crimes and Property Crime Rates: 1977 - 1996

Year	Number				Rate per 100,000 population			
	City	Suburbs[2]	MSA[1]	U.S.	City	Suburbs[3]	MSA[1]	U.S.
1977	31,828	6,312	38,140	9,955,000	6,028.0	3,935.3	5,540.4	4,601.7
1978	31,906	7,768	39,674	10,123,400	6,020.0	4,924.0	5,768.6	4,642.5
1979	34,446	8,499	42,945	11,041,500	6,304.0	4,747.0	5,919.7	5,016.6
1980	38,042	8,662	46,704	12,063,700	7,008.5	4,475.4	6,342.7	5,353.3
1981	39,436	9,285	48,721	12,061,900	6,856.6	4,479.4	6,226.8	5,263.9
1982	39,512	9,875	49,387	11,652,000	6,686.1	4,686.3	6,160.4	5,032.5
1983	36,660	9,091	45,751	10,850,500	6,050.2	4,568.3	5,683.8	4,637.4
1984	36,431	9,605	46,036	10,608,500	6,255.1	4,593.8	5,816.2	4,492.1
1985	41,623	10,734	52,357	11,102,600	6,925.5	4,822.3	6,357.1	4,650.5
1986	51,407	13,285	64,692	11,722,700	8,336.3	5,793.1	7,646.9	4,862.6
1987	64,650	14,675	79,325	12,024,700	10,263.7	5,911.7	9,033.5	4,940.3
1988	n/a	n/a	n/a	12,356,900	n/a	n/a	n/a	5,027.1
1989	58,202	12,658	70,860	12,605,400	8,889.4	4,726.3	7,680.8	5,077.9
1990	54,964	14,287	69,251	12,655,500	8,632.9	5,290.6	7,637.5	5,088.5
1991	57,712	14,415	72,127	12,961,100	8,831.0	5,201.8	7,750.3	5,139.7
1992	58,229	14,838	73,067	12,505,900	8,770.8	5,270.8	7,728.6	4,902.7
1993	56,096	13,274	69,370	12,218,800	8,343.8	4,513.4	7,178.1	4,737.6
1994	55,574	12,087	67,661	12,131,900	8,103.8	4,029.2	6,863.8	4,660.0
1995	51,533	11,659	63,192	12,063,900	7,587.9	3,762.3	6,389.2	4,591.3
1996	49,769	n/a	n/a	11,791,300	7,209.1	n/a	n/a	4,444.8

Notes: Property crimes include burglary, larceny-theft and motor vehicle theft; n/a not available; (1) Metropolitan Statistical Area - see Appendix A for areas included; (2) calculated by the editors using the following formula: (number of crimes in the MSA minus number of crimes in the city); (3) calculated by the editors using the following formula: ((number of crimes in the MSA minus number of crimes in the city) ÷ (population of the MSA minus population of the city)) x 100,000
Source: U.S. Department of Justice, FBI Uniform Crime Reports, 1977 - 1996

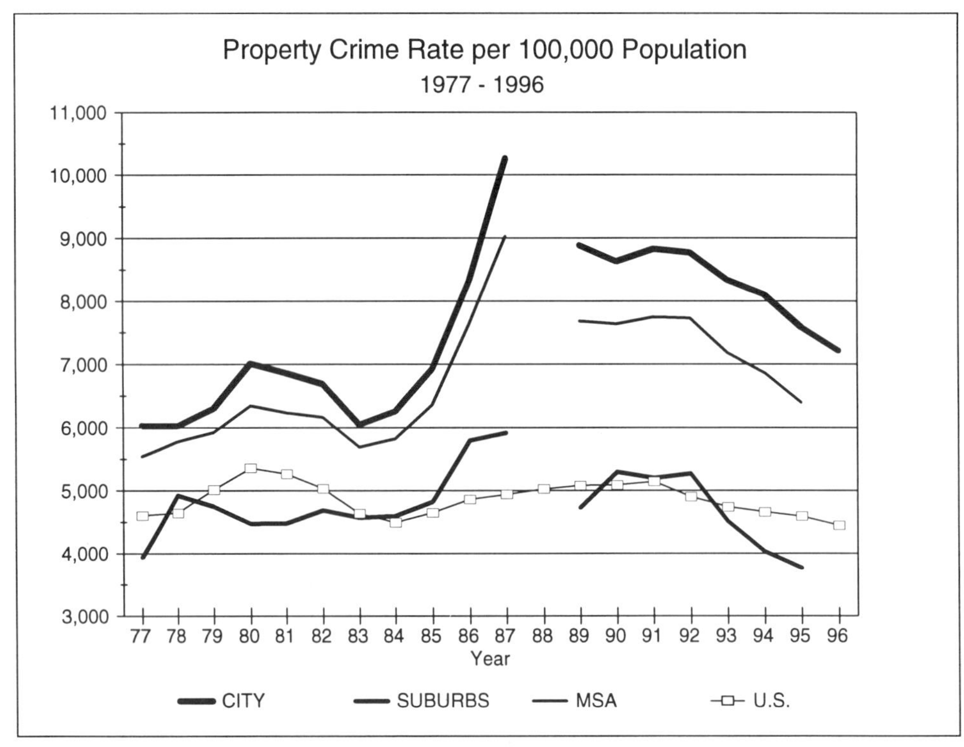

Note: Missing line segments indicate data not available.

Murders and Murder Rates: 1977 - 1996

Year	Number				Rate per 100,000 population			
	City	Suburbs[2]	MSA[1]	U.S.	City	Suburbs[3]	MSA[1]	U.S.
1977	77	14	91	19,120	14.6	8.7	13.2	8.8
1978	79	15	94	19,560	14.9	9.5	13.7	9.0
1979	73	14	87	21,460	13.4	7.8	12.0	9.7
1980	70	21	91	23,040	12.9	10.9	12.4	10.2
1981	89	14	103	22,520	15.5	6.8	13.2	9.8
1982	83	21	104	21,010	14.0	10.0	13.0	9.1
1983	82	14	96	19,310	13.5	7.0	11.9	8.3
1984	103	14	117	18,690	17.7	6.7	14.8	7.9
1985	90	17	107	18,980	15.0	7.6	13.0	7.9
1986	119	20	139	20,610	19.3	8.7	16.4	8.6
1987	147	15	162	20,100	23.3	6.0	18.4	8.3
1988	n/a	n/a	n/a	20,680	n/a	n/a	n/a	8.4
1989	165	12	177	21,500	25.2	4.5	19.2	8.7
1990	176	16	192	23,440	27.6	5.9	21.2	9.4
1991	128	23	151	24,700	19.6	8.3	16.2	9.8
1992	123	19	142	23,760	18.5	6.7	15.0	9.3
1993	125	21	146	24,530	18.6	7.1	15.1	9.5
1994	106	17	123	23,330	15.5	5.7	12.5	9.0
1995	86	7	93	21,610	12.7	2.3	9.4	8.2
1996	85	n/a	n/a	19,650	12.3	n/a	n/a	7.4

Notes: (1) Metropolitan Statistical Area - see Appendix A for areas included; (2) calculated by the editors using the following formula: (number of crimes in the MSA minus number of crimes in the city); (3) calculated by the editors using the following formula: ((number of crimes in the MSA minus number of crimes in the city) ÷ (population of the MSA minus population of the city)) x 100,000; n/a not avail.
Source: U.S. Department of Justice, FBI Uniform Crime Reports, 1977 - 1996

Forcible Rapes and Forcible Rape Rates: 1977 - 1996

Year	Number				Rate per 100,000 population			
	City	Suburbs[2]	MSA[1]	U.S.	City	Suburbs[3]	MSA[1]	U.S.
1977	299	42	341	63,500	56.6	26.2	49.5	29.4
1978	278	52	330	67,610	52.5	33.0	48.0	31.0
1979	372	68	440	76,390	68.1	38.0	60.7	34.7
1980	414	62	476	82,990	76.3	32.0	64.6	36.8
1981	410	70	480	82,500	71.3	33.8	61.3	36.0
1982	422	64	486	78,770	71.4	30.4	60.6	34.0
1983	411	85	496	78,920	67.8	42.7	61.6	33.7
1984	587	107	694	84,230	100.8	51.2	87.7	35.7
1985	705	72	777	88,670	117.3	32.3	94.3	37.1
1986	618	83	701	91,460	100.2	36.2	82.9	37.9
1987	609	98	707	91,110	96.7	39.5	80.5	37.4
1988	n/a	n/a	n/a	92,490	n/a	n/a	n/a	37.6
1989	609	80	689	94,500	93.0	29.9	74.7	38.1
1990	704	91	795	102,560	110.6	33.7	87.7	41.2
1991	798	99	897	106,590	122.1	35.7	96.4	42.3
1992	713	127	840	109,060	107.4	45.1	88.9	42.8
1993	699	125	824	106,010	104.0	42.5	85.3	41.1
1994	648	120	768	102,220	94.5	40.0	77.9	39.3
1995	625	148	773	97,470	92.0	47.8	78.2	37.1
1996	681	n/a	n/a	95,770	98.6	n/a	n/a	36.1

Notes: (1) Metropolitan Statistical Area - see Appendix A for areas included; (2) calculated by the editors using the following formula: (number of crimes in the MSA minus number of crimes in the city); (3) calculated by the editors using the following formula: ((number of crimes in the MSA minus number of crimes in the city) ÷ (population of the MSA minus population of the city)) x 100,000; n/a not avail.
Source: U.S. Department of Justice, FBI Uniform Crime Reports, 1977 - 1996

Robberies and Robbery Rates: 1977 - 1996

Year	Number				Rate per 100,000 population			
	City	Suburbs[2]	MSA[1]	U.S.	City	Suburbs[3]	MSA[1]	U.S.
1977	1,466	145	1,611	412,610	277.7	90.4	234.0	190.7
1978	1,347	155	1,502	426,930	254.2	98.3	218.4	195.8
1979	1,555	253	1,808	480,700	284.6	141.3	249.2	218.4
1980	1,631	213	1,844	565,840	300.5	110.1	250.4	251.1
1981	2,340	235	2,575	592,910	406.8	113.4	329.1	258.7
1982	2,152	211	2,363	553,130	364.2	100.1	294.8	238.9
1983	2,288	203	2,491	506,570	377.6	102.0	309.5	216.5
1984	2,134	235	2,369	485,010	366.4	112.4	299.3	205.4
1985	2,693	234	2,927	497,870	448.1	105.1	355.4	208.5
1986	2,985	316	3,301	542,780	484.1	137.8	390.2	225.1
1987	3,876	382	4,258	517,700	615.3	153.9	484.9	212.7
1988	n/a	n/a	n/a	542,970	n/a	n/a	n/a	220.9
1989	3,940	309	4,249	578,330	601.8	115.4	460.6	233.0
1990	3,963	357	4,320	639,270	622.4	132.2	476.4	257.0
1991	4,131	374	4,505	687,730	632.1	135.0	484.1	272.7
1992	3,614	356	3,970	672,480	544.4	126.5	419.9	263.6
1993	3,604	320	3,924	659,870	536.1	108.8	406.0	255.9
1994	3,427	279	3,706	618,950	499.7	93.0	376.0	237.7
1995	2,920	252	3,172	580,510	430.0	81.3	320.7	220.9
1996	2,792	n/a	n/a	537,050	404.4	n/a	n/a	202.4

Notes: (1) Metropolitan Statistical Area - see Appendix A for areas included; (2) calculated by the editors using the following formula: (number of crimes in the MSA minus number of crimes in the city); (3) calculated by the editors using the following formula: ((number of crimes in the MSA minus number of crimes in the city) ÷ (population of the MSA minus population of the city)) x 100,000; n/a not avail.
Source: U.S. Department of Justice, FBI Uniform Crime Reports, 1977 - 1996

Aggravated Assaults and Aggravated Assault Rates: 1977 - 1996

Year	Number				Rate per 100,000 population			
	City	Suburbs[2]	MSA[1]	U.S.	City	Suburbs[3]	MSA[1]	U.S.
1977	2,329	498	2,827	534,350	441.1	310.5	410.7	247.0
1978	2,664	573	3,237	571,460	502.6	363.2	470.7	262.1
1979	2,903	565	3,468	629,480	531.3	315.6	478.0	286.0
1980	2,733	704	3,437	672,650	503.5	363.7	466.8	298.5
1981	2,795	589	3,384	663,900	486.0	284.2	432.5	289.7
1982	2,986	803	3,789	669,480	505.3	381.1	472.6	289.2
1983	2,889	621	3,510	653,290	476.8	312.1	436.1	279.2
1984	3,404	805	4,209	685,350	584.5	385.0	531.8	290.2
1985	3,813	1,154	4,967	723,250	634.4	518.4	603.1	302.9
1986	4,281	1,480	5,761	834,320	694.2	645.4	681.0	346.1
1987	4,945	1,169	6,114	855,090	785.1	470.9	696.3	351.3
1988	n/a	n/a	n/a	910,090	n/a	n/a	n/a	370.2
1989	4,735	975	5,710	951,710	723.2	364.1	618.9	383.4
1990	6,811	1,566	8,377	1,054,860	1,069.8	579.9	923.9	424.1
1991	6,448	1,467	7,915	1,092,740	986.7	529.4	850.5	433.3
1992	7,098	1,569	8,667	1,126,970	1,069.1	557.3	916.7	441.8
1993	6,989	1,839	8,828	1,135,610	1,039.6	625.3	913.5	440.3
1994	6,242	1,538	7,780	1,113,180	910.2	512.7	789.2	427.6
1995	5,965	1,555	7,520	1,099,210	878.3	501.8	760.3	418.3
1996	6,207	n/a	n/a	1,029,810	899.1	n/a	n/a	388.2

Notes: (1) Metropolitan Statistical Area - see Appendix A for areas included; (2) calculated by the editors using the following formula: (number of crimes in the MSA minus number of crimes in the city); (3) calculated by the editors using the following formula: ((number of crimes in the MSA minus number of crimes in the city) ÷ (population of the MSA minus population of the city)) x 100,000; n/a not avail.
Source: U.S. Department of Justice, FBI Uniform Crime Reports, 1977 - 1996

Burglaries and Burglary Rates: 1977 - 1996

Year	Number				Rate per 100,000 population			
	City	Suburbs[2]	MSA[1]	U.S.	City	Suburbs[3]	MSA[1]	U.S.
1977	9,961	1,909	11,870	3,071,500	1,886.6	1,190.2	1,724.3	1,419.8
1978	10,385	2,467	12,852	3,128,300	1,959.4	1,563.8	1,868.7	1,434.6
1979	11,450	2,362	13,812	3,327,700	2,095.5	1,319.3	1,903.9	1,511.9
1980	13,568	2,835	16,403	3,795,200	2,499.7	1,464.8	2,227.6	1,684.1
1981	13,096	3,129	16,225	3,779,700	2,276.9	1,509.6	2,073.6	1,649.5
1982	12,830	2,729	15,559	3,447,100	2,171.1	1,295.1	1,940.8	1,488.8
1983	12,509	2,210	14,719	3,129,900	2,064.4	1,110.5	1,828.6	1,337.7
1984	11,630	2,426	14,056	2,984,400	1,996.8	1,160.3	1,775.9	1,263.7
1985	13,663	2,744	16,407	3,073,300	2,273.4	1,232.8	1,992.1	1,287.3
1986	16,498	3,364	19,862	3,241,400	2,675.3	1,466.9	2,347.8	1,344.6
1987	20,745	3,736	24,481	3,236,200	3,293.4	1,505.0	2,787.9	1,329.6
1988	n/a	n/a	n/a	3,218,100	n/a	n/a	n/a	1,309.2
1989	19,708	3,389	23,097	3,168,200	3,010.1	1,265.4	2,503.6	1,276.3
1990	17,529	3,772	21,301	3,073,900	2,753.2	1,396.8	2,349.2	1,235.9
1991	17,301	3,550	20,851	3,157,200	2,647.4	1,281.0	2,240.5	1,252.0
1992	16,304	3,225	19,529	2,979,900	2,455.8	1,145.6	2,065.7	1,168.2
1993	15,127	3,206	18,333	2,834,800	2,250.0	1,090.1	1,897.0	1,099.2
1994	14,327	2,667	16,994	2,712,800	2,089.2	889.0	1,723.9	1,042.0
1995	12,491	2,603	15,094	2,593,800	1,839.2	840.0	1,526.1	987.1
1996	13,171	n/a	n/a	2,501,500	1,907.8	n/a	n/a	943.0

Notes: (1) Metropolitan Statistical Area - see Appendix A for areas included; (2) calculated by the editors using the following formula: (number of crimes in the MSA minus number of crimes in the city); (3) calculated by the editors using the following formula: ((number of crimes in the MSA minus number of crimes in the city) ÷ (population of the MSA minus population of the city)) x 100,000; n/a not avail.
Source: U.S. Department of Justice, FBI Uniform Crime Reports, 1977 - 1996

Larceny-Thefts and Larceny-Theft Rates: 1977 - 1996

Year	Number				Rate per 100,000 population			
	City	Suburbs[2]	MSA[1]	U.S.	City	Suburbs[3]	MSA[1]	U.S.
1977	20,176	4,017	24,193	5,905,700	3,821.2	2,504.4	3,514.4	2,729.9
1978	19,707	4,825	24,532	5,991,000	3,718.3	3,058.5	3,567.0	2,747.4
1979	21,013	5,589	26,602	6,601,000	3,845.6	3,121.6	3,666.9	2,999.1
1980	22,668	5,395	28,063	7,136,900	4,176.2	2,787.4	3,811.1	3,167.0
1981	24,469	5,693	30,162	7,194,400	4,254.3	2,746.5	3,854.9	3,139.7
1982	25,005	6,652	31,657	7,142,500	4,231.3	3,156.8	3,948.8	3,084.8
1983	22,634	6,451	29,085	6,712,800	3,735.4	3,241.7	3,613.3	2,868.9
1984	22,936	6,676	29,612	6,591,900	3,938.0	3,192.9	3,741.2	2,791.3
1985	25,806	7,398	33,204	6,926,400	4,293.8	3,323.6	4,031.6	2,901.2
1986	31,668	9,158	40,826	7,257,200	5,135.3	3,993.5	4,825.8	3,010.3
1987	38,820	10,096	48,916	7,499,900	6,163.0	4,067.1	5,570.5	3,081.3
1988	n/a	n/a	n/a	7,705,900	n/a	n/a	n/a	3,134.9
1989	33,267	8,522	41,789	7,872,400	5,081.0	3,182.0	4,529.7	3,171.3
1990	31,392	9,540	40,932	7,945,700	4,930.6	3,532.7	4,514.3	3,194.8
1991	34,594	10,034	44,628	8,142,200	5,293.5	3,620.9	4,795.5	3,228.8
1992	33,138	10,647	43,785	7,915,200	4,991.4	3,782.0	4,631.3	3,103.0
1993	31,936	9,346	41,282	7,820,900	4,750.2	3,177.8	4,271.7	3,032.4
1994	34,453	8,674	43,127	7,879,800	5,023.9	2,891.5	4,375.0	3,026.7
1995	33,306	8,397	41,703	7,997,700	4,904.1	2,709.7	4,216.5	3,043.8
1996	31,852	n/a	n/a	7,894,600	4,613.8	n/a	n/a	2,975.9

Notes: (1) Metropolitan Statistical Area - see Appendix A for areas included; (2) calculated by the editors using the following formula: (number of crimes in the MSA minus number of crimes in the city); (3) calculated by the editors using the following formula: ((number of crimes in the MSA minus number of crimes in the city) ÷ (population of the MSA minus population of the city)) x 100,000; n/a not avail.
Source: U.S. Department of Justice, FBI Uniform Crime Reports, 1977 - 1996

Motor Vehicle Thefts and Motor Vehicle Theft Rates: 1977 - 1996

Year	Number				Rate per 100,000 population			
	City	Suburbs[2]	MSA[1]	U.S.	City	Suburbs[3]	MSA[1]	U.S.
1977	1,691	386	2,077	977,700	320.3	240.7	301.7	451.9
1978	1,814	476	2,290	1,004,100	342.3	301.7	333.0	460.5
1979	1,983	548	2,531	1,112,800	362.9	306.1	348.9	505.6
1980	1,806	432	2,238	1,131,700	332.7	223.2	303.9	502.2
1981	1,871	463	2,334	1,087,800	325.3	223.4	298.3	474.7
1982	1,677	494	2,171	1,062,400	283.8	234.4	270.8	458.8
1983	1,517	430	1,947	1,007,900	250.4	216.1	241.9	430.8
1984	1,865	503	2,368	1,032,200	320.2	240.6	299.2	437.1
1985	2,154	592	2,746	1,102,900	358.4	266.0	333.4	462.0
1986	3,241	763	4,004	1,224,100	525.6	332.7	473.3	507.8
1987	5,085	843	5,928	1,288,700	807.3	339.6	675.1	529.4
1988	n/a	n/a	n/a	1,432,900	n/a	n/a	n/a	582.9
1989	5,227	747	5,974	1,564,800	798.3	278.9	647.5	630.4
1990	6,043	975	7,018	1,635,900	949.1	361.0	774.0	657.8
1991	5,817	831	6,648	1,661,700	890.1	299.9	714.4	659.0
1992	8,787	966	9,753	1,610,800	1,323.5	343.1	1,031.6	631.5
1993	9,033	722	9,755	1,563,100	1,343.6	245.5	1,009.4	606.1
1994	6,794	746	7,540	1,539,300	990.7	248.7	764.9	591.3
1995	5,736	659	6,395	1,472,400	844.6	212.7	646.6	560.4
1996	4,746	n/a	n/a	1,395,200	687.5	n/a	n/a	525.9

Notes: (1) Metropolitan Statistical Area - see Appendix A for areas included; (2) calculated by the editors using the following formula: (number of crimes in the MSA minus number of crimes in the city); (3) calculated by the editors using the following formula: ((number of crimes in the MSA minus number of crimes in the city) ÷ (population of the MSA minus population of the city)) x 100,000; n/a not avail.
Source: U.S. Department of Justice, FBI Uniform Crime Reports, 1977 - 1996

HATE CRIMES

Criminal Incidents by Bias Motivation

Area	Race	Ethnicity	Religion	Sexual Orientation
Jacksonville	1	0	0	0

Notes: Figures include both violent and property crimes. Law enforcement agencies must have submitted data for at least one quarter of calendar year 1995 to be included in this report, therefore figures shown may not represent complete 12-month totals; n/a not available
Source: U.S. Department of Justice, FBI Uniform Crime Reports, Hate Crime Statistics 1995

LAW ENFORCEMENT

Full-Time Law Enforcement Employees

Jurisdiction	Police Employees			Police Officers per 100,000 population
	Total	Officers	Civilians	
Jacksonville	2,362	1,394	968	201.9

Notes: Data as of October 31, 1996
Source: U.S. Department of Justice, FBI Uniform Crime Reports, 1996

Number of Police Officers by Race

Race	Police Officers				Index of Representation[1]		
	1983		1992				
	Number	Pct.	Number	Pct.	1983	1992	% Chg.
Black	78	6.2	232	19.3	0.24	0.76	216.7
Hispanic[2]	9	0.7	0	0.0	0.38	0.00	-100.0

Notes: (1) The index of representation is calculated by dividing the percent of black/hispanic police officers by the percent of corresponding blacks/hispanics in the local population. An index approaching 1.0 indicates that a city is closer to achieving a representation of police officers equal to their proportion in the local population; (2) Hispanic officers can be of any race ; Data for 1983 is based on 1980-81 information from the Police Executive Research Forum, Survey of Operational and Administrative Practices 1981
Source: Bureau of Justice Statistics, Sourcebook of Criminal Justice Statistics, 1994

CORRECTIONS

Federal Correctional Facilities

Type	Year Opened	Security Level	Sex of Inmates	Rated Capacity	Population on 7/1/95	Number of Staff
None listed						

Notes: Data as of 1995
Source: Bureau of Justice Statistics, Sourcebook of Criminal Justice Statistics Online

City/County/Regional Correctional Facilities

Name	Year Opened	Year Renov.	Rated Capacity	1995 Pop.	Number of COs[1]	Number of Staff	ACA[2] Accred.
Duval County - J.I. Montgomery Corr Ctr	1956	1995	611	554	120	130	No
Duval County Corr Div	1989	--	300	n/a	n/a	n/a	No
Duval County Jails and Prisons Division	1991	--	2,189	n/a	n/a	n/a	No

Notes: Data as of April 1996; (1) Correctional Officers; (2) American Correctional Assn. Accreditation
Source: American Correctional Association, 1996-1998 National Jail and Adult Detention Directory

Private Adult Correctional Facilities

Name	Date Opened	Rated Capacity	Present Pop.	Security Level	Facility Construct.	Expans. Plans	ACA[1] Accred.
None listed							

Notes: Data as of December 1996; (1) American Correctional Association Accreditation
Source: University of Florida, Center for Studies in Criminology and Law, Private Adult Correctional Facility Census, 10th Ed., March 15, 1997

Characteristics of Shock Incarceration Programs

Jurisdiction	Year Program Began	Number of Camps	Average Num. of Inmates	Number of Beds	Program Length	Voluntary/ Mandatory
Florida	1987	1	94	112	120 days min.	n/a

Note: Data as of July 1996;
Source: Sourcebook of Criminal Justice Statistics Online

INMATES AND HIV/AIDS

HIV Testing Policies for Inmates

Jurisdiction	All Inmates at Some Time	All Convicted Inmates at Admission	Random Samples While in Custody	High-risk Groups	Upon Inmate Request	Upon Court Order	Upon Involve-ment in Incident
Duval Co.	No	No	No	Yes	Yes	Yes	Yes

Source: HIV in Prisons and Jails, 1993 (released August 1995)

Inmates Known to be Positive for HIV

Jurisdiction	Number of Jail Inmates in Facilities Providing Data	Type of HIV Infection/AIDS Cases				HIV/AIDS Cases as a Percent of Tot. Custody Pop.
		Total	Asymp-tomatic	Symp-tomatic	Confirmed AIDS	
Duval Co.	2,423	12	0	0	12	0.5

Source: HIV in Prisons and Jails, 1993 (released August, 1995)

DEATH PENALTY

Death Penalty Statistics

State	Prisoners Executed		Prisoners Under Sentence of Death					Avg. No. of Years on Death Row[4]
	1930-1995	1996[1]	Total[2]	White[3]	Black[3]	Hisp.	Women	
Florida	206	2	362	228	134	35	6	6.9

Notes: Data as of 12/31/95 unless otherwise noted; (1) Data as of 7/31/97; (2) Includes persons of other races; (3) Includes people of Hispanic origin; (4) Covers prisoners sentenced 1974 through 1995
Source: Bureau of Justice Statistics, Capital Punishment 1995 (released 12/96); Death Penalty Information Center Web Site, 9/30/97

Capital Offenses and Methods of Execution

Capital Offenses in Florida	Minimum Age for Imposition of Death Penalty	Mentally Retarded Excluded	Methods of Execution[1]
First-degree murder; felony murder; capital drug-trafficking.	16	No	Electrocution

Notes: Data as of 12/31/95 unless otherwise noted; (1) Data as of 7/31/97
Source: Bureau of Justice Statistics, Capital Punishment 1995 (released 12/96); Death Penalty Information Center Web Site, 9/30/97

LAWS

Statutory Provisions Relating to the Purchase, Ownership and Use of Handguns

Jurisdiction	Instant Background Check	Federal Waiting Period Applies[1]	State Waiting Period (days)	License or Permit to Purchase	Regis-tration	Record of Sale Sent to Police	Concealed Carry Law
Florida	Yes[a]	No	3[b,c]	No	No	No	Yes[d]

Note: Data as of 1996; (1) The Federal 5-day waiting period for handgun purchases applies to states that don't have instant background checks, waiting period requirements, or licensing procedures exempting them from the Federal requirement; (a) Concealed firearm carry permit holders are exempt from Instant Check; (b) The State waiting period does not apply to a person holding a valid permit or license to carry a firearm; (c) Purchases from licensed dealers only; (d) "Shall issue" permit system, liberally administered discretion by local authorities over permit issuance, or no permit required
Source: Sourcebook of Criminal Justice Statistics Online

Statutory Provisions Relating to Alcohol Use and Driving

Jurisdiction	Drinking Age	Blood Alcohol Concentration Levels as Evidence in State Courts[1]		Open Container Law[1]	Anti-Consump-tion Law[1]	Dram Shop Law[1]
		Illegal per se at 0.10%	Presumption at 0.10%			
Florida	21	(a)	(a,b)	Yes	No	Yes[c]

Note: Data as of January 1, 1997; (1) See Appendix C for an explanation of terms; (a) 0.08%; (b) Constitutes prima facie evidence; (c) Applies only to the actions of intoxicated minors or persons known to be habitually addicted to alcohol
Source: Sourcebook of Criminal Justice Statistics Online

Statutory Provisions Relating to Curfews

Jurisdiction	Year Enacted	Latest Revision	Age Group(s)	Curfew Provisions
Jacksonville	1991	-	17 and under	11 pm to 6 am weekday nights midnight to 6 am weekend nights

Note: Data as of February 1996
Source: Sourcebook of Criminal Justice Statistics Online

Statutory Provisions Relating to Hate Crimes

Jurisdiction	Bias-Motivated Violence and Intimidation						Institutional Vandalism
		Criminal Penalty					
	Civil Action	Race/ Religion/ Ethnicity	Sexual Orientation	Mental/ Physical Disability	Gender	Age	
Florida	Yes	Yes	Yes	No	No	No	Yes

Source: Anti-Defamation League, 1997 Hate Crimes Laws

Kansas City, Missouri

OVERVIEW

The total crime rate for the city increased 37.4% between 1977 and 1996. During that same period, the violent crime rate increased 61.9% and the property crime rate increased 33.3%.

Among violent crimes, the rates for: Murders increased 10.0%; Forcible Rapes increased 29.8%; Robberies increased 26.8%; and Aggravated Assaults increased 95.9%.

Among property crimes, the rates for: Burglaries decreased 18.6%; Larceny-Thefts increased 51.9%; and Motor Vehicle Thefts increased 106.4%.

ANTI-CRIME PROGRAMS

An anti-drug tax which was approved by Kansas City voters in 1989 (and renewed in 1995) in response to a rise in violent crime linked to crack cocaine, has allowed the Police Department to make more arrests of drug criminals. The tax has also paid for more prosecutors to expedite criminal cases through the courts. Nearly $7 million in additional revenue raised by the tax, is spent on drug treatment and prevention as forms of crime deterrence including a drug court that offers nonviolent felons with addiction problems the option of drug treatment instead of prison. The anti-drug tax has helped cut violent crime since 1991; the number of drug cases filed for prosecution and risen dramatically and nearly 700 people a month have entered or returned to drug treatment. *New York Times, 5/5/97*

CRIME RISK

Your Chances of Becoming a Victim[1]

Area	Any Crime	Violent Crime					Property Crime			
		Any	Murder	Forcible Rape[2]	Robbery	Aggrav. Assault	Any	Burglary	Larceny -Theft	Motor Vehicle Theft
City	1:9	1:50	1:4,312	1:572	1:156	1:82	1:10	1:50	1:16	1:71

Note: (1) Figures have been calculated by dividing the population of the city by the number of crimes reported to the FBI during 1996 and are expressed as odds (eg. 1:20 should be read as 1 in 20).
(2) Figures have been calculated by dividing the female population of the city by the number of forcible rapes reported to the FBI during 1996. The female population of the city was estimated by calculating the ratio of females to males reported in the 1990 Census and applying that ratio to 1996 population estimate.
Source: FBI Uniform Crime Reports 1996

CRIME STATISTICS

Total Crimes and Total Crime Rates: 1977 - 1996

Year	Number				Rate per 100,000 population			
	City	Suburbs[2]	MSA[1]	U.S.	City	Suburbs[3]	MSA[1]	U.S.
1977	38,960	42,550	81,510	10,984,500	8,488.0	4,949.1	6,180.8	5,077.6
1978	37,729	44,089	81,818	11,209,000	8,237.8	5,154.8	6,230.0	5,140.3
1979	42,065	47,221	89,286	12,249,500	9,087.0	5,445.7	6,713.0	5,565.5
1980	49,275	52,800	102,075	13,408,300	11,026.8	6,032.3	7,720.3	5,950.0
1981	51,005	52,409	103,414	13,423,800	11,329.1	5,932.3	7,754.2	5,858.2
1982	45,503	46,988	92,491	12,974,400	10,080.5	5,281.7	6,897.0	5,603.6
1983	45,388	48,771	94,159	12,108,600	10,016.6	4,860.4	6,464.5	5,175.0
1984	45,416	46,618	92,034	11,881,800	10,081.5	4,572.7	6,260.9	5,031.3
1985	46,616	46,241	92,857	12,431,400	10,476.9	4,453.0	6,259.9	5,207.1
1986	54,378	52,648	107,026	13,211,900	12,131.5	5,040.7	7,170.0	5,480.4
1987	52,777	55,408	108,185	13,508,700	11,876.5	5,111.7	7,078.6	5,550.0
1988	53,487	57,773	111,260	13,923,100	11,953.4	5,213.6	7,152.3	5,664.2
1989	56,028	59,222	115,250	14,251,400	12,721.1	5,182.6	7,279.8	5,741.0
1990	56,308	60,151	116,459	14,475,600	12,953.0	5,315.7	7,435.4	5,820.3
1991	57,834	60,191	118,025	14,872,900	13,198.4	5,279.9	7,478.5	5,897.8
1992	55,033	58,176	113,209	14,438,200	12,474.6	4,984.0	7,038.6	5,660.2
1993	55,165	n/a	n/a	14,144,800	12,669.1	n/a	n/a	5,484.4
1994	55,112	n/a	n/a	13,989,500	12,551.4	n/a	n/a	5,373.5
1995	52,575	n/a	n/a	13,862,700	11,800.0	n/a	n/a	5,275.9
1996	52,300	n/a	n/a	13,473,600	11,661.8	n/a	n/a	5,078.9

Notes: (1) Metropolitan Statistical Area - see Appendix A for areas included; (2) calculated by the editors using the following formula: (number of crimes in the MSA minus number of crimes in the city); (3) calculated by the editors using the following formula: ((number of crimes in the MSA minus number of crimes in the city) ÷ (population of the MSA minus population of the city)) x 100,000; n/a not avail.
Source: U.S. Department of Justice, FBI Uniform Crime Reports, 1977 - 1996

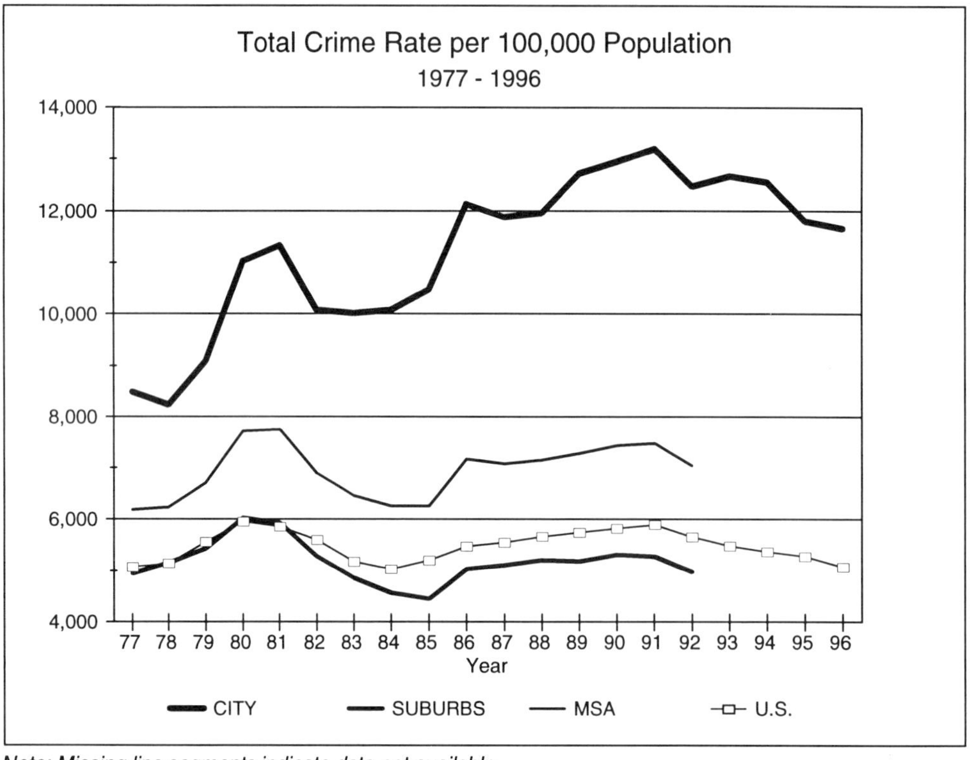

Note: Missing line segments indicate data not available.

Violent Crimes and Violent Crime Rates: 1977 - 1996

Year	Number				Rate per 100,000 population			
	City	Suburbs[2]	MSA[1]	U.S.	City	Suburbs[3]	MSA[1]	U.S.
1977	5,616	3,566	9,182	1,029,580	1,223.5	414.8	696.3	475.9
1978	5,029	4,003	9,032	1,085,550	1,098.0	468.0	687.7	497.8
1979	5,942	4,061	10,003	1,208,030	1,283.6	468.3	752.1	548.9
1980	7,014	4,481	11,495	1,344,520	1,569.6	511.9	869.4	596.6
1981	7,714	4,136	11,850	1,361,820	1,713.4	468.2	888.5	594.3
1982	6,729	3,682	10,411	1,322,390	1,490.7	413.9	776.3	571.1
1983	7,452	3,938	11,390	1,258,090	1,644.6	392.5	782.0	537.7
1984	7,167	4,101	11,268	1,273,280	1,590.9	402.3	766.5	539.2
1985	8,012	4,235	12,247	1,328,800	1,800.7	407.8	825.6	556.6
1986	9,673	4,754	14,427	1,489,170	2,158.0	455.2	966.5	617.7
1987	8,423	4,887	13,310	1,484,000	1,895.4	450.9	870.9	609.7
1988	8,316	4,796	13,112	1,566,220	1,858.5	432.8	842.9	637.2
1989	8,996	5,052	14,048	1,646,040	2,042.5	442.1	887.3	663.1
1990	11,087	5,830	16,917	1,820,130	2,550.4	515.2	1,080.1	731.8
1991	12,413	6,130	18,543	1,911,770	2,832.8	537.7	1,175.0	758.1
1992	12,594	6,000	18,594	1,932,270	2,854.7	514.0	1,156.0	757.5
1993	10,961	n/a	n/a	1,926,020	2,517.3	n/a	n/a	746.8
1994	10,693	n/a	n/a	1,857,670	2,435.3	n/a	n/a	713.6
1995	9,734	n/a	n/a	1,798,790	2,184.7	n/a	n/a	684.6
1996	8,885	n/a	n/a	1,682,280	1,981.2	n/a	n/a	634.1

Notes: Violent crimes include murder, forcible rape, robbery and aggravated assault; n/a not available; (1) Metropolitan Statistical Area - see Appendix A for areas included; (2) calculated by the editors using the following formula: (number of crimes in the MSA minus number of crimes in the city); (3) calculated by the editors using the following formula: ((number of crimes in the MSA minus number of crimes in the city) ÷ (population of the MSA minus population of the city)) x 100,000
Source: U.S. Department of Justice, FBI Uniform Crime Reports, 1977 - 1996

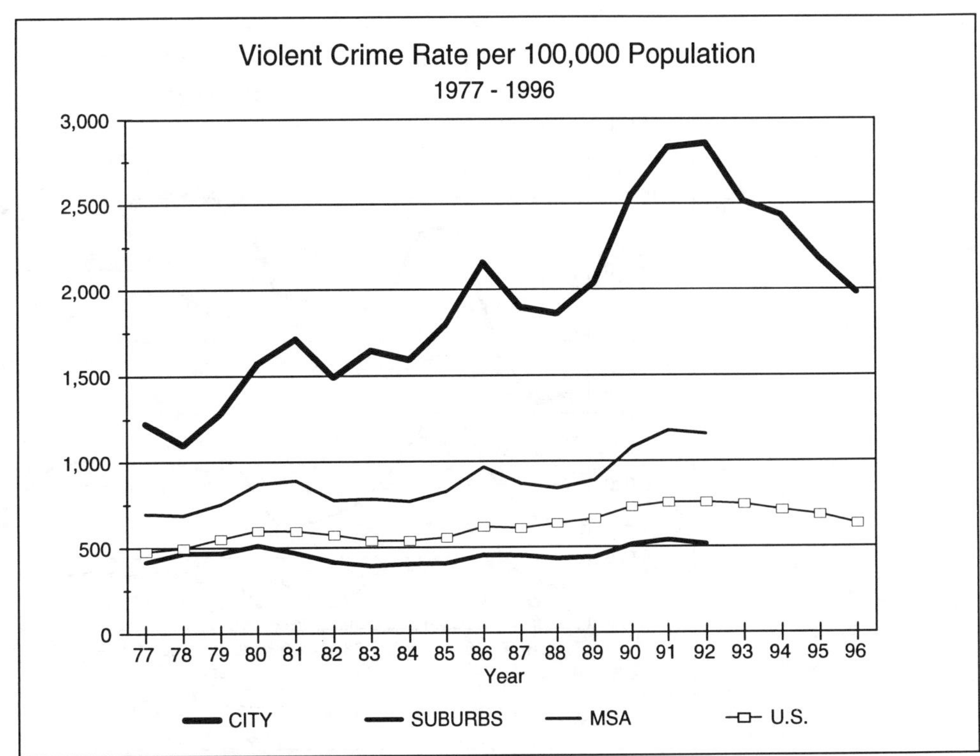

Note: Missing line segments indicate data not available.

Property Crimes and Property Crime Rates: 1977 - 1996

Year	Number				Rate per 100,000 population			
	City	Suburbs[2]	MSA[1]	U.S.	City	Suburbs[3]	MSA[1]	U.S.
1977	33,344	38,984	72,328	9,955,000	7,264.5	4,534.3	5,484.6	4,601.7
1978	32,700	40,086	72,786	10,123,400	7,139.7	4,686.8	5,542.2	4,642.5
1979	36,123	43,160	79,283	11,041,500	7,803.4	4,977.4	5,960.9	5,016.6
1980	42,261	48,319	90,580	12,063,700	9,457.2	5,520.3	6,850.9	5,353.3
1981	43,291	48,273	91,564	12,061,900	9,615.7	5,464.2	6,865.6	5,263.9
1982	38,774	43,306	82,080	11,652,000	8,589.8	4,867.8	6,120.6	5,032.5
1983	37,936	44,833	82,769	10,850,500	8,372.0	4,468.0	5,682.5	4,637.4
1984	38,249	42,517	80,766	10,608,500	8,490.6	4,170.4	5,494.4	4,492.1
1985	38,604	42,006	80,610	11,102,600	8,676.2	4,045.2	5,434.3	4,650.5
1986	44,705	47,894	92,599	11,722,700	9,973.5	4,585.6	6,203.5	4,862.6
1987	44,354	50,521	94,875	12,024,700	9,981.1	4,660.8	6,207.8	4,940.3
1988	45,171	52,977	98,148	12,356,900	10,095.0	4,780.8	6,309.4	5,027.1
1989	47,032	54,170	101,202	12,605,400	10,678.5	4,740.5	6,392.5	5,077.9
1990	45,221	54,321	99,542	12,655,500	10,402.5	4,800.5	6,355.3	5,088.5
1991	45,421	54,061	99,482	12,961,100	10,365.6	4,742.2	6,303.5	5,139.7
1992	42,439	52,176	94,615	12,505,900	9,619.8	4,470.0	5,882.5	4,902.7
1993	44,204	n/a	n/a	12,218,800	10,151.9	n/a	n/a	4,737.6
1994	44,419	n/a	n/a	12,131,900	10,116.2	n/a	n/a	4,660.0
1995	42,841	n/a	n/a	12,063,900	9,615.3	n/a	n/a	4,591.3
1996	43,415	n/a	n/a	11,791,300	9,680.6	n/a	n/a	4,444.8

Notes: Property crimes include burglary, larceny-theft and motor vehicle theft; n/a not available; (1) Metropolitan Statistical Area - see Appendix A for areas included; (2) calculated by the editors using the following formula: (number of crimes in the MSA minus number of crimes in the city); (3) calculated by the editors using the following formula: ((number of crimes in the MSA minus number of crimes in the city) ÷ (population of the MSA minus population of the city)) x 100,000
Source: U.S. Department of Justice, FBI Uniform Crime Reports, 1977 - 1996

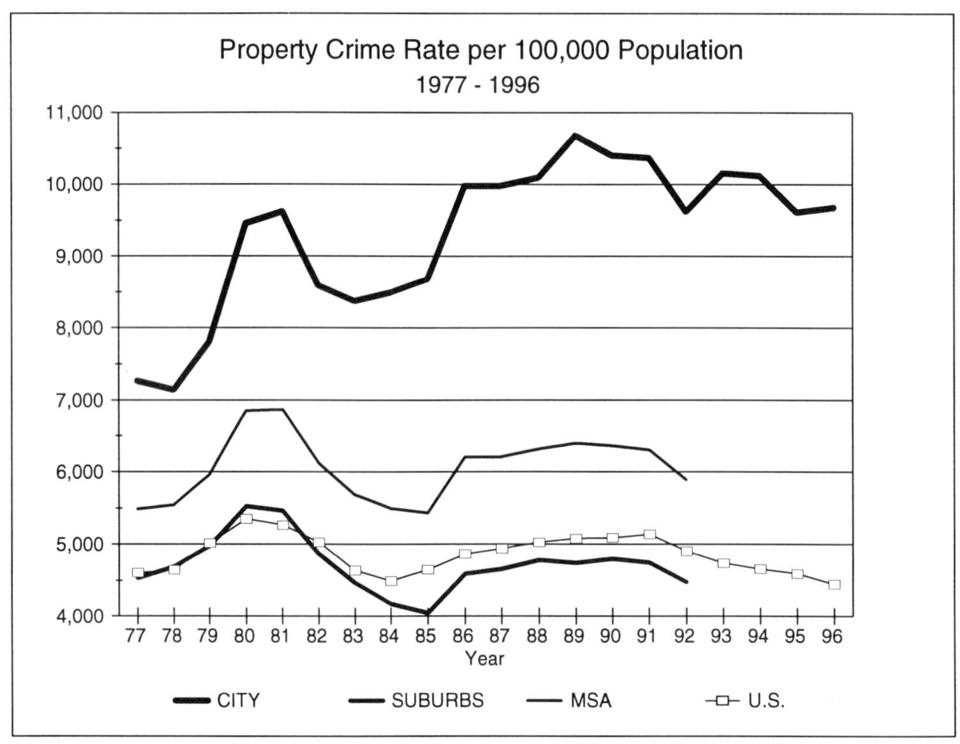

Note: Missing line segments indicate data not available.

Murders and Murder Rates: 1977 - 1996

Year	Number				Rate per 100,000 population			
	City	Suburbs[2]	MSA[1]	U.S.	City	Suburbs[3]	MSA[1]	U.S.
1977	97	54	151	19,120	21.1	6.3	11.5	8.8
1978	115	51	166	19,560	25.1	6.0	12.6	9.0
1979	119	51	170	21,460	25.7	5.9	12.8	9.7
1980	133	65	198	23,040	29.8	7.4	15.0	10.2
1981	115	57	172	22,520	25.5	6.5	12.9	9.8
1982	93	41	134	21,010	20.6	4.6	10.0	9.1
1983	106	68	174	19,310	23.4	6.8	11.9	8.3
1984	88	52	140	18,690	19.5	5.1	9.5	7.9
1985	91	42	133	18,980	20.5	4.0	9.0	7.9
1986	116	44	160	20,610	25.9	4.2	10.7	8.6
1987	131	46	177	20,100	29.5	4.2	11.6	8.3
1988	134	60	194	20,680	29.9	5.4	12.5	8.4
1989	140	68	208	21,500	31.8	6.0	13.1	8.7
1990	121	57	178	23,440	27.8	5.0	11.4	9.4
1991	135	71	206	24,700	30.8	6.2	13.1	9.8
1992	150	79	229	23,760	34.0	6.8	14.2	9.3
1993	153	n/a	n/a	24,530	35.1	n/a	n/a	9.5
1994	142	n/a	n/a	23,330	32.3	n/a	n/a	9.0
1995	107	n/a	n/a	21,610	24.0	n/a	n/a	8.2
1996	104	n/a	n/a	19,650	23.2	n/a	n/a	7.4

Notes: (1) Metropolitan Statistical Area - see Appendix A for areas included; (2) calculated by the editors using the following formula: (number of crimes in the MSA minus number of crimes in the city); (3) calculated by the editors using the following formula: ((number of crimes in the MSA minus number of crimes in the city) ÷ (population of the MSA minus population of the city)) x 100,000; n/a not avail.
Source: U.S. Department of Justice, FBI Uniform Crime Reports, 1977 - 1996

Forcible Rapes and Forcible Rape Rates: 1977 - 1996

Year	Number				Rate per 100,000 population			
	City	Suburbs[2]	MSA[1]	U.S.	City	Suburbs[3]	MSA[1]	U.S.
1977	325	229	554	63,500	70.8	26.6	42.0	29.4
1978	342	252	594	67,610	74.7	29.5	45.2	31.0
1979	436	269	705	76,390	94.2	31.0	53.0	34.7
1980	518	295	813	82,990	115.9	33.7	61.5	36.8
1981	429	286	715	82,500	95.3	32.4	53.6	36.0
1982	376	225	601	78,770	83.3	25.3	44.8	34.0
1983	425	261	686	78,920	93.8	26.0	47.1	33.7
1984	372	283	655	84,230	82.6	27.8	44.6	35.7
1985	424	277	701	88,670	95.3	26.7	47.3	37.1
1986	460	295	755	91,460	102.6	28.2	50.6	37.9
1987	486	331	817	91,110	109.4	30.5	53.5	37.4
1988	473	315	788	92,490	105.7	28.4	50.7	37.6
1989	507	353	860	94,500	115.1	30.9	54.3	38.1
1990	517	381	898	102,560	118.9	33.7	57.3	41.2
1991	477	433	910	106,590	108.9	38.0	57.7	42.3
1992	564	430	994	109,060	127.8	36.8	61.8	42.8
1993	515	n/a	n/a	106,010	118.3	n/a	n/a	41.1
1994	490	n/a	n/a	102,220	111.6	n/a	n/a	39.3
1995	470	n/a	n/a	97,470	105.5	n/a	n/a	37.1
1996	412	n/a	n/a	95,770	91.9	n/a	n/a	36.1

Notes: (1) Metropolitan Statistical Area - see Appendix A for areas included; (2) calculated by the editors using the following formula: (number of crimes in the MSA minus number of crimes in the city); (3) calculated by the editors using the following formula: ((number of crimes in the MSA minus number of crimes in the city) ÷ (population of the MSA minus population of the city)) x 100,000; n/a not avail.
Source: U.S. Department of Justice, FBI Uniform Crime Reports, 1977 - 1996

Robberies and Robbery Rates: 1977 - 1996

Year	Number				Rate per 100,000 population			
	City	Suburbs[2]	MSA[1]	U.S.	City	Suburbs[3]	MSA[1]	U.S.
1977	2,326	1,049	3,375	412,610	506.8	122.0	255.9	190.7
1978	1,864	1,097	2,961	426,930	407.0	128.3	225.5	195.8
1979	2,651	1,198	3,849	480,700	572.7	138.2	289.4	218.4
1980	2,889	1,340	4,229	565,840	646.5	153.1	319.9	251.1
1981	3,235	1,176	4,411	592,910	718.6	133.1	330.7	258.7
1982	2,756	967	3,723	553,130	610.5	108.7	277.6	238.9
1983	2,876	1,029	3,905	506,570	634.7	102.5	268.1	216.5
1984	2,440	892	3,332	485,010	541.6	87.5	226.7	205.4
1985	2,646	913	3,559	497,870	594.7	87.9	239.9	208.5
1986	3,442	1,149	4,591	542,780	767.9	110.0	307.6	225.1
1987	3,279	1,234	4,513	517,700	737.9	113.8	295.3	212.7
1988	3,479	1,250	4,729	542,970	777.5	112.8	304.0	220.9
1989	3,824	1,319	5,143	578,330	868.2	115.4	324.9	233.0
1990	4,492	1,553	6,045	639,270	1,033.3	137.2	385.9	257.0
1991	4,955	1,735	6,690	687,730	1,130.8	152.2	423.9	272.7
1992	4,494	1,532	6,026	672,480	1,018.7	131.2	374.7	263.6
1993	3,891	n/a	n/a	659,870	893.6	n/a	n/a	255.9
1994	3,727	n/a	n/a	618,950	848.8	n/a	n/a	237.7
1995	3,346	n/a	n/a	580,510	751.0	n/a	n/a	220.9
1996	2,881	n/a	n/a	537,050	642.4	n/a	n/a	202.4

Notes: (1) Metropolitan Statistical Area - see Appendix A for areas included; (2) calculated by the editors using the following formula: (number of crimes in the MSA minus number of crimes in the city); (3) calculated by the editors using the following formula: ((number of crimes in the MSA minus number of crimes in the city) ÷ (population of the MSA minus population of the city)) x 100,000; n/a not avail.
Source: U.S. Department of Justice, FBI Uniform Crime Reports, 1977 - 1996

Aggravated Assaults and Aggravated Assault Rates: 1977 - 1996

Year	Number				Rate per 100,000 population			
	City	Suburbs[2]	MSA[1]	U.S.	City	Suburbs[3]	MSA[1]	U.S.
1977	2,868	2,234	5,102	534,350	624.8	259.8	386.9	247.0
1978	2,708	2,603	5,311	571,460	591.3	304.3	404.4	262.1
1979	2,736	2,543	5,279	629,480	591.0	293.3	396.9	286.0
1980	3,474	2,781	6,255	672,650	777.4	317.7	473.1	298.5
1981	3,935	2,617	6,552	663,900	874.0	296.2	491.3	289.7
1982	3,504	2,449	5,953	669,480	776.3	275.3	443.9	289.2
1983	4,045	2,580	6,625	653,290	892.7	257.1	454.8	279.2
1984	4,267	2,874	7,141	685,350	947.2	281.9	485.8	290.2
1985	4,851	3,003	7,854	723,250	1,090.3	289.2	529.5	302.9
1986	5,655	3,266	8,921	834,320	1,261.6	312.7	597.6	346.1
1987	4,527	3,276	7,803	855,090	1,018.7	302.2	510.6	351.3
1988	4,230	3,171	7,401	910,090	945.3	286.2	475.8	370.2
1989	4,525	3,312	7,837	951,710	1,027.4	289.8	495.0	383.4
1990	5,957	3,839	9,796	1,054,860	1,370.3	339.3	625.4	424.1
1991	6,846	3,891	10,737	1,092,740	1,562.3	341.3	680.3	433.3
1992	7,386	3,959	11,345	1,126,970	1,674.2	339.2	705.4	441.8
1993	6,402	n/a	n/a	1,135,610	1,470.3	n/a	n/a	440.3
1994	6,334	n/a	n/a	1,113,180	1,442.5	n/a	n/a	427.6
1995	5,811	n/a	n/a	1,099,210	1,304.2	n/a	n/a	418.3
1996	5,488	n/a	n/a	1,029,810	1,223.7	n/a	n/a	388.2

Notes: (1) Metropolitan Statistical Area - see Appendix A for areas included; (2) calculated by the editors using the following formula: (number of crimes in the MSA minus number of crimes in the city); (3) calculated by the editors using the following formula: ((number of crimes in the MSA minus number of crimes in the city) ÷ (population of the MSA minus population of the city)) x 100,000; n/a not avail.
Source: U.S. Department of Justice, FBI Uniform Crime Reports, 1977 - 1996

Burglaries and Burglary Rates: 1977 - 1996

Year	Number				Rate per 100,000 population			
	City	Suburbs[2]	MSA[1]	U.S.	City	Suburbs[3]	MSA[1]	U.S.
1977	11,248	12,310	23,558	3,071,500	2,450.5	1,431.8	1,786.4	1,419.8
1978	11,478	12,747	24,225	3,128,300	2,506.1	1,490.4	1,844.6	1,434.6
1979	12,254	13,136	25,390	3,327,700	2,647.1	1,514.9	1,909.0	1,511.9
1980	15,210	15,493	30,703	3,795,200	3,403.7	1,770.0	2,322.2	1,684.1
1981	14,839	14,929	29,768	3,779,700	3,296.0	1,689.9	2,232.1	1,649.5
1982	12,864	13,306	26,170	3,447,100	2,849.8	1,495.7	1,951.5	1,488.8
1983	11,636	13,338	24,974	3,129,900	2,567.9	1,329.2	1,714.6	1,337.7
1984	11,182	11,629	22,811	2,984,400	2,482.2	1,140.7	1,551.8	1,263.7
1985	11,164	11,061	22,225	3,073,300	2,509.1	1,065.2	1,498.3	1,287.3
1986	13,525	12,930	26,455	3,241,400	3,017.4	1,238.0	1,772.3	1,344.6
1987	13,767	12,891	26,658	3,236,200	3,098.0	1,189.3	1,744.3	1,329.6
1988	13,409	14,305	27,714	3,218,100	2,996.7	1,290.9	1,781.6	1,309.2
1989	12,104	13,015	25,119	3,168,200	2,748.2	1,139.0	1,586.7	1,276.3
1990	11,640	12,164	23,804	3,073,900	2,677.6	1,075.0	1,519.8	1,235.9
1991	13,008	13,027	26,035	3,157,200	2,968.6	1,142.7	1,649.7	1,252.0
1992	12,551	13,667	26,218	2,979,900	2,845.0	1,170.9	1,630.1	1,168.2
1993	12,106	n/a	n/a	2,834,800	2,780.3	n/a	n/a	1,099.2
1994	11,958	n/a	n/a	2,712,800	2,723.4	n/a	n/a	1,042.0
1995	9,748	n/a	n/a	2,593,800	2,187.9	n/a	n/a	987.1
1996	8,947	n/a	n/a	2,501,500	1,995.0	n/a	n/a	943.0

Notes: (1) Metropolitan Statistical Area - see Appendix A for areas included; (2) calculated by the editors using the following formula: (number of crimes in the MSA minus number of crimes in the city); (3) calculated by the editors using the following formula: ((number of crimes in the MSA minus number of crimes in the city) ÷ (population of the MSA minus population of the city)) x 100,000; n/a not avail.
Source: U.S. Department of Justice, FBI Uniform Crime Reports, 1977 - 1996

Larceny-Thefts and Larceny-Theft Rates: 1977 - 1996

Year	Number				Rate per 100,000 population			
	City	Suburbs[2]	MSA[1]	U.S.	City	Suburbs[3]	MSA[1]	U.S.
1977	18,950	23,997	42,947	5,905,700	4,128.5	2,791.1	3,256.6	2,729.9
1978	18,117	24,521	42,638	5,991,000	3,955.7	2,867.0	3,246.6	2,747.4
1979	20,275	26,605	46,880	6,601,000	4,379.9	3,068.2	3,524.7	2,999.1
1980	23,231	29,590	52,821	7,136,900	5,198.7	3,380.6	3,995.1	3,167.0
1981	24,690	30,246	54,936	7,194,400	5,484.1	3,423.6	4,119.2	3,139.7
1982	22,766	27,173	49,939	7,142,500	5,043.5	3,054.4	3,723.9	3,084.8
1983	23,244	28,588	51,832	6,712,800	5,129.7	2,849.0	3,558.5	2,868.9
1984	22,729	27,713	50,442	6,591,900	5,045.4	2,718.3	3,431.5	2,791.3
1985	21,888	27,750	49,638	6,926,400	4,919.3	2,672.3	3,346.3	2,901.2
1986	24,375	30,880	55,255	7,257,200	5,438.0	2,956.6	3,701.7	3,010.3
1987	24,224	33,523	57,747	7,499,900	5,451.2	3,092.7	3,778.4	3,081.3
1988	24,578	34,592	59,170	7,705,900	5,492.8	3,121.7	3,803.7	3,134.9
1989	25,853	35,960	61,813	7,872,400	5,869.9	3,146.9	3,904.5	3,171.3
1990	23,229	36,273	59,502	7,945,700	5,343.6	3,205.5	3,798.9	3,194.8
1991	22,527	35,745	58,272	8,142,200	5,140.9	3,135.5	3,692.3	3,228.8
1992	21,846	33,605	55,451	7,915,200	4,951.9	2,879.0	3,447.6	3,103.0
1993	23,611	n/a	n/a	7,820,900	5,422.5	n/a	n/a	3,032.4
1994	25,109	n/a	n/a	7,879,800	5,718.4	n/a	n/a	3,026.7
1995	26,301	n/a	n/a	7,997,700	5,903.1	n/a	n/a	3,043.8
1996	28,124	n/a	n/a	7,894,600	6,271.0	n/a	n/a	2,975.9

Notes: (1) Metropolitan Statistical Area - see Appendix A for areas included; (2) calculated by the editors using the following formula: (number of crimes in the MSA minus number of crimes in the city); (3) calculated by the editors using the following formula: ((number of crimes in the MSA minus number of crimes in the city) ÷ (population of the MSA minus population of the city)) x 100,000; n/a not avail.
Source: U.S. Department of Justice, FBI Uniform Crime Reports, 1977 - 1996

Motor Vehicle Thefts and Motor Vehicle Theft Rates: 1977 - 1996

Year	Number				Rate per 100,000 population			
	City	Suburbs[2]	MSA[1]	U.S.	City	Suburbs[3]	MSA[1]	U.S.
1977	3,146	2,677	5,823	977,700	685.4	311.4	441.6	451.9
1978	3,105	2,818	5,923	1,004,100	677.9	329.5	451.0	460.5
1979	3,594	3,419	7,013	1,112,800	776.4	394.3	527.3	505.6
1980	3,820	3,236	7,056	1,131,700	854.8	369.7	533.7	502.2
1981	3,762	3,098	6,860	1,087,800	835.6	350.7	514.4	474.7
1982	3,144	2,827	5,971	1,062,400	696.5	317.8	445.3	458.8
1983	3,056	2,907	5,963	1,007,900	674.4	289.7	409.4	430.8
1984	4,338	3,175	7,513	1,032,200	963.0	311.4	511.1	437.1
1985	5,552	3,195	8,747	1,102,900	1,247.8	307.7	589.7	462.0
1986	6,805	4,084	10,889	1,224,100	1,518.2	391.0	729.5	507.8
1987	6,363	4,107	10,470	1,288,700	1,431.9	378.9	685.1	529.4
1988	7,184	4,080	11,264	1,432,900	1,605.5	368.2	724.1	582.9
1989	9,075	5,195	14,270	1,564,800	2,060.5	454.6	901.4	630.4
1990	10,352	5,884	16,236	1,635,900	2,381.4	520.0	1,036.6	657.8
1991	9,886	5,289	15,175	1,661,700	2,256.1	463.9	961.5	659.0
1992	8,042	4,904	12,946	1,610,800	1,822.9	420.1	804.9	631.5
1993	8,487	n/a	n/a	1,563,100	1,949.1	n/a	n/a	606.1
1994	7,352	n/a	n/a	1,539,300	1,674.4	n/a	n/a	591.3
1995	6,792	n/a	n/a	1,472,400	1,524.4	n/a	n/a	560.4
1996	6,344	n/a	n/a	1,395,200	1,414.6	n/a	n/a	525.9

Notes: (1) Metropolitan Statistical Area - see Appendix A for areas included; (2) calculated by the editors using the following formula: (number of crimes in the MSA minus number of crimes in the city); (3) calculated by the editors using the following formula: ((number of crimes in the MSA minus number of crimes in the city) ÷ (population of the MSA minus population of the city)) x 100,000; n/a not avail.
Source: U.S. Department of Justice, FBI Uniform Crime Reports, 1977 - 1996

HATE CRIMES

Criminal Incidents by Bias Motivation

Area	Race	Ethnicity	Religion	Sexual Orientation
Kansas City	27	0	1	2

Notes: Figures include both violent and property crimes. Law enforcement agencies must have submitted data for at least one quarter of calendar year 1995 to be included in this report, therefore figures shown may not represent complete 12-month totals; n/a not available
Source: U.S. Department of Justice, FBI Uniform Crime Reports, Hate Crime Statistics 1995

LAW ENFORCEMENT

Full-Time Law Enforcement Employees

Jurisdiction	Police Employees			Police Officers per 100,000 population
	Total	Officers	Civilians	
Kansas City	1,849	1,179	670	262.9

Notes: Data as of October 31, 1996
Source: U.S. Department of Justice, FBI Uniform Crime Reports, 1996

Number of Police Officers by Race

Race	Police Officers				Index of Representation[1]		
	1983		1992				
	Number	Pct.	Number	Pct.	1983	1992	% Chg.
Black	123	10.8	156	13.4	0.39	0.45	15.4
Hispanic[2]	18	1.6	32	2.7	0.45	0.69	53.3

Notes: (1) The index of representation is calculated by dividing the percent of black/hispanic police officers by the percent of corresponding blacks/hispanics in the local population. An index approaching 1.0 indicates that a city is closer to achieving a representation of police officers equal to their proportion in the local population; (2) Hispanic officers can be of any race
Source: Bureau of Justice Statistics, Sourcebook of Criminal Justice Statistics, 1994

CORRECTIONS

Federal Correctional Facilities

Type	Year Opened	Security Level	Sex of Inmates	Rated Capacity	Population on 7/1/95	Number of Staff
None listed						

Notes: Data as of 1995
Source: Bureau of Justice Statistics, Sourcebook of Criminal Justice Statistics Online

City/County/Regional Correctional Facilities

Name	Year Opened	Year Renov.	Rated Capacity	1995 Pop.	Number of COs[1]	Number of Staff	ACA[2] Accred.
Jackson Co Detention Ctr	1983	1993	520	576	191	243	No
Jackson Co Municipal Correctional Institution	1971	1995	358	358	48	80	Yes

Notes: Data as of April 1996; (1) Correctional Officers; (2) American Correctional Assn. Accreditation
Source: American Correctional Association, 1996-1998 National Jail and Adult Detention Directory

Private Adult Correctional Facilities

Name	Date Opened	Rated Capacity	Present Pop.	Security Level	Facility Construct.	Expans. Plans	ACA[1] Accred.
None listed							

Notes: Data as of December 1996; (1) American Correctional Association Accreditation
Source: University of Florida, Center for Studies in Criminology and Law, Private Adult Correctional Facility Census, 10th Ed., March 15, 1997

Characteristics of Shock Incarceration Programs

Jurisdiction	Year Program Began	Number of Camps	Average Num. of Inmates	Number of Beds	Program Length	Voluntary/ Mandatory
Missouri	1994	1	40 to 45	50	90 days	Mandatory

Note: Data as of July 1996;
Source: Sourcebook of Criminal Justice Statistics Online

DEATH PENALTY

Death Penalty Statistics

State	Prisoners Executed		Prisoners Under Sentence of Death					Avg. No. of Years on Death Row[4]
	1930-1995	1996[1]	Total[2]	White[3]	Black[3]	Hisp.	Women	
Missouri	79	6	92	51	41	0	2	6.1

Notes: Data as of 12/31/95 unless otherwise noted; (1) Data as of 7/31/97; (2) Includes persons of other races; (3) Includes people of Hispanic origin; (4) Covers prisoners sentenced 1974 through 1995
Source: Bureau of Justice Statistics, Capital Punishment 1995 (released 12/96); Death Penalty Information Center Web Site, 9/30/97

Capital Offenses and Methods of Execution

Capital Offenses in Missouri	Minimum Age for Imposition of Death Penalty	Mentally Retarded Excluded	Methods of Execution[1]
First-degree murder (565.020 RSMO).	16	No	Lethal injection; lethal gas

Notes: Data as of 12/31/95 unless otherwise noted; (1) Data as of 7/31/97
Source: Bureau of Justice Statistics, Capital Punishment 1995 (released 12/96); Death Penalty Information Center Web Site, 9/30/97

LAWS

Statutory Provisions Relating to the Purchase, Ownership and Use of Handguns

Jurisdiction	Instant Background Check	Federal Waiting Period Applies[1]	State Waiting Period (days)	License or Permit to Purchase	Regis-tration	Record of Sale Sent to Police	Concealed Carry Law
Missouri	No	No	7	Yes[a]	No	Yes	Yes[b]

Note: Data as of 1996; (1) The Federal 5-day waiting period for handgun purchases applies to states that don't have instant background checks, waiting period requirements, or licensing procedures exempting them from the Federal requirement; (a) A purchase permit is required for a handgun, must be issued to qualified applicants within 7 days, and is valid for 30 days; (b) No permit system exists and concealed carry is prohibited
Source: Sourcebook of Criminal Justice Statistics Online

Statutory Provisions Relating to Alcohol Use and Driving

Jurisdiction	Drinking Age	Blood Alcohol Concentration Levels as Evidence in State Courts[1]		Open Container Law[1]	Anti-Consumption Law[1]	Dram Shop Law[1]
		Illegal per se at 0.10%	Presumption at 0.10%			
Missouri	21	Yes	No	No	(a)	(b)

Note: Data as of January 1, 1997; (1) See Appendix C for an explanation of terms; (a) Applies to drivers only; (b) Cause of action limited to licensees who have been convicted of selling alcoholic beverages to minors or intoxicated individuals
Source: Sourcebook of Criminal Justice Statistics Online

Statutory Provisions Relating to Curfews

Jurisdiction	Year Enacted	Latest Revision	Age Group(s)	Curfew Provisions
Kansas City	1991	-	17 and under	11 pm to 6 am weekday nights midnight to 6 am weekend nights

Note: Data as of February 1996
Source: Sourcebook of Criminal Justice Statistics Online

Statutory Provisions Relating to Hate Crimes

Jurisdiction	Bias-Motivated Violence and Intimidation						Institutional Vandalism
	Civil Action	Criminal Penalty					
		Race/ Religion/ Ethnicity	Sexual Orientation	Mental/ Physical Disability	Gender	Age	
Missouri	Yes	Yes	No	No	No	No	Yes

Source: Anti-Defamation League, 1997 Hate Crimes Laws

Knoxville, Tennessee

OVERVIEW

The total crime rate for the city increased 5.4% between 1977 and 1996. During that same period, the violent crime rate increased 70.0% and the property crime rate decreased 0.8%.

Among violent crimes, the rates for: Murders increased 63.0%; Forcible Rapes increased 16.7%; Robberies increased 65.9%; and Aggravated Assaults increased 79.8%.

Among property crimes, the rates for: Burglaries decreased 29.8%; Larceny-Thefts increased 8.8%; and Motor Vehicle Thefts increased 44.2%.

ANTI-CRIME PROGRAMS

Among the special anticrime programs instituted are:

- Neighborhood Watch and Business Watch where individuals at home or at work report suspicious activities to the police
- Home or Business Security Survey conducted by a Crime Prevention staff member to determine security deficiencies of a home or business
- Operation Identification where items which are more likely to be stolen are marked
- Rape Prevention & Personal Protection where tips on how to avoid becoming a victim are offered along with how to cope with ramifications of the incident
- Senior Citizens Programs which offer safety tips for the senior citizens
- Youth Safety programs such as "Stranger Danger" and "Youth Fingerprint Program". The Police Department will also develop programs to suit specific needs. *Knoxville Chief of Police, 7/97*

The city instituted a program which the National League of Cities (1993) considers among those which are innovative for combatting crime and violence:

- The Systems Approach to Community Crime Prevention—community-wide profiles are used to develop short and long-term strategies for dealing with crime and violence. Neighborhood self-help networks are established. The results have been a reduction in the number of crimes as well as in emergency calls. *Exemplary Programs in Criminal Justice, National League of Cities, 1994*

CRIME RISK

Your Chances of Becoming a Victim[1]

Area	Any Crime	Violent Crime					Property Crime			
		Any	Murder	Forcible Rape[2]	Robbery	Aggrav. Assault	Any	Burglary	Larceny -Theft	Motor Vehicle Theft
City	1:16	1:114	1:7,568	1:1,391	1:294	1:206	1:19	1:74	1:33	1:109

Note: (1) Figures have been calculated by dividing the population of the city by the number of crimes reported to the FBI during 1996 and are expressed as odds (eg. 1:20 should be read as 1 in 20). (2) Figures have been calculated by dividing the female population of the city by the number of forcible rapes reported to the FBI during 1996. The female population of the city was estimated by calculating the ratio of females to males reported in the 1990 Census and applying that ratio to 1996 population estimate.
Source: FBI Uniform Crime Reports 1996

CRIME STATISTICS

Total Crimes and Total Crime Rates: 1977 - 1996

Year	Number				Rate per 100,000 population			
	City	Suburbs[2]	MSA[1]	U.S.	City	Suburbs[3]	MSA[1]	U.S.
1977	10,860	6,736	17,596	10,984,500	5,870.3	2,568.3	3,934.0	5,077.6
1978	11,031	7,621	18,652	11,209,000	5,962.7	2,832.9	4,108.2	5,140.3
1979	11,237	9,161	20,398	12,249,500	5,954.2	3,422.7	4,469.5	5,565.5
1980	12,423	8,770	21,193	13,408,300	6,816.5	2,996.9	4,462.7	5,950.0
1981	12,527	8,438	20,965	13,423,800	6,777.5	2,843.1	4,353.0	5,858.2
1982	11,863	8,561	20,424	12,974,400	6,361.7	2,859.1	4,203.3	5,603.6
1983	9,994	10,422	20,416	12,108,600	5,320.5	2,647.9	3,511.3	5,175.0
1984	9,796	9,209	19,005	11,881,800	5,512.2	2,245.8	3,233.5	5,031.3
1985	10,838	10,189	21,027	12,431,400	6,170.5	2,431.7	3,536.0	5,207.1
1986	11,872	11,574	23,446	13,211,900	6,701.6	2,739.3	3,909.8	5,480.4
1987	11,728	10,702	22,430	13,508,700	6,698.3	2,697.8	3,922.8	5,550.0
1988	11,059	12,064	23,123	13,923,100	6,303.4	3,015.2	4,017.5	5,664.2
1989	12,523	13,146	25,669	14,251,400	7,211.6	3,247.4	4,437.4	5,741.0
1990	13,113	14,121	27,234	14,475,600	7,941.4	3,411.5	4,703.3	5,820.3
1991	15,529	14,997	30,526	14,872,900	9,260.8	3,567.8	5,191.3	5,897.8
1992	15,231	n/a	n/a	14,438,200	8,954.8	n/a	n/a	5,660.2
1993	13,365	n/a	n/a	14,144,800	7,873.3	n/a	n/a	5,484.4
1994	13,261	n/a	n/a	13,989,500	7,697.4	n/a	n/a	5,373.5
1995	13,667	n/a	n/a	13,862,700	7,947.8	n/a	n/a	5,275.9
1996	10,767	n/a	n/a	13,473,600	6,186.0	n/a	n/a	5,078.9

Notes: (1) Metropolitan Statistical Area - see Appendix A for areas included; (2) calculated by the editors using the following formula: (number of crimes in the MSA minus number of crimes in the city); (3) calculated by the editors using the following formula: ((number of crimes in the MSA minus number of crimes in the city) ÷ (population of the MSA minus population of the city)) x 100,000; n/a not avail.
Source: U.S. Department of Justice, FBI Uniform Crime Reports, 1977 - 1996

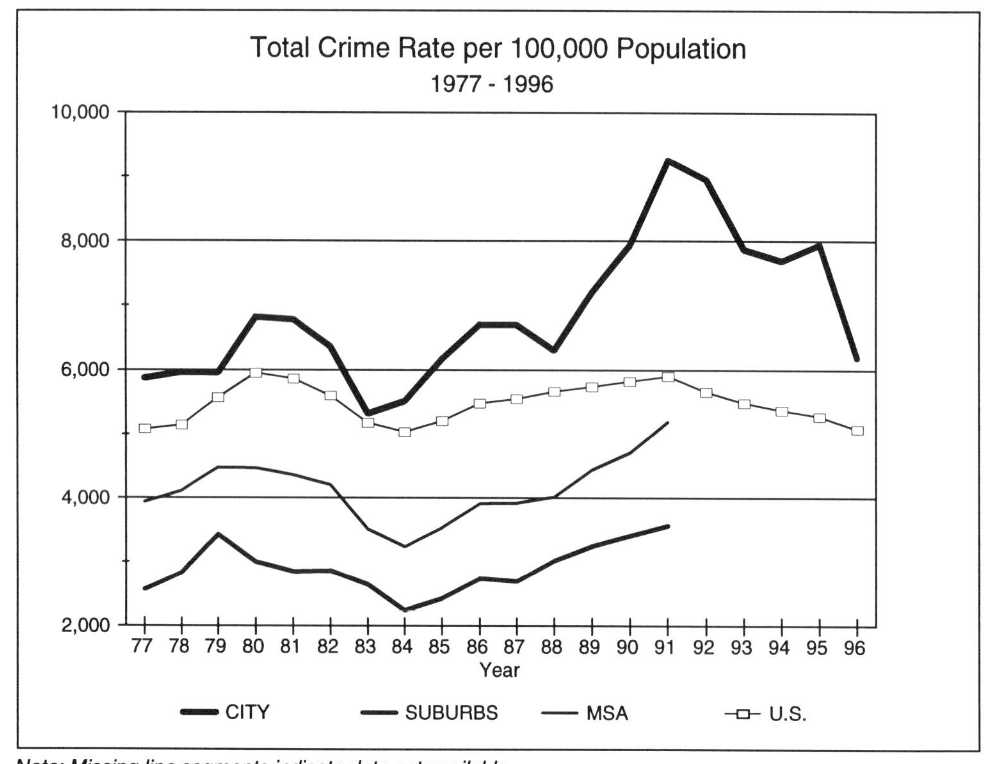

Note: Missing line segments indicate data not available.

Violent Crimes and Violent Crime Rates: 1977 - 1996

Year	Number				Rate per 100,000 population			
	City	Suburbs[2]	MSA[1]	U.S.	City	Suburbs[3]	MSA[1]	U.S.
1977	955	391	1,346	1,029,580	516.2	149.1	300.9	475.9
1978	1,215	465	1,680	1,085,550	656.8	172.9	370.0	497.8
1979	1,135	574	1,709	1,208,030	601.4	214.5	374.5	548.9
1980	1,347	570	1,917	1,344,520	739.1	194.8	403.7	596.6
1981	1,094	424	1,518	1,361,820	591.9	142.9	315.2	594.3
1982	1,030	473	1,503	1,322,390	552.4	158.0	309.3	571.1
1983	957	581	1,538	1,258,090	509.5	147.6	264.5	537.7
1984	879	548	1,427	1,273,280	494.6	133.6	242.8	539.2
1985	1,078	604	1,682	1,328,800	613.7	144.1	282.9	556.6
1986	1,437	805	2,242	1,489,170	811.2	190.5	373.9	617.7
1987	1,376	761	2,137	1,484,000	785.9	191.8	373.7	609.7
1988	1,260	776	2,036	1,566,220	718.2	193.9	353.7	637.2
1989	1,607	825	2,432	1,646,040	925.4	203.8	420.4	663.1
1990	1,973	842	2,815	1,820,130	1,194.9	203.4	486.2	731.8
1991	2,764	928	3,692	1,911,770	1,648.3	220.8	627.9	758.1
1992	3,107	n/a	n/a	1,932,270	1,826.7	n/a	n/a	757.5
1993	2,912	n/a	n/a	1,926,020	1,715.5	n/a	n/a	746.8
1994	3,031	n/a	n/a	1,857,670	1,759.3	n/a	n/a	713.6
1995	3,180	n/a	n/a	1,798,790	1,849.3	n/a	n/a	684.6
1996	1,527	n/a	n/a	1,682,280	877.3	n/a	n/a	634.1

Notes: Violent crimes include murder, forcible rape, robbery and aggravated assault; n/a not available; (1) Metropolitan Statistical Area - see Appendix A for areas included; (2) calculated by the editors using the following formula: (number of crimes in the MSA minus number of crimes in the city); (3) calculated by the editors using the following formula: ((number of crimes in the MSA minus number of crimes in the city) ÷ (population of the MSA minus population of the city)) x 100,000
Source: U.S. Department of Justice, FBI Uniform Crime Reports, 1977 - 1996

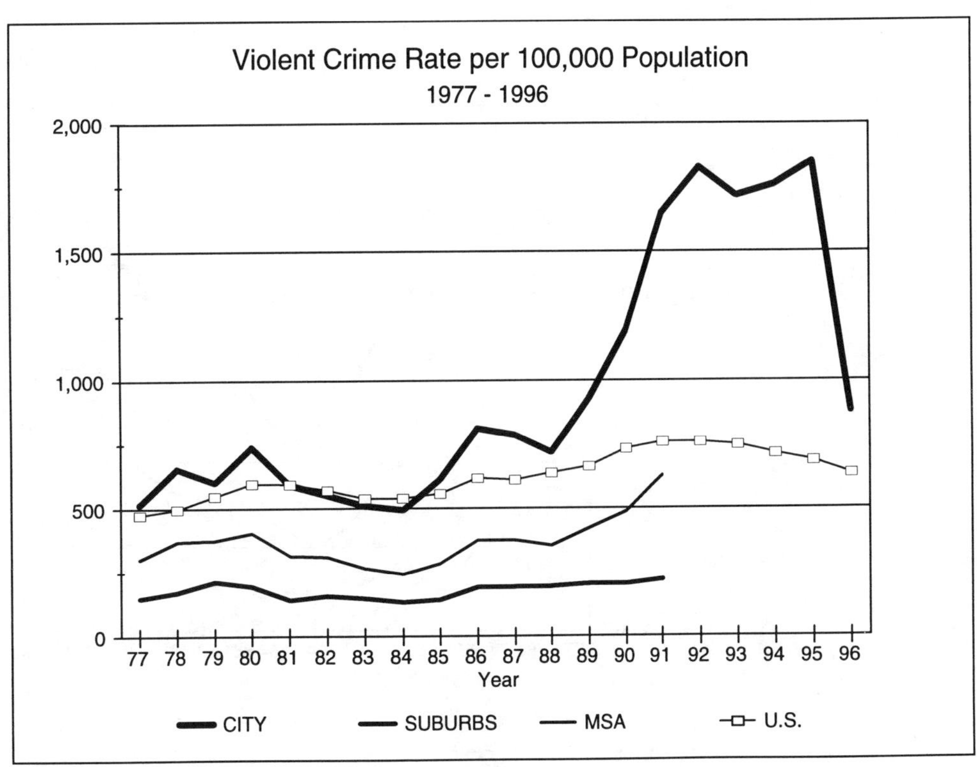

Note: Missing line segments indicate data not available.

Property Crimes and Property Crime Rates: 1977 - 1996

Year	Number				Rate per 100,000 population			
	City	Suburbs[2]	MSA[1]	U.S.	City	Suburbs[3]	MSA[1]	U.S.
1977	9,905	6,345	16,250	9,955,000	5,354.1	2,419.2	3,633.1	4,601.7
1978	9,816	7,156	16,972	10,123,400	5,305.9	2,660.1	3,738.2	4,642.5
1979	10,102	8,587	18,689	11,041,500	5,352.8	3,208.2	4,095.1	5,016.6
1980	11,076	8,200	19,276	12,063,700	6,077.4	2,802.1	4,059.1	5,353.3
1981	11,433	8,014	19,447	12,061,900	6,185.6	2,700.3	4,037.9	5,263.9
1982	10,833	8,088	18,921	11,652,000	5,809.4	2,701.2	3,894.0	5,032.5
1983	9,037	9,841	18,878	10,850,500	4,811.1	2,500.2	3,246.8	4,637.4
1984	8,917	8,661	17,578	10,608,500	5,017.6	2,112.2	2,990.7	4,492.1
1985	9,760	9,585	19,345	11,102,600	5,556.7	2,287.5	3,253.1	4,650.5
1986	10,435	10,769	21,204	11,722,700	5,890.4	2,548.8	3,535.9	4,862.6
1987	10,352	9,941	20,293	12,024,700	5,912.4	2,506.0	3,549.1	4,940.3
1988	9,799	11,288	21,087	12,356,900	5,585.3	2,821.2	3,663.8	5,027.1
1989	10,916	12,321	23,237	12,605,400	6,286.2	3,043.6	4,017.0	5,077.9
1990	11,140	13,279	24,419	12,655,500	6,746.6	3,208.1	4,217.2	5,088.5
1991	12,765	14,069	26,834	12,961,100	7,612.4	3,347.1	4,563.4	5,139.7
1992	12,124	n/a	n/a	12,505,900	7,128.1	n/a	n/a	4,902.7
1993	10,453	n/a	n/a	12,218,800	6,157.8	n/a	n/a	4,737.6
1994	10,230	n/a	n/a	12,131,900	5,938.0	n/a	n/a	4,660.0
1995	10,487	n/a	n/a	12,063,900	6,098.5	n/a	n/a	4,591.3
1996	9,240	n/a	n/a	11,791,300	5,308.7	n/a	n/a	4,444.8

Notes: Property crimes include burglary, larceny-theft and motor vehicle theft; n/a not available; (1) Metropolitan Statistical Area - see Appendix A for areas included; (2) calculated by the editors using the following formula: (number of crimes in the MSA minus number of crimes in the city); (3) calculated by the editors using the following formula: ((number of crimes in the MSA minus number of crimes in the city) ÷ (population of the MSA minus population of the city)) x 100,000
Source: U.S. Department of Justice, FBI Uniform Crime Reports, 1977 - 1996

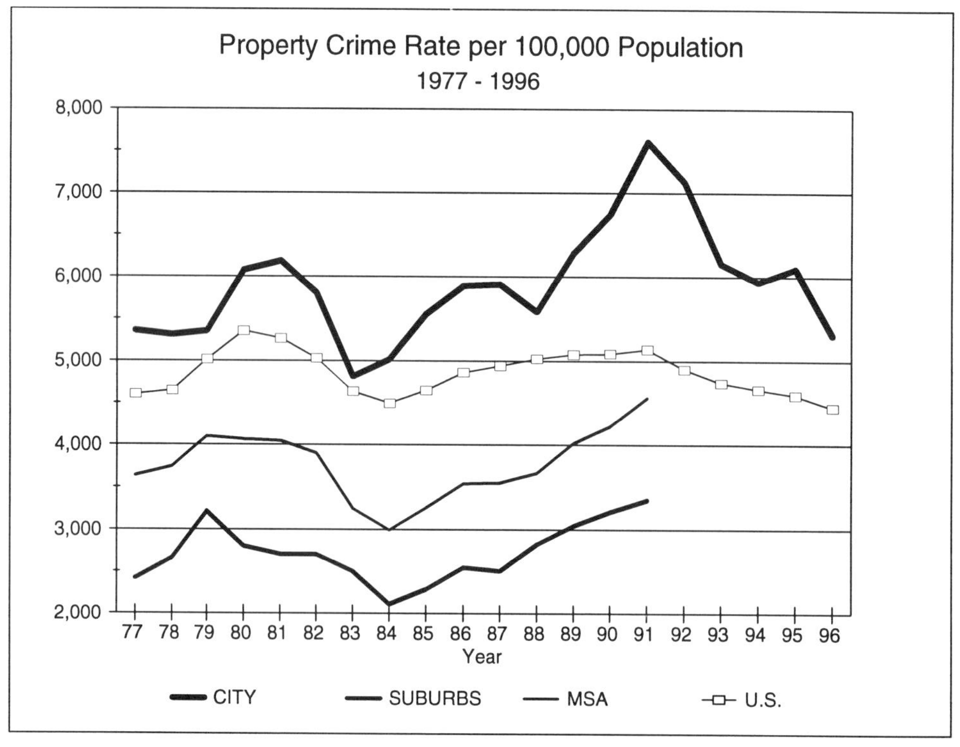

Note: Missing line segments indicate data not available.

Murders and Murder Rates: 1977 - 1996

Year	Number				Rate per 100,000 population			
	City	Suburbs[2]	MSA[1]	U.S.	City	Suburbs[3]	MSA[1]	U.S.
1977	15	16	31	19,120	8.1	6.1	6.9	8.8
1978	18	12	30	19,560	9.7	4.5	6.6	9.0
1979	25	12	37	21,460	13.2	4.5	8.1	9.7
1980	21	14	35	23,040	11.5	4.8	7.4	10.2
1981	25	16	41	22,520	13.5	5.4	8.5	9.8
1982	19	16	35	21,010	10.2	5.3	7.2	9.1
1983	19	12	31	19,310	10.1	3.0	5.3	8.3
1984	20	10	30	18,690	11.3	2.4	5.1	7.9
1985	16	20	36	18,980	9.1	4.8	6.1	7.9
1986	29	22	51	20,610	16.4	5.2	8.5	8.6
1987	20	20	40	20,100	11.4	5.0	7.0	8.3
1988	21	11	32	20,680	12.0	2.7	5.6	8.4
1989	26	15	41	21,500	15.0	3.7	7.1	8.7
1990	25	20	45	23,440	15.1	4.8	7.8	9.4
1991	35	24	59	24,700	20.9	5.7	10.0	9.8
1992	35	n/a	n/a	23,760	20.6	n/a	n/a	9.3
1993	14	n/a	n/a	24,530	8.2	n/a	n/a	9.5
1994	24	n/a	n/a	23,330	13.9	n/a	n/a	9.0
1995	19	n/a	n/a	21,610	11.0	n/a	n/a	8.2
1996	23	n/a	n/a	19,650	13.2	n/a	n/a	7.4

Notes: (1) Metropolitan Statistical Area - see Appendix A for areas included; (2) calculated by the editors using the following formula: (number of crimes in the MSA minus number of crimes in the city); (3) calculated by the editors using the following formula: ((number of crimes in the MSA minus number of crimes in the city) ÷ (population of the MSA minus population of the city)) x 100,000; n/a not avail.
Source: U.S. Department of Justice, FBI Uniform Crime Reports, 1977 - 1996

Forcible Rapes and Forcible Rape Rates: 1977 - 1996

Year	Number				Rate per 100,000 population			
	City	Suburbs[2]	MSA[1]	U.S.	City	Suburbs[3]	MSA[1]	U.S.
1977	61	39	100	63,500	33.0	14.9	22.4	29.4
1978	65	48	113	67,610	35.1	17.8	24.9	31.0
1979	63	63	126	76,390	33.4	23.5	27.6	34.7
1980	91	64	155	82,990	49.9	21.9	32.6	36.8
1981	88	43	131	82,500	47.6	14.5	27.2	36.0
1982	88	62	150	78,770	47.2	20.7	30.9	34.0
1983	83	72	155	78,920	44.2	18.3	26.7	33.7
1984	86	61	147	84,230	48.4	14.9	25.0	35.7
1985	63	73	136	88,670	35.9	17.4	22.9	37.1
1986	87	75	162	91,460	49.1	17.8	27.0	37.9
1987	86	61	147	91,110	49.1	15.4	25.7	37.4
1988	66	72	138	92,490	37.6	18.0	24.0	37.6
1989	79	81	160	94,500	45.5	20.0	27.7	38.1
1990	111	73	184	102,560	67.2	17.6	31.8	41.2
1991	123	94	217	106,590	73.4	22.4	36.9	42.3
1992	116	n/a	n/a	109,060	68.2	n/a	n/a	42.8
1993	102	n/a	n/a	106,010	60.1	n/a	n/a	41.1
1994	109	n/a	n/a	102,220	63.3	n/a	n/a	39.3
1995	110	n/a	n/a	97,470	64.0	n/a	n/a	37.1
1996	67	n/a	n/a	95,770	38.5	n/a	n/a	36.1

Notes: (1) Metropolitan Statistical Area - see Appendix A for areas included; (2) calculated by the editors using the following formula: (number of crimes in the MSA minus number of crimes in the city); (3) calculated by the editors using the following formula: ((number of crimes in the MSA minus number of crimes in the city) ÷ (population of the MSA minus population of the city)) x 100,000; n/a not avail.
Source: U.S. Department of Justice, FBI Uniform Crime Reports, 1977 - 1996

Robberies and Robbery Rates: 1977 - 1996

Year	Number				Rate per 100,000 population			
	City	Suburbs[2]	MSA[1]	U.S.	City	Suburbs[3]	MSA[1]	U.S.
1977	380	97	477	412,610	205.4	37.0	106.6	190.7
1978	426	147	573	426,930	230.3	54.6	126.2	195.8
1979	461	178	639	480,700	244.3	66.5	140.0	218.4
1980	528	160	688	565,840	289.7	54.7	144.9	251.1
1981	474	129	603	592,910	256.4	43.5	125.2	258.7
1982	446	172	618	553,130	239.2	57.4	127.2	238.9
1983	370	173	543	506,570	197.0	44.0	93.4	216.5
1984	281	127	408	485,010	158.1	31.0	69.4	205.4
1985	420	146	566	497,870	239.1	34.8	95.2	208.5
1986	496	167	663	542,780	280.0	39.5	110.6	225.1
1987	439	152	591	517,700	250.7	38.3	103.4	212.7
1988	360	148	508	542,970	205.2	37.0	88.3	220.9
1989	442	186	628	578,330	254.5	45.9	108.6	233.0
1990	601	166	767	639,270	364.0	40.1	132.5	257.0
1991	668	162	830	687,730	398.4	38.5	141.2	272.7
1992	792	n/a	n/a	672,480	465.6	n/a	n/a	263.6
1993	596	n/a	n/a	659,870	351.1	n/a	n/a	255.9
1994	632	n/a	n/a	618,950	366.8	n/a	n/a	237.7
1995	716	n/a	n/a	580,510	416.4	n/a	n/a	220.9
1996	593	n/a	n/a	537,050	340.7	n/a	n/a	202.4

Notes: (1) Metropolitan Statistical Area - see Appendix A for areas included; (2) calculated by the editors using the following formula: (number of crimes in the MSA minus number of crimes in the city); (3) calculated by the editors using the following formula: ((number of crimes in the MSA minus number of crimes in the city) ÷ (population of the MSA minus population of the city)) x 100,000; n/a not avail.
Source: U.S. Department of Justice, FBI Uniform Crime Reports, 1977 - 1996

Aggravated Assaults and Aggravated Assault Rates: 1977 - 1996

Year	Number				Rate per 100,000 population			
	City	Suburbs[2]	MSA[1]	U.S.	City	Suburbs[3]	MSA[1]	U.S.
1977	499	239	738	534,350	269.7	91.1	165.0	247.0
1978	706	258	964	571,460	381.6	95.9	212.3	262.1
1979	586	321	907	629,480	310.5	119.9	198.7	286.0
1980	707	332	1,039	672,650	387.9	113.5	218.8	298.5
1981	507	236	743	663,900	274.3	79.5	154.3	289.7
1982	477	223	700	669,480	255.8	74.5	144.1	289.2
1983	485	324	809	653,290	258.2	82.3	139.1	279.2
1984	492	350	842	685,350	276.8	85.4	143.3	290.2
1985	579	365	944	723,250	329.6	87.1	158.7	302.9
1986	825	541	1,366	834,320	465.7	128.0	227.8	346.1
1987	831	528	1,359	855,090	474.6	133.1	237.7	351.3
1988	813	545	1,358	910,090	463.4	136.2	235.9	370.2
1989	1,060	543	1,603	951,710	610.4	134.1	277.1	383.4
1990	1,236	583	1,819	1,054,860	748.5	140.8	314.1	424.1
1991	1,938	648	2,586	1,092,740	1,155.7	154.2	439.8	433.3
1992	2,164	n/a	n/a	1,126,970	1,272.3	n/a	n/a	441.8
1993	2,200	n/a	n/a	1,135,610	1,296.0	n/a	n/a	440.3
1994	2,266	n/a	n/a	1,113,180	1,315.3	n/a	n/a	427.6
1995	2,335	n/a	n/a	1,099,210	1,357.9	n/a	n/a	418.3
1996	844	n/a	n/a	1,029,810	484.9	n/a	n/a	388.2

Notes: (1) Metropolitan Statistical Area - see Appendix A for areas included; (2) calculated by the editors using the following formula: (number of crimes in the MSA minus number of crimes in the city); (3) calculated by the editors using the following formula: ((number of crimes in the MSA minus number of crimes in the city) ÷ (population of the MSA minus population of the city)) x 100,000; n/a not avail.
Source: U.S. Department of Justice, FBI Uniform Crime Reports, 1977 - 1996

Burglaries and Burglary Rates: 1977 - 1996

Year	Number				Rate per 100,000 population			
	City	Suburbs[2]	MSA[1]	U.S.	City	Suburbs[3]	MSA[1]	U.S.
1977	3,546	2,365	5,911	3,071,500	1,916.8	901.7	1,321.6	1,419.8
1978	3,794	2,312	6,106	3,128,300	2,050.8	859.4	1,344.9	1,434.6
1979	4,052	3,231	7,283	3,327,700	2,147.1	1,207.1	1,595.8	1,511.9
1980	4,374	2,773	7,147	3,795,200	2,400.0	947.6	1,505.0	1,684.1
1981	4,232	3,004	7,236	3,779,700	2,289.6	1,012.2	1,502.4	1,649.5
1982	3,605	3,061	6,666	3,447,100	1,933.2	1,022.3	1,371.9	1,488.8
1983	2,984	3,586	6,570	3,129,900	1,588.6	911.1	1,130.0	1,337.7
1984	3,192	3,137	6,329	2,984,400	1,796.1	765.0	1,076.8	1,263.7
1985	3,302	3,458	6,760	3,073,300	1,879.9	825.3	1,136.8	1,287.3
1986	4,079	3,996	8,075	3,241,400	2,302.5	945.8	1,346.6	1,344.6
1987	4,008	3,821	7,829	3,236,200	2,289.1	963.2	1,369.2	1,329.6
1988	3,700	3,908	7,608	3,218,100	2,108.9	976.7	1,321.9	1,309.2
1989	3,989	4,048	8,037	3,168,200	2,297.1	1,000.0	1,389.4	1,276.3
1990	3,637	3,809	7,446	3,073,900	2,202.6	920.2	1,285.9	1,235.9
1991	3,984	4,667	8,651	3,157,200	2,375.9	1,110.3	1,471.2	1,252.0
1992	3,340	n/a	n/a	2,979,900	1,963.7	n/a	n/a	1,168.2
1993	2,817	n/a	n/a	2,834,800	1,659.5	n/a	n/a	1,099.2
1994	2,688	n/a	n/a	2,712,800	1,560.3	n/a	n/a	1,042.0
1995	2,810	n/a	n/a	2,593,800	1,634.1	n/a	n/a	987.1
1996	2,341	n/a	n/a	2,501,500	1,345.0	n/a	n/a	943.0

Notes: (1) Metropolitan Statistical Area - see Appendix A for areas included; (2) calculated by the editors using the following formula: (number of crimes in the MSA minus number of crimes in the city); (3) calculated by the editors using the following formula: ((number of crimes in the MSA minus number of crimes in the city) ÷ (population of the MSA minus population of the city)) x 100,000; n/a not avail.
Source: U.S. Department of Justice, FBI Uniform Crime Reports, 1977 - 1996

Larceny-Thefts and Larceny-Theft Rates: 1977 - 1996

Year	Number				Rate per 100,000 population			
	City	Suburbs[2]	MSA[1]	U.S.	City	Suburbs[3]	MSA[1]	U.S.
1977	5,183	3,310	8,493	5,905,700	2,801.6	1,262.0	1,898.8	2,729.9
1978	4,891	4,082	8,973	5,991,000	2,643.8	1,517.4	1,976.4	2,747.4
1979	4,729	4,521	9,250	6,601,000	2,505.8	1,689.1	2,026.8	2,999.1
1980	5,193	4,534	9,727	7,136,900	2,849.4	1,549.4	2,048.3	3,167.0
1981	5,602	4,296	9,898	7,194,400	3,030.9	1,447.5	2,055.2	3,139.7
1982	5,695	4,063	9,758	7,142,500	3,054.0	1,356.9	2,008.2	3,084.8
1983	4,768	5,328	10,096	6,712,800	2,538.4	1,353.7	1,736.4	2,868.9
1984	4,450	4,737	9,187	6,591,900	2,504.0	1,155.2	1,563.0	2,791.3
1985	4,956	5,220	10,176	6,926,400	2,821.6	1,245.8	1,711.2	2,901.2
1986	4,906	5,803	10,709	7,257,200	2,769.4	1,373.4	1,785.8	3,010.3
1987	4,854	5,249	10,103	7,499,900	2,772.3	1,323.2	1,766.9	3,081.3
1988	4,525	6,489	11,014	7,705,900	2,579.2	1,621.8	1,913.6	3,134.9
1989	4,986	7,207	12,193	7,872,400	2,871.3	1,780.3	2,107.8	3,171.3
1990	5,660	8,632	14,292	7,945,700	3,427.8	2,085.4	2,468.2	3,194.8
1991	6,639	8,359	14,998	8,142,200	3,959.2	1,988.6	2,550.6	3,228.8
1992	6,903	n/a	n/a	7,915,200	4,058.5	n/a	n/a	3,103.0
1993	6,027	n/a	n/a	7,820,900	3,550.5	n/a	n/a	3,032.4
1994	5,925	n/a	n/a	7,879,800	3,439.2	n/a	n/a	3,026.7
1995	5,898	n/a	n/a	7,997,700	3,429.9	n/a	n/a	3,043.8
1996	5,304	n/a	n/a	7,894,600	3,047.3	n/a	n/a	2,975.9

Notes: (1) Metropolitan Statistical Area - see Appendix A for areas included; (2) calculated by the editors using the following formula: (number of crimes in the MSA minus number of crimes in the city); (3) calculated by the editors using the following formula: ((number of crimes in the MSA minus number of crimes in the city) ÷ (population of the MSA minus population of the city)) x 100,000; n/a not avail.
Source: U.S. Department of Justice, FBI Uniform Crime Reports, 1977 - 1996

Motor Vehicle Thefts and Motor Vehicle Theft Rates: 1977 - 1996

Year	Number				Rate per 100,000 population			
	City	Suburbs[2]	MSA[1]	U.S.	City	Suburbs[3]	MSA[1]	U.S.
1977	1,176	670	1,846	977,700	635.7	255.5	412.7	451.9
1978	1,131	762	1,893	1,004,100	611.4	283.3	416.9	460.5
1979	1,321	835	2,156	1,112,800	700.0	312.0	472.4	505.6
1980	1,509	893	2,402	1,131,700	828.0	305.2	505.8	502.2
1981	1,599	714	2,313	1,087,800	865.1	240.6	480.3	474.7
1982	1,533	964	2,497	1,062,400	822.1	322.0	513.9	458.8
1983	1,285	927	2,212	1,007,900	684.1	235.5	380.4	430.8
1984	1,275	787	2,062	1,032,200	717.4	191.9	350.8	437.1
1985	1,502	907	2,409	1,102,900	855.1	216.5	405.1	462.0
1986	1,450	970	2,420	1,224,100	818.5	229.6	403.6	507.8
1987	1,490	871	2,361	1,288,700	851.0	219.6	412.9	529.4
1988	1,574	891	2,465	1,432,900	897.2	222.7	428.3	582.9
1989	1,941	1,066	3,007	1,564,800	1,117.8	263.3	519.8	630.4
1990	1,843	838	2,681	1,635,900	1,116.2	202.5	463.0	657.8
1991	2,142	1,043	3,185	1,661,700	1,277.4	248.1	541.6	659.0
1992	1,881	n/a	n/a	1,610,800	1,105.9	n/a	n/a	631.5
1993	1,609	n/a	n/a	1,563,100	947.9	n/a	n/a	606.1
1994	1,617	n/a	n/a	1,539,300	938.6	n/a	n/a	591.3
1995	1,779	n/a	n/a	1,472,400	1,034.5	n/a	n/a	560.4
1996	1,595	n/a	n/a	1,395,200	916.4	n/a	n/a	525.9

Notes: (1) Metropolitan Statistical Area - see Appendix A for areas included; (2) calculated by the editors using the following formula: (number of crimes in the MSA minus number of crimes in the city); (3) calculated by the editors using the following formula: ((number of crimes in the MSA minus number of crimes in the city) ÷ (population of the MSA minus population of the city)) x 100,000; n/a not avail.
Source: U.S. Department of Justice, FBI Uniform Crime Reports, 1977 - 1996

HATE CRIMES

Criminal Incidents by Bias Motivation

Area	Race	Ethnicity	Religion	Sexual Orientation
Knoxville	n/a	n/a	n/a	n/a

Notes: Figures include both violent and property crimes. Law enforcement agencies must have submitted data for at least one quarter of calendar year 1995 to be included in this report, therefore figures shown may not represent complete 12-month totals; n/a not available
Source: U.S. Department of Justice, FBI Uniform Crime Reports, Hate Crime Statistics 1995

LAW ENFORCEMENT

Full-Time Law Enforcement Employees

Jurisdiction	Police Employees			Police Officers per 100,000 population
	Total	Officers	Civilians	
Knoxville	474	383	91	220.0

Notes: Data as of October 31, 1996
Source: U.S. Department of Justice, FBI Uniform Crime Reports, 1996

CORRECTIONS

Federal Correctional Facilities

Type	Year Opened	Security Level	Sex of Inmates	Rated Capacity	Population on 7/1/95	Number of Staff
None listed						

Notes: Data as of 1995
Source: Bureau of Justice Statistics, Sourcebook of Criminal Justice Statistics Online

City/County/Regional Correctional Facilities

Name	Year Opened	Year Renov.	Rated Capacity	1995 Pop.	Number of COs[1]	Number of Staff	ACA[2] Accred.
Knox County Jail	1979	1990	645	n/a	n/a	n/a	No

Notes: Data as of April 1996; (1) Correctional Officers; (2) American Correctional Assn. Accreditation
Source: American Correctional Association, 1996-1998 National Jail and Adult Detention Directory

Private Adult Correctional Facilities

Name	Date Opened	Rated Capacity	Present Pop.	Security Level	Facility Construct.	Expans. Plans	ACA[1] Accred.
None listed							

Notes: Data as of December 1996; (1) American Correctional Association Accreditation
Source: University of Florida, Center for Studies in Criminology and Law, Private Adult Correctional Facility Census, 10th Ed., March 15, 1997

Characteristics of Shock Incarceration Programs

Jurisdiction	Year Program Began	Number of Camps	Average Num. of Inmates	Number of Beds	Program Length	Voluntary/ Mandatory
Tennessee	1989	1	142	150	90 to 120 days	Mandatory

Note: Data as of July 1996;
Source: Sourcebook of Criminal Justice Statistics Online

DEATH PENALTY

Death Penalty Statistics

State	Prisoners Executed		Prisoners Under Sentence of Death					Avg. No. of Years on Death Row[4]
	1930-1995	1996[1]	Total[2]	White[3]	Black[3]	Hisp.	Women	
Tennessee	93	0	96	64	30	1	1	8.5

Notes: Data as of 12/31/95 unless otherwise noted; (1) Data as of 7/31/97; (2) Includes persons of other races; (3) Includes people of Hispanic origin; (4) Covers prisoners sentenced 1974 through 1995
Source: Bureau of Justice Statistics, Capital Punishment 1995 (released 12/96); Death Penalty Information Center Web Site, 9/30/97

Capital Offenses and Methods of Execution

Capital Offenses in Tennessee	Minimum Age for Imposition of Death Penalty	Mentally Retarded Excluded	Methods of Execution[1]
First-degree murder.	18	No	Electrocution

Notes: Data as of 12/31/95 unless otherwise noted; (1) Data as of 7/31/97
Source: Bureau of Justice Statistics, Capital Punishment 1995 (released 12/96); Death Penalty Information Center Web Site, 9/30/97

LAWS

Statutory Provisions Relating to the Purchase, Ownership and Use of Handguns

Jurisdiction	Instant Background Check	Federal Waiting Period Applies[1]	State Waiting Period (days)	License or Permit to Purchase	Regis-tration	Record of Sale Sent to Police	Concealed Carry Law
Tennessee	No	No	15	No	No	Yes	Yes[a]

Note: Data as of 1996; (1) The Federal 5-day waiting period for handgun purchases applies to states that don't have instant background checks, waiting period requirements, or licensing procedures exempting them from the Federal requirement; (a) "Shall issue" permit system, liberally administered discretion by local authorities over permit issuance, or no permit required
Source: Sourcebook of Criminal Justice Statistics Online

Statutory Provisions Relating to Alcohol Use and Driving

Jurisdiction	Drinking Age	Blood Alcohol Concentration Levels as Evidence in State Courts[1]		Open Container Law[1]	Anti-Consump-tion Law[1]	Dram Shop Law[1]
		Illegal per se at 0.10%	Presumption at 0.10%			
Tennessee	21	Yes	Yes[a]	Yes[b]	Yes[b]	Yes

Note: Data as of January 1, 1997; (1) See Appendix C for an explanation of terms; (a) For a first offense, an alcohol concentration of 0.10% or more; for a subsequent offense, an alcohol concentration of 0.08% or more; (b) Applies to drivers only
Source: Sourcebook of Criminal Justice Statistics Online

Statutory Provisions Relating to Curfews

Jurisdiction	Year Enacted	Latest Revision	Age Group(s)	Curfew Provisions
Knoxville	1979	-	17 and under	Midnight to 6 am every night

Note: Data as of February 1996
Source: Sourcebook of Criminal Justice Statistics Online

Statutory Provisions Relating to Hate Crimes

Jurisdiction	Bias-Motivated Violence and Intimidation						Institutional Vandalism
	Civil Action	Criminal Penalty					
		Race/ Religion/ Ethnicity	Sexual Orientation	Mental/ Physical Disability	Gender	Age	
Tennessee	No	Yes	No	No	No	No	Yes

Source: Anti-Defamation League, 1997 Hate Crimes Laws

Lansing, Michigan

OVERVIEW

The total crime rate for the city increased 24.7% between 1977 and 1996. During that same period, the violent crime rate increased 204.1% and the property crime rate increased 11.3%.

Among violent crimes, the rates for: Murders decreased 18.6%; Forcible Rapes increased 201.7%; Robberies increased 101.5%; and Aggravated Assaults increased 271.5%.

Among property crimes, the rates for: Burglaries decreased 16.9%; Larceny-Thefts increased 19.8%; and Motor Vehicle Thefts increased 43.7%.

ANTI-CRIME PROGRAMS

Information not available at time of publication.

CRIME RISK

Your Chances of Becoming a Victim[1]

Area	Any Crime	Violent Crime					Property Crime			
		Any	Murder	Forcible Rape[2]	Robbery	Aggrav. Assault	Any	Burglary	Larceny -Theft	Motor Vehicle Theft
City	1:12	1:73	1:12,082	1:370	1:352	1:107	1:15	1:75	1:20	1:225

Note: (1) Figures have been calculated by dividing the population of the city by the number of crimes reported to the FBI during 1996 and are expressed as odds (eg. 1:20 should be read as 1 in 20). (2) Figures have been calculated by dividing the female population of the city by the number of forcible rapes reported to the FBI during 1996. The female population of the city was estimated by calculating the ratio of females to males reported in the 1990 Census and applying that ratio to 1996 population estimate.
Source: FBI Uniform Crime Reports 1996

CRIME STATISTICS

Total Crimes and Total Crime Rates: 1977 - 1996

Year	Number				Rate per 100,000 population			
	City	Suburbs[2]	MSA[1]	U.S.	City	Suburbs[3]	MSA[1]	U.S.
1977	8,216	11,837	20,053	10,984,500	6,469.3	3,703.0	4,489.6	5,077.6
1978	8,385	12,071	20,456	11,209,000	6,708.0	3,694.6	4,528.5	5,140.3
1979	8,468	13,668	22,136	12,249,500	6,721.9	4,107.5	4,825.5	5,565.5
1980	9,515	15,678	25,193	13,408,300	7,565.0	4,586.8	5,387.9	5,950.0
1981	10,008	15,997	26,005	13,423,800	7,980.4	4,693.9	5,577.9	5,858.2
1982	10,766	n/a	n/a	12,974,400	8,671.6	n/a	n/a	5,603.6
1983	9,965	11,899	21,864	12,108,600	8,061.9	4,173.7	5,349.6	5,175.0
1984	9,438	11,511	20,949	11,881,800	7,386.9	4,032.7	5,069.8	5,031.3
1985	9,877	12,694	22,571	12,431,400	7,706.7	4,396.1	5,413.8	5,207.1
1986	11,683	13,437	25,120	13,211,900	9,063.0	4,627.3	5,991.0	5,480.4
1987	10,996	13,876	24,872	13,508,700	8,483.9	4,669.5	5,827.9	5,550.0
1988	10,506	14,004	24,510	13,923,100	8,005.2	4,647.4	5,666.1	5,664.2
1989	10,089	13,716	23,805	14,251,400	8,044.2	4,505.6	5,538.1	5,741.0
1990	10,574	14,504	25,078	14,475,600	8,305.0	4,749.9	5,796.0	5,820.3
1991	10,340	15,442	25,782	14,872,900	8,058.3	5,018.1	5,912.7	5,897.8
1992	9,257	13,853	23,110	14,438,200	7,161.6	4,468.9	5,261.3	5,660.2
1993	n/a	n/a	n/a	14,144,800	n/a	n/a	n/a	5,484.4
1994	10,250	13,391	23,641	13,989,500	8,036.0	4,295.6	5,381.6	5,373.5
1995	9,784	12,609	22,393	13,862,700	8,136.0	3,961.4	5,106.1	5,275.9
1996	9,744	12,659	22,403	13,473,600	8,064.8	3,958.6	5,084.6	5,078.9

Notes: (1) Metropolitan Statistical Area - see Appendix A for areas included; (2) calculated by the editors using the following formula: (number of crimes in the MSA minus number of crimes in the city); (3) calculated by the editors using the following formula: ((number of crimes in the MSA minus number of crimes in the city) ÷ (population of the MSA minus population of the city)) x 100,000; n/a not avail.
Source: U.S. Department of Justice, FBI Uniform Crime Reports, 1977 - 1996

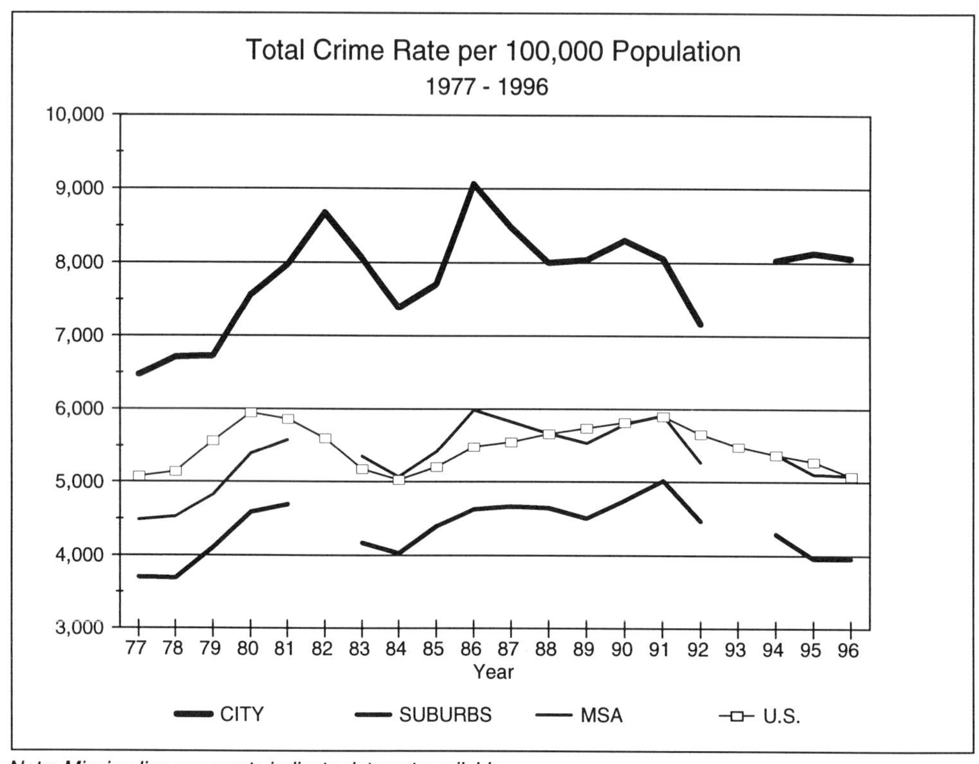

Note: Missing line segments indicate data not available.

Violent Crimes and Violent Crime Rates: 1977 - 1996

Year	Number				Rate per 100,000 population			
	City	Suburbs[2]	MSA[1]	U.S.	City	Suburbs[3]	MSA[1]	U.S.
1977	570	492	1,062	1,029,580	448.8	153.9	237.8	475.9
1978	695	583	1,278	1,085,550	556.0	178.4	282.9	497.8
1979	689	651	1,340	1,208,030	546.9	195.6	292.1	548.9
1980	735	773	1,508	1,344,520	584.4	226.2	322.5	596.6
1981	893	733	1,626	1,361,820	712.1	215.1	348.8	594.3
1982	1,012	n/a	n/a	1,322,390	815.1	n/a	n/a	571.1
1983	914	525	1,439	1,258,090	739.4	184.1	352.1	537.7
1984	1,102	559	1,661	1,273,280	862.5	195.8	402.0	539.2
1985	1,064	628	1,692	1,328,800	830.2	217.5	405.8	556.6
1986	1,501	683	2,184	1,489,170	1,164.4	235.2	520.9	617.7
1987	1,684	761	2,445	1,484,000	1,299.3	256.1	572.9	609.7
1988	1,602	891	2,493	1,566,220	1,220.7	295.7	576.3	637.2
1989	1,591	953	2,544	1,646,040	1,268.5	313.1	591.8	663.1
1990	1,874	1,043	2,917	1,820,130	1,471.9	341.6	674.2	731.8
1991	1,768	1,110	2,878	1,911,770	1,377.9	360.7	660.0	758.1
1992	1,782	898	2,680	1,932,270	1,378.6	289.7	610.1	757.5
1993	n/a	n/a	n/a	1,926,020	n/a	n/a	n/a	746.8
1994	1,613	972	2,585	1,857,670	1,264.6	311.8	588.4	713.6
1995	1,643	840	2,483	1,798,790	1,366.3	263.9	566.2	684.6
1996	1,649	845	2,494	1,682,280	1,364.8	264.2	566.0	634.1

Notes: Violent crimes include murder, forcible rape, robbery and aggravated assault; n/a not available; (1) Metropolitan Statistical Area - see Appendix A for areas included; (2) calculated by the editors using the following formula: (number of crimes in the MSA minus number of crimes in the city); (3) calculated by the editors using the following formula: ((number of crimes in the MSA minus number of crimes in the city) ÷ (population of the MSA minus population of the city)) x 100,000
Source: U.S. Department of Justice, FBI Uniform Crime Reports, 1977 - 1996

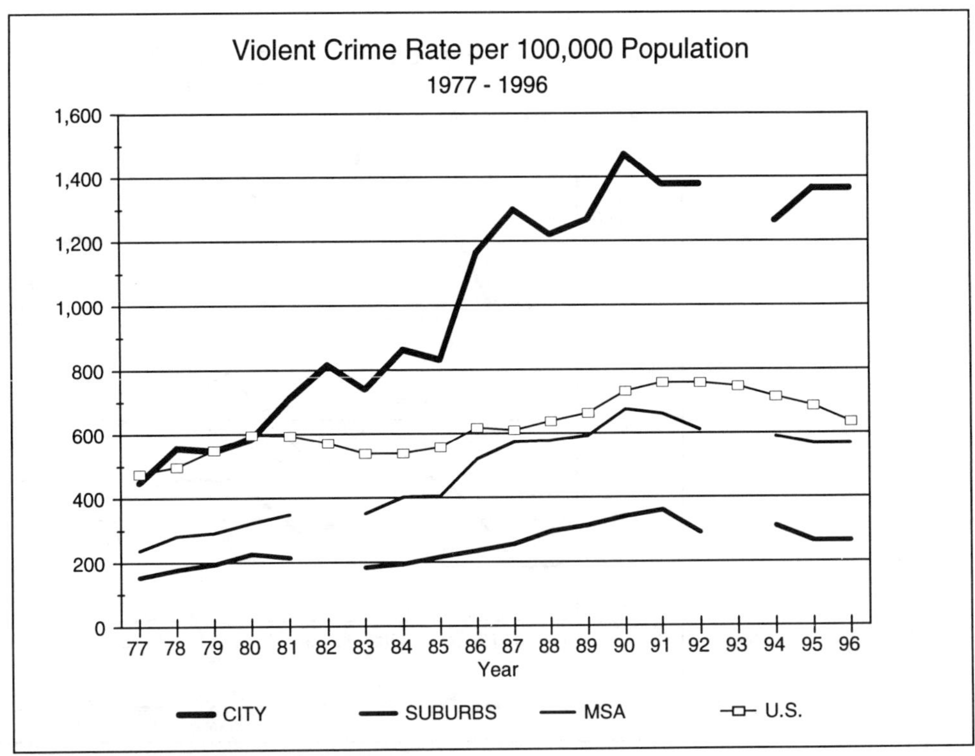

Note: Missing line segments indicate data not available.

Property Crimes and Property Crime Rates: 1977 - 1996

Year	Number				Rate per 100,000 population			
	City	Suburbs[2]	MSA[1]	U.S.	City	Suburbs[3]	MSA[1]	U.S.
1977	7,646	11,345	18,991	9,955,000	6,020.5	3,549.1	4,251.8	4,601.7
1978	7,690	11,488	19,178	10,123,400	6,152.0	3,516.2	4,245.6	4,642.5
1979	7,779	13,017	20,796	11,041,500	6,175.0	3,911.9	4,533.4	5,016.6
1980	8,780	14,905	23,685	12,063,700	6,980.7	4,360.6	5,065.4	5,353.3
1981	9,115	15,264	24,379	12,061,900	7,268.3	4,478.8	5,229.2	5,263.9
1982	9,754	n/a	n/a	11,652,000	7,856.5	n/a	n/a	5,032.5
1983	9,051	11,374	20,425	10,850,500	7,322.5	3,989.5	4,997.5	4,637.4
1984	8,336	10,952	19,288	10,608,500	6,524.4	3,836.8	4,667.8	4,492.1
1985	8,813	12,066	20,879	11,102,600	6,876.5	4,178.6	5,008.0	4,650.5
1986	10,182	12,754	22,936	11,722,700	7,898.6	4,392.1	5,470.1	4,862.6
1987	9,312	13,115	22,427	12,024,700	7,184.6	4,413.4	5,255.0	4,940.3
1988	8,904	13,113	22,017	12,356,900	6,784.6	4,351.7	5,089.8	5,027.1
1989	8,498	12,763	21,261	12,605,400	6,775.7	4,192.6	4,946.3	5,077.9
1990	8,700	13,461	22,161	12,655,500	6,833.1	4,408.3	5,121.9	5,088.5
1991	8,572	14,332	22,904	12,961,100	6,680.4	4,657.4	5,252.7	5,139.7
1992	7,475	12,955	20,430	12,505,900	5,783.0	4,179.2	4,651.2	4,902.7
1993	7,367	11,950	19,317	12,218,800	5,786.6	3,840.5	4,405.5	4,737.6
1994	8,637	12,419	21,056	12,131,900	6,771.4	3,983.8	4,793.2	4,660.0
1995	8,141	11,769	19,910	12,063,900	6,769.7	3,697.5	4,540.0	4,591.3
1996	8,095	11,814	19,909	11,791,300	6,700.0	3,694.4	4,518.5	4,444.8

Notes: Property crimes include burglary, larceny-theft and motor vehicle theft; n/a not available; (1) Metropolitan Statistical Area - see Appendix A for areas included; (2) calculated by the editors using the following formula: (number of crimes in the MSA minus number of crimes in the city); (3) calculated by the editors using the following formula: ((number of crimes in the MSA minus number of crimes in the city) ÷ (population of the MSA minus population of the city)) x 100,000
Source: U.S. Department of Justice, FBI Uniform Crime Reports, 1977 - 1996

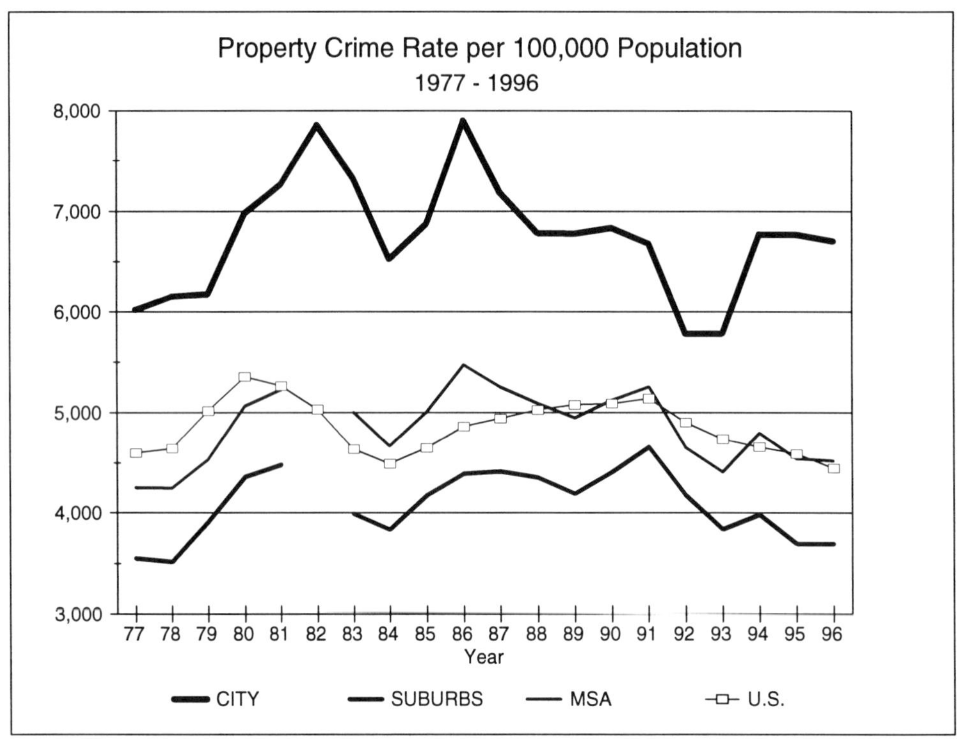

Note: Missing line segments indicate data not available.

Murders and Murder Rates: 1977 - 1996

Year	Number				Rate per 100,000 population			
	City	Suburbs[2]	MSA[1]	U.S.	City	Suburbs[3]	MSA[1]	U.S.
1977	13	9	22	19,120	10.2	2.8	4.9	8.8
1978	13	5	18	19,560	10.4	1.5	4.0	9.0
1979	7	8	15	21,460	5.6	2.4	3.3	9.7
1980	4	11	15	23,040	3.2	3.2	3.2	10.2
1981	9	8	17	22,520	7.2	2.3	3.6	9.8
1982	8	n/a	n/a	21,010	6.4	n/a	n/a	9.1
1983	5	2	7	19,310	4.0	0.7	1.7	8.3
1984	17	13	30	18,690	13.3	4.6	7.3	7.9
1985	6	5	11	18,980	4.7	1.7	2.6	7.9
1986	6	4	10	20,610	4.7	1.4	2.4	8.6
1987	8	3	11	20,100	6.2	1.0	2.6	8.3
1988	11	4	15	20,680	8.4	1.3	3.5	8.4
1989	16	6	22	21,500	12.8	2.0	5.1	8.7
1990	11	3	14	23,440	8.6	1.0	3.2	9.4
1991	12	4	16	24,700	9.4	1.3	3.7	9.8
1992	7	4	11	23,760	5.4	1.3	2.5	9.3
1993	14	7	21	24,530	11.0	2.2	4.8	9.5
1994	10	4	14	23,330	7.8	1.3	3.2	9.0
1995	13	6	19	21,610	10.8	1.9	4.3	8.2
1996	10	3	13	19,650	8.3	0.9	3.0	7.4

Notes: (1) Metropolitan Statistical Area - see Appendix A for areas included; (2) calculated by the editors using the following formula: (number of crimes in the MSA minus number of crimes in the city); (3) calculated by the editors using the following formula: ((number of crimes in the MSA minus number of crimes in the city) ÷ (population of the MSA minus population of the city)) x 100,000; n/a not avail.
Source: U.S. Department of Justice, FBI Uniform Crime Reports, 1977 - 1996

Forcible Rapes and Forcible Rape Rates: 1977 - 1996

Year	Number				Rate per 100,000 population			
	City	Suburbs[2]	MSA[1]	U.S.	City	Suburbs[3]	MSA[1]	U.S.
1977	60	81	141	63,500	47.2	25.3	31.6	29.4
1978	67	78	145	67,610	53.6	23.9	32.1	31.0
1979	54	76	130	76,390	42.9	22.8	28.3	34.7
1980	53	103	156	82,990	42.1	30.1	33.4	36.8
1981	111	101	212	82,500	88.5	29.6	45.5	36.0
1982	181	n/a	n/a	78,770	145.8	n/a	n/a	34.0
1983	76	92	168	78,920	61.5	32.3	41.1	33.7
1984	92	135	227	84,230	72.0	47.3	54.9	35.7
1985	75	160	235	88,670	58.5	55.4	56.4	37.1
1986	145	149	294	91,460	112.5	51.3	70.1	37.9
1987	164	154	318	91,110	126.5	51.8	74.5	37.4
1988	136	221	357	92,490	103.6	73.3	82.5	37.6
1989	148	254	402	94,500	118.0	83.4	93.5	38.1
1990	163	216	379	102,560	128.0	70.7	87.6	41.2
1991	188	255	443	106,590	146.5	82.9	101.6	42.3
1992	184	245	429	109,060	142.3	79.0	97.7	42.8
1993	n/a	n/a	n/a	106,010	n/a	n/a	n/a	41.1
1994	156	257	413	102,220	122.3	82.4	94.0	39.3
1995	148	200	348	97,470	123.1	62.8	79.4	37.1
1996	172	138	310	95,770	142.4	43.2	70.4	36.1

Notes: (1) Metropolitan Statistical Area - see Appendix A for areas included; (2) calculated by the editors using the following formula: (number of crimes in the MSA minus number of crimes in the city); (3) calculated by the editors using the following formula: ((number of crimes in the MSA minus number of crimes in the city) ÷ (population of the MSA minus population of the city)) x 100,000; n/a not avail.
Source: U.S. Department of Justice, FBI Uniform Crime Reports, 1977 - 1996

Robberies and Robbery Rates: 1977 - 1996

Year	Number				Rate per 100,000 population			
	City	Suburbs[2]	MSA[1]	U.S.	City	Suburbs[3]	MSA[1]	U.S.
1977	179	105	284	412,610	140.9	32.8	63.6	190.7
1978	149	105	254	426,930	119.2	32.1	56.2	195.8
1979	180	126	306	480,700	142.9	37.9	66.7	218.4
1980	216	180	396	565,840	171.7	52.7	84.7	251.1
1981	153	128	281	592,910	122.0	37.6	60.3	258.7
1982	250	n/a	n/a	553,130	201.4	n/a	n/a	238.9
1983	247	140	387	506,570	199.8	49.1	94.7	216.5
1984	180	102	282	485,010	140.9	35.7	68.2	205.4
1985	210	103	313	497,870	163.9	35.7	75.1	208.5
1986	293	133	426	542,780	227.3	45.8	101.6	225.1
1987	336	163	499	517,700	259.2	54.9	116.9	212.7
1988	398	216	614	542,970	303.3	71.7	141.9	220.9
1989	360	162	522	578,330	287.0	53.2	121.4	233.0
1990	309	159	468	639,270	242.7	52.1	108.2	257.0
1991	294	163	457	687,730	229.1	53.0	104.8	272.7
1992	312	92	404	672,480	241.4	29.7	92.0	263.6
1993	302	124	426	659,870	237.2	39.9	97.2	255.9
1994	349	170	519	618,950	273.6	54.5	118.1	237.7
1995	344	94	438	580,510	286.1	29.5	99.9	220.9
1996	343	163	506	537,050	283.9	51.0	114.8	202.4

Notes: (1) Metropolitan Statistical Area - see Appendix A for areas included; (2) calculated by the editors using the following formula: (number of crimes in the MSA minus number of crimes in the city); (3) calculated by the editors using the following formula: ((number of crimes in the MSA minus number of crimes in the city) ÷ (population of the MSA minus population of the city)) x 100,000; n/a not avail.
Source: U.S. Department of Justice, FBI Uniform Crime Reports, 1977 - 1996

Aggravated Assaults and Aggravated Assault Rates: 1977 - 1996

Year	Number				Rate per 100,000 population			
	City	Suburbs[2]	MSA[1]	U.S.	City	Suburbs[3]	MSA[1]	U.S.
1977	318	297	615	534,350	250.4	92.9	137.7	247.0
1978	466	395	861	571,460	372.8	120.9	190.6	262.1
1979	448	441	889	629,480	355.6	132.5	193.8	286.0
1980	462	479	941	672,650	367.3	140.1	201.2	298.5
1981	620	496	1,116	663,900	494.4	145.5	239.4	289.7
1982	573	n/a	n/a	669,480	461.5	n/a	n/a	289.2
1983	586	291	877	653,290	474.1	102.1	214.6	279.2
1984	813	309	1,122	685,350	636.3	108.3	271.5	290.2
1985	773	360	1,133	723,250	603.1	124.7	271.8	302.9
1986	1,057	397	1,454	834,320	820.0	136.7	346.8	346.1
1987	1,176	441	1,617	855,090	907.3	148.4	378.9	351.3
1988	1,057	450	1,507	910,090	805.4	149.3	348.4	370.2
1989	1,067	531	1,598	951,710	850.7	174.4	371.8	383.4
1990	1,391	665	2,056	1,054,860	1,092.5	217.8	475.2	424.1
1991	1,274	688	1,962	1,092,740	992.9	223.6	450.0	433.3
1992	1,279	557	1,836	1,126,970	989.5	179.7	418.0	441.8
1993	1,066	574	1,640	1,135,610	837.3	184.5	374.0	440.3
1994	1,098	541	1,639	1,113,180	860.8	173.5	373.1	427.6
1995	1,138	540	1,678	1,099,210	946.3	169.7	382.6	418.3
1996	1,124	541	1,665	1,029,810	930.3	169.2	377.9	388.2

Notes: (1) Metropolitan Statistical Area - see Appendix A for areas included; (2) calculated by the editors using the following formula: (number of crimes in the MSA minus number of crimes in the city); (3) calculated by the editors using the following formula: ((number of crimes in the MSA minus number of crimes in the city) ÷ (population of the MSA minus population of the city)) x 100,000; n/a not avail.
Source: U.S. Department of Justice, FBI Uniform Crime Reports, 1977 - 1996

Burglaries and Burglary Rates: 1977 - 1996

Year	Number				Rate per 100,000 population			
	City	Suburbs[2]	MSA[1]	U.S.	City	Suburbs[3]	MSA[1]	U.S.
1977	2,033	2,733	4,766	3,071,500	1,600.8	855.0	1,067.0	1,419.8
1978	2,235	2,610	4,845	3,128,300	1,788.0	798.9	1,072.6	1,434.6
1979	2,029	2,617	4,646	3,327,700	1,610.6	786.5	1,012.8	1,511.9
1980	2,534	3,098	5,632	3,795,200	2,014.7	906.4	1,204.5	1,684.1
1981	2,696	3,254	5,950	3,779,700	2,149.8	954.8	1,276.2	1,649.5
1982	3,264	n/a	n/a	3,447,100	2,629.0	n/a	n/a	1,488.8
1983	2,914	2,830	5,744	3,129,900	2,357.5	992.7	1,405.4	1,337.7
1984	2,383	2,525	4,908	2,984,400	1,865.1	884.6	1,187.8	1,263.7
1985	2,391	2,738	5,129	3,073,300	1,865.6	948.2	1,230.2	1,287.3
1986	3,107	2,817	5,924	3,241,400	2,410.2	970.1	1,412.8	1,344.6
1987	2,612	2,720	5,332	3,236,200	2,015.3	915.3	1,249.4	1,329.6
1988	2,309	2,526	4,835	3,218,100	1,759.4	838.3	1,117.7	1,309.2
1989	1,963	2,441	4,404	3,168,200	1,565.2	801.9	1,024.6	1,276.3
1990	1,748	2,355	4,103	3,073,900	1,372.9	771.2	948.3	1,235.9
1991	1,759	2,523	4,282	3,157,200	1,370.8	819.9	982.0	1,252.0
1992	1,488	2,052	3,540	2,979,900	1,151.2	662.0	805.9	1,168.2
1993	1,372	1,953	3,325	2,834,800	1,077.7	627.7	758.3	1,099.2
1994	1,539	2,003	3,542	2,712,800	1,206.6	642.5	806.3	1,042.0
1995	1,502	2,066	3,568	2,593,800	1,249.0	649.1	813.6	987.1
1996	1,607	2,024	3,631	2,501,500	1,330.1	632.9	824.1	943.0

Notes: (1) Metropolitan Statistical Area - see Appendix A for areas included; (2) calculated by the editors using the following formula: (number of crimes in the MSA minus number of crimes in the city); (3) calculated by the editors using the following formula: ((number of crimes in the MSA minus number of crimes in the city) ÷ (population of the MSA minus population of the city)) x 100,000; n/a not avail.
Source: U.S. Department of Justice, FBI Uniform Crime Reports, 1977 - 1996

Larceny-Thefts and Larceny-Theft Rates: 1977 - 1996

Year	Number				Rate per 100,000 population			
	City	Suburbs[2]	MSA[1]	U.S.	City	Suburbs[3]	MSA[1]	U.S.
1977	5,221	8,110	13,331	5,905,700	4,111.0	2,537.1	2,984.6	2,729.9
1978	5,013	8,396	13,409	5,991,000	4,010.4	2,569.8	2,968.4	2,747.4
1979	5,241	9,775	15,016	6,601,000	4,160.3	2,937.6	3,273.4	2,999.1
1980	5,881	11,177	17,058	7,136,900	4,675.8	3,270.0	3,648.1	3,167.0
1981	6,139	11,482	17,621	7,194,400	4,895.3	3,369.1	3,779.6	3,139.7
1982	6,168	n/a	n/a	7,142,500	4,968.1	n/a	n/a	3,084.8
1983	5,854	8,137	13,991	6,712,800	4,736.0	2,854.1	3,423.3	2,868.9
1984	5,493	7,999	13,492	6,591,900	4,299.2	2,802.3	3,265.2	2,791.3
1985	5,998	8,807	14,805	6,926,400	4,680.1	3,050.0	3,551.1	2,901.2
1986	6,607	9,337	15,944	7,257,200	5,125.3	3,215.4	3,802.6	3,010.3
1987	6,043	9,523	15,566	7,499,900	4,662.4	3,204.6	3,647.4	3,081.3
1988	5,910	9,689	15,599	7,705,900	4,503.2	3,215.4	3,606.1	3,134.9
1989	5,915	9,443	15,358	7,872,400	4,716.2	3,102.0	3,573.0	3,171.3
1990	6,376	10,240	16,616	7,945,700	5,007.8	3,353.5	3,840.3	3,194.8
1991	6,218	10,872	17,090	8,142,200	4,845.9	3,533.0	3,919.3	3,228.8
1992	5,253	10,199	15,452	7,915,200	4,063.9	3,290.2	3,517.9	3,103.0
1993	5,295	9,363	14,658	7,820,900	4,159.1	3,009.1	3,343.0	3,032.4
1994	6,121	9,693	15,814	7,879,800	4,798.9	3,109.3	3,599.9	3,026.7
1995	5,940	9,017	14,957	7,997,700	4,939.5	2,832.9	3,410.5	3,043.8
1996	5,952	9,026	14,978	7,894,600	4,926.3	2,822.5	3,399.4	2,975.9

Notes: (1) Metropolitan Statistical Area - see Appendix A for areas included; (2) calculated by the editors using the following formula: (number of crimes in the MSA minus number of crimes in the city); (3) calculated by the editors using the following formula: ((number of crimes in the MSA minus number of crimes in the city) ÷ (population of the MSA minus population of the city)) x 100,000; n/a not avail.
Source: U.S. Department of Justice, FBI Uniform Crime Reports, 1977 - 1996

Motor Vehicle Thefts and Motor Vehicle Theft Rates: 1977 - 1996

Year	Number				Rate per 100,000 population			
	City	Suburbs[2]	MSA[1]	U.S.	City	Suburbs[3]	MSA[1]	U.S.
1977	392	502	894	977,700	308.7	157.0	200.2	451.9
1978	442	482	924	1,004,100	353.6	147.5	204.6	460.5
1979	509	625	1,134	1,112,800	404.0	187.8	247.2	505.6
1980	365	630	995	1,131,700	290.2	184.3	212.8	502.2
1981	280	528	808	1,087,800	223.3	154.9	173.3	474.7
1982	322	n/a	n/a	1,062,400	259.4	n/a	n/a	458.8
1983	283	407	690	1,007,900	229.0	142.8	168.8	430.8
1984	460	428	888	1,032,200	360.0	149.9	214.9	437.1
1985	424	521	945	1,102,900	330.8	180.4	226.7	462.0
1986	468	600	1,068	1,224,100	363.0	206.6	254.7	507.8
1987	657	872	1,529	1,288,700	506.9	293.4	358.3	529.4
1988	685	898	1,583	1,432,900	521.9	298.0	366.0	582.9
1989	620	879	1,499	1,564,800	494.3	288.7	348.7	630.4
1990	576	866	1,442	1,635,900	452.4	283.6	333.3	657.8
1991	595	937	1,532	1,661,700	463.7	304.5	351.3	659.0
1992	734	704	1,438	1,610,800	567.9	227.1	327.4	631.5
1993	700	634	1,334	1,563,100	549.8	203.8	304.2	606.1
1994	977	723	1,700	1,539,300	766.0	231.9	387.0	591.3
1995	699	686	1,385	1,472,400	581.3	215.5	315.8	560.4
1996	536	764	1,300	1,395,200	443.6	238.9	295.0	525.9

Notes: (1) Metropolitan Statistical Area - see Appendix A for areas included; (2) calculated by the editors using the following formula: (number of crimes in the MSA minus number of crimes in the city); (3) calculated by the editors using the following formula: ((number of crimes in the MSA minus number of crimes in the city) ÷ (population of the MSA minus population of the city)) x 100,000; n/a not avail.
Source: U.S. Department of Justice, FBI Uniform Crime Reports, 1977 - 1996

HATE CRIMES

Criminal Incidents by Bias Motivation

Area	Race	Ethnicity	Religion	Sexual Orientation
Lansing	n/a	n/a	n/a	n/a

Notes: Figures include both violent and property crimes. Law enforcement agencies must have submitted data for at least one quarter of calendar year 1995 to be included in this report, therefore figures shown may not represent complete 12-month totals; n/a not available
Source: U.S. Department of Justice, FBI Uniform Crime Reports, Hate Crime Statistics 1995

LAW ENFORCEMENT

Full-Time Law Enforcement Employees

Jurisdiction	Police Employees			Police Officers per 100,000 population
	Total	Officers	Civilians	
Lansing	344	254	90	210.2

Notes: Data as of October 31, 1996
Source: U.S. Department of Justice, FBI Uniform Crime Reports, 1996

CORRECTIONS

Federal Correctional Facilities

Type	Year Opened	Security Level	Sex of Inmates	Rated Capacity	Population on 7/1/95	Number of Staff
None listed						

Notes: Data as of 1995
Source: Bureau of Justice Statistics, Sourcebook of Criminal Justice Statistics Online

City/County/Regional Correctional Facilities

Name	Year Opened	Year Renov.	Rated Capacity	1995 Pop.	Number of COs[1]	Number of Staff	ACA[2] Accred.
None listed							

Notes: Data as of April 1996; (1) Correctional Officers; (2) American Correctional Assn. Accreditation
Source: American Correctional Association, 1996-1998 National Jail and Adult Detention Directory

Private Adult Correctional Facilities

Name	Date Opened	Rated Capacity	Present Pop.	Security Level	Facility Construct.	Expans. Plans	ACA[1] Accred.
None listed							

Notes: Data as of December 1996; (1) American Correctional Association Accreditation
Source: University of Florida, Center for Studies in Criminology and Law, Private Adult Correctional Facility Census, 10th Ed., March 15, 1997

Characteristics of Shock Incarceration Programs

Jurisdiction	Year Program Began	Number of Camps	Average Num. of Inmates	Number of Beds	Program Length	Voluntary/ Mandatory
Michigan	1988	1	319	360	90 days	Voluntary

Note: Data as of July 1996;
Source: Sourcebook of Criminal Justice Statistics Online

DEATH PENALTY

Michigan did not have the death penalty as of July 31, 1997.
Source: Death Penalty Information Center Web Site, 9/30/97

LAWS

Statutory Provisions Relating to the Purchase, Ownership and Use of Handguns

Jurisdiction	Instant Background Check	Federal Waiting Period Applies[1]	State Waiting Period (days)	License or Permit to Purchase	Regis-tration	Record of Sale Sent to Police	Concealed Carry Law
Michigan	No	No	No	Yes[a]	Yes	Yes	Yes[b]

Note: Data as of 1996; (1) The Federal 5-day waiting period for handgun purchases applies to states that don't have instant background checks, waiting period requirements, or licensing procedures exempting them from the Federal requirement; (a) A handgun purchaser must obtain a license to purchase from local law enforcement, and within 10 days present to such official the license and handgun purchased to obtain a certificate of inspection; (b) Restrictively administered discretion by local authorities over permit issuance, or permits are unavailable and carrying is prohibited in most circumstances
Source: Sourcebook of Criminal Justice Statistics Online

Statutory Provisions Relating to Alcohol Use and Driving

Jurisdiction	Drinking Age	Blood Alcohol Concentration Levels as Evidence in State Courts[1]		Open Container Law[1]	Anti-Consump-tion Law[1]	Dram Shop Law[1]
		Illegal per se at 0.10%	Presumption at 0.10%			
Michigan	21	Yes	(a)	Yes	Yes	Yes

Note: Data as of January 1, 1997; (1) See Appendix C for an explanation of terms; (a) Presumption of driving while impaired at 0.07%; presumption of driving under the influence at 0.10%
Source: Sourcebook of Criminal Justice Statistics Online

Statutory Provisions Relating to Curfews

Jurisdiction	Year Enacted	Latest Revision	Age Group(s)	Curfew Provisions
Lansing	1986	-	13 through 16 12 and under	Midnight to 6 am every night 10 pm to 6 am every night

Note: Data as of February 1996
Source: Sourcebook of Criminal Justice Statistics Online

Statutory Provisions Relating to Hate Crimes

Jurisdiction	Bias-Motivated Violence and Intimidation						Institutional Vandalism
	Civil Action	Criminal Penalty					
		Race/ Religion/ Ethnicity	Sexual Orientation	Mental/ Physical Disability	Gender	Age	
Michigan	Yes	Yes	No	No	Yes	No	No

Source: Anti-Defamation League, 1997 Hate Crimes Laws

Las Vegas, Nevada

OVERVIEW

The total crime rate for the city decreased 60.0% between 1977 and 1996. During that same period, the violent crime rate decreased 40.3% and the property crime rate decreased 62.2%.

Among violent crimes, the rates for: Murders decreased 47.0%; Forcible Rapes decreased 49.8%; Robberies decreased 50.2%; and Aggravated Assaults decreased 25.2%.

Among property crimes, the rates for: Burglaries decreased 74.7%; Larceny-Thefts decreased 59.5%; and Motor Vehicle Thefts decreased 27.4%.

ANTI-CRIME PROGRAMS

Information not available at time of publication.

CRIME RISK

Your Chances of Becoming a Victim[1]

Area	Any Crime	Violent Crime					Property Crime			
		Any	Murder	Forcible Rape[2]	Robbery	Aggrav. Assault	Any	Burglary	Larceny -Theft	Motor Vehicle Theft
City	1:15	1:99	1:5,163	1:866	1:228	1:202	1:17	1:71	1:29	1:105

Note: (1) Figures have been calculated by dividing the population of the city by the number of crimes reported to the FBI during 1996 and are expressed as odds (eg. 1:20 should be read as 1 in 20).
(2) Figures have been calculated by dividing the female population of the city by the number of forcible rapes reported to the FBI during 1996. The female population of the city was estimated by calculating the ratio of females to males reported in the 1990 Census and applying that ratio to 1996 population estimate.
Source: FBI Uniform Crime Reports 1996

CRIME STATISTICS

Total Crimes and Total Crime Rates: 1977 - 1996

Year	Number				Rate per 100,000 population			
	City	Suburbs[2]	MSA[1]	U.S.	City	Suburbs[3]	MSA[1]	U.S.
1977	27,595	6,092	33,687	10,984,500	17,139.8	3,118.5	9,453.4	5,077.6
1978	29,371	5,276	34,647	11,209,000	17,379.3	2,652.5	9,417.4	5,140.3
1979	34,133	5,596	39,729	12,249,500	10,527.7	7,586.5	9,982.6	5,565.5
1980	41,405	6,168	47,573	13,408,300	10,743.5	8,029.0	10,292.3	5,950.0
1981	43,376	6,876	50,252	13,423,800	10,659.7	8,477.2	10,297.0	5,858.2
1982	42,144	6,776	48,920	12,974,400	9,933.7	8,012.5	9,614.4	5,603.6
1983	35,225	5,913	41,138	12,108,600	8,209.4	6,913.6	7,994.1	5,175.0
1984	34,813	5,338	40,151	11,881,800	7,943.4	5,799.1	7,571.2	5,031.3
1985	35,191	5,213	40,404	12,431,400	7,704.7	5,510.9	7,328.3	5,207.1
1986	35,841	5,429	41,270	13,211,900	7,738.4	5,217.7	7,276.0	5,480.4
1987	37,020	6,223	43,243	13,508,700	7,690.2	5,491.3	7,271.2	5,550.0
1988	37,461	7,799	45,260	13,923,100	7,331.8	6,484.0	7,170.2	5,664.2
1989	39,624	5,070	44,694	14,251,400	7,390.5	3,923.3	6,717.1	5,741.0
1990	43,944	5,402	49,346	14,475,600	7,131.0	4,314.1	6,655.3	5,820.3
1991	48,779	6,857	55,636	14,872,900	7,431.4	5,050.3	7,023.3	5,897.8
1992	49,880	13,302	63,182	14,438,200	7,352.8	5,161.8	6,749.6	5,660.2
1993	48,365	18,044	66,409	14,144,800	6,741.3	6,211.3	6,588.6	5,484.4
1994	58,161	21,584	79,745	13,989,500	7,728.2	7,117.9	7,553.0	5,373.5
1995	60,178	23,421	83,599	13,862,700	7,584.5	6,991.8	7,408.6	5,275.9
1996	56,943	22,315	79,258	13,473,600	6,849.8	6,353.8	6,702.5	5,078.9

Notes: (1) Metropolitan Statistical Area - see Appendix A for areas included; (2) calculated by the editors using the following formula: (number of crimes in the MSA minus number of crimes in the city); (3) calculated by the editors using the following formula: ((number of crimes in the MSA minus number of crimes in the city) ÷ (population of the MSA minus population of the city)) x 100,000; n/a not avail.
Source: U.S. Department of Justice, FBI Uniform Crime Reports, 1977 - 1996

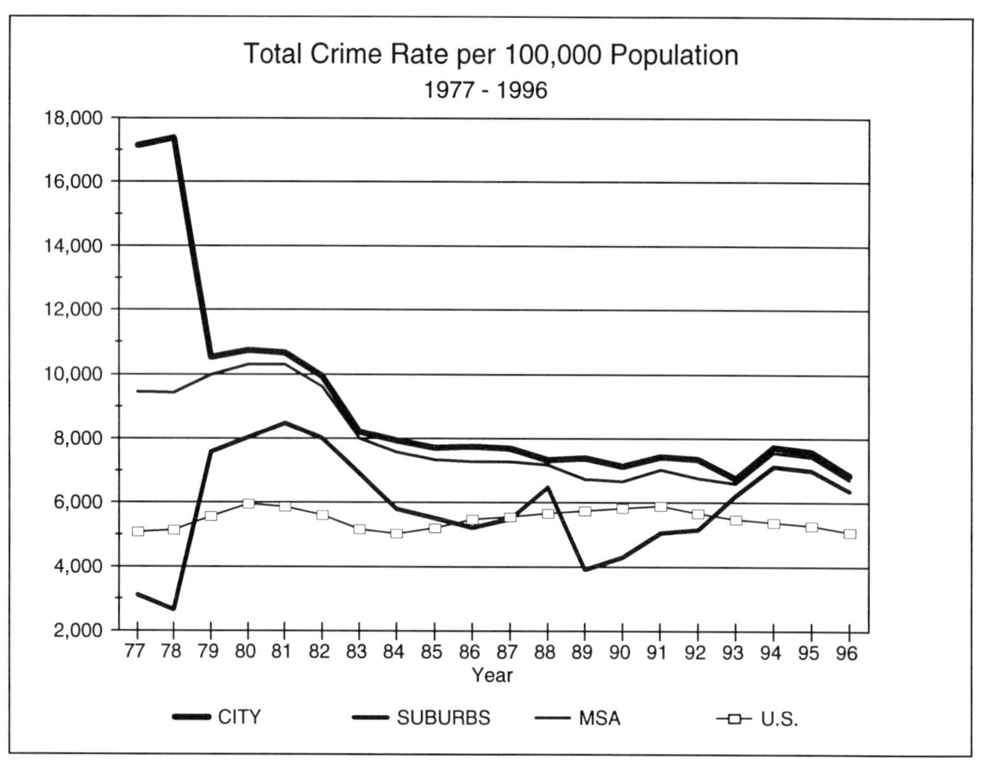

Note: Missing line segments indicate data not available.

Violent Crimes and Violent Crime Rates: 1977 - 1996

Year	Number				Rate per 100,000 population			
	City	Suburbs[2]	MSA[1]	U.S.	City	Suburbs[3]	MSA[1]	U.S.
1977	2,729	696	3,425	1,029,580	1,695.0	356.3	961.1	475.9
1978	2,886	712	3,598	1,085,550	1,707.7	358.0	978.0	497.8
1979	3,210	867	4,077	1,208,030	990.1	1,175.4	1,024.4	548.9
1980	4,421	886	5,307	1,344,520	1,147.1	1,153.3	1,148.2	596.6
1981	4,648	1,136	5,784	1,361,820	1,142.3	1,400.5	1,185.2	594.3
1982	4,470	908	5,378	1,322,390	1,053.6	1,073.7	1,057.0	571.1
1983	3,564	745	4,309	1,258,090	830.6	871.1	837.3	537.7
1984	3,309	700	4,009	1,273,280	755.0	760.5	756.0	539.2
1985	3,624	803	4,427	1,328,800	793.4	848.9	802.9	556.6
1986	3,947	943	4,890	1,489,170	852.2	906.3	862.1	617.7
1987	3,884	984	4,868	1,484,000	806.8	868.3	818.5	609.7
1988	4,024	1,435	5,459	1,566,220	787.6	1,193.0	864.8	637.2
1989	4,094	375	4,469	1,646,040	763.6	290.2	671.6	663.1
1990	4,510	392	4,902	1,820,130	731.9	313.1	661.1	731.8
1991	5,661	582	6,243	1,911,770	862.4	428.7	788.1	758.1
1992	6,027	1,031	7,058	1,932,270	888.4	400.1	754.0	757.5
1993	7,281	2,390	9,671	1,926,020	1,014.9	822.7	959.5	746.8
1994	9,418	3,036	12,454	1,857,670	1,251.4	1,001.2	1,179.6	713.6
1995	9,523	2,730	12,253	1,798,790	1,200.2	815.0	1,085.9	684.6
1996	8,409	2,550	10,959	1,682,280	1,011.5	726.1	926.8	634.1

Notes: Violent crimes include murder, forcible rape, robbery and aggravated assault; n/a not available; (1) Metropolitan Statistical Area - see Appendix A for areas included; (2) calculated by the editors using the following formula: (number of crimes in the MSA minus number of crimes in the city); (3) calculated by the editors using the following formula: ((number of crimes in the MSA minus number of crimes in the city) ÷ (population of the MSA minus population of the city)) x 100,000
Source: U.S. Department of Justice, FBI Uniform Crime Reports, 1977 - 1996

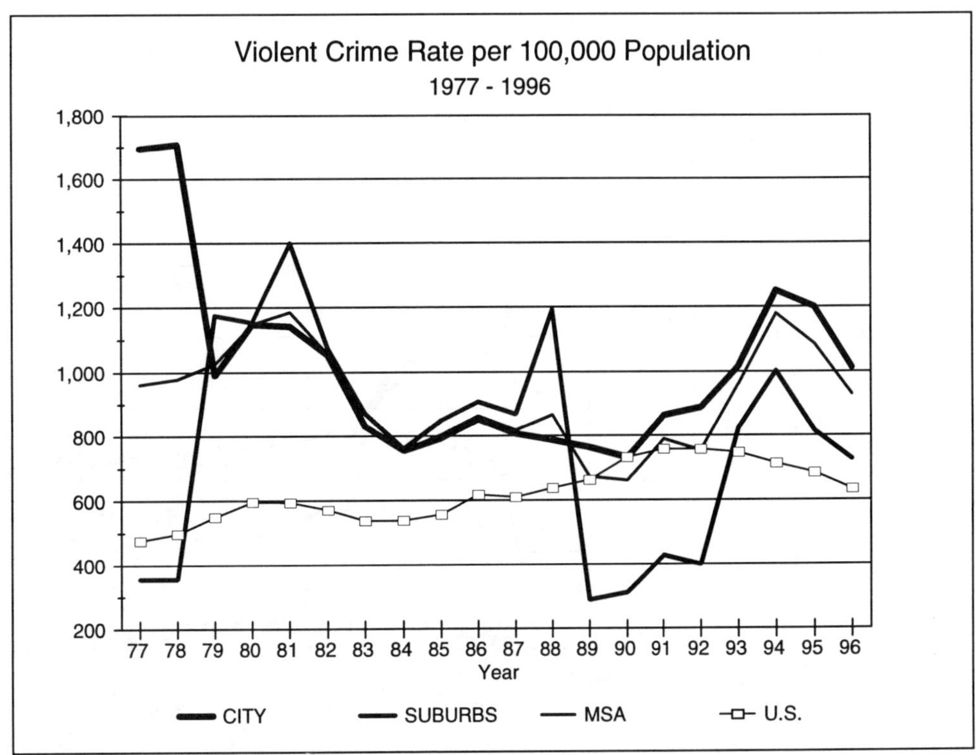

Note: Missing line segments indicate data not available.

Property Crimes and Property Crime Rates: 1977 - 1996

Year	Number				Rate per 100,000 population			
	City	Suburbs[2]	MSA[1]	U.S.	City	Suburbs[3]	MSA[1]	U.S.
1977	24,866	5,396	30,262	9,955,000	15,444.7	2,762.2	8,492.3	4,601.7
1978	26,485	4,564	31,049	10,123,400	15,671.6	2,294.6	8,439.4	4,642.5
1979	30,923	4,729	35,652	11,041,500	9,537.7	6,411.1	8,958.2	5,016.6
1980	36,984	5,282	42,266	12,063,700	9,596.4	6,875.6	9,144.2	5,353.3
1981	38,728	5,740	44,468	12,061,900	9,517.5	7,076.6	9,111.8	5,263.9
1982	37,674	5,868	43,542	11,652,000	8,880.1	6,938.8	8,557.4	5,032.5
1983	31,661	5,168	36,829	10,850,500	7,378.8	6,042.5	7,156.7	4,637.4
1984	31,504	4,638	36,142	10,608,500	7,188.4	5,038.7	6,815.2	4,492.1
1985	31,567	4,410	35,977	11,102,600	6,911.2	4,662.0	6,525.3	4,650.5
1986	31,894	4,486	36,380	11,722,700	6,886.2	4,311.4	6,413.9	4,862.6
1987	33,136	5,239	38,375	12,024,700	6,883.4	4,623.0	6,452.6	4,940.3
1988	33,437	6,364	39,801	12,356,900	6,544.2	5,290.9	6,305.4	5,027.1
1989	35,530	4,695	40,225	12,605,400	6,626.9	3,633.1	6,045.4	5,077.9
1990	39,434	5,010	44,444	12,655,500	6,399.1	4,001.1	5,994.1	5,088.5
1991	43,118	6,275	49,393	12,961,100	6,569.0	4,621.7	6,235.2	5,139.7
1992	43,853	12,271	56,124	12,505,900	6,464.3	4,761.8	5,995.6	4,902.7
1993	41,084	15,654	56,738	12,218,800	5,726.5	5,388.6	5,629.1	4,737.6
1994	48,743	18,548	67,291	12,131,900	6,476.8	6,116.7	6,373.4	4,660.0
1995	50,655	20,691	71,346	12,063,900	6,384.3	6,176.8	6,322.7	4,591.3
1996	48,534	19,765	68,299	11,791,300	5,838.3	5,627.8	5,775.8	4,444.8

Notes: Property crimes include burglary, larceny-theft and motor vehicle theft; n/a not available; (1) Metropolitan Statistical Area - see Appendix A for areas included; (2) calculated by the editors using the following formula: (number of crimes in the MSA minus number of crimes in the city); (3) calculated by the editors using the following formula: ((number of crimes in the MSA minus number of crimes in the city) ÷ (population of the MSA minus population of the city)) x 100,000
Source: U.S. Department of Justice, FBI Uniform Crime Reports, 1977 - 1996

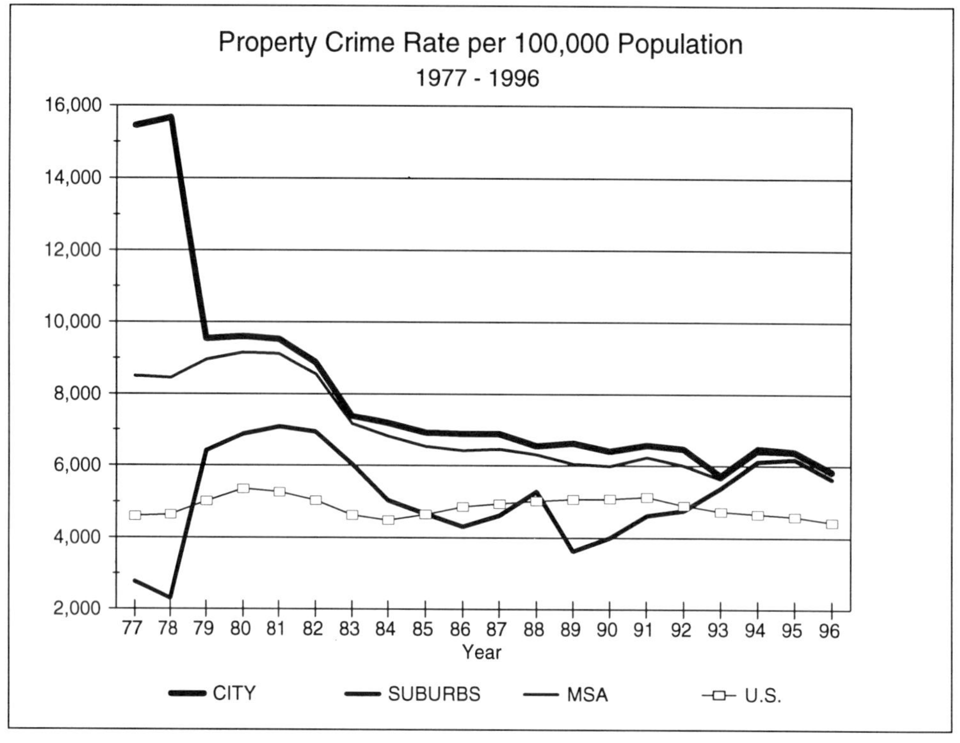

Note: Missing line segments indicate data not available.

Murders and Murder Rates: 1977 - 1996

Year	Number				Rate per 100,000 population			
	City	Suburbs[2]	MSA[1]	U.S.	City	Suburbs[3]	MSA[1]	U.S.
1977	59	14	73	19,120	36.6	7.2	20.5	8.8
1978	54	11	65	19,560	32.0	5.5	17.7	9.0
1979	75	14	89	21,460	23.1	19.0	22.4	9.7
1980	92	16	108	23,040	23.9	20.8	23.4	10.2
1981	106	9	115	22,520	26.0	11.1	23.6	9.8
1982	88	13	101	21,010	20.7	15.4	19.8	9.1
1983	74	10	84	19,310	17.2	11.7	16.3	8.3
1984	67	7	74	18,690	15.3	7.6	14.0	7.9
1985	57	14	71	18,980	12.5	14.8	12.9	7.9
1986	75	13	88	20,610	16.2	12.5	15.5	8.6
1987	47	12	59	20,100	9.8	10.6	9.9	8.3
1988	54	23	77	20,680	10.6	19.1	12.2	8.4
1989	67	3	70	21,500	12.5	2.3	10.5	8.7
1990	79	12	91	23,440	12.8	9.6	12.3	9.4
1991	103	2	105	24,700	15.7	1.5	13.3	9.8
1992	99	30	129	23,760	14.6	11.6	13.8	9.3
1993	91	41	132	24,530	12.7	14.1	13.1	9.5
1994	105	40	145	23,330	14.0	13.2	13.7	9.0
1995	118	20	138	21,610	14.9	6.0	12.2	8.2
1996	161	48	209	19,650	19.4	13.7	17.7	7.4

Notes: (1) Metropolitan Statistical Area - see Appendix A for areas included; (2) calculated by the editors using the following formula: (number of crimes in the MSA minus number of crimes in the city); (3) calculated by the editors using the following formula: ((number of crimes in the MSA minus number of crimes in the city) ÷ (population of the MSA minus population of the city)) x 100,000; n/a not avail.
Source: U.S. Department of Justice, FBI Uniform Crime Reports, 1977 - 1996

Forcible Rapes and Forcible Rape Rates: 1977 - 1996

Year	Number				Rate per 100,000 population			
	City	Suburbs[2]	MSA[1]	U.S.	City	Suburbs[3]	MSA[1]	U.S.
1977	183	47	230	63,500	113.7	24.1	64.5	29.4
1978	192	57	249	67,610	113.6	28.7	67.7	31.0
1979	198	71	269	76,390	61.1	96.3	67.6	34.7
1980	291	61	352	82,990	75.5	79.4	76.2	36.8
1981	310	71	381	82,500	76.2	87.5	78.1	36.0
1982	286	71	357	78,770	67.4	84.0	70.2	34.0
1983	244	63	307	78,920	56.9	73.7	59.7	33.7
1984	245	89	334	84,230	55.9	96.7	63.0	35.7
1985	278	90	368	88,670	60.9	95.1	66.7	37.1
1986	323	110	433	91,460	69.7	105.7	76.3	37.9
1987	308	96	404	91,110	64.0	84.7	67.9	37.4
1988	363	143	506	92,490	71.0	118.9	80.2	37.6
1989	305	68	373	94,500	56.9	52.6	56.1	38.1
1990	371	96	467	102,560	60.2	76.7	63.0	41.2
1991	433	122	555	106,590	66.0	89.9	70.1	42.3
1992	393	168	561	109,060	57.9	65.2	59.9	42.8
1993	435	168	603	106,010	60.6	57.8	59.8	41.1
1994	574	216	790	102,220	76.3	71.2	74.8	39.3
1995	571	179	750	97,470	72.0	53.4	66.5	37.1
1996	475	149	624	95,770	57.1	42.4	52.8	36.1

Notes: (1) Metropolitan Statistical Area - see Appendix A for areas included; (2) calculated by the editors using the following formula: (number of crimes in the MSA minus number of crimes in the city); (3) calculated by the editors using the following formula: ((number of crimes in the MSA minus number of crimes in the city) ÷ (population of the MSA minus population of the city)) x 100,000; n/a not avail.
Source: U.S. Department of Justice, FBI Uniform Crime Reports, 1977 - 1996

Robberies and Robbery Rates: 1977 - 1996

Year	Number				Rate per 100,000 population			
	City	Suburbs[2]	MSA[1]	U.S.	City	Suburbs[3]	MSA[1]	U.S.
1977	1,419	193	1,612	412,610	881.4	98.8	452.4	190.7
1978	1,548	183	1,731	426,930	916.0	92.0	470.5	195.8
1979	1,891	219	2,110	480,700	583.2	296.9	530.2	218.4
1980	2,636	279	2,915	565,840	684.0	363.2	630.7	251.1
1981	2,778	407	3,185	592,910	682.7	501.8	652.6	258.7
1982	2,739	330	3,069	553,130	645.6	390.2	603.2	238.9
1983	1,985	249	2,234	506,570	462.6	291.1	434.1	216.5
1984	1,767	253	2,020	485,010	403.2	274.9	380.9	205.4
1985	1,755	237	1,992	497,870	384.2	250.5	361.3	208.5
1986	1,933	297	2,230	542,780	417.4	285.4	393.2	225.1
1987	1,837	313	2,150	517,700	381.6	276.2	361.5	212.7
1988	1,887	506	2,393	542,970	369.3	420.7	379.1	220.9
1989	2,046	90	2,136	578,330	381.6	69.6	321.0	233.0
1990	2,229	108	2,337	639,270	361.7	86.3	315.2	257.0
1991	3,193	190	3,383	687,730	486.4	139.9	427.1	272.7
1992	3,609	222	3,831	672,480	532.0	86.1	409.3	263.6
1993	3,572	600	4,172	659,870	497.9	206.5	413.9	255.9
1994	3,805	709	4,514	618,950	505.6	233.8	427.5	237.7
1995	3,712	738	4,450	580,510	467.8	220.3	394.4	220.9
1996	3,650	672	4,322	537,050	439.1	191.3	365.5	202.4

Notes: (1) Metropolitan Statistical Area - see Appendix A for areas included; (2) calculated by the editors using the following formula: (number of crimes in the MSA minus number of crimes in the city); (3) calculated by the editors using the following formula: ((number of crimes in the MSA minus number of crimes in the city) ÷ (population of the MSA minus population of the city)) x 100,000; n/a not avail.
Source: U.S. Department of Justice, FBI Uniform Crime Reports, 1977 - 1996

Aggravated Assaults and Aggravated Assault Rates: 1977 - 1996

Year	Number				Rate per 100,000 population			
	City	Suburbs[2]	MSA[1]	U.S.	City	Suburbs[3]	MSA[1]	U.S.
1977	1,068	442	1,510	534,350	663.4	226.3	423.7	247.0
1978	1,092	461	1,553	571,460	646.2	231.8	422.1	262.1
1979	1,046	563	1,609	629,480	322.6	763.3	404.3	286.0
1980	1,402	530	1,932	672,650	363.8	689.9	418.0	298.5
1981	1,454	649	2,103	663,900	357.3	800.1	430.9	289.7
1982	1,357	494	1,851	669,480	319.9	584.1	363.8	289.2
1983	1,261	423	1,684	653,290	293.9	494.6	327.2	279.2
1984	1,230	351	1,581	685,350	280.7	381.3	298.1	290.2
1985	1,534	462	1,996	723,250	335.9	488.4	362.0	302.9
1986	1,616	523	2,139	834,320	348.9	502.6	377.1	346.1
1987	1,692	563	2,255	855,090	351.5	496.8	379.2	351.3
1988	1,720	763	2,483	910,090	336.6	634.3	393.4	370.2
1989	1,676	214	1,890	951,710	312.6	165.6	284.0	383.4
1990	1,831	176	2,007	1,054,860	297.1	140.6	270.7	424.1
1991	1,932	268	2,200	1,092,740	294.3	197.4	277.7	433.3
1992	1,926	611	2,537	1,126,970	283.9	237.1	271.0	441.8
1993	3,183	1,581	4,764	1,135,610	443.7	544.2	472.6	440.3
1994	4,934	2,071	7,005	1,113,180	655.6	683.0	663.5	427.6
1995	5,122	1,793	6,915	1,099,210	645.5	535.3	612.8	418.3
1996	4,123	1,681	5,804	1,029,810	496.0	478.6	490.8	388.2

Notes: (1) Metropolitan Statistical Area - see Appendix A for areas included; (2) calculated by the editors using the following formula: (number of crimes in the MSA minus number of crimes in the city); (3) calculated by the editors using the following formula: ((number of crimes in the MSA minus number of crimes in the city) ÷ (population of the MSA minus population of the city)) x 100,000; n/a not avail.
Source: U.S. Department of Justice, FBI Uniform Crime Reports, 1977 - 1996

Burglaries and Burglary Rates: 1977 - 1996

Year	Number				Rate per 100,000 population			
	City	Suburbs[2]	MSA[1]	U.S.	City	Suburbs[3]	MSA[1]	U.S.
1977	8,922	2,171	11,093	3,071,500	5,541.6	1,111.4	3,113.0	1,419.8
1978	10,308	1,709	12,017	3,128,300	6,099.4	859.2	3,266.3	1,434.6
1979	11,709	1,696	13,405	3,327,700	3,611.4	2,299.3	3,368.2	1,511.9
1980	14,526	2,155	16,681	3,795,200	3,769.1	2,805.2	3,608.9	1,684.1
1981	14,418	2,400	16,818	3,779,700	3,543.2	2,958.9	3,446.1	1,649.5
1982	13,463	2,193	15,656	3,447,100	3,173.3	2,593.2	3,076.9	1,488.8
1983	11,250	2,013	13,263	3,129,900	2,621.9	2,353.6	2,577.3	1,337.7
1984	10,874	1,962	12,836	2,984,400	2,481.2	2,131.5	2,420.5	1,263.7
1985	9,975	1,695	11,670	3,073,300	2,183.9	1,791.8	2,116.6	1,287.3
1986	9,077	1,540	10,617	3,241,400	1,959.8	1,480.1	1,871.8	1,344.6
1987	9,395	1,930	11,325	3,236,200	1,951.6	1,703.1	1,904.3	1,329.6
1988	8,965	2,080	11,045	3,218,100	1,754.6	1,729.3	1,749.8	1,309.2
1989	9,019	1,215	10,234	3,168,200	1,682.2	940.2	1,538.1	1,276.3
1990	10,176	1,308	11,484	3,073,900	1,651.3	1,044.6	1,548.8	1,235.9
1991	10,743	1,620	12,363	3,157,200	1,636.7	1,193.2	1,560.7	1,252.0
1992	10,337	3,379	13,716	2,979,900	1,523.8	1,311.2	1,465.3	1,168.2
1993	9,783	4,468	14,251	2,834,800	1,363.6	1,538.0	1,413.9	1,099.2
1994	11,657	4,851	16,508	2,712,800	1,548.9	1,599.7	1,563.5	1,042.0
1995	12,219	5,281	17,500	2,593,800	1,540.0	1,576.5	1,550.9	987.1
1996	11,656	5,273	16,929	2,501,500	1,402.1	1,501.4	1,431.6	943.0

Notes: (1) Metropolitan Statistical Area - see Appendix A for areas included; (2) calculated by the editors using the following formula: (number of crimes in the MSA minus number of crimes in the city); (3) calculated by the editors using the following formula: ((number of crimes in the MSA minus number of crimes in the city) ÷ (population of the MSA minus population of the city)) x 100,000; n/a not avail.
Source: U.S. Department of Justice, FBI Uniform Crime Reports, 1977 - 1996

Larceny-Thefts and Larceny-Theft Rates: 1977 - 1996

Year	Number				Rate per 100,000 population			
	City	Suburbs[2]	MSA[1]	U.S.	City	Suburbs[3]	MSA[1]	U.S.
1977	13,830	2,917	16,747	5,905,700	8,590.1	1,493.2	4,699.6	2,729.9
1978	13,818	2,599	16,417	5,991,000	8,176.3	1,306.7	4,462.3	2,747.4
1979	16,288	2,695	18,983	6,601,000	5,023.7	3,653.6	4,769.8	2,999.1
1980	19,019	2,762	21,781	7,136,900	4,934.9	3,595.3	4,712.3	3,167.0
1981	21,107	2,982	24,089	7,194,400	5,187.1	3,676.4	4,936.0	3,139.7
1982	20,747	3,284	24,031	7,142,500	4,890.3	3,883.3	4,722.9	3,084.8
1983	17,611	2,838	20,449	6,712,800	4,104.4	3,318.3	3,973.7	2,868.9
1984	17,622	2,389	20,011	6,591,900	4,020.9	2,595.4	3,773.4	2,791.3
1985	18,533	2,408	20,941	6,926,400	4,057.6	2,545.6	3,798.2	2,901.2
1986	19,689	2,608	22,297	7,257,200	4,251.0	2,506.5	3,931.0	3,010.3
1987	20,069	2,852	22,921	7,499,900	4,168.9	2,516.7	3,854.1	3,081.3
1988	20,341	3,590	23,931	7,705,900	3,981.1	2,984.7	3,791.2	3,134.9
1989	21,930	3,131	25,061	7,872,400	4,090.3	2,422.8	3,766.4	3,171.3
1990	24,009	3,260	27,269	7,945,700	3,896.0	2,603.5	3,677.7	3,194.8
1991	25,828	4,115	29,943	8,142,200	3,934.8	3,030.8	3,779.9	3,228.8
1992	26,116	7,887	34,003	7,915,200	3,849.7	3,060.5	3,632.5	3,103.0
1993	23,855	9,331	33,186	7,820,900	3,325.0	3,212.0	3,292.4	3,032.4
1994	29,351	11,470	40,821	7,879,800	3,900.1	3,782.5	3,866.3	3,026.7
1995	30,445	13,021	43,466	7,997,700	3,837.1	3,887.1	3,852.0	3,043.8
1996	28,952	12,253	41,205	7,894,600	3,482.7	3,488.8	3,484.5	2,975.9

Notes: (1) Metropolitan Statistical Area - see Appendix A for areas included; (2) calculated by the editors using the following formula: (number of crimes in the MSA minus number of crimes in the city); (3) calculated by the editors using the following formula: ((number of crimes in the MSA minus number of crimes in the city) ÷ (population of the MSA minus population of the city)) x 100,000; n/a not avail.
Source: U.S. Department of Justice, FBI Uniform Crime Reports, 1977 - 1996

Motor Vehicle Thefts and Motor Vehicle Theft Rates: 1977 - 1996

Year	Number				Rate per 100,000 population			
	City	Suburbs[2]	MSA[1]	U.S.	City	Suburbs[3]	MSA[1]	U.S.
1977	2,114	308	2,422	977,700	1,313.0	157.7	679.7	451.9
1978	2,359	256	2,615	1,004,100	1,395.9	128.7	710.8	460.5
1979	2,926	338	3,264	1,112,800	902.5	458.2	820.1	505.6
1980	3,439	365	3,804	1,131,700	892.3	475.1	823.0	502.2
1981	3,203	358	3,561	1,087,800	787.1	441.4	729.7	474.7
1982	3,464	391	3,855	1,062,400	816.5	462.3	757.6	458.8
1983	2,800	317	3,117	1,007,900	652.6	370.6	605.7	430.8
1984	3,008	287	3,295	1,032,200	686.3	311.8	621.3	437.1
1985	3,059	307	3,366	1,102,900	669.7	324.5	610.5	462.0
1986	3,128	338	3,466	1,224,100	675.4	324.8	611.1	507.8
1987	3,672	457	4,129	1,288,700	762.8	403.3	694.3	529.4
1988	4,131	694	4,825	1,432,900	808.5	577.0	764.4	582.9
1989	4,581	349	4,930	1,564,800	854.4	270.1	740.9	630.4
1990	5,249	442	5,691	1,635,900	851.8	353.0	767.5	657.8
1991	6,547	540	7,087	1,661,700	997.4	397.7	894.6	659.0
1992	7,400	1,005	8,405	1,610,800	1,090.8	390.0	897.9	631.5
1993	7,446	1,855	9,301	1,563,100	1,037.9	638.5	922.8	606.1
1994	7,735	2,227	9,962	1,539,300	1,027.8	734.4	943.5	591.3
1995	7,991	2,389	10,380	1,472,400	1,007.1	713.2	919.9	560.4
1996	7,926	2,239	10,165	1,395,200	953.4	637.5	859.6	525.9

Notes: (1) Metropolitan Statistical Area - see Appendix A for areas included; (2) calculated by the editors using the following formula: (number of crimes in the MSA minus number of crimes in the city); (3) calculated by the editors using the following formula: ((number of crimes in the MSA minus number of crimes in the city) ÷ (population of the MSA minus population of the city)) x 100,000; n/a not avail.
Source: U.S. Department of Justice, FBI Uniform Crime Reports, 1977 - 1996

HATE CRIMES

Criminal Incidents by Bias Motivation

Area	Race	Ethnicity	Religion	Sexual Orientation
Las Vegas	41	3	7	5

Notes: Figures include both violent and property crimes. Law enforcement agencies must have submitted data for at least one quarter of calendar year 1995 to be included in this report, therefore figures shown may not represent complete 12-month totals; n/a not available
Source: U.S. Department of Justice, FBI Uniform Crime Reports, Hate Crime Statistics 1995

LAW ENFORCEMENT

Full-Time Law Enforcement Employees

Jurisdiction	Police Employees			Police Officers per 100,000 population
	Total	Officers	Civilians	
Las Vegas	2,520	1,666	854	200.4

Notes: Data as of October 31, 1996
Source: U.S. Department of Justice, FBI Uniform Crime Reports, 1996

CORRECTIONS

Federal Correctional Facilities

Type	Year Opened	Security Level	Sex of Inmates	Rated Capacity	Population on 7/1/95	Number of Staff
None listed						

Notes: Data as of 1995
Source: Bureau of Justice Statistics, Sourcebook of Criminal Justice Statistics Online

City/County/Regional Correctional Facilities

Name	Year Opened	Year Renov.	Rated Capacity	1995 Pop.	Number of COs[1]	Number of Staff	ACA[2] Accred.
Clark Co - Dept of Det and Enf	1982	1990	750	464	105	147	Yes
Clark Co Detention Center	1984	--	1,487	1,649	n/a	451	No

Notes: Data as of April 1996; (1) Correctional Officers; (2) American Correctional Assn. Accreditation
Source: American Correctional Association, 1996-1998 National Jail and Adult Detention Directory

Private Adult Correctional Facilities

Name	Date Opened	Rated Capacity	Present Pop.	Security Level	Facility Construct.	Expans. Plans	ACA[1] Accred.
Nevada Women's Pris	9/97	500	n/a	Med.	New	None	Will be sought

Notes: Data as of December 1996; (1) American Correctional Association Accreditation
Source: University of Florida, Center for Studies in Criminology and Law, Private Adult Correctional Facility Census, 10th Ed., March 15, 1997

Characteristics of Shock Incarceration Programs

Jurisdiction	Year Program Began	Number of Camps	Average Num. of Inmates	Number of Beds	Program Length	Voluntary/ Mandatory
Nevada	1991	1	73	73	190 days	Voluntary

Note: Data as of July 1996;
Source: Sourcebook of Criminal Justice Statistics Online

INMATES AND HIV/AIDS

HIV Testing Policies for Inmates

Jurisdiction	All Inmates at Some Time	All Convicted Inmates at Admission	Random Samples While in Custody	High-risk Groups	Upon Inmate Request	Upon Court Order	Upon Involvement in Incident
Clark Co.[1]	No	No	No	No	Yes	Yes	No

Notes: (1) All facilities reported following the same testing policy or authorities reported the policy to be jurisdiction-wide
Source: HIV in Prisons and Jails, 1993 (released August 1995)

Inmates Known to be Positive for HIV

Jurisdiction	Number of Jail Inmates in Facilities Providing Data	Type of HIV Infection/AIDS Cases				HIV/AIDS Cases as a Percent of Tot. Custody Pop.
		Total	Asymptomatic	Symptomatic	Confirmed AIDS	
Clark Co.	1,376	22	2	10	10	1.6

Source: HIV in Prisons and Jails, 1993 (released August, 1995)

DEATH PENALTY

Death Penalty Statistics

State	Prisoners Executed		Prisoners Under Sentence of Death					Avg. No. of Years on Death Row[4]
	1930-1995	1996[1]	Total[2]	White[3]	Black[3]	Hisp.	Women	
Nevada	34	1	75	48	26	10	1	7.1

Notes: Data as of 12/31/95 unless otherwise noted; (1) Data as of 7/31/97; (2) Includes persons of other races; (3) Includes people of Hispanic origin; (4) Covers prisoners sentenced 1974 through 1995
Source: Bureau of Justice Statistics, Capital Punishment 1995 (released 12/96); Death Penalty Information Center Web Site, 9/30/97

Capital Offenses and Methods of Execution

Capital Offenses in Nevada	Minimum Age for Imposition of Death Penalty	Mentally Retarded Excluded	Methods of Execution[1]
First-degree murder with 10 aggravating circumstances.	16	No	Lethal injection

Notes: Data as of 12/31/95 unless otherwise noted; (1) Data as of 7/31/97
Source: Bureau of Justice Statistics, Capital Punishment 1995 (released 12/96); Death Penalty Information Center Web Site, 9/30/97

LAWS

Statutory Provisions Relating to the Purchase, Ownership and Use of Handguns

Jurisdiction	Instant Background Check	Federal Waiting Period Applies[1]	State Waiting Period (days)	License or Permit to Purchase	Regis-tration	Record of Sale Sent to Police	Concealed Carry Law
Nevada	Yes[a]	Yes	(b)	No	(b)	No	Yes[c]

Note: Data as of 1996; (1) The Federal 5-day waiting period for handgun purchases applies to states that don't have instant background checks, waiting period requirements, or licensing procedures exempting them from the Federal requirement; (a) Nevada has, but does not use, its Instant Check system; (b) Local ordinance in certain cities or counties; (c) "Shall issue" permit system, liberally administered discretion by local authorities over permit issuance, or no permit required
Source: Sourcebook of Criminal Justice Statistics Online

Statutory Provisions Relating to Alcohol Use and Driving

Jurisdiction	Drinking Age	Blood Alcohol Concentration Levels as Evidence in State Courts[1]		Open Container Law[1]	Anti-Consump-tion Law[1]	Dram Shop Law[1]
		Illegal per se at 0.10%	Presumption at 0.10%			
Nevada	21	Yes	No	Yes	(a)	No

Note: Data as of January 1, 1997; (1) See Appendix C for an explanation of terms; (a) Applies to drivers only
Source: Sourcebook of Criminal Justice Statistics Online

Statutory Provisions Relating to Curfews

Jurisdiction	Year Enacted	Latest Revision	Age Group(s)	Curfew Provisions
Las Vegas	1955	1992	H.S. students	10 pm to 5 am weekday nights 11 pm to 5 am weekend nights Special "Las Vegas Strip" curfew: 9 pm to 5 am every night

Note: Data as of February 1996
Source: Sourcebook of Criminal Justice Statistics Online

Statutory Provisions Relating to Hate Crimes

Jurisdiction	Bias-Motivated Violence and Intimidation						Institutional Vandalism
		Criminal Penalty					
	Civil Action	Race/ Religion/ Ethnicity	Sexual Orientation	Mental/ Physical Disability	Gender	Age	
Nevada	No	Yes	Yes	No	No	No	Yes

Source: Anti-Defamation League, 1997 Hate Crimes Laws

Lexington, Kentucky

OVERVIEW

The total crime rate for the city decreased 12.3% between 1977 and 1996. During that same period, the violent crime rate increased 78.5% and the property crime rate decreased 18.5%.

Among violent crimes, the rates for: Murders decreased 42.0%; Forcible Rapes increased 30.1%; Robberies increased 48.1%; and Aggravated Assaults increased 110.1%.

Among property crimes, the rates for: Burglaries decreased 31.5%; Larceny-Thefts decreased 16.5%; and Motor Vehicle Thefts increased 23.9%.

ANTI-CRIME PROGRAMS

Information not available at time of publication.

CRIME RISK

Your Chances of Becoming a Victim[1]

Area	Any Crime	Violent Crime					Property Crime			
		Any	Murder	Forcible Rape[2]	Robbery	Aggrav. Assault	Any	Burglary	Larceny -Theft	Motor Vehicle Theft
City	1:16	1:121	1:17,225	1:1,031	1:416	1:188	1:18	1:83	1:25	1:264

Note: (1) Figures have been calculated by dividing the population of the city by the number of crimes reported to the FBI during 1996 and are expressed as odds (eg. 1:20 should be read as 1 in 20). (2) Figures have been calculated by dividing the female population of the city by the number of forcible rapes reported to the FBI during 1996. The female population of the city was estimated by calculating the ratio of females to males reported in the 1990 Census and applying that ratio to 1996 population estimate.
Source: FBI Uniform Crime Reports 1996

CRIME STATISTICS

Total Crimes and Total Crime Rates: 1977 - 1996

Year	Number				Rate per 100,000 population			
	City	Suburbs[2]	MSA[1]	U.S.	City	Suburbs[3]	MSA[1]	U.S.
1977	13,774	2,097	15,871	10,984,500	7,249.5	2,315.6	5,656.9	5,077.6
1978	13,594	2,122	15,716	11,209,000	7,117.3	2,064.6	5,349.5	5,140.3
1979	13,537	2,229	15,766	12,249,500	7,007.7	2,045.2	5,217.8	5,565.5
1980	15,566	2,722	18,288	13,408,300	7,664.9	2,422.6	5,797.6	5,950.0
1981	14,967	4,958	19,925	13,423,800	7,330.6	4,389.0	6,282.8	5,858.2
1982	16,810	3,725	20,535	12,974,400	8,219.8	3,292.1	6,464.6	5,603.6
1983	13,826	5,155	18,981	12,108,600	6,675.2	4,498.5	5,899.9	5,175.0
1984	12,026	3,741	15,767	11,881,800	5,736.0	3,233.1	4,845.9	5,031.3
1985	12,711	3,901	16,612	12,431,400	6,042.4	3,334.4	5,074.6	5,207.1
1986	13,486	4,268	17,754	13,211,900	6,408.7	3,642.4	5,419.3	5,480.4
1987	14,056	4,446	18,502	13,508,700	6,601.1	3,732.4	5,572.0	5,550.0
1988	n/a	n/a	n/a	13,923,100	n/a	n/a	n/a	5,664.2
1989	14,983	4,967	19,950	14,251,400	6,632.1	4,057.4	5,727.2	5,741.0
1990	16,245	5,684	21,929	14,475,600	7,208.3	4,618.8	6,293.7	5,820.3
1991	15,936	5,637	21,573	14,872,900	7,018.4	4,546.7	6,145.4	5,897.8
1992	14,782	5,541	20,323	14,438,200	6,437.4	4,419.4	5,724.7	5,660.2
1993	15,641	5,538	21,179	14,144,800	6,653.1	4,288.9	5,814.9	5,484.4
1994	16,146	8,587	24,733	13,989,500	6,799.7	4,491.3	5,770.1	5,373.5
1995	15,933	7,844	23,777	13,862,700	6,648.2	4,024.8	5,471.6	5,275.9
1996	15,328	n/a	n/a	13,473,600	6,356.2	n/a	n/a	5,078.9

Notes: (1) Metropolitan Statistical Area - see Appendix A for areas included; (2) calculated by the editors using the following formula: (number of crimes in the MSA minus number of crimes in the city); (3) calculated by the editors using the following formula: ((number of crimes in the MSA minus number of crimes in the city) ÷ (population of the MSA minus population of the city)) x 100,000; n/a not avail.
Source: U.S. Department of Justice, FBI Uniform Crime Reports, 1977 - 1996

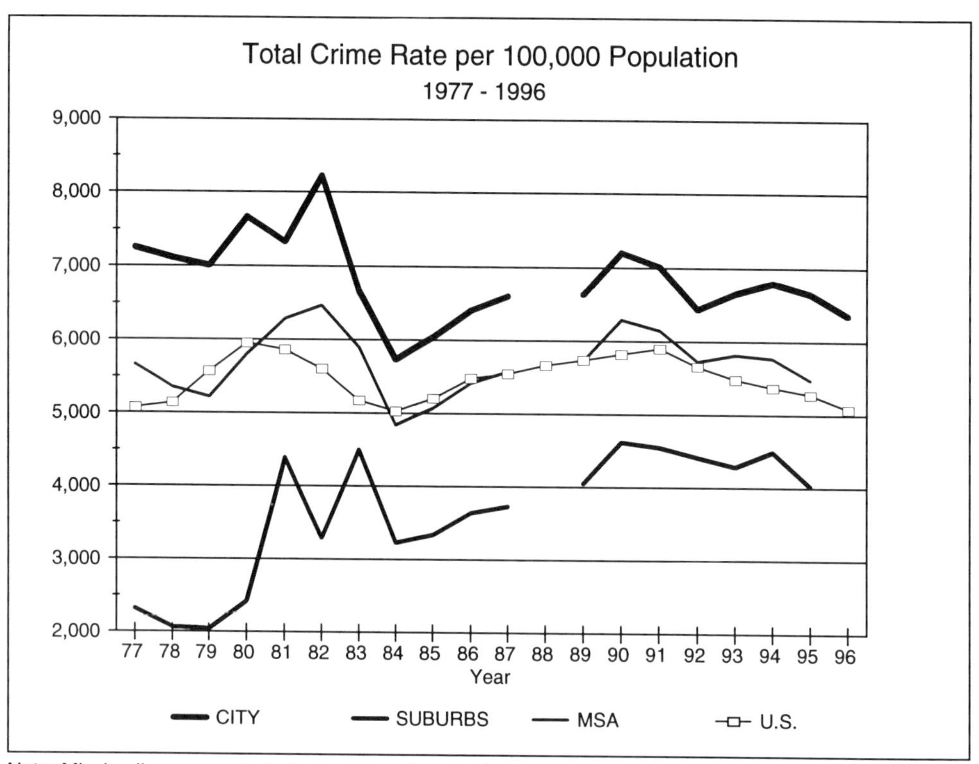

Note: Missing line segments indicate data not available.

Violent Crimes and Violent Crime Rates: 1977 - 1996

Year	Number				Rate per 100,000 population			
	City	Suburbs[2]	MSA[1]	U.S.	City	Suburbs[3]	MSA[1]	U.S.
1977	882	147	1,029	1,029,580	464.2	162.3	366.8	475.9
1978	915	111	1,026	1,085,550	479.1	108.0	349.2	497.8
1979	873	149	1,022	1,208,030	451.9	136.7	338.2	548.9
1980	981	185	1,166	1,344,520	483.1	164.6	369.6	596.6
1981	1,102	249	1,351	1,361,820	539.7	220.4	426.0	594.3
1982	1,163	279	1,442	1,322,390	568.7	246.6	454.0	571.1
1983	998	324	1,322	1,258,090	481.8	282.7	410.9	537.7
1984	1,019	249	1,268	1,273,280	486.0	215.2	389.7	539.2
1985	1,121	274	1,395	1,328,800	532.9	234.2	426.1	556.6
1986	1,275	321	1,596	1,489,170	605.9	273.9	487.2	617.7
1987	1,037	367	1,404	1,484,000	487.0	308.1	422.8	609.7
1988	n/a	n/a	n/a	1,566,220	n/a	n/a	n/a	637.2
1989	1,386	534	1,920	1,646,040	613.5	436.2	551.2	663.1
1990	1,770	635	2,405	1,820,130	785.4	516.0	690.2	731.8
1991	1,802	695	2,497	1,911,770	793.6	560.6	711.3	758.1
1992	1,977	767	2,744	1,932,270	861.0	611.8	772.9	757.5
1993	2,160	605	2,765	1,926,020	918.8	468.5	759.2	746.8
1994	2,328	1,622	3,950	1,857,670	980.4	848.4	921.5	713.6
1995	2,099	401	2,500	1,798,790	875.8	205.8	575.3	684.6
1996	1,998	n/a	n/a	1,682,280	828.5	n/a	n/a	634.1

Notes: Violent crimes include murder, forcible rape, robbery and aggravated assault; n/a not available; (1) Metropolitan Statistical Area - see Appendix A for areas included; (2) calculated by the editors using the following formula: (number of crimes in the MSA minus number of crimes in the city); (3) calculated by the editors using the following formula: ((number of crimes in the MSA minus number of crimes in the city) ÷ (population of the MSA minus population of the city)) x 100,000
Source: U.S. Department of Justice, FBI Uniform Crime Reports, 1977 - 1996

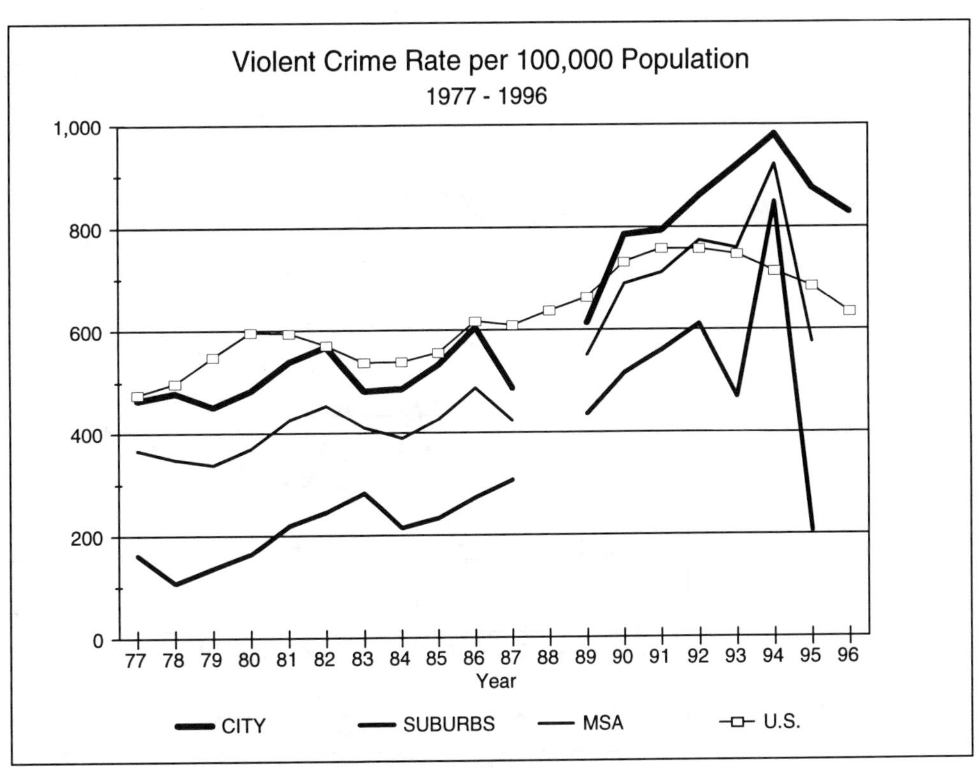

Note: Missing line segments indicate data not available.

Property Crimes and Property Crime Rates: 1977 - 1996

Year	Number				Rate per 100,000 population			
	City	Suburbs[2]	MSA[1]	U.S.	City	Suburbs[3]	MSA[1]	U.S.
1977	12,892	1,950	14,842	9,955,000	6,785.3	2,153.3	5,290.2	4,601.7
1978	12,679	2,011	14,690	10,123,400	6,638.2	1,956.6	5,000.3	4,642.5
1979	12,664	2,080	14,744	11,041,500	6,555.8	1,908.5	4,879.6	5,016.6
1980	14,585	2,537	17,122	12,063,700	7,181.8	2,257.9	5,427.9	5,353.3
1981	13,865	4,709	18,574	12,061,900	6,790.9	4,168.6	5,856.8	5,263.9
1982	15,647	3,446	19,093	11,652,000	7,651.2	3,045.5	6,010.6	5,032.5
1983	12,828	4,831	17,659	10,850,500	6,193.3	4,215.8	5,489.0	4,637.4
1984	11,007	3,492	14,499	10,608,500	5,249.9	3,017.9	4,456.2	4,492.1
1985	11,590	3,627	15,217	11,102,600	5,509.5	3,100.2	4,648.5	4,650.5
1986	12,211	3,947	16,158	11,722,700	5,802.8	3,368.5	4,932.1	4,862.6
1987	13,019	4,079	17,098	12,024,700	6,114.1	3,424.3	5,149.2	4,940.3
1988	n/a	n/a	n/a	12,356,900	n/a	n/a	n/a	5,027.1
1989	13,597	4,433	18,030	12,605,400	6,018.6	3,621.2	5,176.0	5,077.9
1990	14,475	5,049	19,524	12,655,500	6,422.9	4,102.8	5,603.5	5,088.5
1991	14,134	4,942	19,076	12,961,100	6,224.8	3,986.1	5,434.1	5,139.7
1992	12,805	4,774	17,579	12,505,900	5,576.4	3,807.7	4,951.7	4,902.7
1993	13,481	4,933	18,414	12,218,800	5,734.3	3,820.4	5,055.8	4,737.6
1994	13,818	6,965	20,783	12,131,900	5,819.3	3,643.0	4,848.6	4,660.0
1995	13,834	7,443	21,277	12,063,900	5,772.3	3,819.1	4,896.3	4,591.3
1996	13,330	n/a	n/a	11,791,300	5,527.7	n/a	n/a	4,444.8

Notes: Property crimes include burglary, larceny-theft and motor vehicle theft; n/a not available; (1) Metropolitan Statistical Area - see Appendix A for areas included; (2) calculated by the editors using the following formula: (number of crimes in the MSA minus number of crimes in the city); (3) calculated by the editors using the following formula: ((number of crimes in the MSA minus number of crimes in the city) ÷ (population of the MSA minus population of the city)) x 100,000
Source: U.S. Department of Justice, FBI Uniform Crime Reports, 1977 - 1996

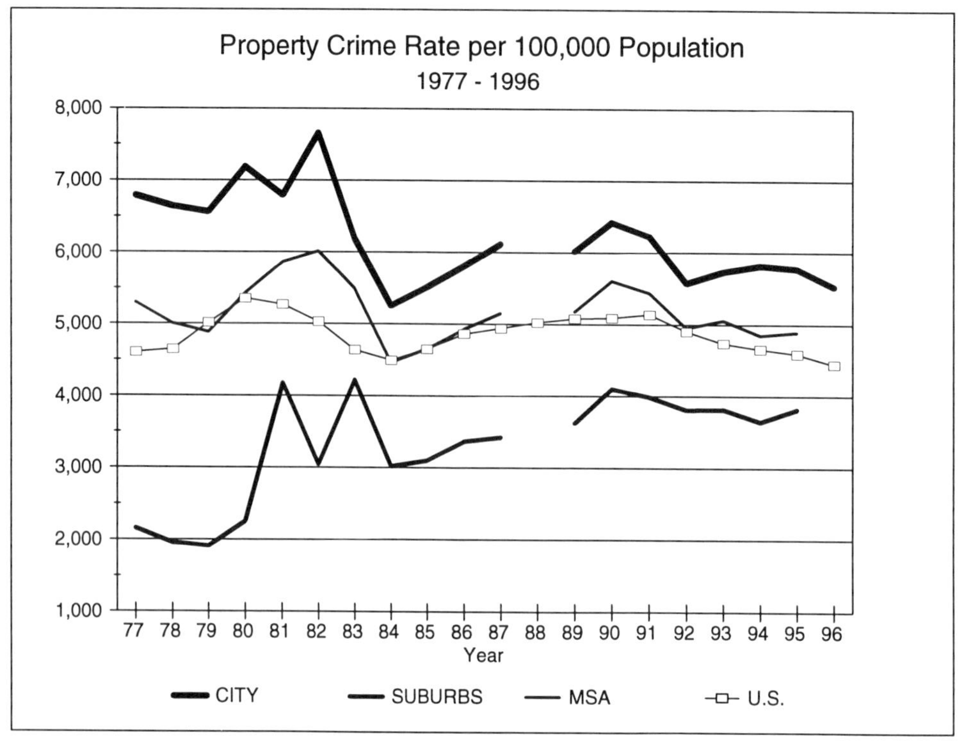

Note: Missing line segments indicate data not available.

Murders and Murder Rates: 1977 - 1996

Year	Number				Rate per 100,000 population			
	City	Suburbs[2]	MSA[1]	U.S.	City	Suburbs[3]	MSA[1]	U.S.
1977	19	2	21	19,120	10.0	2.2	7.5	8.8
1978	11	6	17	19,560	5.8	5.8	5.8	9.0
1979	18	7	25	21,460	9.3	6.4	8.3	9.7
1980	11	8	19	23,040	5.4	7.1	6.0	10.2
1981	18	3	21	22,520	8.8	2.7	6.6	9.8
1982	19	21	40	21,010	9.3	18.6	12.6	9.1
1983	12	10	22	19,310	5.8	8.7	6.8	8.3
1984	12	4	16	18,690	5.7	3.5	4.9	7.9
1985	7	5	12	18,980	3.3	4.3	3.7	7.9
1986	24	3	27	20,610	11.4	2.6	8.2	8.6
1987	12	5	17	20,100	5.6	4.2	5.1	8.3
1988	n/a	n/a	n/a	20,680	n/a	n/a	n/a	8.4
1989	11	6	17	21,500	4.9	4.9	4.9	8.7
1990	20	6	26	23,440	8.9	4.9	7.5	9.4
1991	13	8	21	24,700	5.7	6.5	6.0	9.8
1992	18	10	28	23,760	7.8	8.0	7.9	9.3
1993	8	3	11	24,530	3.4	2.3	3.0	9.5
1994	23	15	38	23,330	9.7	7.8	8.9	9.0
1995	14	9	23	21,610	5.8	4.6	5.3	8.2
1996	14	n/a	n/a	19,650	5.8	n/a	n/a	7.4

Notes: (1) Metropolitan Statistical Area - see Appendix A for areas included; (2) calculated by the editors using the following formula: (number of crimes in the MSA minus number of crimes in the city); (3) calculated by the editors using the following formula: ((number of crimes in the MSA minus number of crimes in the city) ÷ (population of the MSA minus population of the city)) x 100,000; n/a not avail.
Source: U.S. Department of Justice, FBI Uniform Crime Reports, 1977 - 1996

Forcible Rapes and Forcible Rape Rates: 1977 - 1996

Year	Number				Rate per 100,000 population			
	City	Suburbs[2]	MSA[1]	U.S.	City	Suburbs[3]	MSA[1]	U.S.
1977	74	13	87	63,500	38.9	14.4	31.0	29.4
1978	67	17	84	67,610	35.1	16.5	28.6	31.0
1979	68	16	84	76,390	35.2	14.7	27.8	34.7
1980	71	18	89	82,990	35.0	16.0	28.2	36.8
1981	87	29	116	82,500	42.6	25.7	36.6	36.0
1982	71	26	97	78,770	34.7	23.0	30.5	34.0
1983	90	30	120	78,920	43.5	26.2	37.3	33.7
1984	89	14	103	84,230	42.4	12.1	31.7	35.7
1985	96	26	122	88,670	45.6	22.2	37.3	37.1
1986	89	15	104	91,460	42.3	12.8	31.7	37.9
1987	104	31	135	91,110	48.8	26.0	40.7	37.4
1988	n/a	n/a	n/a	92,490	n/a	n/a	n/a	37.6
1989	104	29	133	94,500	46.0	23.7	38.2	38.1
1990	141	36	177	102,560	62.6	29.3	50.8	41.2
1991	164	44	208	106,590	72.2	35.5	59.3	42.3
1992	151	58	209	109,060	65.8	46.3	58.9	42.8
1993	139	69	208	106,010	59.1	53.4	57.1	41.1
1994	116	69	185	102,220	48.9	36.1	43.2	39.3
1995	131	57	188	97,470	54.7	29.2	43.3	37.1
1996	122	n/a	n/a	95,770	50.6	n/a	n/a	36.1

Notes: (1) Metropolitan Statistical Area - see Appendix A for areas included; (2) calculated by the editors using the following formula: (number of crimes in the MSA minus number of crimes in the city); (3) calculated by the editors using the following formula: ((number of crimes in the MSA minus number of crimes in the city) ÷ (population of the MSA minus population of the city)) x 100,000; n/a not avail.
Source: U.S. Department of Justice, FBI Uniform Crime Reports, 1977 - 1996

Robberies and Robbery Rates: 1977 - 1996

Year	Number				Rate per 100,000 population			
	City	Suburbs[2]	MSA[1]	U.S.	City	Suburbs[3]	MSA[1]	U.S.
1977	308	40	348	412,610	162.1	44.2	124.0	190.7
1978	311	16	327	426,930	162.8	15.6	111.3	195.8
1979	275	42	317	480,700	142.4	38.5	104.9	218.4
1980	351	24	375	565,840	172.8	21.4	118.9	251.1
1981	447	49	496	592,910	218.9	43.4	156.4	258.7
1982	414	53	467	553,130	202.4	46.8	147.0	238.9
1983	349	63	412	506,570	168.5	55.0	128.1	216.5
1984	304	33	337	485,010	145.0	28.5	103.6	205.4
1985	308	29	337	497,870	146.4	24.8	102.9	208.5
1986	386	23	409	542,780	183.4	19.6	124.8	225.1
1987	373	23	396	517,700	175.2	19.3	119.3	212.7
1988	n/a	n/a	n/a	542,970	n/a	n/a	n/a	220.9
1989	364	45	409	578,330	161.1	36.8	117.4	233.0
1990	452	44	496	639,270	200.6	35.8	142.4	257.0
1991	453	53	506	687,730	199.5	42.7	144.1	272.7
1992	525	42	567	672,480	228.6	33.5	159.7	263.6
1993	558	48	606	659,870	237.4	37.2	166.4	255.9
1994	699	116	815	618,950	294.4	60.7	190.1	237.7
1995	636	94	730	580,510	265.4	48.2	168.0	220.9
1996	579	n/a	n/a	537,050	240.1	n/a	n/a	202.4

Notes: (1) Metropolitan Statistical Area - see Appendix A for areas included; (2) calculated by the editors using the following formula: (number of crimes in the MSA minus number of crimes in the city); (3) calculated by the editors using the following formula: ((number of crimes in the MSA minus number of crimes in the city) ÷ (population of the MSA minus population of the city)) x 100,000; n/a not avail.
Source: U.S. Department of Justice, FBI Uniform Crime Reports, 1977 - 1996

Aggravated Assaults and Aggravated Assault Rates: 1977 - 1996

Year	Number				Rate per 100,000 population			
	City	Suburbs[2]	MSA[1]	U.S.	City	Suburbs[3]	MSA[1]	U.S.
1977	481	92	573	534,350	253.2	101.6	204.2	247.0
1978	526	72	598	571,460	275.4	70.1	203.6	262.1
1979	512	84	596	629,480	265.0	77.1	197.2	286.0
1980	548	135	683	672,650	269.8	120.1	216.5	298.5
1981	550	168	718	663,900	269.4	148.7	226.4	289.7
1982	659	179	838	669,480	322.2	158.2	263.8	289.2
1983	547	221	768	653,290	264.1	192.9	238.7	279.2
1984	614	198	812	685,350	292.9	171.1	249.6	290.2
1985	710	214	924	723,250	337.5	182.9	282.3	302.9
1986	776	280	1,056	834,320	368.8	239.0	322.3	346.1
1987	548	308	856	855,090	257.4	258.6	257.8	351.3
1988	n/a	n/a	n/a	910,090	n/a	n/a	n/a	370.2
1989	907	454	1,361	951,710	401.5	370.9	390.7	383.4
1990	1,157	549	1,706	1,054,860	513.4	446.1	489.6	424.1
1991	1,172	590	1,762	1,092,740	516.2	475.9	501.9	433.3
1992	1,283	657	1,940	1,126,970	558.7	524.0	546.5	441.8
1993	1,455	485	1,940	1,135,610	618.9	375.6	532.6	440.3
1994	1,490	1,422	2,912	1,113,180	627.5	743.8	679.4	427.6
1995	1,318	241	1,559	1,099,210	549.9	123.7	358.8	418.3
1996	1,283	n/a	n/a	1,029,810	532.0	n/a	n/a	388.2

Notes: (1) Metropolitan Statistical Area - see Appendix A for areas included; (2) calculated by the editors using the following formula: (number of crimes in the MSA minus number of crimes in the city); (3) calculated by the editors using the following formula: ((number of crimes in the MSA minus number of crimes in the city) ÷ (population of the MSA minus population of the city)) x 100,000; n/a not avail.
Source: U.S. Department of Justice, FBI Uniform Crime Reports, 1977 - 1996

Burglaries and Burglary Rates: 1977 - 1996

Year	Number				Rate per 100,000 population			
	City	Suburbs[2]	MSA[1]	U.S.	City	Suburbs[3]	MSA[1]	U.S.
1977	3,330	604	3,934	3,071,500	1,752.6	667.0	1,402.2	1,419.8
1978	3,416	648	4,064	3,128,300	1,788.5	630.5	1,383.3	1,434.6
1979	3,446	612	4,058	3,327,700	1,783.9	561.5	1,343.0	1,511.9
1980	4,015	808	4,823	3,795,200	1,977.0	719.1	1,529.0	1,684.1
1981	4,122	1,132	5,254	3,779,700	2,018.9	1,002.1	1,656.7	1,649.5
1982	3,878	1,037	4,915	3,447,100	1,896.3	916.5	1,547.3	1,488.8
1983	3,708	1,090	4,798	3,129,900	1,790.2	951.2	1,491.4	1,337.7
1984	2,983	607	3,590	2,984,400	1,422.8	524.6	1,103.4	1,263.7
1985	2,965	687	3,652	3,073,300	1,409.5	587.2	1,115.6	1,287.3
1986	3,202	855	4,057	3,241,400	1,521.6	729.7	1,238.4	1,344.6
1987	2,860	907	3,767	3,236,200	1,343.1	761.4	1,134.5	1,329.6
1988	n/a	n/a	n/a	3,218,100	n/a	n/a	n/a	1,309.2
1989	3,354	798	4,152	3,168,200	1,484.6	651.9	1,191.9	1,276.3
1990	3,177	987	4,164	3,073,900	1,409.7	802.0	1,195.1	1,235.9
1991	3,211	1,030	4,241	3,157,200	1,414.2	830.8	1,208.1	1,252.0
1992	2,831	831	3,662	2,979,900	1,232.9	662.8	1,031.5	1,168.2
1993	3,187	898	4,085	2,834,800	1,355.6	695.5	1,121.6	1,099.2
1994	3,089	1,416	4,505	2,712,800	1,300.9	740.6	1,051.0	1,042.0
1995	2,978	1,410	4,388	2,593,800	1,242.6	723.5	1,009.8	987.1
1996	2,893	n/a	n/a	2,501,500	1,199.7	n/a	n/a	943.0

Notes: (1) Metropolitan Statistical Area - see Appendix A for areas included; (2) calculated by the editors using the following formula: (number of crimes in the MSA minus number of crimes in the city); (3) calculated by the editors using the following formula: ((number of crimes in the MSA minus number of crimes in the city) ÷ (population of the MSA minus population of the city)) x 100,000; n/a not avail.
Source: U.S. Department of Justice, FBI Uniform Crime Reports, 1977 - 1996

Larceny-Thefts and Larceny-Theft Rates: 1977 - 1996

Year	Number				Rate per 100,000 population			
	City	Suburbs[2]	MSA[1]	U.S.	City	Suburbs[3]	MSA[1]	U.S.
1977	8,980	1,233	10,213	5,905,700	4,726.3	1,361.6	3,640.2	2,729.9
1978	8,679	1,249	9,928	5,991,000	4,544.0	1,215.2	3,379.4	2,747.4
1979	8,582	1,323	9,905	6,601,000	4,442.7	1,213.9	3,278.1	2,999.1
1980	9,744	1,587	11,331	7,136,900	4,798.1	1,412.4	3,592.1	3,167.0
1981	8,790	3,379	12,169	7,194,400	4,305.2	2,991.2	3,837.2	3,139.7
1982	10,949	2,217	13,166	7,142,500	5,353.9	1,959.4	4,144.8	3,084.8
1983	8,407	3,543	11,950	6,712,800	4,058.9	3,091.8	3,714.4	2,868.9
1984	7,332	2,729	10,061	6,591,900	3,497.1	2,358.5	3,092.2	2,791.3
1985	7,946	2,771	10,717	6,926,400	3,777.3	2,368.6	3,273.8	2,901.2
1986	8,285	2,904	11,189	7,257,200	3,937.1	2,478.3	3,415.4	3,010.3
1987	9,372	3,024	12,396	7,499,900	4,401.4	2,538.6	3,733.1	3,081.3
1988	n/a	n/a	n/a	7,705,900	n/a	n/a	n/a	3,134.9
1989	9,458	3,420	12,878	7,872,400	4,186.5	2,793.7	3,697.0	3,171.3
1990	10,538	3,806	14,344	7,945,700	4,675.9	3,092.7	4,116.8	3,194.8
1991	10,075	3,729	13,804	8,142,200	4,437.2	3,007.7	3,932.3	3,228.8
1992	9,319	3,764	13,083	7,915,200	4,058.3	3,002.1	3,685.3	3,103.0
1993	9,684	3,821	13,505	7,820,900	4,119.2	2,959.2	3,707.9	3,032.4
1994	10,058	5,188	15,246	7,879,800	4,235.8	2,713.5	3,556.8	3,026.7
1995	9,912	5,607	15,519	7,997,700	4,135.9	2,877.0	3,571.3	3,043.8
1996	9,522	n/a	n/a	7,894,600	3,948.6	n/a	n/a	2,975.9

Notes: (1) Metropolitan Statistical Area - see Appendix A for areas included; (2) calculated by the editors using the following formula: (number of crimes in the MSA minus number of crimes in the city); (3) calculated by the editors using the following formula: ((number of crimes in the MSA minus number of crimes in the city) ÷ (population of the MSA minus population of the city)) x 100,000; n/a not avail.
Source: U.S. Department of Justice, FBI Uniform Crime Reports, 1977 - 1996

Motor Vehicle Thefts and Motor Vehicle Theft Rates: 1977 - 1996

Year	Number				Rate per 100,000 population			
	City	Suburbs[2]	MSA[1]	U.S.	City	Suburbs[3]	MSA[1]	U.S.
1977	582	113	695	977,700	306.3	124.8	247.7	451.9
1978	584	114	698	1,004,100	305.8	110.9	237.6	460.5
1979	636	145	781	1,112,800	329.2	133.0	258.5	505.6
1980	826	142	968	1,131,700	406.7	126.4	306.9	502.2
1981	953	198	1,151	1,087,800	466.8	175.3	362.9	474.7
1982	820	192	1,012	1,062,400	401.0	169.7	318.6	458.8
1983	713	198	911	1,007,900	344.2	172.8	283.2	430.8
1984	692	156	848	1,032,200	330.1	134.8	260.6	437.1
1985	679	169	848	1,102,900	322.8	144.5	259.0	462.0
1986	724	188	912	1,224,100	344.1	160.4	278.4	507.8
1987	787	148	935	1,288,700	369.6	124.2	281.6	529.4
1988	n/a	n/a	n/a	1,432,900	n/a	n/a	n/a	582.9
1989	785	215	1,000	1,564,800	347.5	175.6	287.1	630.4
1990	760	256	1,016	1,635,900	337.2	208.0	291.6	657.8
1991	848	183	1,031	1,661,700	373.5	147.6	293.7	659.0
1992	655	179	834	1,610,800	285.2	142.8	234.9	631.5
1993	610	214	824	1,563,100	259.5	165.7	226.2	606.1
1994	671	361	1,032	1,539,300	282.6	188.8	240.8	591.3
1995	944	426	1,370	1,472,400	393.9	218.6	315.3	560.4
1996	915	n/a	n/a	1,395,200	379.4	n/a	n/a	525.9

Notes: (1) Metropolitan Statistical Area - see Appendix A for areas included; (2) calculated by the editors using the following formula: (number of crimes in the MSA minus number of crimes in the city); (3) calculated by the editors using the following formula: ((number of crimes in the MSA minus number of crimes in the city) ÷ (population of the MSA minus population of the city)) x 100,000; n/a not avail.
Source: U.S. Department of Justice, FBI Uniform Crime Reports, 1977 - 1996

HATE CRIMES

Criminal Incidents by Bias Motivation

Area	Race	Ethnicity	Religion	Sexual Orientation
Lexington	11	0	4	0

Notes: Figures include both violent and property crimes. Law enforcement agencies must have submitted data for at least one quarter of calendar year 1995 to be included in this report, therefore figures shown may not represent complete 12-month totals; n/a not available
Source: U.S. Department of Justice, FBI Uniform Crime Reports, Hate Crime Statistics 1995

LAW ENFORCEMENT

Full-Time Law Enforcement Employees

Jurisdiction	Police Employees			Police Officers per 100,000 population
	Total	Officers	Civilians	
Lexington	553	403	150	167.1

Notes: Data as of October 31, 1996
Source: U.S. Department of Justice, FBI Uniform Crime Reports, 1996

CORRECTIONS

Federal Correctional Facilities

Type	Year Opened	Security Level	Sex of Inmates	Rated Capacity	Population on 7/1/95	Number of Staff
None listed						

Notes: Data as of 1995
Source: Bureau of Justice Statistics, Sourcebook of Criminal Justice Statistics Online

City/County/Regional Correctional Facilities

Name	Year Opened	Year Renov.	Rated Capacity	1995 Pop.	Number of COs[1]	Number of Staff	ACA[2] Accred.
Lexington-Fayette Det Ctr	1976	1992	500	n/a	n/a	n/a	No

Notes: Data as of April 1996; (1) Correctional Officers; (2) American Correctional Assn. Accreditation
Source: American Correctional Association, 1996-1998 National Jail and Adult Detention Directory

Private Adult Correctional Facilities

Name	Date Opened	Rated Capacity	Present Pop.	Security Level	Facility Construct.	Expans. Plans	ACA[1] Accred.
None listed							

Notes: Data as of December 1996; (1) American Correctional Association Accreditation
Source: University of Florida, Center for Studies in Criminology and Law, Private Adult Correctional Facility Census, 10th Ed., March 15, 1997

Characteristics of Shock Incarceration Programs

Jurisdiction	Year Program Began	Number of Camps	Average Num. of Inmates	Number of Beds	Program Length	Voluntary/ Mandatory
Kentucky	1993	1	42	40-50 male; 10 female	17 weeks	Voluntary

Note: Data as of July 1996;
Source: Sourcebook of Criminal Justice Statistics Online

DEATH PENALTY

Death Penalty Statistics

State	Prisoners Executed		Prisoners Under Sentence of Death					Avg. No. of Years on Death Row[4]
	1930-1995	1996[1]	Total[2]	White[3]	Black[3]	Hisp.	Women	
Kentucky	103	0	28	22	6	0	0	8.8

Notes: Data as of 12/31/95 unless otherwise noted; (1) Data as of 7/31/97; (2) Includes persons of other races; (3) Includes people of Hispanic origin; (4) Covers prisoners sentenced 1974 through 1995
Source: Bureau of Justice Statistics, Capital Punishment 1995 (released 12/96); Death Penalty Information Center Web Site, 9/30/97

Capital Offenses and Methods of Execution

Capital Offenses in Kentucky	Minimum Age for Imposition of Death Penalty	Mentally Retarded Excluded	Methods of Execution[1]
Murder with aggravating factors; kidnaping with aggravating factors.	16	No	Electrocution

Notes: Data as of 12/31/95 unless otherwise noted; (1) Data as of 7/31/97
Source: Bureau of Justice Statistics, Capital Punishment 1995 (released 12/96); Death Penalty Information Center Web Site, 9/30/97

LAWS

Statutory Provisions Relating to the Purchase, Ownership and Use of Handguns

Jurisdiction	Instant Background Check	Federal Waiting Period Applies[1]	State Waiting Period (days)	License or Permit to Purchase	Regis-tration	Record of Sale Sent to Police	Concealed Carry Law
Kentucky	No	Yes	No	No	No	No	Yes[a]

Note: Data as of 1996; (1) The Federal 5-day waiting period for handgun purchases applies to states that don't have instant background checks, waiting period requirements, or licensing procedures exempting them from the Federal requirement; (a) "Shall issue" permit system, liberally administered discretion by local authorities over permit issuance, or no permit required
Source: Sourcebook of Criminal Justice Statistics Online

Statutory Provisions Relating to Alcohol Use and Driving

Jurisdiction	Drinking Age	Blood Alcohol Concentration Levels as Evidence in State Courts[1]		Open Container Law[1]	Anti-Consump-tion Law[1]	Dram Shop Law[1]
		Illegal per se at 0.10%	Presumption at 0.10%			
Kentucky	21	Yes	No	No	Yes	Yes

Note: Data as of January 1, 1997; (1) See Appendix C for an explanation of terms
Source: Sourcebook of Criminal Justice Statistics Online

Statutory Provisions Relating to Curfews

Jurisdiction	Year Enacted	Latest Revision	Age Group(s)	Curfew Provisions
Lexington	1995	-	17 and under	11 pm to 5 am weekday nights 1 am to 5 am weekend nights

Note: Data as of February 1996
Source: Sourcebook of Criminal Justice Statistics Online

Statutory Provisions Relating to Hate Crimes

Jurisdiction	Bias-Motivated Violence and Intimidation						Institutional Vandalism
		Criminal Penalty					
	Civil Action	Race/ Religion/ Ethnicity	Sexual Orientation	Mental/ Physical Disability	Gender	Age	
Kentucky	No	No	No	No	No	No	Yes

Source: Anti-Defamation League, 1997 Hate Crimes Laws

Los Angeles, California

OVERVIEW

The total crime rate for the city decreased 14.8% between 1977 and 1996. During that same period, the violent crime rate increased 47.3% and the property crime rate decreased 26.1%.

Among violent crimes, the rates for: Murders decreased 2.9%; Forcible Rapes decreased 50.6%; Robberies increased 30.4%; and Aggravated Assaults increased 80.5%.

Among property crimes, the rates for: Burglaries decreased 55.7%; Larceny-Thefts decreased 14.2%; and Motor Vehicle Thefts decreased 0.1%.

ANTI-CRIME PROGRAMS

The city is attempting to implement CPTED (Crime Prevention Through Environmental Design) which explores ways in which security can be heightened through the study of the physical environment at crime locations in order to identify potential crime hazards and to help prepare remedies for urban areas.

Some programs which have been implemented include:

- Basic Car Plan—Each of 18 geographical areas are sub-divided into several defined parts called a Basic Car area with a senior lead officer assigned to each. The lead officer unites the Department and the Community. In this way the officers become more sensitive to the community's needs.
- Neighborhood Watch—This is the cornerstone of the Department's crime prevention programs. It enlists the active participation of residents in reducing crime in their communities.
- Apartment Watch—Residents, building owners and local law enforcement join to reduce crime.
- Business Watch—Business owners, managers and employers are educated in techniques which help to reduce losses.
- PACE (Police Assisted Community Enhancement)—Recognizes the relationship between the appearance of community neglect and lawlessness. PACE uses Los Angeles Police Department resources to coordinate the efforts of involved city departments to alleviate adverse conditions which affect the quality of city life such as graffiti, abandoned vehicles, decaying structures, trash, and road decay.
- Jeopardy Program—Counseling and referrals for youth in jeopardy of becoming gang members. *Los Angeles Police Department, 8/97*

By early 1998 the Los Angeles Police Department gang database along with other police and sheriff departments will be hooked by CAL/GANG to the California Department of Justice central gang database. 200,000 gang member records will be tracked including information on physical attributes, firearm and vehicle data and other information. *Governing, 7/97*

CRIME RISK

Your Chances of Becoming a Victim[1]

Area	Any Crime	Violent Crime						Property Crime			
		Any	Murder	Forcible Rape[2]	Robbery	Aggrav. Assault		Any	Burglary	Larceny -Theft	Motor Vehicle Theft
City	1:15	1:56	1:4,920	1:1,191	1:139	1:99		1:20	1:98	1:37	1:84

Note: (1) Figures have been calculated by dividing the population of the city by the number of crimes reported to the FBI during 1996 and are expressed as odds (eg. 1:20 should be read as 1 in 20).
(2) Figures have been calculated by dividing the female population of the city by the number of forcible rapes reported to the FBI during 1996. The female population of the city was estimated by calculating the ratio of females to males reported in the 1990 Census and applying that ratio to 1996 population estimate.
Source: FBI Uniform Crime Reports 1996

CRIME STATISTICS

Total Crimes and Total Crime Rates: 1977 - 1996

Year	Number				Rate per 100,000 population			
	City	Suburbs[2]	MSA[1]	U.S.	City	Suburbs[3]	MSA[1]	U.S.
1977	217,834	281,979	499,813	10,984,500	7,889.7	6,458.7	7,013.1	5,077.6
1978	233,344	288,453	521,797	11,209,000	8,372.6	6,676.6	7,341.7	5,140.3
1979	258,635	304,090	562,725	12,249,500	9,032.4	6,998.3	7,806.3	5,565.5
1980	293,837	332,893	626,730	13,408,300	9,952.1	7,410.8	8,418.7	5,950.0
1981	304,100	330,112	634,212	13,423,800	10,032.7	7,158.4	8,298.3	5,858.2
1982	320,372	318,805	639,177	12,974,400	10,328.0	6,755.2	8,172.2	5,603.6
1983	307,511	296,902	604,413	12,108,600	9,735.4	6,178.7	7,589.4	5,175.0
1984	297,183	285,224	582,407	11,881,800	9,451.6	5,888.4	7,291.0	5,031.3
1985	294,404	290,015	584,419	12,431,400	9,239.2	5,866.4	7,188.3	5,207.1
1986	311,420	304,761	616,181	13,211,900	9,550.3	6,023.8	7,405.9	5,480.4
1987	288,509	288,518	577,027	13,508,700	8,633.5	5,587.2	6,784.1	5,550.0
1988	295,181	298,958	594,139	13,923,100	8,675.8	5,686.3	6,860.8	5,664.2
1989	319,097	335,353	654,450	14,251,400	9,272.2	6,240.7	7,424.2	5,741.0
1990	321,536	340,372	661,908	14,475,600	9,225.2	6,329.2	7,468.1	5,820.3
1991	346,224	343,471	689,695	14,872,900	9,730.0	6,256.6	7,622.6	5,897.8
1992	338,531	342,477	681,008	14,438,200	9,363.7	6,139.8	7,407.6	5,660.2
1993	312,789	331,969	644,758	14,144,800	8,872.6	5,906.1	7,049.6	5,484.4
1994	278,351	313,444	591,795	13,989,500	7,840.0	5,537.6	6,425.1	5,373.5
1995	266,204	298,599	564,803	13,862,700	7,680.0	5,211.3	6,141.8	5,275.9
1996	235,260	269,811	505,071	13,473,600	6,725.3	4,666.2	5,442.4	5,078.9

Notes: (1) Metropolitan Statistical Area - see Appendix A for areas included; (2) calculated by the editors using the following formula: (number of crimes in the MSA minus number of crimes in the city); (3) calculated by the editors using the following formula: ((number of crimes in the MSA minus number of crimes in the city) ÷ (population of the MSA minus population of the city)) x 100,000; n/a not avail.
Source: U.S. Department of Justice, FBI Uniform Crime Reports, 1977 - 1996

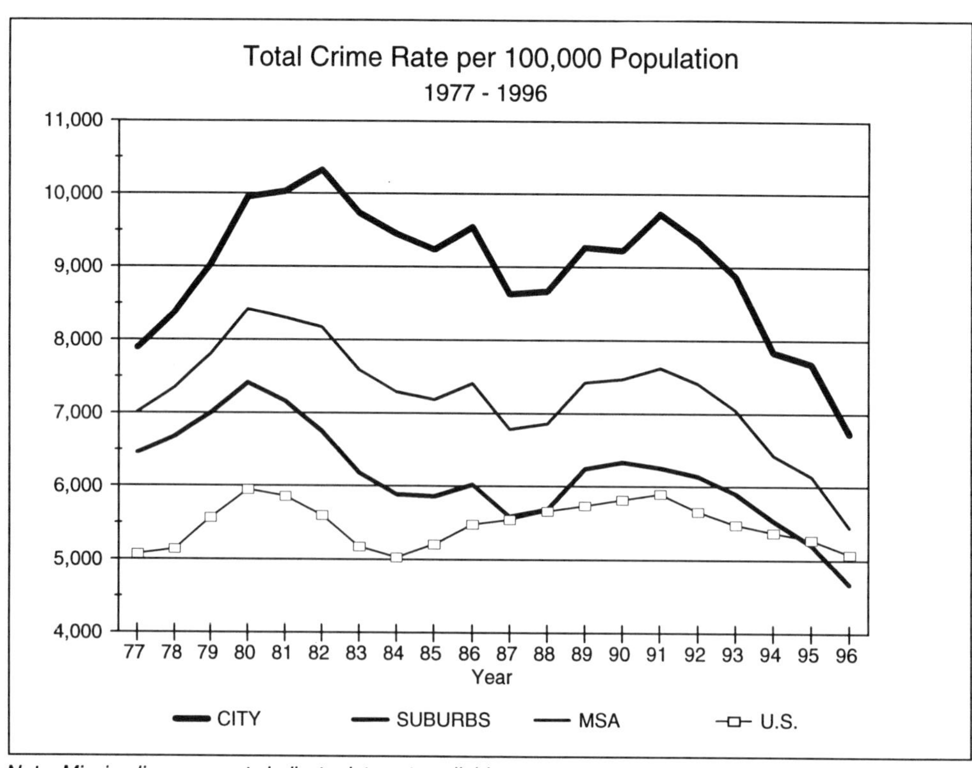

Note: Missing line segments indicate data not available.

Violent Crimes and Violent Crime Rates: 1977 - 1996

Year	Number				Rate per 100,000 population			
	City	Suburbs[2]	MSA[1]	U.S.	City	Suburbs[3]	MSA[1]	U.S.
1977	33,676	37,883	71,559	1,029,580	1,219.7	867.7	1,004.1	475.9
1978	36,797	40,159	76,956	1,085,550	1,320.3	929.5	1,082.8	497.8
1979	43,372	43,500	86,872	1,208,030	1,514.7	1,001.1	1,205.1	548.9
1980	51,447	48,277	99,724	1,344,520	1,742.5	1,074.7	1,339.6	596.6
1981	52,818	46,574	99,392	1,361,820	1,742.5	1,009.9	1,300.5	594.3
1982	53,957	45,373	99,330	1,322,390	1,739.4	961.4	1,270.0	571.1
1983	53,435	43,980	97,415	1,258,090	1,691.7	915.2	1,223.2	537.7
1984	51,442	43,312	94,754	1,273,280	1,636.1	894.2	1,186.2	539.2
1985	52,832	43,062	95,894	1,328,800	1,658.0	871.0	1,179.5	556.6
1986	66,378	49,441	115,819	1,489,170	2,035.6	977.2	1,392.0	617.7
1987	63,833	51,159	114,992	1,484,000	1,910.2	990.7	1,352.0	609.7
1988	66,736	53,932	120,668	1,566,220	1,961.5	1,025.8	1,393.4	637.2
1989	77,297	63,840	141,137	1,646,040	2,246.1	1,188.0	1,601.1	663.1
1990	83,809	72,043	155,852	1,820,130	2,404.6	1,339.6	1,758.4	731.8
1991	89,875	72,622	162,497	1,911,770	2,525.8	1,322.9	1,795.9	758.1
1992	88,919	74,594	163,513	1,932,270	2,459.5	1,337.3	1,778.6	757.5
1993	83,701	70,175	153,876	1,926,020	2,374.3	1,248.5	1,682.4	746.8
1994	73,102	64,897	137,999	1,857,670	2,059.0	1,146.5	1,498.2	713.6
1995	70,518	60,306	130,824	1,798,790	2,034.4	1,052.5	1,422.6	684.6
1996	62,840	55,760	118,600	1,682,280	1,796.4	964.3	1,278.0	634.1

Notes: Violent crimes include murder, forcible rape, robbery and aggravated assault; n/a not available; (1) Metropolitan Statistical Area - see Appendix A for areas included; (2) calculated by the editors using the following formula: (number of crimes in the MSA minus number of crimes in the city); (3) calculated by the editors using the following formula: ((number of crimes in the MSA minus number of crimes in the city) ÷ (population of the MSA minus population of the city)) x 100,000

Source: U.S. Department of Justice, FBI Uniform Crime Reports, 1977 - 1996

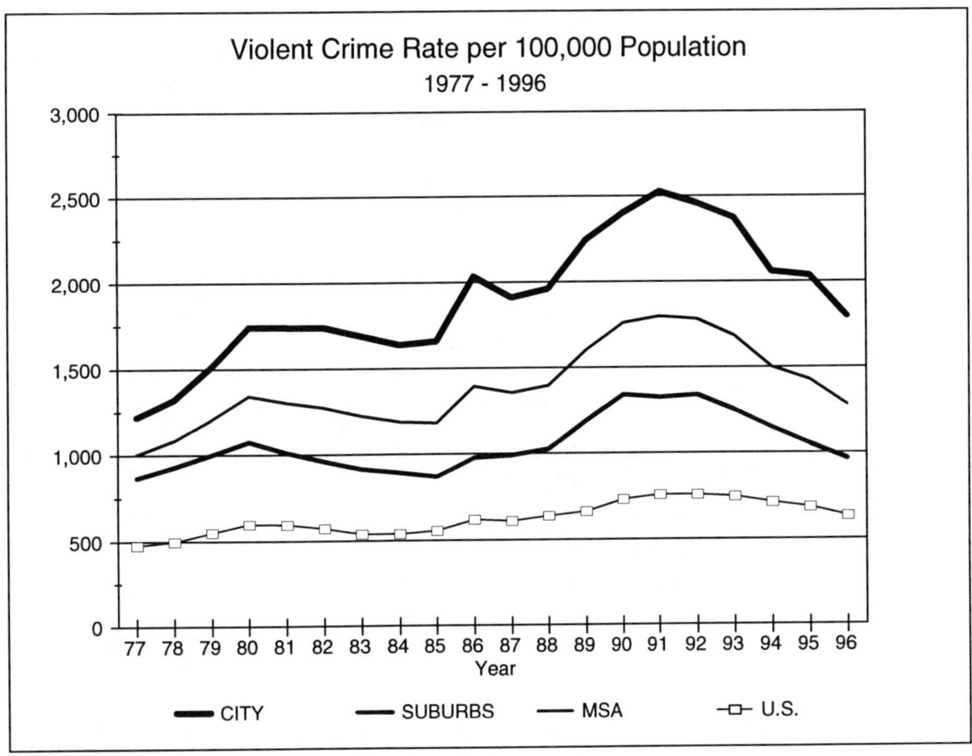

Note: Missing line segments indicate data not available.

Property Crimes and Property Crime Rates: 1977 - 1996

Year	Number				Rate per 100,000 population			
	City	Suburbs[2]	MSA[1]	U.S.	City	Suburbs[3]	MSA[1]	U.S.
1977	184,158	244,096	428,254	9,955,000	6,670.0	5,591.0	6,009.0	4,601.7
1978	196,547	248,294	444,841	10,123,400	7,052.3	5,747.1	6,258.9	4,642.5
1979	215,263	260,590	475,853	11,041,500	7,517.7	5,997.2	6,601.2	5,016.6
1980	242,390	284,616	527,006	12,063,700	8,209.6	6,336.1	7,079.1	5,353.3
1981	251,282	283,538	534,820	12,061,900	8,290.2	6,148.4	6,997.8	5,263.9
1982	266,415	273,432	539,847	11,652,000	8,588.5	5,793.8	6,902.2	5,032.5
1983	254,076	252,922	506,998	10,850,500	8,043.7	5,263.4	6,366.2	4,637.4
1984	245,741	241,912	487,653	10,608,500	7,815.6	4,994.3	6,104.8	4,492.1
1985	241,572	246,953	488,525	11,102,600	7,581.2	4,995.3	6,008.8	4,650.5
1986	245,042	255,320	500,362	11,722,700	7,514.7	5,046.6	6,013.9	4,862.6
1987	224,676	237,359	462,035	12,024,700	6,723.4	4,596.5	5,432.1	4,940.3
1988	228,445	245,026	473,471	12,356,900	6,714.3	4,660.5	5,467.4	5,027.1
1989	241,800	271,513	513,313	12,605,400	7,026.1	5,052.7	5,823.1	5,077.9
1990	237,727	268,329	506,056	12,655,500	6,820.7	4,989.6	5,709.7	5,088.5
1991	256,349	270,849	527,198	12,961,100	7,204.2	4,933.7	5,826.6	5,139.7
1992	249,612	267,883	517,495	12,505,900	6,904.2	4,802.5	5,629.0	4,902.7
1993	229,088	261,794	490,882	12,218,800	6,498.4	4,657.6	5,367.1	4,737.6
1994	205,249	248,547	453,796	12,131,900	5,781.0	4,391.0	4,926.8	4,660.0
1995	195,686	238,293	433,979	12,063,900	5,645.5	4,158.8	4,719.2	4,591.3
1996	172,420	214,051	386,471	11,791,300	4,928.9	3,701.9	4,164.4	4,444.8

Notes: Property crimes include burglary, larceny-theft and motor vehicle theft; n/a not available; (1) Metropolitan Statistical Area - see Appendix A for areas included; (2) calculated by the editors using the following formula: (number of crimes in the MSA minus number of crimes in the city); (3) calculated by the editors using the following formula: ((number of crimes in the MSA minus number of crimes in the city) ÷ (population of the MSA minus population of the city)) x 100,000
Source: U.S. Department of Justice, FBI Uniform Crime Reports, 1977 - 1996

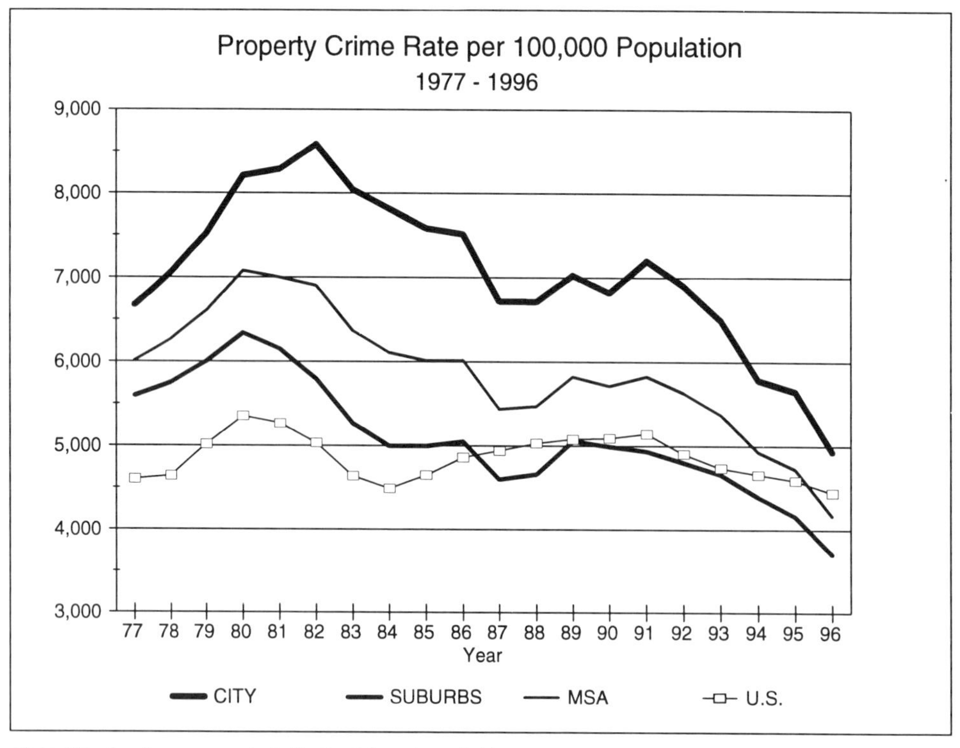

Note: Missing line segments indicate data not available.

Murders and Murder Rates: 1977 - 1996

Year	Number				Rate per 100,000 population			
	City	Suburbs[2]	MSA[1]	U.S.	City	Suburbs[3]	MSA[1]	U.S.
1977	576	562	1,138	19,120	20.9	12.9	16.0	8.8
1978	651	586	1,237	19,560	23.4	13.6	17.4	9.0
1979	786	653	1,439	21,460	27.4	15.0	20.0	9.7
1980	1,010	721	1,731	23,040	34.2	16.1	23.3	10.2
1981	879	621	1,500	22,520	29.0	13.5	19.6	9.8
1982	849	567	1,416	21,010	27.4	12.0	18.1	9.1
1983	820	528	1,348	19,310	26.0	11.0	16.9	8.3
1984	759	542	1,301	18,690	24.1	11.2	16.3	7.9
1985	777	549	1,326	18,980	24.4	11.1	16.3	7.9
1986	834	575	1,409	20,610	25.6	11.4	16.9	8.6
1987	811	601	1,412	20,100	24.3	11.6	16.6	8.3
1988	736	610	1,346	20,680	21.6	11.6	15.5	8.4
1989	877	710	1,587	21,500	25.5	13.2	18.0	8.7
1990	983	785	1,768	23,440	28.2	14.6	19.9	9.4
1991	1,027	829	1,856	24,700	28.9	15.1	20.5	9.8
1992	1,094	825	1,919	23,760	30.3	14.8	20.9	9.3
1993	1,076	868	1,944	24,530	30.5	15.4	21.3	9.5
1994	845	824	1,669	23,330	23.8	14.6	18.1	9.0
1995	849	833	1,682	21,610	24.5	14.5	18.3	8.2
1996	711	690	1,401	19,650	20.3	11.9	15.1	7.4

Notes: (1) Metropolitan Statistical Area - see Appendix A for areas included; (2) calculated by the editors using the following formula: (number of crimes in the MSA minus number of crimes in the city); (3) calculated by the editors using the following formula: ((number of crimes in the MSA minus number of crimes in the city) ÷ (population of the MSA minus population of the city)) x 100,000; n/a not avail.
Source: U.S. Department of Justice, FBI Uniform Crime Reports, 1977 - 1996

Forcible Rapes and Forcible Rape Rates: 1977 - 1996

Year	Number				Rate per 100,000 population			
	City	Suburbs[2]	MSA[1]	U.S.	City	Suburbs[3]	MSA[1]	U.S.
1977	2,339	2,287	4,626	63,500	84.7	52.4	64.9	29.4
1978	2,467	2,291	4,758	67,610	88.5	53.0	66.9	31.0
1979	2,508	2,631	5,139	76,390	87.6	60.5	71.3	34.7
1980	2,813	2,799	5,612	82,990	95.3	62.3	75.4	36.8
1981	2,666	2,705	5,371	82,500	88.0	58.7	70.3	36.0
1982	2,706	2,592	5,298	78,770	87.2	54.9	67.7	34.0
1983	2,494	2,355	4,849	78,920	79.0	49.0	60.9	33.7
1984	2,347	2,196	4,543	84,230	74.6	45.3	56.9	35.7
1985	2,318	2,130	4,448	88,670	72.7	43.1	54.7	37.1
1986	2,330	2,098	4,428	91,460	71.5	41.5	53.2	37.9
1987	2,169	2,107	4,276	91,110	64.9	40.8	50.3	37.4
1988	2,006	1,966	3,972	92,490	59.0	37.4	45.9	37.6
1989	1,996	2,010	4,006	94,500	58.0	37.4	45.4	38.1
1990	2,014	2,201	4,215	102,560	57.8	40.9	47.6	41.2
1991	1,966	2,148	4,114	106,590	55.3	39.1	45.5	42.3
1992	1,872	1,993	3,865	109,060	51.8	35.7	42.0	42.8
1993	1,773	1,915	3,688	106,010	50.3	34.1	40.3	41.1
1994	1,554	1,634	3,188	102,220	43.8	28.9	34.6	39.3
1995	1,590	1,589	3,179	97,470	45.9	27.7	34.6	37.1
1996	1,463	1,571	3,034	95,770	41.8	27.2	32.7	36.1

Notes: (1) Metropolitan Statistical Area - see Appendix A for areas included; (2) calculated by the editors using the following formula: (number of crimes in the MSA minus number of crimes in the city); (3) calculated by the editors using the following formula: ((number of crimes in the MSA minus number of crimes in the city) ÷ (population of the MSA minus population of the city)) x 100,000; n/a not avail.
Source: U.S. Department of Justice, FBI Uniform Crime Reports, 1977 - 1996

Robberies and Robbery Rates: 1977 - 1996

Year	Number				Rate per 100,000 population			
	City	Suburbs[2]	MSA[1]	U.S.	City	Suburbs[3]	MSA[1]	U.S.
1977	15,246	15,330	30,576	412,610	552.2	351.1	429.0	190.7
1978	17,105	16,096	33,201	426,930	613.7	372.6	467.1	195.8
1979	20,454	17,695	38,149	480,700	714.3	407.2	529.2	218.4
1980	25,637	21,114	46,751	565,840	868.3	470.0	628.0	251.1
1981	28,152	21,703	49,855	592,910	928.8	470.6	652.3	258.7
1982	30,029	20,954	50,983	553,130	968.1	444.0	651.8	238.9
1983	29,243	20,039	49,282	506,570	925.8	417.0	618.8	216.5
1984	27,323	19,929	47,252	485,010	869.0	411.4	591.5	205.4
1985	27,938	19,385	47,323	497,870	876.8	392.1	582.1	208.5
1986	29,930	19,446	49,376	542,780	917.9	384.4	593.5	225.1
1987	26,192	18,126	44,318	517,700	783.8	351.0	521.0	212.7
1988	26,182	19,824	46,006	542,970	769.5	377.1	531.3	220.9
1989	31,063	23,277	54,340	578,330	902.6	433.2	616.4	233.0
1990	36,098	26,996	63,094	639,270	1,035.7	502.0	711.9	257.0
1991	39,778	28,098	67,876	687,730	1,117.9	511.8	750.2	272.7
1992	39,508	29,451	68,959	672,480	1,092.8	528.0	750.1	263.6
1993	38,415	27,579	65,994	659,870	1,089.7	490.7	721.6	255.9
1994	30,817	25,299	56,116	618,950	868.0	447.0	609.2	237.7
1995	29,134	23,255	52,389	580,510	840.5	405.9	569.7	220.9
1996	25,189	20,983	46,172	537,050	720.1	362.9	497.5	202.4

Notes: (1) Metropolitan Statistical Area - see Appendix A for areas included; (2) calculated by the editors using the following formula: (number of crimes in the MSA minus number of crimes in the city); (3) calculated by the editors using the following formula: ((number of crimes in the MSA minus number of crimes in the city) ÷ (population of the MSA minus population of the city)) x 100,000; n/a not avail.
Source: U.S. Department of Justice, FBI Uniform Crime Reports, 1977 - 1996

Aggravated Assaults and Aggravated Assault Rates: 1977 - 1996

Year	Number				Rate per 100,000 population			
	City	Suburbs[2]	MSA[1]	U.S.	City	Suburbs[3]	MSA[1]	U.S.
1977	15,515	19,704	35,219	534,350	561.9	451.3	494.2	247.0
1978	16,574	21,186	37,760	571,460	594.7	490.4	531.3	262.1
1979	19,624	22,521	42,145	629,480	685.3	518.3	584.7	286.0
1980	21,987	23,643	45,630	672,650	744.7	526.3	612.9	298.5
1981	21,121	21,545	42,666	663,900	696.8	467.2	558.3	289.7
1982	20,373	21,260	41,633	669,480	656.8	450.5	532.3	289.2
1983	20,878	21,058	41,936	653,290	661.0	438.2	526.6	279.2
1984	21,013	20,645	41,658	685,350	668.3	426.2	521.5	290.2
1985	21,799	20,998	42,797	723,250	684.1	424.7	526.4	302.9
1986	33,284	27,322	60,606	834,320	1,020.7	540.0	728.4	346.1
1987	34,661	30,325	64,986	855,090	1,037.2	587.3	764.0	351.3
1988	37,812	31,532	69,344	910,090	1,111.4	599.7	800.8	370.2
1989	43,361	37,843	81,204	951,710	1,260.0	704.2	921.2	383.4
1990	44,714	42,061	86,775	1,054,860	1,282.9	782.1	979.1	424.1
1991	47,104	41,547	88,651	1,092,740	1,323.8	756.8	979.8	433.3
1992	46,445	42,325	88,770	1,126,970	1,284.7	758.8	965.6	441.8
1993	42,437	39,813	82,250	1,135,610	1,203.8	708.3	899.3	440.3
1994	39,886	37,140	77,026	1,113,180	1,123.4	656.1	836.3	427.6
1995	38,945	34,629	73,574	1,099,210	1,123.6	604.4	800.1	418.3
1996	35,477	32,516	67,993	1,029,810	1,014.2	562.3	732.7	388.2

Notes: (1) Metropolitan Statistical Area - see Appendix A for areas included; (2) calculated by the editors using the following formula: (number of crimes in the MSA minus number of crimes in the city); (3) calculated by the editors using the following formula: ((number of crimes in the MSA minus number of crimes in the city) ÷ (population of the MSA minus population of the city)) x 100,000; n/a not avail.
Source: U.S. Department of Justice, FBI Uniform Crime Reports, 1977 - 1996

Burglaries and Burglary Rates: 1977 - 1996

Year	Number				Rate per 100,000 population			
	City	Suburbs[2]	MSA[1]	U.S.	City	Suburbs[3]	MSA[1]	U.S.
1977	63,928	92,854	156,782	3,071,500	2,315.4	2,126.8	2,199.9	1,419.8
1978	69,876	96,005	165,881	3,128,300	2,507.2	2,222.2	2,333.9	1,434.6
1979	74,339	97,788	172,127	3,327,700	2,596.2	2,250.5	2,387.8	1,511.9
1980	86,525	107,216	193,741	3,795,200	2,930.6	2,386.8	2,602.5	1,684.1
1981	86,783	104,817	191,600	3,779,700	2,863.1	2,272.9	2,507.0	1,649.5
1982	85,000	94,988	179,988	3,447,100	2,740.2	2,012.7	2,301.2	1,488.8
1983	79,691	85,741	165,432	3,129,900	2,522.9	1,784.3	2,077.3	1,337.7
1984	68,696	80,339	149,035	2,984,400	2,184.8	1,658.6	1,865.7	1,263.7
1985	63,963	79,559	143,522	3,073,300	2,007.3	1,609.3	1,765.3	1,287.3
1986	64,201	79,327	143,528	3,241,400	1,968.8	1,567.9	1,725.1	1,344.6
1987	52,927	68,912	121,839	3,236,200	1,583.8	1,334.5	1,432.5	1,329.6
1988	50,988	67,310	118,298	3,218,100	1,498.6	1,280.3	1,366.0	1,309.2
1989	51,209	71,196	122,405	3,168,200	1,488.0	1,324.9	1,388.6	1,276.3
1990	51,482	71,680	123,162	3,073,900	1,477.1	1,332.9	1,389.6	1,235.9
1991	57,460	71,664	129,124	3,157,200	1,614.8	1,305.4	1,427.1	1,252.0
1992	57,771	70,961	128,732	2,979,900	1,597.9	1,272.2	1,400.3	1,168.2
1993	50,232	66,142	116,374	2,834,800	1,424.9	1,176.7	1,272.4	1,099.2
1994	43,535	60,476	104,011	2,712,800	1,226.2	1,068.4	1,129.2	1,042.0
1995	41,325	55,443	96,768	2,593,800	1,192.2	967.6	1,052.3	987.1
1996	35,865	51,453	87,318	2,501,500	1,025.3	889.8	940.9	943.0

Notes: (1) Metropolitan Statistical Area - see Appendix A for areas included; (2) calculated by the editors using the following formula: (number of crimes in the MSA minus number of crimes in the city); (3) calculated by the editors using the following formula: ((number of crimes in the MSA minus number of crimes in the city) ÷ (population of the MSA minus population of the city)) x 100,000; n/a not avail.
Source: U.S. Department of Justice, FBI Uniform Crime Reports, 1977 - 1996

Larceny-Thefts and Larceny-Theft Rates: 1977 - 1996

Year	Number				Rate per 100,000 population			
	City	Suburbs[2]	MSA[1]	U.S.	City	Suburbs[3]	MSA[1]	U.S.
1977	87,439	119,223	206,662	5,905,700	3,166.9	2,730.8	2,899.8	2,729.9
1978	90,240	118,582	208,822	5,991,000	3,237.9	2,744.7	2,938.1	2,747.4
1979	101,623	125,932	227,555	6,601,000	3,549.0	2,898.2	3,156.7	2,999.1
1980	112,982	138,025	251,007	7,136,900	3,826.6	3,072.7	3,371.7	3,167.0
1981	121,997	141,152	263,149	7,194,400	4,024.9	3,060.8	3,443.2	3,139.7
1982	132,544	140,953	273,497	7,142,500	4,272.9	2,986.7	3,496.8	3,084.8
1983	125,276	130,055	255,331	6,712,800	3,966.1	2,706.5	3,206.1	2,868.9
1984	128,538	125,460	253,998	6,591,900	4,088.0	2,590.1	3,179.7	2,791.3
1985	125,968	128,985	254,953	6,926,400	3,953.2	2,609.1	3,135.9	2,901.2
1986	124,518	130,333	254,851	7,257,200	3,818.6	2,576.1	3,063.1	3,010.3
1987	114,643	119,585	234,228	7,499,900	3,430.7	2,315.8	2,753.8	3,081.3
1988	120,126	123,065	243,191	7,705,900	3,530.7	2,340.7	2,808.2	3,134.9
1989	126,600	137,552	264,152	7,872,400	3,678.7	2,559.7	2,996.6	3,171.3
1990	122,632	133,339	255,971	7,945,700	3,518.5	2,479.4	2,888.0	3,194.8
1991	130,234	135,432	265,666	8,142,200	3,660.0	2,467.0	2,936.2	3,228.8
1992	123,860	131,646	255,506	7,915,200	3,425.9	2,360.1	2,779.3	3,103.0
1993	119,092	129,363	248,455	7,820,900	3,378.2	2,301.5	2,716.5	3,032.4
1994	110,791	125,967	236,758	7,879,800	3,120.5	2,225.4	2,570.5	3,026.7
1995	108,149	126,742	234,891	7,997,700	3,120.1	2,212.0	2,554.3	3,043.8
1996	95,069	113,542	208,611	7,894,600	2,717.7	1,963.6	2,247.9	2,975.9

Notes: (1) Metropolitan Statistical Area - see Appendix A for areas included; (2) calculated by the editors using the following formula: (number of crimes in the MSA minus number of crimes in the city); (3) calculated by the editors using the following formula: ((number of crimes in the MSA minus number of crimes in the city) ÷ (population of the MSA minus population of the city)) x 100,000; n/a not avail.
Source: U.S. Department of Justice, FBI Uniform Crime Reports, 1977 - 1996

Motor Vehicle Thefts and Motor Vehicle Theft Rates: 1977 - 1996

Year	Number				Rate per 100,000 population			
	City	Suburbs[2]	MSA[1]	U.S.	City	Suburbs[3]	MSA[1]	U.S.
1977	32,791	32,019	64,810	977,700	1,187.6	733.4	909.4	451.9
1978	36,431	33,707	70,138	1,004,100	1,307.2	780.2	986.8	460.5
1979	39,301	36,870	76,171	1,112,800	1,372.5	848.5	1,056.7	505.6
1980	42,883	39,375	82,258	1,131,700	1,452.4	876.6	1,104.9	502.2
1981	42,502	37,569	80,071	1,087,800	1,402.2	814.7	1,047.7	474.7
1982	48,871	37,491	86,362	1,062,400	1,575.5	794.4	1,104.2	458.8
1983	49,109	37,126	86,235	1,007,900	1,554.7	772.6	1,082.8	430.8
1984	48,507	36,113	84,620	1,032,200	1,542.7	745.6	1,059.3	437.1
1985	51,641	38,409	90,050	1,102,900	1,620.6	776.9	1,107.6	462.0
1986	56,323	45,660	101,983	1,224,100	1,727.2	902.5	1,225.7	507.8
1987	57,106	48,862	105,968	1,288,700	1,708.9	946.2	1,245.9	529.4
1988	57,331	54,651	111,982	1,432,900	1,685.0	1,039.5	1,293.1	582.9
1989	63,991	62,765	126,756	1,564,800	1,859.4	1,168.0	1,437.9	630.4
1990	63,613	63,310	126,923	1,635,900	1,825.1	1,177.3	1,432.0	657.8
1991	68,655	63,753	132,408	1,661,700	1,929.4	1,161.3	1,463.4	659.0
1992	67,981	65,276	133,257	1,610,800	1,880.3	1,170.2	1,449.5	631.5
1993	59,764	66,289	126,053	1,563,100	1,695.3	1,179.4	1,378.2	606.1
1994	50,923	62,104	113,027	1,539,300	1,434.3	1,097.2	1,227.1	591.3
1995	46,212	56,108	102,320	1,472,400	1,333.2	979.2	1,112.7	560.4
1996	41,486	49,056	90,542	1,395,200	1,185.9	848.4	975.6	525.9

Notes: (1) Metropolitan Statistical Area - see Appendix A for areas included; (2) calculated by the editors using the following formula: (number of crimes in the MSA minus number of crimes in the city); (3) calculated by the editors using the following formula: ((number of crimes in the MSA minus number of crimes in the city) ÷ (population of the MSA minus population of the city)) x 100,000; n/a not avail.
Source: U.S. Department of Justice, FBI Uniform Crime Reports, 1977 - 1996

HATE CRIMES

Criminal Incidents by Bias Motivation

Area	Race	Ethnicity	Religion	Sexual Orientation
Los Angeles	235	73	80	49

Notes: Figures include both violent and property crimes. Law enforcement agencies must have submitted data for at least one quarter of calendar year 1995 to be included in this report, therefore figures shown may not represent complete 12-month totals; n/a not available
Source: U.S. Department of Justice, FBI Uniform Crime Reports, Hate Crime Statistics 1995

ILLEGAL DRUGS

Drug Use by Adult Arrestees

Sex	Percent Testing Positive by Urinalysis (%)				
	Any Drug[1]	Cocaine	Marijuana	Opiates	Multiple Drugs
Male	64	44	30	6	20
Female	74	49	20	12	24

Notes: The catchment area is part of city and part of county; (1) Includes cocaine, opiates, marijuana, methadone, phencyclidine (PCP), benzodiazepines, methaqualone, propoxyphene, barbiturates & amphetamines
Source: National Institute of Justice, 1996 Drug Use Forecasting, Annual Report on Adult and Juvenile Arrestees (released June 1997)

LAW ENFORCEMENT

Full-Time Law Enforcement Employees

Jurisdiction	Police Employees			Police Officers per 100,000 population
	Total	Officers	Civilians	
Los Angeles	12,204	9,148	3,056	261.5

Notes: Data as of October 31, 1996
Source: U.S. Department of Justice, FBI Uniform Crime Reports, 1996

Number of Police Officers by Race

Race	Police Officers 1983		Police Officers 1992		Index of Representation[1]		
	Number	Pct.	Number	Pct.	1983	1992	% Chg.
Black	657	9.5	1,127	14.1	0.55	1.00	81.8
Hispanic[2]	943	13.6	1,787	22.3	0.49	0.56	14.3

Notes: (1) The index of representation is calculated by dividing the percent of black/hispanic police officers by the percent of corresponding blacks/hispanics in the local population. An index approaching 1.0 indicates that a city is closer to achieving a representation of police officers equal to their proportion in the local population; (2) Hispanic officers can be of any race
Source: Bureau of Justice Statistics, Sourcebook of Criminal Justice Statistics, 1994

CORRECTIONS

Federal Correctional Facilities

Type	Year Opened	Security Level	Sex of Inmates	Rated Capacity	Population on 7/1/95	Number of Staff
Metro Corr/Detention Ctr	1988	Admin.	Both	728	1,049	295

Notes: Data as of 1995
Source: Bureau of Justice Statistics, Sourcebook of Criminal Justice Statistics Online

City/County/Regional Correctional Facilities

Name	Year Opened	Year Renov.	Rated Capacity	1995 Pop.	Number of COs[1]	Number of Staff	ACA[2] Accred.
LA Co-Custody Division South	n/a	--	n/a	n/a	n/a	n/a	No
LA Co-Inmate Reception Ctr	1975	--	700	230	n/a	n/a	No
LA Co-Men's Central Jail	1963	1976	6,800	6,391	n/a	n/a	No
LA Co-Sybil Brand Inst	1963	1991	2,175	2,127	n/a	n/a	No
LA Co-Twin Towers Corr Facil	n/a	--	4,192	n/a	n/a	n/a	No

Notes: Data as of April 1996; (1) Correctional Officers; (2) American Correctional Assn. Accreditation
Source: American Correctional Association, 1996-1998 National Jail and Adult Detention Directory

Private Adult Correctional Facilities

None listed

Notes: Data as of December 1996
Source: University of Florida, Center for Studies in Criminology and Law, Private Adult Correctional Facility Census, 10th Ed., March 15, 1997

Characteristics of Shock Incarceration Programs

Jurisdiction	Year Program Began	Number of Camps	Average Num. of Inmates	Number of Beds	Program Length	Voluntary/ Mandatory
California	1993	3[a]	350	200[b]	4 months[c]	Voluntary

Note: Data as of July 1996; (a) One boot camp; two work training and parole camps; (b) 200 program beds at San Quentin shock incarceration facility. Work training beds vary with each facility; (c) Shock incarceration and intensive parole programs: 4 months; Work training program: 2 months
Source: Sourcebook of Criminal Justice Statistics Online

INMATES AND HIV/AIDS

HIV Testing Policies for Inmates

Jurisdiction	All Inmates at Some Time	All Convicted Inmates at Admission	Random Samples While in Custody	High-risk Groups	Upon Inmate Request	Upon Court Order	Upon Involvement in Incident
Los Angeles Co.[1]	No	No	No	Yes	Yes	Yes	No

Notes: (1) All facilities reported following the same testing policy or authorities reported the policy to be jurisdiction-wide
Source: HIV in Prisons and Jails, 1993 (released August 1995)

Inmates Known to be Positive for HIV

Jurisdiction	Number of Jail Inmates in Facilities Providing Data	Type of HIV Infection/AIDS Cases: Total	Asymptomatic	Symptomatic	Confirmed AIDS	HIV/AIDS Cases as a Percent of Tot. Custody Pop.
Los Angeles Co.	20,065	83	0	0	83	0.4

Source: HIV in Prisons and Jails, 1993 (released August, 1995)

DEATH PENALTY

Death Penalty Statistics

State	Prisoners Executed		Prisoners Under Sentence of Death					Avg. No. of Years on Death Row[4]
	1930-1995	1996[1]	Total[2]	White[3]	Black[3]	Hisp.	Women	
California	294	2	420	251	160	61	8	7.0

Notes: Data as of 12/31/95 unless otherwise noted; (1) Data as of 7/31/97; (2) Includes persons of other races; (3) Includes people of Hispanic origin; (4) Covers prisoners sentenced 1974 through 1995
Source: Bureau of Justice Statistics, Capital Punishment 1995 (released 12/96); Death Penalty Information Center Web Site, 9/30/97

Capital Offenses and Methods of Execution

Capital Offenses in California	Minimum Age for Imposition of Death Penalty	Mentally Retarded Excluded	Methods of Execution[1]
First-degree murder with special circumstances; train-wrecking; treason; perjury causing execution.	18	No	Lethal injection; lethal gas

Notes: Data as of 12/31/95 unless otherwise noted; (1) Data as of 7/31/97
Source: Bureau of Justice Statistics, Capital Punishment 1995 (released 12/96); Death Penalty Information Center Web Site, 9/30/97

LAWS

Statutory Provisions Relating to the Purchase, Ownership and Use of Handguns

Jurisdiction	Instant Background Check	Federal Waiting Period Applies[1]	State Waiting Period (days)	License or Permit to Purchase	Registration	Record of Sale Sent to Police	Concealed Carry Law
California	No	No	15	No	No	Yes	Yes[a]

Note: Data as of 1996; (1) The Federal 5-day waiting period for handgun purchases applies to states that don't have instant background checks, waiting period requirements, or licensing procedures exempting them from the Federal requirement; (a) Restrictively administered discretion by local authorities over permit issuance, or permits are unavailable and carrying is prohibited in most circumstances
Source: Sourcebook of Criminal Justice Statistics Online

Statutory Provisions Relating to Alcohol Use and Driving

Jurisdiction	Drinking Age	Blood Alcohol Concentration Levels as Evidence in State Courts[1]		Open Container Law[1]	Anti-Consumption Law[1]	Dram Shop Law[1]
		Illegal per se at 0.10%	Presumption at 0.10%			
California	21	(a)	(a)	Yes	Yes	Yes[b]

Note: Data as of January 1, 1997; (1) See Appendix C for an explanation of terms; (a) 0.08%; (b) Applies only to the actions of intoxicated minors
Source: Sourcebook of Criminal Justice Statistics Online

Statutory Provisions Relating to Curfews

Jurisdiction	Year Enacted	Latest Revision	Age Group(s)	Curfew Provisions
Los Angeles	1988	1989	17 and under	10 pm to dawn every night

Note: Data as of February 1996
Source: Sourcebook of Criminal Justice Statistics Online

Statutory Provisions Relating to Hate Crimes

Jurisdiction	Bias-Motivated Violence and Intimidation						Institutional Vandalism
	Civil Action	Criminal Penalty					
		Race/ Religion/ Ethnicity	Sexual Orientation	Mental/ Physical Disability	Gender	Age	
California	Yes	Yes	Yes	Yes	Yes	No	Yes

Source: Anti-Defamation League, 1997 Hate Crimes Laws

Lubbock, Texas

OVERVIEW

The total crime rate for the city decreased 20.4% between 1977 and 1996. During that same period, the violent crime rate increased 74.0% and the property crime rate decreased 27.8%.

Among violent crimes, the rates for: Murders decreased 62.8%; Forcible Rapes increased 32.6%; Robberies decreased 19.4%; and Aggravated Assaults increased 132.4%.

Among property crimes, the rates for: Burglaries decreased 54.3%; Larceny-Thefts decreased 15.7%; and Motor Vehicle Thefts increased 14.4%.

ANTI-CRIME PROGRAMS

Information not available at time of publication.

CRIME RISK

Your Chances of Becoming a Victim[1]

Area	Any Crime	Violent Crime					Property Crime			
		Any	Murder	Forcible Rape[2]	Robbery	Aggrav. Assault	Any	Burglary	Larceny -Theft	Motor Vehicle Theft
City	1:16	1:98	1:13,494	1:818	1:733	1:123	1:19	1:82	1:27	1:212

Note: (1) Figures have been calculated by dividing the population of the city by the number of crimes reported to the FBI during 1996 and are expressed as odds (eg. 1:20 should be read as 1 in 20). (2) Figures have been calculated by dividing the female population of the city by the number of forcible rapes reported to the FBI during 1996. The female population of the city was estimated by calculating the ratio of females to males reported in the 1990 Census and applying that ratio to 1996 population estimate.
Source: FBI Uniform Crime Reports 1996

CRIME STATISTICS

Total Crimes and Total Crime Rates: 1977 - 1996

Year	Number				Rate per 100,000 population			
	City	Suburbs[2]	MSA[1]	U.S.	City	Suburbs[3]	MSA[1]	U.S.
1977	13,339	1,446	14,785	10,984,500	8,035.5	5,130.0	7,613.8	5,077.6
1978	14,259	1,907	16,166	11,209,000	8,487.5	5,002.9	7,843.1	5,140.3
1979	13,332	1,809	15,141	12,249,500	7,679.0	5,767.6	7,386.5	5,565.5
1980	13,491	1,794	15,285	13,408,300	7,745.8	4,850.7	7,238.7	5,950.0
1981	15,418	1,782	17,200	13,423,800	8,501.1	4,627.1	7,822.6	5,858.2
1982	17,637	1,742	19,379	12,974,400	9,390.5	4,367.9	8,510.8	5,603.6
1983	17,647	1,927	19,574	12,108,600	9,130.5	4,695.5	8,353.7	5,175.0
1984	18,246	2,197	20,443	11,881,800	9,873.8	5,585.8	9,121.3	5,031.3
1985	17,579	2,139	19,718	12,431,400	9,617.2	5,266.0	8,826.1	5,207.1
1986	19,222	2,439	21,661	13,211,900	10,319.3	5,896.7	9,515.7	5,480.4
1987	18,594	2,664	21,258	13,508,700	9,911.7	7,047.6	9,431.4	5,550.0
1988	17,666	2,573	20,239	13,923,100	9,359.5	6,765.4	8,924.5	5,664.2
1989	14,411	2,284	16,695	14,251,400	7,592.8	5,964.4	7,319.4	5,741.0
1990	12,302	1,944	14,246	14,475,600	6,606.7	5,453.9	6,421.5	5,820.3
1991	12,442	2,050	14,492	14,872,900	6,542.3	5,631.6	6,395.9	5,897.8
1992	13,366	2,066	15,432	14,438,200	6,905.9	5,577.3	6,692.5	5,660.2
1993	12,353	1,837	14,190	14,144,800	6,446.0	5,017.5	6,216.8	5,484.4
1994	12,639	1,990	14,629	13,989,500	6,470.7	5,333.4	6,288.3	5,373.5
1995	13,406	2,120	15,526	13,862,700	6,766.3	5,898.2	6,633.0	5,275.9
1996	12,948	1,787	14,735	13,473,600	6,397.1	4,867.1	6,162.2	5,078.9

Notes: (1) Metropolitan Statistical Area - see Appendix A for areas included; (2) calculated by the editors using the following formula: (number of crimes in the MSA minus number of crimes in the city); (3) calculated by the editors using the following formula: ((number of crimes in the MSA minus number of crimes in the city) ÷ (population of the MSA minus population of the city)) x 100,000; n/a not avail.
Source: U.S. Department of Justice, FBI Uniform Crime Reports, 1977 - 1996

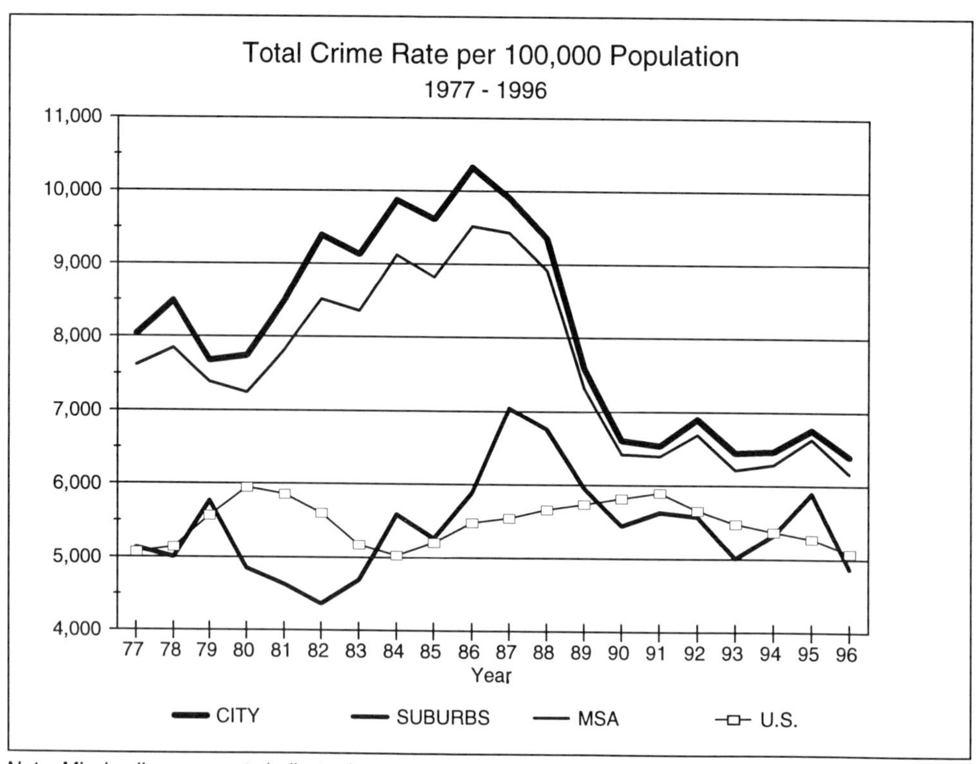

Note: Missing line segments indicate data not available.

Violent Crimes and Violent Crime Rates: 1977 - 1996

Year	Number				Rate per 100,000 population			
	City	Suburbs[2]	MSA[1]	U.S.	City	Suburbs[3]	MSA[1]	U.S.
1977	974	111	1,085	1,029,580	586.7	393.8	558.7	475.9
1978	1,043	104	1,147	1,085,550	620.8	272.8	556.5	497.8
1979	1,101	112	1,213	1,208,030	634.2	357.1	591.8	548.9
1980	1,199	139	1,338	1,344,520	688.4	375.8	633.7	596.6
1981	1,598	115	1,713	1,361,820	881.1	298.6	779.1	594.3
1982	1,798	116	1,914	1,322,390	957.3	290.9	840.6	571.1
1983	1,709	96	1,805	1,258,090	884.2	233.9	770.3	537.7
1984	1,706	99	1,805	1,273,280	923.2	251.7	805.4	539.2
1985	1,522	166	1,688	1,328,800	832.7	408.7	755.6	556.6
1986	1,741	180	1,921	1,489,170	934.7	435.2	843.9	617.7
1987	1,107	124	1,231	1,484,000	590.1	328.0	546.1	609.7
1988	997	133	1,130	1,566,220	528.2	349.7	498.3	637.2
1989	978	138	1,116	1,646,040	515.3	360.4	489.3	663.1
1990	1,116	164	1,280	1,820,130	599.3	460.1	577.0	731.8
1991	1,065	149	1,214	1,911,770	560.0	409.3	535.8	758.1
1992	1,223	237	1,460	1,932,270	631.9	639.8	633.2	757.5
1993	1,275	190	1,465	1,926,020	665.3	519.0	641.8	746.8
1994	1,349	198	1,547	1,857,670	690.6	530.7	665.0	713.6
1995	1,905	224	2,129	1,798,790	961.5	623.2	909.6	684.6
1996	2,066	150	2,216	1,682,280	1,020.7	408.5	926.7	634.1

Notes: Violent crimes include murder, forcible rape, robbery and aggravated assault; n/a not available; (1) Metropolitan Statistical Area - see Appendix A for areas included; (2) calculated by the editors using the following formula: (number of crimes in the MSA minus number of crimes in the city); (3) calculated by the editors using the following formula: ((number of crimes in the MSA minus number of crimes in the city) ÷ (population of the MSA minus population of the city)) x 100,000
Source: U.S. Department of Justice, FBI Uniform Crime Reports, 1977 - 1996

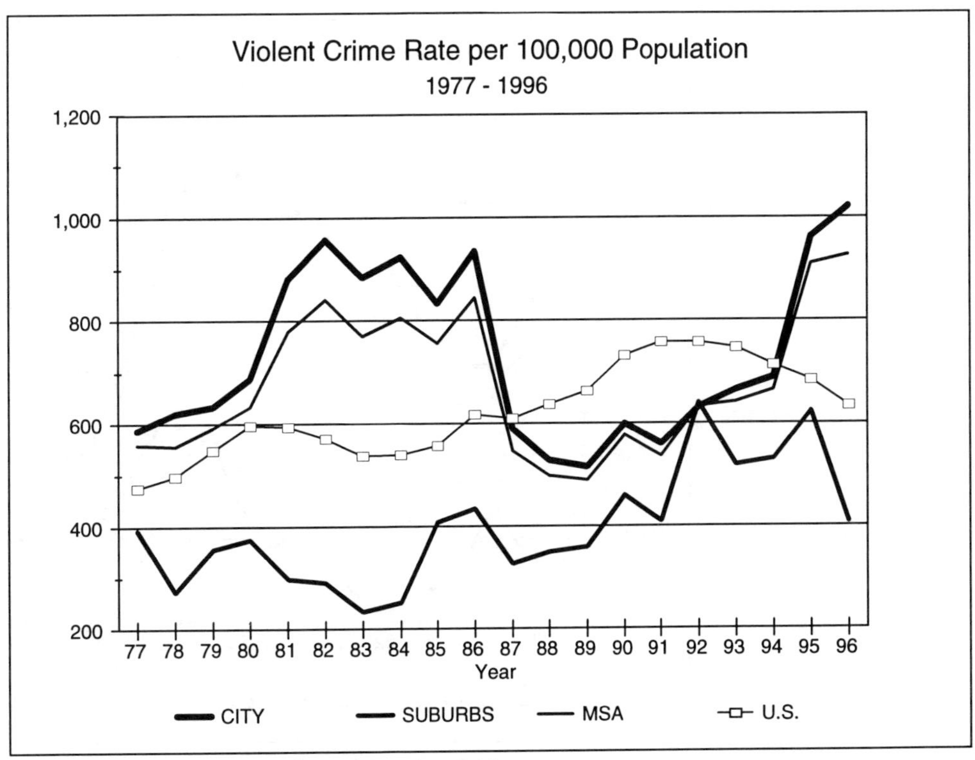

Note: Missing line segments indicate data not available.

Property Crimes and Property Crime Rates: 1977 - 1996

Year	Number				Rate per 100,000 population			
	City	Suburbs[2]	MSA[1]	U.S.	City	Suburbs[3]	MSA[1]	U.S.
1977	12,365	1,335	13,700	9,955,000	7,448.8	4,736.2	7,055.1	4,601.7
1978	13,216	1,803	15,019	10,123,400	7,866.7	4,730.0	7,286.6	4,642.5
1979	12,231	1,697	13,928	11,041,500	7,044.9	5,410.5	6,794.8	5,016.6
1980	12,292	1,655	13,947	12,063,700	7,057.4	4,474.9	6,605.1	5,353.3
1981	13,820	1,667	15,487	12,061,900	7,620.0	4,328.5	7,043.5	5,263.9
1982	15,839	1,626	17,465	11,652,000	8,433.2	4,077.0	7,670.2	5,032.5
1983	15,938	1,831	17,769	10,850,500	8,246.3	4,461.6	7,583.4	4,637.4
1984	16,540	2,098	18,638	10,608,500	8,950.6	5,334.1	8,315.9	4,492.1
1985	16,057	1,973	18,030	11,102,600	8,784.5	4,857.3	8,070.5	4,650.5
1986	17,481	2,259	19,740	11,722,700	9,384.7	5,461.5	8,671.8	4,862.6
1987	17,487	2,540	20,027	12,024,700	9,321.6	6,719.6	8,885.3	4,940.3
1988	16,669	2,440	19,109	12,356,900	8,831.3	6,415.6	8,426.2	5,027.1
1989	13,433	2,146	15,579	12,605,400	7,077.6	5,604.0	6,830.2	5,077.9
1990	11,186	1,780	12,966	12,655,500	6,007.3	4,993.8	5,844.5	5,088.5
1991	11,377	1,901	13,278	12,961,100	5,982.3	5,222.2	5,860.2	5,139.7
1992	12,143	1,829	13,972	12,505,900	6,274.0	4,937.5	6,059.3	4,902.7
1993	11,078	1,647	12,725	12,218,800	5,780.7	4,498.5	5,575.0	4,737.6
1994	11,290	1,792	13,082	12,131,900	5,780.1	4,802.7	5,623.3	4,660.0
1995	11,501	1,896	13,397	12,063,900	5,804.8	5,275.0	5,723.5	4,591.3
1996	10,882	1,637	12,519	11,791,300	5,376.4	4,458.5	5,235.5	4,444.8

Notes: Property crimes include burglary, larceny-theft and motor vehicle theft; n/a not available; (1) Metropolitan Statistical Area - see Appendix A for areas included; (2) calculated by the editors using the following formula: (number of crimes in the MSA minus number of crimes in the city); (3) calculated by the editors using the following formula: ((number of crimes in the MSA minus number of crimes in the city) ÷ (population of the MSA minus population of the city)) x 100,000
Source: U.S. Department of Justice, FBI Uniform Crime Reports, 1977 - 1996

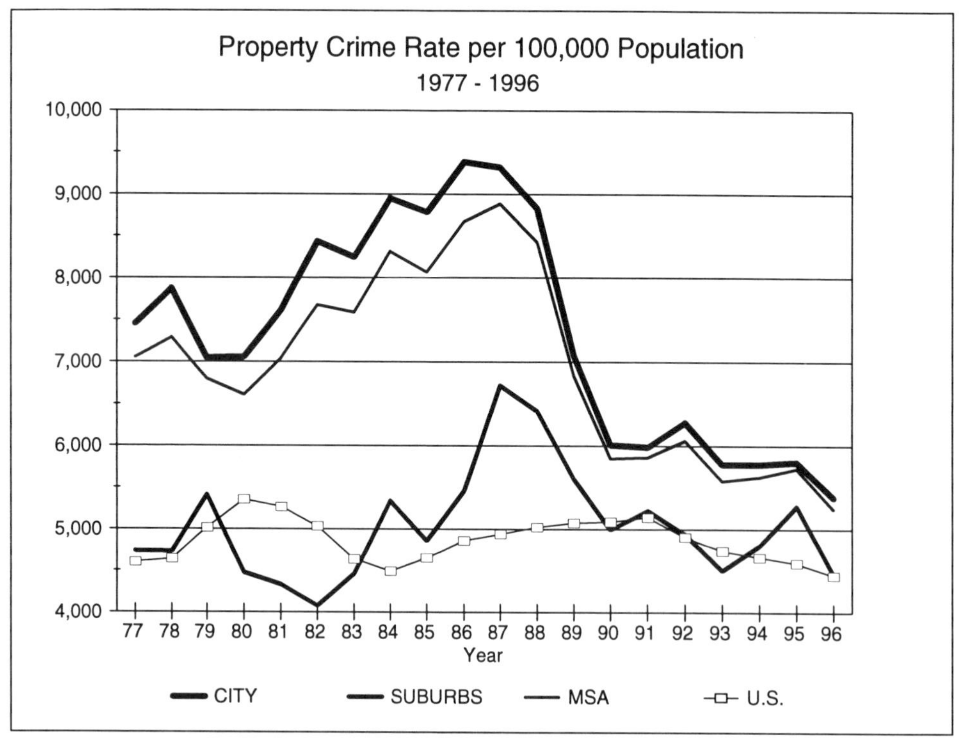

Note: Missing line segments indicate data not available.

Murders and Murder Rates: 1977 - 1996

Year	Number				Rate per 100,000 population			
	City	Suburbs[2]	MSA[1]	U.S.	City	Suburbs[3]	MSA[1]	U.S.
1977	33	4	37	19,120	19.9	14.2	19.1	8.8
1978	31	8	39	19,560	18.5	21.0	18.9	9.0
1979	31	14	45	21,460	17.9	44.6	22.0	9.7
1980	28	8	36	23,040	16.1	21.6	17.0	10.2
1981	34	2	36	22,520	18.7	5.2	16.4	9.8
1982	24	2	26	21,010	12.8	5.0	11.4	9.1
1983	35	3	38	19,310	18.1	7.3	16.2	8.3
1984	27	2	29	18,690	14.6	5.1	12.9	7.9
1985	20	2	22	18,980	10.9	4.9	9.8	7.9
1986	28	2	30	20,610	15.0	4.8	13.2	8.6
1987	24	5	29	20,100	12.8	13.2	12.9	8.3
1988	24	1	25	20,680	12.7	2.6	11.0	8.4
1989	15	1	16	21,500	7.9	2.6	7.0	8.7
1990	16	0	16	23,440	8.6	0.0	7.2	9.4
1991	18	5	23	24,700	9.5	13.7	10.2	9.8
1992	14	3	17	23,760	7.2	8.1	7.4	9.3
1993	17	2	19	24,530	8.9	5.5	8.3	9.5
1994	20	6	26	23,330	10.2	16.1	11.2	9.0
1995	19	1	20	21,610	9.6	2.8	8.5	8.2
1996	15	0	15	19,650	7.4	0.0	6.3	7.4

Notes: (1) Metropolitan Statistical Area - see Appendix A for areas included; (2) calculated by the editors using the following formula: (number of crimes in the MSA minus number of crimes in the city); (3) calculated by the editors using the following formula: ((number of crimes in the MSA minus number of crimes in the city) ÷ (population of the MSA minus population of the city)) x 100,000; n/a not avail.
Source: U.S. Department of Justice, FBI Uniform Crime Reports, 1977 - 1996

Forcible Rapes and Forcible Rape Rates: 1977 - 1996

Year	Number				Rate per 100,000 population			
	City	Suburbs[2]	MSA[1]	U.S.	City	Suburbs[3]	MSA[1]	U.S.
1977	78	15	93	63,500	47.0	53.2	47.9	29.4
1978	111	18	129	67,610	66.1	47.2	62.6	31.0
1979	127	13	140	76,390	73.1	41.4	68.3	34.7
1980	121	16	137	82,990	69.5	43.3	64.9	36.8
1981	143	18	161	82,500	78.8	46.7	73.2	36.0
1982	150	10	160	78,770	79.9	25.1	70.3	34.0
1983	125	4	129	78,920	64.7	9.7	55.1	33.7
1984	100	11	111	84,230	54.1	28.0	49.5	35.7
1985	96	17	113	88,670	52.5	41.9	50.6	37.1
1986	105	28	133	91,460	56.4	67.7	58.4	37.9
1987	130	29	159	91,110	69.3	76.7	70.5	37.4
1988	106	36	142	92,490	56.2	94.7	62.6	37.6
1989	119	38	157	94,500	62.7	99.2	68.8	38.1
1990	160	26	186	102,560	85.9	72.9	83.8	41.2
1991	137	6	143	106,590	72.0	16.5	63.1	42.3
1992	158	12	170	109,060	81.6	32.4	73.7	42.8
1993	136	19	155	106,010	71.0	51.9	67.9	41.1
1994	139	16	155	102,220	71.2	42.9	66.6	39.3
1995	122	15	137	97,470	61.6	41.7	58.5	37.1
1996	126	14	140	95,770	62.3	38.1	58.5	36.1

Notes: (1) Metropolitan Statistical Area - see Appendix A for areas included; (2) calculated by the editors using the following formula: (number of crimes in the MSA minus number of crimes in the city); (3) calculated by the editors using the following formula: ((number of crimes in the MSA minus number of crimes in the city) ÷ (population of the MSA minus population of the city)) x 100,000; n/a not avail.
Source: U.S. Department of Justice, FBI Uniform Crime Reports, 1977 - 1996

Robberies and Robbery Rates: 1977 - 1996

Year	Number				Rate per 100,000 population			
	City	Suburbs[2]	MSA[1]	U.S.	City	Suburbs[3]	MSA[1]	U.S.
1977	281	12	293	412,610	169.3	42.6	150.9	190.7
1978	299	18	317	426,930	178.0	47.2	153.8	195.8
1979	232	7	239	480,700	133.6	22.3	116.6	218.4
1980	223	8	231	565,840	128.0	21.6	109.4	251.1
1981	314	9	323	592,910	173.1	23.4	146.9	258.7
1982	315	11	326	553,130	167.7	27.6	143.2	238.9
1983	303	13	316	506,570	156.8	31.7	134.9	216.5
1984	341	13	354	485,010	184.5	33.1	157.9	205.4
1985	280	9	289	497,870	153.2	22.2	129.4	208.5
1986	324	15	339	542,780	173.9	36.3	148.9	225.1
1987	359	13	372	517,700	191.4	34.4	165.0	212.7
1988	327	15	342	542,970	173.2	39.4	150.8	220.9
1989	268	11	279	578,330	141.2	28.7	122.3	233.0
1990	304	10	314	639,270	163.3	28.1	141.5	257.0
1991	276	9	285	687,730	145.1	24.7	125.8	272.7
1992	352	11	363	672,480	181.9	29.7	157.4	263.6
1993	282	5	287	659,870	147.2	13.7	125.7	255.9
1994	324	6	330	618,950	165.9	16.1	141.9	237.7
1995	297	8	305	580,510	149.9	22.3	130.3	220.9
1996	276	12	288	537,050	136.4	32.7	120.4	202.4

Notes: (1) Metropolitan Statistical Area - see Appendix A for areas included; (2) calculated by the editors using the following formula: (number of crimes in the MSA minus number of crimes in the city); (3) calculated by the editors using the following formula: ((number of crimes in the MSA minus number of crimes in the city) ÷ (population of the MSA minus population of the city)) x 100,000; n/a not avail.
Source: U.S. Department of Justice, FBI Uniform Crime Reports, 1977 - 1996

Aggravated Assaults and Aggravated Assault Rates: 1977 - 1996

Year	Number				Rate per 100,000 population			
	City	Suburbs[2]	MSA[1]	U.S.	City	Suburbs[3]	MSA[1]	U.S.
1977	582	80	662	534,350	350.6	283.8	340.9	247.0
1978	602	60	662	571,460	358.3	157.4	321.2	262.1
1979	711	78	789	629,480	409.5	248.7	384.9	286.0
1980	827	107	934	672,650	474.8	289.3	442.3	298.5
1981	1,107	86	1,193	663,900	610.4	223.3	542.6	289.7
1982	1,309	93	1,402	669,480	697.0	233.2	615.7	289.2
1983	1,246	76	1,322	653,290	644.7	185.2	564.2	279.2
1984	1,238	73	1,311	685,350	669.9	185.6	584.9	290.2
1985	1,126	138	1,264	723,250	616.0	339.7	565.8	302.9
1986	1,284	135	1,419	834,320	689.3	326.4	623.4	346.1
1987	594	77	671	855,090	316.6	203.7	297.7	351.3
1988	540	81	621	910,090	286.1	213.0	273.8	370.2
1989	576	88	664	951,710	303.5	229.8	291.1	383.4
1990	636	128	764	1,054,860	341.6	359.1	344.4	424.1
1991	634	129	763	1,092,740	333.4	354.4	336.7	433.3
1992	699	211	910	1,126,970	361.2	569.6	394.6	441.8
1993	840	164	1,004	1,135,610	438.3	447.9	439.9	440.3
1994	866	170	1,036	1,113,180	443.4	455.6	445.3	427.6
1995	1,467	200	1,667	1,099,210	740.4	556.4	712.2	418.3
1996	1,649	124	1,773	1,029,810	814.7	337.7	741.5	388.2

Notes: (1) Metropolitan Statistical Area - see Appendix A for areas included; (2) calculated by the editors using the following formula: (number of crimes in the MSA minus number of crimes in the city); (3) calculated by the editors using the following formula: ((number of crimes in the MSA minus number of crimes in the city) ÷ (population of the MSA minus population of the city)) x 100,000; n/a not avail.
Source: U.S. Department of Justice, FBI Uniform Crime Reports, 1977 - 1996

Burglaries and Burglary Rates: 1977 - 1996

Year	Number				Rate per 100,000 population			
	City	Suburbs[2]	MSA[1]	U.S.	City	Suburbs[3]	MSA[1]	U.S.
1977	4,412	451	4,863	3,071,500	2,657.8	1,600.0	2,504.3	1,419.8
1978	4,119	600	4,719	3,128,300	2,451.8	1,574.1	2,289.5	1,434.6
1979	4,150	537	4,687	3,327,700	2,390.3	1,712.1	2,286.6	1,511.9
1980	3,798	452	4,250	3,795,200	2,180.6	1,222.2	2,012.7	1,684.1
1981	4,649	482	5,131	3,779,700	2,563.4	1,251.6	2,333.6	1,649.5
1982	5,196	450	5,646	3,447,100	2,766.5	1,128.3	2,479.6	1,488.8
1983	5,139	602	5,741	3,129,900	2,658.9	1,466.9	2,450.1	1,337.7
1984	6,006	786	6,792	2,984,400	3,250.1	1,998.4	3,030.5	1,263.7
1985	5,679	688	6,367	3,073,300	3,106.9	1,693.8	2,850.0	1,287.3
1986	6,146	705	6,851	3,241,400	3,299.5	1,704.5	3,009.7	1,344.6
1987	5,891	912	6,803	3,236,200	3,140.3	2,412.7	3,018.2	1,329.6
1988	4,687	826	5,513	3,218,100	2,483.2	2,171.9	2,431.0	1,309.2
1989	3,520	613	4,133	3,168,200	1,854.6	1,600.8	1,812.0	1,276.3
1990	2,893	450	3,343	3,073,900	1,553.7	1,262.5	1,506.9	1,235.9
1991	3,034	464	3,498	3,157,200	1,595.3	1,274.7	1,543.8	1,252.0
1992	2,919	391	3,310	2,979,900	1,508.2	1,055.5	1,435.5	1,168.2
1993	2,541	351	2,892	2,834,800	1,325.9	958.7	1,267.0	1,099.2
1994	2,499	335	2,834	2,712,800	1,279.4	897.8	1,218.2	1,042.0
1995	2,441	323	2,764	2,593,800	1,232.0	898.6	1,180.8	987.1
1996	2,456	306	2,762	2,501,500	1,213.4	833.4	1,155.1	943.0

Notes: (1) Metropolitan Statistical Area - see Appendix A for areas included; (2) calculated by the editors using the following formula: (number of crimes in the MSA minus number of crimes in the city); (3) calculated by the editors using the following formula: ((number of crimes in the MSA minus number of crimes in the city) ÷ (population of the MSA minus population of the city)) x 100,000; n/a not avail.
Source: U.S. Department of Justice, FBI Uniform Crime Reports, 1977 - 1996

Larceny-Thefts and Larceny-Theft Rates: 1977 - 1996

Year	Number				Rate per 100,000 population			
	City	Suburbs[2]	MSA[1]	U.S.	City	Suburbs[3]	MSA[1]	U.S.
1977	7,269	823	8,092	5,905,700	4,378.9	2,919.8	4,167.1	2,729.9
1978	8,223	1,156	9,379	5,991,000	4,894.6	3,032.7	4,550.3	2,747.4
1979	7,294	1,060	8,354	6,601,000	4,201.2	3,379.6	4,075.5	2,999.1
1980	7,724	1,118	8,842	7,136,900	4,434.7	3,022.9	4,187.4	3,167.0
1981	8,378	1,109	9,487	7,194,400	4,619.4	2,879.6	4,314.7	3,139.7
1982	9,811	1,096	10,907	7,142,500	5,223.7	2,748.1	4,790.1	3,084.8
1983	10,030	1,166	11,196	6,712,800	5,189.5	2,841.2	4,778.2	2,868.9
1984	9,680	1,225	10,905	6,591,900	5,238.3	3,114.5	4,865.6	2,791.3
1985	9,662	1,192	10,854	6,926,400	5,285.9	2,934.6	4,858.4	2,901.2
1986	10,458	1,435	11,893	7,257,200	5,614.4	3,469.4	5,224.6	3,010.3
1987	10,783	1,531	12,314	7,499,900	5,748.0	4,050.3	5,463.3	3,081.3
1988	11,200	1,529	12,729	7,705,900	5,933.8	4,020.3	5,612.9	3,134.9
1989	9,222	1,437	10,659	7,872,400	4,858.9	3,752.5	4,673.1	3,171.3
1990	7,516	1,263	8,779	7,945,700	4,036.4	3,543.4	3,957.2	3,194.8
1991	7,691	1,407	9,098	8,142,200	4,044.1	3,865.2	4,015.3	3,228.8
1992	8,506	1,373	9,879	7,915,200	4,394.8	3,706.5	4,284.3	3,103.0
1993	7,927	1,248	9,175	7,820,900	4,136.4	3,408.7	4,019.7	3,032.4
1994	7,926	1,400	9,326	7,879,800	4,057.8	3,752.1	4,008.8	3,026.7
1995	8,086	1,487	9,573	7,997,700	4,081.2	4,137.1	4,089.8	3,043.8
1996	7,472	1,260	8,732	7,894,600	3,691.6	3,431.7	3,651.7	2,975.9

Notes: (1) Metropolitan Statistical Area - see Appendix A for areas included; (2) calculated by the editors using the following formula: (number of crimes in the MSA minus number of crimes in the city); (3) calculated by the editors using the following formula: ((number of crimes in the MSA minus number of crimes in the city) ÷ (population of the MSA minus population of the city)) x 100,000; n/a not avail.
Source: U.S. Department of Justice, FBI Uniform Crime Reports, 1977 - 1996

Motor Vehicle Thefts and Motor Vehicle Theft Rates: 1977 - 1996

Year	Number				Rate per 100,000 population			
	City	Suburbs[2]	MSA[1]	U.S.	City	Suburbs[3]	MSA[1]	U.S.
1977	684	61	745	977,700	412.0	216.4	383.7	451.9
1978	874	47	921	1,004,100	520.2	123.3	446.8	460.5
1979	787	100	887	1,112,800	453.3	318.8	432.7	505.6
1980	770	85	855	1,131,700	442.1	229.8	404.9	502.2
1981	793	76	869	1,087,800	437.2	197.3	395.2	474.7
1982	832	80	912	1,062,400	443.0	200.6	400.5	458.8
1983	769	63	832	1,007,900	397.9	153.5	355.1	430.8
1984	854	87	941	1,032,200	462.1	221.2	419.9	437.1
1985	716	93	809	1,102,900	391.7	229.0	362.1	462.0
1986	877	119	996	1,224,100	470.8	287.7	437.5	507.8
1987	813	97	910	1,288,700	433.4	256.6	403.7	529.4
1988	782	85	867	1,432,900	414.3	223.5	382.3	582.9
1989	691	96	787	1,564,800	364.1	250.7	345.0	630.4
1990	777	67	844	1,635,900	417.3	188.0	380.4	657.8
1991	652	30	682	1,661,700	342.8	82.4	301.0	659.0
1992	718	65	783	1,610,800	371.0	175.5	339.6	631.5
1993	610	48	658	1,563,100	318.3	131.1	288.3	606.1
1994	865	57	922	1,539,300	442.8	152.8	396.3	591.3
1995	974	86	1,060	1,472,400	491.6	239.3	452.9	560.4
1996	954	71	1,025	1,395,200	471.3	193.4	428.7	525.9

Notes: (1) Metropolitan Statistical Area - see Appendix A for areas included; (2) calculated by the editors using the following formula: (number of crimes in the MSA minus number of crimes in the city); (3) calculated by the editors using the following formula: ((number of crimes in the MSA minus number of crimes in the city) ÷ (population of the MSA minus population of the city)) x 100,000; n/a not avail.
Source: U.S. Department of Justice, FBI Uniform Crime Reports, 1977 - 1996

HATE CRIMES

Criminal Incidents by Bias Motivation

Area	Race	Ethnicity	Religion	Sexual Orientation
Lubbock	0	0	0	0

Notes: Figures include both violent and property crimes. Law enforcement agencies must have submitted data for at least one quarter of calendar year 1995 to be included in this report, therefore figures shown may not represent complete 12-month totals; n/a not available
Source: U.S. Department of Justice, FBI Uniform Crime Reports, Hate Crime Statistics 1995

LAW ENFORCEMENT

Full-Time Law Enforcement Employees

Jurisdiction	Police Employees			Police Officers per 100,000 population
	Total	Officers	Civilians	
Lubbock	340	299	41	147.7

Notes: Data as of October 31, 1996
Source: U.S. Department of Justice, FBI Uniform Crime Reports, 1996

CORRECTIONS

Federal Correctional Facilities

Type	Year Opened	Security Level	Sex of Inmates	Rated Capacity	Population on 7/1/95	Number of Staff
None listed						

Notes: Data as of 1995
Source: Bureau of Justice Statistics, Sourcebook of Criminal Justice Statistics Online

City/County/Regional Correctional Facilities

Name	Year Opened	Year Renov.	Rated Capacity	1995 Pop.	Number of COs[1]	Number of Staff	ACA[2] Accred.
Lubbock County Jail	1981	1990	733	n/a	n/a	n/a	No

Notes: Data as of April 1996; (1) Correctional Officers; (2) American Correctional Assn. Accreditation
Source: American Correctional Association, 1996-1998 National Jail and Adult Detention Directory

Private Adult Correctional Facilities

Name	Date Opened	Rated Capacity	Present Pop.	Security Level	Facility Construct.	Expans. Plans	ACA[1] Accred.
None listed							

Notes: Data as of December 1996; (1) American Correctional Association Accreditation
Source: University of Florida, Center for Studies in Criminology and Law, Private Adult Correctional Facility Census, 10th Ed., March 15, 1997

Characteristics of Shock Incarceration Programs

Jurisdiction	Year Program Began	Number of Camps	Average Num. of Inmates	Number of Beds	Program Length	Voluntary/ Mandatory
Texas	1989	2	250	500 male; 20 female	75 to 90 days	Mandatory

Note: Data as of July 1996;
Source: Sourcebook of Criminal Justice Statistics Online

DEATH PENALTY

Death Penalty Statistics

State	Prisoners Executed		Prisoners Under Sentence of Death					Avg. No. of Years on Death Row[4]
	1930-1995	1996[1]	Total[2]	White[3]	Black[3]	Hisp.	Women	
Texas	401	3	404	241	158	68	6	6.5

Notes: Data as of 12/31/95 unless otherwise noted; (1) Data as of 7/31/97; (2) Includes persons of other races; (3) Includes people of Hispanic origin; (4) Covers prisoners sentenced 1974 through 1995
Source: Bureau of Justice Statistics, Capital Punishment 1995 (released 12/96); Death Penalty Information Center Web Site, 9/30/97

Capital Offenses and Methods of Execution

Capital Offenses in Texas	Minimum Age for Imposition of Death Penalty	Mentally Retarded Excluded	Methods of Execution[1]
Criminal homicide with 1 of 8 aggravating circumstances.	17	No	Lethal injection

Notes: Data as of 12/31/95 unless otherwise noted; (1) Data as of 7/31/97
Source: Bureau of Justice Statistics, Capital Punishment 1995 (released 12/96); Death Penalty Information Center Web Site, 9/30/97

LAWS

Statutory Provisions Relating to the Purchase, Ownership and Use of Handguns

Jurisdiction	Instant Background Check	Federal Waiting Period Applies[1]	State Waiting Period (days)	License or Permit to Purchase	Regis-tration	Record of Sale Sent to Police	Concealed Carry Law
Texas	No	Yes[a]	No	No	No	No	Yes[b]

Note: Data as of 1996; (1) The Federal 5-day waiting period for handgun purchases applies to states that don't have instant background checks, waiting period requirements, or licensing procedures exempting them from the Federal requirement; (a) The Federal waiting period does not apply to a person holding a valid permit or license to carry a firearm, issued within 5 years of proposed purchase; (b) "Shall issue" permit system, liberally administered discretion by local authorities over permit issuance, or no permit required
Source: Sourcebook of Criminal Justice Statistics Online

Statutory Provisions Relating to Alcohol Use and Driving

Jurisdiction	Drinking Age	Blood Alcohol Concentration Levels as Evidence in State Courts[1]		Open Container Law[1]	Anti-Consump-tion Law[1]	Dram Shop Law[1]
		Illegal per se at 0.10%	Presumption at 0.10%			
Texas	21	Yes	No	No	Yes[a]	Yes[b]

Note: Data as of January 1, 1997; (1) See Appendix C for an explanation of terms; (a) Applies to drivers only; (b) Statutory law has limited dram shop actions
Source: Sourcebook of Criminal Justice Statistics Online

Statutory Provisions Relating to Hate Crimes

Jurisdiction	Bias-Motivated Violence and Intimidation						Institutional Vandalism
	Civil Action	Criminal Penalty					
		Race/ Religion/ Ethnicity	Sexual Orientation	Mental/ Physical Disability	Gender	Age	
Texas	No	No	No	No	No	No	Yes

Source: Anti-Defamation League, 1997 Hate Crimes Laws

Madison, Wisconsin

OVERVIEW

The total crime rate for the city decreased 35.9% between 1977 and 1996. During that same period, the violent crime rate increased 193.5% and the property crime rate decreased 40.2%.

Among violent crimes, the rates for: Murders decreased 79.2%; Forcible Rapes increased 8.9%; Robberies increased 109.6%; and Aggravated Assaults increased 747.7%.

Among property crimes, the rates for: Burglaries decreased 51.3%; Larceny-Thefts decreased 39.9%; and Motor Vehicle Thefts increased 7.5%.

ANTI-CRIME PROGRAMS

Information not available at time of publication.

CRIME RISK

Your Chances of Becoming a Victim[1]

Area	Any Crime	Violent Crime					Property Crime			
		Any	Murder	Forcible Rape[2]	Robbery	Aggrav. Assault	Any	Burglary	Larceny -Theft	Motor Vehicle Theft
City	1:22	1:256	1:197,572	1:1,341	1:661	1:498	1:24	1:142	1:31	1:308

Note: (1) Figures have been calculated by dividing the population of the city by the number of crimes reported to the FBI during 1996 and are expressed as odds (eg. 1:20 should be read as 1 in 20). (2) Figures have been calculated by dividing the female population of the city by the number of forcible rapes reported to the FBI during 1996. The female population of the city was estimated by calculating the ratio of females to males reported in the 1990 Census and applying that ratio to 1996 population estimate.
Source: FBI Uniform Crime Reports 1996

CRIME STATISTICS

Total Crimes and Total Crime Rates: 1977 - 1996

Year	Number				Rate per 100,000 population			
	City	Suburbs[2]	MSA[1]	U.S.	City	Suburbs[3]	MSA[1]	U.S.
1977	12,136	6,540	18,676	10,984,500	7,181.1	4,462.9	5,918.7	5,077.6
1978	12,294	6,521	18,815	11,209,000	7,231.8	4,325.5	5,865.8	5,140.3
1979	13,663	7,955	21,618	12,249,500	7,958.1	5,297.3	6,716.6	5,565.5
1980	14,796	8,796	23,592	13,408,300	8,721.9	5,894.5	7,398.7	5,950.0
1981	14,898	8,373	23,271	13,423,800	8,674.4	5,542.2	7,208.6	5,858.2
1982	12,623	6,532	19,155	12,974,400	7,309.7	4,444.9	5,992.6	5,603.6
1983	12,486	5,818	18,304	12,108,600	7,251.7	3,970.8	5,743.4	5,175.0
1984	12,322	6,196	18,518	11,881,800	7,126.7	4,031.8	5,670.3	5,031.3
1985	12,358	6,034	18,392	12,431,400	7,224.7	3,864.9	5,621.4	5,207.1
1986	11,161	5,647	16,808	13,211,900	6,510.8	3,611.2	5,127.6	5,480.4
1987	11,960	5,441	17,401	13,508,700	6,770.8	3,334.4	5,120.6	5,550.0
1988	11,783	5,407	17,190	13,923,100	6,582.3	3,269.7	4,991.6	5,664.2
1989	12,556	5,873	18,429	14,251,400	7,028.6	3,490.5	5,312.5	5,741.0
1990	12,620	6,067	18,687	14,475,600	6,598.3	3,589.8	5,187.0	5,820.3
1991	12,884	6,691	19,575	14,872,900	6,650.3	3,908.7	5,364.2	5,897.8
1992	11,508	7,087	18,595	14,438,200	5,878.4	4,092.9	5,040.4	5,660.2
1993	10,616	6,479	17,095	14,144,800	5,391.0	3,604.2	4,538.3	5,484.4
1994	9,619	6,212	15,831	13,989,500	4,842.5	3,425.9	4,166.5	5,373.5
1995	9,287	6,079	15,366	13,862,700	4,734.5	3,198.0	3,978.3	5,275.9
1996	9,096	6,826	15,922	13,473,600	4,603.9	3,565.5	4,092.8	5,078.9

Notes: (1) Metropolitan Statistical Area - see Appendix A for areas included; (2) calculated by the editors using the following formula: (number of crimes in the MSA minus number of crimes in the city); (3) calculated by the editors using the following formula: ((number of crimes in the MSA minus number of crimes in the city) ÷ (population of the MSA minus population of the city)) x 100,000; n/a not avail.
Source: U.S. Department of Justice, FBI Uniform Crime Reports, 1977 - 1996

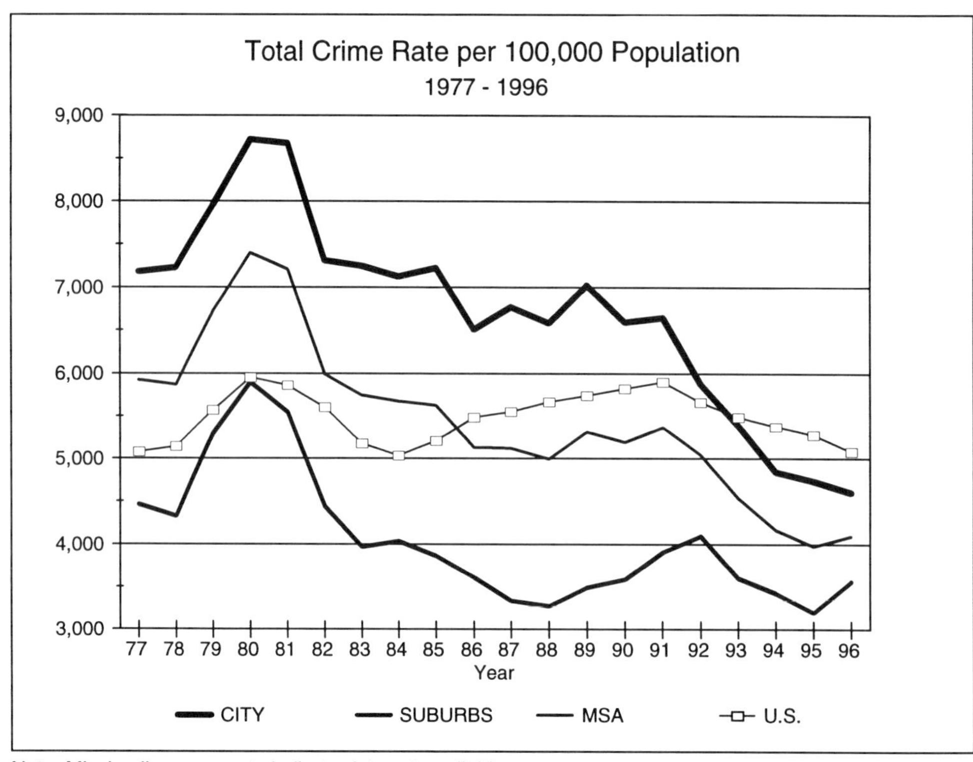

Note: Missing line segments indicate data not available.

Violent Crimes and Violent Crime Rates: 1977 - 1996

Year	Number				Rate per 100,000 population			
	City	Suburbs[2]	MSA[1]	U.S.	City	Suburbs[3]	MSA[1]	U.S.
1977	225	184	409	1,029,580	133.1	125.6	129.6	475.9
1978	230	176	406	1,085,550	135.3	116.7	126.6	497.8
1979	342	229	571	1,208,030	199.2	152.5	177.4	548.9
1980	435	240	675	1,344,520	256.4	160.8	211.7	596.6
1981	463	253	716	1,361,820	269.6	167.5	221.8	594.3
1982	419	219	638	1,322,390	242.6	149.0	199.6	571.1
1983	433	201	634	1,258,090	251.5	137.2	198.9	537.7
1984	439	230	669	1,273,280	253.9	149.7	204.9	539.2
1985	445	227	672	1,328,800	260.2	145.4	205.4	556.6
1986	458	283	741	1,489,170	267.2	181.0	226.1	617.7
1987	377	227	604	1,484,000	213.4	139.1	177.7	609.7
1988	440	283	723	1,566,220	245.8	171.1	209.9	637.2
1989	504	301	805	1,646,040	282.1	178.9	232.1	663.1
1990	596	430	1,026	1,820,130	311.6	254.4	284.8	731.8
1991	770	471	1,241	1,911,770	397.5	275.1	340.1	758.1
1992	713	473	1,186	1,932,270	364.2	273.2	321.5	757.5
1993	631	481	1,112	1,926,020	320.4	267.6	295.2	746.8
1994	624	439	1,063	1,857,670	314.1	242.1	279.8	713.6
1995	617	384	1,001	1,798,790	314.5	202.0	259.2	684.6
1996	772	373	1,145	1,682,280	390.7	194.8	294.3	634.1

Notes: Violent crimes include murder, forcible rape, robbery and aggravated assault; n/a not available; (1) Metropolitan Statistical Area - see Appendix A for areas included; (2) calculated by the editors using the following formula: (number of crimes in the MSA minus number of crimes in the city); (3) calculated by the editors using the following formula: ((number of crimes in the MSA minus number of crimes in the city) ÷ (population of the MSA minus population of the city)) x 100,000
Source: U.S. Department of Justice, FBI Uniform Crime Reports, 1977 - 1996

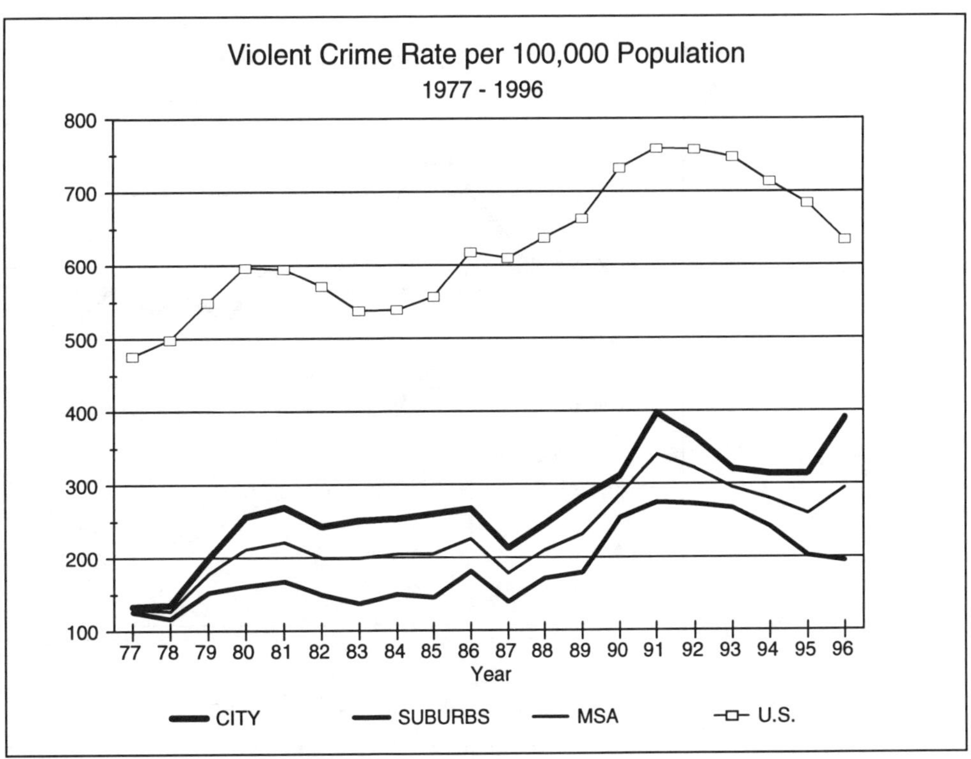

Note: Missing line segments indicate data not available.

Property Crimes and Property Crime Rates: 1977 - 1996

Year	Number				Rate per 100,000 population			
	City	Suburbs[2]	MSA[1]	U.S.	City	Suburbs[3]	MSA[1]	U.S.
1977	11,911	6,356	18,267	9,955,000	7,047.9	4,337.4	5,789.1	4,601.7
1978	12,064	6,345	18,409	10,123,400	7,096.5	4,208.8	5,739.2	4,642.5
1979	13,321	7,726	21,047	11,041,500	7,758.9	5,144.8	6,539.2	5,016.6
1980	14,361	8,556	22,917	12,063,700	8,465.5	5,733.6	7,187.0	5,353.3
1981	14,435	8,120	22,555	12,061,900	8,404.9	5,374.8	6,986.8	5,263.9
1982	12,204	6,313	18,517	11,652,000	7,067.1	4,295.8	5,793.0	5,032.5
1983	12,053	5,617	17,670	10,850,500	7,000.2	3,833.7	5,544.4	4,637.4
1984	11,883	5,966	17,849	10,608,500	6,872.8	3,882.1	5,465.4	4,492.1
1985	11,913	5,807	17,720	11,102,600	6,964.5	3,719.5	5,416.0	4,650.5
1986	10,703	5,364	16,067	11,722,700	6,243.6	3,430.3	4,901.5	4,862.6
1987	11,583	5,214	16,797	12,024,700	6,557.3	3,195.2	4,942.9	4,940.3
1988	11,343	5,124	16,467	12,356,900	6,336.5	3,098.6	4,781.7	5,027.1
1989	12,052	5,572	17,624	12,605,400	6,746.5	3,311.6	5,080.5	5,077.9
1990	12,024	5,637	17,661	12,655,500	6,286.7	3,335.4	4,902.2	5,088.5
1991	12,114	6,220	18,334	12,961,100	6,252.9	3,633.5	5,024.1	5,139.7
1992	10,795	6,614	17,409	12,505,900	5,514.2	3,819.7	4,718.9	4,902.7
1993	9,985	5,998	15,983	12,218,800	5,070.6	3,336.6	4,243.1	4,737.6
1994	8,995	5,773	14,768	12,131,900	4,528.3	3,183.8	3,886.7	4,660.0
1995	8,670	5,695	14,365	12,063,900	4,420.0	2,996.0	3,719.2	4,591.3
1996	8,324	6,453	14,777	11,791,300	4,213.1	3,370.6	3,798.5	4,444.8

Notes: Property crimes include burglary, larceny-theft and motor vehicle theft; n/a not available; (1) Metropolitan Statistical Area - see Appendix A for areas included; (2) calculated by the editors using the following formula: (number of crimes in the MSA minus number of crimes in the city); (3) calculated by the editors using the following formula: ((number of crimes in the MSA minus number of crimes in the city) ÷ (population of the MSA minus population of the city)) x 100,000
Source: U.S. Department of Justice, FBI Uniform Crime Reports, 1977 - 1996

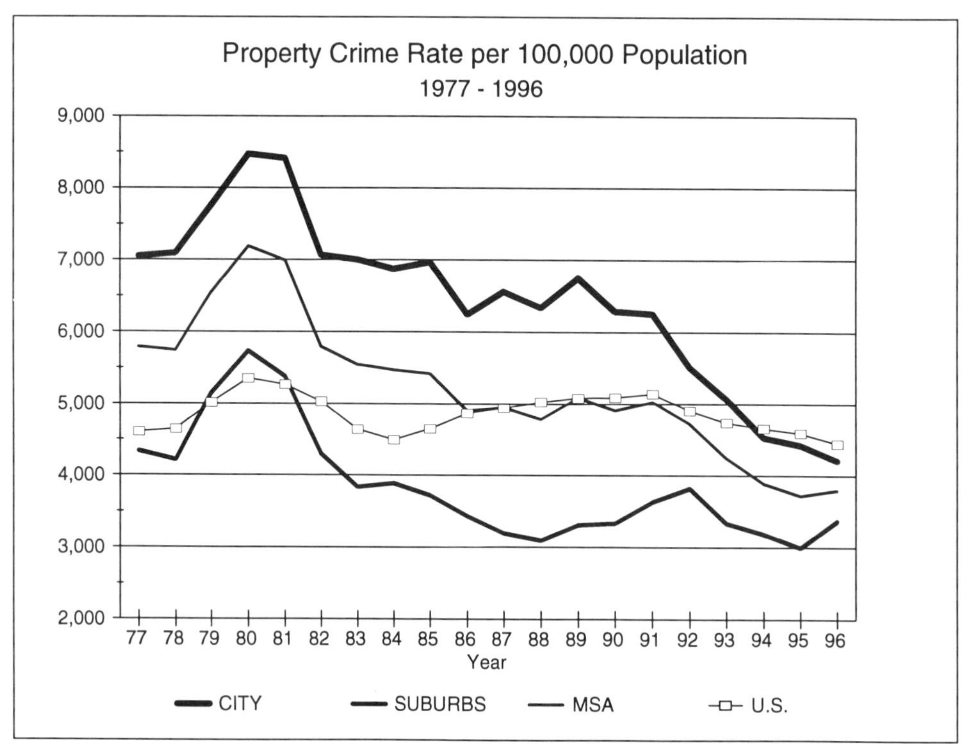

Note: Missing line segments indicate data not available.

Murders and Murder Rates: 1977 - 1996

Year	Number				Rate per 100,000 population			
	City	Suburbs[2]	MSA[1]	U.S.	City	Suburbs[3]	MSA[1]	U.S.
1977	4	3	7	19,120	2.4	2.0	2.2	8.8
1978	2	2	4	19,560	1.2	1.3	1.2	9.0
1979	5	2	7	21,460	2.9	1.3	2.2	9.7
1980	4	1	5	23,040	2.4	0.7	1.6	10.2
1981	6	2	8	22,520	3.5	1.3	2.5	9.8
1982	3	4	7	21,010	1.7	2.7	2.2	9.1
1983	5	3	8	19,310	2.9	2.0	2.5	8.3
1984	6	0	6	18,690	3.5	0.0	1.8	7.9
1985	4	1	5	18,980	2.3	0.6	1.5	7.9
1986	3	1	4	20,610	1.8	0.6	1.2	8.6
1987	6	0	6	20,100	3.4	0.0	1.8	8.3
1988	6	1	7	20,680	3.4	0.6	2.0	8.4
1989	7	5	12	21,500	3.9	3.0	3.5	8.7
1990	3	1	4	23,440	1.6	0.6	1.1	9.4
1991	2	2	4	24,700	1.0	1.2	1.1	9.8
1992	3	1	4	23,760	1.5	0.6	1.1	9.3
1993	2	1	3	24,530	1.0	0.6	0.8	9.5
1994	4	3	7	23,330	2.0	1.7	1.8	9.0
1995	5	0	5	21,610	2.5	0.0	1.3	8.2
1996	1	1	2	19,650	0.5	0.5	0.5	7.4

Notes: (1) Metropolitan Statistical Area - see Appendix A for areas included; (2) calculated by the editors using the following formula: (number of crimes in the MSA minus number of crimes in the city); (3) calculated by the editors using the following formula: ((number of crimes in the MSA minus number of crimes in the city) ÷ (population of the MSA minus population of the city)) x 100,000; n/a not avail.
Source: U.S. Department of Justice, FBI Uniform Crime Reports, 1977 - 1996

Forcible Rapes and Forcible Rape Rates: 1977 - 1996

Year	Number				Rate per 100,000 population			
	City	Suburbs[2]	MSA[1]	U.S.	City	Suburbs[3]	MSA[1]	U.S.
1977	59	15	74	63,500	34.9	10.2	23.5	29.4
1978	55	12	67	67,610	32.4	8.0	20.9	31.0
1979	67	15	82	76,390	39.0	10.0	25.5	34.7
1980	76	24	100	82,990	44.8	16.1	31.4	36.8
1981	66	22	88	82,500	38.4	14.6	27.3	36.0
1982	63	21	84	78,770	36.5	14.3	26.3	34.0
1983	81	49	130	78,920	47.0	33.4	40.8	33.7
1984	64	24	88	84,230	37.0	15.6	26.9	35.7
1985	63	33	96	88,670	36.8	21.1	29.3	37.1
1986	67	13	80	91,460	39.1	8.3	24.4	37.9
1987	48	11	59	91,110	27.2	6.7	17.4	37.4
1988	62	11	73	92,490	34.6	6.7	21.2	37.6
1989	53	12	65	94,500	29.7	7.1	18.7	38.1
1990	62	16	78	102,560	32.4	9.5	21.7	41.2
1991	93	33	126	106,590	48.0	19.3	34.5	42.3
1992	81	29	110	109,060	41.4	16.7	29.8	42.8
1993	99	18	117	106,010	50.3	10.0	31.1	41.1
1994	80	30	110	102,220	40.3	16.5	29.0	39.3
1995	67	33	100	97,470	34.2	17.4	25.9	37.1
1996	75	28	103	95,770	38.0	14.6	26.5	36.1

Notes: (1) Metropolitan Statistical Area - see Appendix A for areas included; (2) calculated by the editors using the following formula: (number of crimes in the MSA minus number of crimes in the city); (3) calculated by the editors using the following formula: ((number of crimes in the MSA minus number of crimes in the city) ÷ (population of the MSA minus population of the city)) x 100,000; n/a not avail.
Source: U.S. Department of Justice, FBI Uniform Crime Reports, 1977 - 1996

Robberies and Robbery Rates: 1977 - 1996

Year	Number				Rate per 100,000 population			
	City	Suburbs[2]	MSA[1]	U.S.	City	Suburbs[3]	MSA[1]	U.S.
1977	122	37	159	412,610	72.2	25.2	50.4	190.7
1978	124	46	170	426,930	72.9	30.5	53.0	195.8
1979	184	49	233	480,700	107.2	32.6	72.4	218.4
1980	244	55	299	565,840	143.8	36.9	93.8	251.1
1981	221	57	278	592,910	128.7	37.7	86.1	258.7
1982	164	38	202	553,130	95.0	25.9	63.2	238.9
1983	162	20	182	506,570	94.1	13.7	57.1	216.5
1984	171	28	199	485,010	98.9	18.2	60.9	205.4
1985	205	29	234	497,870	119.8	18.6	71.5	208.5
1986	211	24	235	542,780	123.1	15.3	71.7	225.1
1987	185	40	225	517,700	104.7	24.5	66.2	212.7
1988	214	33	247	542,970	119.5	20.0	71.7	220.9
1989	198	24	222	578,330	110.8	14.3	64.0	233.0
1990	230	34	264	639,270	120.3	20.1	73.3	257.0
1991	325	29	354	687,730	167.8	16.9	97.0	272.7
1992	281	42	323	672,480	143.5	24.3	87.6	263.6
1993	316	50	366	659,870	160.5	27.8	97.2	255.9
1994	310	46	356	618,950	156.1	25.4	93.7	237.7
1995	282	56	338	580,510	143.8	29.5	87.5	220.9
1996	299	29	328	537,050	151.3	15.1	84.3	202.4

Notes: (1) Metropolitan Statistical Area - see Appendix A for areas included; (2) calculated by the editors using the following formula: (number of crimes in the MSA minus number of crimes in the city); (3) calculated by the editors using the following formula: ((number of crimes in the MSA minus number of crimes in the city) ÷ (population of the MSA minus population of the city)) x 100,000; n/a not avail.
Source: U.S. Department of Justice, FBI Uniform Crime Reports, 1977 - 1996

Aggravated Assaults and Aggravated Assault Rates: 1977 - 1996

Year	Number				Rate per 100,000 population			
	City	Suburbs[2]	MSA[1]	U.S.	City	Suburbs[3]	MSA[1]	U.S.
1977	40	129	169	534,350	23.7	88.0	53.6	247.0
1978	49	116	165	571,460	28.8	76.9	51.4	262.1
1979	86	163	249	629,480	50.1	108.5	77.4	286.0
1980	111	160	271	672,650	65.4	107.2	85.0	298.5
1981	170	172	342	663,900	99.0	113.8	105.9	289.7
1982	189	156	345	669,480	109.4	106.2	107.9	289.2
1983	185	129	314	653,290	107.4	88.0	98.5	279.2
1984	198	178	376	685,350	114.5	115.8	115.1	290.2
1985	173	164	337	723,250	101.1	105.0	103.0	302.9
1986	177	245	422	834,320	103.3	156.7	128.7	346.1
1987	138	176	314	855,090	78.1	107.9	92.4	351.3
1988	158	238	396	910,090	88.3	143.9	115.0	370.2
1989	246	260	506	951,710	137.7	154.5	145.9	383.4
1990	301	379	680	1,054,860	157.4	224.3	188.7	424.1
1991	350	407	757	1,092,740	180.7	237.8	207.4	433.3
1992	348	401	749	1,126,970	177.8	231.6	203.0	441.8
1993	214	412	626	1,135,610	108.7	229.2	166.2	440.3
1994	230	360	590	1,113,180	115.8	198.5	155.3	427.6
1995	263	295	558	1,099,210	134.1	155.2	144.5	418.3
1996	397	315	712	1,029,810	200.9	164.5	183.0	388.2

Notes: (1) Metropolitan Statistical Area - see Appendix A for areas included; (2) calculated by the editors using the following formula: (number of crimes in the MSA minus number of crimes in the city); (3) calculated by the editors using the following formula: ((number of crimes in the MSA minus number of crimes in the city) ÷ (population of the MSA minus population of the city)) x 100,000; n/a not avail.
Source: U.S. Department of Justice, FBI Uniform Crime Reports, 1977 - 1996

Burglaries and Burglary Rates: 1977 - 1996

Year	Number				Rate per 100,000 population			
	City	Suburbs[2]	MSA[1]	U.S.	City	Suburbs[3]	MSA[1]	U.S.
1977	2,440	1,376	3,816	3,071,500	1,443.8	939.0	1,209.4	1,419.8
1978	2,853	1,371	4,224	3,128,300	1,678.2	909.4	1,316.9	1,434.6
1979	3,308	1,589	4,897	3,327,700	1,926.8	1,058.1	1,521.5	1,511.9
1980	3,646	1,853	5,499	3,795,200	2,149.2	1,241.7	1,724.5	1,684.1
1981	3,381	1,594	4,975	3,779,700	1,968.6	1,055.1	1,541.1	1,649.5
1982	2,721	1,404	4,125	3,447,100	1,575.7	955.4	1,290.5	1,488.8
1983	2,678	1,206	3,884	3,129,900	1,555.3	823.1	1,218.7	1,337.7
1984	2,693	1,079	3,772	2,984,400	1,557.5	702.1	1,155.0	1,263.7
1985	2,492	1,043	3,535	3,073,300	1,456.9	668.1	1,080.5	1,287.3
1986	1,988	943	2,931	3,241,400	1,159.7	603.0	894.2	1,344.6
1987	2,370	823	3,193	3,236,200	1,341.7	504.4	939.6	1,329.6
1988	2,063	832	2,895	3,218,100	1,152.4	503.1	840.6	1,309.2
1989	2,521	913	3,434	3,168,200	1,411.2	542.6	989.9	1,276.3
1990	2,334	850	3,184	3,073,900	1,220.3	502.9	883.8	1,235.9
1991	2,273	1,003	3,276	3,157,200	1,173.3	585.9	897.7	1,252.0
1992	1,956	861	2,817	2,979,900	999.1	497.2	763.6	1,168.2
1993	1,606	819	2,425	2,834,800	815.6	455.6	643.8	1,099.2
1994	1,537	811	2,348	2,712,800	773.8	447.3	618.0	1,042.0
1995	1,459	702	2,161	2,593,800	743.8	369.3	559.5	987.1
1996	1,389	834	2,223	2,501,500	703.0	435.6	571.4	943.0

Notes: (1) Metropolitan Statistical Area - see Appendix A for areas included; (2) calculated by the editors using the following formula: (number of crimes in the MSA minus number of crimes in the city); (3) calculated by the editors using the following formula: ((number of crimes in the MSA minus number of crimes in the city) ÷ (population of the MSA minus population of the city)) x 100,000; n/a not avail.
Source: U.S. Department of Justice, FBI Uniform Crime Reports, 1977 - 1996

Larceny-Thefts and Larceny-Theft Rates: 1977 - 1996

Year	Number				Rate per 100,000 population			
	City	Suburbs[2]	MSA[1]	U.S.	City	Suburbs[3]	MSA[1]	U.S.
1977	8,961	4,720	13,681	5,905,700	5,302.4	3,220.9	4,335.7	2,729.9
1978	8,650	4,742	13,392	5,991,000	5,088.2	3,145.5	4,175.1	2,747.4
1979	9,354	5,811	15,165	6,601,000	5,448.3	3,869.6	4,711.7	2,999.1
1980	10,125	6,344	16,469	7,136,900	5,968.5	4,251.3	5,164.9	3,167.0
1981	10,471	6,219	16,690	7,194,400	6,096.8	4,116.5	5,170.0	3,139.7
1982	9,073	4,747	13,820	7,142,500	5,254.0	3,230.2	4,323.6	3,084.8
1983	9,016	4,246	13,262	6,712,800	5,236.4	2,897.9	4,161.3	2,868.9
1984	8,754	4,657	13,411	6,591,900	5,063.0	3,030.3	4,106.5	2,791.3
1985	8,896	4,510	13,406	6,926,400	5,200.7	2,888.7	4,097.5	2,901.2
1986	8,207	4,206	12,413	7,257,200	4,787.6	2,689.7	3,786.8	3,010.3
1987	8,574	4,171	12,745	7,499,900	4,853.9	2,556.1	3,750.5	3,081.3
1988	8,503	4,030	12,533	7,705,900	4,750.0	2,437.0	3,639.3	3,134.9
1989	8,817	4,421	13,238	7,872,400	4,935.6	2,627.5	3,816.1	3,171.3
1990	8,957	4,566	13,523	7,945,700	4,683.1	2,701.7	3,753.6	3,194.8
1991	9,089	4,981	14,070	8,142,200	4,691.5	2,909.7	3,855.7	3,228.8
1992	8,209	5,565	13,774	7,915,200	4,193.3	3,213.9	3,733.6	3,103.0
1993	7,466	4,938	12,404	7,820,900	3,791.4	2,747.0	3,293.0	3,032.4
1994	6,571	4,654	11,225	7,879,800	3,308.0	2,566.7	2,954.3	3,026.7
1995	6,478	4,774	11,252	7,997,700	3,302.5	2,511.5	2,913.2	3,043.8
1996	6,294	5,392	11,686	7,894,600	3,185.7	2,816.4	3,004.0	2,975.9

Notes: (1) Metropolitan Statistical Area - see Appendix A for areas included; (2) calculated by the editors using the following formula: (number of crimes in the MSA minus number of crimes in the city); (3) calculated by the editors using the following formula: ((number of crimes in the MSA minus number of crimes in the city) ÷ (population of the MSA minus population of the city)) x 100,000; n/a not avail.
Source: U.S. Department of Justice, FBI Uniform Crime Reports, 1977 - 1996

Motor Vehicle Thefts and Motor Vehicle Theft Rates: 1977 - 1996

Year	Number				Rate per 100,000 population			
	City	Suburbs[2]	MSA[1]	U.S.	City	Suburbs[3]	MSA[1]	U.S.
1977	510	260	770	977,700	301.8	177.4	244.0	451.9
1978	561	232	793	1,004,100	330.0	153.9	247.2	460.5
1979	659	326	985	1,112,800	383.8	217.1	306.0	505.6
1980	590	359	949	1,131,700	347.8	240.6	297.6	502.2
1981	583	307	890	1,087,800	339.5	203.2	275.7	474.7
1982	410	162	572	1,062,400	237.4	110.2	178.9	458.8
1983	359	165	524	1,007,900	208.5	112.6	164.4	430.8
1984	436	230	666	1,032,200	252.2	149.7	203.9	437.1
1985	525	254	779	1,102,900	306.9	162.7	238.1	462.0
1986	508	215	723	1,224,100	296.3	137.5	220.6	507.8
1987	639	220	859	1,288,700	361.7	134.8	252.8	529.4
1988	777	262	1,039	1,432,900	434.1	158.4	301.7	582.9
1989	714	238	952	1,564,800	399.7	141.5	274.4	630.4
1990	733	221	954	1,635,900	383.2	130.8	264.8	657.8
1991	752	236	988	1,661,700	388.2	137.9	270.7	659.0
1992	630	188	818	1,610,800	321.8	108.6	221.7	631.5
1993	913	241	1,154	1,563,100	463.6	134.1	306.4	606.1
1994	887	308	1,195	1,539,300	446.5	169.9	314.5	591.3
1995	733	219	952	1,472,400	373.7	115.2	246.5	560.4
1996	641	227	868	1,395,200	324.4	118.6	223.1	525.9

Notes: (1) Metropolitan Statistical Area - see Appendix A for areas included; (2) calculated by the editors using the following formula: (number of crimes in the MSA minus number of crimes in the city); (3) calculated by the editors using the following formula: ((number of crimes in the MSA minus number of crimes in the city) ÷ (population of the MSA minus population of the city)) x 100,000; n/a not avail.
Source: U.S. Department of Justice, FBI Uniform Crime Reports, 1977 - 1996

HATE CRIMES

Criminal Incidents by Bias Motivation

Area	Race	Ethnicity	Religion	Sexual Orientation
Madison	4	0	1	1

Notes: Figures include both violent and property crimes. Law enforcement agencies must have submitted data for at least one quarter of calendar year 1995 to be included in this report, therefore figures shown may not represent complete 12-month totals; n/a not available
Source: U.S. Department of Justice, FBI Uniform Crime Reports, Hate Crime Statistics 1995

LAW ENFORCEMENT

Full-Time Law Enforcement Employees

Jurisdiction	Police Employees			Police Officers per 100,000 population
	Total	Officers	Civilians	
Madison	395	333	62	168.5

Notes: Data as of October 31, 1996
Source: U.S. Department of Justice, FBI Uniform Crime Reports, 1996

CORRECTIONS

Federal Correctional Facilities

Type	Year Opened	Security Level	Sex of Inmates	Rated Capacity	Population on 7/1/95	Number of Staff
None listed						

Notes: Data as of 1995
Source: Bureau of Justice Statistics, Sourcebook of Criminal Justice Statistics Online

City/County/Regional Correctional Facilities

Name	Year Opened	Year Renov.	Rated Capacity	1995 Pop.	Number of COs[1]	Number of Staff	ACA[2] Accred.
Dane Co. Public Safety Building Jail	1957	1994	942	767	136	216	No
Dane County City/County Building Jail	1956	1985	338	n/a	n/a	n/a	No

Notes: Data as of April 1996; (1) Correctional Officers; (2) American Correctional Assn. Accreditation
Source: American Correctional Association, 1996-1998 National Jail and Adult Detention Directory

Private Adult Correctional Facilities

Name	Date Opened	Rated Capacity	Present Pop.	Security Level	Facility Construct.	Expans. Plans	ACA[1] Accred.
None listed							

Notes: Data as of December 1996; (1) American Correctional Association Accreditation
Source: University of Florida, Center for Studies in Criminology and Law, Private Adult Correctional Facility Census, 10th Ed., March 15, 1997

Characteristics of Shock Incarceration Programs

Jurisdiction	Year Program Began	Number of Camps	Average Num. of Inmates	Number of Beds	Program Length	Voluntary/ Mandatory
Wisconsin	1991	1	70	75	6 months	Voluntary

Note: Data as of July 1996;
Source: Sourcebook of Criminal Justice Statistics Online

DEATH PENALTY

Wisconsin did not have the death penalty as of July 31, 1997.
Source: Death Penalty Information Center Web Site, 9/30/97

LAWS

Statutory Provisions Relating to the Purchase, Ownership and Use of Handguns

Jurisdiction	Instant Background Check	Federal Waiting Period Applies[1]	State Waiting Period (days)	License or Permit to Purchase	Registration	Record of Sale Sent to Police	Concealed Carry Law
Wisconsin	Yes	No	2	No	No	Yes	Yes[a]

Note: Data as of 1996; (1) The Federal 5-day waiting period for handgun purchases applies to states that don't have instant background checks, waiting period requirements, or licensing procedures exempting them from the Federal requirement; (a) No permit system exists and concealed carry is prohibited
Source: Sourcebook of Criminal Justice Statistics Online

Statutory Provisions Relating to Alcohol Use and Driving

Jurisdiction	Drinking Age	Blood Alcohol Concentration Levels as Evidence in State Courts[1]		Open Container Law[1]	Anti-Consumption Law[1]	Dram Shop Law[1]
		Illegal per se at 0.10%	Presumption at 0.10%			
Wisconsin	21	Yes[a]	Yes[b]	Yes	Yes	Yes[c]

Note: Data as of January 1, 1997; (1) See Appendix C for an explanation of terms; (a) First and second offense 0.10%; third or subsequent offenses 0.08%; (b) 0.10% is prima facie evidence for first and second offenses. 0.08% is prima facie evidence for third and subsequent offenses; (c) Applies only to the actions of intoxicated minors
Source: Sourcebook of Criminal Justice Statistics Online

Statutory Provisions Relating to Curfews

Jurisdiction	Year Enacted	Latest Revision	Age Group(s)	Curfew Provisions
Madison	1973	1992	15 through 17	11 pm to 4 am weekday nights midnight to 4 am weekend nights
			14 and under	10 pm to 4 am every night

Note: Data as of February 1996
Source: Sourcebook of Criminal Justice Statistics Online

Statutory Provisions Relating to Hate Crimes

Jurisdiction	Bias-Motivated Violence and Intimidation						Institutional Vandalism
		Criminal Penalty					
	Civil Action	Race/ Religion/ Ethnicity	Sexual Orientation	Mental/ Physical Disability	Gender	Age	
Wisconsin	Yes	Yes	Yes	Yes	No	No	Yes

Source: Anti-Defamation League, 1997 Hate Crimes Laws

Manchester, New Hampshire

OVERVIEW

The total crime rate for the city increased 0.1% between 1977 and 1996. During that same period, the violent crime rate increased 146.5% and the property crime rate decreased 2.7%.

Among violent crimes, the rates for: Murders decreased 16.7%; Forcible Rapes increased 1,485.7%; Robberies increased 279.9%; and Aggravated Assaults decreased 19.5%.

Among property crimes, the rates for: Burglaries decreased 44.1%; Larceny-Thefts increased 20.1%; and Motor Vehicle Thefts decreased 16.4%.

ANTI-CRIME PROGRAMS

Information not available at time of publication.

CRIME RISK

Your Chances of Becoming a Victim[1]

Area	Any Crime	Violent Crime					Property Crime			
		Any	Murder	Forcible Rape[2]	Robbery	Aggrav. Assault	Any	Burglary	Larceny -Theft	Motor Vehicle Theft
City	1:19	1:416	1:99,036	1:938	1:723	1:2,201	1:20	1:118	1:27	1:233

Note: (1) Figures have been calculated by dividing the population of the city by the number of crimes reported to the FBI during 1996 and are expressed as odds (eg. 1:20 should be read as 1 in 20). (2) Figures have been calculated by dividing the female population of the city by the number of forcible rapes reported to the FBI during 1996. The female population of the city was estimated by calculating the ratio of females to males reported in the 1990 Census and applying that ratio to 1996 population estimate.
Source: FBI Uniform Crime Reports 1996

CRIME STATISTICS

Total Crimes and Total Crime Rates: 1977 - 1996

Year	Number				Rate per 100,000 population			
	City	Suburbs[2]	MSA[1]	U.S.	City	Suburbs[3]	MSA[1]	U.S.
1977	4,403	5,389	9,792	10,984,500	5,172.8	3,208.9	3,869.5	5,077.6
1978	5,214	5,710	10,924	11,209,000	6,062.8	3,251.0	4,175.2	5,140.3
1979	5,867	7,174	13,041	12,249,500	6,675.2	4,057.2	4,926.4	5,565.5
1980	6,417	8,030	14,447	13,408,300	7,070.5	4,326.9	5,228.0	5,950.0
1981	6,490	6,650	13,140	13,423,800	7,029.6	3,522.4	4,674.2	5,858.2
1982	5,825	6,361	12,186	12,974,400	6,203.0	3,312.6	4,261.9	5,603.6
1983	5,616	1,097	6,713	12,108,600	5,930.6	2,972.3	5,100.9	5,175.0
1984	5,544	1,177	6,721	11,881,800	5,849.6	3,095.3	5,060.9	5,031.3
1985	5,591	1,209	6,800	12,431,400	5,774.5	3,112.2	5,012.2	5,207.1
1986	5,495	1,436	6,931	13,211,900	5,504.7	4,244.0	5,185.5	5,480.4
1987	5,935	1,437	7,372	13,508,700	5,927.2	3,318.5	5,139.6	5,550.0
1988	7,024	1,579	8,603	13,923,100	6,776.1	3,508.1	5,786.7	5,664.2
1989	7,295	1,709	9,004	14,251,400	7,273.5	3,671.6	6,131.8	5,741.0
1990	7,427	1,475	8,902	14,475,600	7,459.3	3,300.9	6,171.1	5,820.3
1991	7,013	1,337	8,350	14,872,900	7,066.7	3,003.7	5,808.6	5,897.8
1992	5,773	n/a	n/a	14,438,200	5,785.8	n/a	n/a	5,660.2
1993	5,480	1,651	7,131	14,144,800	5,583.6	2,402.1	4,273.2	5,484.4
1994	4,781	1,570	6,351	13,989,500	4,817.1	2,260.2	3,764.4	5,373.5
1995	4,349	1,373	5,722	13,862,700	4,447.5	1,957.8	3,407.7	5,275.9
1996	5,129	1,717	6,846	13,473,600	5,178.9	2,418.9	4,026.6	5,078.9

Notes: (1) Metropolitan Statistical Area - see Appendix A for areas included; (2) calculated by the editors using the following formula: (number of crimes in the MSA minus number of crimes in the city); (3) calculated by the editors using the following formula: ((number of crimes in the MSA minus number of crimes in the city) ÷ (population of the MSA minus population of the city)) x 100,000; n/a not avail.
Source: U.S. Department of Justice, FBI Uniform Crime Reports, 1977 - 1996

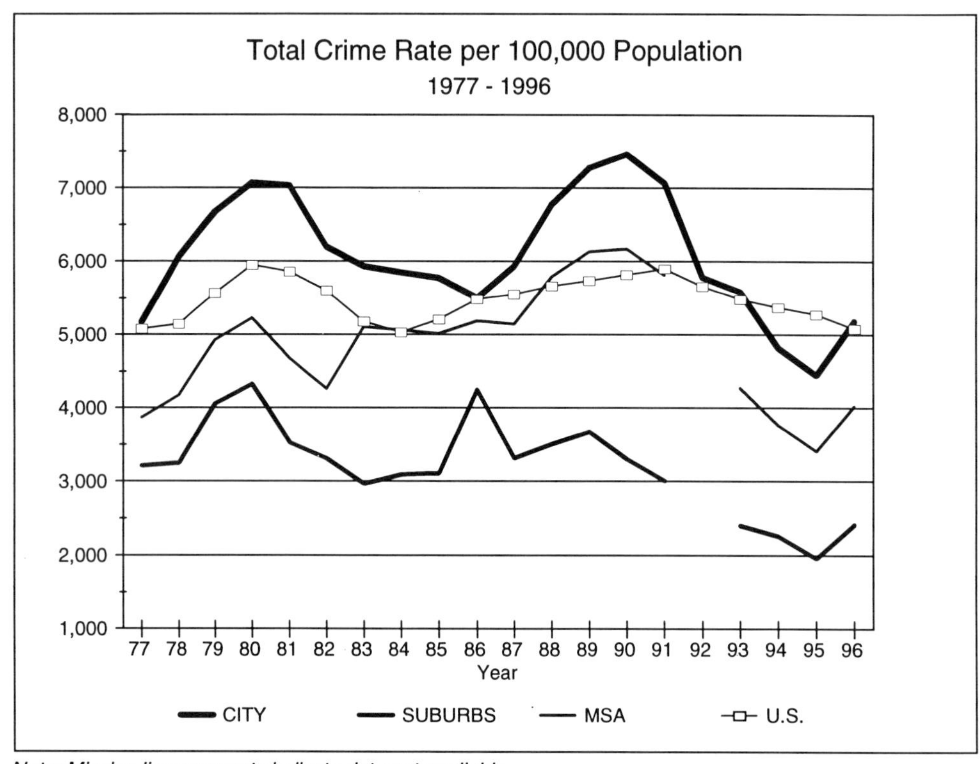

Note: Missing line segments indicate data not available.

Violent Crimes and Violent Crime Rates: 1977 - 1996

Year	Number				Rate per 100,000 population			
	City	Suburbs[2]	MSA[1]	U.S.	City	Suburbs[3]	MSA[1]	U.S.
1977	83	192	275	1,029,580	97.5	114.3	108.7	475.9
1978	121	164	285	1,085,550	140.7	93.4	108.9	497.8
1979	158	213	371	1,208,030	179.8	120.5	140.2	548.9
1980	177	468	645	1,344,520	195.0	252.2	233.4	596.6
1981	163	293	456	1,361,820	176.6	155.2	162.2	594.3
1982	154	225	379	1,322,390	164.0	117.2	132.6	571.1
1983	139	46	185	1,258,090	146.8	124.6	140.6	537.7
1984	353	76	429	1,273,280	372.5	199.9	323.0	539.2
1985	200	62	262	1,328,800	206.6	159.6	193.1	556.6
1986	176	42	218	1,489,170	176.3	124.1	163.1	617.7
1987	193	48	241	1,484,000	192.7	110.8	168.0	609.7
1988	187	98	285	1,566,220	180.4	217.7	191.7	637.2
1989	186	105	291	1,646,040	185.5	225.6	198.2	663.1
1990	197	40	237	1,820,130	197.9	89.5	164.3	731.8
1991	240	33	273	1,911,770	241.8	74.1	189.9	758.1
1992	223	n/a	n/a	1,932,270	223.5	n/a	n/a	757.5
1993	219	57	276	1,926,020	223.1	82.9	165.4	746.8
1994	219	47	266	1,857,670	220.7	67.7	157.7	713.6
1995	227	30	257	1,798,790	232.1	42.8	153.1	684.6
1996	238	57	295	1,682,280	240.3	80.3	173.5	634.1

Notes: Violent crimes include murder, forcible rape, robbery and aggravated assault; n/a not available; (1) Metropolitan Statistical Area - see Appendix A for areas included; (2) calculated by the editors using the following formula: (number of crimes in the MSA minus number of crimes in the city); (3) calculated by the editors using the following formula: ((number of crimes in the MSA minus number of crimes in the city) ÷ (population of the MSA minus population of the city)) x 100,000
Source: U.S. Department of Justice, FBI Uniform Crime Reports, 1977 - 1996

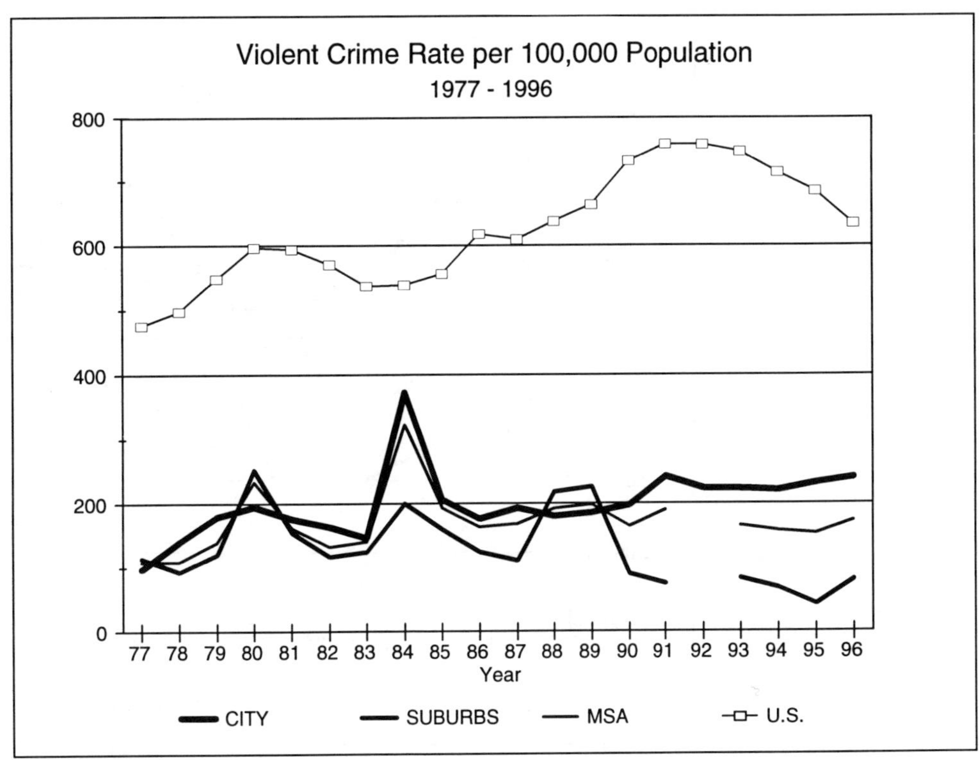

Note: Missing line segments indicate data not available.

Property Crimes and Property Crime Rates: 1977 - 1996

Year	Number				Rate per 100,000 population			
	City	Suburbs[2]	MSA[1]	U.S.	City	Suburbs[3]	MSA[1]	U.S.
1977	4,320	5,197	9,517	9,955,000	5,075.2	3,094.6	3,760.8	4,601.7
1978	5,093	5,546	10,639	10,123,400	5,922.1	3,157.6	4,066.3	4,642.5
1979	5,709	6,961	12,670	11,041,500	6,495.4	3,936.7	4,786.3	5,016.6
1980	6,240	7,562	13,802	12,063,700	6,875.5	4,074.7	4,994.6	5,353.3
1981	6,327	6,357	12,684	12,061,900	6,853.0	3,367.2	4,512.0	5,263.9
1982	5,671	6,136	11,807	11,652,000	6,039.0	3,195.5	4,129.3	5,032.5
1983	5,477	1,051	6,528	10,850,500	5,783.8	2,847.6	4,960.4	4,637.4
1984	5,191	1,101	6,292	10,608,500	5,477.1	2,895.4	4,737.9	4,492.1
1985	5,391	1,147	6,538	11,102,600	5,567.9	2,952.6	4,819.0	4,650.5
1986	5,319	1,394	6,713	11,722,700	5,328.4	4,119.9	5,022.4	4,862.6
1987	5,742	1,389	7,131	12,024,700	5,734.5	3,207.6	4,971.6	4,940.3
1988	6,837	1,481	8,318	12,356,900	6,595.7	3,290.4	5,595.0	5,027.1
1989	7,109	1,604	8,713	12,605,400	7,088.1	3,446.1	5,933.6	5,077.9
1990	7,230	1,435	8,665	12,655,500	7,261.4	3,211.4	6,006.8	5,088.5
1991	6,773	1,304	8,077	12,961,100	6,824.9	2,929.5	5,618.7	5,139.7
1992	5,550	n/a	n/a	12,505,900	5,562.3	n/a	n/a	4,902.7
1993	5,261	1,594	6,855	12,218,800	5,360.4	2,319.2	4,107.8	4,737.6
1994	4,562	1,523	6,085	12,131,900	4,596.4	2,192.6	3,606.7	4,660.0
1995	4,122	1,343	5,465	12,063,900	4,215.4	1,915.0	3,254.6	4,591.3
1996	4,891	1,660	6,551	11,791,300	4,938.6	2,338.6	3,853.1	4,444.8

Notes: Property crimes include burglary, larceny-theft and motor vehicle theft; n/a not available; (1) Metropolitan Statistical Area - see Appendix A for areas included; (2) calculated by the editors using the following formula: (number of crimes in the MSA minus number of crimes in the city); (3) calculated by the editors using the following formula: ((number of crimes in the MSA minus number of crimes in the city) ÷ (population of the MSA minus population of the city)) x 100,000
Source: U.S. Department of Justice, FBI Uniform Crime Reports, 1977 - 1996

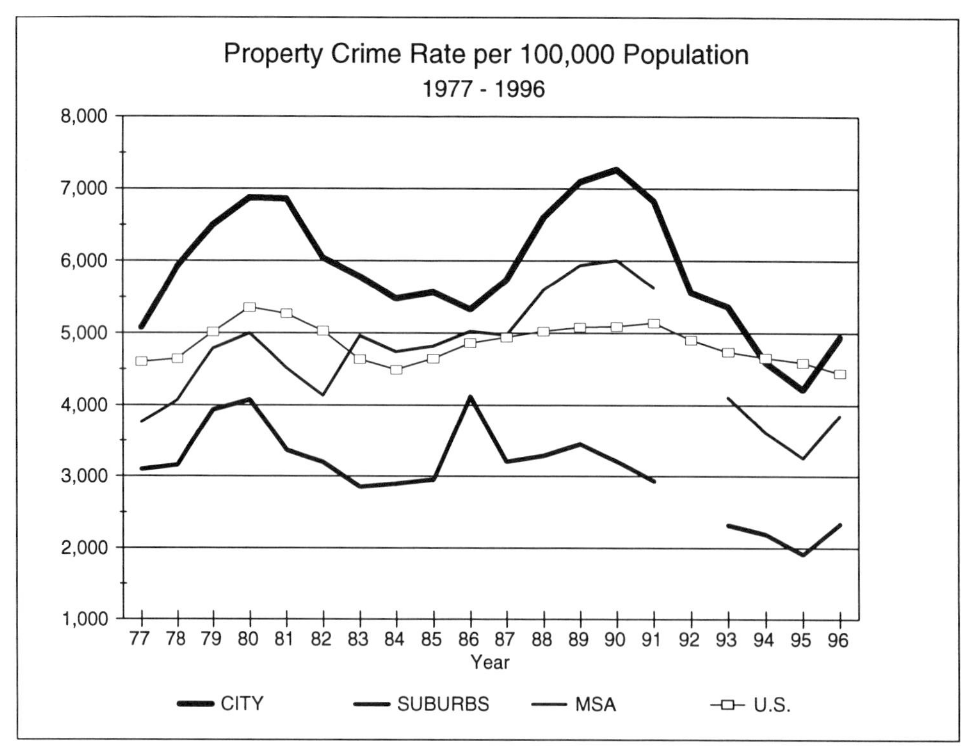

Note: Missing line segments indicate data not available.

Murders and Murder Rates: 1977 - 1996

Year	Number				Rate per 100,000 population			
	City	Suburbs[2]	MSA[1]	U.S.	City	Suburbs[3]	MSA[1]	U.S.
1977	1	4	5	19,120	1.2	2.4	2.0	8.8
1978	1	0	1	19,560	1.2	0.0	0.4	9.0
1979	1	5	6	21,460	1.1	2.8	2.3	9.7
1980	1	3	4	23,040	1.1	1.6	1.4	10.2
1981	2	6	8	22,520	2.2	3.2	2.8	9.8
1982	1	1	2	21,010	1.1	0.5	0.7	9.1
1983	6	0	6	19,310	6.3	0.0	4.6	8.3
1984	2	0	2	18,690	2.1	0.0	1.5	7.9
1985	4	3	7	18,980	4.1	7.7	5.2	7.9
1986	2	0	2	20,610	2.0	0.0	1.5	8.6
1987	4	1	5	20,100	4.0	2.3	3.5	8.3
1988	6	1	7	20,680	5.8	2.2	4.7	8.4
1989	5	0	5	21,500	5.0	0.0	3.4	8.7
1990	2	1	3	23,440	2.0	2.2	2.1	9.4
1991	6	0	6	24,700	6.0	0.0	4.2	9.8
1992	1	n/a	n/a	23,760	1.0	n/a	n/a	9.3
1993	5	2	7	24,530	5.1	2.9	4.2	9.5
1994	2	0	2	23,330	2.0	0.0	1.2	9.0
1995	3	1	4	21,610	3.1	1.4	2.4	8.2
1996	1	1	2	19,650	1.0	1.4	1.2	7.4

Notes: (1) Metropolitan Statistical Area - see Appendix A for areas included; (2) calculated by the editors using the following formula: (number of crimes in the MSA minus number of crimes in the city); (3) calculated by the editors using the following formula: ((number of crimes in the MSA minus number of crimes in the city) ÷ (population of the MSA minus population of the city)) x 100,000; n/a not avail.
Source: U.S. Department of Justice, FBI Uniform Crime Reports, 1977 - 1996

Forcible Rapes and Forcible Rape Rates: 1977 - 1996

Year	Number				Rate per 100,000 population			
	City	Suburbs[2]	MSA[1]	U.S.	City	Suburbs[3]	MSA[1]	U.S.
1977	3	17	20	63,500	3.5	10.1	7.9	29.4
1978	6	22	28	67,610	7.0	12.5	10.7	31.0
1979	21	25	46	76,390	23.9	14.1	17.4	34.7
1980	20	46	66	82,990	22.0	24.8	23.9	36.8
1981	15	39	54	82,500	16.2	20.7	19.2	36.0
1982	25	28	53	78,770	26.6	14.6	18.5	34.0
1983	17	1	18	78,920	18.0	2.7	13.7	33.7
1984	45	4	49	84,230	47.5	10.5	36.9	35.7
1985	19	6	25	88,670	19.6	15.4	18.4	37.1
1986	8	2	10	91,460	8.0	5.9	7.5	37.9
1987	22	4	26	91,110	22.0	9.2	18.1	37.4
1988	34	1	35	92,490	32.8	2.2	23.5	37.6
1989	28	3	31	94,500	27.9	6.4	21.1	38.1
1990	21	1	22	102,560	21.1	2.2	15.3	41.2
1991	23	3	26	106,590	23.2	6.7	18.1	42.3
1992	27	n/a	n/a	109,060	27.1	n/a	n/a	42.8
1993	33	7	40	106,010	33.6	10.2	24.0	41.1
1994	30	3	33	102,220	30.2	4.3	19.6	39.3
1995	29	3	32	97,470	29.7	4.3	19.1	37.1
1996	55	11	66	95,770	55.5	15.5	38.8	36.1

Notes: (1) Metropolitan Statistical Area - see Appendix A for areas included; (2) calculated by the editors using the following formula: (number of crimes in the MSA minus number of crimes in the city); (3) calculated by the editors using the following formula: ((number of crimes in the MSA minus number of crimes in the city) ÷ (population of the MSA minus population of the city)) x 100,000; n/a not avail.
Source: U.S. Department of Justice, FBI Uniform Crime Reports, 1977 - 1996

Robberies and Robbery Rates: 1977 - 1996

Year	Number				Rate per 100,000 population			
	City	Suburbs[2]	MSA[1]	U.S.	City	Suburbs[3]	MSA[1]	U.S.
1977	31	36	67	412,610	36.4	21.4	26.5	190.7
1978	57	32	89	426,930	66.3	18.2	34.0	195.8
1979	68	38	106	480,700	77.4	21.5	40.0	218.4
1980	104	69	173	565,840	114.6	37.2	62.6	251.1
1981	104	47	151	592,910	112.6	24.9	53.7	258.7
1982	72	69	141	553,130	76.7	35.9	49.3	238.9
1983	67	6	73	506,570	70.8	16.3	55.5	216.5
1984	87	4	91	485,010	91.8	10.5	68.5	205.4
1985	108	7	115	497,870	111.5	18.0	84.8	208.5
1986	103	5	108	542,780	103.2	14.8	80.8	225.1
1987	104	3	107	517,700	103.9	6.9	74.6	212.7
1988	74	4	78	542,970	71.4	8.9	52.5	220.9
1989	94	6	100	578,330	93.7	12.9	68.1	233.0
1990	116	2	118	639,270	116.5	4.5	81.8	257.0
1991	165	11	176	687,730	166.3	24.7	122.4	272.7
1992	156	n/a	n/a	672,480	156.3	n/a	n/a	263.6
1993	140	13	153	659,870	142.6	18.9	91.7	255.9
1994	136	10	146	618,950	137.0	14.4	86.5	237.7
1995	160	11	171	580,510	163.6	15.7	101.8	220.9
1996	137	11	148	537,050	138.3	15.5	87.0	202.4

Notes: (1) Metropolitan Statistical Area - see Appendix A for areas included; (2) calculated by the editors using the following formula: (number of crimes in the MSA minus number of crimes in the city); (3) calculated by the editors using the following formula: ((number of crimes in the MSA minus number of crimes in the city) ÷ (population of the MSA minus population of the city)) x 100,000; n/a not avail.
Source: U.S. Department of Justice, FBI Uniform Crime Reports, 1977 - 1996

Aggravated Assaults and Aggravated Assault Rates: 1977 - 1996

Year	Number				Rate per 100,000 population			
	City	Suburbs[2]	MSA[1]	U.S.	City	Suburbs[3]	MSA[1]	U.S.
1977	48	135	183	534,350	56.4	80.4	72.3	247.0
1978	57	110	167	571,460	66.3	62.6	63.8	262.1
1979	68	145	213	629,480	77.4	82.0	80.5	286.0
1980	52	350	402	672,650	57.3	188.6	145.5	298.5
1981	42	201	243	663,900	45.5	106.5	86.4	289.7
1982	56	127	183	669,480	59.6	66.1	64.0	289.2
1983	49	39	88	653,290	51.7	105.7	66.9	279.2
1984	219	68	287	685,350	231.1	178.8	216.1	290.2
1985	69	46	115	723,250	71.3	118.4	84.8	302.9
1986	63	35	98	834,320	63.1	103.4	73.3	346.1
1987	63	40	103	855,090	62.9	92.4	71.8	351.3
1988	73	92	165	910,090	70.4	204.4	111.0	370.2
1989	59	96	155	951,710	58.8	206.2	105.6	383.4
1990	58	36	94	1,054,860	58.3	80.6	65.2	424.1
1991	46	19	65	1,092,740	46.4	42.7	45.2	433.3
1992	39	n/a	n/a	1,126,970	39.1	n/a	n/a	441.8
1993	41	35	76	1,135,610	41.8	50.9	45.5	440.3
1994	51	34	85	1,113,180	51.4	48.9	50.4	427.6
1995	35	15	50	1,099,210	35.8	21.4	29.8	418.3
1996	45	34	79	1,029,810	45.4	47.9	46.5	388.2

Notes: (1) Metropolitan Statistical Area - see Appendix A for areas included; (2) calculated by the editors using the following formula: (number of crimes in the MSA minus number of crimes in the city); (3) calculated by the editors using the following formula: ((number of crimes in the MSA minus number of crimes in the city) ÷ (population of the MSA minus population of the city)) x 100,000; n/a not avail.
Source: U.S. Department of Justice, FBI Uniform Crime Reports, 1977 - 1996

Burglaries and Burglary Rates: 1977 - 1996

Year	Number				Rate per 100,000 population			
	City	Suburbs[2]	MSA[1]	U.S.	City	Suburbs[3]	MSA[1]	U.S.
1977	1,287	1,237	2,524	3,071,500	1,512.0	736.6	997.4	1,419.8
1978	1,437	1,724	3,161	3,128,300	1,670.9	981.6	1,208.1	1,434.6
1979	1,388	1,827	3,215	3,327,700	1,579.2	1,033.2	1,214.5	1,511.9
1980	1,721	2,653	4,374	3,795,200	1,896.3	1,429.5	1,582.8	1,684.1
1981	2,030	1,940	3,970	3,779,700	2,198.8	1,027.6	1,412.2	1,649.5
1982	1,343	1,755	3,098	3,447,100	1,430.2	914.0	1,083.5	1,488.8
1983	1,397	252	1,649	3,129,900	1,475.3	682.8	1,253.0	1,337.7
1984	1,439	292	1,731	2,984,400	1,518.3	767.9	1,303.4	1,263.7
1985	1,402	280	1,682	3,073,300	1,448.0	720.8	1,239.8	1,287.3
1986	1,288	327	1,615	3,241,400	1,290.3	966.4	1,208.3	1,344.6
1987	1,298	295	1,593	3,236,200	1,296.3	681.2	1,110.6	1,329.6
1988	1,742	287	2,029	3,218,100	1,680.5	637.6	1,364.8	1,309.2
1989	1,917	373	2,290	3,168,200	1,911.4	801.4	1,559.5	1,276.3
1990	1,887	380	2,267	3,073,900	1,895.2	850.4	1,571.6	1,235.9
1991	2,040	348	2,388	3,157,200	2,055.6	781.8	1,661.2	1,252.0
1992	1,501	n/a	n/a	2,979,900	1,504.3	n/a	n/a	1,168.2
1993	1,277	289	1,566	2,834,800	1,301.1	420.5	938.4	1,099.2
1994	1,068	287	1,355	2,712,800	1,076.1	413.2	803.1	1,042.0
1995	886	274	1,160	2,593,800	906.1	390.7	690.8	987.1
1996	837	283	1,120	2,501,500	845.1	398.7	658.7	943.0

Notes: (1) Metropolitan Statistical Area - see Appendix A for areas included; (2) calculated by the editors using the following formula: (number of crimes in the MSA minus number of crimes in the city); (3) calculated by the editors using the following formula: ((number of crimes in the MSA minus number of crimes in the city) ÷ (population of the MSA minus population of the city)) x 100,000; n/a not avail.
Source: U.S. Department of Justice, FBI Uniform Crime Reports, 1977 - 1996

Larceny-Thefts and Larceny-Theft Rates: 1977 - 1996

Year	Number				Rate per 100,000 population			
	City	Suburbs[2]	MSA[1]	U.S.	City	Suburbs[3]	MSA[1]	U.S.
1977	2,596	3,539	6,135	5,905,700	3,049.8	2,107.3	2,424.3	2,729.9
1978	3,168	3,414	6,582	5,991,000	3,683.7	1,943.7	2,515.7	2,747.4
1979	3,806	4,627	8,433	6,601,000	4,330.3	2,616.7	3,185.7	2,999.1
1980	3,992	4,397	8,389	7,136,900	4,398.6	2,369.3	3,035.7	3,167.0
1981	3,896	4,048	7,944	7,194,400	4,219.9	2,144.1	2,825.9	3,139.7
1982	3,881	4,022	7,903	7,142,500	4,132.9	2,094.5	2,764.0	3,084.8
1983	3,736	729	4,465	6,712,800	3,945.3	1,975.2	3,392.8	2,868.9
1984	3,344	752	4,096	6,591,900	3,528.3	1,977.6	3,084.3	2,791.3
1985	3,615	790	4,405	6,926,400	3,733.6	2,033.6	3,246.8	2,901.2
1986	3,613	977	4,590	7,257,200	3,619.4	2,887.5	3,434.1	3,010.3
1987	4,063	1,011	5,074	7,499,900	4,057.7	2,334.7	3,537.5	3,081.3
1988	4,593	1,108	5,701	7,705,900	4,430.9	2,461.7	3,834.7	3,134.9
1989	4,584	1,111	5,695	7,872,400	4,570.5	2,386.9	3,878.3	3,171.3
1990	4,762	976	5,738	7,945,700	4,782.7	2,184.2	3,977.8	3,194.8
1991	4,306	887	5,193	8,142,200	4,339.0	1,992.7	3,612.5	3,228.8
1992	3,698	n/a	n/a	7,915,200	3,706.2	n/a	n/a	3,103.0
1993	3,536	1,195	4,731	7,820,900	3,602.8	1,738.7	2,835.0	3,032.4
1994	3,080	1,130	4,210	7,879,800	3,103.2	1,626.8	2,495.4	3,026.7
1995	2,930	992	3,922	7,997,700	2,996.4	1,414.5	2,335.7	3,043.8
1996	3,629	1,284	4,913	7,894,600	3,664.3	1,808.9	2,889.7	2,975.9

Notes: (1) Metropolitan Statistical Area - see Appendix A for areas included; (2) calculated by the editors using the following formula: (number of crimes in the MSA minus number of crimes in the city); (3) calculated by the editors using the following formula: ((number of crimes in the MSA minus number of crimes in the city) ÷ (population of the MSA minus population of the city)) x 100,000; n/a not avail.
Source: U.S. Department of Justice, FBI Uniform Crime Reports, 1977 - 1996

Motor Vehicle Thefts and Motor Vehicle Theft Rates: 1977 - 1996

Year	Number				Rate per 100,000 population			
	City	Suburbs[2]	MSA[1]	U.S.	City	Suburbs[3]	MSA[1]	U.S.
1977	437	421	858	977,700	513.4	250.7	339.1	451.9
1978	488	408	896	1,004,100	567.4	232.3	342.5	460.5
1979	515	507	1,022	1,112,800	585.9	286.7	386.1	505.6
1980	527	512	1,039	1,131,700	580.7	275.9	376.0	502.2
1981	401	369	770	1,087,800	434.3	195.5	273.9	474.7
1982	447	359	806	1,062,400	476.0	187.0	281.9	458.8
1983	344	70	414	1,007,900	363.3	189.7	314.6	430.8
1984	408	57	465	1,032,200	430.5	149.9	350.1	437.1
1985	374	77	451	1,102,900	386.3	198.2	332.4	462.0
1986	418	90	508	1,224,100	418.7	266.0	380.1	507.8
1987	381	83	464	1,288,700	380.5	191.7	323.5	529.4
1988	502	86	588	1,432,900	484.3	191.1	395.5	582.9
1989	608	120	728	1,564,800	606.2	257.8	495.8	630.4
1990	581	79	660	1,635,900	583.5	176.8	457.5	657.8
1991	427	69	496	1,661,700	430.3	155.0	345.0	659.0
1992	351	n/a	n/a	1,610,800	351.8	n/a	n/a	631.5
1993	448	110	558	1,563,100	456.5	160.0	334.4	606.1
1994	414	106	520	1,539,300	417.1	152.6	308.2	591.3
1995	306	77	383	1,472,400	312.9	109.8	228.1	560.4
1996	425	93	518	1,395,200	429.1	131.0	304.7	525.9

Notes: (1) Metropolitan Statistical Area - see Appendix A for areas included; (2) calculated by the editors using the following formula: (number of crimes in the MSA minus number of crimes in the city); (3) calculated by the editors using the following formula: ((number of crimes in the MSA minus number of crimes in the city) ÷ (population of the MSA minus population of the city)) x 100,000; n/a not avail.
Source: U.S. Department of Justice, FBI Uniform Crime Reports, 1977 - 1996

HATE CRIMES

Criminal Incidents by Bias Motivation

Area	Race	Ethnicity	Religion	Sexual Orientation
Manchester	n/a	n/a	n/a	n/a

Notes: Figures include both violent and property crimes. Law enforcement agencies must have submitted data for at least one quarter of calendar year 1995 to be included in this report, therefore figures shown may not represent complete 12-month totals; n/a not available
Source: U.S. Department of Justice, FBI Uniform Crime Reports, Hate Crime Statistics 1995

LAW ENFORCEMENT

Full-Time Law Enforcement Employees

Jurisdiction	Police Employees			Police Officers per 100,000 population
	Total	Officers	Civilians	
Manchester	245	185	60	186.8

Notes: Data as of October 31, 1996
Source: U.S. Department of Justice, FBI Uniform Crime Reports, 1996

CORRECTIONS

Federal Correctional Facilities

Type	Year Opened	Security Level	Sex of Inmates	Rated Capacity	Population on 7/1/95	Number of Staff
None listed						

Notes: Data as of 1995
Source: Bureau of Justice Statistics, Sourcebook of Criminal Justice Statistics Online

City/County/Regional Correctional Facilities

Name	Year Opened	Year Renov.	Rated Capacity	1995 Pop.	Number of COs[1]	Number of Staff	ACA[2] Accred.
Hillsborough Co Dept of Corr	1989	--	577	425	138	169	No

Notes: Data as of April 1996; (1) Correctional Officers; (2) American Correctional Assn. Accreditation
Source: American Correctional Association, 1996-1998 National Jail and Adult Detention Directory

Private Adult Correctional Facilities

Name	Date Opened	Rated Capacity	Present Pop.	Security Level	Facility Construct.	Expans. Plans	ACA[1] Accred.
None listed							

Notes: Data as of December 1996; (1) American Correctional Association Accreditation
Source: University of Florida, Center for Studies in Criminology and Law, Private Adult Correctional Facility Census, 10th Ed., March 15, 1997

Characteristics of Shock Incarceration Programs

Jurisdiction	Year Program Began	Number of Camps	Average Num. of Inmates	Number of Beds	Program Length	Voluntary/ Mandatory
New Hampshire did not have a shock incarceration program as of July 1996						

Source: Sourcebook of Criminal Justice Statistics Online

DEATH PENALTY

Death Penalty Statistics

State	Prisoners Executed		Prisoners Under Sentence of Death					Avg. No. of Years on Death Row[4]
	1930-1995	1996[1]	Total[2]	White[3]	Black[3]	Hisp.	Women	
New Hampshire	1	0	0	0	0	0	0	0.0

Notes: Data as of 12/31/95 unless otherwise noted; (1) Data as of 7/31/97; (2) Includes persons of other races; (3) Includes people of Hispanic origin; (4) Covers prisoners sentenced 1974 through 1995
Source: Bureau of Justice Statistics, Capital Punishment 1995 (released 12/96); Death Penalty Information Center Web Site, 9/30/97

Capital Offenses and Methods of Execution

Capital Offenses in New Hampshire	Minimum Age for Imposition of Death Penalty	Mentally Retarded Excluded	Methods of Execution[1]
Capital murder.	17	No	Lethal injection; hanging

Notes: Data as of 12/31/95 unless otherwise noted; (1) Data as of 7/31/97
Source: Bureau of Justice Statistics, Capital Punishment 1995 (released 12/96); Death Penalty Information Center Web Site, 9/30/97

LAWS

Statutory Provisions Relating to the Purchase, Ownership and Use of Handguns

Jurisdiction	Instant Background Check	Federal Waiting Period Applies[1]	State Waiting Period (days)	License or Permit to Purchase	Registration	Record of Sale Sent to Police	Concealed Carry Law
New Hampshire	Yes	No	No	No	No	Yes	Yes[a]

Note: Data as of 1996; (1) The Federal 5-day waiting period for handgun purchases applies to states that don't have instant background checks, waiting period requirements, or licensing procedures exempting them from the Federal requirement; (a) "Shall issue" permit system, liberally administered discretion by local authorities over permit issuance, or no permit required
Source: Sourcebook of Criminal Justice Statistics Online

Statutory Provisions Relating to Alcohol Use and Driving

Jurisdiction	Drinking Age	Blood Alcohol Concentration Levels as Evidence in State Courts[1]		Open Container Law[1]	Anti-Consumption Law[1]	Dram Shop Law[1]
		Illegal per se at 0.10%	Presumption at 0.10%			
New Hampshire	21	(a)	(a,b)	Yes	No	Yes

Note: Data as of January 1, 1997; (1) See Appendix C for an explanation of terms; (a) 0.08%; (b) Constitutes prima facie evidence
Source: Sourcebook of Criminal Justice Statistics Online

Statutory Provisions Relating to Hate Crimes

Jurisdiction	Bias-Motivated Violence and Intimidation						Institutional Vandalism
	Civil Action	Criminal Penalty					
		Race/ Religion/ Ethnicity	Sexual Orientation	Mental/ Physical Disability	Gender	Age	
New Hampshire	No	Yes	Yes	No	Yes	No	No

Source: Anti-Defamation League, 1997 Hate Crimes Laws

Miami, Florida

OVERVIEW

The total crime rate for the city increased 39.9% between 1977 and 1996. During that same period, the violent crime rate increased 102.2% and the property crime rate increased 28.3%.

Among violent crimes, the rates for: Murders increased 33.1%; Forcible Rapes increased 1.8%; Robberies increased 89.3%; and Aggravated Assaults increased 123.1%.

Among property crimes, the rates for: Burglaries decreased 11.5%; Larceny-Thefts increased 28.1%; and Motor Vehicle Thefts increased 204.4%.

ANTI-CRIME PROGRAMS

The city instituted two programs which the National League of Cities (1993) considers among those which are innovative for combatting crime and violence:

- "Do The Right Thing" Program—Designed to reward model students living in low-income communities. The ultimate reward is higher self-esteem.
- The Dade County Drug Court—Its underlying belief is that "a flexible program of court-supervised treatment can reduce the demand for illicit drugs and, hence, the incidence of drug-related crime and prosecution." Drug Court defendants have shorter sentences and fewer rearrests than other felony drug and non-drug related defendants who did not participate. *Exemplary Programs in Criminal Justice, National League of Cities, 1994*

CRIME RISK

Your Chances of Becoming a Victim[1]

Area	Any Crime	Violent Crime					Property Crime			
		Any	Murder	Forcible Rape[2]	Robbery	Aggrav. Assault	Any	Burglary	Larceny -Theft	Motor Vehicle Theft
City	1:7	1:32	1:3,105	1:994	1:75	1:59	1:9	1:39	1:16	1:50

Note: (1) Figures have been calculated by dividing the population of the city by the number of crimes reported to the FBI during 1996 and are expressed as odds (eg. 1:20 should be read as 1 in 20). (2) Figures have been calculated by dividing the female population of the city by the number of forcible rapes reported to the FBI during 1996. The female population of the city was estimated by calculating the ratio of females to males reported in the 1990 Census and applying that ratio to 1996 population estimate.
Source: FBI Uniform Crime Reports 1996

CRIME STATISTICS

Total Crimes and Total Crime Rates: 1977 - 1996

Year	Number				Rate per 100,000 population			
	City	Suburbs[2]	MSA[1]	U.S.	City	Suburbs[3]	MSA[1]	U.S.
1977	34,099	82,205	116,304	10,984,500	9,826.8	7,635.8	8,169.8	5,077.6
1978	34,860	85,528	120,388	11,209,000	10,017.2	7,889.4	8,406.5	5,140.3
1979	37,180	102,386	139,566	12,249,500	10,246.9	8,995.9	9,298.3	5,565.5
1980	52,540	129,624	182,164	13,408,300	15,650.0	10,477.9	11,581.8	5,950.0
1981	52,911	127,930	180,841	13,423,800	14,832.1	9,731.7	10,820.4	5,858.2
1982	52,901	123,294	176,195	12,974,400	14,473.4	9,154.0	10,289.4	5,603.6
1983	49,799	117,242	167,041	12,108,600	13,287.9	8,488.4	9,512.8	5,175.0
1984	51,893	125,885	177,778	11,881,800	12,952.3	9,015.6	9,893.3	5,031.3
1985	58,355	140,753	199,108	12,431,400	15,122.1	10,193.5	11,270.1	5,207.1
1986	58,728	154,485	213,213	13,211,900	14,816.3	10,892.3	11,749.4	5,480.4
1987	58,791	166,928	225,719	13,508,700	15,266.9	11,615.1	12,386.8	5,550.0
1988	n/a	n/a	n/a	13,923,100	n/a	n/a	n/a	5,664.2
1989	70,053	190,976	261,029	14,251,400	18,376.7	12,889.2	14,012.1	5,741.0
1990	68,209	191,601	259,810	14,475,600	19,023.7	12,137.8	13,412.4	5,820.3
1991	67,678	186,490	254,168	14,872,900	18,393.5	11,512.4	12,786.1	5,897.8
1992	65,369	183,756	249,125	14,438,200	17,488.1	11,166.3	12,336.4	5,660.2
1993	69,828	205,252	275,080	14,144,800	18,744.8	12,327.1	13,500.4	5,484.4
1994	65,269	201,603	266,872	13,989,500	17,177.0	11,869.0	12,839.3	5,373.5
1995	59,170	194,106	253,276	13,862,700	15,623.7	11,573.0	12,319.2	5,275.9
1996	52,918	n/a	n/a	13,473,600	13,745.8	n/a	n/a	5,078.9

Notes: (1) Metropolitan Statistical Area - see Appendix A for areas included; (2) calculated by the editors using the following formula: (number of crimes in the MSA minus number of crimes in the city); (3) calculated by the editors using the following formula: ((number of crimes in the MSA minus number of crimes in the city) ÷ (population of the MSA minus population of the city)) x 100,000; n/a not avail.
Source: U.S. Department of Justice, FBI Uniform Crime Reports, 1977 - 1996

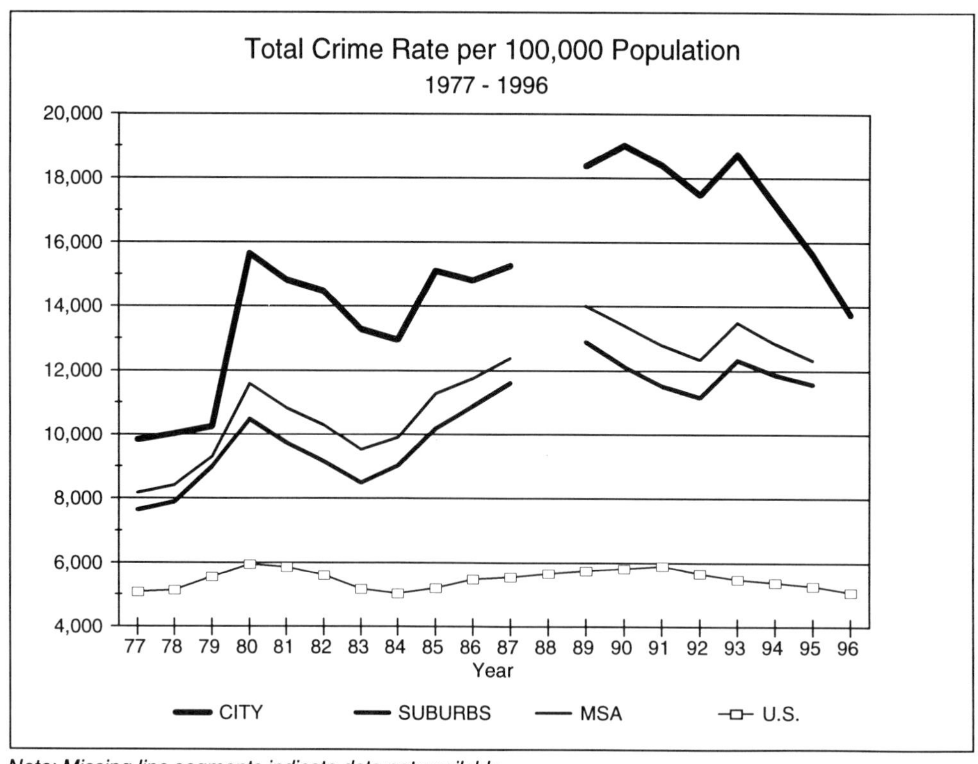

Note: Missing line segments indicate data not available.

Violent Crimes and Violent Crime Rates: 1977 - 1996

Year	Number				Rate per 100,000 population			
	City	Suburbs[2]	MSA[1]	U.S.	City	Suburbs[3]	MSA[1]	U.S.
1977	5,346	10,097	15,443	1,029,580	1,540.6	937.9	1,084.8	475.9
1978	6,272	11,981	18,253	1,085,550	1,802.3	1,105.2	1,274.6	497.8
1979	6,825	13,777	20,602	1,208,030	1,881.0	1,210.5	1,372.6	548.9
1980	11,474	18,717	30,191	1,344,520	3,417.7	1,512.9	1,919.5	596.6
1981	11,211	18,741	29,952	1,361,820	3,142.7	1,425.6	1,792.1	594.3
1982	9,963	17,243	27,206	1,322,390	2,725.8	1,280.2	1,588.8	571.1
1983	9,784	16,662	26,446	1,258,090	2,610.7	1,206.3	1,506.1	537.7
1984	10,928	18,128	29,056	1,273,280	2,727.6	1,298.3	1,617.0	539.2
1985	11,186	18,707	29,893	1,328,800	2,898.7	1,354.8	1,692.0	556.6
1986	11,676	20,829	32,505	1,489,170	2,945.7	1,468.6	1,791.2	617.7
1987	11,309	21,751	33,060	1,484,000	2,936.7	1,513.5	1,814.2	609.7
1988	n/a	n/a	n/a	1,566,220	n/a	n/a	n/a	637.2
1989	14,093	26,964	41,057	1,646,040	3,697.0	1,819.8	2,204.0	663.1
1990	15,607	28,914	44,521	1,820,130	4,352.8	1,831.7	2,298.3	731.8
1991	15,645	27,987	43,632	1,911,770	4,252.0	1,727.7	2,194.9	758.1
1992	13,945	27,190	41,135	1,932,270	3,730.7	1,652.2	2,037.0	757.5
1993	14,502	29,024	43,526	1,926,020	3,893.0	1,743.1	2,136.2	746.8
1994	12,971	26,817	39,788	1,857,670	3,413.6	1,578.8	1,914.2	713.6
1995	12,927	25,855	38,782	1,798,790	3,413.3	1,541.5	1,886.3	684.6
1996	11,990	n/a	n/a	1,682,280	3,114.5	n/a	n/a	634.1

Notes: Violent crimes include murder, forcible rape, robbery and aggravated assault; n/a not available; (1) Metropolitan Statistical Area - see Appendix A for areas included; (2) calculated by the editors using the following formula: (number of crimes in the MSA minus number of crimes in the city); (3) calculated by the editors using the following formula: ((number of crimes in the MSA minus number of crimes in the city) ÷ (population of the MSA minus population of the city)) x 100,000
Source: U.S. Department of Justice, FBI Uniform Crime Reports, 1977 - 1996

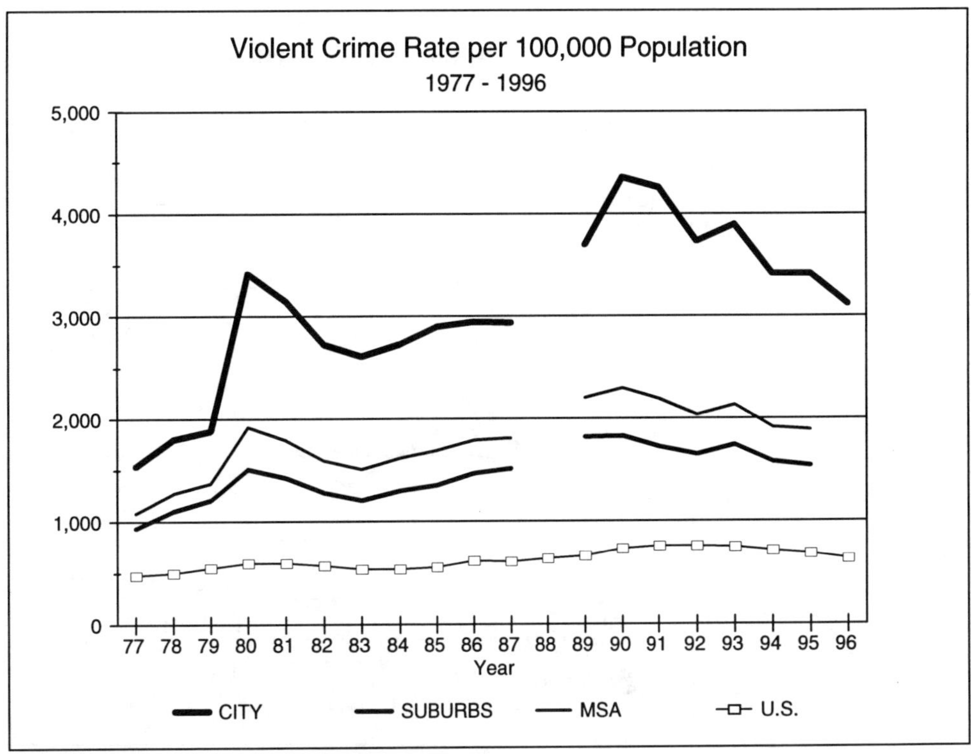

Note: Missing line segments indicate data not available.

Property Crimes and Property Crime Rates: 1977 - 1996

Year	Number				Rate per 100,000 population			
	City	Suburbs[2]	MSA[1]	U.S.	City	Suburbs[3]	MSA[1]	U.S.
1977	28,753	72,108	100,861	9,955,000	8,286.2	6,697.9	7,085.0	4,601.7
1978	28,588	73,547	102,135	10,123,400	8,214.9	6,784.2	7,131.9	4,642.5
1979	30,355	88,609	118,964	11,041,500	8,365.9	7,785.4	7,925.8	5,016.6
1980	41,066	110,907	151,973	12,063,700	12,232.3	8,964.9	9,662.3	5,353.3
1981	41,700	109,189	150,889	12,061,900	11,689.4	8,306.1	9,028.2	5,263.9
1982	42,938	106,051	148,989	11,652,000	11,747.5	7,873.8	8,700.6	5,032.5
1983	40,015	100,580	140,595	10,850,500	10,677.2	7,282.1	8,006.7	4,637.4
1984	40,965	107,757	148,722	10,608,500	10,224.7	7,717.3	8,276.4	4,492.1
1985	47,169	122,046	169,215	11,102,600	12,223.4	8,838.8	9,578.0	4,650.5
1986	47,052	133,656	180,708	11,722,700	11,870.6	9,423.7	9,958.2	4,862.6
1987	47,482	145,177	192,659	12,024,700	12,330.1	10,101.6	10,572.6	4,940.3
1988	n/a	n/a	n/a	12,356,900	n/a	n/a	n/a	5,027.1
1989	55,960	164,012	219,972	12,605,400	14,679.7	11,069.4	11,808.2	5,077.9
1990	52,602	162,687	215,289	12,655,500	14,670.8	10,306.1	11,114.0	5,088.5
1991	52,033	158,503	210,536	12,961,100	14,141.5	9,784.7	10,591.1	5,139.7
1992	51,424	156,566	207,990	12,505,900	13,757.4	9,514.0	10,299.5	4,902.7
1993	55,326	176,228	231,554	12,218,800	14,851.9	10,584.0	11,364.2	4,737.6
1994	52,298	174,786	227,084	12,131,900	13,763.4	10,290.2	10,925.1	4,660.0
1995	46,243	168,251	214,494	12,063,900	12,210.3	10,031.5	10,432.8	4,591.3
1996	40,928	n/a	n/a	11,791,300	10,631.3	n/a	n/a	4,444.8

Notes: Property crimes include burglary, larceny-theft and motor vehicle theft; n/a not available; (1) Metropolitan Statistical Area - see Appendix A for areas included; (2) calculated by the editors using the following formula: (number of crimes in the MSA minus number of crimes in the city); (3) calculated by the editors using the following formula: ((number of crimes in the MSA minus number of crimes in the city) ÷ (population of the MSA minus population of the city)) x 100,000
Source: U.S. Department of Justice, FBI Uniform Crime Reports, 1977 - 1996

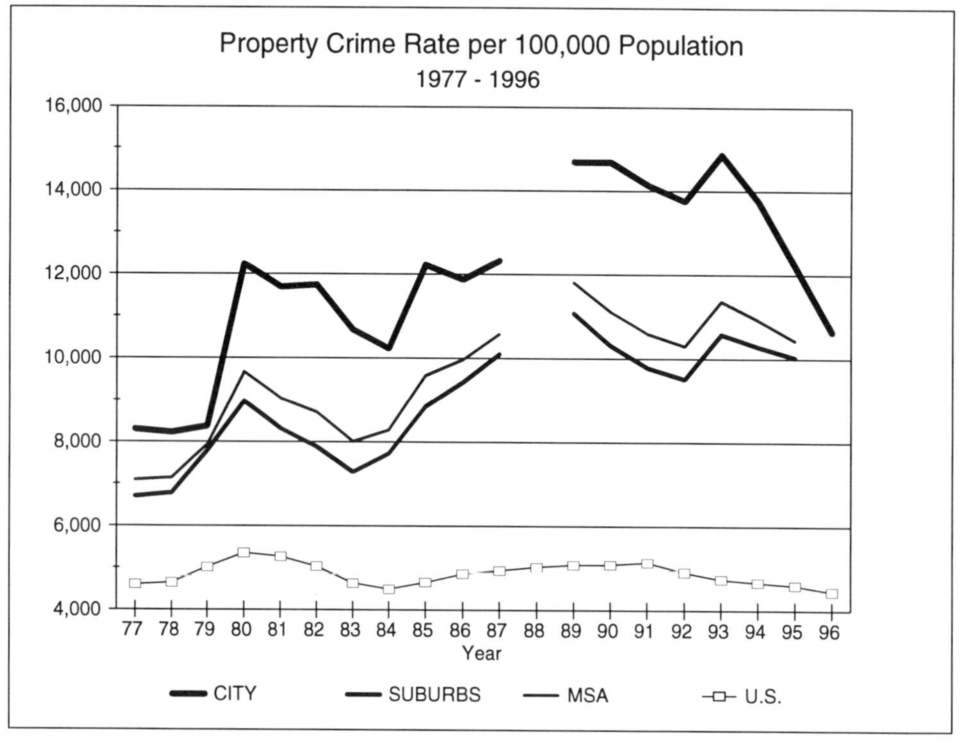

Note: Missing line segments indicate data not available.

Murders and Murder Rates: 1977 - 1996

Year	Number				Rate per 100,000 population			
	City	Suburbs[2]	MSA[1]	U.S.	City	Suburbs[3]	MSA[1]	U.S.
1977	84	138	222	19,120	24.2	12.8	15.6	8.8
1978	96	147	243	19,560	27.6	13.6	17.0	9.0
1979	134	186	320	21,460	36.9	16.3	21.3	9.7
1980	220	295	515	23,040	65.5	23.8	32.7	10.2
1981	210	366	576	22,520	58.9	27.8	34.5	9.8
1982	190	318	508	21,010	52.0	23.6	29.7	9.1
1983	144	246	390	19,310	38.4	17.8	22.2	8.3
1984	170	255	425	18,690	42.4	18.3	23.7	7.9
1985	131	255	386	18,980	33.9	18.5	21.8	7.9
1986	148	244	392	20,610	37.3	17.2	21.6	8.6
1987	128	239	367	20,100	33.2	16.6	20.1	8.3
1988	n/a	n/a	n/a	20,680	n/a	n/a	n/a	8.4
1989	132	275	407	21,500	34.6	18.6	21.8	8.7
1990	129	257	386	23,440	36.0	16.3	19.9	9.4
1991	134	227	361	24,700	36.4	14.0	18.2	9.8
1992	128	216	344	23,760	34.2	13.1	17.0	9.3
1993	127	241	368	24,530	34.1	14.5	18.1	9.5
1994	116	207	323	23,330	30.5	12.2	15.5	9.0
1995	110	201	311	21,610	29.0	12.0	15.1	8.2
1996	124	n/a	n/a	19,650	32.2	n/a	n/a	7.4

Notes: (1) Metropolitan Statistical Area - see Appendix A for areas included; (2) calculated by the editors using the following formula: (number of crimes in the MSA minus number of crimes in the city); (3) calculated by the editors using the following formula: ((number of crimes in the MSA minus number of crimes in the city) ÷ (population of the MSA minus population of the city)) x 100,000; n/a not avail.
Source: U.S. Department of Justice, FBI Uniform Crime Reports, 1977 - 1996

Forcible Rapes and Forcible Rape Rates: 1977 - 1996

Year	Number				Rate per 100,000 population			
	City	Suburbs[2]	MSA[1]	U.S.	City	Suburbs[3]	MSA[1]	U.S.
1977	178	360	538	63,500	51.3	33.4	37.8	29.4
1978	207	435	642	67,610	59.5	40.1	44.8	31.0
1979	261	591	852	76,390	71.9	51.9	56.8	34.7
1980	325	729	1,054	82,990	96.8	58.9	67.0	36.8
1981	382	762	1,144	82,500	107.1	58.0	68.4	36.0
1982	349	605	954	78,770	95.5	44.9	55.7	34.0
1983	365	569	934	78,920	97.4	41.2	53.2	33.7
1984	273	557	830	84,230	68.1	39.9	46.2	35.7
1985	284	695	979	88,670	73.6	50.3	55.4	37.1
1986	221	710	931	91,460	55.8	50.1	51.3	37.9
1987	202	712	914	91,110	52.5	49.5	50.2	37.4
1988	n/a	n/a	n/a	92,490	n/a	n/a	n/a	37.6
1989	285	918	1,203	94,500	74.8	62.0	64.6	38.1
1990	299	1,015	1,314	102,560	83.4	64.3	67.8	41.2
1991	253	979	1,232	106,590	68.8	60.4	62.0	42.3
1992	272	823	1,095	109,060	72.8	50.0	54.2	42.8
1993	204	876	1,080	106,010	54.8	52.6	53.0	41.1
1994	221	945	1,166	102,220	58.2	55.6	56.1	39.3
1995	198	871	1,069	97,470	52.3	51.9	52.0	37.1
1996	201	n/a	n/a	95,770	52.2	n/a	n/a	36.1

Notes: (1) Metropolitan Statistical Area - see Appendix A for areas included; (2) calculated by the editors using the following formula: (number of crimes in the MSA minus number of crimes in the city); (3) calculated by the editors using the following formula: ((number of crimes in the MSA minus number of crimes in the city) ÷ (population of the MSA minus population of the city)) x 100,000; n/a not avail.
Source: U.S. Department of Justice, FBI Uniform Crime Reports, 1977 - 1996

Robberies and Robbery Rates: 1977 - 1996

Year	Number				Rate per 100,000 population			
	City	Suburbs[2]	MSA[1]	U.S.	City	Suburbs[3]	MSA[1]	U.S.
1977	2,447	3,112	5,559	412,610	705.2	289.1	390.5	190.7
1978	2,832	3,553	6,385	426,930	813.8	327.7	445.9	195.8
1979	3,390	4,796	8,186	480,700	934.3	421.4	545.4	218.4
1980	6,890	8,762	15,652	565,840	2,052.3	708.3	995.1	251.1
1981	6,196	8,231	14,427	592,910	1,736.9	626.1	863.2	258.7
1982	5,123	7,423	12,546	553,130	1,401.6	551.1	732.7	238.9
1983	4,719	7,031	11,750	506,570	1,259.2	509.1	669.1	216.5
1984	5,705	6,814	12,519	485,010	1,424.0	488.0	696.7	205.4
1985	5,768	7,380	13,148	497,870	1,494.7	534.5	744.2	208.5
1986	5,767	8,852	14,619	542,780	1,454.9	624.1	805.6	225.1
1987	5,594	8,943	14,537	517,700	1,452.7	622.3	797.7	212.7
1988	n/a	n/a	n/a	542,970	n/a	n/a	n/a	220.9
1989	7,289	11,678	18,967	578,330	1,912.1	788.2	1,018.2	233.0
1990	8,172	12,682	20,854	639,270	2,279.2	803.4	1,076.6	257.0
1991	8,542	12,687	21,229	687,730	2,321.5	783.2	1,067.9	272.7
1992	7,065	11,160	18,225	672,480	1,890.1	678.2	902.5	263.6
1993	7,082	11,528	18,610	659,870	1,901.1	692.4	913.3	255.9
1994	5,841	9,934	15,775	618,950	1,537.2	584.8	758.9	237.7
1995	5,676	9,605	15,281	580,510	1,498.7	572.7	743.3	220.9
1996	5,139	n/a	n/a	537,050	1,334.9	n/a	n/a	202.4

Notes: (1) Metropolitan Statistical Area - see Appendix A for areas included; (2) calculated by the editors using the following formula: (number of crimes in the MSA minus number of crimes in the city); (3) calculated by the editors using the following formula: ((number of crimes in the MSA minus number of crimes in the city) ÷ (population of the MSA minus population of the city)) x 100,000; n/a not avail.
Source: U.S. Department of Justice, FBI Uniform Crime Reports, 1977 - 1996

Aggravated Assaults and Aggravated Assault Rates: 1977 - 1996

Year	Number				Rate per 100,000 population			
	City	Suburbs[2]	MSA[1]	U.S.	City	Suburbs[3]	MSA[1]	U.S.
1977	2,637	6,487	9,124	534,350	759.9	602.6	640.9	247.0
1978	3,137	7,846	10,983	571,460	901.4	723.7	766.9	262.1
1979	3,040	8,204	11,244	629,480	837.8	720.8	749.1	286.0
1980	4,039	8,931	12,970	672,650	1,203.1	721.9	824.6	298.5
1981	4,423	9,382	13,805	663,900	1,239.9	713.7	826.0	289.7
1982	4,301	8,897	13,198	669,480	1,176.7	660.6	770.7	289.2
1983	4,556	8,816	13,372	653,290	1,215.7	638.3	761.5	279.2
1984	4,780	10,502	15,282	685,350	1,193.1	752.1	850.4	290.2
1985	5,003	10,377	15,380	723,250	1,296.5	751.5	870.6	302.9
1986	5,540	11,023	16,563	834,320	1,397.7	777.2	912.7	346.1
1987	5,385	11,857	17,242	855,090	1,398.4	825.0	946.2	351.3
1988	n/a	n/a	n/a	910,090	n/a	n/a	n/a	370.2
1989	6,387	14,093	20,480	951,710	1,675.5	951.2	1,099.4	383.4
1990	7,007	14,960	21,967	1,054,860	1,954.3	947.7	1,134.0	424.1
1991	6,716	14,094	20,810	1,092,740	1,825.3	870.0	1,046.9	433.3
1992	6,480	14,991	21,471	1,126,970	1,733.6	911.0	1,063.2	441.8
1993	7,089	16,379	23,468	1,135,610	1,903.0	983.7	1,151.8	440.3
1994	6,793	15,731	22,524	1,113,180	1,787.7	926.1	1,083.6	427.6
1995	6,943	15,178	22,121	1,099,210	1,833.3	904.9	1,075.9	418.3
1996	6,526	n/a	n/a	1,029,810	1,695.2	n/a	n/a	388.2

Notes: (1) Metropolitan Statistical Area - see Appendix A for areas included; (2) calculated by the editors using the following formula: (number of crimes in the MSA minus number of crimes in the city); (3) calculated by the editors using the following formula: ((number of crimes in the MSA minus number of crimes in the city) ÷ (population of the MSA minus population of the city)) x 100,000; n/a not avail.
Source: U.S. Department of Justice, FBI Uniform Crime Reports, 1977 - 1996

Burglaries and Burglary Rates: 1977 - 1996

Year	Number				Rate per 100,000 population			
	City	Suburbs[2]	MSA[1]	U.S.	City	Suburbs[3]	MSA[1]	U.S.
1977	9,989	20,257	30,246	3,071,500	2,878.7	1,881.6	2,124.6	1,419.8
1978	9,635	22,222	31,857	3,128,300	2,768.7	2,049.8	2,224.5	1,434.6
1979	10,364	29,210	39,574	3,327,700	2,856.4	2,566.5	2,636.5	1,511.9
1980	13,729	37,900	51,629	3,795,200	4,089.4	3,063.6	3,282.5	1,684.1
1981	12,570	36,329	48,899	3,779,700	3,523.6	2,763.6	2,925.8	1,649.5
1982	11,130	31,187	42,317	3,447,100	3,045.1	2,315.5	2,471.2	1,488.8
1983	9,984	27,964	37,948	3,129,900	2,664.0	2,024.6	2,161.1	1,337.7
1984	10,682	30,901	41,583	2,984,400	2,666.2	2,213.1	2,314.1	1,263.7
1985	11,789	34,111	45,900	3,073,300	3,055.0	2,470.4	2,598.1	1,287.3
1986	12,371	37,777	50,148	3,241,400	3,121.0	2,663.5	2,763.5	1,344.6
1987	11,875	40,732	52,607	3,236,200	3,083.7	2,834.2	2,886.9	1,329.6
1988	n/a	n/a	n/a	3,218,100	n/a	n/a	n/a	1,309.2
1989	15,350	44,082	59,432	3,168,200	4,026.7	2,975.1	3,190.3	1,276.3
1990	13,507	43,383	56,890	3,073,900	3,767.1	2,748.3	2,936.9	1,235.9
1991	12,601	38,474	51,075	3,157,200	3,424.7	2,375.1	2,569.4	1,252.0
1992	12,081	35,348	47,429	2,979,900	3,232.0	2,148.0	2,348.6	1,168.2
1993	12,277	40,603	52,880	2,834,800	3,295.7	2,438.5	2,595.3	1,099.2
1994	11,277	35,256	46,533	2,712,800	2,967.8	2,075.6	2,238.7	1,042.0
1995	9,874	31,819	41,693	2,593,800	2,607.2	1,897.1	2,027.9	987.1
1996	9,804	n/a	n/a	2,501,500	2,546.7	n/a	n/a	943.0

Notes: (1) Metropolitan Statistical Area - see Appendix A for areas included; (2) calculated by the editors using the following formula: (number of crimes in the MSA minus number of crimes in the city); (3) calculated by the editors using the following formula: ((number of crimes in the MSA minus number of crimes in the city) ÷ (population of the MSA minus population of the city)) x 100,000; n/a not avail.
Source: U.S. Department of Justice, FBI Uniform Crime Reports, 1977 - 1996

Larceny-Thefts and Larceny-Theft Rates: 1977 - 1996

Year	Number				Rate per 100,000 population			
	City	Suburbs[2]	MSA[1]	U.S.	City	Suburbs[3]	MSA[1]	U.S.
1977	16,486	46,064	62,550	5,905,700	4,751.0	4,278.7	4,393.9	2,729.9
1978	16,473	45,372	61,845	5,991,000	4,733.6	4,185.3	4,318.5	2,747.4
1979	17,044	52,397	69,441	6,601,000	4,697.4	4,603.7	4,626.4	2,999.1
1980	22,577	63,176	85,753	7,136,900	6,725.0	5,106.7	5,452.1	3,167.0
1981	24,388	62,964	87,352	7,194,400	6,836.5	4,789.7	5,226.6	3,139.7
1982	26,329	64,969	91,298	7,142,500	7,203.4	4,823.6	5,331.6	3,084.8
1983	24,729	61,932	86,661	6,712,800	6,598.5	4,483.9	4,935.2	2,868.9
1984	24,738	64,835	89,573	6,591,900	6,174.5	4,643.3	4,984.7	2,791.3
1985	28,093	71,210	99,303	6,926,400	7,280.0	5,157.1	5,620.8	2,901.2
1986	26,265	76,471	102,736	7,257,200	6,626.3	5,391.7	5,661.4	3,010.3
1987	27,548	81,540	109,088	7,499,900	7,153.7	5,673.7	5,986.4	3,081.3
1988	n/a	n/a	n/a	7,705,900	n/a	n/a	n/a	3,134.9
1989	31,268	91,363	122,631	7,872,400	8,202.4	6,166.2	6,582.9	3,171.3
1990	29,518	92,316	121,834	7,945,700	8,232.6	5,848.2	6,289.5	3,194.8
1991	30,751	93,218	123,969	8,142,200	8,357.5	5,754.5	6,236.3	3,228.8
1992	30,633	94,015	124,648	7,915,200	8,195.2	5,713.0	6,172.4	3,103.0
1993	31,871	103,736	135,607	7,820,900	8,555.5	6,230.2	6,655.3	3,032.4
1994	30,645	107,386	138,031	7,879,800	8,064.9	6,322.1	6,640.7	3,026.7
1995	27,537	105,094	132,631	7,997,700	7,271.1	6,265.9	6,451.1	3,043.8
1996	23,431	n/a	n/a	7,894,600	6,086.4	n/a	n/a	2,975.9

Notes: (1) Metropolitan Statistical Area - see Appendix A for areas included; (2) calculated by the editors using the following formula: (number of crimes in the MSA minus number of crimes in the city); (3) calculated by the editors using the following formula: ((number of crimes in the MSA minus number of crimes in the city) ÷ (population of the MSA minus population of the city)) x 100,000; n/a not avail.
Source: U.S. Department of Justice, FBI Uniform Crime Reports, 1977 - 1996

Motor Vehicle Thefts and Motor Vehicle Theft Rates: 1977 - 1996

Year	Number				Rate per 100,000 population			
	City	Suburbs[2]	MSA[1]	U.S.	City	Suburbs[3]	MSA[1]	U.S.
1977	2,278	5,787	8,065	977,700	656.5	537.5	566.5	451.9
1978	2,480	5,953	8,433	1,004,100	712.6	549.1	588.9	460.5
1979	2,947	7,002	9,949	1,112,800	812.2	615.2	662.8	505.6
1980	4,760	9,831	14,591	1,131,700	1,417.9	794.7	927.7	502.2
1981	4,742	9,896	14,638	1,087,800	1,329.3	752.8	875.8	474.7
1982	5,479	9,895	15,374	1,062,400	1,499.0	734.7	897.8	458.8
1983	5,302	10,684	15,986	1,007,900	1,414.7	773.5	910.4	430.8
1984	5,545	12,021	17,566	1,032,200	1,384.0	860.9	977.5	437.1
1985	7,287	16,725	24,012	1,102,900	1,888.4	1,211.2	1,359.1	462.0
1986	8,416	19,408	27,824	1,224,100	2,123.2	1,368.4	1,533.3	507.8
1987	8,059	22,905	30,964	1,288,700	2,092.8	1,593.8	1,699.2	529.4
1988	n/a	n/a	n/a	1,432,900	n/a	n/a	n/a	582.9
1989	9,342	28,567	37,909	1,564,800	2,450.6	1,928.0	2,035.0	630.4
1990	9,577	26,988	36,565	1,635,900	2,671.1	1,709.7	1,887.6	657.8
1991	8,681	26,811	35,492	1,661,700	2,359.3	1,655.1	1,785.4	659.0
1992	8,710	27,203	35,913	1,610,800	2,330.2	1,653.0	1,778.4	631.5
1993	11,178	31,889	43,067	1,563,100	3,000.7	1,915.2	2,113.6	606.1
1994	10,376	32,144	42,520	1,539,300	2,730.7	1,892.4	2,045.7	591.3
1995	8,832	31,338	40,170	1,472,400	2,332.1	1,868.4	1,953.8	560.4
1996	7,693	n/a	n/a	1,395,200	1,998.3	n/a	n/a	525.9

Notes: (1) Metropolitan Statistical Area - see Appendix A for areas included; (2) calculated by the editors using the following formula: (number of crimes in the MSA minus number of crimes in the city); (3) calculated by the editors using the following formula: ((number of crimes in the MSA minus number of crimes in the city) ÷ (population of the MSA minus population of the city)) x 100,000; n/a not avail.
Source: U.S. Department of Justice, FBI Uniform Crime Reports, 1977 - 1996

HATE CRIMES

Criminal Incidents by Bias Motivation

Area	Race	Ethnicity	Religion	Sexual Orientation
Miami	0	0	0	0

Notes: Figures include both violent and property crimes. Law enforcement agencies must have submitted data for at least one quarter of calendar year 1995 to be included in this report, therefore figures shown may not represent complete 12-month totals; n/a not available
Source: U.S. Department of Justice, FBI Uniform Crime Reports, Hate Crime Statistics 1995

ILLEGAL DRUGS

Drug Use by Adult Arrestees

Sex	Percent Testing Positive by Urinalysis (%)				
	Any Drug[1]	Cocaine	Marijuana	Opiates	Multiple Drugs
Male	67	52	34	1	22
Female	n/a	n/a	n/a	n/a	n/a

Notes: n/a not available; The catchment area is the entire county; (1) Includes cocaine, opiates, marijuana, methadone, phencyclidine (PCP), benzodiazepines, methaqualone, propoxyphene, barbiturates & amphetamines
Source: National Institute of Justice, 1996 Drug Use Forecasting, Annual Report on Adult and Juvenile Arrestees (released June 1997)

LAW ENFORCEMENT

Full-Time Law Enforcement Employees

Jurisdiction	Police Employees			Police Officers per 100,000 population
	Total	Officers	Civilians	
Miami	1,427	1,027	400	266.8

Notes: Data as of October 31, 1996
Source: U.S. Department of Justice, FBI Uniform Crime Reports, 1996

Number of Police Officers by Race

Race	Police Officers 1983 Number	1983 Pct.	1992 Number	1992 Pct.	Index of Representation[1] 1983	1992	% Chg.
Black	181	17.2	231	22.4	0.69	0.81	17.4
Hispanic[2]	413	39.3	487	47.2	0.70	0.75	7.1

Notes: (1) The index of representation is calculated by dividing the percent of black/hispanic police officers by the percent of corresponding blacks/hispanics in the local population. An index approaching 1.0 indicates that a city is closer to achieving a representation of police officers equal to their proportion in the local population; (2) Hispanic officers can be of any race
Source: Bureau of Justice Statistics, Sourcebook of Criminal Justice Statistics, 1994

CORRECTIONS

Federal Correctional Facilities

Type	Year Opened	Security Level	Sex of Inmates	Rated Capacity	Population on 7/1/95	Number of Staff
Fed Correctional Inst.[1]	n/a	Medium	Male	525	723	342
Metro Corr/Detention Ctr	1976	Admin.	Both	1,226	1,188	261

Notes: Data as of 1995; (1) A minimum security satellite camp is operated adjacent to this facility
Source: Bureau of Justice Statistics, Sourcebook of Criminal Justice Statistics Online

City/County/Regional Correctional Facilities

Name	Year Opened	Year Renov.	Rated Capacity	1995 Pop.	Number of COs[1]	Number of Staff	ACA[2] Accred.
Dade Co-Boot Camp	1985	1996	120	42	36	38	No
Dade Co-Corr/ Rehab Hdqts	1957	1996	1,000	6,622	1,808	2,175	No
Dade Co-Interim Central Detention Ctr	1956	1981	321	261	71	75	No
Dade Co-Metro West Det Ctr	1992	1995	2,376	1,968	371	422	No
Dade Co-North Dade Det Ctr	1974	1996	171	131	42	50	No
Dade Co-Pre-Trial Det Ctr	1959	1991	1,338	1,586	303	316	No
Dade Co-TG Knight Corr Ctr	1989	1996	994	781	219	347	No
Dade Co-Train & Treat Ctr	1957	1996	1,250	1,114	155	186	No
Dade Co-Women's Det Ctr	1978	1996	203	344	117	119	Yes

Notes: Data as of April 1996; (1) Correctional Officers; (2) American Correctional Assn. Accreditation
Source: American Correctional Association, 1996-1998 National Jail and Adult Detention Directory

Private Adult Correctional Facilities

None listed

Source: University of Florida, Center for Studies in Criminology and Law, Private Adult Correctional Facility Census, 10th Ed., March 15, 1997

Characteristics of Shock Incarceration Programs

Jurisdiction	Year Program Began	Number of Camps	Average Num. of Inmates	Number of Beds	Program Length	Voluntary/ Mandatory
Florida	1987	1	94	112	120 days min.	n/a

Note: Data as of July 1996; Source: Sourcebook of Criminal Justice Statistics Online

INMATES AND HIV/AIDS

HIV Testing Policies for Inmates

Jurisdiction	All Inmates at Some Time	All Convicted Inmates at Admission	Random Samples While in Custody	High-risk Groups	Upon Inmate Request	Upon Court Order	Upon Involvement in Incident
Dade Co.	No	No	No	No	Yes	Yes	No

Source: HIV in Prisons and Jails, 1993 (released August 1995)

Inmates Known to be Positive for HIV

Jurisdiction	Number of Jail Inmates in Facilities Providing Data	Type of HIV Infection/AIDS Cases: Total	Asymptomatic	Symptomatic	Confirmed AIDS	HIV/AIDS Cases as a Percent of Tot. Custody Pop.
Dade Co.	5,553	350	285	52	13	6.3

Source: HIV in Prisons and Jails, 1993 (released August, 1995)

DEATH PENALTY

Death Penalty Statistics

State	Prisoners Executed		Prisoners Under Sentence of Death					Avg. No. of Years on Death Row[4]
	1930-1995	1996[1]	Total[2]	White[3]	Black[3]	Hisp.	Women	
Florida	206	2	362	228	134	35	6	6.9

Notes: Data as of 12/31/95 unless otherwise noted; (1) Data as of 7/31/97; (2) Includes persons of other races; (3) Includes people of Hispanic origin; (4) Covers prisoners sentenced 1974 through 1995
Source: Bureau of Justice Statistics, Capital Punishment 1995 (released 12/96); Death Penalty Information Center Web Site, 9/30/97

Capital Offenses and Methods of Execution

Capital Offenses in Florida	Minimum Age for Imposition of Death Penalty	Mentally Retarded Excluded	Methods of Execution[1]
First-degree murder; felony murder; capital drug-trafficking.	16	No	Electrocution

Notes: Data as of 12/31/95 unless otherwise noted; (1) Data as of 7/31/97
Source: Bureau of Justice Statistics, Capital Punishment 1995 (released 12/96); Death Penalty Information Center Web Site, 9/30/97

LAWS

Statutory Provisions Relating to the Purchase, Ownership and Use of Handguns

Jurisdiction	Instant Background Check	Federal Waiting Period Applies[1]	State Waiting Period (days)	License or Permit to Purchase	Regis-tration	Record of Sale Sent to Police	Concealed Carry Law
Florida	Yes[a]	No	3[b,c]	No	No	No	Yes[d]

Note: Data as of 1996; (1) The Federal 5-day waiting period for handgun purchases applies to states that don't have instant background checks, waiting period requirements, or licensing procedures exempting them from the Federal requirement; (a) Concealed firearm carry permit holders are exempt from Instant Check; (b) The State waiting period does not apply to a person holding a valid permit or license to carry a firearm; (c) Purchases from licensed dealers only; (d) "Shall issue" permit system, liberally administered discretion by local authorities over permit issuance, or no permit required
Source: Sourcebook of Criminal Justice Statistics Online

Statutory Provisions Relating to Alcohol Use and Driving

Jurisdiction	Drinking Age	Blood Alcohol Concentration Levels as Evidence in State Courts[1]		Open Container Law[1]	Anti-Consump-tion Law[1]	Dram Shop Law[1]
		Illegal per se at 0.10%	Presumption at 0.10%			
Florida	21	(a)	(a,b)	Yes	No	Yes[c]

Note: Data as of January 1, 1997; (1) See Appendix C for an explanation of terms; (a) 0.08%; (b) Constitutes prima facie evidence; (c) Applies only to the actions of intoxicated minors or persons known to be habitually addicted to alcohol
Source: Sourcebook of Criminal Justice Statistics Online

Statutory Provisions Relating to Curfews

Jurisdiction	Year Enacted	Latest Revision	Age Group(s)	Curfew Provisions
Miami	1994	1996	16 and under	11 pm to 6 am weekday nights midnight to 6 am weekend nights

Note: Data as of February 1996
Source: Sourcebook of Criminal Justice Statistics Online

Statutory Provisions Relating to Hate Crimes

Jurisdiction	Bias-Motivated Violence and Intimidation						Institutional Vandalism
	Civil Action	Criminal Penalty					
		Race/ Religion/ Ethnicity	Sexual Orientation	Mental/ Physical Disability	Gender	Age	
Florida	Yes	Yes	Yes	No	No	No	Yes

Source: Anti-Defamation League, 1997 Hate Crimes Laws

Milwaukee, Wisconsin

OVERVIEW

The total crime rate for the city increased 49.6% between 1977 and 1996. During that same period, the violent crime rate increased 145.4% and the property crime rate increased 42.0%.

Among violent crimes, the rates for: Murders increased 149.4%; Forcible Rapes increased 37.4%; Robberies increased 151.4%; and Aggravated Assaults increased 161.8%.

Among property crimes, the rates for: Burglaries increased 12.1%; Larceny-Thefts increased 26.5%; and Motor Vehicle Thefts increased 194.0%.

ANTI-CRIME PROGRAMS

Information not available at time of publication.

CRIME RISK

Your Chances of Becoming a Victim[1]

Area	Any Crime	Violent Crime					Property Crime			
		Any	Murder	Forcible Rape[2]	Robbery	Aggrav. Assault	Any	Burglary	Larceny -Theft	Motor Vehicle Theft
City	1:13	1:105	1:4,824	1:1,177	1:187	1:284	1:14	1:82	1:24	1:62

Note: (1) Figures have been calculated by dividing the population of the city by the number of crimes reported to the FBI during 1996 and are expressed as odds (eg. 1:20 should be read as 1 in 20). (2) Figures have been calculated by dividing the female population of the city by the number of forcible rapes reported to the FBI during 1996. The female population of the city was estimated by calculating the ratio of females to males reported in the 1990 Census and applying that ratio to 1996 population estimate.
Source: FBI Uniform Crime Reports 1996

CRIME STATISTICS

Total Crimes and Total Crime Rates: 1977 - 1996

Year	Number				Rate per 100,000 population			
	City	Suburbs[2]	MSA[1]	U.S.	City	Suburbs[3]	MSA[1]	U.S.
1977	34,547	29,148	63,695	10,984,500	5,290.5	3,836.9	4,508.8	5,077.6
1978	33,822	29,702	63,524	11,209,000	5,343.1	3,836.6	4,514.3	5,140.3
1979	38,370	31,708	70,078	12,249,500	5,947.9	4,040.8	4,901.3	5,565.5
1980	41,446	33,271	74,717	13,408,300	6,538.8	4,383.4	5,364.2	5,950.0
1981	44,775	32,864	77,639	13,423,800	6,977.4	4,276.7	5,505.7	5,858.2
1982	45,851	31,136	76,987	12,974,400	7,106.1	4,029.7	5,429.7	5,603.6
1983	47,408	28,459	75,867	12,108,600	7,367.5	3,694.2	5,366.0	5,175.0
1984	47,846	27,079	74,925	11,881,800	7,565.1	3,526.1	5,350.2	5,031.3
1985	43,943	27,213	71,156	12,431,400	7,065.6	3,513.7	5,095.6	5,207.1
1986	48,909	25,974	74,883	13,211,900	7,847.1	3,346.8	5,351.2	5,480.4
1987	50,398	25,677	76,075	13,508,700	8,290.7	3,299.6	5,488.5	5,550.0
1988	49,424	24,925	74,349	13,923,100	8,087.2	3,143.5	5,295.4	5,664.2
1989	52,644	27,162	79,806	14,251,400	8,760.9	3,393.0	5,694.6	5,741.0
1990	58,406	28,470	86,876	14,475,600	9,298.8	3,540.8	6,066.1	5,820.3
1991	57,551	29,706	87,257	14,872,900	9,044.0	3,647.5	6,014.6	5,897.8
1992	55,742	28,860	84,602	14,438,200	8,668.8	3,548.9	5,809.7	5,660.2
1993	50,432	27,422	77,854	14,144,800	8,093.5	3,301.7	5,355.8	5,484.4
1994	51,241	27,314	78,555	13,989,500	8,149.8	3,260.4	5,356.6	5,373.5
1995	52,679	26,331	79,010	13,862,700	8,462.9	3,152.3	5,419.9	5,275.9
1996	49,623	26,837	76,460	13,473,600	7,912.6	3,189.9	5,206.8	5,078.9

Notes: (1) Metropolitan Statistical Area - see Appendix A for areas included; (2) calculated by the editors using the following formula: (number of crimes in the MSA minus number of crimes in the city); (3) calculated by the editors using the following formula: ((number of crimes in the MSA minus number of crimes in the city) ÷ (population of the MSA minus population of the city)) x 100,000; n/a not avail.
Source: U.S. Department of Justice, FBI Uniform Crime Reports, 1977 - 1996

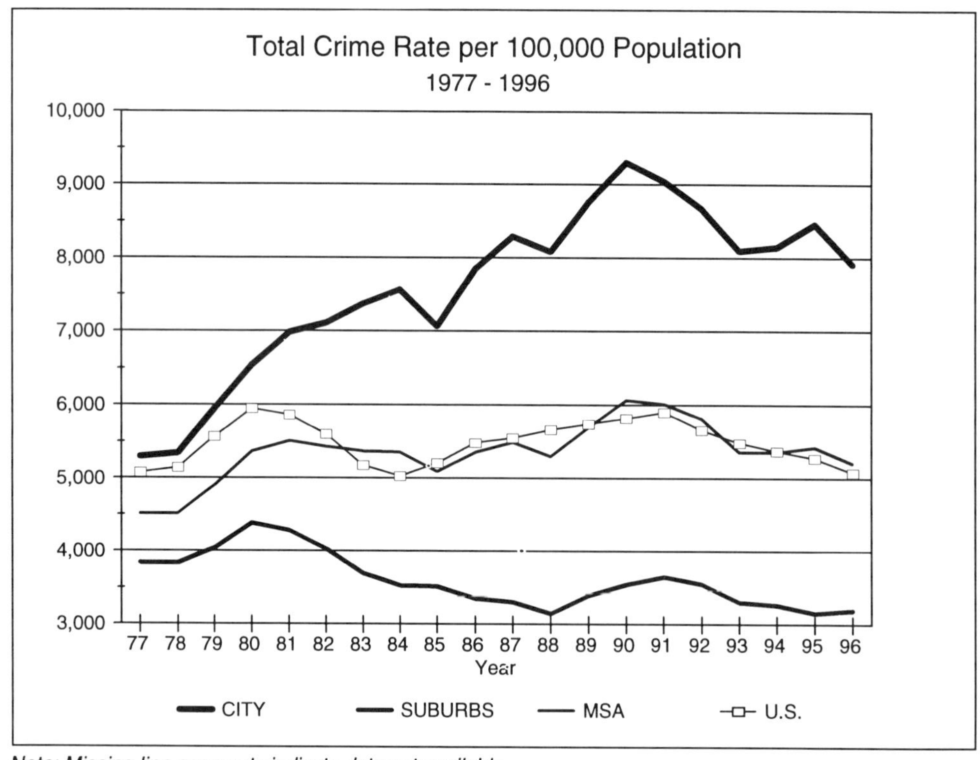

Note: Missing line segments indicate data not available.

Violent Crimes and Violent Crime Rates: 1977 - 1996

Year	Number				Rate per 100,000 population			
	City	Suburbs[2]	MSA[1]	U.S.	City	Suburbs[3]	MSA[1]	U.S.
1977	2,535	687	3,222	1,029,580	388.2	90.4	228.1	475.9
1978	2,438	756	3,194	1,085,550	385.2	97.7	227.0	497.8
1979	3,039	925	3,964	1,208,030	471.1	117.9	277.2	548.9
1980	3,310	953	4,263	1,344,520	522.2	125.6	306.1	596.6
1981	3,424	915	4,339	1,361,820	533.6	119.1	307.7	594.3
1982	3,593	872	4,465	1,322,390	556.9	112.9	314.9	571.1
1983	3,720	782	4,502	1,258,090	578.1	101.5	318.4	537.7
1984	3,456	904	4,360	1,273,280	546.4	117.7	311.3	539.2
1985	4,056	1,022	5,078	1,328,800	652.2	132.0	363.6	556.6
1986	6,135	1,060	7,195	1,489,170	984.3	136.6	514.2	617.7
1987	6,008	995	7,003	1,484,000	988.3	127.9	505.2	609.7
1988	5,037	869	5,906	1,566,220	824.2	109.6	420.6	637.2
1989	4,269	1,070	5,339	1,646,040	710.4	133.7	381.0	663.1
1990	6,282	1,198	7,480	1,820,130	1,000.2	149.0	522.3	731.8
1991	6,228	1,321	7,549	1,911,770	978.7	162.2	520.3	758.1
1992	6,322	1,195	7,517	1,932,270	983.2	146.9	516.2	757.5
1993	6,014	995	7,009	1,926,020	965.2	119.8	482.2	746.8
1994	6,562	1,048	7,610	1,857,670	1,043.7	125.1	518.9	713.6
1995	6,737	1,038	7,775	1,798,790	1,082.3	124.3	533.3	684.6
1996	5,974	996	6,970	1,682,280	952.6	118.4	474.6	634.1

Notes: Violent crimes include murder, forcible rape, robbery and aggravated assault; n/a not available; (1) Metropolitan Statistical Area - see Appendix A for areas included; (2) calculated by the editors using the following formula: (number of crimes in the MSA minus number of crimes in the city); (3) calculated by the editors using the following formula: ((number of crimes in the MSA minus number of crimes in the city) ÷ (population of the MSA minus population of the city)) x 100,000
Source: U.S. Department of Justice, FBI Uniform Crime Reports, 1977 - 1996

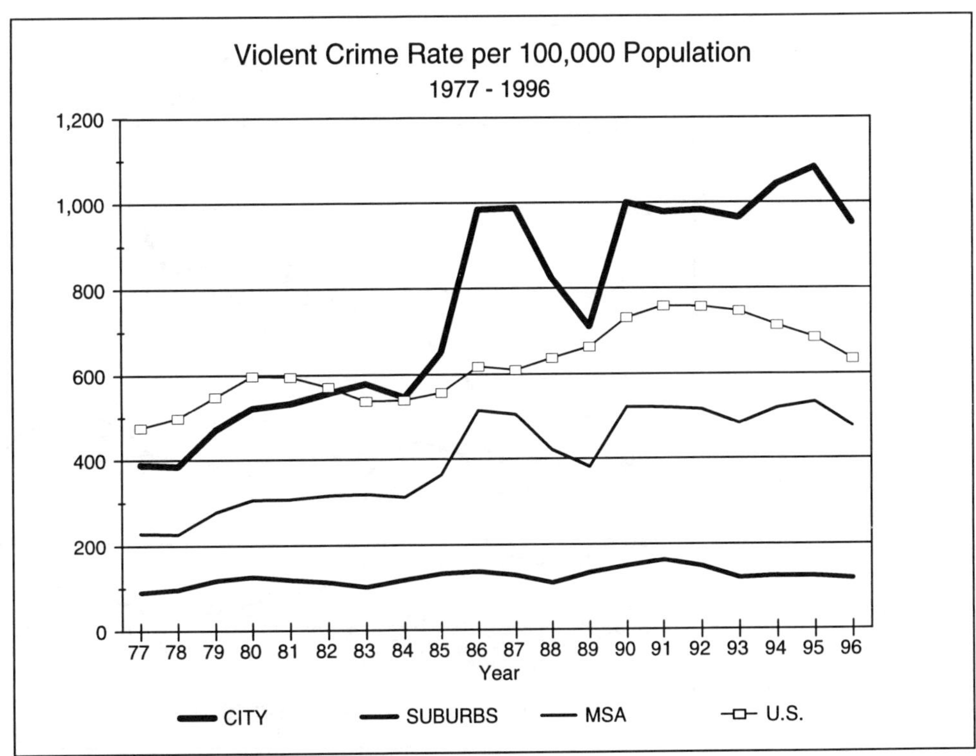

Note: Missing line segments indicate data not available.

Property Crimes and Property Crime Rates: 1977 - 1996

Year	Number				Rate per 100,000 population			
	City	Suburbs[2]	MSA[1]	U.S.	City	Suburbs[3]	MSA[1]	U.S.
1977	32,012	28,461	60,473	9,955,000	4,902.3	3,746.5	4,280.8	4,601.7
1978	31,384	28,946	60,330	10,123,400	4,958.0	3,738.9	4,287.3	4,642.5
1979	35,331	30,783	66,114	11,041,500	5,476.9	3,922.9	4,624.0	5,016.6
1980	38,136	32,318	70,454	12,063,700	6,016.6	4,257.8	5,058.2	5,353.3
1981	41,351	31,949	73,300	12,061,900	6,443.8	4,157.6	5,198.0	5,263.9
1982	42,258	30,264	72,522	11,652,000	6,549.3	3,916.8	5,114.8	5,032.5
1983	43,688	27,677	71,365	10,850,500	6,789.4	3,592.7	5,047.6	4,637.4
1984	44,390	26,175	70,565	10,608,500	7,018.6	3,408.4	5,038.9	4,492.1
1985	39,887	26,191	66,078	11,102,600	6,413.4	3,381.7	4,732.0	4,650.5
1986	42,774	24,914	67,688	11,722,700	6,862.7	3,210.2	4,837.0	4,862.6
1987	44,390	24,682	69,072	12,024,700	7,302.4	3,171.7	4,983.3	4,940.3
1988	44,387	24,056	68,443	12,356,900	7,263.0	3,033.9	4,874.7	5,027.1
1989	48,375	26,092	74,467	12,605,400	8,050.5	3,259.3	5,313.7	5,077.9
1990	52,124	27,272	79,396	12,655,500	8,298.7	3,391.8	5,543.8	5,088.5
1991	51,323	28,385	79,708	12,961,100	8,065.3	3,485.3	5,494.2	5,139.7
1992	49,420	27,665	77,085	12,505,900	7,685.6	3,401.9	5,293.5	4,902.7
1993	44,418	26,427	70,845	12,218,800	7,128.4	3,181.9	4,873.6	4,737.6
1994	44,679	26,266	70,945	12,131,900	7,106.2	3,135.3	4,837.7	4,660.0
1995	45,942	25,293	71,235	12,063,900	7,380.6	3,028.0	4,886.6	4,591.3
1996	43,649	25,841	69,490	11,791,300	6,960.0	3,071.5	4,732.2	4,444.8

Notes: Property crimes include burglary, larceny-theft and motor vehicle theft; n/a not available; (1) Metropolitan Statistical Area - see Appendix A for areas included; (2) calculated by the editors using the following formula: (number of crimes in the MSA minus number of crimes in the city); (3) calculated by the editors using the following formula: ((number of crimes in the MSA minus number of crimes in the city) ÷ (population of the MSA minus population of the city)) x 100,000
Source: U.S. Department of Justice, FBI Uniform Crime Reports, 1977 - 1996

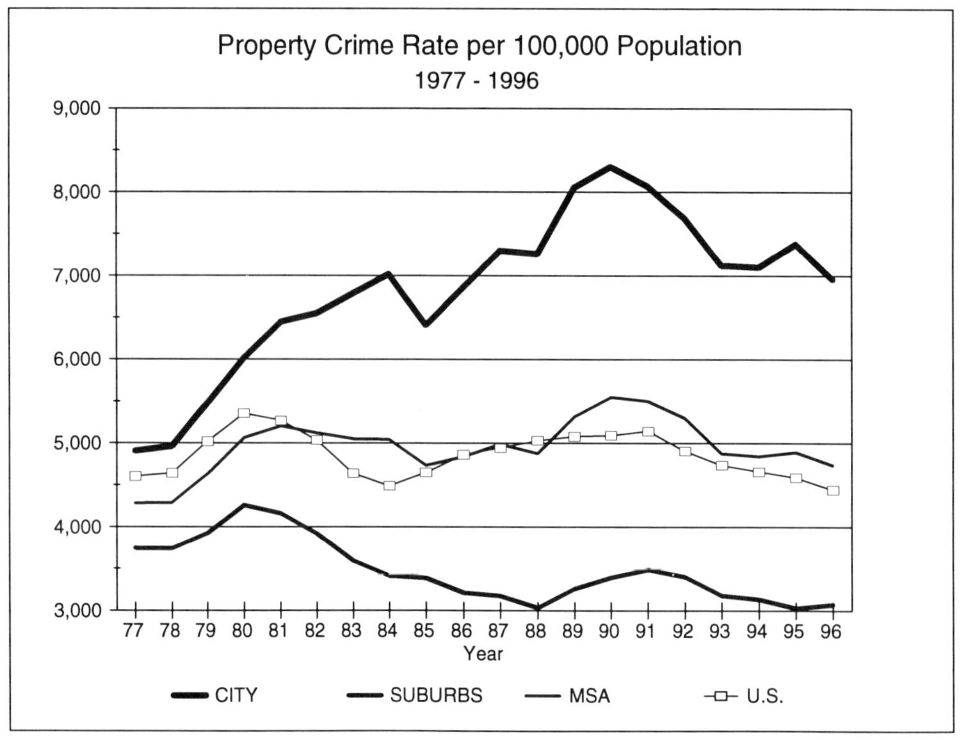

Note: Missing line segments indicate data not available.

Murders and Murder Rates: 1977 - 1996

Year	Number				Rate per 100,000 population			
	City	Suburbs[2]	MSA[1]	U.S.	City	Suburbs[3]	MSA[1]	U.S.
1977	54	9	63	19,120	8.3	1.2	4.5	8.8
1978	48	12	60	19,560	7.6	1.6	4.3	9.0
1979	63	14	77	21,460	9.8	1.8	5.4	9.7
1980	74	5	79	23,040	11.7	0.7	5.7	10.2
1981	71	7	78	22,520	11.1	0.9	5.5	9.8
1982	62	15	77	21,010	9.6	1.9	5.4	9.1
1983	51	8	59	19,310	7.9	1.0	4.2	8.3
1984	44	5	49	18,690	7.0	0.7	3.5	7.9
1985	68	8	76	18,980	10.9	1.0	5.4	7.9
1986	83	10	93	20,610	13.3	1.3	6.6	8.6
1987	92	13	105	20,100	15.1	1.7	7.6	8.3
1988	81	7	88	20,680	13.3	0.9	6.3	8.4
1989	112	7	119	21,500	18.6	0.9	8.5	8.7
1990	155	5	160	23,440	24.7	0.6	11.2	9.4
1991	163	12	175	24,700	25.6	1.5	12.1	9.8
1992	146	13	159	23,760	22.7	1.6	10.9	9.3
1993	157	9	166	24,530	25.2	1.1	11.4	9.5
1994	139	8	147	23,330	22.1	1.0	10.0	9.0
1995	138	8	146	21,610	22.2	1.0	10.0	8.2
1996	130	8	138	19,650	20.7	1.0	9.4	7.4

Notes: (1) Metropolitan Statistical Area - see Appendix A for areas included; (2) calculated by the editors using the following formula: (number of crimes in the MSA minus number of crimes in the city); (3) calculated by the editors using the following formula: ((number of crimes in the MSA minus number of crimes in the city) ÷ (population of the MSA minus population of the city)) x 100,000; n/a not avail.
Source: U.S. Department of Justice, FBI Uniform Crime Reports, 1977 - 1996

Forcible Rapes and Forcible Rape Rates: 1977 - 1996

Year	Number				Rate per 100,000 population			
	City	Suburbs[2]	MSA[1]	U.S.	City	Suburbs[3]	MSA[1]	U.S.
1977	213	61	274	63,500	32.6	8.0	19.4	29.4
1978	288	56	344	67,610	45.5	7.2	24.4	31.0
1979	283	50	333	76,390	43.9	6.4	23.3	34.7
1980	213	48	261	82,990	33.6	6.3	18.7	36.8
1981	290	36	326	82,500	45.2	4.7	23.1	36.0
1982	194	58	252	78,770	30.1	7.5	17.8	34.0
1983	235	70	305	78,920	36.5	9.1	21.6	33.7
1984	292	53	345	84,230	46.2	6.9	24.6	35.7
1985	390	38	428	88,670	62.7	4.9	30.6	37.1
1986	444	52	496	91,460	71.2	6.7	35.4	37.9
1987	437	43	480	91,110	71.9	5.5	34.6	37.4
1988	400	68	468	92,490	65.5	8.6	33.3	37.6
1989	461	64	525	94,500	76.7	8.0	37.5	38.1
1990	495	74	569	102,560	78.8	9.2	39.7	41.2
1991	502	103	605	106,590	78.9	12.6	41.7	42.3
1992	514	109	623	109,060	79.9	13.4	42.8	42.8
1993	424	91	515	106,010	68.0	11.0	35.4	41.1
1994	429	94	523	102,220	68.2	11.2	35.7	39.3
1995	370	73	443	97,470	59.4	8.7	30.4	37.1
1996	281	81	362	95,770	44.8	9.6	24.7	36.1

Notes: (1) Metropolitan Statistical Area - see Appendix A for areas included; (2) calculated by the editors using the following formula: (number of crimes in the MSA minus number of crimes in the city); (3) calculated by the editors using the following formula: ((number of crimes in the MSA minus number of crimes in the city) ÷ (population of the MSA minus population of the city)) x 100,000; n/a not avail.
Source: U.S. Department of Justice, FBI Uniform Crime Reports, 1977 - 1996

Robberies and Robbery Rates: 1977 - 1996

Year	Number				Rate per 100,000 population			
	City	Suburbs[2]	MSA[1]	U.S.	City	Suburbs[3]	MSA[1]	U.S.
1977	1,389	196	1,585	412,610	212.7	25.8	112.2	190.7
1978	1,212	236	1,448	426,930	191.5	30.5	102.9	195.8
1979	1,592	252	1,844	480,700	246.8	32.1	129.0	218.4
1980	1,796	295	2,091	565,840	283.4	38.9	150.1	251.1
1981	1,806	281	2,087	592,910	281.4	36.6	148.0	258.7
1982	2,087	254	2,341	553,130	323.5	32.9	165.1	238.9
1983	2,198	221	2,419	506,570	341.6	28.7	171.1	216.5
1984	1,871	250	2,121	485,010	295.8	32.6	151.5	205.4
1985	2,086	248	2,334	497,870	335.4	32.0	167.1	208.5
1986	2,207	272	2,479	542,780	354.1	35.0	177.2	225.1
1987	1,984	240	2,224	517,700	326.4	30.8	160.5	212.7
1988	2,111	208	2,319	542,970	345.4	26.2	165.2	220.9
1989	2,415	277	2,692	578,330	401.9	34.6	192.1	233.0
1990	4,146	331	4,477	639,270	660.1	41.2	312.6	257.0
1991	4,252	368	4,620	687,730	668.2	45.2	318.5	272.7
1992	4,334	419	4,753	672,480	674.0	51.5	326.4	263.6
1993	4,022	355	4,377	659,870	645.5	42.7	301.1	255.9
1994	4,017	355	4,372	618,950	638.9	42.4	298.1	237.7
1995	3,650	397	4,047	580,510	586.4	47.5	277.6	220.9
1996	3,353	351	3,704	537,050	534.7	41.7	252.2	202.4

Notes: (1) Metropolitan Statistical Area - see Appendix A for areas included; (2) calculated by the editors using the following formula: (number of crimes in the MSA minus number of crimes in the city); (3) calculated by the editors using the following formula: ((number of crimes in the MSA minus number of crimes in the city) ÷ (population of the MSA minus population of the city)) x 100,000; n/a not avail.
Source: U.S. Department of Justice, FBI Uniform Crime Reports, 1977 - 1996

Aggravated Assaults and Aggravated Assault Rates: 1977 - 1996

Year	Number				Rate per 100,000 population			
	City	Suburbs[2]	MSA[1]	U.S.	City	Suburbs[3]	MSA[1]	U.S.
1977	879	421	1,300	534,350	134.6	55.4	92.0	247.0
1978	890	452	1,342	571,460	140.6	58.4	95.4	262.1
1979	1,101	609	1,710	629,480	170.7	77.6	119.6	286.0
1980	1,227	605	1,832	672,650	193.6	79.7	131.5	298.5
1981	1,257	591	1,848	663,900	195.9	76.9	131.0	289.7
1982	1,250	545	1,795	669,480	193.7	70.5	126.6	289.2
1983	1,236	483	1,719	653,290	192.1	62.7	121.6	279.2
1984	1,249	596	1,845	685,350	197.5	77.6	131.7	290.2
1985	1,512	728	2,240	723,250	243.1	94.0	160.4	302.9
1986	3,401	726	4,127	834,320	545.7	93.5	294.9	346.1
1987	3,495	699	4,194	855,090	574.9	89.8	302.6	351.3
1988	2,445	586	3,031	910,090	400.1	73.9	215.9	370.2
1989	1,281	722	2,003	951,710	213.2	90.2	142.9	383.4
1990	1,486	788	2,274	1,054,860	236.6	98.0	158.8	424.1
1991	1,311	838	2,149	1,092,740	206.0	102.9	148.1	433.3
1992	1,328	654	1,982	1,126,970	206.5	80.4	136.1	441.8
1993	1,411	540	1,951	1,135,610	226.4	65.0	134.2	440.3
1994	1,977	591	2,568	1,113,180	314.4	70.5	175.1	427.6
1995	2,579	560	3,139	1,099,210	414.3	67.0	215.3	418.3
1996	2,210	556	2,766	1,029,810	352.4	66.1	188.4	388.2

Notes: (1) Metropolitan Statistical Area - see Appendix A for areas included; (2) calculated by the editors using the following formula: (number of crimes in the MSA minus number of crimes in the city); (3) calculated by the editors using the following formula: ((number of crimes in the MSA minus number of crimes in the city) ÷ (population of the MSA minus population of the city)) x 100,000; n/a not avail.
Source: U.S. Department of Justice, FBI Uniform Crime Reports, 1977 - 1996

Burglaries and Burglary Rates: 1977 - 1996

Year	Number				Rate per 100,000 population			
	City	Suburbs[2]	MSA[1]	U.S.	City	Suburbs[3]	MSA[1]	U.S.
1977	7,077	4,618	11,695	3,071,500	1,083.8	607.9	827.9	1,419.8
1978	7,209	4,644	11,853	3,128,300	1,138.9	599.9	842.3	1,434.6
1979	8,546	5,032	13,578	3,327,700	1,324.8	641.3	949.6	1,511.9
1980	9,638	5,868	15,506	3,795,200	1,520.6	773.1	1,113.2	1,684.1
1981	10,293	6,035	16,328	3,779,700	1,604.0	785.3	1,157.9	1,649.5
1982	10,183	5,835	16,018	3,447,100	1,578.2	755.2	1,129.7	1,488.8
1983	8,873	5,671	14,544	3,129,900	1,378.9	736.1	1,028.7	1,337.7
1984	8,201	4,893	13,094	2,984,400	1,296.7	637.2	935.0	1,263.7
1985	7,782	4,595	12,377	3,073,300	1,251.3	593.3	886.3	1,287.3
1986	8,417	4,392	12,809	3,241,400	1,350.4	565.9	915.3	1,344.6
1987	9,964	4,636	14,600	3,236,200	1,639.1	595.7	1,053.3	1,329.6
1988	8,787	4,009	12,796	3,218,100	1,437.8	505.6	911.4	1,309.2
1989	9,175	3,983	13,158	3,168,200	1,526.9	497.5	938.9	1,276.3
1990	9,311	4,242	13,553	3,073,900	1,482.4	527.6	946.3	1,235.9
1991	9,431	4,266	13,697	3,157,200	1,482.1	523.8	944.1	1,252.0
1992	8,742	3,945	12,687	2,979,900	1,359.5	485.1	871.2	1,168.2
1993	8,250	3,840	12,090	2,834,800	1,324.0	462.4	831.7	1,099.2
1994	8,461	3,636	12,097	2,712,800	1,345.7	434.0	824.9	1,042.0
1995	8,366	3,299	11,665	2,593,800	1,344.0	394.9	800.2	987.1
1996	7,622	3,186	10,808	2,501,500	1,215.4	378.7	736.0	943.0

Notes: (1) Metropolitan Statistical Area - see Appendix A for areas included; (2) calculated by the editors using the following formula: (number of crimes in the MSA minus number of crimes in the city); (3) calculated by the editors using the following formula: ((number of crimes in the MSA minus number of crimes in the city) ÷ (population of the MSA minus population of the city)) x 100,000; n/a not avail.
Source: U.S. Department of Justice, FBI Uniform Crime Reports, 1977 - 1996

Larceny-Thefts and Larceny-Theft Rates: 1977 - 1996

Year	Number				Rate per 100,000 population			
	City	Suburbs[2]	MSA[1]	U.S.	City	Suburbs[3]	MSA[1]	U.S.
1977	21,365	22,600	43,965	5,905,700	3,271.8	2,975.0	3,112.2	2,729.9
1978	20,556	22,935	43,491	5,991,000	3,247.4	2,962.5	3,090.6	2,747.4
1979	22,563	24,218	46,781	6,601,000	3,497.6	3,086.3	3,271.9	2,999.1
1980	24,726	25,124	49,850	7,136,900	3,901.0	3,310.0	3,578.9	3,167.0
1981	27,512	24,736	52,248	7,194,400	4,287.3	3,219.0	3,705.1	3,139.7
1982	28,794	23,441	52,235	7,142,500	4,462.6	3,033.8	3,684.0	3,084.8
1983	30,216	20,997	51,213	6,712,800	4,695.8	2,725.6	3,622.3	2,868.9
1984	30,618	20,041	50,659	6,591,900	4,841.1	2,609.7	3,617.4	2,791.3
1985	27,151	20,432	47,583	6,926,400	4,365.6	2,638.1	3,407.5	2,901.2
1986	28,051	19,296	47,347	7,257,200	4,500.6	2,486.3	3,383.5	3,010.3
1987	28,680	18,870	47,550	7,499,900	4,718.0	2,424.9	3,430.6	3,081.3
1988	28,924	18,809	47,733	7,705,900	4,732.8	2,372.2	3,399.7	3,134.9
1989	30,063	20,561	50,624	7,872,400	5,003.0	2,568.4	3,612.3	3,171.3
1990	29,575	21,319	50,894	7,945,700	4,708.6	2,651.5	3,553.7	3,194.8
1991	28,322	22,288	50,610	8,142,200	4,450.8	2,736.7	3,488.5	3,228.8
1992	26,437	21,864	48,301	7,915,200	4,111.4	2,688.6	3,316.8	3,103.0
1993	25,553	20,761	46,314	7,820,900	4,100.9	2,499.7	3,186.1	3,032.4
1994	25,532	20,986	46,518	7,879,800	4,060.8	2,505.0	3,172.0	3,026.7
1995	26,231	20,403	46,634	7,997,700	4,214.0	2,442.6	3,199.0	3,043.8
1996	25,948	20,945	46,893	7,894,600	4,137.5	2,489.6	3,193.4	2,975.9

Notes: (1) Metropolitan Statistical Area - see Appendix A for areas included; (2) calculated by the editors using the following formula: (number of crimes in the MSA minus number of crimes in the city); (3) calculated by the editors using the following formula: ((number of crimes in the MSA minus number of crimes in the city) ÷ (population of the MSA minus population of the city)) x 100,000; n/a not avail.
Source: U.S. Department of Justice, FBI Uniform Crime Reports, 1977 - 1996

Motor Vehicle Thefts and Motor Vehicle Theft Rates: 1977 - 1996

Year	Number				Rate per 100,000 population			
	City	Suburbs[2]	MSA[1]	U.S.	City	Suburbs[3]	MSA[1]	U.S.
1977	3,570	1,243	4,813	977,700	546.7	163.6	340.7	451.9
1978	3,619	1,367	4,986	1,004,100	571.7	176.6	354.3	460.5
1979	4,222	1,533	5,755	1,112,800	654.5	195.4	402.5	505.6
1980	3,772	1,326	5,098	1,131,700	595.1	174.7	366.0	502.2
1981	3,546	1,178	4,724	1,087,800	552.6	153.3	335.0	474.7
1982	3,281	988	4,269	1,062,400	508.5	127.9	301.1	458.8
1983	4,599	1,009	5,608	1,007,900	714.7	131.0	396.6	430.8
1984	5,571	1,241	6,812	1,032,200	880.8	161.6	486.4	437.1
1985	4,954	1,164	6,118	1,102,900	796.6	150.3	438.1	462.0
1986	6,306	1,226	7,532	1,224,100	1,011.7	158.0	538.2	507.8
1987	5,746	1,176	6,922	1,288,700	945.2	151.1	499.4	529.4
1988	6,676	1,238	7,914	1,432,900	1,092.4	156.1	563.7	582.9
1989	9,137	1,548	10,685	1,564,800	1,520.6	193.4	762.4	630.4
1990	13,238	1,711	14,949	1,635,900	2,107.6	212.8	1,043.8	657.8
1991	13,570	1,831	15,401	1,661,700	2,132.5	224.8	1,061.6	659.0
1992	14,241	1,856	16,097	1,610,800	2,214.7	228.2	1,105.4	631.5
1993	10,615	1,826	12,441	1,563,100	1,703.5	219.9	855.8	606.1
1994	10,686	1;644	12,330	1,539,300	1,699.6	196.2	840.8	591.3
1995	11,345	1,591	12,936	1,472,400	1,822.6	190.5	887.4	560.4
1996	10,079	1,710	11,789	1,395,200	1,607.1	203.3	802.8	525.9

Notes: (1) Metropolitan Statistical Area - see Appendix A for areas included; (2) calculated by the editors using the following formula: (number of crimes in the MSA minus number of crimes in the city); (3) calculated by the editors using the following formula: ((number of crimes in the MSA minus number of crimes in the city) ÷ (population of the MSA minus population of the city)) x 100,000; n/a not avail.
Source: U.S. Department of Justice, FBI Uniform Crime Reports, 1977 - 1996

HATE CRIMES

Criminal Incidents by Bias Motivation

Area	Race	Ethnicity	Religion	Sexual Orientation
Milwaukee	3	1	1	0

Notes: Figures include both violent and property crimes. Law enforcement agencies must have submitted data for at least one quarter of calendar year 1995 to be included in this report, therefore figures shown may not represent complete 12-month totals; n/a not available
Source: U.S. Department of Justice, FBI Uniform Crime Reports, Hate Crime Statistics 1995

LAW ENFORCEMENT

Full-Time Law Enforcement Employees

Jurisdiction	Police Employees			Police Officers per 100,000 population
	Total	Officers	Civilians	
Milwaukee	2,848	2,130	718	339.6

Notes: Data as of October 31, 1996
Source: U.S. Department of Justice, FBI Uniform Crime Reports, 1996

Number of Police Officers by Race

Race	Police Officers				Index of Representation[1]		
	1983		1992				
	Number	Pct.	Number	Pct.	1983	1992	% Chg.
Black	168	11.7	283	14.4	0.50	0.47	-6.0
Hispanic[2]	66	4.6	109	5.5	1.09	0.87	-20.2

Notes: (1) The index of representation is calculated by dividing the percent of black/hispanic police officers by the percent of corresponding blacks/hispanics in the local population. An index approaching 1.0 indicates that a city is closer to achieving a representation of police officers equal to their proportion in the local population; (2) Hispanic officers can be of any race
Source: Bureau of Justice Statistics, Sourcebook of Criminal Justice Statistics, 1994

CORRECTIONS

Federal Correctional Facilities

Type	Year Opened	Security Level	Sex of Inmates	Rated Capacity	Population on 7/1/95	Number of Staff
None listed						

Notes: Data as of 1995
Source: Bureau of Justice Statistics, Sourcebook of Criminal Justice Statistics Online

City/County/Regional Correctional Facilities

Name	Year Opened	Year Renov.	Rated Capacity	1995 Pop.	Number of COs[1]	Number of Staff	ACA[2] Accred.
Milwaukee Co House of Corr	1953	1993	1,106	n/a	n/a	n/a	No
Milwaukee Co Jail	1992	-	798	1,170	290	438	No

Notes: Data as of April 1996; (1) Correctional Officers; (2) American Correctional Assn. Accreditation
Source: American Correctional Association, 1996-1998 National Jail and Adult Detention Directory

Private Adult Correctional Facilities

Name	Date Opened	Rated Capacity	Present Pop.	Security Level	Facility Construct.	Expans. Plans	ACA[1] Accred.
None listed							

Notes: Data as of December 1996; (1) American Correctional Association Accreditation
Source: University of Florida, Center for Studies in Criminology and Law, Private Adult Correctional Facility Census, 10th Ed., March 15, 1997

Characteristics of Shock Incarceration Programs

Jurisdiction	Year Program Began	Number of Camps	Average Num. of Inmates	Number of Beds	Program Length	Voluntary/ Mandatory
Wisconsin	1991	1	70	75	6 months	Voluntary

Note: Data as of July 1996;
Source: Sourcebook of Criminal Justice Statistics Online

INMATES AND HIV/AIDS

HIV Testing Policies for Inmates

Jurisdiction	All Inmates at Some Time	All Convicted Inmates at Admission	Random Samples While in Custody	High-risk Groups	Upon Inmate Request	Upon Court Order	Upon Involvement in Incident
Milwaukee Co.[1]	No	No	No	No	Yes	Yes	Yes

Notes: (1) All facilities reported following the same testing policy or authorities reported the policy to be jurisdiction-wide
Source: HIV in Prisons and Jails, 1993 (released August 1995)

Inmates Known to be Positive for HIV

Jurisdiction	Number of Jail Inmates in Facilities Providing Data	Type of HIV Infection/AIDS Cases				HIV/AIDS Cases as a Percent of Tot. Custody Pop.
		Total	Asymptomatic	Symptomatic	Confirmed AIDS	
Milwaukee Co.	2,292	25	20	2	3	1.1

Source: HIV in Prisons and Jails, 1993 (released August, 1995)

DEATH PENALTY

Wisconsin did not have the death penalty as of July 31, 1997.
Source: Death Penalty Information Center Web Site, 9/30/97

LAWS

Statutory Provisions Relating to the Purchase, Ownership and Use of Handguns

Jurisdiction	Instant Background Check	Federal Waiting Period Applies[1]	State Waiting Period (days)	License or Permit to Purchase	Registration	Record of Sale Sent to Police	Concealed Carry Law
Wisconsin	Yes	No	2	No	No	Yes	Yes[a]

Note: Data as of 1996; (1) The Federal 5-day waiting period for handgun purchases applies to states that don't have instant background checks, waiting period requirements, or licensing procedures exempting them from the Federal requirement; (a) No permit system exists and concealed carry is prohibited
Source: Sourcebook of Criminal Justice Statistics Online

Statutory Provisions Relating to Alcohol Use and Driving

Jurisdiction	Drinking Age	Blood Alcohol Concentration Levels as Evidence in State Courts[1]		Open Container Law[1]	Anti-Consumption Law[1]	Dram Shop Law[1]
		Illegal per se at 0.10%	Presumption at 0.10%			
Wisconsin	21	Yes[a]	Yes[b]	Yes	Yes	Yes[c]

Note: Data as of January 1, 1997; (1) See Appendix C for an explanation of terms; (a) First and second offense 0.10%; third or subsequent offenses 0.08%; (b) 0.10% is prima facie evidence for first and second offenses. 0.08% is prima facie evidence for third and subsequent offenses; (c) Applies only to the actions of intoxicated minors
Source: Sourcebook of Criminal Justice Statistics Online

Statutory Provisions Relating to Curfews

Jurisdiction	Year Enacted	Latest Revision	Age Group(s)	Curfew Provisions
Milwaukee	1942	-	16 and under	10 pm to 5 am weekday nights 11 pm to 5 am weekend nights

Note: Data as of February 1996
Source: Sourcebook of Criminal Justice Statistics Online

Statutory Provisions Relating to Hate Crimes

Jurisdiction	Bias-Motivated Violence and Intimidation						Institutional Vandalism
	Civil Action	Criminal Penalty					
		Race/ Religion/ Ethnicity	Sexual Orientation	Mental/ Physical Disability	Gender	Age	
Wisconsin	Yes	Yes	Yes	Yes	No	No	Yes

Source: Anti-Defamation League, 1997 Hate Crimes Laws

Minneapolis, Minnesota

OVERVIEW

The total crime rate for the city increased 25.8% between 1977 and 1996. During that same period, the violent crime rate increased 116.6% and the property crime rate increased 16.1%.

Among violent crimes, the rates for: Murders increased 117.0%; Forcible Rapes increased 58.6%; Robberies increased 95.4%; and Aggravated Assaults increased 164.7%.

Among property crimes, the rates for: Burglaries decreased 21.5%; Larceny-Thefts increased 30.9%; and Motor Vehicle Thefts increased 52.6%.

ANTI-CRIME PROGRAMS

Crime prevention activities and programs include:

- Neighborhood Watch—Citizens report crime and suspicious activity to the police.
- RECAP—Program which addresses chronic problems which result in many calls to police in an effort to reduce the number of calls.
- McGruff Houses—Screened and trained volunteers let young children into their homes in emergency situations.
- Personal Safety Workshops—Two-hour workshops on street safety.
- Security Surveys—Trained officers visit homes and offices to assess security and make recommendations.
- Operation Identification—Personal identification codes are engraved on valuable possessions which aids in recovery of stolen goods.
  Minneapolis Police Department, 7/97

The city instituted a program which the National League of Cities (1993) considers among those which are innovative for combatting crime and violence:

- Community Crime Prevention/S.A.F.E. (Safety for Everyone), which added more civilian crime prevention specialists and police officers to the Community Crime Prevention Team, and has also strengthened the collaboration between the police department and city residents. As a result of the program citizens' trust of government has increased and there has been greater community participation in local events. *Exemplary Programs in Criminal Justice, National League of Cities, 1994*

CRIME RISK

Your Chances of Becoming a Victim[1]

Area	Any Crime	Violent Crime					Property Crime			
		Any	Murder	Forcible Rape[2]	Robbery	Aggrav. Assault	Any	Burglary	Larceny -Theft	Motor Vehicle Theft
City	1:9	1:53	1:4,357	1:361	1:112	1:122	1:11	1:47	1:17	1:64

Note: (1) Figures have been calculated by dividing the population of the city by the number of crimes reported to the FBI during 1996 and are expressed as odds (eg. 1:20 should be read as 1 in 20). (2) Figures have been calculated by dividing the female population of the city by the number of forcible rapes reported to the FBI during 1996. The female population of the city was estimated by calculating the ratio of females to males reported in the 1990 Census and applying that ratio to 1996 population estimate.
Source: FBI Uniform Crime Reports 1996

CRIME STATISTICS

Total Crimes and Total Crime Rates: 1977 - 1996

Year	Number				Rate per 100,000 population			
	City	Suburbs[2]	MSA[1]	U.S.	City	Suburbs[3]	MSA[1]	U.S.
1977	32,298	80,344	112,642	10,984,500	8,971.7	4,646.4	5,391.7	5,077.6
1978	30,542	80,795	111,337	11,209,000	8,627.7	4,618.9	5,293.6	5,140.3
1979	32,406	86,035	118,441	12,249,500	8,905.2	4,985.9	5,668.5	5,565.5
1980	35,820	93,579	129,399	13,408,300	9,676.8	5,383.3	6,137.1	5,950.0
1981	38,215	92,990	131,205	13,423,800	10,251.2	5,311.1	6,178.3	5,858.2
1982	37,259	89,284	126,543	12,974,400	9,890.8	5,047.0	5,897.3	5,603.6
1983	34,948	79,144	114,092	12,108,600	9,249.2	4,403.3	5,245.0	5,175.0
1984	31,635	76,473	108,108	11,881,800	8,530.0	4,173.7	4,907.1	5,031.3
1985	37,977	81,897	119,874	12,431,400	10,519.3	4,342.6	5,335.0	5,207.1
1986	41,794	86,646	128,440	13,211,900	11,518.4	4,586.8	5,703.7	5,480.4
1987	45,356	93,365	138,721	13,508,700	12,620.9	4,784.8	6,003.5	5,550.0
1988	40,004	90,139	130,143	13,923,100	10,967.7	4,499.8	5,496.0	5,664.2
1989	42,145	93,454	135,599	14,251,400	12,097.3	4,523.8	5,616.7	5,741.0
1990	n/a	n/a	n/a	14,475,600	n/a	n/a	n/a	5,820.3
1991	42,115	96,963	139,078	14,872,900	11,281.7	4,568.7	5,572.8	5,897.8
1992	41,898	103,397	145,295	14,438,200	11,103.4	4,650.0	5,586.3	5,660.2
1993	40,463	n/a	n/a	14,144,800	11,036.1	n/a	n/a	5,484.4
1994	41,411	98,242	139,653	13,989,500	11,167.0	4,259.0	5,215.8	5,373.5
1995	41,299	102,264	143,563	13,862,700	11,545.4	4,337.6	5,287.2	5,275.9
1996	40,826	105,840	146,666	13,473,600	11,290.5	4,443.7	5,346.1	5,078.9

Notes: (1) Metropolitan Statistical Area - see Appendix A for areas included; (2) calculated by the editors using the following formula: (number of crimes in the MSA minus number of crimes in the city); (3) calculated by the editors using the following formula: ((number of crimes in the MSA minus number of crimes in the city) ÷ (population of the MSA minus population of the city)) x 100,000; n/a not avail.
Source: U.S. Department of Justice, FBI Uniform Crime Reports, 1977 - 1996

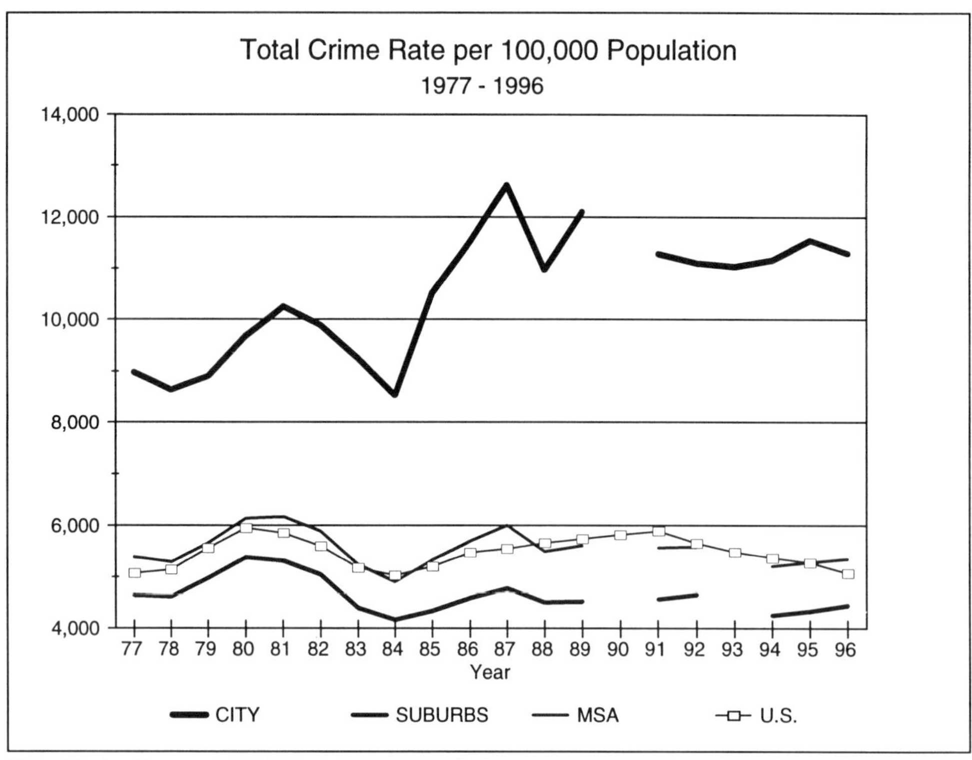

Note: Missing line segments indicate data not available.

Violent Crimes and Violent Crime Rates: 1977 - 1996

Year	Number				Rate per 100,000 population			
	City	Suburbs[2]	MSA[1]	U.S.	City	Suburbs[3]	MSA[1]	U.S.
1977	3,130	3,330	6,460	1,029,580	869.4	192.6	309.2	475.9
1978	3,098	3,231	6,329	1,085,550	875.1	184.7	300.9	497.8
1979	3,899	3,539	7,438	1,208,030	1,071.5	205.1	356.0	548.9
1980	3,917	3,702	7,619	1,344,520	1,058.2	213.0	361.3	596.6
1981	3,883	3,963	7,846	1,361,820	1,041.6	226.3	369.5	594.3
1982	4,247	3,473	7,720	1,322,390	1,127.4	196.3	359.8	571.1
1983	3,487	3,125	6,612	1,258,090	922.9	173.9	304.0	537.7
1984	3,883	3,532	7,415	1,273,280	1,047.0	192.8	336.6	539.2
1985	5,135	3,872	9,007	1,328,800	1,422.4	205.3	400.9	556.6
1986	5,959	4,255	10,214	1,489,170	1,642.3	225.2	453.6	617.7
1987	5,538	4,540	10,078	1,484,000	1,541.0	232.7	436.2	609.7
1988	5,500	4,811	10,311	1,566,220	1,507.9	240.2	435.4	637.2
1989	5,367	5,057	10,424	1,646,040	1,540.5	244.8	431.8	663.1
1990	n/a	n/a	n/a	1,820,130	n/a	n/a	n/a	731.8
1991	5,889	5,840	11,729	1,911,770	1,577.5	275.2	470.0	758.1
1992	6,199	6,233	12,432	1,932,270	1,642.8	280.3	478.0	757.5
1993	6,481	n/a	n/a	1,926,020	1,767.7	n/a	n/a	746.8
1994	7,074	6,220	13,294	1,857,670	1,907.6	269.7	496.5	713.6
1995	7,076	6,225	13,301	1,798,790	1,978.1	264.0	489.9	684.6
1996	6,808	6,046	12,854	1,682,280	1,882.8	253.8	468.5	634.1

Notes: Violent crimes include murder, forcible rape, robbery and aggravated assault; n/a not available; (1) Metropolitan Statistical Area - see Appendix A for areas included; (2) calculated by the editors using the following formula: (number of crimes in the MSA minus number of crimes in the city); (3) calculated by the editors using the following formula: ((number of crimes in the MSA minus number of crimes in the city) ÷ (population of the MSA minus population of the city)) x 100,000
Source: U.S. Department of Justice, FBI Uniform Crime Reports, 1977 - 1996

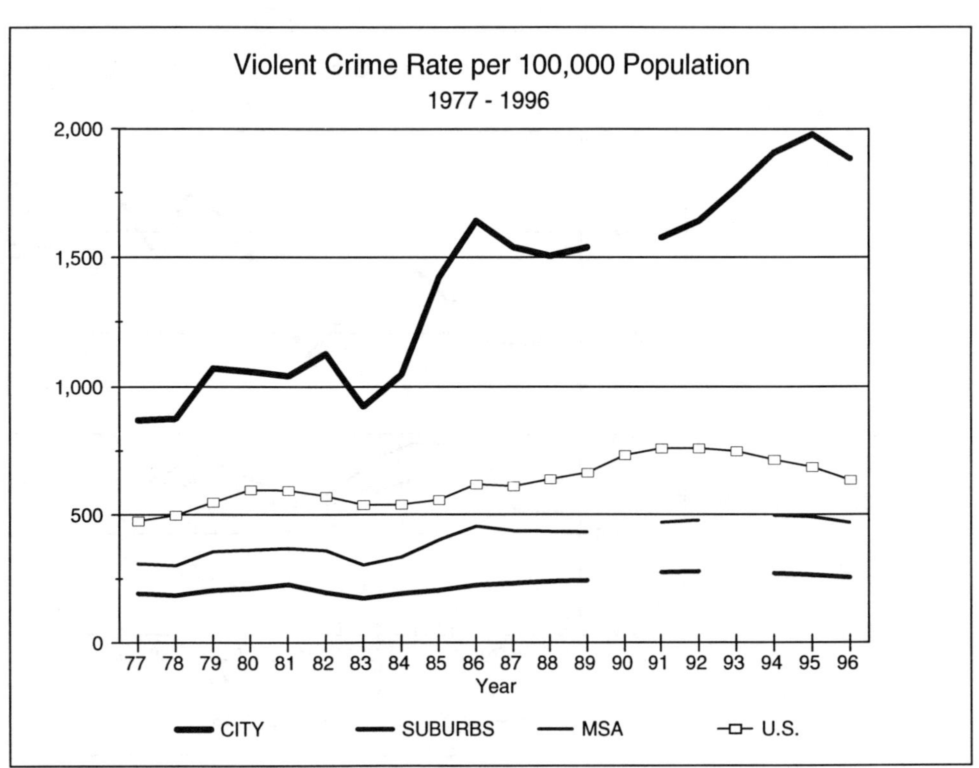

Note: Missing line segments indicate data not available.

Property Crimes and Property Crime Rates: 1977 - 1996

Year	Number				Rate per 100,000 population			
	City	Suburbs[2]	MSA[1]	U.S.	City	Suburbs[3]	MSA[1]	U.S.
1977	29,168	77,014	106,182	9,955,000	8,102.2	4,453.8	5,082.5	4,601.7
1978	27,444	77,564	105,008	10,123,400	7,752.5	4,434.2	4,992.7	4,642.5
1979	28,507	82,496	111,003	11,041,500	7,833.8	4,780.8	5,312.5	5,016.6
1980	31,903	89,877	121,780	12,063,700	8,618.6	5,170.3	5,775.7	5,353.3
1981	34,332	89,027	123,359	12,061,900	9,209.6	5,084.8	5,808.8	5,263.9
1982	33,012	85,811	118,823	11,652,000	8,763.4	4,850.7	5,537.6	5,032.5
1983	31,461	76,019	107,480	10,850,500	8,326.3	4,229.4	4,941.1	4,637.4
1984	27,752	72,941	100,693	10,608,500	7,483.0	3,981.0	4,570.5	4,492.1
1985	32,842	78,025	110,867	11,102,600	9,097.0	4,137.3	4,934.1	4,650.5
1986	35,835	82,391	118,226	11,722,700	9,876.1	4,361.6	5,250.1	4,862.6
1987	39,818	88,825	128,643	12,024,700	11,079.9	4,552.1	5,567.3	4,940.3
1988	34,504	85,328	119,832	12,356,900	9,459.8	4,259.6	5,060.6	5,027.1
1989	36,778	88,397	125,175	12,605,400	10,556.7	4,279.0	5,184.9	5,077.9
1990	n/a	n/a	n/a	12,655,500	n/a	n/a	n/a	5,088.5
1991	36,226	91,123	127,349	12,961,100	9,704.2	4,293.5	5,102.9	5,139.7
1992	35,699	97,164	132,863	12,505,900	9,460.6	4,369.7	5,108.3	4,902.7
1993	33,982	93,949	127,931	12,218,800	9,268.4	4,117.5	4,830.6	4,737.6
1994	34,337	92,022	126,359	12,131,900	9,259.4	3,989.4	4,719.3	4,660.0
1995	34,223	96,039	130,262	12,063,900	9,567.3	4,073.6	4,797.3	4,591.3
1996	34,018	99,794	133,812	11,791,300	9,407.8	4,189.8	4,877.6	4,444.8

Notes: Property crimes include burglary, larceny-theft and motor vehicle theft; n/a not available; (1) Metropolitan Statistical Area - see Appendix A for areas included; (2) calculated by the editors using the following formula: (number of crimes in the MSA minus number of crimes in the city); (3) calculated by the editors using the following formula: ((number of crimes in the MSA minus number of crimes in the city) ÷ (population of the MSA minus population of the city)) x 100,000
Source: U.S. Department of Justice, FBI Uniform Crime Reports, 1977 - 1996

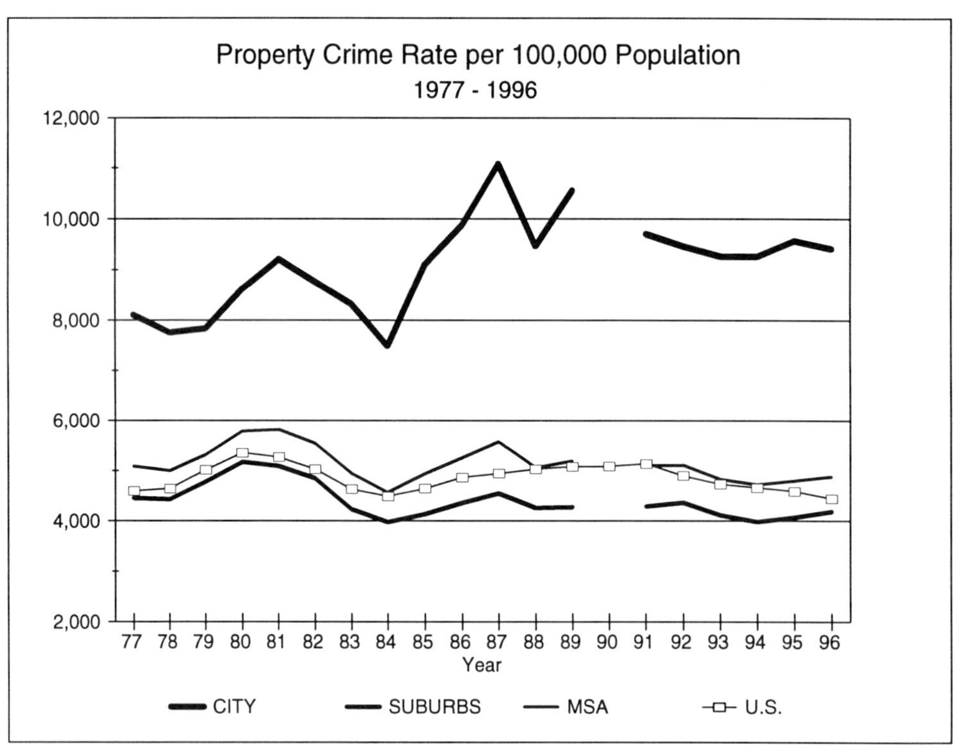

Note: Missing line segments indicate data not available.

Murders and Murder Rates: 1977 - 1996

Year	Number				Rate per 100,000 population			
	City	Suburbs[2]	MSA[1]	U.S.	City	Suburbs[3]	MSA[1]	U.S.
1977	38	37	75	19,120	10.6	2.1	3.6	8.8
1978	26	31	57	19,560	7.3	1.8	2.7	9.0
1979	30	36	66	21,460	8.2	2.1	3.2	9.7
1980	36	35	71	23,040	9.7	2.0	3.4	10.2
1981	28	29	57	22,520	7.5	1.7	2.7	9.8
1982	36	34	70	21,010	9.6	1.9	3.3	9.1
1983	16	29	45	19,310	4.2	1.6	2.1	8.3
1984	27	23	50	18,690	7.3	1.3	2.3	7.9
1985	29	28	57	18,980	8.0	1.5	2.5	7.9
1986	44	33	77	20,610	12.1	1.7	3.4	8.6
1987	38	40	78	20,100	10.6	2.0	3.4	8.3
1988	55	34	89	20,680	15.1	1.7	3.8	8.4
1989	46	38	84	21,500	13.2	1.8	3.5	8.7
1990	n/a	n/a	n/a	23,440	n/a	n/a	n/a	9.4
1991	64	32	96	24,700	17.1	1.5	3.8	9.8
1992	60	53	113	23,760	15.9	2.4	4.3	9.3
1993	58	58	116	24,530	15.8	2.5	4.4	9.5
1994	62	55	117	23,330	16.7	2.4	4.4	9.0
1995	96	60	156	21,610	26.8	2.5	5.7	8.2
1996	83	40	123	19,650	23.0	1.7	4.5	7.4

Notes: (1) Metropolitan Statistical Area - see Appendix A for areas included; (2) calculated by the editors using the following formula: (number of crimes in the MSA minus number of crimes in the city); (3) calculated by the editors using the following formula: ((number of crimes in the MSA minus number of crimes in the city) ÷ (population of the MSA minus population of the city)) x 100,000; n/a not avail.
Source: U.S. Department of Justice, FBI Uniform Crime Reports, 1977 - 1996

Forcible Rapes and Forcible Rape Rates: 1977 - 1996

Year	Number				Rate per 100,000 population			
	City	Suburbs[2]	MSA[1]	U.S.	City	Suburbs[3]	MSA[1]	U.S.
1977	324	268	592	63,500	90.0	15.5	28.3	29.4
1978	307	316	623	67,610	86.7	18.1	29.6	31.0
1979	327	335	662	76,390	89.9	19.4	31.7	34.7
1980	373	365	738	82,990	100.8	21.0	35.0	36.8
1981	367	432	799	82,500	98.4	24.7	37.6	36.0
1982	314	409	723	78,770	83.4	23.1	33.7	34.0
1983	316	425	741	78,920	83.6	23.6	34.1	33.7
1984	392	428	820	84,230	105.7	23.4	37.2	35.7
1985	419	486	905	88,670	116.1	25.8	40.3	37.1
1986	492	482	974	91,460	135.6	25.5	43.3	37.9
1987	520	538	1,058	91,110	144.7	27.6	45.8	37.4
1988	460	533	993	92,490	126.1	26.6	41.9	37.6
1989	462	497	959	94,500	132.6	24.1	39.7	38.1
1990	n/a	n/a	n/a	102,560	n/a	n/a	n/a	41.2
1991	744	656	1,400	106,590	199.3	30.9	56.1	42.3
1992	600	791	1,391	109,060	159.0	35.6	53.5	42.8
1993	518	n/a	n/a	106,010	141.3	n/a	n/a	41.1
1994	578	1,091	1,669	102,220	155.9	47.3	62.3	39.3
1995	578	974	1,552	97,470	161.6	41.3	57.2	37.1
1996	516	932	1,448	95,770	142.7	39.1	52.8	36.1

Notes: (1) Metropolitan Statistical Area - see Appendix A for areas included; (2) calculated by the editors using the following formula: (number of crimes in the MSA minus number of crimes in the city); (3) calculated by the editors using the following formula: ((number of crimes in the MSA minus number of crimes in the city) ÷ (population of the MSA minus population of the city)) x 100,000; n/a not avail.
Source: U.S. Department of Justice, FBI Uniform Crime Reports, 1977 - 1996

Robberies and Robbery Rates: 1977 - 1996

Year	Number				Rate per 100,000 population			
	City	Suburbs[2]	MSA[1]	U.S.	City	Suburbs[3]	MSA[1]	U.S.
1977	1,652	1,457	3,109	412,610	458.9	84.3	148.8	190.7
1978	1,688	1,398	3,086	426,930	476.8	79.9	146.7	195.8
1979	1,988	1,458	3,446	480,700	546.3	84.5	164.9	218.4
1980	2,267	1,463	3,730	565,840	612.4	84.2	176.9	251.1
1981	2,296	1,703	3,999	592,910	615.9	97.3	188.3	258.7
1982	2,583	1,351	3,934	553,130	685.7	76.4	183.3	238.9
1983	2,001	1,074	3,075	506,570	529.6	59.8	141.4	216.5
1984	1,740	1,025	2,765	485,010	469.2	55.9	125.5	205.4
1985	2,326	1,094	3,420	497,870	644.3	58.0	152.2	208.5
1986	2,801	1,299	4,100	542,780	772.0	68.8	182.1	225.1
1987	2,866	1,279	4,145	517,700	797.5	65.5	179.4	212.7
1988	2,565	1,331	3,896	542,970	703.2	66.4	164.5	220.9
1989	2,524	1,419	3,943	578,330	724.5	68.7	163.3	233.0
1990	n/a	n/a	n/a	639,270	n/a	n/a	n/a	257.0
1991	2,610	1,536	4,146	687,730	699.2	72.4	166.1	272.7
1992	3,075	1,616	4,691	672,480	814.9	72.7	180.4	263.6
1993	3,178	1,703	4,881	659,870	866.8	74.6	184.3	255.9
1994	3,444	1,671	5,115	618,950	928.7	72.4	191.0	237.7
1995	3,550	1,840	5,390	580,510	992.4	78.0	198.5	220.9
1996	3,242	1,794	5,036	537,050	896.6	75.3	183.6	202.4

Notes: (1) Metropolitan Statistical Area - see Appendix A for areas included; (2) calculated by the editors using the following formula: (number of crimes in the MSA minus number of crimes in the city); (3) calculated by the editors using the following formula: ((number of crimes in the MSA minus number of crimes in the city) ÷ (population of the MSA minus population of the city)) x 100,000; n/a not avail.
Source: U.S. Department of Justice, FBI Uniform Crime Reports, 1977 - 1996

Aggravated Assaults and Aggravated Assault Rates: 1977 - 1996

Year	Number				Rate per 100,000 population			
	City	Suburbs[2]	MSA[1]	U.S.	City	Suburbs[3]	MSA[1]	U.S.
1977	1,116	1,568	2,684	534,350	310.0	90.7	128.5	247.0
1978	1,077	1,486	2,563	571,460	304.2	85.0	121.9	262.1
1979	1,554	1,710	3,264	629,480	427.0	99.1	156.2	286.0
1980	1,241	1,839	3,080	672,650	335.3	105.8	146.1	298.5
1981	1,192	1,799	2,991	663,900	319.8	102.7	140.8	289.7
1982	1,314	1,679	2,993	669,480	348.8	94.9	139.5	289.2
1983	1,154	1,597	2,751	653,290	305.4	88.9	126.5	279.2
1984	1,724	2,056	3,780	685,350	464.9	112.2	171.6	290.2
1985	2,361	2,264	4,625	723,250	654.0	120.0	205.8	302.9
1986	2,622	2,441	5,063	834,320	722.6	129.2	224.8	346.1
1987	2,114	2,683	4,797	855,090	588.3	137.5	207.6	351.3
1988	2,420	2,913	5,333	910,090	663.5	145.4	225.2	370.2
1989	2,335	3,103	5,438	951,710	670.2	150.2	225.2	383.4
1990	n/a	n/a	n/a	1,054,860	n/a	n/a	n/a	424.1
1991	2,471	3,616	6,087	1,092,740	661.9	170.4	243.9	433.3
1992	2,464	3,773	6,237	1,126,970	653.0	169.7	239.8	441.8
1993	2,727	3,516	6,243	1,135,610	743.8	154.1	235.7	440.3
1994	2,990	3,403	6,393	1,113,180	806.3	147.5	238.8	427.6
1995	2,852	3,351	6,203	1,099,210	797.3	142.1	228.4	418.3
1996	2,967	3,280	6,247	1,029,810	820.5	137.7	227.7	388.2

Notes: (1) Metropolitan Statistical Area - see Appendix A for areas included; (2) calculated by the editors using the following formula: (number of crimes in the MSA minus number of crimes in the city); (3) calculated by the editors using the following formula: ((number of crimes in the MSA minus number of crimes in the city) ÷ (population of the MSA minus population of the city)) x 100,000; n/a not avail.
Source: U.S. Department of Justice, FBI Uniform Crime Reports, 1977 - 1996

Burglaries and Burglary Rates: 1977 - 1996

Year	Number				Rate per 100,000 population			
	City	Suburbs[2]	MSA[1]	U.S.	City	Suburbs[3]	MSA[1]	U.S.
1977	9,743	21,115	30,858	3,071,500	2,706.4	1,221.1	1,477.1	1,419.8
1978	10,353	19,920	30,273	3,128,300	2,924.6	1,138.8	1,439.4	1,434.6
1979	9,979	20,476	30,455	3,327,700	2,742.2	1,186.6	1,457.5	1,511.9
1980	11,609	22,882	34,491	3,795,200	3,136.2	1,316.3	1,635.8	1,684.1
1981	12,543	24,162	36,705	3,779,700	3,364.7	1,380.0	1,728.4	1,649.5
1982	11,467	23,341	34,808	3,447,100	3,044.0	1,319.4	1,622.2	1,488.8
1983	10,887	21,065	31,952	3,129,900	2,881.3	1,172.0	1,468.9	1,337.7
1984	9,413	19,827	29,240	2,984,400	2,538.1	1,082.1	1,327.2	1,263.7
1985	10,983	19,503	30,486	3,073,300	3,042.2	1,034.1	1,356.8	1,287.3
1986	10,750	19,655	30,405	3,241,400	2,962.7	1,040.5	1,350.2	1,344.6
1987	11,987	20,838	32,825	3,236,200	3,335.6	1,067.9	1,420.6	1,329.6
1988	9,386	18,210	27,596	3,218,100	2,573.3	909.0	1,165.4	1,309.2
1989	9,842	18,121	27,963	3,168,200	2,825.0	877.2	1,158.3	1,276.3
1990	n/a	n/a	n/a	3,073,900	n/a	n/a	n/a	1,235.9
1991	8,990	16,466	25,456	3,157,200	2,408.2	775.8	1,020.0	1,252.0
1992	9,307	18,041	27,348	2,979,900	2,466.4	811.3	1,051.5	1,168.2
1993	9,358	16,847	26,205	2,834,800	2,552.4	738.4	989.5	1,099.2
1994	8,854	15,829	24,683	2,712,800	2,387.6	686.2	921.9	1,042.0
1995	8,024	15,823	23,847	2,593,800	2,243.2	671.1	878.2	987.1
1996	7,678	15,992	23,670	2,501,500	2,123.4	671.4	862.8	943.0

Notes: (1) Metropolitan Statistical Area - see Appendix A for areas included; (2) calculated by the editors using the following formula: (number of crimes in the MSA minus number of crimes in the city); (3) calculated by the editors using the following formula: ((number of crimes in the MSA minus number of crimes in the city) ÷ (population of the MSA minus population of the city)) x 100,000; n/a not avail.
Source: U.S. Department of Justice, FBI Uniform Crime Reports, 1977 - 1996

Larceny-Thefts and Larceny-Theft Rates: 1977 - 1996

Year	Number				Rate per 100,000 population			
	City	Suburbs[2]	MSA[1]	U.S.	City	Suburbs[3]	MSA[1]	U.S.
1977	15,738	49,639	65,377	5,905,700	4,371.7	2,870.7	3,129.3	2,729.9
1978	14,072	51,483	65,555	5,991,000	3,975.1	2,943.2	3,116.9	2,747.4
1979	15,243	55,776	71,019	6,601,000	4,188.8	3,232.3	3,398.9	2,999.1
1980	17,504	61,431	78,935	7,136,900	4,728.7	3,533.9	3,743.7	3,167.0
1981	18,943	60,380	79,323	7,194,400	5,081.5	3,448.6	3,735.2	3,139.7
1982	19,058	57,848	76,906	7,142,500	5,059.1	3,270.0	3,584.1	3,084.8
1983	18,416	50,937	69,353	6,712,800	4,873.9	2,834.0	3,188.3	2,868.9
1984	16,194	49,159	65,353	6,591,900	4,366.5	2,683.0	2,966.4	2,791.3
1985	18,448	53,712	72,160	6,926,400	5,110.0	2,848.1	3,211.5	2,901.2
1986	20,917	57,575	78,492	7,257,200	5,764.7	3,047.9	3,485.6	3,010.3
1987	23,254	62,533	85,787	7,499,900	6,470.8	3,204.7	3,712.6	3,081.3
1988	20,004	60,515	80,519	7,705,900	5,484.4	3,020.9	3,400.4	3,134.9
1989	21,448	62,407	83,855	7,872,400	6,156.4	3,020.9	3,473.4	3,171.3
1990	n/a	n/a	n/a	7,945,700	n/a	n/a	n/a	3,194.8
1991	22,155	67,107	89,262	8,142,200	5,934.9	3,161.9	3,576.7	3,228.8
1992	21,223	71,787	93,010	7,915,200	5,624.3	3,228.4	3,576.0	3,103.0
1993	19,952	69,539	89,491	7,820,900	5,441.8	3,047.7	3,379.2	3,032.4
1994	21,279	69,251	90,530	7,879,800	5,738.1	3,002.2	3,381.1	3,026.7
1995	21,710	72,628	94,338	7,997,700	6,069.2	3,080.6	3,474.3	3,043.8
1996	20,690	75,508	96,198	7,894,600	5,721.9	3,170.2	3,506.5	2,975.9

Notes: (1) Metropolitan Statistical Area - see Appendix A for areas included; (2) calculated by the editors using the following formula: (number of crimes in the MSA minus number of crimes in the city); (3) calculated by the editors using the following formula: ((number of crimes in the MSA minus number of crimes in the city) ÷ (population of the MSA minus population of the city)) x 100,000; n/a not avail.
Source: U.S. Department of Justice, FBI Uniform Crime Reports, 1977 - 1996

Motor Vehicle Thefts and Motor Vehicle Theft Rates: 1977 - 1996

Year	Number				Rate per 100,000 population			
	City	Suburbs[2]	MSA[1]	U.S.	City	Suburbs[3]	MSA[1]	U.S.
1977	3,687	6,260	9,947	977,700	1,024.2	362.0	476.1	451.9
1978	3,019	6,161	9,180	1,004,100	852.8	352.2	436.5	460.5
1979	3,285	6,244	9,529	1,112,800	902.7	361.9	456.0	505.6
1980	2,790	5,564	8,354	1,131,700	753.7	320.1	396.2	502.2
1981	2,846	4,485	7,331	1,087,800	763.4	256.2	345.2	474.7
1982	2,487	4,622	7,109	1,062,400	660.2	261.3	331.3	458.8
1983	2,158	4,017	6,175	1,007,900	571.1	223.5	283.9	430.8
1984	2,145	3,955	6,100	1,032,200	578.4	215.9	276.9	437.1
1985	3,411	4,810	8,221	1,102,900	944.8	255.0	365.9	462.0
1986	4,168	5,161	9,329	1,224,100	1,148.7	273.2	414.3	507.8
1987	4,577	5,454	10,031	1,288,700	1,273.6	279.5	434.1	529.4
1988	5,114	6,603	11,717	1,432,900	1,402.1	329.6	494.8	582.9
1989	5,488	7,869	13,357	1,564,800	1,575.3	380.9	553.3	630.4
1990	n/a	n/a	n/a	1,635,900	n/a	n/a	n/a	657.8
1991	5,081	7,550	12,631	1,661,700	1,361.1	355.7	506.1	659.0
1992	5,169	7,336	12,505	1,610,800	1,369.8	329.9	480.8	631.5
1993	4,672	7,563	12,235	1,563,100	1,274.3	331.5	462.0	606.1
1994	4,204	6,942	11,146	1,539,300	1,133.7	301.0	416.3	591.3
1995	4,489	7,588	12,077	1,472,400	1,254.9	321.9	444.8	560.4
1996	5,650	8,294	13,944	1,395,200	1,562.5	348.2	508.3	525.9

Notes: (1) Metropolitan Statistical Area - see Appendix A for areas included; (2) calculated by the editors using the following formula: (number of crimes in the MSA minus number of crimes in the city); (3) calculated by the editors using the following formula: ((number of crimes in the MSA minus number of crimes in the city) ÷ (population of the MSA minus population of the city)) x 100,000; n/a not avail.
Source: U.S. Department of Justice, FBI Uniform Crime Reports, 1977 - 1996

HATE CRIMES

Criminal Incidents by Bias Motivation

Area	Race	Ethnicity	Religion	Sexual Orientation
Minneapolis	35	0	0	9

Notes: Figures include both violent and property crimes. Law enforcement agencies must have submitted data for at least one quarter of calendar year 1995 to be included in this report, therefore figures shown may not represent complete 12-month totals; n/a not available
Source: U.S. Department of Justice, FBI Uniform Crime Reports, Hate Crime Statistics 1995

LAW ENFORCEMENT

Full-Time Law Enforcement Employees

Jurisdiction	Police Employees			Police Officers per 100,000 population
	Total	Officers	Civilians	
Minneapolis	1,081	913	168	252.5

Notes: Data as of October 31, 1996
Source: U.S. Department of Justice, FBI Uniform Crime Reports, 1996

Number of Police Officers by Race

Race	Police Officers				Index of Representation[1]		
	1983		1992				
	Number	Pct.	Number	Pct.	1983	1992	% Chg.
Black	20	3.0	46	5.5	0.38	0.42	10.5
Hispanic[2]	8	1.2	24	2.9	0.85	1.38	62.4

Notes: (1) The index of representation is calculated by dividing the percent of black/hispanic police officers by the percent of corresponding blacks/hispanics in the local population. An index approaching 1.0 indicates that a city is closer to achieving a representation of police officers equal to their proportion in the local population; (2) Hispanic officers can be of any race
Source: Bureau of Justice Statistics, Sourcebook of Criminal Justice Statistics, 1994

CORRECTIONS

Federal Correctional Facilities

Type	Year Opened	Security Level	Sex of Inmates	Rated Capacity	Population on 7/1/95	Number of Staff
None listed						

Notes: Data as of 1995
Source: Bureau of Justice Statistics, Sourcebook of Criminal Justice Statistics Online

City/County/Regional Correctional Facilities

Name	Year Opened	Year Renov.	Rated Capacity	1995 Pop.	Number of COs[1]	Number of Staff	ACA[2] Accred.
Hennepin Co Adult Det Ctr	1896	1987	509	499	181	238	Yes

Notes: Data as of April 1996; (1) Correctional Officers; (2) American Correctional Assn. Accreditation
Source: American Correctional Association, 1996-1998 National Jail and Adult Detention Directory

Private Adult Correctional Facilities

Name	Date Opened	Rated Capacity	Present Pop.	Security Level	Facility Construct.	Expans. Plans	ACA[1] Accred.
None listed							

Notes: Data as of December 1996; (1) American Correctional Association Accreditation
Source: University of Florida, Center for Studies in Criminology and Law, Private Adult Correctional Facility Census, 10th Ed., March 15, 1997

Characteristics of Shock Incarceration Programs

Jurisdiction	Year Program Began	Number of Camps	Average Num. of Inmates	Number of Beds	Program Length	Voluntary/ Mandatory
Minnesota	1992	1	51[a]	72 male; 8 female	6 months	Voluntary

Note: Data as of July 1996; (a) Varies
Source: Sourcebook of Criminal Justice Statistics Online

DEATH PENALTY

Minnesota did not have the death penalty as of July 31, 1997.
Source: Death Penalty Information Center Web Site, 9/30/97

LAWS

Statutory Provisions Relating to the Purchase, Ownership and Use of Handguns

Jurisdiction	Instant Background Check	Federal Waiting Period Applies[1]	State Waiting Period (days)	License or Permit to Purchase	Regis-tration	Record of Sale Sent to Police	Concealed Carry Law
Minnesota	No	No	7[a]	Yes[a]	No	Yes	Yes[b]

Note: Data as of 1996; (1) The Federal 5-day waiting period for handgun purchases applies to states that don't have instant background checks, waiting period requirements, or licensing procedures exempting them from the Federal requirement; (a) A handgun transfer or carrying permit, or a 7-day waiting period and handgun transfer report, is required to purchase handguns from a dealer; (b) Restrictively administered discretion by local authorities over permit issuance, or permits are unavailable and carrying is prohibited in most circumstances
Source: Sourcebook of Criminal Justice Statistics Online

Statutory Provisions Relating to Alcohol Use and Driving

Jurisdiction	Drinking Age	Blood Alcohol Concentration Levels as Evidence in State Courts[1]		Open Container Law[1]	Anti-Consump-tion Law[1]	Dram Shop Law[1]
		Illegal per se at 0.10%	Presumption at 0.10%			
Minnesota	21	Yes	No	Yes	Yes	Yes

Note: Data as of January 1, 1997; (1) See Appendix C for an explanation of terms
Source: Sourcebook of Criminal Justice Statistics Online

Statutory Provisions Relating to Curfews

Jurisdiction	Year Enacted	Latest Revision	Age Group(s)	Curfew Provisions
Minneapolis	1960	-	15 through 17 14 and under	Midnight to 4 am every night 10 pm to 4 am weekday nights 11 pm to 4 am weekend nights

Note: Data as of February 1996
Source: Sourcebook of Criminal Justice Statistics Online

Statutory Provisions Relating to Hate Crimes

Jurisdiction	Bias-Motivated Violence and Intimidation						Institutional Vandalism
		Criminal Penalty					
	Civil Action	Race/ Religion/ Ethnicity	Sexual Orientation	Mental/ Physical Disability	Gender	Age	
Minnesota	No	Yes	Yes	Yes	Yes	No	Yes

Source: Anti-Defamation League, 1997 Hate Crimes Laws

Mobile, Alabama

OVERVIEW

The total crime rate for the city increased 35.3% between 1977 and 1996. During that same period, the violent crime rate increased 21.6% and the property crime rate increased 37.3%.

Among violent crimes, the rates for: Murders increased 0.8%; Forcible Rapes decreased 4.2%; Robberies increased 101.3%; and Aggravated Assaults decreased 25.7%.

Among property crimes, the rates for: Burglaries decreased 4.6%; Larceny-Thefts increased 53.7%; and Motor Vehicle Thefts increased 126.1%.

ANTI-CRIME PROGRAMS

Among their programs:

- Penelope House—provides a safe shelter for women in danger. Clients are offered case management counseling in order to promote independence.
- Enhanced Truancy Enforcement—increases the level of law enforcement's participation in the reduction of truancy in order to impact the number of crimes committed by juvenile offenders.
- Academy of Public Service—provides a pool of minority candidates for area public safety agencies. The academy prepares students for careers in public service/safety organizations such as police and fire departments, as well as government agencies.
  Mobile Police Department, 6/97

CRIME RISK

Your Chances of Becoming a Victim[1]

Area	Any Crime	Violent Crime					Property Crime			
		Any	Murder	Forcible Rape[2]	Robbery	Aggrav. Assault	Any	Burglary	Larceny -Theft	Motor Vehicle Theft
City	1:11	1:95	1:4,061	1:934	1:161	1:283	1:12	1:47	1:19	1:107

Note: (1) Figures have been calculated by dividing the population of the city by the number of crimes reported to the FBI during 1996 and are expressed as odds (eg. 1:20 should be read as 1 in 20).
(2) Figures have been calculated by dividing the female population of the city by the number of forcible rapes reported to the FBI during 1996. The female population of the city was estimated by calculating the ratio of females to males reported in the 1990 Census and applying that ratio to 1996 population estimate.
Source: FBI Uniform Crime Reports 1996

CRIME STATISTICS

Total Crimes and Total Crime Rates: 1977 - 1996

Year	Number				Rate per 100,000 population			
	City	Suburbs[2]	MSA[1]	U.S.	City	Suburbs[3]	MSA[1]	U.S.
1977	14,272	8,102	22,374	10,984,500	6,962.0	3,795.3	5,346.6	5,077.6
1978	15,210	9,091	24,301	11,209,000	7,312.5	4,114.2	5,665.0	5,140.3
1979	16,580	8,633	25,213	12,249,500	7,913.3	3,769.5	5,749.3	5,565.5
1980	21,088	11,243	32,331	13,408,300	10,575.1	4,674.3	7,348.9	5,950.0
1981	21,998	11,542	33,540	13,423,800	10,877.9	4,731.7	7,517.6	5,858.2
1982	22,344	11,773	34,117	12,974,400	10,973.3	4,793.4	7,594.6	5,603.6
1983	19,731	10,287	30,018	12,108,600	9,650.9	4,171.6	6,655.2	5,175.0
1984	16,782	9,413	26,195	11,881,800	8,111.9	3,676.2	5,658.5	5,031.3
1985	16,707	9,122	25,829	12,431,400	8,090.4	3,471.2	5,503.8	5,207.1
1986	20,133	10,564	30,697	13,211,900	9,672.4	3,988.6	6,489.8	5,480.4
1987	21,623	11,011	32,634	13,508,700	10,558.1	4,097.0	6,891.2	5,550.0
1988	21,852	11,156	33,008	13,923,100	10,346.3	4,026.3	6,760.0	5,664.2
1989	21,686	10,478	32,164	14,251,400	10,351.0	3,773.3	6,601.8	5,741.0
1990	22,379	8,873	31,252	14,475,600	11,401.7	3,161.6	6,552.8	5,820.3
1991	n/a	n/a	n/a	14,872,900	n/a	n/a	n/a	5,897.8
1992	26,257	n/a	n/a	14,438,200	13,069.0	n/a	n/a	5,660.2
1993	18,567	12,446	31,013	14,144,800	9,088.7	4,188.4	6,184.8	5,484.4
1994	20,525	13,090	33,615	13,989,500	9,971.0	4,371.8	6,653.0	5,373.5
1995	18,915	13,019	31,934	13,862,700	9,175.9	4,197.9	6,185.6	5,275.9
1996	19,512	12,705	32,217	13,473,600	9,421.3	4,077.6	6,211.3	5,078.9

Notes: (1) Metropolitan Statistical Area - see Appendix A for areas included; (2) calculated by the editors using the following formula: (number of crimes in the MSA minus number of crimes in the city); (3) calculated by the editors using the following formula: ((number of crimes in the MSA minus number of crimes in the city) ÷ (population of the MSA minus population of the city)) x 100,000; n/a not avail.
Source: U.S. Department of Justice, FBI Uniform Crime Reports, 1977 - 1996

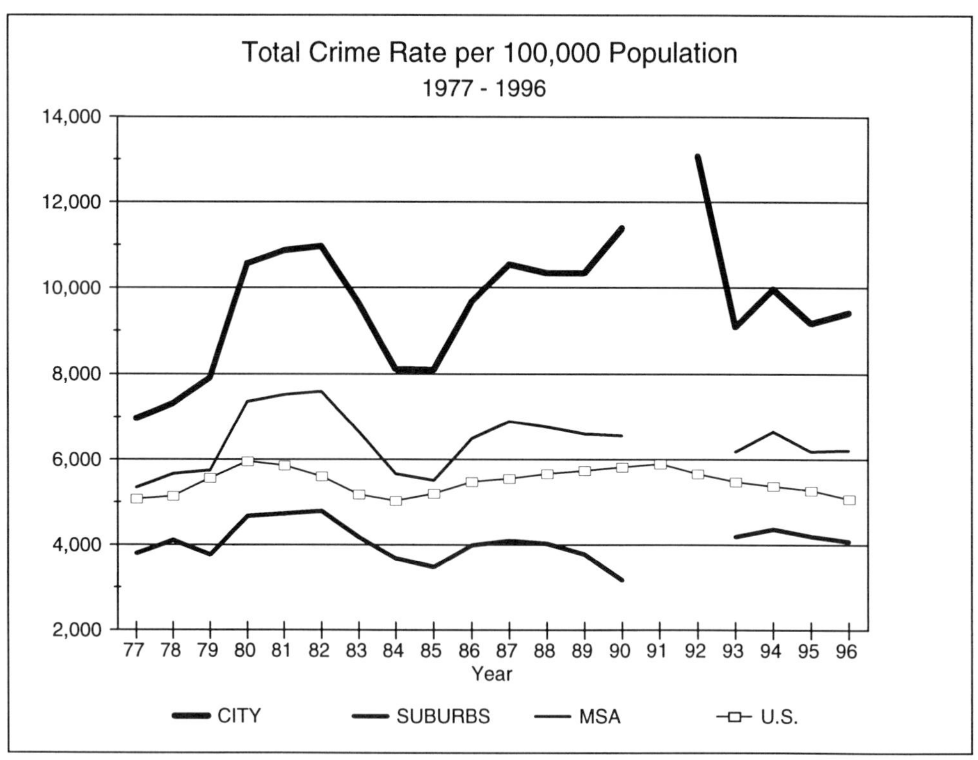

Note: Missing line segments indicate data not available.

Violent Crimes and Violent Crime Rates: 1977 - 1996

Year	Number				Rate per 100,000 population			
	City	Suburbs[2]	MSA[1]	U.S.	City	Suburbs[3]	MSA[1]	U.S.
1977	1,779	927	2,706	1,029,580	867.8	434.2	646.6	475.9
1978	1,938	1,077	3,015	1,085,550	931.7	487.4	702.8	497.8
1979	1,763	888	2,651	1,208,030	841.4	387.7	604.5	548.9
1980	2,675	986	3,661	1,344,520	1,341.5	409.9	832.2	596.6
1981	2,629	1,101	3,730	1,361,820	1,300.0	451.4	836.0	594.3
1982	2,436	1,313	3,749	1,322,390	1,196.3	534.6	834.5	571.1
1983	2,225	1,277	3,502	1,258,090	1,088.3	517.8	776.4	537.7
1984	2,185	1,414	3,599	1,273,280	1,056.2	552.2	777.4	539.2
1985	2,177	1,180	3,357	1,328,800	1,054.2	449.0	715.3	556.6
1986	3,525	1,525	5,050	1,489,170	1,693.5	575.8	1,067.6	617.7
1987	2,972	1,621	4,593	1,484,000	1,451.2	603.1	969.9	609.7
1988	3,392	1,516	4,908	1,566,220	1,606.0	547.1	1,005.2	637.2
1989	3,553	1,383	4,936	1,646,040	1,695.9	498.0	1,013.1	663.1
1990	5,898	1,337	7,235	1,820,130	3,004.9	476.4	1,517.0	731.8
1991	n/a	n/a	n/a	1,911,770	n/a	n/a	n/a	758.1
1992	7,163	n/a	n/a	1,932,270	3,565.3	n/a	n/a	757.5
1993	2,220	2,069	4,289	1,926,020	1,086.7	696.3	855.3	746.8
1994	2,297	1,931	4,228	1,857,670	1,115.9	644.9	836.8	713.6
1995	2,332	1,797	4,129	1,798,790	1,131.3	579.4	799.8	684.6
1996	2,185	1,679	3,864	1,682,280	1,055.0	538.9	745.0	634.1

Notes: Violent crimes include murder, forcible rape, robbery and aggravated assault; n/a not available; (1) Metropolitan Statistical Area - see Appendix A for areas included; (2) calculated by the editors using the following formula: (number of crimes in the MSA minus number of crimes in the city); (3) calculated by the editors using the following formula: ((number of crimes in the MSA minus number of crimes in the city) ÷ (population of the MSA minus population of the city)) x 100,000
Source: U.S. Department of Justice, FBI Uniform Crime Reports, 1977 - 1996

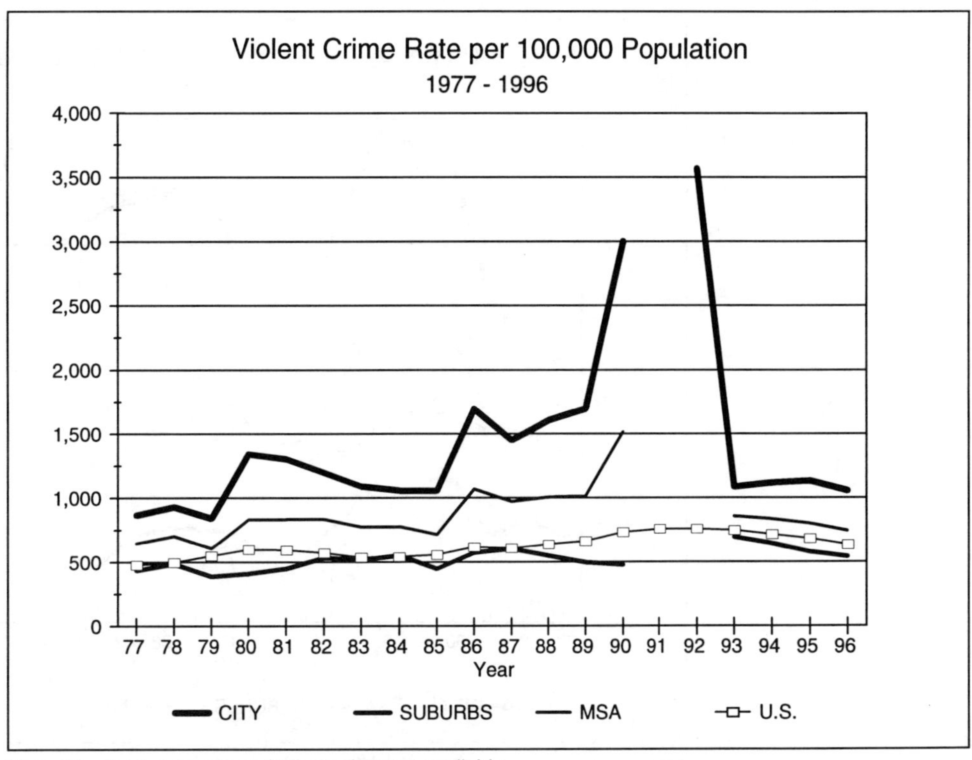

Note: Missing line segments indicate data not available.

Property Crimes and Property Crime Rates: 1977 - 1996

Year	Number				Rate per 100,000 population			
	City	Suburbs[2]	MSA[1]	U.S.	City	Suburbs[3]	MSA[1]	U.S.
1977	12,493	7,175	19,668	9,955,000	6,094.1	3,361.1	4,699.9	4,601.7
1978	13,272	8,014	21,286	10,123,400	6,380.8	3,626.8	4,962.1	4,642.5
1979	14,817	7,745	22,562	11,041,500	7,071.9	3,381.8	5,144.8	5,016.6
1980	18,413	10,257	28,670	12,063,700	9,233.7	4,264.3	6,516.8	5,353.3
1981	19,369	10,441	29,810	12,061,900	9,577.9	4,280.4	6,681.5	5,263.9
1982	19,908	10,460	30,368	11,652,000	9,776.9	4,258.8	6,760.0	5,032.5
1983	17,506	9,010	26,516	10,850,500	8,562.6	3,653.7	5,878.8	4,637.4
1984	14,597	7,999	22,596	10,608,500	7,055.7	3,124.0	4,881.1	4,492.1
1985	14,530	7,942	22,472	11,102,600	7,036.1	3,022.2	4,788.5	4,650.5
1986	16,608	9,039	25,647	11,722,700	7,978.9	3,412.8	5,422.1	4,862.6
1987	18,651	9,390	28,041	12,024,700	9,106.9	3,493.8	5,921.3	4,940.3
1988	18,460	9,640	28,100	12,356,900	8,740.3	3,479.2	5,754.9	5,027.1
1989	18,133	9,095	27,228	12,605,400	8,655.1	3,275.2	5,588.7	5,077.9
1990	16,481	7,536	24,017	12,655,500	8,396.8	2,685.2	5,035.8	5,088.5
1991	n/a	n/a	n/a	12,961,100	n/a	n/a	n/a	5,139.7
1992	19,094	n/a	n/a	12,505,900	9,503.7	n/a	n/a	4,902.7
1993	16,347	10,377	26,724	12,218,800	8,002.0	3,492.1	5,329.5	4,737.6
1994	18,228	11,159	29,387	12,131,900	8,855.2	3,726.9	5,816.2	4,660.0
1995	16,583	11,222	27,805	12,063,900	8,044.6	3,618.5	5,385.8	4,591.3
1996	17,327	11,026	28,353	11,791,300	8,366.2	3,538.8	5,466.3	4,444.8

Notes: Property crimes include burglary, larceny-theft and motor vehicle theft; n/a not available; (1) Metropolitan Statistical Area - see Appendix A for areas included; (2) calculated by the editors using the following formula: (number of crimes in the MSA minus number of crimes in the city); (3) calculated by the editors using the following formula: ((number of crimes in the MSA minus number of crimes in the city) ÷ (population of the MSA minus population of the city)) x 100,000
Source: U.S. Department of Justice, FBI Uniform Crime Reports, 1977 - 1996

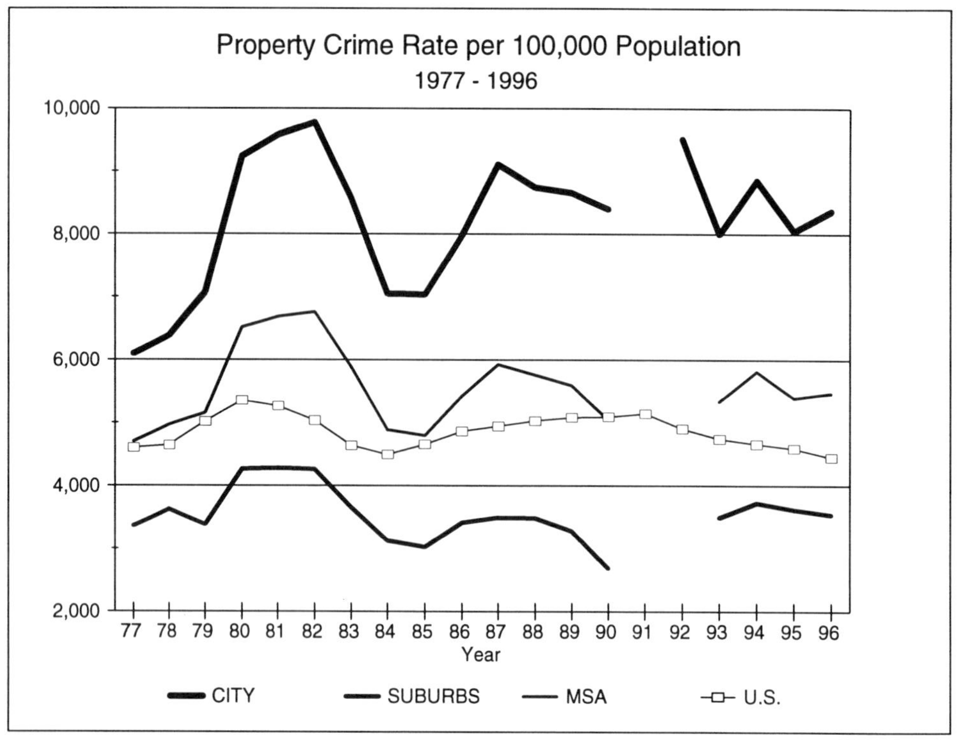

Note: Missing line segments indicate data not available.

Murders and Murder Rates: 1977 - 1996

Year	Number				Rate per 100,000 population			
	City	Suburbs[2]	MSA[1]	U.S.	City	Suburbs[3]	MSA[1]	U.S.
1977	50	43	93	19,120	24.4	20.1	22.2	8.8
1978	44	36	80	19,560	21.2	16.3	18.6	9.0
1979	52	36	88	21,460	24.8	15.7	20.1	9.7
1980	54	36	90	23,040	27.1	15.0	20.5	10.2
1981	39	45	84	22,520	19.3	18.4	18.8	9.8
1982	46	27	73	21,010	22.6	11.0	16.3	9.1
1983	36	17	53	19,310	17.6	6.9	11.8	8.3
1984	36	25	61	18,690	17.4	9.8	13.2	7.9
1985	26	27	53	18,980	12.6	10.3	11.3	7.9
1986	47	26	73	20,610	22.6	9.8	15.4	8.6
1987	32	23	55	20,100	15.6	8.6	11.6	8.3
1988	37	18	55	20,680	17.5	6.5	11.3	8.4
1989	40	18	58	21,500	19.1	6.5	11.9	8.7
1990	41	16	57	23,440	20.9	5.7	12.0	9.4
1991	n/a	n/a	n/a	24,700	n/a	n/a	n/a	9.8
1992	35	n/a	n/a	23,760	17.4	n/a	n/a	9.3
1993	42	23	65	24,530	20.6	7.7	13.0	9.5
1994	39	34	73	23,330	18.9	11.4	14.4	9.0
1995	56	35	91	21,610	27.2	11.3	17.6	8.2
1996	51	29	80	19,650	24.6	9.3	15.4	7.4

Notes: (1) Metropolitan Statistical Area - see Appendix A for areas included; (2) calculated by the editors using the following formula: (number of crimes in the MSA minus number of crimes in the city); (3) calculated by the editors using the following formula: ((number of crimes in the MSA minus number of crimes in the city) ÷ (population of the MSA minus population of the city)) x 100,000; n/a not avail.
Source: U.S. Department of Justice, FBI Uniform Crime Reports, 1977 - 1996

Forcible Rapes and Forcible Rape Rates: 1977 - 1996

Year	Number				Rate per 100,000 population			
	City	Suburbs[2]	MSA[1]	U.S.	City	Suburbs[3]	MSA[1]	U.S.
1977	123	72	195	63,500	60.0	33.7	46.6	29.4
1978	119	76	195	67,610	57.2	34.4	45.5	31.0
1979	120	70	190	76,390	57.3	30.6	43.3	34.7
1980	144	77	221	82,990	72.2	32.0	50.2	36.8
1981	123	58	181	82,500	60.8	23.8	40.6	36.0
1982	153	79	232	78,770	75.1	32.2	51.6	34.0
1983	84	76	160	78,920	41.1	30.8	35.5	33.7
1984	115	83	198	84,230	55.6	32.4	42.8	35.7
1985	126	55	181	88,670	61.0	20.9	38.6	37.1
1986	124	67	191	91,460	59.6	25.3	40.4	37.9
1987	127	79	206	91,110	62.0	29.4	43.5	37.4
1988	126	75	201	92,490	59.7	27.1	41.2	37.6
1989	133	66	199	94,500	63.5	23.8	40.8	38.1
1990	146	60	206	102,560	74.4	21.4	43.2	41.2
1991	n/a	n/a	n/a	106,590	n/a	n/a	n/a	42.3
1992	172	n/a	n/a	109,060	85.6	n/a	n/a	42.8
1993	122	78	200	106,010	59.7	26.2	39.9	41.1
1994	125	96	221	102,220	60.7	32.1	43.7	39.3
1995	106	94	200	97,470	51.4	30.3	38.7	37.1
1996	119	117	236	95,770	57.5	37.6	45.5	36.1

Notes: (1) Metropolitan Statistical Area - see Appendix A for areas included; (2) calculated by the editors using the following formula: (number of crimes in the MSA minus number of crimes in the city); (3) calculated by the editors using the following formula: ((number of crimes in the MSA minus number of crimes in the city) ÷ (population of the MSA minus population of the city)) x 100,000; n/a not avail.
Source: U.S. Department of Justice, FBI Uniform Crime Reports, 1977 - 1996

Robberies and Robbery Rates: 1977 - 1996

Year	Number				Rate per 100,000 population			
	City	Suburbs[2]	MSA[1]	U.S.	City	Suburbs[3]	MSA[1]	U.S.
1977	631	232	863	412,610	307.8	108.7	206.2	190.7
1978	668	266	934	426,930	321.2	120.4	217.7	195.8
1979	564	216	780	480,700	269.2	94.3	177.9	218.4
1980	956	285	1,241	565,840	479.4	118.5	282.1	251.1
1981	938	328	1,266	592,910	463.8	134.5	283.8	258.7
1982	823	353	1,176	553,130	404.2	143.7	261.8	238.9
1983	790	213	1,003	506,570	386.4	86.4	222.4	216.5
1984	686	236	922	485,010	331.6	92.2	199.2	205.4
1985	726	247	973	497,870	351.6	94.0	207.3	208.5
1986	798	254	1,052	542,780	383.4	95.9	222.4	225.1
1987	775	239	1,014	517,700	378.4	88.9	214.1	212.7
1988	932	287	1,219	542,970	441.3	103.6	249.7	220.9
1989	847	231	1,078	578,330	404.3	83.2	221.3	233.0
1990	842	171	1,013	639,270	429.0	60.9	212.4	257.0
1991	n/a	n/a	n/a	687,730	n/a	n/a	n/a	272.7
1992	1,188	n/a	n/a	672,480	591.3	n/a	n/a	263.6
1993	1,186	460	1,646	659,870	580.6	154.8	328.3	255.9
1994	1,259	517	1,776	618,950	611.6	172.7	351.5	237.7
1995	1,384	512	1,896	580,510	671.4	165.1	367.3	220.9
1996	1,283	393	1,676	537,050	619.5	126.1	323.1	202.4

Notes: (1) Metropolitan Statistical Area - see Appendix A for areas included; (2) calculated by the editors using the following formula: (number of crimes in the MSA minus number of crimes in the city); (3) calculated by the editors using the following formula: ((number of crimes in the MSA minus number of crimes in the city) ÷ (population of the MSA minus population of the city)) x 100,000; n/a not avail.
Source: U.S. Department of Justice, FBI Uniform Crime Reports, 1977 - 1996

Aggravated Assaults and Aggravated Assault Rates: 1977 - 1996

Year	Number				Rate per 100,000 population			
	City	Suburbs[2]	MSA[1]	U.S.	City	Suburbs[3]	MSA[1]	U.S.
1977	975	580	1,555	534,350	475.6	271.7	371.6	247.0
1978	1,107	699	1,806	571,460	532.2	316.3	421.0	262.1
1979	1,027	566	1,593	629,480	490.2	247.1	363.2	286.0
1980	1,521	588	2,109	672,650	762.7	244.5	479.4	298.5
1981	1,529	670	2,199	663,900	756.1	274.7	492.9	289.7
1982	1,414	854	2,268	669,480	694.4	347.7	504.9	289.2
1983	1,315	971	2,286	653,290	643.2	393.8	506.8	279.2
1984	1,348	1,070	2,418	685,350	651.6	417.9	522.3	290.2
1985	1,299	851	2,150	723,250	629.0	323.8	458.1	302.9
1986	2,556	1,178	3,734	834,320	1,228.0	444.8	789.4	346.1
1987	2,038	1,280	3,318	855,090	995.1	476.3	700.7	351.3
1988	2,297	1,136	3,433	910,090	1,087.6	410.0	703.1	370.2
1989	2,533	1,068	3,601	951,710	1,209.0	384.6	739.1	383.4
1990	4,869	1,090	5,959	1,054,860	2,480.7	388.4	1,249.5	424.1
1991	n/a	n/a	n/a	1,092,740	n/a	n/a	n/a	433.3
1992	5,768	n/a	n/a	1,126,970	2,870.9	n/a	n/a	441.8
1993	870	1,508	2,378	1,135,610	425.9	507.5	474.2	440.3
1994	874	1,284	2,158	1,113,180	424.6	428.8	427.1	427.6
1995	786	1,156	1,942	1,099,210	381.3	372.7	376.2	418.3
1996	732	1,140	1,872	1,029,810	353.4	365.9	360.9	388.2

Notes: (1) Metropolitan Statistical Area - see Appendix A for areas included; (2) calculated by the editors using the following formula: (number of crimes in the MSA minus number of crimes in the city); (3) calculated by the editors using the following formula: ((number of crimes in the MSA minus number of crimes in the city) ÷ (population of the MSA minus population of the city)) x 100,000; n/a not avail.
Source: U.S. Department of Justice, FBI Uniform Crime Reports, 1977 - 1996

Burglaries and Burglary Rates: 1977 - 1996

Year	Number				Rate per 100,000 population			
	City	Suburbs[2]	MSA[1]	U.S.	City	Suburbs[3]	MSA[1]	U.S.
1977	4,570	3,405	7,975	3,071,500	2,229.3	1,595.0	1,905.7	1,419.8
1978	4,960	3,840	8,800	3,128,300	2,384.6	1,737.8	2,051.4	1,434.6
1979	5,130	3,195	8,325	3,327,700	2,448.5	1,395.1	1,898.3	1,511.9
1980	7,130	4,637	11,767	3,795,200	3,575.5	1,927.8	2,674.7	1,684.1
1981	7,439	4,575	12,014	3,779,700	3,678.5	1,875.6	2,692.8	1,649.5
1982	6,416	4,087	10,503	3,447,100	3,150.9	1,664.0	2,338.0	1,488.8
1983	5,370	3,247	8,617	3,129,900	2,626.6	1,316.7	1,910.5	1,337.7
1984	4,932	2,693	7,625	2,984,400	2,384.0	1,051.7	1,647.1	1,263.7
1985	6,157	2,845	9,002	3,073,300	2,981.5	1,082.6	1,918.2	1,287.3
1986	7,949	3,194	11,143	3,241,400	3,818.9	1,205.9	2,355.8	1,344.6
1987	9,429	3,458	12,887	3,236,200	4,604.0	1,286.6	2,721.3	1,329.6
1988	9,569	3,337	12,906	3,218,100	4,530.6	1,204.4	2,643.1	1,309.2
1989	6,429	2,966	9,395	3,168,200	3,068.6	1,068.1	1,928.4	1,276.3
1990	4,580	2,320	6,900	3,073,900	2,333.4	826.7	1,446.8	1,235.9
1991	n/a	n/a	n/a	3,157,200	n/a	n/a	n/a	1,252.0
1992	5,056	n/a	n/a	2,979,900	2,516.5	n/a	n/a	1,168.2
1993	4,884	3,648	8,532	2,834,800	2,390.8	1,227.6	1,701.5	1,099.2
1994	4,712	3,416	8,128	2,712,800	2,289.1	1,140.9	1,608.7	1,042.0
1995	4,236	3,231	7,467	2,593,800	2,054.9	1,041.8	1,446.3	987.1
1996	4,404	3,044	7,448	2,501,500	2,126.4	977.0	1,435.9	943.0

Notes: (1) Metropolitan Statistical Area - see Appendix A for areas included; (2) calculated by the editors using the following formula: (number of crimes in the MSA minus number of crimes in the city); (3) calculated by the editors using the following formula: ((number of crimes in the MSA minus number of crimes in the city) ÷ (population of the MSA minus population of the city)) x 100,000; n/a not avail.
Source: U.S. Department of Justice, FBI Uniform Crime Reports, 1977 - 1996

Larceny-Thefts and Larceny-Theft Rates: 1977 - 1996

Year	Number				Rate per 100,000 population			
	City	Suburbs[2]	MSA[1]	U.S.	City	Suburbs[3]	MSA[1]	U.S.
1977	7,077	3,357	10,434	5,905,700	3,452.2	1,572.6	2,493.4	2,729.9
1978	7,420	3,685	11,105	5,991,000	3,567.3	1,667.7	2,588.8	2,747.4
1979	8,742	4,034	12,776	6,601,000	4,172.4	1,761.4	2,913.3	2,999.1
1980	10,189	5,025	15,214	7,136,900	5,109.5	2,089.1	3,458.2	3,167.0
1981	10,961	5,359	16,320	7,194,400	5,420.1	2,197.0	3,657.9	3,139.7
1982	12,657	5,870	18,527	7,142,500	6,215.9	2,390.0	4,124.2	3,084.8
1983	11,264	5,343	16,607	6,712,800	5,509.5	2,166.7	3,681.9	2,868.9
1984	8,901	4,887	13,788	6,591,900	4,302.5	1,908.6	2,978.4	2,791.3
1985	7,480	4,734	12,214	6,926,400	3,622.2	1,801.4	2,602.6	2,901.2
1986	7,683	5,360	13,043	7,257,200	3,691.1	2,023.7	2,757.5	3,010.3
1987	8,280	5,464	13,744	7,499,900	4,043.0	2,033.0	2,902.3	3,081.3
1988	7,952	5,780	13,732	7,705,900	3,765.0	2,086.1	2,812.3	3,134.9
1989	10,613	5,629	16,242	7,872,400	5,065.7	2,027.1	3,333.8	3,171.3
1990	10,741	4,785	15,526	7,945,700	5,472.3	1,705.0	3,255.5	3,194.8
1991	n/a	n/a	n/a	8,142,200	n/a	n/a	n/a	3,228.8
1992	11,754	n/a	n/a	7,915,200	5,850.4	n/a	n/a	3,103.0
1993	9,926	5,983	15,909	7,820,900	4,858.9	2,013.4	3,172.7	3,032.4
1994	11,787	7,054	18,841	7,879,800	5,726.1	2,355.9	3,729.0	3,026.7
1995	10,416	7,074	17,490	7,997,700	5,052.9	2,281.0	3,387.8	3,043.8
1996	10,990	7,108	18,098	7,894,600	5,306.5	2,281.3	3,489.2	2,975.9

Notes: (1) Metropolitan Statistical Area - see Appendix A for areas included; (2) calculated by the editors using the following formula: (number of crimes in the MSA minus number of crimes in the city); (3) calculated by the editors using the following formula: ((number of crimes in the MSA minus number of crimes in the city) ÷ (population of the MSA minus population of the city)) x 100,000; n/a not avail.
Source: U.S. Department of Justice, FBI Uniform Crime Reports, 1977 - 1996

Motor Vehicle Thefts and Motor Vehicle Theft Rates: 1977 - 1996

Year	Number				Rate per 100,000 population			
	City	Suburbs[2]	MSA[1]	U.S.	City	Suburbs[3]	MSA[1]	U.S.
1977	846	413	1,259	977,700	412.7	193.5	300.9	451.9
1978	892	489	1,381	1,004,100	428.8	221.3	321.9	460.5
1979	945	516	1,461	1,112,800	451.0	225.3	333.2	505.6
1980	1,094	595	1,689	1,131,700	548.6	247.4	383.9	502.2
1981	969	507	1,476	1,087,800	479.2	207.8	330.8	474.7
1982	835	503	1,338	1,062,400	410.1	204.8	297.8	458.8
1983	872	420	1,292	1,007,900	426.5	170.3	286.4	430.8
1984	764	419	1,183	1,032,200	369.3	163.6	255.5	437.1
1985	893	363	1,256	1,102,900	432.4	138.1	267.6	462.0
1986	976	485	1,461	1,224,100	468.9	183.1	308.9	507.8
1987	942	468	1,410	1,288,700	460.0	174.1	297.7	529.4
1988	939	523	1,462	1,432,900	444.6	188.8	299.4	582.9
1989	1,091	500	1,591	1,564,800	520.7	180.1	326.6	630.4
1990	1,160	431	1,591	1,635,900	591.0	153.6	333.6	657.8
1991	n/a	n/a	n/a	1,661,700	n/a	n/a	n/a	659.0
1992	2,284	n/a	n/a	1,610,800	1,136.8	n/a	n/a	631.5
1993	1,537	746	2,283	1,563,100	752.4	251.0	455.3	606.1
1994	1,729	689	2,418	1,539,300	839.9	230.1	478.6	591.3
1995	1,931	917	2,848	1,472,400	936.8	295.7	551.7	560.4
1996	1,933	874	2,807	1,395,200	933.3	280.5	541.2	525.9

Notes: (1) Metropolitan Statistical Area - see Appendix A for areas included; (2) calculated by the editors using the following formula: (number of crimes in the MSA minus number of crimes in the city); (3) calculated by the editors using the following formula: ((number of crimes in the MSA minus number of crimes in the city) ÷ (population of the MSA minus population of the city)) x 100,000; n/a not avail.
Source: U.S. Department of Justice, FBI Uniform Crime Reports, 1977 - 1996

HATE CRIMES

Criminal Incidents by Bias Motivation

Area	Race	Ethnicity	Religion	Sexual Orientation
Mobile	n/a	n/a	n/a	n/a

Notes: Figures include both violent and property crimes. Law enforcement agencies must have submitted data for at least one quarter of calendar year 1995 to be included in this report, therefore figures shown may not represent complete 12-month totals; n/a not available
Source: U.S. Department of Justice, FBI Uniform Crime Reports, Hate Crime Statistics 1995

LAW ENFORCEMENT

Full-Time Law Enforcement Employees

Jurisdiction	Police Employees			Police Officers per 100,000 population
	Total	Officers	Civilians	
Mobile	641	456	185	220.2

Notes: Data as of October 31, 1996
Source: U.S. Department of Justice, FBI Uniform Crime Reports, 1996

CORRECTIONS

Federal Correctional Facilities

Type	Year Opened	Security Level	Sex of Inmates	Rated Capacity	Population on 7/1/95	Number of Staff
None listed						

Notes: Data as of 1995
Source: Bureau of Justice Statistics, Sourcebook of Criminal Justice Statistics Online

City/County/Regional Correctional Facilities

Name	Year Opened	Year Renov.	Rated Capacity	1995 Pop.	Number of COs[1]	Number of Staff	ACA[2] Accred.
Mobile County Metro Jail	1984	1992	816	n/a	n/a	n/a	No

Notes: Data as of April 1996; (1) Correctional Officers; (2) American Correctional Assn. Accreditation
Source: American Correctional Association, 1996-1998 National Jail and Adult Detention Directory

Private Adult Correctional Facilities

Name	Date Opened	Rated Capacity	Present Pop.	Security Level	Facility Construct.	Expans. Plans	ACA[1] Accred.
None listed							

Notes: Data as of December 1996; (1) American Correctional Association Accreditation
Source: University of Florida, Center for Studies in Criminology and Law, Private Adult Correctional Facility Census, 10th Ed., March 15, 1997

Characteristics of Shock Incarceration Programs

Jurisdiction	Year Program Began	Number of Camps	Average Num. of Inmates	Number of Beds	Program Length	Voluntary/ Mandatory
Alabama	1988	1	120	150	90 to 180 days	Voluntary

Note: Data as of July 1996;
Source: Sourcebook of Criminal Justice Statistics Online

DEATH PENALTY

Death Penalty Statistics

State	Prisoners Executed		Prisoners Under Sentence of Death					Avg. No. of Years on Death Row[4]
	1930-1995	1996[1]	Total[2]	White[3]	Black[3]	Hisp.	Women	
Alabama	147	1	143	82	59	0	4	6.3

Notes: Data as of 12/31/95 unless otherwise noted; (1) Data as of 7/31/97; (2) Includes persons of other races; (3) Includes people of Hispanic origin; (4) Covers prisoners sentenced 1974 through 1995
Source: Bureau of Justice Statistics, Capital Punishment 1995 (released 12/96); Death Penalty Information Center Web Site, 9/30/97

Capital Offenses and Methods of Execution

Capital Offenses in Alabama	Minimum Age for Imposition of Death Penalty	Mentally Retarded Excluded	Methods of Execution[1]
Intentional murder with 18 aggravating factors (13A-5-40).	16	No	Electrocution

Notes: Data as of 12/31/95 unless otherwise noted; (1) Data as of 7/31/97
Source: Bureau of Justice Statistics, Capital Punishment 1995 (released 12/96); Death Penalty Information Center Web Site, 9/30/97

LAWS

Statutory Provisions Relating to the Purchase, Ownership and Use of Handguns

Jurisdiction	Instant Background Check	Federal Waiting Period Applies[1]	State Waiting Period (days)	License or Permit to Purchase	Regis-tration	Record of Sale Sent to Police	Concealed Carry Law
Alabama	No	Yes	2	No	No	Yes	Yes[a]

Note: Data as of 1996; (1) The Federal 5-day waiting period for handgun purchases applies to states that don't have instant background checks, waiting period requirements, or licensing procedures exempting them from the Federal requirement; (a) "Shall issue" permit system, liberally administered discretion by local authorities over permit issuance, or no permit required
Source: Sourcebook of Criminal Justice Statistics Online

Statutory Provisions Relating to Alcohol Use and Driving

Jurisdiction	Drinking Age	Blood Alcohol Concentration Levels as Evidence in State Courts[1]		Open Container Law[1]	Anti-Consump-tion Law[1]	Dram Shop Law[1]
		Illegal per se at 0.10%	Presumption at 0.10%			
Alabama	21	(a)	(a)	No	No	Yes

Note: Data as of January 1, 1997; (1) See Appendix C for an explanation of terms; (a) 0.08%
Source: Sourcebook of Criminal Justice Statistics Online

Statutory Provisions Relating to Hate Crimes

Jurisdiction	Bias-Motivated Violence and Intimidation						Institutional Vandalism
	Civil Action	Criminal Penalty					
		Race/ Religion/ Ethnicity	Sexual Orientation	Mental/ Physical Disability	Gender	Age	
Alabama	No	Yes	No	No	No	No	Yes

Source: Anti-Defamation League, 1997 Hate Crimes Laws

Nashville, Tennessee

OVERVIEW

The total crime rate for the city increased 84.4% between 1977 and 1996. During that same period, the violent crime rate increased 174.3% and the property crime rate increased 72.9%.

Among violent crimes, the rates for: Murders decreased 12.0%; Forcible Rapes increased 110.8%; Robberies increased 39.5%; and Aggravated Assaults increased 428.9%.

Among property crimes, the rates for: Burglaries decreased 25.6%; Larceny-Thefts increased 121.1%; and Motor Vehicle Thefts increased 194.7%.

ANTI-CRIME PROGRAMS

Programs include:

- Domestic Violence Division—which exists to reduce homicides, assaults, spousal rapes, domestic hostage situations, stalkings and other crimes through quality investigations.
- School Services Division—places public uniformed officers in public high and middle school hallways.
- Join Hands With the Badge—encourages citizens to come forward with crime-related information.
- Officer Bill Program—works with area children to promote safety, build self-esteem and strengthen ties with law enforcement officials.
- Neighborhood Watch Groups—volunteer to report crimes and emergencies to the police.
- Combat Auto Theft (CAT)—A voluntary decal program designed to reduce auto theft. Those cars with decals authorize the police to stop the car between the hours of 1:00 A.M. to 5:00 A.M. *Metro Nashville Police Department, 7/97*

Nashville received one of the National Institute of Justice's awards to receive funding for projects to improve police-citizen cooperation. The project: Metropolitan Nashville Police Department's Palm Top Project which will create an onsite system for law enforcement officers to conduct up-to-date warrant, arrest history, and stolen vehicle checks; access mug shots; and complete reports onsite and online. *National Institute of Justice Journal, 6/97*

Another highly-regarded violence-prevention program, FAST (Fast Track), is being used in selected schools. The program combines training for parents and special enrichment classes for selected students, the 10% seen as most troubled. *New York Times, 12/30/94*

CRIME RISK

Your Chances of Becoming a Victim[1]

Area	Any Crime	Violent Crime					Property Crime			
		Any	Murder	Forcible Rape[2]	Robbery	Aggrav. Assault	Any	Burglary	Larceny -Theft	Motor Vehicle Theft
City	1:9	1:53	1:5,956	1:572	1:182	1:81	1:11	1:66	1:16	1:64

Note: (1) Figures have been calculated by dividing the population of the city by the number of crimes reported to the FBI during 1996 and are expressed as odds (eg. 1:20 should be read as 1 in 20). (2) Figures have been calculated by dividing the female population of the city by the number of forcible rapes reported to the FBI during 1996. The female population of the city was estimated by calculating the ratio of females to males reported in the 1990 Census and applying that ratio to 1996 population estimate.
Source: FBI Uniform Crime Reports 1996

CRIME STATISTICS

Total Crimes and Total Crime Rates: 1977 - 1996

Year	Number				Rate per 100,000 population			
	City	Suburbs[2]	MSA[1]	U.S.	City	Suburbs[3]	MSA[1]	U.S.
1977	26,096	7,840	33,936	10,984,500	6,083.0	2,265.3	4,378.3	5,077.6
1978	26,444	8,719	35,163	11,209,000	6,222.1	2,433.1	4,488.8	5,140.3
1979	28,612	9,951	38,563	12,249,500	6,437.7	2,875.6	4,878.3	5,565.5
1980	34,886	12,852	47,738	13,408,300	7,717.7	3,413.4	5,761.7	5,950.0
1981	33,604	11,310	44,914	13,423,800	7,330.2	2,961.9	5,345.1	5,858.2
1982	35,206	11,520	46,726	12,974,400	7,612.0	2,990.3	5,511.7	5,603.6
1983	31,213	9,924	41,137	12,108,600	6,699.7	2,557.4	4,817.3	5,175.0
1984	31,125	10,203	41,328	11,881,800	6,542.4	2,545.5	4,714.8	5,031.3
1985	31,863	12,387	44,250	12,431,400	6,620.4	2,965.8	4,922.4	5,207.1
1986	38,240	13,834	52,074	13,211,900	8,120.5	3,283.5	5,836.4	5,480.4
1987	43,001	14,791	57,792	13,508,700	8,828.0	3,308.7	6,186.7	5,550.0
1988	37,185	14,826	52,011	13,923,100	7,396.2	3,181.1	5,368.5	5,664.2
1989	34,950	15,304	50,254	14,251,400	6,970.5	3,191.8	5,123.4	5,741.0
1990	39,360	18,066	57,426	14,475,600	7,878.9	3,721.4	5,829.9	5,820.3
1991	43,958	20,336	64,294	14,872,900	8,664.6	4,125.0	6,427.3	5,897.8
1992	49,864	19,907	69,771	14,438,200	9,686.6	3,981.0	6,875.2	5,660.2
1993	55,500	20,642	76,142	14,144,800	10,805.1	3,932.8	7,331.8	5,484.4
1994	52,469	20,398	72,867	13,989,500	10,065.0	3,829.4	6,913.6	5,373.5
1995	56,090	22,831	78,921	13,862,700	10,710.7	4,055.0	7,262.3	5,275.9
1996	59,467	24,061	83,528	13,473,600	11,218.9	4,222.1	7,593.9	5,078.9

Notes: (1) Metropolitan Statistical Area - see Appendix A for areas included; (2) calculated by the editors using the following formula: (number of crimes in the MSA minus number of crimes in the city); (3) calculated by the editors using the following formula: ((number of crimes in the MSA minus number of crimes in the city) ÷ (population of the MSA minus population of the city)) x 100,000; n/a not avail.
Source: U.S. Department of Justice, FBI Uniform Crime Reports, 1977 - 1996

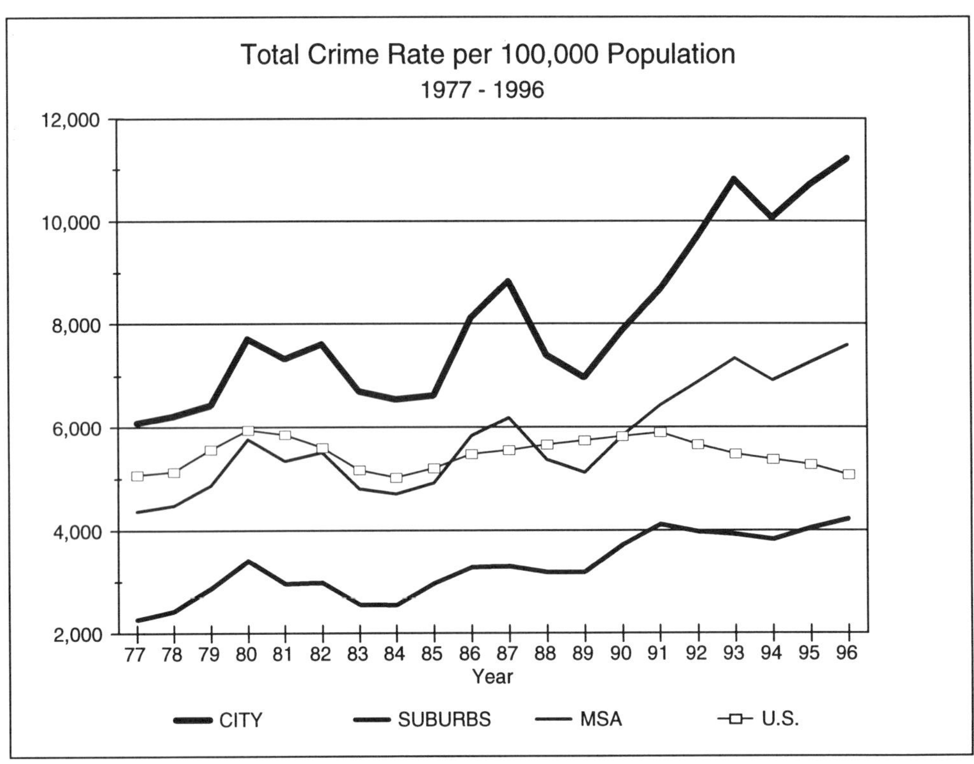

Note: Missing line segments indicate data not available.

Violent Crimes and Violent Crime Rates: 1977 - 1996

Year	Number				Rate per 100,000 population			
	City	Suburbs[2]	MSA[1]	U.S.	City	Suburbs[3]	MSA[1]	U.S.
1977	2,957	790	3,747	1,029,580	689.3	228.3	483.4	475.9
1978	3,153	760	3,913	1,085,550	741.9	212.1	499.5	497.8
1979	3,251	844	4,095	1,208,030	731.5	243.9	518.0	548.9
1980	3,634	921	4,555	1,344,520	803.9	244.6	549.8	596.6
1981	3,087	1,040	4,127	1,361,820	673.4	272.4	491.1	594.3
1982	3,248	833	4,081	1,322,390	702.3	216.2	481.4	571.1
1983	3,289	725	4,014	1,258,090	706.0	186.8	470.1	537.7
1984	3,104	960	4,064	1,273,280	652.5	239.5	463.6	539.2
1985	3,376	1,204	4,580	1,328,800	701.5	288.3	509.5	556.6
1986	4,218	1,305	5,523	1,489,170	895.7	309.7	619.0	617.7
1987	5,253	1,550	6,803	1,484,000	1,078.4	346.7	728.3	609.7
1988	5,290	1,676	6,966	1,566,220	1,052.2	359.6	719.0	637.2
1989	5,230	1,584	6,814	1,646,040	1,043.1	330.4	694.7	663.1
1990	6,886	1,901	8,787	1,820,130	1,378.4	391.6	892.1	731.8
1991	7,989	2,159	10,148	1,911,770	1,574.7	437.9	1,014.5	758.1
1992	8,382	2,182	10,564	1,932,270	1,628.3	436.4	1,041.0	757.5
1993	9,164	2,246	11,410	1,926,020	1,784.1	427.9	1,098.7	746.8
1994	9,375	2,561	11,936	1,857,670	1,798.4	480.8	1,132.5	713.6
1995	9,376	2,450	11,826	1,798,790	1,790.4	435.1	1,088.2	684.6
1996	10,021	2,622	12,643	1,682,280	1,890.5	460.1	1,149.4	634.1

Notes: Violent crimes include murder, forcible rape, robbery and aggravated assault; n/a not available; (1) Metropolitan Statistical Area - see Appendix A for areas included; (2) calculated by the editors using the following formula: (number of crimes in the MSA minus number of crimes in the city); (3) calculated by the editors using the following formula: ((number of crimes in the MSA minus number of crimes in the city) ÷ (population of the MSA minus population of the city)) x 100,000
Source: U.S. Department of Justice, FBI Uniform Crime Reports, 1977 - 1996

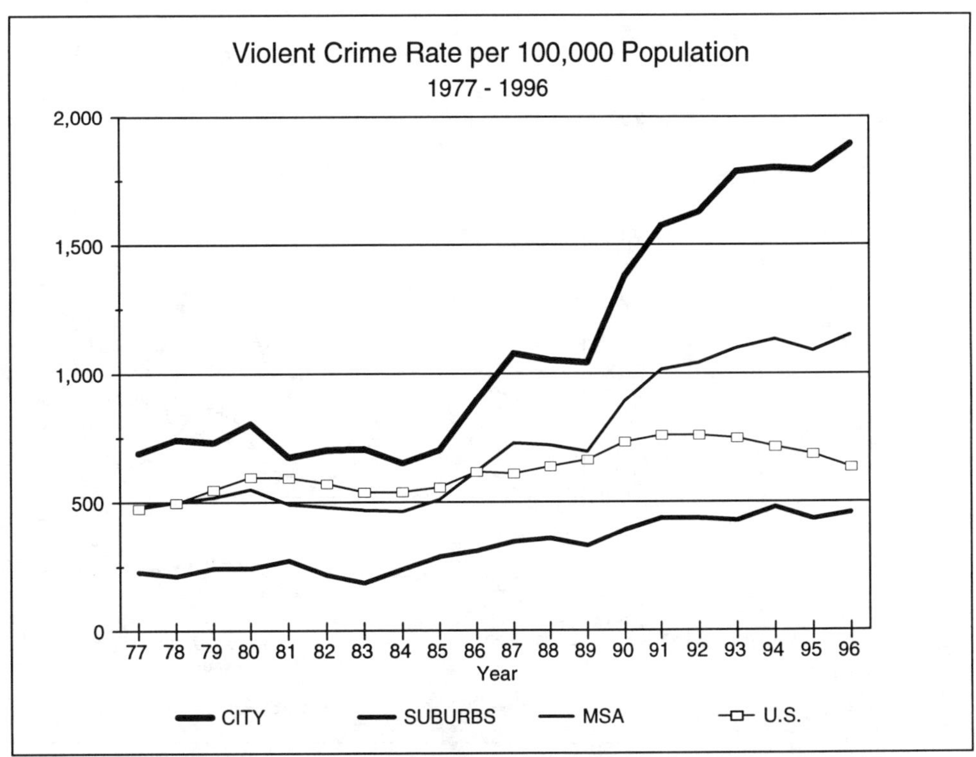

Note: Missing line segments indicate data not available.

Property Crimes and Property Crime Rates: 1977 - 1996

Year	Number				Rate per 100,000 population			
	City	Suburbs[2]	MSA[1]	U.S.	City	Suburbs[3]	MSA[1]	U.S.
1977	23,139	7,050	30,189	9,955,000	5,393.7	2,037.1	3,894.9	4,601.7
1978	23,291	7,959	31,250	10,123,400	5,480.2	2,221.0	3,989.3	4,642.5
1979	25,361	9,107	34,468	11,041,500	5,706.2	2,631.7	4,360.3	5,016.6
1980	31,252	11,931	43,183	12,063,700	6,913.8	3,168.8	5,211.9	5,353.3
1981	30,517	10,270	40,787	12,061,900	6,656.9	2,689.5	4,854.0	5,263.9
1982	31,958	10,687	42,645	11,652,000	6,909.7	2,774.1	5,030.4	5,032.5
1983	27,924	9,199	37,123	10,850,500	5,993.7	2,370.6	4,347.3	4,637.4
1984	28,021	9,243	37,264	10,608,500	5,889.9	2,306.0	4,251.1	4,492.1
1985	28,487	11,183	39,670	11,102,600	5,918.9	2,677.5	4,412.9	4,650.5
1986	34,022	12,529	46,551	11,722,700	7,224.8	2,973.7	5,217.4	4,862.6
1987	37,748	13,241	50,989	12,024,700	7,749.6	2,961.9	5,458.4	4,940.3
1988	31,895	13,150	45,045	12,356,900	6,344.0	2,821.5	4,649.4	5,027.1
1989	29,720	13,720	43,440	12,605,400	5,927.4	2,861.4	4,428.7	5,077.9
1990	32,474	16,165	48,639	12,655,500	6,500.5	3,329.8	4,937.8	5,088.5
1991	35,969	18,177	54,146	12,961,100	7,089.9	3,687.1	5,412.9	5,139.7
1992	41,482	17,725	59,207	12,505,900	8,058.3	3,544.7	5,834.3	4,902.7
1993	46,336	18,396	64,732	12,218,800	9,021.0	3,504.9	6,233.1	4,737.6
1994	43,094	17,837	60,931	12,131,900	8,266.6	3,348.6	5,781.1	4,660.0
1995	46,714	20,381	67,095	12,063,900	8,920.3	3,619.9	6,174.1	4,591.3
1996	49,446	21,439	70,885	11,791,300	9,328.4	3,762.0	6,444.4	4,444.8

Notes: Property crimes include burglary, larceny-theft and motor vehicle theft; n/a not available; (1) Metropolitan Statistical Area - see Appendix A for areas included; (2) calculated by the editors using the following formula: (number of crimes in the MSA minus number of crimes in the city); (3) calculated by the editors using the following formula: ((number of crimes in the MSA minus number of crimes in the city) ÷ (population of the MSA minus population of the city)) x 100,000
Source: U.S. Department of Justice, FBI Uniform Crime Reports, 1977 - 1996

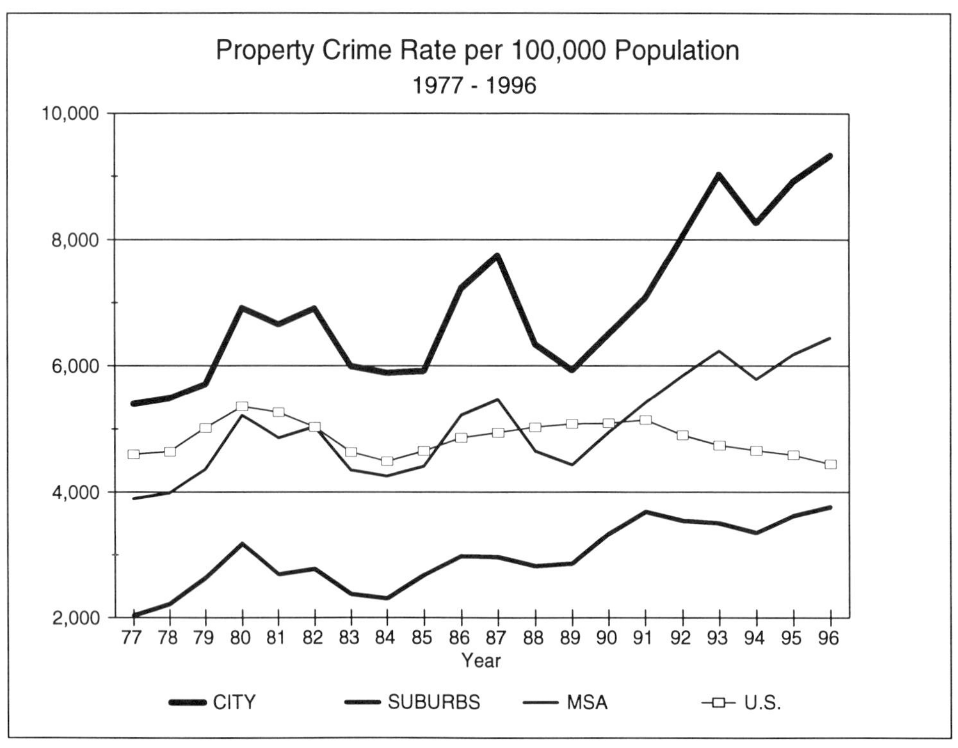

Note: Missing line segments indicate data not available.

Murders and Murder Rates: 1977 - 1996

Year	Number				Rate per 100,000 population			
	City	Suburbs[2]	MSA[1]	U.S.	City	Suburbs[3]	MSA[1]	U.S.
1977	82	12	94	19,120	19.1	3.5	12.1	8.8
1978	81	20	101	19,560	19.1	5.6	12.9	9.0
1979	89	18	107	21,460	20.0	5.2	13.5	9.7
1980	87	25	112	23,040	19.2	6.6	13.5	10.2
1981	79	20	99	22,520	17.2	5.2	11.8	9.8
1982	67	34	101	21,010	14.5	8.8	11.9	9.1
1983	81	18	99	19,310	17.4	4.6	11.6	8.3
1984	72	23	95	18,690	15.1	5.7	10.8	7.9
1985	81	17	98	18,980	16.8	4.1	10.9	7.9
1986	93	28	121	20,610	19.7	6.6	13.6	8.6
1987	99	16	115	20,100	20.3	3.6	12.3	8.3
1988	79	21	100	20,680	15.7	4.5	10.3	8.4
1989	69	24	93	21,500	13.8	5.0	9.5	8.7
1990	67	26	93	23,440	13.4	5.4	9.4	9.4
1991	88	32	120	24,700	17.3	6.5	12.0	9.8
1992	90	24	114	23,760	17.5	4.8	11.2	9.3
1993	87	20	107	24,530	16.9	3.8	10.3	9.5
1994	73	21	94	23,330	14.0	3.9	8.9	9.0
1995	105	25	130	21,610	20.1	4.4	12.0	8.2
1996	89	25	114	19,650	16.8	4.4	10.4	7.4

Notes: (1) Metropolitan Statistical Area - see Appendix A for areas included; (2) calculated by the editors using the following formula: (number of crimes in the MSA minus number of crimes in the city); (3) calculated by the editors using the following formula: ((number of crimes in the MSA minus number of crimes in the city) ÷ (population of the MSA minus population of the city)) x 100,000; n/a not avail.
Source: U.S. Department of Justice, FBI Uniform Crime Reports, 1977 - 1996

Forcible Rapes and Forcible Rape Rates: 1977 - 1996

Year	Number				Rate per 100,000 population			
	City	Suburbs[2]	MSA[1]	U.S.	City	Suburbs[3]	MSA[1]	U.S.
1977	187	38	225	63,500	43.6	11.0	29.0	29.4
1978	217	44	261	67,610	51.1	12.3	33.3	31.0
1979	266	55	321	76,390	59.9	15.9	40.6	34.7
1980	295	53	348	82,990	65.3	14.1	42.0	36.8
1981	363	65	428	82,500	79.2	17.0	50.9	36.0
1982	321	56	377	78,770	69.4	14.5	44.5	34.0
1983	324	44	368	78,920	69.5	11.3	43.1	33.7
1984	410	60	470	84,230	86.2	15.0	53.6	35.7
1985	348	80	428	88,670	72.3	19.2	47.6	37.1
1986	410	113	523	91,460	87.1	26.8	58.6	37.9
1987	509	92	601	91,110	104.5	20.6	64.3	37.4
1988	464	96	560	92,490	92.3	20.6	57.8	37.6
1989	478	129	607	94,500	95.3	26.9	61.9	38.1
1990	553	123	676	102,560	110.7	25.3	68.6	41.2
1991	514	162	676	106,590	101.3	32.9	67.6	42.3
1992	498	255	753	109,060	96.7	51.0	74.2	42.8
1993	577	192	769	106,010	112.3	36.6	74.0	41.1
1994	508	218	726	102,220	97.4	40.9	68.9	39.3
1995	487	174	661	97,470	93.0	30.9	60.8	37.1
1996	487	159	646	95,770	91.9	27.9	58.7	36.1

Notes: (1) Metropolitan Statistical Area - see Appendix A for areas included; (2) calculated by the editors using the following formula: (number of crimes in the MSA minus number of crimes in the city); (3) calculated by the editors using the following formula: ((number of crimes in the MSA minus number of crimes in the city) ÷ (population of the MSA minus population of the city)) x 100,000; n/a not avail.
Source: U.S. Department of Justice, FBI Uniform Crime Reports, 1977 - 1996

Robberies and Robbery Rates: 1977 - 1996

Year	Number				Rate per 100,000 population			
	City	Suburbs[2]	MSA[1]	U.S.	City	Suburbs[3]	MSA[1]	U.S.
1977	1,688	157	1,845	412,610	393.5	45.4	238.0	190.7
1978	1,772	155	1,927	426,930	416.9	43.3	246.0	195.8
1979	1,716	186	1,902	480,700	386.1	53.7	240.6	218.4
1980	2,027	231	2,258	565,840	448.4	61.4	272.5	251.1
1981	1,594	179	1,773	592,910	347.7	46.9	211.0	258.7
1982	1,662	167	1,829	553,130	359.3	43.3	215.7	238.9
1983	1,713	166	1,879	506,570	367.7	42.8	220.0	216.5
1984	1,438	156	1,594	485,010	302.3	38.9	181.8	205.4
1985	1,588	198	1,786	497,870	329.9	47.4	198.7	208.5
1986	1,953	218	2,171	542,780	414.7	51.7	243.3	225.1
1987	2,350	259	2,609	517,700	482.5	57.9	279.3	212.7
1988	1,954	254	2,208	542,970	388.7	54.5	227.9	220.9
1989	1,608	201	1,809	578,330	320.7	41.9	184.4	233.0
1990	2,164	215	2,379	639,270	433.2	44.3	241.5	257.0
1991	2,648	277	2,925	687,730	522.0	56.2	292.4	272.7
1992	2,668	235	2,903	672,480	518.3	47.0	286.1	263.6
1993	2,709	333	3,042	659,870	527.4	63.4	292.9	255.9
1994	2,652	283	2,935	618,950	508.7	53.1	278.5	237.7
1995	2,675	297	2,972	580,510	510.8	52.7	273.5	220.9
1996	2,910	317	3,227	537,050	549.0	55.6	293.4	202.4

Notes: (1) Metropolitan Statistical Area - see Appendix A for areas included; (2) calculated by the editors using the following formula: (number of crimes in the MSA minus number of crimes in the city); (3) calculated by the editors using the following formula: ((number of crimes in the MSA minus number of crimes in the city) ÷ (population of the MSA minus population of the city)) x 100,000; n/a not avail.
Source: U.S. Department of Justice, FBI Uniform Crime Reports, 1977 - 1996

Aggravated Assaults and Aggravated Assault Rates: 1977 - 1996

Year	Number				Rate per 100,000 population			
	City	Suburbs[2]	MSA[1]	U.S.	City	Suburbs[3]	MSA[1]	U.S.
1977	1,000	583	1,583	534,350	233.1	168.5	204.2	247.0
1978	1,083	541	1,624	571,460	254.8	151.0	207.3	262.1
1979	1,180	585	1,765	629,480	265.5	169.1	223.3	286.0
1980	1,225	612	1,837	672,650	271.0	162.5	221.7	298.5
1981	1,051	776	1,827	663,900	229.3	203.2	217.4	289.7
1982	1,198	576	1,774	669,480	259.0	149.5	209.3	289.2
1983	1,171	497	1,668	653,290	251.3	128.1	195.3	279.2
1984	1,184	721	1,905	685,350	248.9	179.9	217.3	290.2
1985	1,359	909	2,268	723,250	282.4	217.6	252.3	302.9
1986	1,762	946	2,708	834,320	374.2	224.5	303.5	346.1
1987	2,295	1,183	3,478	855,090	471.2	264.6	372.3	351.3
1988	2,793	1,305	4,098	910,090	555.5	280.0	423.0	370.2
1989	3,075	1,230	4,305	951,710	613.3	256.5	438.9	383.4
1990	4,102	1,537	5,639	1,054,860	821.1	316.6	572.5	424.1
1991	4,739	1,688	6,427	1,092,740	934.1	342.4	642.5	433.3
1992	5,126	1,668	6,794	1,126,970	995.8	333.6	669.5	441.8
1993	5,791	1,701	7,492	1,135,610	1,127.4	324.1	721.4	440.3
1994	6,142	2,039	8,181	1,113,180	1,178.2	382.8	776.2	427.6
1995	6,109	1,954	8,063	1,099,210	1,166.5	347.0	742.0	418.3
1996	6,535	2,121	8,656	1,029,810	1,232.9	372.2	787.0	388.2

Notes: (1) Metropolitan Statistical Area - see Appendix A for areas included; (2) calculated by the editors using the following formula: (number of crimes in the MSA minus number of crimes in the city); (3) calculated by the editors using the following formula: ((number of crimes in the MSA minus number of crimes in the city) ÷ (population of the MSA minus population of the city)) x 100,000; n/a not avail.
Source: U.S. Department of Justice, FBI Uniform Crime Reports, 1977 - 1996

Burglaries and Burglary Rates: 1977 - 1996

Year	Number				Rate per 100,000 population			
	City	Suburbs[2]	MSA[1]	U.S.	City	Suburbs[3]	MSA[1]	U.S.
1977	8,729	2,586	11,315	3,071,500	2,034.7	747.2	1,459.8	1,419.8
1978	8,613	2,859	11,472	3,128,300	2,026.6	797.8	1,464.5	1,434.6
1979	9,349	3,289	12,638	3,327,700	2,103.5	950.4	1,598.7	1,511.9
1980	11,482	4,727	16,209	3,795,200	2,540.1	1,255.5	1,956.3	1,684.1
1981	10,358	3,654	14,012	3,779,700	2,259.5	956.9	1,667.5	1,649.5
1982	9,530	3,471	13,001	3,447,100	2,060.5	901.0	1,533.6	1,488.8
1983	8,601	3,005	11,606	3,129,900	1,846.2	774.4	1,359.1	1,337.7
1984	8,788	3,142	11,930	2,984,400	1,847.2	783.9	1,361.0	1,263.7
1985	8,587	3,399	11,986	3,073,300	1,784.2	813.8	1,333.3	1,287.3
1986	11,380	3,928	15,308	3,241,400	2,416.6	932.3	1,715.7	1,344.6
1987	11,358	4,128	15,486	3,236,200	2,331.8	923.4	1,657.8	1,329.6
1988	8,866	3,893	12,759	3,218,100	1,763.5	835.3	1,317.0	1,309.2
1989	8,062	3,795	11,857	3,168,200	1,607.9	791.5	1,208.8	1,276.3
1990	8,892	4,038	12,930	3,073,900	1,779.9	831.8	1,312.7	1,235.9
1991	10,321	4,745	15,066	3,157,200	2,034.4	962.5	1,506.1	1,252.0
1992	10,238	4,554	14,792	2,979,900	1,988.8	910.7	1,457.6	1,168.2
1993	9,149	4,218	13,367	2,834,800	1,781.2	803.6	1,287.1	1,099.2
1994	8,342	4,145	12,487	2,712,800	1,600.2	778.2	1,184.8	1,042.0
1995	8,236	4,458	12,694	2,593,800	1,572.7	791.8	1,168.1	987.1
1996	8,025	4,751	12,776	2,501,500	1,514.0	833.7	1,161.5	943.0

Notes: (1) Metropolitan Statistical Area - see Appendix A for areas included; (2) calculated by the editors using the following formula: (number of crimes in the MSA minus number of crimes in the city); (3) calculated by the editors using the following formula: ((number of crimes in the MSA minus number of crimes in the city) ÷ (population of the MSA minus population of the city)) x 100,000; n/a not avail.
Source: U.S. Department of Justice, FBI Uniform Crime Reports, 1977 - 1996

Larceny-Thefts and Larceny-Theft Rates: 1977 - 1996

Year	Number				Rate per 100,000 population			
	City	Suburbs[2]	MSA[1]	U.S.	City	Suburbs[3]	MSA[1]	U.S.
1977	12,151	3,983	16,134	5,905,700	2,832.4	1,150.9	2,081.6	2,729.9
1978	12,263	4,543	16,806	5,991,000	2,885.4	1,267.7	2,145.4	2,747.4
1979	13,420	5,153	18,573	6,601,000	3,019.5	1,489.1	2,349.5	2,999.1
1980	17,189	6,501	23,690	7,136,900	3,802.7	1,726.6	2,859.2	3,167.0
1981	17,968	6,065	24,033	7,194,400	3,919.5	1,588.3	2,860.1	3,139.7
1982	20,379	6,693	27,072	7,142,500	4,406.2	1,737.3	3,193.4	3,084.8
1983	17,598	5,685	23,283	6,712,800	3,777.3	1,465.0	2,726.6	2,868.9
1984	17,379	5,543	22,922	6,591,900	3,653.0	1,382.9	2,615.0	2,791.3
1985	17,764	7,002	24,766	6,926,400	3,690.9	1,676.5	2,755.0	2,901.2
1986	19,730	7,671	27,401	7,257,200	4,189.8	1,820.7	3,071.1	3,010.3
1987	22,602	8,170	30,772	7,499,900	4,640.1	1,827.6	3,294.2	3,081.3
1988	20,213	8,429	28,642	7,705,900	4,020.4	1,808.5	2,956.4	3,134.9
1989	18,989	9,067	28,056	7,872,400	3,787.2	1,891.0	2,860.3	3,171.3
1990	20,115	11,057	31,172	7,945,700	4,026.5	2,277.6	3,164.6	3,194.8
1991	21,807	12,326	34,133	8,142,200	4,298.4	2,500.2	3,412.2	3,228.8
1992	26,106	12,199	38,305	7,915,200	5,071.4	2,439.6	3,774.6	3,103.0
1993	32,456	12,963	45,419	7,820,900	6,318.7	2,469.8	4,373.5	3,032.4
1994	28,779	12,564	41,343	7,879,800	5,520.6	2,358.7	3,922.6	3,026.7
1995	30,363	14,557	44,920	7,997,700	5,798.0	2,585.5	4,133.6	3,043.8
1996	33,195	15,197	48,392	7,894,600	6,262.5	2,666.7	4,399.5	2,975.9

Notes: (1) Metropolitan Statistical Area - see Appendix A for areas included; (2) calculated by the editors using the following formula: (number of crimes in the MSA minus number of crimes in the city); (3) calculated by the editors using the following formula: ((number of crimes in the MSA minus number of crimes in the city) ÷ (population of the MSA minus population of the city)) x 100,000; n/a not avail.
Source: U.S. Department of Justice, FBI Uniform Crime Reports, 1977 - 1996

Motor Vehicle Thefts and Motor Vehicle Theft Rates: 1977 - 1996

Year	Number				Rate per 100,000 population			
	City	Suburbs[2]	MSA[1]	U.S.	City	Suburbs[3]	MSA[1]	U.S.
1977	2,259	481	2,740	977,700	526.6	139.0	353.5	451.9
1978	2,415	557	2,972	1,004,100	568.2	155.4	379.4	460.5
1979	2,592	665	3,257	1,112,800	583.2	192.2	412.0	505.6
1980	2,581	703	3,284	1,131,700	571.0	186.7	396.4	502.2
1981	2,191	551	2,742	1,087,800	477.9	144.3	326.3	474.7
1982	2,049	523	2,572	1,062,400	443.0	135.8	303.4	458.8
1983	1,725	509	2,234	1,007,900	370.3	131.2	261.6	430.8
1984	1,854	558	2,412	1,032,200	389.7	139.2	275.2	437.1
1985	2,136	782	2,918	1,102,900	443.8	187.2	324.6	462.0
1986	2,912	930	3,842	1,224,100	618.4	220.7	430.6	507.8
1987	3,788	943	4,731	1,288,700	777.7	210.9	506.5	529.4
1988	2,816	828	3,644	1,432,900	560.1	177.7	376.1	582.9
1989	2,669	858	3,527	1,564,800	532.3	178.9	359.6	630.4
1990	3,467	1,070	4,537	1,635,900	694.0	220.4	460.6	657.8
1991	3,841	1,106	4,947	1,661,700	757.1	224.3	494.5	659.0
1992	5,138	972	6,110	1,610,800	998.1	194.4	602.1	631.5
1993	4,731	1,215	5,946	1,563,100	921.1	231.5	572.5	606.1
1994	5,973	1,128	7,101	1,539,300	1,145.8	211.8	673.7	591.3
1995	8,115	1,366	9,481	1,472,400	1,549.6	242.6	872.4	560.4
1996	8,226	1,491	9,717	1,395,200	1,551.9	261.6	883.4	525.9

Notes: (1) Metropolitan Statistical Area - see Appendix A for areas included; (2) calculated by the editors using the following formula: (number of crimes in the MSA minus number of crimes in the city); (3) calculated by the editors using the following formula: ((number of crimes in the MSA minus number of crimes in the city) ÷ (population of the MSA minus population of the city)) x 100,000; n/a not avail.
Source: U.S. Department of Justice, FBI Uniform Crime Reports, 1977 - 1996

HATE CRIMES

Criminal Incidents by Bias Motivation

Area	Race	Ethnicity	Religion	Sexual Orientation
Nashville	n/a	n/a	n/a	n/a

Notes: Figures include both violent and property crimes. Law enforcement agencies must have submitted data for at least one quarter of calendar year 1995 to be included in this report, therefore figures shown may not represent complete 12-month totals; n/a not available
Source: U.S. Department of Justice, FBI Uniform Crime Reports, Hate Crime Statistics 1995

LAW ENFORCEMENT

Full-Time Law Enforcement Employees

Jurisdiction	Police Employees			Police Officers per 100,000 population
	Total	Officers	Civilians	
Nashville	1,563	1,166	397	220.0

Notes: Data as of October 31, 1996
Source: U.S. Department of Justice, FBI Uniform Crime Reports, 1996

Number of Police Officers by Race

Race	Police Officers				Index of Representation[1]		
	1983		1992				
	Number	Pct.	Number	Pct.	1983	1992	% Chg.
Black	114	11.8	139	13.1	0.50	0.54	8.0
Hispanic[2]	3	0.3	6	0.6	0.38	0.56	47.4

Notes: (1) The index of representation is calculated by dividing the percent of black/hispanic police officers by the percent of corresponding blacks/hispanics in the local population. An index approaching 1.0 indicates that a city is closer to achieving a representation of police officers equal to their proportion in the local population; (2) Hispanic officers can be of any race
Source: Bureau of Justice Statistics, Sourcebook of Criminal Justice Statistics, 1994

CORRECTIONS

Federal Correctional Facilities

Type	Year Opened	Security Level	Sex of Inmates	Rated Capacity	Population on 7/1/95	Number of Staff
None listed						

Notes: Data as of 1995
Source: Bureau of Justice Statistics, Sourcebook of Criminal Justice Statistics Online

City/County/Regional Correctional Facilities

Name	Year Opened	Year Renov.	Rated Capacity	1995 Pop.	Number of COs[1]	Number of Staff	ACA[2] Accred.
Davidson Co Criminal Just Ctr	1940	1992	179	169	9	63	No
Davidson Co DUI Det Ctr	1946	1987	169	n/a	n/a	n/a	No
Davidson Co Hill Det I	1972	1992	179	171	34	42	No
Davidson Co Hill Det II	1988	1996	163	117	16	19	No
Davidson Co Pre-Release Ctr	1988	1993	163	n/a	n/a	n/a	No

Notes: Data as of April 1996; (1) Correctional Officers; (2) American Correctional Assn. Accreditation
Source: American Correctional Association, 1996-1998 National Jail and Adult Detention Directory

Private Adult Correctional Facilities

Name	Date Opened	Rated Capacity	Present Pop.	Security Level	Facility Construct.	Expans. Plans	ACA[1] Accred.
Metro-Davidson Co. Detention Center	2/92	1,092	1,002	Med.	New	None	Yes-1/94

Notes: Data as of December 1996; (1) American Correctional Association Accreditation
Source: University of Florida, Center for Studies in Criminology and Law, Private Adult Correctional Facility Census, 10th Ed., March 15, 1997

Characteristics of Shock Incarceration Programs

Jurisdiction	Year Program Began	Number of Camps	Average Num. of Inmates	Number of Beds	Program Length	Voluntary/ Mandatory
Tennessee	1989	1	142	150	90 to 120 days	Mandatory

Note: Data as of July 1996;
Source: Sourcebook of Criminal Justice Statistics Online

INMATES AND HIV/AIDS

HIV Testing Policies for Inmates

Jurisdiction	All Inmates at Some Time	All Convicted Inmates at Admission	Random Samples While in Custody	High-risk Groups	Upon Inmate Request	Upon Court Order	Upon Involvement in Incident
Davidson Co.[1]	No	Yes	No	No	Yes	Yes	Yes

Notes: (1) Includes inmates held by the city of Nashville
Source: HIV in Prisons and Jails, 1993 (released August 1995)

Inmates Known to be Positive for HIV

Jurisdiction	Number of Jail Inmates in Facilities Providing Data	Type of HIV Infection/AIDS Cases				HIV/AIDS Cases as a Percent of Tot. Custody Pop.
		Total	Asymp-tomatic	Symp-tomatic	Confirmed AIDS	
Davidson Co.[1]	1,220	12	12	0	0	1.0

Note: (1) Some but not all facilities reported data on HIV/AIDS cases. Excludes inmates in facilities that did not report data.
Source: HIV in Prisons and Jails, 1993 (released August, 1995)

DEATH PENALTY

Death Penalty Statistics

State	Prisoners Executed		Prisoners Under Sentence of Death					Avg. No. of Years on Death Row[4]
	1930-1995	1996[1]	Total[2]	White[3]	Black[3]	Hisp.	Women	
Tennessee	93	0	96	64	30	1	1	8.5

Notes: Data as of 12/31/95 unless otherwise noted; (1) Data as of 7/31/97; (2) Includes persons of other races; (3) Includes people of Hispanic origin; (4) Covers prisoners sentenced 1974 through 1995
Source: Bureau of Justice Statistics, Capital Punishment 1995 (released 12/96); Death Penalty Information Center Web Site, 9/30/97

Capital Offenses and Methods of Execution

Capital Offenses in Tennessee	Minimum Age for Imposition of Death Penalty	Mentally Retarded Excluded	Methods of Execution[1]
First-degree murder.	18	No	Electrocution

Notes: Data as of 12/31/95 unless otherwise noted; (1) Data as of 7/31/97
Source: Bureau of Justice Statistics, Capital Punishment 1995 (released 12/96); Death Penalty Information Center Web Site, 9/30/97

LAWS

Statutory Provisions Relating to the Purchase, Ownership and Use of Handguns

Jurisdiction	Instant Background Check	Federal Waiting Period Applies[1]	State Waiting Period (days)	License or Permit to Purchase	Regis-tration	Record of Sale Sent to Police	Concealed Carry Law
Tennessee	No	No	15	No	No	Yes	Yes[a]

Note: Data as of 1996; (1) The Federal 5-day waiting period for handgun purchases applies to states that don't have instant background checks, waiting period requirements, or licensing procedures exempting them from the Federal requirement; (a) "Shall issue" permit system, liberally administered discretion by local authorities over permit issuance, or no permit required
Source: Sourcebook of Criminal Justice Statistics Online

Statutory Provisions Relating to Alcohol Use and Driving

Jurisdiction	Drinking Age	Blood Alcohol Concentration Levels as Evidence in State Courts[1]		Open Container Law[1]	Anti-Consump-tion Law[1]	Dram Shop Law[1]
		Illegal per se at 0.10%	Presumption at 0.10%			
Tennessee	21	Yes	Yes[a]	Yes[b]	Yes[b]	Yes

Note: Data as of January 1, 1997; (1) See Appendix C for an explanation of terms; (a) For a first offense, an alcohol concentration of 0.10% or more; for a subsequent offense, an alcohol concentration of 0.08% or more; (b) Applies to drivers only
Source: Sourcebook of Criminal Justice Statistics Online

Statutory Provisions Relating to Curfews

Jurisdiction	Year Enacted	Latest Revision	Age Group(s)	Curfew Provisions
Nashville	1965	-	17 and under	Midnight to 5 am every night

Note: Data as of February 1996
Source: Sourcebook of Criminal Justice Statistics Online

Statutory Provisions Relating to Hate Crimes

Jurisdiction	Bias-Motivated Violence and Intimidation						Institutional Vandalism
	Civil Action	Criminal Penalty					
		Race/ Religion/ Ethnicity	Sexual Orientation	Mental/ Physical Disability	Gender	Age	
Tennessee	No	Yes	No	No	No	No	Yes

Source: Anti-Defamation League, 1997 Hate Crimes Laws

New Orleans, Louisiana

OVERVIEW

The total crime rate for the city increased 55.3% between 1977 and 1996. During that same period, the violent crime rate increased 112.9% and the property crime rate increased 45.2%.

Among violent crimes, the rates for: Murders increased 133.4%; Forcible Rapes increased 24.5%; Robberies increased 99.7%; and Aggravated Assaults increased 146.4%.

Among property crimes, the rates for: Burglaries increased 31.6%; Larceny-Thefts increased 32.5%; and Motor Vehicle Thefts increased 112.3%.

ANTI-CRIME PROGRAMS

New Orleans anti-crime programs include:

- Truancy Task Force—targets school aged youths who habitually skip school thus reducing the instances of juvenile-related crime.
- Curfew Task Force—targets juveniles under the age of 16 who are out in the streets during the late hours when the opportunities are greater to become victims and/or perpetrators of violent crimes.
- NUMBY (Not In My Back Yard)—increased police presence in eight housing developments to reduce crimes in these developments.
- Rapid Response Units—two-person uniformed units which respond to calls regarding crimes in progress.
- Crimestoppers—uses the reward system to obtain information which leads to the arrest of persons wanted for crimes.
- New Orleans Most Wanted Program—news media is used to broadcast names and descriptions of persons wanted for serious crimes.
- Mobile Sub-Station—targets various high-crime areas by increasing police presence within these areas.
- Print Track—computer-operated fingerprinting classification, storage and retrieval system.
- T.R.A.C.E. Unit (Telephonic Reporting and Computer Entry)—process by which victims can report property crimes by telephone thus relieving the need for a field patrol unit to write a report at the scene.
- Gun Buy-Backs—weapons are exchanged for cash or merchandise.
- C.O.P.S. (Community Oriented Police)— primary responsibilities are patrolling housing developments and interacting with its residents. *New Orleans Police Department, 7/97*

The police department received one of the National Institute of Justice's awards to receive funding for projects which improve police-citizens cooperation. The project: Affordable Crime Mapping and Information Sharing Technology for Community Police Officers.
National Institute of Justice, 6/97

CRIME RISK

Your Chances of Becoming a Victim[1]

Area	Any Crime	Violent Crime						Property Crime			
		Any	Murder	Forcible Rape[2]	Robbery	Aggrav. Assault		Any	Burglary	Larceny -Theft	Motor Vehicle Theft
City	1:9	1:44	1:1,391	1:671	1:86	1:107		1:11	1:49	1:21	1:48

Note: (1) Figures have been calculated by dividing the population of the city by the number of crimes reported to the FBI during 1996 and are expressed as odds (eg. 1:20 should be read as 1 in 20). (2) Figures have been calculated by dividing the female population of the city by the number of forcible rapes reported to the FBI during 1996. The female population of the city was estimated by calculating the ratio of females to males reported in the 1990 Census and applying that ratio to 1996 population estimate.
Source: FBI Uniform Crime Reports 1996

CRIME STATISTICS

Total Crimes and Total Crime Rates: 1977 - 1996

Year	Number: City	Number: Suburbs[2]	Number: MSA[1]	Number: U.S.	Rate per 100,000 population: City	Rate: Suburbs[3]	Rate: MSA[1]	Rate: U.S.
1977	39,897	29,388	69,285	10,984,500	7,111.8	4,954.8	6,003.2	5,077.6
1978	45,823	32,461	78,284	11,209,000	8,241.5	5,548.9	6,861.0	5,140.3
1979	52,479	39,804	92,283	12,249,500	9,244.9	6,738.4	7,966.7	5,565.5
1980	53,575	39,814	93,389	13,408,300	9,605.4	6,361.6	7,890.2	5,950.0
1981	52,158	40,094	92,252	13,423,800	9,122.2	6,249.4	7,603.2	5,858.2
1982	49,483	43,433	92,916	12,974,400	8,541.3	6,681.4	7,557.9	5,603.6
1983	44,523	41,837	86,360	12,108,600	7,552.6	5,694.6	6,521.8	5,175.0
1984	46,980	41,844	88,824	11,881,800	8,155.2	5,576.7	6,696.6	5,031.3
1985	48,732	46,585	95,317	12,431,400	8,681.0	6,106.4	7,197.8	5,207.1
1986	56,889	50,180	107,069	13,211,900	10,088.0	6,549.1	8,049.4	5,480.4
1987	51,001	49,774	100,775	13,508,700	9,280.7	6,438.9	7,619.7	5,550.0
1988	52,460	48,599	101,059	13,923,100	9,750.1	6,305.0	7,721.2	5,664.2
1989	59,534	53,331	112,865	14,251,400	11,262.8	6,920.1	8,686.9	5,741.0
1990	61,799	53,437	115,236	14,475,600	12,436.0	7,202.9	9,302.1	5,820.3
1991	54,238	56,105	110,343	14,872,900	10,830.5	7,505.7	8,839.5	5,897.8
1992	50,441	56,707	107,148	14,438,200	9,988.2	7,524.3	8,512.9	5,660.2
1993	52,773	54,555	107,328	14,144,800	10,734.5	7,091.2	8,511.7	5,484.4
1994	49,842	55,818	105,660	13,989,500	10,089.7	6,807.7	8,041.6	5,373.5
1995	53,399	54,741	108,140	13,862,700	10,960.9	6,596.0	8,210.5	5,275.9
1996	53,919	55,208	109,127	13,473,600	11,042.2	6,638.6	8,267.7	5,078.9

Notes: (1) Metropolitan Statistical Area - see Appendix A for areas included; (2) calculated by the editors using the following formula: (number of crimes in the MSA minus number of crimes in the city); (3) calculated by the editors using the following formula: ((number of crimes in the MSA minus number of crimes in the city) ÷ (population of the MSA minus population of the city)) x 100,000; n/a not avail.
Source: U.S. Department of Justice, FBI Uniform Crime Reports, 1977 - 1996

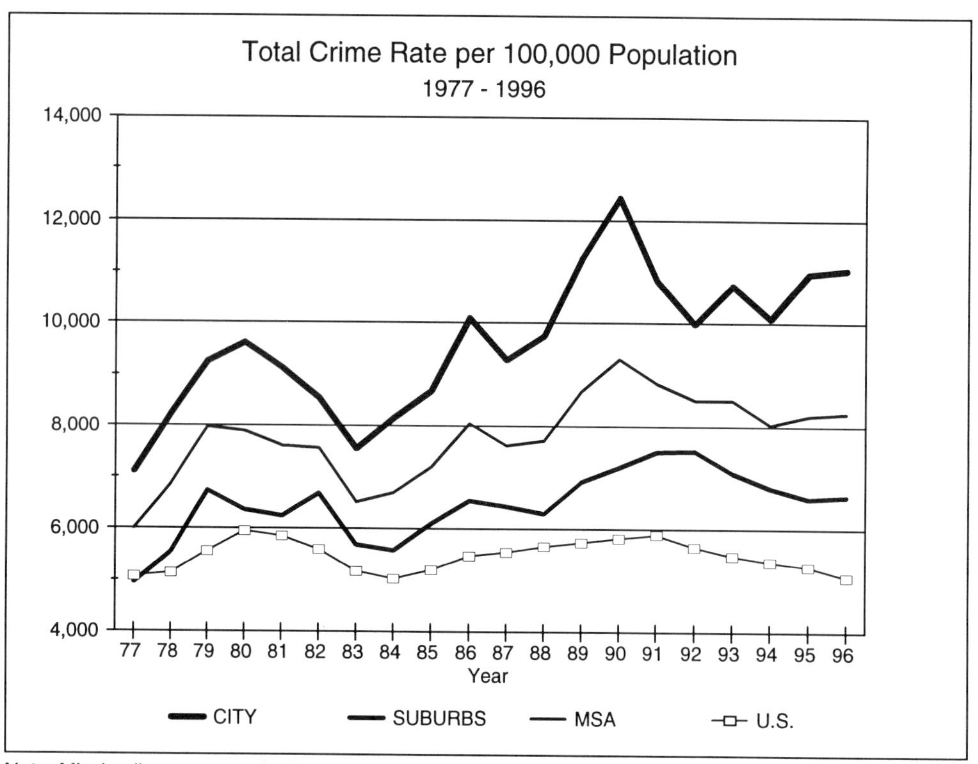

Note: Missing line segments indicate data not available.

Violent Crimes and Violent Crime Rates: 1977 - 1996

Year	Number				Rate per 100,000 population			
	City	Suburbs[2]	MSA[1]	U.S.	City	Suburbs[3]	MSA[1]	U.S.
1977	5,947	2,740	8,687	1,029,580	1,060.1	462.0	752.7	475.9
1978	7,635	3,080	10,715	1,085,550	1,373.2	526.5	939.1	497.8
1979	8,894	3,786	12,680	1,208,030	1,566.8	640.9	1,094.7	548.9
1980	8,172	3,500	11,672	1,344,520	1,465.1	559.2	986.1	596.6
1981	8,121	3,661	11,782	1,361,820	1,420.3	570.6	971.0	594.3
1982	8,604	4,481	13,085	1,322,390	1,485.1	689.3	1,064.3	571.1
1983	8,049	4,187	12,236	1,258,090	1,365.4	569.9	924.0	537.7
1984	8,687	4,493	13,180	1,273,280	1,508.0	598.8	993.7	539.2
1985	8,222	4,730	12,952	1,328,800	1,464.6	620.0	978.1	556.6
1986	9,165	5,252	14,417	1,489,170	1,625.2	685.4	1,083.9	617.7
1987	7,678	4,717	12,395	1,484,000	1,397.2	610.2	937.2	609.7
1988	8,923	5,017	13,940	1,566,220	1,658.4	650.9	1,065.1	637.2
1989	10,203	5,479	15,682	1,646,040	1,930.2	710.9	1,207.0	663.1
1990	11,227	6,218	17,445	1,820,130	2,259.2	838.1	1,408.2	731.8
1991	10,969	6,603	17,572	1,911,770	2,190.3	883.3	1,407.7	758.1
1992	10,007	6,691	16,698	1,932,270	1,981.6	887.8	1,326.7	757.5
1993	10,024	6,527	16,551	1,926,020	2,039.0	848.4	1,312.6	746.8
1994	9,321	6,804	16,125	1,857,670	1,886.9	829.8	1,227.2	713.6
1995	10,876	6,701	17,577	1,798,790	2,232.4	807.4	1,334.5	684.6
1996	11,021	6,481	17,502	1,682,280	2,257.0	779.3	1,326.0	634.1

Notes: Violent crimes include murder, forcible rape, robbery and aggravated assault; n/a not available; (1) Metropolitan Statistical Area - see Appendix A for areas included; (2) calculated by the editors using the following formula: (number of crimes in the MSA minus number of crimes in the city); (3) calculated by the editors using the following formula: ((number of crimes in the MSA minus number of crimes in the city) ÷ (population of the MSA minus population of the city)) x 100,000
Source: U.S. Department of Justice, FBI Uniform Crime Reports, 1977 - 1996

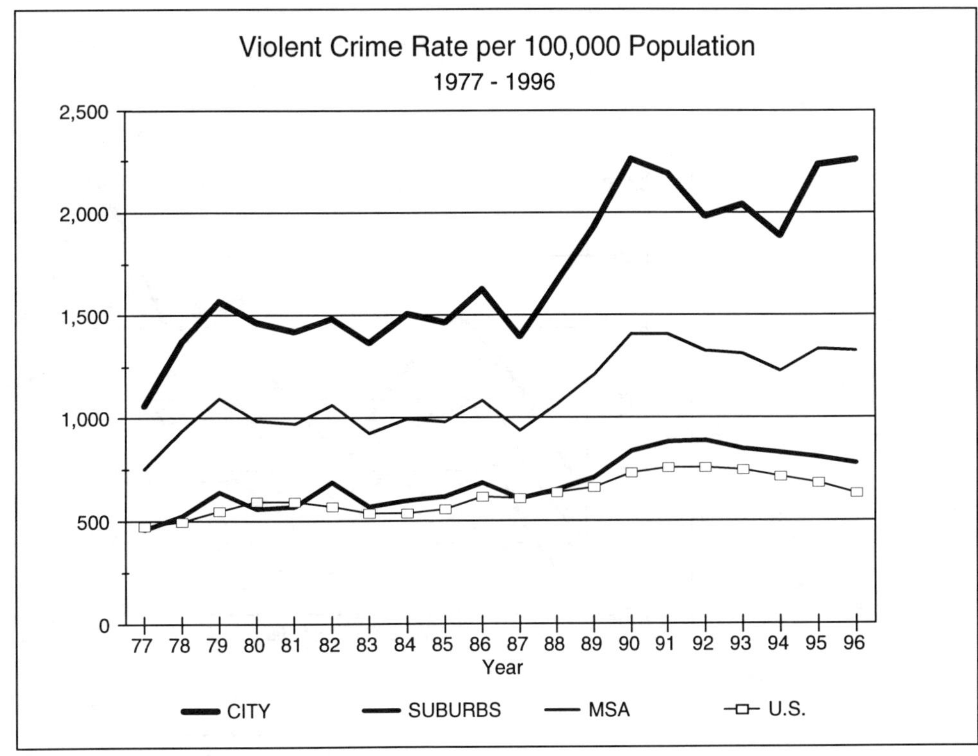

Note: Missing line segments indicate data not available.

Property Crimes and Property Crime Rates: 1977 - 1996

Year	Number				Rate per 100,000 population			
	City	Suburbs[2]	MSA[1]	U.S.	City	Suburbs[3]	MSA[1]	U.S.
1977	33,950	26,648	60,598	9,955,000	6,051.7	4,492.8	5,250.6	4,601.7
1978	38,188	29,381	67,569	10,123,400	6,868.3	5,022.4	5,921.9	4,642.5
1979	43,585	36,018	79,603	11,041,500	7,678.1	6,097.5	6,872.0	5,016.6
1980	45,403	36,314	81,717	12,063,700	8,140.2	5,802.4	6,904.1	5,353.3
1981	44,037	36,433	80,470	12,061,900	7,701.9	5,678.8	6,632.2	5,263.9
1982	40,879	38,952	79,831	11,652,000	7,056.2	5,992.1	6,493.5	5,032.5
1983	36,474	37,650	74,124	10,850,500	6,187.2	5,124.7	5,597.7	4,637.4
1984	38,293	37,351	75,644	10,608,500	6,647.3	4,977.9	5,702.9	4,492.1
1985	40,510	41,855	82,365	11,102,600	7,216.4	5,486.4	6,219.8	4,650.5
1986	47,724	44,928	92,652	11,722,700	8,462.8	5,863.6	6,965.6	4,862.6
1987	43,323	45,057	88,380	12,024,700	7,883.6	5,828.7	6,682.5	4,940.3
1988	43,537	43,582	87,119	12,356,900	8,091.7	5,654.1	6,656.2	5,027.1
1989	49,331	47,852	97,183	12,605,400	9,332.6	6,209.2	7,479.9	5,077.9
1990	50,572	47,219	97,791	12,655,500	10,176.7	6,364.8	7,893.9	5,088.5
1991	43,269	49,502	92,771	12,961,100	8,640.1	6,622.3	7,431.8	5,139.7
1992	40,434	50,016	90,450	12,505,900	8,006.6	6,636.5	7,186.2	4,902.7
1993	42,749	48,028	90,777	12,218,800	8,695.6	6,242.8	7,199.1	4,737.6
1994	40,521	49,014	89,535	12,131,900	8,202.8	5,977.8	6,814.3	4,660.0
1995	42,523	48,040	90,563	12,063,900	8,728.4	5,788.6	6,876.0	4,591.3
1996	42,898	48,727	91,625	11,791,300	8,785.2	5,859.3	6,941.7	4,444.8

Notes: Property crimes include burglary, larceny-theft and motor vehicle theft; n/a not available; (1) Metropolitan Statistical Area - see Appendix A for areas included; (2) calculated by the editors using the following formula: (number of crimes in the MSA minus number of crimes in the city); (3) calculated by the editors using the following formula: ((number of crimes in the MSA minus number of crimes in the city) ÷ (population of the MSA minus population of the city)) x 100,000
Source: U.S. Department of Justice, FBI Uniform Crime Reports, 1977 - 1996

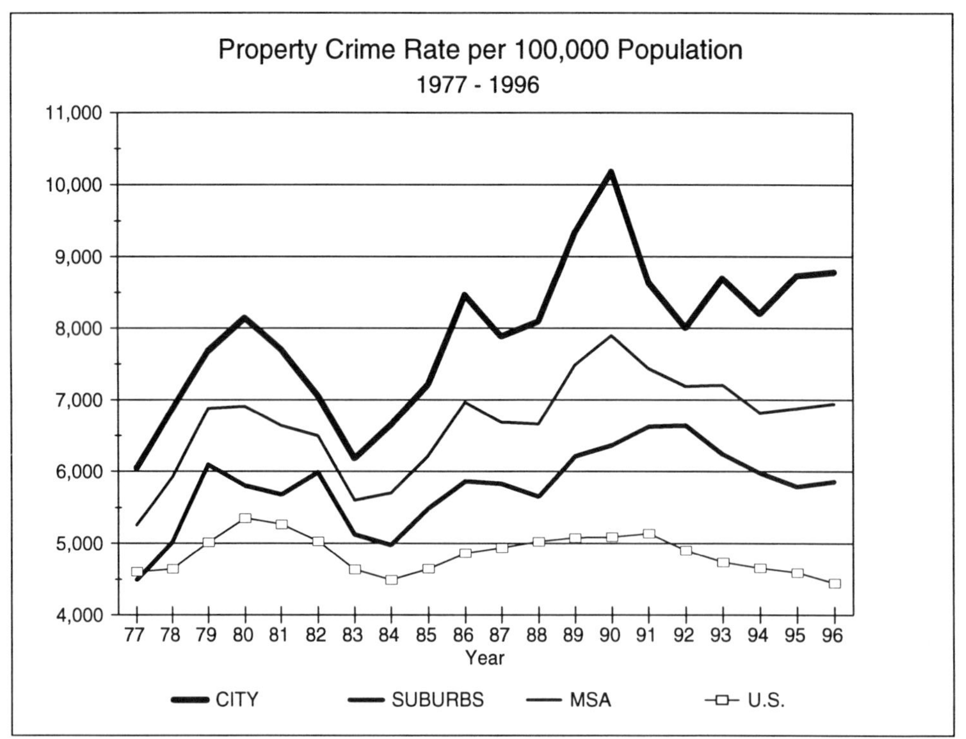

Note: Missing line segments indicate data not available.

Murders and Murder Rates: 1977 - 1996

Year	Number				Rate per 100,000 population			
	City	Suburbs[2]	MSA[1]	U.S.	City	Suburbs[3]	MSA[1]	U.S.
1977	173	49	222	19,120	30.8	8.3	19.2	8.8
1978	216	56	272	19,560	38.8	9.6	23.8	9.0
1979	242	66	308	21,460	42.6	11.2	26.6	9.7
1980	218	46	264	23,040	39.1	7.4	22.3	10.2
1981	217	68	285	22,520	38.0	10.6	23.5	9.8
1982	233	78	311	21,010	40.2	12.0	25.3	9.1
1983	211	65	276	19,310	35.8	8.8	20.8	8.3
1984	214	84	298	18,690	37.1	11.2	22.5	7.9
1985	152	55	207	18,980	27.1	7.2	15.6	7.9
1986	197	69	266	20,610	34.9	9.0	20.0	8.6
1987	205	34	239	20,100	37.3	4.4	18.1	8.3
1988	228	34	262	20,680	42.4	4.4	20.0	8.4
1989	251	70	321	21,500	47.5	9.1	24.7	8.7
1990	304	83	387	23,440	61.2	11.2	31.2	9.4
1991	345	94	439	24,700	68.9	12.6	35.2	9.8
1992	279	77	356	23,760	55.2	10.2	28.3	9.3
1993	395	80	475	24,530	80.3	10.4	37.7	9.5
1994	424	79	503	23,330	85.8	9.6	38.3	9.0
1995	363	68	431	21,610	74.5	8.2	32.7	8.2
1996	351	70	421	19,650	71.9	8.4	31.9	7.4

Notes: (1) Metropolitan Statistical Area - see Appendix A for areas included; (2) calculated by the editors using the following formula: (number of crimes in the MSA minus number of crimes in the city); (3) calculated by the editors using the following formula: ((number of crimes in the MSA minus number of crimes in the city) ÷ (population of the MSA minus population of the city)) x 100,000; n/a not avail.
Source: U.S. Department of Justice, FBI Uniform Crime Reports, 1977 - 1996

Forcible Rapes and Forcible Rape Rates: 1977 - 1996

Year	Number				Rate per 100,000 population			
	City	Suburbs[2]	MSA[1]	U.S.	City	Suburbs[3]	MSA[1]	U.S.
1977	360	154	514	63,500	64.2	26.0	44.5	29.4
1978	406	183	589	67,610	73.0	31.3	51.6	31.0
1979	423	237	660	76,390	74.5	40.1	57.0	34.7
1980	588	285	873	82,990	105.4	45.5	73.8	36.8
1981	453	284	737	82,500	79.2	44.3	60.7	36.0
1982	488	294	782	78,770	84.2	45.2	63.6	34.0
1983	536	294	830	78,920	90.9	40.0	62.7	33.7
1984	555	314	869	84,230	96.3	41.8	65.5	35.7
1985	451	312	763	88,670	80.3	40.9	57.6	37.1
1986	456	299	755	91,460	80.9	39.0	56.8	37.9
1987	359	267	626	91,110	65.3	34.5	47.3	37.4
1988	403	264	667	92,490	74.9	34.3	51.0	37.6
1989	388	317	705	94,500	73.4	41.1	54.3	38.1
1990	361	331	692	102,560	72.6	44.6	55.9	41.2
1991	302	364	666	106,590	60.3	48.7	53.4	42.3
1992	287	342	629	109,060	56.8	45.4	50.0	42.8
1993	298	361	659	106,010	60.6	46.9	52.3	41.1
1994	436	321	757	102,220	88.3	39.1	57.6	39.3
1995	487	327	814	97,470	100.0	39.4	61.8	37.1
1996	390	269	659	95,770	79.9	32.3	49.9	36.1

Notes: (1) Metropolitan Statistical Area - see Appendix A for areas included; (2) calculated by the editors using the following formula: (number of crimes in the MSA minus number of crimes in the city); (3) calculated by the editors using the following formula: ((number of crimes in the MSA minus number of crimes in the city) ÷ (population of the MSA minus population of the city)) x 100,000; n/a not avail.
Source: U.S. Department of Justice, FBI Uniform Crime Reports, 1977 - 1996

Robberies and Robbery Rates: 1977 - 1996

Year	Number				Rate per 100,000 population			
	City	Suburbs[2]	MSA[1]	U.S.	City	Suburbs[3]	MSA[1]	U.S.
1977	3,279	719	3,998	412,610	584.5	121.2	346.4	190.7
1978	4,164	909	5,073	426,930	748.9	155.4	444.6	195.8
1979	5,276	1,224	6,500	480,700	929.4	207.2	561.1	218.4
1980	4,647	900	5,547	565,840	833.2	143.8	468.7	251.1
1981	4,950	1,087	6,037	592,910	865.7	169.4	497.6	258.7
1982	5,106	1,307	6,413	553,130	881.4	201.1	521.6	238.9
1983	4,550	1,147	5,697	506,570	771.8	156.1	430.2	216.5
1984	4,705	1,337	6,042	485,010	816.7	178.2	455.5	205.4
1985	4,142	1,315	5,457	497,870	737.8	172.4	412.1	208.5
1986	5,165	1,488	6,653	542,780	915.9	194.2	500.2	225.1
1987	3,786	1,344	5,130	517,700	688.9	173.9	387.9	212.7
1988	4,729	1,439	6,168	542,970	878.9	186.7	471.3	220.9
1989	5,449	1,694	7,143	578,330	1,030.9	219.8	549.8	233.0
1990	6,048	1,940	7,988	639,270	1,217.1	261.5	644.8	257.0
1991	5,969	2,069	8,038	687,730	1,191.9	276.8	643.9	272.7
1992	5,341	1,812	7,153	672,480	1,057.6	240.4	568.3	263.6
1993	5,179	1,868	7,047	659,870	1,053.5	242.8	558.9	255.9
1994	4,822	1,871	6,693	618,950	976.1	228.2	509.4	237.7
1995	5,349	1,886	7,235	580,510	1,098.0	227.3	549.3	220.9
1996	5,700	1,789	7,489	537,050	1,167.3	215.1	567.4	202.4

Notes: (1) Metropolitan Statistical Area - see Appendix A for areas included; (2) calculated by the editors using the following formula: (number of crimes in the MSA minus number of crimes in the city); (3) calculated by the editors using the following formula: ((number of crimes in the MSA minus number of crimes in the city) ÷ (population of the MSA minus population of the city)) x 100,000; n/a not avail.
Source: U.S. Department of Justice, FBI Uniform Crime Reports, 1977 - 1996

Aggravated Assaults and Aggravated Assault Rates: 1977 - 1996

Year	Number				Rate per 100,000 population			
	City	Suburbs[2]	MSA[1]	U.S.	City	Suburbs[3]	MSA[1]	U.S.
1977	2,135	1,818	3,953	534,350	380.6	306.5	342.5	247.0
1978	2,849	1,932	4,781	571,460	512.4	330.3	419.0	262.1
1979	2,953	2,259	5,212	629,480	520.2	382.4	449.9	286.0
1980	2,719	2,269	4,988	672,650	487.5	362.5	421.4	298.5
1981	2,501	2,222	4,723	663,900	437.4	346.3	389.3	289.7
1982	2,777	2,802	5,579	669,480	479.3	431.0	453.8	289.2
1983	2,752	2,681	5,433	653,290	466.8	364.9	410.3	279.2
1984	3,213	2,758	5,971	685,350	557.7	367.6	450.2	290.2
1985	3,477	3,048	6,525	723,250	619.4	399.5	492.7	302.9
1986	3,347	3,396	6,743	834,320	593.5	443.2	506.9	346.1
1987	3,328	3,072	6,400	855,090	605.6	397.4	483.9	351.3
1988	3,563	3,280	6,843	910,090	662.2	425.5	522.8	370.2
1989	4,115	3,398	7,513	951,710	778.5	440.9	578.3	383.4
1990	4,514	3,864	8,378	1,054,860	908.4	520.8	676.3	424.1
1991	4,353	4,076	8,429	1,092,740	869.2	545.3	675.2	433.3
1992	4,100	4,460	8,560	1,126,970	811.9	591.8	680.1	441.8
1993	4,152	4,218	8,370	1,135,610	844.6	548.3	663.8	440.3
1994	3,639	4,533	8,172	1,113,180	736.7	552.9	622.0	427.6
1995	4,677	4,420	9,097	1,099,210	960.0	532.6	690.7	418.3
1996	4,580	4,353	8,933	1,029,810	937.9	523.4	676.8	388.2

Notes: (1) Metropolitan Statistical Area - see Appendix A for areas included; (2) calculated by the editors using the following formula: (number of crimes in the MSA minus number of crimes in the city); (3) calculated by the editors using the following formula: ((number of crimes in the MSA minus number of crimes in the city) ÷ (population of the MSA minus population of the city)) x 100,000; n/a not avail.
Source: U.S. Department of Justice, FBI Uniform Crime Reports, 1977 - 1996

Burglaries and Burglary Rates: 1977 - 1996

Year	Number				Rate per 100,000 population			
	City	Suburbs[2]	MSA[1]	U.S.	City	Suburbs[3]	MSA[1]	U.S.
1977	8,692	8,261	16,953	3,071,500	1,549.4	1,392.8	1,468.9	1,419.8
1978	10,514	9,331	19,845	3,128,300	1,891.0	1,595.0	1,739.3	1,434.6
1979	12,810	10,879	23,689	3,327,700	2,256.6	1,841.7	2,045.0	1,511.9
1980	14,154	11,613	25,767	3,795,200	2,537.6	1,855.6	2,177.0	1,684.1
1981	13,117	10,969	24,086	3,779,700	2,294.1	1,709.7	1,985.1	1,649.5
1982	12,320	11,106	23,426	3,447,100	2,126.6	1,708.5	1,905.5	1,488.8
1983	10,782	10,391	21,173	3,129,900	1,829.0	1,414.4	1,598.9	1,337.7
1984	10,821	10,509	21,330	2,984,400	1,878.4	1,400.6	1,608.1	1,263.7
1985	10,383	10,773	21,156	3,073,300	1,849.6	1,412.1	1,597.6	1,287.3
1986	11,561	11,973	23,534	3,241,400	2,050.1	1,562.6	1,769.3	1,344.6
1987	11,999	12,009	24,008	3,236,200	2,183.5	1,553.5	1,815.3	1,329.6
1988	12,322	11,957	24,279	3,218,100	2,290.1	1,551.2	1,855.0	1,309.2
1989	12,925	12,122	25,047	3,168,200	2,445.2	1,572.9	1,927.8	1,276.3
1990	13,624	11,278	24,902	3,073,900	2,741.6	1,520.2	2,010.1	1,235.9
1991	12,400	11,391	23,791	3,157,200	2,476.1	1,523.9	1,905.9	1,252.0
1992	10,967	10,945	21,912	2,979,900	2,171.6	1,452.3	1,740.9	1,168.2
1993	11,184	9,502	20,686	2,834,800	2,274.9	1,235.1	1,640.5	1,099.2
1994	10,064	9,654	19,718	2,712,800	2,037.3	1,177.4	1,500.7	1,042.0
1995	10,236	9,121	19,357	2,593,800	2,101.1	1,099.0	1,469.7	987.1
1996	9,954	9,038	18,992	2,501,500	2,038.5	1,086.8	1,438.9	943.0

Notes: (1) Metropolitan Statistical Area - see Appendix A for areas included; (2) calculated by the editors using the following formula: (number of crimes in the MSA minus number of crimes in the city); (3) calculated by the editors using the following formula: ((number of crimes in the MSA minus number of crimes in the city) ÷ (population of the MSA minus population of the city)) x 100,000; n/a not avail.
Source: U.S. Department of Justice, FBI Uniform Crime Reports, 1977 - 1996

Larceny-Thefts and Larceny-Theft Rates: 1977 - 1996

Year	Number				Rate per 100,000 population			
	City	Suburbs[2]	MSA[1]	U.S.	City	Suburbs[3]	MSA[1]	U.S.
1977	19,754	15,822	35,576	5,905,700	3,521.2	2,667.6	3,082.5	2,729.9
1978	22,183	17,066	39,249	5,991,000	3,989.7	2,917.2	3,439.9	2,747.4
1979	24,687	21,396	46,083	6,601,000	4,348.9	3,622.1	3,978.3	2,999.1
1980	25,668	21,409	47,077	7,136,900	4,602.0	3,420.8	3,977.4	3,167.0
1981	25,305	22,175	47,480	7,194,400	4,425.7	3,456.4	3,913.2	3,139.7
1982	23,613	24,484	48,097	7,142,500	4,075.9	3,766.5	3,912.3	3,084.8
1983	20,847	24,061	44,908	6,712,800	3,536.3	3,275.1	3,391.4	2,868.9
1984	22,238	23,762	46,000	6,591,900	3,860.3	3,166.8	3,468.0	2,791.3
1985	23,433	27,651	51,084	6,926,400	4,174.3	3,624.5	3,857.6	2,901.2
1986	26,697	29,397	56,094	7,257,200	4,734.1	3,836.6	4,217.1	3,010.3
1987	22,365	29,950	52,315	7,499,900	4,069.8	3,874.4	3,955.6	3,081.3
1988	21,534	27,951	49,485	7,705,900	4,002.3	3,626.2	3,780.8	3,134.9
1989	24,935	31,435	56,370	7,872,400	4,717.3	4,079.0	4,338.7	3,171.3
1990	24,806	31,027	55,833	7,945,700	4,991.8	4,182.2	4,507.0	3,194.8
1991	20,977	32,393	53,370	8,142,200	4,188.8	4,333.5	4,275.4	3,228.8
1992	20,343	33,143	53,486	7,915,200	4,028.3	4,397.7	4,249.5	3,103.0
1993	22,019	33,015	55,034	7,820,900	4,478.9	4,291.4	4,364.5	3,032.4
1994	21,890	33,625	55,515	7,879,800	4,431.3	4,101.0	4,225.1	3,026.7
1995	22,454	33,387	55,841	7,997,700	4,609.0	4,023.0	4,239.7	3,043.8
1996	22,774	34,236	57,010	7,894,600	4,663.9	4,116.8	4,319.2	2,975.9

Notes: (1) Metropolitan Statistical Area - see Appendix A for areas included; (2) calculated by the editors using the following formula: (number of crimes in the MSA minus number of crimes in the city); (3) calculated by the editors using the following formula: ((number of crimes in the MSA minus number of crimes in the city) ÷ (population of the MSA minus population of the city)) x 100,000; n/a not avail.
Source: U.S. Department of Justice, FBI Uniform Crime Reports, 1977 - 1996

Motor Vehicle Thefts and Motor Vehicle Theft Rates: 1977 - 1996

Year	Number				Rate per 100,000 population			
	City	Suburbs[2]	MSA[1]	U.S.	City	Suburbs[3]	MSA[1]	U.S.
1977	5,504	2,565	8,069	977,700	981.1	432.5	699.1	451.9
1978	5,491	2,984	8,475	1,004,100	987.6	510.1	742.8	460.5
1979	6,088	3,743	9,831	1,112,800	1,072.5	633.7	848.7	505.6
1980	5,581	3,292	8,873	1,131,700	1,000.6	526.0	749.7	502.2
1981	5,615	3,289	8,904	1,087,800	982.0	512.7	733.8	474.7
1982	4,946	3,362	8,308	1,062,400	853.7	517.2	675.8	458.8
1983	4,845	3,198	8,043	1,007,900	821.9	435.3	607.4	430.8
1984	5,234	3,080	8,314	1,032,200	908.6	410.5	626.8	437.1
1985	6,694	3,431	10,125	1,102,900	1,192.5	449.7	764.6	462.0
1986	9,466	3,558	13,024	1,224,100	1,678.6	464.4	979.1	507.8
1987	8,959	3,098	12,057	1,288,700	1,630.3	400.8	911.6	529.4
1988	9,681	3,674	13,355	1,432,900	1,799.3	476.6	1,020.4	582.9
1989	11,471	4,295	15,766	1,564,800	2,170.1	557.3	1,213.5	630.4
1990	12,142	4,914	17,056	1,635,900	2,443.4	662.4	1,376.8	657.8
1991	9,892	5,718	15,610	1,661,700	1,975.3	764.9	1,250.5	659.0
1992	9,124	5,928	15,052	1,610,800	1,806.7	786.6	1,195.9	631.5
1993	9,546	5,511	15,057	1,563,100	1,941.7	716.3	1,194.1	606.1
1994	8,567	5,735	14,302	1,539,300	1,734.2	699.5	1,088.5	591.3
1995	9,833	5,532	15,365	1,472,400	2,018.4	666.6	1,166.6	560.4
1996	10,170	5,453	15,623	1,395,200	2,082.7	655.7	1,183.6	525.9

Notes: (1) Metropolitan Statistical Area - see Appendix A for areas included; (2) calculated by the editors using the following formula: (number of crimes in the MSA minus number of crimes in the city); (3) calculated by the editors using the following formula: ((number of crimes in the MSA minus number of crimes in the city) ÷ (population of the MSA minus population of the city)) x 100,000; n/a not avail.
Source: U.S. Department of Justice, FBI Uniform Crime Reports, 1977 - 1996

HATE CRIMES

Criminal Incidents by Bias Motivation

Area	Race	Ethnicity	Religion	Sexual Orientation
New Orleans	0	0	0	0

Notes: Figures include both violent and property crimes. Law enforcement agencies must have submitted data for at least one quarter of calendar year 1995 to be included in this report, therefore figures shown may not represent complete 12-month totals; n/a not available
Source: U.S. Department of Justice, FBI Uniform Crime Reports, Hate Crime Statistics 1995

ILLEGAL DRUGS

Drug Use by Adult Arrestees

Sex	Percent Testing Positive by Urinalysis (%)				
	Any Drug[1]	Cocaine	Marijuana	Opiates	Multiple Drugs
Male	67	46	40	7	26
Female	35	26	13	3	10

Notes: The catchment area is the entire parish; (1) Includes cocaine, opiates, marijuana, methadone, phencyclidine (PCP), benzodiazepines, methaqualone, propoxyphene, barbiturates & amphetamines
Source: National Institute of Justice, 1996 Drug Use Forecasting, Annual Report on Adult and Juvenile Arrestees (released June 1997)

LAW ENFORCEMENT

Full-Time Law Enforcement Employees

Jurisdiction	Police Employees			Police Officers per 100,000 population
	Total	Officers	Civilians	
New Orleans	1,613	1,302	311	266.6

Notes: Data as of October 31, 1996
Source: U.S. Department of Justice, FBI Uniform Crime Reports, 1996

Number of Police Officers by Race

Race	Police Officers				Index of Representation[1]		
	1983		1992				
	Number	Pct.	Number	Pct.	1983	1992	% Chg.
Black	276	21.0	608	39.2	0.38	0.63	65.8
Hispanic[2]	26	2.0	25	1.6	0.56	0.46	-17.9

Notes: (1) The index of representation is calculated by dividing the percent of black/hispanic police officers by the percent of corresponding blacks/hispanics in the local population. An index approaching 1.0 indicates that a city is closer to achieving a representation of police officers equal to their proportion in the local population; (2) Hispanic officers can be of any race
Source: Bureau of Justice Statistics, Sourcebook of Criminal Justice Statistics, 1994

CORRECTIONS

Federal Correctional Facilities

Type	Year Opened	Security Level	Sex of Inmates	Rated Capacity	Population on 7/1/95	Number of Staff
None listed						

Notes: Data as of 1995
Source: Bureau of Justice Statistics, Sourcebook of Criminal Justice Statistics Online

City/County/Regional Correctional Facilities

Name	Year Opened	Year Renov.	Rated Capacity	1995 Pop.	Number of COs[1]	Number of Staff	ACA[2] Accred.
New Orleans Parish Prison System	1929	1993	3,455	n/a	n/a	n/a	No

Notes: Data as of April 1996; (1) Correctional Officers; (2) American Correctional Assn. Accreditation
Source: American Correctional Association, 1996-1998 National Jail and Adult Detention Directory

Private Adult Correctional Facilities

Name	Date Opened	Rated Capacity	Present Pop.	Security Level	Facility Construct.	Expans. Plans	ACA[1] Accred.
None listed							

Notes: Data as of December 1996; (1) American Correctional Association Accreditation
Source: University of Florida, Center for Studies in Criminology and Law, Private Adult Correctional Facility Census, 10th Ed., March 15, 1997

Characteristics of Shock Incarceration Programs

Jurisdiction	Year Program Began	Number of Camps	Average Num. of Inmates	Number of Beds	Program Length	Voluntary/ Mandatory
Louisiana	1987	1	130	136	90 to 180	Voluntary

Note: Data as of July 1996;
Source: Sourcebook of Criminal Justice Statistics Online

INMATES AND HIV/AIDS

HIV Testing Policies for Inmates

Jurisdiction	All Inmates at Some Time	All Convicted Inmates at Admission	Random Samples While in Custody	High-risk Groups	Upon Inmate Request	Upon Court Order	Upon Involvement in Incident
Orleans Parish[1]	n/a	n/a	n/a	n/a	n/a	n/a	n/a

Notes: (1) Provided no data on AIDS testing policies
Source: HIV in Prisons and Jails, 1993 (released August 1995)

Inmates Known to be Positive for HIV

Jurisdiction	Number of Jail Inmates in Facilities Providing Data	Type of HIV Infection/AIDS Cases				HIV/AIDS Cases as a Percent of Tot. Custody Pop.
		Total	Asymptomatic	Symptomatic	Confirmed AIDS	
Orleans Parish[1]	5,351	n/a	n/a	n/a	n/a	n/a

Note: (1) Jurisdiction did not provide data on HIV/AIDS cases; n/a not available
Source: HIV in Prisons and Jails, 1993 (released August, 1995)

DEATH PENALTY

Death Penalty Statistics

State	Prisoners Executed		Prisoners Under Sentence of Death					Avg. No. of Years on Death Row[4]
	1930-1995	1996[1]	Total[2]	White[3]	Black[3]	Hisp.	Women	
Louisiana	155	1	57	20	37	1	0	5.0

Notes: Data as of 12/31/95 unless otherwise noted; (1) Data as of 7/31/97; (2) Includes persons of other races; (3) Includes people of Hispanic origin; (4) Covers prisoners sentenced 1974 through 1995
Source: Bureau of Justice Statistics, Capital Punishment 1995 (released 12/96); Death Penalty Information Center Web Site, 9/30/97

Capital Offenses and Methods of Execution

Capital Offenses in Louisiana	Minimum Age for Imposition of Death Penalty	Mentally Retarded Excluded	Methods of Execution[1]
First-degree murder; aggravated rape of victim under age 12; treason (La. R.S. 14:30, 14:42, and 14:113).	None	No	Lethal injection

Notes: Data as of 12/31/95 unless otherwise noted; (1) Data as of 7/31/97
Source: Bureau of Justice Statistics, Capital Punishment 1995 (released 12/96); Death Penalty Information Center Web Site, 9/30/97

LAWS

Statutory Provisions Relating to the Purchase, Ownership and Use of Handguns

Jurisdiction	Instant Background Check	Federal Waiting Period Applies[1]	State Waiting Period (days)	License or Permit to Purchase	Regis-tration	Record of Sale Sent to Police	Concealed Carry Law
Louisiana	No	Yes[a]	No	No	No	No	Yes[b]

Note: Data as of 1996; (1) The Federal 5-day waiting period for handgun purchases applies to states that don't have instant background checks, waiting period requirements, or licensing procedures exempting them from the Federal requirement; (a) The Federal waiting period does not apply to a person holding a valid permit or license to carry a firearm, issued within 5 years of proposed purchase; (b) "Shall issue" permit system, liberally administered discretion by local authorities over permit issuance, or no permit required
Source: Sourcebook of Criminal Justice Statistics Online

Statutory Provisions Relating to Alcohol Use and Driving

Jurisdiction	Drinking Age	Blood Alcohol Concentration Levels as Evidence in State Courts[1]		Open Container Law[1]	Anti-Consump-tion Law[1]	Dram Shop Law[1]
		Illegal per se at 0.10%	Presumption at 0.10%			
Louisiana	21	Yes	Yes	No	No	(a)

Note: Data as of January 1, 1997; (1) See Appendix C for an explanation of terms; (a) The statue appears to have limited actions to those committed by minors
Source: Sourcebook of Criminal Justice Statistics Online

Statutory Provisions Relating to Curfews

Jurisdiction	Year Enacted	Latest Revision	Age Group(s)	Curfew Provisions
New Orleans	1994	-	17 and under	8 pm to 6 am school nights 9 pm to 6 am summer weekday nights 11 pm to 6 am weekend nights 9 am to 3:15 pm school days

Note: Data as of February 1996
Source: Sourcebook of Criminal Justice Statistics Online

Statutory Provisions Relating to Hate Crimes

Jurisdiction	Bias-Motivated Violence and Intimidation						Institutional Vandalism
	Civil Action	Criminal Penalty					
		Race/ Religion/ Ethnicity	Sexual Orientation	Mental/ Physical Disability	Gender	Age	
Louisiana	Yes	No	No	No	No	No	Yes

Source: Anti-Defamation League, 1997 Hate Crimes Laws

New York, New York

OVERVIEW

The total crime rate for the city decreased 37.6% between 1977 and 1996. During that same period, the violent crime rate decreased 19.5% and the property crime rate decreased 42.2%.

Among violent crimes, the rates for: Murders decreased 37.1%; Forcible Rapes decreased 40.4%; Robberies decreased 33.6%; and Aggravated Assaults increased 8.0%.

Among property crimes, the rates for: Burglaries decreased 65.9%; Larceny-Thefts decreased 24.9%; and Motor Vehicle Thefts decreased 36.4%.

ANTI-CRIME PROGRAMS

Police strategies include:

- Getting Guns Off the Streets of New York by identifying and pursuing all accomplices involved in the commission of violent crimes; identifying and pursuing gun traffickers inside and outside the city; utilization of detectives in precincts to strengthen every gun arrest, et. al.
- Curbing Youth Violence in the schools and on the streets by making schools the focal points of youth violence reduction efforts.
- Driving Drug Dealers out of New York by driving open-air drug activity off the streets of targeted areas, confiscating and tracing guns; preventing the return of drug activity through the deployment of uniformed personnel; targeting mid-level dealers and suppliers more aggressively; and strengthening the Narcotics District Major Case Squads, the Drug Enforcement Task Force, and the joint FBI/NYPD Task Force to pursue and apprehend local high-level narcotics suppliers.
- Breaking the Cycle of Domestic Violence by tracking and recording all calls for domestic incidents; establishing a Domestic Violence Investigator in every precinct detective squad and greater use of technology.
- Reclaiming the public spaces of New York by empowering precinct commanders to respond to disorderly and persistent quality of life conditions. Some of the specific targets include prostitution, sale of liquor to minors, unlicensed vendors, graffiti, and "squeegee cleaners".
- Reducing auto-related crime in New York by having Precinct Detective Squads interview all suspects arrested for auto-related crimes; undercover sting operations against those buying and selling property stolen from cars; securing of civil closing order for chop shops; and expanding (CAT) Combat Auto-Theft Program and Operation Identification.
- Reclaiming the Roads of New York-addresses traffic congestion and the environmental, commercial and quality-of-life problems it engenders.
- Bringing fugitives to justice-increases fugitive apprehension efforts. *The City of New York Police Department, Crime Analysis and Program Planning Section, 8/97*

CRIME RISK

Your Chances of Becoming a Victim[1]

Area	Any Crime	Violent Crime					Property Crime			
		Any	Murder	Forcible Rape[2]	Robbery	Aggrav. Assault	Any	Burglary	Larceny -Theft	Motor Vehicle Theft
City	1:19	1:74	1:7,467	1:1,673	1:148	1:161	1:26	1:120	1:45	1:122

Note: (1) Figures have been calculated by dividing the population of the city by the number of crimes reported to the FBI during 1996 and are expressed as odds (eg. 1:20 should be read as 1 in 20). (2) Figures have been calculated by dividing the female population of the city by the number of forcible rapes reported to the FBI during 1996. The female population of the city was estimated by calculating the ratio of females to males reported in the 1990 Census and applying that ratio to 1996 population estimate.
Source: FBI Uniform Crime Reports 1996

CRIME STATISTICS

Total Crimes and Total Crime Rates: 1977 - 1996

Year	Number				Rate per 100,000 population			
	City	Suburbs[2]	MSA[1]	U.S.	City	Suburbs[3]	MSA[1]	U.S.
1977	610,077	99,157	709,234	10,984,500	8,359.5	4,443.9	7,442.7	5,077.6
1978	570,354	89,060	659,414	11,209,000	7,993.7	4,112.2	7,089.9	5,140.3
1979	621,110	95,087	716,197	12,249,500	8,736.4	4,601.7	7,805.3	5,565.5
1980	710,151	102,836	812,987	13,408,300	10,094.0	5,027.6	8,952.8	5,950.0
1981	725,846	98,796	824,642	13,423,800	10,265.9	4,800.1	9,033.6	5,858.2
1982	688,567	90,019	778,586	12,974,400	9,702.8	4,355.3	8,496.6	5,603.6
1983	622,877	49,607	672,484	12,108,600	8,772.8	4,094.2	8,090.8	5,175.0
1984	600,216	48,675	648,891	11,881,800	8,374.6	4,010.8	7,742.7	5,031.3
1985	601,467	46,898	648,365	12,431,400	8,372.3	3,858.8	7,719.2	5,207.1
1986	635,199	46,501	681,700	13,211,900	8,847.3	3,828.4	8,121.0	5,480.4
1987	656,505	49,711	706,216	13,508,700	9,012.6	4,093.8	8,309.8	5,550.0
1988	718,483	50,636	769,119	13,923,100	9,780.1	4,161.1	8,981.6	5,664.2
1989	712,419	48,435	760,854	14,251,400	9,667.2	3,980.0	8,861.1	5,741.0
1990	710,222	50,416	760,638	14,475,600	9,699.1	4,118.0	8,899.6	5,820.3
1991	678,855	49,015	727,870	14,872,900	9,236.1	3,988.7	8,484.4	5,897.8
1992	626,182	431,747	1,057,929	14,438,200	8,490.5	4,457.2	6,200.6	5,660.2
1993	600,346	48,963	649,309	14,144,800	8,171.0	3,848.1	7,532.9	5,484.4
1994	530,120	41,252	571,372	13,989,500	7,226.1	3,280.6	6,648.7	5,373.5
1995	444,758	42,554	487,312	13,862,700	6,076.3	3,335.6	5,669.5	5,275.9
1996	382,555	39,469	422,024	13,473,600	5,212.2	3,085.6	4,896.6	5,078.9

Notes: (1) Metropolitan Statistical Area - see Appendix A for areas included; (2) calculated by the editors using the following formula: (number of crimes in the MSA minus number of crimes in the city); (3) calculated by the editors using the following formula: ((number of crimes in the MSA minus number of crimes in the city) ÷ (population of the MSA minus population of the city)) x 100,000; n/a not avail.
Source: U.S. Department of Justice, FBI Uniform Crime Reports, 1977 - 1996

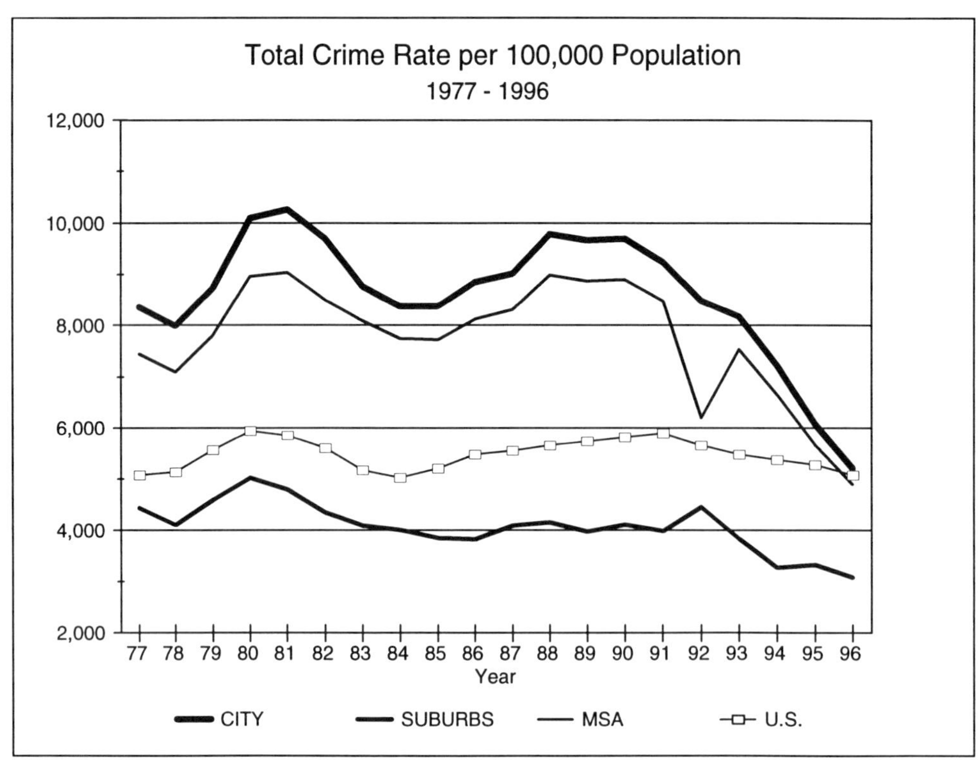

Note: Missing line segments indicate data not available.

Violent Crimes and Violent Crime Rates: 1977 - 1996

Year	Number				Rate per 100,000 population			
	City	Suburbs[2]	MSA[1]	U.S.	City	Suburbs[3]	MSA[1]	U.S.
1977	121,912	5,713	127,625	1,029,580	1,670.5	256.0	1,339.3	475.9
1978	122,685	4,795	127,480	1,085,550	1,719.5	221.4	1,370.6	497.8
1979	132,383	4,971	137,354	1,208,030	1,862.1	240.6	1,496.9	548.9
1980	149,549	5,784	155,333	1,344,520	2,125.7	282.8	1,710.6	596.6
1981	156,946	6,046	162,992	1,361,820	2,219.8	293.8	1,785.5	594.3
1982	143,943	5,703	149,646	1,322,390	2,028.3	275.9	1,633.1	571.1
1983	132,653	3,988	136,641	1,258,090	1,868.3	329.1	1,644.0	537.7
1984	132,292	4,406	136,698	1,273,280	1,845.8	363.1	1,631.1	539.2
1985	135,152	4,112	139,264	1,328,800	1,881.3	338.3	1,658.0	556.6
1986	143,251	4,029	147,280	1,489,170	1,995.2	331.7	1,754.5	617.7
1987	148,313	4,098	152,411	1,484,000	2,036.1	337.5	1,793.4	609.7
1988	162,916	4,021	166,937	1,566,220	2,217.6	330.4	1,949.5	637.2
1989	169,487	4,059	173,546	1,646,040	2,299.9	333.5	2,021.2	663.1
1990	174,542	4,840	179,382	1,820,130	2,383.6	395.3	2,098.8	731.8
1991	170,390	4,981	175,371	1,911,770	2,318.2	405.3	2,044.2	758.1
1992	159,578	51,702	211,280	1,932,270	2,163.7	533.7	1,238.3	757.5
1993	153,543	7,261	160,804	1,926,020	2,089.8	570.7	1,865.5	746.8
1994	136,522	4,463	140,985	1,857,670	1,860.9	354.9	1,640.6	713.6
1995	115,153	4,561	119,714	1,798,790	1,573.2	357.5	1,392.8	684.6
1996	98,659	4,067	102,726	1,682,280	1,344.2	317.9	1,191.9	634.1

Notes: Violent crimes include murder, forcible rape, robbery and aggravated assault; n/a not available; (1) Metropolitan Statistical Area - see Appendix A for areas included; (2) calculated by the editors using the following formula: (number of crimes in the MSA minus number of crimes in the city); (3) calculated by the editors using the following formula: ((number of crimes in the MSA minus number of crimes in the city) ÷ (population of the MSA minus population of the city)) x 100,000
Source: U.S. Department of Justice, FBI Uniform Crime Reports, 1977 - 1996

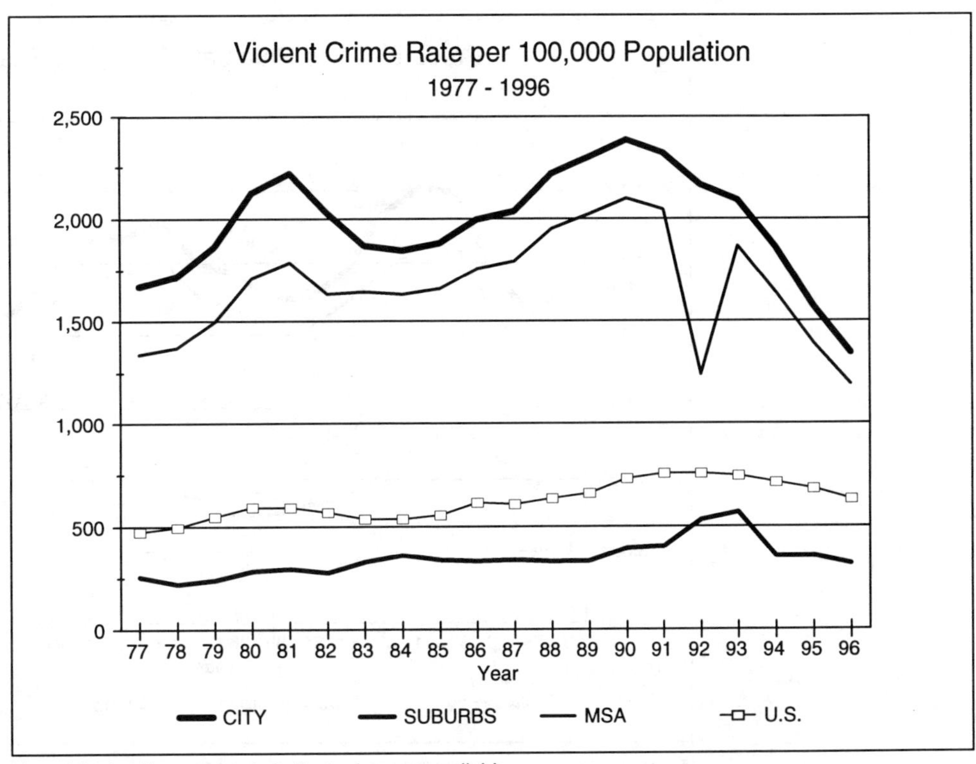

Note: Missing line segments indicate data not available.

Property Crimes and Property Crime Rates: 1977 - 1996

Year	Number				Rate per 100,000 population			
	City	Suburbs[2]	MSA[1]	U.S.	City	Suburbs[3]	MSA[1]	U.S.
1977	488,165	93,444	581,609	9,955,000	6,689.0	4,187.8	6,103.4	4,601.7
1978	447,669	84,265	531,934	10,123,400	6,274.3	3,890.8	5,719.3	4,642.5
1979	488,727	90,116	578,843	11,041,500	6,874.4	4,361.1	6,308.4	5,016.6
1980	560,602	97,052	657,654	12,063,700	7,968.4	4,744.8	7,242.3	5,353.3
1981	568,900	92,750	661,650	12,061,900	8,046.2	4,506.4	7,248.1	5,263.9
1982	544,624	84,316	628,940	11,652,000	7,674.5	4,079.3	6,863.6	5,032.5
1983	490,224	45,619	535,843	10,850,500	6,904.5	3,765.0	6,446.8	4,637.4
1984	467,924	44,269	512,193	10,608,500	6,528.8	3,647.8	6,111.6	4,492.1
1985	466,315	42,786	509,101	11,102,600	6,491.0	3,520.5	6,061.2	4,650.5
1986	491,948	42,472	534,420	11,722,700	6,852.0	3,496.7	6,366.5	4,862.6
1987	508,192	45,613	553,805	12,024,700	6,976.5	3,756.3	6,516.4	4,940.3
1988	555,567	46,615	602,182	12,356,900	7,562.5	3,830.6	7,032.2	5,027.1
1989	542,932	44,376	587,308	12,605,400	7,367.3	3,646.4	6,840.0	5,077.9
1990	535,680	45,576	581,256	12,655,500	7,315.5	3,722.7	6,800.8	5,088.5
1991	508,465	44,034	552,499	12,961,100	6,917.9	3,583.4	6,440.2	5,139.7
1992	466,604	380,045	846,649	12,505,900	6,326.8	3,923.4	4,962.3	4,902.7
1993	446,803	41,702	488,505	12,218,800	6,081.2	3,277.4	5,667.3	4,737.6
1994	393,598	36,789	430,387	12,131,900	5,365.1	2,925.7	5,008.2	4,660.0
1995	329,605	37,993	367,598	12,063,900	4,503.1	2,978.1	4,276.7	4,591.3
1996	283,896	35,402	319,298	11,791,300	3,868.0	2,767.6	3,704.7	4,444.8

Notes: Property crimes include burglary, larceny-theft and motor vehicle theft; n/a not available; (1) Metropolitan Statistical Area - see Appendix A for areas included; (2) calculated by the editors using the following formula: (number of crimes in the MSA minus number of crimes in the city); (3) calculated by the editors using the following formula: ((number of crimes in the MSA minus number of crimes in the city) ÷ (population of the MSA minus population of the city)) x 100,000
Source: U.S. Department of Justice, FBI Uniform Crime Reports, 1977 - 1996

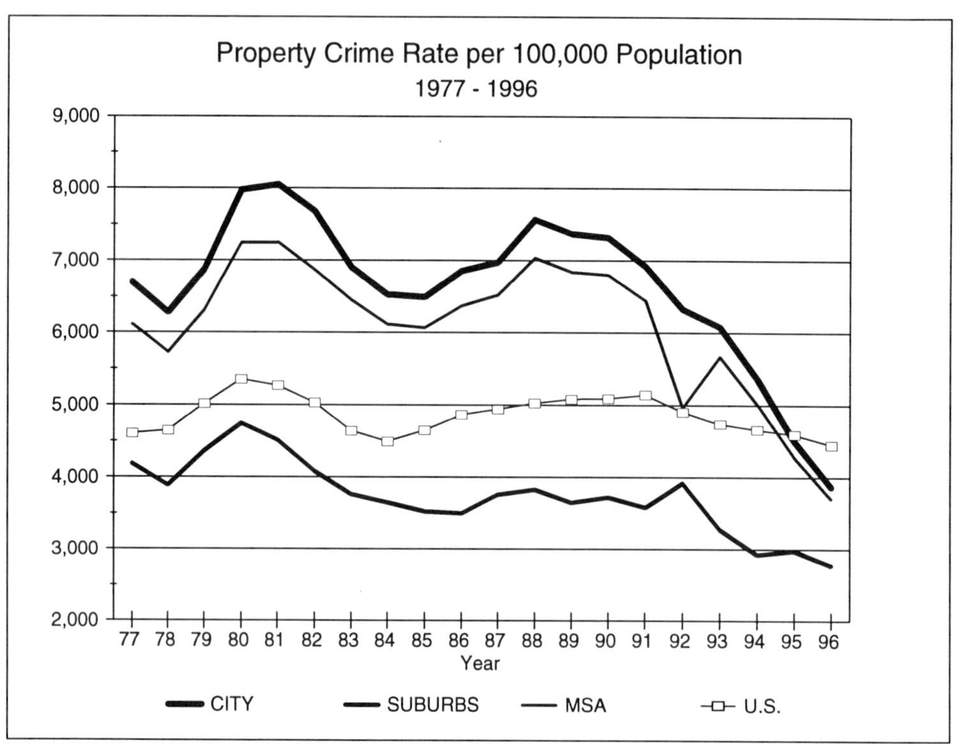

Note: Missing line segments indicate data not available.

Murders and Murder Rates: 1977 - 1996

Year	Number				Rate per 100,000 population			
	City	Suburbs[2]	MSA[1]	U.S.	City	Suburbs[3]	MSA[1]	U.S.
1977	1,553	75	1,628	19,120	21.3	3.4	17.1	8.8
1978	1,503	58	1,561	19,560	21.1	2.7	16.8	9.0
1979	1,733	81	1,814	21,460	24.4	3.9	19.8	9.7
1980	1,812	91	1,903	23,040	25.8	4.4	21.0	10.2
1981	1,826	67	1,893	22,520	25.8	3.3	20.7	9.8
1982	1,668	81	1,749	21,010	23.5	3.9	19.1	9.1
1983	1,622	43	1,665	19,310	22.8	3.5	20.0	8.3
1984	1,450	42	1,492	18,690	20.2	3.5	17.8	7.9
1985	1,384	48	1,432	18,980	19.3	3.9	17.0	7.9
1986	1,582	34	1,616	20,610	22.0	2.8	19.3	8.6
1987	1,672	61	1,733	20,100	23.0	5.0	20.4	8.3
1988	1,896	50	1,946	20,680	25.8	4.1	22.7	8.4
1989	1,905	46	1,951	21,500	25.8	3.8	22.7	8.7
1990	2,245	57	2,302	23,440	30.7	4.7	26.9	9.4
1991	2,154	48	2,202	24,700	29.3	3.9	25.7	9.8
1992	1,995	408	2,403	23,760	27.1	4.2	14.1	9.3
1993	1,946	55	2,001	24,530	26.5	4.3	23.2	9.5
1994	1,561	38	1,599	23,330	21.3	3.0	18.6	9.0
1995	1,177	43	1,220	21,610	16.1	3.4	14.2	8.2
1996	983	47	1,030	19,650	13.4	3.7	12.0	7.4

Notes: (1) Metropolitan Statistical Area - see Appendix A for areas included; (2) calculated by the editors using the following formula: (number of crimes in the MSA minus number of crimes in the city); (3) calculated by the editors using the following formula: ((number of crimes in the MSA minus number of crimes in the city) ÷ (population of the MSA minus population of the city)) x 100,000; n/a not avail.
Source: U.S. Department of Justice, FBI Uniform Crime Reports, 1977 - 1996

Forcible Rapes and Forcible Rape Rates: 1977 - 1996

Year	Number				Rate per 100,000 population			
	City	Suburbs[2]	MSA[1]	U.S.	City	Suburbs[3]	MSA[1]	U.S.
1977	3,899	181	4,080	63,500	53.4	8.1	42.8	29.4
1978	3,882	196	4,078	67,610	54.4	9.1	43.8	31.0
1979	3,875	207	4,082	76,390	54.5	10.0	44.5	34.7
1980	3,711	220	3,931	82,990	52.7	10.8	43.3	36.8
1981	3,862	225	4,087	82,500	54.6	10.9	44.8	36.0
1982	3,547	254	3,801	78,770	50.0	12.3	41.5	34.0
1983	3,662	144	3,806	78,920	51.6	11.9	45.8	33.7
1984	3,829	147	3,976	84,230	53.4	12.1	47.4	35.7
1985	3,880	175	4,055	88,670	54.0	14.4	48.3	37.1
1986	3,536	162	3,698	91,460	49.3	13.3	44.1	37.9
1987	3,507	166	3,673	91,110	48.1	13.7	43.2	37.4
1988	3,412	165	3,577	92,490	46.4	13.6	41.8	37.6
1989	3,254	144	3,398	94,500	44.2	11.8	39.6	38.1
1990	3,126	182	3,308	102,560	42.7	14.9	38.7	41.2
1991	2,892	170	3,062	106,590	39.3	13.8	35.7	42.3
1992	2,815	1,971	4,786	109,060	38.2	20.3	28.1	42.8
1993	2,818	178	2,996	106,010	38.4	14.0	34.8	41.1
1994	2,666	163	2,829	102,220	36.3	13.0	32.9	39.3
1995	2,374	131	2,505	97,470	32.4	10.3	29.1	37.1
1996	2,332	135	2,467	95,770	31.8	10.6	28.6	36.1

Notes: (1) Metropolitan Statistical Area - see Appendix A for areas included; (2) calculated by the editors using the following formula: (number of crimes in the MSA minus number of crimes in the city); (3) calculated by the editors using the following formula: ((number of crimes in the MSA minus number of crimes in the city) ÷ (population of the MSA minus population of the city)) x 100,000; n/a not avail.
Source: U.S. Department of Justice, FBI Uniform Crime Reports, 1977 - 1996

Robberies and Robbery Rates: 1977 - 1996

Year	Number				Rate per 100,000 population			
	City	Suburbs[2]	MSA[1]	U.S.	City	Suburbs[3]	MSA[1]	U.S.
1977	74,404	2,804	77,208	412,610	1,019.5	125.7	810.2	190.7
1978	74,029	2,143	76,172	426,930	1,037.5	98.9	819.0	195.8
1979	82,572	2,456	85,028	480,700	1,161.4	118.9	926.7	218.4
1980	100,550	2,944	103,494	565,840	1,429.2	143.9	1,139.7	251.1
1981	107,475	3,210	110,685	592,910	1,520.1	156.0	1,212.5	258.7
1982	95,944	2,806	98,750	553,130	1,352.0	135.8	1,077.6	238.9
1983	84,043	1,783	85,826	506,570	1,183.7	147.2	1,032.6	216.5
1984	79,541	2,064	81,605	485,010	1,109.8	170.1	973.7	205.4
1985	79,532	1,913	81,445	497,870	1,107.1	157.4	969.7	208.5
1986	80,827	1,756	82,583	542,780	1,125.8	144.6	983.8	225.1
1987	78,890	1,936	80,826	517,700	1,083.0	159.4	951.0	212.7
1988	86,578	1,854	88,432	542,970	1,178.5	152.4	1,032.7	220.9
1989	93,377	1,742	95,119	578,330	1,267.1	143.1	1,107.8	233.0
1990	100,280	2,170	102,450	639,270	1,369.5	177.2	1,198.7	257.0
1991	98,512	2,346	100,858	687,730	1,340.3	190.9	1,175.7	272.7
1992	91,239	25,682	116,921	672,480	1,237.1	265.1	685.3	263.6
1993	86,001	4,309	90,310	659,870	1,170.5	338.7	1,047.7	255.9
1994	72,540	2,052	74,592	618,950	988.8	163.2	868.0	237.7
1995	59,280	2,132	61,412	580,510	809.9	167.1	714.5	220.9
1996	49,670	1,781	51,451	537,050	676.7	139.2	597.0	202.4

Notes: (1) Metropolitan Statistical Area - see Appendix A for areas included; (2) calculated by the editors using the following formula: (number of crimes in the MSA minus number of crimes in the city); (3) calculated by the editors using the following formula: ((number of crimes in the MSA minus number of crimes in the city) ÷ (population of the MSA minus population of the city)) x 100,000; n/a not avail.
Source: U.S. Department of Justice, FBI Uniform Crime Reports, 1977 - 1996

Aggravated Assaults and Aggravated Assault Rates: 1977 - 1996

Year	Number				Rate per 100,000 population			
	City	Suburbs[2]	MSA[1]	U.S.	City	Suburbs[3]	MSA[1]	U.S.
1977	42,056	2,653	44,709	534,350	576.3	118.9	469.2	247.0
1978	43,271	2,398	45,669	571,460	606.5	110.7	491.0	262.1
1979	44,203	2,227	46,430	629,480	621.8	107.8	506.0	286.0
1980	43,476	2,529	46,005	672,650	618.0	123.6	506.6	298.5
1981	43,783	2,544	46,327	663,900	619.2	123.6	507.5	289.7
1982	42,784	2,562	45,346	669,480	602.9	124.0	494.9	289.2
1983	43,326	2,018	45,344	653,290	610.2	166.6	545.5	279.2
1984	47,472	2,153	49,625	685,350	662.4	177.4	592.1	290.2
1985	50,356	1,976	52,332	723,250	700.9	162.6	623.0	302.9
1986	57,306	2,077	59,383	834,320	798.2	171.0	707.4	346.1
1987	64,244	1,935	66,179	855,090	881.9	159.4	778.7	351.3
1988	71,030	1,952	72,982	910,090	966.9	160.4	852.3	370.2
1989	70,951	2,127	73,078	951,710	962.8	174.8	851.1	383.4
1990	68,891	2,431	71,322	1,054,860	940.8	198.6	834.5	424.1
1991	66,832	2,417	69,249	1,092,740	909.3	196.7	807.2	433.3
1992	63,529	23,641	87,170	1,126,970	861.4	244.1	510.9	441.8
1993	62,778	2,719	65,497	1,135,610	854.4	213.7	759.9	440.3
1994	59,755	2,210	61,965	1,113,180	814.5	175.8	721.1	427.6
1995	52,322	2,255	54,577	1,099,210	714.8	176.8	635.0	418.3
1996	45,674	2,104	47,778	1,029,810	622.3	164.5	554.4	388.2

Notes: (1) Metropolitan Statistical Area - see Appendix A for areas included; (2) calculated by the editors using the following formula: (number of crimes in the MSA minus number of crimes in the city); (3) calculated by the editors using the following formula: ((number of crimes in the MSA minus number of crimes in the city) ÷ (population of the MSA minus population of the city)) x 100,000; n/a not avail.
Source: U.S. Department of Justice, FBI Uniform Crime Reports, 1977 - 1996

Burglaries and Burglary Rates: 1977 - 1996

Year	Number				Rate per 100,000 population			
	City	Suburbs[2]	MSA[1]	U.S.	City	Suburbs[3]	MSA[1]	U.S.
1977	178,907	22,421	201,328	3,071,500	2,451.5	1,004.8	2,112.7	1,419.8
1978	164,447	22,056	186,503	3,128,300	2,304.8	1,018.4	2,005.2	1,434.6
1979	178,162	25,258	203,420	3,327,700	2,506.0	1,222.3	2,216.9	1,511.9
1980	210,703	30,909	241,612	3,795,200	2,994.9	1,511.1	2,660.7	1,684.1
1981	205,825	27,465	233,290	3,779,700	2,911.1	1,334.4	2,555.6	1,649.5
1982	172,794	22,234	195,028	3,447,100	2,434.9	1,075.7	2,128.3	1,488.8
1983	143,698	11,840	155,538	3,129,900	2,023.9	977.2	1,871.3	1,337.7
1984	128,687	10,648	139,335	2,984,400	1,795.5	877.4	1,662.6	1,263.7
1985	124,838	10,389	135,227	3,073,300	1,737.7	854.8	1,610.0	1,287.3
1986	124,382	9,688	134,070	3,241,400	1,732.4	797.6	1,597.2	1,344.6
1987	123,412	9,758	133,170	3,236,200	1,694.2	803.6	1,567.0	1,329.6
1988	127,148	9,646	136,794	3,218,100	1,730.8	792.7	1,597.5	1,309.2
1989	121,322	8,872	130,194	3,168,200	1,646.3	729.0	1,516.3	1,276.3
1990	119,937	8,590	128,527	3,073,900	1,637.9	701.6	1,503.8	1,235.9
1991	112,015	8,604	120,619	3,157,200	1,524.0	700.2	1,406.0	1,252.0
1992	103,476	81,725	185,201	2,979,900	1,403.0	843.7	1,085.5	1,168.2
1993	99,207	7,499	106,706	2,834,800	1,350.3	589.4	1,237.9	1,099.2
1994	88,370	6,791	95,161	2,712,800	1,204.6	540.1	1,107.3	1,042.0
1995	73,889	6,566	80,455	2,593,800	1,009.5	514.7	936.0	987.1
1996	61,270	6,173	67,443	2,501,500	834.8	482.6	782.5	943.0

Notes: (1) Metropolitan Statistical Area - see Appendix A for areas included; (2) calculated by the editors using the following formula: (number of crimes in the MSA minus number of crimes in the city); (3) calculated by the editors using the following formula: ((number of crimes in the MSA minus number of crimes in the city) ÷ (population of the MSA minus population of the city)) x 100,000; n/a not avail.
Source: U.S. Department of Justice, FBI Uniform Crime Reports, 1977 - 1996

Larceny-Thefts and Larceny-Theft Rates: 1977 - 1996

Year	Number				Rate per 100,000 population			
	City	Suburbs[2]	MSA[1]	U.S.	City	Suburbs[3]	MSA[1]	U.S.
1977	214,838	61,296	276,134	5,905,700	2,943.8	2,747.1	2,897.7	2,729.9
1978	200,110	53,212	253,322	5,991,000	2,804.6	2,457.0	2,723.7	2,747.4
1979	220,817	55,554	276,371	6,601,000	3,106.0	2,688.5	3,012.0	2,999.1
1980	249,421	56,526	305,947	7,136,900	3,545.3	2,763.5	3,369.2	3,167.0
1981	258,369	55,670	314,039	7,194,400	3,654.2	2,704.8	3,440.2	3,139.7
1982	264,400	53,020	317,420	7,142,500	3,725.7	2,565.2	3,464.0	3,084.8
1983	253,801	29,358	283,159	6,712,800	3,574.6	2,423.0	3,406.7	2,868.9
1984	250,759	29,182	279,941	6,591,900	3,498.7	2,404.6	3,340.3	2,791.3
1985	262,051	28,206	290,257	6,926,400	3,647.7	2,320.8	3,455.7	2,901.2
1986	281,713	28,334	310,047	7,257,200	3,923.8	2,332.7	3,693.6	3,010.3
1987	289,126	30,724	319,850	7,499,900	3,969.2	2,530.2	3,763.6	3,081.3
1988	308,479	30,832	339,311	7,705,900	4,199.1	2,533.7	3,962.4	3,134.9
1989	287,749	28,970	316,719	7,872,400	3,904.6	2,380.5	3,688.6	3,171.3
1990	268,620	29,915	298,535	7,945,700	3,668.4	2,443.5	3,492.9	3,194.8
1991	256,473	28,379	284,852	8,142,200	3,489.4	2,309.4	3,320.4	3,228.8
1992	236,169	223,887	460,056	7,915,200	3,202.2	2,311.3	2,696.4	3,103.0
1993	235,132	28,678	263,810	7,820,900	3,200.3	2,253.8	3,060.6	3,032.4
1994	209,808	24,781	234,589	7,879,800	2,859.9	1,970.7	2,729.8	3,026.7
1995	183,037	26,751	209,788	7,997,700	2,500.7	2,096.9	2,440.7	3,043.8
1996	162,246	24,764	187,010	7,894,600	2,210.6	1,936.0	2,169.8	2,975.9

Notes: (1) Metropolitan Statistical Area - see Appendix A for areas included; (2) calculated by the editors using the following formula: (number of crimes in the MSA minus number of crimes in the city); (3) calculated by the editors using the following formula: ((number of crimes in the MSA minus number of crimes in the city) ÷ (population of the MSA minus population of the city)) x 100,000; n/a not avail.
Source: U.S. Department of Justice, FBI Uniform Crime Reports, 1977 - 1996

Motor Vehicle Thefts and Motor Vehicle Theft Rates: 1977 - 1996

Year	Number				Rate per 100,000 population			
	City	Suburbs[2]	MSA[1]	U.S.	City	Suburbs[3]	MSA[1]	U.S.
1977	94,420	9,727	104,147	977,700	1,293.8	435.9	1,092.9	451.9
1978	83,112	8,997	92,109	1,004,100	1,164.8	415.4	990.3	460.5
1979	89,748	9,304	99,052	1,112,800	1,262.4	450.3	1,079.5	505.6
1980	100,478	9,617	110,095	1,131,700	1,428.2	470.2	1,212.4	502.2
1981	104,706	9,615	114,321	1,087,800	1,480.9	467.2	1,252.3	474.7
1982	107,430	9,062	116,492	1,062,400	1,513.8	438.4	1,271.3	458.8
1983	92,725	4,421	97,146	1,007,900	1,306.0	364.9	1,168.8	430.8
1984	88,478	4,439	92,917	1,032,200	1,234.5	365.8	1,108.7	437.1
1985	79,426	4,191	83,617	1,102,900	1,105.6	344.8	995.5	462.0
1986	85,853	4,450	90,303	1,224,100	1,195.8	366.4	1,075.8	507.8
1987	95,654	5,131	100,785	1,288,700	1,313.1	422.5	1,185.9	529.4
1988	119,940	6,137	126,077	1,432,900	1,632.6	504.3	1,472.3	582.9
1989	133,861	6,534	140,395	1,564,800	1,816.4	536.9	1,635.1	630.4
1990	147,123	7,071	154,194	1,635,900	2,009.2	577.6	1,804.1	657.8
1991	139,977	7,051	147,028	1,661,700	1,904.4	573.8	1,713.8	659.0
1992	126,959	74,433	201,392	1,610,800	1,721.5	768.4	1,180.4	631.5
1993	112,464	5,525	117,989	1,563,100	1,530.7	434.2	1,368.8	606.1
1994	95,420	5,217	100,637	1,539,300	1,300.7	414.9	1,171.1	591.3
1995	72,679	4,676	77,355	1,472,400	992.9	366.5	900.0	560.4
1996	60,380	4,465	64,845	1,395,200	822.7	349.1	752.4	525.9

Notes: (1) Metropolitan Statistical Area - see Appendix A for areas included; (2) calculated by the editors using the following formula: (number of crimes in the MSA minus number of crimes in the city); (3) calculated by the editors using the following formula: ((number of crimes in the MSA minus number of crimes in the city) ÷ (population of the MSA minus population of the city)) x 100,000; n/a not avail.
Source: U.S. Department of Justice, FBI Uniform Crime Reports, 1977 - 1996

HATE CRIMES

Criminal Incidents by Bias Motivation

Area	Race	Ethnicity	Religion	Sexual Orientation
New York	135	33	169	79

Notes: Figures include both violent and property crimes. Law enforcement agencies must have submitted data for at least one quarter of calendar year 1995 to be included in this report, therefore figures shown may not represent complete 12-month totals; n/a not available
Source: U.S. Department of Justice, FBI Uniform Crime Reports, Hate Crime Statistics 1995

ILLEGAL DRUGS

Drug Use by Adult Arrestees

Sex	Percent Testing Positive by Urinalysis (%)				
	Any Drug[1]	Cocaine	Marijuana	Opiates	Multiple Drugs
Male	78	56	38	17	35
Female	83	69	19	27	37

Notes: The catchment area is Manhattan; (1) Includes cocaine, opiates, marijuana, methadone, phencyclidine (PCP), benzodiazepines, methaqualone, propoxyphene, barbiturates & amphetamines
Source: National Institute of Justice, 1996 Drug Use Forecasting, Annual Report on Adult and Juvenile Arrestees (released June 1997)

LAW ENFORCEMENT

Number of Police Officers by Race

Race	Police Officers				Index of Representation[1]		
	1983		1992				
	Number	Pct.	Number	Pct.	1983	1992	% Chg.
Black	2,395	10.2	3,121	11.5	0.40	0.40	0.0
Hispanic[2]	1,704	7.3	3,688	13.6	0.36	0.55	52.8

Notes: (1) The index of representation is calculated by dividing the percent of black/hispanic police officers by the percent of corresponding blacks/hispanics in the local population. An index approaching 1.0 indicates that a city is closer to achieving a representation of police officers equal to their proportion in the local population; (2) Hispanic officers can be of any race
Source: Bureau of Justice Statistics, Sourcebook of Criminal Justice Statistics, 1994

Full-Time Law Enforcement Employees

Jurisdiction	Police Employees			Police Officers per 100,000 population
	Total	Officers	Civilians	
New York	48,441	37,090	11,351	505.3

Notes: Data as of October 31, 1996
Source: U.S. Department of Justice, FBI Uniform Crime Reports, 1996

CORRECTIONS

Federal Correctional Facilities

Type	Year Opened	Security Level	Sex of Inmates	Rated Capacity	Population on 7/1/95	Number of Staff
Metro Corr/Detention Ctr	1996	Admin.	Both	578	942	310
Metro Corr/Detention Ctr	1975	Admin.	Both	507	788	320

Notes: Data as of 1995
Source: Bureau of Justice Statistics, Sourcebook of Criminal Justice Statistics Online

City/County/Regional Correctional Facilities

Name	Year Opened	Year Renov.	Rated Capacity	1995 Pop.	Number of COs[1]	Number of Staff	ACA[2] Accred.
Adolescent Reception/Det Ctr	1972	--	2,848	2,128	n/a	1,030	No
Anna M. Kross Center	1978	--	2,734	2,260	n/a	1,246	No
Bellevue Hosp Pris Ward	n/a	--	n/a	71	n/a	248	No
Bronx House of Det-Men	1938	--	469	449	n/a	420	No
Brooklyn Corr Facility	1984	--	1,353	809	n/a	730	No
Brooklyn House of Det-Men	1957	--	1,957	768	n/a	511	No
Correctional Inst for Men	1964	--	2,304	2,079	n/a	1,017	No
Elmhurst Hosp Pris Ward	n/a	--	n/a	20	n/a	70	No
George Motchan Det Ctr	1971	--	2,555	2,404	n/a	1,045	No
George R. Vierno Center	1991	--	782	1,207	n/a	525	No
James A. Thomas Center	1933	--	1,050	1,105	n/a	548	No
Kings Co Hosp Pris Ward	n/a	--	n/a	53	n/a	171	No
Manhattan Detention Complex	1941	--	881	790	n/a	872	No
North Infirmary Command	1933	--	498	414	n/a	356	No
Otis Bantum Corr Ctr	1985	--	1,025	1,718	n/a	475	No
Queens House of Det-Men	1961	--	502	477	n/a	357	No
Rose M. Singer Center	1988	--	1,799	1,669	n/a	815	No
V.C. Bain Maritime Facil	1992	--	800	412	n/a	319	No
West Facility	1991	--	200	308	n/a	396	No

Notes: Data as of April 1996; (1) Correctional Officers; (2) American Correctional Assn. Accreditation
Source: American Correctional Association, 1996-1998 National Jail and Adult Detention Directory

Private Adult Correctional Facilities

Name	Date Opened	Rated Capacity	Present Pop.	Security Level	Facility Construct.	Expans. Plans	ACA Accred.[1]
NY INS Proc Ctr	3/97	200	n/a	Min.	Renov.	None	Will be sought

Notes: Data as of December 1996; (1) American Correctional Association Accreditation
Source: University of Florida, Center for Studies in Criminology and Law, Private Adult Correctional Facility Census, 10th Ed., March 15, 1997

Characteristics of Shock Incarceration Programs

Jurisdiction	Year Program Began	Number of Camps	Average Num. of Inmates	Number of Beds	Program Length	Voluntary/ Mandatory
New York	1987	4	1450	1,390 male/180 fem.	180 days	Voluntary

Note: Data as of July 1996;
Source: Sourcebook of Criminal Justice Statistics Online

INMATES AND HIV/AIDS

HIV Testing Policies for Inmates

Jurisdiction	All Inmates at Some Time	All Convicted Inmates at Admission	Random Samples While in Custody	High-risk Groups	Upon Inmate Request	Upon Court Order	Upon Involvement in Incident
New York City	Yes	No	Yes	No	Yes	Yes	No

Source: HIV in Prisons and Jails, 1993 (released August 1995)

Inmates Known to be Positive for HIV

Jurisdiction	Number of Jail Inmates in Facilities Providing Data	Type of HIV Infection/AIDS Cases				HIV/AIDS Cases as a Percent of Tot. Custody Pop.
		Total	Asymp-tomatic	Symp-tomatic	Confirmed AIDS	
New York City[1,2]	9,361	1,070	258	350	186	11.4

Note: (1) Detail does not add to total; (2) Some but not all facilities reported data on HIV/AIDS cases. Excludes inmates in facilities that did not report data.
Source: HIV in Prisons and Jails, 1993 (released August, 1995)

DEATH PENALTY

Death Penalty Statistics

State	Prisoners Executed		Prisoners Under Sentence of Death					Avg. No. of Years on Death Row[4]
	1930-1995	1996[1]	Total[2]	White[3]	Black[3]	Hisp.	Women	
New York	329	0	0	0	0	0	0	0.0

Notes: Data as of 12/31/95 unless otherwise noted; (1) Data as of 7/31/97; (2) Includes persons of other races; (3) Includes people of Hispanic origin; (4) Covers prisoners sentenced 1974 through 1995
Source: Bureau of Justice Statistics, Capital Punishment 1995 (released 12/96); Death Penalty Information Center Web Site, 9/30/97

Capital Offenses and Methods of Execution

Capital Offenses in New York	Minimum Age for Imposition of Death Penalty	Mentally Retarded Excluded	Methods of Execution[1]
First-degree murder with 1 of 10 aggravating factors.	19	Yes	Lethal injection

Notes: Data as of 12/31/95 unless otherwise noted; (1) Data as of 7/31/97
Source: Bureau of Justice Statistics, Capital Punishment 1995 (released 12/96); Death Penalty Information Center Web Site, 9/30/97

LAWS

Statutory Provisions Relating to the Purchase, Ownership and Use of Handguns

Jurisdiction	Instant Background Check	Federal Waiting Period Applies[1]	State Waiting Period (days)	License or Permit to Purchase	Regis-tration	Record of Sale Sent to Police	Concealed Carry Law
New York	No	No	No	Yes[a]	Yes	Yes	Yes[a,b]

Note: Data as of 1996; (1) The Federal 5-day waiting period for handgun purchases applies to states that don't have instant background checks, waiting period requirements, or licensing procedures exempting them from the Federal requirement; (a) Purchase, possession and/or carrying of a handgun require a single license, which includes and restrictions made upon the bearer; (b) Restrictively administered discretion by local authorities over permit issuance, or permits are unavailable and carrying is prohibited in most circumstances
Source: Sourcebook of Criminal Justice Statistics Online

Statutory Provisions Relating to Alcohol Use and Driving

Jurisdiction	Drinking Age	Blood Alcohol Concentration Levels as Evidence in State Courts[1]		Open Container Law[1]	Anti-Consump-tion Law[1]	Dram Shop Law[1]
		Illegal per se at 0.10%	Presumption at 0.10%			
New York	21	Yes	(a)	No	Yes	Yes

Note: Data as of January 1, 1997; (1) See Appendix C for an explanation of terms; (a) Greater than 0.07% but less than 0.10% constitutes prima facie evidence of impairment
Source: Sourcebook of Criminal Justice Statistics Online

Statutory Provisions Relating to Hate Crimes

Jurisdiction	Bias-Motivated Violence and Intimidation						Institutional Vandalism
		Criminal Penalty					
	Civil Action	Race/ Religion/ Ethnicity	Sexual Orientation	Mental/ Physical Disability	Gender	Age	
New York	Yes	Yes	No	Yes	Yes	No	No

Source: Anti-Defamation League, 1997 Hate Crimes Laws

Norfolk, Virginia

OVERVIEW

The total crime rate for the city increased 11.2% between 1977 and 1996. During that same period, the violent crime rate increased 30.6% and the property crime rate increased 8.9%.

Among violent crimes, the rates for: Murders increased 48.5%; Forcible Rapes increased 7.9%; Robberies increased 95.8%; and Aggravated Assaults decreased 1.2%.

Among property crimes, the rates for: Burglaries decreased 25.8%; Larceny-Thefts increased 14.4%; and Motor Vehicle Thefts increased 87.6%.

ANTI-CRIME PROGRAMS

Under the city's Police Assisted Community Enforcement (PACE) program which seeks to resolve community problems and to improve the quality of life through partnerships with the people of Norfolk, several teams are dedicated to reaching specific goals:

- Neighborhood Environmental Assessment Teams (NEATS)—which identify and respond to environmental problems and conditions that lead to blight and decay; and implement new strategies to insure safe and healthy neighborhoods.
- Family Assessment Services Teams (FAST)—whose primary function is the interagency, collaborative delivery of human services to families experiencing domestic violence, substance abuse problems, truancy, teen pregnancy, et al.
- SAFE (Spiritual Action for Empowerment)—a cooperative venture between the city and religious organizations which seeks to provide resources, training and support to local communities in addressing the problems of violence and drugs.
Norfolk Police Department, 6/97

CRIME RISK

Your Chances of Becoming a Victim[1]

Area	Any Crime	Violent Crime					Property Crime			
		Any	Murder	Forcible Rape[2]	Robbery	Aggrav. Assault	Any	Burglary	Larceny -Theft	Motor Vehicle Theft
City	1:13	1:105	1:4,032	1:809	1:228	1:234	1:15	1:89	1:20	1:144

Note: (1) Figures have been calculated by dividing the population of the city by the number of crimes reported to the FBI during 1996 and are expressed as odds (eg. 1:20 should be read as 1 in 20).
(2) Figures have been calculated by dividing the female population of the city by the number of forcible rapes reported to the FBI during 1996. The female population of the city was estimated by calculating the ratio of females to males reported in the 1990 Census and applying that ratio to 1996 population estimate.
Source: FBI Uniform Crime Reports 1996

CRIME STATISTICS

Total Crimes and Total Crime Rates: 1977 - 1996

Year	Number				Rate per 100,000 population			
	City	Suburbs[2]	MSA[1]	U.S.	City	Suburbs[3]	MSA[1]	U.S.
1977	19,443	24,001	43,444	10,984,500	6,894.7	4,701.2	5,481.7	5,077.6
1978	19,472	25,201	44,673	11,209,000	6,929.5	4,911.5	5,625.6	5,140.3
1979	19,907	25,944	45,851	12,249,500	7,037.4	4,943.5	5,676.8	5,565.5
1980	20,183	28,824	49,007	13,408,300	7,679.9	5,367.1	6,127.0	5,950.0
1981	20,769	29,372	50,141	13,423,800	7,753.4	5,365.8	6,150.3	5,858.2
1982	20,934	28,214	49,148	12,974,400	7,722.6	5,093.3	5,957.2	5,603.6
1983	19,951	44,316	64,267	12,108,600	7,278.1	4,777.2	5,347.7	5,175.0
1984	18,601	46,621	65,222	11,881,800	6,776.1	4,849.8	5,277.7	5,031.3
1985	18,427	47,073	65,500	12,431,400	6,506.3	4,736.0	5,128.5	5,207.1
1986	19,255	51,710	70,965	13,211,900	6,704.4	5,130.6	5,479.6	5,480.4
1987	20,732	54,916	75,648	13,508,700	7,394.5	5,202.5	5,662.5	5,550.0
1988	22,129	58,371	80,500	13,923,100	7,759.7	5,395.1	5,888.4	5,664.2
1989	24,000	61,352	85,352	14,251,400	8,263.5	5,533.1	6,099.8	5,741.0
1990	26,786	65,653	92,439	14,475,600	10,253.8	5,785.0	6,621.2	5,820.3
1991	24,529	70,320	94,849	14,872,900	9,242.6	6,099.1	6,687.3	5,897.8
1992	22,643	69,133	91,776	14,438,200	8,406.6	5,674.8	6,169.4	5,660.2
1993	22,209	66,994	89,203	14,144,800	8,620.9	5,309.6	5,871.0	5,484.4
1994	19,854	66,635	86,489	13,989,500	7,635.0	5,231.0	5,638.5	5,373.5
1995	20,602	65,255	85,857	13,862,700	8,448.4	5,011.2	5,553.3	5,275.9
1996	18,854	64,403	83,257	13,473,600	7,665.6	4,902.5	5,338.2	5,078.9

Notes: (1) Metropolitan Statistical Area - see Appendix A for areas included; (2) calculated by the editors using the following formula: (number of crimes in the MSA minus number of crimes in the city); (3) calculated by the editors using the following formula: ((number of crimes in the MSA minus number of crimes in the city) ÷ (population of the MSA minus population of the city)) x 100,000; n/a not avail.
Source: U.S. Department of Justice, FBI Uniform Crime Reports, 1977 - 1996

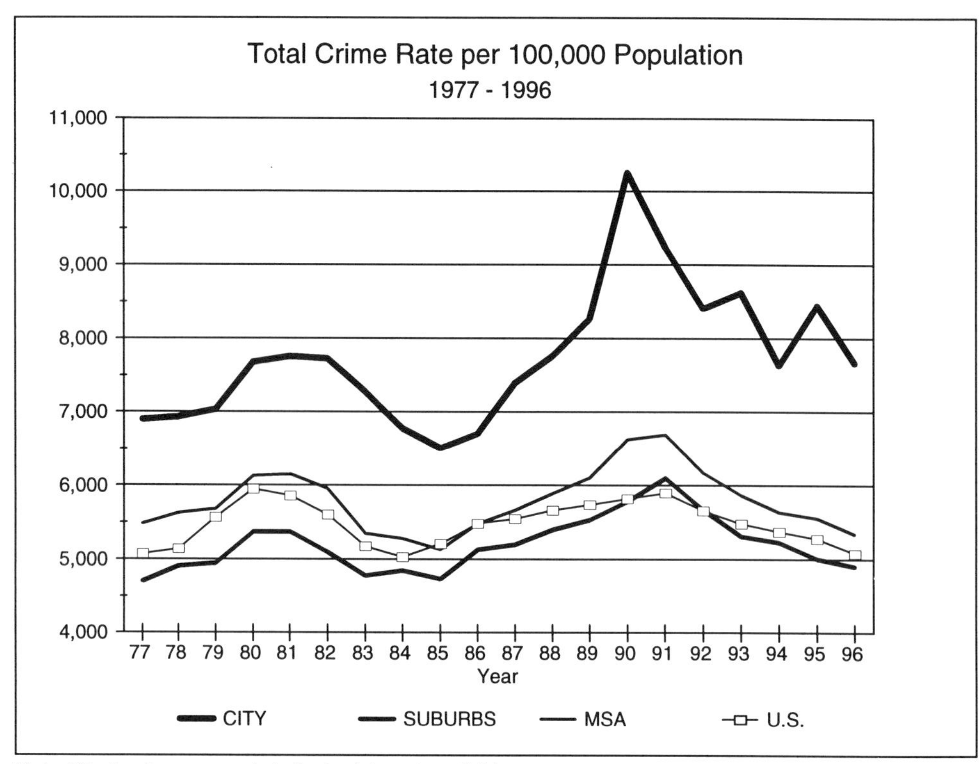

Note: Missing line segments indicate data not available.

Violent Crimes and Violent Crime Rates: 1977 - 1996

Year	Number				Rate per 100,000 population			
	City	Suburbs[2]	MSA[1]	U.S.	City	Suburbs[3]	MSA[1]	U.S.
1977	2,048	2,000	4,048	1,029,580	726.2	391.8	510.8	475.9
1978	2,166	1,857	4,023	1,085,550	770.8	361.9	506.6	497.8
1979	2,127	1,919	4,046	1,208,030	751.9	365.7	500.9	548.9
1980	2,171	1,830	4,001	1,344,520	826.1	340.8	500.2	596.6
1981	2,441	2,036	4,477	1,361,820	911.3	371.9	549.2	594.3
1982	2,375	1,918	4,293	1,322,390	876.1	346.2	520.4	571.1
1983	2,159	3,023	5,182	1,258,090	787.6	325.9	431.2	537.7
1984	1,975	3,506	5,481	1,273,280	719.5	364.7	443.5	539.2
1985	2,064	3,286	5,350	1,328,800	728.8	330.6	418.9	556.6
1986	2,207	3,912	6,119	1,489,170	768.5	388.1	472.5	617.7
1987	2,140	3,921	6,061	1,484,000	763.3	371.5	453.7	609.7
1988	2,207	4,133	6,340	1,566,220	773.9	382.0	463.8	637.2
1989	2,180	4,349	6,529	1,646,040	750.6	392.2	466.6	663.1
1990	2,851	5,244	8,095	1,820,130	1,091.4	462.1	579.8	731.8
1991	3,074	5,945	9,019	1,911,770	1,158.3	515.6	635.9	758.1
1992	2,707	6,781	9,488	1,932,270	1,005.0	556.6	637.8	757.5
1993	2,769	7,146	9,915	1,926,020	1,074.9	566.3	652.6	746.8
1994	2,382	6,525	8,907	1,857,670	916.0	512.2	580.7	713.6
1995	2,393	6,472	8,865	1,798,790	981.3	497.0	573.4	684.6
1996	2,332	5,578	7,910	1,682,280	948.1	424.6	507.2	634.1

Notes: Violent crimes include murder, forcible rape, robbery and aggravated assault; n/a not available; (1) Metropolitan Statistical Area - see Appendix A for areas included; (2) calculated by the editors using the following formula: (number of crimes in the MSA minus number of crimes in the city); (3) calculated by the editors using the following formula: ((number of crimes in the MSA minus number of crimes in the city) ÷ (population of the MSA minus population of the city)) x 100,000
Source: U.S. Department of Justice, FBI Uniform Crime Reports, 1977 - 1996

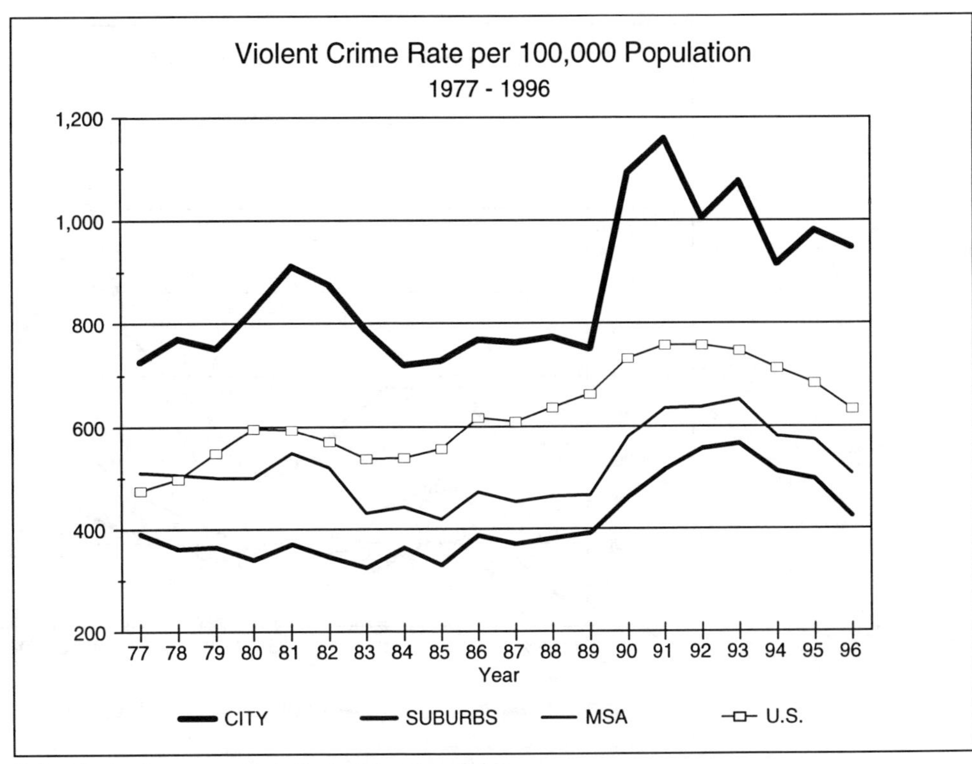

Note: Missing line segments indicate data not available.

Property Crimes and Property Crime Rates: 1977 - 1996

Year	Number				Rate per 100,000 population			
	City	Suburbs[2]	MSA[1]	U.S.	City	Suburbs[3]	MSA[1]	U.S.
1977	17,395	22,001	39,396	9,955,000	6,168.4	4,309.5	4,970.9	4,601.7
1978	17,306	23,344	40,650	10,123,400	6,158.7	4,549.6	5,119.0	4,642.5
1979	17,780	24,025	41,805	11,041,500	6,285.5	4,577.8	5,175.9	5,016.6
1980	18,012	26,994	45,006	12,063,700	6,853.8	5,026.3	5,626.8	5,353.3
1981	18,328	27,336	45,664	12,061,900	6,842.2	4,993.9	5,601.2	5,263.9
1982	18,559	26,296	44,855	11,652,000	6,846.4	4,747.1	5,436.9	5,032.5
1983	17,792	41,293	59,085	10,850,500	6,490.5	4,451.3	4,916.5	4,637.4
1984	16,626	43,115	59,741	10,608,500	6,056.6	4,485.1	4,834.2	4,492.1
1985	16,363	43,787	60,150	11,102,600	5,777.5	4,405.4	4,709.6	4,650.5
1986	17,048	47,798	64,846	11,722,700	5,936.0	4,742.5	5,007.2	4,862.6
1987	18,592	50,995	69,587	12,024,700	6,631.2	4,831.0	5,208.8	4,940.3
1988	19,922	54,238	74,160	12,356,900	6,985.8	5,013.1	5,424.6	5,027.1
1989	21,820	57,003	78,823	12,605,400	7,512.9	5,140.9	5,633.2	5,077.9
1990	23,935	60,409	84,344	12,655,500	9,162.5	5,323.0	6,041.4	5,088.5
1991	21,455	64,375	85,830	12,961,100	8,084.3	5,583.4	6,051.4	5,139.7
1992	19,936	62,352	82,288	12,505,900	7,401.6	5,118.1	5,531.6	4,902.7
1993	19,440	59,848	79,288	12,218,800	7,546.1	4,743.2	5,218.4	4,737.6
1994	17,472	60,110	77,582	12,131,900	6,719.0	4,718.8	5,057.9	4,660.0
1995	18,209	58,783	76,992	12,063,900	7,467.1	4,514.2	4,979.9	4,591.3
1996	16,522	58,825	75,347	11,791,300	6,717.5	4,477.9	4,831.1	4,444.8

Notes: Property crimes include burglary, larceny-theft and motor vehicle theft; n/a not available; (1) Metropolitan Statistical Area - see Appendix A for areas included; (2) calculated by the editors using the following formula: (number of crimes in the MSA minus number of crimes in the city); (3) calculated by the editors using the following formula: ((number of crimes in the MSA minus number of crimes in the city) ÷ (population of the MSA minus population of the city)) x 100,000
Source: U.S. Department of Justice, FBI Uniform Crime Reports, 1977 - 1996

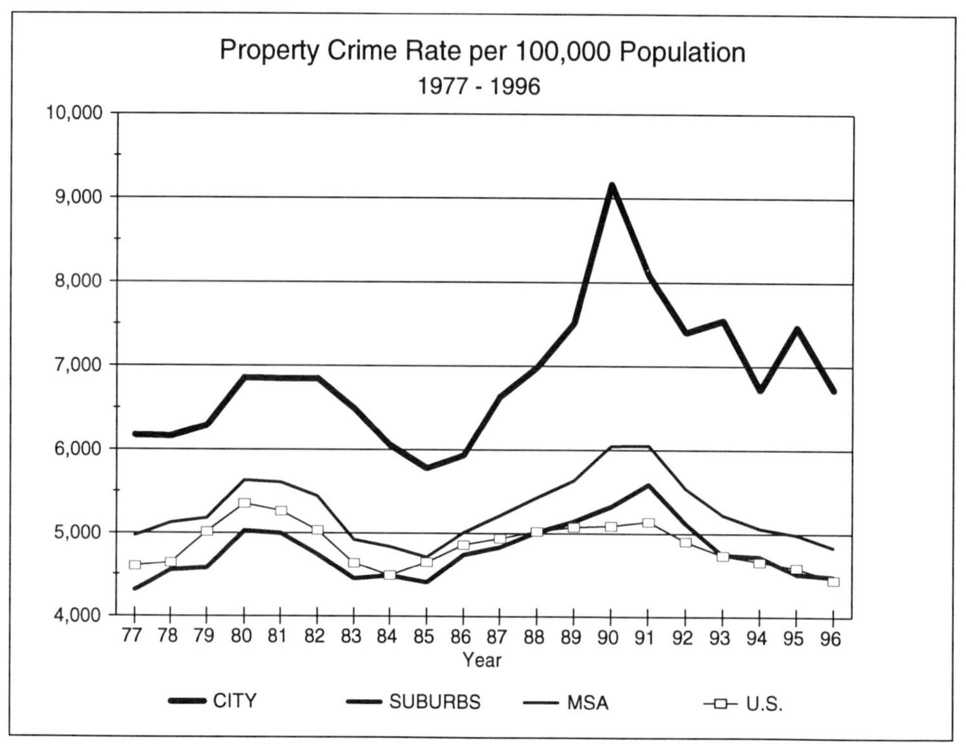

Note: Missing line segments indicate data not available.

Murders and Murder Rates: 1977 - 1996

Year	Number				Rate per 100,000 population			
	City	Suburbs[2]	MSA[1]	U.S.	City	Suburbs[3]	MSA[1]	U.S.
1977	47	53	100	19,120	16.7	10.4	12.6	8.8
1978	45	32	77	19,560	16.0	6.2	9.7	9.0
1979	48	48	96	21,460	17.0	9.1	11.9	9.7
1980	36	48	84	23,040	13.7	8.9	10.5	10.2
1981	43	46	89	22,520	16.1	8.4	10.9	9.8
1982	36	51	87	21,010	13.3	9.2	10.5	9.1
1983	31	78	109	19,310	11.3	8.4	9.1	8.3
1984	36	81	117	18,690	13.1	8.4	9.5	7.9
1985	38	74	112	18,980	13.4	7.4	8.8	7.9
1986	46	85	131	20,610	16.0	8.4	10.1	8.6
1987	50	87	137	20,100	17.8	8.2	10.3	8.3
1988	48	100	148	20,680	16.8	9.2	10.8	8.4
1989	55	86	141	21,500	18.9	7.8	10.1	8.7
1990	63	104	167	23,440	24.1	9.2	12.0	9.4
1991	86	129	215	24,700	32.4	11.2	15.2	9.8
1992	79	133	212	23,760	29.3	10.9	14.3	9.3
1993	62	122	184	24,530	24.1	9.7	12.1	9.5
1994	61	127	188	23,330	23.5	10.0	12.3	9.0
1995	53	110	163	21,610	21.7	8.4	10.5	8.2
1996	61	103	164	19,650	24.8	7.8	10.5	7.4

Notes: (1) Metropolitan Statistical Area - see Appendix A for areas included; (2) calculated by the editors using the following formula: (number of crimes in the MSA minus number of crimes in the city); (3) calculated by the editors using the following formula: ((number of crimes in the MSA minus number of crimes in the city) ÷ (population of the MSA minus population of the city)) x 100,000; n/a not avail.
Source: U.S. Department of Justice, FBI Uniform Crime Reports, 1977 - 1996

Forcible Rapes and Forcible Rape Rates: 1977 - 1996

Year	Number				Rate per 100,000 population			
	City	Suburbs[2]	MSA[1]	U.S.	City	Suburbs[3]	MSA[1]	U.S.
1977	151	202	353	63,500	53.5	39.6	44.5	29.4
1978	138	184	322	67,610	49.1	35.9	40.5	31.0
1979	133	223	356	76,390	47.0	42.5	44.1	34.7
1980	111	236	347	82,990	42.2	43.9	43.4	36.8
1981	189	197	386	82,500	70.6	36.0	47.3	36.0
1982	170	194	364	78,770	62.7	35.0	44.1	34.0
1983	150	283	433	78,920	54.7	30.5	36.0	33.7
1984	174	382	556	84,230	63.4	39.7	45.0	35.7
1985	178	355	533	88,670	62.8	35.7	41.7	37.1
1986	177	371	548	91,460	61.6	36.8	42.3	37.9
1987	181	398	579	91,110	64.6	37.7	43.3	37.4
1988	200	354	554	92,490	70.1	32.7	40.5	37.6
1989	189	393	582	94,500	65.1	35.4	41.6	38.1
1990	218	487	705	102,560	83.5	42.9	50.5	41.2
1991	205	498	703	106,590	77.2	43.2	49.6	42.3
1992	260	521	781	109,060	96.5	42.8	52.5	42.8
1993	204	524	728	106,010	79.2	41.5	47.9	41.1
1994	157	495	652	102,220	60.4	38.9	42.5	39.3
1995	177	484	661	97,470	72.6	37.2	42.8	37.1
1996	142	470	612	95,770	57.7	35.8	39.2	36.1

Notes: (1) Metropolitan Statistical Area - see Appendix A for areas included; (2) calculated by the editors using the following formula: (number of crimes in the MSA minus number of crimes in the city); (3) calculated by the editors using the following formula: ((number of crimes in the MSA minus number of crimes in the city) ÷ (population of the MSA minus population of the city)) x 100,000; n/a not avail.
Source: U.S. Department of Justice, FBI Uniform Crime Reports, 1977 - 1996

Robberies and Robbery Rates: 1977 - 1996

Year	Number				Rate per 100,000 population			
	City	Suburbs[2]	MSA[1]	U.S.	City	Suburbs[3]	MSA[1]	U.S.
1977	632	592	1,224	412,610	224.1	116.0	154.4	190.7
1978	794	629	1,423	426,930	282.6	122.6	179.2	195.8
1979	1,021	637	1,658	480,700	360.9	121.4	205.3	218.4
1980	1,016	686	1,702	565,840	386.6	127.7	212.8	251.1
1981	1,085	973	2,058	592,910	405.1	177.8	252.4	258.7
1982	1,104	776	1,880	553,130	407.3	140.1	227.9	238.9
1983	1,063	1,145	2,208	506,570	387.8	123.4	183.7	216.5
1984	780	1,229	2,009	485,010	284.1	127.8	162.6	205.4
1985	928	1,074	2,002	497,870	327.7	108.1	156.8	208.5
1986	1,050	1,435	2,485	542,780	365.6	142.4	191.9	225.1
1987	1,007	1,432	2,439	517,700	359.2	135.7	182.6	212.7
1988	1,104	1,723	2,827	542,970	387.1	159.3	206.8	220.9
1989	950	1,653	2,603	578,330	327.1	149.1	186.0	233.0
1990	1,393	2,006	3,399	639,270	533.2	176.8	243.5	257.0
1991	1,530	2,461	3,991	687,730	576.5	213.5	281.4	272.7
1992	1,215	2,818	4,033	672,480	451.1	231.3	271.1	263.6
1993	1,428	3,032	4,460	659,870	554.3	240.3	293.5	255.9
1994	1,197	2,783	3,980	618,950	460.3	218.5	259.5	237.7
1995	1,293	2,700	3,993	580,510	530.2	207.3	258.3	220.9
1996	1,079	2,146	3,225	537,050	438.7	163.4	206.8	202.4

Notes: (1) Metropolitan Statistical Area - see Appendix A for areas included; (2) calculated by the editors using the following formula: (number of crimes in the MSA minus number of crimes in the city); (3) calculated by the editors using the following formula: ((number of crimes in the MSA minus number of crimes in the city) ÷ (population of the MSA minus population of the city)) x 100,000; n/a not avail.
Source: U.S. Department of Justice, FBI Uniform Crime Reports, 1977 - 1996

Aggravated Assaults and Aggravated Assault Rates: 1977 - 1996

Year	Number				Rate per 100,000 population			
	City	Suburbs[2]	MSA[1]	U.S.	City	Suburbs[3]	MSA[1]	U.S.
1977	1,218	1,153	2,371	534,350	431.9	225.8	299.2	247.0
1978	1,189	1,012	2,201	571,460	423.1	197.2	277.2	262.1
1979	925	1,011	1,936	629,480	327.0	192.6	239.7	286.0
1980	1,008	860	1,868	672,650	383.6	160.1	233.5	298.5
1981	1,124	820	1,944	663,900	419.6	149.8	238.5	289.7
1982	1,065	897	1,962	669,480	392.9	161.9	237.8	289.2
1983	915	1,517	2,432	653,290	333.8	163.5	202.4	279.2
1984	985	1,814	2,799	685,350	358.8	188.7	226.5	290.2
1985	920	1,783	2,703	723,250	324.8	179.4	211.6	302.9
1986	934	2,021	2,955	834,320	325.2	200.5	228.2	346.1
1987	902	2,004	2,906	855,090	321.7	189.8	217.5	351.3
1988	855	1,956	2,811	910,090	299.8	180.8	205.6	370.2
1989	986	2,217	3,203	951,710	339.5	199.9	228.9	383.4
1990	1,177	2,647	3,824	1,054,860	450.6	233.2	273.9	424.1
1991	1,253	2,857	4,110	1,092,740	472.1	247.8	289.8	433.3
1992	1,153	3,309	4,462	1,126,970	428.1	271.6	299.9	441.8
1993	1,075	3,468	4,543	1,135,610	417.3	274.9	299.0	440.3
1994	967	3,120	4,087	1,113,180	371.9	244.9	266.4	427.6
1995	870	3,178	4,048	1,099,210	356.8	244.0	261.8	418.3
1996	1,050	2,859	3,909	1,029,810	426.9	217.6	250.6	388.2

Notes: (1) Metropolitan Statistical Area - see Appendix A for areas included; (2) calculated by the editors using the following formula: (number of crimes in the MSA minus number of crimes in the city); (3) calculated by the editors using the following formula: ((number of crimes in the MSA minus number of crimes in the city) ÷ (population of the MSA minus population of the city)) x 100,000; n/a not avail.
Source: U.S. Department of Justice, FBI Uniform Crime Reports, 1977 - 1996

Burglaries and Burglary Rates: 1977 - 1996

Year	Number				Rate per 100,000 population			
	City	Suburbs[2]	MSA[1]	U.S.	City	Suburbs[3]	MSA[1]	U.S.
1977	4,275	5,506	9,781	3,071,500	1,516.0	1,078.5	1,234.2	1,419.8
1978	4,346	5,885	10,231	3,128,300	1,546.6	1,146.9	1,288.4	1,434.6
1979	4,500	6,190	10,690	3,327,700	1,590.8	1,179.5	1,323.5	1,511.9
1980	5,275	7,149	12,424	3,795,200	2,007.2	1,331.2	1,553.3	1,684.1
1981	4,793	7,366	12,159	3,779,700	1,789.3	1,345.7	1,491.4	1,649.5
1982	4,088	6,517	10,605	3,447,100	1,508.1	1,176.5	1,285.4	1,488.8
1983	4,219	10,045	14,264	3,129,900	1,539.1	1,082.8	1,186.9	1,337.7
1984	3,937	10,612	14,549	2,984,400	1,434.2	1,103.9	1,177.3	1,263.7
1985	3,620	10,162	13,782	3,073,300	1,278.2	1,022.4	1,079.1	1,287.3
1986	4,236	12,123	16,359	3,241,400	1,474.9	1,202.8	1,263.2	1,344.6
1987	4,645	11,867	16,512	3,236,200	1,656.7	1,124.2	1,236.0	1,329.6
1988	4,234	12,120	16,354	3,218,100	1,484.7	1,120.2	1,196.3	1,309.2
1989	3,876	11,477	15,353	3,168,200	1,334.6	1,035.1	1,097.2	1,276.3
1990	4,200	11,404	15,604	3,073,900	1,607.8	1,004.9	1,117.7	1,235.9
1991	4,571	12,691	17,262	3,157,200	1,722.4	1,100.7	1,217.0	1,252.0
1992	3,787	11,682	15,469	2,979,900	1,406.0	958.9	1,039.9	1,168.2
1993	3,732	11,158	14,890	2,834,800	1,448.7	884.3	980.0	1,099.2
1994	3,120	10,735	13,855	2,712,800	1,199.8	842.7	903.3	1,042.0
1995	3,134	9,848	12,982	2,593,800	1,285.2	756.3	839.7	987.1
1996	2,766	9,735	12,501	2,501,500	1,124.6	741.0	801.5	943.0

Notes: (1) Metropolitan Statistical Area - see Appendix A for areas included; (2) calculated by the editors using the following formula: (number of crimes in the MSA minus number of crimes in the city); (3) calculated by the editors using the following formula: ((number of crimes in the MSA minus number of crimes in the city) ÷ (population of the MSA minus population of the city)) x 100,000; n/a not avail.
Source: U.S. Department of Justice, FBI Uniform Crime Reports, 1977 - 1996

Larceny-Thefts and Larceny-Theft Rates: 1977 - 1996

Year	Number				Rate per 100,000 population			
	City	Suburbs[2]	MSA[1]	U.S.	City	Suburbs[3]	MSA[1]	U.S.
1977	12,079	15,356	27,435	5,905,700	4,283.3	3,007.9	3,461.7	2,729.9
1978	11,800	16,153	27,953	5,991,000	4,199.3	3,148.1	3,520.1	2,747.4
1979	12,096	16,522	28,618	6,601,000	4,276.1	3,148.2	3,543.2	2,999.1
1980	11,759	18,583	30,342	7,136,900	4,474.5	3,460.2	3,793.4	3,167.0
1981	12,656	18,869	31,525	7,194,400	4,724.7	3,447.1	3,866.9	3,139.7
1982	13,440	18,732	32,172	7,142,500	4,958.0	3,381.6	3,899.6	3,084.8
1983	12,593	29,380	41,973	6,712,800	4,593.9	3,167.1	3,492.6	2,868.9
1984	11,584	30,579	42,163	6,591,900	4,219.9	3,181.0	3,411.8	2,791.3
1985	11,578	31,665	43,243	6,926,400	4,088.0	3,185.8	3,385.9	2,901.2
1986	11,644	33,188	44,832	7,257,200	4,054.3	3,292.9	3,461.8	3,010.3
1987	12,713	36,569	49,282	7,499,900	4,534.4	3,464.4	3,688.9	3,081.3
1988	13,908	38,423	52,331	7,705,900	4,876.9	3,551.4	3,827.9	3,134.9
1989	15,496	41,433	56,929	7,872,400	5,335.5	3,736.7	4,068.5	3,171.3
1990	16,941	43,748	60,689	7,945,700	6,485.1	3,854.9	4,347.0	3,194.8
1991	13,935	46,313	60,248	8,142,200	5,250.7	4,016.9	4,247.7	3,228.8
1992	13,967	45,521	59,488	7,915,200	5,185.5	3,736.6	3,998.9	3,103.0
1993	13,535	43,961	57,496	7,820,900	5,253.9	3,484.1	3,784.2	3,032.4
1994	12,542	45,238	57,780	7,879,800	4,823.1	3,551.3	3,766.9	3,026.7
1995	12,747	44,795	57,542	7,997,700	5,227.2	3,440.0	3,721.9	3,043.8
1996	12,053	45,096	57,149	7,894,600	4,900.5	3,432.8	3,664.2	2,975.9

Notes: (1) Metropolitan Statistical Area - see Appendix A for areas included; (2) calculated by the editors using the following formula: (number of crimes in the MSA minus number of crimes in the city); (3) calculated by the editors using the following formula: ((number of crimes in the MSA minus number of crimes in the city) ÷ (population of the MSA minus population of the city)) x 100,000; n/a not avail.
Source: U.S. Department of Justice, FBI Uniform Crime Reports, 1977 - 1996

Motor Vehicle Thefts and Motor Vehicle Theft Rates: 1977 - 1996

Year	Number				Rate per 100,000 population			
	City	Suburbs[2]	MSA[1]	U.S.	City	Suburbs[3]	MSA[1]	U.S.
1977	1,041	1,139	2,180	977,700	369.1	223.1	275.1	451.9
1978	1,160	1,306	2,466	1,004,100	412.8	254.5	310.5	460.5
1979	1,184	1,313	2,497	1,112,800	418.6	250.2	309.2	505.6
1980	978	1,262	2,240	1,131,700	372.1	235.0	280.1	502.2
1981	879	1,101	1,980	1,087,800	328.1	201.1	242.9	474.7
1982	1,031	1,047	2,078	1,062,400	380.3	189.0	251.9	458.8
1983	980	1,868	2,848	1,007,900	357.5	201.4	237.0	430.8
1984	1,105	1,924	3,029	1,032,200	402.5	200.1	245.1	437.1
1985	1,165	1,960	3,125	1,102,900	411.3	197.2	244.7	462.0
1986	1,168	2,487	3,655	1,224,100	406.7	246.8	282.2	507.8
1987	1,234	2,559	3,793	1,288,700	440.1	242.4	283.9	529.4
1988	1,780	3,695	5,475	1,432,900	624.2	341.5	400.5	582.9
1989	2,448	4,093	6,541	1,564,800	842.9	369.1	467.5	630.4
1990	2,794	5,257	8,051	1,635,900	1,069.6	463.2	576.7	657.8
1991	2,949	5,371	8,320	1,661,700	1,111.2	465.8	586.6	659.0
1992	2,182	5,149	7,331	1,610,800	810.1	422.7	492.8	631.5
1993	2,173	4,729	6,902	1,563,100	843.5	374.8	454.3	606.1
1994	1,810	4,137	5,947	1,539,300	696.1	324.8	387.7	591.3
1995	2,328	4,140	6,468	1,472,400	954.7	317.9	418.4	560.4
1996	1,703	3,994	5,697	1,395,200	692.4	304.0	365.3	525.9

Notes: (1) Metropolitan Statistical Area - see Appendix A for areas included; (2) calculated by the editors using the following formula: (number of crimes in the MSA minus number of crimes in the city); (3) calculated by the editors using the following formula: ((number of crimes in the MSA minus number of crimes in the city) ÷ (population of the MSA minus population of the city)) x 100,000; n/a not avail.
Source: U.S. Department of Justice, FBI Uniform Crime Reports, 1977 - 1996

HATE CRIMES

Criminal Incidents by Bias Motivation

Area	Race	Ethnicity	Religion	Sexual Orientation
Norfolk	n/a	n/a	n/a	n/a

Notes: Figures include both violent and property crimes. Law enforcement agencies must have submitted data for at least one quarter of calendar year 1995 to be included in this report, therefore figures shown may not represent complete 12-month totals; n/a not available
Source: U.S. Department of Justice, FBI Uniform Crime Reports, Hate Crime Statistics 1995

LAW ENFORCEMENT

Full-Time Law Enforcement Employees

Jurisdiction	Police Employees			Police Officers per 100,000 population
	Total	Officers	Civilians	
Norfolk	854	731	123	297.2

Notes: Data as of October 31, 1996
Source: U.S. Department of Justice, FBI Uniform Crime Reports, 1996

CORRECTIONS

Federal Correctional Facilities

Type	Year Opened	Security Level	Sex of Inmates	Rated Capacity	Population on 7/1/95	Number of Staff
None listed						

Notes: Data as of 1995
Source: Bureau of Justice Statistics, Sourcebook of Criminal Justice Statistics Online

City/County/Regional Correctional Facilities

Name	Year Opened	Year Renov.	Rated Capacity	1995 Pop.	Number of COs[1]	Number of Staff	ACA[2] Accred.
Norfolk City Jail	1961	1989	579	1,122	296	354	No

Notes: Data as of April 1996; (1) Correctional Officers; (2) American Correctional Assn. Accreditation
Source: American Correctional Association, 1996-1998 National Jail and Adult Detention Directory

Private Adult Correctional Facilities

Name	Date Opened	Rated Capacity	Present Pop.	Security Level	Facility Construct.	Expans. Plans	ACA[1] Accred.
None listed							

Notes: Data as of December 1996; (1) American Correctional Association Accreditation
Source: University of Florida, Center for Studies in Criminology and Law, Private Adult Correctional Facility Census, 10th Ed., March 15, 1997

Characteristics of Shock Incarceration Programs

Jurisdiction	Year Program Began	Number of Camps	Average Num. of Inmates	Number of Beds	Program Length	Voluntary/ Mandatory
Virginia	1991	1	57	100	89 days	Voluntary

Note: Data as of July 1996;
Source: Sourcebook of Criminal Justice Statistics Online

DEATH PENALTY

Death Penalty Statistics

State	Prisoners Executed		Prisoners Under Sentence of Death					Avg. No. of Years on Death Row[4]
	1930-1995	1996[1]	Total[2]	White[3]	Black[3]	Hisp.	Women	
Virginia	121	8	56	28	28	2	0	4.5

Notes: Data as of 12/31/95 unless otherwise noted; (1) Data as of 7/31/97; (2) Includes persons of other races; (3) Includes people of Hispanic origin; (4) Covers prisoners sentenced 1974 through 1995
Source: Bureau of Justice Statistics, Capital Punishment 1995 (released 12/96); Death Penalty Information Center Web Site, 9/30/97

Capital Offenses and Methods of Execution

Capital Offenses in Virginia	Minimum Age for Imposition of Death Penalty	Mentally Retarded Excluded	Methods of Execution[1]
First-degree murder with 1 of 9 aggravating circumstances.	14[a]	No	Lethal injection; electrocution

Notes: Data as of 12/31/95 unless otherwise noted; (1) Data as of 7/31/97; (a) The minimum age for transfer to adult court is 14 by statute, but the effective age for a capital sentence is 16 based on interpretation of a U.S. Supreme Court decision by the State attorney general's office.
Source: Bureau of Justice Statistics, Capital Punishment 1995 (released 12/96); Death Penalty Information Center Web Site, 9/30/97

LAWS

Statutory Provisions Relating to the Purchase, Ownership and Use of Handguns

Jurisdiction	Instant Background Check	Federal Waiting Period Applies[1]	State Waiting Period (days)	License or Permit to Purchase	Regis-tration	Record of Sale Sent to Police	Concealed Carry Law
Virginia	Yes	No	(a,b)	Yes[a]	No	(b)	Yes[c]

Note: Data as of 1996; (1) The Federal 5-day waiting period for handgun purchases applies to states that don't have instant background checks, waiting period requirements, or licensing procedures exempting them from the Federal requirement; (a) A permit is required to acquire another handgun before 30 days have elapsed following the acquisition of a handgun; (b) Local ordinance in certain cities or counties; (c) "Shall issue" permit system, liberally administered discretion by local authorities over permit issuance, or no permit required
Source: Sourcebook of Criminal Justice Statistics Online

Statutory Provisions Relating to Alcohol Use and Driving

Jurisdiction	Drinking Age	Blood Alcohol Concentration Levels as Evidence in State Courts[1]		Open Container Law[1]	Anti-Consump-tion Law[1]	Dram Shop Law[1]
		Illegal per se at 0.10%	Presumption at 0.10%			
Virginia	21	(a)	(a)	No	Yes[b]	No

Note: Data as of January 1, 1997; (1) See Appendix C for an explanation of terms; (a) 0.08%; (b) Applies to drivers only
Source: Sourcebook of Criminal Justice Statistics Online

Statutory Provisions Relating to Curfews

Jurisdiction	Year Enacted	Latest Revision	Age Group(s)	Curfew Provisions
Norfolk	1993	-	17 and under	11 pm to 5 am every night

Note: Data as of February 1996
Source: Sourcebook of Criminal Justice Statistics Online

Statutory Provisions Relating to Hate Crimes

Jurisdiction	Bias-Motivated Violence and Intimidation						Institutional Vandalism
		Criminal Penalty					
	Civil Action	Race/ Religion/ Ethnicity	Sexual Orientation	Mental/ Physical Disability	Gender	Age	
Virginia	Yes	Yes	No	No	No	No	Yes

Source: Anti-Defamation League, 1997 Hate Crimes Laws

Oakland, California

OVERVIEW

The total crime rate for the city decreased 12.0% between 1977 and 1996. During that same period, the violent crime rate increased 26.4% and the property crime rate decreased 18.5%.

Among violent crimes, the rates for: Murders decreased 11.7%; Forcible Rapes decreased 21.5%; Robberies increased 6.4%; and Aggravated Assaults increased 62.6%.

Among property crimes, the rates for: Burglaries decreased 57.6%; Larceny-Thefts increased 1.3%; and Motor Vehicle Thefts increased 22.2%.

ANTI-CRIME PROGRAMS

Drug trafficking has been a serious problem in Oakland for over 10 years. From 1984 to 1987 drug-related homicides rose from 22.0% to nearly 48.2%. With the introduction of crack cocaine, controlling street-level drug trafficking became much harder for the Oakland Police Department. The Department created a "Special Duty Unit", a group of hand- picked, specially trained patrol officers who engaged in undercover buy-and-bust operations, aggressive patrol, and motor vehicle stops. Community residents were enlisted to join the police in controlling the retail trade of illegal drugs on the street. *Police Department, 7/97*

CRIME RISK

Your Chances of Becoming a Victim[1]

Area	Any Crime	Violent Crime					Property Crime			
		Any	Murder	Forcible Rape[2]	Robbery	Aggrav. Assault	Any	Burglary	Larceny -Theft	Motor Vehicle Theft
City	1:9	1:46	1:4,002	1:604	1:103	1:90	1:12	1:61	1:19	1:73

Note: (1) Figures have been calculated by dividing the population of the city by the number of crimes reported to the FBI during 1996 and are expressed as odds (eg. 1:20 should be read as 1 in 20). (2) Figures have been calculated by dividing the female population of the city by the number of forcible rapes reported to the FBI during 1996. The female population of the city was estimated by calculating the ratio of females to males reported in the 1990 Census and applying that ratio to 1996 population estimate.
Source: FBI Uniform Crime Reports 1996

CRIME STATISTICS

Total Crimes and Total Crime Rates: 1977 - 1996

Year	Number				Rate per 100,000 population			
	City	Suburbs[2]	MSA[1]	U.S.	City	Suburbs[3]	MSA[1]	U.S.
1977	39,713	215,449	255,162	10,984,500	11,961.7	7,475.6	7,939.0	5,077.6
1978	38,854	217,161	256,015	11,209,000	11,703.0	7,620.8	8,046.8	5,140.3
1979	41,269	225,094	266,363	12,249,500	11,972.9	7,771.2	8,218.0	5,565.5
1980	44,152	231,365	275,517	13,408,300	13,034.9	8,013.3	8,540.6	5,950.0
1981	44,678	232,705	277,383	13,423,800	12,848.3	7,850.8	8,375.5	5,858.2
1982	43,343	220,185	263,528	12,974,400	12,179.5	7,258.6	7,775.3	5,603.6
1983	40,166	n/a	n/a	12,108,600	11,085.0	n/a	n/a	5,175.0
1984	41,268	100,419	141,687	11,881,800	11,509.2	6,559.7	7,499.0	5,031.3
1985	42,823	103,082	145,905	12,431,400	11,826.5	6,592.9	7,577.0	5,207.1
1986	45,947	102,854	148,801	13,211,900	12,399.5	6,428.1	7,550.9	5,480.4
1987	44,535	102,952	147,487	13,508,700	12,168.6	6,368.0	7,438.8	5,550.0
1988	46,615	107,396	154,011	13,923,100	12,674.6	6,563.9	7,685.4	5,664.2
1989	45,914	107,710	153,624	14,251,400	12,534.4	6,361.7	7,459.6	5,741.0
1990	40,595	102,856	143,451	14,475,600	10,905.5	6,012.6	6,887.0	5,820.3
1991	46,308	112,278	158,586	14,872,900	12,186.5	6,429.5	7,458.4	5,897.8
1992	48,086	110,998	159,084	14,438,200	12,454.7	6,256.0	7,363.8	5,660.2
1993	44,927	114,134	159,061	14,144,800	11,915.8	6,365.3	7,329.6	5,484.4
1994	40,373	114,054	154,427	13,989,500	10,633.0	6,316.3	7,066.3	5,373.5
1995	n/a	n/a	n/a	13,862,700	n/a	n/a	n/a	5,275.9
1996	39,174	99,172	138,346	13,473,600	10,526.5	5,386.0	6,250.3	5,078.9

Notes: (1) Metropolitan Statistical Area - see Appendix A for areas included; (2) calculated by the editors using the following formula: (number of crimes in the MSA minus number of crimes in the city); (3) calculated by the editors using the following formula: ((number of crimes in the MSA minus number of crimes in the city) ÷ (population of the MSA minus population of the city)) x 100,000; n/a not avail.
Source: U.S. Department of Justice, FBI Uniform Crime Reports, 1977 - 1996

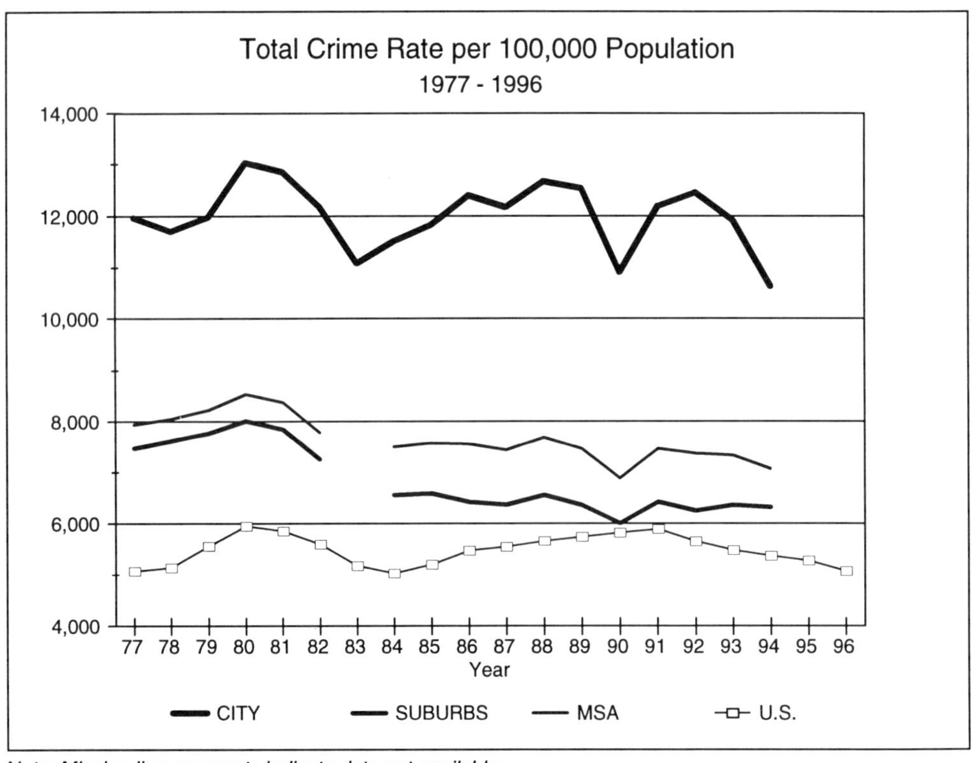

Note: Missing line segments indicate data not available.

Violent Crimes and Violent Crime Rates: 1977 - 1996

Year	Number				Rate per 100,000 population			
	City	Suburbs[2]	MSA[1]	U.S.	City	Suburbs[3]	MSA[1]	U.S.
1977	5,764	18,946	24,710	1,029,580	1,736.1	657.4	768.8	475.9
1978	5,374	20,706	26,080	1,085,550	1,618.7	726.6	819.7	497.8
1979	6,064	21,887	27,951	1,208,030	1,759.3	755.6	862.4	548.9
1980	7,536	24,872	32,408	1,344,520	2,224.8	861.4	1,004.6	596.6
1981	7,036	23,828	30,864	1,361,820	2,023.4	803.9	931.9	594.3
1982	6,609	23,061	29,670	1,322,390	1,857.1	760.2	875.4	571.1
1983	6,777	n/a	n/a	1,258,090	1,870.3	n/a	n/a	537.7
1984	6,388	9,470	15,858	1,273,280	1,781.5	618.6	839.3	539.2
1985	6,703	9,820	16,523	1,328,800	1,851.2	628.1	858.1	556.6
1986	6,985	10,739	17,724	1,489,170	1,885.0	671.2	899.4	617.7
1987	6,485	10,520	17,005	1,484,000	1,771.9	650.7	857.7	609.7
1988	6,049	10,605	16,654	1,566,220	1,644.7	648.2	831.1	637.2
1989	5,555	11,295	16,850	1,646,040	1,516.5	667.1	818.2	663.1
1990	5,845	12,308	18,153	1,820,130	1,570.2	719.5	871.5	731.8
1991	9,484	12,571	22,055	1,911,770	2,495.8	719.9	1,037.3	758.1
1992	10,140	13,870	24,010	1,932,270	2,626.4	781.7	1,111.4	757.5
1993	9,809	14,876	24,685	1,926,020	2,601.6	829.6	1,137.5	746.8
1994	8,330	14,341	22,671	1,857,670	2,193.9	794.2	1,037.4	713.6
1995	n/a	n/a	n/a	1,798,790	n/a	n/a	n/a	684.6
1996	8,168	11,115	19,283	1,682,280	2,194.8	603.7	871.2	634.1

Notes: Violent crimes include murder, forcible rape, robbery and aggravated assault; n/a not available; (1) Metropolitan Statistical Area - see Appendix A for areas included; (2) calculated by the editors using the following formula: (number of crimes in the MSA minus number of crimes in the city); (3) calculated by the editors using the following formula: ((number of crimes in the MSA minus number of crimes in the city) ÷ (population of the MSA minus population of the city)) x 100,000
Source: U.S. Department of Justice, FBI Uniform Crime Reports, 1977 - 1996

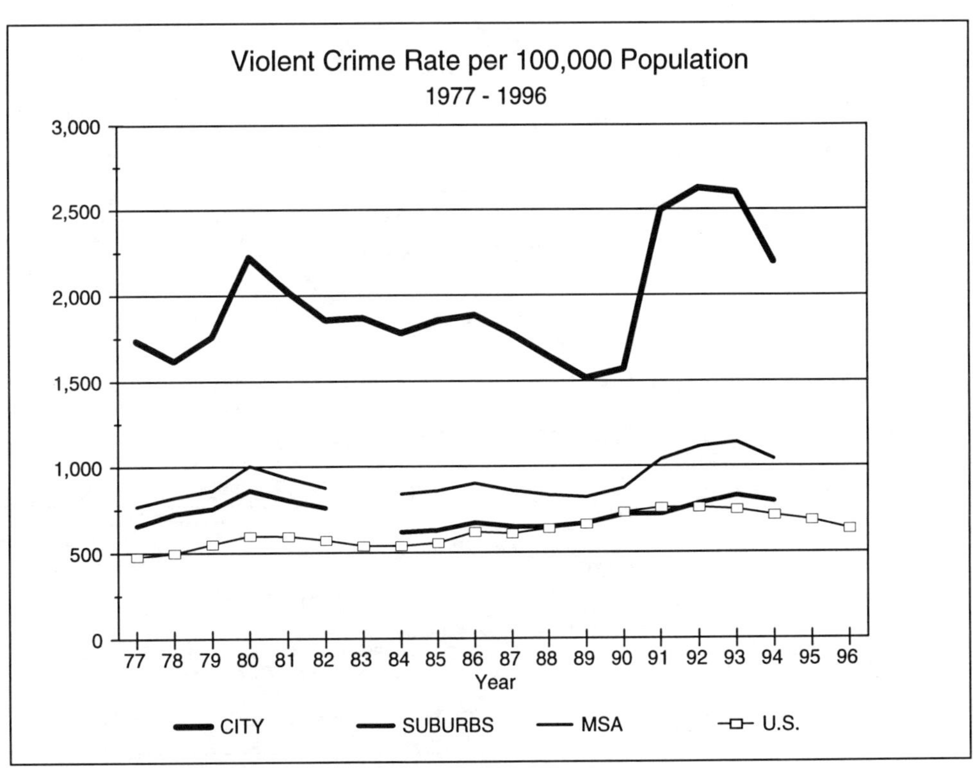

Note: Missing line segments indicate data not available.

Property Crimes and Property Crime Rates: 1977 - 1996

Year	Number				Rate per 100,000 population			
	City	Suburbs[2]	MSA[1]	U.S.	City	Suburbs[3]	MSA[1]	U.S.
1977	33,949	196,503	230,452	9,955,000	10,225.6	6,818.2	7,170.2	4,601.7
1978	33,480	196,455	229,935	10,123,400	10,084.3	6,894.2	7,227.1	4,642.5
1979	35,205	203,207	238,412	11,041,500	10,213.6	7,015.5	7,355.6	5,016.6
1980	36,616	206,493	243,109	12,063,700	10,810.1	7,151.9	7,536.0	5,353.3
1981	37,642	208,877	246,519	12,061,900	10,824.9	7,046.9	7,443.6	5,263.9
1982	36,734	197,124	233,858	11,652,000	10,322.4	6,498.4	6,899.9	5,032.5
1983	33,389	n/a	n/a	10,850,500	9,214.7	n/a	n/a	4,637.4
1984	34,880	90,949	125,829	10,608,500	9,727.6	5,941.1	6,659.7	4,492.1
1985	36,120	93,262	129,382	11,102,600	9,975.3	5,964.8	6,718.9	4,650.5
1986	38,962	92,115	131,077	11,722,700	10,514.5	5,756.9	6,651.5	4,862.6
1987	38,050	92,432	130,482	12,024,700	10,396.7	5,717.3	6,581.1	4,940.3
1988	40,566	96,791	137,357	12,356,900	11,029.9	5,915.7	6,854.3	5,027.1
1989	40,359	96,415	136,774	12,605,400	11,017.9	5,694.6	6,641.4	5,077.9
1990	34,750	90,548	125,298	12,655,500	9,335.3	5,293.1	6,015.5	5,088.5
1991	36,824	99,707	136,531	12,961,100	9,690.7	5,709.7	6,421.1	5,139.7
1992	37,946	97,128	135,074	12,505,900	9,828.4	5,474.3	6,252.4	4,902.7
1993	35,118	99,258	134,376	12,218,800	9,314.2	5,535.6	6,192.1	4,737.6
1994	32,043	99,713	131,756	12,131,900	8,439.1	5,522.1	6,028.9	4,660.0
1995	n/a	n/a	n/a	12,063,900	n/a	n/a	n/a	4,591.3
1996	31,006	88,057	119,063	11,791,300	8,331.7	4,782.4	5,379.1	4,444.8

Notes: Property crimes include burglary, larceny-theft and motor vehicle theft; n/a not available; (1) Metropolitan Statistical Area - see Appendix A for areas included; (2) calculated by the editors using the following formula: (number of crimes in the MSA minus number of crimes in the city); (3) calculated by the editors using the following formula: ((number of crimes in the MSA minus number of crimes in the city) ÷ (population of the MSA minus population of the city)) x 100,000
Source: U.S. Department of Justice, FBI Uniform Crime Reports, 1977 - 1996

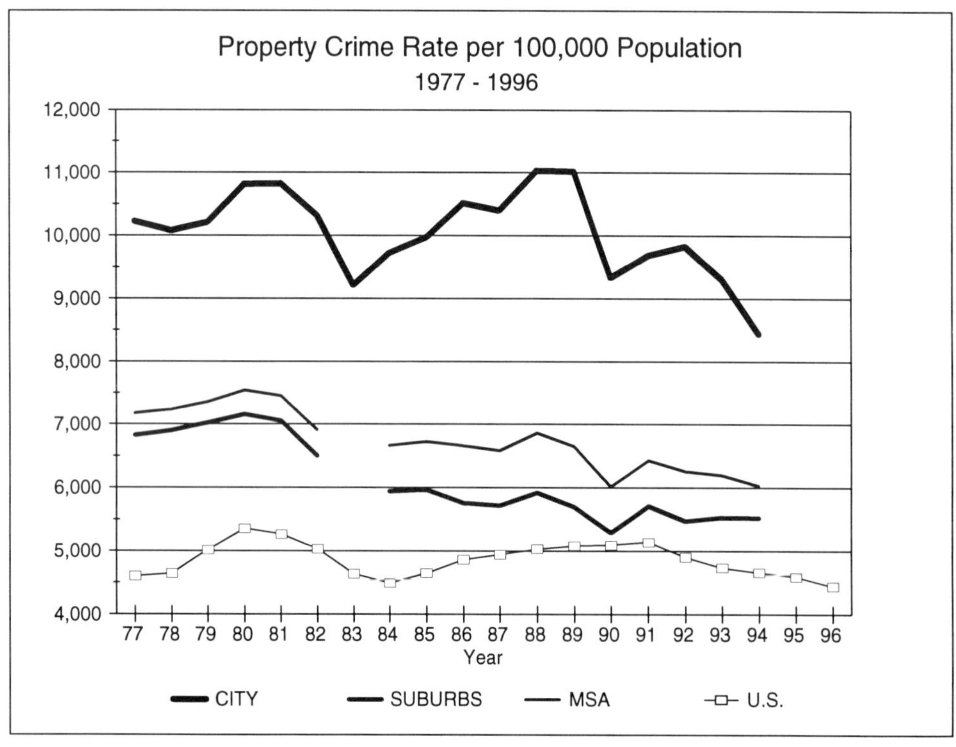

Note: Missing line segments indicate data not available.

Murders and Murder Rates: 1977 - 1996

Year	Number				Rate per 100,000 population			
	City	Suburbs[2]	MSA[1]	U.S.	City	Suburbs[3]	MSA[1]	U.S.
1977	94	288	382	19,120	28.3	10.0	11.9	8.8
1978	97	258	355	19,560	29.2	9.1	11.2	9.0
1979	106	251	357	21,460	30.8	8.7	11.0	9.7
1980	132	247	379	23,040	39.0	8.6	11.7	10.2
1981	118	294	412	22,520	33.9	9.9	12.4	9.8
1982	94	244	338	21,010	26.4	8.0	10.0	9.1
1983	98	n/a	n/a	19,310	27.0	n/a	n/a	8.3
1984	115	116	231	18,690	32.1	7.6	12.2	7.9
1985	95	110	205	18,980	26.2	7.0	10.6	7.9
1986	129	99	228	20,610	34.8	6.2	11.6	8.6
1987	114	84	198	20,100	31.1	5.2	10.0	8.3
1988	112	122	234	20,680	30.5	7.5	11.7	8.4
1989	129	121	250	21,500	35.2	7.1	12.1	8.7
1990	146	112	258	23,440	39.2	6.5	12.4	9.4
1991	149	157	306	24,700	39.2	9.0	14.4	9.8
1992	165	135	300	23,760	42.7	7.6	13.9	9.3
1993	154	158	312	24,530	40.8	8.8	14.4	9.5
1994	140	167	307	23,330	36.9	9.2	14.0	9.0
1995	n/a	n/a	n/a	21,610	n/a	n/a	n/a	8.2
1996	93	120	213	19,650	25.0	6.5	9.6	7.4

Notes: (1) Metropolitan Statistical Area - see Appendix A for areas included; (2) calculated by the editors using the following formula: (number of crimes in the MSA minus number of crimes in the city); (3) calculated by the editors using the following formula: ((number of crimes in the MSA minus number of crimes in the city) ÷ (population of the MSA minus population of the city)) x 100,000; n/a not avail.
Source: U.S. Department of Justice, FBI Uniform Crime Reports, 1977 - 1996

Forcible Rapes and Forcible Rape Rates: 1977 - 1996

Year	Number				Rate per 100,000 population			
	City	Suburbs[2]	MSA[1]	U.S.	City	Suburbs[3]	MSA[1]	U.S.
1977	366	1,301	1,667	63,500	110.2	45.1	51.9	29.4
1978	351	1,335	1,686	67,610	105.7	46.8	53.0	31.0
1979	373	1,442	1,815	76,390	108.2	49.8	56.0	34.7
1980	434	1,631	2,065	82,990	128.1	56.5	64.0	36.8
1981	430	1,492	1,922	82,500	123.7	50.3	58.0	36.0
1982	441	1,291	1,732	78,770	123.9	42.6	51.1	34.0
1983	478	n/a	n/a	78,920	131.9	n/a	n/a	33.7
1984	426	538	964	84,230	118.8	35.1	51.0	35.7
1985	531	563	1,094	88,670	146.6	36.0	56.8	37.1
1986	538	543	1,081	91,460	145.2	33.9	54.9	37.9
1987	538	559	1,097	91,110	147.0	34.6	55.3	37.4
1988	498	517	1,015	92,490	135.4	31.6	50.6	37.6
1989	442	533	975	94,500	120.7	31.5	47.3	38.1
1990	517	579	1,096	102,560	138.9	33.8	52.6	41.2
1991	460	561	1,021	106,590	121.1	32.1	48.0	42.3
1992	418	562	980	109,060	108.3	31.7	45.4	42.8
1993	353	581	934	106,010	93.6	32.4	43.0	41.1
1994	323	570	893	102,220	85.1	31.6	40.9	39.3
1995	n/a	n/a	n/a	97,470	n/a	n/a	n/a	37.1
1996	322	496	818	95,770	86.5	26.9	37.0	36.1

Notes: (1) Metropolitan Statistical Area - see Appendix A for areas included; (2) calculated by the editors using the following formula: (number of crimes in the MSA minus number of crimes in the city); (3) calculated by the editors using the following formula: ((number of crimes in the MSA minus number of crimes in the city) ÷ (population of the MSA minus population of the city)) x 100,000; n/a not avail.
Source: U.S. Department of Justice, FBI Uniform Crime Reports, 1977 - 1996

Robberies and Robbery Rates: 1977 - 1996

Year	Number				Rate per 100,000 population			
	City	Suburbs[2]	MSA[1]	U.S.	City	Suburbs[3]	MSA[1]	U.S.
1977	3,037	9,130	12,167	412,610	914.8	316.8	378.6	190.7
1978	2,774	10,409	13,183	426,930	835.5	365.3	414.4	195.8
1979	3,072	10,740	13,812	480,700	891.2	370.8	426.1	218.4
1980	4,248	12,546	16,794	565,840	1,254.1	434.5	520.6	251.1
1981	3,836	12,198	16,034	592,910	1,103.1	411.5	484.1	258.7
1982	3,194	11,836	15,030	553,130	897.5	390.2	443.5	238.9
1983	3,289	n/a	n/a	506,570	907.7	n/a	n/a	216.5
1984	3,170	3,352	6,522	485,010	884.1	219.0	345.2	205.4
1985	3,316	3,986	7,302	497,870	915.8	254.9	379.2	208.5
1986	3,787	3,966	7,753	542,780	1,022.0	247.9	393.4	225.1
1987	3,176	3,403	6,579	517,700	867.8	210.5	331.8	212.7
1988	3,141	3,287	6,428	542,970	854.0	200.9	320.8	220.9
1989	3,224	3,375	6,599	578,330	880.1	199.3	320.4	233.0
1990	3,230	3,901	7,131	639,270	867.7	228.0	342.4	257.0
1991	3,933	4,394	8,327	687,730	1,035.0	251.6	391.6	272.7
1992	4,610	5,172	9,782	672,480	1,194.0	291.5	452.8	263.6
1993	4,559	5,273	9,832	659,870	1,209.2	294.1	453.1	255.9
1994	3,877	4,847	8,724	618,950	1,021.1	268.4	399.2	237.7
1995	n/a	n/a	n/a	580,510	n/a	n/a	n/a	220.9
1996	3,622	4,057	7,679	537,050	973.3	220.3	346.9	202.4

Notes: (1) Metropolitan Statistical Area - see Appendix A for areas included; (2) calculated by the editors using the following formula: (number of crimes in the MSA minus number of crimes in the city); (3) calculated by the editors using the following formula: ((number of crimes in the MSA minus number of crimes in the city) ÷ (population of the MSA minus population of the city)) x 100,000; n/a not avail.
Source: U.S. Department of Justice, FBI Uniform Crime Reports, 1977 - 1996

Aggravated Assaults and Aggravated Assault Rates: 1977 - 1996

Year	Number				Rate per 100,000 population			
	City	Suburbs[2]	MSA[1]	U.S.	City	Suburbs[3]	MSA[1]	U.S.
1977	2,267	8,227	10,494	534,350	682.8	285.5	326.5	247.0
1978	2,152	8,704	10,856	571,460	648.2	305.4	341.2	262.1
1979	2,513	9,454	11,967	629,480	729.1	326.4	369.2	286.0
1980	2,722	10,448	13,170	672,650	803.6	361.9	408.2	298.5
1981	2,652	9,844	12,496	663,900	762.6	332.1	377.3	289.7
1982	2,880	9,690	12,570	669,480	809.3	319.4	370.9	289.2
1983	2,912	n/a	n/a	653,290	803.7	n/a	n/a	279.2
1984	2,677	5,464	8,141	685,350	746.6	356.9	430.9	290.2
1985	2,761	5,161	7,922	723,250	762.5	330.1	411.4	302.9
1986	2,531	6,131	8,662	834,320	683.0	383.2	439.6	346.1
1987	2,657	6,474	9,131	855,090	726.0	400.4	460.5	351.3
1988	2,298	6,679	8,977	910,090	624.8	408.2	448.0	370.2
1989	1,760	7,266	9,026	951,710	480.5	429.2	438.3	383.4
1990	1,952	7,716	9,668	1,054,860	524.4	451.1	464.2	424.1
1991	4,942	7,459	12,401	1,092,740	1,300.5	427.1	583.2	433.3
1992	4,947	8,001	12,948	1,126,970	1,281.3	450.9	599.3	441.8
1993	4,743	8,864	13,607	1,135,610	1,258.0	494.3	627.0	440.3
1994	3,990	8,757	12,747	1,113,180	1,050.8	485.0	583.3	427.6
1995	n/a	n/a	n/a	1,099,210	n/a	n/a	n/a	418.3
1996	4,131	6,442	10,573	1,029,810	1,110.1	349.9	477.7	388.2

Notes: (1) Metropolitan Statistical Area - see Appendix A for areas included; (2) calculated by the editors using the following formula: (number of crimes in the MSA minus number of crimes in the city); (3) calculated by the editors using the following formula: ((number of crimes in the MSA minus number of crimes in the city) ÷ (population of the MSA minus population of the city)) x 100,000; n/a not avail.
Source: U.S. Department of Justice, FBI Uniform Crime Reports, 1977 - 1996

Burglaries and Burglary Rates: 1977 - 1996

Year	Number				Rate per 100,000 population			
	City	Suburbs[2]	MSA[1]	U.S.	City	Suburbs[3]	MSA[1]	U.S.
1977	12,750	59,729	72,479	3,071,500	3,840.4	2,072.5	2,255.1	1,419.8
1978	12,501	59,054	71,555	3,128,300	3,765.4	2,072.4	2,249.0	1,434.6
1979	12,351	58,952	71,303	3,327,700	3,583.3	2,035.3	2,199.9	1,511.9
1980	13,124	60,025	73,149	3,795,200	3,874.6	2,079.0	2,267.5	1,684.1
1981	14,171	60,127	74,298	3,779,700	4,075.2	2,028.5	2,243.4	1,649.5
1982	12,780	50,981	63,761	3,447,100	3,591.2	1,680.6	1,881.2	1,488.8
1983	11,647	n/a	n/a	3,129,900	3,214.3	n/a	n/a	1,337.7
1984	12,413	24,611	37,024	2,984,400	3,461.8	1,607.7	1,959.6	1,263.7
1985	11,846	25,092	36,938	3,073,300	3,271.5	1,604.8	1,918.2	1,287.3
1986	12,231	24,348	36,579	3,241,400	3,300.7	1,521.7	1,856.2	1,344.6
1987	10,793	23,082	33,875	3,236,200	2,949.0	1,427.7	1,708.5	1,329.6
1988	10,962	22,635	33,597	3,218,100	2,980.6	1,383.4	1,676.5	1,309.2
1989	9,874	22,337	32,211	3,168,200	2,695.6	1,319.3	1,564.1	1,276.3
1990	8,500	19,364	27,864	3,073,900	2,283.5	1,132.0	1,337.7	1,235.9
1991	8,848	21,889	30,737	3,157,200	2,328.5	1,253.5	1,445.6	1,252.0
1992	8,870	21,386	30,256	2,979,900	2,297.4	1,205.3	1,400.5	1,168.2
1993	8,355	22,443	30,798	2,834,800	2,216.0	1,251.6	1,419.2	1,099.2
1994	7,026	20,795	27,821	2,712,800	1,850.4	1,151.6	1,273.0	1,042.0
1995	n/a	n/a	n/a	2,593,800	n/a	n/a	n/a	987.1
1996	6,058	16,575	22,633	2,501,500	1,627.9	900.2	1,022.5	943.0

Notes: (1) Metropolitan Statistical Area - see Appendix A for areas included; (2) calculated by the editors using the following formula: (number of crimes in the MSA minus number of crimes in the city); (3) calculated by the editors using the following formula: ((number of crimes in the MSA minus number of crimes in the city) ÷ (population of the MSA minus population of the city)) x 100,000; n/a not avail.
Source: U.S. Department of Justice, FBI Uniform Crime Reports, 1977 - 1996

Larceny-Thefts and Larceny-Theft Rates: 1977 - 1996

Year	Number				Rate per 100,000 population			
	City	Suburbs[2]	MSA[1]	U.S.	City	Suburbs[3]	MSA[1]	U.S.
1977	17,498	116,526	134,024	5,905,700	5,270.5	4,043.2	4,170.0	2,729.9
1978	17,790	118,356	136,146	5,991,000	5,358.4	4,153.5	4,279.2	2,747.4
1979	18,924	124,470	143,394	6,601,000	5,490.2	4,297.2	4,424.1	2,999.1
1980	20,093	127,373	147,466	7,136,900	5,932.0	4,411.6	4,571.2	3,167.0
1981	20,070	132,284	152,354	7,194,400	5,771.6	4,462.9	4,600.3	3,139.7
1982	20,947	131,260	152,207	7,142,500	5,886.2	4,327.1	4,490.8	3,084.8
1983	19,000	n/a	n/a	6,712,800	5,243.6	n/a	n/a	2,868.9
1984	19,544	60,484	80,028	6,591,900	5,450.6	3,951.0	4,235.6	2,791.3
1985	20,866	61,492	82,358	6,926,400	5,762.6	3,932.9	4,276.9	2,901.2
1986	22,672	60,594	83,266	7,257,200	6,118.4	3,786.9	4,225.3	3,010.3
1987	22,448	61,444	83,892	7,499,900	6,133.6	3,800.6	4,231.2	3,081.3
1988	23,661	63,875	87,536	7,705,900	6,433.4	3,903.9	4,368.2	3,134.9
1989	23,941	62,656	86,597	7,872,400	6,535.8	3,700.7	4,205.0	3,171.3
1990	19,077	59,963	79,040	7,945,700	5,124.9	3,505.2	3,794.7	3,194.8
1991	20,695	65,699	86,394	8,142,200	5,446.1	3,762.2	4,063.1	3,228.8
1992	21,310	64,862	86,172	7,915,200	5,519.5	3,655.7	3,988.8	3,103.0
1993	18,991	65,244	84,235	7,820,900	5,036.9	3,638.7	3,881.6	3,032.4
1994	17,800	66,540	84,340	7,879,800	4,688.0	3,685.0	3,859.3	3,026.7
1995	n/a	n/a	n/a	7,997,700	n/a	n/a	n/a	3,043.8
1996	19,878	60,298	80,176	7,894,600	5,341.5	3,274.8	3,622.3	2,975.9

Notes: (1) Metropolitan Statistical Area - see Appendix A for areas included; (2) calculated by the editors using the following formula: (number of crimes in the MSA minus number of crimes in the city); (3) calculated by the editors using the following formula: ((number of crimes in the MSA minus number of crimes in the city) ÷ (population of the MSA minus population of the city)) x 100,000; n/a not avail.
Source: U.S. Department of Justice, FBI Uniform Crime Reports, 1977 - 1996

Motor Vehicle Thefts and Motor Vehicle Theft Rates: 1977 - 1996

Year	Number				Rate per 100,000 population			
	City	Suburbs[2]	MSA[1]	U.S.	City	Suburbs[3]	MSA[1]	U.S.
1977	3,701	20,248	23,949	977,700	1,114.8	702.6	745.1	451.9
1978	3,189	19,045	22,234	1,004,100	960.5	668.3	698.8	460.5
1979	3,930	19,785	23,715	1,112,800	1,140.2	683.1	731.7	505.6
1980	3,399	19,095	22,494	1,131,700	1,003.5	661.4	697.3	502.2
1981	3,401	16,466	19,867	1,087,800	978.0	555.5	599.9	474.7
1982	3,007	14,883	17,890	1,062,400	845.0	490.6	527.8	458.8
1983	2,742	n/a	n/a	1,007,900	756.7	n/a	n/a	430.8
1984	2,923	5,854	8,777	1,032,200	815.2	382.4	464.5	437.1
1985	3,408	6,678	10,086	1,102,900	941.2	427.1	523.8	462.0
1986	4,059	7,173	11,232	1,224,100	1,095.4	448.3	570.0	507.8
1987	4,809	7,906	12,715	1,288,700	1,314.0	489.0	641.3	529.4
1988	5,943	10,281	16,224	1,432,900	1,615.9	628.4	809.6	582.9
1989	6,544	11,422	17,966	1,564,800	1,786.5	674.6	872.4	630.4
1990	7,173	11,221	18,394	1,635,900	1,927.0	655.9	883.1	657.8
1991	7,281	12,119	19,400	1,661,700	1,916.1	694.0	912.4	659.0
1992	7,766	10,880	18,646	1,610,800	2,011.5	613.2	863.1	631.5
1993	7,772	11,571	19,343	1,563,100	2,061.3	645.3	891.3	606.1
1994	7,217	12,378	19,595	1,539,300	1,900.7	685.5	896.6	591.3
1995	n/a	n/a	n/a	1,472,400	n/a	n/a	n/a	560.4
1996	5,070	11,184	16,254	1,395,200	1,362.4	607.4	734.3	525.9

Notes: (1) Metropolitan Statistical Area - see Appendix A for areas included; (2) calculated by the editors using the following formula: (number of crimes in the MSA minus number of crimes in the city); (3) calculated by the editors using the following formula: ((number of crimes in the MSA minus number of crimes in the city) ÷ (population of the MSA minus population of the city)) x 100,000; n/a not avail.
Source: U.S. Department of Justice, FBI Uniform Crime Reports, 1977 - 1996

HATE CRIMES

Criminal Incidents by Bias Motivation

Area	Race	Ethnicity	Religion	Sexual Orientation
Oakland	9	0	0	1

Notes: Figures include both violent and property crimes. Law enforcement agencies must have submitted data for at least one quarter of calendar year 1995 to be included in this report, therefore figures shown may not represent complete 12-month totals; n/a not available
Source: U.S. Department of Justice, FBI Uniform Crime Reports, Hate Crime Statistics 1995

LAW ENFORCEMENT

Full-Time Law Enforcement Employees

Jurisdiction	Police Employees			Police Officers per 100,000 population
	Total	Officers	Civilians	
Oakland	1,024	626	398	168.2

Notes: Data as of October 31, 1996
Source: U.S. Department of Justice, FBI Uniform Crime Reports, 1996

Number of Police Officers by Race

Race	Police Officers				Index of Representation[1]		
	1983		1992				
	Number	Pct.	Number	Pct.	1983	1992	% Chg.
Black	147	23.1	144	26.2	0.49	0.60	22.4
Hispanic[2]	59	9.3	61	11.1	0.96	0.80	-16.7

Notes: (1) The index of representation is calculated by dividing the percent of black/hispanic police officers by the percent of corresponding blacks/hispanics in the local population. An index approaching 1.0 indicates that a city is closer to achieving a representation of police officers equal to their proportion in the local population; (2) Hispanic officers can be of any race
Source: Bureau of Justice Statistics, Sourcebook of Criminal Justice Statistics, 1994

CORRECTIONS

Federal Correctional Facilities

Type	Year Opened	Security Level	Sex of Inmates	Rated Capacity	Population on 7/1/95	Number of Staff
None listed						

Notes: Data as of 1995
Source: Bureau of Justice Statistics, Sourcebook of Criminal Justice Statistics Online

City/County/Regional Correctional Facilities

Name	Year Opened	Year Renov.	Rated Capacity	1995 Pop.	Number of COs[1]	Number of Staff	ACA[2] Accred.
Alameda Co Jail North	1984	--	693	546	88	147	No

Notes: Data as of April 1996; (1) Correctional Officers; (2) American Correctional Assn. Accreditation
Source: American Correctional Association, 1996-1998 National Jail and Adult Detention Directory

Private Adult Correctional Facilities

Name	Date Opened	Rated Capacity	Present Pop.	Security Level	Facility Construct.	Expans. Plans	ACA[1] Accred.
None listed							

Notes: Data as of December 1996; (1) American Correctional Association Accreditation
Source: University of Florida, Center for Studies in Criminology and Law, Private Adult Correctional Facility Census, 10th Ed., March 15, 1997

Characteristics of Shock Incarceration Programs

Jurisdiction	Year Program Began	Number of Camps	Average Num. of Inmates	Number of Beds	Program Length	Voluntary/ Mandatory
California	1993	3[a]	350	200[b]	4 months[c]	Voluntary

Note: Data as of July 1996; (a) One boot camp; two work training and parole camps; (b) 200 program beds at San Quentin shock incarceration facility. Work training beds vary with each facility; (c) Shock incarceration and intensive parole programs: 4 months; Work training program: 2 months
Source: Sourcebook of Criminal Justice Statistics Online

INMATES AND HIV/AIDS

HIV Testing Policies for Inmates

Jurisdiction	All Inmates at Some Time	All Convicted Inmates at Admission	Random Samples While in Custody	High-risk Groups	Upon Inmate Request	Upon Court Order	Upon Involvement in Incident
Alameda Co.[1]	No	No	No	No	Yes	Yes	Yes

Notes: (1) All facilities reported following the same testing policy or authorities reported the policy to be jurisdiction-wide
Source: HIV in Prisons and Jails, 1993 (released August 1995)

Inmates Known to be Positive for HIV

Jurisdiction	Number of Jail Inmates in Facilities Providing Data	Type of HIV Infection/AIDS Cases				HIV/AIDS Cases as a Percent of Tot. Custody Pop.
		Total	Asymptomatic	Symptomatic	Confirmed AIDS	
Alameda Co.	3,281	27	10	6	11	0.8

Source: HIV in Prisons and Jails, 1993 (released August, 1995)

DEATH PENALTY

Death Penalty Statistics

State	Prisoners Executed		Prisoners Under Sentence of Death					Avg. No. of Years on Death Row[4]
	1930-1995	1996[1]	Total[2]	White[3]	Black[3]	Hisp.	Women	
California	294	2	420	251	160	61	8	7.0

Notes: Data as of 12/31/95 unless otherwise noted; (1) Data as of 7/31/97; (2) Includes persons of other races; (3) Includes people of Hispanic origin; (4) Covers prisoners sentenced 1974 through 1995
Source: Bureau of Justice Statistics, Capital Punishment 1995 (released 12/96); Death Penalty Information Center Web Site, 9/30/97

Capital Offenses and Methods of Execution

Capital Offenses in California	Minimum Age for Imposition of Death Penalty	Mentally Retarded Excluded	Methods of Execution[1]
First-degree murder with special circumstances; train-wrecking; treason; perjury causing execution.	18	No	Lethal injection; lethal gas

Notes: Data as of 12/31/95 unless otherwise noted; (1) Data as of 7/31/97
Source: Bureau of Justice Statistics, Capital Punishment 1995 (released 12/96); Death Penalty Information Center Web Site, 9/30/97

LAWS

Statutory Provisions Relating to the Purchase, Ownership and Use of Handguns

Jurisdiction	Instant Background Check	Federal Waiting Period Applies[1]	State Waiting Period (days)	License or Permit to Purchase	Registration	Record of Sale Sent to Police	Concealed Carry Law
California	No	No	15	No	No	Yes	Yes[a]

Note: Data as of 1996; (1) The Federal 5-day waiting period for handgun purchases applies to states that don't have instant background checks, waiting period requirements, or licensing procedures exempting them from the Federal requirement; (a) Restrictively administered discretion by local authorities over permit issuance, or permits are unavailable and carrying is prohibited in most circumstances
Source: Sourcebook of Criminal Justice Statistics Online

Statutory Provisions Relating to Alcohol Use and Driving

Jurisdiction	Drinking Age	Blood Alcohol Concentration Levels as Evidence in State Courts[1]		Open Container Law[1]	Anti-Consumption Law[1]	Dram Shop Law[1]
		Illegal per se at 0.10%	Presumption at 0.10%			
California	21	(a)	(a)	Yes	Yes	Yes[b]

Note: Data as of January 1, 1997; (1) See Appendix C for an explanation of terms; (a) 0.08%; (b) Applies only to the actions of intoxicated minors
Source: Sourcebook of Criminal Justice Statistics Online

Statutory Provisions Relating to Curfews

Jurisdiction	Year Enacted	Latest Revision	Age Group(s)	Curfew Provisions
Oakland	1965	-	15 and under	10 pm to 6 am weekday nights 11 pm to 6 am weekend nights

Note: Data as of February 1996
Source: Sourcebook of Criminal Justice Statistics Online

Statutory Provisions Relating to Hate Crimes

Jurisdiction	Bias-Motivated Violence and Intimidation						Institutional Vandalism
	Civil Action	Criminal Penalty					
		Race/ Religion/ Ethnicity	Sexual Orientation	Mental/ Physical Disability	Gender	Age	
California	Yes	Yes	Yes	Yes	Yes	No	Yes

Source: Anti-Defamation League, 1997 Hate Crimes Laws

Omaha, Nebraska

OVERVIEW

The total crime rate for the city increased 27.7% between 1977 and 1996. During that same period, the violent crime rate increased 158.1% and the property crime rate increased 15.3%.

Among violent crimes, the rates for: Murders decreased 9.4%; Forcible Rapes increased 25.5%; Robberies increased 0.9%; and Aggravated Assaults increased 329.4%.

Among property crimes, the rates for: Burglaries decreased 24.8%; Larceny-Thefts increased 21.4%; and Motor Vehicle Thefts increased 67.2%.

ANTI-CRIME PROGRAMS

The Omaha Police Prevention Programs Unit manages the following:

- Business Watch—a formal network for concerned businesses to communicate with other businesses and the police regarding crime related problems.
- McGruff House Program—adults volunteer their homes to provide emergency assistance for children as they go to and from school.
- D.A.R.E. (Drug Abuse Resistance Education)—a curriculum for 5th and 6th graders.
- Neighborhood Watch Program—residents of a community share information regarding neighborhood safety and home security.
- Explorers—a training program for young men and women interested in the law enforcement profession.
- Public presentations regarding public safety, police service and crime prevention methods. *Omaha Police Department, 7/97*

CRIME RISK

Your Chances of Becoming a Victim[1]

Area	Any Crime	Violent Crime					Property Crime			
		Any	Murder	Forcible Rape[2]	Robbery	Aggrav. Assault	Any	Burglary	Larceny -Theft	Motor Vehicle Theft
City	1:13	1:74	1:12,985	1:886	1:448	1:94	1:16	1:99	1:23	1:96

Note: (1) Figures have been calculated by dividing the population of the city by the number of crimes reported to the FBI during 1996 and are expressed as odds (eg. 1:20 should be read as 1 in 20). (2) Figures have been calculated by dividing the female population of the city by the number of forcible rapes reported to the FBI during 1996. The female population of the city was estimated by calculating the ratio of females to males reported in the 1990 Census and applying that ratio to 1996 population estimate.
Source: FBI Uniform Crime Reports 1996

CRIME STATISTICS

Total Crimes and Total Crime Rates: 1977 - 1996

Year	Number				Rate per 100,000 population			
	City	Suburbs[2]	MSA[1]	U.S.	City	Suburbs[3]	MSA[1]	U.S.
1977	22,020	10,251	32,271	10,984,500	6,016.4	5,094.4	5,689.3	5,077.6
1978	21,459	9,891	31,350	11,209,000	5,831.3	4,669.6	5,406.9	5,140.3
1979	24,352	10,751	35,103	12,249,500	6,575.8	5,012.8	6,002.6	5,565.5
1980	24,430	10,855	35,285	13,408,300	7,807.1	4,286.8	6,232.6	5,950.0
1981	24,351	11,282	35,633	13,423,800	7,541.7	4,574.3	6,256.7	5,858.2
1982	24,377	8,693	33,070	12,974,400	7,502.1	3,506.8	5,773.1	5,603.6
1983	24,259	8,049	32,308	12,108,600	7,412.4	3,039.0	5,456.2	5,175.0
1984	21,867	7,505	29,372	11,881,800	6,111.7	3,094.4	4,892.7	5,031.3
1985	22,720	8,336	31,056	12,431,400	6,261.0	3,420.1	5,119.5	5,207.1
1986	22,511	8,604	31,115	13,211,900	6,772.9	3,178.6	5,159.6	5,480.4
1987	24,383	9,601	33,984	13,508,700	6,502.6	4,041.6	5,548.2	5,550.0
1988	23,944	9,876	33,820	13,923,100	6,335.1	4,104.0	5,467.2	5,664.2
1989	23,345	10,790	34,135	14,251,400	6,574.0	4,002.2	5,464.1	5,741.0
1990	23,673	10,438	34,111	14,475,600	7,049.8	3,695.3	5,517.2	5,820.3
1991	24,004	4,992	28,996	14,872,900	7,081.1	1,752.5	4,648.0	5,897.8
1992	n/a	n/a	n/a	14,438,200	n/a	n/a	n/a	5,660.2
1993	n/a	n/a	n/a	14,144,800	n/a	n/a	n/a	5,484.4
1994	27,541	10,209	37,750	13,989,500	7,983.5	3,183.1	5,670.7	5,373.5
1995	27,324	10,116	37,440	13,862,700	7,849.7	3,159.5	5,602.6	5,275.9
1996	26,939	7,013	33,952	13,473,600	7,683.5	2,173.7	5,043.1	5,078.9

Notes: (1) Metropolitan Statistical Area - see Appendix A for areas included; (2) calculated by the editors using the following formula: (number of crimes in the MSA minus number of crimes in the city); (3) calculated by the editors using the following formula: ((number of crimes in the MSA minus number of crimes in the city) ÷ (population of the MSA minus population of the city)) x 100,000; n/a not avail.
Source: U.S. Department of Justice, FBI Uniform Crime Reports, 1977 - 1996

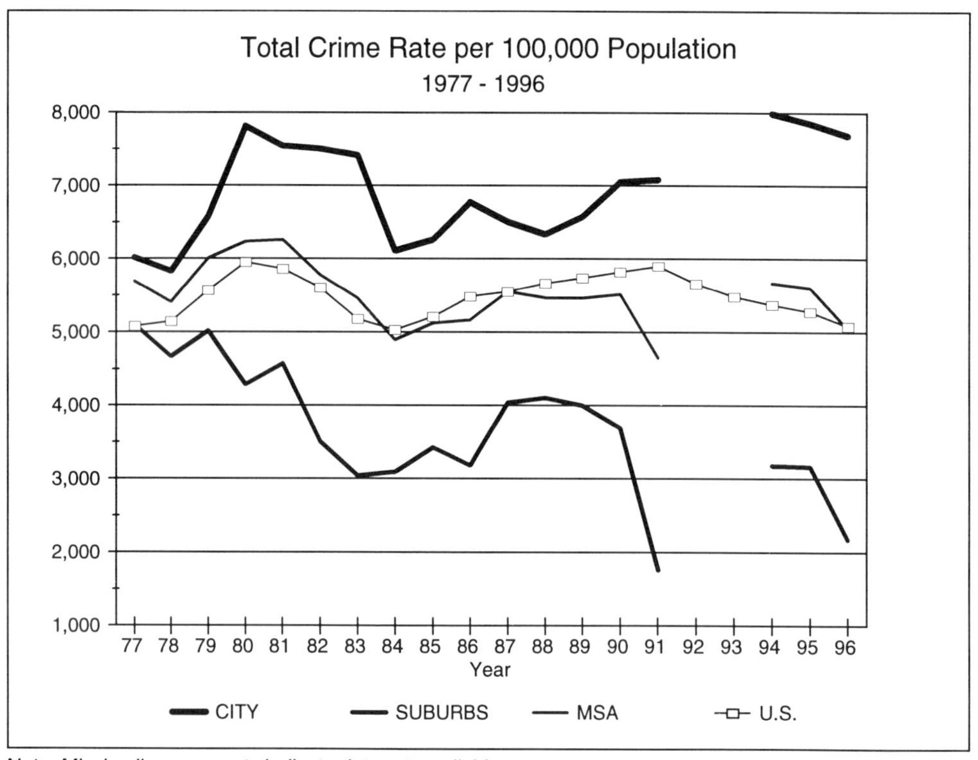

Note: Missing line segments indicate data not available.

Violent Crimes and Violent Crime Rates: 1977 - 1996

Year	Number				Rate per 100,000 population			
	City	Suburbs[2]	MSA[1]	U.S.	City	Suburbs[3]	MSA[1]	U.S.
1977	1,918	526	2,444	1,029,580	524.0	261.4	430.9	475.9
1978	1,856	571	2,427	1,085,550	504.3	269.6	418.6	497.8
1979	2,017	557	2,574	1,208,030	544.7	259.7	440.2	548.9
1980	1,983	575	2,558	1,344,520	633.7	227.1	451.8	596.6
1981	1,583	605	2,188	1,361,820	490.3	245.3	384.2	594.3
1982	2,450	440	2,890	1,322,390	754.0	177.5	504.5	571.1
1983	2,390	430	2,820	1,258,090	730.3	162.4	476.2	537.7
1984	2,410	366	2,776	1,273,280	673.6	150.9	462.4	539.2
1985	2,498	490	2,988	1,328,800	688.4	201.0	492.6	556.6
1986	2,726	541	3,267	1,489,170	820.2	199.9	541.7	617.7
1987	2,536	432	2,968	1,484,000	676.3	181.9	484.6	609.7
1988	2,774	418	3,192	1,566,220	733.9	173.7	516.0	637.2
1989	2,751	565	3,316	1,646,040	774.7	209.6	530.8	663.1
1990	3,139	647	3,786	1,820,130	934.8	229.1	612.4	731.8
1991	3,242	170	3,412	1,911,770	956.4	59.7	546.9	758.1
1992	n/a	n/a	n/a	1,932,270	n/a	n/a	n/a	757.5
1993	n/a	n/a	n/a	1,926,020	n/a	n/a	n/a	746.8
1994	3,930	851	4,781	1,857,670	1,139.2	265.3	718.2	713.6
1995	3,585	583	4,168	1,798,790	1,029.9	182.1	623.7	684.6
1996	4,742	332	5,074	1,682,280	1,352.5	102.9	753.7	634.1

Notes: Violent crimes include murder, forcible rape, robbery and aggravated assault; n/a not available; (1) Metropolitan Statistical Area - see Appendix A for areas included; (2) calculated by the editors using the following formula: (number of crimes in the MSA minus number of crimes in the city); (3) calculated by the editors using the following formula: ((number of crimes in the MSA minus number of crimes in the city) ÷ (population of the MSA minus population of the city)) x 100,000
Source: U.S. Department of Justice, FBI Uniform Crime Reports, 1977 - 1996

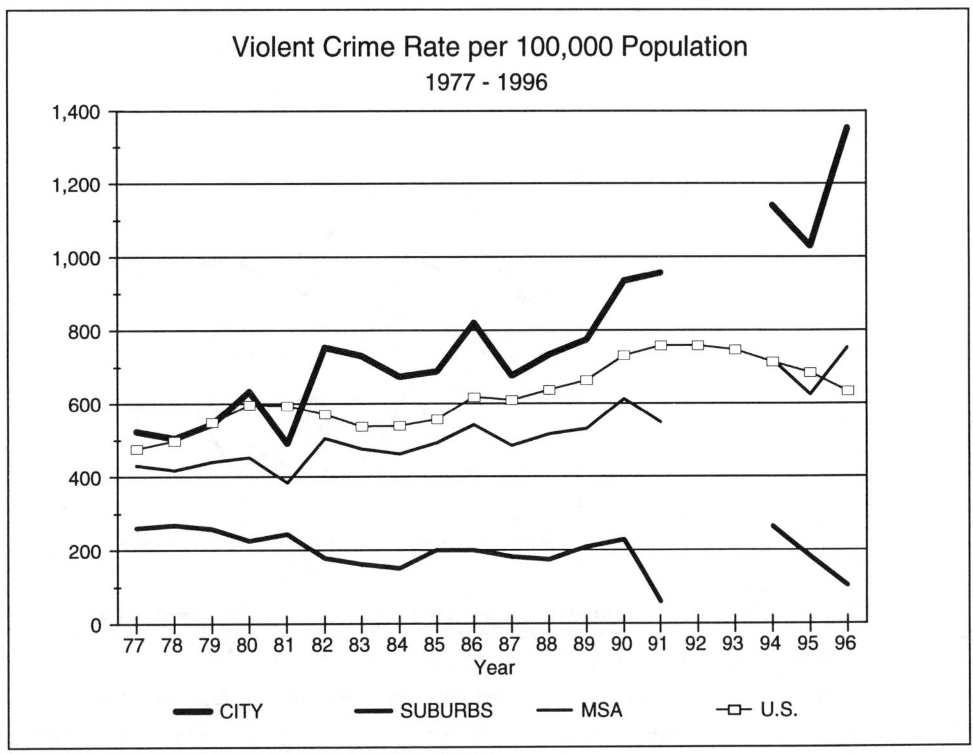

Note: Missing line segments indicate data not available.

Property Crimes and Property Crime Rates: 1977 - 1996

Year	Number				Rate per 100,000 population			
	City	Suburbs[2]	MSA[1]	U.S.	City	Suburbs[3]	MSA[1]	U.S.
1977	20,102	9,725	29,827	9,955,000	5,492.3	4,833.0	5,258.4	4,601.7
1978	19,603	9,320	28,923	10,123,400	5,326.9	4,400.0	4,988.3	4,642.5
1979	22,335	10,194	32,529	11,041,500	6,031.2	4,753.1	5,562.5	5,016.6
1980	22,447	10,280	32,727	12,063,700	7,173.4	4,059.7	5,780.7	5,353.3
1981	22,768	10,677	33,445	12,061,900	7,051.5	4,329.0	5,872.5	5,263.9
1982	21,927	8,253	30,180	11,652,000	6,748.1	3,329.3	5,268.6	5,032.5
1983	21,869	7,619	29,488	10,850,500	6,682.1	2,876.7	4,980.0	4,637.4
1984	19,457	7,139	26,596	10,608,500	5,438.1	2,943.5	4,430.3	4,492.1
1985	20,222	7,846	28,068	11,102,600	5,572.6	3,219.1	4,627.0	4,650.5
1986	19,785	8,063	27,848	11,722,700	5,952.7	2,978.8	4,617.9	4,862.6
1987	21,847	9,169	31,016	12,024,700	5,826.3	3,859.8	5,063.6	4,940.3
1988	21,170	9,458	30,628	12,356,900	5,601.2	3,930.3	4,951.2	5,027.1
1989	20,594	10,225	30,819	12,605,400	5,799.3	3,792.6	4,933.3	5,077.9
1990	20,534	9,791	30,325	12,655,500	6,115.0	3,466.2	4,904.9	5,088.5
1991	20,762	4,822	25,584	12,961,100	6,124.7	1,692.8	4,101.1	5,139.7
1992	n/a	n/a	n/a	12,505,900	n/a	n/a	n/a	4,902.7
1993	n/a	n/a	n/a	12,218,800	n/a	n/a	n/a	4,737.6
1994	23,611	9,358	32,969	12,131,900	6,844.3	2,917.7	4,952.5	4,660.0
1995	23,739	9,533	33,272	12,063,900	6,819.8	2,977.4	4,978.8	4,591.3
1996	22,197	6,681	28,878	11,791,300	6,331.0	2,070.8	4,289.4	4,444.8

Notes: Property crimes include burglary, larceny-theft and motor vehicle theft; n/a not available; (1) Metropolitan Statistical Area - see Appendix A for areas included; (2) calculated by the editors using the following formula: (number of crimes in the MSA minus number of crimes in the city); (3) calculated by the editors using the following formula: ((number of crimes in the MSA minus number of crimes in the city) ÷ (population of the MSA minus population of the city)) x 100,000
Source: U.S. Department of Justice, FBI Uniform Crime Reports, 1977 - 1996

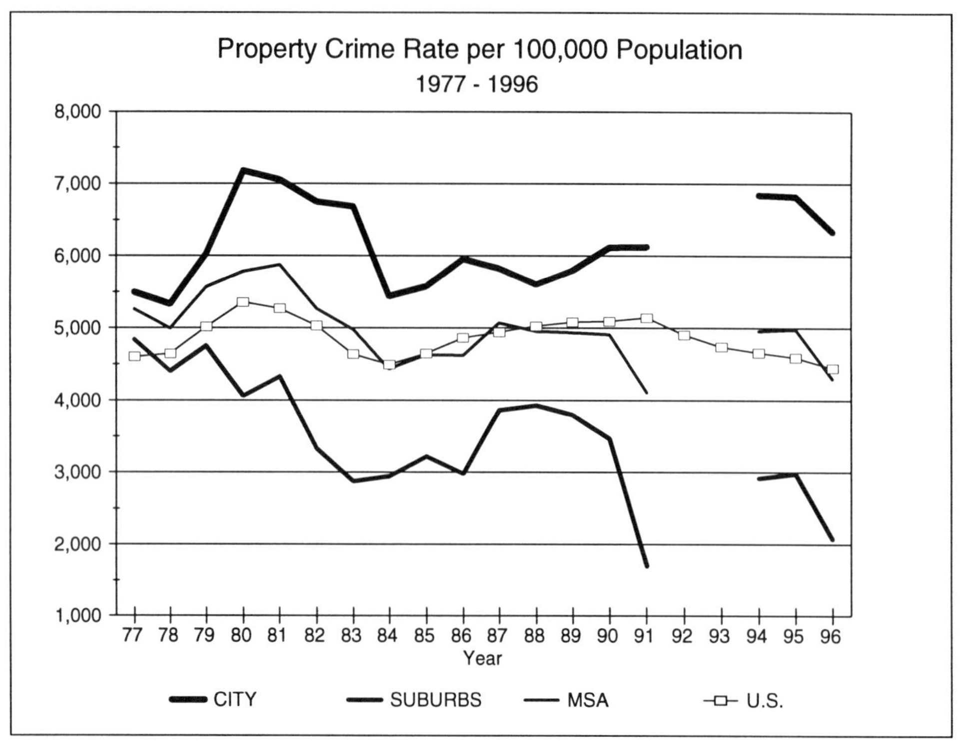

Note: Missing line segments indicate data not available.

Murders and Murder Rates: 1977 - 1996

Year	Number				Rate per 100,000 population			
	City	Suburbs[2]	MSA[1]	U.S.	City	Suburbs[3]	MSA[1]	U.S.
1977	31	6	37	19,120	8.5	3.0	6.5	8.8
1978	24	8	32	19,560	6.5	3.8	5.5	9.0
1979	40	9	49	21,460	10.8	4.2	8.4	9.7
1980	38	6	44	23,040	12.1	2.4	7.8	10.2
1981	28	6	34	22,520	8.7	2.4	6.0	9.8
1982	20	8	28	21,010	6.2	3.2	4.9	9.1
1983	27	13	40	19,310	8.2	4.9	6.8	8.3
1984	24	9	33	18,690	6.7	3.7	5.5	7.9
1985	24	3	27	18,980	6.6	1.2	4.5	7.9
1986	30	8	38	20,610	9.0	3.0	6.3	8.6
1987	28	2	30	20,100	7.5	0.8	4.9	8.3
1988	28	4	32	20,680	7.4	1.7	5.2	8.4
1989	23	3	26	21,500	6.5	1.1	4.2	8.7
1990	11	11	22	23,440	3.3	3.9	3.6	9.4
1991	35	1	36	24,700	10.3	0.4	5.8	9.8
1992	n/a	n/a	n/a	23,760	n/a	n/a	n/a	9.3
1993	n/a	n/a	n/a	24,530	n/a	n/a	n/a	9.5
1994	33	7	40	23,330	9.6	2.2	6.0	9.0
1995	27	3	30	21,610	7.8	0.9	4.5	8.2
1996	27	5	32	19,650	7.7	1.5	4.8	7.4

Notes: (1) Metropolitan Statistical Area - see Appendix A for areas included; (2) calculated by the editors using the following formula: (number of crimes in the MSA minus number of crimes in the city); (3) calculated by the editors using the following formula: ((number of crimes in the MSA minus number of crimes in the city) ÷ (population of the MSA minus population of the city)) x 100,000; n/a not avail.
Source: U.S. Department of Justice, FBI Uniform Crime Reports, 1977 - 1996

Forcible Rapes and Forcible Rape Rates: 1977 - 1996

Year	Number				Rate per 100,000 population			
	City	Suburbs[2]	MSA[1]	U.S.	City	Suburbs[3]	MSA[1]	U.S.
1977	172	37	209	63,500	47.0	18.4	36.8	29.4
1978	162	37	199	67,610	44.0	17.5	34.3	31.0
1979	193	45	238	76,390	52.1	21.0	40.7	34.7
1980	213	49	262	82,990	68.1	19.4	46.3	36.8
1981	186	50	236	82,500	57.6	20.3	41.4	36.0
1982	175	34	209	78,770	53.9	13.7	36.5	34.0
1983	157	47	204	78,920	48.0	17.7	34.5	33.7
1984	202	44	246	84,230	56.5	18.1	41.0	35.7
1985	214	42	256	88,670	59.0	17.2	42.2	37.1
1986	225	48	273	91,460	67.7	17.7	45.3	37.9
1987	189	43	232	91,110	50.4	18.1	37.9	37.4
1988	216	37	253	92,490	57.1	15.4	40.9	37.6
1989	188	52	240	94,500	52.9	19.3	38.4	38.1
1990	217	49	266	102,560	64.6	17.3	43.0	41.2
1991	207	24	231	106,590	61.1	8.4	37.0	42.3
1992	n/a	n/a	n/a	109,060	n/a	n/a	n/a	42.8
1993	n/a	n/a	n/a	106,010	n/a	n/a	n/a	41.1
1994	217	50	267	102,220	62.9	15.6	40.1	39.3
1995	80	49	129	97,470	23.0	15.3	19.3	37.1
1996	207	29	236	95,770	59.0	9.0	35.1	36.1

Notes: (1) Metropolitan Statistical Area - see Appendix A for areas included; (2) calculated by the editors using the following formula: (number of crimes in the MSA minus number of crimes in the city); (3) calculated by the editors using the following formula: ((number of crimes in the MSA minus number of crimes in the city) ÷ (population of the MSA minus population of the city)) x 100,000; n/a not avail.
Source: U.S. Department of Justice, FBI Uniform Crime Reports, 1977 - 1996

Robberies and Robbery Rates: 1977 - 1996

Year	Number				Rate per 100,000 population			
	City	Suburbs[2]	MSA[1]	U.S.	City	Suburbs[3]	MSA[1]	U.S.
1977	809	131	940	412,610	221.0	65.1	165.7	190.7
1978	878	125	1,003	426,930	238.6	59.0	173.0	195.8
1979	954	118	1,072	480,700	257.6	55.0	183.3	218.4
1980	1,053	163	1,216	565,840	336.5	64.4	214.8	251.1
1981	899	142	1,041	592,910	278.4	57.6	182.8	258.7
1982	743	71	814	553,130	228.7	28.6	142.1	238.9
1983	622	94	716	506,570	190.1	35.5	120.9	216.5
1984	530	61	591	485,010	148.1	25.2	98.4	205.4
1985	591	89	680	497,870	162.9	36.5	112.1	208.5
1986	627	138	765	542,780	188.6	51.0	126.9	225.1
1987	570	105	675	517,700	152.0	44.2	110.2	212.7
1988	710	98	808	542,970	187.9	40.7	130.6	220.9
1989	639	104	743	578,330	179.9	38.6	118.9	233.0
1990	604	104	708	639,270	179.9	36.8	114.5	257.0
1991	634	29	663	687,730	187.0	10.2	106.3	272.7
1992	n/a	n/a	n/a	672,480	n/a	n/a	n/a	263.6
1993	n/a	n/a	n/a	659,870	n/a	n/a	n/a	255.9
1994	918	137	1,055	618,950	266.1	42.7	158.5	237.7
1995	808	102	910	580,510	232.1	31.9	136.2	220.9
1996	782	47	829	537,050	223.0	14.6	123.1	202.4

Notes: (1) Metropolitan Statistical Area - see Appendix A for areas included; (2) calculated by the editors using the following formula: (number of crimes in the MSA minus number of crimes in the city); (3) calculated by the editors using the following formula: ((number of crimes in the MSA minus number of crimes in the city) ÷ (population of the MSA minus population of the city)) x 100,000; n/a not avail.
Source: U.S. Department of Justice, FBI Uniform Crime Reports, 1977 - 1996

Aggravated Assaults and Aggravated Assault Rates: 1977 - 1996

Year	Number				Rate per 100,000 population			
	City	Suburbs[2]	MSA[1]	U.S.	City	Suburbs[3]	MSA[1]	U.S.
1977	906	352	1,258	534,350	247.5	174.9	221.8	247.0
1978	792	401	1,193	571,460	215.2	189.3	205.8	262.1
1979	830	385	1,215	629,480	224.1	179.5	207.8	286.0
1980	679	357	1,036	672,650	217.0	141.0	183.0	298.5
1981	470	407	877	663,900	145.6	165.0	154.0	289.7
1982	1,512	327	1,839	669,480	465.3	131.9	321.0	289.2
1983	1,584	276	1,860	653,290	484.0	104.2	314.1	279.2
1984	1,654	252	1,906	685,350	462.3	103.9	317.5	290.2
1985	1,669	356	2,025	723,250	459.9	146.1	333.8	302.9
1986	1,844	347	2,191	834,320	554.8	128.2	363.3	346.1
1987	1,749	282	2,031	855,090	466.4	118.7	331.6	351.3
1988	1,820	279	2,099	910,090	481.5	115.9	339.3	370.2
1989	1,901	406	2,307	951,710	535.3	150.6	369.3	383.4
1990	2,307	483	2,790	1,054,860	687.0	171.0	451.3	424.1
1991	2,366	116	2,482	1,092,740	698.0	40.7	397.9	433.3
1992	n/a	n/a	n/a	1,126,970	n/a	n/a	n/a	441.8
1993	n/a	n/a	n/a	1,135,610	n/a	n/a	n/a	440.3
1994	2,762	657	3,419	1,113,180	800.6	204.8	513.6	427.6
1995	2,670	429	3,099	1,099,210	767.0	134.0	463.7	418.3
1996	3,726	251	3,977	1,029,810	1,062.7	77.8	590.7	388.2

Notes: (1) Metropolitan Statistical Area - see Appendix A for areas included; (2) calculated by the editors using the following formula: (number of crimes in the MSA minus number of crimes in the city); (3) calculated by the editors using the following formula: ((number of crimes in the MSA minus number of crimes in the city) ÷ (population of the MSA minus population of the city)) x 100,000; n/a not avail.
Source: U.S. Department of Justice, FBI Uniform Crime Reports, 1977 - 1996

Burglaries and Burglary Rates: 1977 - 1996

Year	Number				Rate per 100,000 population			
	City	Suburbs[2]	MSA[1]	U.S.	City	Suburbs[3]	MSA[1]	U.S.
1977	4,930	2,683	7,613	3,071,500	1,347.0	1,333.4	1,342.2	1,419.8
1978	5,048	2,534	7,582	3,128,300	1,371.7	1,196.3	1,307.7	1,434.6
1979	5,140	2,716	7,856	3,327,700	1,388.0	1,266.4	1,343.4	1,511.9
1980	5,351	2,751	8,102	3,795,200	1,710.0	1,086.4	1,431.1	1,684.1
1981	5,933	2,957	8,890	3,779,700	1,837.5	1,198.9	1,561.0	1,649.5
1982	5,352	2,228	7,580	3,447,100	1,647.1	898.8	1,323.3	1,488.8
1983	5,393	1,952	7,345	3,129,900	1,647.8	737.0	1,240.4	1,337.7
1984	4,045	1,792	5,837	2,984,400	1,130.6	738.9	972.3	1,263.7
1985	4,751	1,917	6,668	3,073,300	1,309.2	786.5	1,099.2	1,287.3
1986	4,643	2,004	6,647	3,241,400	1,396.9	740.3	1,102.2	1,344.6
1987	5,338	2,208	7,546	3,236,200	1,423.6	929.5	1,231.9	1,329.6
1988	4,580	2,146	6,726	3,218,100	1,211.8	891.8	1,087.3	1,309.2
1989	4,760	2,237	6,997	3,168,200	1,340.4	829.7	1,120.0	1,276.3
1990	4,190	2,090	6,280	3,073,900	1,247.8	739.9	1,015.8	1,235.9
1991	3,986	875	4,861	3,157,200	1,175.9	307.2	779.2	1,252.0
1992	n/a	n/a	n/a	2,979,900	n/a	n/a	n/a	1,168.2
1993	n/a	n/a	n/a	2,834,800	n/a	n/a	n/a	1,099.2
1994	4,398	1,795	6,193	2,712,800	1,274.9	559.7	930.3	1,042.0
1995	3,883	1,455	5,338	2,593,800	1,115.5	454.4	798.8	987.1
1996	3,552	1,110	4,662	2,501,500	1,013.1	344.0	692.5	943.0

Notes: (1) Metropolitan Statistical Area - see Appendix A for areas included; (2) calculated by the editors using the following formula: (number of crimes in the MSA minus number of crimes in the city); (3) calculated by the editors using the following formula: ((number of crimes in the MSA minus number of crimes in the city) ÷ (population of the MSA minus population of the city)) x 100,000; n/a not avail.
Source: U.S. Department of Justice, FBI Uniform Crime Reports, 1977 - 1996

Larceny-Thefts and Larceny-Theft Rates: 1977 - 1996

Year	Number				Rate per 100,000 population			
	City	Suburbs[2]	MSA[1]	U.S.	City	Suburbs[3]	MSA[1]	U.S.
1977	12,895	6,277	19,172	5,905,700	3,523.2	3,119.4	3,380.0	2,729.9
1978	12,811	6,049	18,860	5,991,000	3,481.3	2,855.8	3,252.7	2,747.4
1979	14,875	6,695	21,570	6,601,000	4,016.7	3,121.6	3,688.5	2,999.1
1980	15,138	6,834	21,972	7,136,900	4,837.7	2,698.8	3,881.0	3,167.0
1981	15,239	7,062	22,301	7,194,400	4,719.7	2,863.3	3,915.7	3,139.7
1982	15,345	5,466	20,811	7,142,500	4,722.5	2,205.0	3,633.0	3,084.8
1983	15,246	5,209	20,455	6,712,800	4,658.5	1,966.8	3,454.5	2,868.9
1984	14,365	4,863	19,228	6,591,900	4,014.9	2,005.1	3,202.9	2,791.3
1985	14,279	5,387	19,666	6,926,400	3,934.9	2,210.2	3,241.9	2,901.2
1986	13,927	5,529	19,456	7,257,200	4,190.2	2,042.6	3,226.3	3,010.3
1987	15,292	6,480	21,772	7,499,900	4,078.1	2,727.8	3,554.5	3,081.3
1988	15,185	6,767	21,952	7,705,900	4,017.6	2,812.0	3,548.6	3,134.9
1989	14,368	7,376	21,744	7,872,400	4,046.1	2,735.9	3,480.6	3,171.3
1990	14,997	7,146	22,143	7,945,700	4,466.1	2,529.9	3,581.5	3,194.8
1991	15,040	3,736	18,776	8,142,200	4,436.7	1,311.6	3,009.7	3,228.8
1992	n/a	n/a	n/a	7,915,200	n/a	n/a	n/a	3,103.0
1993	n/a	n/a	n/a	7,820,900	n/a	n/a	n/a	3,032.4
1994	14,843	6,938	21,781	7,879,800	4,302.6	2,163.2	3,271.9	3,026.7
1995	16,071	7,487	23,558	7,997,700	4,616.9	2,338.4	3,525.2	3,043.8
1996	14,999	5,118	20,117	7,894,600	4,278.0	1,586.3	2,988.1	2,975.9

Notes: (1) Metropolitan Statistical Area - see Appendix A for areas included; (2) calculated by the editors using the following formula: (number of crimes in the MSA minus number of crimes in the city); (3) calculated by the editors using the following formula: ((number of crimes in the MSA minus number of crimes in the city) ÷ (population of the MSA minus population of the city)) x 100,000; n/a not avail.
Source: U.S. Department of Justice, FBI Uniform Crime Reports, 1977 - 1996

Motor Vehicle Thefts and Motor Vehicle Theft Rates: 1977 - 1996

Year	Number				Rate per 100,000 population			
	City	Suburbs[2]	MSA[1]	U.S.	City	Suburbs[3]	MSA[1]	U.S.
1977	2,277	765	3,042	977,700	622.1	380.2	536.3	451.9
1978	1,744	737	2,481	1,004,100	473.9	347.9	427.9	460.5
1979	2,320	783	3,103	1,112,800	626.5	365.1	530.6	505.6
1980	1,958	695	2,653	1,131,700	625.7	274.5	468.6	502.2
1981	1,596	658	2,254	1,087,800	494.3	266.8	395.8	474.7
1982	1,230	559	1,789	1,062,400	378.5	225.5	312.3	458.8
1983	1,230	458	1,688	1,007,900	375.8	172.9	285.1	430.8
1984	1,047	484	1,531	1,032,200	292.6	199.6	255.0	437.1
1985	1,192	542	1,734	1,102,900	328.5	222.4	285.8	462.0
1986	1,215	530	1,745	1,224,100	365.6	195.8	289.4	507.8
1987	1,217	481	1,698	1,288,700	324.6	202.5	277.2	529.4
1988	1,405	545	1,950	1,432,900	371.7	226.5	315.2	582.9
1989	1,466	612	2,078	1,564,800	412.8	227.0	332.6	630.4
1990	1,347	555	1,902	1,635,900	401.1	196.5	307.6	657.8
1991	1,736	211	1,947	1,661,700	512.1	74.1	312.1	659.0
1992	n/a	n/a	n/a	1,610,800	n/a	n/a	n/a	631.5
1993	n/a	n/a	n/a	1,563,100	n/a	n/a	n/a	606.1
1994	4,370	625	4,995	1,539,300	1,266.8	194.9	750.3	591.3
1995	3,785	591	4,376	1,472,400	1,087.4	184.6	654.8	560.4
1996	3,646	453	4,099	1,395,200	1,039.9	140.4	608.8	525.9

Notes: (1) Metropolitan Statistical Area - see Appendix A for areas included; (2) calculated by the editors using the following formula: (number of crimes in the MSA minus number of crimes in the city); (3) calculated by the editors using the following formula: ((number of crimes in the MSA minus number of crimes in the city) ÷ (population of the MSA minus population of the city)) x 100,000; n/a not avail.
Source: U.S. Department of Justice, FBI Uniform Crime Reports, 1977 - 1996

HATE CRIMES

Criminal Incidents by Bias Motivation

Area	Race	Ethnicity	Religion	Sexual Orientation
Omaha	n/a	n/a	n/a	n/a

Notes: Figures include both violent and property crimes. Law enforcement agencies must have submitted data for at least one quarter of calendar year 1995 to be included in this report, therefore figures shown may not represent complete 12-month totals; n/a not available
Source: U.S. Department of Justice, FBI Uniform Crime Reports, Hate Crime Statistics 1995

ILLEGAL DRUGS

Drug Use by Adult Arrestees

Sex	Percent Testing Positive by Urinalysis (%)				
	Any Drug[1]	Cocaine	Marijuana	Opiates	Multiple Drugs
Male	63	24	52	1	18
Female	51	28	33	3	16

Notes: The catchment area is the entire city; (1) Includes cocaine, opiates, marijuana, methadone, phencyclidine (PCP), benzodiazepines, methaqualone, propoxyphene, barbiturates & amphetamines
Source: National Institute of Justice, 1996 Drug Use Forecasting, Annual Report on Adult and Juvenile Arrestees (released June 1997)

LAW ENFORCEMENT

Full-Time Law Enforcement Employees

Jurisdiction	Police Employees			Police Officers per 100,000 population
	Total	Officers	Civilians	
Omaha	879	702	177	200.2

Notes: Data as of October 31, 1996
Source: U.S. Department of Justice, FBI Uniform Crime Reports, 1996

Number of Police Officers by Race

Race	Police Officers				Index of Representation[1]		
	1983		1992				
	Number	Pct.	Number	Pct.	1983	1992	% Chg.
Black	46	8.3	70	11.5	0.69	0.87	26.1
Hispanic[2]	12	2.2	18	3.0	0.91	0.94	3.3

Notes: (1) The index of representation is calculated by dividing the percent of black/hispanic police officers by the percent of corresponding blacks/hispanics in the local population. An index approaching 1.0 indicates that a city is closer to achieving a representation of police officers equal to their proportion in the local population; (2) Hispanic officers can be of any race
Source: Bureau of Justice Statistics, Sourcebook of Criminal Justice Statistics, 1994

CORRECTIONS

Federal Correctional Facilities

Type	Year Opened	Security Level	Sex of Inmates	Rated Capacity	Population on 7/1/95	Number of Staff
None listed						

Notes: Data as of 1995
Source: Bureau of Justice Statistics, Sourcebook of Criminal Justice Statistics Online

City/County/Regional Correctional Facilities

Name	Year Opened	Year Renov.	Rated Capacity	1995 Pop.	Number of COs[1]	Number of Staff	ACA[2] Accred.
Douglas Co Correctional Ctr	1979	1989	761	754	227	236	No
Douglas Co Work Release Ctr	1983	--	45	45	6	7	No

Notes: Data as of April 1996; (1) Correctional Officers; (2) American Correctional Assn. Accreditation
Source: American Correctional Association, 1996-1998 National Jail and Adult Detention Directory

Private Adult Correctional Facilities

Name	Date Opened	Rated Capacity	Present Pop.	Security Level	Facility Construct.	Expans. Plans	ACA[1] Accred.
None listed							

Notes: Data as of December 1996; (1) American Correctional Association Accreditation
Source: University of Florida, Center for Studies in Criminology and Law, Private Adult Correctional Facility Census, 10th Ed., March 15, 1997

Characteristics of Shock Incarceration Programs

Jurisdiction	Year Program Began	Number of Camps	Average Num. of Inmates	Number of Beds	Program Length	Voluntary/ Mandatory
Nebraska did not have a shock incarceration program as of July 1996						

Source: Sourcebook of Criminal Justice Statistics Online

DEATH PENALTY

Death Penalty Statistics

State	Prisoners Executed		Prisoners Under Sentence of Death					Avg. No. of Years on Death Row[4]
	1930-1995	1996[1]	Total[2]	White[3]	Black[3]	Hisp.	Women	
Nebraska	5	1	10	7	2	0	0	12.2

Notes: Data as of 12/31/95 unless otherwise noted; (1) Data as of 7/31/97; (2) Includes persons of other races; (3) Includes people of Hispanic origin; (4) Covers prisoners sentenced 1974 through 1995
Source: Bureau of Justice Statistics, Capital Punishment 1995 (released 12/96); Death Penalty Information Center Web Site, 9/30/97

Capital Offenses and Methods of Execution

Capital Offenses in Nebraska	Minimum Age for Imposition of Death Penalty	Mentally Retarded Excluded	Methods of Execution[1]
First-degree murder.	18	No	Electrocution

Notes: Data as of 12/31/95 unless otherwise noted; (1) Data as of 7/31/97
Source: Bureau of Justice Statistics, Capital Punishment 1995 (released 12/96); Death Penalty Information Center Web Site, 9/30/97

LAWS

Statutory Provisions Relating to the Purchase, Ownership and Use of Handguns

Jurisdiction	Instant Background Check	Federal Waiting Period Applies[1]	State Waiting Period (days)	License or Permit to Purchase	Regis-tration	Record of Sale Sent to Police	Concealed Carry Law
Nebraska	(a)	No	No	Yes[a]	No	No	Yes[b]

Note: Data as of 1996; (1) The Federal 5-day waiting period for handgun purchases applies to states that don't have instant background checks, waiting period requirements, or licensing procedures exempting them from the Federal requirement; (a) Instant Check is not yet operational. When operational, firearm purchases from licensed dealers will be subject either to it or the current permit-to-purchase, at the purchaser's option; (b) No permit system exists and concealed carry is prohibited
Source: Sourcebook of Criminal Justice Statistics Online

Statutory Provisions Relating to Alcohol Use and Driving

Jurisdiction	Drinking Age	Blood Alcohol Concentration Levels as Evidence in State Courts[1]		Open Container Law[1]	Anti-Consump-tion Law[1]	Dram Shop Law[1]
		Illegal per se at 0.10%	Presumption at 0.10%			
Nebraska	21	Yes	No	No	Yes	No

Note: Data as of January 1, 1997; (1) See Appendix C for an explanation of terms
Source: Sourcebook of Criminal Justice Statistics Online

Statutory Provisions Relating to Hate Crimes

Jurisdiction	Bias-Motivated Violence and Intimidation						Institutional Vandalism
	Civil Action	Criminal Penalty					
		Race/ Religion/ Ethnicity	Sexual Orientation	Mental/ Physical Disability	Gender	Age	
Nebraska	No	No	No	No	No	No	No

Source: Anti-Defamation League, 1997 Hate Crimes Laws

Orlando, Florida

OVERVIEW

The total crime rate for the city increased 36.6% between 1977 and 1996. During that same period, the violent crime rate increased 120.5% and the property crime rate increased 27.0%.

Among violent crimes, the rates for: Murders decreased 45.4%; Forcible Rapes increased 22.3%; Robberies increased 148.2%; and Aggravated Assaults increased 124.7%.

Among property crimes, the rates for: Burglaries decreased 5.9%; Larceny-Thefts increased 31.2%; and Motor Vehicle Thefts increased 156.0%.

ANTI-CRIME PROGRAMS

The police department is addressing crime problems through the redeployment of patrol officers on bicycles, prostitution decoy operations, reverse drug stings, uniform drug enforcement, community problem solving meetings and crime prevention/target hardening through the completion of security surveys. Partnerships, such as with the Parramore Heritage Resource Center (a neighborhood in West Orlando), the Callahan Neighborhood Association and the Orlando Housing Authority have been formed to implement the above activities.

The department has used the Department of Justice supplemental grant to enhance police patrols resulting in a reduction of violent crime by 7.09%.

The "I-Team" was formed to improve communications between city, county and private industry in the International Drive Community. *Orlando Police Department, Crime Prevention Division, 6/97*

CRIME RISK

Your Chances of Becoming a Victim[1]

Area	Any Crime	Violent Crime					Property Crime			
		Any	Murder	Forcible Rape[2]	Robbery	Aggrav. Assault	Any	Burglary	Larceny -Theft	Motor Vehicle Theft
City	1:8	1:46	1:14,047	1:551	1:169	1:67	1:9	1:41	1:14	1:83

Note: (1) Figures have been calculated by dividing the population of the city by the number of crimes reported to the FBI during 1996 and are expressed as odds (eg. 1:20 should be read as 1 in 20).
(2) Figures have been calculated by dividing the female population of the city by the number of forcible rapes reported to the FBI during 1996. The female population of the city was estimated by calculating the ratio of females to males reported in the 1990 Census and applying that ratio to 1996 population estimate.
Source: FBI Uniform Crime Reports 1996

CRIME STATISTICS

Total Crimes and Total Crime Rates: 1977 - 1996

Year	Number				Rate per 100,000 population			
	City	Suburbs[2]	MSA[1]	U.S.	City	Suburbs[3]	MSA[1]	U.S.
1977	11,090	33,352	44,442	10,984,500	9,643.5	7,065.8	7,570.8	5,077.6
1978	12,992	37,015	50,007	11,209,000	11,010.2	7,795.6	8,435.4	5,140.3
1979	14,022	40,793	54,815	12,249,500	11,539.3	8,009.5	8,689.5	5,565.5
1980	17,532	48,539	66,071	13,408,300	13,717.1	8,563.2	9,511.5	5,950.0
1981	17,469	49,704	67,173	13,423,800	12,862.6	8,252.1	9,100.4	5,858.2
1982	17,154	44,186	61,340	12,974,400	12,327.5	7,159.9	8,110.7	5,603.6
1983	13,682	39,719	53,401	12,108,600	9,589.4	6,277.1	6,886.6	5,175.0
1984	13,678	38,899	52,577	11,881,800	9,732.4	5,916.9	6,588.9	5,031.3
1985	16,122	43,819	59,941	12,431,400	11,351.5	6,159.6	7,023.6	5,207.1
1986	17,797	49,155	66,952	13,211,900	12,199.6	6,726.7	7,637.4	5,480.4
1987	18,884	51,923	70,807	13,508,700	12,568.4	6,700.3	7,653.3	5,550.0
1988	n/a	n/a	n/a	13,923,100	n/a	n/a	n/a	5,664.2
1989	21,200	65,047	86,247	14,251,400	13,233.7	7,768.2	8,645.9	5,741.0
1990	23,750	65,952	89,702	14,475,600	14,420.8	7,263.0	8,361.9	5,820.3
1991	n/a	n/a	n/a	14,872,900	n/a	n/a	n/a	5,897.8
1992	20,433	78,132	98,565	14,438,200	11,900.8	7,069.5	7,719.1	5,660.2
1993	21,953	77,495	99,448	14,144,800	12,420.5	6,756.9	7,513.2	5,484.4
1994	21,836	81,156	102,992	13,989,500	12,111.7	6,937.2	7,628.2	5,373.5
1995	20,750	77,716	98,466	13,862,700	11,550.3	6,462.3	7,123.5	5,275.9
1996	24,055	n/a	n/a	13,473,600	13,172.4	n/a	n/a	5,078.9

Notes: (1) Metropolitan Statistical Area - see Appendix A for areas included; (2) calculated by the editors using the following formula: (number of crimes in the MSA minus number of crimes in the city); (3) calculated by the editors using the following formula: ((number of crimes in the MSA minus number of crimes in the city) ÷ (population of the MSA minus population of the city)) x 100,000; n/a not avail.
Source: U.S. Department of Justice, FBI Uniform Crime Reports, 1977 - 1996

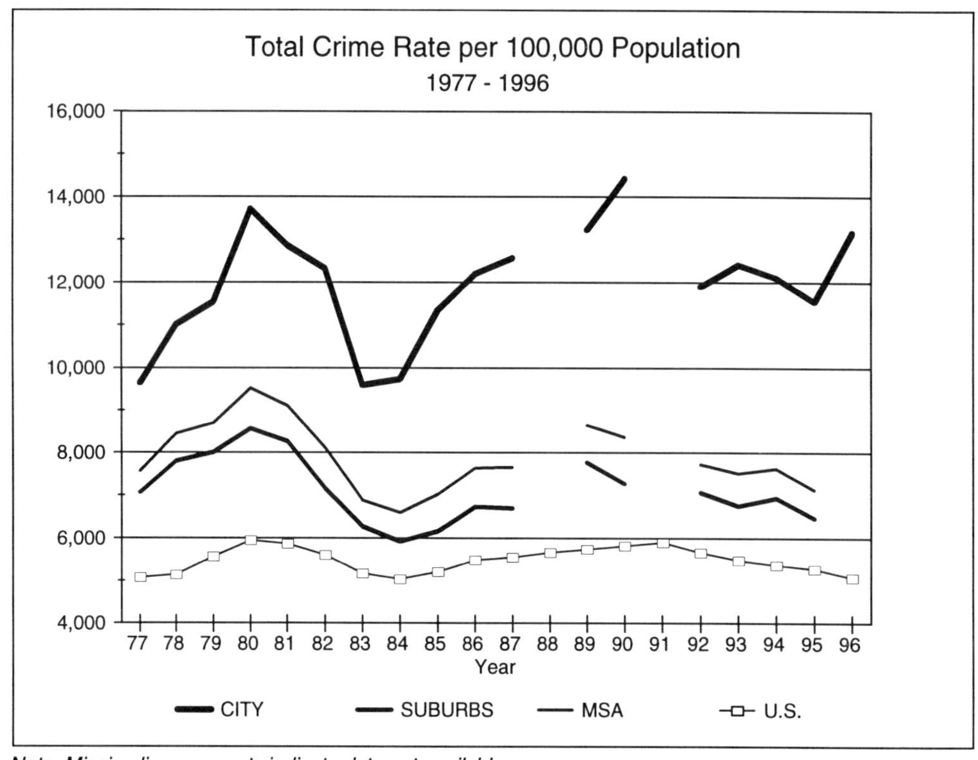

Note: Missing line segments indicate data not available.

Violent Crimes and Violent Crime Rates: 1977 - 1996

Year	Number				Rate per 100,000 population			
	City	Suburbs[2]	MSA[1]	U.S.	City	Suburbs[3]	MSA[1]	U.S.
1977	1,143	3,737	4,880	1,029,580	993.9	791.7	831.3	475.9
1978	1,620	3,702	5,322	1,085,550	1,372.9	779.7	897.7	497.8
1979	1,726	4,005	5,731	1,208,030	1,420.4	786.4	908.5	548.9
1980	2,350	4,747	7,097	1,344,520	1,838.7	837.5	1,021.7	596.6
1981	2,373	4,961	7,334	1,361,820	1,747.3	823.7	993.6	594.3
1982	2,662	4,568	7,230	1,322,390	1,913.0	740.2	956.0	571.1
1983	2,215	4,197	6,412	1,258,090	1,552.4	663.3	826.9	537.7
1984	2,387	4,083	6,470	1,273,280	1,698.4	621.1	810.8	539.2
1985	2,931	4,562	7,493	1,328,800	2,063.7	641.3	878.0	556.6
1986	3,416	5,779	9,195	1,489,170	2,341.6	790.8	1,048.9	617.7
1987	3,411	5,060	8,471	1,484,000	2,270.2	653.0	915.6	609.7
1988	n/a	n/a	n/a	1,566,220	n/a	n/a	n/a	637.2
1989	3,343	6,604	9,947	1,646,040	2,086.8	788.7	997.1	663.1
1990	4,109	7,427	11,536	1,820,130	2,494.9	817.9	1,075.4	731.8
1991	n/a	n/a	n/a	1,911,770	n/a	n/a	n/a	758.1
1992	3,232	10,571	13,803	1,932,270	1,882.4	956.5	1,081.0	757.5
1993	4,140	10,661	14,801	1,926,020	2,342.3	929.5	1,118.2	746.8
1994	4,109	11,106	15,215	1,857,670	2,279.1	949.3	1,126.9	713.6
1995	3,772	10,148	13,920	1,798,790	2,099.6	843.8	1,007.0	684.6
1996	4,002	n/a	n/a	1,682,280	2,191.5	n/a	n/a	634.1

Notes: Violent crimes include murder, forcible rape, robbery and aggravated assault; n/a not available; (1) Metropolitan Statistical Area - see Appendix A for areas included; (2) calculated by the editors using the following formula: (number of crimes in the MSA minus number of crimes in the city); (3) calculated by the editors using the following formula: ((number of crimes in the MSA minus number of crimes in the city) ÷ (population of the MSA minus population of the city)) x 100,000
Source: U.S. Department of Justice, FBI Uniform Crime Reports, 1977 - 1996

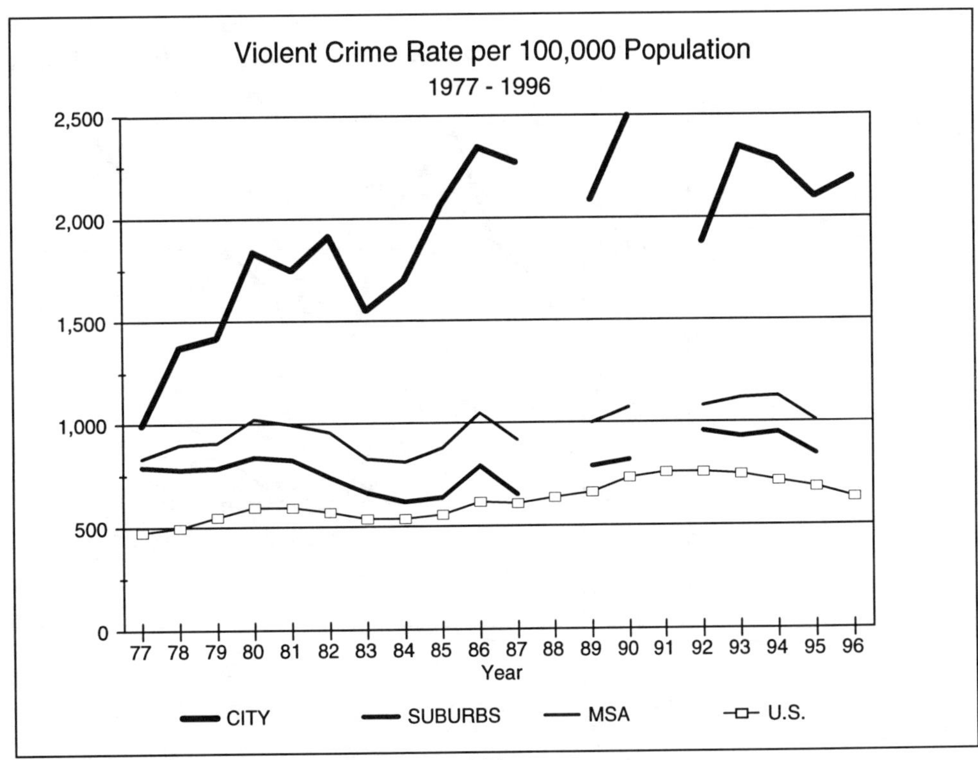

Note: Missing line segments indicate data not available.

Property Crimes and Property Crime Rates: 1977 - 1996

Year	Number				Rate per 100,000 population			
	City	Suburbs[2]	MSA[1]	U.S.	City	Suburbs[3]	MSA[1]	U.S.
1977	9,947	29,615	39,562	9,955,000	8,649.6	6,274.1	6,739.5	4,601.7
1978	11,372	33,313	44,685	10,123,400	9,637.3	7,015.9	7,537.7	4,642.5
1979	12,296	36,788	49,084	11,041,500	10,118.9	7,223.2	7,781.0	5,016.6
1980	15,182	43,792	58,974	12,063,700	11,878.5	7,725.7	8,489.8	5,353.3
1981	15,096	44,743	59,839	12,061,900	11,115.4	7,428.5	8,106.8	5,263.9
1982	14,492	39,618	54,110	11,652,000	10,414.5	6,419.7	7,154.7	5,032.5
1983	11,467	35,522	46,989	10,850,500	8,037.0	5,613.8	6,059.7	4,637.4
1984	11,291	34,816	46,107	10,608,500	8,034.0	5,295.9	5,778.1	4,492.1
1985	13,191	39,257	52,448	11,102,600	9,287.8	5,518.3	6,145.6	4,650.5
1986	14,381	43,376	57,757	11,722,700	9,858.0	5,935.8	6,588.5	4,862.6
1987	15,473	46,863	62,336	12,024,700	10,298.2	6,047.3	6,737.7	4,940.3
1988	n/a	n/a	n/a	12,356,900	n/a	n/a	n/a	5,027.1
1989	17,857	58,443	76,300	12,605,400	11,146.9	6,979.5	7,648.8	5,077.9
1990	19,641	58,525	78,166	12,655,500	11,925.8	6,445.1	7,286.5	5,088.5
1991	n/a	n/a	n/a	12,961,100	n/a	n/a	n/a	5,139.7
1992	17,201	67,561	84,762	12,505,900	10,018.4	6,113.0	6,638.1	4,902.7
1993	17,813	66,834	84,647	12,218,800	10,078.2	5,827.3	6,395.0	4,737.6
1994	17,727	70,050	87,777	12,131,900	9,832.6	5,987.9	6,501.3	4,660.0
1995	16,978	67,568	84,546	12,063,900	9,450.7	5,618.4	6,116.5	4,591.3
1996	20,053	n/a	n/a	11,791,300	10,981.0	n/a	n/a	4,444.8

Notes: Property crimes include burglary, larceny-theft and motor vehicle theft; n/a not available; (1) Metropolitan Statistical Area - see Appendix A for areas included; (2) calculated by the editors using the following formula: (number of crimes in the MSA minus number of crimes in the city); (3) calculated by the editors using the following formula: ((number of crimes in the MSA minus number of crimes in the city) ÷ (population of the MSA minus population of the city)) x 100,000
Source: U.S. Department of Justice, FBI Uniform Crime Reports, 1977 - 1996

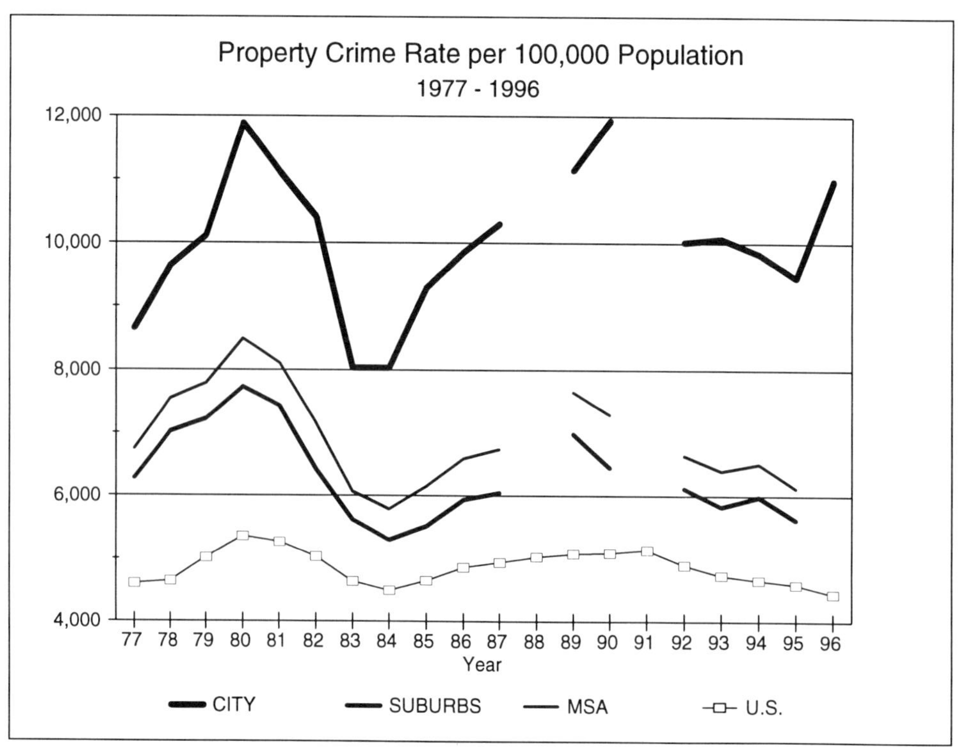

Note: Missing line segments indicate data not available.

Murders and Murder Rates: 1977 - 1996

Year	Number				Rate per 100,000 population			
	City	Suburbs[2]	MSA[1]	U.S.	City	Suburbs[3]	MSA[1]	U.S.
1977	15	29	44	19,120	13.0	6.1	7.5	8.8
1978	13	53	66	19,560	11.0	11.2	11.1	9.0
1979	17	44	61	21,460	14.0	8.6	9.7	9.7
1980	17	51	68	23,040	13.3	9.0	9.8	10.2
1981	25	55	80	22,520	18.4	9.1	10.8	9.8
1982	34	45	79	21,010	24.4	7.3	10.4	9.1
1983	14	41	55	19,310	9.8	6.5	7.1	8.3
1984	18	30	48	18,690	12.8	4.6	6.0	7.9
1985	24	54	78	18,980	16.9	7.6	9.1	7.9
1986	14	49	63	20,610	9.6	6.7	7.2	8.6
1987	27	55	82	20,100	18.0	7.1	8.9	8.3
1988	n/a	n/a	n/a	20,680	n/a	n/a	n/a	8.4
1989	19	49	68	21,500	11.9	5.9	6.8	8.7
1990	30	29	59	23,440	18.2	3.2	5.5	9.4
1991	n/a	n/a	n/a	24,700	n/a	n/a	n/a	9.8
1992	13	53	66	23,760	7.6	4.8	5.2	9.3
1993	15	54	69	24,530	8.5	4.7	5.2	9.5
1994	17	65	82	23,330	9.4	5.6	6.1	9.0
1995	19	60	79	21,610	10.6	5.0	5.7	8.2
1996	13	n/a	n/a	19,650	7.1	n/a	n/a	7.4

Notes: (1) Metropolitan Statistical Area - see Appendix A for areas included; (2) calculated by the editors using the following formula: (number of crimes in the MSA minus number of crimes in the city); (3) calculated by the editors using the following formula: ((number of crimes in the MSA minus number of crimes in the city) ÷ (population of the MSA minus population of the city)) x 100,000; n/a not avail.
Source: U.S. Department of Justice, FBI Uniform Crime Reports, 1977 - 1996

Forcible Rapes and Forcible Rape Rates: 1977 - 1996

Year	Number				Rate per 100,000 population			
	City	Suburbs[2]	MSA[1]	U.S.	City	Suburbs[3]	MSA[1]	U.S.
1977	85	301	386	63,500	73.9	63.8	65.8	29.4
1978	107	259	366	67,610	90.7	54.5	61.7	31.0
1979	133	295	428	76,390	109.5	57.9	67.8	34.7
1980	190	338	528	82,990	148.7	59.6	76.0	36.8
1981	154	340	494	82,500	113.4	56.4	66.9	36.0
1982	160	328	488	78,770	115.0	53.1	64.5	34.0
1983	141	283	424	78,920	98.8	44.7	54.7	33.7
1984	146	237	383	84,230	103.9	36.1	48.0	35.7
1985	154	276	430	88,670	108.4	38.8	50.4	37.1
1986	172	279	451	91,460	117.9	38.2	51.4	37.9
1987	181	289	470	91,110	120.5	37.3	50.8	37.4
1988	n/a	n/a	n/a	92,490	n/a	n/a	n/a	37.6
1989	176	338	514	94,500	109.9	40.4	51.5	38.1
1990	181	281	462	102,560	109.9	30.9	43.1	41.2
1991	n/a	n/a	n/a	106,590	n/a	n/a	n/a	42.3
1992	140	538	678	109,060	81.5	48.7	53.1	42.8
1993	209	540	749	106,010	118.2	47.1	56.6	41.1
1994	144	560	704	102,220	79.9	47.9	52.1	39.3
1995	141	521	662	97,470	78.5	43.3	47.9	37.1
1996	165	n/a	n/a	95,770	90.4	n/a	n/a	36.1

Notes: (1) Metropolitan Statistical Area - see Appendix A for areas included; (2) calculated by the editors using the following formula: (number of crimes in the MSA minus number of crimes in the city); (3) calculated by the editors using the following formula: ((number of crimes in the MSA minus number of crimes in the city) ÷ (population of the MSA minus population of the city)) x 100,000; n/a not avail.
Source: U.S. Department of Justice, FBI Uniform Crime Reports, 1977 - 1996

Robberies and Robbery Rates: 1977 - 1996

Year	Number				Rate per 100,000 population			
	City	Suburbs[2]	MSA[1]	U.S.	City	Suburbs[3]	MSA[1]	U.S.
1977	274	564	838	412,610	238.3	119.5	142.8	190.7
1978	410	701	1,111	426,930	347.5	147.6	187.4	195.8
1979	496	848	1,344	480,700	408.2	166.5	213.1	218.4
1980	742	1,102	1,844	565,840	580.5	194.4	265.5	251.1
1981	885	1,407	2,292	592,910	651.6	233.6	310.5	258.7
1982	809	1,229	2,038	553,130	581.4	199.1	269.5	238.9
1983	768	999	1,767	506,570	538.3	157.9	227.9	216.5
1984	802	939	1,741	485,010	570.7	142.8	218.2	205.4
1985	902	1,012	1,914	497,870	635.1	142.3	224.3	208.5
1986	1,229	1,604	2,833	542,780	842.5	219.5	323.2	225.1
1987	1,029	1,445	2,474	517,700	684.9	186.5	267.4	212.7
1988	n/a	n/a	n/a	542,970	n/a	n/a	n/a	220.9
1989	1,189	1,860	3,049	578,330	742.2	222.1	305.7	233.0
1990	1,449	1,579	3,028	639,270	879.8	173.9	282.3	257.0
1991	n/a	n/a	n/a	687,730	n/a	n/a	n/a	272.7
1992	808	2,414	3,222	672,480	470.6	218.4	252.3	263.6
1993	1,107	2,133	3,240	659,870	626.3	186.0	244.8	255.9
1994	1,095	2,455	3,550	618,950	607.4	209.9	262.9	237.7
1995	1,048	2,333	3,381	580,510	583.4	194.0	244.6	220.9
1996	1,080	n/a	n/a	537,050	591.4	n/a	n/a	202.4

Notes: (1) Metropolitan Statistical Area - see Appendix A for areas included; (2) calculated by the editors using the following formula: (number of crimes in the MSA minus number of crimes in the city); (3) calculated by the editors using the following formula: ((number of crimes in the MSA minus number of crimes in the city) ÷ (population of the MSA minus population of the city)) x 100,000; n/a not avail.
Source: U.S. Department of Justice, FBI Uniform Crime Reports, 1977 - 1996

Aggravated Assaults and Aggravated Assault Rates: 1977 - 1996

Year	Number				Rate per 100,000 population			
	City	Suburbs[2]	MSA[1]	U.S.	City	Suburbs[3]	MSA[1]	U.S.
1977	769	2,843	3,612	534,350	668.7	602.3	615.3	247.0
1978	1,090	2,689	3,779	571,460	923.7	566.3	637.5	262.1
1979	1,080	2,818	3,898	629,480	888.8	553.3	617.9	286.0
1980	1,401	3,256	4,657	672,650	1,096.1	574.4	670.4	298.5
1981	1,309	3,159	4,468	663,900	963.8	524.5	605.3	289.7
1982	1,659	2,966	4,625	669,480	1,192.2	480.6	611.5	289.2
1983	1,292	2,874	4,166	653,290	905.5	454.2	537.2	279.2
1984	1,421	2,877	4,298	685,350	1,011.1	437.6	538.6	290.2
1985	1,851	3,220	5,071	723,250	1,303.3	452.6	594.2	302.9
1986	2,001	3,847	5,848	834,320	1,371.7	526.4	667.1	346.1
1987	2,174	3,271	5,445	855,090	1,446.9	422.1	588.5	351.3
1988	n/a	n/a	n/a	910,090	n/a	n/a	n/a	370.2
1989	1,959	4,357	6,316	951,710	1,222.9	520.3	633.2	383.4
1990	2,449	5,538	7,987	1,054,860	1,487.0	609.9	744.5	424.1
1991	n/a	n/a	n/a	1,092,740	n/a	n/a	n/a	433.3
1992	2,271	7,566	9,837	1,126,970	1,322.7	684.6	770.4	441.8
1993	2,809	7,934	10,743	1,135,610	1,589.3	691.8	811.6	440.3
1994	2,853	8,026	10,879	1,113,180	1,582.5	686.1	805.8	427.6
1995	2,564	7,234	9,798	1,099,210	1,427.2	601.5	708.8	418.3
1996	2,744	n/a	n/a	1,029,810	1,502.6	n/a	n/a	388.2

Notes: (1) Metropolitan Statistical Area - see Appendix A for areas included; (2) calculated by the editors using the following formula: (number of crimes in the MSA minus number of crimes in the city); (3) calculated by the editors using the following formula: ((number of crimes in the MSA minus number of crimes in the city) ÷ (population of the MSA minus population of the city)) x 100,000; n/a not avail.
Source: U.S. Department of Justice, FBI Uniform Crime Reports, 1977 - 1996

Burglaries and Burglary Rates: 1977 - 1996

Year	Number				Rate per 100,000 population			
	City	Suburbs[2]	MSA[1]	U.S.	City	Suburbs[3]	MSA[1]	U.S.
1977	2,957	9,811	12,768	3,071,500	2,571.3	2,078.5	2,175.0	1,419.8
1978	3,372	11,175	14,547	3,128,300	2,857.6	2,353.5	2,453.9	1,434.6
1979	3,787	12,219	16,006	3,327,700	3,116.5	2,399.2	2,537.3	1,511.9
1980	5,264	16,905	22,169	3,795,200	4,118.6	2,982.4	3,191.4	1,684.1
1981	5,180	17,373	22,553	3,779,700	3,814.1	2,884.4	3,055.4	1,649.5
1982	4,473	14,043	18,516	3,447,100	3,214.5	2,275.5	2,448.3	1,488.8
1983	3,490	11,406	14,896	3,129,900	2,446.1	1,802.6	1,921.0	1,337.7
1984	3,790	11,178	14,968	2,984,400	2,696.7	1,700.3	1,875.8	1,263.7
1985	4,011	11,760	15,771	3,073,300	2,824.2	1,653.1	1,848.0	1,287.3
1986	4,335	13,162	17,497	3,241,400	2,971.6	1,801.2	1,995.9	1,344.6
1987	4,515	15,519	20,034	3,236,200	3,005.0	2,002.6	2,165.4	1,329.6
1988	n/a	n/a	n/a	3,218,100	n/a	n/a	n/a	1,309.2
1989	5,854	19,806	25,660	3,168,200	3,654.3	2,365.3	2,572.3	1,276.3
1990	5,453	18,117	23,570	3,073,900	3,311.0	1,995.1	2,197.2	1,235.9
1991	n/a	n/a	n/a	3,157,200	n/a	n/a	n/a	1,252.0
1992	4,497	19,652	24,149	2,979,900	2,619.2	1,778.1	1,891.2	1,168.2
1993	4,352	19,917	24,269	2,834,800	2,462.3	1,736.6	1,833.5	1,099.2
1994	3,975	18,999	22,974	2,712,800	2,204.8	1,624.0	1,701.6	1,042.0
1995	3,862	17,052	20,914	2,593,800	2,149.7	1,417.9	1,513.0	987.1
1996	4,418	n/a	n/a	2,501,500	2,419.3	n/a	n/a	943.0

Notes: (1) Metropolitan Statistical Area - see Appendix A for areas included; (2) calculated by the editors using the following formula: (number of crimes in the MSA minus number of crimes in the city); (3) calculated by the editors using the following formula: ((number of crimes in the MSA minus number of crimes in the city) ÷ (population of the MSA minus population of the city)) x 100,000; n/a not avail.
Source: U.S. Department of Justice, FBI Uniform Crime Reports, 1977 - 1996

Larceny-Thefts and Larceny-Theft Rates: 1977 - 1996

Year	Number				Rate per 100,000 population			
	City	Suburbs[2]	MSA[1]	U.S.	City	Suburbs[3]	MSA[1]	U.S.
1977	6,451	18,289	24,740	5,905,700	5,609.6	3,874.6	4,214.5	2,729.9
1978	7,318	20,356	27,674	5,991,000	6,201.7	4,287.1	4,668.2	2,747.4
1979	7,740	22,535	30,275	6,601,000	6,369.6	4,424.7	4,799.3	2,999.1
1980	9,022	24,728	33,750	7,136,900	7,058.9	4,362.5	4,858.6	3,167.0
1981	9,061	25,312	34,373	7,194,400	6,671.7	4,202.4	4,656.8	3,139.7
1982	9,184	23,462	32,646	7,142,500	6,600.0	3,801.8	4,316.6	3,084.8
1983	7,276	22,072	29,348	6,712,800	5,099.6	3,488.2	3,784.7	2,868.9
1984	6,817	21,496	28,313	6,591,900	4,850.5	3,269.8	3,548.2	2,791.3
1985	8,306	25,136	33,442	6,926,400	5,848.3	3,533.3	3,918.6	2,901.2
1986	9,134	27,501	36,635	7,257,200	6,261.2	3,763.4	4,179.1	3,010.3
1987	9,853	28,227	38,080	7,499,900	6,557.7	3,642.5	4,115.9	3,081.3
1988	n/a	n/a	n/a	7,705,900	n/a	n/a	n/a	3,134.9
1989	10,220	33,406	43,626	7,872,400	6,379.6	3,989.5	4,373.3	3,171.3
1990	12,662	34,838	47,500	7,945,700	7,688.2	3,836.6	4,427.9	3,194.8
1991	n/a	n/a	n/a	8,142,200	n/a	n/a	n/a	3,228.8
1992	10,816	41,693	52,509	7,915,200	6,299.6	3,772.4	4,112.2	3,103.0
1993	11,655	40,894	52,549	7,820,900	6,594.1	3,565.6	3,970.0	3,032.4
1994	11,631	44,428	56,059	7,879,800	6,451.3	3,797.7	4,152.1	3,026.7
1995	11,255	44,411	55,666	7,997,700	6,265.0	3,692.9	4,027.2	3,043.8
1996	13,444	n/a	n/a	7,894,600	7,361.9	n/a	n/a	2,975.9

Notes: (1) Metropolitan Statistical Area - see Appendix A for areas included; (2) calculated by the editors using the following formula: (number of crimes in the MSA minus number of crimes in the city); (3) calculated by the editors using the following formula: ((number of crimes in the MSA minus number of crimes in the city) ÷ (population of the MSA minus population of the city)) x 100,000; n/a not avail.
Source: U.S. Department of Justice, FBI Uniform Crime Reports, 1977 - 1996

Motor Vehicle Thefts and Motor Vehicle Theft Rates: 1977 - 1996

Year	Number				Rate per 100,000 population			
	City	Suburbs[2]	MSA[1]	U.S.	City	Suburbs[3]	MSA[1]	U.S.
1977	539	1,515	2,054	977,700	468.7	321.0	349.9	451.9
1978	682	1,782	2,464	1,004,100	578.0	375.3	415.6	460.5
1979	769	2,034	2,803	1,112,800	632.8	399.4	444.3	505.6
1980	896	2,159	3,055	1,131,700	701.0	380.9	439.8	502.2
1981	855	2,058	2,913	1,087,800	629.5	341.7	394.6	474.7
1982	835	2,113	2,948	1,062,400	600.1	342.4	389.8	458.8
1983	701	2,044	2,745	1,007,900	491.3	323.0	354.0	430.8
1984	684	2,142	2,826	1,032,200	486.7	325.8	354.2	437.1
1985	874	2,361	3,235	1,102,900	615.4	331.9	379.1	462.0
1986	912	2,713	3,625	1,224,100	625.2	371.3	413.5	507.8
1987	1,105	3,117	4,222	1,288,700	735.4	402.2	456.3	529.4
1988	n/a	n/a	n/a	1,432,900	n/a	n/a	n/a	582.9
1989	1,783	5,231	7,014	1,564,800	1,113.0	624.7	703.1	630.4
1990	1,526	5,570	7,096	1,635,900	926.6	613.4	661.5	657.8
1991	n/a	n/a	n/a	1,661,700	n/a	n/a	n/a	659.0
1992	1,888	6,216	8,104	1,610,800	1,099.6	562.4	634.7	631.5
1993	1,806	6,023	7,829	1,563,100	1,021.8	525.2	591.5	606.1
1994	2,121	6,623	8,744	1,539,300	1,176.5	566.1	647.6	591.3
1995	1,861	6,105	7,966	1,472,400	1,035.9	507.6	576.3	560.4
1996	2,191	n/a	n/a	1,395,200	1,199.8	n/a	n/a	525.9

Notes: (1) Metropolitan Statistical Area - see Appendix A for areas included; (2) calculated by the editors using the following formula: (number of crimes in the MSA minus number of crimes in the city); (3) calculated by the editors using the following formula: ((number of crimes in the MSA minus number of crimes in the city) ÷ (population of the MSA minus population of the city)) x 100,000; n/a not avail.
Source: U.S. Department of Justice, FBI Uniform Crime Reports, 1977 - 1996

HATE CRIMES

Criminal Incidents by Bias Motivation

Area	Race	Ethnicity	Religion	Sexual Orientation
Orlando	4	0	0	6

Notes: Figures include both violent and property crimes. Law enforcement agencies must have submitted data for at least one quarter of calendar year 1995 to be included in this report, therefore figures shown may not represent complete 12-month totals; n/a not available
Source: U.S. Department of Justice, FBI Uniform Crime Reports, Hate Crime Statistics 1995

LAW ENFORCEMENT

Full-Time Law Enforcement Employees

Jurisdiction	Police Employees			Police Officers per 100,000 population
	Total	Officers	Civilians	
Orlando	859	609	250	333.5

Notes: Data as of October 31, 1996
Source: U.S. Department of Justice, FBI Uniform Crime Reports, 1996

CORRECTIONS

Federal Correctional Facilities

Type	Year Opened	Security Level	Sex of Inmates	Rated Capacity	Population on 7/1/95	Number of Staff
None listed						

Notes: Data as of 1995
Source: Bureau of Justice Statistics, Sourcebook of Criminal Justice Statistics Online

City/County/Regional Correctional Facilities

Name	Year Opened	Year Renov.	Rated Capacity	1995 Pop.	Number of COs[1]	Number of Staff	ACA[2] Accred.
Orange Co Corrections Div	1971	--	3,329	2,861	788	1,380	Yes

Notes: Data as of April 1996; (1) Correctional Officers; (2) American Correctional Assn. Accreditation
Source: American Correctional Association, 1996-1998 National Jail and Adult Detention Directory

Private Adult Correctional Facilities

Name	Date Opened	Rated Capacity	Present Pop.	Security Level	Facility Construct.	Expans. Plans	ACA[1] Accred.
None listed							

Notes: Data as of December 1996; (1) American Correctional Association Accreditation
Source: University of Florida, Center for Studies in Criminology and Law, Private Adult Correctional Facility Census, 10th Ed., March 15, 1997

Characteristics of Shock Incarceration Programs

Jurisdiction	Year Program Began	Number of Camps	Average Num. of Inmates	Number of Beds	Program Length	Voluntary/ Mandatory
Florida	1987	1	94	112	120 days min.	n/a

Note: Data as of July 1996;
Source: Sourcebook of Criminal Justice Statistics Online

INMATES AND HIV/AIDS

HIV Testing Policies for Inmates

Jurisdiction	All Inmates at Some Time	All Convicted Inmates at Admission	Random Samples While in Custody	High-risk Groups	Upon Inmate Request	Upon Court Order	Upon Involvement in Incident
Orange Co.[1]	No	No	No	No	Yes	Yes	Yes

Notes: (1) All facilities reported following the same testing policy or authorities reported the policy to be jurisdiction-wide
Source: HIV in Prisons and Jails, 1993 (released August 1995)

Inmates Known to be Positive for HIV

Jurisdiction	Number of Jail Inmates in Facilities Providing Data	Type of HIV Infection/AIDS Cases				HIV/AIDS Cases as a Percent of Tot. Custody Pop.
		Total	Asymptomatic	Symptomatic	Confirmed AIDS	
Orange Co.	3,096	51	14	28	9	1.6

Source: HIV in Prisons and Jails, 1993 (released August, 1995)

DEATH PENALTY

Death Penalty Statistics

State	Prisoners Executed		Prisoners Under Sentence of Death					Avg. No. of Years on Death Row[4]
	1930-1995	1996[1]	Total[2]	White[3]	Black[3]	Hisp.	Women	
Florida	206	2	362	228	134	35	6	6.9

Notes: Data as of 12/31/95 unless otherwise noted; (1) Data as of 7/31/97; (2) Includes persons of other races; (3) Includes people of Hispanic origin; (4) Covers prisoners sentenced 1974 through 1995
Source: Bureau of Justice Statistics, Capital Punishment 1995 (released 12/96); Death Penalty Information Center Web Site, 9/30/97

Capital Offenses and Methods of Execution

Capital Offenses in Florida	Minimum Age for Imposition of Death Penalty	Mentally Retarded Excluded	Methods of Execution[1]
First-degree murder; felony murder; capital drug-trafficking.	16	No	Electrocution

Notes: Data as of 12/31/95 unless otherwise noted; (1) Data as of 7/31/97
Source: Bureau of Justice Statistics, Capital Punishment 1995 (released 12/96); Death Penalty Information Center Web Site, 9/30/97

LAWS

Statutory Provisions Relating to the Purchase, Ownership and Use of Handguns

Jurisdiction	Instant Background Check	Federal Waiting Period Applies[1]	State Waiting Period (days)	License or Permit to Purchase	Registration	Record of Sale Sent to Police	Concealed Carry Law
Florida	Yes[a]	No	3[b,c]	No	No	No	Yes[d]

Note: Data as of 1996; (1) The Federal 5-day waiting period for handgun purchases applies to states that don't have instant background checks, waiting period requirements, or licensing procedures exempting them from the Federal requirement; (a) Concealed firearm carry permit holders are exempt from Instant Check; (b) The State waiting period does not apply to a person holding a valid permit or license to carry a firearm; (c) Purchases from licensed dealers only; (d) "Shall issue" permit system, liberally administered discretion by local authorities over permit issuance, or no permit required
Source: Sourcebook of Criminal Justice Statistics Online

Statutory Provisions Relating to Alcohol Use and Driving

Jurisdiction	Drinking Age	Blood Alcohol Concentration Levels as Evidence in State Courts[1]		Open Container Law[1]	Anti-Consumption Law[1]	Dram Shop Law[1]
		Illegal per se at 0.10%	Presumption at 0.10%			
Florida	21	(a)	(a,b)	Yes	No	Yes[c]

Note: Data as of January 1, 1997; (1) See Appendix C for an explanation of terms; (a) 0.08%; (b) Constitutes prima facie evidence; (c) Applies only to the actions of intoxicated minors or persons known to be habitually addicted to alcohol
Source: Sourcebook of Criminal Justice Statistics Online

Statutory Provisions Relating to Curfews

Jurisdiction	Year Enacted	Latest Revision	Age Group(s)	Curfew Provisions
Orlando	1994	-	17 and under	Special downtown tourist dist. curfew: midnight to 5 am every night

Note: Data as of February 1996
Source: Sourcebook of Criminal Justice Statistics Online

Statutory Provisions Relating to Hate Crimes

Jurisdiction	Bias-Motivated Violence and Intimidation						Institutional Vandalism
	Civil Action	Criminal Penalty					
		Race/Religion/Ethnicity	Sexual Orientation	Mental/Physical Disability	Gender	Age	
Florida	Yes	Yes	Yes	No	No	No	Yes

Source: Anti-Defamation League, 1997 Hate Crimes Laws

Philadelphia, Pennsylvania

OVERVIEW

The total crime rate for the city increased 71.3% between 1977 and 1996. During that same period, the violent crime rate increased 125.6% and the property crime rate increased 60.3%.

Among violent crimes, the rates for: Murders increased 48.9%; Forcible Rapes increased 6.2%; Robberies increased 157.4%; and Aggravated Assaults increased 99.0%.

Among property crimes, the rates for: Burglaries decreased 1.3%; Larceny-Thefts increased 77.0%; and Motor Vehicle Thefts increased 117.5%.

ANTI-CRIME PROGRAMS

Some of the city's numerous programs include:

- District mini-stations—which are police substations staffed by police and volunteer community members.
- Drug Task Force and Weed & Seed Program—these identify and target areas of the city which are in need of additional police drug enforcement efforts and other city agency efforts.
- Police/Clergy Program—clergy members ride along with officers in an attempt to ease community tensions.
- Footbeat Program—increased footbeats make police more accessible to the community.
- D.A.R.E. (Drug Abuse Resistance Education Program)—classroom instruction regarding the dangers of drug abuse is provided to public and private school children.
- Youth Aid Panels—selected community volunteers mediate non-judicial punishment to juvenile offenders who commit certain designated crimes. It serves as an alternative to the traditional juvenile system and helps to alleviate court backup.
- G.R.E.A.T. (Gang Resistance Education And Training)—classroom instruction regarding anti-violence and anti-gang curriculum.
- Cops Ahead Program—federally funded program for footbeat officers, deployed city-wide to reduce drug trafficking and other illict activity.
- Town Watch—city patrol teams provide the Police Department with additional eyes and ears to ensure safer neighborhoods.
- D.U.I. Sobriety Checkpoints—designed to reduce D.U.I. incidents through pre-scheduled routine car stops on major highways by specially trained police officers and supervisors.
- Anti-Graffiti Program—police officers from each division are assigned to enforce vandalism laws.
- Bicycle Patrol—instituted in the Center City District to provide a conspicuous police presence, increase mobility, and effectiveness.
- S.A.V.E. Program (Stolen Auto Verification Efforts)—voluntary program whereby the owner gives the police permission to stop his or her vehicle during certain hours of the day when the vehicle is not normally being operated.
- Citizen's Police Academy—citizens take part in a program designed to familiarize the community with the Police Department's training practices.
  Philadelphia Police Department, 6/97

CRIME RISK

Your Chances of Becoming a Victim[1]

Area	Any Crime	Violent Crime					Property Crime			
		Any	Murder	Forcible Rape[2]	Robbery	Aggrav. Assault	Any	Burglary	Larceny -Theft	Motor Vehicle Theft
City	1:14	1:65	1:3,692	1:1,162	1:99	1:226	1:19	1:94	1:35	1:66

Note: (1) Figures have been calculated by dividing the population of the city by the number of crimes reported to the FBI during 1996 and are expressed as odds (eg. 1:20 should be read as 1 in 20). (2) Figures have been calculated by dividing the female population of the city by the number of forcible rapes reported to the FBI during 1996. The female population of the city was estimated by calculating the ratio of females to males reported in the 1990 Census and applying that ratio to 1996 population estimate.
Source: FBI Uniform Crime Reports 1996

CRIME STATISTICS

Total Crimes and Total Crime Rates: 1977 - 1996

Year	Number				Rate per 100,000 population			
	City	Suburbs[2]	MSA[1]	U.S.	City	Suburbs[3]	MSA[1]	U.S.
1977	71,827	126,275	198,102	10,984,500	4,039.8	4,034.3	4,036.3	5,077.6
1978	72,948	129,763	202,711	11,209,000	4,156.6	4,106.5	4,124.4	5,140.3
1979	82,586	138,446	221,032	12,249,500	4,699.4	4,603.2	4,638.7	5,565.5
1980	101,144	150,724	251,868	13,408,300	6,016.3	4,991.2	5,357.8	5,950.0
1981	100,592	149,972	250,564	13,423,800	5,963.4	4,941.8	5,306.7	5,858.2
1982	94,641	138,765	233,406	12,974,400	5,608.2	4,564.7	4,937.2	5,603.6
1983	89,764	125,031	214,795	12,108,600	5,304.1	4,100.6	4,530.1	5,175.0
1984	82,529	115,662	198,191	11,881,800	4,949.1	3,739.0	4,162.8	5,031.3
1985	83,667	116,436	200,103	12,431,400	5,101.3	3,731.6	4,203.5	5,207.1
1986	86,094	118,048	204,142	13,211,900	5,233.2	3,766.1	4,271.1	5,480.4
1987	94,575	120,028	214,603	13,508,700	5,734.0	3,752.5	4,426.6	5,550.0
1988	100,051	114,406	214,457	13,923,100	6,037.0	3,526.1	4,375.0	5,664.2
1989	115,602	115,674	231,276	14,251,400	6,996.9	3,524.1	4,686.9	5,741.0
1990	114,032	119,378	233,410	14,475,600	7,191.8	3,649.2	4,805.8	5,820.3
1991	109,139	128,082	237,221	14,872,900	6,835.3	3,893.3	4,854.6	5,897.8
1992	97,359	123,501	220,860	14,438,200	6,071.1	3,666.5	4,442.1	5,660.2
1993	97,659	118,770	216,429	14,144,800	6,262.1	3,483.2	4,355.3	5,484.4
1994	100,417	119,586	220,003	13,989,500	6,434.6	3,502.6	4,422.3	5,373.5
1995	108,278	n/a	n/a	13,862,700	7,077.7	n/a	n/a	5,275.9
1996	105,766	124,232	229,998	13,473,600	6,920.0	3,613.2	4,630.8	5,078.9

Notes: (1) Metropolitan Statistical Area - see Appendix A for areas included; (2) calculated by the editors using the following formula: (number of crimes in the MSA minus number of crimes in the city); (3) calculated by the editors using the following formula: ((number of crimes in the MSA minus number of crimes in the city) ÷ (population of the MSA minus population of the city)) x 100,000; n/a not avail.
Source: U.S. Department of Justice, FBI Uniform Crime Reports, 1977 - 1996

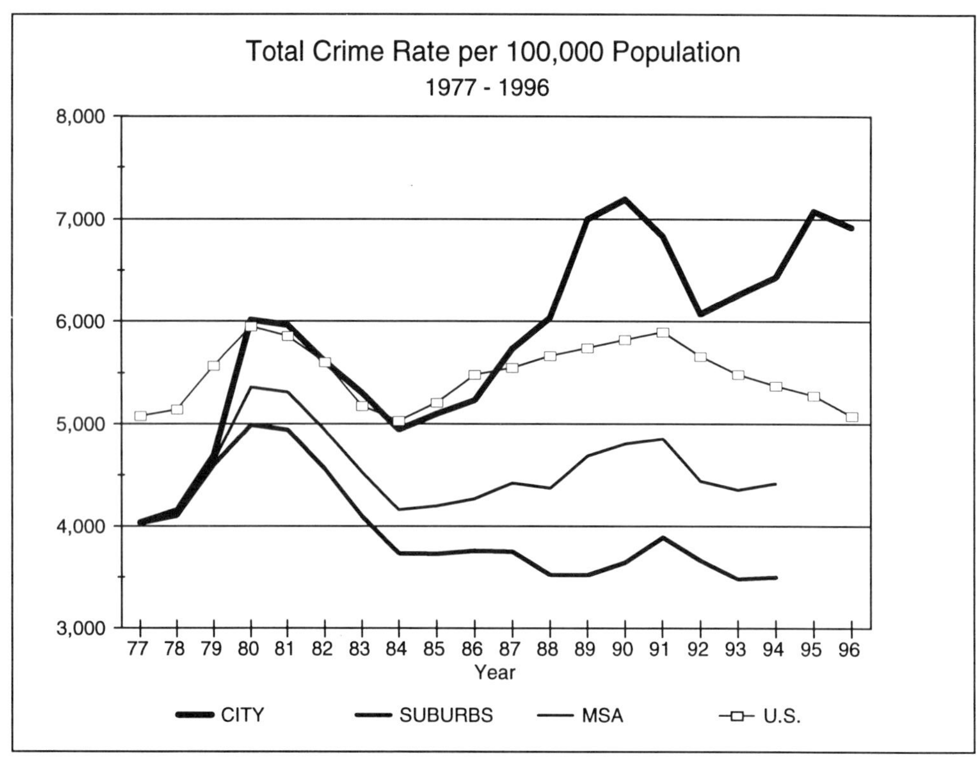

Note: Missing line segments indicate data not available.

Violent Crimes and Violent Crime Rates: 1977 - 1996

Year	Number				Rate per 100,000 population			
	City	Suburbs[2]	MSA[1]	U.S.	City	Suburbs[3]	MSA[1]	U.S.
1977	12,047	9,073	21,120	1,029,580	677.6	289.9	430.3	475.9
1978	12,368	9,908	22,276	1,085,550	704.7	313.6	453.2	497.8
1979	14,537	10,664	25,201	1,208,030	827.2	354.6	528.9	548.9
1980	17,299	12,690	29,989	1,344,520	1,029.0	420.2	637.9	596.6
1981	17,616	12,080	29,696	1,361,820	1,044.3	398.1	628.9	594.3
1982	17,509	12,172	29,681	1,322,390	1,037.5	400.4	627.8	571.1
1983	16,973	11,240	28,213	1,258,090	1,002.9	368.6	595.0	537.7
1984	15,600	11,012	26,612	1,273,280	935.5	356.0	559.0	539.2
1985	16,209	11,019	27,228	1,328,800	988.3	353.1	572.0	556.6
1986	17,207	11,901	29,108	1,489,170	1,045.9	379.7	609.0	617.7
1987	17,398	12,477	29,875	1,484,000	1,054.8	390.1	616.2	609.7
1988	17,159	12,509	29,668	1,566,220	1,035.4	385.5	605.2	637.2
1989	18,054	11,974	30,028	1,646,040	1,092.7	364.8	608.5	663.1
1990	21,387	14,328	35,715	1,820,130	1,348.8	438.0	735.3	731.8
1991	22,481	14,606	37,087	1,911,770	1,408.0	444.0	759.0	758.1
1992	19,067	14,399	33,466	1,932,270	1,189.0	427.5	673.1	757.5
1993	19,576	13,332	32,908	1,926,020	1,255.2	391.0	662.2	746.8
1994	20,638	13,868	34,506	1,857,670	1,322.5	406.2	693.6	713.6
1995	21,972	n/a	n/a	1,798,790	1,436.2	n/a	n/a	684.6
1996	23,367	13,051	36,418	1,682,280	1,528.9	379.6	733.2	634.1

Notes: Violent crimes include murder, forcible rape, robbery and aggravated assault; n/a not available; (1) Metropolitan Statistical Area - see Appendix A for areas included; (2) calculated by the editors using the following formula: (number of crimes in the MSA minus number of crimes in the city); (3) calculated by the editors using the following formula: ((number of crimes in the MSA minus number of crimes in the city) ÷ (population of the MSA minus population of the city)) x 100,000
Source: U.S. Department of Justice, FBI Uniform Crime Reports, 1977 - 1996

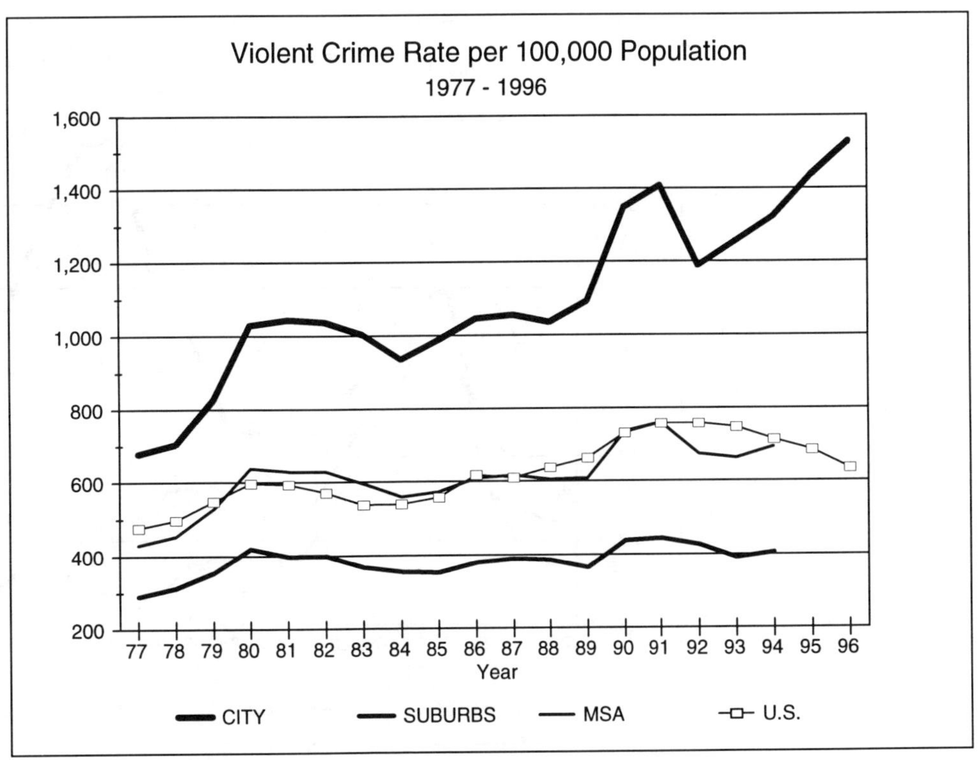

Note: Missing line segments indicate data not available.

Property Crimes and Property Crime Rates: 1977 - 1996

Year	Number				Rate per 100,000 population			
	City	Suburbs[2]	MSA[1]	U.S.	City	Suburbs[3]	MSA[1]	U.S.
1977	59,780	117,202	176,982	9,955,000	3,362.2	3,744.5	3,606.0	4,601.7
1978	60,580	119,855	180,435	10,123,400	3,451.9	3,793.0	3,671.2	4,642.5
1979	68,049	127,782	195,831	11,041,500	3,872.2	4,248.6	4,109.8	5,016.6
1980	83,845	138,034	221,879	12,063,700	4,987.3	4,570.9	4,719.8	5,353.3
1981	82,976	137,892	220,868	12,061,900	4,919.0	4,543.7	4,677.8	5,263.9
1982	77,132	126,593	203,725	11,652,000	4,570.6	4,164.3	4,309.3	5,032.5
1983	72,791	113,791	186,582	10,850,500	4,301.1	3,731.9	3,935.1	4,637.4
1984	66,929	104,650	171,579	10,608,500	4,013.6	3,383.0	3,603.9	4,492.1
1985	67,458	105,417	172,875	11,102,600	4,113.0	3,378.5	3,631.6	4,650.5
1986	68,887	106,147	175,034	11,722,700	4,187.3	3,386.4	3,662.1	4,862.6
1987	77,177	107,551	184,728	12,024,700	4,679.2	3,362.4	3,810.4	4,940.3
1988	82,892	101,897	184,789	12,356,900	5,001.7	3,140.5	3,769.8	5,027.1
1989	97,548	103,700	201,248	12,605,400	5,904.2	3,159.3	4,078.4	5,077.9
1990	92,645	105,050	197,695	12,655,500	5,843.0	3,211.3	4,070.4	5,088.5
1991	86,658	113,476	200,134	12,961,100	5,427.3	3,449.3	4,095.6	5,139.7
1992	78,292	109,102	187,394	12,505,900	4,882.1	3,239.0	3,769.0	4,902.7
1993	78,083	105,438	183,521	12,218,800	5,006.8	3,092.2	3,693.1	4,737.6
1994	79,779	105,718	185,497	12,131,900	5,112.2	3,096.4	3,728.7	4,660.0
1995	86,306	n/a	n/a	12,063,900	5,641.5	n/a	n/a	4,591.3
1996	82,399	111,181	193,580	11,791,300	5,391.2	3,233.6	3,897.5	4,444.8

Notes: Property crimes include burglary, larceny-theft and motor vehicle theft; n/a not available; (1) Metropolitan Statistical Area - see Appendix A for areas included; (2) calculated by the editors using the following formula: (number of crimes in the MSA minus number of crimes in the city); (3) calculated by the editors using the following formula: ((number of crimes in the MSA minus number of crimes in the city) ÷ (population of the MSA minus population of the city)) x 100,000
Source: U.S. Department of Justice, FBI Uniform Crime Reports, 1977 - 1996

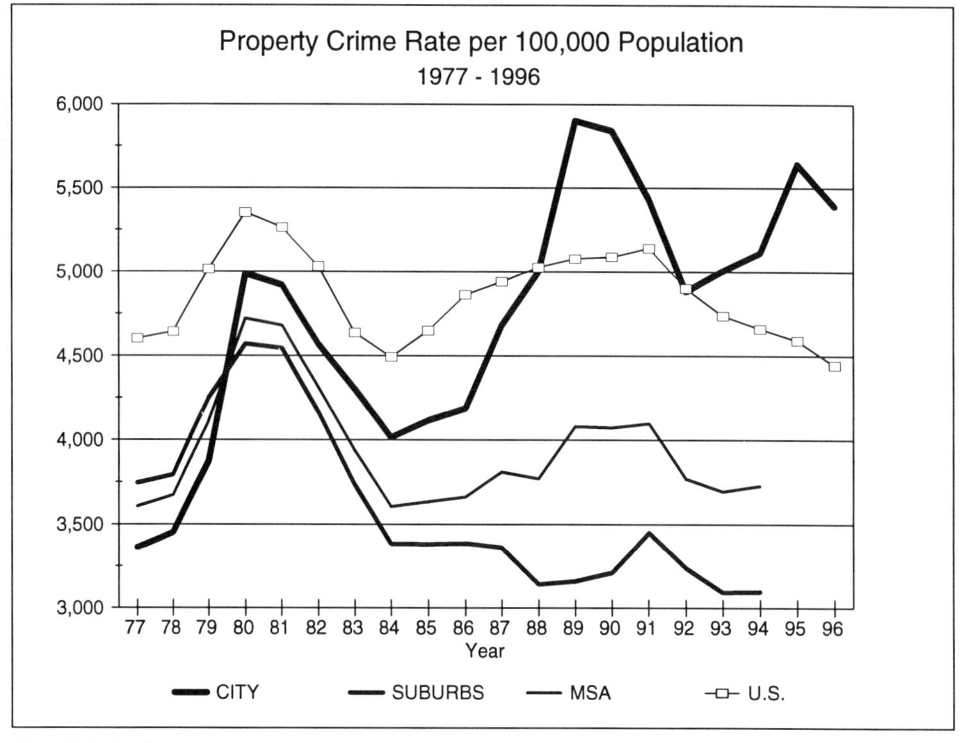

Note: Missing line segments indicate data not available.

Murders and Murder Rates: 1977 - 1996

Year	Number				Rate per 100,000 population			
	City	Suburbs[2]	MSA[1]	U.S.	City	Suburbs[3]	MSA[1]	U.S.
1977	323	114	437	19,120	18.2	3.6	8.9	8.8
1978	351	129	480	19,560	20.0	4.1	9.8	9.0
1979	385	120	505	21,460	21.9	4.0	10.6	9.7
1980	436	131	567	23,040	25.9	4.3	12.1	10.2
1981	362	148	510	22,520	21.5	4.9	10.8	9.8
1982	332	145	477	21,010	19.7	4.8	10.1	9.1
1983	311	102	413	19,310	18.4	3.3	8.7	8.3
1984	264	104	368	18,690	15.8	3.4	7.7	7.9
1985	273	109	382	18,980	16.6	3.5	8.0	7.9
1986	343	122	465	20,610	20.8	3.9	9.7	8.6
1987	338	115	453	20,100	20.5	3.6	9.3	8.3
1988	371	131	502	20,680	22.4	4.0	10.2	8.4
1989	475	106	581	21,500	28.7	3.2	11.8	8.7
1990	503	140	643	23,440	31.7	4.3	13.2	9.4
1991	440	117	557	24,700	27.6	3.6	11.4	9.8
1992	425	121	546	23,760	26.5	3.6	11.0	9.3
1993	439	157	596	24,530	28.1	4.6	12.0	9.5
1994	404	131	535	23,330	25.9	3.8	10.8	9.0
1995	432	n/a	n/a	21,610	28.2	n/a	n/a	8.2
1996	414	92	506	19,650	27.1	2.7	10.2	7.4

Notes: (1) Metropolitan Statistical Area - see Appendix A for areas included; (2) calculated by the editors using the following formula: (number of crimes in the MSA minus number of crimes in the city); (3) calculated by the editors using the following formula: ((number of crimes in the MSA minus number of crimes in the city) ÷ (population of the MSA minus population of the city)) x 100,000; n/a not avail.
Source: U.S. Department of Justice, FBI Uniform Crime Reports, 1977 - 1996

Forcible Rapes and Forcible Rape Rates: 1977 - 1996

Year	Number				Rate per 100,000 population			
	City	Suburbs[2]	MSA[1]	U.S.	City	Suburbs[3]	MSA[1]	U.S.
1977	771	564	1,335	63,500	43.4	18.0	27.2	29.4
1978	724	619	1,343	67,610	41.3	19.6	27.3	31.0
1979	838	692	1,530	76,390	47.7	23.0	32.1	34.7
1980	937	773	1,710	82,990	55.7	25.6	36.4	36.8
1981	936	739	1,675	82,500	55.5	24.4	35.5	36.0
1982	839	651	1,490	78,770	49.7	21.4	31.5	34.0
1983	822	622	1,444	78,920	48.6	20.4	30.5	33.7
1984	937	736	1,673	84,230	56.2	23.8	35.1	35.7
1985	1,021	727	1,748	88,670	62.3	23.3	36.7	37.1
1986	1,086	732	1,818	91,460	66.0	23.4	38.0	37.9
1987	1,102	737	1,839	91,110	66.8	23.0	37.9	37.4
1988	916	727	1,643	92,490	55.3	22.4	33.5	37.6
1989	784	801	1,585	94,500	47.5	24.4	32.1	38.1
1990	734	810	1,544	102,560	46.3	24.8	31.8	41.2
1991	904	834	1,738	106,590	56.6	25.4	35.6	42.3
1992	781	890	1,671	109,060	48.7	26.4	33.6	42.8
1993	785	754	1,539	106,010	50.3	22.1	31.0	41.1
1994	721	761	1,482	102,220	46.2	22.3	29.8	39.3
1995	773	n/a	n/a	97,470	50.5	n/a	n/a	37.1
1996	704	724	1,428	95,770	46.1	21.1	28.8	36.1

Notes: (1) Metropolitan Statistical Area - see Appendix A for areas included; (2) calculated by the editors using the following formula: (number of crimes in the MSA minus number of crimes in the city); (3) calculated by the editors using the following formula: ((number of crimes in the MSA minus number of crimes in the city) ÷ (population of the MSA minus population of the city)) x 100,000; n/a not avail.
Source: U.S. Department of Justice, FBI Uniform Crime Reports, 1977 - 1996

Robberies and Robbery Rates: 1977 - 1996

Year	Number				Rate per 100,000 population			
	City	Suburbs[2]	MSA[1]	U.S.	City	Suburbs[3]	MSA[1]	U.S.
1977	6,999	3,414	10,413	412,610	393.6	109.1	212.2	190.7
1978	7,069	3,411	10,480	426,930	402.8	107.9	213.2	195.8
1979	8,838	3,433	12,271	480,700	502.9	114.1	257.5	218.4
1980	10,883	4,853	15,736	565,840	647.3	160.7	334.7	251.1
1981	10,816	4,558	15,374	592,910	641.2	150.2	325.6	258.7
1982	10,604	4,540	15,144	553,130	628.4	149.3	320.3	238.9
1983	10,744	4,026	14,770	506,570	634.9	132.0	311.5	216.5
1984	9,365	3,572	12,937	485,010	561.6	115.5	271.7	205.4
1985	9,381	3,562	12,943	497,870	572.0	114.2	271.9	208.5
1986	9,647	3,436	13,083	542,780	586.4	109.6	273.7	225.1
1987	9,302	3,254	12,556	517,700	564.0	101.7	259.0	212.7
1988	8,901	3,556	12,457	542,970	537.1	109.6	254.1	220.9
1989	10,233	3,643	13,876	578,330	619.4	111.0	281.2	233.0
1990	12,806	4,258	17,064	639,270	807.7	130.2	351.3	257.0
1991	13,921	4,858	18,779	687,730	871.9	147.7	384.3	272.7
1992	11,681	4,706	16,387	672,480	728.4	139.7	329.6	263.6
1993	11,531	4,730	16,261	659,870	739.4	138.7	327.2	255.9
1994	12,706	4,765	17,471	618,950	814.2	139.6	351.2	237.7
1995	13,612	n/a	n/a	580,510	889.8	n/a	n/a	220.9
1996	15,485	4,470	19,955	537,050	1,013.1	130.0	401.8	202.4

Notes: (1) Metropolitan Statistical Area - see Appendix A for areas included; (2) calculated by the editors using the following formula: (number of crimes in the MSA minus number of crimes in the city); (3) calculated by the editors using the following formula: ((number of crimes in the MSA minus number of crimes in the city) ÷ (population of the MSA minus population of the city)) x 100,000; n/a not avail.
Source: U.S. Department of Justice, FBI Uniform Crime Reports, 1977 - 1996

Aggravated Assaults and Aggravated Assault Rates: 1977 - 1996

Year	Number				Rate per 100,000 population			
	City	Suburbs[2]	MSA[1]	U.S.	City	Suburbs[3]	MSA[1]	U.S.
1977	3,954	4,981	8,935	534,350	222.4	159.1	182.0	247.0
1978	4,224	5,749	9,973	571,460	240.7	181.9	202.9	262.1
1979	4,476	6,419	10,895	629,480	254.7	213.4	228.6	286.0
1980	5,043	6,933	11,976	672,650	300.0	229.6	254.8	298.5
1981	5,502	6,635	12,137	663,900	326.2	218.6	257.1	289.7
1982	5,734	6,836	12,570	669,480	339.8	224.9	265.9	289.2
1983	5,096	6,490	11,586	653,290	301.1	212.8	244.4	279.2
1984	5,034	6,600	11,634	685,350	301.9	213.4	244.4	290.2
1985	5,534	6,621	12,155	723,250	337.4	212.2	255.3	302.9
1986	6,131	7,611	13,742	834,320	372.7	242.8	287.5	346.1
1987	6,656	8,371	15,027	855,090	403.5	261.7	310.0	351.3
1988	6,971	8,095	15,066	910,090	420.6	249.5	307.4	370.2
1989	6,562	7,424	13,986	951,710	397.2	226.2	283.4	383.4
1990	7,344	9,120	16,464	1,054,860	463.2	278.8	339.0	424.1
1991	7,216	8,797	16,013	1,092,740	451.9	267.4	327.7	433.3
1992	6,180	8,682	14,862	1,126,970	385.4	257.7	298.9	441.8
1993	6,821	7,691	14,512	1,135,610	437.4	225.6	292.0	440.3
1994	6,807	8,211	15,018	1,113,180	436.2	240.5	301.9	427.6
1995	7,155	n/a	n/a	1,099,210	467.7	n/a	n/a	418.3
1996	6,764	7,765	14,529	1,029,810	442.6	225.8	292.5	388.2

Notes: (1) Metropolitan Statistical Area - see Appendix A for areas included; (2) calculated by the editors using the following formula: (number of crimes in the MSA minus number of crimes in the city); (3) calculated by the editors using the following formula: ((number of crimes in the MSA minus number of crimes in the city) ÷ (population of the MSA minus population of the city)) x 100,000; n/a not avail.
Source: U.S. Department of Justice, FBI Uniform Crime Reports, 1977 - 1996

Burglaries and Burglary Rates: 1977 - 1996

Year	Number				Rate per 100,000 population			
	City	Suburbs[2]	MSA[1]	U.S.	City	Suburbs[3]	MSA[1]	U.S.
1977	19,108	35,762	54,870	3,071,500	1,074.7	1,142.6	1,118.0	1,419.8
1978	19,154	36,229	55,383	3,128,300	1,091.4	1,146.5	1,126.8	1,434.6
1979	20,965	37,146	58,111	3,327,700	1,193.0	1,235.1	1,219.5	1,511.9
1980	24,940	42,877	67,817	3,795,200	1,483.5	1,419.9	1,442.6	1,684.1
1981	26,676	43,502	70,178	3,779,700	1,581.4	1,433.4	1,486.3	1,649.5
1982	23,127	35,772	58,899	3,447,100	1,370.4	1,176.7	1,245.9	1,488.8
1983	21,254	30,823	52,077	3,129,900	1,255.9	1,010.9	1,098.3	1,337.7
1984	18,318	25,903	44,221	2,984,400	1,098.5	837.4	928.8	1,263.7
1985	19,007	26,233	45,240	3,073,300	1,158.9	840.7	950.3	1,287.3
1986	19,174	25,656	44,830	3,241,400	1,165.5	818.5	937.9	1,344.6
1987	20,070	24,573	44,643	3,236,200	1,216.8	768.2	920.9	1,329.6
1988	20,403	22,046	42,449	3,218,100	1,231.1	679.5	866.0	1,309.2
1989	21,896	22,816	44,712	3,168,200	1,325.3	695.1	906.1	1,276.3
1990	24,144	22,252	46,396	3,073,900	1,522.7	680.2	955.3	1,235.9
1991	21,460	23,277	44,737	3,157,200	1,344.0	707.5	915.5	1,252.0
1992	16,199	22,796	38,995	2,979,900	1,010.1	676.8	784.3	1,168.2
1993	15,117	22,917	38,034	2,834,800	969.3	672.1	765.4	1,099.2
1994	14,106	21,330	35,436	2,712,800	903.9	624.7	712.3	1,042.0
1995	16,165	n/a	n/a	2,593,800	1,056.6	n/a	n/a	987.1
1996	16,204	20,153	36,357	2,501,500	1,060.2	586.1	732.0	943.0

Notes: (1) Metropolitan Statistical Area - see Appendix A for areas included; (2) calculated by the editors using the following formula: (number of crimes in the MSA minus number of crimes in the city); (3) calculated by the editors using the following formula: ((number of crimes in the MSA minus number of crimes in the city) ÷ (population of the MSA minus population of the city)) x 100,000; n/a not avail.
Source: U.S. Department of Justice, FBI Uniform Crime Reports, 1977 - 1996

Larceny-Thefts and Larceny-Theft Rates: 1977 - 1996

Year	Number				Rate per 100,000 population			
	City	Suburbs[2]	MSA[1]	U.S.	City	Suburbs[3]	MSA[1]	U.S.
1977	28,301	70,041	98,342	5,905,700	1,591.7	2,237.7	2,003.7	2,729.9
1978	29,690	71,802	101,492	5,991,000	1,691.7	2,272.3	2,065.0	2,747.4
1979	33,863	77,176	111,039	6,601,000	1,926.9	2,566.0	2,330.3	2,999.1
1980	40,910	80,171	121,081	7,136,900	2,433.4	2,654.8	2,575.6	3,167.0
1981	39,731	80,696	120,427	7,194,400	2,355.4	2,659.0	2,550.5	3,139.7
1982	40,099	77,312	117,411	7,142,500	2,376.2	2,543.2	2,483.6	3,084.8
1983	37,611	69,451	107,062	6,712,800	2,222.4	2,277.7	2,258.0	2,868.9
1984	35,286	67,024	102,310	6,591,900	2,116.0	2,166.7	2,148.9	2,791.3
1985	35,815	67,364	103,179	6,926,400	2,183.7	2,158.9	2,167.5	2,901.2
1986	36,619	68,563	105,182	7,257,200	2,225.9	2,187.4	2,200.6	3,010.3
1987	41,784	69,877	111,661	7,499,900	2,533.3	2,184.6	2,303.2	3,081.3
1988	42,161	65,686	107,847	7,705,900	2,544.0	2,024.5	2,200.1	3,134.9
1989	50,609	65,639	116,248	7,872,400	3,063.2	1,999.8	2,355.8	3,171.3
1990	42,633	66,725	109,358	7,945,700	2,688.8	2,039.7	2,251.6	3,194.8
1991	40,880	73,334	114,214	8,142,200	2,560.3	2,229.1	2,337.3	3,228.8
1992	39,677	70,959	110,636	7,915,200	2,474.2	2,106.6	2,225.2	3,103.0
1993	39,181	68,639	107,820	7,820,900	2,512.4	2,013.0	2,169.7	3,032.4
1994	40,392	69,756	110,148	7,879,800	2,588.3	2,043.1	2,214.1	3,026.7
1995	46,332	n/a	n/a	7,997,700	3,028.5	n/a	n/a	3,043.8
1996	43,064	76,452	119,516	7,894,600	2,817.6	2,223.5	2,406.3	2,975.9

Notes: (1) Metropolitan Statistical Area - see Appendix A for areas included; (2) calculated by the editors using the following formula: (number of crimes in the MSA minus number of crimes in the city); (3) calculated by the editors using the following formula: ((number of crimes in the MSA minus number of crimes in the city) ÷ (population of the MSA minus population of the city)) x 100,000; n/a not avail.
Source: U.S. Department of Justice, FBI Uniform Crime Reports, 1977 - 1996

Motor Vehicle Thefts and Motor Vehicle Theft Rates: 1977 - 1996

Year	Number				Rate per 100,000 population			
	City	Suburbs[2]	MSA[1]	U.S.	City	Suburbs[3]	MSA[1]	U.S.
1977	12,371	11,399	23,770	977,700	695.8	364.2	484.3	451.9
1978	11,736	11,824	23,560	1,004,100	668.7	374.2	479.4	460.5
1979	13,221	13,460	26,681	1,112,800	752.3	447.5	559.9	505.6
1980	17,995	14,986	32,981	1,131,700	1,070.4	496.3	701.6	502.2
1981	16,569	13,694	30,263	1,087,800	982.3	451.2	640.9	474.7
1982	13,906	13,509	27,415	1,062,400	824.0	444.4	579.9	458.8
1983	13,926	13,517	27,443	1,007,900	822.9	443.3	578.8	430.8
1984	13,325	11,723	25,048	1,032,200	799.1	379.0	526.1	437.1
1985	12,636	11,820	24,456	1,102,900	770.4	378.8	513.7	462.0
1986	13,094	11,928	25,022	1,224,100	795.9	380.5	523.5	507.8
1987	15,323	13,101	28,424	1,288,700	929.0	409.6	586.3	529.4
1988	20,328	14,165	34,493	1,432,900	1,226.6	436.6	703.7	582.9
1989	25,043	15,245	40,288	1,564,800	1,515.7	464.5	816.5	630.4
1990	25,868	16,073	41,941	1,635,900	1,631.5	491.3	863.5	657.8
1991	24,318	16,865	41,183	1,661,700	1,523.0	512.6	842.8	659.0
1992	22,416	15,347	37,763	1,610,800	1,397.8	455.6	759.5	631.5
1993	23,785	13,882	37,667	1,563,100	1,525.1	407.1	758.0	606.1
1994	25,281	14,632	39,913	1,539,300	1,620.0	428.6	802.3	591.3
1995	23,809	n/a	n/a	1,472,400	1,556.3	n/a	n/a	560.4
1996	23,131	14,576	37,707	1,395,200	1,513.4	423.9	759.2	525.9

Notes: (1) Metropolitan Statistical Area - see Appendix A for areas included; (2) calculated by the editors using the following formula: (number of crimes in the MSA minus number of crimes in the city); (3) calculated by the editors using the following formula: ((number of crimes in the MSA minus number of crimes in the city) ÷ (population of the MSA minus population of the city)) x 100,000; n/a not avail.
Source: U.S. Department of Justice, FBI Uniform Crime Reports, 1977 - 1996

HATE CRIMES

Criminal Incidents by Bias Motivation

Area	Race	Ethnicity	Religion	Sexual Orientation
Philadelphia	111	25	8	1

Notes: Figures include both violent and property crimes. Law enforcement agencies must have submitted data for at least one quarter of calendar year 1995 to be included in this report, therefore figures shown may not represent complete 12-month totals; n/a not available
Source: U.S. Department of Justice, FBI Uniform Crime Reports, Hate Crime Statistics 1995

ILLEGAL DRUGS

Drug Use by Adult Arrestees

Sex	Percent Testing Positive by Urinalysis (%)				
	Any Drug[1]	Cocaine	Marijuana	Opiates	Multiple Drugs
Male	69	40	39	11	27
Female	81	69	21	16	34

Notes: The catchment area is the entire city; (1) Includes cocaine, opiates, marijuana, methadone, phencyclidine (PCP), benzodiazepines, methaqualone, propoxyphene, barbiturates & amphetamines
Source: National Institute of Justice, 1996 Drug Use Forecasting, Annual Report on Adult and Juvenile Arrestees (released June 1997)

LAW ENFORCEMENT

Full-Time Law Enforcement Employees

Jurisdiction	Police Employees			Police Officers per 100,000 population
	Total	Officers	Civilians	
Philadelphia	7,410	6,455	955	422.3

Notes: Data as of October 31, 1996
Source: U.S. Department of Justice, FBI Uniform Crime Reports, 1996

Number of Police Officers by Race

Race	Police Officers				Index of Representation[1]		
	1983		1992				
	Number	Pct.	Number	Pct.	1983	1992	% Chg.
Black	1,201	16.5	1,615	25.7	0.44	0.64	45.5
Hispanic[2]	46	0.6	202	3.2	0.16	0.57	256.2

Notes: (1) The index of representation is calculated by dividing the percent of black/hispanic police officers by the percent of corresponding blacks/hispanics in the local population. An index approaching 1.0 indicates that a city is closer to achieving a representation of police officers equal to their proportion in the local population; (2) Hispanic officers can be of any race
Source: Bureau of Justice Statistics, Sourcebook of Criminal Justice Statistics, 1994

CORRECTIONS

Federal Correctional Facilities

Type	Year Opened	Security Level	Sex of Inmates	Rated Capacity	Population on 7/1/95	Number of Staff
None listed						

Notes: Data as of 1995
Source: Bureau of Justice Statistics, Sourcebook of Criminal Justice Statistics Online

City/County/Regional Correctional Facilities

Name	Year Opened	Year Renov.	Rated Capacity	1995 Pop.	Number of COs[1]	Number of Staff	ACA[2] Accred.
Philadelphia Alt & Spec Det	1981	--	185	n/a	n/a	n/a	No
Philadelphia Detention Ctr	1963	1988	920	n/a	n/a	n/a	No
Philadelphia House of Corr	1928	1984	797	n/a	n/a	n/a	No
Philadelphia Indust Corr Ctr	1986	--	920	n/a	n/a	n/a	No

Notes: Data as of April 1996; (1) Correctional Officers; (2) American Correctional Assn. Accreditation
Source: American Correctional Association, 1996-1998 National Jail and Adult Detention Directory

Private Adult Correctional Facilities

Name	Date Opened	Rated Capacity	Present Pop.	Security Level	Facility Construct.	Expans. Plans	ACA[1] Accred.
None listed							

Notes: Data as of December 1996; (1) American Correctional Association Accreditation
Source: University of Florida, Center for Studies in Criminology and Law, Private Adult Correctional Facility Census, 10th Ed., March 15, 1997

Characteristics of Shock Incarceration Programs

Jurisdiction	Year Program Began	Number of Camps	Average Num. of Inmates	Number of Beds	Program Length	Voluntary/ Mandatory
Pennsylvania	1992	1	130	158	6 months	Voluntary

Note: Data as of July 1996;
Source: Sourcebook of Criminal Justice Statistics Online

INMATES AND HIV/AIDS

HIV Testing Policies for Inmates

Jurisdiction	All Inmates at Some Time	All Convicted Inmates at Admission	Random Samples While in Custody	High-risk Groups	Upon Inmate Request	Upon Court Order	Upon Involvement in Incident
Philadelphia Co.	No	No	No	No	Yes	No	No

Source: HIV in Prisons and Jails, 1993 (released August 1995)

Inmates Known to be Positive for HIV

Jurisdiction	Number of Jail Inmates in Facilities Providing Data	Type of HIV Infection/AIDS Cases				HIV/AIDS Cases as a Percent of Tot. Custody Pop.
		Total	Asymptomatic	Symptomatic	Confirmed AIDS	
Philadelphia[1]	1,049	124	80	44	0	11.8

Note: (1) Some but not all facilities reported data on HIV/AIDS cases. Excludes inmates in facilities that did not report data.
Source: HIV in Prisons and Jails, 1993 (released August, 1995)

DEATH PENALTY

Death Penalty Statistics

State	Prisoners Executed		Prisoners Under Sentence of Death					Avg. No. of Years on Death Row[4]
	1930-1995	1996[1]	Total[2]	White[3]	Black[3]	Hisp.	Women	
Pennsylvania	154	0	196	67	122	11	4	6.1

Notes: Data as of 12/31/95 unless otherwise noted; (1) Data as of 7/31/97; (2) Includes persons of other races; (3) Includes people of Hispanic origin; (4) Covers prisoners sentenced 1974 through 1995
Source: Bureau of Justice Statistics, Capital Punishment 1995 (released 12/96); Death Penalty Information Center Web Site, 9/30/97

Capital Offenses and Methods of Execution

Capital Offenses in Pennsylvania	Minimum Age for Imposition of Death Penalty	Mentally Retarded Excluded	Methods of Execution[1]
First-degree murder with 16 aggravating circumstances.	None	No	Lethal injection

Notes: Data as of 12/31/95 unless otherwise noted; (1) Data as of 7/31/97
Source: Bureau of Justice Statistics, Capital Punishment 1995 (released 12/96); Death Penalty Information Center Web Site, 9/30/97

LAWS

Statutory Provisions Relating to the Purchase, Ownership and Use of Handguns

Jurisdiction	Instant Background Check	Federal Waiting Period Applies[1]	State Waiting Period (days)	License or Permit to Purchase	Regis-tration	Record of Sale Sent to Police	Concealed Carry Law
Pennsylvania	(a)	Yes[a,b]	2[a]	No	No	Yes	Yes[c,d]

Note: Data as of 1996; (1) The Federal 5-day waiting period for handgun purchases applies to states that don't have instant background checks, waiting period requirements, or licensing procedures exempting them from the Federal requirement; (a) Instant Check is not yet operational. When operational, the State waiting period will end and the Federal waiting period will no longer apply. Carry permit holders will be exempt from Instant Check; (b) The Federal waiting period does not apply to a person holding a valid permit or license to carry a firearm, issued within 5 years of proposed purchase; (c) "Shall issue" permit system, liberally administered discretion by local authorities over permit issuance, or no permit required; (d) Prior to 1995, the law did not apply to Philadelphia
Source: Sourcebook of Criminal Justice Statistics Online

Statutory Provisions Relating to Alcohol Use and Driving

Jurisdiction	Drinking Age	Blood Alcohol Concentration Levels as Evidence in State Courts[1]		Open Container Law[1]	Anti-Consump-tion Law[1]	Dram Shop Law[1]
		Illegal per se at 0.10%	Presumption at 0.10%			
Pennsylvania	21	Yes	No	No	Yes[a]	Yes

Note: Data as of January 1, 1997; (1) See Appendix C for an explanation of terms; (a) Applies to drivers only
Source: Sourcebook of Criminal Justice Statistics Online

Statutory Provisions Relating to Curfews

Jurisdiction	Year Enacted	Latest Revision	Age Group(s)	Curfew Provisions
Philadelphia	1956	-	17 and under	10:30 pm to 6 am weekday nights midnight to 6 am weekend nights

Note: Data as of February 1996
Source: Sourcebook of Criminal Justice Statistics Online

Statutory Provisions Relating to Hate Crimes

Jurisdiction	Bias-Motivated Violence and Intimidation						Institutional Vandalism
	Civil Action	Criminal Penalty					
		Race/ Religion/ Ethnicity	Sexual Orientation	Mental/ Physical Disability	Gender	Age	
Pennsylvania	Yes	Yes	No	No	No	No	Yes

Source: Anti-Defamation League, 1997 Hate Crimes Laws

Phoenix, Arizona

OVERVIEW

The total crime rate for the city decreased 4.3% between 1977 and 1996. During that same period, the violent crime rate increased 47.3% and the property crime rate decreased 7.8%.

Among violent crimes, the rates for: Murders increased 59.8%; Forcible Rapes decreased 12.4%; Robberies increased 41.6%; and Aggravated Assaults increased 59.0%.

Among property crimes, the rates for: Burglaries decreased 43.3%; Larceny-Thefts decreased 7.0%; and Motor Vehicle Thefts increased 161.5%.

ANTI-CRIME PROGRAMS

Block Watchers on Patrol is a program in which citizens assist neighbors in crime prevention by acting as additional eyes and ears for the Police Department. The Department provides training and support for citizens to conduct crime prevention patrols in their neighborhoods.
Phoenix Police Department, 8/97

The city instituted a program which the National League of Cities (1993) considers among those which are innovative for combatting crime and violence:

- Gang Resistance Education and Training (G.R.E.A.T.) the goals of which are to reduce gang activity and violence by providing youths with skills and strategies to resist gang involvement or pressures. Three full-time police officers present G.R.E.A.T. to about 3,000 students per school semester. *Exemplary Programs in Criminal Justice, National League of Cities, 1994*

CRIME RISK

Your Chances of Becoming a Victim[1]

Area	Any Crime	Violent Crime					Property Crime			
		Any	Murder	Forcible Rape[2]	Robbery	Aggrav. Assault	Any	Burglary	Larceny -Theft	Motor Vehicle Theft
City	1:10	1:108	1:6,128	1:1,252	1:303	1:186	1:12	1:58	1:19	1:63

Note: (1) Figures have been calculated by dividing the population of the city by the number of crimes reported to the FBI during 1996 and are expressed as odds (eg. 1:20 should be read as 1 in 20).
(2) Figures have been calculated by dividing the female population of the city by the number of forcible rapes reported to the FBI during 1996. The female population of the city was estimated by calculating the ratio of females to males reported in the 1990 Census and applying that ratio to 1996 population estimate.
Source: FBI Uniform Crime Reports 1996

CRIME STATISTICS

Total Crimes and Total Crime Rates: 1977 - 1996

Year	Number				Rate per 100,000 population			
	City	Suburbs[2]	MSA[1]	U.S.	City	Suburbs[3]	MSA[1]	U.S.
1977	68,324	39,046	107,370	10,984,500	9,974.3	6,432.6	8,310.4	5,077.6
1978	71,575	41,218	112,793	11,209,000	10,510.3	6,723.4	8,716.3	5,140.3
1979	75,147	46,178	121,325	12,249,500	10,463.0	7,355.1	9,013.4	5,565.5
1980	88,523	52,178	140,701	13,408,300	11,453.6	7,063.8	9,308.4	5,950.0
1981	81,370	50,107	131,477	13,423,800	10,235.4	6,594.9	8,456.4	5,858.2
1982	75,654	48,836	124,490	12,974,400	9,293.5	6,277.0	7,819.4	5,603.6
1983	68,692	44,153	112,845	12,108,600	8,144.5	5,477.9	6,841.4	5,175.0
1984	71,279	48,052	119,331	11,881,800	8,190.4	5,797.0	7,022.8	5,031.3
1985	82,523	59,178	141,701	12,431,400	9,264.5	6,579.9	7,915.7	5,207.1
1986	89,374	63,630	153,004	13,211,900	9,640.6	6,797.7	8,212.3	5,480.4
1987	83,960	65,398	149,358	13,508,700	8,997.2	6,320.5	7,589.8	5,550.0
1988	87,080	68,862	155,942	13,923,100	9,149.8	6,525.7	7,770.0	5,664.2
1989	102,359	75,433	177,792	14,251,400	10,866.7	6,690.1	8,591.1	5,741.0
1990	105,779	78,491	184,270	14,475,600	10,756.4	6,893.0	8,683.4	5,820.3
1991	99,172	78,421	177,593	14,872,900	9,958.1	6,672.3	8,179.4	5,897.8
1992	92,213	82,488	174,701	14,438,200	9,222.2	6,153.6	7,464.6	5,660.2
1993	96,476	89,908	186,384	14,144,800	9,282.2	6,640.8	7,787.9	5,484.4
1994	108,131	97,286	205,417	13,989,500	10,048.3	6,940.6	8,290.3	5,373.5
1995	118,126	107,382	225,508	13,862,700	10,880.1	7,283.1	8,808.5	5,275.9
1996	108,749	99,007	207,756	13,473,600	9,541.1	6,396.6	7,730.2	5,078.9

Notes: (1) Metropolitan Statistical Area - see Appendix A for areas included; (2) calculated by the editors using the following formula: (number of crimes in the MSA minus number of crimes in the city); (3) calculated by the editors using the following formula: ((number of crimes in the MSA minus number of crimes in the city) ÷ (population of the MSA minus population of the city)) x 100,000; n/a not avail.
Source: U.S. Department of Justice, FBI Uniform Crime Reports, 1977 - 1996

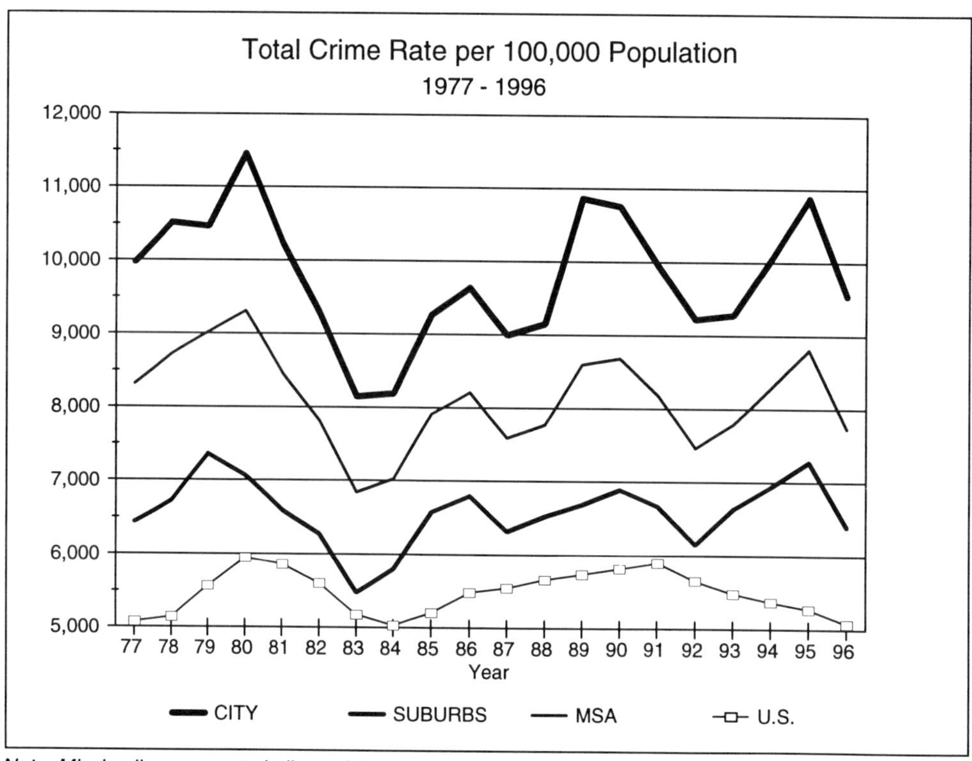

Note: Missing line segments indicate data not available.

Violent Crimes and Violent Crime Rates: 1977 - 1996

Year	Number				Rate per 100,000 population			
	City	Suburbs[2]	MSA[1]	U.S.	City	Suburbs[3]	MSA[1]	U.S.
1977	4,295	2,131	6,426	1,029,580	627.0	351.1	497.4	475.9
1978	5,401	2,636	8,037	1,085,550	793.1	430.0	621.1	497.8
1979	5,803	3,268	9,071	1,208,030	808.0	520.5	673.9	548.9
1980	7,020	4,222	11,242	1,344,520	908.3	571.6	743.7	596.6
1981	6,319	3,523	9,842	1,361,820	794.9	463.7	633.0	594.3
1982	5,431	3,159	8,590	1,322,390	667.2	406.0	539.5	571.1
1983	5,270	3,089	8,359	1,258,090	624.8	383.2	506.8	537.7
1984	6,372	2,978	9,350	1,273,280	732.2	359.3	550.3	539.2
1985	7,521	3,982	11,503	1,328,800	844.3	442.8	642.6	556.6
1986	9,238	4,446	13,684	1,489,170	996.5	475.0	734.5	617.7
1987	8,181	4,578	12,759	1,484,000	876.7	442.5	648.4	609.7
1988	8,477	4,398	12,875	1,566,220	890.7	416.8	641.5	637.2
1989	8,481	4,349	12,830	1,646,040	900.4	385.7	620.0	663.1
1990	10,665	5,006	15,671	1,820,130	1,084.5	439.6	738.5	731.8
1991	11,010	5,739	16,749	1,911,770	1,105.5	488.3	771.4	758.1
1992	10,907	6,644	17,551	1,932,270	1,090.8	495.6	749.9	757.5
1993	11,911	7,397	19,308	1,926,020	1,146.0	546.4	806.8	746.8
1994	11,627	7,402	19,029	1,857,670	1,080.5	528.1	768.0	713.6
1995	11,590	7,995	19,585	1,798,790	1,067.5	542.3	765.0	684.6
1996	10,529	7,425	17,954	1,682,280	923.8	479.7	668.0	634.1

Notes: Violent crimes include murder, forcible rape, robbery and aggravated assault; n/a not available; (1) Metropolitan Statistical Area - see Appendix A for areas included; (2) calculated by the editors using the following formula: (number of crimes in the MSA minus number of crimes in the city); (3) calculated by the editors using the following formula: ((number of crimes in the MSA minus number of crimes in the city) ÷ (population of the MSA minus population of the city)) x 100,000
Source: U.S. Department of Justice, FBI Uniform Crime Reports, 1977 - 1996

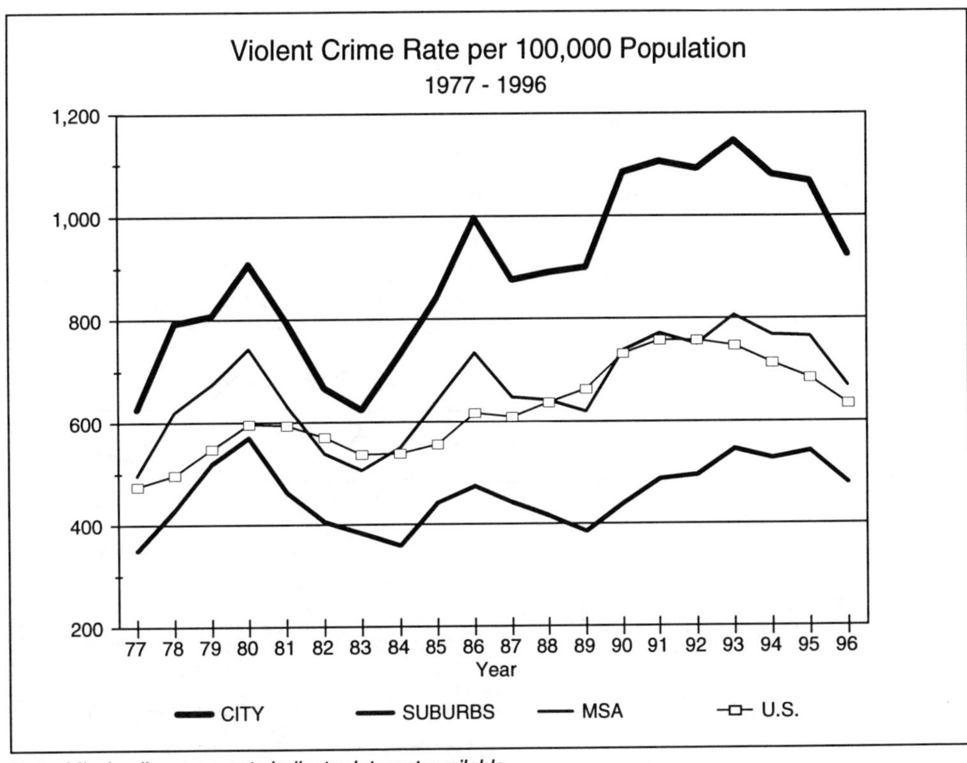

Note: Missing line segments indicate data not available.

Property Crimes and Property Crime Rates: 1977 - 1996

Year	Number				Rate per 100,000 population			
	City	Suburbs[2]	MSA[1]	U.S.	City	Suburbs[3]	MSA[1]	U.S.
1977	64,029	36,915	100,944	9,955,000	9,347.3	6,081.5	7,813.0	4,601.7
1978	66,174	38,582	104,756	10,123,400	9,717.2	6,293.4	8,095.2	4,642.5
1979	69,344	42,910	112,254	11,041,500	9,655.0	6,834.6	8,339.5	5,016.6
1980	81,503	47,956	129,459	12,063,700	10,545.3	6,492.2	8,564.6	5,353.3
1981	75,051	46,584	121,635	12,061,900	9,440.6	6,131.2	7,823.3	5,263.9
1982	70,223	45,677	115,900	11,652,000	8,626.3	5,871.0	7,279.8	5,032.5
1983	63,422	41,064	104,486	10,850,500	7,519.7	5,094.6	6,334.6	4,637.4
1984	64,907	45,074	109,981	10,608,500	7,458.2	5,437.7	6,472.6	4,492.1
1985	75,002	55,196	130,198	11,102,600	8,420.1	6,137.1	7,273.1	4,650.5
1986	80,136	59,184	139,320	11,722,700	8,644.1	6,322.8	7,477.9	4,862.6
1987	75,779	60,820	136,599	12,024,700	8,120.5	5,878.1	6,941.5	4,940.3
1988	78,603	64,464	143,067	12,356,900	8,259.1	6,108.9	7,128.5	5,027.1
1989	93,878	71,084	164,962	12,605,400	9,966.4	6,304.4	7,971.2	5,077.9
1990	95,114	73,485	168,599	12,655,500	9,671.9	6,453.4	7,944.9	5,088.5
1991	88,162	72,682	160,844	12,961,100	8,852.5	6,184.0	7,408.0	5,139.7
1992	81,306	75,844	157,150	12,505,900	8,131.4	5,657.9	6,714.7	4,902.7
1993	84,565	82,511	167,076	12,218,800	8,136.2	6,094.4	6,981.1	4,737.6
1994	96,504	89,884	186,388	12,131,900	8,967.9	6,412.6	7,522.3	4,660.0
1995	106,536	99,387	205,923	12,063,900	9,812.6	6,740.8	8,043.5	4,591.3
1996	98,220	91,582	189,802	11,791,300	8,617.4	5,916.9	7,062.2	4,444.8

Notes: Property crimes include burglary, larceny-theft and motor vehicle theft; n/a not available; (1) Metropolitan Statistical Area - see Appendix A for areas included; (2) calculated by the editors using the following formula: (number of crimes in the MSA minus number of crimes in the city); (3) calculated by the editors using the following formula: ((number of crimes in the MSA minus number of crimes in the city) ÷ (population of the MSA minus population of the city)) x 100,000
Source: U.S. Department of Justice, FBI Uniform Crime Reports, 1977 - 1996

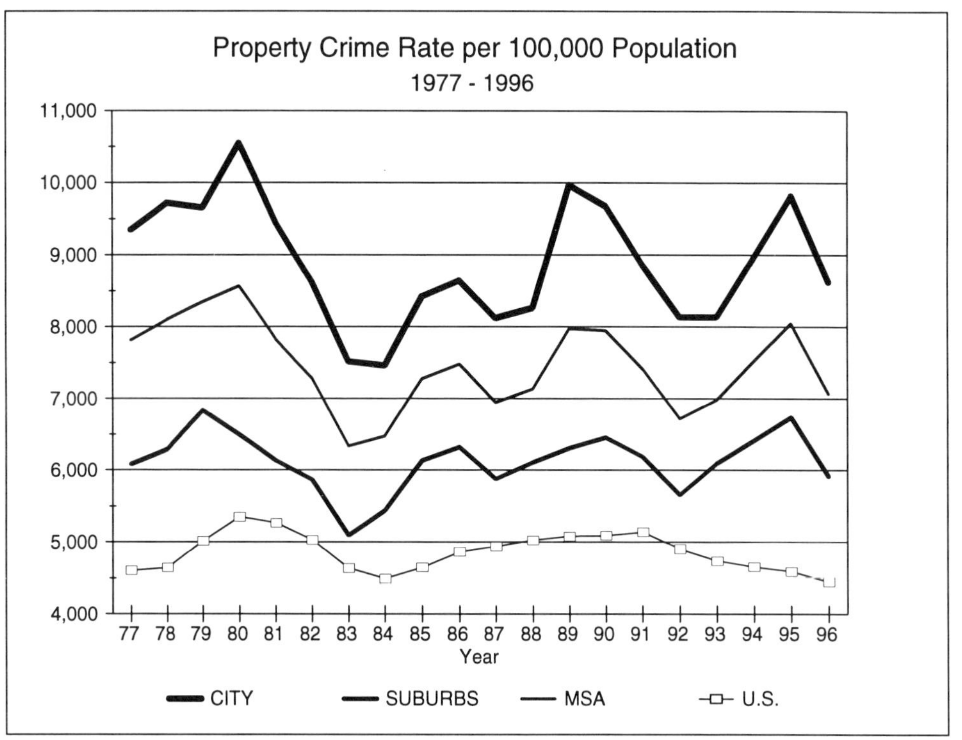

Note: Missing line segments indicate data not available.

Murders and Murder Rates: 1977 - 1996

Year	Number				Rate per 100,000 population			
	City	Suburbs[2]	MSA[1]	U.S.	City	Suburbs[3]	MSA[1]	U.S.
1977	70	37	107	19,120	10.2	6.1	8.3	8.8
1978	88	42	130	19,560	12.9	6.9	10.0	9.0
1979	91	46	137	21,460	12.7	7.3	10.2	9.7
1980	103	55	158	23,040	13.3	7.4	10.5	10.2
1981	96	47	143	22,520	12.1	6.2	9.2	9.8
1982	95	40	135	21,010	11.7	5.1	8.5	9.1
1983	83	53	136	19,310	9.8	6.6	8.2	8.3
1984	101	38	139	18,690	11.6	4.6	8.2	7.9
1985	89	52	141	18,980	10.0	5.8	7.9	7.9
1986	122	64	186	20,610	13.2	6.8	10.0	8.6
1987	111	57	168	20,100	11.9	5.5	8.5	8.3
1988	106	68	174	20,680	11.1	6.4	8.7	8.4
1989	126	44	170	21,500	13.4	3.9	8.2	8.7
1990	128	47	175	23,440	13.0	4.1	8.2	9.4
1991	128	75	203	24,700	12.9	6.4	9.3	9.8
1992	136	71	207	23,760	13.6	5.3	8.8	9.3
1993	158	71	229	24,530	15.2	5.2	9.6	9.5
1994	231	77	308	23,330	21.5	5.5	12.4	9.0
1995	214	91	305	21,610	19.7	6.2	11.9	8.2
1996	186	81	267	19,650	16.3	5.2	9.9	7.4

Notes: (1) Metropolitan Statistical Area - see Appendix A for areas included; (2) calculated by the editors using the following formula: (number of crimes in the MSA minus number of crimes in the city); (3) calculated by the editors using the following formula: ((number of crimes in the MSA minus number of crimes in the city) ÷ (population of the MSA minus population of the city)) x 100,000; n/a not avail.
Source: U.S. Department of Justice, FBI Uniform Crime Reports, 1977 - 1996

Forcible Rapes and Forcible Rape Rates: 1977 - 1996

Year	Number				Rate per 100,000 population			
	City	Suburbs[2]	MSA[1]	U.S.	City	Suburbs[3]	MSA[1]	U.S.
1977	316	157	473	63,500	46.1	25.9	36.6	29.4
1978	463	222	685	67,610	68.0	36.2	52.9	31.0
1979	477	241	718	76,390	66.4	38.4	53.3	34.7
1980	485	300	785	82,990	62.8	40.6	51.9	36.8
1981	408	240	648	82,500	51.3	31.6	41.7	36.0
1982	431	207	638	78,770	52.9	26.6	40.1	34.0
1983	499	230	729	78,920	59.2	28.5	44.2	33.7
1984	525	252	777	84,230	60.3	30.4	45.7	35.7
1985	635	287	922	88,670	71.3	31.9	51.5	37.1
1986	567	321	888	91,460	61.2	34.3	47.7	37.9
1987	503	338	841	91,110	53.9	32.7	42.7	37.4
1988	445	343	788	92,490	46.8	32.5	39.3	37.6
1989	399	329	728	94,500	42.4	29.2	35.2	38.1
1990	512	363	875	102,560	52.1	31.9	41.2	41.2
1991	480	422	902	106,590	48.2	35.9	41.5	42.3
1992	476	500	976	109,060	47.6	37.3	41.7	42.8
1993	444	437	881	106,010	42.7	32.3	36.8	41.1
1994	438	396	834	102,220	40.7	28.3	33.7	39.3
1995	411	417	828	97,470	37.9	28.3	32.3	37.1
1996	460	378	838	95,770	40.4	24.4	31.2	36.1

Notes: (1) Metropolitan Statistical Area - see Appendix A for areas included; (2) calculated by the editors using the following formula: (number of crimes in the MSA minus number of crimes in the city); (3) calculated by the editors using the following formula: ((number of crimes in the MSA minus number of crimes in the city) ÷ (population of the MSA minus population of the city)) x 100,000; n/a not avail.
Source: U.S. Department of Justice, FBI Uniform Crime Reports, 1977 - 1996

Robberies and Robbery Rates: 1977 - 1996

Year	Number				Rate per 100,000 population			
	City	Suburbs[2]	MSA[1]	U.S.	City	Suburbs[3]	MSA[1]	U.S.
1977	1,594	451	2,045	412,610	232.7	74.3	158.3	190.7
1978	2,031	668	2,699	426,930	298.2	109.0	208.6	195.8
1979	2,337	735	3,072	480,700	325.4	117.1	228.2	218.4
1980	3,037	981	4,018	565,840	392.9	132.8	265.8	251.1
1981	2,696	781	3,477	592,910	339.1	102.8	223.6	258.7
1982	2,402	682	3,084	553,130	295.1	87.7	193.7	238.9
1983	1,971	657	2,628	506,570	233.7	81.5	159.3	216.5
1984	2,106	581	2,687	485,010	242.0	70.1	158.1	205.4
1985	2,425	693	3,118	497,870	272.2	77.1	174.2	208.5
1986	2,972	1,025	3,997	542,780	320.6	109.5	214.5	225.1
1987	2,287	910	3,197	517,700	245.1	87.9	162.5	212.7
1988	2,518	910	3,428	542,970	264.6	86.2	170.8	220.9
1989	2,615	952	3,567	578,330	277.6	84.4	172.4	233.0
1990	3,383	1,082	4,465	639,270	344.0	95.0	210.4	257.0
1991	3,448	1,279	4,727	687,730	346.2	108.8	217.7	272.7
1992	3,140	1,192	4,332	672,480	314.0	88.9	185.1	263.6
1993	3,437	1,471	4,908	659,870	330.7	108.7	205.1	255.9
1994	3,451	1,450	4,901	618,950	320.7	103.4	197.8	237.7
1995	3,693	1,670	5,363	580,510	340.1	113.3	209.5	220.9
1996	3,757	1,710	5,467	537,050	329.6	110.5	203.4	202.4

Notes: (1) Metropolitan Statistical Area - see Appendix A for areas included; (2) calculated by the editors using the following formula: (number of crimes in the MSA minus number of crimes in the city); (3) calculated by the editors using the following formula: ((number of crimes in the MSA minus number of crimes in the city) ÷ (population of the MSA minus population of the city)) x 100,000; n/a not avail.
Source: U.S. Department of Justice, FBI Uniform Crime Reports, 1977 - 1996

Aggravated Assaults and Aggravated Assault Rates: 1977 - 1996

Year	Number				Rate per 100,000 population			
	City	Suburbs[2]	MSA[1]	U.S.	City	Suburbs[3]	MSA[1]	U.S.
1977	2,315	1,486	3,801	534,350	338.0	244.8	294.2	247.0
1978	2,819	1,704	4,523	571,460	414.0	278.0	349.5	262.1
1979	2,898	2,246	5,144	629,480	403.5	357.7	382.2	286.0
1980	3,395	2,886	6,281	672,650	439.3	390.7	415.5	298.5
1981	3,119	2,455	5,574	663,900	392.3	323.1	358.5	289.7
1982	2,503	2,230	4,733	669,480	307.5	286.6	297.3	289.2
1983	2,717	2,149	4,866	653,290	322.1	266.6	295.0	279.2
1984	3,640	2,107	5,747	685,350	418.3	254.2	338.2	290.2
1985	4,372	2,950	7,322	723,250	490.8	328.0	409.0	302.9
1986	5,577	3,036	8,613	834,320	601.6	324.3	462.3	346.1
1987	5,280	3,273	8,553	855,090	565.8	316.3	434.6	351.3
1988	5,408	3,077	8,485	910,090	568.2	291.6	422.8	370.2
1989	5,341	3,024	8,365	951,710	567.0	268.2	404.2	383.4
1990	6,642	3,514	10,156	1,054,860	675.4	308.6	478.6	424.1
1991	6,954	3,963	10,917	1,092,740	698.3	337.2	502.8	433.3
1992	7,155	4,881	12,036	1,126,970	715.6	364.1	514.3	441.8
1993	7,872	5,418	13,290	1,135,610	757.4	400.2	555.3	440.3
1994	7,507	5,479	12,986	1,113,180	697.6	390.9	524.1	427.6
1995	7,272	5,817	13,089	1,099,210	669.8	394.5	511.3	418.3
1996	6,126	5,256	11,382	1,029,810	537.5	339.6	423.5	388.2

Notes: (1) Metropolitan Statistical Area - see Appendix A for areas included; (2) calculated by the editors using the following formula: (number of crimes in the MSA minus number of crimes in the city); (3) calculated by the editors using the following formula: ((number of crimes in the MSA minus number of crimes in the city) ÷ (population of the MSA minus population of the city)) x 100,000; n/a not avail.
Source: U.S. Department of Justice, FBI Uniform Crime Reports, 1977 - 1996

Burglaries and Burglary Rates: 1977 - 1996

Year	Number				Rate per 100,000 population			
	City	Suburbs[2]	MSA[1]	U.S.	City	Suburbs[3]	MSA[1]	U.S.
1977	20,714	11,332	32,046	3,071,500	3,023.9	1,866.9	2,480.3	1,419.8
1978	20,340	10,381	30,721	3,128,300	2,986.8	1,693.3	2,374.0	1,434.6
1979	19,715	11,511	31,226	3,327,700	2,745.0	1,833.4	2,319.8	1,511.9
1980	24,137	13,230	37,367	3,795,200	3,123.0	1,791.1	2,472.1	1,684.1
1981	23,052	12,638	35,690	3,779,700	2,899.7	1,663.4	2,295.5	1,649.5
1982	21,482	11,707	33,189	3,447,100	2,638.9	1,504.7	2,084.6	1,488.8
1983	18,771	10,224	28,995	3,129,900	2,225.6	1,268.4	1,757.9	1,337.7
1984	19,340	11,691	31,031	2,984,400	2,222.3	1,410.4	1,826.2	1,263.7
1985	23,346	14,012	37,358	3,073,300	2,620.9	1,558.0	2,086.9	1,287.3
1986	25,586	14,660	40,246	3,241,400	2,759.9	1,566.2	2,160.2	1,344.6
1987	21,185	13,973	35,158	3,236,200	2,270.2	1,350.5	1,786.6	1,329.6
1988	20,841	13,811	34,652	3,218,100	2,189.8	1,308.8	1,726.6	1,309.2
1989	23,013	15,860	38,873	3,168,200	2,443.1	1,406.6	1,878.4	1,276.3
1990	24,682	16,688	41,370	3,073,900	2,509.9	1,465.5	1,949.5	1,235.9
1991	24,219	16,277	40,496	3,157,200	2,431.9	1,384.9	1,865.1	1,252.0
1992	20,317	16,770	37,087	2,979,900	2,031.9	1,251.0	1,584.7	1,168.2
1993	20,617	18,359	38,976	2,834,800	1,983.6	1,356.0	1,628.6	1,099.2
1994	21,347	19,773	41,120	2,712,800	1,983.7	1,410.7	1,659.5	1,042.0
1995	20,953	20,473	41,426	2,593,800	1,929.9	1,388.6	1,618.1	987.1
1996	19,559	18,200	37,759	2,501,500	1,716.0	1,175.9	1,404.9	943.0

Notes: (1) Metropolitan Statistical Area - see Appendix A for areas included; (2) calculated by the editors using the following formula: (number of crimes in the MSA minus number of crimes in the city); (3) calculated by the editors using the following formula: ((number of crimes in the MSA minus number of crimes in the city) ÷ (population of the MSA minus population of the city)) x 100,000; n/a not avail.
Source: U.S. Department of Justice, FBI Uniform Crime Reports, 1977 - 1996

Larceny-Thefts and Larceny-Theft Rates: 1977 - 1996

Year	Number				Rate per 100,000 population			
	City	Suburbs[2]	MSA[1]	U.S.	City	Suburbs[3]	MSA[1]	U.S.
1977	39,156	23,668	62,824	5,905,700	5,716.2	3,899.2	4,862.5	2,729.9
1978	41,125	26,004	67,129	5,991,000	6,038.9	4,241.7	5,187.5	2,747.4
1979	44,344	28,961	73,305	6,601,000	6,174.2	4,612.8	5,445.9	2,999.1
1980	51,598	31,968	83,566	7,136,900	6,676.0	4,327.8	5,528.5	3,167.0
1981	46,977	31,450	78,427	7,194,400	5,909.2	4,139.3	5,044.3	3,139.7
1982	44,347	31,561	75,908	7,142,500	5,447.7	4,056.6	4,767.9	3,084.8
1983	39,933	28,557	68,490	6,712,800	4,734.7	3,542.9	4,152.3	2,868.9
1984	41,128	30,677	71,805	6,591,900	4,725.8	3,700.9	4,225.8	2,791.3
1985	46,743	38,210	84,953	6,926,400	5,247.6	4,248.5	4,745.7	2,901.2
1986	48,896	41,066	89,962	7,257,200	5,274.3	4,387.2	4,828.6	3,010.3
1987	48,700	43,039	91,739	7,499,900	5,218.7	4,159.6	4,661.8	3,081.3
1988	51,147	46,228	97,375	7,705,900	5,374.2	4,380.8	4,851.9	3,134.9
1989	58,160	48,760	106,920	7,872,400	6,174.4	4,324.5	5,166.5	3,171.3
1990	52,912	48,288	101,200	7,945,700	5,380.5	4,240.6	4,768.9	3,194.8
1991	47,338	47,701	95,039	8,142,200	4,753.3	4,058.6	4,377.2	3,228.8
1992	46,006	50,604	96,610	7,915,200	4,601.1	3,775.0	4,127.9	3,103.0
1993	48,382	54,695	103,077	7,820,900	4,654.9	4,039.9	4,307.0	3,032.4
1994	54,493	58,046	112,539	7,879,800	5,063.9	4,141.2	4,541.9	3,026.7
1995	62,422	63,852	126,274	7,997,700	5,749.4	4,330.7	4,932.4	3,043.8
1996	60,565	60,926	121,491	7,894,600	5,313.7	3,936.3	4,520.4	2,975.9

Notes: (1) Metropolitan Statistical Area - see Appendix A for areas included; (2) calculated by the editors using the following formula: (number of crimes in the MSA minus number of crimes in the city); (3) calculated by the editors using the following formula: ((number of crimes in the MSA minus number of crimes in the city) ÷ (population of the MSA minus population of the city)) x 100,000; n/a not avail.
Source: U.S. Department of Justice, FBI Uniform Crime Reports, 1977 - 1996

Motor Vehicle Thefts and Motor Vehicle Theft Rates: 1977 - 1996

Year	Number				Rate per 100,000 population			
	City	Suburbs[2]	MSA[1]	U.S.	City	Suburbs[3]	MSA[1]	U.S.
1977	4,159	1,915	6,074	977,700	607.2	315.5	470.1	451.9
1978	4,709	2,197	6,906	1,004,100	691.5	358.4	533.7	460.5
1979	5,285	2,438	7,723	1,112,800	735.9	388.3	573.8	505.6
1980	5,768	2,758	8,526	1,131,700	746.3	373.4	564.1	502.2
1981	5,022	2,496	7,518	1,087,800	631.7	328.5	483.5	474.7
1982	4,394	2,409	6,803	1,062,400	539.8	309.6	427.3	458.8
1983	4,718	2,283	7,001	1,007,900	559.4	283.2	424.4	430.8
1984	4,439	2,706	7,145	1,032,200	510.1	326.5	420.5	437.1
1985	4,913	2,974	7,887	1,102,900	551.6	330.7	440.6	462.0
1986	5,654	3,458	9,112	1,224,100	609.9	369.4	489.1	507.8
1987	5,894	3,808	9,702	1,288,700	631.6	368.0	493.0	529.4
1988	6,615	4,425	11,040	1,432,900	695.1	419.3	550.1	582.9
1989	12,705	6,464	19,169	1,564,800	1,348.8	573.3	926.3	630.4
1990	17,520	8,509	26,029	1,635,900	1,781.6	747.3	1,226.6	657.8
1991	16,605	8,704	25,309	1,661,700	1,667.3	740.6	1,165.7	659.0
1992	14,983	8,470	23,453	1,610,800	1,498.4	631.9	1,002.1	631.5
1993	15,566	9,457	25,023	1,563,100	1,497.6	698.5	1,045.6	606.1
1994	20,664	12,065	32,729	1,539,300	1,920.3	860.7	1,320.9	591.3
1995	23,161	15,062	38,223	1,472,400	2,133.3	1,021.6	1,493.0	560.4
1996	18,096	12,456	30,552	1,395,200	1,587.7	804.8	1,136.8	525.9

Notes: (1) Metropolitan Statistical Area - see Appendix A for areas included; (2) calculated by the editors using the following formula: (number of crimes in the MSA minus number of crimes in the city); (3) calculated by the editors using the following formula: ((number of crimes in the MSA minus number of crimes in the city) ÷ (population of the MSA minus population of the city)) x 100,000; n/a not avail.
Source: U.S. Department of Justice, FBI Uniform Crime Reports, 1977 - 1996

HATE CRIMES

Criminal Incidents by Bias Motivation

Area	Race	Ethnicity	Religion	Sexual Orientation
Phoenix	75	8	13	29

Notes: Figures include both violent and property crimes. Law enforcement agencies must have submitted data for at least one quarter of calendar year 1995 to be included in this report, therefore figures shown may not represent complete 12-month totals; n/a not available
Source: U.S. Department of Justice, FBI Uniform Crime Reports, Hate Crime Statistics 1995

ILLEGAL DRUGS

Drug Use by Adult Arrestees

Sex	Percent Testing Positive by Urinalysis (%)				
	Any Drug[1]	Cocaine	Marijuana	Opiates	Multiple Drugs
Male	59	32	28	9	22
Female	65	42	22	13	27

Notes: The catchment area is the entire county; (1) Includes cocaine, opiates, marijuana, methadone, phencyclidine (PCP), benzodiazepines, methaqualone, propoxyphene, barbiturates & amphetamines
Source: National Institute of Justice, 1996 Drug Use Forecasting, Annual Report on Adult and Juvenile Arrestees (released June 1997)

LAW ENFORCEMENT

Full-Time Law Enforcement Employees

Jurisdiction	Police Employees			Police Officers per 100,000 population
	Total	Officers	Civilians	
Phoenix	3,140	2,255	885	197.8

Notes: Data as of October 31, 1996
Source: U.S. Department of Justice, FBI Uniform Crime Reports, 1996

Number of Police Officers by Race

Race	Police Officers 1983 Number	1983 Pct.	1992 Number	1992 Pct.	Index of Representation[1] 1983	1992	% Chg.
Black	48	2.9	66	4.0	0.58	0.77	32.8
Hispanic[2]	156	9.4	211	12.8	0.63	0.64	1.6

Notes: (1) The index of representation is calculated by dividing the percent of black/hispanic police officers by the percent of corresponding blacks/hispanics in the local population. An index approaching 1.0 indicates that a city is closer to achieving a representation of police officers equal to their proportion in the local population; (2) Hispanic officers can be of any race
Source: Bureau of Justice Statistics, Sourcebook of Criminal Justice Statistics, 1994

CORRECTIONS

Federal Correctional Facilities

Type	Year Opened	Security Level	Sex of Inmates	Rated Capacity	Population on 7/1/95	Number of Staff
Federal Correctional Inst.[1]	1985	Medium	Male	740	1,144	370

Notes: Data as of 1995; (1) A minimum security satellite camp is operated adjacent to this facility.
Source: Bureau of Justice Statistics, Sourcebook of Criminal Justice Statistics Online

City/County/Regional Correctional Facilities

Name	Year Opened	Year Renov.	Rated Capacity	1995 Pop.	Number of COs[1]	Number of Staff	ACA[2] Accred.
Maricopa Co 1st Ave Jail	1964	--	420	n/a	n/a	n/a	No
Maricopa Co Central Jail	1976	--	847	n/a	n/a	n/a	No
Maricopa Co Estrella Jail	1993	--	600	n/a	n/a	n/a	No
Maricopa Co Madison St Jail	1985	--	1,500	n/a	n/a	n/a	No
Maricopa Co Towers Jail	1982	--	720	n/a	n/a	n/a	No

Notes: Data as of April 1996; (1) Correctional Officers; (2) American Correctional Assn. Accreditation
Source: American Correctional Association, 1996-1998 National Jail and Adult Detention Directory

Private Adult Correctional Facilities

Name	Date Opened	Rated Capacity	Present Pop.	Security Level	Facility Construct.	Expans. Plans	ACA[1] Accred.
Arizona State Prison (Phoenix-West)	4/96	400	400	Min.	Renov.	None	In prog.

Notes: Data as of December 1996; (1) American Correctional Association Accreditation
Source: University of Florida, Center for Studies in Criminology and Law, Private Adult Correctional Facility Census, 10th Ed., March 15, 1997

Characteristics of Shock Incarceration Programs

Arizona did not have a shock incarceration program as of July 1996

Source: Sourcebook of Criminal Justice Statistics Online

INMATES AND HIV/AIDS

HIV Testing Policies for Inmates

Jurisdiction	All Inmates at Some Time	All Convicted Inmates at Admission	Random Samples While in Custody	High-risk Groups	Upon Inmate Request	Upon Court Order	Upon Involvement in Incident
Maricopa Co.[1]	No	No	No	No	Yes	No	No

Notes: (1) All facilities reported following the same testing policy or authorities reported the policy to be jurisdiction-wide
Source: HIV in Prisons and Jails, 1993 (released August 1995)

Inmates Known to be Positive for HIV

Jurisdiction	Number of Jail Inmates in Facilities Providing Data	Type of HIV Infection/AIDS Cases Total	Asymptomatic	Symptomatic	Confirmed AIDS	HIV/AIDS Cases as a Percent of Tot. Custody Pop.
Maricopa Co.[1,2]	1,773	1	0	0	0	0.1

Note: (1) Detail does not add to total; (2) Some but not all facilities reported data on HIV/AIDS cases. Excludes inmates in facilities that did not report data.
Source: HIV in Prisons and Jails, 1993 (released August, 1995)

DEATH PENALTY

Death Penalty Statistics

State	Prisoners Executed		Prisoners Under Sentence of Death					Avg. No. of Years on Death Row[4]
	1930-1995	1996[1]	Total[2]	White[3]	Black[3]	Hisp.	Women	
Arizona	42	2	117	97	14	18	1	7.2

Notes: Data as of 12/31/95 unless otherwise noted; (1) Data as of 7/31/97; (2) Includes persons of other races; (3) Includes people of Hispanic origin; (4) Covers prisoners sentenced 1974 through 1995
Source: Bureau of Justice Statistics, Capital Punishment 1995 (released 12/96); Death Penalty Information Center Web Site, 9/30/97

Capital Offenses and Methods of Execution

Capital Offenses in Arizona	Minimum Age for Imposition of Death Penalty	Mentally Retarded Excluded	Methods of Execution[1]
First-degree murder accompanied by at least 1 of 10 aggravating factors.	None	No	Lethal injection; lethal gas

Notes: Data as of 12/31/95 unless otherwise noted; (1) Data as of 7/31/97
Source: Bureau of Justice Statistics, Capital Punishment 1995 (released 12/96); Death Penalty Information Center Web Site, 9/30/97

LAWS

Statutory Provisions Relating to the Purchase, Ownership and Use of Handguns

Jurisdiction	Instant Background Check	Federal Waiting Period Applies[1]	State Waiting Period (days)	License or Permit to Purchase	Regis-tration	Record of Sale Sent to Police	Concealed Carry Law
Arizona	Yes[a]	Yes[b]	No	No	No	No	Yes[c]

Note: Data as of 1996; (1) The Federal 5-day waiting period for handgun purchases applies to states that don't have instant background checks, waiting period requirements, or licensing procedures exempting them from the Federal requirement; (a) Concealed firearm carry permit holders are exempt from Instant Check; (b) The Federal waiting period does not apply to a person holding a valid permit or license to carry a firearm, issued within 5 years of proposed purchase; (c) "Shall issue" permit system, liberally administered discretion by local authorities over permit issuance, or no permit required
Source: Sourcebook of Criminal Justice Statistics Online

Statutory Provisions Relating to Alcohol Use and Driving

Jurisdiction	Drinking Age	Blood Alcohol Concentration Levels as Evidence in State Courts[1]		Open Container Law[1]	Anti-Consump-tion Law[1]	Dram Shop Law[1]
		Illegal per se at 0.10%	Presumption at 0.10%			
Arizona	21	Yes	Yes	No	Yes	Yes

Note: Data as of January 1, 1997; (1) See Appendix C for an explanation of terms
Source: Sourcebook of Criminal Justice Statistics Online

Statutory Provisions Relating to Curfews

Jurisdiction	Year Enacted	Latest Revision	Age Group(s)	Curfew Provisions
Phoenix	1968	1993	16 and 17	Midnight to 5 am every night
			15 and under	10 pm to 5 am every night

Note: Data as of February 1996
Source: Sourcebook of Criminal Justice Statistics Online

Statutory Provisions Relating to Hate Crimes

Jurisdiction	Bias-Motivated Violence and Intimidation						Institutional Vandalism
	Civil Action	Criminal Penalty					
		Race/ Religion/ Ethnicity	Sexual Orientation	Mental/ Physical Disability	Gender	Age	
Arizona	No	No	No	No	No	No	Yes

Source: Anti-Defamation League, 1997 Hate Crimes Laws

Pittsburgh, Pennsylvania

OVERVIEW

The total crime rate for the city decreased 12.6% between 1977 and 1996. During that same period, the violent crime rate decreased 22.3% and the property crime rate decreased 10.6%.

Among violent crimes, the rates for: Murders increased 12.7%; Forcible Rapes increased 1.9%; Robberies decreased 23.1%; and Aggravated Assaults decreased 25.7%.

Among property crimes, the rates for: Burglaries decreased 47.3%; Larceny-Thefts increased 28.3%; and Motor Vehicle Thefts decreased 32.7%.

ANTI-CRIME PROGRAMS

Among the programs are:

- Business and Neighborhood Watch—which is considered proactive prevention. Residents, employers and employees help to identify problems in their neighborhoods and report them to the police.
- Green Circle—an educational program for grades K-3 which seeks to teach children to recognize and accept differences among people and to develop positive relationships with the police.
- D.A.R.E. (Drug Abuse Resistance Education)—a curriculum for schools.
- McGruff Safe House—provides a temporary haven for children who find themselves in an emergency. The homes are volunteered by neighborhood residents.
  Pittsburgh Bureau of Police, 8/97

CRIME RISK

Your Chances of Becoming a Victim[1]

Area	Any Crime	Violent Crime					Property Crime			
		Any	Murder	Forcible Rape[2]	Robbery	Aggrav. Assault	Any	Burglary	Larceny -Theft	Motor Vehicle Theft
City	1:19	1:124	1:7,538	1:921	1:226	1:344	1:22	1:116	1:35	1:126

Note: (1) Figures have been calculated by dividing the population of the city by the number of crimes reported to the FBI during 1996 and are expressed as odds (eg. 1:20 should be read as 1 in 20). (2) Figures have been calculated by dividing the female population of the city by the number of forcible rapes reported to the FBI during 1996. The female population of the city was estimated by calculating the ratio of females to males reported in the 1990 Census and applying that ratio to 1996 population estimate.
Source: FBI Uniform Crime Reports 1996

CRIME STATISTICS

Total Crimes and Total Crime Rates: 1977 - 1996

Year	Number				Rate per 100,000 population			
	City	Suburbs[2]	MSA[1]	U.S.	City	Suburbs[3]	MSA[1]	U.S.
1977	26,776	43,213	69,989	10,984,500	6,057.9	2,255.8	2,968.6	5,077.6
1978	26,776	42,669	69,445	11,209,000	6,183.8	2,232.3	2,962.1	5,140.3
1979	27,958	46,619	74,577	12,249,500	6,362.7	2,543.1	3,281.7	5,565.5
1980	30,399	48,353	78,752	13,408,300	7,166.1	2,634.6	3,485.3	5,950.0
1981	31,384	45,032	76,416	13,423,800	7,373.5	2,445.4	3,370.6	5,858.2
1982	29,913	43,243	73,156	12,974,400	7,024.9	2,348.2	3,226.5	5,603.6
1983	30,842	39,727	70,569	12,108,600	7,224.8	2,206.4	3,168.1	5,175.0
1984	31,445	39,969	71,414	11,881,800	7,568.4	2,237.8	3,243.8	5,031.3
1985	28,931	36,470	65,401	12,431,400	7,215.3	2,070.3	3,024.2	5,207.1
1986	32,008	37,369	69,377	13,211,900	7,958.2	2,114.7	3,198.2	5,480.4
1987	30,836	35,844	66,680	13,508,700	7,926.7	2,058.9	3,130.6	5,550.0
1988	31,904	34,692	66,596	13,923,100	8,239.9	2,002.2	3,141.5	5,664.2
1989	33,407	37,840	71,247	14,251,400	8,875.1	2,196.0	3,393.5	5,741.0
1990	32,386	37,778	70,164	14,475,600	8,755.8	2,241.2	3,413.5	5,820.3
1991	30,603	41,868	72,471	14,872,900	8,218.9	2,467.5	3,502.5	5,897.8
1992	30,694	48,963	79,657	14,438,200	8,210.4	2,384.5	3,281.8	5,660.2
1993	28,613	46,801	75,414	14,144,800	7,765.3	2,276.9	3,111.2	5,484.4
1994	26,350	46,403	72,753	13,989,500	7,148.8	2,256.9	3,000.6	5,373.5
1995	21,748	n/a	n/a	13,862,700	6,130.0	n/a	n/a	5,275.9
1996	18,764	45,454	64,218	13,473,600	5,296.0	2,211.6	2,665.1	5,078.9

Notes: (1) Metropolitan Statistical Area - see Appendix A for areas included; (2) calculated by the editors using the following formula: (number of crimes in the MSA minus number of crimes in the city); (3) calculated by the editors using the following formula: ((number of crimes in the MSA minus number of crimes in the city) ÷ (population of the MSA minus population of the city)) x 100,000; n/a not avail.
Source: U.S. Department of Justice, FBI Uniform Crime Reports, 1977 - 1996

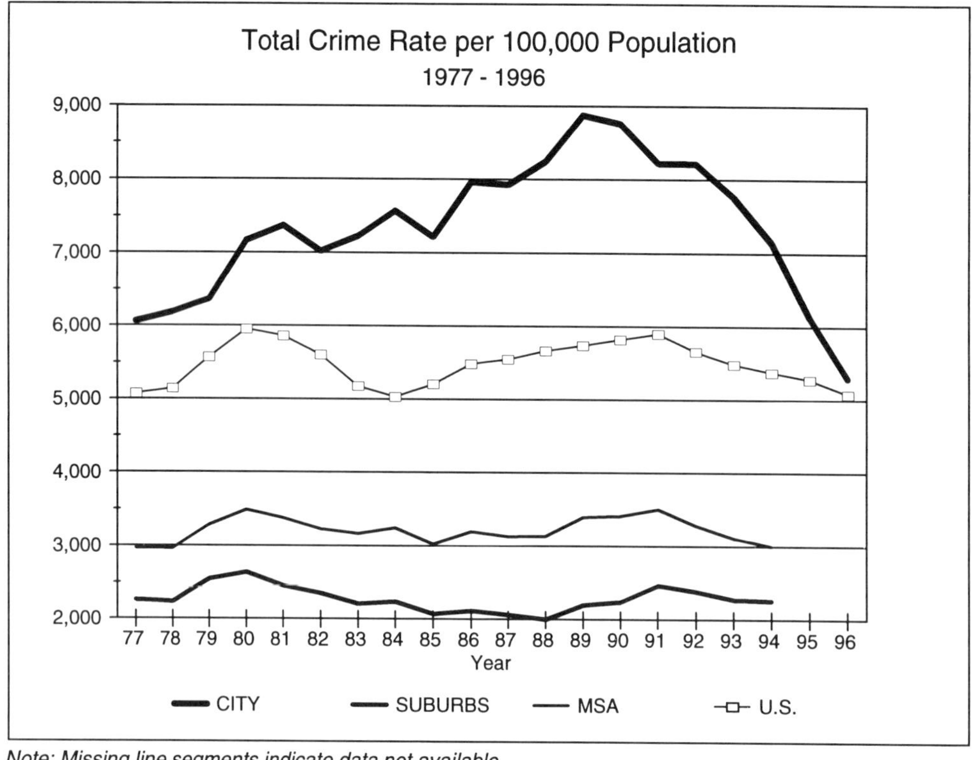

Note: Missing line segments indicate data not available.

Violent Crimes and Violent Crime Rates: 1977 - 1996

Year	Number				Rate per 100,000 population			
	City	Suburbs[2]	MSA[1]	U.S.	City	Suburbs[3]	MSA[1]	U.S.
1977	4,572	2,949	7,521	1,029,580	1,034.4	153.9	319.0	475.9
1978	4,818	3,216	8,034	1,085,550	1,112.7	168.3	342.7	497.8
1979	4,649	3,591	8,240	1,208,030	1,058.0	195.9	362.6	548.9
1980	5,120	3,508	8,628	1,344,520	1,207.0	191.1	381.8	596.6
1981	5,983	3,666	9,649	1,361,820	1,405.7	199.1	425.6	594.3
1982	5,391	3,342	8,733	1,322,390	1,266.0	181.5	385.2	571.1
1983	5,605	3,003	8,608	1,258,090	1,313.0	166.8	386.4	537.7
1984	4,564	2,845	7,409	1,273,280	1,098.5	159.3	336.5	539.2
1985	4,353	2,978	7,331	1,328,800	1,085.6	169.0	339.0	556.6
1986	4,707	3,205	7,912	1,489,170	1,170.3	181.4	364.7	617.7
1987	4,318	3,262	7,580	1,484,000	1,110.0	187.4	355.9	609.7
1988	4,117	3,116	7,233	1,566,220	1,063.3	179.8	341.2	637.2
1989	4,579	3,655	8,234	1,646,040	1,216.5	212.1	392.2	663.1
1990	4,893	3,795	8,688	1,820,130	1,322.9	225.1	422.7	731.8
1991	4,294	4,584	8,878	1,911,770	1,153.2	270.2	429.1	758.1
1992	4,495	5,449	9,944	1,932,270	1,202.4	265.4	409.7	757.5
1993	4,479	5,056	9,535	1,926,020	1,215.6	246.0	393.4	746.8
1994	4,105	5,160	9,265	1,857,670	1,113.7	251.0	382.1	713.6
1995	3,474	n/a	n/a	1,798,790	979.2	n/a	n/a	684.6
1996	2,848	4,458	7,306	1,682,280	803.8	216.9	303.2	634.1

Notes: Violent crimes include murder, forcible rape, robbery and aggravated assault; n/a not available; (1) Metropolitan Statistical Area - see Appendix A for areas included; (2) calculated by the editors using the following formula: (number of crimes in the MSA minus number of crimes in the city); (3) calculated by the editors using the following formula: ((number of crimes in the MSA minus number of crimes in the city) ÷ (population of the MSA minus population of the city)) x 100,000
Source: U.S. Department of Justice, FBI Uniform Crime Reports, 1977 - 1996

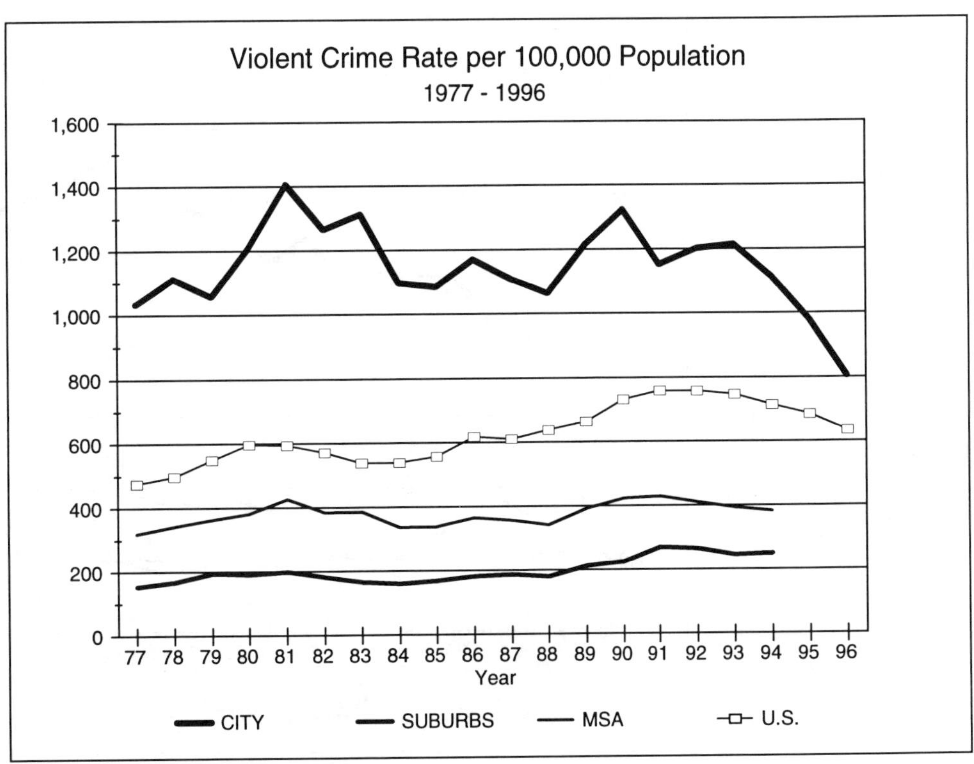

Note: Missing line segments indicate data not available.

Property Crimes and Property Crime Rates: 1977 - 1996

Year	Number				Rate per 100,000 population			
	City	Suburbs[2]	MSA[1]	U.S.	City	Suburbs[3]	MSA[1]	U.S.
1977	22,204	40,264	62,468	9,955,000	5,023.5	2,101.8	2,649.6	4,601.7
1978	21,958	39,453	61,411	10,123,400	5,071.1	2,064.0	2,619.4	4,642.5
1979	23,309	43,028	66,337	11,041,500	5,304.6	2,347.2	2,919.1	5,016.6
1980	25,279	44,845	70,124	12,063,700	5,959.1	2,443.4	3,103.5	5,353.3
1981	25,401	41,366	66,767	12,061,900	5,967.8	2,246.3	2,945.0	5,263.9
1982	24,522	39,901	64,423	11,652,000	5,758.9	2,166.8	2,841.4	5,032.5
1983	25,237	36,724	61,961	10,850,500	5,911.8	2,039.6	2,781.7	4,637.4
1984	26,881	37,124	64,005	10,608,500	6,469.9	2,078.5	2,907.3	4,492.1
1985	24,578	33,492	58,070	11,102,600	6,129.7	1,901.2	2,685.2	4,650.5
1986	27,301	34,164	61,465	11,722,700	6,787.8	1,933.4	2,833.4	4,862.6
1987	26,518	32,582	59,100	12,024,700	6,816.7	1,871.6	2,774.8	4,940.3
1988	27,787	31,576	59,363	12,356,900	7,176.6	1,822.4	2,800.3	5,027.1
1989	28,828	34,185	63,013	12,605,400	7,658.6	1,983.9	3,001.3	5,077.9
1990	27,493	33,983	61,476	12,655,500	7,433.0	2,016.1	2,990.8	5,088.5
1991	26,309	37,284	63,593	12,961,100	7,065.7	2,197.3	3,073.4	5,139.7
1992	26,199	43,514	69,713	12,505,900	7,008.0	2,119.1	2,872.1	4,902.7
1993	24,134	41,745	65,879	12,218,800	6,549.7	2,030.9	2,717.8	4,737.6
1994	22,245	41,243	63,488	12,131,900	6,035.1	2,005.9	2,618.4	4,660.0
1995	18,274	n/a	n/a	12,063,900	5,150.8	n/a	n/a	4,591.3
1996	15,916	40,996	56,912	11,791,300	4,492.1	1,994.7	2,361.9	4,444.8

Notes: Property crimes include burglary, larceny-theft and motor vehicle theft; n/a not available; (1) Metropolitan Statistical Area - see Appendix A for areas included; (2) calculated by the editors using the following formula: (number of crimes in the MSA minus number of crimes in the city); (3) calculated by the editors using the following formula: ((number of crimes in the MSA minus number of crimes in the city) ÷ (population of the MSA minus population of the city)) x 100,000
Source: U.S. Department of Justice, FBI Uniform Crime Reports, 1977 - 1996

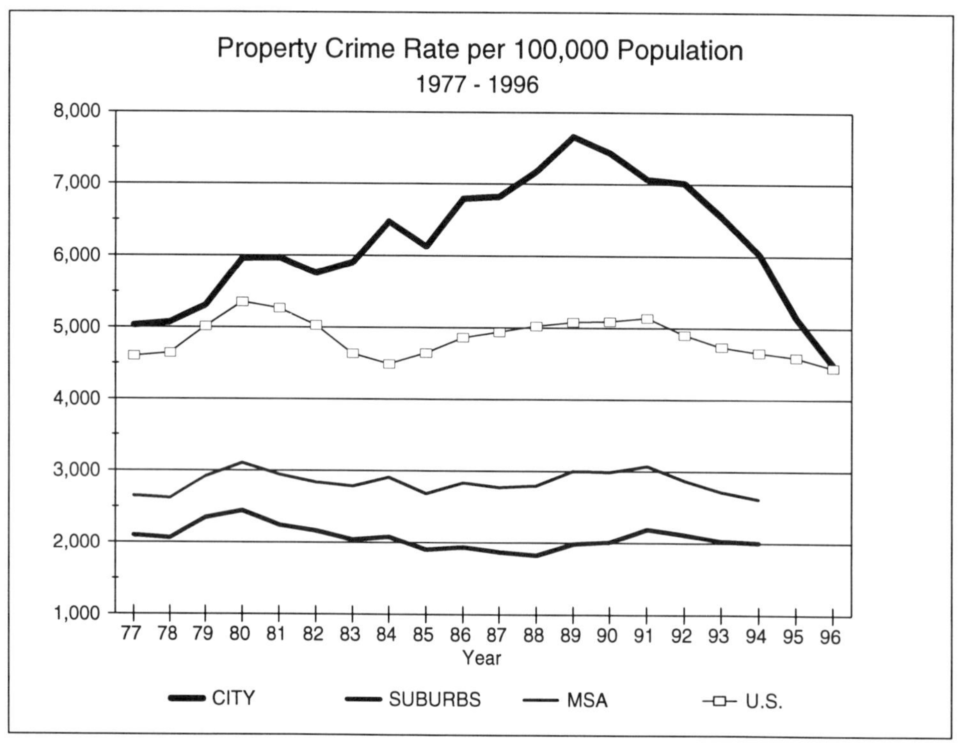

Note: Missing line segments indicate data not available.

Murders and Murder Rates: 1977 - 1996

Year	Number				Rate per 100,000 population			
	City	Suburbs[2]	MSA[1]	U.S.	City	Suburbs[3]	MSA[1]	U.S.
1977	52	60	112	19,120	11.8	3.1	4.8	8.8
1978	66	57	123	19,560	15.2	3.0	5.2	9.0
1979	68	50	118	21,460	15.5	2.7	5.2	9.7
1980	50	51	101	23,040	11.8	2.8	4.5	10.2
1981	49	49	98	22,520	11.5	2.7	4.3	9.8
1982	51	52	103	21,010	12.0	2.8	4.5	9.1
1983	42	35	77	19,310	9.8	1.9	3.5	8.3
1984	47	41	88	18,690	11.3	2.3	4.0	7.9
1985	34	42	76	18,980	8.5	2.4	3.5	7.9
1986	47	38	85	20,610	11.7	2.2	3.9	8.6
1987	37	30	67	20,100	9.5	1.7	3.1	8.3
1988	18	35	53	20,680	4.6	2.0	2.5	8.4
1989	31	36	67	21,500	8.2	2.1	3.2	8.7
1990	35	32	67	23,440	9.5	1.9	3.3	9.4
1991	36	32	68	24,700	9.7	1.9	3.3	9.8
1992	44	60	104	23,760	11.8	2.9	4.3	9.3
1993	80	48	128	24,530	21.7	2.3	5.3	9.5
1994	64	46	110	23,330	17.4	2.2	4.5	9.0
1995	58	n/a	n/a	21,610	16.3	n/a	n/a	8.2
1996	47	36	83	19,650	13.3	1.8	3.4	7.4

Notes: (1) Metropolitan Statistical Area - see Appendix A for areas included; (2) calculated by the editors using the following formula: (number of crimes in the MSA minus number of crimes in the city); (3) calculated by the editors using the following formula: ((number of crimes in the MSA minus number of crimes in the city) ÷ (population of the MSA minus population of the city)) x 100,000; n/a not avail.
Source: U.S. Department of Justice, FBI Uniform Crime Reports, 1977 - 1996

Forcible Rapes and Forcible Rape Rates: 1977 - 1996

Year	Number				Rate per 100,000 population			
	City	Suburbs[2]	MSA[1]	U.S.	City	Suburbs[3]	MSA[1]	U.S.
1977	252	240	492	63,500	57.0	12.5	20.9	29.4
1978	231	237	468	67,610	53.3	12.4	20.0	31.0
1979	263	319	582	76,390	59.9	17.4	25.6	34.7
1980	299	270	569	82,990	70.5	14.7	25.2	36.8
1981	213	296	509	82,500	50.0	16.1	22.5	36.0
1982	236	247	483	78,770	55.4	13.4	21.3	34.0
1983	214	269	483	78,920	50.1	14.9	21.7	33.7
1984	224	296	520	84,230	53.9	16.6	23.6	35.7
1985	188	297	485	88,670	46.9	16.9	22.4	37.1
1986	253	273	526	91,460	62.9	15.4	24.2	37.9
1987	263	320	583	91,110	67.6	18.4	27.4	37.4
1988	234	290	524	92,490	60.4	16.7	24.7	37.6
1989	219	360	579	94,500	58.2	20.9	27.6	38.1
1990	302	324	626	102,560	81.6	19.2	30.5	41.2
1991	300	401	701	106,590	80.6	23.6	33.9	42.3
1992	221	489	710	109,060	59.1	23.8	29.3	42.8
1993	226	433	659	106,010	61.3	21.1	27.2	41.1
1994	261	412	673	102,220	70.8	20.0	27.8	39.3
1995	243	n/a	n/a	97,470	68.5	n/a	n/a	37.1
1996	206	348	554	95,770	58.1	16.9	23.0	36.1

Notes: (1) Metropolitan Statistical Area - see Appendix A for areas included; (2) calculated by the editors using the following formula: (number of crimes in the MSA minus number of crimes in the city); (3) calculated by the editors using the following formula: ((number of crimes in the MSA minus number of crimes in the city) ÷ (population of the MSA minus population of the city)) x 100,000; n/a not avail.
Source: U.S. Department of Justice, FBI Uniform Crime Reports, 1977 - 1996

Robberies and Robbery Rates: 1977 - 1996

Year	Number				Rate per 100,000 population			
	City	Suburbs[2]	MSA[1]	U.S.	City	Suburbs[3]	MSA[1]	U.S.
1977	2,539	1,120	3,659	412,610	574.4	58.5	155.2	190.7
1978	3,046	1,119	4,165	426,930	703.5	58.5	177.7	195.8
1979	2,752	1,142	3,894	480,700	626.3	62.3	171.3	218.4
1980	3,252	1,288	4,540	565,840	766.6	70.2	200.9	251.1
1981	4,288	1,368	5,656	592,910	1,007.4	74.3	249.5	258.7
1982	3,841	1,181	5,022	553,130	902.0	64.1	221.5	238.9
1983	4,198	1,176	5,374	506,570	983.4	65.3	241.3	216.5
1984	3,212	974	4,186	485,010	773.1	54.5	190.1	205.4
1985	3,016	873	3,889	497,870	752.2	49.6	179.8	208.5
1986	3,253	855	4,108	542,780	808.8	48.4	189.4	225.1
1987	2,834	849	3,683	517,700	728.5	48.8	172.9	212.7
1988	2,537	695	3,232	542,970	655.2	40.1	152.5	220.9
1989	2,471	834	3,305	578,330	656.5	48.4	157.4	233.0
1990	2,319	784	3,103	639,270	627.0	46.5	151.0	257.0
1991	2,704	1,095	3,799	687,730	726.2	64.5	183.6	272.7
1992	2,989	1,359	4,348	672,480	799.5	66.2	179.1	263.6
1993	2,784	1,269	4,053	659,870	755.6	61.7	167.2	255.9
1994	2,469	1,254	3,723	618,950	669.8	61.0	153.5	237.7
1995	2,077	n/a	n/a	580,510	585.4	n/a	n/a	220.9
1996	1,565	1,049	2,614	537,050	441.7	51.0	108.5	202.4

Notes: (1) Metropolitan Statistical Area - see Appendix A for areas included; (2) calculated by the editors using the following formula: (number of crimes in the MSA minus number of crimes in the city); (3) calculated by the editors using the following formula: ((number of crimes in the MSA minus number of crimes in the city) ÷ (population of the MSA minus population of the city)) x 100,000; n/a not avail.
Source: U.S. Department of Justice, FBI Uniform Crime Reports, 1977 - 1996

Aggravated Assaults and Aggravated Assault Rates: 1977 - 1996

Year	Number				Rate per 100,000 population			
	City	Suburbs[2]	MSA[1]	U.S.	City	Suburbs[3]	MSA[1]	U.S.
1977	1,729	1,529	3,258	534,350	391.2	79.8	138.2	247.0
1978	1,475	1,803	3,278	571,460	340.6	94.3	139.8	262.1
1979	1,566	2,080	3,646	629,480	356.4	113.5	160.4	286.0
1980	1,519	1,899	3,418	672,650	358.1	103.5	151.3	298.5
1981	1,433	1,953	3,386	663,900	336.7	106.1	149.4	289.7
1982	1,263	1,862	3,125	669,480	296.6	101.1	137.8	289.2
1983	1,151	1,523	2,674	653,290	269.6	84.6	120.0	279.2
1984	1,081	1,534	2,615	685,350	260.2	85.9	118.8	290.2
1985	1,115	1,766	2,881	723,250	278.1	100.2	133.2	302.9
1986	1,154	2,039	3,193	834,320	286.9	115.4	147.2	346.1
1987	1,184	2,063	3,247	855,090	304.4	118.5	152.4	351.3
1988	1,328	2,096	3,424	910,090	343.0	121.0	161.5	370.2
1989	1,858	2,425	4,283	951,710	493.6	140.7	204.0	383.4
1990	2,237	2,655	4,892	1,054,860	604.8	157.5	238.0	424.1
1991	1,254	3,056	4,310	1,092,740	336.8	180.1	208.3	433.3
1992	1,241	3,541	4,782	1,126,970	332.0	172.4	197.0	441.8
1993	1,389	3,306	4,695	1,135,610	377.0	160.8	193.7	440.3
1994	1,311	3,448	4,759	1,113,180	355.7	167.7	196.3	427.6
1995	1,096	n/a	n/a	1,099,210	308.9	n/a	n/a	418.3
1996	1,030	3,025	4,055	1,029,810	290.7	147.2	168.3	388.2

Notes: (1) Metropolitan Statistical Area - see Appendix A for areas included; (2) calculated by the editors using the following formula: (number of crimes in the MSA minus number of crimes in the city); (3) calculated by the editors using the following formula: ((number of crimes in the MSA minus number of crimes in the city) ÷ (population of the MSA minus population of the city)) x 100,000; n/a not avail.
Source: U.S. Department of Justice, FBI Uniform Crime Reports, 1977 - 1996

Burglaries and Burglary Rates: 1977 - 1996

Year	Number				Rate per 100,000 population			
	City	Suburbs[2]	MSA[1]	U.S.	City	Suburbs[3]	MSA[1]	U.S.
1977	7,213	12,252	19,465	3,071,500	1,631.9	639.6	825.6	1,419.8
1978	7,808	11,574	19,382	3,128,300	1,803.2	605.5	826.7	1,434.6
1979	7,397	11,870	19,267	3,327,700	1,683.4	647.5	847.8	1,511.9
1980	8,997	13,399	22,396	3,795,200	2,120.9	730.1	991.2	1,684.1
1981	8,843	12,709	21,552	3,779,700	2,077.6	690.1	950.6	1,649.5
1982	8,096	11,849	19,945	3,447,100	1,901.3	643.4	879.7	1,488.8
1983	7,377	10,533	17,910	3,129,900	1,728.1	585.0	804.1	1,337.7
1984	7,450	10,247	17,697	2,984,400	1,793.1	573.7	803.8	1,263.7
1985	7,243	9,406	16,649	3,073,300	1,806.4	533.9	769.9	1,287.3
1986	6,980	8,985	15,965	3,241,400	1,735.4	508.5	736.0	1,344.6
1987	7,647	8,489	16,136	3,236,200	1,965.7	487.6	757.6	1,329.6
1988	7,444	8,219	15,663	3,218,100	1,922.6	474.4	738.9	1,309.2
1989	8,109	8,704	16,813	3,168,200	2,154.3	505.1	800.8	1,276.3
1990	5,988	7,605	13,593	3,073,900	1,618.9	451.2	661.3	1,235.9
1991	5,891	8,872	14,763	3,157,200	1,582.1	522.9	713.5	1,252.0
1992	5,201	9,670	14,871	2,979,900	1,391.2	470.9	612.7	1,168.2
1993	4,611	8,919	13,530	2,834,800	1,251.4	433.9	558.2	1,099.2
1994	4,335	8,269	12,604	2,712,800	1,176.1	402.2	519.8	1,042.0
1995	3,598	n/a	n/a	2,593,800	1,014.1	n/a	n/a	987.1
1996	3,049	7,661	10,710	2,501,500	860.6	372.7	444.5	943.0

Notes: (1) Metropolitan Statistical Area - see Appendix A for areas included; (2) calculated by the editors using the following formula: (number of crimes in the MSA minus number of crimes in the city); (3) calculated by the editors using the following formula: ((number of crimes in the MSA minus number of crimes in the city) ÷ (population of the MSA minus population of the city)) x 100,000; n/a not avail.
Source: U.S. Department of Justice, FBI Uniform Crime Reports, 1977 - 1996

Larceny-Thefts and Larceny-Theft Rates: 1977 - 1996

Year	Number				Rate per 100,000 population			
	City	Suburbs[2]	MSA[1]	U.S.	City	Suburbs[3]	MSA[1]	U.S.
1977	9,781	23,137	32,918	5,905,700	2,212.9	1,207.8	1,396.2	2,729.9
1978	8,803	22,356	31,159	5,991,000	2,033.0	1,169.6	1,329.1	2,747.4
1979	9,725	24,548	34,273	6,601,000	2,213.2	1,339.1	1,508.1	2,999.1
1980	10,721	25,023	35,744	7,136,900	2,527.3	1,363.4	1,581.9	3,167.0
1981	11,661	23,177	34,838	7,194,400	2,739.7	1,258.6	1,536.7	3,139.7
1982	11,769	22,682	34,451	7,142,500	2,763.9	1,231.7	1,519.5	3,084.8
1983	12,690	21,296	33,986	6,712,800	2,972.7	1,182.7	1,525.8	2,868.9
1984	11,754	20,560	32,314	6,591,900	2,829.1	1,151.1	1,467.8	2,791.3
1985	10,569	18,654	29,223	6,926,400	2,635.9	1,058.9	1,351.3	2,901.2
1986	11,137	19,179	30,316	7,257,200	2,769.0	1,085.4	1,397.5	3,010.3
1987	11,723	19,455	31,178	7,499,900	3,013.5	1,117.5	1,463.8	3,081.3
1988	10,973	18,479	29,452	7,705,900	2,834.0	1,066.5	1,389.3	3,134.9
1989	12,669	19,473	32,142	7,872,400	3,365.7	1,130.1	1,530.9	3,171.3
1990	12,871	19,300	32,171	7,945,700	3,479.8	1,145.0	1,565.1	3,194.8
1991	12,942	21,811	34,753	8,142,200	3,475.8	1,285.4	1,679.6	3,228.8
1992	12,874	26,519	39,393	7,915,200	3,443.7	1,291.5	1,623.0	3,103.0
1993	13,017	26,739	39,756	7,820,900	3,532.7	1,300.9	1,640.1	3,032.4
1994	12,568	27,493	40,061	7,879,800	3,409.7	1,337.2	1,652.2	3,026.7
1995	11,289	n/a	n/a	7,997,700	3,182.0	n/a	n/a	3,043.8
1996	10,057	29,008	39,065	7,894,600	2,838.5	1,411.4	1,621.2	2,975.9

Notes: (1) Metropolitan Statistical Area - see Appendix A for areas included; (2) calculated by the editors using the following formula: (number of crimes in the MSA minus number of crimes in the city); (3) calculated by the editors using the following formula: ((number of crimes in the MSA minus number of crimes in the city) ÷ (population of the MSA minus population of the city)) x 100,000; n/a not avail.
Source: U.S. Department of Justice, FBI Uniform Crime Reports, 1977 - 1996

Motor Vehicle Thefts and Motor Vehicle Theft Rates: 1977 - 1996

Year	Number				Rate per 100,000 population			
	City	Suburbs[2]	MSA[1]	U.S.	City	Suburbs[3]	MSA[1]	U.S.
1977	5,210	4,875	10,085	977,700	1,178.7	254.5	427.8	451.9
1978	5,347	5,523	10,870	1,004,100	1,234.9	288.9	463.6	460.5
1979	6,187	6,610	12,797	1,112,800	1,408.0	360.6	563.1	505.6
1980	5,561	6,423	11,984	1,131,700	1,310.9	350.0	530.4	502.2
1981	4,897	5,480	10,377	1,087,800	1,150.5	297.6	457.7	474.7
1982	4,657	5,370	10,027	1,062,400	1,093.7	291.6	442.2	458.8
1983	5,170	4,895	10,065	1,007,900	1,211.1	271.9	451.9	430.8
1984	7,677	6,317	13,994	1,032,200	1,847.8	353.7	635.6	437.1
1985	6,766	5,432	12,198	1,102,900	1,687.4	308.4	564.0	462.0
1986	9,184	6,000	15,184	1,224,100	2,283.4	339.5	700.0	507.8
1987	7,148	4,638	11,786	1,288,700	1,837.5	266.4	553.4	529.4
1988	9,370	4,878	14,248	1,432,900	2,420.0	281.5	672.1	582.9
1989	8,050	6,008	14,058	1,564,800	2,138.6	348.7	669.6	630.4
1990	8,634	7,078	15,712	1,635,900	2,334.3	419.9	764.4	657.8
1991	7,476	6,601	14,077	1,661,700	2,007.8	389.0	680.3	659.0
1992	8,124	7,325	15,449	1,610,800	2,173.1	356.7	636.5	631.5
1993	6,506	6,087	12,593	1,563,100	1,765.7	296.1	519.5	606.1
1994	5,342	5,481	10,823	1,539,300	1,449.3	266.6	446.4	591.3
1995	3,387	n/a	n/a	1,472,400	954.7	n/a	n/a	560.4
1996	2,810	4,327	7,137	1,395,200	793.1	210.5	296.2	525.9

Notes: (1) Metropolitan Statistical Area - see Appendix A for areas included; (2) calculated by the editors using the following formula: (number of crimes in the MSA minus number of crimes in the city); (3) calculated by the editors using the following formula: ((number of crimes in the MSA minus number of crimes in the city) ÷ (population of the MSA minus population of the city)) x 100,000; n/a not avail.
Source: U.S. Department of Justice, FBI Uniform Crime Reports, 1977 - 1996

HATE CRIMES

Criminal Incidents by Bias Motivation

Area	Race	Ethnicity	Religion	Sexual Orientation
Pittsburgh	38	4	2	2

Notes: Figures include both violent and property crimes. Law enforcement agencies must have submitted data for at least one quarter of calendar year 1995 to be included in this report, therefore figures shown may not represent complete 12-month totals; n/a not available
Source: U.S. Department of Justice, FBI Uniform Crime Reports, Hate Crime Statistics 1995

LAW ENFORCEMENT

Full-Time Law Enforcement Employees

Jurisdiction	Police Employees			Police Officers per 100,000 population
	Total	Officers	Civilians	
Pittsburgh	1,209	1,148	61	324.0

Notes: Data as of October 31, 1996
Source: U.S. Department of Justice, FBI Uniform Crime Reports, 1996

Number of Police Officers by Race

Race	Police Officers				Index of Representation[1]		
	1983		1992				
	Number	Pct.	Number	Pct.	1983	1992	% Chg.
Black	175	14.3	289	25.6	0.60	0.99	65.0
Hispanic[2]	4	0.3	0	0.0	0.38	0.00	-100.0

Notes: (1) The index of representation is calculated by dividing the percent of black/hispanic police officers by the percent of corresponding blacks/hispanics in the local population. An index approaching 1.0 indicates that a city is closer to achieving a representation of police officers equal to their proportion in the local population; (2) Hispanic officers can be of any race
Source: Bureau of Justice Statistics, Sourcebook of Criminal Justice Statistics, 1994

CORRECTIONS

Federal Correctional Facilities

Type	Year Opened	Security Level	Sex of Inmates	Rated Capacity	Population on 7/1/95	Number of Staff
None listed						

Notes: Data as of 1995
Source: Bureau of Justice Statistics, Sourcebook of Criminal Justice Statistics Online

City/County/Regional Correctional Facilities

Name	Year Opened	Year Renov.	Rated Capacity	1995 Pop.	Number of COs[1]	Number of Staff	ACA[2] Accred.
Allegheny County Jail	1995	--	2,400	1,507	436	471	No

Notes: Data as of April 1996; (1) Correctional Officers; (2) American Correctional Assn. Accreditation
Source: American Correctional Association, 1996-1998 National Jail and Adult Detention Directory

Private Adult Correctional Facilities

Name	Date Opened	Rated Capacity	Present Pop.	Security Level	Facility Construct.	Expans. Plans	ACA[1] Accred.
None listed							

Notes: Data as of December 1996; (1) American Correctional Association Accreditation
Source: University of Florida, Center for Studies in Criminology and Law, Private Adult Correctional Facility Census, 10th Ed., March 15, 1997

Characteristics of Shock Incarceration Programs

Jurisdiction	Year Program Began	Number of Camps	Average Num. of Inmates	Number of Beds	Program Length	Voluntary/ Mandatory
Pennsylvania	1992	1	130	158	6 months	Voluntary

Note: Data as of July 1996;
Source: Sourcebook of Criminal Justice Statistics Online

DEATH PENALTY

Death Penalty Statistics

State	Prisoners Executed		Prisoners Under Sentence of Death					Avg. No. of Years on Death Row[4]
	1930-1995	1996[1]	Total[2]	White[3]	Black[3]	Hisp.	Women	
Pennsylvania	154	0	196	67	122	11	4	6.1

Notes: Data as of 12/31/95 unless otherwise noted; (1) Data as of 7/31/97; (2) Includes persons of other races; (3) Includes people of Hispanic origin; (4) Covers prisoners sentenced 1974 through 1995
Source: Bureau of Justice Statistics, Capital Punishment 1995 (released 12/96); Death Penalty Information Center Web Site, 9/30/97

Capital Offenses and Methods of Execution

Capital Offenses in Pennsylvania	Minimum Age for Imposition of Death Penalty	Mentally Retarded Excluded	Methods of Execution[1]
First-degree murder with 16 aggravating circumstances.	None	No	Lethal injection

Notes: Data as of 12/31/95 unless otherwise noted; (1) Data as of 7/31/97
Source: Bureau of Justice Statistics, Capital Punishment 1995 (released 12/96); Death Penalty Information Center Web Site, 9/30/97

LAWS

Statutory Provisions Relating to the Purchase, Ownership and Use of Handguns

Jurisdiction	Instant Background Check	Federal Waiting Period Applies[1]	State Waiting Period (days)	License or Permit to Purchase	Regis- tration	Record of Sale Sent to Police	Concealed Carry Law
Pennsylvania	(a)	Yes[a,b]	2[a]	No	No	Yes	Yes[c,d]

Note: Data as of 1996; (1) The Federal 5-day waiting period for handgun purchases applies to states that don't have instant background checks, waiting period requirements, or licensing procedures exempting them from the Federal requirement; (a) Instant Check is not yet operational. When operational, the State waiting period will end and the Federal waiting period will no longer apply. Carry permit holders will be exempt from Instant Check; (b) The Federal waiting period does not apply to a person holding a valid permit or license to carry a firearm, issued within 5 years of proposed purchase; (c) "Shall issue" permit system, liberally administered discretion by local authorities over permit issuance, or no permit required; (d) Prior to 1995, the law did not apply to Philadelphia
Source: Sourcebook of Criminal Justice Statistics Online

Statutory Provisions Relating to Alcohol Use and Driving

Jurisdiction	Drinking Age	Blood Alcohol Concentration Levels as Evidence in State Courts[1]		Open Container Law[1]	Anti-Consumption Law[1]	Dram Shop Law[1]
		Illegal per se at 0.10%	Presumption at 0.10%			
Pennsylvania	21	Yes	No	No	Yes[a]	Yes

Note: Data as of January 1, 1997; (1) See Appendix C for an explanation of terms; (a) Applies to drivers only
Source: Sourcebook of Criminal Justice Statistics Online

Statutory Provisions Relating to Hate Crimes

Jurisdiction	Bias-Motivated Violence and Intimidation						Institutional Vandalism
	Civil Action	Criminal Penalty					
		Race/ Religion/ Ethnicity	Sexual Orientation	Mental/ Physical Disability	Gender	Age	
Pennsylvania	Yes	Yes	No	No	No	No	Yes

Source: Anti-Defamation League, 1997 Hate Crimes Laws

Portland, Oregon

OVERVIEW

The total crime rate for the city increased 12.1% between 1977 and 1996. During that same period, the violent crime rate increased 61.8% and the property crime rate increased 6.1%.

Among violent crimes, the rates for: Murders increased 1.9%; Forcible Rapes decreased 2.2%; Robberies decreased 0.9%; and Aggravated Assaults increased 131.0%.

Among property crimes, the rates for: Burglaries decreased 47.4%; Larceny-Thefts increased 24.2%; and Motor Vehicle Thefts increased 101.4%.

ANTI-CRIME PROGRAMS

Special anti-crime programs which have been instituted include:

- WomenStrength—self-defense classes designed to introduce teenage and adult women to a variety of sexual assault prevention and protection strategies.
- Block Homes—adult volunteers serve as a link between emergency services and children.
- Sexual Minorities Partnerships Agreement—whose goal is to protect people in the gay, lesbian and "transgender" community.
- Anti-graffiti Program—supports a graffiti hotline which can be called to report graffiti, receive information on prevention techniques, and to volunteer to help clean up graffiti.
- Auto Theft Task Force—multi-agency interdisciplinary task force to reduce auto theft through targeted arrests; work with District Attorney to enhance prosecutions; conduct prevention program.
- Crisis Intervention Team—on-call officers trained to defuse situations where a person with mental illness is involved in a crisis that warrants police response.
- Crisis Response Teams—community volunteers respond to critical incidents and work with families and communities to curb retaliatory violence and aid families affected by violence.
- Domestic Violence Reduction Unit—follow-up on misdemeanor domestic violence cases to ensure prosecution; seek resources for victims; provide referral information; expand outreach to non-English speaking communities.
- Elder Safety Program—officers in each precinct designated as the elder crimes officer to better respond to the needs of this growing population.
- Neighborhood Liaison Teams—officers who work districts within a certain neighborhood, together with the precinct sergeant to provide for better information sharing and problem-solving among shifts.
- Neighborhood Response Teams (NRT)—work with district officers and staff from other agencies, identify and address chronic problem locations with problem solving meetings and partnership agreements. *Portland Bureau of Police, 6/97*

CRIME RISK

Your Chances of Becoming a Victim[1]

Area	Any Crime	Violent Crime					Property Crime			
		Any	Murder	Forcible Rape[2]	Robbery	Aggrav. Assault	Any	Burglary	Larceny -Theft	Motor Vehicle Theft
City	1:9	1:60	1:9,175	1:600	1:227	1:88	1:11	1:66	1:16	1:72

Note: (1) Figures have been calculated by dividing the population of the city by the number of crimes reported to the FBI during 1996 and are expressed as odds (eg. 1:20 should be read as 1 in 20). (2) Figures have been calculated by dividing the female population of the city by the number of forcible rapes reported to the FBI during 1996. The female population of the city was estimated by calculating the ratio of females to males reported in the 1990 Census and applying that ratio to 1996 population estimate.
Source: FBI Uniform Crime Reports 1996

CRIME STATISTICS

Total Crimes and Total Crime Rates: 1977 - 1996

Year	Number				Rate per 100,000 population			
	City	Suburbs[2]	MSA[1]	U.S.	City	Suburbs[3]	MSA[1]	U.S.
1977	36,821	40,495	77,316	10,984,500	9,588.8	5,468.6	6,875.6	5,077.6
1978	35,614	42,979	78,593	11,209,000	9,250.4	5,672.7	6,878.2	5,140.3
1979	36,078	46,259	82,337	12,249,500	8,874.7	5,982.1	6,978.8	5,565.5
1980	40,833	49,550	90,383	13,408,300	11,205.0	5,698.7	7,324.9	5,950.0
1981	50,432	54,665	105,097	13,423,800	13,648.0	6,186.7	8,386.9	5,858.2
1982	48,092	51,529	99,621	12,974,400	13,005.0	5,818.2	7,935.1	5,603.6
1983	48,318	42,560	90,878	12,108,600	12,999.0	5,695.9	8,122.0	5,175.0
1984	50,267	40,700	90,967	11,881,800	13,694.7	5,323.2	8,038.6	5,031.3
1985	62,255	39,145	101,400	12,431,400	16,936.9	5,055.9	8,880.6	5,207.1
1986	65,654	39,915	105,569	13,211,900	17,819.5	5,129.6	9,207.4	5,480.4
1987	64,802	38,149	102,951	13,508,700	16,580.0	4,934.5	8,844.9	5,550.0
1988	67,681	39,176	106,857	13,923,100	17,458.9	4,975.0	9,093.3	5,664.2
1989	54,301	35,338	89,639	14,251,400	12,753.1	4,500.6	7,402.2	5,741.0
1990	48,545	33,159	81,704	14,475,600	11,100.6	4,131.8	6,589.9	5,820.3
1991	50,281	36,126	86,407	14,872,900	11,181.7	4,378.9	6,778.8	5,897.8
1992	51,613	50,313	101,926	14,438,200	11,266.0	4,437.9	6,403.1	5,660.2
1993	51,765	50,699	102,464	14,144,800	11,379.7	4,274.9	6,244.5	5,484.4
1994	54,715	54,493	109,208	13,989,500	11,815.7	4,515.5	6,539.9	5,373.5
1995	55,348	59,785	115,133	13,862,700	12,068.3	4,782.6	6,738.1	5,275.9
1996	50,306	56,949	107,255	13,473,600	10,751.3	4,467.5	6,154.7	5,078.9

Notes: (1) Metropolitan Statistical Area - see Appendix A for areas included; (2) calculated by the editors using the following formula: (number of crimes in the MSA minus number of crimes in the city); (3) calculated by the editors using the following formula: ((number of crimes in the MSA minus number of crimes in the city) ÷ (population of the MSA minus population of the city)) x 100,000; n/a not avail.
Source: U.S. Department of Justice, FBI Uniform Crime Reports, 1977 - 1996

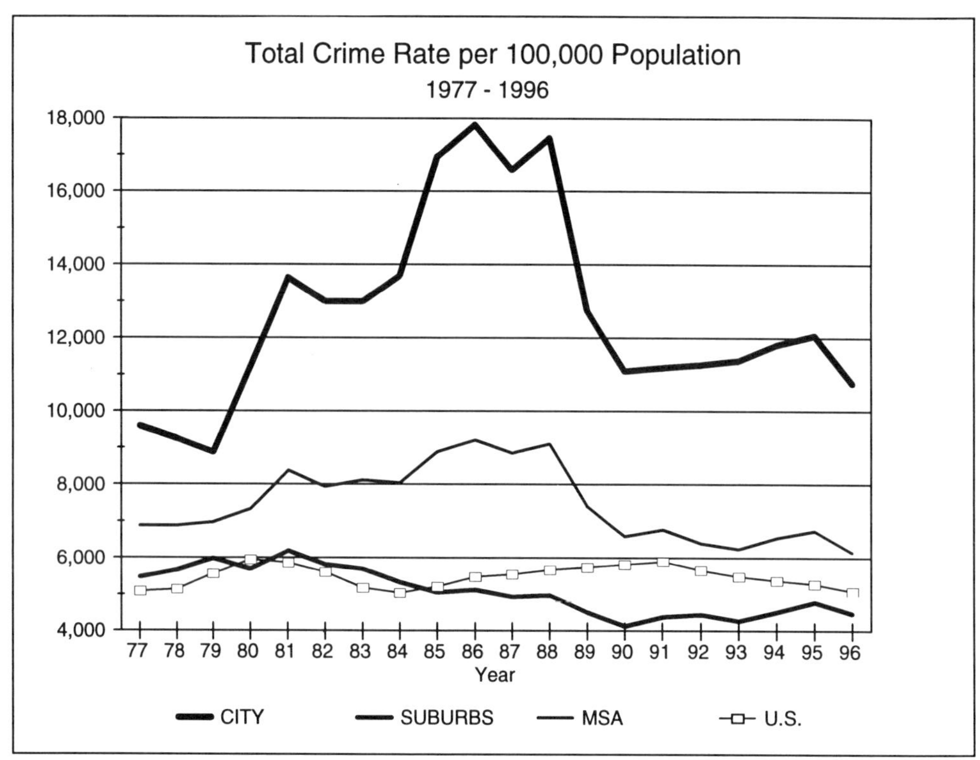

Note: Missing line segments indicate data not available.

Violent Crimes and Violent Crime Rates: 1977 - 1996

Year	Number				Rate per 100,000 population			
	City	Suburbs[2]	MSA[1]	U.S.	City	Suburbs[3]	MSA[1]	U.S.
1977	3,973	2,436	6,409	1,029,580	1,034.6	329.0	569.9	475.9
1978	4,017	2,969	6,986	1,085,550	1,043.4	391.9	611.4	497.8
1979	4,558	3,553	8,111	1,208,030	1,121.2	459.5	687.5	548.9
1980	4,957	3,026	7,983	1,344,520	1,360.2	348.0	647.0	596.6
1981	6,452	2,382	8,834	1,361,820	1,746.1	269.6	705.0	594.3
1982	6,484	2,282	8,766	1,322,390	1,753.4	257.7	698.2	571.1
1983	6,879	2,330	9,209	1,258,090	1,850.7	311.8	823.0	537.7
1984	7,408	2,264	9,672	1,273,280	2,018.2	296.1	854.7	539.2
1985	8,634	2,219	10,853	1,328,800	2,348.9	286.6	950.5	556.6
1986	8,804	1,839	10,643	1,489,170	2,389.5	236.3	928.3	617.7
1987	8,763	1,822	10,585	1,484,000	2,242.1	235.7	909.4	609.7
1988	8,686	1,886	10,572	1,566,220	2,240.6	239.5	899.7	637.2
1989	8,052	1,834	9,886	1,646,040	1,891.1	233.6	816.4	663.1
1990	7,836	1,829	9,665	1,820,130	1,791.8	227.9	779.5	731.8
1991	8,121	2,055	10,176	1,911,770	1,806.0	249.1	798.3	758.1
1992	8,389	3,249	11,638	1,932,270	1,831.1	286.6	731.1	757.5
1993	8,445	3,234	11,679	1,926,020	1,856.5	272.7	711.8	746.8
1994	8,808	3,242	12,050	1,857,670	1,902.1	268.6	721.6	713.6
1995	8,833	3,587	12,420	1,798,790	1,926.0	286.9	726.9	684.6
1996	7,835	3,397	11,232	1,682,280	1,674.5	266.5	644.5	634.1

Notes: Violent crimes include murder, forcible rape, robbery and aggravated assault; n/a not available; (1) Metropolitan Statistical Area - see Appendix A for areas included; (2) calculated by the editors using the following formula: (number of crimes in the MSA minus number of crimes in the city); (3) calculated by the editors using the following formula: ((number of crimes in the MSA minus number of crimes in the city) ÷ (population of the MSA minus population of the city)) x 100,000
Source: U.S. Department of Justice, FBI Uniform Crime Reports, 1977 - 1996

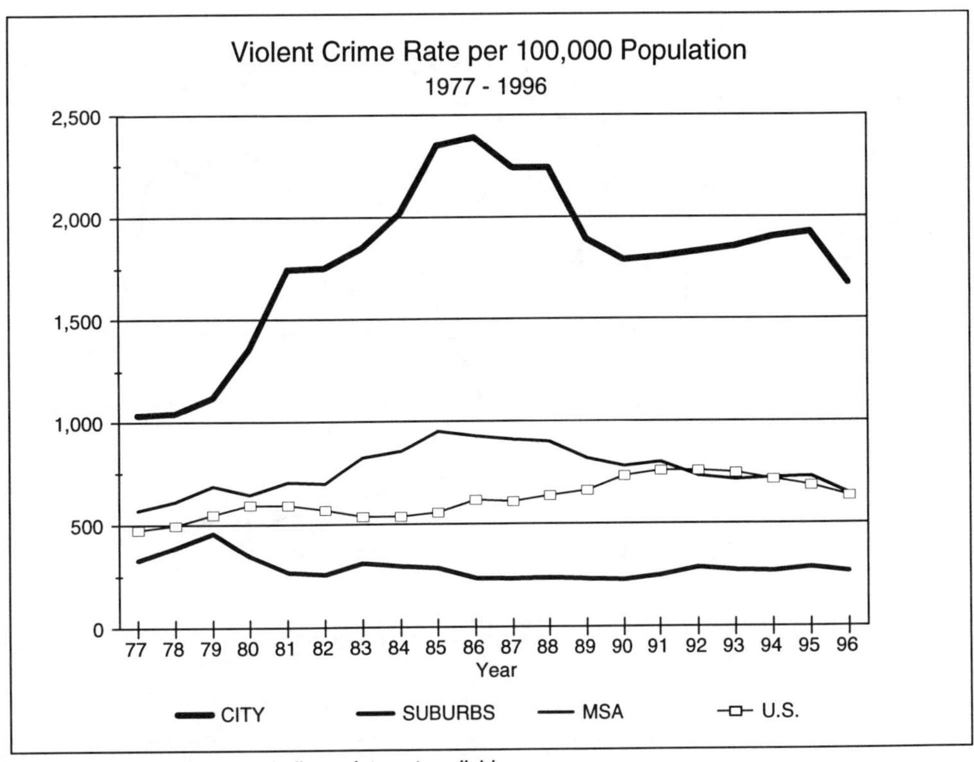

Note: Missing line segments indicate data not available.

Property Crimes and Property Crime Rates: 1977 - 1996

Year	Number				Rate per 100,000 population			
	City	Suburbs[2]	MSA[1]	U.S.	City	Suburbs[3]	MSA[1]	U.S.
1977	32,848	38,059	70,907	9,955,000	8,554.2	5,139.6	6,305.6	4,601.7
1978	31,597	40,010	71,607	10,123,400	8,207.0	5,280.8	6,266.8	4,642.5
1979	31,520	42,706	74,226	11,041,500	7,753.5	5,522.6	6,291.3	5,016.6
1980	35,876	46,524	82,400	12,063,700	9,844.7	5,350.6	6,677.9	5,353.3
1981	43,980	52,283	96,263	12,061,900	11,902.0	5,917.1	7,682.0	5,263.9
1982	41,608	49,247	90,855	11,652,000	11,251.6	5,560.6	7,236.9	5,032.5
1983	41,439	40,230	81,669	10,850,500	11,148.3	5,384.1	7,299.0	4,637.4
1984	42,859	38,436	81,295	10,608,500	11,676.5	5,027.1	7,183.9	4,492.1
1985	53,621	36,926	90,547	11,102,600	14,587.9	4,769.3	7,930.1	4,650.5
1986	56,850	38,076	94,926	11,722,700	15,430.0	4,893.3	8,279.2	4,862.6
1987	56,039	36,327	92,366	12,024,700	14,337.9	4,698.8	7,935.5	4,940.3
1988	58,995	37,290	96,285	12,356,900	15,218.3	4,735.5	8,193.6	5,027.1
1989	46,249	33,504	79,753	12,605,400	10,862.0	4,267.0	6,585.9	5,077.9
1990	40,709	31,330	72,039	12,655,500	9,308.8	3,903.9	5,810.3	5,088.5
1991	42,160	34,071	76,231	12,961,100	9,375.7	4,129.8	5,980.4	5,139.7
1992	43,224	47,064	90,288	12,505,900	9,434.8	4,151.4	5,671.9	4,902.7
1993	43,320	47,465	90,785	12,218,800	9,523.2	4,002.2	5,532.8	4,737.6
1994	45,907	51,251	97,158	12,131,900	9,913.6	4,246.9	5,818.3	4,660.0
1995	46,515	56,198	102,713	12,063,900	10,142.3	4,495.6	6,011.3	4,591.3
1996	42,471	53,552	96,023	11,791,300	9,076.8	4,201.0	5,510.2	4,444.8

Notes: Property crimes include burglary, larceny-theft and motor vehicle theft; n/a not available; (1) Metropolitan Statistical Area - see Appendix A for areas included; (2) calculated by the editors using the following formula: (number of crimes in the MSA minus number of crimes in the city); (3) calculated by the editors using the following formula: ((number of crimes in the MSA minus number of crimes in the city) ÷ (population of the MSA minus population of the city)) x 100,000
Source: U.S. Department of Justice, FBI Uniform Crime Reports, 1977 - 1996

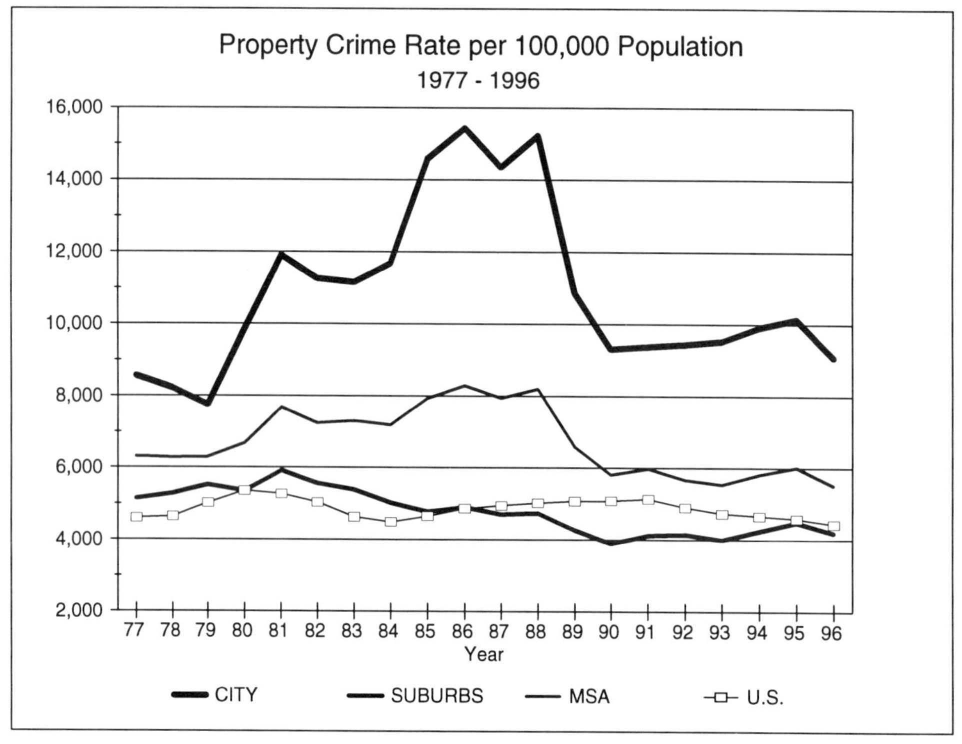

Note: Missing line segments indicate data not available.

Murders and Murder Rates: 1977 - 1996

Year	Number				Rate per 100,000 population			
	City	Suburbs[2]	MSA[1]	U.S.	City	Suburbs[3]	MSA[1]	U.S.
1977	41	27	68	19,120	10.7	3.6	6.0	8.8
1978	34	20	54	19,560	8.8	2.6	4.7	9.0
1979	39	17	56	21,460	9.6	2.2	4.7	9.7
1980	46	30	76	23,040	12.6	3.5	6.2	10.2
1981	38	31	69	22,520	10.3	3.5	5.5	9.8
1982	36	38	74	21,010	9.7	4.3	5.9	9.1
1983	36	29	65	19,310	9.7	3.9	5.8	8.3
1984	34	28	62	18,690	9.3	3.7	5.5	7.9
1985	43	20	63	18,980	11.7	2.6	5.5	7.9
1986	46	35	81	20,610	12.5	4.5	7.1	8.6
1987	66	27	93	20,100	16.9	3.5	8.0	8.3
1988	45	27	72	20,680	11.6	3.4	6.1	8.4
1989	38	26	64	21,500	8.9	3.3	5.3	8.7
1990	33	22	55	23,440	7.5	2.7	4.4	9.4
1991	53	22	75	24,700	11.8	2.7	5.9	9.8
1992	46	28	74	23,760	10.0	2.5	4.6	9.3
1993	58	35	93	24,530	12.8	3.0	5.7	9.5
1994	50	43	93	23,330	10.8	3.6	5.6	9.0
1995	43	21	64	21,610	9.4	1.7	3.7	8.2
1996	51	24	75	19,650	10.9	1.9	4.3	7.4

Notes: (1) Metropolitan Statistical Area - see Appendix A for areas included; (2) calculated by the editors using the following formula: (number of crimes in the MSA minus number of crimes in the city); (3) calculated by the editors using the following formula: ((number of crimes in the MSA minus number of crimes in the city) ÷ (population of the MSA minus population of the city)) x 100,000; n/a not avail.
Source: U.S. Department of Justice, FBI Uniform Crime Reports, 1977 - 1996

Forcible Rapes and Forcible Rape Rates: 1977 - 1996

Year	Number				Rate per 100,000 population			
	City	Suburbs[2]	MSA[1]	U.S.	City	Suburbs[3]	MSA[1]	U.S.
1977	337	262	599	63,500	87.8	35.4	53.3	29.4
1978	371	243	614	67,610	96.4	32.1	53.7	31.0
1979	435	298	733	76,390	107.0	38.5	62.1	34.7
1980	364	329	693	82,990	99.9	37.8	56.2	36.8
1981	403	307	710	82,500	109.1	34.7	56.7	36.0
1982	392	324	716	78,770	106.0	36.6	57.0	34.0
1983	377	231	608	78,920	101.4	30.9	54.3	33.7
1984	370	204	574	84,230	100.8	26.7	50.7	35.7
1985	469	267	736	88,670	127.6	34.5	64.5	37.1
1986	438	290	728	91,460	118.9	37.3	63.5	37.9
1987	407	264	671	91,110	104.1	34.1	57.6	37.4
1988	372	187	559	92,490	96.0	23.7	47.6	37.6
1989	415	227	642	94,500	97.5	28.9	53.0	38.1
1990	424	248	672	102,560	97.0	30.9	54.2	41.2
1991	464	361	825	106,590	103.2	43.8	64.7	42.3
1992	490	492	982	109,060	107.0	43.4	61.7	42.8
1993	479	449	928	106,010	105.3	37.9	56.6	41.1
1994	400	398	798	102,220	86.4	33.0	47.8	39.3
1995	426	475	901	97,470	92.9	38.0	52.7	37.1
1996	402	429	831	95,770	85.9	33.7	47.7	36.1

Notes: (1) Metropolitan Statistical Area - see Appendix A for areas included; (2) calculated by the editors using the following formula: (number of crimes in the MSA minus number of crimes in the city); (3) calculated by the editors using the following formula: ((number of crimes in the MSA minus number of crimes in the city) ÷ (population of the MSA minus population of the city)) x 100,000; n/a not avail.
Source: U.S. Department of Justice, FBI Uniform Crime Reports, 1977 - 1996

Robberies and Robbery Rates: 1977 - 1996

Year	Number				Rate per 100,000 population			
	City	Suburbs[2]	MSA[1]	U.S.	City	Suburbs[3]	MSA[1]	U.S.
1977	1,703	603	2,306	412,610	443.5	81.4	205.1	190.7
1978	1,774	683	2,457	426,930	460.8	90.1	215.0	195.8
1979	1,787	686	2,473	480,700	439.6	88.7	209.6	218.4
1980	2,249	818	3,067	565,840	617.1	94.1	248.6	251.1
1981	3,072	895	3,967	592,910	831.4	101.3	316.6	258.7
1982	2,811	854	3,665	553,130	760.1	96.4	291.9	238.9
1983	2,964	786	3,750	506,570	797.4	105.2	335.1	216.5
1984	3,042	704	3,746	485,010	828.8	92.1	331.0	205.4
1985	3,508	691	4,199	497,870	954.4	89.2	367.7	208.5
1986	3,887	623	4,510	542,780	1,055.0	80.1	393.3	225.1
1987	3,667	702	4,369	517,700	938.2	90.8	375.4	212.7
1988	3,632	725	4,357	542,970	936.9	92.1	370.8	220.9
1989	2,667	603	3,270	578,330	626.4	76.8	270.0	233.0
1990	2,541	562	3,103	639,270	581.0	70.0	250.3	257.0
1991	2,723	649	3,372	687,730	605.6	78.7	264.5	272.7
1992	2,686	935	3,621	672,480	586.3	82.5	227.5	263.6
1993	2,305	913	3,218	659,870	506.7	77.0	196.1	255.9
1994	2,344	1,031	3,375	618,950	506.2	85.4	202.1	237.7
1995	2,298	1,056	3,354	580,510	501.1	84.5	196.3	220.9
1996	2,057	988	3,045	537,050	439.6	77.5	174.7	202.4

Notes: (1) Metropolitan Statistical Area - see Appendix A for areas included; (2) calculated by the editors using the following formula: (number of crimes in the MSA minus number of crimes in the city); (3) calculated by the editors using the following formula: ((number of crimes in the MSA minus number of crimes in the city) ÷ (population of the MSA minus population of the city)) x 100,000; n/a not avail.
Source: U.S. Department of Justice, FBI Uniform Crime Reports, 1977 - 1996

Aggravated Assaults and Aggravated Assault Rates: 1977 - 1996

Year	Number				Rate per 100,000 population			
	City	Suburbs[2]	MSA[1]	U.S.	City	Suburbs[3]	MSA[1]	U.S.
1977	1,892	1,544	3,436	534,350	492.7	208.5	305.6	247.0
1978	1,838	2,023	3,861	571,460	477.4	267.0	337.9	262.1
1979	2,297	2,552	4,849	629,480	565.0	330.0	411.0	286.0
1980	2,298	1,849	4,147	672,650	630.6	212.7	336.1	298.5
1981	2,939	1,149	4,088	663,900	795.4	130.0	326.2	289.7
1982	3,245	1,066	4,311	669,480	877.5	120.4	343.4	289.2
1983	3,502	1,284	4,786	653,290	942.1	171.8	427.7	279.2
1984	3,962	1,328	5,290	685,350	1,079.4	173.7	467.5	290.2
1985	4,614	1,241	5,855	723,250	1,255.3	160.3	512.8	302.9
1986	4,433	891	5,324	834,320	1,203.2	114.5	464.3	346.1
1987	4,623	829	5,452	855,090	1,182.8	107.2	468.4	351.3
1988	4,637	947	5,584	910,090	1,196.2	120.3	475.2	370.2
1989	4,932	978	5,910	951,710	1,158.3	124.6	488.0	383.4
1990	4,838	997	5,835	1,054,860	1,106.3	124.2	470.6	424.1
1991	4,881	1,023	5,904	1,092,740	1,085.5	124.0	463.2	433.3
1992	5,167	1,794	6,961	1,126,970	1,127.8	158.2	437.3	441.8
1993	5,603	1,837	7,440	1,135,610	1,231.7	154.9	453.4	440.3
1994	6,014	1,770	7,784	1,113,180	1,298.7	146.7	466.1	427.6
1995	6,066	2,035	8,101	1,099,210	1,322.7	162.8	474.1	418.3
1996	5,325	1,956	7,281	1,029,810	1,138.0	153.4	417.8	388.2

Notes: (1) Metropolitan Statistical Area - see Appendix A for areas included; (2) calculated by the editors using the following formula: (number of crimes in the MSA minus number of crimes in the city); (3) calculated by the editors using the following formula: ((number of crimes in the MSA minus number of crimes in the city) ÷ (population of the MSA minus population of the city)) x 100,000; n/a not avail.
Source: U.S. Department of Justice, FBI Uniform Crime Reports, 1977 - 1996

Burglaries and Burglary Rates: 1977 - 1996

Year	Number				Rate per 100,000 population			
	City	Suburbs[2]	MSA[1]	U.S.	City	Suburbs[3]	MSA[1]	U.S.
1977	11,150	11,828	22,978	3,071,500	2,903.6	1,597.3	2,043.4	1,419.8
1978	9,734	12,603	22,337	3,128,300	2,528.3	1,663.4	1,954.8	1,434.6
1979	9,373	13,062	22,435	3,327,700	2,305.6	1,689.1	1,901.6	1,511.9
1980	10,979	14,289	25,268	3,795,200	3,012.7	1,643.4	2,047.8	1,684.1
1981	14,395	17,840	32,235	3,779,700	3,895.6	2,019.0	2,572.4	1,649.5
1982	13,728	16,183	29,911	3,447,100	3,712.3	1,827.2	2,382.5	1,488.8
1983	13,222	14,128	27,350	3,129,900	3,557.1	1,890.8	2,444.3	1,337.7
1984	14,630	14,244	28,874	2,984,400	3,985.8	1,863.0	2,551.5	1,263.7
1985	17,148	13,003	30,151	3,073,300	4,665.2	1,679.5	2,640.6	1,287.3
1986	17,236	12,539	29,775	3,241,400	4,678.1	1,611.4	2,596.9	1,344.6
1987	15,185	11,200	26,385	3,236,200	3,885.2	1,448.7	2,266.8	1,329.6
1988	15,236	11,261	26,497	3,218,100	3,930.3	1,430.0	2,254.8	1,309.2
1989	12,380	8,882	21,262	3,168,200	2,907.6	1,131.2	1,755.8	1,276.3
1990	8,967	7,295	16,262	3,073,900	2,050.4	909.0	1,311.6	1,235.9
1991	9,503	7,685	17,188	3,157,200	2,113.3	931.5	1,348.4	1,252.0
1992	8,761	10,468	19,229	2,979,900	1,912.3	923.3	1,208.0	1,168.2
1993	7,845	9,534	17,379	2,834,800	1,724.6	803.9	1,059.1	1,099.2
1994	8,001	9,936	17,937	2,712,800	1,727.8	823.3	1,074.2	1,042.0
1995	7,813	10,416	18,229	2,593,800	1,703.6	833.2	1,066.8	987.1
1996	7,142	9,645	16,787	2,501,500	1,526.4	756.6	963.3	943.0

Notes: (1) Metropolitan Statistical Area - see Appendix A for areas included; (2) calculated by the editors using the following formula: (number of crimes in the MSA minus number of crimes in the city); (3) calculated by the editors using the following formula: ((number of crimes in the MSA minus number of crimes in the city) ÷ (population of the MSA minus population of the city)) x 100,000; n/a not avail.
Source: U.S. Department of Justice, FBI Uniform Crime Reports, 1977 - 1996

Larceny-Thefts and Larceny-Theft Rates: 1977 - 1996

Year	Number				Rate per 100,000 population			
	City	Suburbs[2]	MSA[1]	U.S.	City	Suburbs[3]	MSA[1]	U.S.
1977	19,047	23,054	42,101	5,905,700	4,960.2	3,113.3	3,744.0	2,729.9
1978	19,411	24,280	43,691	5,991,000	5,041.8	3,204.7	3,823.7	2,747.4
1979	19,783	26,342	46,125	6,601,000	4,866.4	3,406.5	3,909.5	2,999.1
1980	22,649	28,987	51,636	7,136,900	6,215.1	3,333.7	4,184.7	3,167.0
1981	27,141	31,337	58,478	7,194,400	7,345.0	3,546.6	4,666.7	3,139.7
1982	25,632	30,223	55,855	7,142,500	6,931.4	3,412.5	4,449.0	3,084.8
1983	25,813	23,624	49,437	6,712,800	6,944.5	3,161.6	4,418.3	2,868.9
1984	25,884	21,867	47,751	6,591,900	7,051.8	2,860.0	4,219.7	2,791.3
1985	33,086	21,545	54,631	6,926,400	9,001.3	2,782.7	4,784.6	2,901.2
1986	35,722	22,741	58,463	7,257,200	9,695.5	2,922.5	5,099.0	3,010.3
1987	35,695	22,148	57,843	7,499,900	9,132.8	2,864.8	4,969.5	3,081.3
1988	35,601	22,692	58,293	7,705,900	9,183.6	2,881.7	4,960.6	3,134.9
1989	26,903	21,181	48,084	7,872,400	6,318.4	2,697.6	3,970.7	3,171.3
1990	25,933	21,149	47,082	7,945,700	5,930.0	2,635.3	3,797.4	3,194.8
1991	26,250	23,195	49,445	8,142,200	5,837.6	2,811.5	3,879.0	3,228.8
1992	26,562	32,104	58,666	7,915,200	5,797.9	2,831.8	3,685.4	3,103.0
1993	27,016	32,713	59,729	7,820,900	5,939.0	2,758.3	3,640.1	3,032.4
1994	28,363	34,879	63,242	7,879,800	6,125.0	2,890.2	3,787.3	3,026.7
1995	29,589	38,837	68,426	7,997,700	6,451.7	3,106.8	4,004.6	3,043.8
1996	28,823	38,287	67,110	7,894,600	6,160.0	3,003.5	3,851.1	2,975.9

Notes: (1) Metropolitan Statistical Area - see Appendix A for areas included; (2) calculated by the editors using the following formula: (number of crimes in the MSA minus number of crimes in the city); (3) calculated by the editors using the following formula: ((number of crimes in the MSA minus number of crimes in the city) ÷ (population of the MSA minus population of the city)) x 100,000; n/a not avail.
Source: U.S. Department of Justice, FBI Uniform Crime Reports, 1977 - 1996

Motor Vehicle Thefts and Motor Vehicle Theft Rates: 1977 - 1996

Year	Number				Rate per 100,000 population			
	City	Suburbs[2]	MSA[1]	U.S.	City	Suburbs[3]	MSA[1]	U.S.
1977	2,651	3,177	5,828	977,700	690.4	429.0	518.3	451.9
1978	2,452	3,127	5,579	1,004,100	636.9	412.7	488.3	460.5
1979	2,364	3,302	5,666	1,112,800	581.5	427.0	480.2	505.6
1980	2,248	3,248	5,496	1,131,700	616.9	373.5	445.4	502.2
1981	2,444	3,106	5,550	1,087,800	661.4	351.5	442.9	474.7
1982	2,248	2,841	5,089	1,062,400	607.9	320.8	405.4	458.8
1983	2,404	2,478	4,882	1,007,900	646.7	331.6	436.3	430.8
1984	2,345	2,325	4,670	1,032,200	638.9	304.1	412.7	437.1
1985	3,387	2,378	5,765	1,102,900	921.5	307.1	504.9	462.0
1986	3,892	2,796	6,688	1,224,100	1,056.3	359.3	583.3	507.8
1987	5,159	2,979	8,138	1,288,700	1,320.0	385.3	699.2	529.4
1988	8,158	3,337	11,495	1,432,900	2,104.4	423.8	978.2	582.9
1989	6,966	3,441	10,407	1,564,800	1,636.0	438.2	859.4	630.4
1990	5,809	2,886	8,695	1,635,900	1,328.3	359.6	701.3	657.8
1991	6,407	3,191	9,598	1,661,700	1,424.8	386.8	753.0	659.0
1992	7,901	4,492	12,393	1,610,800	1,724.6	396.2	778.5	631.5
1993	8,459	5,218	13,677	1,563,100	1,859.6	440.0	833.5	606.1
1994	9,543	6,436	15,979	1,539,300	2,060.8	533.3	956.9	591.3
1995	9,113	6,945	16,058	1,472,400	1,987.0	555.6	939.8	560.4
1996	6,506	5,620	12,126	1,395,200	1,390.5	440.9	695.8	525.9

Notes: (1) Metropolitan Statistical Area - see Appendix A for areas included; (2) calculated by the editors using the following formula: (number of crimes in the MSA minus number of crimes in the city); (3) calculated by the editors using the following formula: ((number of crimes in the MSA minus number of crimes in the city) ÷ (population of the MSA minus population of the city)) x 100,000; n/a not avail.
Source: U.S. Department of Justice, FBI Uniform Crime Reports, 1977 - 1996

HATE CRIMES

Criminal Incidents by Bias Motivation

Area	Race	Ethnicity	Religion	Sexual Orientation
Portland	45	8	6	31

Notes: Figures include both violent and property crimes. Law enforcement agencies must have submitted data for at least one quarter of calendar year 1995 to be included in this report, therefore figures shown may not represent complete 12-month totals; n/a not available
Source: U.S. Department of Justice, FBI Uniform Crime Reports, Hate Crime Statistics 1995

ILLEGAL DRUGS

Drug Use by Adult Arrestees

Sex	Percent Testing Positive by Urinalysis (%)				
	Any Drug[1]	Cocaine	Marijuana	Opiates	Multiple Drugs
Male	66	34	35	13	25
Female	74	46	26	26	33

Notes: The catchment area is the entire county; (1) Includes cocaine, opiates, marijuana, methadone, phencyclidine (PCP), benzodiazepines, methaqualone, propoxyphene, barbiturates & amphetamines
Source: National Institute of Justice, 1996 Drug Use Forecasting, Annual Report on Adult and Juvenile Arrestees (released June 1997)

LAW ENFORCEMENT

Full-Time Law Enforcement Employees

Jurisdiction	Police Employees			Police Officers per 100,000 population
	Total	Officers	Civilians	
Portland	1,247	979	268	209.2

Notes: Data as of October 31, 1996
Source: U.S. Department of Justice, FBI Uniform Crime Reports, 1996

Number of Police Officers by Race

Race	Police Officers 1983		Police Officers 1992		Index of Representation[1]		
	Number	Pct.	Number	Pct.	1983	1992	% Chg.
Black	19	2.8	32	3.6	0.36	0.46	27.8
Hispanic[2]	9	1.3	20	2.3	0.68	0.69	1.5

Notes: (1) The index of representation is calculated by dividing the percent of black/hispanic police officers by the percent of corresponding blacks/hispanics in the local population. An index approaching 1.0 indicates that a city is closer to achieving a representation of police officers equal to their proportion in the local population; (2) Hispanic officers can be of any race
Source: Bureau of Justice Statistics, Sourcebook of Criminal Justice Statistics, 1994

CORRECTIONS

Federal Correctional Facilities

Type	Year Opened	Security Level	Sex of Inmates	Rated Capacity	Population on 7/1/95	Number of Staff
None listed						

Notes: Data as of 1995
Source: Bureau of Justice Statistics, Sourcebook of Criminal Justice Statistics Online

City/County/Regional Correctional Facilities

Name	Year Opened	Year Renov.	Rated Capacity	1995 Pop.	Number of COs[1]	Number of Staff	ACA[2] Accred.
Multnomah Co Courthouse	1911	1987	71	70	n/a	n/a	No
Multnomah Co Detention Ctr	1983	--	476	476	162	273	Yes
Multnomah Co Inverness Facil	1988	1991	604	592	n/a	n/a	No
Multnomah Co Restitution Ctr	1923	1987	160	130	23	33	No

Notes: Data as of April 1996; (1) Correctional Officers; (2) American Correctional Assn. Accreditation
Source: American Correctional Association, 1996-1998 National Jail and Adult Detention Directory

Private Adult Correctional Facilities

Name	Date Opened	Rated Capacity	Present Pop.	Security Level	Facility Construct.	Expans. Plans	ACA[1] Accred.
None listed							

Notes: Data as of December 1996; (1) American Correctional Association Accreditation
Source: University of Florida, Center for Studies in Criminology and Law, Private Adult Correctional Facility Census, 10th Ed., March 15, 1997

Characteristics of Shock Incarceration Programs

Jurisdiction	Year Program Began	Number of Camps	Average Num. of Inmates	Number of Beds	Program Length	Voluntary/ Mandatory
Oregon did not have a shock incarceration program as of July 1996						

Source: Sourcebook of Criminal Justice Statistics Online

DEATH PENALTY

Death Penalty Statistics

State	Prisoners Executed 1930-1995	Prisoners Executed 1996[1]	Prisoners Under Sentence of Death Total[2]	White[3]	Black[3]	Hisp.	Women	Avg. No. of Years on Death Row[4]
Oregon	19	1	20	18	1	1	0	2.5

Notes: Data as of 12/31/95 unless otherwise noted; (1) Data as of 7/31/97; (2) Includes persons of other races; (3) Includes people of Hispanic origin; (4) Covers prisoners sentenced 1974 through 1995
Source: Bureau of Justice Statistics, Capital Punishment 1995 (released 12/96); Death Penalty Information Center Web Site, 9/30/97

Capital Offenses and Methods of Execution

Capital Offenses in Oregon	Minimum Age for Imposition of Death Penalty	Mentally Retarded Excluded	Methods of Execution[1]
Aggravated murder (ORS 163.095).	18	No	Lethal injection

Notes: Data as of 12/31/95 unless otherwise noted; (1) Data as of 7/31/97
Source: Bureau of Justice Statistics, Capital Punishment 1995 (released 12/96); Death Penalty Information Center Web Site, 9/30/97

LAWS

Statutory Provisions Relating to the Purchase, Ownership and Use of Handguns

Jurisdiction	Instant Background Check	Federal Waiting Period Applies[1]	State Waiting Period (days)	License or Permit to Purchase	Regis-tration	Record of Sale Sent to Police	Concealed Carry Law
Oregon	Yes	No	No	No	No	Yes	Yes[a]

Note: Data as of 1996; (1) The Federal 5-day waiting period for handgun purchases applies to states that don't have instant background checks, waiting period requirements, or licensing procedures exempting them from the Federal requirement; (a) "Shall issue" permit system, liberally administered discretion by local authorities over permit issuance, or no permit required
Source: Sourcebook of Criminal Justice Statistics Online

Statutory Provisions Relating to Alcohol Use and Driving

Jurisdiction	Drinking Age	Blood Alcohol Concentration Levels as Evidence in State Courts[1]		Open Container Law[1]	Anti-Consump-tion Law[1]	Dram Shop Law[1]
		Illegal per se at 0.10%	Presumption at 0.10%			
Oregon	21	(a)	(b)	Yes	Yes	Yes

Note: Data as of January 1, 1997; (1) See Appendix C for an explanation of terms; (a) 0.08%; (b) Not less than 0.08% constitutes being under the influence of intoxicating liquor
Source: Sourcebook of Criminal Justice Statistics Online

Statutory Provisions Relating to Curfews

Jurisdiction	Year Enacted	Latest Revision	Age Group(s)	Curfew Provisions
Portland	1906	-	15 through 17	10:15 pm to 6 am school nights midnight to 6 am non-school nights
			14 and under	9:15 pm to 6 am school nights 10:15 pm to 6 am non-school nights

Note: Data as of February 1996
Source: Sourcebook of Criminal Justice Statistics Online

Statutory Provisions Relating to Hate Crimes

Jurisdiction	Bias-Motivated Violence and Intimidation						Institutional Vandalism
		Criminal Penalty					
	Civil Action	Race/ Religion/ Ethnicity	Sexual Orientation	Mental/ Physical Disability	Gender	Age	
Oregon	Yes	Yes	Yes	No	No	No	Yes

Source: Anti-Defamation League, 1997 Hate Crimes Laws

Raleigh, North Carolina

OVERVIEW

The total crime rate for the city increased 15.3% between 1977 and 1996. During that same period, the violent crime rate increased 107.9% and the property crime rate increased 8.5%.

Among violent crimes, the rates for: Murders increased 41.7%; Forcible Rapes increased 29.7%; Robberies increased 243.2%; and Aggravated Assaults increased 76.7%.

Among property crimes, the rates for: Burglaries decreased 11.9%; Larceny-Thefts increased 11.9%; and Motor Vehicle Thefts increased 54.3%.

ANTI-CRIME PROGRAMS

The Raleigh Police Department has implemented several programs:

- MOVE (Mobile Operation Vice Enforcement) has a number of aspects: a) Roadblocks and floodlights are used to dissuade potential drug activity; b) A beat officer keeps close tabs on MOVE locations and documents criminal activity or other unusual activity; c) Selective Enforcement Units provide a covert police presence, observe criminal activity and take appropriate action.
- CLEAN (Community and Law Enforcement Against Narcotics) project which consists of officers assigned to target areas that are likely to be involved in drug activity. The officers encourage community residents to contact them in a confidential manner.
- Operation Crackdown—begun in 1992, employs officers to work four hour shifts several times a week in Raleigh Housing Authority areas with the specific intent of curbing drug-related activity.
- COPE (Community Oriented Police Enforcement)—officers act as a link to various resources available to alleviate neighborhood concerns which have been elicited through surveys.
- Downtown East Drug Enforcement—uniform officers and narcotics investigators work jointly in areas known for high drug-related traffic.
  Raleigh Police Department, Research & Planning, 8/97

CRIME RISK

Your Chances of Becoming a Victim[1]

Area	Any Crime	Violent Crime					Property Crime			
		Any	Murder	Forcible Rape[2]	Robbery	Aggrav. Assault	Any	Burglary	Larceny -Theft	Motor Vehicle Theft
City	1:14	1:116	1:9,807	1:1,407	1:335	1:194	1:16	1:78	1:23	1:178

Note: (1) Figures have been calculated by dividing the population of the city by the number of crimes reported to the FBI during 1996 and are expressed as odds (eg. 1:20 should be read as 1 in 20). (2) Figures have been calculated by dividing the female population of the city by the number of forcible rapes reported to the FBI during 1996. The female population of the city was estimated by calculating the ratio of females to males reported in the 1990 Census and applying that ratio to 1996 population estimate.
Source: FBI Uniform Crime Reports 1996

CRIME STATISTICS

Total Crimes and Total Crime Rates: 1977 - 1996

Year	Number				Rate per 100,000 population			
	City	Suburbs[2]	MSA[1]	U.S.	City	Suburbs[3]	MSA[1]	U.S.
1977	8,336	15,933	24,269	10,984,500	6,040.6	4,596.4	5,007.6	5,077.6
1978	8,448	16,095	24,543	11,209,000	6,121.7	4,554.7	4,994.8	5,140.3
1979	9,701	20,977	30,678	12,249,500	6,915.2	5,896.2	6,184.4	5,565.5
1980	10,681	22,644	33,325	13,408,300	7,196.0	6,018.3	6,351.5	5,950.0
1981	11,085	24,065	35,150	13,423,800	7,333.5	6,280.6	6,578.5	5,858.2
1982	11,224	23,092	34,316	12,974,400	7,341.6	5,958.6	6,349.9	5,603.6
1983	9,765	22,645	32,410	12,108,600	6,321.1	5,358.3	5,616.1	5,175.0
1984	9,552	22,021	31,573	11,881,800	6,044.5	5,058.7	5,321.2	5,031.3
1985	10,280	21,906	32,186	12,431,400	5,983.2	4,911.3	5,209.4	5,207.1
1986	11,896	23,161	35,057	13,211,900	6,840.7	5,130.6	5,606.2	5,480.4
1987	12,669	25,429	38,098	13,508,700	6,932.4	5,343.7	5,784.5	5,550.0
1988	12,504	25,220	37,724	13,923,100	6,640.2	5,163.2	5,574.2	5,664.2
1989	14,248	26,624	40,872	14,251,400	7,533.4	5,297.5	5,908.8	5,741.0
1990	13,844	28,338	42,182	14,475,600	6,657.3	5,377.5	5,739.6	5,820.3
1991	16,464	32,799	49,263	14,872,900	7,789.9	6,124.1	6,595.4	5,897.8
1992	16,237	41,831	58,068	14,438,200	7,563.6	6,262.9	6,579.2	5,660.2
1993	15,255	40,332	55,587	14,144,800	6,808.5	5,769.5	6,021.7	5,484.4
1994	16,522	41,728	58,250	13,989,500	7,243.6	5,863.8	6,198.7	5,373.5
1995	17,523	41,642	59,165	13,862,700	7,274.2	5,622.2	6,027.6	5,275.9
1996	17,080	43,624	60,704	13,473,600	6,966.4	5,787.0	6,076.4	5,078.9

Notes: (1) Metropolitan Statistical Area - see Appendix A for areas included; (2) calculated by the editors using the following formula: (number of crimes in the MSA minus number of crimes in the city); (3) calculated by the editors using the following formula: ((number of crimes in the MSA minus number of crimes in the city) ÷ (population of the MSA minus population of the city)) x 100,000; n/a not avail.
Source: U.S. Department of Justice, FBI Uniform Crime Reports, 1977 - 1996

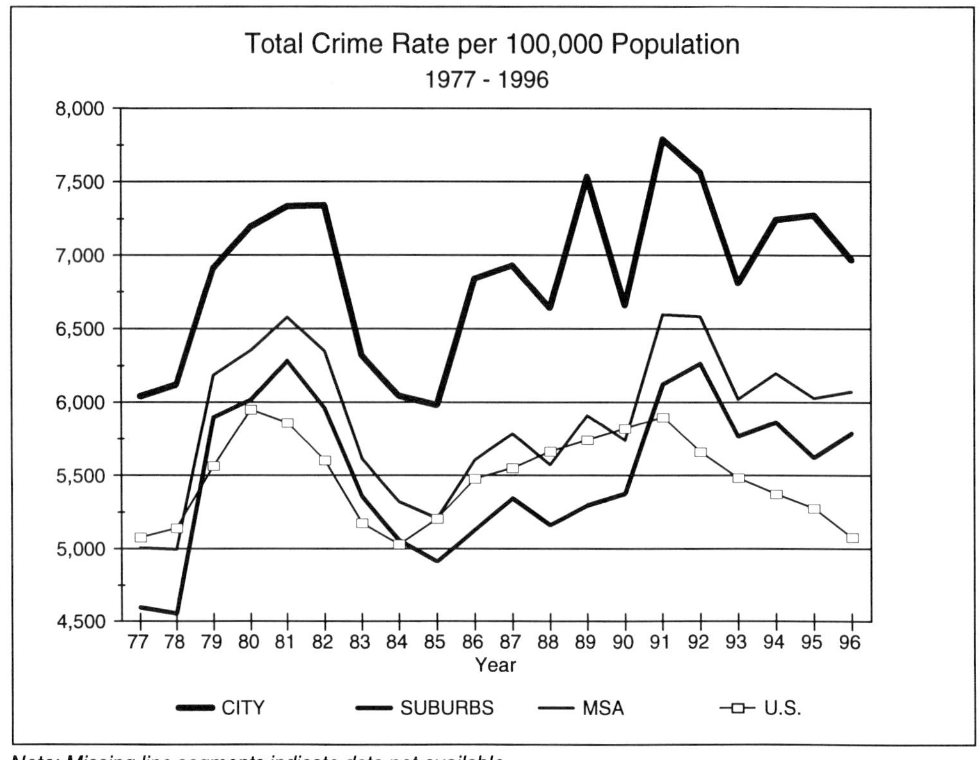

Note: Missing line segments indicate data not available.

Violent Crimes and Violent Crime Rates: 1977 - 1996

Year	Number				Rate per 100,000 population			
	City	Suburbs[2]	MSA[1]	U.S.	City	Suburbs[3]	MSA[1]	U.S.
1977	571	1,108	1,679	1,029,580	413.8	319.6	346.4	475.9
1978	645	1,120	1,765	1,085,550	467.4	316.9	359.2	497.8
1979	804	1,368	2,172	1,208,030	573.1	384.5	437.9	548.9
1980	784	1,385	2,169	1,344,520	528.2	368.1	413.4	596.6
1981	719	1,363	2,082	1,361,820	475.7	355.7	389.7	594.3
1982	886	1,380	2,266	1,322,390	579.5	356.1	419.3	571.1
1983	879	1,464	2,343	1,258,090	569.0	346.4	406.0	537.7
1984	947	1,326	2,273	1,273,280	599.3	304.6	383.1	539.2
1985	1,035	1,366	2,401	1,328,800	602.4	306.3	388.6	556.6
1986	1,163	1,496	2,659	1,489,170	668.8	331.4	425.2	617.7
1987	1,124	1,593	2,717	1,484,000	615.0	334.8	412.5	609.7
1988	1,177	1,601	2,778	1,566,220	625.0	327.8	410.5	637.2
1989	1,248	1,785	3,033	1,646,040	659.9	355.2	438.5	663.1
1990	1,179	2,138	3,317	1,820,130	567.0	405.7	451.3	731.8
1991	1,761	3,013	4,774	1,911,770	833.2	562.6	639.2	758.1
1992	2,171	3,980	6,151	1,932,270	1,011.3	595.9	696.9	757.5
1993	2,030	3,792	5,822	1,926,020	906.0	542.4	630.7	746.8
1994	2,170	3,794	5,964	1,857,670	951.4	533.1	634.7	713.6
1995	2,039	3,850	5,889	1,798,790	846.4	519.8	600.0	684.6
1996	2,109	3,594	5,703	1,682,280	860.2	476.8	570.9	634.1

Notes: Violent crimes include murder, forcible rape, robbery and aggravated assault; n/a not available; (1) Metropolitan Statistical Area - see Appendix A for areas included; (2) calculated by the editors using the following formula: (number of crimes in the MSA minus number of crimes in the city); (3) calculated by the editors using the following formula: ((number of crimes in the MSA minus number of crimes in the city) ÷ (population of the MSA minus population of the city)) x 100,000
Source: U.S. Department of Justice, FBI Uniform Crime Reports, 1977 - 1996

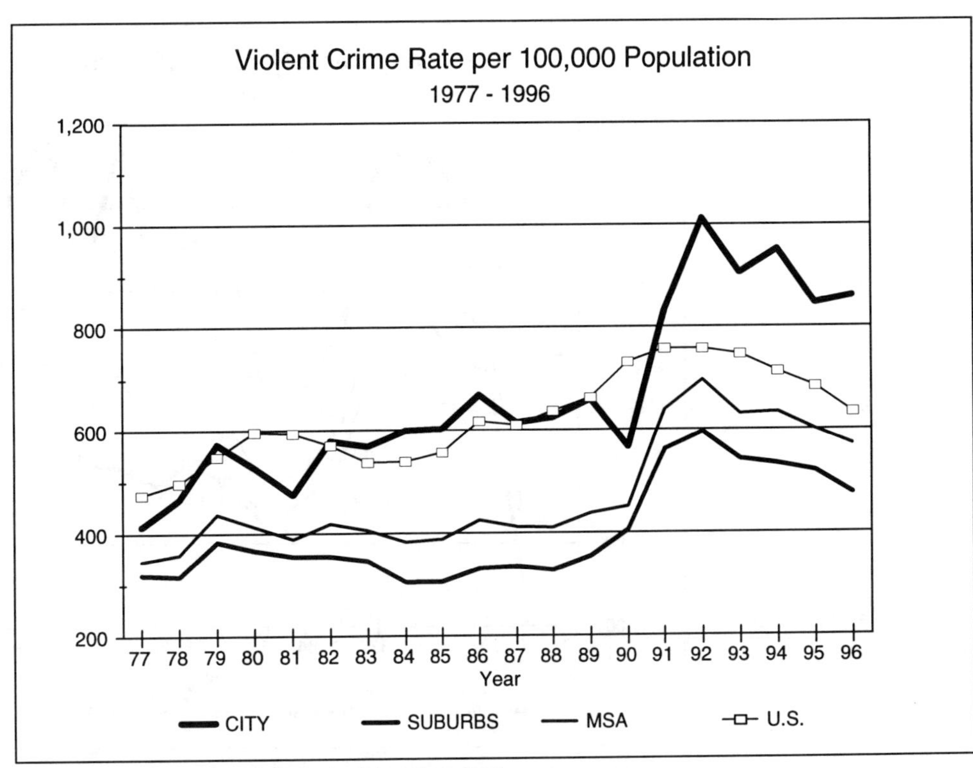

Note: Missing line segments indicate data not available.

Property Crimes and Property Crime Rates: 1977 - 1996

Year	Number				Rate per 100,000 population			
	City	Suburbs[2]	MSA[1]	U.S.	City	Suburbs[3]	MSA[1]	U.S.
1977	7,765	14,825	22,590	9,955,000	5,626.8	4,276.7	4,661.2	4,601.7
1978	7,803	14,975	22,778	10,123,400	5,654.3	4,237.7	4,635.6	4,642.5
1979	8,897	19,609	28,506	11,041,500	6,342.1	5,511.7	5,746.5	5,016.6
1980	9,897	21,259	31,156	12,063,700	6,667.8	5,650.2	5,938.1	5,353.3
1981	10,366	22,702	33,068	12,061,900	6,857.9	5,924.9	6,188.8	5,263.9
1982	10,338	21,712	32,050	11,652,000	6,762.1	5,602.5	5,930.6	5,032.5
1983	8,886	21,181	30,067	10,850,500	5,752.1	5,011.9	5,210.1	4,637.4
1984	8,605	20,695	29,300	10,608,500	5,445.2	4,754.1	4,938.1	4,492.1
1985	9,245	20,540	29,785	11,102,600	5,380.8	4,605.1	4,820.8	4,650.5
1986	10,733	21,665	32,398	11,722,700	6,171.9	4,799.2	5,181.0	4,862.6
1987	11,545	23,836	35,381	12,024,700	6,317.4	5,008.9	5,372.0	4,940.3
1988	11,327	23,619	34,946	12,356,900	6,015.1	4,835.5	5,163.7	5,027.1
1989	13,000	24,839	37,839	12,605,400	6,873.5	4,942.3	5,470.4	5,077.9
1990	12,665	26,200	38,865	12,655,500	6,090.4	4,971.8	5,288.3	5,088.5
1991	14,703	29,786	44,489	12,961,100	6,956.7	5,561.5	5,956.3	5,139.7
1992	14,066	37,851	51,917	12,505,900	6,552.3	5,667.0	5,882.3	4,902.7
1993	13,225	36,540	49,765	12,218,800	5,902.5	5,227.1	5,391.0	4,737.6
1994	14,352	37,934	52,286	12,131,900	6,292.3	5,330.7	5,564.1	4,660.0
1995	15,484	37,792	53,276	12,063,900	6,427.8	5,102.4	5,427.7	4,591.3
1996	14,971	40,030	55,001	11,791,300	6,106.2	5,310.2	5,505.6	4,444.8

Notes: Property crimes include burglary, larceny-theft and motor vehicle theft; n/a not available; (1) Metropolitan Statistical Area - see Appendix A for areas included; (2) calculated by the editors using the following formula: (number of crimes in the MSA minus number of crimes in the city); (3) calculated by the editors using the following formula: ((number of crimes in the MSA minus number of crimes in the city) ÷ (population of the MSA minus population of the city)) x 100,000
Source: U.S. Department of Justice, FBI Uniform Crime Reports, 1977 - 1996

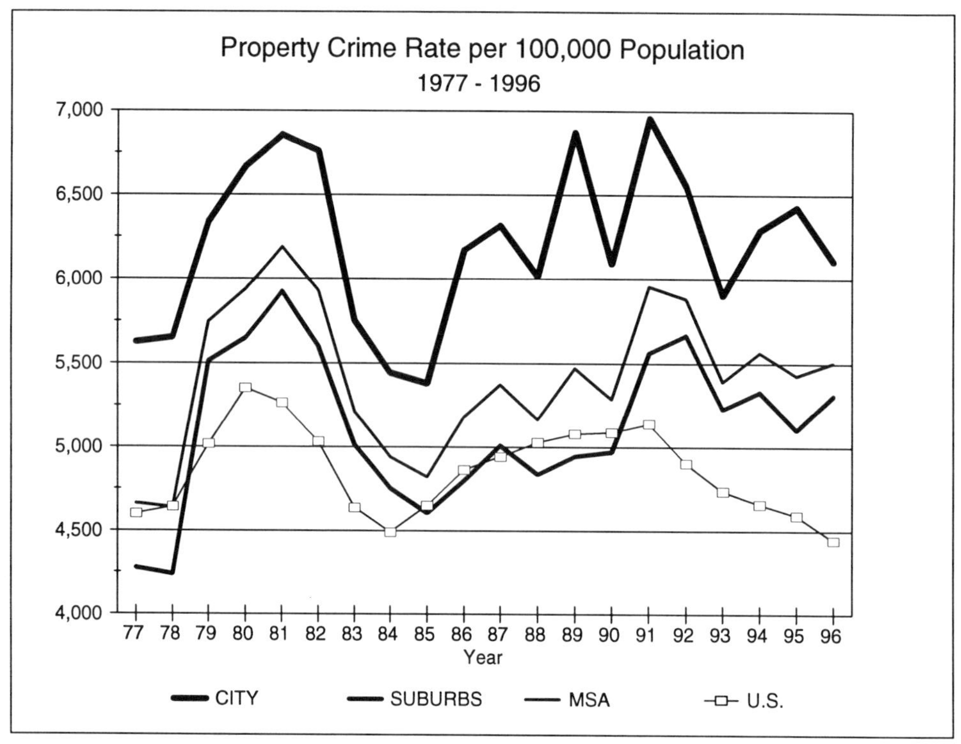

Note: Missing line segments indicate data not available.

Murders and Murder Rates: 1977 - 1996

Year	Number				Rate per 100,000 population			
	City	Suburbs[2]	MSA[1]	U.S.	City	Suburbs[3]	MSA[1]	U.S.
1977	10	28	38	19,120	7.2	8.1	7.8	8.8
1978	12	35	47	19,560	8.7	9.9	9.6	9.0
1979	17	30	47	21,460	12.1	8.4	9.5	9.7
1980	12	38	50	23,040	8.1	10.1	9.5	10.2
1981	11	25	36	22,520	7.3	6.5	6.7	9.8
1982	20	39	59	21,010	13.1	10.1	10.9	9.1
1983	12	38	50	19,310	7.8	9.0	8.7	8.3
1984	8	33	41	18,690	5.1	7.6	6.9	7.9
1985	13	56	69	18,980	7.6	12.6	11.2	7.9
1986	16	47	63	20,610	9.2	10.4	10.1	8.6
1987	15	37	52	20,100	8.2	7.8	7.9	8.3
1988	11	36	47	20,680	5.8	7.4	6.9	8.4
1989	15	31	46	21,500	7.9	6.2	6.7	8.7
1990	24	45	69	23,440	11.5	8.5	9.4	9.4
1991	25	52	77	24,700	11.8	9.7	10.3	9.8
1992	19	61	80	23,760	8.9	9.1	9.1	9.3
1993	27	59	86	24,530	12.1	8.4	9.3	9.5
1994	30	69	99	23,330	13.2	9.7	10.5	9.0
1995	18	70	88	21,610	7.5	9.5	9.0	8.2
1996	25	74	99	19,650	10.2	9.8	9.9	7.4

Notes: (1) Metropolitan Statistical Area - see Appendix A for areas included; (2) calculated by the editors using the following formula: (number of crimes in the MSA minus number of crimes in the city); (3) calculated by the editors using the following formula: ((number of crimes in the MSA minus number of crimes in the city) ÷ (population of the MSA minus population of the city)) x 100,000; n/a not avail.
Source: U.S. Department of Justice, FBI Uniform Crime Reports, 1977 - 1996

Forcible Rapes and Forcible Rape Rates: 1977 - 1996

Year	Number				Rate per 100,000 population			
	City	Suburbs[2]	MSA[1]	U.S.	City	Suburbs[3]	MSA[1]	U.S.
1977	39	100	139	63,500	28.3	28.8	28.7	29.4
1978	48	111	159	67,610	34.8	31.4	32.4	31.0
1979	46	121	167	76,390	32.8	34.0	33.7	34.7
1980	64	143	207	82,990	43.1	38.0	39.5	36.8
1981	56	142	198	82,500	37.0	37.1	37.1	36.0
1982	62	115	177	78,770	40.6	29.7	32.8	34.0
1983	46	129	175	78,920	29.8	30.5	30.3	33.7
1984	47	143	190	84,230	29.7	32.9	32.0	35.7
1985	57	124	181	88,670	33.2	27.8	29.3	37.1
1986	76	122	198	91,460	43.7	27.0	31.7	37.9
1987	78	128	206	91,110	42.7	26.9	31.3	37.4
1988	65	165	230	92,490	34.5	33.8	34.0	37.6
1989	102	134	236	94,500	53.9	26.7	34.1	38.1
1990	96	163	259	102,560	46.2	30.9	35.2	41.2
1991	120	173	293	106,590	56.8	32.3	39.2	42.3
1992	120	274	394	109,060	55.9	41.0	44.6	42.8
1993	94	223	317	106,010	42.0	31.9	34.3	41.1
1994	89	195	284	102,220	39.0	27.4	30.2	39.3
1995	104	193	297	97,470	43.2	26.1	30.3	37.1
1996	90	182	272	95,770	36.7	24.1	27.2	36.1

Notes: (1) Metropolitan Statistical Area - see Appendix A for areas included; (2) calculated by the editors using the following formula: (number of crimes in the MSA minus number of crimes in the city); (3) calculated by the editors using the following formula: ((number of crimes in the MSA minus number of crimes in the city) ÷ (population of the MSA minus population of the city)) x 100,000; n/a not avail.
Source: U.S. Department of Justice, FBI Uniform Crime Reports, 1977 - 1996

Robberies and Robbery Rates: 1977 - 1996

Year	Number				Rate per 100,000 population			
	City	Suburbs[2]	MSA[1]	U.S.	City	Suburbs[3]	MSA[1]	U.S.
1977	120	292	412	412,610	87.0	84.2	85.0	190.7
1978	173	252	425	426,930	125.4	71.3	86.5	195.8
1979	202	365	567	480,700	144.0	102.6	114.3	218.4
1980	260	382	642	565,840	175.2	101.5	122.4	251.1
1981	288	374	662	592,910	190.5	97.6	123.9	258.7
1982	322	411	733	553,130	210.6	106.1	135.6	238.9
1983	289	430	719	506,570	187.1	101.7	124.6	216.5
1984	306	341	647	485,010	193.6	78.3	109.0	205.4
1985	307	373	680	497,870	178.7	83.6	110.1	208.5
1986	339	417	756	542,780	194.9	92.4	120.9	225.1
1987	384	487	871	517,700	210.1	102.3	132.2	212.7
1988	335	460	795	542,970	177.9	94.2	117.5	220.9
1989	380	483	863	578,330	200.9	96.1	124.8	233.0
1990	388	613	1,001	639,270	186.6	116.3	136.2	257.0
1991	652	1,073	1,725	687,730	308.5	200.3	230.9	272.7
1992	887	1,305	2,192	672,480	413.2	195.4	248.4	263.6
1993	795	1,342	2,137	659,870	354.8	192.0	231.5	255.9
1994	825	1,362	2,187	618,950	361.7	191.4	232.7	237.7
1995	648	1,397	2,045	580,510	269.0	188.6	208.3	220.9
1996	732	1,278	2,010	537,050	298.6	169.5	201.2	202.4

Notes: (1) Metropolitan Statistical Area - see Appendix A for areas included; (2) calculated by the editors using the following formula: (number of crimes in the MSA minus number of crimes in the city); (3) calculated by the editors using the following formula: ((number of crimes in the MSA minus number of crimes in the city) ÷ (population of the MSA minus population of the city)) x 100,000; n/a not avail.
Source: U.S. Department of Justice, FBI Uniform Crime Reports, 1977 - 1996

Aggravated Assaults and Aggravated Assault Rates: 1977 - 1996

Year	Number				Rate per 100,000 population			
	City	Suburbs[2]	MSA[1]	U.S.	City	Suburbs[3]	MSA[1]	U.S.
1977	402	688	1,090	534,350	291.3	198.5	224.9	247.0
1978	412	722	1,134	571,460	298.6	204.3	230.8	262.1
1979	539	852	1,391	629,480	384.2	239.5	280.4	286.0
1980	448	822	1,270	672,650	301.8	218.5	242.1	298.5
1981	364	822	1,186	663,900	240.8	214.5	222.0	289.7
1982	482	815	1,297	669,480	315.3	210.3	240.0	289.2
1983	532	867	1,399	653,290	344.4	205.2	242.4	279.2
1984	586	809	1,395	685,350	370.8	185.8	235.1	290.2
1985	658	813	1,471	723,250	383.0	182.3	238.1	302.9
1986	732	910	1,642	834,320	420.9	201.6	262.6	346.1
1987	647	941	1,588	855,090	354.0	197.7	241.1	351.3
1988	766	940	1,706	910,090	406.8	192.4	252.1	370.2
1989	751	1,137	1,888	951,710	397.1	226.2	272.9	383.4
1990	671	1,317	1,988	1,054,860	322.7	249.9	270.5	424.1
1991	964	1,715	2,679	1,092,740	456.1	320.2	358.7	433.3
1992	1,145	2,340	3,485	1,126,970	533.4	350.3	394.9	441.8
1993	1,114	2,168	3,282	1,135,610	497.2	310.1	355.5	440.3
1994	1,226	2,168	3,394	1,113,180	537.5	304.7	361.2	427.6
1995	1,269	2,190	3,459	1,099,210	526.8	295.7	352.4	418.3
1996	1,262	2,060	3,322	1,029,810	514.7	273.3	332.5	388.2

Notes: (1) Metropolitan Statistical Area - see Appendix A for areas included; (2) calculated by the editors using the following formula: (number of crimes in the MSA minus number of crimes in the city); (3) calculated by the editors using the following formula: ((number of crimes in the MSA minus number of crimes in the city) ÷ (population of the MSA minus population of the city)) x 100,000; n/a not avail.
Source: U.S. Department of Justice, FBI Uniform Crime Reports, 1977 - 1996

Burglaries and Burglary Rates: 1977 - 1996

Year	Number				Rate per 100,000 population			
	City	Suburbs[2]	MSA[1]	U.S.	City	Suburbs[3]	MSA[1]	U.S.
1977	2,005	4,813	6,818	3,071,500	1,452.9	1,388.5	1,406.8	1,419.8
1978	1,996	4,771	6,767	3,128,300	1,446.4	1,350.1	1,377.2	1,434.6
1979	2,043	6,015	8,058	3,327,700	1,456.3	1,690.7	1,624.4	1,511.9
1980	2,378	6,760	9,138	3,795,200	1,602.1	1,796.7	1,741.6	1,684.1
1981	2,599	6,454	9,053	3,779,700	1,719.4	1,684.4	1,694.3	1,649.5
1982	2,730	6,191	8,921	3,447,100	1,785.7	1,597.5	1,650.7	1,488.8
1983	2,379	6,320	8,699	3,129,900	1,540.0	1,495.5	1,507.4	1,337.7
1984	1,950	6,153	8,103	2,984,400	1,234.0	1,413.5	1,365.7	1,263.7
1985	2,061	6,294	8,355	3,073,300	1,199.6	1,411.1	1,352.3	1,287.3
1986	2,284	6,425	8,709	3,241,400	1,313.4	1,423.3	1,392.7	1,344.6
1987	3,240	7,648	10,888	3,236,200	1,772.9	1,607.2	1,653.2	1,329.6
1988	2,742	7,468	10,210	3,218,100	1,456.1	1,528.9	1,508.7	1,309.2
1989	3,042	7,723	10,765	3,168,200	1,608.4	1,536.7	1,556.3	1,276.3
1990	2,856	8,178	11,034	3,073,900	1,373.4	1,551.9	1,501.4	1,235.9
1991	3,934	10,398	14,332	3,157,200	1,861.4	1,941.5	1,918.8	1,252.0
1992	3,775	13,031	16,806	2,979,900	1,758.5	1,951.0	1,904.2	1,168.2
1993	2,947	11,318	14,265	2,834,800	1,315.3	1,619.0	1,545.3	1,099.2
1994	3,546	10,977	14,523	2,712,800	1,554.6	1,542.5	1,545.5	1,042.0
1995	3,682	10,398	14,080	2,593,800	1,528.5	1,403.9	1,434.4	987.1
1996	3,139	9,946	13,085	2,501,500	1,280.3	1,319.4	1,309.8	943.0

Notes: (1) Metropolitan Statistical Area - see Appendix A for areas included; (2) calculated by the editors using the following formula: (number of crimes in the MSA minus number of crimes in the city); (3) calculated by the editors using the following formula: ((number of crimes in the MSA minus number of crimes in the city) ÷ (population of the MSA minus population of the city)) x 100,000; n/a not avail.
Source: U.S. Department of Justice, FBI Uniform Crime Reports, 1977 - 1996

Larceny-Thefts and Larceny-Theft Rates: 1977 - 1996

Year	Number				Rate per 100,000 population			
	City	Suburbs[2]	MSA[1]	U.S.	City	Suburbs[3]	MSA[1]	U.S.
1977	5,258	9,124	14,382	5,905,700	3,810.1	2,632.1	2,967.5	2,729.9
1978	5,366	9,369	14,735	5,991,000	3,888.4	2,651.3	2,998.7	2,747.4
1979	6,356	12,483	18,839	6,601,000	4,530.8	3,508.7	3,797.8	2,999.1
1980	7,068	13,468	20,536	7,136,900	4,761.9	3,579.5	3,914.0	3,167.0
1981	7,345	15,349	22,694	7,194,400	4,859.3	4,005.9	4,247.3	3,139.7
1982	7,195	14,618	21,813	7,142,500	4,706.2	3,772.0	4,036.3	3,084.8
1983	6,120	13,963	20,083	6,712,800	3,961.6	3,304.0	3,480.0	2,868.9
1984	6,075	13,622	19,697	6,591,900	3,844.3	3,129.2	3,319.7	2,791.3
1985	6,498	13,183	19,681	6,926,400	3,782.0	2,955.6	3,185.4	2,901.2
1986	7,712	14,088	21,800	7,257,200	4,434.7	3,120.8	3,486.2	3,010.3
1987	7,640	14,991	22,631	7,499,900	4,180.6	3,150.2	3,436.1	3,081.3
1988	7,860	14,872	22,732	7,705,900	4,174.0	3,044.7	3,358.9	3,134.9
1989	9,061	15,640	24,701	7,872,400	4,790.8	3,112.0	3,571.0	3,171.3
1990	9,021	16,503	25,524	7,945,700	4,338.0	3,131.7	3,473.0	3,194.8
1991	9,881	17,724	27,605	8,142,200	4,675.2	3,309.3	3,695.8	3,228.8
1992	9,343	22,794	32,137	7,915,200	4,352.2	3,412.7	3,641.2	3,103.0
1993	9,395	23,193	32,588	7,820,900	4,193.1	3,317.8	3,530.2	3,032.4
1994	9,791	24,600	34,391	7,879,800	4,292.6	3,456.9	3,659.7	3,026.7
1995	10,565	24,999	35,564	7,997,700	4,385.8	3,375.2	3,623.2	3,043.8
1996	10,456	27,104	37,560	7,894,600	4,264.7	3,595.5	3,759.7	2,975.9

Notes: (1) Metropolitan Statistical Area - see Appendix A for areas included; (2) calculated by the editors using the following formula: (number of crimes in the MSA minus number of crimes in the city); (3) calculated by the editors using the following formula: ((number of crimes in the MSA minus number of crimes in the city) ÷ (population of the MSA minus population of the city)) x 100,000; n/a not avail.
Source: U.S. Department of Justice, FBI Uniform Crime Reports, 1977 - 1996

Motor Vehicle Thefts and Motor Vehicle Theft Rates: 1977 - 1996

Year	Number				Rate per 100,000 population			
	City	Suburbs[2]	MSA[1]	U.S.	City	Suburbs[3]	MSA[1]	U.S.
1977	502	888	1,390	977,700	363.8	256.2	286.8	451.9
1978	441	835	1,276	1,004,100	319.6	236.3	259.7	460.5
1979	498	1,111	1,609	1,112,800	355.0	312.3	324.4	505.6
1980	451	1,031	1,482	1,131,700	303.8	274.0	282.5	502.2
1981	422	899	1,321	1,087,800	279.2	234.6	247.2	474.7
1982	413	903	1,316	1,062,400	270.1	233.0	243.5	458.8
1983	387	898	1,285	1,007,900	250.5	212.5	222.7	430.8
1984	580	920	1,500	1,032,200	367.0	211.3	252.8	437.1
1985	686	1,063	1,749	1,102,900	399.3	238.3	283.1	462.0
1986	737	1,152	1,889	1,224,100	423.8	255.2	302.1	507.8
1987	665	1,197	1,862	1,288,700	363.9	251.5	282.7	529.4
1988	725	1,279	2,004	1,432,900	385.0	261.8	296.1	582.9
1989	897	1,476	2,373	1,564,800	474.3	293.7	343.1	630.4
1990	788	1,519	2,307	1,635,900	378.9	288.3	313.9	657.8
1991	888	1,664	2,552	1,661,700	420.2	310.7	341.7	659.0
1992	948	2,026	2,974	1,610,800	441.6	303.3	337.0	631.5
1993	883	2,029	2,912	1,563,100	394.1	290.2	315.5	606.1
1994	1,015	2,357	3,372	1,539,300	445.0	331.2	358.8	591.3
1995	1,237	2,395	3,632	1,472,400	513.5	323.4	370.0	560.4
1996	1,376	2,980	4,356	1,395,200	561.2	395.3	436.0	525.9

Notes: (1) Metropolitan Statistical Area - see Appendix A for areas included; (2) calculated by the editors using the following formula: (number of crimes in the MSA minus number of crimes in the city); (3) calculated by the editors using the following formula: ((number of crimes in the MSA minus number of crimes in the city) ÷ (population of the MSA minus population of the city)) x 100,000; n/a not avail.
Source: U.S. Department of Justice, FBI Uniform Crime Reports, 1977 - 1996

HATE CRIMES

Criminal Incidents by Bias Motivation

Area	Race	Ethnicity	Religion	Sexual Orientation
Raleigh	0	0	0	0

Notes: Figures include both violent and property crimes. Law enforcement agencies must have submitted data for at least one quarter of calendar year 1995 to be included in this report, therefore figures shown may not represent complete 12-month totals; n/a not available
Source: U.S. Department of Justice, FBI Uniform Crime Reports, Hate Crime Statistics 1995

LAW ENFORCEMENT

Full-Time Law Enforcement Employees

Jurisdiction	Police Employees			Police Officers per 100,000 population
	Total	Officers	Civilians	
Raleigh	640	573	67	233.7

Notes: Data as of October 31, 1996
Source: U.S. Department of Justice, FBI Uniform Crime Reports, 1996

CORRECTIONS

Federal Correctional Facilities

Type	Year Opened	Security Level	Sex of Inmates	Rated Capacity	Population on 7/1/95	Number of Staff
None listed						

Notes: Data as of 1995
Source: Bureau of Justice Statistics, Sourcebook of Criminal Justice Statistics Online

City/County/Regional Correctional Facilities

Name	Year Opened	Year Renov.	Rated Capacity	1995 Pop.	Number of COs[1]	Number of Staff	ACA[2] Accred.
Wake Co Detention Facility	1991	--	480	n/a	n/a	n/a	No

Notes: Data as of April 1996; (1) Correctional Officers; (2) American Correctional Assn. Accreditation
Source: American Correctional Association, 1996-1998 National Jail and Adult Detention Directory

Private Adult Correctional Facilities

Name	Date Opened	Rated Capacity	Present Pop.	Security Level	Facility Construct.	Expans. Plans	ACA[1] Accred.
None listed							

Notes: Data as of December 1996; (1) American Correctional Association Accreditation
Source: University of Florida, Center for Studies in Criminology and Law, Private Adult Correctional Facility Census, 10th Ed., March 15, 1997

Characteristics of Shock Incarceration Programs

Jurisdiction	Year Program Began	Number of Camps	Average Num. of Inmates	Number of Beds	Program Length	Voluntary/ Mandatory
North Carolina	1989	2	240	360	90 to 120 days	Voluntary

Note: Data as of July 1996;
Source: Sourcebook of Criminal Justice Statistics Online

DEATH PENALTY

Death Penalty Statistics

State	Prisoners Executed		Prisoners Under Sentence of Death					Avg. No. of Years on Death Row[4]
	1930-1995	1996[1]	Total[2]	White[3]	Black[3]	Hisp.	Women	
North Carolina	271	0	139	68	69	1	2	3.3

Notes: Data as of 12/31/95 unless otherwise noted; (1) Data as of 7/31/97; (2) Includes persons of other races; (3) Includes people of Hispanic origin; (4) Covers prisoners sentenced 1974 through 1995
Source: Bureau of Justice Statistics, Capital Punishment 1995 (released 12/96); Death Penalty Information Center Web Site, 9/30/97

Capital Offenses and Methods of Execution

Capital Offenses in North Carolina	Minimum Age for Imposition of Death Penalty	Mentally Retarded Excluded	Methods of Execution[1]
First-degree murder (N.C.G.S. 14-17).	17	No	Lethal injection; lethal gas

Notes: Data as of 12/31/95 unless otherwise noted; (1) Data as of 7/31/97
Source: Bureau of Justice Statistics, Capital Punishment 1995 (released 12/96); Death Penalty Information Center Web Site, 9/30/97

LAWS

Statutory Provisions Relating to the Purchase, Ownership and Use of Handguns

Jurisdiction	Instant Background Check	Federal Waiting Period Applies[1]	State Waiting Period (days)	License or Permit to Purchase	Regis- tration	Record of Sale Sent to Police	Concealed Carry Law
North Carolina	No	No	No	Yes[a]	No	Yes	Yes[b]

Note: Data as of 1996; (1) The Federal 5-day waiting period for handgun purchases applies to states that don't have instant background checks, waiting period requirements, or licensing procedures exempting them from the Federal requirement; (a) To purchase a handgun, a license or permit is required, which must be issued to qualified applicants within 30 days; (b) "Shall issue" permit system, liberally administered discretion by local authorities over permit issuance, or no permit required
Source: Sourcebook of Criminal Justice Statistics Online

Statutory Provisions Relating to Alcohol Use and Driving

Jurisdiction	Drinking Age	Blood Alcohol Concentration Levels as Evidence in State Courts[1]		Open Container Law[1]	Anti- Consump- tion Law[1]	Dram Shop Law[1]
		Illegal per se at 0.10%	Presumption at 0.10%			
North Carolina	21	(a)	No	Yes[b]	Yes[b,c]	Yes[d,e]

Note: Data as of January 1, 1997; (1) See Appendix C for an explanation of terms; (a) 0.08%; (b) Limited application; (c) Applies to drivers only; (d) State has a statute that places a monetary limit on the amount of damages that can be awarded in dram shop liability actions; (e) Applies specifically to the actions of intoxicated minors, but the law does not foreclose developing case law as to other types of dram shop action
Source: Sourcebook of Criminal Justice Statistics Online

Statutory Provisions Relating to Hate Crimes

Jurisdiction	Bias-Motivated Violence and Intimidation						Institutional Vandalism
		Criminal Penalty					
	Civil Action	Race/ Religion/ Ethnicity	Sexual Orientation	Mental/ Physical Disability	Gender	Age	
North Carolina	No	Yes	No	No	No	No	Yes

Source: Anti-Defamation League, 1997 Hate Crimes Laws

Reno, Nevada

OVERVIEW

The total crime rate for the city decreased 10.0% between 1977 and 1996. During that same period, the violent crime rate increased 50.4% and the property crime rate decreased 13.9%.

Among violent crimes, the rates for: Murders decreased 22.7%; Forcible Rapes increased 98.3%; Robberies increased 6.5%; and Aggravated Assaults increased 147.5%.

Among property crimes, the rates for: Burglaries decreased 47.5%; Larceny-Thefts increased 1.7%; and Motor Vehicle Thefts decreased 20.2%.

ANTI-CRIME PROGRAMS

Information not available at time of publication.

CRIME RISK

Your Chances of Becoming a Victim[1]

Area	Any Crime	Violent Crime					Property Crime			
		Any	Murder	Forcible Rape[2]	Robbery	Aggrav. Assault	Any	Burglary	Larceny -Theft	Motor Vehicle Theft
City	1:15	1:142	1:13,297	1:698	1:315	1:325	1:16	1:95	1:22	1:220

Note: (1) Figures have been calculated by dividing the population of the city by the number of crimes reported to the FBI during 1996 and are expressed as odds (eg. 1:20 should be read as 1 in 20).
(2) Figures have been calculated by dividing the female population of the city by the number of forcible rapes reported to the FBI during 1996. The female population of the city was estimated by calculating the ratio of females to males reported in the 1990 Census and applying that ratio to 1996 population estimate.
Source: FBI Uniform Crime Reports 1996

CRIME STATISTICS

Total Crimes and Total Crime Rates: 1977 - 1996

Year	Number				Rate per 100,000 population			
	City	Suburbs[2]	MSA[1]	U.S.	City	Suburbs[3]	MSA[1]	U.S.
1977	6,990	4,325	11,315	10,984,500	7,555.2	6,964.7	7,318.0	5,077.6
1978	8,882	5,350	14,232	11,209,000	9,317.4	7,651.5	8,612.5	5,140.3
1979	10,215	5,907	16,122	12,249,500	10,409.1	7,956.6	9,352.9	5,565.5
1980	9,980	6,084	16,064	13,408,300	9,886.8	6,547.1	8,286.0	5,950.0
1981	9,775	5,795	15,570	13,423,800	9,171.6	5,906.3	7,606.4	5,858.2
1982	9,118	5,004	14,122	12,974,400	8,205.5	4,891.7	6,617.1	5,603.6
1983	8,308	4,466	12,774	12,108,600	7,392.7	4,316.8	5,918.4	5,175.0
1984	9,467	4,675	14,142	11,881,800	8,541.5	4,439.8	6,543.2	5,031.3
1985	10,333	5,166	15,499	12,431,400	9,520.3	4,747.6	7,130.9	5,207.1
1986	9,819	5,098	14,917	13,211,900	8,793.3	4,552.6	6,669.9	5,480.4
1987	9,806	5,380	15,186	13,508,700	8,503.3	4,512.5	6,474.7	5,550.0
1988	10,673	5,904	16,577	13,923,100	8,888.5	4,755.8	6,787.8	5,664.2
1989	11,426	6,556	17,982	14,251,400	9,416.1	4,993.4	7,117.7	5,741.0
1990	11,558	5,982	17,540	14,475,600	8,635.0	4,951.3	6,887.4	5,820.3
1991	12,089	6,742	18,831	14,872,900	8,453.8	5,223.3	6,921.2	5,897.8
1992	11,766	6,113	17,879	14,438,200	7,961.3	4,582.5	6,358.4	5,660.2
1993	11,571	6,508	18,079	14,144,800	7,956.2	4,865.5	6,475.5	5,484.4
1994	10,950	6,738	17,688	13,989,500	7,177.8	4,802.4	6,039.8	5,373.5
1995	10,947	6,662	17,609	13,862,700	7,188.1	4,600.4	5,926.8	5,275.9
1996	10,854	6,173	17,027	13,473,600	6,802.5	4,068.6	5,470.0	5,078.9

Notes: (1) Metropolitan Statistical Area - see Appendix A for areas included; (2) calculated by the editors using the following formula: (number of crimes in the MSA minus number of crimes in the city); (3) calculated by the editors using the following formula: ((number of crimes in the MSA minus number of crimes in the city) ÷ (population of the MSA minus population of the city)) x 100,000; n/a not avail.
Source: U.S. Department of Justice, FBI Uniform Crime Reports, 1977 - 1996

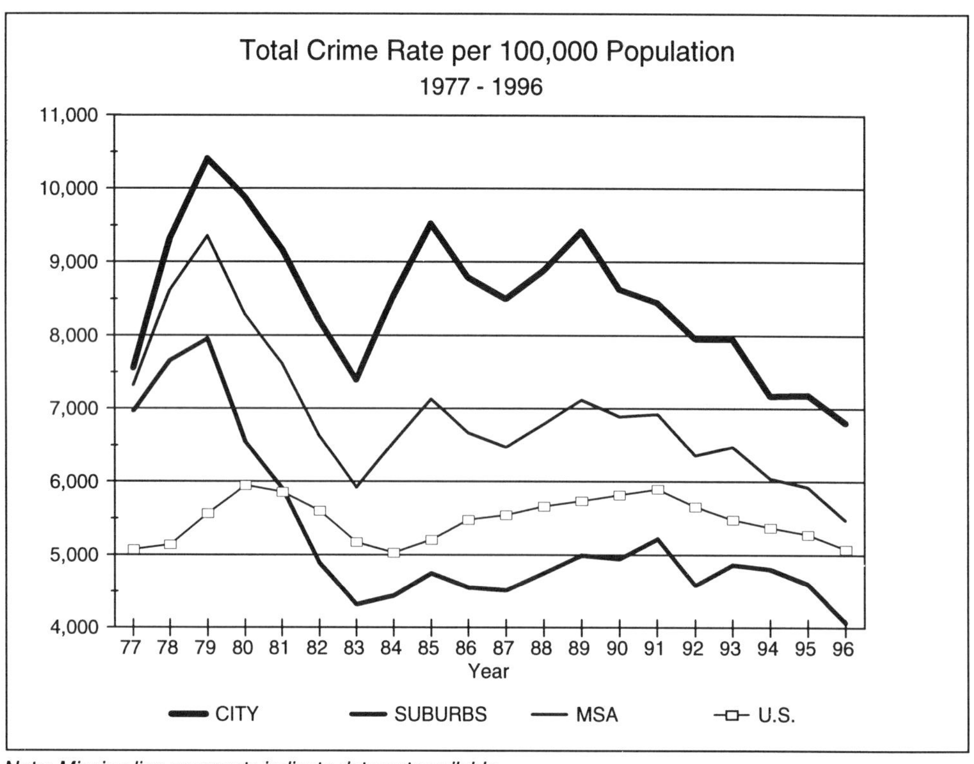

Note: Missing line segments indicate data not available.

Violent Crimes and Violent Crime Rates: 1977 - 1996

Year	Number				Rate per 100,000 population			
	City	Suburbs[2]	MSA[1]	U.S.	City	Suburbs[3]	MSA[1]	U.S.
1977	433	242	675	1,029,580	468.0	389.7	436.6	475.9
1978	645	337	982	1,085,550	676.6	482.0	594.3	497.8
1979	764	376	1,140	1,208,030	778.5	506.5	661.3	548.9
1980	830	443	1,273	1,344,520	822.2	476.7	656.6	596.6
1981	760	415	1,175	1,361,820	713.1	423.0	574.0	594.3
1982	668	408	1,076	1,322,390	601.2	398.8	504.2	571.1
1983	637	369	1,006	1,258,090	566.8	356.7	466.1	537.7
1984	719	458	1,177	1,273,280	648.7	435.0	544.6	539.2
1985	865	450	1,315	1,328,800	797.0	413.5	605.0	556.6
1986	872	491	1,363	1,489,170	780.9	438.5	609.4	617.7
1987	903	465	1,368	1,484,000	783.0	390.0	583.3	609.7
1988	1,159	836	1,995	1,566,220	965.2	673.4	816.9	637.2
1989	1,123	705	1,828	1,646,040	925.5	537.0	723.6	663.1
1990	1,061	543	1,604	1,820,130	792.7	449.4	629.8	731.8
1991	1,134	699	1,833	1,911,770	793.0	541.5	673.7	758.1
1992	1,038	580	1,618	1,932,270	702.3	434.8	575.4	757.5
1993	1,047	569	1,616	1,926,020	719.9	425.4	578.8	746.8
1994	1,152	536	1,688	1,857,670	755.1	382.0	576.4	713.6
1995	1,097	609	1,706	1,798,790	720.3	420.5	574.2	684.6
1996	1,123	583	1,706	1,682,280	703.8	384.3	548.1	634.1

Notes: Violent crimes include murder, forcible rape, robbery and aggravated assault; n/a not available; (1) Metropolitan Statistical Area - see Appendix A for areas included; (2) calculated by the editors using the following formula: (number of crimes in the MSA minus number of crimes in the city); (3) calculated by the editors using the following formula: ((number of crimes in the MSA minus number of crimes in the city) ÷ (population of the MSA minus population of the city)) x 100,000
Source: U.S. Department of Justice, FBI Uniform Crime Reports, 1977 - 1996

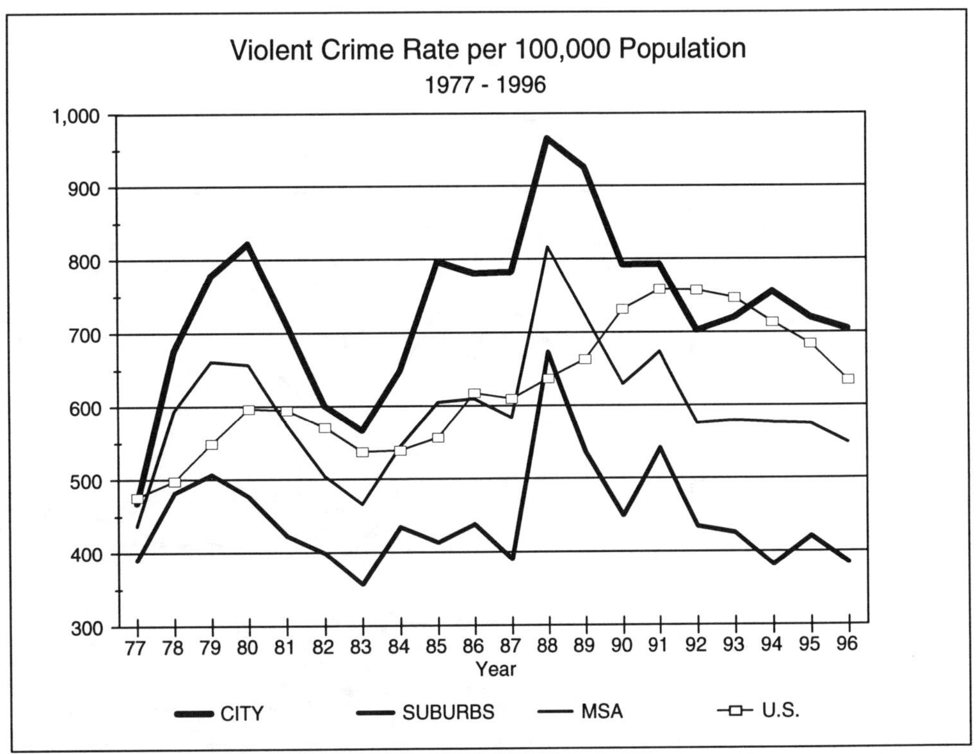

Note: Missing line segments indicate data not available.

Property Crimes and Property Crime Rates: 1977 - 1996

Year	Number				Rate per 100,000 population			
	City	Suburbs[2]	MSA[1]	U.S.	City	Suburbs[3]	MSA[1]	U.S.
1977	6,557	4,083	10,640	9,955,000	7,087.2	6,575.0	6,881.5	4,601.7
1978	8,237	5,013	13,250	10,123,400	8,640.8	7,169.5	8,018.3	4,642.5
1979	9,452	5,530	14,982	11,041,500	9,631.6	7,448.8	8,691.5	5,016.6
1980	9,150	5,641	14,791	12,063,700	9,064.5	6,070.4	7,629.3	5,353.3
1981	9,015	5,380	14,395	12,061,900	8,458.5	5,483.3	7,032.4	5,263.9
1982	8,450	4,596	13,046	11,652,000	7,604.4	4,492.8	6,112.9	5,032.5
1983	7,671	4,097	11,768	10,850,500	6,825.9	3,960.1	5,452.3	4,637.4
1984	8,748	4,217	12,965	10,608,500	7,892.8	4,004.9	5,998.6	4,492.1
1985	9,468	4,716	14,184	11,102,600	8,723.3	4,334.0	6,525.8	4,650.5
1986	8,947	4,607	13,554	11,722,700	8,012.4	4,114.1	6,060.5	4,862.6
1987	8,903	4,915	13,818	12,024,700	7,720.3	4,122.5	5,891.4	4,940.3
1988	9,514	5,068	14,582	12,356,900	7,923.3	4,082.4	5,970.9	5,027.1
1989	10,303	5,851	16,154	12,605,400	8,490.7	4,456.4	6,394.1	5,077.9
1990	10,497	5,439	15,936	12,655,500	7,842.4	4,501.8	6,257.6	5,088.5
1991	10,955	6,043	16,998	12,961,100	7,660.8	4,681.7	6,247.5	5,139.7
1992	10,728	5,533	16,261	12,505,900	7,258.9	4,147.7	5,783.0	4,902.7
1993	10,524	5,939	16,463	12,218,800	7,236.3	4,440.1	5,896.7	4,737.6
1994	9,798	6,202	16,000	12,131,900	6,422.7	4,420.3	5,463.4	4,660.0
1995	9,850	6,053	15,903	12,063,900	6,467.8	4,179.8	5,352.6	4,591.3
1996	9,731	5,590	15,321	11,791,300	6,098.7	3,684.3	4,921.9	4,444.8

Notes: Property crimes include burglary, larceny-theft and motor vehicle theft; n/a not available; (1) Metropolitan Statistical Area - see Appendix A for areas included; (2) calculated by the editors using the following formula: (number of crimes in the MSA minus number of crimes in the city); (3) calculated by the editors using the following formula: ((number of crimes in the MSA minus number of crimes in the city) ÷ (population of the MSA minus population of the city)) x 100,000
Source: U.S. Department of Justice, FBI Uniform Crime Reports, 1977 - 1996

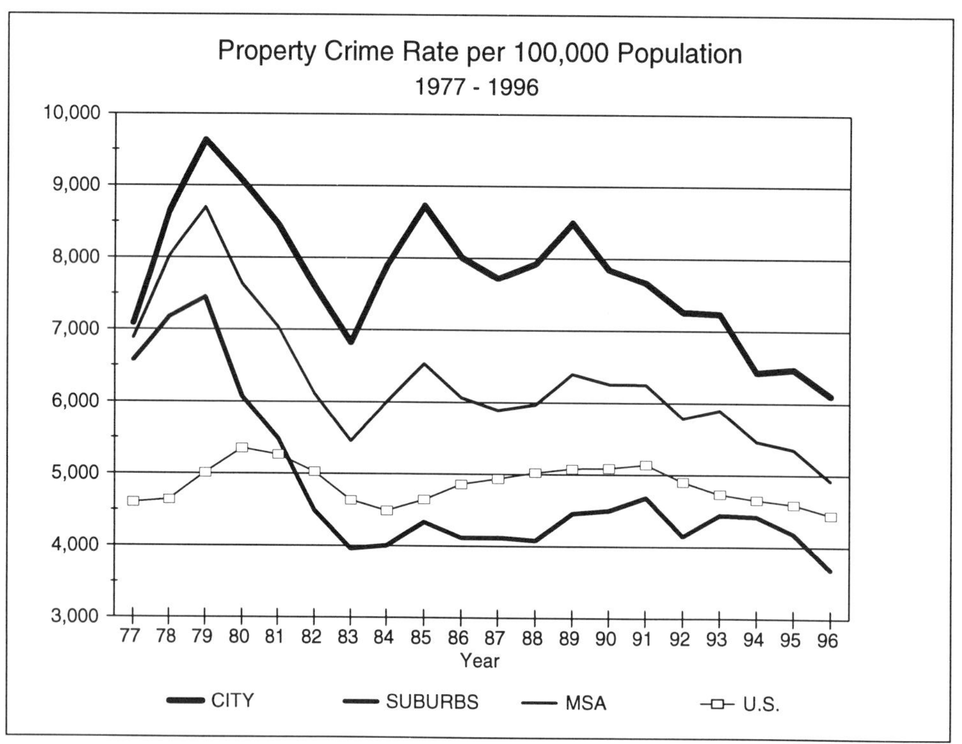

Note: Missing line segments indicate data not available.

Murders and Murder Rates: 1977 - 1996

Year	Number				Rate per 100,000 population			
	City	Suburbs[2]	MSA[1]	U.S.	City	Suburbs[3]	MSA[1]	U.S.
1977	9	5	14	19,120	9.7	8.1	9.1	8.8
1978	12	14	26	19,560	12.6	20.0	15.7	9.0
1979	8	13	21	21,460	8.2	17.5	12.2	9.7
1980	16	9	25	23,040	15.9	9.7	12.9	10.2
1981	11	9	20	22,520	10.3	9.2	9.8	9.8
1982	7	9	16	21,010	6.3	8.8	7.5	9.1
1983	9	9	18	19,310	8.0	8.7	8.3	8.3
1984	8	3	11	18,690	7.2	2.8	5.1	7.9
1985	9	10	19	18,980	8.3	9.2	8.7	7.9
1986	8	8	16	20,610	7.2	7.1	7.2	8.6
1987	12	4	16	20,100	10.4	3.4	6.8	8.3
1988	14	5	19	20,680	11.7	4.0	7.8	8.4
1989	8	8	16	21,500	6.6	6.1	6.3	8.7
1990	11	2	13	23,440	8.2	1.7	5.1	9.4
1991	9	12	21	24,700	6.3	9.3	7.7	9.8
1992	13	7	20	23,760	8.8	5.2	7.1	9.3
1993	16	7	23	24,530	11.0	5.2	8.2	9.5
1994	21	7	28	23,330	13.8	5.0	9.6	9.0
1995	14	7	21	21,610	9.2	4.8	7.1	8.2
1996	12	2	14	19,650	7.5	1.3	4.5	7.4

Notes: (1) Metropolitan Statistical Area - see Appendix A for areas included; (2) calculated by the editors using the following formula: (number of crimes in the MSA minus number of crimes in the city); (3) calculated by the editors using the following formula: ((number of crimes in the MSA minus number of crimes in the city) ÷ (population of the MSA minus population of the city)) x 100,000; n/a not avail.
Source: U.S. Department of Justice, FBI Uniform Crime Reports, 1977 - 1996

Forcible Rapes and Forcible Rape Rates: 1977 - 1996

Year	Number				Rate per 100,000 population			
	City	Suburbs[2]	MSA[1]	U.S.	City	Suburbs[3]	MSA[1]	U.S.
1977	33	22	55	63,500	35.7	35.4	35.6	29.4
1978	53	32	85	67,610	55.6	45.8	51.4	31.0
1979	79	46	125	76,390	80.5	62.0	72.5	34.7
1980	86	60	146	82,990	85.2	64.6	75.3	36.8
1981	89	50	139	82,500	83.5	51.0	67.9	36.0
1982	106	42	148	78,770	95.4	41.1	69.3	34.0
1983	76	50	126	78,920	67.6	48.3	58.4	33.7
1984	87	85	172	84,230	78.5	80.7	79.6	35.7
1985	83	75	158	88,670	76.5	68.9	72.7	37.1
1986	79	102	181	91,460	70.7	91.1	80.9	37.9
1987	115	87	202	91,110	99.7	73.0	86.1	37.4
1988	151	98	249	92,490	125.8	78.9	102.0	37.6
1989	137	113	250	94,500	112.9	86.1	99.0	38.1
1990	143	103	246	102,560	106.8	85.3	96.6	41.2
1991	167	87	254	106,590	116.8	67.4	93.4	42.3
1992	130	92	222	109,060	88.0	69.0	79.0	42.8
1993	129	62	191	106,010	88.7	46.4	68.4	41.1
1994	121	59	180	102,220	79.3	42.1	61.5	39.3
1995	94	44	138	97,470	61.7	30.4	46.4	37.1
1996	113	60	173	95,770	70.8	39.5	55.6	36.1

Notes: (1) Metropolitan Statistical Area - see Appendix A for areas included; (2) calculated by the editors using the following formula: (number of crimes in the MSA minus number of crimes in the city); (3) calculated by the editors using the following formula: ((number of crimes in the MSA minus number of crimes in the city) ÷ (population of the MSA minus population of the city)) x 100,000; n/a not avail.
Source: U.S. Department of Justice, FBI Uniform Crime Reports, 1977 - 1996

Robberies and Robbery Rates: 1977 - 1996

Year	Number				Rate per 100,000 population			
	City	Suburbs[2]	MSA[1]	U.S.	City	Suburbs[3]	MSA[1]	U.S.
1977	276	88	364	412,610	298.3	141.7	235.4	190.7
1978	433	115	548	426,930	454.2	164.5	331.6	195.6
1979	509	127	636	480,700	518.7	171.1	369.0	218.4
1980	480	147	627	565,840	475.5	158.2	323.4	251.1
1981	395	110	505	592,910	370.6	112.1	246.7	258.7
1982	366	106	472	553,130	329.4	103.6	221.2	238.9
1983	297	88	385	506,570	264.3	85.1	178.4	216.5
1984	362	65	427	485,010	326.6	61.7	197.6	205.4
1985	424	74	498	497,870	390.7	68.0	229.1	208.5
1986	375	101	476	542,780	335.8	90.2	212.8	225.1
1987	408	113	521	517,700	353.8	94.8	222.1	212.7
1988	464	135	599	542,970	386.4	108.7	245.3	220.9
1989	458	102	560	578,330	377.4	77.7	221.7	233.0
1990	370	92	462	639,270	276.4	76.1	181.4	257.0
1991	427	128	555	687,730	298.6	99.2	204.0	272.7
1992	413	129	542	672,480	279.5	96.7	192.8	263.6
1993	432	122	554	659,870	297.0	91.2	198.4	255.9
1994	507	110	617	618,950	332.3	78.4	210.7	237.7
1995	421	121	542	580,510	276.4	83.6	182.4	220.9
1996	507	102	609	537,050	317.8	67.2	195.6	202.4

Notes: (1) Metropolitan Statistical Area - see Appendix A for areas included; (2) calculated by the editors using the following formula: (number of crimes in the MSA minus number of crimes in the city); (3) calculated by the editors using the following formula: ((number of crimes in the MSA minus number of crimes in the city) ÷ (population of the MSA minus population of the city)) x 100,000; n/a not avail.
Source: U.S. Department of Justice, FBI Uniform Crime Reports, 1977 - 1996

Aggravated Assaults and Aggravated Assault Rates: 1977 - 1996

Year	Number				Rate per 100,000 population			
	City	Suburbs[2]	MSA[1]	U.S.	City	Suburbs[3]	MSA[1]	U.S.
1977	115	127	242	534,350	124.3	204.5	156.5	247.0
1978	147	176	323	571,460	154.2	251.7	195.5	262.1
1979	168	190	358	629,480	171.2	255.9	207.7	286.0
1980	248	227	475	672,650	245.7	244.3	245.0	298.5
1981	265	246	511	663,900	248.6	250.7	249.6	289.7
1982	189	251	440	669,480	170.1	245.4	206.2	289.2
1983	255	222	477	653,290	226.9	214.6	221.0	279.2
1984	262	305	567	685,350	236.4	289.7	262.3	290.2
1985	349	291	640	723,250	321.5	267.4	294.5	302.9
1986	410	280	690	834,320	367.2	250.0	308.5	346.1
1987	368	261	629	855,090	319.1	218.9	268.2	351.3
1988	530	598	1,128	910,090	441.4	481.7	461.9	370.2
1989	520	482	1,002	951,710	428.5	367.1	396.6	383.4
1990	537	346	883	1,054,860	401.2	286.4	346.7	424.1
1991	531	472	1,003	1,092,740	371.3	365.7	368.6	433.3
1992	482	352	834	1,126,970	326.1	263.9	296.6	441.8
1993	470	378	848	1,135,610	323.2	282.6	303.7	440.3
1994	503	360	863	1,113,180	329.7	256.6	294.7	427.6
1995	568	437	1,005	1,099,210	373.0	301.8	338.3	418.3
1996	491	419	910	1,029,810	307.7	276.2	292.3	388.2

Notes: (1) Metropolitan Statistical Area - see Appendix A for areas included; (2) calculated by the editors using the following formula: (number of crimes in the MSA minus number of crimes in the city); (3) calculated by the editors using the following formula: ((number of crimes in the MSA minus number of crimes in the city) ÷ (population of the MSA minus population of the city)) x 100,000; n/a not avail.
Source: U.S. Department of Justice, FBI Uniform Crime Reports, 1977 - 1996

Burglaries and Burglary Rates: 1977 - 1996

Year	Number				Rate per 100,000 population			
	City	Suburbs[2]	MSA[1]	U.S.	City	Suburbs[3]	MSA[1]	U.S.
1977	1,851	1,243	3,094	3,071,500	2,000.7	2,001.6	2,001.1	1,419.8
1978	2,449	1,526	3,975	3,128,300	2,569.1	2,182.5	2,405.5	1,434.6
1979	3,038	1,728	4,766	3,327,700	3,095.7	2,327.6	2,764.9	1,511.9
1980	2,897	1,701	4,598	3,795,200	2,869.9	1,830.5	2,371.7	1,684.1
1981	2,835	1,487	4,322	3,779,700	2,660.0	1,515.6	2,111.4	1,649.5
1982	2,478	1,414	3,892	3,447,100	2,230.0	1,382.3	1,823.7	1,488.8
1983	2,030	1,110	3,140	3,129,900	1,806.4	1,072.9	1,454.8	1,337.7
1984	2,566	1,168	3,734	2,984,400	2,315.2	1,109.2	1,727.6	1,263.7
1985	2,787	1,373	4,160	3,073,300	2,567.8	1,261.8	1,914.0	1,287.3
1986	2,470	1,194	3,664	3,241,400	2,212.0	1,066.3	1,638.3	1,344.6
1987	2,134	1,337	3,471	3,236,200	1,850.5	1,121.4	1,479.9	1,329.6
1988	2,266	1,408	3,674	3,218,100	1,887.1	1,134.2	1,504.4	1,309.2
1989	2,194	1,370	3,564	3,168,200	1,808.1	1,043.5	1,410.7	1,276.3
1990	1,812	1,289	3,101	3,073,900	1,353.8	1,066.9	1,217.7	1,235.9
1991	2,155	1,462	3,617	3,157,200	1,507.0	1,132.7	1,329.4	1,252.0
1992	1,852	1,319	3,171	2,979,900	1,253.1	988.8	1,127.7	1,168.2
1993	1,837	1,321	3,158	2,834,800	1,263.1	987.6	1,131.1	1,099.2
1994	1,952	1,517	3,469	2,712,800	1,279.6	1,081.2	1,184.5	1,042.0
1995	1,846	1,384	3,230	2,593,800	1,212.1	955.7	1,087.1	987.1
1996	1,676	1,331	3,007	2,501,500	1,050.4	877.3	966.0	943.0

Notes: (1) Metropolitan Statistical Area - see Appendix A for areas included; (2) calculated by the editors using the following formula: (number of crimes in the MSA minus number of crimes in the city); (3) calculated by the editors using the following formula: ((number of crimes in the MSA minus number of crimes in the city) ÷ (population of the MSA minus population of the city)) x 100,000; n/a not avail.
Source: U.S. Department of Justice, FBI Uniform Crime Reports, 1977 - 1996

Larceny-Thefts and Larceny-Theft Rates: 1977 - 1996

Year	Number				Rate per 100,000 population			
	City	Suburbs[2]	MSA[1]	U.S.	City	Suburbs[3]	MSA[1]	U.S.
1977	4,179	2,592	6,771	5,905,700	4,516.9	4,174.0	4,379.2	2,729.9
1978	5,129	3,168	8,297	5,991,000	5,380.4	4,530.8	5,020.9	2,747.4
1979	5,565	3,409	8,974	6,601,000	5,670.8	4,591.9	5,206.1	2,999.1
1980	5,520	3,577	9,097	7,136,900	5,468.4	3,849.3	4,692.3	3,167.0
1981	5,511	3,559	9,070	7,194,400	5,170.8	3,627.3	4,431.0	3,139.7
1982	5,416	2,954	8,370	7,142,500	4,874.0	2,887.7	3,921.9	3,084.8
1983	5,073	2,769	7,842	6,712,800	4,514.1	2,676.5	3,633.3	2,868.9
1984	5,577	2,767	8,344	6,591,900	5,031.8	2,627.8	3,860.6	2,791.3
1985	6,012	3,042	9,054	6,926,400	5,539.1	2,795.6	4,165.6	2,901.2
1986	5,855	3,132	8,987	7,257,200	5,243.4	2,796.9	4,018.4	3,010.3
1987	6,031	3,270	9,301	7,499,900	5,229.8	2,742.7	3,965.6	3,081.3
1988	6,471	3,316	9,787	7,705,900	5,389.1	2,671.1	4,007.5	3,134.9
1989	7,381	4,114	11,495	7,872,400	6,082.7	3,133.4	4,550.0	3,171.3
1990	7,961	3,781	11,742	7,945,700	5,947.7	3,129.5	4,610.7	3,194.8
1991	8,168	4,207	12,375	8,142,200	5,711.8	3,259.3	4,548.3	3,228.8
1992	8,301	3,907	12,208	7,915,200	5,616.8	2,928.8	4,341.6	3,103.0
1993	8,006	4,206	12,212	7,820,900	5,504.9	3,144.5	4,374.1	3,032.4
1994	7,109	4,186	11,295	7,879,800	4,660.0	2,983.5	3,856.8	3,026.7
1995	7,193	4,206	11,399	7,997,700	4,723.1	2,904.4	3,836.6	3,043.8
1996	7,330	3,839	11,169	7,894,600	4,593.9	2,530.3	3,588.1	2,975.9

Notes: (1) Metropolitan Statistical Area - see Appendix A for areas included; (2) calculated by the editors using the following formula: (number of crimes in the MSA minus number of crimes in the city); (3) calculated by the editors using the following formula: ((number of crimes in the MSA minus number of crimes in the city) ÷ (population of the MSA minus population of the city)) x 100,000; n/a not avail.
Source: U.S. Department of Justice, FBI Uniform Crime Reports, 1977 - 1996

Motor Vehicle Thefts and Motor Vehicle Theft Rates: 1977 - 1996

Year	Number				Rate per 100,000 population			
	City	Suburbs[2]	MSA[1]	U.S.	City	Suburbs[3]	MSA[1]	U.S.
1977	527	248	775	977,700	569.6	399.4	501.2	451.9
1978	659	319	978	1,004,100	691.3	456.2	591.8	460.5
1979	850	392	1,242	1,112,800	866.2	528.0	720.5	505.6
1980	733	363	1,096	1,131,700	726.2	390.6	565.3	502.2
1981	669	334	1,003	1,087,800	627.7	340.4	490.0	474.7
1982	556	228	784	1,062,400	500.4	222.9	367.4	458.8
1983	568	218	786	1,007,900	505.4	210.7	364.2	430.8
1984	605	282	887	1,032,200	545.9	267.8	410.4	437.1
1985	669	301	970	1,102,900	616.4	276.6	446.3	462.0
1986	622	281	903	1,224,100	557.0	250.9	403.8	507.8
1987	738	308	1,046	1,288,700	640.0	258.3	446.0	529.4
1988	777	344	1,121	1,432,900	647.1	277.1	459.0	582.9
1989	728	367	1,095	1,564,800	599.9	279.5	433.4	630.4
1990	724	369	1,093	1,635,900	540.9	305.4	429.2	657.8
1991	632	374	1,006	1,661,700	442.0	289.8	369.7	659.0
1992	575	307	882	1,610,800	389.1	230.1	313.7	631.5
1993	681	412	1,093	1,563,100	468.3	308.0	391.5	606.1
1994	737	499	1,236	1,539,300	483.1	355.7	422.0	591.3
1995	811	463	1,274	1,472,400	532.5	319.7	428.8	560.4
1996	725	420	1,145	1,395,200	454.4	276.8	367.8	525.9

Notes: (1) Metropolitan Statistical Area - see Appendix A for areas included; (2) calculated by the editors using the following formula: (number of crimes in the MSA minus number of crimes in the city); (3) calculated by the editors using the following formula: ((number of crimes in the MSA minus number of crimes in the city) ÷ (population of the MSA minus population of the city)) x 100,000; n/a not avail.
Source: U.S. Department of Justice, FBI Uniform Crime Reports, 1977 - 1996

HATE CRIMES

Criminal Incidents by Bias Motivation

Area	Race	Ethnicity	Religion	Sexual Orientation
Reno	7	1	0	2

Notes: Figures include both violent and property crimes. Law enforcement agencies must have submitted data for at least one quarter of calendar year 1995 to be included in this report, therefore figures shown may not represent complete 12-month totals; n/a not available
Source: U.S. Department of Justice, FBI Uniform Crime Reports, Hate Crime Statistics 1995

LAW ENFORCEMENT

Full-Time Law Enforcement Employees

Jurisdiction	Police Employees			Police Officers per 100,000 population
	Total	Officers	Civilians	
Reno	447	310	137	194.3

Notes: Data as of October 31, 1996
Source: U.S. Department of Justice, FBI Uniform Crime Reports, 1996

CORRECTIONS

Federal Correctional Facilities

Type	Year Opened	Security Level	Sex of Inmates	Rated Capacity	Population on 7/1/95	Number of Staff
None listed						

Notes: Data as of 1995
Source: Bureau of Justice Statistics, Sourcebook of Criminal Justice Statistics Online

City/County/Regional Correctional Facilities

Name	Year Opened	Year Renov.	Rated Capacity	1995 Pop.	Number of COs[1]	Number of Staff	ACA[2] Accred.
None listed							

Notes: Data as of April 1996; (1) Correctional Officers; (2) American Correctional Assn. Accreditation
Source: American Correctional Association, 1996-1998 National Jail and Adult Detention Directory

Private Adult Correctional Facilities

Name	Date Opened	Rated Capacity	Present Pop.	Security Level	Facility Construct.	Expans. Plans	ACA[1] Accred.
None listed							

Notes: Data as of December 1996; (1) American Correctional Association Accreditation
Source: University of Florida, Center for Studies in Criminology and Law, Private Adult Correctional Facility Census, 10th Ed., March 15, 1997

Characteristics of Shock Incarceration Programs

Jurisdiction	Year Program Began	Number of Camps	Average Num. of Inmates	Number of Beds	Program Length	Voluntary/ Mandatory
Nevada	1991	1	73	73	190 days	Voluntary

Note: Data as of July 1996;
Source: Sourcebook of Criminal Justice Statistics Online

DEATH PENALTY

Death Penalty Statistics

State	Prisoners Executed		Prisoners Under Sentence of Death					Avg. No. of Years on Death Row[4]
	1930-1995	1996[1]	Total[2]	White[3]	Black[3]	Hisp.	Women	
Nevada	34	1	75	48	26	10	1	7.1

Notes: Data as of 12/31/95 unless otherwise noted; (1) Data as of 7/31/97; (2) Includes persons of other races; (3) Includes people of Hispanic origin; (4) Covers prisoners sentenced 1974 through 1995
Source: Bureau of Justice Statistics, Capital Punishment 1995 (released 12/96); Death Penalty Information Center Web Site, 9/30/97

Capital Offenses and Methods of Execution

Capital Offenses in Nevada	Minimum Age for Imposition of Death Penalty	Mentally Retarded Excluded	Methods of Execution[1]
First-degree murder with 10 aggravating circumstances.	16	No	Lethal injection

Notes: Data as of 12/31/95 unless otherwise noted; (1) Data as of 7/31/97
Source: Bureau of Justice Statistics, Capital Punishment 1995 (released 12/96); Death Penalty Information Center Web Site, 9/30/97

LAWS

Statutory Provisions Relating to the Purchase, Ownership and Use of Handguns

Jurisdiction	Instant Background Check	Federal Waiting Period Applies[1]	State Waiting Period (days)	License or Permit to Purchase	Regis-tration	Record of Sale Sent to Police	Concealed Carry Law
Nevada	Yes[a]	Yes	(b)	No	(b)	No	Yes[c]

Note: Data as of 1996; (1) The Federal 5-day waiting period for handgun purchases applies to states that don't have instant background checks, waiting period requirements, or licensing procedures exempting them from the Federal requirement; (a) Nevada has, but does not use, its Instant Check system; (b) Local ordinance in certain cities or counties; (c) "Shall issue" permit system, liberally administered discretion by local authorities over permit issuance, or no permit required
Source: Sourcebook of Criminal Justice Statistics Online

Statutory Provisions Relating to Alcohol Use and Driving

Jurisdiction	Drinking Age	Blood Alcohol Concentration Levels as Evidence in State Courts[1]		Open Container Law[1]	Anti-Consump-tion Law[1]	Dram Shop Law[1]
		Illegal per se at 0.10%	Presumption at 0.10%			
Nevada	21	Yes	No	Yes	(a)	No

Note: Data as of January 1, 1997; (1) See Appendix C for an explanation of terms; (a) Applies to drivers only
Source: Sourcebook of Criminal Justice Statistics Online

Statutory Provisions Relating to Curfews

Jurisdiction	Year Enacted	Latest Revision	Age Group(s)	Curfew Provisions
Reno	1950	1994	16 and 17	Midnight to 5 am weekday nights 1 am to 5 am weekend nights
			15 and under	11 pm to 5 am weekday nights midnight to 5 am weekend nights 1 am to 5 am on "special event" nights[1]

Note: Data as of February 1996; (1) "Special events" nights are designated as such by the city council
Source: Sourcebook of Criminal Justice Statistics Online

Statutory Provisions Relating to Hate Crimes

Jurisdiction	Bias-Motivated Violence and Intimidation						Institutional Vandalism
		Criminal Penalty					
	Civil Action	Race/ Religion/ Ethnicity	Sexual Orientation	Mental/ Physical Disability	Gender	Age	
Nevada	No	Yes	Yes	No	No	No	Yes

Source: Anti-Defamation League, 1997 Hate Crimes Laws

Richmond, Virginia

OVERVIEW

The total crime rate for the city increased 19.5% between 1977 and 1996. During that same period, the violent crime rate increased 79.9% and the property crime rate increased 11.7%.

Among violent crimes, the rates for: Murders increased 90.6%; Forcible Rapes increased 10.4%; Robberies increased 95.3%; and Aggravated Assaults increased 75.6%.

Among property crimes, the rates for: Burglaries decreased 7.2%; Larceny-Thefts increased 10.6%; and Motor Vehicle Thefts increased 106.3%.

ANTI-CRIME PROGRAMS

Information not available at time of publication.

CRIME RISK

Your Chances of Becoming a Victim[1]

Area	Any Crime	Violent Crime					Property Crime			
		Any	Murder	Forcible Rape[2]	Robbery	Aggrav. Assault	Any	Burglary	Larceny -Theft	Motor Vehicle Theft
City	1:10	1:61	1:1,829	1:779	1:133	1:129	1:13	1:51	1:20	1:101

Note: (1) Figures have been calculated by dividing the population of the city by the number of crimes reported to the FBI during 1996 and are expressed as odds (eg. 1:20 should be read as 1 in 20). (2) Figures have been calculated by dividing the female population of the city by the number of forcible rapes reported to the FBI during 1996. The female population of the city was estimated by calculating the ratio of females to males reported in the 1990 Census and applying that ratio to 1996 population estimate.
Source: FBI Uniform Crime Reports 1996

CRIME STATISTICS

Total Crimes and Total Crime Rates: 1977 - 1996

Year	Number				Rate per 100,000 population			
	City	Suburbs[2]	MSA[1]	U.S.	City	Suburbs[3]	MSA[1]	U.S.
1977	18,014	15,497	33,511	10,984,500	8,078.0	4,178.8	5,643.1	5,077.6
1978	16,943	15,803	32,746	11,209,000	7,701.4	4,215.1	5,504.4	5,140.3
1979	18,828	17,167	35,995	12,249,500	8,492.7	4,423.7	5,903.1	5,565.5
1980	21,493	19,273	40,766	13,408,300	9,795.0	4,782.6	6,549.7	5,950.0
1981	24,766	21,177	45,943	13,423,800	11,073.2	5,155.7	7,241.9	5,858.2
1982	22,464	18,473	40,937	12,974,400	9,925.0	4,444.2	6,376.4	5,603.6
1983	23,079	23,191	46,270	12,108,600	10,088.4	4,116.9	5,841.6	5,175.0
1984	19,274	22,133	41,407	11,881,800	8,586.0	3,845.3	5,175.5	5,031.3
1985	17,596	22,578	40,174	12,431,400	7,931.2	3,865.1	4,984.3	5,207.1
1986	18,257	22,756	41,013	13,211,900	8,116.3	3,840.6	5,017.1	5,480.4
1987	18,564	23,390	41,954	13,508,700	8,357.9	3,869.2	5,075.3	5,550.0
1988	20,114	26,459	46,573	13,923,100	9,143.6	4,278.6	5,555.1	5,664.2
1989	21,367	26,596	47,963	14,251,400	9,881.7	4,157.8	5,603.8	5,741.0
1990	23,043	28,779	51,822	14,475,600	11,348.1	4,343.4	5,986.6	5,820.3
1991	23,917	30,912	54,829	14,872,900	11,593.8	4,592.2	6,234.6	5,897.8
1992	22,246	29,443	51,689	14,438,200	10,629.8	4,311.6	5,793.7	5,660.2
1993	22,142	29,100	51,242	14,144,800	10,783.6	4,131.6	5,633.1	5,484.4
1994	21,939	29,705	51,644	13,989,500	10,585.2	4,178.3	5,624.5	5,373.5
1995	20,984	28,518	49,502	13,862,700	10,330.2	3,945.7	5,346.4	5,275.9
1996	19,771	31,173	50,944	13,473,600	9,650.0	4,276.2	5,455.2	5,078.9

Notes: (1) Metropolitan Statistical Area - see Appendix A for areas included; (2) calculated by the editors using the following formula: (number of crimes in the MSA minus number of crimes in the city); (3) calculated by the editors using the following formula: ((number of crimes in the MSA minus number of crimes in the city) ÷ (population of the MSA minus population of the city)) x 100,000; n/a not avail.
Source: U.S. Department of Justice, FBI Uniform Crime Reports, 1977 - 1996

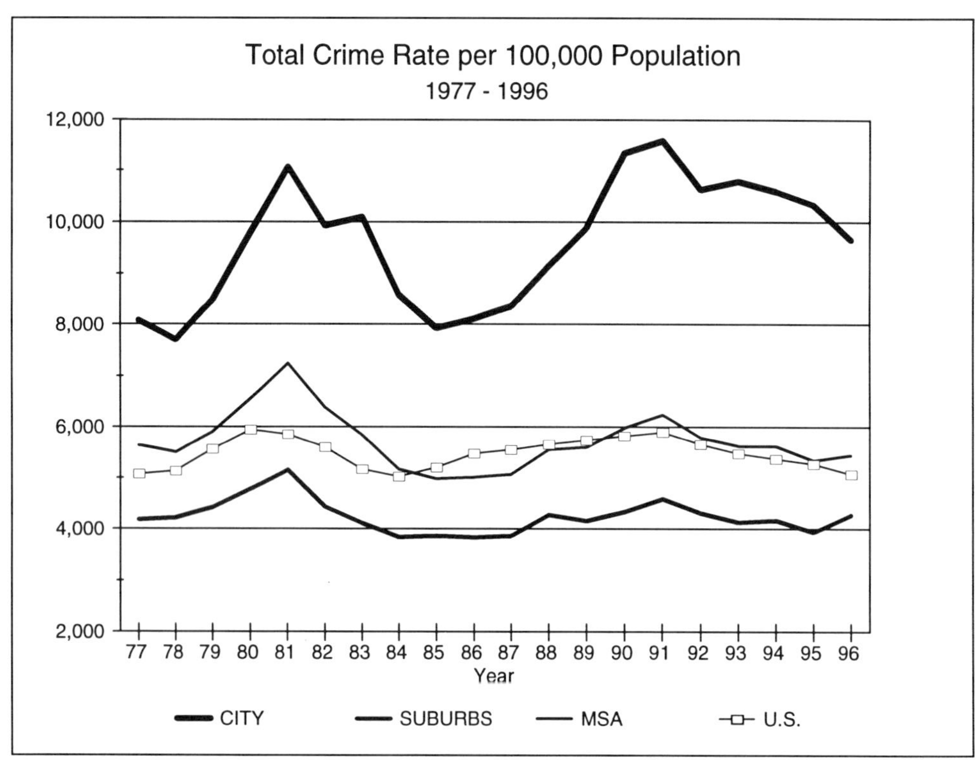

Note: Missing line segments indicate data not available.

Violent Crimes and Violent Crime Rates: 1977 - 1996

Year	Number				Rate per 100,000 population			
	City	Suburbs[2]	MSA[1]	U.S.	City	Suburbs[3]	MSA[1]	U.S.
1977	2,047	668	2,715	1,029,580	917.9	180.1	457.2	475.9
1978	1,836	551	2,387	1,085,550	834.5	147.0	401.2	497.8
1979	2,234	699	2,933	1,208,030	1,007.7	180.1	481.0	548.9
1980	2,430	675	3,105	1,344,520	1,107.4	167.5	498.9	596.6
1981	2,668	827	3,495	1,361,820	1,192.9	201.3	550.9	594.3
1982	2,774	739	3,513	1,322,390	1,225.6	177.8	547.2	571.1
1983	2,937	1,184	4,121	1,258,090	1,283.8	210.2	520.3	537.7
1984	2,757	1,305	4,062	1,273,280	1,228.2	226.7	507.7	539.2
1985	2,647	1,389	4,036	1,328,800	1,193.1	237.8	500.7	556.6
1986	2,586	1,376	3,962	1,489,170	1,149.6	232.2	484.7	617.7
1987	2,614	1,399	4,013	1,484,000	1,176.9	231.4	485.5	609.7
1988	2,584	1,536	4,120	1,566,220	1,174.7	248.4	491.4	637.2
1989	2,928	1,751	4,679	1,646,040	1,354.1	273.7	546.7	663.1
1990	3,229	1,887	5,116	1,820,130	1,590.2	284.8	591.0	731.8
1991	3,414	1,789	5,203	1,911,770	1,654.9	265.8	591.6	758.1
1992	3,110	1,963	5,073	1,932,270	1,486.1	287.5	568.6	757.5
1993	3,275	1,987	5,262	1,926,020	1,595.0	282.1	578.5	746.8
1994	3,534	1,949	5,483	1,857,670	1,705.1	274.1	597.1	713.6
1995	3,500	2,086	5,586	1,798,790	1,723.0	288.6	603.3	684.6
1996	3,383	2,188	5,571	1,682,280	1,651.2	300.1	596.6	634.1

Notes: Violent crimes include murder, forcible rape, robbery and aggravated assault; n/a not available; (1) Metropolitan Statistical Area - see Appendix A for areas included; (2) calculated by the editors using the following formula: (number of crimes in the MSA minus number of crimes in the city); (3) calculated by the editors using the following formula: ((number of crimes in the MSA minus number of crimes in the city) ÷ (population of the MSA minus population of the city)) x 100,000
Source: U.S. Department of Justice, FBI Uniform Crime Reports, 1977 - 1996

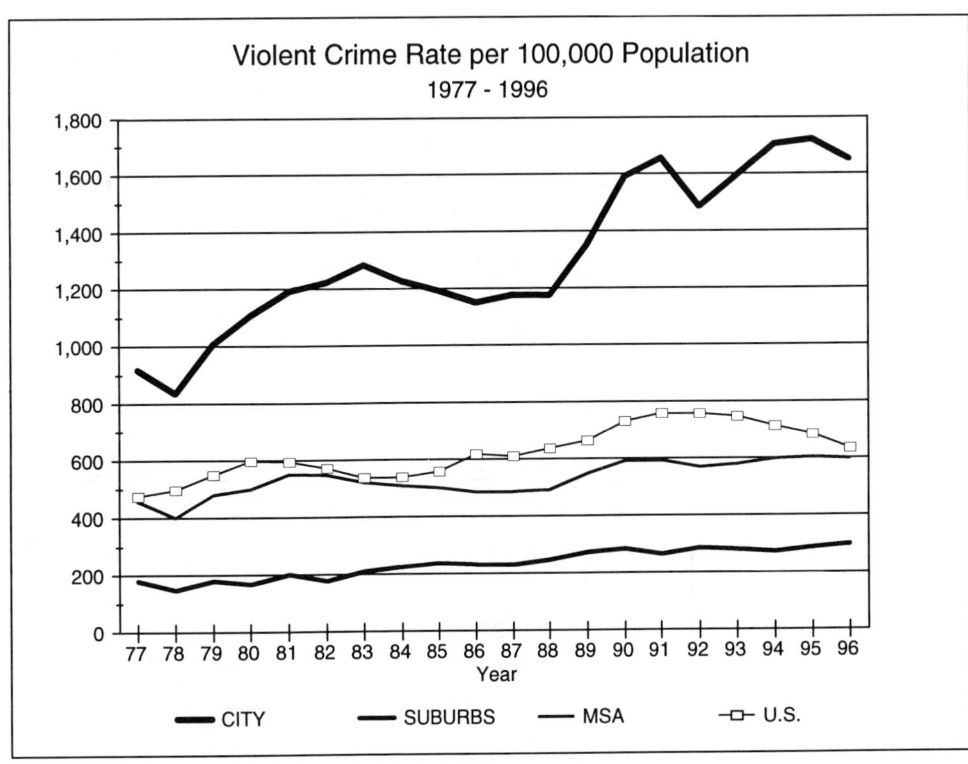

Note: Missing line segments indicate data not available.

Property Crimes and Property Crime Rates: 1977 - 1996

Year	Number				Rate per 100,000 population			
	City	Suburbs[2]	MSA[1]	U.S.	City	Suburbs[3]	MSA[1]	U.S.
1977	15,967	14,829	30,796	9,955,000	7,160.1	3,998.7	5,185.9	4,601.7
1978	15,107	15,252	30,359	10,123,400	6,866.8	4,068.2	5,103.1	4,642.5
1979	16,594	16,468	33,062	11,041,500	7,485.1	4,243.6	5,422.1	5,016.6
1980	19,063	18,598	37,661	12,063,700	8,687.5	4,615.1	6,050.8	5,353.3
1981	22,098	20,350	42,448	12,061,900	9,880.3	4,954.4	6,691.0	5,263.9
1982	19,690	17,734	37,424	11,652,000	8,699.4	4,266.4	5,829.2	5,032.5
1983	20,142	22,007	42,149	10,850,500	8,804.6	3,906.7	5,321.3	4,637.4
1984	16,517	20,828	37,345	10,608,500	7,357.9	3,618.6	4,667.7	4,492.1
1985	14,949	21,189	36,138	11,102,600	6,738.1	3,627.3	4,483.5	4,650.5
1986	15,671	21,380	37,051	11,722,700	6,966.7	3,608.3	4,532.4	4,862.6
1987	15,950	21,991	37,941	12,024,700	7,181.0	3,637.8	4,589.9	4,940.3
1988	17,530	24,923	42,453	12,356,900	7,968.9	4,030.2	5,063.7	5,027.1
1989	18,439	24,845	43,284	12,605,400	8,527.5	3,884.1	5,057.2	5,077.9
1990	19,814	26,892	46,706	12,655,500	9,757.9	4,058.7	5,395.5	5,088.5
1991	20,503	29,123	49,626	12,961,100	9,938.8	4,326.4	5,643.0	5,139.7
1992	19,136	27,480	46,616	12,505,900	9,143.8	4,024.1	5,225.1	4,902.7
1993	18,867	27,113	45,980	12,218,800	9,188.6	3,849.5	5,054.7	4,737.6
1994	18,405	27,756	46,161	12,131,900	8,880.1	3,904.1	5,027.3	4,660.0
1995	17,484	26,432	43,916	12,063,900	8,607.2	3,657.1	4,743.1	4,591.3
1996	16,388	28,985	45,373	11,791,300	7,998.8	3,976.1	4,858.6	4,444.8

Notes: Property crimes include burglary, larceny-theft and motor vehicle theft; n/a not available; (1) Metropolitan Statistical Area - see Appendix A for areas included; (2) calculated by the editors using the following formula: (number of crimes in the MSA minus number of crimes in the city); (3) calculated by the editors using the following formula: ((number of crimes in the MSA minus number of crimes in the city) ÷ (population of the MSA minus population of the city)) x 100,000
Source: U.S. Department of Justice, FBI Uniform Crime Reports, 1977 - 1996

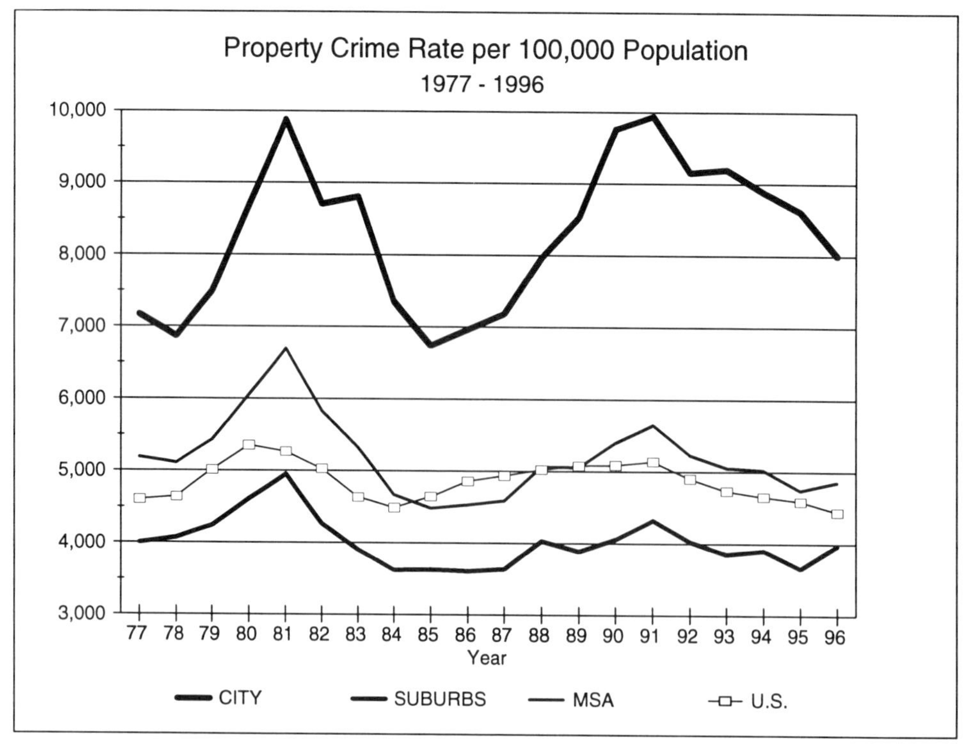

Note: Missing line segments indicate data not available.

Murders and Murder Rates: 1977 - 1996

Year	Number				Rate per 100,000 population			
	City	Suburbs[2]	MSA[1]	U.S.	City	Suburbs[3]	MSA[1]	U.S.
1977	64	16	80	19,120	28.7	4.3	13.5	8.8
1978	52	22	74	19,560	23.6	5.9	12.4	9.0
1979	52	29	81	21,460	23.5	7.5	13.3	9.7
1980	57	20	77	23,040	26.0	5.0	12.4	10.2
1981	48	34	82	22,520	21.5	8.3	12.9	9.8
1982	69	20	89	21,010	30.5	4.8	13.9	9.1
1983	61	37	98	19,310	26.7	6.6	12.4	8.3
1984	76	42	118	18,690	33.9	7.3	14.7	7.9
1985	92	25	117	18,980	41.5	4.3	14.5	7.9
1986	82	26	108	20,610	36.5	4.4	13.2	8.6
1987	78	40	118	20,100	35.1	6.6	14.3	8.3
1988	99	29	128	20,680	45.0	4.7	15.3	8.4
1989	98	37	135	21,500	45.3	5.8	15.8	8.7
1990	113	49	162	23,440	55.6	7.4	18.7	9.4
1991	116	41	157	24,700	56.2	6.1	17.9	9.8
1992	117	32	149	23,760	55.9	4.7	16.7	9.3
1993	112	46	158	24,530	54.5	6.5	17.4	9.5
1994	160	49	209	23,330	77.2	6.9	22.8	9.0
1995	120	36	156	21,610	59.1	5.0	16.8	8.2
1996	112	37	149	19,650	54.7	5.1	16.0	7.4

Notes: (1) Metropolitan Statistical Area - see Appendix A for areas included; (2) calculated by the editors using the following formula: (number of crimes in the MSA minus number of crimes in the city); (3) calculated by the editors using the following formula: ((number of crimes in the MSA minus number of crimes in the city) ÷ (population of the MSA minus population of the city)) x 100,000; n/a not avail.
Source: U.S. Department of Justice, FBI Uniform Crime Reports, 1977 - 1996

Forcible Rapes and Forcible Rape Rates: 1977 - 1996

Year	Number				Rate per 100,000 population			
	City	Suburbs[2]	MSA[1]	U.S.	City	Suburbs[3]	MSA[1]	U.S.
1977	141	45	186	63,500	63.2	12.1	31.3	29.4
1978	126	64	190	67,610	57.3	17.1	31.9	31.0
1979	161	99	260	76,390	72.6	25.5	42.6	34.7
1980	157	100	257	82,990	71.5	24.8	41.3	36.8
1981	195	102	297	82,500	87.2	24.8	46.8	36.0
1982	171	88	259	78,770	75.6	21.2	40.3	34.0
1983	194	142	336	78,920	84.8	25.2	42.4	33.7
1984	205	156	361	84,230	91.3	27.1	45.1	35.7
1985	213	147	360	88,670	96.0	25.2	44.7	37.1
1986	207	160	367	91,460	92.0	27.0	44.9	37.9
1987	182	143	325	91,110	81.9	23.7	39.3	37.4
1988	202	174	376	92,490	91.8	28.1	44.8	37.6
1989	180	166	346	94,500	83.2	26.0	40.4	38.1
1990	180	186	366	102,560	88.6	28.1	42.3	41.2
1991	150	176	326	106,590	72.7	26.1	37.1	42.3
1992	178	201	379	109,060	85.1	29.4	42.5	42.8
1993	174	207	381	106,010	84.7	29.4	41.9	41.1
1994	169	179	348	102,220	81.5	25.2	37.9	39.3
1995	171	184	355	97,470	84.2	25.5	38.3	37.1
1996	143	160	303	95,770	69.8	21.9	32.4	36.1

Notes: (1) Metropolitan Statistical Area - see Appendix A for areas included; (2) calculated by the editors using the following formula: (number of crimes in the MSA minus number of crimes in the city); (3) calculated by the editors using the following formula: ((number of crimes in the MSA minus number of crimes in the city) ÷ (population of the MSA minus population of the city)) x 100,000; n/a not avail.
Source: U.S. Department of Justice, FBI Uniform Crime Reports, 1977 - 1996

Robberies and Robbery Rates: 1977 - 1996

Year	Number				Rate per 100,000 population			
	City	Suburbs[2]	MSA[1]	U.S.	City	Suburbs[3]	MSA[1]	U.S.
1977	861	220	1,081	412,610	386.1	59.3	182.0	190.7
1978	807	184	991	426,930	366.8	49.1	166.6	195.8
1979	985	225	1,210	480,700	444.3	58.0	198.4	218.4
1980	1,130	237	1,367	565,840	515.0	58.8	219.6	251.1
1981	1,364	301	1,665	592,910	609.9	73.3	262.5	258.7
1982	1,395	273	1,668	553,130	616.3	65.7	259.8	238.9
1983	1,489	440	1,929	506,570	650.9	78.1	243.5	216.5
1984	1,278	452	1,730	485,010	569.3	78.5	216.2	205.4
1985	1,081	502	1,583	497,870	487.3	85.9	196.4	208.5
1986	1,017	401	1,418	542,780	452.1	67.7	173.5	225.1
1987	1,083	505	1,588	517,700	487.6	83.5	192.1	212.7
1988	982	573	1,555	542,970	446.4	92.7	185.5	220.9
1989	1,085	497	1,582	578,330	501.8	77.7	184.8	233.0
1990	1,281	549	1,830	639,270	630.9	82.9	211.4	257.0
1991	1,449	637	2,086	687,730	702.4	94.6	237.2	272.7
1992	1,459	747	2,206	672,480	697.2	109.4	247.3	263.6
1993	1,578	704	2,282	659,870	768.5	100.0	250.9	255.9
1994	1,586	662	2,248	618,950	765.2	93.1	244.8	237.7
1995	1,491	667	2,158	580,510	734.0	92.3	233.1	220.9
1996	1,545	742	2,287	537,050	754.1	101.8	244.9	202.4

Notes: (1) Metropolitan Statistical Area - see Appendix A for areas included; (2) calculated by the editors using the following formula: (number of crimes in the MSA minus number of crimes in the city); (3) calculated by the editors using the following formula: ((number of crimes in the MSA minus number of crimes in the city) ÷ (population of the MSA minus population of the city)) x 100,000; n/a not avail.
Source: U.S. Department of Justice, FBI Uniform Crime Reports, 1977 - 1996

Aggravated Assaults and Aggravated Assault Rates: 1977 - 1996

Year	Number				Rate per 100,000 population			
	City	Suburbs[2]	MSA[1]	U.S.	City	Suburbs[3]	MSA[1]	U.S.
1977	981	387	1,368	534,350	439.9	104.4	230.4	247.0
1978	851	281	1,132	571,460	386.8	75.0	190.3	262.1
1979	1,036	346	1,382	629,480	467.3	89.2	226.6	286.0
1980	1,086	318	1,404	672,650	494.9	78.9	225.6	298.5
1981	1,061	390	1,451	663,900	474.4	94.9	228.7	289.7
1982	1,139	358	1,497	669,480	503.2	86.1	233.2	289.2
1983	1,193	565	1,758	653,290	521.5	100.3	221.9	279.2
1984	1,198	655	1,853	685,350	533.7	113.8	231.6	290.2
1985	1,261	715	1,976	723,250	568.4	122.4	245.2	302.9
1986	1,280	789	2,069	834,320	569.0	133.2	253.1	346.1
1987	1,271	711	1,982	855,090	572.2	117.6	239.8	351.3
1988	1,301	760	2,061	910,090	591.4	122.9	245.8	370.2
1989	1,565	1,051	2,616	951,710	723.8	164.3	305.6	383.4
1990	1,655	1,103	2,758	1,054,860	815.0	166.5	318.6	424.1
1991	1,699	935	2,634	1,092,740	823.6	138.9	299.5	433.3
1992	1,356	983	2,339	1,126,970	647.9	143.9	262.2	441.8
1993	1,411	1,030	2,441	1,135,610	687.2	146.2	268.3	440.3
1994	1,619	1,059	2,678	1,113,180	781.1	149.0	291.7	427.6
1995	1,718	1,199	2,917	1,099,210	845.8	165.9	315.0	418.3
1996	1,583	1,249	2,832	1,029,810	772.6	171.3	303.3	388.2

Notes: (1) Metropolitan Statistical Area - see Appendix A for areas included; (2) calculated by the editors using the following formula: (number of crimes in the MSA minus number of crimes in the city); (3) calculated by the editors using the following formula: ((number of crimes in the MSA minus number of crimes in the city) ÷ (population of the MSA minus population of the city)) x 100,000; n/a not avail.
Source: U.S. Department of Justice, FBI Uniform Crime Reports, 1977 - 1996

Burglaries and Burglary Rates: 1977 - 1996

Year	Number				Rate per 100,000 population			
	City	Suburbs[2]	MSA[1]	U.S.	City	Suburbs[3]	MSA[1]	U.S.
1977	4,719	4,180	8,899	3,071,500	2,116.1	1,127.2	1,498.5	1,419.8
1978	4,447	4,015	8,462	3,128,300	2,021.4	1,070.9	1,422.4	1,434.6
1979	5,192	4,261	9,453	3,327,700	2,342.0	1,098.0	1,550.3	1,511.9
1980	6,601	4,981	11,582	3,795,200	3,008.3	1,236.0	1,860.8	1,684.1
1981	7,412	5,286	12,698	3,779,700	3,314.0	1,286.9	2,001.6	1,649.5
1982	6,824	4,547	11,371	3,447,100	3,015.0	1,093.9	1,771.2	1,488.8
1983	7,487	5,492	12,979	3,129,900	3,272.7	974.9	1,638.6	1,337.7
1984	5,465	5,489	10,954	2,984,400	2,434.5	953.6	1,369.1	1,263.7
1985	4,307	5,212	9,519	3,073,300	1,941.3	892.2	1,181.0	1,287.3
1986	4,481	4,729	9,210	3,241,400	1,992.1	798.1	1,126.7	1,344.6
1987	4,143	5,054	9,197	3,236,200	1,865.3	836.0	1,112.6	1,329.6
1988	4,773	5,348	10,121	3,218,100	2,169.8	864.8	1,207.2	1,309.2
1989	4,656	4,818	9,474	3,168,200	2,153.3	753.2	1,106.9	1,276.3
1990	4,396	4,926	9,322	3,073,900	2,164.9	743.5	1,076.9	1,235.9
1991	4,822	5,220	10,042	3,157,200	2,337.5	775.5	1,141.9	1,252.0
1992	4,677	5,327	10,004	2,979,900	2,234.8	780.1	1,121.3	1,168.2
1993	5,081	5,163	10,244	2,834,800	2,474.5	733.0	1,126.1	1,099.2
1994	4,927	5,151	10,078	2,712,800	2,377.2	724.5	1,097.6	1,042.0
1995	4,260	4,437	8,697	2,593,800	2,097.1	613.9	939.3	987.1
1996	4,022	4,624	8,646	2,501,500	1,963.1	634.3	925.8	943.0

Notes: (1) Metropolitan Statistical Area - see Appendix A for areas included; (2) calculated by the editors using the following formula: (number of crimes in the MSA minus number of crimes in the city); (3) calculated by the editors using the following formula: ((number of crimes in the MSA minus number of crimes in the city) ÷ (population of the MSA minus population of the city)) x 100,000; n/a not avail.
Source: U.S. Department of Justice, FBI Uniform Crime Reports, 1977 - 1996

Larceny-Thefts and Larceny-Theft Rates: 1977 - 1996

Year	Number				Rate per 100,000 population			
	City	Suburbs[2]	MSA[1]	U.S.	City	Suburbs[3]	MSA[1]	U.S.
1977	10,178	9,945	20,123	5,905,700	4,564.1	2,681.7	3,388.6	2,729.9
1978	9,439	10,392	19,831	5,991,000	4,290.5	2,771.9	3,333.4	2,747.4
1979	10,184	11,338	21,522	6,601,000	4,593.7	2,921.7	3,529.6	2,999.1
1980	11,231	12,766	23,997	7,136,900	5,118.3	3,167.9	3,855.5	3,167.0
1981	13,649	14,343	27,992	7,194,400	6,102.6	3,491.9	4,412.3	3,139.7
1982	11,870	12,466	24,336	7,142,500	5,244.4	2,999.0	3,790.6	3,084.8
1983	11,754	15,648	27,402	6,712,800	5,138.0	2,777.9	3,459.5	2,868.9
1984	10,149	14,464	24,613	6,591,900	4,521.1	2,512.9	3,076.4	2,791.3
1985	9,622	14,932	24,554	6,926,400	4,337.0	2,556.2	3,046.3	2,901.2
1986	10,051	15,582	25,633	7,257,200	4,468.2	2,629.8	3,135.7	3,010.3
1987	9,969	15,759	25,728	7,499,900	4,488.3	2,606.9	3,112.4	3,081.3
1988	10,554	18,093	28,647	7,705,900	4,797.7	2,925.8	3,417.0	3,134.9
1989	11,763	18,594	30,357	7,872,400	5,440.1	2,906.8	3,546.8	3,171.3
1990	13,001	20,576	33,577	7,945,700	6,402.7	3,105.4	3,878.9	3,194.8
1991	12,941	22,377	35,318	8,142,200	6,273.1	3,324.3	4,016.0	3,228.8
1992	12,046	20,705	32,751	7,915,200	5,756.0	3,032.0	3,671.0	3,103.0
1993	11,571	20,506	32,077	7,820,900	5,635.3	2,911.4	3,526.3	3,032.4
1994	10,837	21,147	31,984	7,879,800	5,228.7	2,974.5	3,483.3	3,026.7
1995	10,848	20,589	31,437	7,997,700	5,340.3	2,848.6	3,395.3	3,043.8
1996	10,338	22,745	33,083	7,894,600	5,045.9	3,120.1	3,542.6	2,975.9

Notes: (1) Metropolitan Statistical Area - see Appendix A for areas included; (2) calculated by the editors using the following formula: (number of crimes in the MSA minus number of crimes in the city); (3) calculated by the editors using the following formula: ((number of crimes in the MSA minus number of crimes in the city) ÷ (population of the MSA minus population of the city)) x 100,000; n/a not avail.
Source: U.S. Department of Justice, FBI Uniform Crime Reports, 1977 - 1996

Motor Vehicle Thefts and Motor Vehicle Theft Rates: 1977 - 1996

Year	Number				Rate per 100,000 population			
	City	Suburbs[2]	MSA[1]	U.S.	City	Suburbs[3]	MSA[1]	U.S.
1977	1,070	704	1,774	977,700	479.8	189.8	298.7	451.9
1978	1,221	845	2,066	1,004,100	555.0	225.4	347.3	460.5
1979	1,218	869	2,087	1,112,800	549.4	223.9	342.3	505.6
1980	1,231	851	2,082	1,131,700	561.0	211.2	334.5	502.2
1981	1,037	721	1,758	1,087,800	463.7	175.5	277.1	474.7
1982	996	721	1,717	1,062,400	440.1	173.5	267.4	458.8
1983	901	867	1,768	1,007,900	393.8	153.9	223.2	430.8
1984	903	875	1,778	1,032,200	402.3	152.0	222.2	437.1
1985	1,020	1,045	2,065	1,102,900	459.8	178.9	256.2	462.0
1986	1,139	1,069	2,208	1,224,100	506.4	180.4	270.1	507.8
1987	1,838	1,178	3,016	1,288,700	827.5	194.9	364.9	529.4
1988	2,203	1,482	3,685	1,432,900	1,001.5	239.7	439.5	582.9
1989	2,020	1,433	3,453	1,564,800	934.2	224.0	403.4	630.4
1990	2,417	1,390	3,807	1,635,900	1,190.3	209.8	439.8	657.8
1991	2,740	1,526	4,266	1,661,700	1,328.2	226.7	485.1	659.0
1992	2,413	1,448	3,861	1,610,800	1,153.0	212.0	432.8	631.5
1993	2,215	1,444	3,659	1,563,100	1,078.7	205.0	402.2	606.1
1994	2,641	1,458	4,099	1,539,300	1,274.2	205.1	446.4	591.3
1995	2,376	1,406	3,782	1,472,400	1,169.7	194.5	408.5	560.4
1996	2,028	1,616	3,644	1,395,200	989.8	221.7	390.2	525.9

Notes: (1) Metropolitan Statistical Area - see Appendix A for areas included; (2) calculated by the editors using the following formula: (number of crimes in the MSA minus number of crimes in the city); (3) calculated by the editors using the following formula: ((number of crimes in the MSA minus number of crimes in the city) ÷ (population of the MSA minus population of the city)) x 100,000; n/a not avail.
Source: U.S. Department of Justice, FBI Uniform Crime Reports, 1977 - 1996

HATE CRIMES

Criminal Incidents by Bias Motivation

Area	Race	Ethnicity	Religion	Sexual Orientation
Richmond	1	0	0	0

Notes: Figures include both violent and property crimes. Law enforcement agencies must have submitted data for at least one quarter of calendar year 1995 to be included in this report, therefore figures shown may not represent complete 12-month totals; n/a not available
Source: U.S. Department of Justice, FBI Uniform Crime Reports, Hate Crime Statistics 1995

LAW ENFORCEMENT

Full-Time Law Enforcement Employees

Jurisdiction	Police Employees			Police Officers per 100,000 population
	Total	Officers	Civilians	
Richmond	759	667	92	325.6

Notes: Data as of October 31, 1996
Source: U.S. Department of Justice, FBI Uniform Crime Reports, 1996

CORRECTIONS

Federal Correctional Facilities

Type	Year Opened	Security Level	Sex of Inmates	Rated Capacity	Population on 7/1/95	Number of Staff
None listed						

Notes: Data as of 1995
Source: Bureau of Justice Statistics, Sourcebook of Criminal Justice Statistics Online

City/County/Regional Correctional Facilities

Name	Year Opened	Year Renov.	Rated Capacity	1995 Pop.	Number of COs[1]	Number of Staff	ACA[2] Accred.
Henrico County Reg Jail	1979	1996	185	574	238	269	No
Richmond City Jail	1964	1991	729	n/a	n/a	n/a	No

Notes: Data as of April 1996; (1) Correctional Officers; (2) American Correctional Assn. Accreditation
Source: American Correctional Association, 1996-1998 National Jail and Adult Detention Directory

Private Adult Correctional Facilities

Name	Date Opened	Rated Capacity	Present Pop.	Security Level	Facility Construct.	Expans. Plans	ACA[1] Accred.
None listed							

Notes: Data as of December 1996; (1) American Correctional Association Accreditation
Source: University of Florida, Center for Studies in Criminology and Law, Private Adult Correctional Facility Census, 10th Ed., March 15, 1997

Characteristics of Shock Incarceration Programs

Jurisdiction	Year Program Began	Number of Camps	Average Num. of Inmates	Number of Beds	Program Length	Voluntary/ Mandatory
Virginia	1991	1	57	100	89 days	Voluntary

Note: Data as of July 1996;
Source: Sourcebook of Criminal Justice Statistics Online

INMATES AND HIV/AIDS

HIV Testing Policies for Inmates

Jurisdiction	All Inmates at Some Time	All Convicted Inmates at Admission	Random Samples While in Custody	High-risk Groups	Upon Inmate Request	Upon Court Order	Upon Involvement in Incident
Richmond[1]	No	No	No	Yes	No	Yes	Yes

Notes: (1) All facilities reported following the same testing policy or authorities reported the policy to be jurisdiction-wide
Source: HIV in Prisons and Jails, 1993 (released August 1995)

Inmates Known to be Positive for HIV

Jurisdiction	Number of Jail Inmates in Facilities Providing Data	Type of HIV Infection/AIDS Cases				HIV/AIDS Cases as a Percent of Tot. Custody Pop.
		Total	Asymptomatic	Symptomatic	Confirmed AIDS	
Richmond[1]	1,478	62	0	0	0	4.2

Note: (1) Detail does not add to total.
Source: HIV in Prisons and Jails, 1993 (released August, 1995)

DEATH PENALTY

Death Penalty Statistics

State	Prisoners Executed		Prisoners Under Sentence of Death					Avg. No. of Years on Death Row[4]
	1930-1995	1996[1]	Total[2]	White[3]	Black[3]	Hisp.	Women	
Virginia	121	8	56	28	28	2	0	4.5

Notes: Data as of 12/31/95 unless otherwise noted; (1) Data as of 7/31/97; (2) Includes persons of other races; (3) Includes people of Hispanic origin; (4) Covers prisoners sentenced 1974 through 1995
Source: Bureau of Justice Statistics, Capital Punishment 1995 (released 12/96); Death Penalty Information Center Web Site, 9/30/97

Capital Offenses and Methods of Execution

Capital Offenses in Virginia	Minimum Age for Imposition of Death Penalty	Mentally Retarded Excluded	Methods of Execution[1]
First-degree murder with 1 of 9 aggravating circumstances.	14[a]	No	Lethal injection; electrocution

Notes: Data as of 12/31/95 unless otherwise noted; (1) Data as of 7/31/97; (a) The minimum age for transfer to adult court is 14 by statute, but the effective age for a capital sentence is 16 based on interpretation of a U.S. Supreme Court decision by the State attorney general's office.
Source: Bureau of Justice Statistics, Capital Punishment 1995 (released 12/96); Death Penalty Information Center Web Site, 9/30/97

LAWS

Statutory Provisions Relating to the Purchase, Ownership and Use of Handguns

Jurisdiction	Instant Background Check	Federal Waiting Period Applies[1]	State Waiting Period (days)	License or Permit to Purchase	Registration	Record of Sale Sent to Police	Concealed Carry Law
Virginia	Yes	No	(a,b)	Yes[a]	No	(b)	Yes[c]

Note: Data as of 1996; (1) The Federal 5-day waiting period for handgun purchases applies to states that don't have instant background checks, waiting period requirements, or licensing procedures exempting them from the Federal requirement; (a) A permit is required to acquire another handgun before 30 days have elapsed following the acquisition of a handgun; (b) Local ordinance in certain cities or counties; (c) "Shall issue" permit system, liberally administered discretion by local authorities over permit issuance, or no permit required
Source: Sourcebook of Criminal Justice Statistics Online

Statutory Provisions Relating to Alcohol Use and Driving

Jurisdiction	Drinking Age	Blood Alcohol Concentration Levels as Evidence in State Courts[1]		Open Container Law[1]	Anti-Consumption Law[1]	Dram Shop Law[1]
		Illegal per se at 0.10%	Presumption at 0.10%			
Virginia	21	(a)	(a)	No	Yes[b]	No

Note: Data as of January 1, 1997; (1) See Appendix C for an explanation of terms; (a) 0.08%; (b) Applies to drivers only
Source: Sourcebook of Criminal Justice Statistics Online

Statutory Provisions Relating to Curfews

Jurisdiction	Year Enacted	Latest Revision	Age Group(s)	Curfew Provisions
Richmond	1992	1994	17 year olds 16 and under	Midnight to 5 am every night 11 pm to 5 am every night

Note: Data as of February 1996
Source: Sourcebook of Criminal Justice Statistics Online

Statutory Provisions Relating to Hate Crimes

Jurisdiction	Bias-Motivated Violence and Intimidation						Institutional Vandalism
	Civil Action	Criminal Penalty					
		Race/ Religion/ Ethnicity	Sexual Orientation	Mental/ Physical Disability	Gender	Age	
Virginia	Yes	Yes	No	No	No	No	Yes

Source: Anti-Defamation League, 1997 Hate Crimes Laws

Sacramento, California

OVERVIEW

The total crime rate for the city decreased 12.6% between 1977 and 1996. During that same period, the violent crime rate decreased 11.1% and the property crime rate decreased 12.8%.

Among violent crimes, the rates for: Murders decreased 27.1%; Forcible Rapes decreased 47.5%; Robberies increased 2.6%; and Aggravated Assaults decreased 18.0%.

Among property crimes, the rates for: Burglaries decreased 40.2%; Larceny-Thefts decreased 10.0%; and Motor Vehicle Thefts increased 59.9%.

ANTI-CRIME PROGRAMS

Information not available at time of publication.

CRIME RISK

Your Chances of Becoming a Victim[1]

Area	Any Crime	Violent Crime					Property Crime			
		Any	Murder	Forcible Rape[2]	Robbery	Aggrav. Assault	Any	Burglary	Larceny -Theft	Motor Vehicle Theft
City	1:11	1:102	1:8,821	1:1,283	1:202	1:232	1:13	1:53	1:23	1:62

Note: (1) Figures have been calculated by dividing the population of the city by the number of crimes reported to the FBI during 1996 and are expressed as odds (eg. 1:20 should be read as 1 in 20).
(2) Figures have been calculated by dividing the female population of the city by the number of forcible rapes reported to the FBI during 1996. The female population of the city was estimated by calculating the ratio of females to males reported in the 1990 Census and applying that ratio to 1996 population estimate.
Source: FBI Uniform Crime Reports 1996

CRIME STATISTICS

Total Crimes and Total Crime Rates: 1977 - 1996

Year	Number				Rate per 100,000 population			
	City	Suburbs[2]	MSA[1]	U.S.	City	Suburbs[3]	MSA[1]	U.S.
1977	26,998	45,412	72,410	10,984,500	10,187.9	6,943.8	7,879.3	5,077.6
1978	29,188	49,851	79,039	11,209,000	11,056.1	7,255.6	8,310.5	5,140.3
1979	31,652	53,653	85,305	12,249,500	11,539.2	7,733.8	8,812.1	5,565.5
1980	34,699	60,062	94,761	13,408,300	12,638.6	8,155.7	9,373.1	5,950.0
1981	36,661	59,162	95,823	13,423,800	13,007.1	7,825.2	9,232.4	5,858.2
1982	31,202	57,557	88,759	12,974,400	10,817.3	7,439.0	8,356.4	5,603.6
1983	30,505	56,586	87,091	12,108,600	10,386.6	6,434.0	7,423.5	5,175.0
1984	30,499	57,068	87,567	11,881,800	10,157.9	6,255.7	7,222.0	5,031.3
1985	33,908	59,569	93,477	12,431,400	10,835.2	6,323.7	7,448.7	5,207.1
1986	35,069	60,439	95,508	13,211,900	10,950.3	6,269.5	7,436.8	5,480.4
1987	34,355	61,425	95,780	13,508,700	10,356.4	6,190.1	7,233.9	5,550.0
1988	35,143	63,416	98,559	13,923,100	10,321.5	6,214.6	7,242.1	5,664.2
1989	35,825	63,919	99,744	14,251,400	10,319.1	5,947.7	7,015.0	5,741.0
1990	33,710	64,383	98,093	14,475,600	9,126.5	5,791.2	6,623.0	5,820.3
1991	38,076	70,935	109,011	14,872,900	10,098.2	6,250.4	7,210.0	5,897.8
1992	38,374	58,300	96,674	14,438,200	10,016.7	5,791.0	6,955.8	5,660.2
1993	39,485	61,380	100,865	14,144,800	10,209.9	5,866.2	7,038.4	5,484.4
1994	40,218	n/a	n/a	13,989,500	10,326.7	n/a	n/a	5,373.5
1995	38,803	64,290	103,093	13,862,700	10,324.2	5,992.3	7,116.1	5,275.9
1996	33,780	58,018	91,798	13,473,600	8,906.3	5,358.7	6,279.1	5,078.9

Notes: (1) Metropolitan Statistical Area - see Appendix A for areas included; (2) calculated by the editors using the following formula: (number of crimes in the MSA minus number of crimes in the city); (3) calculated by the editors using the following formula: ((number of crimes in the MSA minus number of crimes in the city) ÷ (population of the MSA minus population of the city)) x 100,000; n/a not avail.
Source: U.S. Department of Justice, FBI Uniform Crime Reports, 1977 - 1996

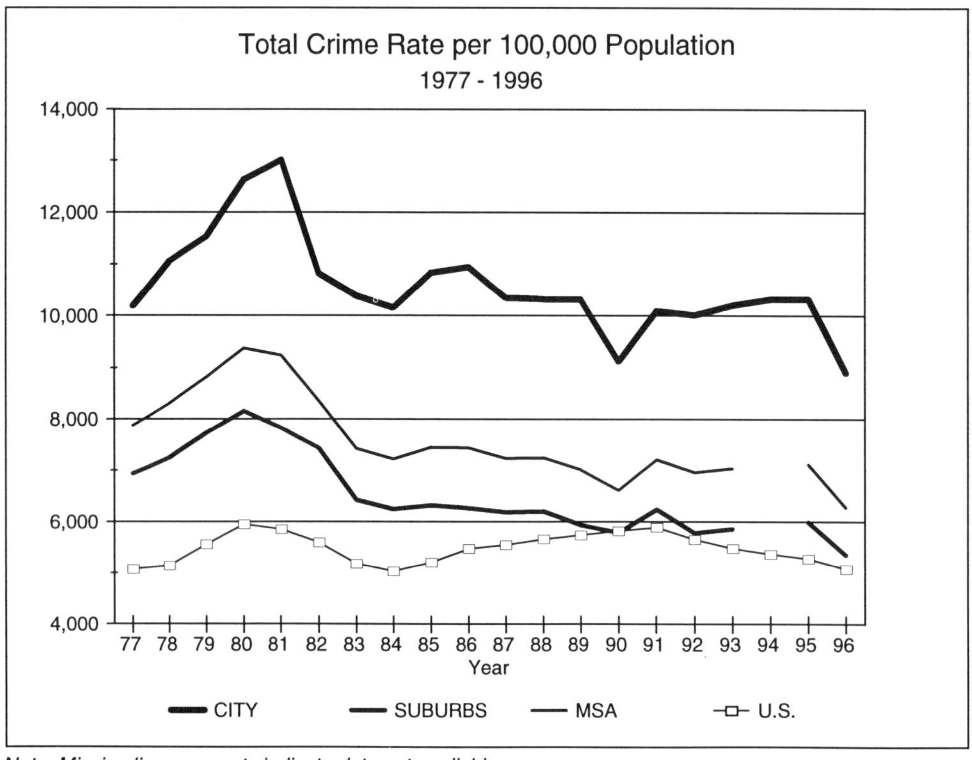

Note: Missing line segments indicate data not available.

Violent Crimes and Violent Crime Rates: 1977 - 1996

Year	Number				Rate per 100,000 population			
	City	Suburbs[2]	MSA[1]	U.S.	City	Suburbs[3]	MSA[1]	U.S.
1977	2,915	3,167	6,082	1,029,580	1,100.0	484.3	661.8	475.9
1978	3,198	3,739	6,937	1,085,550	1,211.4	544.2	729.4	497.8
1979	3,212	3,803	7,015	1,208,030	1,171.0	548.2	724.7	548.9
1980	3,221	3,949	7,170	1,344,520	1,173.2	536.2	709.2	596.6
1981	3,535	4,017	7,552	1,361,820	1,254.2	531.3	727.6	594.3
1982	2,988	3,819	6,807	1,322,390	1,035.9	493.6	640.9	571.1
1983	3,080	3,851	6,931	1,258,090	1,048.7	437.9	590.8	537.7
1984	3,252	3,885	7,137	1,273,280	1,083.1	425.9	588.6	539.2
1985	3,681	4,293	7,974	1,328,800	1,176.2	455.7	635.4	556.6
1986	4,238	5,746	9,984	1,489,170	1,323.3	596.1	777.4	617.7
1987	3,836	5,624	9,460	1,484,000	1,156.4	566.8	714.5	609.7
1988	3,582	5,801	9,383	1,566,220	1,052.0	568.5	689.5	637.2
1989	3,658	5,663	9,321	1,646,040	1,053.7	526.9	655.5	663.1
1990	3,978	6,663	10,641	1,820,130	1,077.0	599.3	718.5	731.8
1991	4,896	7,115	12,011	1,911,770	1,298.5	626.9	794.4	758.1
1992	4,674	6,249	10,923	1,932,270	1,220.0	620.7	785.9	757.5
1993	4,850	6,694	11,544	1,926,020	1,254.1	639.8	805.5	746.8
1994	4,698	n/a	n/a	1,857,670	1,206.3	n/a	n/a	713.6
1995	4,280	7,549	11,829	1,798,790	1,138.8	703.6	816.5	684.6
1996	3,707	6,539	10,246	1,682,280	977.4	604.0	700.8	634.1

Notes: Violent crimes include murder, forcible rape, robbery and aggravated assault; n/a not available; (1) Metropolitan Statistical Area - see Appendix A for areas included; (2) calculated by the editors using the following formula: (number of crimes in the MSA minus number of crimes in the city); (3) calculated by the editors using the following formula: ((number of crimes in the MSA minus number of crimes in the city) ÷ (population of the MSA minus population of the city)) x 100,000
Source: U.S. Department of Justice, FBI Uniform Crime Reports, 1977 - 1996

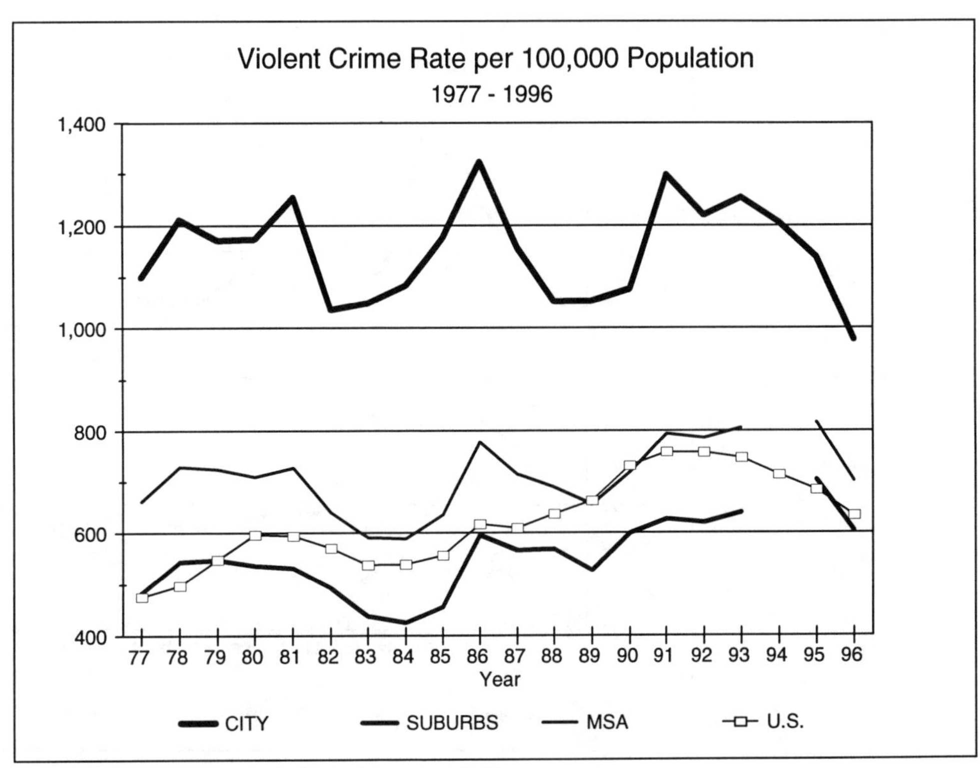

Note: Missing line segments indicate data not available.

Property Crimes and Property Crime Rates: 1977 - 1996

Year	Number				Rate per 100,000 population			
	City	Suburbs[2]	MSA[1]	U.S.	City	Suburbs[3]	MSA[1]	U.S.
1977	24,083	42,245	66,328	9,955,000	9,087.9	6,459.6	7,217.5	4,601.7
1978	25,990	46,112	72,102	10,123,400	9,844.7	6,711.4	7,581.1	4,642.5
1979	28,440	49,850	78,290	11,041,500	10,368.2	7,185.6	8,087.4	5,016.6
1980	31,478	56,113	87,591	12,063,700	11,465.4	7,619.5	8,663.9	5,353.3
1981	33,126	55,145	88,271	12,061,900	11,752.9	7,293.9	8,504.8	5,263.9
1982	28,214	53,738	81,952	11,652,000	9,781.4	6,945.4	7,715.5	5,032.5
1983	27,425	52,735	80,160	10,850,500	9,337.9	5,996.1	6,832.7	4,637.4
1984	27,247	53,183	80,430	10,608,500	9,074.8	5,829.8	6,633.4	4,492.1
1985	30,227	55,276	85,503	11,102,600	9,658.9	5,867.9	6,813.3	4,650.5
1986	30,831	54,693	85,524	11,722,700	9,627.0	5,673.5	6,659.4	4,862.6
1987	30,519	55,801	86,320	12,024,700	9,200.0	5,623.3	6,519.4	4,940.3
1988	31,561	57,615	89,176	12,356,900	9,269.5	5,646.1	6,552.6	5,027.1
1989	32,167	58,256	90,423	12,605,400	9,265.4	5,420.7	6,359.5	5,077.9
1990	29,732	57,720	87,452	12,655,500	8,049.5	5,191.9	5,904.5	5,088.5
1991	33,180	63,820	97,000	12,961,100	8,799.7	5,623.5	6,415.6	5,139.7
1992	33,700	52,051	85,751	12,505,900	8,796.6	5,170.3	6,169.9	4,902.7
1993	34,635	54,686	89,321	12,218,800	8,955.8	5,226.4	6,232.9	4,737.6
1994	35,520	n/a	n/a	12,131,900	9,120.4	n/a	n/a	4,660.0
1995	34,523	56,741	91,264	12,063,900	9,185.4	5,288.7	6,299.6	4,591.3
1996	30,073	51,479	81,552	11,791,300	7,928.9	4,754.7	5,578.2	4,444.8

Notes: Property crimes include burglary, larceny-theft and motor vehicle theft; n/a not available; (1) Metropolitan Statistical Area - see Appendix A for areas included; (2) calculated by the editors using the following formula: (number of crimes in the MSA minus number of crimes in the city); (3) calculated by the editors using the following formula: ((number of crimes in the MSA minus number of crimes in the city) ÷ (population of the MSA minus population of the city)) x 100,000
Source: U.S. Department of Justice, FBI Uniform Crime Reports, 1977 - 1996

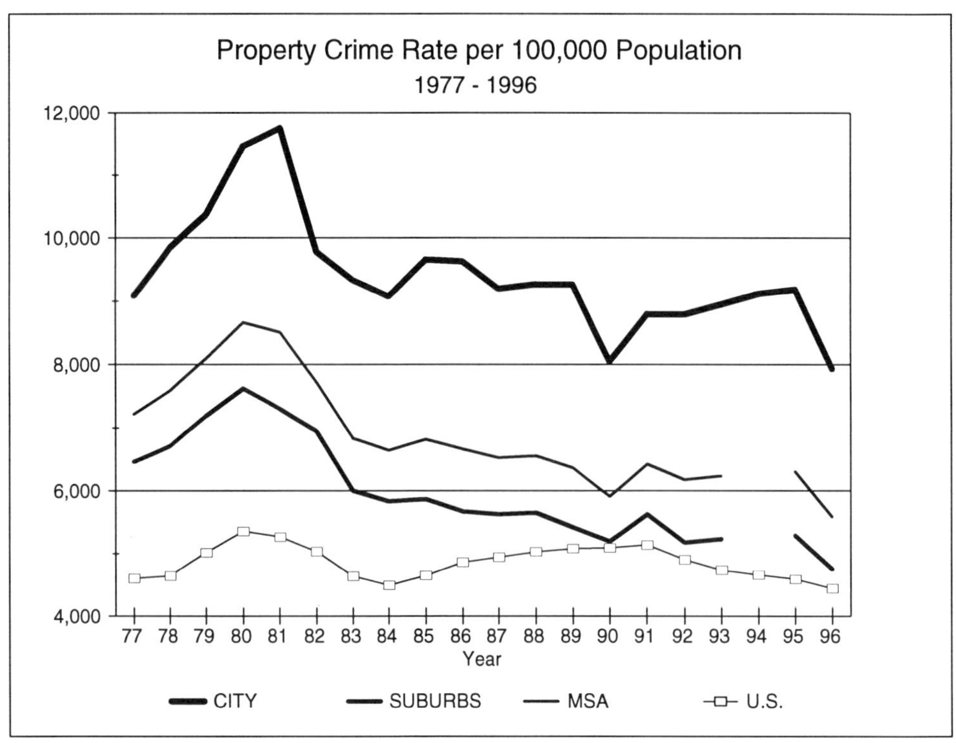

Note: Missing line segments indicate data not available.

Murders and Murder Rates: 1977 - 1996

Year	Number				Rate per 100,000 population			
	City	Suburbs[2]	MSA[1]	U.S.	City	Suburbs[3]	MSA[1]	U.S.
1977	41	45	86	19,120	15.5	6.9	9.4	8.8
1978	61	48	109	19,560	23.1	7.0	11.5	9.0
1979	44	52	96	21,460	16.0	7.5	9.9	9.7
1980	45	46	91	23,040	16.4	6.2	9.0	10.2
1981	53	38	91	22,520	18.8	5.0	8.8	9.8
1982	43	41	84	21,010	14.9	5.3	7.9	9.1
1983	52	48	100	19,310	17.7	5.5	8.5	8.3
1984	45	59	104	18,690	15.0	6.5	8.6	7.9
1985	39	51	90	18,980	12.5	5.4	7.2	7.9
1986	70	64	134	20,610	21.9	6.6	10.4	8.6
1987	78	62	140	20,100	23.5	6.2	10.6	8.3
1988	68	60	128	20,680	20.0	5.9	9.4	8.4
1989	44	45	89	21,500	12.7	4.2	6.3	8.7
1990	43	76	119	23,440	11.6	6.8	8.0	9.4
1991	66	81	147	24,700	17.5	7.1	9.7	9.8
1992	45	56	101	23,760	11.7	5.6	7.3	9.3
1993	85	74	159	24,530	22.0	7.1	11.1	9.5
1994	62	n/a	n/a	23,330	15.9	n/a	n/a	9.0
1995	57	57	114	21,610	15.2	5.3	7.9	8.2
1996	43	58	101	19,650	11.3	5.4	6.9	7.4

Notes: (1) Metropolitan Statistical Area - see Appendix A for areas included; (2) calculated by the editors using the following formula: (number of crimes in the MSA minus number of crimes in the city); (3) calculated by the editors using the following formula: ((number of crimes in the MSA minus number of crimes in the city) ÷ (population of the MSA minus population of the city)) x 100,000; n/a not avail.
Source: U.S. Department of Justice, FBI Uniform Crime Reports, 1977 - 1996

Forcible Rapes and Forcible Rape Rates: 1977 - 1996

Year	Number				Rate per 100,000 population			
	City	Suburbs[2]	MSA[1]	U.S.	City	Suburbs[3]	MSA[1]	U.S.
1977	205	264	469	63,500	77.4	40.4	51.0	29.4
1978	218	260	478	67,610	82.6	37.8	50.3	31.0
1979	219	304	523	76,390	79.8	43.8	54.0	34.7
1980	217	314	531	82,990	79.0	42.6	52.5	36.8
1981	228	353	581	82,500	80.9	46.7	56.0	36.0
1982	191	311	502	78,770	66.2	40.2	47.3	34.0
1983	217	333	550	78,920	73.9	37.9	46.9	33.7
1984	248	357	605	84,230	82.6	39.1	49.9	35.7
1985	209	336	545	88,670	66.8	35.7	43.4	37.1
1986	258	385	643	91,460	80.6	39.9	50.1	37.9
1987	241	366	607	91,110	72.6	36.9	45.8	37.4
1988	188	383	571	92,490	55.2	37.5	42.0	37.6
1989	187	396	583	94,500	53.9	36.8	41.0	38.1
1990	211	458	669	102,560	57.1	41.2	45.2	41.2
1991	221	470	691	106,590	58.6	41.4	45.7	42.3
1992	237	392	629	109,060	61.9	38.9	45.3	42.8
1993	167	383	550	106,010	43.2	36.6	38.4	41.1
1994	174	n/a	n/a	102,220	44.7	n/a	n/a	39.3
1995	158	391	549	97,470	42.0	36.4	37.9	37.1
1996	154	343	497	95,770	40.6	31.7	34.0	36.1

Notes: (1) Metropolitan Statistical Area - see Appendix A for areas included; (2) calculated by the editors using the following formula: (number of crimes in the MSA minus number of crimes in the city); (3) calculated by the editors using the following formula: ((number of crimes in the MSA minus number of crimes in the city) ÷ (population of the MSA minus population of the city)) x 100,000; n/a not avail.
Source: U.S. Department of Justice, FBI Uniform Crime Reports, 1977 - 1996

Robberies and Robbery Rates: 1977 - 1996

Year	Number				Rate per 100,000 population			
	City	Suburbs[2]	MSA[1]	U.S.	City	Suburbs[3]	MSA[1]	U.S.
1977	1,276	1,083	2,359	412,610	481.5	165.6	256.7	190.7
1978	1,582	1,366	2,948	426,930	599.2	198.8	310.0	195.8
1979	1,640	1,297	2,937	480,700	597.9	187.0	303.4	218.4
1980	1,604	1,453	3,057	565,840	584.2	197.3	302.4	251.1
1981	1,833	1,741	3,574	592,910	650.3	230.3	344.4	258.7
1982	1,543	1,527	3,070	553,130	534.9	197.4	289.0	238.9
1983	1,553	1,402	2,955	506,570	528.8	159.4	251.9	216.5
1984	1,645	1,386	3,031	485,010	547.9	151.9	250.0	205.4
1985	2,083	1,523	3,606	497,870	665.6	161.7	287.3	208.5
1986	2,214	1,677	3,891	542,780	691.3	174.0	303.0	225.1
1987	1,841	1,451	3,292	517,700	555.0	146.2	248.6	212.7
1988	1,612	1,513	3,125	542,970	473.4	148.3	229.6	220.9
1989	1,654	1,468	3,122	578,330	476.4	136.6	219.6	233.0
1990	1,790	1,593	3,383	639,270	484.6	143.3	228.4	257.0
1991	2,280	2,024	4,304	687,730	604.7	178.3	284.7	272.7
1992	2,322	1,766	4,088	672,480	606.1	175.4	294.1	263.6
1993	2,310	1,791	4,101	659,870	597.3	171.2	286.2	255.9
1994	2,292	n/a	n/a	618,950	588.5	n/a	n/a	237.7
1995	2,129	2,082	4,211	580,510	566.5	194.1	290.7	220.9
1996	1,874	1,770	3,644	537,050	494.1	163.5	249.3	202.4

Notes: (1) Metropolitan Statistical Area - see Appendix A for areas included; (2) calculated by the editors using the following formula: (number of crimes in the MSA minus number of crimes in the city); (3) calculated by the editors using the following formula: ((number of crimes in the MSA minus number of crimes in the city) ÷ (population of the MSA minus population of the city)) x 100,000; n/a not avail.
Source: U.S. Department of Justice, FBI Uniform Crime Reports, 1977 - 1996

Aggravated Assaults and Aggravated Assault Rates: 1977 - 1996

Year	Number				Rate per 100,000 population			
	City	Suburbs[2]	MSA[1]	U.S.	City	Suburbs[3]	MSA[1]	U.S.
1977	1,393	1,775	3,168	534,350	525.7	271.4	344.7	247.0
1978	1,337	2,065	3,402	571,460	506.4	300.6	357.7	262.1
1979	1,309	2,150	3,459	629,480	477.2	309.9	357.3	286.0
1980	1,355	2,136	3,491	672,650	493.5	290.0	345.3	298.5
1981	1,421	1,885	3,306	663,900	504.2	249.3	318.5	289.7
1982	1,211	1,940	3,151	669,480	419.8	250.7	296.7	289.2
1983	1,258	2,068	3,326	653,290	428.3	235.1	283.5	279.2
1984	1,314	2,083	3,397	685,350	437.6	228.3	280.2	290.2
1985	1,350	2,383	3,733	723,250	431.4	253.0	297.5	302.9
1986	1,696	3,620	5,316	834,320	529.6	375.5	413.9	346.1
1987	1,676	3,745	5,421	855,090	505.2	377.4	409.4	351.3
1988	1,714	3,845	5,559	910,090	503.4	376.8	408.5	370.2
1989	1,773	3,754	5,527	951,710	510.7	349.3	388.7	383.4
1990	1,934	4,536	6,470	1,054,860	523.6	408.0	436.8	424.1
1991	2,329	4,540	6,869	1,092,740	617.7	400.0	454.3	433.3
1992	2,070	4,035	6,105	1,126,970	540.3	400.8	439.3	441.8
1993	2,288	4,446	6,734	1,135,610	591.6	424.9	469.9	440.3
1994	2,170	n/a	n/a	1,113,180	557.2	n/a	n/a	427.6
1995	1,936	5,019	6,955	1,099,210	515.1	467.8	480.1	418.3
1996	1,636	4,368	6,004	1,029,810	431.3	403.4	410.7	388.2

Notes: (1) Metropolitan Statistical Area - see Appendix A for areas included; (2) calculated by the editors using the following formula: (number of crimes in the MSA minus number of crimes in the city); (3) calculated by the editors using the following formula: ((number of crimes in the MSA minus number of crimes in the city) ÷ (population of the MSA minus population of the city)) x 100,000; n/a not avail.
Source: U.S. Department of Justice, FBI Uniform Crime Reports, 1977 - 1996

Burglaries and Burglary Rates: 1977 - 1996

Year	Number				Rate per 100,000 population			
	City	Suburbs[2]	MSA[1]	U.S.	City	Suburbs[3]	MSA[1]	U.S.
1977	8,348	12,266	20,614	3,071,500	3,150.2	1,875.6	2,243.1	1,419.8
1978	9,460	13,458	22,918	3,128,300	3,583.3	1,958.7	2,409.7	1,434.6
1979	9,728	13,396	23,124	3,327,700	3,546.5	1,931.0	2,388.7	1,511.9
1980	10,401	15,477	25,878	3,795,200	3,788.4	2,101.6	2,559.7	1,684.1
1981	10,835	16,016	26,851	3,779,700	3,844.2	2,118.4	2,587.1	1,649.5
1982	9,230	14,558	23,788	3,447,100	3,199.9	1,881.5	2,239.6	1,488.8
1983	9,339	15,258	24,597	3,129,900	3,179.8	1,734.9	2,096.6	1,337.7
1984	9,408	15,108	24,516	2,984,400	3,133.4	1,656.1	2,021.9	1,263.7
1985	9,975	16,234	26,209	3,073,300	3,187.5	1,723.4	2,088.5	1,287.3
1986	9,983	14,950	24,933	3,241,400	3,117.2	1,550.8	1,941.4	1,344.6
1987	8,800	14,128	22,928	3,236,200	2,652.8	1,423.7	1,731.7	1,329.6
1988	7,701	15,009	22,710	3,218,100	2,261.8	1,470.8	1,668.7	1,309.2
1989	7,481	14,795	22,276	3,168,200	2,154.8	1,376.7	1,566.7	1,276.3
1990	6,966	15,195	22,161	3,073,900	1,885.9	1,366.8	1,496.3	1,235.9
1991	7,753	16,123	23,876	3,157,200	2,056.2	1,420.7	1,579.2	1,252.0
1992	7,305	14,075	21,380	2,979,900	1,906.8	1,398.1	1,538.3	1,168.2
1993	8,080	15,280	23,360	2,834,800	2,089.3	1,460.3	1,630.1	1,099.2
1994	8,076	n/a	n/a	2,712,800	2,073.7	n/a	n/a	1,042.0
1995	8,003	14,814	22,817	2,593,800	2,129.3	1,380.8	1,575.0	987.1
1996	7,148	12,122	19,270	2,501,500	1,884.6	1,119.6	1,318.1	943.0

Notes: (1) Metropolitan Statistical Area - see Appendix A for areas included; (2) calculated by the editors using the following formula: (number of crimes in the MSA minus number of crimes in the city); (3) calculated by the editors using the following formula: ((number of crimes in the MSA minus number of crimes in the city) ÷ (population of the MSA minus population of the city)) x 100,000; n/a not avail.
Source: U.S. Department of Justice, FBI Uniform Crime Reports, 1977 - 1996

Larceny-Thefts and Larceny-Theft Rates: 1977 - 1996

Year	Number				Rate per 100,000 population			
	City	Suburbs[2]	MSA[1]	U.S.	City	Suburbs[3]	MSA[1]	U.S.
1977	13,077	26,729	39,806	5,905,700	4,934.7	4,087.1	4,331.5	2,729.9
1978	13,799	29,075	42,874	5,991,000	5,226.9	4,231.7	4,508.0	2,747.4
1979	16,040	32,203	48,243	6,601,000	5,847.6	4,641.9	4,983.5	2,999.1
1980	18,451	36,250	54,701	7,136,900	6,720.5	4,922.3	5,410.6	3,167.0
1981	19,981	35,151	55,132	7,194,400	7,089.1	4,649.3	5,311.9	3,139.7
1982	16,932	35,339	52,271	7,142,500	5,870.1	4,567.4	4,921.2	3,084.8
1983	16,074	33,995	50,069	6,712,800	5,473.0	3,865.3	4,267.8	2,868.9
1984	15,604	34,508	50,112	6,591,900	5,197.0	3,782.7	4,132.9	2,791.3
1985	17,334	35,014	52,348	6,926,400	5,539.0	3,717.0	4,171.3	2,901.2
1986	17,643	35,436	53,079	7,257,200	5,509.0	3,675.9	4,133.0	3,010.3
1987	17,856	36,281	54,137	7,499,900	5,382.7	3,656.2	4,088.8	3,081.3
1988	18,086	35,832	53,918	7,705,900	5,311.9	3,511.4	3,961.9	3,134.9
1989	17,952	36,242	54,194	7,872,400	5,170.9	3,372.3	3,811.5	3,171.3
1990	16,219	35,073	51,292	7,945,700	4,391.0	3,154.8	3,463.1	3,194.8
1991	17,870	38,392	56,262	8,142,200	4,739.3	3,382.9	3,721.2	3,228.8
1992	18,216	29,545	47,761	7,915,200	4,754.9	2,934.7	3,436.4	3,103.0
1993	18,670	29,514	48,184	7,820,900	4,827.6	2,820.7	3,362.3	3,032.4
1994	18,598	n/a	n/a	7,879,800	4,775.4	n/a	n/a	3,026.7
1995	18,538	31,427	49,965	7,997,700	4,932.4	2,929.2	3,448.9	3,043.8
1996	16,842	28,955	45,797	7,894,600	4,440.5	2,674.4	3,132.6	2,975.9

Notes: (1) Metropolitan Statistical Area - see Appendix A for areas included; (2) calculated by the editors using the following formula: (number of crimes in the MSA minus number of crimes in the city); (3) calculated by the editors using the following formula: ((number of crimes in the MSA minus number of crimes in the city) ÷ (population of the MSA minus population of the city)) x 100,000; n/a not avail.
Source: U.S. Department of Justice, FBI Uniform Crime Reports, 1977 - 1996

Motor Vehicle Thefts and Motor Vehicle Theft Rates: 1977 - 1996

Year	Number				Rate per 100,000 population			
	City	Suburbs[2]	MSA[1]	U.S.	City	Suburbs[3]	MSA[1]	U.S.
1977	2,658	3,250	5,908	977,700	1,003.0	497.0	642.9	451.9
1978	2,731	3,579	6,310	1,004,100	1,034.5	520.9	663.5	460.5
1979	2,672	4,251	6,923	1,112,800	974.1	612.8	715.2	505.6
1980	2,626	4,386	7,012	1,131,700	956.5	595.6	693.6	502.2
1981	2,310	3,978	6,288	1,087,800	819.6	526.2	605.8	474.7
1982	2,052	3,841	5,893	1,062,400	711.4	496.4	554.8	458.8
1983	2,012	3,482	5,494	1,007,900	685.1	395.9	468.3	430.8
1984	2,235	3,567	5,802	1,032,200	744.4	391.0	478.5	437.1
1985	2,918	4,028	6,946	1,102,900	932.4	427.6	553.5	462.0
1986	3,205	4,307	7,512	1,224,100	1,000.8	446.8	584.9	507.8
1987	3,863	5,392	9,255	1,288,700	1,164.5	543.4	699.0	529.4
1988	5,774	6,774	12,548	1,432,900	1,695.8	663.8	922.0	582.9
1989	6,734	7,219	13,953	1,564,800	1,939.7	671.7	981.3	630.4
1990	6,547	7,452	13,999	1,635,900	1,772.5	670.3	945.2	657.8
1991	7,557	9,305	16,862	1,661,700	2,004.2	819.9	1,115.3	659.0
1992	8,179	8,431	16,610	1,610,800	2,134.9	837.5	1,195.1	631.5
1993	7,885	9,892	17,777	1,563,100	2,038.9	945.4	1,240.5	606.1
1994	8,846	n/a	n/a	1,539,300	2,271.4	n/a	n/a	591.3
1995	7,982	10,500	18,482	1,472,400	2,123.7	978.7	1,275.7	560.4
1996	6,083	10,402	16,485	1,395,200	1,603.8	960.8	1,127.6	525.9

Notes: (1) Metropolitan Statistical Area - see Appendix A for areas included; (2) calculated by the editors using the following formula: (number of crimes in the MSA minus number of crimes in the city); (3) calculated by the editors using the following formula: ((number of crimes in the MSA minus number of crimes in the city) ÷ (population of the MSA minus population of the city)) x 100,000; n/a not avail.
Source: U.S. Department of Justice, FBI Uniform Crime Reports, 1977 - 1996

HATE CRIMES

Criminal Incidents by Bias Motivation

Area	Race	Ethnicity	Religion	Sexual Orientation
Sacramento	25	4	0	7

Notes: Figures include both violent and property crimes. Law enforcement agencies must have submitted data for at least one quarter of calendar year 1995 to be included in this report, therefore figures shown may not represent complete 12-month totals; n/a not available
Source: U.S. Department of Justice, FBI Uniform Crime Reports, Hate Crime Statistics 1995

LAW ENFORCEMENT

Full-Time Law Enforcement Employees

Jurisdiction	Police Employees			Police Officers per 100,000 population
	Total	Officers	Civilians	
Sacramento	1,044	638	406	168.2

Notes: Data as of October 31, 1996
Source: U.S. Department of Justice, FBI Uniform Crime Reports, 1996

Number of Police Officers by Race

Race	Police Officers				Index of Representation[1]		
	1983		1992				
	Number	Pct.	Number	Pct.	1983	1992	% Chg.
Black	n/a	n/a	38	n/a	n/a	0.41	n/a
Hispanic[2]	n/a	n/a	70	n/a	n/a	0.71	n/a

Notes: (1) The index of representation is calculated by dividing the percent of black/hispanic police officers by the percent of corresponding blacks/hispanics in the local population. An index approaching 1.0 indicates that a city is closer to achieving a representation of police officers equal to their proportion in the local population; (2) Hispanic officers can be of any race ; n/a not available
Source: Bureau of Justice Statistics, Sourcebook of Criminal Justice Statistics, 1994

CORRECTIONS

Federal Correctional Facilities

Type	Year Opened	Security Level	Sex of Inmates	Rated Capacity	Population on 7/1/95	Number of Staff
None listed						

Notes: Data as of 1995
Source: Bureau of Justice Statistics, Sourcebook of Criminal Justice Statistics Online

City/County/Regional Correctional Facilities

Name	Year Opened	Year Renov.	Rated Capacity	1995 Pop.	Number of COs[1]	Number of Staff	ACA[2] Accred.
Sacramento Co-Lorenzo E. Patino Hall of Justice	1989	--	2,000	1,663	210	299	No

Notes: Data as of April 1996; (1) Correctional Officers; (2) American Correctional Assn. Accreditation
Source: American Correctional Association, 1996-1998 National Jail and Adult Detention Directory

Private Adult Correctional Facilities

Name	Date Opened	Rated Capacity	Present Pop.	Security Level	Facility Construct.	Expans. Plans	ACA[1] Accred.
None listed							

Notes: Data as of December 1996; (1) American Correctional Association Accreditation
Source: University of Florida, Center for Studies in Criminology and Law, Private Adult Correctional Facility Census, 10th Ed., March 15, 1997

Characteristics of Shock Incarceration Programs

Jurisdiction	Year Program Began	Number of Camps	Average Num. of Inmates	Number of Beds	Program Length	Voluntary/ Mandatory
California	1993	3[a]	350	200[b]	4 months[c]	Voluntary

Note: Data as of July 1996; (a) One boot camp; two work training and parole camps; (b) 200 program beds at San Quentin shock incarceration facility. Work training beds vary with each facility; (c) Shock incarceration and intensive parole programs: 4 months; Work training program: 2 months
Source: Sourcebook of Criminal Justice Statistics Online

INMATES AND HIV/AIDS

HIV Testing Policies for Inmates

Jurisdiction	All Inmates at Some Time	All Convicted Inmates at Admission	Random Samples While in Custody	High-risk Groups	Upon Inmate Request	Upon Court Order	Upon Involvement in Incident
Sacramento Co.[1]	No	No	No	No	Yes	Yes	Yes

Notes: (1) All facilities reported following the same testing policy or authorities reported the policy to be jurisdiction-wide
Source: HIV in Prisons and Jails, 1993 (released August 1995)

Inmates Known to be Positive for HIV

Jurisdiction	Number of Jail Inmates in Facilities Providing Data	Type of HIV Infection/AIDS Cases: Total	Asymptomatic	Symptomatic	Confirmed AIDS	HIV/AIDS Cases as a Percent of Tot. Custody Pop.
Sacramento Co.	2,741	17	17	0	0	0.6

Source: HIV in Prisons and Jails, 1993 (released August, 1995)

DEATH PENALTY

Death Penalty Statistics

State	Prisoners Executed		Prisoners Under Sentence of Death					Avg. No. of Years on Death Row[4]
	1930-1995	1996[1]	Total[2]	White[3]	Black[3]	Hisp.	Women	
California	294	2	420	251	160	61	8	7.0

Notes: Data as of 12/31/95 unless otherwise noted; (1) Data as of 7/31/97; (2) Includes persons of other races; (3) Includes people of Hispanic origin; (4) Covers prisoners sentenced 1974 through 1995
Source: Bureau of Justice Statistics, Capital Punishment 1995 (released 12/96); Death Penalty Information Center Web Site, 9/30/97

Capital Offenses and Methods of Execution

Capital Offenses in California	Minimum Age for Imposition of Death Penalty	Mentally Retarded Excluded	Methods of Execution[1]
First-degree murder with special circumstances; train-wrecking; treason; perjury causing execution.	18	No	Lethal injection; lethal gas

Notes: Data as of 12/31/95 unless otherwise noted; (1) Data as of 7/31/97
Source: Bureau of Justice Statistics, Capital Punishment 1995 (released 12/96); Death Penalty Information Center Web Site, 9/30/97

LAWS

Statutory Provisions Relating to the Purchase, Ownership and Use of Handguns

Jurisdiction	Instant Background Check	Federal Waiting Period Applies[1]	State Waiting Period (days)	License or Permit to Purchase	Regis-tration	Record of Sale Sent to Police	Concealed Carry Law
California	No	No	15	No	No	Yes	Yes[a]

Note: Data as of 1996; (1) The Federal 5-day waiting period for handgun purchases applies to states that don't have instant background checks, waiting period requirements, or licensing procedures exempting them from the Federal requirement; (a) Restrictively administered discretion by local authorities over permit issuance, or permits are unavailable and carrying is prohibited in most circumstances
Source: Sourcebook of Criminal Justice Statistics Online

Statutory Provisions Relating to Alcohol Use and Driving

Jurisdiction	Drinking Age	Blood Alcohol Concentration Levels as Evidence in State Courts[1]		Open Container Law[1]	Anti-Consump-tion Law[1]	Dram Shop Law[1]
		Illegal per se at 0.10%	Presumption at 0.10%			
California	21	(a)	(a)	Yes	Yes	Yes[b]

Note: Data as of January 1, 1997; (1) See Appendix C for an explanation of terms; (a) 0.08%; (b) Applies only to the actions of intoxicated minors
Source: Sourcebook of Criminal Justice Statistics Online

Statutory Provisions Relating to Curfews

Jurisdiction	Year Enacted	Latest Revision	Age Group(s)	Curfew Provisions
Sacramento	1994	-	17 and under	10 pm to daylight every night

Note: Data as of February 1996
Source: Sourcebook of Criminal Justice Statistics Online

Statutory Provisions Relating to Hate Crimes

Jurisdiction	Bias-Motivated Violence and Intimidation						Institutional Vandalism
	Civil Action	Criminal Penalty					
		Race/ Religion/ Ethnicity	Sexual Orientation	Mental/ Physical Disability	Gender	Age	
California	Yes	Yes	Yes	Yes	Yes	No	Yes

Source: Anti-Defamation League, 1997 Hate Crimes Laws

Saint Louis, Missouri

OVERVIEW

The total crime rate for the city increased 41.3% between 1977 and 1996. During that same period, the violent crime rate increased 45.3% and the property crime rate increased 40.5%.

Among violent crimes, the rates for: Murders increased 18.1%; Forcible Rapes decreased 21.2%; Robberies increased 14.5%; and Aggravated Assaults increased 91.2%.

Among property crimes, the rates for: Burglaries decreased 10.0%; Larceny-Thefts increased 70.1%; and Motor Vehicle Thefts increased 49.8%.

ANTI-CRIME PROGRAMS

Programs include:

- Youth/Young Adult Summit & Job Symposium—business and corporate leaders provide employment opportunities for qualified applicants in attendance. The overall job placement rate has been 67%.
- St. Louis City Out-Post Site Program—recreational outlets for youth/young adults are provided which has resulted in crime dropping from 10%-20% or higher.
- Adopt-A-Lot Program—businesses, social/civic organizations and churches are encouraged to adopt city-owned vacant lots and be responsible for the maintenance and upkeep.
- Midnite Basketball Program—crime has dropped as much as 15% in neighborhoods during game times. *Office of the Mayor, City of St. Louis, 7/97*

CRIME RISK

Your Chances of Becoming a Victim[1]

Area	Any Crime	Violent Crime					Property Crime			
		Any	Murder	Forcible Rape[2]	Robbery	Aggrav. Assault	Any	Burglary	Larceny -Theft	Motor Vehicle Theft
City	1:7	1:37	1:2,253	1:757	1:92	1:66	1:8	1:38	1:13	1:51

Note: (1) Figures have been calculated by dividing the population of the city by the number of crimes reported to the FBI during 1996 and are expressed as odds (eg. 1:20 should be read as 1 in 20). (2) Figures have been calculated by dividing the female population of the city by the number of forcible rapes reported to the FBI during 1996. The female population of the city was estimated by calculating the ratio of females to males reported in the 1990 Census and applying that ratio to 1996 population estimate.
Source: FBI Uniform Crime Reports 1996

CRIME STATISTICS

Total Crimes and Total Crime Rates: 1977 - 1996

Year	Number				Rate per 100,000 population			
	City	Suburbs[2]	MSA[1]	U.S.	City	Suburbs[3]	MSA[1]	U.S.
1977	55,450	82,029	137,479	10,984,500	10,704.6	4,434.7	5,806.4	5,077.6
1978	54,485	84,685	139,170	11,209,000	10,810.5	4,461.2	5,793.3	5,140.3
1979	57,213	83,791	141,004	12,249,500	11,319.2	4,455.3	5,909.2	5,565.5
1980	64,631	87,121	151,752	13,408,300	14,337.3	4,614.0	6,488.0	5,950.0
1981	62,654	85,777	148,431	13,423,800	13,795.4	4,507.3	6,296.8	5,858.2
1982	60,136	81,278	141,414	12,974,400	13,206.2	4,263.8	5,988.0	5,603.6
1983	50,987	50,295	101,282	12,108,600	11,150.5	3,612.5	5,476.2	5,175.0
1984	47,232	48,926	96,158	11,881,800	10,673.2	3,460.9	5,180.4	5,031.3
1985	49,113	49,919	99,032	12,431,400	11,392.2	3,492.3	5,322.8	5,207.1
1986	51,188	77,191	128,379	13,211,900	11,786.4	3,860.0	5,274.3	5,480.4
1987	54,408	76,268	130,676	13,508,700	12,670.3	3,746.5	5,301.0	5,550.0
1988	57,215	80,810	138,025	13,923,100	13,456.4	3,931.3	5,563.9	5,664.2
1989	62,082	83,081	145,163	14,251,400	15,326.4	3,992.0	5,838.6	5,741.0
1990	58,199	83,387	141,586	14,475,600	14,671.3	4,051.3	5,767.3	5,820.3
1991	64,103	91,976	156,079	14,872,900	16,031.4	4,430.9	6,304.6	5,897.8
1992	59,579	n/a	n/a	14,438,200	14,799.6	n/a	n/a	5,660.2
1993	64,438	n/a	n/a	14,144,800	16,648.4	n/a	n/a	5,484.4
1994	63,839	n/a	n/a	13,989,500	16,350.7	n/a	n/a	5,373.5
1995	59,736	n/a	n/a	13,862,700	16,082.9	n/a	n/a	5,275.9
1996	56,588	n/a	n/a	13,473,600	15,128.8	n/a	n/a	5,078.9

Notes: (1) Metropolitan Statistical Area - see Appendix A for areas included; (2) calculated by the editors using the following formula: (number of crimes in the MSA minus number of crimes in the city); (3) calculated by the editors using the following formula: ((number of crimes in the MSA minus number of crimes in the city) ÷ (population of the MSA minus population of the city)) x 100,000; n/a not avail.
Source: U.S. Department of Justice, FBI Uniform Crime Reports, 1977 - 1996

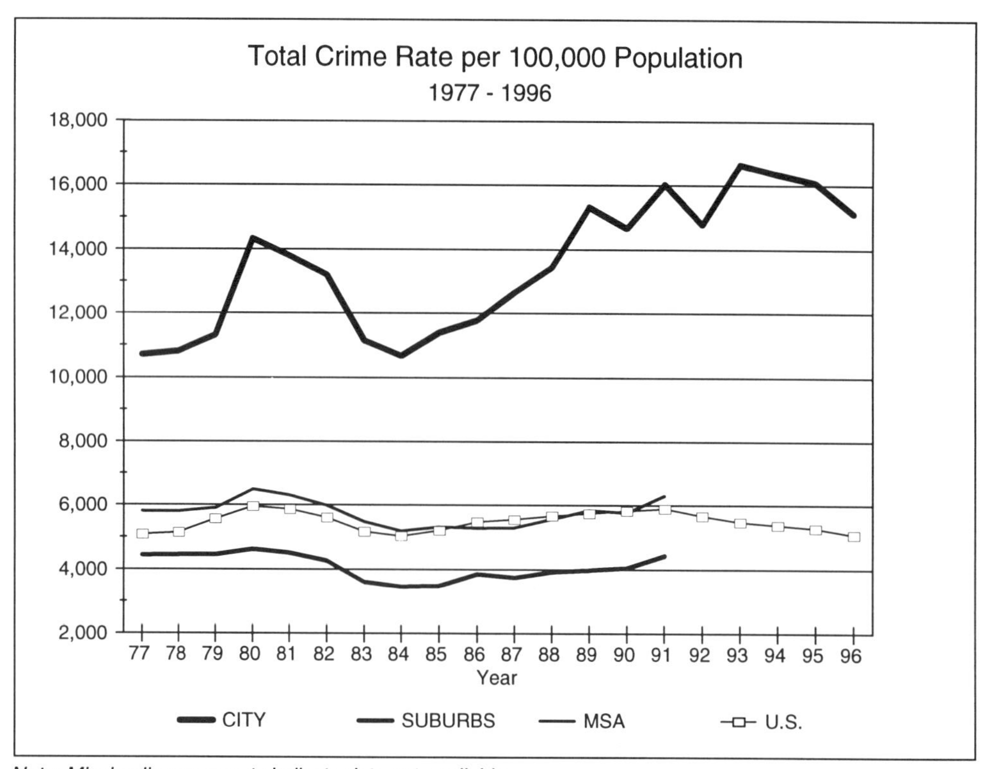

Note: Missing line segments indicate data not available.

Violent Crimes and Violent Crime Rates: 1977 - 1996

Year	Number				Rate per 100,000 population			
	City	Suburbs[2]	MSA[1]	U.S.	City	Suburbs[3]	MSA[1]	U.S.
1977	9,726	5,993	15,719	1,029,580	1,877.6	324.0	663.9	475.9
1978	10,095	6,671	16,766	1,085,550	2,003.0	351.4	697.9	497.8
1979	10,774	6,443	17,217	1,208,030	2,131.6	342.6	721.5	548.9
1980	10,983	6,926	17,909	1,344,520	2,436.4	366.8	765.7	596.6
1981	10,364	5,992	16,356	1,361,820	2,282.0	314.9	693.9	594.3
1982	10,069	6,254	16,323	1,322,390	2,211.2	328.1	691.2	571.1
1983	8,461	3,094	11,555	1,258,090	1,850.4	222.2	624.8	537.7
1984	7,729	3,516	11,245	1,273,280	1,746.6	248.7	605.8	539.2
1985	8,642	3,631	12,273	1,328,800	2,004.6	254.0	659.7	556.6
1986	9,889	7,076	16,965	1,489,170	2,277.0	353.8	697.0	617.7
1987	9,778	7,238	17,016	1,484,000	2,277.1	355.6	690.3	609.7
1988	10,481	7,389	17,870	1,566,220	2,465.0	359.5	720.3	637.2
1989	12,644	8,024	20,668	1,646,040	3,121.5	385.5	831.3	663.1
1990	13,682	8,714	22,396	1,820,130	3,449.1	423.4	912.3	731.8
1991	14,076	9,132	23,208	1,911,770	3,520.2	439.9	937.5	758.1
1992	13,247	n/a	n/a	1,932,270	3,290.6	n/a	n/a	757.5
1993	14,998	n/a	n/a	1,926,020	3,874.9	n/a	n/a	746.8
1994	14,644	n/a	n/a	1,857,670	3,750.7	n/a	n/a	713.6
1995	12,452	n/a	n/a	1,798,790	3,352.5	n/a	n/a	684.6
1996	10,203	n/a	n/a	1,682,280	2,727.8	n/a	n/a	634.1

Notes: Violent crimes include murder, forcible rape, robbery and aggravated assault; n/a not available; (1) Metropolitan Statistical Area - see Appendix A for areas included; (2) calculated by the editors using the following formula: (number of crimes in the MSA minus number of crimes in the city); (3) calculated by the editors using the following formula: ((number of crimes in the MSA minus number of crimes in the city) ÷ (population of the MSA minus population of the city)) x 100,000
Source: U.S. Department of Justice, FBI Uniform Crime Reports, 1977 - 1996

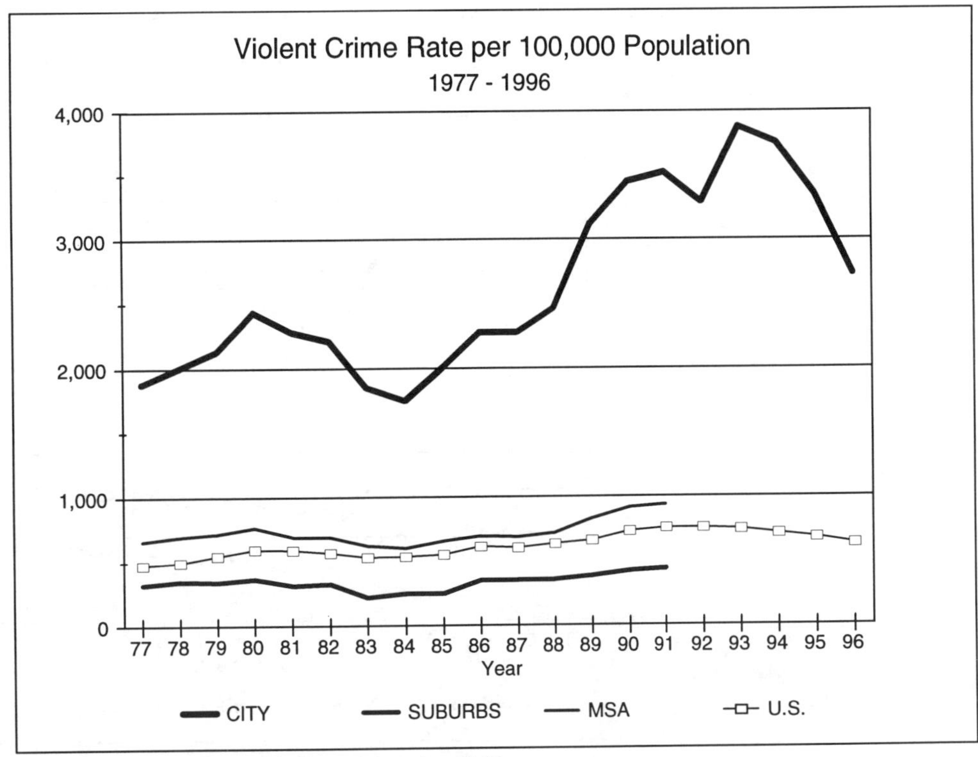

Note: Missing line segments indicate data not available.

Property Crimes and Property Crime Rates: 1977 - 1996

Year	Number				Rate per 100,000 population			
	City	Suburbs[2]	MSA[1]	U.S.	City	Suburbs[3]	MSA[1]	U.S.
1977	45,724	76,036	121,760	9,955,000	8,827.0	4,110.7	5,142.5	4,601.7
1978	44,390	78,014	122,404	10,123,400	8,807.5	4,109.8	5,095.4	4,642.5
1979	46,439	77,348	123,787	11,041,500	9,187.6	4,112.7	5,187.7	5,016.6
1980	53,648	80,195	133,843	12,063,700	11,900.9	4,247.2	5,722.3	5,353.3
1981	52,290	79,785	132,075	12,061,900	11,513.4	4,192.4	5,603.0	5,263.9
1982	50,067	75,024	125,091	11,652,000	10,995.0	3,935.7	5,296.9	5,032.5
1983	42,526	47,201	89,727	10,850,500	9,300.1	3,390.3	4,851.4	4,637.4
1984	39,503	45,410	84,913	10,608,500	8,926.7	3,212.2	4,574.6	4,492.1
1985	40,471	46,288	86,759	11,102,600	9,387.6	3,238.3	4,663.2	4,650.5
1986	41,299	70,115	111,414	11,722,700	9,509.4	3,506.2	4,577.3	4,862.6
1987	44,630	69,030	113,660	12,024,700	10,393.2	3,391.0	4,610.7	4,940.3
1988	46,734	73,421	120,155	12,356,900	10,991.4	3,571.8	4,843.5	5,027.1
1989	49,438	75,057	124,495	12,605,400	12,204.9	3,606.4	5,007.3	5,077.9
1990	44,517	74,673	119,190	12,655,500	11,222.3	3,627.9	4,855.0	5,088.5
1991	50,027	82,844	132,871	12,961,100	12,511.2	3,991.0	5,367.1	5,139.7
1992	46,332	78,351	124,683	12,505,900	11,509.0	3,662.0	4,904.6	4,902.7
1993	49,440	n/a	n/a	12,218,800	12,773.4	n/a	n/a	4,737.6
1994	49,195	n/a	n/a	12,131,900	12,600.0	n/a	n/a	4,660.0
1995	47,284	n/a	n/a	12,063,900	12,730.4	n/a	n/a	4,591.3
1996	46,385	n/a	n/a	11,791,300	12,401.0	n/a	n/a	4,444.8

Notes: Property crimes include burglary, larceny-theft and motor vehicle theft; n/a not available; (1) Metropolitan Statistical Area - see Appendix A for areas included; (2) calculated by the editors using the following formula: (number of crimes in the MSA minus number of crimes in the city); (3) calculated by the editors using the following formula: ((number of crimes in the MSA minus number of crimes in the city) ÷ (population of the MSA minus population of the city)) x 100,000
Source: U.S. Department of Justice, FBI Uniform Crime Reports, 1977 - 1996

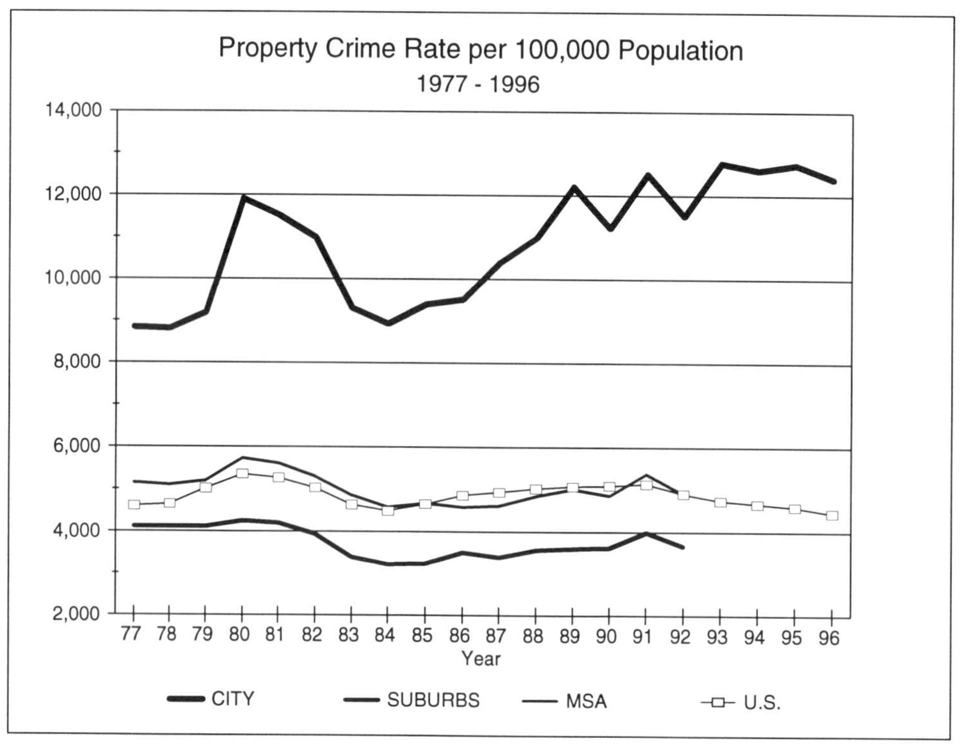

Note: Missing line segments indicate data not available.

Murders and Murder Rates: 1977 - 1996

Year	Number				Rate per 100,000 population			
	City	Suburbs[2]	MSA[1]	U.S.	City	Suburbs[3]	MSA[1]	U.S.
1977	195	112	307	19,120	37.6	6.1	13.0	8.8
1978	210	137	347	19,560	41.7	7.2	14.4	9.0
1979	265	117	382	21,460	52.4	6.2	16.0	9.7
1980	225	131	356	23,040	49.9	6.9	15.2	10.2
1981	265	106	371	22,520	58.3	5.6	15.7	9.8
1982	226	123	349	21,010	49.6	6.5	14.8	9.1
1983	152	49	201	19,310	33.2	3.5	10.9	8.3
1984	128	43	171	18,690	28.9	3.0	9.2	7.9
1985	169	44	213	18,980	39.2	3.1	11.4	7.9
1986	195	133	328	20,610	44.9	6.7	13.5	8.6
1987	153	103	256	20,100	35.6	5.1	10.4	8.3
1988	140	141	281	20,680	32.9	6.9	11.3	8.4
1989	158	121	279	21,500	39.0	5.8	11.2	8.7
1990	177	139	316	23,440	44.6	6.8	12.9	9.4
1991	260	148	408	24,700	65.0	7.1	16.5	9.8
1992	231	169	400	23,760	57.4	7.9	15.7	9.3
1993	267	n/a	n/a	24,530	69.0	n/a	n/a	9.5
1994	248	n/a	n/a	23,330	63.5	n/a	n/a	9.0
1995	204	n/a	n/a	21,610	54.9	n/a	n/a	8.2
1996	166	n/a	n/a	19,650	44.4	n/a	n/a	7.4

Notes: (1) Metropolitan Statistical Area - see Appendix A for areas included; (2) calculated by the editors using the following formula: (number of crimes in the MSA minus number of crimes in the city); (3) calculated by the editors using the following formula: ((number of crimes in the MSA minus number of crimes in the city) ÷ (population of the MSA minus population of the city)) x 100,000; n/a not avail.
Source: U.S. Department of Justice, FBI Uniform Crime Reports, 1977 - 1996

Forcible Rapes and Forcible Rape Rates: 1977 - 1996

Year	Number				Rate per 100,000 population			
	City	Suburbs[2]	MSA[1]	U.S.	City	Suburbs[3]	MSA[1]	U.S.
1977	473	447	920	63,500	91.3	24.2	38.9	29.4
1978	497	482	979	67,610	98.6	25.4	40.8	31.0
1979	555	503	1,058	76,390	109.8	26.7	44.3	34.7
1980	392	492	884	82,990	87.0	26.1	37.8	36.8
1981	413	416	829	82,500	90.9	21.9	35.2	36.0
1982	316	421	737	78,770	69.4	22.1	31.2	34.0
1983	323	242	565	78,920	70.6	17.4	30.5	33.7
1984	349	240	589	84,230	78.9	17.0	31.7	35.7
1985	384	238	622	88,670	89.1	16.7	33.4	37.1
1986	373	284	657	91,460	85.9	14.2	27.0	37.9
1987	332	242	574	91,110	77.3	11.9	23.3	37.4
1988	305	268	573	92,490	71.7	13.0	23.1	37.6
1989	330	264	594	94,500	81.5	12.7	23.9	38.1
1990	331	326	657	102,560	83.4	15.8	26.8	41.2
1991	342	354	696	106,590	85.5	17.1	28.1	42.3
1992	349	n/a	n/a	109,060	86.7	n/a	n/a	42.8
1993	319	n/a	n/a	106,010	82.4	n/a	n/a	41.1
1994	304	n/a	n/a	102,220	77.9	n/a	n/a	39.3
1995	273	n/a	n/a	97,470	73.5	n/a	n/a	37.1
1996	269	n/a	n/a	95,770	71.9	n/a	n/a	36.1

Notes: (1) Metropolitan Statistical Area - see Appendix A for areas included; (2) calculated by the editors using the following formula: (number of crimes in the MSA minus number of crimes in the city); (3) calculated by the editors using the following formula: ((number of crimes in the MSA minus number of crimes in the city) ÷ (population of the MSA minus population of the city)) x 100,000; n/a not avail.
Source: U.S. Department of Justice, FBI Uniform Crime Reports, 1977 - 1996

Robberies and Robbery Rates: 1977 - 1996

Year	Number				Rate per 100,000 population			
	City	Suburbs[2]	MSA[1]	U.S.	City	Suburbs[3]	MSA[1]	U.S.
1977	4,943	2,433	7,376	412,610	954.2	131.5	311.5	190.7
1978	5,025	2,375	7,400	426,930	997.0	125.1	308.0	195.8
1979	5,386	2,238	7,624	480,700	1,065.6	119.0	319.5	218.4
1980	5,938	2,019	7,957	565,840	1,317.2	106.9	340.2	251.1
1981	5,365	1,657	7,022	592,910	1,181.3	87.1	297.9	258.7
1982	4,899	1,629	6,528	553,130	1,075.8	85.5	276.4	238.9
1983	3,840	870	4,710	506,570	839.8	62.5	254.7	216.5
1984	3,112	807	3,919	485,010	703.2	57.1	211.1	205.4
1985	3,136	858	3,994	497,870	727.4	60.0	214.7	208.5
1986	3,326	1,976	5,302	542,780	765.8	98.8	217.8	225.1
1987	3,296	1,747	5,043	517,700	767.6	85.8	204.6	212.7
1988	3,327	1,876	5,203	542,970	782.5	91.3	209.7	220.9
1989	4,220	2,052	6,272	578,330	1,041.8	98.6	252.3	233.0
1990	4,708	2,029	6,737	639,270	1,186.8	98.6	274.4	257.0
1991	5,294	2,561	7,855	687,730	1,324.0	123.4	317.3	272.7
1992	4,936	2,093	7,029	672,480	1,226.1	97.8	276.5	263.6
1993	6,223	n/a	n/a	659,870	1,607.8	n/a	n/a	255.9
1994	6,025	n/a	n/a	618,950	1,543.1	n/a	n/a	237.7
1995	5,136	n/a	n/a	580,510	1,382.8	n/a	n/a	220.9
1996	4,086	n/a	n/a	537,050	1,092.4	n/a	n/a	202.4

Notes: (1) Metropolitan Statistical Area - see Appendix A for areas included; (2) calculated by the editors using the following formula: (number of crimes in the MSA minus number of crimes in the city); (3) calculated by the editors using the following formula: ((number of crimes in the MSA minus number of crimes in the city) ÷ (population of the MSA minus population of the city)) x 100,000; n/a not avail.
Source: U.S. Department of Justice, FBI Uniform Crime Reports, 1977 - 1996

Aggravated Assaults and Aggravated Assault Rates: 1977 - 1996

Year	Number				Rate per 100,000 population			
	City	Suburbs[2]	MSA[1]	U.S.	City	Suburbs[3]	MSA[1]	U.S.
1977	4,115	3,001	7,116	534,350	794.4	162.2	300.5	247.0
1978	4,363	3,677	8,040	571,460	865.7	193.7	334.7	262.1
1979	4,568	3,585	8,153	629,480	903.7	190.6	341.7	286.0
1980	4,428	4,284	8,712	672,650	982.3	226.9	372.5	298.5
1981	4,321	3,813	8,134	663,900	951.4	200.4	345.1	289.7
1982	4,628	4,081	8,709	669,480	1,016.3	214.1	368.8	289.2
1983	4,146	1,933	6,079	653,290	906.7	138.8	328.7	279.2
1984	4,140	2,426	6,566	685,350	935.5	171.6	353.7	290.2
1985	4,953	2,491	7,444	723,250	1,148.9	174.3	400.1	302.9
1986	5,995	4,683	10,678	834,320	1,380.4	234.2	438.7	346.1
1987	5,997	5,146	11,143	855,090	1,396.6	252.8	452.0	351.3
1988	6,709	5,104	11,813	910,090	1,577.9	248.3	476.2	370.2
1989	7,936	5,587	13,523	951,710	1,959.2	268.5	543.9	383.4
1990	8,466	6,220	14,686	1,054,860	2,134.2	302.2	598.2	424.1
1991	8,180	6,069	14,249	1,092,740	2,045.7	292.4	575.6	433.3
1992	7,731	5,943	13,674	1,126,970	1,920.4	277.8	537.9	441.8
1993	8,189	n/a	n/a	1,135,610	2,115.7	n/a	n/a	440.3
1994	8,067	n/a	n/a	1,113,180	2,066.1	n/a	n/a	427.6
1995	6,839	n/a	n/a	1,099,210	1,841.3	n/a	n/a	418.3
1996	5,682	n/a	n/a	1,029,810	1,519.1	n/a	n/a	388.2

Notes: (1) Metropolitan Statistical Area - see Appendix A for areas included; (2) calculated by the editors using the following formula: (number of crimes in the MSA minus number of crimes in the city); (3) calculated by the editors using the following formula: ((number of crimes in the MSA minus number of crimes in the city) ÷ (population of the MSA minus population of the city)) x 100,000; n/a not avail.
Source: U.S. Department of Justice, FBI Uniform Crime Reports, 1977 - 1996

Burglaries and Burglary Rates: 1977 - 1996

Year	Number				Rate per 100,000 population			
	City	Suburbs[2]	MSA[1]	U.S.	City	Suburbs[3]	MSA[1]	U.S.
1977	15,215	22,923	38,138	3,071,500	2,937.3	1,239.3	1,610.8	1,419.8
1978	16,688	23,166	39,854	3,128,300	3,311.1	1,220.4	1,659.0	1,434.6
1979	17,263	23,965	41,228	3,327,700	3,415.4	1,274.2	1,727.8	1,511.9
1980	20,184	25,513	45,697	3,795,200	4,477.5	1,351.2	1,953.7	1,684.1
1981	19,214	24,481	43,695	3,779,700	4,230.6	1,286.4	1,853.7	1,649.5
1982	17,149	22,255	39,404	3,447,100	3,766.0	1,167.5	1,668.5	1,488.8
1983	14,199	12,641	26,840	3,129,900	3,105.2	908.0	1,451.2	1,337.7
1984	13,256	12,254	25,510	2,984,400	2,995.5	866.8	1,374.3	1,263.7
1985	13,498	11,665	25,163	3,073,300	3,131.0	816.1	1,352.5	1,287.3
1986	12,523	18,664	31,187	3,241,400	2,883.5	933.3	1,281.3	1,344.6
1987	11,796	18,320	30,116	3,236,200	2,747.0	899.9	1,221.7	1,329.6
1988	12,541	19,999	32,540	3,218,100	2,949.5	972.9	1,311.7	1,309.2
1989	13,837	18,721	32,558	3,168,200	3,416.0	899.5	1,309.5	1,276.3
1990	11,531	17,174	28,705	3,073,900	2,906.8	834.4	1,169.3	1,235.9
1991	13,396	22,542	35,938	3,157,200	3,350.2	1,086.0	1,451.7	1,252.0
1992	12,303	18,059	30,362	2,979,900	3,056.1	844.0	1,194.3	1,168.2
1993	12,400	n/a	n/a	2,834,800	3,203.7	n/a	n/a	1,099.2
1994	12,522	n/a	n/a	2,712,800	3,207.2	n/a	n/a	1,042.0
1995	10,692	n/a	n/a	2,593,800	2,878.6	n/a	n/a	987.1
1996	9,887	n/a	n/a	2,501,500	2,643.3	n/a	n/a	943.0

Notes: (1) Metropolitan Statistical Area - see Appendix A for areas included; (2) calculated by the editors using the following formula: (number of crimes in the MSA minus number of crimes in the city); (3) calculated by the editors using the following formula: ((number of crimes in the MSA minus number of crimes in the city) ÷ (population of the MSA minus population of the city)) x 100,000; n/a not avail.
Source: U.S. Department of Justice, FBI Uniform Crime Reports, 1977 - 1996

Larceny-Thefts and Larceny-Theft Rates: 1977 - 1996

Year	Number				Rate per 100,000 population			
	City	Suburbs[2]	MSA[1]	U.S.	City	Suburbs[3]	MSA[1]	U.S.
1977	23,790	45,849	69,639	5,905,700	4,592.7	2,478.7	2,941.2	2,729.9
1978	22,151	47,137	69,288	5,991,000	4,395.0	2,483.2	2,884.3	2,747.4
1979	23,103	45,694	68,797	6,601,000	4,570.8	2,429.6	2,883.2	2,999.1
1980	27,043	47,430	74,473	7,136,900	5,999.0	2,511.9	3,184.0	3,167.0
1981	27,195	48,446	75,641	7,194,400	5,987.9	2,545.7	3,208.9	3,139.7
1982	27,638	46,642	74,280	7,142,500	6,069.5	2,446.8	3,145.3	3,084.8
1983	22,974	30,473	53,447	6,712,800	5,024.3	2,188.8	2,889.8	2,868.9
1984	21,051	29,376	50,427	6,591,900	4,757.0	2,078.0	2,716.7	2,791.3
1985	21,390	30,732	52,122	6,926,400	4,961.6	2,150.0	2,801.5	2,901.2
1986	21,641	45,264	66,905	7,257,200	4,983.0	2,263.5	2,748.7	3,010.3
1987	25,157	45,448	70,605	7,499,900	5,858.4	2,232.5	2,864.2	3,081.3
1988	26,735	48,058	74,793	7,705,900	6,287.8	2,338.0	3,014.9	3,134.9
1989	26,669	49,797	76,466	7,872,400	6,583.9	2,392.7	3,075.5	3,171.3
1990	24,564	51,099	75,663	7,945,700	6,192.3	2,482.6	3,082.0	3,194.8
1991	27,381	53,126	80,507	8,142,200	6,847.7	2,559.3	3,252.0	3,228.8
1992	25,600	53,349	78,949	7,915,200	6,359.1	2,493.4	3,105.6	3,103.0
1993	26,975	n/a	n/a	7,820,900	6,969.3	n/a	n/a	3,032.4
1994	27,744	n/a	n/a	7,879,800	7,105.9	n/a	n/a	3,026.7
1995	28,587	n/a	n/a	7,997,700	7,696.6	n/a	n/a	3,043.8
1996	29,228	n/a	n/a	7,894,600	7,814.1	n/a	n/a	2,975.9

Notes: (1) Metropolitan Statistical Area - see Appendix A for areas included; (2) calculated by the editors using the following formula: (number of crimes in the MSA minus number of crimes in the city); (3) calculated by the editors using the following formula: ((number of crimes in the MSA minus number of crimes in the city) ÷ (population of the MSA minus population of the city)) x 100,000; n/a not avail.
Source: U.S. Department of Justice, FBI Uniform Crime Reports, 1977 - 1996

Motor Vehicle Thefts and Motor Vehicle Theft Rates: 1977 - 1996

Year	Number				Rate per 100,000 population			
	City	Suburbs[2]	MSA[1]	U.S.	City	Suburbs[3]	MSA[1]	U.S.
1977	6,719	7,264	13,983	977,700	1,297.1	392.7	590.6	451.9
1978	5,551	7,711	13,262	1,004,100	1,101.4	406.2	552.1	460.5
1979	6,073	7,689	13,762	1,112,800	1,201.5	408.8	576.7	505.6
1980	6,421	7,252	13,673	1,131,700	1,424.4	384.1	584.6	502.2
1981	5,881	6,858	12,739	1,087,800	1,294.9	360.4	540.4	474.7
1982	5,280	6,127	11,407	1,062,400	1,159.5	321.4	483.0	458.8
1983	5,353	4,087	9,440	1,007,900	1,170.7	293.6	510.4	430.8
1984	5,196	3,780	8,976	1,032,200	1,174.2	267.4	483.6	437.1
1985	5,583	3,891	9,474	1,102,900	1,295.0	272.2	509.2	462.0
1986	7,135	6,187	13,322	1,224,100	1,642.9	309.4	547.3	507.8
1987	7,677	5,262	12,939	1,288,700	1,787.8	258.5	524.9	529.4
1988	7,458	5,364	12,822	1,432,900	1,754.1	261.0	516.9	582.9
1989	8,932	6,539	15,471	1,564,800	2,205.1	314.2	622.3	630.4
1990	8,422	6,400	14,822	1,635,900	2,123.1	310.9	603.8	657.8
1991	9,250	7,176	16,426	1,661,700	2,313.3	345.7	663.5	659.0
1992	8,429	6,943	15,372	1,610,800	2,093.8	324.5	604.7	631.5
1993	10,065	n/a	n/a	1,563,100	2,600.4	n/a	n/a	606.1
1994	8,929	n/a	n/a	1,539,300	2,286.9	n/a	n/a	591.3
1995	8,005	n/a	n/a	1,472,400	2,155.2	n/a	n/a	560.4
1996	7,270	n/a	n/a	1,395,200	1,943.6	n/a	n/a	525.9

Notes: (1) Metropolitan Statistical Area - see Appendix A for areas included; (2) calculated by the editors using the following formula: (number of crimes in the MSA minus number of crimes in the city); (3) calculated by the editors using the following formula: ((number of crimes in the MSA minus number of crimes in the city) ÷ (population of the MSA minus population of the city)) x 100,000; n/a not avail.
Source: U.S. Department of Justice, FBI Uniform Crime Reports, 1977 - 1996

HATE CRIMES

Criminal Incidents by Bias Motivation

Area	Race	Ethnicity	Religion	Sexual Orientation
Saint Louis	34	1	0	4

Notes: Figures include both violent and property crimes. Law enforcement agencies must have submitted data for at least one quarter of calendar year 1995 to be included in this report, therefore figures shown may not represent complete 12-month totals; n/a not available
Source: U.S. Department of Justice, FBI Uniform Crime Reports, Hate Crime Statistics 1995

ILLEGAL DRUGS

Drug Use by Adult Arrestees

Sex	Percent Testing Positive by Urinalysis (%)				
	Any Drug[1]	Cocaine	Marijuana	Opiates	Multiple Drugs
Male	75	43	52	10	29
Female	73	55	29	7	20

Notes: The catchment area is the entire city; (1) Includes cocaine, opiates, marijuana, methadone, phencyclidine (PCP), benzodiazepines, methaqualone, propoxyphene, barbiturates & amphetamines
Source: National Institute of Justice, 1996 Drug Use Forecasting, Annual Report on Adult and Juvenile Arrestees (released June 1997)

LAW ENFORCEMENT

Full-Time Law Enforcement Employees

Jurisdiction	Police Employees			Police Officers per 100,000 population
	Total	Officers	Civilians	
Saint Louis	2,281	1,625	656	434.4

Notes: Data as of October 31, 1996
Source: U.S. Department of Justice, FBI Uniform Crime Reports, 1996

Number of Police Officers by Race

Race	Police Officers 1983		Police Officers 1992		Index of Representation[1]		
	Number	Pct.	Number	Pct.	1983	1992	% Chg.
Black	346	19.6	437	28.2	0.43	0.59	37.2
Hispanic[2]	0	0.0	7	0.5	0.00	0.31	--

Notes: (1) The index of representation is calculated by dividing the percent of black/hispanic police officers by the percent of corresponding blacks/hispanics in the local population. An index approaching 1.0 indicates that a city is closer to achieving a representation of police officers equal to their proportion in the local population; (2) Hispanic officers can be of any race
Source: Bureau of Justice Statistics, Sourcebook of Criminal Justice Statistics, 1994

CORRECTIONS

Federal Correctional Facilities

Type	Year Opened	Security Level	Sex of Inmates	Rated Capacity	Population on 7/1/95	Number of Staff
None listed						

Notes: Data as of 1995
Source: Bureau of Justice Statistics, Sourcebook of Criminal Justice Statistics Online

City/County/Regional Correctional Facilities

Name	Year Opened	Year Renov.	Rated Capacity	1995 Pop.	Number of COs[1]	Number of Staff	ACA[2] Accred.
St Louis Med Sec Inst	1966	--	610	606	239	287	No
St Louis Municipal Jail	1920	1973	228	n/a	108	122	No

Notes: Data as of April 1996; (1) Correctional Officers; (2) American Correctional Assn. Accreditation
Source: American Correctional Association, 1996-1998 National Jail and Adult Detention Directory

Private Adult Correctional Facilities

Name	Date Opened	Rated Capacity	Present Pop.	Security Level	Facility Construct.	Expans. Plans	ACA[1] Accred.
None listed							

Notes: Data as of December 1996; (1) American Correctional Association Accreditation
Source: University of Florida, Center for Studies in Criminology and Law, Private Adult Correctional Facility Census, 10th Ed., March 15, 1997

Characteristics of Shock Incarceration Programs

Jurisdiction	Year Program Began	Number of Camps	Average Num. of Inmates	Number of Beds	Program Length	Voluntary/ Mandatory
Missouri	1994	1	40 to 45	50	90 days	Mandatory

Note: Data as of July 1996;
Source: Sourcebook of Criminal Justice Statistics Online

DEATH PENALTY

Death Penalty Statistics

State	Prisoners Executed 1930-1995	Prisoners Executed 1996[1]	Prisoners Under Sentence of Death Total[2]	White[3]	Black[3]	Hisp.	Women	Avg. No. of Years on Death Row[4]
Missouri	79	6	92	51	41	0	2	6.1

Notes: Data as of 12/31/95 unless otherwise noted; (1) Data as of 7/31/97; (2) Includes persons of other races; (3) Includes people of Hispanic origin; (4) Covers prisoners sentenced 1974 through 1995
Source: Bureau of Justice Statistics, Capital Punishment 1995 (released 12/96); Death Penalty Information Center Web Site, 9/30/97

Capital Offenses and Methods of Execution

Capital Offenses in Missouri	Minimum Age for Imposition of Death Penalty	Mentally Retarded Excluded	Methods of Execution[1]
First-degree murder (565.020 RSMO).	16	No	Lethal injection; lethal gas

Notes: Data as of 12/31/95 unless otherwise noted; (1) Data as of 7/31/97
Source: Bureau of Justice Statistics, Capital Punishment 1995 (released 12/96); Death Penalty Information Center Web Site, 9/30/97

LAWS

Statutory Provisions Relating to the Purchase, Ownership and Use of Handguns

Jurisdiction	Instant Background Check	Federal Waiting Period Applies[1]	State Waiting Period (days)	License or Permit to Purchase	Registration	Record of Sale Sent to Police	Concealed Carry Law
Missouri	No	No	7	Yes[a]	No	Yes	Yes[b]

Note: Data as of 1996; (1) The Federal 5-day waiting period for handgun purchases applies to states that don't have instant background checks, waiting period requirements, or licensing procedures exempting them from the Federal requirement; (a) A purchase permit is required for a handgun, must be issued to qualified applicants within 7 days, and is valid for 30 days; (b) No permit system exists and concealed carry is prohibited
Source: Sourcebook of Criminal Justice Statistics Online

Statutory Provisions Relating to Alcohol Use and Driving

Jurisdiction	Drinking Age	Blood Alcohol Concentration Levels as Evidence in State Courts[1]		Open Container Law[1]	Anti-Consumption Law[1]	Dram Shop Law[1]
		Illegal per se at 0.10%	Presumption at 0.10%			
Missouri	21	Yes	No	No	(a)	(b)

Note: Data as of January 1, 1997; (1) See Appendix C for an explanation of terms; (a) Applies to drivers only; (b) Cause of action limited to licensees who have been convicted of selling alcoholic beverages to minors or intoxicated individuals
Source: Sourcebook of Criminal Justice Statistics Online

Statutory Provisions Relating to Curfews

Jurisdiction	Year Enacted	Latest Revision	Age Group(s)	Curfew Provisions
Saint Louis	1955	-	16 and under	11 pm to 6 am weekday nights midnight to 6 am weekend nights

Note: Data as of February 1996
Source: Sourcebook of Criminal Justice Statistics Online

Statutory Provisions Relating to Hate Crimes

Jurisdiction	Bias-Motivated Violence and Intimidation						Institutional Vandalism
	Civil Action	Criminal Penalty					
		Race/ Religion/ Ethnicity	Sexual Orientation	Mental/ Physical Disability	Gender	Age	
Missouri	Yes	Yes	No	No	No	No	Yes

Source: Anti-Defamation League, 1997 Hate Crimes Laws

Saint Paul, Minnesota

OVERVIEW

The total crime rate for the city decreased 3.7% between 1977 and 1996. During that same period, the violent crime rate increased 28.1% and the property crime rate decreased 6.8%.

Among violent crimes, the rates for: Murders increased 51.6%; Forcible Rapes increased 97.1%; Robberies decreased 1.7%; and Aggravated Assaults increased 48.6%.

Among property crimes, the rates for: Burglaries decreased 46.0%; Larceny-Thefts increased 17.1%; and Motor Vehicle Thefts increased 23.6%.

ANTI-CRIME PROGRAMS

Among the city's anti-crime programs are:

- Gun Interdiction Program—identifies, incarcerates, and prosecutes to the fullest extent of the law those individuals who illegally possess and carry firearms.
- A Community Outreach Program (ACOP)—provides individualized police services to Public Housing residents and Southeast Asian citizens of Saint Paul.
- Bike Patrol—introduced in 1994, officers are assigned to high density/high crime areas and have been very successful in combating street-level narcotics and disorderly groups.
- Mobile Crisis Team—reaches out to families in crisis by providing teams which are available to accompany police officers as they are called to homes or sites requiring emergency assistance. The team provides assessment, mediation, and consultation to poor families, especially those unlikely to use mental health services.
- Graffiti, Inc.—vandals are identified and redirected to legal and safe environments to paint; community education and involvement in addressing the graffiti problem through the formation of community advisory groups; and the ongoing removal of illegal graffiti as quickly as it appears. *City of Saint Paul, Department of Police, 6/97*

CRIME RISK

Your Chances of Becoming a Victim[1]

Area	Any Crime	Violent Crime					Property Crime			
		Any	Murder	Forcible Rape[2]	Robbery	Aggrav. Assault	Any	Burglary	Larceny -Theft	Motor Vehicle Theft
City	1:13	1:110	1:10,280	1:605	1:305	1:205	1:15	1:65	1:23	1:101

Note: (1) Figures have been calculated by dividing the population of the city by the number of crimes reported to the FBI during 1996 and are expressed as odds (eg. 1:20 should be read as 1 in 20). (2) Figures have been calculated by dividing the female population of the city by the number of forcible rapes reported to the FBI during 1996. The female population of the city was estimated by calculating the ratio of females to males reported in the 1990 Census and applying that ratio to 1996 population estimate.
Source: FBI Uniform Crime Reports 1996

CRIME STATISTICS

Total Crimes and Total Crime Rates: 1977 - 1996

Year	Number				Rate per 100,000 population			
	City	Suburbs[2]	MSA[1]	U.S.	City	Suburbs[3]	MSA[1]	U.S.
1977	21,403	91,239	112,642	10,984,500	8,046.2	5,004.4	5,391.7	5,077.6
1978	20,162	91,175	111,337	11,209,000	7,666.2	4,954.6	5,293.6	5,140.3
1979	21,001	97,440	118,441	12,249,500	7,817.2	5,351.4	5,668.5	5,565.5
1980	22,134	107,265	129,399	13,408,300	8,245.3	5,829.5	6,137.1	5,950.0
1981	22,799	108,406	131,205	13,423,800	8,433.3	5,849.4	6,178.3	5,858.2
1982	24,413	102,130	126,543	12,974,400	8,936.4	5,454.0	5,897.3	5,603.6
1983	21,899	92,193	114,092	12,108,600	7,994.9	4,848.9	5,245.0	5,175.0
1984	21,147	86,961	108,108	11,881,800	7,783.4	4,502.4	4,907.1	5,031.3
1985	20,854	99,020	119,874	12,431,400	7,784.4	5,003.4	5,335.0	5,207.1
1986	21,326	107,114	128,440	13,211,900	7,920.5	5,402.7	5,703.7	5,480.4
1987	21,360	117,361	138,721	13,508,700	8,043.7	5,738.6	6,003.5	5,550.0
1988	20,512	109,631	130,143	13,923,100	7,655.3	5,220.5	5,496.0	5,664.2
1989	21,796	113,803	135,599	14,251,400	8,322.2	5,292.4	5,621.4	5,741.0
1990	22,144	n/a	n/a	14,475,600	8,134.1	n/a	n/a	5,820.3
1991	21,765	117,313	139,078	14,872,900	7,892.3	5,284.7	5,572.8	5,897.8
1992	21,398	123,897	145,295	14,438,200	7,676.1	5,335.4	5,586.3	5,660.2
1993	20,382	n/a	n/a	14,144,800	7,515.3	n/a	n/a	5,484.4
1994	19,472	120,181	139,653	13,989,500	7,101.1	5,000.7	5,215.8	5,373.5
1995	20,256	123,307	143,563	13,862,700	7,657.1	5,031.3	5,287.2	5,275.9
1996	20,704	125,962	146,666	13,473,600	7,745.8	5,087.1	5,346.1	5,078.9

Notes: (1) Metropolitan Statistical Area - see Appendix A for areas included; (2) calculated by the editors using the following formula: (number of crimes in the MSA minus number of crimes in the city); (3) calculated by the editors using the following formula: ((number of crimes in the MSA minus number of crimes in the city) ÷ (population of the MSA minus population of the city)) x 100,000; n/a not avail.
Source: U.S. Department of Justice, FBI Uniform Crime Reports, 1977 - 1996

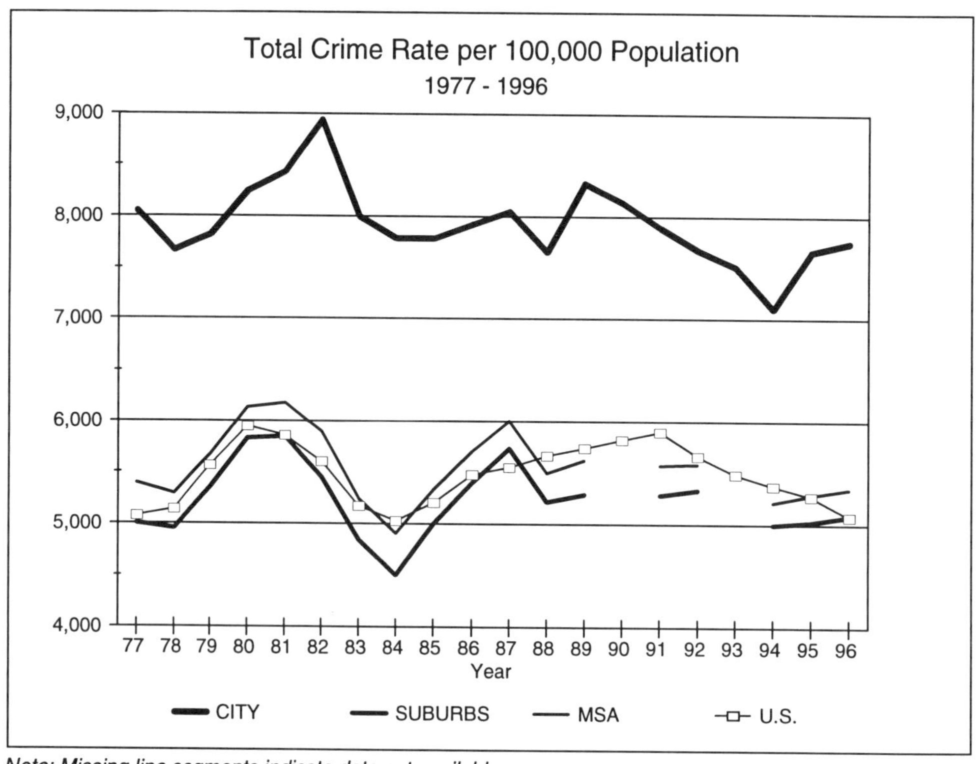

Note: Missing line segments indicate data not available.

Violent Crimes and Violent Crime Rates: 1977 - 1996

Year	Number				Rate per 100,000 population			
	City	Suburbs[2]	MSA[1]	U.S.	City	Suburbs[3]	MSA[1]	U.S.
1977	1,893	4,567	6,460	1,029,580	711.7	250.5	309.2	475.9
1978	1,752	4,577	6,329	1,085,550	666.2	248.7	300.9	497.8
1979	1,882	5,556	7,438	1,208,030	700.5	305.1	356.0	548.9
1980	2,032	5,587	7,619	1,344,520	757.0	303.6	361.3	596.6
1981	2,309	5,537	7,846	1,361,820	854.1	298.8	369.5	594.3
1982	2,046	5,674	7,720	1,322,390	748.9	303.0	359.8	571.1
1983	1,820	4,792	6,612	1,258,090	664.4	252.0	304.0	537.7
1984	2,093	5,322	7,415	1,273,280	770.4	275.5	336.6	539.2
1985	2,095	6,912	9,007	1,328,800	782.0	349.3	400.9	556.6
1986	2,401	7,813	10,214	1,489,170	891.7	394.1	453.6	617.7
1987	2,289	7,789	10,078	1,484,000	862.0	380.9	436.2	609.7
1988	2,468	7,843	10,311	1,566,220	921.1	373.5	435.4	637.2
1989	2,463	7,961	10,424	1,646,040	940.4	370.2	432.1	663.1
1990	2,763	n/a	n/a	1,820,130	1,014.9	n/a	n/a	731.8
1991	2,731	8,998	11,729	1,911,770	990.3	405.3	470.0	758.1
1992	2,619	9,813	12,432	1,932,270	939.5	422.6	478.0	757.5
1993	2,704	n/a	n/a	1,926,020	997.0	n/a	n/a	746.8
1994	2,730	10,564	13,294	1,857,670	995.6	439.6	496.5	713.6
1995	2,536	10,765	13,301	1,798,790	958.6	439.2	489.9	684.6
1996	2,437	10,417	12,854	1,682,280	911.7	420.7	468.5	634.1

Notes: Violent crimes include murder, forcible rape, robbery and aggravated assault; n/a not available; (1) Metropolitan Statistical Area - see Appendix A for areas included; (2) calculated by the editors using the following formula: (number of crimes in the MSA minus number of crimes in the city); (3) calculated by the editors using the following formula: ((number of crimes in the MSA minus number of crimes in the city) ÷ (population of the MSA minus population of the city)) x 100,000
Source: U.S. Department of Justice, FBI Uniform Crime Reports, 1977 - 1996

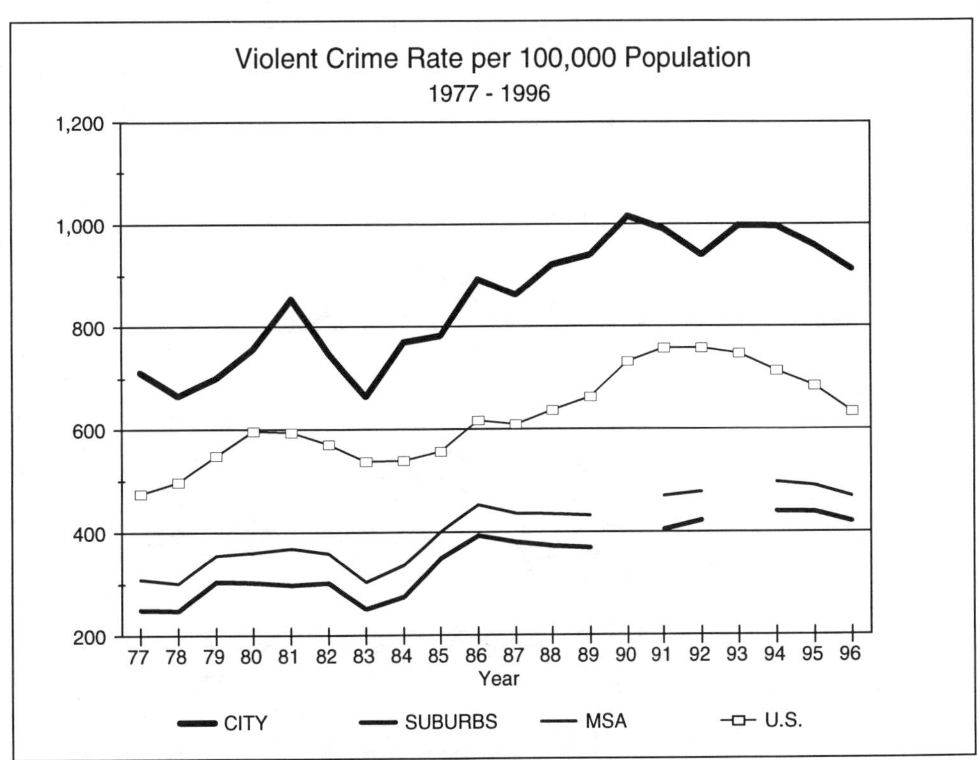

Note: Missing line segments indicate data not available.

Property Crimes and Property Crime Rates: 1977 - 1996

Year	Number				Rate per 100,000 population			
	City	Suburbs[2]	MSA[1]	U.S.	City	Suburbs[3]	MSA[1]	U.S.
1977	19,510	86,672	106,182	9,955,000	7,334.6	4,753.9	5,082.5	4,601.7
1978	18,410	86,598	105,008	10,123,400	7,000.0	4,705.8	4,992.7	4,642.5
1979	19,119	91,884	111,003	11,041,500	7,116.7	5,046.3	5,312.5	5,016.6
1980	20,102	101,678	121,780	12,063,700	7,488.4	5,525.8	5,775.7	5,353.3
1981	20,490	102,869	123,359	12,061,900	7,579.2	5,550.6	5,808.8	5,263.9
1982	22,367	96,456	118,823	11,652,000	8,187.4	5,151.0	5,537.6	5,032.5
1983	20,079	87,401	107,480	10,850,500	7,330.4	4,596.9	4,941.1	4,637.4
1984	19,054	81,639	100,693	10,608,500	7,013.1	4,226.9	4,570.5	4,492.1
1985	18,759	92,108	110,867	11,102,600	7,002.3	4,654.2	4,934.1	4,650.5
1986	18,925	99,301	118,226	11,722,700	7,028.8	5,008.6	5,250.1	4,862.6
1987	19,071	109,572	128,643	12,024,700	7,181.7	5,357.7	5,567.3	4,940.3
1988	18,044	101,788	119,832	12,356,900	6,734.2	4,847.1	5,060.6	5,027.1
1989	19,333	105,842	125,175	12,605,400	7,381.8	4,922.2	5,189.2	5,077.9
1990	19,381	n/a	n/a	12,655,500	7,119.2	n/a	n/a	5,088.5
1991	19,034	108,315	127,349	12,961,100	6,902.0	4,879.4	5,102.9	5,139.7
1992	18,779	114,084	132,863	12,505,900	6,736.6	4,912.8	5,108.3	4,902.7
1993	17,678	110,253	127,931	12,218,800	6,518.2	4,638.1	4,830.6	4,737.6
1994	16,742	109,617	126,359	12,131,900	6,105.5	4,561.1	4,719.3	4,660.0
1995	17,720	112,542	130,262	12,063,900	6,698.4	4,592.1	4,797.3	4,591.3
1996	18,267	115,545	133,812	11,791,300	6,834.1	4,666.4	4,877.6	4,444.8

Notes: Property crimes include burglary, larceny-theft and motor vehicle theft; n/a not available; (1) Metropolitan Statistical Area - see Appendix A for areas included; (2) calculated by the editors using the following formula: (number of crimes in the MSA minus number of crimes in the city); (3) calculated by the editors using the following formula: ((number of crimes in the MSA minus number of crimes in the city) ÷ (population of the MSA minus population of the city)) x 100,000
Source: U.S. Department of Justice, FBI Uniform Crime Reports, 1977 - 1996

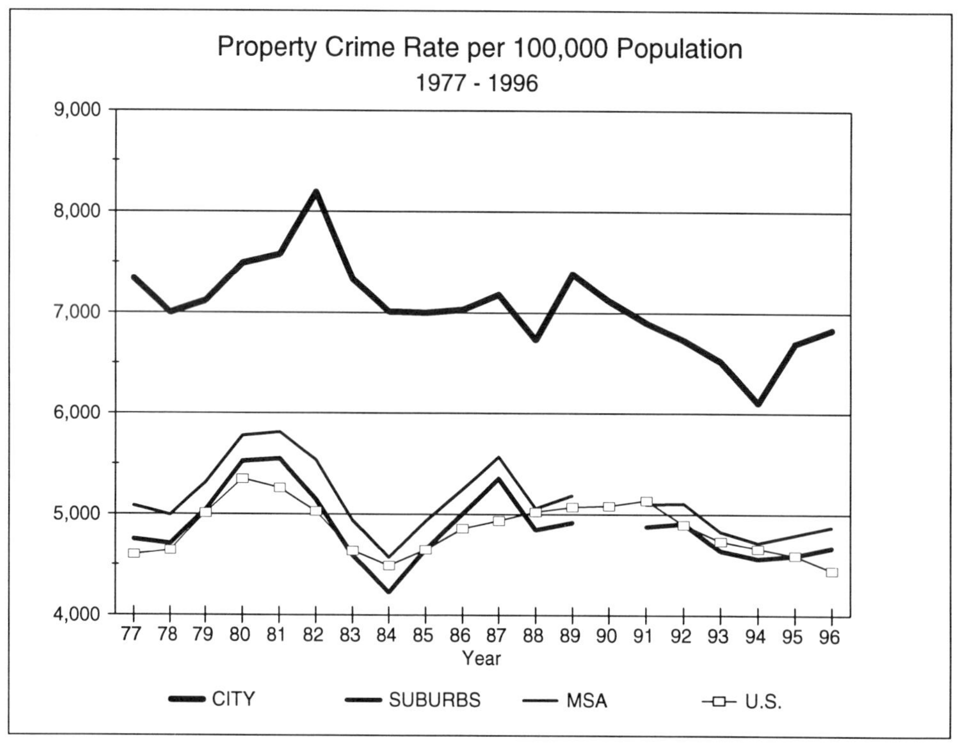

Note: Missing line segments indicate data not available.

Murders and Murder Rates: 1977 - 1996

Year	Number				Rate per 100,000 population			
	City	Suburbs[2]	MSA[1]	U.S.	City	Suburbs[3]	MSA[1]	U.S.
1977	17	58	75	19,120	6.4	3.2	3.6	8.8
1978	15	42	57	19,560	5.7	2.3	2.7	9.0
1979	16	50	66	21,460	6.0	2.7	3.2	9.7
1980	16	55	71	23,040	6.0	3.0	3.4	10.2
1981	13	44	57	22,520	4.8	2.4	2.7	9.8
1982	9	61	70	21,010	3.3	3.3	3.3	9.1
1983	12	33	45	19,310	4.4	1.7	2.1	8.3
1984	15	35	50	18,690	5.5	1.8	2.3	7.9
1985	17	40	57	18,980	6.3	2.0	2.5	7.9
1986	12	65	77	20,610	4.5	3.3	3.4	8.6
1987	12	66	78	20,100	4.5	3.2	3.4	8.3
1988	17	72	89	20,680	6.3	3.4	3.8	8.4
1989	15	69	84	21,500	5.7	3.2	3.5	8.7
1990	18	n/a	n/a	23,440	6.6	n/a	n/a	9.4
1991	12	84	96	24,700	4.4	3.8	3.8	9.8
1992	33	80	113	23,760	11.8	3.4	4.3	9.3
1993	22	94	116	24,530	8.1	4.0	4.4	9.5
1994	29	88	117	23,330	10.6	3.7	4.4	9.0
1995	25	131	156	21,610	9.5	5.3	5.7	8.2
1996	26	97	123	19,650	9.7	3.9	4.5	7.4

Notes: (1) Metropolitan Statistical Area - see Appendix A for areas included; (2) calculated by the editors using the following formula: (number of crimes in the MSA minus number of crimes in the city); (3) calculated by the editors using the following formula: ((number of crimes in the MSA minus number of crimes in the city) ÷ (population of the MSA minus population of the city)) x 100,000; n/a not avail.
Source: U.S. Department of Justice, FBI Uniform Crime Reports, 1977 - 1996

Forcible Rapes and Forcible Rape Rates: 1977 - 1996

Year	Number				Rate per 100,000 population			
	City	Suburbs[2]	MSA[1]	U.S.	City	Suburbs[3]	MSA[1]	U.S.
1977	118	474	592	63,500	44.4	26.0	28.3	29.4
1978	139	484	623	67,610	52.9	26.3	29.6	31.0
1979	125	537	662	76,390	46.5	29.5	31.7	34.7
1980	140	598	738	82,990	52.2	32.5	35.0	36.8
1981	197	602	799	82,500	72.9	32.5	37.6	36.0
1982	216	507	723	78,770	79.1	27.1	33.7	34.0
1983	220	521	741	78,920	80.3	27.4	34.1	33.7
1984	217	603	820	84,230	79.9	31.2	37.2	35.7
1985	233	672	905	88,670	87.0	34.0	40.3	37.1
1986	239	735	974	91,460	88.8	37.1	43.3	37.9
1987	218	840	1,058	91,110	82.1	41.1	45.8	37.4
1988	237	756	993	92,490	88.5	36.0	41.9	37.6
1989	189	770	959	94,500	72.2	35.8	39.8	38.1
1990	269	n/a	n/a	102,560	98.8	n/a	n/a	41.2
1991	286	1,114	1,400	106,590	103.7	50.2	56.1	42.3
1992	237	1,154	1,391	109,060	85.0	49.7	53.5	42.8
1993	242	n/a	n/a	106,010	89.2	n/a	n/a	41.1
1994	269	1,400	1,669	102,220	98.1	58.3	62.3	39.3
1995	233	1,319	1,552	97,470	88.1	53.8	57.2	37.1
1996	234	1,214	1,448	95,770	87.5	49.0	52.8	36.1

Notes: (1) Metropolitan Statistical Area - see Appendix A for areas included; (2) calculated by the editors using the following formula: (number of crimes in the MSA minus number of crimes in the city); (3) calculated by the editors using the following formula: ((number of crimes in the MSA minus number of crimes in the city) ÷ (population of the MSA minus population of the city)) x 100,000; n/a not avail.
Source: U.S. Department of Justice, FBI Uniform Crime Reports, 1977 - 1996

Robberies and Robbery Rates: 1977 - 1996

Year	Number				Rate per 100,000 population			
	City	Suburbs[2]	MSA[1]	U.S.	City	Suburbs[3]	MSA[1]	U.S.
1977	886	2,223	3,109	412,610	333.1	121.9	148.8	190.7
1978	790	2,296	3,086	426,930	300.4	124.8	146.7	195.8
1979	894	2,552	3,446	480,700	332.8	140.2	164.9	218.4
1980	876	2,854	3,730	565,840	326.3	155.1	176.9	251.1
1981	1,061	2,938	3,999	592,910	392.5	158.5	188.3	258.7
1982	846	3,088	3,934	553,130	309.7	164.9	183.3	238.9
1983	681	2,394	3,075	506,570	248.6	125.9	141.4	216.5
1984	666	2,099	2,765	485,010	245.1	108.7	125.5	205.4
1985	645	2,775	3,420	497,870	240.8	140.2	152.2	208.5
1986	794	3,306	4,100	542,780	294.9	166.7	182.1	225.1
1987	746	3,399	4,145	517,700	280.9	166.2	179.4	212.7
1988	787	3,109	3,896	542,970	293.7	148.0	164.5	220.9
1989	856	3,087	3,943	578,330	326.8	143.6	163.5	233.0
1990	780	n/a	n/a	639,270	286.5	n/a	n/a	257.0
1991	850	3,296	4,146	687,730	308.2	148.5	166.1	272.7
1992	835	3,856	4,691	672,480	299.5	166.1	180.4	263.6
1993	954	3,927	4,881	659,870	351.8	165.2	184.3	255.9
1994	872	4,243	5,115	618,950	318.0	176.5	191.0	237.7
1995	930	4,460	5,390	580,510	351.6	182.0	198.5	220.9
1996	875	4,161	5,036	537,050	327.4	168.0	183.6	202.4

Notes: (1) Metropolitan Statistical Area - see Appendix A for areas included; (2) calculated by the editors using the following formula: (number of crimes in the MSA minus number of crimes in the city); (3) calculated by the editors using the following formula: ((number of crimes in the MSA minus number of crimes in the city) ÷ (population of the MSA minus population of the city)) x 100,000; n/a not avail.
Source: U.S. Department of Justice, FBI Uniform Crime Reports, 1977 - 1996

Aggravated Assaults and Aggravated Assault Rates: 1977 - 1996

Year	Number				Rate per 100,000 population			
	City	Suburbs[2]	MSA[1]	U.S.	City	Suburbs[3]	MSA[1]	U.S.
1977	872	1,812	2,684	534,350	327.8	99.4	128.5	247.0
1978	808	1,755	2,563	571,460	307.2	95.4	121.9	262.1
1979	847	2,417	3,264	629,480	315.3	132.7	156.2	286.0
1980	1,000	2,080	3,080	672,650	372.5	113.0	146.1	298.5
1981	1,038	1,953	2,991	663,900	384.0	105.4	140.8	289.7
1982	975	2,018	2,993	669,480	356.9	107.8	139.5	289.2
1983	907	1,844	2,751	653,290	331.1	97.0	126.5	279.2
1984	1,195	2,585	3,780	685,350	439.8	133.8	171.6	290.2
1985	1,200	3,425	4,625	723,250	447.9	173.1	205.8	302.9
1986	1,356	3,707	5,063	834,320	503.6	187.0	224.8	346.1
1987	1,313	3,484	4,797	855,090	494.4	170.4	207.6	351.3
1988	1,427	3,906	5,333	910,090	532.6	186.0	225.2	370.2
1989	1,403	4,035	5,438	951,710	535.7	187.6	225.4	383.4
1990	1,696	n/a	n/a	1,054,860	623.0	n/a	n/a	424.1
1991	1,583	4,504	6,087	1,092,740	574.0	202.9	243.9	433.3
1992	1,514	4,723	6,237	1,126,970	543.1	203.4	239.8	441.8
1993	1,486	4,757	6,243	1,135,610	547.9	200.1	235.7	440.3
1994	1,560	4,833	6,393	1,113,180	568.9	201.1	238.8	427.6
1995	1,348	4,855	6,203	1,099,210	509.6	198.1	228.4	418.3
1996	1,302	4,945	6,247	1,029,810	487.1	199.7	227.7	388.2

Notes: (1) Metropolitan Statistical Area - see Appendix A for areas included; (2) calculated by the editors using the following formula: (number of crimes in the MSA minus number of crimes in the city); (3) calculated by the editors using the following formula: ((number of crimes in the MSA minus number of crimes in the city) ÷ (population of the MSA minus population of the city)) x 100,000; n/a not avail.
Source: U.S. Department of Justice, FBI Uniform Crime Reports, 1977 - 1996

Burglaries and Burglary Rates: 1977 - 1996

Year	Number				Rate per 100,000 population			
	City	Suburbs[2]	MSA[1]	U.S.	City	Suburbs[3]	MSA[1]	U.S.
1977	7,608	23,250	30,858	3,071,500	2,860.2	1,275.3	1,477.1	1,419.8
1978	7,145	23,128	30,273	3,128,300	2,716.7	1,256.8	1,439.4	1,434.6
1979	7,135	23,320	30,455	3,327,700	2,655.9	1,280.7	1,457.5	1,511.9
1980	7,297	27,194	34,491	3,795,200	2,718.3	1,477.9	1,635.8	1,684.1
1981	7,964	28,741	36,705	3,779,700	2,945.9	1,550.8	1,728.4	1,649.5
1982	8,341	26,467	34,808	3,447,100	3,053.2	1,413.4	1,622.2	1,488.8
1983	8,005	23,947	31,952	3,129,900	2,922.5	1,259.5	1,468.9	1,337.7
1984	7,260	21,980	29,240	2,984,400	2,672.1	1,138.0	1,327.2	1,263.7
1985	6,729	23,757	30,486	3,073,300	2,511.8	1,200.4	1,356.8	1,287.3
1986	6,605	23,800	30,405	3,241,400	2,453.1	1,200.4	1,350.2	1,344.6
1987	6,183	26,642	32,825	3,236,200	2,328.4	1,302.7	1,420.6	1,329.6
1988	5,160	22,436	27,596	3,218,100	1,925.8	1,068.4	1,165.4	1,309.2
1989	5,065	22,898	27,963	3,168,200	1,933.9	1,064.9	1,159.2	1,276.3
1990	5,075	n/a	n/a	3,073,900	1,864.2	n/a	n/a	1,235.9
1991	4,583	20,873	25,456	3,157,200	1,661.9	940.3	1,020.0	1,252.0
1992	4,661	22,687	27,348	2,979,900	1,672.0	977.0	1,051.5	1,168.2
1993	4,023	22,182	26,205	2,834,800	1,483.4	933.1	989.5	1,099.2
1994	4,074	20,609	24,683	2,712,800	1,485.7	857.5	921.9	1,042.0
1995	4,272	19,575	23,847	2,593,800	1,614.9	798.7	878.2	987.1
1996	4,127	19,543	23,670	2,501,500	1,544.0	789.3	862.8	943.0

Notes: (1) Metropolitan Statistical Area - see Appendix A for areas included; (2) calculated by the editors using the following formula: (number of crimes in the MSA minus number of crimes in the city); (3) calculated by the editors using the following formula: ((number of crimes in the MSA minus number of crimes in the city) ÷ (population of the MSA minus population of the city)) x 100,000; n/a not avail.
Source: U.S. Department of Justice, FBI Uniform Crime Reports, 1977 - 1996

Larceny-Thefts and Larceny-Theft Rates: 1977 - 1996

Year	Number				Rate per 100,000 population			
	City	Suburbs[2]	MSA[1]	U.S.	City	Suburbs[3]	MSA[1]	U.S.
1977	9,779	55,598	65,377	5,905,700	3,676.3	3,049.5	3,129.3	2,729.9
1978	9,449	56,106	65,555	5,991,000	3,592.8	3,048.9	3,116.9	2,747.4
1979	10,146	60,873	71,019	6,601,000	3,776.6	3,343.2	3,398.9	2,999.1
1980	11,443	67,492	78,935	7,136,900	4,262.7	3,668.0	3,743.7	3,167.0
1981	11,364	67,959	79,323	7,194,400	4,203.5	3,666.9	3,735.2	3,139.7
1982	12,729	64,177	76,906	7,142,500	4,659.4	3,427.2	3,584.1	3,084.8
1983	11,024	58,329	69,353	6,712,800	4,024.6	3,067.8	3,188.3	2,868.9
1984	10,707	54,646	65,353	6,591,900	3,940.9	2,829.3	2,966.4	2,791.3
1985	10,901	61,259	72,160	6,926,400	4,069.1	3,095.4	3,211.5	2,901.2
1986	10,994	67,498	78,492	7,257,200	4,083.2	3,404.5	3,485.6	3,010.3
1987	11,578	74,209	85,787	7,499,900	4,360.0	3,628.6	3,712.6	3,081.3
1988	11,096	69,423	80,519	7,705,900	4,141.1	3,305.9	3,400.4	3,134.9
1989	11,528	72,327	83,855	7,872,400	4,401.6	3,363.6	3,476.3	3,171.3
1990	11,990	n/a	n/a	7,945,700	4,404.3	n/a	n/a	3,194.8
1991	12,124	77,138	89,262	8,142,200	4,396.3	3,474.9	3,576.7	3,228.8
1992	11,732	81,278	93,010	7,915,200	4,208.6	3,500.1	3,576.0	3,103.0
1993	11,329	78,162	89,491	7,820,900	4,177.2	3,288.1	3,379.2	3,032.4
1994	10,642	79,888	90,530	7,879,800	3,881.0	3,324.1	3,381.1	3,026.7
1995	11,219	83,119	94,338	7,997,700	4,241.0	3,391.5	3,474.3	3,043.8
1996	11,504	84,694	96,198	7,894,600	4,303.9	3,420.4	3,506.5	2,975.9

Notes: (1) Metropolitan Statistical Area - see Appendix A for areas included; (2) calculated by the editors using the following formula: (number of crimes in the MSA minus number of crimes in the city); (3) calculated by the editors using the following formula: ((number of crimes in the MSA minus number of crimes in the city) ÷ (population of the MSA minus population of the city)) x 100,000; n/a not avail.
Source: U.S. Department of Justice, FBI Uniform Crime Reports, 1977 - 1996

Motor Vehicle Thefts and Motor Vehicle Theft Rates: 1977 - 1996

Year	Number				Rate per 100,000 population			
	City	Suburbs[2]	MSA[1]	U.S.	City	Suburbs[3]	MSA[1]	U.S.
1977	2,123	7,824	9,947	977,700	798.1	429.1	476.1	451.9
1978	1,816	7,364	9,180	1,004,100	690.5	400.2	436.5	460.5
1979	1,838	7,691	9,529	1,112,800	684.2	422.4	456.0	505.6
1980	1,362	6,992	8,354	1,131,700	507.4	380.0	396.2	502.2
1981	1,162	6,169	7,331	1,087,800	429.8	332.9	345.2	474.7
1982	1,297	5,812	7,109	1,062,400	474.8	310.4	331.3	458.8
1983	1,050	5,125	6,175	1,007,900	383.3	269.5	283.9	430.8
1984	1,087	5,013	6,100	1,032,200	400.1	259.5	276.9	437.1
1985	1,129	7,092	8,221	1,102,900	421.4	358.4	365.9	462.0
1986	1,326	8,003	9,329	1,224,100	492.5	403.7	414.3	507.8
1987	1,310	8,721	10,031	1,288,700	493.3	426.4	434.1	529.4
1988	1,788	9,929	11,717	1,432,900	667.3	472.8	494.8	582.9
1989	2,740	10,617	13,357	1,564,800	1,046.2	493.7	553.7	630.4
1990	2,316	n/a	n/a	1,635,900	850.7	n/a	n/a	657.8
1991	2,327	10,304	12,631	1,661,700	843.8	464.2	506.1	659.0
1992	2,386	10,119	12,505	1,610,800	855.9	435.8	480.8	631.5
1993	2,326	9,909	12,235	1,563,100	857.6	416.9	462.0	606.1
1994	2,026	9,120	11,146	1,539,300	738.8	379.5	416.3	591.3
1995	2,229	9,848	12,077	1,472,400	842.6	401.8	444.8	560.4
1996	2,636	11,308	13,944	1,395,200	986.2	456.7	508.3	525.9

Notes: (1) Metropolitan Statistical Area - see Appendix A for areas included; (2) calculated by the editors using the following formula: (number of crimes in the MSA minus number of crimes in the city); (3) calculated by the editors using the following formula: ((number of crimes in the MSA minus number of crimes in the city) ÷ (population of the MSA minus population of the city)) x 100,000; n/a not avail.
Source: U.S. Department of Justice, FBI Uniform Crime Reports, 1977 - 1996

HATE CRIMES

Criminal Incidents by Bias Motivation

Area	Race	Ethnicity	Religion	Sexual Orientation
Saint Paul	40	0	3	0

Notes: Figures include both violent and property crimes. Law enforcement agencies must have submitted data for at least one quarter of calendar year 1995 to be included in this report, therefore figures shown may not represent complete 12-month totals; n/a not available
Source: U.S. Department of Justice, FBI Uniform Crime Reports, Hate Crime Statistics 1995

LAW ENFORCEMENT

Full-Time Law Enforcement Employees

Jurisdiction	Police Employees			Police Officers per 100,000 population
	Total	Officers	Civilians	
Saint Paul	755	578	177	216.2

Notes: Data as of October 31, 1996
Source: U.S. Department of Justice, FBI Uniform Crime Reports, 1996

CORRECTIONS

Federal Correctional Facilities

Type	Year Opened	Security Level	Sex of Inmates	Rated Capacity	Population on 7/1/95	Number of Staff
None listed						

Notes: Data as of 1995
Source: Bureau of Justice Statistics, Sourcebook of Criminal Justice Statistics Online

City/County/Regional Correctional Facilities

Name	Year Opened	Year Renov.	Rated Capacity	1995 Pop.	Number of COs[1]	Number of Staff	ACA[2] Accred.
Ramsey Co Correctional Facil	1959	1996	316	285	69	100	No

Notes: Data as of April 1996; (1) Correctional Officers; (2) American Correctional Assn. Accreditation
Source: American Correctional Association, 1996-1998 National Jail and Adult Detention Directory

Private Adult Correctional Facilities

Name	Date Opened	Rated Capacity	Present Pop.	Security Level	Facility Construct.	Expans. Plans	ACA[1] Accred.
None listed							

Notes: Data as of December 1996; (1) American Correctional Association Accreditation
Source: University of Florida, Center for Studies in Criminology and Law, Private Adult Correctional Facility Census, 10th Ed., March 15, 1997

Characteristics of Shock Incarceration Programs

Jurisdiction	Year Program Began	Number of Camps	Average Num. of Inmates	Number of Beds	Program Length	Voluntary/ Mandatory
Minnesota	1992	1	51[a]	72 male; 8 female	6 months	Voluntary

Note: Data as of July 1996; (a) Varies
Source: Sourcebook of Criminal Justice Statistics Online

DEATH PENALTY

Minnesota did not have the death penalty as of July 31, 1997.
Source: Death Penalty Information Center Web Site, 9/30/97

LAWS

Statutory Provisions Relating to the Purchase, Ownership and Use of Handguns

Jurisdiction	Instant Background Check	Federal Waiting Period Applies[1]	State Waiting Period (days)	License or Permit to Purchase	Regis- tration	Record of Sale Sent to Police	Concealed Carry Law
Minnesota	No	No	7[a]	Yes[a]	No	Yes	Yes[b]

Note: Data as of 1996; (1) The Federal 5-day waiting period for handgun purchases applies to states that don't have instant background checks, waiting period requirements, or licensing procedures exempting them from the Federal requirement; (a) A handgun transfer or carrying permit, or a 7-day waiting period and handgun transfer report, is required to purchase handguns from a dealer; (b) Restrictively administered discretion by local authorities over permit issuance, or permits are unavailable and carrying is prohibited in most circumstances
Source: Sourcebook of Criminal Justice Statistics Online

Statutory Provisions Relating to Alcohol Use and Driving

Jurisdiction	Drinking Age	Blood Alcohol Concentration Levels as Evidence in State Courts[1]		Open Container Law[1]	Anti- Consump- tion Law[1]	Dram Shop Law[1]
		Illegal per se at 0.10%	Presumption at 0.10%			
Minnesota	21	Yes	No	Yes	Yes	Yes

Note: Data as of January 1, 1997; (1) See Appendix C for an explanation of terms
Source: Sourcebook of Criminal Justice Statistics Online

Statutory Provisions Relating to Curfews

Jurisdiction	Year Enacted	Latest Revision	Age Group(s)	Curfew Provisions
Saint Paul	1960	1987	15 through 17 14 and under	Midnight to 6 am every night 10 pm to 6 am weekday nights 11 pm to 6 am weekend nights

Note: Data as of February 1996
Source: Sourcebook of Criminal Justice Statistics Online

Statutory Provisions Relating to Hate Crimes

Jurisdiction	Bias-Motivated Violence and Intimidation						Institutional Vandalism
	Civil Action	Criminal Penalty					
		Race/ Religion/ Ethnicity	Sexual Orientation	Mental/ Physical Disability	Gender	Age	
Minnesota	No	Yes	Yes	Yes	Yes	No	Yes

Source: Anti-Defamation League, 1997 Hate Crimes Laws

Salt Lake City, Utah

OVERVIEW

The total crime rate for the city increased 17.2% between 1977 and 1996. During that same period, the violent crime rate increased 30.8% and the property crime rate increased 16.3%.

Among violent crimes, the rates for: Murders increased 54.2%; Forcible Rapes increased 25.8%; Robberies increased 14.4%; and Aggravated Assaults increased 48.4%.

Among property crimes, the rates for: Burglaries decreased 45.7%; Larceny-Thefts increased 37.9%; and Motor Vehicle Thefts increased 91.0%.

ANTI-CRIME PROGRAMS

Programs include:

- Victim Advocate Program—uses trained volunteers to provide services for victims of domestic violence and information which may prevent revictimization.
- Mobile Neighborhood Watch Programs—citizens report criminal activity to the police.
- Neighborhood Police Offices—smaller visible police offices within communities are growing in numbers.
- Police Volunteer Program—volunteers receive formal training and will be able to handle telephonic police reports and meetings with citizens along with more "behind the scenes" duties.
- Citizen's Academy—30 hours of training by police about police and their challenges.
- Late Night Basketball—initiated in 1992.
- D.A.R.E. (Drug Abuse Resistance Education)—an educational program offered to school children on the hazards of drug abuse.
- G.R.E.A.T. (Gang Resistance Education and Training)—the goals of which are to reduce gang activity and violence by providing youths with skills and strategies to resist gang involvement or pressures.
- Gun Buy-Back Program.
  Salt Lake City, Police Department, 9/97

CRIME RISK

Your Chances of Becoming a Victim[1]

Area	Any Crime	Violent Crime					Property Crime			
		Any	Murder	Forcible Rape[2]	Robbery	Aggrav. Assault	Any	Burglary	Larceny -Theft	Motor Vehicle Theft
City	1:8	1:120	1:9,009	1:602	1:305	1:244	1:9	1:60	1:12	1:63

Note: (1) Figures have been calculated by dividing the population of the city by the number of crimes reported to the FBI during 1996 and are expressed as odds (eg. 1:20 should be read as 1 in 20). (2) Figures have been calculated by dividing the female population of the city by the number of forcible rapes reported to the FBI during 1996. The female population of the city was estimated by calculating the ratio of females to males reported in the 1990 Census and applying that ratio to 1996 population estimate.
Source: FBI Uniform Crime Reports 1996

CRIME STATISTICS

Total Crimes and Total Crime Rates: 1977 - 1996

Year	Number				Rate per 100,000 population			
	City	Suburbs[2]	MSA[1]	U.S.	City	Suburbs[3]	MSA[1]	U.S.
1977	17,622	31,489	49,111	10,984,500	10,552.1	4,912.8	6,078.4	5,077.6
1978	16,103	35,209	51,312	11,209,000	9,818.9	5,208.0	6,108.2	5,140.3
1979	17,453	41,564	59,017	12,249,500	9,685.9	5,931.6	6,699.6	5,565.5
1980	19,086	48,695	67,781	13,408,300	11,710.3	6,305.2	7,247.1	5,950.0
1981	20,849	47,467	68,316	13,423,800	12,308.8	5,914.1	7,028.4	5,858.2
1982	18,915	44,919	63,834	12,974,400	10,893.9	5,459.7	6,406.7	5,603.6
1983	18,763	43,567	62,330	12,108,600	10,372.5	5,259.7	6,176.1	5,175.0
1984	17,674	40,476	58,150	11,881,800	10,208.2	4,753.5	5,675.2	5,031.3
1985	19,037	46,583	65,620	12,431,400	11,592.7	5,434.5	6,424.6	5,207.1
1986	20,282	47,541	67,823	13,211,900	12,204.7	5,480.7	6,561.7	5,480.4
1987	20,873	50,590	71,463	13,508,700	13,058.8	5,679.5	6,802.2	5,550.0
1988	21,764	50,578	72,342	13,923,100	13,434.2	5,625.1	6,817.3	5,664.2
1989	21,781	51,645	73,426	14,251,400	14,115.6	5,603.8	6,824.6	5,741.0
1990	20,002	53,763	73,765	14,475,600	12,506.3	5,893.2	6,879.6	5,820.3
1991	20,835	53,833	74,668	14,872,900	12,680.1	5,743.5	6,778.1	5,897.8
1992	20,345	54,964	75,309	14,438,200	12,088.2	5,724.8	6,673.9	5,660.2
1993	18,453	51,896	70,349	14,144,800	10,830.5	5,252.2	6,072.6	5,484.4
1994	18,992	54,387	73,379	13,989,500	10,863.3	5,365.9	6,174.6	5,373.5
1995	22,115	64,643	86,758	13,862,700	12,582.1	6,281.1	7,200.3	5,275.9
1996	22,283	64,647	86,930	13,473,600	12,367.1	6,127.4	7,037.6	5,078.9

Notes: (1) Metropolitan Statistical Area - see Appendix A for areas included; (2) calculated by the editors using the following formula: (number of crimes in the MSA minus number of crimes in the city); (3) calculated by the editors using the following formula: ((number of crimes in the MSA minus number of crimes in the city) ÷ (population of the MSA minus population of the city)) x 100,000; n/a not avail.
Source: U.S. Department of Justice, FBI Uniform Crime Reports, 1977 - 1996

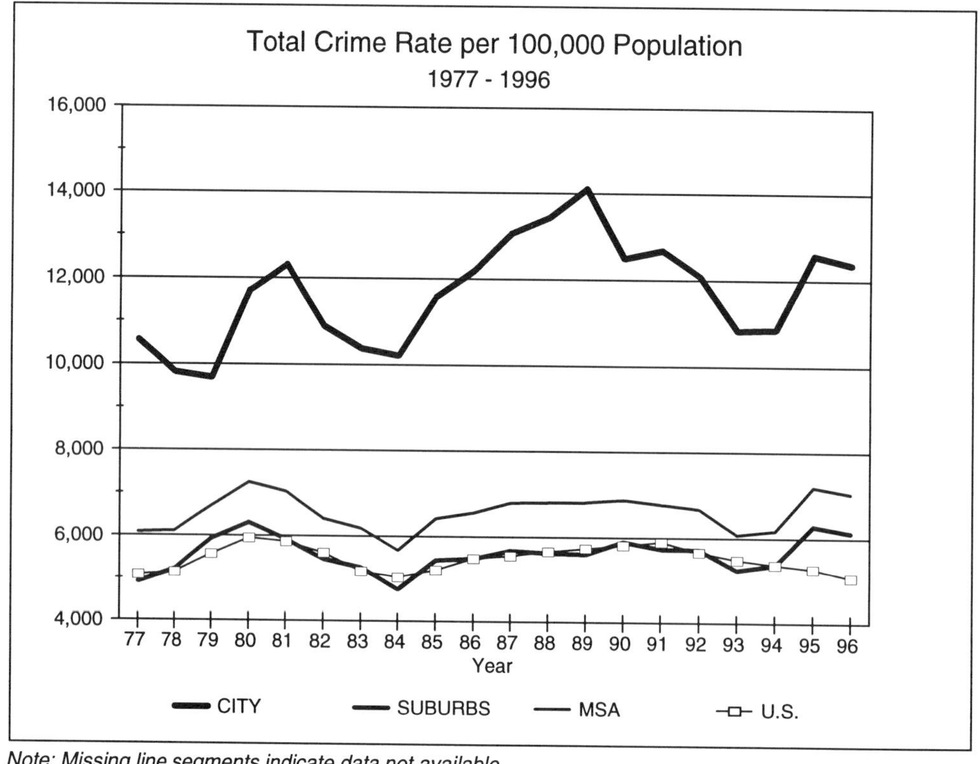

Note: Missing line segments indicate data not available.

Violent Crimes and Violent Crime Rates: 1977 - 1996

Year	Number				Rate per 100,000 population			
	City	Suburbs[2]	MSA[1]	U.S.	City	Suburbs[3]	MSA[1]	U.S.
1977	1,064	1,456	2,520	1,029,580	637.1	227.2	311.9	475.9
1978	1,062	1,865	2,927	1,085,550	647.6	275.9	348.4	497.8
1979	1,119	2,246	3,365	1,208,030	621.0	320.5	382.0	548.9
1980	1,132	2,519	3,651	1,344,520	694.5	326.2	390.4	596.6
1981	1,268	2,371	3,639	1,361,820	748.6	295.4	374.4	594.3
1982	1,279	2,199	3,478	1,322,390	736.6	267.3	349.1	571.1
1983	1,163	1,969	3,132	1,258,090	642.9	237.7	310.3	537.7
1984	1,088	2,126	3,214	1,273,280	628.4	249.7	313.7	539.2
1985	1,083	2,364	3,447	1,328,800	659.5	275.8	337.5	556.6
1986	1,246	2,300	3,546	1,489,170	749.8	265.2	343.1	617.7
1987	1,090	1,970	3,060	1,484,000	681.9	221.2	291.3	609.7
1988	1,036	2,132	3,168	1,566,220	639.5	237.1	298.5	637.2
1989	1,197	2,217	3,414	1,646,040	775.7	240.6	317.3	663.1
1990	1,355	2,661	4,016	1,820,130	847.2	291.7	374.5	731.8
1991	1,319	2,798	4,117	1,911,770	802.7	298.5	373.7	758.1
1992	1,317	2,943	4,260	1,932,270	782.5	306.5	377.5	757.5
1993	1,402	2,977	4,379	1,926,020	822.9	301.3	378.0	746.8
1994	1,320	3,145	4,465	1,857,670	755.0	310.3	375.7	713.6
1995	1,375	3,582	4,957	1,798,790	782.3	348.1	411.4	684.6
1996	1,501	3,706	5,207	1,682,280	833.1	351.3	421.5	634.1

Notes: Violent crimes include murder, forcible rape, robbery and aggravated assault; n/a not available; (1) Metropolitan Statistical Area - see Appendix A for areas included; (2) calculated by the editors using the following formula: (number of crimes in the MSA minus number of crimes in the city); (3) calculated by the editors using the following formula: ((number of crimes in the MSA minus number of crimes in the city) ÷ (population of the MSA minus population of the city)) x 100,000
Source: U.S. Department of Justice, FBI Uniform Crime Reports, 1977 - 1996

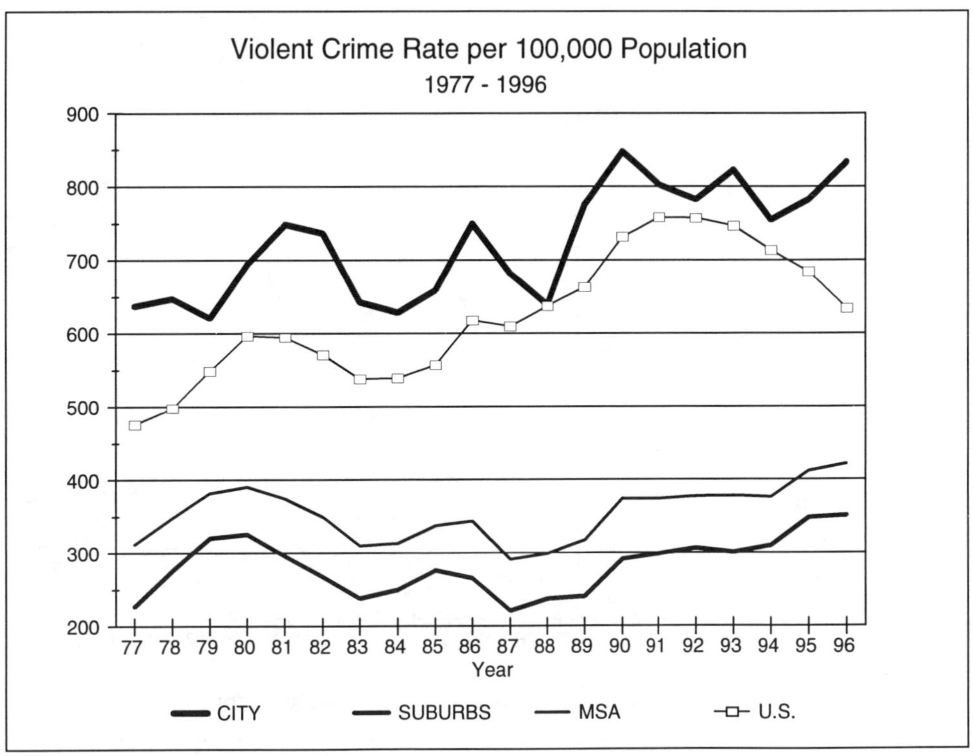

Note: Missing line segments indicate data not available.

Property Crimes and Property Crime Rates: 1977 - 1996

Year	Number				Rate per 100,000 population			
	City	Suburbs[2]	MSA[1]	U.S.	City	Suburbs[3]	MSA[1]	U.S.
1977	16,558	30,033	46,591	9,955,000	9,915.0	4,685.7	5,766.5	4,601.7
1978	15,041	33,344	48,385	10,123,400	9,171.3	4,932.2	5,759.8	4,642.5
1979	16,334	39,318	55,652	11,041,500	9,064.9	5,611.1	6,317.6	5,016.6
1980	17,954	46,176	64,130	12,063,700	11,015.7	5,979.1	6,856.8	5,353.3
1981	19,581	45,096	64,677	12,061,900	11,560.2	5,618.6	6,654.0	5,263.9
1982	17,636	42,720	60,356	11,652,000	10,157.2	5,192.5	6,057.6	5,032.5
1983	17,600	41,598	59,198	10,850,500	9,729.6	5,022.0	5,865.8	4,637.4
1984	16,586	38,350	54,936	10,608,500	9,579.8	4,503.8	5,361.5	4,492.1
1985	17,954	44,219	62,173	11,102,600	10,933.2	5,158.7	6,087.1	4,650.5
1986	19,036	45,241	64,277	11,722,700	11,454.9	5,215.5	6,218.7	4,862.6
1987	19,783	48,620	68,403	12,024,700	12,376.8	5,458.3	6,510.9	4,940.3
1988	20,728	48,446	69,174	12,356,900	12,794.7	5,388.0	6,518.8	5,027.1
1989	20,584	49,428	70,012	12,605,400	13,339.9	5,363.3	6,507.3	5,077.9
1990	18,647	51,102	69,749	12,655,500	11,659.0	5,601.5	6,505.1	5,088.5
1991	19,516	51,035	70,551	12,961,100	11,877.3	5,444.9	6,404.4	5,139.7
1992	19,028	52,021	71,049	12,505,900	11,305.7	5,418.3	6,296.4	4,902.7
1993	17,051	48,919	65,970	12,218,800	10,007.6	4,950.9	5,694.6	4,737.6
1994	17,672	51,242	68,914	12,131,900	10,108.3	5,055.6	5,798.9	4,660.0
1995	20,740	61,061	81,801	12,063,900	11,799.8	5,933.1	6,788.9	4,591.3
1996	20,782	60,941	81,723	11,791,300	11,534.0	5,776.2	6,616.1	4,444.8

Notes: Property crimes include burglary, larceny-theft and motor vehicle theft; n/a not available; (1) Metropolitan Statistical Area - see Appendix A for areas included; (2) calculated by the editors using the following formula: (number of crimes in the MSA minus number of crimes in the city); (3) calculated by the editors using the following formula: ((number of crimes in the MSA minus number of crimes in the city) ÷ (population of the MSA minus population of the city)) x 100,000
Source: U.S. Department of Justice, FBI Uniform Crime Reports, 1977 - 1996

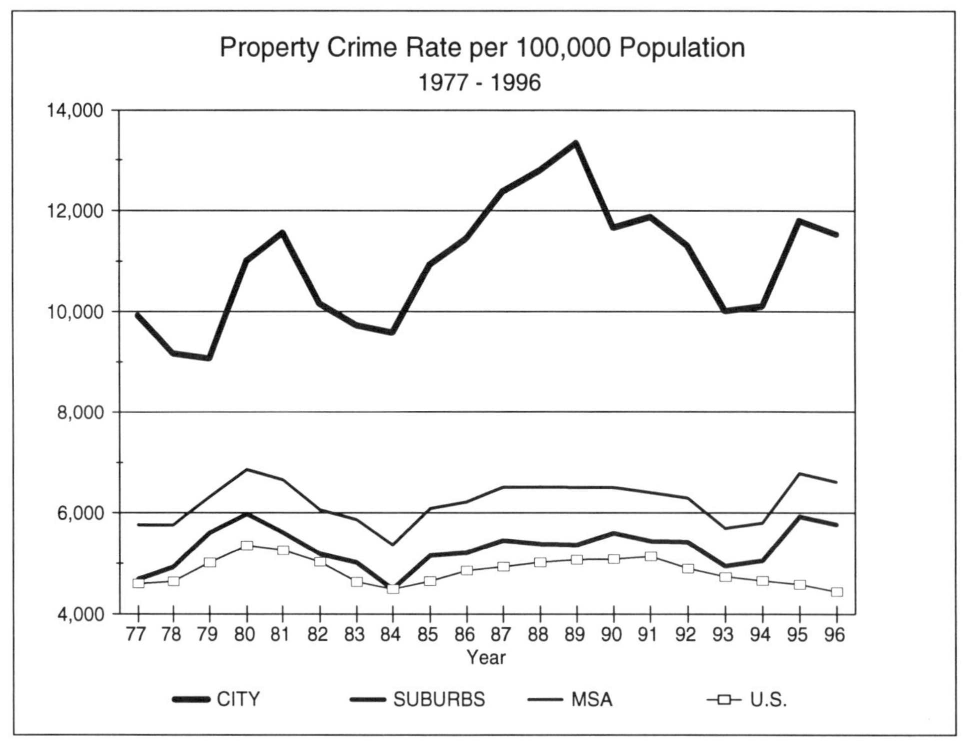

Note: Missing line segments indicate data not available.

Murders and Murder Rates: 1977 - 1996

Year	Number				Rate per 100,000 population			
	City	Suburbs[2]	MSA[1]	U.S.	City	Suburbs[3]	MSA[1]	U.S.
1977	12	27	39	19,120	7.2	4.2	4.8	8.8
1978	21	12	33	19,560	12.8	1.8	3.9	9.0
1979	18	34	52	21,460	10.0	4.9	5.9	9.7
1980	16	28	44	23,040	9.8	3.6	4.7	10.2
1981	14	21	35	22,520	8.3	2.6	3.6	9.8
1982	11	30	41	21,010	6.3	3.6	4.1	9.1
1983	14	28	42	19,310	7.7	3.4	4.2	8.3
1984	8	20	28	18,690	4.6	2.3	2.7	7.9
1985	14	23	37	18,980	8.5	2.7	3.6	7.9
1986	20	21	41	20,610	12.0	2.4	4.0	8.6
1987	13	25	38	20,100	8.1	2.8	3.6	8.3
1988	15	21	36	20,680	9.3	2.3	3.4	8.4
1989	18	19	37	21,500	11.7	2.1	3.4	8.7
1990	25	16	41	23,440	15.6	1.8	3.8	9.4
1991	14	25	39	24,700	8.5	2.7	3.5	9.8
1992	14	26	40	23,760	8.3	2.7	3.5	9.3
1993	19	26	45	24,530	11.2	2.6	3.9	9.5
1994	20	30	50	23,330	11.4	3.0	4.2	9.0
1995	27	22	49	21,610	15.4	2.1	4.1	8.2
1996	20	32	52	19,650	11.1	3.0	4.2	7.4

Notes: (1) Metropolitan Statistical Area - see Appendix A for areas included; (2) calculated by the editors using the following formula: (number of crimes in the MSA minus number of crimes in the city); (3) calculated by the editors using the following formula: ((number of crimes in the MSA minus number of crimes in the city) ÷ (population of the MSA minus population of the city)) x 100,000; n/a not avail.
Source: U.S. Department of Justice, FBI Uniform Crime Reports, 1977 - 1996

Forcible Rapes and Forcible Rape Rates: 1977 - 1996

Year	Number				Rate per 100,000 population			
	City	Suburbs[2]	MSA[1]	U.S.	City	Suburbs[3]	MSA[1]	U.S.
1977	112	105	217	63,500	67.1	16.4	26.9	29.4
1978	131	118	249	67,610	79.9	17.5	29.6	31.0
1979	155	168	323	76,390	86.0	24.0	36.7	34.7
1980	140	206	346	82,990	85.9	26.7	37.0	36.8
1981	137	222	359	82,500	80.9	27.7	36.9	36.0
1982	124	203	327	78,770	71.4	24.7	32.8	34.0
1983	128	193	321	78,920	70.8	23.3	31.8	33.7
1984	98	163	261	84,230	56.6	19.1	25.5	35.7
1985	99	184	283	88,670	60.3	21.5	27.7	37.1
1986	107	220	327	91,460	64.4	25.4	31.6	37.9
1987	94	192	286	91,110	58.8	21.6	27.2	37.4
1988	90	217	307	92,490	55.6	24.1	28.9	37.6
1989	136	217	353	94,500	88.1	23.5	32.8	38.1
1990	167	330	497	102,560	104.4	36.2	46.4	41.2
1991	182	407	589	106,590	110.8	43.4	53.5	42.3
1992	187	429	616	109,060	111.1	44.7	54.6	42.8
1993	204	382	586	106,010	119.7	38.7	50.6	41.1
1994	158	423	581	102,220	90.4	41.7	48.9	39.3
1995	148	472	620	97,470	84.2	45.9	51.5	37.1
1996	152	428	580	95,770	84.4	40.6	47.0	36.1

Notes: (1) Metropolitan Statistical Area - see Appendix A for areas included; (2) calculated by the editors using the following formula: (number of crimes in the MSA minus number of crimes in the city); (3) calculated by the editors using the following formula: ((number of crimes in the MSA minus number of crimes in the city) ÷ (population of the MSA minus population of the city)) x 100,000; n/a not avail.
Source: U.S. Department of Justice, FBI Uniform Crime Reports, 1977 - 1996

Robberies and Robbery Rates: 1977 - 1996

Year	Number				Rate per 100,000 population			
	City	Suburbs[2]	MSA[1]	U.S.	City	Suburbs[3]	MSA[1]	U.S.
1977	479	320	799	412,610	286.8	49.9	98.9	190.7
1978	451	355	806	426,930	275.0	52.5	95.9	195.8
1979	495	484	979	480,700	274.7	69.1	111.1	218.4
1980	528	566	1,094	565,840	324.0	73.3	117.0	251.1
1981	587	597	1,184	592,910	346.6	74.4	121.8	258.7
1982	656	567	1,223	553,130	377.8	68.9	122.7	238.9
1983	523	427	950	506,570	289.1	51.6	94.1	216.5
1984	490	396	886	485,010	283.0	46.5	86.5	205.4
1985	446	410	856	497,870	271.6	47.8	83.8	208.5
1986	506	401	907	542,780	304.5	46.2	87.8	225.1
1987	482	343	825	517,700	301.6	38.5	78.5	212.7
1988	487	371	858	542,970	300.6	41.3	80.9	220.9
1989	484	353	837	578,330	313.7	38.3	77.8	233.0
1990	539	385	924	639,270	337.0	42.2	86.2	257.0
1991	474	429	903	687,730	288.5	45.8	82.0	272.7
1992	470	443	913	672,480	279.3	46.1	80.9	263.6
1993	498	499	997	659,870	292.3	50.5	86.1	255.9
1994	502	597	1,099	618,950	287.1	58.9	92.5	237.7
1995	564	648	1,212	580,510	320.9	63.0	100.6	220.9
1996	591	663	1,254	537,050	328.0	62.8	101.5	202.4

Notes: (1) Metropolitan Statistical Area - see Appendix A for areas included; (2) calculated by the editors using the following formula: (number of crimes in the MSA minus number of crimes in the city); (3) calculated by the editors using the following formula: ((number of crimes in the MSA minus number of crimes in the city) ÷ (population of the MSA minus population of the city)) x 100,000; n/a not avail.
Source: U.S. Department of Justice, FBI Uniform Crime Reports, 1977 - 1996

Aggravated Assaults and Aggravated Assault Rates: 1977 - 1996

Year	Number				Rate per 100,000 population			
	City	Suburbs[2]	MSA[1]	U.S.	City	Suburbs[3]	MSA[1]	U.S.
1977	461	1,004	1,465	534,350	276.0	156.6	181.3	247.0
1978	459	1,380	1,839	571,460	279.9	204.1	218.9	262.1
1979	451	1,560	2,011	629,480	250.3	222.6	228.3	286.0
1980	448	1,719	2,167	672,650	274.9	222.6	231.7	298.5
1981	530	1,531	2,061	663,900	312.9	190.8	212.0	289.7
1982	488	1,399	1,887	669,480	281.1	170.0	189.4	289.2
1983	498	1,321	1,819	653,290	275.3	159.5	180.2	279.2
1984	492	1,547	2,039	685,350	284.2	181.7	199.0	290.2
1985	524	1,747	2,271	723,250	319.1	203.8	222.3	302.9
1986	613	1,658	2,271	834,320	368.9	191.1	219.7	346.1
1987	501	1,410	1,911	855,090	313.4	158.3	181.9	351.3
1988	444	1,523	1,967	910,090	274.1	169.4	185.4	370.2
1989	559	1,628	2,187	951,710	362.3	176.6	203.3	383.4
1990	624	1,930	2,554	1,054,860	390.2	211.6	238.2	424.1
1991	649	1,937	2,586	1,092,740	395.0	206.7	234.7	433.3
1992	646	2,045	2,691	1,126,970	383.8	213.0	238.5	441.8
1993	681	2,070	2,751	1,135,610	399.7	209.5	237.5	440.3
1994	640	2,095	2,735	1,113,180	366.1	206.7	230.1	427.6
1995	636	2,440	3,076	1,099,210	361.8	237.1	255.3	418.3
1996	738	2,583	3,321	1,029,810	409.6	244.8	268.9	388.2

Notes: (1) Metropolitan Statistical Area - see Appendix A for areas included; (2) calculated by the editors using the following formula: (number of crimes in the MSA minus number of crimes in the city); (3) calculated by the editors using the following formula: ((number of crimes in the MSA minus number of crimes in the city) ÷ (population of the MSA minus population of the city)) x 100,000; n/a not avail.
Source: U.S. Department of Justice, FBI Uniform Crime Reports, 1977 - 1996

Burglaries and Burglary Rates: 1977 - 1996

Year	Number				Rate per 100,000 population			
	City	Suburbs[2]	MSA[1]	U.S.	City	Suburbs[3]	MSA[1]	U.S.
1977	5,150	7,406	12,556	3,071,500	3,083.8	1,155.5	1,554.0	1,419.8
1978	4,499	8,415	12,914	3,128,300	2,743.3	1,244.7	1,537.3	1,434.6
1979	4,624	8,660	13,284	3,327,700	2,566.2	1,235.9	1,508.0	1,511.9
1980	5,174	10,907	16,081	3,795,200	3,174.5	1,412.3	1,719.4	1,684.1
1981	5,574	10,385	15,959	3,779,700	3,290.8	1,293.9	1,641.9	1,649.5
1982	4,516	9,545	14,061	3,447,100	2,600.9	1,160.2	1,411.2	1,488.8
1983	4,214	8,871	13,085	3,129,900	2,329.6	1,071.0	1,296.6	1,337.7
1984	3,689	7,204	10,893	2,984,400	2,130.7	846.0	1,063.1	1,263.7
1985	4,002	8,218	12,220	3,073,300	2,437.0	958.7	1,196.4	1,287.3
1986	3,714	7,840	11,554	3,241,400	2,234.9	903.8	1,117.8	1,344.6
1987	3,997	8,372	12,369	3,236,200	2,500.6	939.9	1,177.3	1,329.6
1988	3,594	8,017	11,611	3,218,100	2,218.5	891.6	1,094.2	1,309.2
1989	3,854	7,932	11,786	3,168,200	2,497.7	860.7	1,095.4	1,276.3
1990	3,501	8,160	11,661	3,073,900	2,189.0	894.5	1,087.5	1,235.9
1991	3,460	7,841	11,301	3,157,200	2,105.7	836.6	1,025.9	1,252.0
1992	3,394	8,440	11,834	2,979,900	2,016.6	879.1	1,048.7	1,168.2
1993	2,823	7,736	10,559	2,834,800	1,656.9	782.9	911.5	1,099.2
1994	3,025	7,854	10,879	2,712,800	1,730.3	774.9	915.4	1,042.0
1995	2,950	8,147	11,097	2,593,800	1,678.4	791.6	921.0	987.1
1996	3,015	8,972	11,987	2,501,500	1,673.3	850.4	970.4	943.0

Notes: (1) Metropolitan Statistical Area - see Appendix A for areas included; (2) calculated by the editors using the following formula: (number of crimes in the MSA minus number of crimes in the city); (3) calculated by the editors using the following formula: ((number of crimes in the MSA minus number of crimes in the city) ÷ (population of the MSA minus population of the city)) x 100,000; n/a not avail.
Source: U.S. Department of Justice, FBI Uniform Crime Reports, 1977 - 1996

Larceny-Thefts and Larceny-Theft Rates: 1977 - 1996

Year	Number				Rate per 100,000 population			
	City	Suburbs[2]	MSA[1]	U.S.	City	Suburbs[3]	MSA[1]	U.S.
1977	10,016	20,558	30,574	5,905,700	5,997.6	3,207.4	3,784.1	2,729.9
1978	9,130	22,792	31,922	5,991,000	5,567.1	3,371.3	3,800.0	2,747.4
1979	10,330	28,384	38,714	6,601,000	5,732.9	4,050.7	4,394.8	2,999.1
1980	11,437	32,766	44,203	7,136,900	7,017.2	4,242.7	4,726.2	3,167.0
1981	12,818	32,393	45,211	7,194,400	7,567.5	4,035.9	4,651.4	3,139.7
1982	12,119	31,137	43,256	7,142,500	6,979.8	3,784.6	4,341.4	3,084.8
1983	12,356	30,750	43,106	6,712,800	6,830.6	3,712.4	4,271.3	2,868.9
1984	11,797	29,308	41,105	6,591,900	6,813.7	3,441.9	4,011.7	2,791.3
1985	12,881	34,034	46,915	6,926,400	7,843.9	3,970.5	4,593.3	2,901.2
1986	14,320	35,593	49,913	7,257,200	8,617.1	4,103.3	4,829.0	3,010.3
1987	14,863	38,488	53,351	7,499,900	9,298.7	4,320.8	5,078.2	3,081.3
1988	16,202	38,588	54,790	7,705,900	10,000.9	4,291.6	5,163.3	3,134.9
1989	15,510	39,484	54,994	7,872,400	10,051.6	4,284.3	5,111.4	3,171.3
1990	13,949	40,915	54,864	7,945,700	8,721.6	4,484.9	5,116.8	3,194.8
1991	14,602	41,278	55,880	8,142,200	8,886.7	4,404.0	5,072.6	3,228.8
1992	14,266	41,615	55,881	7,915,200	8,476.3	4,334.4	4,952.2	3,103.0
1993	12,831	39,174	52,005	7,820,900	7,530.8	3,964.7	4,489.1	3,032.4
1994	12,931	40,725	53,656	7,879,800	7,396.5	4,018.0	4,515.0	3,026.7
1995	15,467	49,086	64,553	7,997,700	8,799.8	4,769.5	5,357.4	3,043.8
1996	14,898	47,731	62,629	7,894,600	8,268.4	4,524.1	5,070.3	2,975.9

Notes: (1) Metropolitan Statistical Area - see Appendix A for areas included; (2) calculated by the editors using the following formula: (number of crimes in the MSA minus number of crimes in the city); (3) calculated by the editors using the following formula: ((number of crimes in the MSA minus number of crimes in the city) ÷ (population of the MSA minus population of the city)) x 100,000; n/a not avail.
Source: U.S. Department of Justice, FBI Uniform Crime Reports, 1977 - 1996

Motor Vehicle Thefts and Motor Vehicle Theft Rates: 1977 - 1996

Year	Number				Rate per 100,000 population			
	City	Suburbs[2]	MSA[1]	U.S.	City	Suburbs[3]	MSA[1]	U.S.
1977	1,392	2,069	3,461	977,700	833.5	322.8	428.4	451.9
1978	1,412	2,137	3,549	1,004,100	861.0	316.1	422.5	460.5
1979	1,380	2,274	3,654	1,112,800	765.9	324.5	414.8	505.6
1980	1,343	2,503	3,846	1,131,700	824.0	324.1	411.2	502.2
1981	1,189	2,318	3,507	1,087,800	702.0	288.8	360.8	474.7
1982	1,001	2,038	3,039	1,062,400	576.5	247.7	305.0	458.8
1983	1,030	1,977	3,007	1,007,900	569.4	238.7	298.0	430.8
1984	1,100	1,838	2,938	1,032,200	635.3	215.9	286.7	437.1
1985	1,071	1,967	3,038	1,102,900	652.2	229.5	297.4	462.0
1986	1,002	1,808	2,810	1,224,100	603.0	208.4	271.9	507.8
1987	923	1,760	2,683	1,288,700	577.5	197.6	255.4	529.4
1988	932	1,841	2,773	1,432,900	575.3	204.7	261.3	582.9
1989	1,220	2,012	3,232	1,564,800	790.6	218.3	300.4	630.4
1990	1,197	2,027	3,224	1,635,900	748.4	222.2	300.7	657.8
1991	1,454	1,916	3,370	1,661,700	884.9	204.4	305.9	659.0
1992	1,368	1,966	3,334	1,610,800	812.8	204.8	295.5	631.5
1993	1,397	2,009	3,406	1,563,100	819.9	203.3	294.0	606.1
1994	1,716	2,663	4,379	1,539,300	981.5	262.7	368.5	591.3
1995	2,323	3,828	6,151	1,472,400	1,321.7	372.0	510.5	560.4
1996	2,869	4,238	7,107	1,395,200	1,592.3	401.7	575.4	525.9

Notes: (1) Metropolitan Statistical Area - see Appendix A for areas included; (2) calculated by the editors using the following formula: (number of crimes in the MSA minus number of crimes in the city); (3) calculated by the editors using the following formula: ((number of crimes in the MSA minus number of crimes in the city) ÷ (population of the MSA minus population of the city)) x 100,000; n/a not avail.
Source: U.S. Department of Justice, FBI Uniform Crime Reports, 1977 - 1996

HATE CRIMES

Criminal Incidents by Bias Motivation

Area	Race	Ethnicity	Religion	Sexual Orientation
Salt Lake City	11	4	2	5

Notes: Figures include both violent and property crimes. Law enforcement agencies must have submitted data for at least one quarter of calendar year 1995 to be included in this report, therefore figures shown may not represent complete 12-month totals; n/a not available
Source: U.S. Department of Justice, FBI Uniform Crime Reports, Hate Crime Statistics 1995

LAW ENFORCEMENT

Full-Time Law Enforcement Employees

Jurisdiction	Police Employees			Police Officers per 100,000 population
	Total	Officers	Civilians	
Salt Lake City	542	385	157	213.7

Notes: Data as of October 31, 1996
Source: U.S. Department of Justice, FBI Uniform Crime Reports, 1996

CORRECTIONS

Federal Correctional Facilities

Type	Year Opened	Security Level	Sex of Inmates	Rated Capacity	Population on 7/1/95	Number of Staff
None listed						

Notes: Data as of 1995
Source: Bureau of Justice Statistics, Sourcebook of Criminal Justice Statistics Online

City/County/Regional Correctional Facilities

Name	Year Opened	Year Renov.	Rated Capacity	1995 Pop.	Number of COs[1]	Number of Staff	ACA[2] Accred.
Salt Lake County Jail	1966	1990	575	n/a	n/a	n/a	No
Salt Lake County Oxbow Jail Facility	1991	1996	552	297	68	82	No

Notes: Data as of April 1996; (1) Correctional Officers; (2) American Correctional Assn. Accreditation
Source: American Correctional Association, 1996-1998 National Jail and Adult Detention Directory

Private Adult Correctional Facilities

Name	Date Opened	Rated Capacity	Present Pop.	Security Level	Facility Construct.	Expans. Plans	ACA[1] Accred.
None listed							

Notes: Data as of December 1996; (1) American Correctional Association Accreditation
Source: University of Florida, Center for Studies in Criminology and Law, Private Adult Correctional Facility Census, 10th Ed., March 15, 1997

Characteristics of Shock Incarceration Programs

Jurisdiction	Year Program Began	Number of Camps	Average Num. of Inmates	Number of Beds	Program Length	Voluntary/ Mandatory
Utah did not have a shock incarceration program as of July 1996						

Source: Sourcebook of Criminal Justice Statistics Online

DEATH PENALTY

Death Penalty Statistics

State	Prisoners Executed		Prisoners Under Sentence of Death					Avg. No. of Years on Death Row[4]
	1930-1995	1996[1]	Total[2]	White[3]	Black[3]	Hisp.	Women	
Utah	17	1	10	8	2	2	0	7.6

Notes: Data as of 12/31/95 unless otherwise noted; (1) Data as of 7/31/97; (2) Includes persons of other races; (3) Includes people of Hispanic origin; (4) Covers prisoners sentenced 1974 through 1995
Source: Bureau of Justice Statistics, Capital Punishment 1995 (released 12/96); Death Penalty Information Center Web Site, 9/30/97

Capital Offenses and Methods of Execution

Capital Offenses in Utah	Minimum Age for Imposition of Death Penalty	Mentally Retarded Excluded	Methods of Execution[1]
Aggravated murder; aggravated assault by a prisoner serving a life sentence if serious bodily injury is intentionally caused (76-5-202, Utah Code annotated).	None	No	Lethal injection; firing squad

Notes: Data as of 12/31/95 unless otherwise noted; (1) Data as of 7/31/97
Source: Bureau of Justice Statistics, Capital Punishment 1995 (released 12/96); Death Penalty Information Center Web Site, 9/30/97

LAWS

Statutory Provisions Relating to the Purchase, Ownership and Use of Handguns

Jurisdiction	Instant Background Check	Federal Waiting Period Applies[1]	State Waiting Period (days)	License or Permit to Purchase	Regis- tration	Record of Sale Sent to Police	Concealed Carry Law
Utah	Yes	No	No	No	No	No	Yes[a]

Note: Data as of 1996; (1) The Federal 5-day waiting period for handgun purchases applies to states that don't have instant background checks, waiting period requirements, or licensing procedures exempting them from the Federal requirement; (a) "Shall issue" permit system, liberally administered discretion by local authorities over permit issuance, or no permit required
Source: Sourcebook of Criminal Justice Statistics Online

Statutory Provisions Relating to Alcohol Use and Driving

Jurisdiction	Drinking Age	Blood Alcohol Concentration Levels as Evidence in State Courts[1]		Open Container Law[1]	Anti- Consump- tion Law[1]	Dram Shop Law[1]
		Illegal per se at 0.10%	Presumption at 0.10%			
Utah	21	(a)	No	Yes	Yes	Yes[b]

Note: Data as of January 1, 1997; (1) See Appendix C for an explanation of terms; (a) 0.08%; (b) Utah has a statute that places a monetary limit on the amount of damages that can be awarded in dram shop liability actions
Source: Sourcebook of Criminal Justice Statistics Online

Statutory Provisions Relating to Curfews

Jurisdiction	Year Enacted	Latest Revision	Age Group(s)	Curfew Provisions
Salt Lake City	1994	-	16 and 17 15 and under	1 am to 5 am every night 11 pm to 5 am every night

Note: Data as of February 1996
Source: Sourcebook of Criminal Justice Statistics Online

Statutory Provisions Relating to Hate Crimes

Jurisdiction	Bias-Motivated Violence and Intimidation						Institutional Vandalism
		Criminal Penalty					
	Civil Action	Race/ Religion/ Ethnicity	Sexual Orientation	Mental/ Physical Disability	Gender	Age	
Utah	Yes	Yes	Yes	No	No	No	No

Source: Anti-Defamation League, 1997 Hate Crimes Laws

San Antonio, Texas

OVERVIEW

The total crime rate for the city increased 23.3% between 1977 and 1996. During that same period, the violent crime rate decreased 2.0% and the property crime rate increased 25.2%.

Among violent crimes, the rates for: Murders decreased 37.5%; Forcible Rapes increased 81.4%; Robberies increased 25.0%; and Aggravated Assaults decreased 32.2%.

Among property crimes, the rates for: Burglaries decreased 44.4%; Larceny-Thefts increased 65.3%; and Motor Vehicle Thefts increased 72.9%.

ANTI-CRIME PROGRAMS

Some of the numerous Police Department programs include:

- Crime Stoppers—provides information via the media and manned phones to receive information in solving crimes.
- D.A.R.E. (Drug Abuse Resistance Education)—uniformed officers instruct 5th graders about drugs and gangs.
- Crime Prevention Unit—provides Neighborhood Watch programs, self-defense information, and anti-crime surveys for businesses and homes.
- C.I.O. (Crisis Intervention Officers)—officers, located at substations, aid in resolving neighbor disputes.
- Downtown Foot/Bicycle Patrol—uniformed officers on foot and on bicycles patrol downtown area.
- Storefront Community Services Office—uniformed officers head an office located in a house, shopping center or business to allow for direct contact with the neighborhood.
- Weed and Seed-Volunteers provide 1,700 hours of community service in helping to rid neighborhoods of drug dealers. They receive weekly stipends and an educational incentive of $4,725.00 when completing service.
- Citizens Police Academy—designed to educate citizens about the police department and to develop a better understanding of police officers and the jobs they perform.
  San Antonio Police Department, 8/97

The city instituted a program which the National League of Cities (1993) considers among those which are innovative for combatting crime and violence:

- Family Assistance Crisis Team (FACT) which provides crisis intervention, information, shelter and referrals to victims. who come in or call police. The program combines the efforts of the police, courts and community. *Exemplary Programs in Criminal Justice, National League of Cities, 1994*

CRIME RISK

Your Chances of Becoming a Victim[1]

Area	Any Crime	Violent Crime					Property Crime			
		Any	Murder	Forcible Rape[2]	Robbery	Aggrav. Assault	Any	Burglary	Larceny -Theft	Motor Vehicle Theft
City	1:12	1:215	1:8,731	1:831	1:435	1:624	1:12	1:75	1:17	1:116

Note: (1) Figures have been calculated by dividing the population of the city by the number of crimes reported to the FBI during 1996 and are expressed as odds (eg. 1:20 should be read as 1 in 20).
(2) Figures have been calculated by dividing the female population of the city by the number of forcible rapes reported to the FBI during 1996. The female population of the city was estimated by calculating the ratio of females to males reported in the 1990 Census and applying that ratio to 1996 population estimate.
Source: FBI Uniform Crime Reports 1996

CRIME STATISTICS

Total Crimes and Total Crime Rates: 1977 - 1996

Year	Number				Rate per 100,000 population			
	City	Suburbs[2]	MSA[1]	U.S.	City	Suburbs[3]	MSA[1]	U.S.
1977	55,215	7,479	62,694	10,984,500	6,962.8	3,837.4	6,346.2	5,077.6
1978	52,526	8,250	60,776	11,209,000	6,582.2	3,683.8	5,947.1	5,140.3
1979	54,981	8,771	63,752	12,249,500	6,631.1	3,682.7	5,973.2	5,565.5
1980	57,873	10,742	68,615	13,408,300	7,343.8	3,806.6	6,411.1	5,950.0
1981	62,035	11,213	73,248	13,423,800	7,559.8	3,815.9	6,572.6	5,858.2
1982	66,405	11,376	77,781	12,974,400	7,814.3	3,738.4	6,739.6	5,603.6
1983	70,398	12,869	83,267	12,108,600	8,050.2	4,109.7	7,011.2	5,175.0
1984	75,867	13,976	89,843	11,881,800	8,843.6	4,243.4	7,567.5	5,031.3
1985	83,591	16,401	99,992	12,431,400	9,687.5	4,633.5	8,217.3	5,207.1
1986	100,209	18,743	118,952	13,211,900	11,396.0	5,195.4	9,592.2	5,480.4
1987	118,948	20,638	139,586	13,508,700	12,926.1	5,678.1	10,873.9	5,550.0
1988	116,773	21,840	138,613	13,923,100	12,479.4	5,893.6	10,611.1	5,664.2
1989	120,768	20,745	141,513	14,251,400	12,716.6	5,381.1	10,598.6	5,741.0
1990	116,774	19,683	136,457	14,475,600	12,476.7	5,375.4	10,479.8	5,820.3
1991	117,486	21,526	139,012	14,872,900	12,290.6	5,756.1	10,453.0	5,897.8
1992	109,134	21,512	130,646	14,438,200	11,218.3	5,323.3	9,488.2	5,660.2
1993	97,671	21,127	118,798	14,144,800	9,911.2	5,026.9	8,450.9	5,484.4
1994	87,679	19,446	107,125	13,989,500	8,768.8	4,492.3	7,476.8	5,373.5
1995	79,931	18,143	98,074	13,862,700	7,993.9	3,906.3	6,697.4	5,275.9
1996	87,710	18,213	105,923	13,473,600	8,586.6	3,838.6	7,080.7	5,078.9

Notes: (1) Metropolitan Statistical Area - see Appendix A for areas included; (2) calculated by the editors using the following formula: (number of crimes in the MSA minus number of crimes in the city); (3) calculated by the editors using the following formula: ((number of crimes in the MSA minus number of crimes in the city) ÷ (population of the MSA minus population of the city)) x 100,000; n/a not avail.
Source: U.S. Department of Justice, FBI Uniform Crime Reports, 1977 - 1996

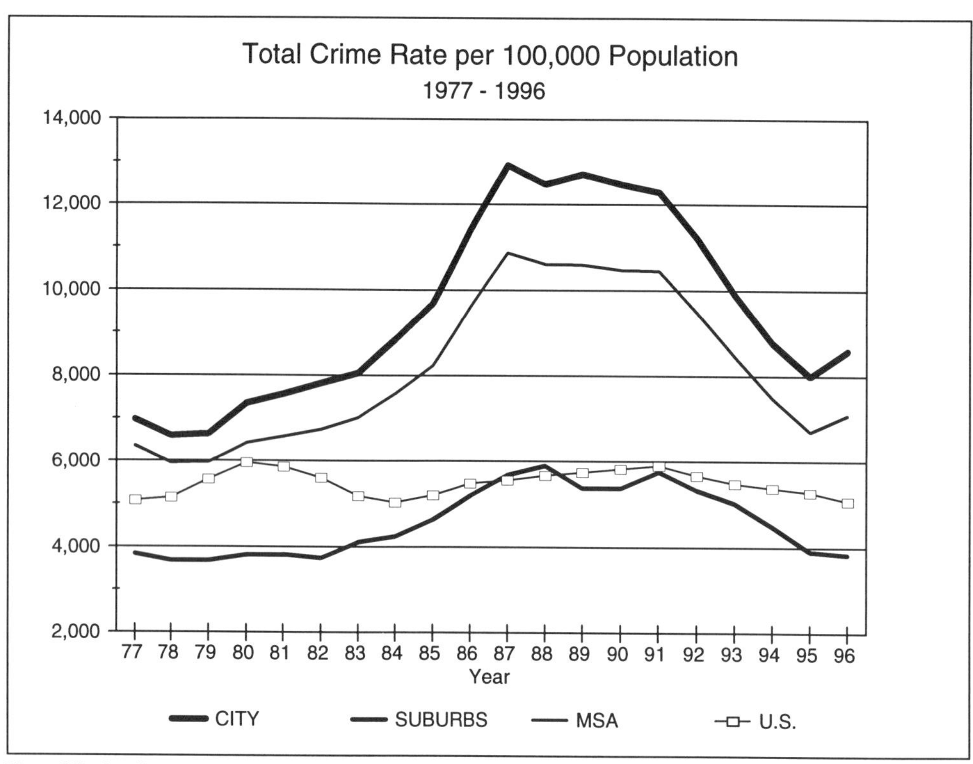

Note: Missing line segments indicate data not available.

Violent Crimes and Violent Crime Rates: 1977 - 1996

Year	Number				Rate per 100,000 population			
	City	Suburbs[2]	MSA[1]	U.S.	City	Suburbs[3]	MSA[1]	U.S.
1977	3,755	530	4,285	1,029,580	473.5	271.9	433.7	475.9
1978	3,446	537	3,983	1,085,550	431.8	239.8	389.7	497.8
1979	4,088	675	4,763	1,208,030	493.0	283.4	446.3	548.9
1980	4,265	741	5,006	1,344,520	541.2	262.6	467.7	596.6
1981	4,651	712	5,363	1,361,820	566.8	242.3	481.2	594.3
1982	5,905	803	6,708	1,322,390	694.9	263.9	581.2	571.1
1983	5,327	861	6,188	1,258,090	609.2	275.0	521.0	537.7
1984	5,388	955	6,343	1,273,280	628.1	290.0	534.3	539.2
1985	5,393	1,226	6,619	1,328,800	625.0	346.4	543.9	556.6
1986	6,237	1,190	7,427	1,489,170	709.3	329.9	598.9	617.7
1987	6,092	1,312	7,404	1,484,000	662.0	361.0	576.8	609.7
1988	5,273	1,322	6,595	1,566,220	563.5	356.7	504.9	637.2
1989	5,253	1,578	6,831	1,646,040	553.1	409.3	511.6	663.1
1990	5,730	1,435	7,165	1,820,130	612.2	391.9	550.3	731.8
1991	7,573	1,899	9,472	1,911,770	792.2	507.8	712.2	758.1
1992	7,131	1,863	8,994	1,932,270	733.0	461.0	653.2	757.5
1993	6,725	2,126	8,851	1,926,020	682.4	505.9	629.6	746.8
1994	6,471	1,748	8,219	1,857,670	647.2	403.8	573.6	713.6
1995	5,178	1,914	7,092	1,798,790	517.9	412.1	484.3	684.6
1996	4,741	1,665	6,406	1,682,280	464.1	350.9	428.2	634.1

Notes: Violent crimes include murder, forcible rape, robbery and aggravated assault; n/a not available; (1) Metropolitan Statistical Area - see Appendix A for areas included; (2) calculated by the editors using the following formula: (number of crimes in the MSA minus number of crimes in the city); (3) calculated by the editors using the following formula: ((number of crimes in the MSA minus number of crimes in the city) ÷ (population of the MSA minus population of the city)) x 100,000
Source: U.S. Department of Justice, FBI Uniform Crime Reports, 1977 - 1996

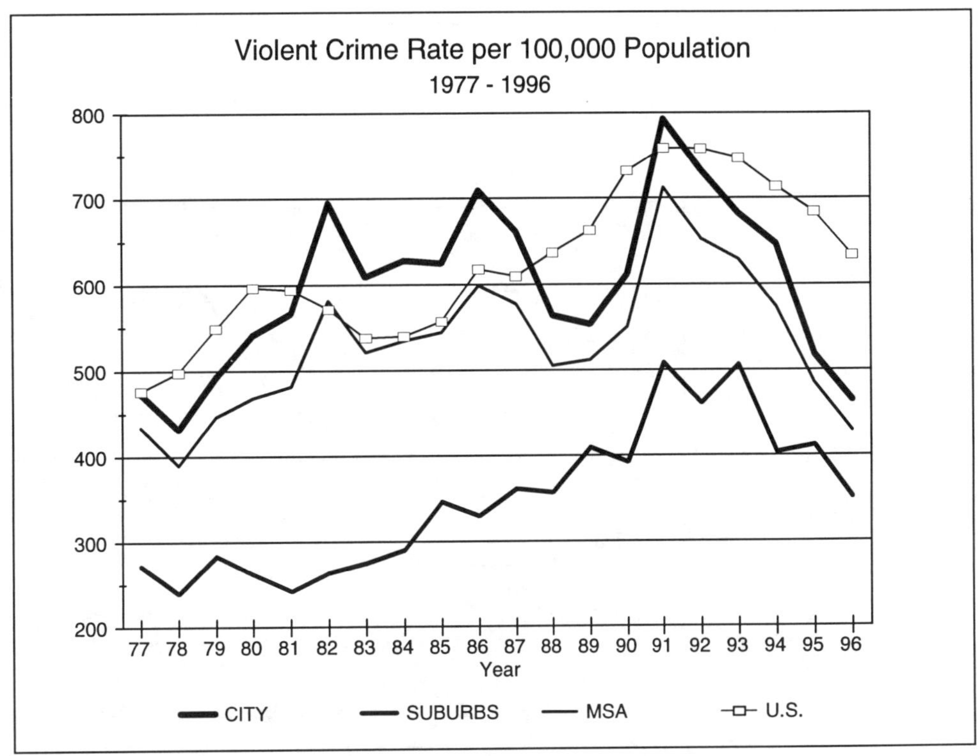

Note: Missing line segments indicate data not available.

Property Crimes and Property Crime Rates: 1977 - 1996

Year	Number				Rate per 100,000 population			
	City	Suburbs[2]	MSA[1]	U.S.	City	Suburbs[3]	MSA[1]	U.S.
1977	51,460	6,949	58,409	9,955,000	6,489.3	3,565.4	5,912.4	4,601.7
1978	49,080	7,713	56,793	10,123,400	6,150.4	3,444.0	5,557.3	4,642.5
1979	50,893	8,096	58,989	11,041,500	6,138.1	3,399.3	5,526.9	5,016.6
1980	53,608	10,001	63,609	12,063,700	6,802.6	3,544.0	5,943.4	5,353.3
1981	57,384	10,501	67,885	12,061,900	6,993.0	3,573.6	6,091.4	5,263.9
1982	60,500	10,573	71,073	11,652,000	7,119.4	3,474.5	6,158.3	5,032.5
1983	65,071	12,008	77,079	10,850,500	7,441.1	3,834.7	6,490.2	4,637.4
1984	70,479	13,021	83,500	10,608,500	8,215.6	3,953.5	7,033.2	4,492.1
1985	78,198	15,175	93,373	11,102,600	9,062.5	4,287.1	7,673.4	4,650.5
1986	93,972	17,553	111,525	11,722,700	10,686.7	4,865.5	8,993.3	4,862.6
1987	112,856	19,326	132,182	12,024,700	12,264.1	5,317.1	10,297.1	4,940.3
1988	111,500	20,518	132,018	12,356,900	11,915.8	5,536.8	10,106.2	5,027.1
1989	115,515	19,167	134,682	12,605,400	12,163.4	4,971.8	10,087.0	5,077.9
1990	111,044	18,248	129,292	12,655,500	11,864.5	4,983.5	9,929.5	5,088.5
1991	109,913	19,627	129,540	12,961,100	11,498.3	5,248.3	9,740.8	5,139.7
1992	102,003	19,649	121,652	12,505,900	10,485.2	4,862.3	8,835.0	4,902.7
1993	90,946	19,001	109,947	12,218,800	9,228.8	4,521.0	7,821.3	4,737.6
1994	81,208	17,698	98,906	12,131,900	8,121.6	4,088.5	6,903.1	4,660.0
1995	74,753	16,229	90,982	12,063,900	7,476.0	3,494.2	6,213.1	4,591.3
1996	82,969	16,548	99,517	11,791,300	8,122.5	3,487.7	6,652.5	4,444.8

Notes: Property crimes include burglary, larceny-theft and motor vehicle theft; n/a not available; (1) Metropolitan Statistical Area - see Appendix A for areas included; (2) calculated by the editors using the following formula: (number of crimes in the MSA minus number of crimes in the city); (3) calculated by the editors using the following formula: ((number of crimes in the MSA minus number of crimes in the city) ÷ (population of the MSA minus population of the city)) x 100,000
Source: U.S. Department of Justice, FBI Uniform Crime Reports, 1977 - 1996

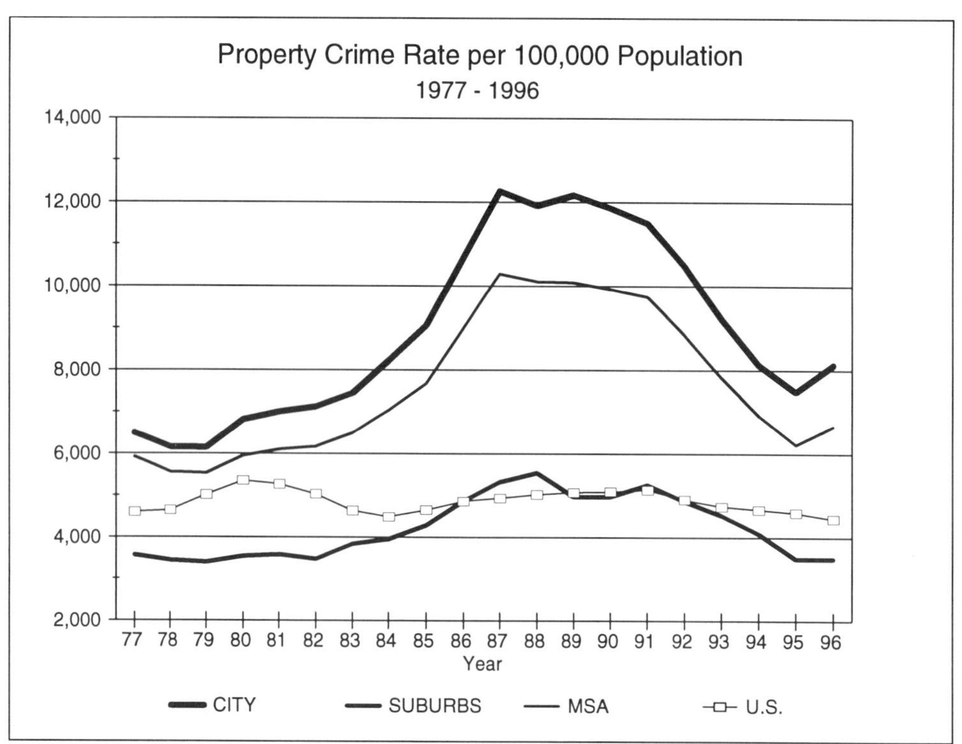

Note: Missing line segments indicate data not available.

Murders and Murder Rates: 1977 - 1996

Year	Number				Rate per 100,000 population			
	City	Suburbs[2]	MSA[1]	U.S.	City	Suburbs[3]	MSA[1]	U.S.
1977	146	20	166	19,120	18.4	10.3	16.8	8.8
1978	136	16	152	19,560	17.0	7.1	14.9	9.0
1979	171	20	191	21,460	20.6	8.4	17.9	9.7
1980	164	23	187	23,040	20.8	8.2	17.5	10.2
1981	185	24	209	22,520	22.5	8.2	18.8	9.8
1982	190	23	213	21,010	22.4	7.6	18.5	9.1
1983	165	15	180	19,310	18.9	4.8	15.2	8.3
1984	160	26	186	18,690	18.7	7.9	15.7	7.9
1985	180	28	208	18,980	20.9	7.9	17.1	7.9
1986	162	34	196	20,610	18.4	9.4	15.8	8.6
1987	174	21	195	20,100	18.9	5.8	15.2	8.3
1988	143	25	168	20,680	15.3	6.7	12.9	8.4
1989	168	18	186	21,500	17.7	4.7	13.9	8.7
1990	208	25	233	23,440	22.2	6.8	17.9	9.4
1991	208	30	238	24,700	21.8	8.0	17.9	9.8
1992	219	35	254	23,760	22.5	8.7	18.4	9.3
1993	220	41	261	24,530	22.3	9.8	18.6	9.5
1994	194	32	226	23,330	19.4	7.4	15.8	9.0
1995	142	17	159	21,610	14.2	3.7	10.9	8.2
1996	117	23	140	19,650	11.5	4.8	9.4	7.4

Notes: (1) Metropolitan Statistical Area - see Appendix A for areas included; (2) calculated by the editors using the following formula: (number of crimes in the MSA minus number of crimes in the city); (3) calculated by the editors using the following formula: ((number of crimes in the MSA minus number of crimes in the city) ÷ (population of the MSA minus population of the city)) x 100,000; n/a not avail.
Source: U.S. Department of Justice, FBI Uniform Crime Reports, 1977 - 1996

Forcible Rapes and Forcible Rape Rates: 1977 - 1996

Year	Number				Rate per 100,000 population			
	City	Suburbs[2]	MSA[1]	U.S.	City	Suburbs[3]	MSA[1]	U.S.
1977	273	47	320	63,500	34.4	24.1	32.4	29.4
1978	304	66	370	67,610	38.1	29.5	36.2	31.0
1979	367	65	432	76,390	44.3	27.3	40.5	34.7
1980	362	63	425	82,990	45.9	22.3	39.7	36.8
1981	376	73	449	82,500	45.8	24.8	40.3	36.0
1982	400	78	478	78,770	47.1	25.6	41.4	34.0
1983	519	95	614	78,920	59.3	30.3	51.7	33.7
1984	745	84	829	84,230	86.8	25.5	69.8	35.7
1985	824	124	948	88,670	95.5	35.0	77.9	37.1
1986	805	117	922	91,460	91.5	32.4	74.3	37.9
1987	849	93	942	91,110	92.3	25.6	73.4	37.4
1988	535	161	696	92,490	57.2	43.4	53.3	37.6
1989	477	100	577	94,500	50.2	25.9	43.2	38.1
1990	430	104	534	102,560	45.9	28.4	41.0	41.2
1991	698	91	789	106,590	73.0	24.3	59.3	42.3
1992	616	116	732	109,060	63.3	28.7	53.2	42.8
1993	553	134	687	106,010	56.1	31.9	48.9	41.1
1994	565	164	729	102,220	56.5	37.9	50.9	39.3
1995	658	137	795	97,470	65.8	29.5	54.3	37.1
1996	637	127	764	95,770	62.4	26.8	51.1	36.1

Notes: (1) Metropolitan Statistical Area - see Appendix A for areas included; (2) calculated by the editors using the following formula: (number of crimes in the MSA minus number of crimes in the city); (3) calculated by the editors using the following formula: ((number of crimes in the MSA minus number of crimes in the city) ÷ (population of the MSA minus population of the city)) x 100,000; n/a not avail.
Source: U.S. Department of Justice, FBI Uniform Crime Reports, 1977 - 1996

Robberies and Robbery Rates: 1977 - 1996

Year	Number				Rate per 100,000 population			
	City	Suburbs[2]	MSA[1]	U.S.	City	Suburbs[3]	MSA[1]	U.S.
1977	1,460	122	1,582	412,610	184.1	62.6	160.1	190.7
1978	1,438	131	1,569	426,930	180.2	58.5	153.5	195.8
1979	1,689	163	1,852	480,700	203.7	68.4	173.5	218.4
1980	1,742	171	1,913	565,840	221.1	60.6	178.7	251.1
1981	1,835	141	1,976	592,910	223.6	48.0	177.3	258.7
1982	2,195	199	2,394	553,130	258.3	65.4	207.4	238.9
1983	2,403	167	2,570	506,570	274.8	53.3	216.4	216.5
1984	2,657	179	2,836	485,010	309.7	54.3	238.9	205.4
1985	2,683	193	2,876	497,870	310.9	54.5	236.3	208.5
1986	3,262	230	3,492	542,780	371.0	63.8	281.6	225.1
1987	3,253	208	3,461	517,700	353.5	57.2	269.6	212.7
1988	2,859	229	3,088	542,970	305.5	61.8	236.4	220.9
1989	2,710	253	2,963	578,330	285.4	65.6	221.9	233.0
1990	2,864	230	3,094	639,270	306.0	62.8	237.6	257.0
1991	3,778	295	4,073	687,730	395.2	78.9	306.3	272.7
1992	3,485	294	3,779	672,480	358.2	72.8	274.4	263.6
1993	2,979	295	3,274	659,870	302.3	70.2	232.9	255.9
1994	2,781	232	3,013	618,950	278.1	53.6	210.3	237.7
1995	2,345	197	2,542	580,510	234.5	42.4	173.6	220.9
1996	2,350	205	2,555	537,050	230.1	43.2	170.8	202.4

Notes: (1) Metropolitan Statistical Area - see Appendix A for areas included; (2) calculated by the editors using the following formula: (number of crimes in the MSA minus number of crimes in the city); (3) calculated by the editors using the following formula: ((number of crimes in the MSA minus number of crimes in the city) ÷ (population of the MSA minus population of the city)) x 100,000; n/a not avail.
Source: U.S. Department of Justice, FBI Uniform Crime Reports, 1977 - 1996

Aggravated Assaults and Aggravated Assault Rates: 1977 - 1996

Year	Number				Rate per 100,000 population			
	City	Suburbs[2]	MSA[1]	U.S.	City	Suburbs[3]	MSA[1]	U.S.
1977	1,876	341	2,217	534,350	236.6	175.0	224.4	247.0
1978	1,568	324	1,892	571,460	196.5	144.7	185.1	262.1
1979	1,861	427	2,288	629,480	224.4	179.3	214.4	286.0
1980	1,997	484	2,481	672,650	253.4	171.5	231.8	298.5
1981	2,255	474	2,729	663,900	274.8	161.3	244.9	289.7
1982	3,120	503	3,623	669,480	367.1	165.3	313.9	289.2
1983	2,240	584	2,824	653,290	256.2	186.5	237.8	279.2
1984	1,826	666	2,492	685,350	212.9	202.2	209.9	290.2
1985	1,706	881	2,587	723,250	197.7	248.9	212.6	302.9
1986	2,008	809	2,817	834,320	228.4	224.2	227.2	346.1
1987	1,816	990	2,806	855,090	197.3	272.4	218.6	351.3
1988	1,736	907	2,643	910,090	185.5	244.8	202.3	370.2
1989	1,898	1,207	3,105	951,710	199.9	313.1	232.5	383.4
1990	2,228	1,076	3,304	1,054,860	238.1	293.9	253.7	424.1
1991	2,889	1,483	4,372	1,092,740	302.2	396.6	328.8	433.3
1992	2,811	1,418	4,229	1,126,970	289.0	350.9	307.1	441.8
1993	2,973	1,656	4,629	1,135,610	301.7	394.0	329.3	440.3
1994	2,931	1,320	4,251	1,113,180	293.1	304.9	296.7	427.6
1995	2,033	1,563	3,596	1,099,210	203.3	336.5	245.6	418.3
1996	1,637	1,310	2,947	1,029,810	160.3	276.1	197.0	388.2

Notes: (1) Metropolitan Statistical Area - see Appendix A for areas included; (2) calculated by the editors using the following formula: (number of crimes in the MSA minus number of crimes in the city); (3) calculated by the editors using the following formula: ((number of crimes in the MSA minus number of crimes in the city) ÷ (population of the MSA minus population of the city)) x 100,000; n/a not avail.
Source: U.S. Department of Justice, FBI Uniform Crime Reports, 1977 - 1996

Burglaries and Burglary Rates: 1977 - 1996

Year	Number				Rate per 100,000 population			
	City	Suburbs[2]	MSA[1]	U.S.	City	Suburbs[3]	MSA[1]	U.S.
1977	19,097	2,006	21,103	3,071,500	2,408.2	1,029.2	2,136.1	1,419.8
1978	16,795	2,567	19,362	3,128,300	2,104.6	1,146.2	1,894.6	1,434.6
1979	16,502	2,602	19,104	3,327,700	1,990.3	1,092.5	1,789.9	1,511.9
1980	17,776	3,709	21,485	3,795,200	2,255.7	1,314.3	2,007.5	1,684.1
1981	20,080	4,002	24,082	3,779,700	2,447.0	1,361.9	2,160.9	1,649.5
1982	20,034	3,601	23,635	3,447,100	2,357.5	1,183.4	2,047.9	1,488.8
1983	22,268	3,827	26,095	3,129,900	2,546.4	1,222.1	2,197.2	1,337.7
1984	23,648	4,009	27,657	2,984,400	2,756.6	1,217.2	2,329.5	1,263.7
1985	24,531	4,426	28,957	3,073,300	2,842.9	1,250.4	2,379.7	1,287.3
1986	29,194	5,273	34,467	3,241,400	3,320.0	1,461.6	2,779.4	1,344.6
1987	33,041	6,075	39,116	3,236,200	3,590.6	1,671.4	3,047.2	1,329.6
1988	27,673	5,858	33,531	3,218,100	2,957.4	1,580.8	2,566.9	1,309.2
1989	28,467	5,379	33,846	3,168,200	2,997.5	1,395.3	2,534.9	1,276.3
1990	26,015	5,733	31,748	3,073,900	2,779.6	1,565.7	2,438.2	1,235.9
1991	24,941	5,652	30,593	3,157,200	2,609.2	1,511.4	2,300.4	1,252.0
1992	21,967	5,066	27,033	2,979,900	2,258.1	1,253.6	1,963.3	1,168.2
1993	17,866	4,208	22,074	2,834,800	1,813.0	1,001.2	1,570.3	1,099.2
1994	16,422	4,035	20,457	2,712,800	1,642.4	932.2	1,427.8	1,042.0
1995	13,961	3,305	17,266	2,593,800	1,396.2	711.6	1,179.1	987.1
1996	13,685	3,576	17,261	2,501,500	1,339.7	753.7	1,153.9	943.0

Notes: (1) Metropolitan Statistical Area - see Appendix A for areas included; (2) calculated by the editors using the following formula: (number of crimes in the MSA minus number of crimes in the city); (3) calculated by the editors using the following formula: ((number of crimes in the MSA minus number of crimes in the city) ÷ (population of the MSA minus population of the city)) x 100,000; n/a not avail.
Source: U.S. Department of Justice, FBI Uniform Crime Reports, 1977 - 1996

Larceny-Thefts and Larceny-Theft Rates: 1977 - 1996

Year	Number				Rate per 100,000 population			
	City	Suburbs[2]	MSA[1]	U.S.	City	Suburbs[3]	MSA[1]	U.S.
1977	28,415	4,530	32,945	5,905,700	3,583.2	2,324.3	3,334.9	2,729.9
1978	28,610	4,779	33,389	5,991,000	3,585.2	2,133.9	3,267.2	2,747.4
1979	29,746	5,026	34,772	6,601,000	3,587.6	2,110.3	3,257.9	2,999.1
1980	31,228	5,749	36,977	7,136,900	3,962.7	2,037.2	3,455.0	3,167.0
1981	32,411	5,946	38,357	7,194,400	3,949.7	2,023.5	3,441.8	3,139.7
1982	35,070	6,326	41,396	7,142,500	4,126.9	2,078.8	3,586.9	3,084.8
1983	37,067	7,375	44,442	6,712,800	4,238.7	2,355.2	3,742.1	2,868.9
1984	39,894	8,112	48,006	6,591,900	4,650.4	2,463.0	4,043.5	2,791.3
1985	46,163	9,715	55,878	6,926,400	5,349.9	2,744.6	4,592.0	2,901.2
1986	56,648	11,185	67,833	7,257,200	6,442.2	3,100.4	5,470.0	3,010.3
1987	66,198	11,677	77,875	7,499,900	7,193.8	3,212.7	6,066.5	3,081.3
1988	70,626	12,730	83,356	7,705,900	7,547.7	3,435.2	6,381.1	3,134.9
1989	71,785	11,689	83,474	7,872,400	7,558.8	3,032.0	6,251.8	3,171.3
1990	70,150	10,692	80,842	7,945,700	7,495.2	2,920.0	6,208.6	3,194.8
1991	70,559	12,093	82,652	8,142,200	7,381.4	3,233.7	6,215.0	3,228.8
1992	65,314	12,834	78,148	7,915,200	6,713.9	3,175.8	5,675.5	3,103.0
1993	61,284	13,190	74,474	7,820,900	6,218.8	3,138.4	5,297.9	3,032.4
1994	54,910	12,401	67,311	7,879,800	5,491.5	2,864.8	4,698.0	3,026.7
1995	52,370	11,861	64,231	7,997,700	5,237.5	2,553.7	4,386.3	3,043.8
1996	60,488	12,030	72,518	7,894,600	5,921.6	2,535.5	4,847.7	2,975.9

Notes: (1) Metropolitan Statistical Area - see Appendix A for areas included; (2) calculated by the editors using the following formula: (number of crimes in the MSA minus number of crimes in the city); (3) calculated by the editors using the following formula: ((number of crimes in the MSA minus number of crimes in the city) ÷ (population of the MSA minus population of the city)) x 100,000; n/a not avail.
Source: U.S. Department of Justice, FBI Uniform Crime Reports, 1977 - 1996

Motor Vehicle Thefts and Motor Vehicle Theft Rates: 1977 - 1996

Year	Number				Rate per 100,000 population			
	City	Suburbs[2]	MSA[1]	U.S.	City	Suburbs[3]	MSA[1]	U.S.
1977	3,948	413	4,361	977,700	497.9	211.9	441.4	451.9
1978	3,675	367	4,042	1,004,100	460.5	163.9	395.5	460.5
1979	4,645	468	5,113	1,112,800	560.2	196.5	479.1	505.6
1980	4,604	543	5,147	1,131,700	584.2	192.4	480.9	502.2
1981	4,893	553	5,446	1,087,800	596.3	188.2	488.7	474.7
1982	5,396	646	6,042	1,062,400	635.0	212.3	523.5	458.8
1983	5,736	806	6,542	1,007,900	655.9	257.4	550.8	430.8
1984	6,937	900	7,837	1,032,200	808.6	273.3	660.1	437.1
1985	7,504	1,034	8,538	1,102,900	869.6	292.1	701.7	462.0
1986	8,130	1,095	9,225	1,224,100	924.6	303.5	743.9	507.8
1987	13,617	1,574	15,191	1,288,700	1,479.8	433.1	1,183.4	529.4
1988	13,201	1,930	15,131	1,432,900	1,410.8	520.8	1,158.3	582.9
1989	15,263	2,099	17,362	1,564,800	1,607.2	544.5	1,300.3	630.4
1990	14,879	1,823	16,702	1,635,900	1,589.8	497.9	1,282.7	657.8
1991	14,413	1,882	16,295	1,661,700	1,507.8	503.3	1,225.3	659.0
1992	14,722	1,749	16,471	1,610,800	1,513.3	432.8	1,196.2	631.5
1993	11,796	1,603	13,399	1,563,100	1,197.0	381.4	953.2	606.1
1994	9,876	1,262	11,138	1,539,300	987.7	291.5	777.4	591.3
1995	8,422	1,063	9,485	1,472,400	842.3	228.9	647.7	560.4
1996	8,796	942	9,738	1,395,200	861.1	198.5	651.0	525.9

Notes: (1) Metropolitan Statistical Area - see Appendix A for areas included; (2) calculated by the editors using the following formula: (number of crimes in the MSA minus number of crimes in the city); (3) calculated by the editors using the following formula: ((number of crimes in the MSA minus number of crimes in the city) ÷ (population of the MSA minus population of the city)) x 100,000; n/a not avail.
Source: U.S. Department of Justice, FBI Uniform Crime Reports, 1977 - 1996

HATE CRIMES

Criminal Incidents by Bias Motivation

Area	Race	Ethnicity	Religion	Sexual Orientation
San Antonio	2	2	1	0

Notes: Figures include both violent and property crimes. Law enforcement agencies must have submitted data for at least one quarter of calendar year 1995 to be included in this report, therefore figures shown may not represent complete 12-month totals; n/a not available
Source: U.S. Department of Justice, FBI Uniform Crime Reports, Hate Crime Statistics 1995

ILLEGAL DRUGS

Drug Use by Adult Arrestees

Sex	Percent Testing Positive by Urinalysis (%)				
	Any Drug[1]	Cocaine	Marijuana	Opiates	Multiple Drugs
Male	57	28	39	10	21
Female	44	23	19	13	20

Notes: The catchment area is the entire county; (1) Includes cocaine, opiates, marijuana, methadone, phencyclidine (PCP), benzodiazepines, methaqualone, propoxyphene, barbiturates & amphetamines
Source: National Institute of Justice, 1996 Drug Use Forecasting, Annual Report on Adult and Juvenile Arrestees (released June 1997)

LAW ENFORCEMENT

Full-Time Law Enforcement Employees

Jurisdiction	Police Employees			Police Officers per 100,000 population
	Total	Officers	Civilians	
San Antonio	2,304	1,868	436	182.9

Notes: Data as of October 31, 1996
Source: U.S. Department of Justice, FBI Uniform Crime Reports, 1996

Number of Police Officers by Race

Race	Police Officers 1983		Police Officers 1992		Index of Representation[1]		
	Number	Pct.	Number	Pct.	1983	1992	% Chg.
Black	54	4.6	90	5.6	n/a	0.80	n/a
Hispanic[2]	384	33.0	583	36.3	n/a	0.65	n/a

Notes: (1) The index of representation is calculated by dividing the percent of black/hispanic police officers by the percent of corresponding blacks/hispanics in the local population. An index approaching 1.0 indicates that a city is closer to achieving a representation of police officers equal to their proportion in the local population; (2) Hispanic officers can be of any race ; n/a not available; Data for 1983 is based on 1980-81 information from the Police Executive Research Forum, Survey of Operational and Administrative Practices 1981
Source: Bureau of Justice Statistics, Sourcebook of Criminal Justice Statistics, 1994

CORRECTIONS

Federal Correctional Facilities

Type	Year Opened	Security Level	Sex of Inmates	Rated Capacity	Population on 7/1/95	Number of Staff
None listed						

Notes: Data as of 1995
Source: Bureau of Justice Statistics, Sourcebook of Criminal Justice Statistics Online

City/County/Regional Correctional Facilities

Name	Year Opened	Year Renov.	Rated Capacity	1995 Pop.	Number of COs[1]	Number of Staff	ACA[2] Accred.
Bexar Co Adult Det Ctr	1988	1993	2,992	3,131	860	918	No

Notes: Data as of April 1996; (1) Correctional Officers; (2) American Correctional Assn. Accreditation
Source: American Correctional Association, 1996-1998 National Jail and Adult Detention Directory

Private Adult Correctional Facilities

Name	Date Opened	Rated Capacity	Present Pop.	Security Level	Facility Construct.	Expans. Plans	ACA[1] Accred.
Central Texas Parole Violator Facility	1/89	623	540	All levels	Take-over	None	In prog.

Notes: Data as of December 1996; (1) American Correctional Association Accreditation
Source: University of Florida, Center for Studies in Criminology and Law, Private Adult Correctional Facility Census, 10th Ed., March 15, 1997

Characteristics of Shock Incarceration Programs

Jurisdiction	Year Program Began	Number of Camps	Average Num. of Inmates	Number of Beds	Program Length	Voluntary/ Mandatory
Texas	1989	2	250	500 male; 20 female	75 to 90 days	Mandatory

Note: Data as of July 1996;
Source: Sourcebook of Criminal Justice Statistics Online

INMATES AND HIV/AIDS

HIV Testing Policies for Inmates

Jurisdiction	All Inmates at Some Time	All Convicted Inmates at Admission	Random Samples While in Custody	High-risk Groups	Upon Inmate Request	Upon Court Order	Upon Involvement in Incident
Bexar Co.[1]	No	No	No	No	Yes	Yes	Yes

Notes: (1) All facilities reported following the same testing policy or authorities reported the policy to be jurisdiction-wide
Source: HIV in Prisons and Jails, 1993 (released August 1995)

Inmates Known to be Positive for HIV

Jurisdiction	Number of Jail Inmates in Facilities Providing Data	Type of HIV Infection/AIDS Cases: Total	Asymptomatic	Symptomatic	Confirmed AIDS	HIV/AIDS Cases as a Percent of Tot. Custody Pop.
Bexar Co.[1]	3,740	8	0	0	0	0.2

Note: (1) Detail does not add to total.
Source: HIV in Prisons and Jails, 1993 (released August, 1995)

DEATH PENALTY

Death Penalty Statistics

State	Prisoners Executed		Prisoners Under Sentence of Death					Avg. No. of Years on Death Row[4]
	1930-1995	1996[1]	Total[2]	White[3]	Black[3]	Hisp.	Women	
Texas	401	3	404	241	158	68	6	6.5

Notes: Data as of 12/31/95 unless otherwise noted; (1) Data as of 7/31/97; (2) Includes persons of other races; (3) Includes people of Hispanic origin; (4) Covers prisoners sentenced 1974 through 1995
Source: Bureau of Justice Statistics, Capital Punishment 1995 (released 12/96); Death Penalty Information Center Web Site, 9/30/97

Capital Offenses and Methods of Execution

Capital Offenses in Texas	Minimum Age for Imposition of Death Penalty	Mentally Retarded Excluded	Methods of Execution[1]
Criminal homicide with 1 of 8 aggravating circumstances.	17	No	Lethal injection

Notes: Data as of 12/31/95 unless otherwise noted; (1) Data as of 7/31/97
Source: Bureau of Justice Statistics, Capital Punishment 1995 (released 12/96); Death Penalty Information Center Web Site, 9/30/97

LAWS

Statutory Provisions Relating to the Purchase, Ownership and Use of Handguns

Jurisdiction	Instant Background Check	Federal Waiting Period Applies[1]	State Waiting Period (days)	License or Permit to Purchase	Regis-tration	Record of Sale Sent to Police	Concealed Carry Law
Texas	No	Yes[a]	No	No	No	No	Yes[b]

Note: Data as of 1996; (1) The Federal 5-day waiting period for handgun purchases applies to states that don't have instant background checks, waiting period requirements, or licensing procedures exempting them from the Federal requirement; (a) The Federal waiting period does not apply to a person holding a valid permit or license to carry a firearm, issued within 5 years of proposed purchase; (b) "Shall issue" permit system, liberally administered discretion by local authorities over permit issuance, or no permit required
Source: Sourcebook of Criminal Justice Statistics Online

Statutory Provisions Relating to Alcohol Use and Driving

Jurisdiction	Drinking Age	Blood Alcohol Concentration Levels as Evidence in State Courts[1]		Open Container Law[1]	Anti-Consump-tion Law[1]	Dram Shop Law[1]
		Illegal per se at 0.10%	Presumption at 0.10%			
Texas	21	Yes	No	No	Yes[a]	Yes[b]

Note: Data as of January 1, 1997; (1) See Appendix C for an explanation of terms; (a) Applies to drivers only; (b) Statutory law has limited dram shop actions
Source: Sourcebook of Criminal Justice Statistics Online

Statutory Provisions Relating to Curfews

Jurisdiction	Year Enacted	Latest Revision	Age Group(s)	Curfew Provisions
San Antonio	1991	1994	16 and under	Midnight to 6 am every night 9 am to 2:30 pm school days

Note: Data as of February 1996
Source: Sourcebook of Criminal Justice Statistics Online

Statutory Provisions Relating to Hate Crimes

Jurisdiction	Bias-Motivated Violence and Intimidation						Institutional Vandalism
		Criminal Penalty					
	Civil Action	Race/ Religion/ Ethnicity	Sexual Orientation	Mental/ Physical Disability	Gender	Age	
Texas	No	No	No	No	No	No	Yes

Source: Anti-Defamation League, 1997 Hate Crimes Laws

San Diego, California

OVERVIEW

The total crime rate for the city decreased 35.6% between 1977 and 1996. During that same period, the violent crime rate increased 57.4% and the property crime rate decreased 42.3%.

Among violent crimes, the rates for: Murders increased 7.9%; Forcible Rapes decreased 15.5%; Robberies decreased 17.3%; and Aggravated Assaults increased 189.6%.

Among property crimes, the rates for: Burglaries decreased 68.7%; Larceny-Thefts decreased 39.5%; and Motor Vehicle Thefts increased 20.5%.

ANTI-CRIME PROGRAMS

Programs include:

- Neighborhood Watch-The Next Generation—focus is on training community coordinators and block captains.
- Safe Streets NOW—a small claims court remedy for neighborhood nuisances.
- San Diego Traffic Offenders Program (STOP Team)—addresses the suspended, revoked and unlicensed drivers in an effort to reduce their involvement in felony hit-and-run, fatal, injury and DUI collisions.
- Daytime Loitering Ordinance—restricts juveniles from loitering, wandering or standing idle in any public or unsupervised place between the hours of 8:30 AM and 1:30 PM on any school day.
- Gang Unit's Violent Crime Task Force—focuses its efforts on hard core gang members. *San Diego Police Department, 7/95*

The San Diego Police Department gang database will be hooked into CAL/GANG, a statewide automated network of databases that will identify and track gang members. The central gang database is in the California Department of Justice and the entire program will be fully operational in early 1998. *Governing, 7/97*

CRIME RISK

Your Chances of Becoming a Victim[1]

Area	Any Crime	Violent Crime					Property Crime			
		Any	Murder	Forcible Rape[2]	Robbery	Aggrav. Assault	Any	Burglary	Larceny -Theft	Motor Vehicle Theft
City	1:19	1:115	1:14,605	1:1,554	1:390	1:174	1:23	1:136	1:37	1:105

Note: (1) Figures have been calculated by dividing the population of the city by the number of crimes reported to the FBI during 1996 and are expressed as odds (eg. 1:20 should be read as 1 in 20). (2) Figures have been calculated by dividing the female population of the city by the number of forcible rapes reported to the FBI during 1996. The female population of the city was estimated by calculating the ratio of females to males reported in the 1990 Census and applying that ratio to 1996 population estimate.
Source: FBI Uniform Crime Reports 1996

CRIME STATISTICS

Total Crimes and Total Crime Rates: 1977 - 1996

Year	Number				Rate per 100,000 population			
	City	Suburbs[2]	MSA[1]	U.S.	City	Suburbs[3]	MSA[1]	U.S.
1977	65,436	46,923	112,359	10,984,500	8,179.5	5,508.8	6,802.3	5,077.6
1978	66,838	50,612	117,450	11,209,000	8,180.9	5,496.7	6,758.7	5,140.3
1979	72,093	55,362	127,455	12,249,500	8,693.0	5,854.0	7,180.4	5,565.5
1980	70,505	60,233	130,738	13,408,300	8,059.3	6,129.5	7,038.4	5,950.0
1981	66,123	56,937	123,060	13,423,800	7,362.5	5,643.9	6,453.3	5,858.2
1982	65,545	53,124	118,669	12,974,400	7,131.3	5,145.6	6,080.8	5,603.6
1983	63,737	50,468	114,205	12,108,600	6,810.7	4,801.0	5,747.5	5,175.0
1984	64,366	49,811	114,177	11,881,800	6,754.5	4,577.8	5,594.1	5,031.3
1985	67,893	52,368	120,261	12,431,400	6,869.8	4,612.2	5,662.8	5,207.1
1986	79,747	60,710	140,457	13,211,900	7,885.0	5,224.8	6,462.7	5,480.4
1987	88,227	69,534	157,761	13,508,700	8,476.4	5,717.8	6,990.0	5,550.0
1988	96,756	75,048	171,804	13,923,100	9,013.4	5,983.7	7,381.0	5,664.2
1989	102,991	76,144	179,135	14,251,400	9,374.4	5,705.8	7,362.3	5,741.0
1990	101,564	77,036	178,600	14,475,600	9,145.4	5,552.3	7,149.7	5,820.3
1991	96,781	77,143	173,924	14,872,900	8,536.9	5,446.6	6,820.4	5,897.8
1992	92,258	78,885	171,143	14,438,200	8,009.5	5,481.7	6,605.5	5,660.2
1993	85,227	76,651	161,878	14,144,800	7,343.3	5,224.8	6,160.5	5,484.4
1994	76,725	76,054	152,779	13,989,500	6,564.5	5,147.8	5,773.6	5,373.5
1995	64,235	68,838	133,073	13,862,700	5,548.2	4,627.6	5,030.5	5,275.9
1996	61,574	61,860	123,434	13,473,600	5,270.1	4,120.8	4,623.8	5,078.9

Notes: (1) Metropolitan Statistical Area - see Appendix A for areas included; (2) calculated by the editors using the following formula: (number of crimes in the MSA minus number of crimes in the city); (3) calculated by the editors using the following formula: ((number of crimes in the MSA minus number of crimes in the city) ÷ (population of the MSA minus population of the city)) x 100,000; n/a not avail.
Source: U.S. Department of Justice, FBI Uniform Crime Reports, 1977 - 1996

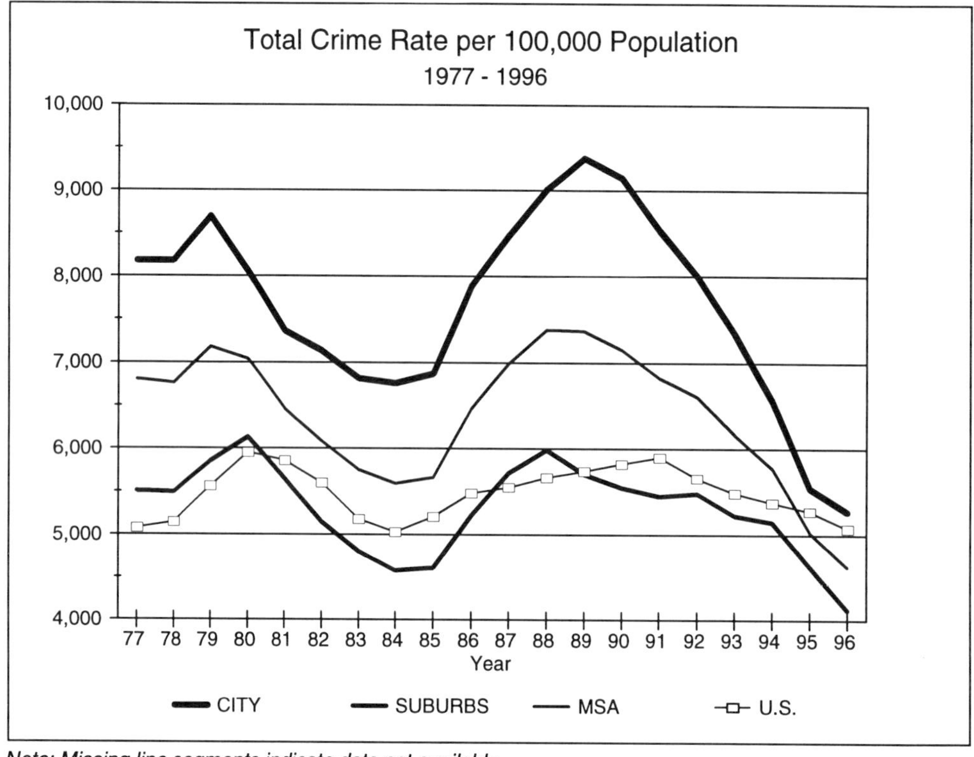

Note: Missing line segments indicate data not available.

Violent Crimes and Violent Crime Rates: 1977 - 1996

Year	Number				Rate per 100,000 population			
	City	Suburbs[2]	MSA[1]	U.S.	City	Suburbs[3]	MSA[1]	U.S.
1977	4,414	3,752	8,166	1,029,580	551.8	440.5	494.4	475.9
1978	4,520	4,215	8,735	1,085,550	553.2	457.8	502.7	497.8
1979	5,436	4,791	10,227	1,208,030	655.5	506.6	576.2	548.9
1980	6,189	5,497	11,686	1,344,520	707.5	559.4	629.1	596.6
1981	6,594	5,354	11,948	1,361,820	734.2	530.7	626.6	594.3
1982	5,835	4,807	10,642	1,322,390	634.9	465.6	545.3	571.1
1983	5,451	4,961	10,412	1,258,090	582.5	471.9	524.0	537.7
1984	5,931	4,788	10,719	1,273,280	622.4	440.0	525.2	539.2
1985	6,250	4,559	10,809	1,328,800	632.4	401.5	509.0	556.6
1986	8,522	6,635	15,157	1,489,170	842.6	571.0	697.4	617.7
1987	9,112	7,172	16,284	1,484,000	875.4	589.8	721.5	609.7
1988	9,171	7,853	17,024	1,566,220	854.3	626.1	731.4	637.2
1989	10,124	8,276	18,400	1,646,040	921.5	620.2	756.2	663.1
1990	12,047	9,166	21,213	1,820,130	1,084.8	660.6	849.2	731.8
1991	13,830	10,823	24,653	1,911,770	1,219.9	764.1	966.8	758.1
1992	14,792	10,408	25,200	1,932,270	1,284.2	723.2	972.6	757.5
1993	13,463	9,496	22,959	1,926,020	1,160.0	647.3	873.7	746.8
1994	12,599	10,762	23,361	1,857,670	1,078.0	728.4	882.8	713.6
1995	11,077	9,941	21,018	1,798,790	956.8	668.3	794.5	684.6
1996	10,149	8,805	18,954	1,682,280	868.7	586.6	710.0	634.1

Notes: Violent crimes include murder, forcible rape, robbery and aggravated assault; n/a not available; (1) Metropolitan Statistical Area - see Appendix A for areas included; (2) calculated by the editors using the following formula: (number of crimes in the MSA minus number of crimes in the city); (3) calculated by the editors using the following formula: ((number of crimes in the MSA minus number of crimes in the city) ÷ (population of the MSA minus population of the city)) x 100,000
Source: U.S. Department of Justice, FBI Uniform Crime Reports, 1977 - 1996

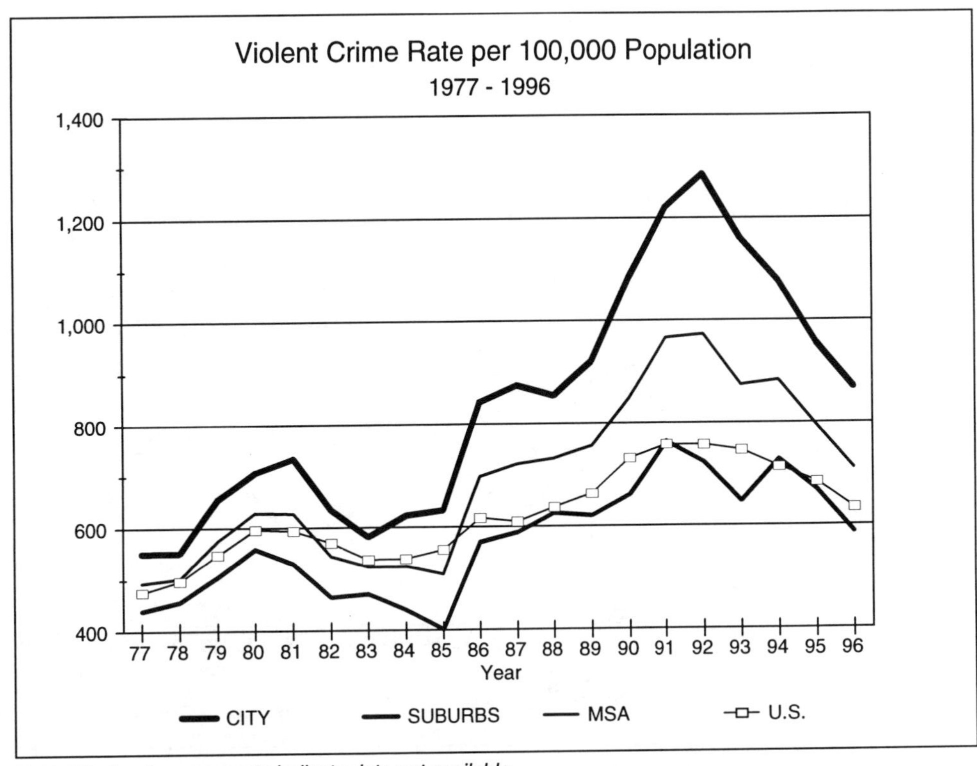

Note: Missing line segments indicate data not available.

Property Crimes and Property Crime Rates: 1977 - 1996

Year	Number				Rate per 100,000 population			
	City	Suburbs[2]	MSA[1]	U.S.	City	Suburbs[3]	MSA[1]	U.S.
1977	61,022	43,171	104,193	9,955,000	7,627.8	5,068.3	6,307.9	4,601.7
1978	62,318	46,397	108,715	10,123,400	7,627.7	5,039.0	6,256.0	4,642.5
1979	66,657	50,571	117,228	11,041,500	8,037.5	5,347.4	6,604.2	5,016.6
1980	64,316	54,736	119,052	12,063,700	7,351.9	5,570.2	6,409.3	5,353.3
1981	59,529	51,583	111,112	12,061,900	6,628.3	5,113.2	5,826.8	5,263.9
1982	59,710	48,317	108,027	11,652,000	6,496.5	4,680.0	5,535.5	5,032.5
1983	58,286	45,507	103,793	10,850,500	6,228.2	4,329.1	5,223.5	4,637.4
1984	58,435	45,023	103,458	10,608,500	6,132.1	4,137.8	5,068.9	4,492.1
1985	61,643	47,809	109,452	11,102,600	6,237.4	4,210.7	5,153.8	4,650.5
1986	71,225	54,075	125,300	11,722,700	7,042.4	4,653.8	5,765.3	4,862.6
1987	79,115	62,362	141,477	12,024,700	7,601.0	5,128.1	6,268.5	4,940.3
1988	87,585	67,195	154,780	12,356,900	8,159.1	5,357.6	6,649.6	5,027.1
1989	92,867	67,868	160,735	12,605,400	8,452.9	5,085.7	6,606.1	5,077.9
1990	89,517	67,870	157,387	12,655,500	8,060.6	4,891.6	6,300.5	5,088.5
1991	82,951	66,320	149,271	12,961,100	7,317.0	4,682.4	5,853.7	5,139.7
1992	77,466	68,477	145,943	12,505,900	6,725.3	4,758.4	5,632.9	4,902.7
1993	71,764	67,155	138,919	12,218,800	6,183.3	4,577.5	5,286.8	4,737.6
1994	64,126	65,292	129,418	12,131,900	5,486.6	4,419.4	4,890.8	4,660.0
1995	53,158	58,897	112,055	12,063,900	4,591.4	3,959.4	4,236.0	4,591.3
1996	51,425	53,055	104,480	11,791,300	4,401.5	3,534.3	3,913.8	4,444.8

Notes: Property crimes include burglary, larceny-theft and motor vehicle theft; n/a not available; (1) Metropolitan Statistical Area - see Appendix A for areas included; (2) calculated by the editors using the following formula: (number of crimes in the MSA minus number of crimes in the city); (3) calculated by the editors using the following formula: ((number of crimes in the MSA minus number of crimes in the city) ÷ (population of the MSA minus population of the city)) x 100,000
Source: U.S. Department of Justice, FBI Uniform Crime Reports, 1977 - 1996

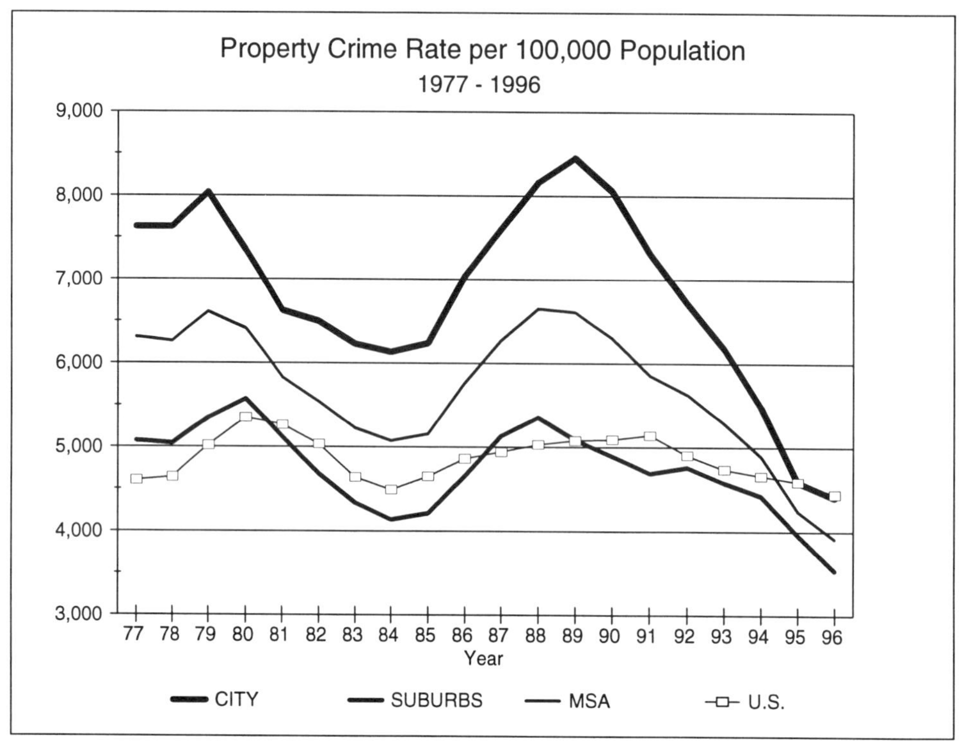

Note: Missing line segments indicate data not available.

Murders and Murder Rates: 1977 - 1996

Year	Number				Rate per 100,000 population			
	City	Suburbs[2]	MSA[1]	U.S.	City	Suburbs[3]	MSA[1]	U.S.
1977	50	63	113	19,120	6.3	7.4	6.8	8.8
1978	68	51	119	19,560	8.3	5.5	6.8	9.0
1979	96	47	143	21,460	11.6	5.0	8.1	9.7
1980	103	80	183	23,040	11.8	8.1	9.9	10.2
1981	94	66	160	22,520	10.5	6.5	8.4	9.8
1982	72	52	124	21,010	7.8	5.0	6.4	9.1
1983	77	54	131	19,310	8.2	5.1	6.6	8.3
1984	103	59	162	18,690	10.8	5.4	7.9	7.9
1985	96	67	163	18,980	9.7	5.9	7.7	7.9
1986	102	95	197	20,610	10.1	8.2	9.1	8.6
1987	96	80	176	20,100	9.2	6.6	7.8	8.3
1988	144	84	228	20,680	13.4	6.7	9.8	8.4
1989	121	70	191	21,500	11.0	5.2	7.8	8.7
1990	135	81	216	23,440	12.2	5.8	8.6	9.4
1991	167	111	278	24,700	14.7	7.8	10.9	9.8
1992	146	99	245	23,760	12.7	6.9	9.5	9.3
1993	133	112	245	24,530	11.5	7.6	9.3	9.5
1994	113	92	205	23,330	9.7	6.2	7.7	9.0
1995	91	107	198	21,610	7.9	7.2	7.5	8.2
1996	80	86	166	19,650	6.8	5.7	6.2	7.4

Notes: (1) Metropolitan Statistical Area - see Appendix A for areas included; (2) calculated by the editors using the following formula: (number of crimes in the MSA minus number of crimes in the city); (3) calculated by the editors using the following formula: ((number of crimes in the MSA minus number of crimes in the city) ÷ (population of the MSA minus population of the city)) x 100,000; n/a not avail.
Source: U.S. Department of Justice, FBI Uniform Crime Reports, 1977 - 1996

Forcible Rapes and Forcible Rape Rates: 1977 - 1996

Year	Number				Rate per 100,000 population			
	City	Suburbs[2]	MSA[1]	U.S.	City	Suburbs[3]	MSA[1]	U.S.
1977	298	342	640	63,500	37.3	40.2	38.7	29.4
1978	316	320	636	67,610	38.7	34.8	36.6	31.0
1979	331	387	718	76,390	39.9	40.9	40.4	34.7
1980	362	425	787	82,990	41.4	43.2	42.4	36.8
1981	559	425	984	82,500	62.2	42.1	51.6	36.0
1982	428	429	857	78,770	46.6	41.6	43.9	34.0
1983	395	430	825	78,920	42.2	40.9	41.5	33.7
1984	393	355	748	84,230	41.2	32.6	36.6	35.7
1985	338	253	591	88,670	34.2	22.3	27.8	37.1
1986	391	382	773	91,460	38.7	32.9	35.6	37.9
1987	410	391	801	91,110	39.4	32.2	35.5	37.4
1988	389	378	767	92,490	36.2	30.1	33.0	37.6
1989	410	425	835	94,500	37.3	31.8	34.3	38.1
1990	439	460	899	102,560	39.5	33.2	36.0	41.2
1991	472	497	969	106,590	41.6	35.1	38.0	42.3
1992	485	472	957	109,060	42.1	32.8	36.9	42.8
1993	396	407	803	106,010	34.1	27.7	30.6	41.1
1994	403	466	869	102,220	34.5	31.5	32.8	39.3
1995	346	378	724	97,470	29.9	25.4	27.4	37.1
1996	368	447	815	95,770	31.5	29.8	30.5	36.1

Notes: (1) Metropolitan Statistical Area - see Appendix A for areas included; (2) calculated by the editors using the following formula: (number of crimes in the MSA minus number of crimes in the city); (3) calculated by the editors using the following formula: ((number of crimes in the MSA minus number of crimes in the city) ÷ (population of the MSA minus population of the city)) x 100,000; n/a not avail.
Source: U.S. Department of Justice, FBI Uniform Crime Reports, 1977 - 1996

Robberies and Robbery Rates: 1977 - 1996

Year	Number				Rate per 100,000 population			
	City	Suburbs[2]	MSA[1]	U.S.	City	Suburbs[3]	MSA[1]	U.S.
1977	2,481	1,118	3,599	412,610	310.1	131.3	217.9	190.7
1978	2,530	1,361	3,891	426,930	309.7	147.8	223.9	195.8
1979	2,884	1,750	4,634	480,700	347.8	185.0	261.1	218.4
1980	2,986	2,040	5,026	565,840	341.3	207.6	270.6	251.1
1981	3,323	1,988	5,311	592,910	370.0	197.1	278.5	258.7
1982	3,142	1,752	4,894	553,130	341.9	169.7	250.8	238.9
1983	2,550	1,483	4,033	506,570	272.5	141.1	203.0	216.5
1984	2,616	1,498	4,114	485,010	274.5	137.7	201.6	205.4
1985	3,062	1,371	4,433	497,870	309.8	120.7	208.7	208.5
1986	3,985	1,923	5,908	542,780	394.0	165.5	271.8	225.1
1987	3,452	1,969	5,421	517,700	331.7	161.9	240.2	212.7
1988	3,204	1,969	5,173	542,970	298.5	157.0	222.2	220.9
1989	3,585	2,053	5,638	578,330	326.3	153.8	231.7	233.0
1990	4,331	2,374	6,705	639,270	390.0	171.1	268.4	257.0
1991	5,331	3,068	8,399	687,730	470.2	216.6	329.4	272.7
1992	5,321	3,233	8,554	672,480	462.0	224.7	330.2	263.6
1993	4,651	2,843	7,494	659,870	400.7	193.8	285.2	255.9
1994	3,845	3,036	6,881	618,950	329.0	205.5	260.0	237.7
1995	3,244	2,648	5,892	580,510	280.2	178.0	222.7	220.9
1996	2,998	2,468	5,466	537,050	256.6	164.4	204.8	202.4

Notes: (1) Metropolitan Statistical Area - see Appendix A for areas included; (2) calculated by the editors using the following formula: (number of crimes in the MSA minus number of crimes in the city); (3) calculated by the editors using the following formula: ((number of crimes in the MSA minus number of crimes in the city) ÷ (population of the MSA minus population of the city)) x 100,000; n/a not avail.
Source: U.S. Department of Justice, FBI Uniform Crime Reports, 1977 - 1996

Aggravated Assaults and Aggravated Assault Rates: 1977 - 1996

Year	Number				Rate per 100,000 population			
	City	Suburbs[2]	MSA[1]	U.S.	City	Suburbs[3]	MSA[1]	U.S.
1977	1,585	2,229	3,814	534,350	198.1	261.7	230.9	247.0
1978	1,606	2,483	4,089	571,460	196.6	269.7	235.3	262.1
1979	2,125	2,607	4,732	629,480	256.2	275.7	266.6	286.0
1980	2,738	2,952	5,690	672,650	313.0	300.4	306.3	298.5
1981	2,618	2,875	5,493	663,900	291.5	285.0	288.1	289.7
1982	2,193	2,574	4,767	669,480	238.6	249.3	244.3	289.2
1983	2,429	2,994	5,423	653,290	259.6	284.8	272.9	279.2
1984	2,819	2,876	5,695	685,350	295.8	264.3	279.0	290.2
1985	2,754	2,868	5,622	723,250	278.7	252.6	264.7	302.9
1986	4,044	4,235	8,279	834,320	399.9	364.5	380.9	346.1
1987	5,154	4,732	9,886	855,090	495.2	389.1	438.0	351.3
1988	5,434	5,422	10,856	910,090	506.2	432.3	466.4	370.2
1989	6,008	5,728	11,736	951,710	546.9	429.2	482.3	383.4
1990	7,142	6,251	13,393	1,054,860	643.1	450.5	536.1	424.1
1991	7,860	7,147	15,007	1,092,740	693.3	504.6	588.5	433.3
1992	8,840	6,604	15,444	1,126,970	767.5	458.9	596.1	441.8
1993	8,283	6,134	14,417	1,135,610	713.7	418.1	548.7	440.3
1994	8,238	7,168	15,406	1,113,180	704.8	485.2	582.2	427.6
1995	7,396	6,808	14,204	1,099,210	638.8	457.7	536.9	418.3
1996	6,703	5,804	12,507	1,029,810	573.7	386.6	468.5	388.2

Notes: (1) Metropolitan Statistical Area - see Appendix A for areas included; (2) calculated by the editors using the following formula: (number of crimes in the MSA minus number of crimes in the city); (3) calculated by the editors using the following formula: ((number of crimes in the MSA minus number of crimes in the city) ÷ (population of the MSA minus population of the city)) x 100,000; n/a not avail.
Source: U.S. Department of Justice, FBI Uniform Crime Reports, 1977 - 1996

Burglaries and Burglary Rates: 1977 - 1996

Year	Number				Rate per 100,000 population			
	City	Suburbs[2]	MSA[1]	U.S.	City	Suburbs[3]	MSA[1]	U.S.
1977	18,809	15,379	34,188	3,071,500	2,351.1	1,805.5	2,069.8	1,419.8
1978	20,158	15,937	36,095	3,128,300	2,467.3	1,730.8	2,077.1	1,434.6
1979	19,952	16,862	36,814	3,327,700	2,405.8	1,783.0	2,074.0	1,511.9
1980	19,960	19,570	39,530	3,795,200	2,281.6	1,991.5	2,128.1	1,684.1
1981	18,708	17,969	36,677	3,779,700	2,083.0	1,781.2	1,923.4	1,649.5
1982	16,214	16,171	32,385	3,447,100	1,764.1	1,566.3	1,659.5	1,488.8
1983	16,157	14,842	30,999	3,129,900	1,726.5	1,411.9	1,560.1	1,337.7
1984	15,248	14,331	29,579	2,984,400	1,600.1	1,317.1	1,449.2	1,263.7
1985	16,363	14,680	31,043	3,073,300	1,655.7	1,292.9	1,461.7	1,287.3
1986	17,533	16,436	33,969	3,241,400	1,733.6	1,414.5	1,563.0	1,344.6
1987	17,370	17,844	35,214	3,236,200	1,668.8	1,467.3	1,560.3	1,329.6
1988	17,536	17,727	35,263	3,218,100	1,633.6	1,413.4	1,515.0	1,309.2
1989	17,495	16,848	34,343	3,168,200	1,592.4	1,262.5	1,411.5	1,276.3
1990	16,691	17,186	33,877	3,073,900	1,503.0	1,238.7	1,356.2	1,235.9
1991	17,088	17,813	34,901	3,157,200	1,507.3	1,257.7	1,368.6	1,252.0
1992	16,437	17,952	34,389	2,979,900	1,427.0	1,247.5	1,327.3	1,168.2
1993	14,583	17,444	32,027	2,834,800	1,256.5	1,189.0	1,218.8	1,099.2
1994	12,889	17,159	30,048	2,712,800	1,102.8	1,161.4	1,135.5	1,042.0
1995	10,311	15,518	25,829	2,593,800	890.6	1,043.2	976.4	987.1
1996	8,608	13,263	21,871	2,501,500	736.8	883.5	819.3	943.0

Notes: (1) Metropolitan Statistical Area - see Appendix A for areas included; (2) calculated by the editors using the following formula: (number of crimes in the MSA minus number of crimes in the city); (3) calculated by the editors using the following formula: ((number of crimes in the MSA minus number of crimes in the city) ÷ (population of the MSA minus population of the city)) x 100,000; n/a not avail.
Source: U.S. Department of Justice, FBI Uniform Crime Reports, 1977 - 1996

Larceny-Thefts and Larceny-Theft Rates: 1977 - 1996

Year	Number				Rate per 100,000 population			
	City	Suburbs[2]	MSA[1]	U.S.	City	Suburbs[3]	MSA[1]	U.S.
1977	35,888	23,995	59,883	5,905,700	4,486.0	2,817.0	3,625.4	2,729.9
1978	35,233	25,944	61,177	5,991,000	4,312.5	2,817.7	3,520.4	2,747.4
1979	39,224	28,757	67,981	6,601,000	4,729.6	3,040.8	3,829.8	2,999.1
1980	36,649	29,761	66,410	7,136,900	4,189.3	3,028.6	3,575.3	3,167.0
1981	33,851	28,441	62,292	7,194,400	3,769.1	2,819.2	3,266.6	3,139.7
1982	35,693	27,524	63,217	7,142,500	3,883.4	2,666.0	3,239.4	3,084.8
1983	34,594	26,103	60,697	6,712,800	3,696.6	2,483.2	3,054.6	2,868.9
1984	34,428	25,587	60,015	6,591,900	3,612.8	2,351.5	2,940.4	2,791.3
1985	35,220	26,762	61,982	6,926,400	3,563.8	2,357.0	2,918.6	2,901.2
1986	40,459	29,109	69,568	7,257,200	4,000.4	2,505.2	3,201.0	3,010.3
1987	43,590	32,993	76,583	7,499,900	4,187.9	2,713.0	3,393.2	3,081.3
1988	45,923	35,118	81,041	7,705,900	4,278.0	2,800.0	3,481.6	3,134.9
1989	49,789	35,703	85,492	7,872,400	4,531.9	2,675.4	3,513.7	3,171.3
1990	48,581	36,051	84,632	7,945,700	4,374.5	2,598.3	3,388.0	3,194.8
1991	44,645	35,322	79,967	8,142,200	3,938.1	2,493.9	3,135.9	3,228.8
1992	40,798	36,749	77,547	7,915,200	3,541.9	2,553.7	2,993.0	3,103.0
1993	37,862	35,832	73,694	7,820,900	3,262.3	2,442.4	2,804.5	3,032.4
1994	35,204	35,406	70,610	7,879,800	3,012.0	2,396.5	2,668.4	3,026.7
1995	30,505	32,324	62,829	7,997,700	2,634.8	2,173.0	2,375.1	3,043.8
1996	31,688	30,326	62,014	7,894,600	2,712.2	2,020.2	2,323.0	2,975.9

Notes: (1) Metropolitan Statistical Area - see Appendix A for areas included; (2) calculated by the editors using the following formula: (number of crimes in the MSA minus number of crimes in the city); (3) calculated by the editors using the following formula: ((number of crimes in the MSA minus number of crimes in the city) ÷ (population of the MSA minus population of the city)) x 100,000; n/a not avail.
Source: U.S. Department of Justice, FBI Uniform Crime Reports, 1977 - 1996

Motor Vehicle Thefts and Motor Vehicle Theft Rates: 1977 - 1996

Year	Number				Rate per 100,000 population			
	City	Suburbs[2]	MSA[1]	U.S.	City	Suburbs[3]	MSA[1]	U.S.
1977	6,325	3,797	10,122	977,700	790.6	445.8	612.8	451.9
1978	6,927	4,516	11,443	1,004,100	847.9	490.5	658.5	460.5
1979	7,481	4,952	12,433	1,112,800	902.1	523.6	700.4	505.6
1980	7,707	5,405	13,112	1,131,700	881.0	550.0	705.9	502.2
1981	6,970	5,173	12,143	1,087,800	776.1	512.8	636.8	474.7
1982	7,803	4,622	12,425	1,062,400	849.0	447.7	636.7	458.8
1983	7,535	4,562	12,097	1,007,900	805.2	434.0	608.8	430.8
1984	8,759	5,105	13,864	1,032,200	919.2	469.2	679.3	437.1
1985	10,060	6,367	16,427	1,102,900	1,017.9	560.8	773.5	462.0
1986	13,233	8,530	21,763	1,224,100	1,308.4	734.1	1,001.4	507.8
1987	18,155	11,525	29,680	1,288,700	1,744.2	947.7	1,315.1	529.4
1988	24,126	14,350	38,476	1,432,900	2,247.5	1,144.2	1,653.0	582.9
1989	25,583	15,317	40,900	1,564,800	2,328.6	1,147.8	1,681.0	630.4
1990	24,245	14,633	38,878	1,635,900	2,183.2	1,054.7	1,556.4	657.8
1991	21,218	13,185	34,403	1,661,700	1,871.6	930.9	1,349.1	659.0
1992	20,231	13,776	34,007	1,610,800	1,756.4	957.3	1,312.5	631.5
1993	19,319	13,879	33,198	1,563,100	1,664.6	946.0	1,263.4	606.1
1994	16,033	12,727	28,760	1,539,300	1,371.8	861.4	1,086.9	591.3
1995	12,342	11,055	23,397	1,472,400	1,066.0	743.2	884.5	560.4
1996	11,129	9,466	20,595	1,395,200	952.5	630.6	771.5	525.9

Notes: (1) Metropolitan Statistical Area - see Appendix A for areas included; (2) calculated by the editors using the following formula: (number of crimes in the MSA minus number of crimes in the city); (3) calculated by the editors using the following formula: ((number of crimes in the MSA minus number of crimes in the city) ÷ (population of the MSA minus population of the city)) x 100,000; n/a not avail.
Source: U.S. Department of Justice, FBI Uniform Crime Reports, 1977 - 1996

HATE CRIMES

Criminal Incidents by Bias Motivation

Area	Race	Ethnicity	Religion	Sexual Orientation
San Diego	54	22	12	31

Notes: Figures include both violent and property crimes. Law enforcement agencies must have submitted data for at least one quarter of calendar year 1995 to be included in this report, therefore figures shown may not represent complete 12-month totals; n/a not available
Source: U.S. Department of Justice, FBI Uniform Crime Reports, Hate Crime Statistics 1995

ILLEGAL DRUGS

Drug Use by Adult Arrestees

Sex	Percent Testing Positive by Urinalysis (%)				
	Any Drug[1]	Cocaine	Marijuana	Opiates	Multiple Drugs
Male	71	27	40	9	31
Female	62	22	23	10	25

Notes: The catchment area is the city and part of the county; (1) Includes cocaine, opiates, marijuana, methadone, phencyclidine (PCP), benzodiazepines, methaqualone, propoxyphene, barbiturates & amphetamines
Source: National Institute of Justice, 1996 Drug Use Forecasting, Annual Report on Adult and Juvenile Arrestees (released June 1997)

LAW ENFORCEMENT

Full-Time Law Enforcement Employees

Jurisdiction	Police Employees			Police Officers per 100,000 population
	Total	Officers	Civilians	
San Diego	2,784	2,002	782	171.4

Notes: Data as of October 31, 1996
Source: U.S. Department of Justice, FBI Uniform Crime Reports, 1996

Number of Police Officers by Race

Race	Police Officers 1983		Police Officers 1992		Index of Representation[1]		
	Number	Pct.	Number	Pct.	1983	1992	% Chg.
Black	76	5.6	146	7.5	0.62	0.80	29.0
Hispanic[2]	107	7.9	226	11.7	0.52	0.56	7.7

Notes: (1) The index of representation is calculated by dividing the percent of black/hispanic police officers by the percent of corresponding blacks/hispanics in the local population. An index approaching 1.0 indicates that a city is closer to achieving a representation of police officers equal to their proportion in the local population; (2) Hispanic officers can be of any race
Source: Bureau of Justice Statistics, Sourcebook of Criminal Justice Statistics, 1994

CORRECTIONS

Federal Correctional Facilities

Type	Year Opened	Security Level	Sex of Inmates	Rated Capacity	Population on 7/1/95	Number of Staff
Metro Corr/Detention Ctr	1974	Admin.	Both	607	995	270

Notes: Data as of 1995
Source: Bureau of Justice Statistics, Sourcebook of Criminal Justice Statistics Online

City/County/Regional Correctional Facilities

Name	Year Opened	Year Renov.	Rated Capacity	1995 Pop.	Number of COs[1]	Number of Staff	ACA[2] Accred.
San Diego Co Jail-Central Detention Facility	1960	--	750	n/a	n/a	n/a	No
San Diego Co-George F. Bailey Detention Facility	1991	--	1,232	1,600	150	225	No
S.D. Co-Work Furlough Ctr	1927	--	128	n/a	n/a	n/a	No

Notes: Data as of April 1996; (1) Correctional Officers; (2) American Correctional Assn. Accreditation
Source: American Correctional Association, 1996-1998 National Jail and Adult Detention Directory

Private Adult Correctional Facilities

Name	Date Opened	Rated Capacity	Present Pop.	Security Level	Facility Construct.	Expans. Plans	ACA[1] Accred.
San Diego City Jail	5/92	200	114	Min.	New	None	No

Notes: Data as of December 1996; (1) American Correctional Association Accreditation
Source: University of Florida, Center for Studies in Criminology and Law, Private Adult Correctional Facility Census, 10th Ed., March 15, 1997

Characteristics of Shock Incarceration Programs

Jurisdiction	Year Program Began	Number of Camps	Average Num. of Inmates	Number of Beds	Program Length	Voluntary/ Mandatory
California	1993	3[a]	350	200[b]	4 months[c]	Voluntary

Note: Data as of July 1996; (a) One boot camp; two work training and parole camps; (b) 200 program beds at San Quentin shock incarceration facility. Work training beds vary with each facility; (c) Shock incarceration and intensive parole programs: 4 months; Work training program: 2 months
Source: Sourcebook of Criminal Justice Statistics Online

INMATES AND HIV/AIDS

HIV Testing Policies for Inmates

Jurisdiction	All Inmates at Some Time	All Convicted Inmates at Admission	Random Samples While in Custody	High-risk Groups	Upon Inmate Request	Upon Court Order	Upon Involvement in Incident
San Diego Co.	No	No	No	Yes	Yes	Yes	Yes

Source: HIV in Prisons and Jails, 1993 (released August 1995)

Inmates Known to be Positive for HIV

Jurisdiction	Number of Jail Inmates in Facilities Providing Data	Type of HIV Infection/AIDS Cases: Total	Asymptomatic	Symptomatic	Confirmed AIDS	HIV/AIDS Cases as a Percent of Tot. Custody Pop.
San Diego Co.[1]	5,374	68	0	0	0	1.3

Note: (1) Detail does not add to total.
Source: HIV in Prisons and Jails, 1993 (released August, 1995)

DEATH PENALTY

Death Penalty Statistics

State	Prisoners Executed		Prisoners Under Sentence of Death					Avg. No. of Years on Death Row[4]
	1930-1995	1996[1]	Total[2]	White[3]	Black[3]	Hisp.	Women	
California	294	2	420	251	160	61	8	7.0

Notes: Data as of 12/31/95 unless otherwise noted; (1) Data as of 7/31/97; (2) Includes persons of other races; (3) Includes people of Hispanic origin; (4) Covers prisoners sentenced 1974 through 1995
Source: Bureau of Justice Statistics, Capital Punishment 1995 (released 12/96); Death Penalty Information Center Web Site, 9/30/97

Capital Offenses and Methods of Execution

Capital Offenses in California	Minimum Age for Imposition of Death Penalty	Mentally Retarded Excluded	Methods of Execution[1]
First-degree murder with special circumstances; train-wrecking; treason; perjury causing execution.	18	No	Lethal injection; lethal gas

Notes: Data as of 12/31/95 unless otherwise noted; (1) Data as of 7/31/97
Source: Bureau of Justice Statistics, Capital Punishment 1995 (released 12/96); Death Penalty Information Center Web Site, 9/30/97

LAWS

Statutory Provisions Relating to the Purchase, Ownership and Use of Handguns

Jurisdiction	Instant Background Check	Federal Waiting Period Applies[1]	State Waiting Period (days)	License or Permit to Purchase	Regis-tration	Record of Sale Sent to Police	Concealed Carry Law
California	No	No	15	No	No	Yes	Yes[a]

Note: Data as of 1996; (1) The Federal 5-day waiting period for handgun purchases applies to states that don't have instant background checks, waiting period requirements, or licensing procedures exempting them from the Federal requirement; (a) Restrictively administered discretion by local authorities over permit issuance, or permits are unavailable and carrying is prohibited in most circumstances
Source: Sourcebook of Criminal Justice Statistics Online

Statutory Provisions Relating to Alcohol Use and Driving

Jurisdiction	Drinking Age	Blood Alcohol Concentration Levels as Evidence in State Courts[1]		Open Container Law[1]	Anti-Consump-tion Law[1]	Dram Shop Law[1]
		Illegal per se at 0.10%	Presumption at 0.10%			
California	21	(a)	(a)	Yes	Yes	Yes[b]

Note: Data as of January 1, 1997; (1) See Appendix C for an explanation of terms; (a) 0.08%; (b) Applies only to the actions of intoxicated minors
Source: Sourcebook of Criminal Justice Statistics Online

Statutory Provisions Relating to Curfews

Jurisdiction	Year Enacted	Latest Revision	Age Group(s)	Curfew Provisions
San Diego	1940	1994	17 and under	10:30 pm to 6 am every night

Note: Data as of February 1996
Source: Sourcebook of Criminal Justice Statistics Online

Statutory Provisions Relating to Hate Crimes

Jurisdiction	Bias-Motivated Violence and Intimidation						Institutional Vandalism
	Civil Action	Criminal Penalty					
		Race/ Religion/ Ethnicity	Sexual Orientation	Mental/ Physical Disability	Gender	Age	
California	Yes	Yes	Yes	Yes	Yes	No	Yes

Source: Anti-Defamation League, 1997 Hate Crimes Laws

San Francisco, California

OVERVIEW

The total crime rate for the city decreased 30.4% between 1977 and 1996. During that same period, the violent crime rate decreased 7.2% and the property crime rate decreased 33.8%.

Among violent crimes, the rates for: Murders decreased 48.8%; Forcible Rapes decreased 55.9%; Robberies decreased 10.2%; and Aggravated Assaults increased 8.7%.

Among property crimes, the rates for: Burglaries decreased 67.7%; Larceny-Thefts decreased 15.1%; and Motor Vehicle Thefts decreased 29.2%.

ANTI-CRIME PROGRAMS

The Police Department has adopted a community policing and problem solving philosophy, an interactive process between police and citizens.

Programs include:

- SAFE (Safety Awareness for Everyone)—a cooperative neighborhood program designed to instruct residents in protecting persons and property.
- Operation I.D.—license numbers are inscribed on property making it easier to catch and prosecute offenders.
- Neighborhood Watch/Business Watch—residents and employers and employees identify problems in community and report them to the police.
- Nightlines—a program designed to promote bus rider safety and convenience at night. Riders can get on or off buses between regular stops from 8:30PM - 6:30AM.
- Senior Escort Program.
  San Francisco Police Department, 9/97

CRIME RISK

Your Chances of Becoming a Victim[1]

Area	Any Crime	Violent Crime					Property Crime			
		Any	Murder	Forcible Rape[2]	Robbery	Aggrav. Assault	Any	Burglary	Larceny -Theft	Motor Vehicle Theft
City	1:13	1:75	1:9,087	1:1,250	1:135	1:188	1:16	1:105	1:24	1:87

Note: (1) Figures have been calculated by dividing the population of the city by the number of crimes reported to the FBI during 1996 and are expressed as odds (eg. 1:20 should be read as 1 in 20).
(2) Figures have been calculated by dividing the female population of the city by the number of forcible rapes reported to the FBI during 1996. The female population of the city was estimated by calculating the ratio of females to males reported in the 1990 Census and applying that ratio to 1996 population estimate.
Source: FBI Uniform Crime Reports 1996

CRIME STATISTICS

Total Crimes and Total Crime Rates: 1977 - 1996

Year	Number				Rate per 100,000 population			
	City	Suburbs[2]	MSA[1]	U.S.	City	Suburbs[3]	MSA[1]	U.S.
1977	71,433	183,729	255,162	10,984,500	10,905.8	7,179.7	7,939.0	5,077.6
1978	70,385	185,630	256,015	11,209,000	10,845.1	7,329.7	8,046.8	5,140.3
1979	70,745	195,618	266,363	12,249,500	10,732.3	7,576.1	8,218.0	5,565.5
1980	70,424	205,093	275,517	13,408,300	10,446.3	8,037.1	8,540.6	5,950.0
1981	71,812	205,571	277,383	13,423,800	10,376.1	7,847.0	8,375.5	5,858.2
1982	68,598	194,930	263,528	12,974,400	9,685.2	7,270.8	7,775.3	5,603.6
1983	62,646	41,460	104,106	12,108,600	8,686.7	4,844.6	6,601.7	5,175.0
1984	59,896	37,690	97,586	11,881,800	8,324.0	4,452.1	6,231.0	5,031.3
1985	58,590	37,332	95,922	12,431,400	7,988.2	4,375.9	6,045.8	5,207.1
1986	56,637	41,641	98,278	13,211,900	7,546.1	4,769.5	6,053.0	5,480.4
1987	57,837	41,738	99,575	13,508,700	7,531.5	4,852.1	6,115.9	5,550.0
1988	66,055	40,477	106,532	13,923,100	8,761.5	4,679.3	6,580.3	5,664.2
1989	67,748	41,428	109,176	14,251,400	9,021.5	4,701.7	6,689.4	5,741.0
1990	69,950	39,575	109,525	14,475,600	9,662.1	4,498.6	6,829.6	5,820.3
1991	69,350	41,817	111,167	14,872,900	9,383.8	4,656.5	6,790.6	5,897.8
1992	76,551	40,644	117,195	14,438,200	10,194.8	4,454.6	7,045.9	5,660.2
1993	70,132	39,890	110,022	14,144,800	9,523.9	4,401.2	6,697.5	5,484.4
1994	61,860	37,378	99,238	13,989,500	8,341.8	4,095.2	5,998.8	5,373.5
1995	60,474	36,029	96,503	13,862,700	8,190.2	3,934.0	5,833.8	5,275.9
1996	56,592	33,245	89,837	13,473,600	7,594.9	3,597.1	5,381.6	5,078.9

Notes: (1) Metropolitan Statistical Area - see Appendix A for areas included; (2) calculated by the editors using the following formula: (number of crimes in the MSA minus number of crimes in the city); (3) calculated by the editors using the following formula: ((number of crimes in the MSA minus number of crimes in the city) ÷ (population of the MSA minus population of the city)) x 100,000; n/a not avail.
Source: U.S. Department of Justice, FBI Uniform Crime Reports, 1977 - 1996

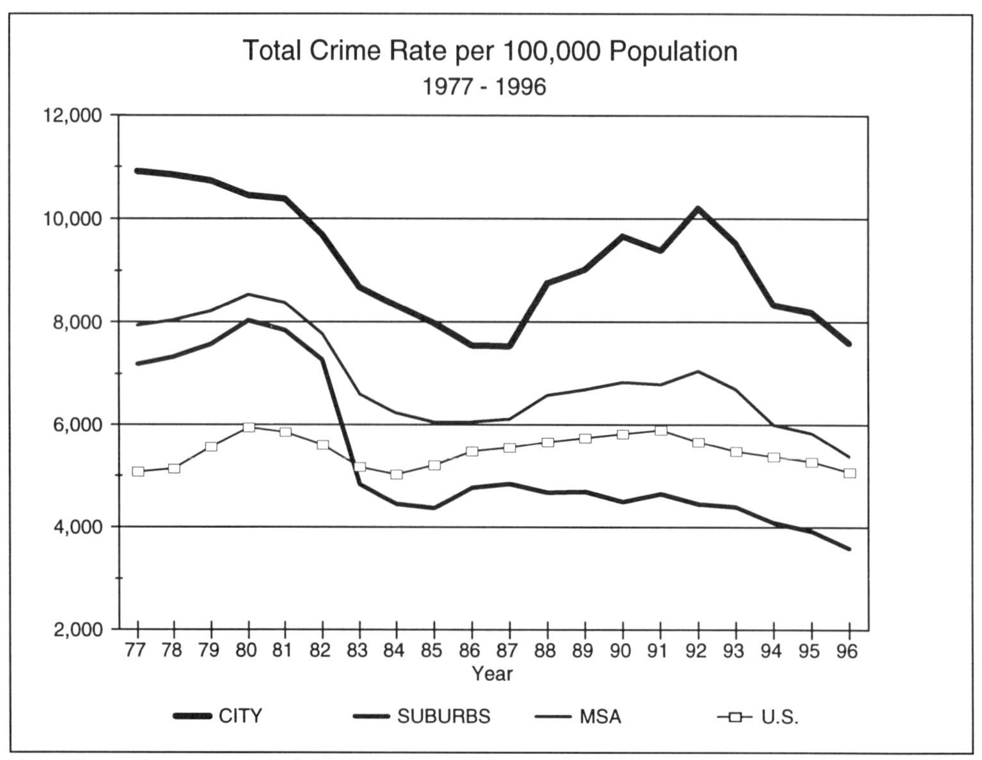

Note: Missing line segments indicate data not available.

Violent Crimes and Violent Crime Rates: 1977 - 1996

Year	Number				Rate per 100,000 population			
	City	Suburbs[2]	MSA[1]	U.S.	City	Suburbs[3]	MSA[1]	U.S.
1977	9,367	15,343	24,710	1,029,580	1,430.1	599.6	768.8	475.9
1978	10,509	15,571	26,080	1,085,550	1,619.3	614.8	819.7	497.8
1979	11,041	16,910	27,951	1,208,030	1,675.0	654.9	862.4	548.9
1980	12,710	19,698	32,408	1,344,520	1,885.3	771.9	1,004.6	596.6
1981	12,011	18,853	30,864	1,361,820	1,735.5	719.6	931.9	594.3
1982	11,615	18,055	29,670	1,322,390	1,639.9	673.4	875.4	571.1
1983	10,117	3,169	13,286	1,258,090	1,402.9	370.3	842.5	537.7
1984	9,372	3,279	12,651	1,273,280	1,302.5	387.3	807.8	539.2
1985	9,502	3,069	12,571	1,328,800	1,295.5	359.7	792.3	556.6
1986	9,506	4,845	14,351	1,489,170	1,266.5	554.9	883.9	617.7
1987	9,298	5,220	14,518	1,484,000	1,210.8	606.8	891.7	609.7
1988	9,667	4,474	14,141	1,566,220	1,282.2	517.2	873.5	637.2
1989	10,064	3,984	14,048	1,646,040	1,340.1	452.2	860.7	663.1
1990	12,388	3,921	16,309	1,820,130	1,711.1	445.7	1,017.0	731.8
1991	12,160	3,944	16,104	1,911,770	1,645.4	439.2	983.7	758.1
1992	13,676	4,385	18,061	1,932,270	1,821.3	480.6	1,085.9	757.5
1993	13,365	4,510	17,875	1,926,020	1,815.0	497.6	1,088.1	746.8
1994	10,837	4,309	15,146	1,857,670	1,461.4	472.1	915.6	713.6
1995	10,903	3,725	14,628	1,798,790	1,476.6	406.7	884.3	684.6
1996	9,886	3,491	13,377	1,682,280	1,326.8	377.7	801.3	634.1

Notes: Violent crimes include murder, forcible rape, robbery and aggravated assault; n/a not available; (1) Metropolitan Statistical Area - see Appendix A for areas included; (2) calculated by the editors using the following formula: (number of crimes in the MSA minus number of crimes in the city); (3) calculated by the editors using the following formula: ((number of crimes in the MSA minus number of crimes in the city) ÷ (population of the MSA minus population of the city)) x 100,000
Source: U.S. Department of Justice, FBI Uniform Crime Reports, 1977 - 1996

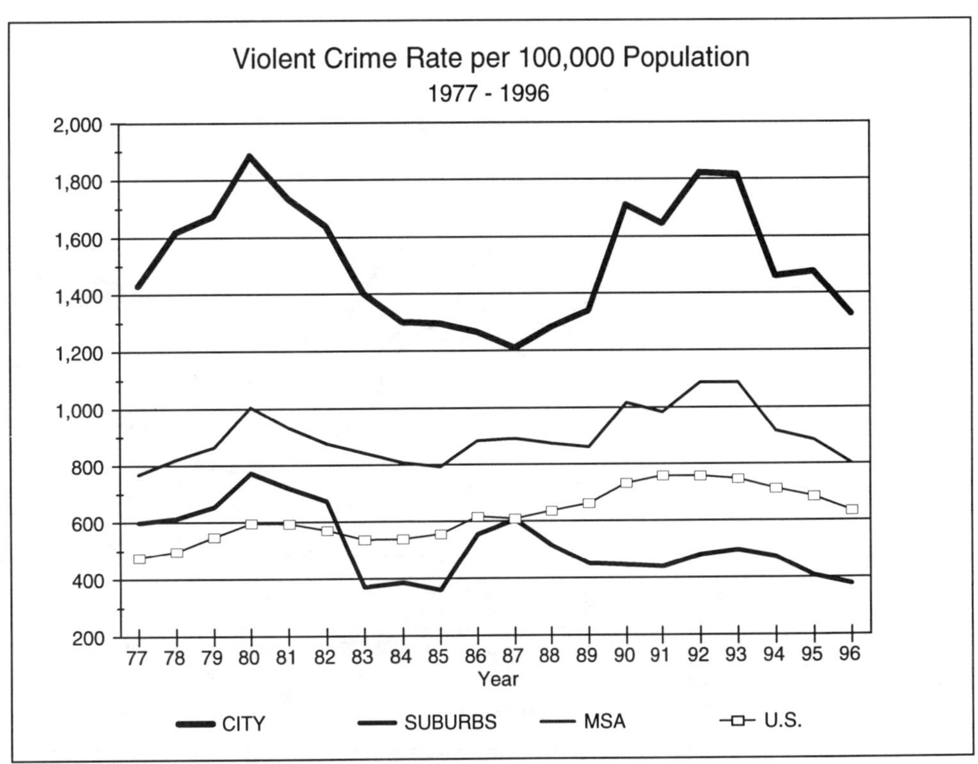

Note: Missing line segments indicate data not available.

Property Crimes and Property Crime Rates: 1977 - 1996

Year	Number				Rate per 100,000 population			
	City	Suburbs[2]	MSA[1]	U.S.	City	Suburbs[3]	MSA[1]	U.S.
1977	62,066	168,386	230,452	9,955,000	9,475.7	6,580.1	7,170.2	4,601.7
1978	59,876	170,059	229,935	10,123,400	9,225.9	6,714.9	7,227.1	4,642.5
1979	59,704	178,708	238,412	11,041,500	9,057.4	6,921.2	7,355.6	5,016.6
1980	57,714	185,395	243,109	12,063,700	8,561.0	7,265.2	7,536.0	5,353.3
1981	59,801	186,718	246,519	12,061,900	8,640.6	7,127.3	7,443.6	5,263.9
1982	56,983	176,875	233,858	11,652,000	8,045.3	6,597.3	6,899.9	5,032.5
1983	52,529	38,291	90,820	10,850,500	7,283.9	4,474.3	5,759.2	4,637.4
1984	50,524	34,411	84,935	10,608,500	7,021.5	4,064.8	5,423.3	4,492.1
1985	49,088	34,263	83,351	11,102,600	6,692.7	4,016.2	5,253.5	4,650.5
1986	47,131	36,796	83,927	11,722,700	6,279.6	4,214.6	5,169.1	4,862.6
1987	48,539	36,518	85,057	12,024,700	6,320.7	4,245.3	5,224.2	4,940.3
1988	56,388	36,003	92,391	12,356,900	7,479.2	4,162.1	5,706.9	5,027.1
1989	57,684	37,444	95,128	12,605,400	7,681.3	4,249.6	5,828.6	5,077.9
1990	57,562	35,654	93,216	12,655,500	7,951.0	4,052.9	5,812.6	5,088.5
1991	57,190	37,873	95,063	12,961,100	7,738.4	4,217.3	5,806.9	5,139.7
1992	62,875	36,259	99,134	12,505,900	8,373.5	3,974.0	5,960.1	4,902.7
1993	56,767	35,380	92,147	12,218,800	7,709.0	3,903.6	5,609.4	4,737.6
1994	51,023	33,069	84,092	12,131,900	6,880.4	3,623.1	5,083.2	4,660.0
1995	49,571	32,304	81,875	12,063,900	6,713.6	3,527.2	4,949.5	4,591.3
1996	46,706	29,754	76,460	11,791,300	6,268.2	3,219.4	4,580.3	4,444.8

Notes: Property crimes include burglary, larceny-theft and motor vehicle theft; n/a not available; (1) Metropolitan Statistical Area - see Appendix A for areas included; (2) calculated by the editors using the following formula: (number of crimes in the MSA minus number of crimes in the city); (3) calculated by the editors using the following formula: ((number of crimes in the MSA minus number of crimes in the city) ÷ (population of the MSA minus population of the city)) x 100,000
Source: U.S. Department of Justice, FBI Uniform Crime Reports, 1977 - 1996

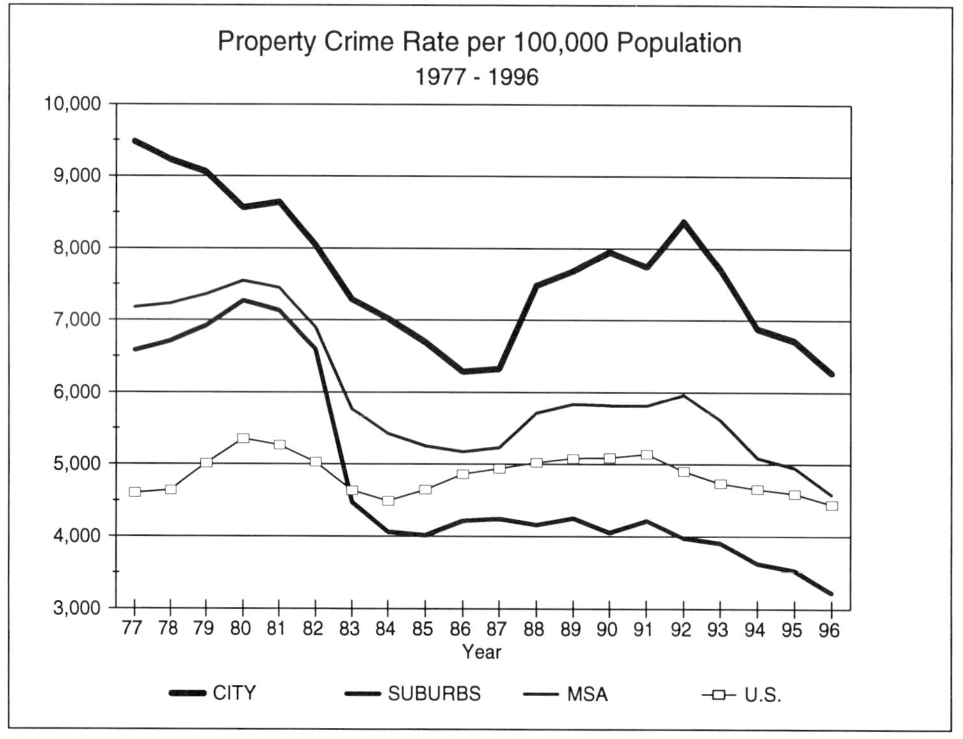

Note: Missing line segments indicate data not available.

Murders and Murder Rates: 1977 - 1996

Year	Number				Rate per 100,000 population			
	City	Suburbs[2]	MSA[1]	U.S.	City	Suburbs[3]	MSA[1]	U.S.
1977	141	241	382	19,120	21.5	9.4	11.9	8.8
1978	118	237	355	19,560	18.2	9.4	11.2	9.0
1979	112	245	357	21,460	17.0	9.5	11.0	9.7
1980	110	269	379	23,040	16.3	10.5	11.7	10.2
1981	126	286	412	22,520	18.2	10.9	12.4	9.8
1982	111	227	338	21,010	15.7	8.5	10.0	9.1
1983	83	43	126	19,310	11.5	5.0	8.0	8.3
1984	73	32	105	18,690	10.1	3.8	6.7	7.9
1985	85	38	123	18,980	11.6	4.5	7.8	7.9
1986	114	47	161	20,610	15.2	5.4	9.9	8.6
1987	103	35	138	20,100	13.4	4.1	8.5	8.3
1988	92	36	128	20,680	12.2	4.2	7.9	8.4
1989	73	41	114	21,500	9.7	4.7	7.0	8.7
1990	101	47	148	23,440	14.0	5.3	9.2	9.4
1991	95	56	151	24,700	12.9	6.2	9.2	9.8
1992	117	66	183	23,760	15.6	7.2	11.0	9.3
1993	129	37	166	24,530	17.5	4.1	10.1	9.5
1994	91	29	120	23,330	12.3	3.2	7.3	9.0
1995	99	42	141	21,610	13.4	4.6	8.5	8.2
1996	82	14	96	19,650	11.0	1.5	5.8	7.4

Notes: (1) Metropolitan Statistical Area - see Appendix A for areas included; (2) calculated by the editors using the following formula: (number of crimes in the MSA minus number of crimes in the city); (3) calculated by the editors using the following formula: ((number of crimes in the MSA minus number of crimes in the city) ÷ (population of the MSA minus population of the city)) x 100,000; n/a not avail.
Source: U.S. Department of Justice, FBI Uniform Crime Reports, 1977 - 1996

Forcible Rapes and Forcible Rape Rates: 1977 - 1996

Year	Number				Rate per 100,000 population			
	City	Suburbs[2]	MSA[1]	U.S.	City	Suburbs[3]	MSA[1]	U.S.
1977	595	1,072	1,667	63,500	90.8	41.9	51.9	29.4
1978	583	1,103	1,686	67,610	89.8	43.6	53.0	31.0
1979	664	1,151	1,815	76,390	100.7	44.6	56.0	34.7
1980	759	1,306	2,065	82,990	112.6	51.2	64.0	36.8
1981	672	1,250	1,922	82,500	97.1	47.7	58.0	36.0
1982	594	1,138	1,732	78,770	83.9	42.4	51.1	34.0
1983	539	199	738	78,920	74.7	23.3	46.8	33.7
1984	495	175	670	84,230	68.8	20.7	42.8	35.7
1985	512	183	695	88,670	69.8	21.5	43.8	37.1
1986	492	197	689	91,460	65.6	22.6	42.4	37.9
1987	452	232	684	91,110	58.9	27.0	42.0	37.4
1988	453	244	697	92,490	60.1	28.2	43.1	37.6
1989	380	200	580	94,500	50.6	22.7	35.5	38.1
1990	419	186	605	102,560	57.9	21.1	37.7	41.2
1991	400	186	586	106,590	54.1	20.7	35.8	42.3
1992	395	241	636	109,060	52.6	26.4	38.2	42.8
1993	361	198	559	106,010	49.0	21.8	34.0	41.1
1994	292	205	497	102,220	39.4	22.5	30.0	39.3
1995	304	196	500	97,470	41.2	21.4	30.2	37.1
1996	298	178	476	95,770	40.0	19.3	28.5	36.1

Notes: (1) Metropolitan Statistical Area - see Appendix A for areas included; (2) calculated by the editors using the following formula: (number of crimes in the MSA minus number of crimes in the city); (3) calculated by the editors using the following formula: ((number of crimes in the MSA minus number of crimes in the city) ÷ (population of the MSA minus population of the city)) x 100,000; n/a not avail.
Source: U.S. Department of Justice, FBI Uniform Crime Reports, 1977 - 1996

Robberies and Robbery Rates: 1977 - 1996

Year	Number				Rate per 100,000 population			
	City	Suburbs[2]	MSA[1]	U.S.	City	Suburbs[3]	MSA[1]	U.S.
1977	5,423	6,744	12,167	412,610	827.9	263.5	378.6	190.7
1978	6,509	6,674	13,183	426,930	1,002.9	263.5	414.4	195.8
1979	6,694	7,118	13,812	480,700	1,015.5	275.7	426.1	218.4
1980	7,527	9,267	16,794	565,840	1,116.5	363.2	520.6	251.1
1981	7,386	8,648	16,034	592,910	1,067.2	330.1	484.1	258.7
1982	7,153	7,877	15,030	553,130	1,009.9	293.8	443.5	238.9
1983	5,945	1,077	7,022	506,570	824.4	125.8	445.3	216.5
1984	5,222	1,009	6,231	485,010	725.7	119.2	397.9	205.4
1985	5,111	897	6,008	497,870	696.8	105.1	378.7	208.5
1986	5,085	1,089	6,174	542,780	677.5	124.7	380.3	225.1
1987	4,654	950	5,604	517,700	606.0	110.4	344.2	212.7
1988	4,867	887	5,754	542,970	645.6	102.5	355.4	220.9
1989	5,005	1,000	6,005	578,330	666.5	113.5	367.9	233.0
1990	7,053	1,143	8,196	639,270	974.2	129.9	511.1	257.0
1991	7,020	1,207	8,227	687,730	949.9	134.4	502.5	272.7
1992	8,278	1,338	9,616	672,480	1,102.4	146.6	578.1	263.6
1993	8,454	1,301	9,755	659,870	1,148.1	143.5	593.8	255.9
1994	6,624	1,196	7,820	618,950	893.2	131.0	472.7	237.7
1995	6,469	1,130	7,599	580,510	876.1	123.4	459.4	220.9
1996	5,539	1,088	6,627	537,050	743.4	117.7	397.0	202.4

Notes: (1) Metropolitan Statistical Area - see Appendix A for areas included; (2) calculated by the editors using the following formula: (number of crimes in the MSA minus number of crimes in the city); (3) calculated by the editors using the following formula: ((number of crimes in the MSA minus number of crimes in the city) ÷ (population of the MSA minus population of the city)) x 100,000; n/a not avail.
Source: U.S. Department of Justice, FBI Uniform Crime Reports, 1977 - 1996

Aggravated Assaults and Aggravated Assault Rates: 1977 - 1996

Year	Number				Rate per 100,000 population			
	City	Suburbs[2]	MSA[1]	U.S.	City	Suburbs[3]	MSA[1]	U.S.
1977	3,208	7,286	10,494	534,350	489.8	284.7	326.5	247.0
1978	3,299	7,557	10,856	571,460	508.3	298.4	341.2	262.1
1979	3,571	8,396	11,967	629,480	541.7	325.2	369.2	286.0
1980	4,314	8,856	13,170	672,650	639.9	347.0	408.2	298.5
1981	3,827	8,669	12,496	663,900	553.0	330.9	377.3	289.7
1982	3,757	8,813	12,570	669,480	530.4	328.7	370.9	289.2
1983	3,550	1,850	5,400	653,290	492.3	216.2	342.4	279.2
1984	3,582	2,063	5,645	685,350	497.8	243.7	360.4	290.2
1985	3,794	1,951	5,745	723,250	517.3	228.7	362.1	302.9
1986	3,815	3,512	7,327	834,320	508.3	402.3	451.3	346.1
1987	4,089	4,003	8,092	855,090	532.5	465.4	497.0	351.3
1988	4,255	3,307	7,562	910,090	564.4	382.3	467.1	370.2
1989	4,606	2,743	7,349	951,710	613.3	311.3	450.3	383.4
1990	4,815	2,545	7,360	1,054,860	665.1	289.3	458.9	424.1
1991	4,645	2,495	7,140	1,092,740	628.5	277.8	436.1	433.3
1992	4,886	2,740	7,626	1,126,970	650.7	300.3	458.5	441.8
1993	4,421	2,974	7,395	1,135,610	600.4	328.1	450.2	440.3
1994	3,830	2,879	6,709	1,113,180	516.5	315.4	405.6	427.6
1995	4,031	2,357	6,388	1,099,210	545.9	257.4	386.2	418.3
1996	3,967	2,211	6,178	1,029,810	532.4	239.2	370.1	388.2

Notes: (1) Metropolitan Statistical Area - see Appendix A for areas included; (2) calculated by the editors using the following formula: (number of crimes in the MSA minus number of crimes in the city); (3) calculated by the editors using the following formula: ((number of crimes in the MSA minus number of crimes in the city) ÷ (population of the MSA minus population of the city)) x 100,000; n/a not avail.
Source: U.S. Department of Justice, FBI Uniform Crime Reports, 1977 - 1996

Burglaries and Burglary Rates: 1977 - 1996

Year	Number				Rate per 100,000 population			
	City	Suburbs[2]	MSA[1]	U.S.	City	Suburbs[3]	MSA[1]	U.S.
1977	19,258	53,221	72,479	3,071,500	2,940.2	2,079.7	2,255.1	1,419.8
1978	18,054	53,501	71,555	3,128,300	2,781.8	2,112.5	2,249.0	1,434.6
1979	17,255	54,048	71,303	3,327,700	2,617.7	2,093.2	2,199.9	1,511.9
1980	16,795	56,354	73,149	3,795,200	2,491.3	2,208.4	2,267.5	1,684.1
1981	17,715	56,583	74,298	3,779,700	2,559.6	2,159.9	2,243.4	1,649.5
1982	13,704	50,057	63,761	3,447,100	1,934.8	1,867.1	1,881.2	1,488.8
1983	12,389	9,376	21,765	3,129,900	1,717.9	1,095.6	1,380.2	1,337.7
1984	13,217	8,552	21,769	2,984,400	1,836.8	1,010.2	1,390.0	1,263.7
1985	11,757	7,680	19,437	3,073,300	1,603.0	900.2	1,225.1	1,287.3
1986	10,076	7,927	18,003	3,241,400	1,342.5	907.9	1,108.8	1,344.6
1987	9,642	7,207	16,849	3,236,200	1,255.6	837.8	1,034.9	1,329.6
1988	10,148	7,173	17,321	3,218,100	1,346.0	829.2	1,069.9	1,309.2
1989	10,692	7,288	17,980	3,168,200	1,423.8	827.1	1,101.7	1,276.3
1990	10,618	6,085	16,703	3,073,900	1,466.7	691.7	1,041.5	1,235.9
1991	10,604	6,876	17,480	3,157,200	1,434.8	765.7	1,067.8	1,252.0
1992	11,831	6,582	18,413	2,979,900	1,575.6	721.4	1,107.0	1,168.2
1993	11,153	6,661	17,814	2,834,800	1,514.6	734.9	1,084.4	1,099.2
1994	8,055	5,947	14,002	2,712,800	1,086.2	651.6	846.4	1,042.0
1995	7,127	5,774	12,901	2,593,800	965.2	630.5	779.9	987.1
1996	7,079	4,597	11,676	2,501,500	950.0	497.4	699.4	943.0

Notes: (1) Metropolitan Statistical Area - see Appendix A for areas included; (2) calculated by the editors using the following formula: (number of crimes in the MSA minus number of crimes in the city); (3) calculated by the editors using the following formula: ((number of crimes in the MSA minus number of crimes in the city) ÷ (population of the MSA minus population of the city)) x 100,000; n/a not avail.
Source: U.S. Department of Justice, FBI Uniform Crime Reports, 1977 - 1996

Larceny-Thefts and Larceny-Theft Rates: 1977 - 1996

Year	Number				Rate per 100,000 population			
	City	Suburbs[2]	MSA[1]	U.S.	City	Suburbs[3]	MSA[1]	U.S.
1977	32,177	101,847	134,024	5,905,700	4,912.5	3,979.9	4,170.0	2,729.9
1978	32,878	103,268	136,146	5,991,000	5,065.9	4,077.6	4,279.2	2,747.4
1979	33,943	109,451	143,394	6,601,000	5,149.3	4,238.9	4,424.1	2,999.1
1980	32,772	114,694	147,466	7,136,900	4,861.2	4,494.6	4,571.2	3,167.0
1981	35,337	117,017	152,354	7,194,400	5,105.8	4,466.7	4,600.3	3,139.7
1982	36,901	115,306	152,207	7,142,500	5,210.0	4,300.8	4,490.8	3,084.8
1983	34,481	26,445	60,926	6,712,800	4,781.3	3,090.1	3,863.5	2,868.9
1984	31,524	23,470	54,994	6,591,900	4,381.0	2,772.4	3,511.5	2,791.3
1985	31,397	23,843	55,240	6,926,400	4,280.7	2,794.8	3,481.7	2,901.2
1986	30,223	25,864	56,087	7,257,200	4,026.8	2,962.4	3,454.5	3,010.3
1987	31,172	26,197	57,369	7,499,900	4,059.2	3,045.4	3,523.6	3,081.3
1988	36,662	25,006	61,668	7,705,900	4,862.8	2,890.8	3,809.1	3,134.9
1989	37,316	25,718	63,034	7,872,400	4,969.1	2,918.8	3,862.2	3,171.3
1990	35,583	25,253	60,836	7,945,700	4,915.1	2,870.6	3,793.5	3,194.8
1991	34,679	26,048	60,727	8,142,200	4,692.4	2,900.6	3,709.5	3,228.8
1992	38,375	25,187	63,562	7,915,200	5,110.6	2,760.5	3,821.4	3,103.0
1993	34,558	24,175	58,733	7,820,900	4,693.0	2,667.3	3,575.3	3,032.4
1994	33,719	23,520	57,239	7,879,800	4,547.0	2,576.9	3,460.0	3,026.7
1995	34,153	23,200	57,353	7,997,700	4,625.5	2,533.2	3,467.1	3,043.8
1996	31,062	21,971	53,033	7,894,600	4,168.7	2,377.3	3,176.9	2,975.9

Notes: (1) Metropolitan Statistical Area - see Appendix A for areas included; (2) calculated by the editors using the following formula: (number of crimes in the MSA minus number of crimes in the city); (3) calculated by the editors using the following formula: ((number of crimes in the MSA minus number of crimes in the city) ÷ (population of the MSA minus population of the city)) x 100,000; n/a not avail.
Source: U.S. Department of Justice, FBI Uniform Crime Reports, 1977 - 1996

Motor Vehicle Thefts and Motor Vehicle Theft Rates: 1977 - 1996

Year	Number				Rate per 100,000 population			
	City	Suburbs[2]	MSA[1]	U.S.	City	Suburbs[3]	MSA[1]	U.S.
1977	10,631	13,318	23,949	977,700	1,623.1	520.4	745.1	451.9
1978	8,944	13,290	22,234	1,004,100	1,378.1	524.8	698.8	460.5
1979	8,506	15,209	23,715	1,112,800	1,290.4	589.0	731.7	505.6
1980	8,147	14,347	22,494	1,131,700	1,208.5	562.2	697.3	502.2
1981	6,749	13,118	19,867	1,087,800	975.2	500.7	599.9	474.7
1982	6,378	11,512	17,890	1,062,400	900.5	429.4	527.8	458.8
1983	5,659	2,470	8,129	1,007,900	784.7	288.6	515.5	430.8
1984	5,783	2,389	8,172	1,032,200	803.7	282.2	521.8	437.1
1985	5,934	2,740	8,674	1,102,900	809.0	321.2	546.7	462.0
1986	6,832	3,005	9,837	1,224,100	910.3	344.2	605.9	507.8
1987	7,725	3,114	10,839	1,288,700	1,005.9	362.0	665.7	529.4
1988	9,578	3,824	13,402	1,432,900	1,270.4	442.1	827.8	582.9
1989	9,676	4,438	14,114	1,564,800	1,288.5	503.7	864.8	630.4
1990	11,361	4,316	15,677	1,635,900	1,569.3	490.6	977.6	657.8
1991	11,907	4,949	16,856	1,661,700	1,611.1	551.1	1,029.6	659.0
1992	12,669	4,490	17,159	1,610,800	1,687.2	492.1	1,031.6	631.5
1993	11,056	4,544	15,600	1,563,100	1,501.4	501.3	949.6	606.1
1994	9,249	3,602	12,851	1,539,300	1,247.2	394.6	776.8	591.3
1995	8,291	3,330	11,621	1,472,400	1,122.9	363.6	702.5	560.4
1996	8,565	3,186	11,751	1,395,200	1,149.5	344.7	703.9	525.9

Notes: (1) Metropolitan Statistical Area - see Appendix A for areas included; (2) calculated by the editors using the following formula: (number of crimes in the MSA minus number of crimes in the city); (3) calculated by the editors using the following formula: ((number of crimes in the MSA minus number of crimes in the city) ÷ (population of the MSA minus population of the city)) x 100,000; n/a not avail.
Source: U.S. Department of Justice, FBI Uniform Crime Reports, 1977 - 1996

HATE CRIMES

Criminal Incidents by Bias Motivation

Area	Race	Ethnicity	Religion	Sexual Orientation
San Francisco	120	14	27	119

Notes: Figures include both violent and property crimes. Law enforcement agencies must have submitted data for at least one quarter of calendar year 1995 to be included in this report, therefore figures shown may not represent complete 12-month totals; n/a not available
Source: U.S. Department of Justice, FBI Uniform Crime Reports, Hate Crime Statistics 1995

LAW ENFORCEMENT

Full-Time Law Enforcement Employees

Jurisdiction	Police Employees			Police Officers per 100,000 population
	Total	Officers	Civilians	
San Francisco	2,416	2,020	396	271.1

Notes: Data as of October 31, 1996
Source: U.S. Department of Justice, FBI Uniform Crime Reports, 1996

Number of Police Officers by Race

Race	Police Officers				Index of Representation[1]		
	1983		1992				
	Number	Pct.	Number	Pct.	1983	1992	% Chg.
Black	159	8.1	170	9.4	0.64	0.85	32.8
Hispanic[2]	159	8.1	189	10.4	0.66	0.74	12.1

Notes: (1) The index of representation is calculated by dividing the percent of black/hispanic police officers by the percent of corresponding blacks/hispanics in the local population. An index approaching 1.0 indicates that a city is closer to achieving a representation of police officers equal to their proportion in the local population; (2) Hispanic officers can be of any race
Source: Bureau of Justice Statistics, Sourcebook of Criminal Justice Statistics, 1994

CORRECTIONS

Federal Correctional Facilities

Type	Year Opened	Security Level	Sex of Inmates	Rated Capacity	Population on 7/1/95	Number of Staff
None listed						

Notes: Data as of 1995
Source: Bureau of Justice Statistics, Sourcebook of Criminal Justice Statistics Online

City/County/Regional Correctional Facilities

Name	Year Opened	Year Renov.	Rated Capacity	1995 Pop.	Number of COs[1]	Number of Staff	ACA[2] Accred.
San Francisco Co Jail 1	1962	--	426	365	87	87	No
San Francisco Co Jail 2	1962	--	372	n/a	n/a	n/a	No
San Francisco Co Jail Hosp	1975	--	22	n/a	n/a	n/a	No

Notes: Data as of April 1996; (1) Correctional Officers; (2) American Correctional Assn. Accreditation
Source: American Correctional Association, 1996-1998 National Jail and Adult Detention Directory

Private Adult Correctional Facilities

Name	Date Opened	Rated Capacity	Present Pop.	Security Level	Facility Construct.	Expans. Plans	ACA[1] Accred.
None listed							

Notes: Data as of December 1996; (1) American Correctional Association Accreditation
Source: University of Florida, Center for Studies in Criminology and Law, Private Adult Correctional Facility Census, 10th Ed., March 15, 1997

Characteristics of Shock Incarceration Programs

Jurisdiction	Year Program Began	Number of Camps	Average Num. of Inmates	Number of Beds	Program Length	Voluntary/ Mandatory
California	1993	3[a]	350	200[b]	4 months[c]	Voluntary

Note: Data as of July 1996; (a) One boot camp; two work training and parole camps; (b) 200 program beds at San Quentin shock incarceration facility. Work training beds vary with each facility; (c) Shock incarceration and intensive parole programs: 4 months; Work training program: 2 months
Source: Sourcebook of Criminal Justice Statistics Online

INMATES AND HIV/AIDS

HIV Testing Policies for Inmates

Jurisdiction	All Inmates at Some Time	All Convicted Inmates at Admission	Random Samples While in Custody	High-risk Groups	Upon Inmate Request	Upon Court Order	Upon Involvement in Incident
San Francisco Co.[1]	n/a	n/a	n/a	n/a	n/a	n/a	n/a

Notes: (1) Provided no data on AIDS testing policies
Source: HIV in Prisons and Jails, 1993 (released August 1995)

Inmates Known to be Positive for HIV

Jurisdiction	Number of Jail Inmates in Facilities Providing Data	Type of HIV Infection/AIDS Cases				HIV/AIDS Cases as a Percent of Tot. Custody Pop.
		Total	Asymptomatic	Symptomatic	Confirmed AIDS	
San Fran. Co.[1]	2,038	n/a	n/a	n/a	n/a	n/a

Note: (1) Jurisdiction did not provide data on HIV/AIDS cases; n/a not available
Source: HIV in Prisons and Jails, 1993 (released August, 1995)

DEATH PENALTY

Death Penalty Statistics

State	Prisoners Executed		Prisoners Under Sentence of Death					Avg. No. of Years on Death Row[4]
	1930-1995	1996[1]	Total[2]	White[3]	Black[3]	Hisp.	Women	
California	294	2	420	251	160	61	8	7.0

Notes: Data as of 12/31/95 unless otherwise noted; (1) Data as of 7/31/97; (2) Includes persons of other races; (3) Includes people of Hispanic origin; (4) Covers prisoners sentenced 1974 through 1995
Source: Bureau of Justice Statistics, Capital Punishment 1995 (released 12/96); Death Penalty Information Center Web Site, 9/30/97

Capital Offenses and Methods of Execution

Capital Offenses in California	Minimum Age for Imposition of Death Penalty	Mentally Retarded Excluded	Methods of Execution[1]
First-degree murder with special circumstances; train-wrecking; treason; perjury causing execution.	18	No	Lethal injection; lethal gas

Notes: Data as of 12/31/95 unless otherwise noted; (1) Data as of 7/31/97
Source: Bureau of Justice Statistics, Capital Punishment 1995 (released 12/96); Death Penalty Information Center Web Site, 9/30/97

LAWS

Statutory Provisions Relating to the Purchase, Ownership and Use of Handguns

Jurisdiction	Instant Background Check	Federal Waiting Period Applies[1]	State Waiting Period (days)	License or Permit to Purchase	Regis-tration	Record of Sale Sent to Police	Concealed Carry Law
California	No	No	15	No	No	Yes	Yes[a]

Note: Data as of 1996; (1) The Federal 5-day waiting period for handgun purchases applies to states that don't have instant background checks, waiting period requirements, or licensing procedures exempting them from the Federal requirement; (a) Restrictively administered discretion by local authorities over permit issuance, or permits are unavailable and carrying is prohibited in most circumstances
Source: Sourcebook of Criminal Justice Statistics Online

Statutory Provisions Relating to Alcohol Use and Driving

Jurisdiction	Drinking Age	Blood Alcohol Concentration Levels as Evidence in State Courts[1]		Open Container Law[1]	Anti-Consump-tion Law[1]	Dram Shop Law[1]
		Illegal per se at 0.10%	Presumption at 0.10%			
California	21	(a)	(a)	Yes	Yes	Yes[b]

Note: Data as of January 1, 1997; (1) See Appendix C for an explanation of terms; (a) 0.08%; (b) Applies only to the actions of intoxicated minors
Source: Sourcebook of Criminal Justice Statistics Online

Statutory Provisions Relating to Curfews

Jurisdiction	Year Enacted	Latest Revision	Age Group(s)	Curfew Provisions
San Francisco	1975	-	17 and under	11 pm to 6 am every night

Note: Data as of February 1996
Source: Sourcebook of Criminal Justice Statistics Online

Statutory Provisions Relating to Hate Crimes

Jurisdiction	Bias-Motivated Violence and Intimidation						Institutional Vandalism
		Criminal Penalty					
	Civil Action	Race/ Religion/ Ethnicity	Sexual Orientation	Mental/ Physical Disability	Gender	Age	
California	Yes	Yes	Yes	Yes	Yes	No	Yes

Source: Anti-Defamation League, 1997 Hate Crimes Laws

San Jose, California

OVERVIEW

The total crime rate for the city decreased 38.6% between 1977 and 1996. During that same period, the violent crime rate increased 59.7% and the property crime rate decreased 45.8%.

Among violent crimes, the rates for: Murders decreased 31.4%; Forcible Rapes decreased 25.5%; Robberies decreased 25.2%; and Aggravated Assaults increased 152.9%.

Among property crimes, the rates for: Burglaries decreased 72.6%; Larceny-Thefts decreased 34.0%; and Motor Vehicle Thefts decreased 24.3%.

ANTI-CRIME PROGRAMS

Programs include:

- Crime Stoppers 947—allows citizens with information about any serious crime to report it anonymously. Cash rewards are provided if the tips result in an arrest and prosecution.
- S.A.V.E.—students referred by Juvenile Probation, along with their parents, must attend a six-hour workshop on alternative ways to handle hostility.
- Youth Court—a pilot program in which high school students are trained in all phases of the justice system. A Juvenile Court Judge presides over all proceedings.
- Business Presentations—custom-designed seminars which provide details on internal theft prevention and security of the business premises.
- Ride-Along Program—adults are given a ride in the front seat of a patrol car.
- Project Crackdown—Comprehensive neighborhood program that helps city, county and private agencies expedite services to areas in which there is much gang and drug activity, blighted conditions and other problems. *San Jose Police Department, 10/97*

CRIME RISK

Your Chances of Becoming a Victim[1]

Area	Any Crime	Violent Crime					Property Crime			
		Any	Murder	Forcible Rape[2]	Robbery	Aggrav. Assault	Any	Burglary	Larceny -Theft	Motor Vehicle Theft
City	1:24	1:137	1:20,759	1:1,200	1:756	1:181	1:29	1:177	1:42	1:223

Note: (1) Figures have been calculated by dividing the population of the city by the number of crimes reported to the FBI during 1996 and are expressed as odds (eg. 1:20 should be read as 1 in 20).
(2) Figures have been calculated by dividing the female population of the city by the number of forcible rapes reported to the FBI during 1996. The female population of the city was estimated by calculating the ratio of females to males reported in the 1990 Census and applying that ratio to 1996 population estimate.
Source: FBI Uniform Crime Reports 1996

CRIME STATISTICS

Total Crimes and Total Crime Rates: 1977 - 1996

Year	Number				Rate per 100,000 population			
	City	Suburbs[2]	MSA[1]	U.S.	City	Suburbs[3]	MSA[1]	U.S.
1977	39,208	37,362	76,570	10,984,500	6,725.2	5,866.6	6,277.0	5,077.6
1978	41,831	37,473	79,304	11,209,000	7,054.1	5,907.4	6,461.5	5,140.3
1979	43,309	40,693	84,002	12,249,500	7,158.6	6,266.0	6,696.5	5,565.5
1980	51,831	46,404	98,235	13,408,300	8,252.0	7,005.6	7,612.2	5,950.0
1981	54,514	43,363	97,877	13,423,800	8,454.1	6,376.8	7,387.9	5,858.2
1982	51,781	39,984	91,765	12,974,400	7,846.8	5,745.5	6,768.2	5,603.6
1983	43,307	35,064	78,371	12,108,600	6,445.3	4,948.5	5,677.1	5,175.0
1984	39,818	31,624	71,442	11,881,800	5,806.1	4,536.2	5,165.9	5,031.3
1985	40,224	34,326	74,550	12,431,400	5,697.0	4,867.7	5,282.6	5,207.1
1986	38,979	34,872	73,851	13,211,900	5,394.6	4,832.1	5,113.5	5,480.4
1987	36,518	33,218	69,736	13,508,700	5,001.9	4,698.8	4,852.8	5,550.0
1988	38,406	32,791	71,197	13,923,100	5,246.6	4,626.1	4,941.3	5,664.2
1989	38,935	32,195	71,130	14,251,400	5,136.8	4,522.2	4,839.1	5,741.0
1990	38,090	31,434	69,524	14,475,600	4,869.3	4,394.3	4,642.4	5,820.3
1991	42,836	34,173	77,009	14,872,900	5,364.3	4,679.8	5,037.3	5,897.8
1992	39,802	34,142	73,944	14,438,200	4,905.7	4,601.9	4,760.6	5,660.2
1993	36,743	34,911	71,654	14,144,800	4,538.8	4,752.2	4,640.3	5,484.4
1994	36,559	31,619	68,178	13,989,500	4,484.5	4,274.0	4,384.3	5,373.5
1995	36,096	30,334	66,430	13,862,700	4,386.7	4,087.0	4,244.6	5,275.9
1996	34,287	29,209	63,496	13,473,600	4,129.1	3,899.7	4,020.3	5,078.9

Notes: (1) Metropolitan Statistical Area - see Appendix A for areas included; (2) calculated by the editors using the following formula: (number of crimes in the MSA minus number of crimes in the city); (3) calculated by the editors using the following formula: ((number of crimes in the MSA minus number of crimes in the city) ÷ (population of the MSA minus population of the city)) x 100,000; n/a not avail.
Source: U.S. Department of Justice, FBI Uniform Crime Reports, 1977 - 1996

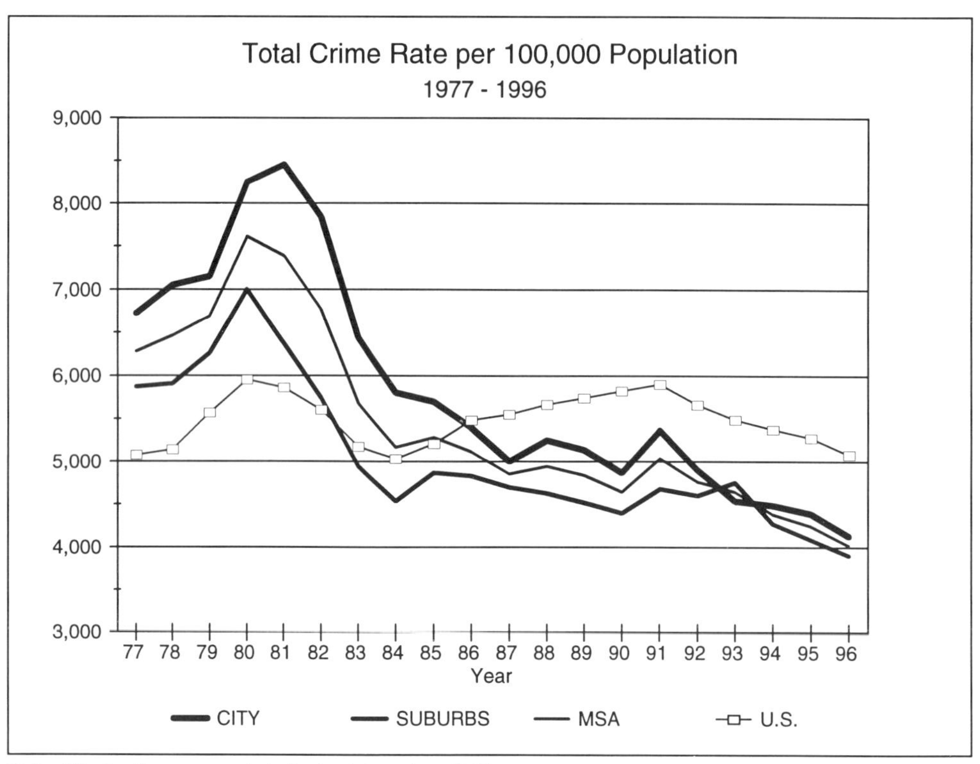

Note: Missing line segments indicate data not available.

Violent Crimes and Violent Crime Rates: 1977 - 1996

Year	Number				Rate per 100,000 population			
	City	Suburbs[2]	MSA[1]	U.S.	City	Suburbs[3]	MSA[1]	U.S.
1977	2,670	2,227	4,897	1,029,580	458.0	349.7	401.4	475.9
1978	2,755	2,212	4,967	1,085,550	464.6	348.7	404.7	497.8
1979	3,236	1,984	5,220	1,208,030	534.9	305.5	416.1	548.9
1980	3,788	2,844	6,632	1,344,520	603.1	429.4	513.9	596.6
1981	4,122	2,952	7,074	1,361,820	639.2	434.1	534.0	594.3
1982	3,616	2,227	5,843	1,322,390	548.0	320.0	431.0	571.1
1983	3,460	2,076	5,536	1,258,090	514.9	293.0	401.0	537.7
1984	3,295	2,207	5,502	1,273,280	480.5	316.6	397.8	539.2
1985	3,470	2,244	5,714	1,328,800	491.5	318.2	404.9	556.6
1986	4,020	2,545	6,565	1,489,170	556.4	352.6	454.6	617.7
1987	4,378	2,794	7,172	1,484,000	599.7	395.2	499.1	609.7
1988	4,689	3,102	7,791	1,566,220	640.6	437.6	540.7	637.2
1989	4,535	2,531	7,066	1,646,040	598.3	355.5	480.7	663.1
1990	4,698	2,569	7,267	1,820,130	600.6	359.1	485.3	731.8
1991	5,258	2,728	7,986	1,911,770	658.5	373.6	522.4	758.1
1992	5,427	2,609	8,036	1,932,270	668.9	351.7	517.4	757.5
1993	5,317	2,785	8,102	1,926,020	656.8	379.1	524.7	746.8
1994	5,915	3,041	8,956	1,857,670	725.6	411.1	575.9	713.6
1995	6,649	2,969	9,618	1,798,790	808.1	400.0	614.5	684.6
1996	6,075	2,802	8,877	1,682,280	731.6	374.1	562.1	634.1

Notes: Violent crimes include murder, forcible rape, robbery and aggravated assault; n/a not available; (1) Metropolitan Statistical Area - see Appendix A for areas included; (2) calculated by the editors using the following formula: (number of crimes in the MSA minus number of crimes in the city); (3) calculated by the editors using the following formula: ((number of crimes in the MSA minus number of crimes in the city) ÷ (population of the MSA minus population of the city)) x 100,000
Source: U.S. Department of Justice, FBI Uniform Crime Reports, 1977 - 1996

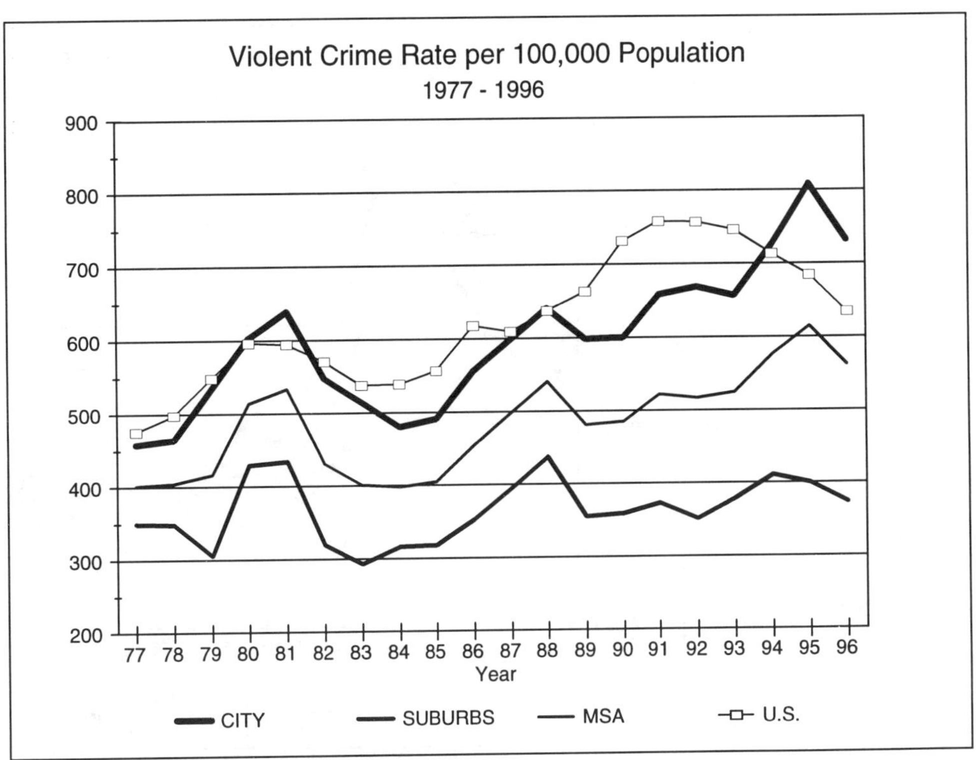

Note: Missing line segments indicate data not available.

Property Crimes and Property Crime Rates: 1977 - 1996

Year	Number				Rate per 100,000 population			
	City	Suburbs[2]	MSA[1]	U.S.	City	Suburbs[3]	MSA[1]	U.S.
1977	36,538	35,135	71,673	9,955,000	6,267.2	5,516.9	5,875.5	4,601.7
1978	39,076	35,261	74,337	10,123,400	6,589.5	5,558.7	6,056.8	4,642.5
1979	40,073	38,709	78,782	11,041,500	6,623.7	5,960.5	6,280.4	5,016.6
1980	48,043	43,560	91,603	12,063,700	7,648.9	6,576.3	7,098.3	5,353.3
1981	50,392	40,411	90,803	12,061,900	7,814.9	5,942.7	6,853.9	5,263.9
1982	48,165	37,757	85,922	11,652,000	7,298.8	5,425.5	6,337.3	5,032.5
1983	39,847	32,988	72,835	10,850,500	5,930.4	4,655.6	5,276.0	4,637.4
1984	36,523	29,417	65,940	10,608,500	5,325.7	4,219.6	4,768.1	4,492.1
1985	36,754	32,082	68,836	11,102,600	5,205.5	4,549.5	4,877.7	4,650.5
1986	34,959	32,327	67,286	11,722,700	4,838.2	4,479.4	4,658.9	4,862.6
1987	32,140	30,424	62,564	12,024,700	4,402.3	4,303.6	4,353.7	4,940.3
1988	33,717	29,689	63,406	12,356,900	4,606.0	4,188.5	4,400.6	5,027.1
1989	34,400	29,664	64,064	12,605,400	4,538.5	4,166.7	4,358.4	5,077.9
1990	33,392	28,865	62,257	12,655,500	4,268.7	4,035.2	4,157.2	5,088.5
1991	37,578	31,445	69,023	12,961,100	4,705.8	4,306.2	4,515.0	5,139.7
1992	34,375	31,533	65,908	12,505,900	4,236.8	4,250.2	4,243.2	4,902.7
1993	31,426	32,126	63,552	12,218,800	3,882.0	4,373.1	4,115.6	4,737.6
1994	30,644	28,578	59,222	12,131,900	3,758.9	3,862.9	3,808.4	4,660.0
1995	29,447	27,365	56,812	12,063,900	3,578.7	3,686.9	3,630.0	4,591.3
1996	28,212	26,407	54,619	11,791,300	3,397.5	3,525.6	3,458.3	4,444.8

Notes: Property crimes include burglary, larceny-theft and motor vehicle theft; n/a not available; (1) Metropolitan Statistical Area - see Appendix A for areas included; (2) calculated by the editors using the following formula: (number of crimes in the MSA minus number of crimes in the city); (3) calculated by the editors using the following formula: ((number of crimes in the MSA minus number of crimes in the city) ÷ (population of the MSA minus population of the city)) x 100,000
Source: U.S. Department of Justice, FBI Uniform Crime Reports, 1977 - 1996

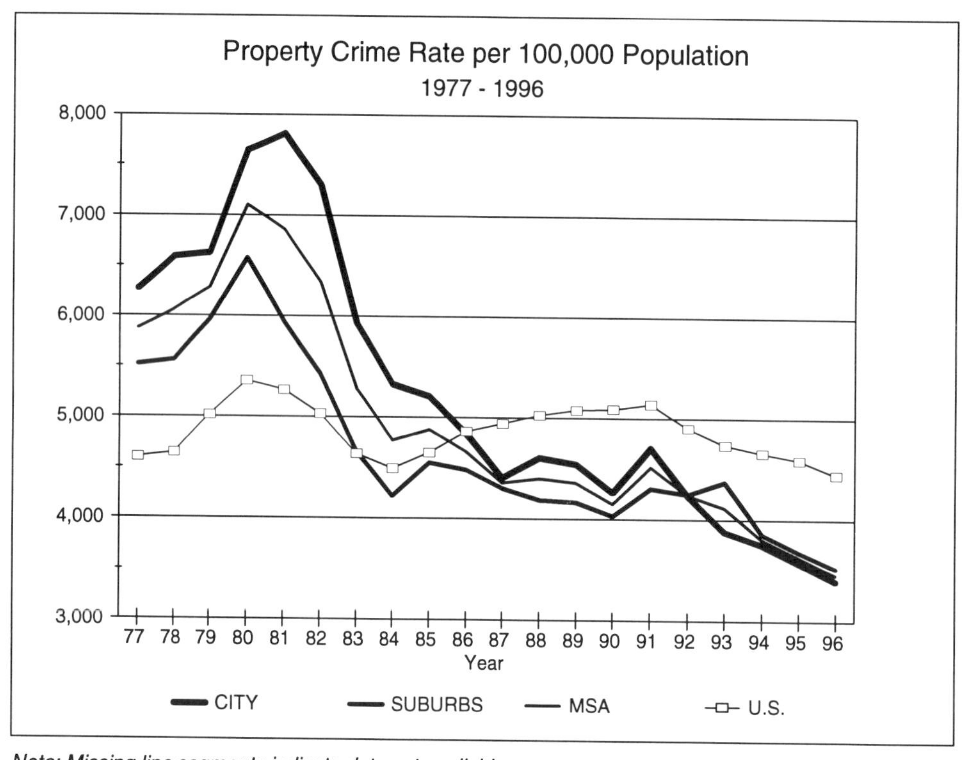

Note: Missing line segments indicate data not available.

Murders and Murder Rates: 1977 - 1996

Year	Number				Rate per 100,000 population			
	City	Suburbs[2]	MSA[1]	U.S.	City	Suburbs[3]	MSA[1]	U.S.
1977	41	27	68	19,120	7.0	4.2	5.6	8.8
1978	44	31	75	19,560	7.4	4.9	6.1	9.0
1979	44	30	74	21,460	7.3	4.6	5.9	9.7
1980	62	36	98	23,040	9.9	5.4	7.6	10.2
1981	68	29	97	22,520	10.5	4.3	7.3	9.8
1982	37	24	61	21,010	5.6	3.4	4.5	9.1
1983	48	24	72	19,310	7.1	3.4	5.2	8.3
1984	48	27	75	18,690	7.0	3.9	5.4	7.9
1985	55	31	86	18,980	7.8	4.4	6.1	7.9
1986	39	20	59	20,610	5.4	2.8	4.1	8.6
1987	24	25	49	20,100	3.3	3.5	3.4	8.3
1988	37	31	68	20,680	5.1	4.4	4.7	8.4
1989	38	18	56	21,500	5.0	2.5	3.8	8.7
1990	35	22	57	23,440	4.5	3.1	3.8	9.4
1991	53	24	77	24,700	6.6	3.3	5.0	9.8
1992	43	25	68	23,760	5.3	3.4	4.4	9.3
1993	41	20	61	24,530	5.1	2.7	4.0	9.5
1994	33	23	56	23,330	4.0	3.1	3.6	9.0
1995	38	18	56	21,610	4.6	2.4	3.6	8.2
1996	40	8	48	19,650	4.8	1.1	3.0	7.4

Notes: (1) Metropolitan Statistical Area - see Appendix A for areas included; (2) calculated by the editors using the following formula: (number of crimes in the MSA minus number of crimes in the city); (3) calculated by the editors using the following formula: ((number of crimes in the MSA minus number of crimes in the city) ÷ (population of the MSA minus population of the city)) x 100,000; n/a not avail.
Source: U.S. Department of Justice, FBI Uniform Crime Reports, 1977 - 1996

Forcible Rapes and Forcible Rape Rates: 1977 - 1996

Year	Number				Rate per 100,000 population			
	City	Suburbs[2]	MSA[1]	U.S.	City	Suburbs[3]	MSA[1]	U.S.
1977	322	230	552	63,500	55.2	36.1	45.3	29.4
1978	367	224	591	67,610	61.9	35.3	48.2	31.0
1979	407	198	605	76,390	67.3	30.5	48.2	34.7
1980	479	277	756	82,990	76.3	41.8	58.6	36.8
1981	465	246	711	82,500	72.1	36.2	53.7	36.0
1982	430	244	674	78,770	65.2	35.1	49.7	34.0
1983	447	255	702	78,920	66.5	36.0	50.9	33.7
1984	421	227	648	84,230	61.4	32.6	46.9	35.7
1985	415	211	626	88,670	58.8	29.9	44.4	37.1
1986	430	241	671	91,460	59.5	33.4	46.5	37.9
1987	393	203	596	91,110	53.8	28.7	41.5	37.4
1988	438	206	644	92,490	59.8	29.1	44.7	37.6
1989	399	226	625	94,500	52.6	31.7	42.5	38.1
1990	416	229	645	102,560	53.2	32.0	43.1	41.2
1991	445	239	684	106,590	55.7	32.7	44.7	42.3
1992	448	211	659	109,060	55.2	28.4	42.4	42.8
1993	391	199	590	106,010	48.3	27.1	38.2	41.1
1994	375	186	561	102,220	46.0	25.1	36.1	39.3
1995	387	181	568	97,470	47.0	24.4	36.3	37.1
1996	341	202	543	95,770	41.1	27.0	34.4	36.1

Notes: (1) Metropolitan Statistical Area - see Appendix A for areas included; (2) calculated by the editors using the following formula: (number of crimes in the MSA minus number of crimes in the city); (3) calculated by the editors using the following formula: ((number of crimes in the MSA minus number of crimes in the city) ÷ (population of the MSA minus population of the city)) x 100,000; n/a not avail.
Source: U.S. Department of Justice, FBI Uniform Crime Reports, 1977 - 1996

Robberies and Robbery Rates: 1977 - 1996

Year	Number				Rate per 100,000 population			
	City	Suburbs[2]	MSA[1]	U.S.	City	Suburbs[3]	MSA[1]	U.S.
1977	1,031	841	1,872	412,610	176.8	132.1	153.5	190.7
1978	1,155	759	1,914	426,930	194.8	119.7	155.9	195.8
1979	1,358	765	2,123	480,700	224.5	117.8	169.2	218.4
1980	1,714	1,003	2,717	565,840	272.9	151.4	210.5	251.1
1981	2,070	1,179	3,249	592,910	321.0	173.4	245.2	258.7
1982	1,701	889	2,590	553,130	257.8	127.7	191.0	238.9
1983	1,461	618	2,079	506,570	217.4	87.2	150.6	216.5
1984	1,175	597	1,772	485,010	171.3	85.6	128.1	205.4
1985	1,237	683	1,920	497,870	175.2	96.9	136.1	208.5
1986	1,126	614	1,740	542,780	155.8	85.1	120.5	225.1
1987	944	572	1,516	517,700	129.3	80.9	105.5	212.7
1988	948	546	1,494	542,970	129.5	77.0	103.7	220.9
1989	995	502	1,497	578,330	131.3	70.5	101.8	233.0
1990	1,034	527	1,561	639,270	132.2	73.7	104.2	257.0
1991	1,328	662	1,990	687,730	166.3	90.7	130.2	272.7
1992	1,231	687	1,918	672,480	151.7	92.6	123.5	263.6
1993	1,186	616	1,802	659,870	146.5	83.9	116.7	255.9
1994	1,109	728	1,837	618,950	136.0	98.4	118.1	237.7
1995	1,209	751	1,960	580,510	146.9	101.2	125.2	220.9
1996	1,098	644	1,742	537,050	132.2	86.0	110.3	202.4

Notes: (1) Metropolitan Statistical Area - see Appendix A for areas included; (2) calculated by the editors using the following formula: (number of crimes in the MSA minus number of crimes in the city); (3) calculated by the editors using the following formula: ((number of crimes in the MSA minus number of crimes in the city) ÷ (population of the MSA minus population of the city)) x 100,000; n/a not avail.
Source: U.S. Department of Justice, FBI Uniform Crime Reports, 1977 - 1996

Aggravated Assaults and Aggravated Assault Rates: 1977 - 1996

Year	Number				Rate per 100,000 population			
	City	Suburbs[2]	MSA[1]	U.S.	City	Suburbs[3]	MSA[1]	U.S.
1977	1,276	1,129	2,405	534,350	218.9	177.3	197.2	247.0
1978	1,189	1,198	2,387	571,460	200.5	188.9	194.5	262.1
1979	1,427	991	2,418	629,480	235.9	152.6	192.8	286.0
1980	1,533	1,528	3,061	672,650	244.1	230.7	237.2	298.5
1981	1,519	1,498	3,017	663,900	235.6	220.3	227.7	289.7
1982	1,448	1,070	2,518	669,480	219.4	153.8	185.7	289.2
1983	1,504	1,179	2,683	653,290	223.8	166.4	194.4	279.2
1984	1,651	1,356	3,007	685,350	240.7	194.5	217.4	290.2
1985	1,763	1,319	3,082	723,250	249.7	187.0	218.4	302.9
1986	2,425	1,670	4,095	834,320	335.6	231.4	283.5	346.1
1987	3,017	1,994	5,011	855,090	413.2	282.1	348.7	351.3
1988	3,266	2,319	5,585	910,090	446.2	327.2	387.6	370.2
1989	3,103	1,785	4,888	951,710	409.4	250.7	332.5	383.4
1990	3,213	1,791	5,004	1,054,860	410.7	250.4	334.1	424.1
1991	3,432	1,803	5,235	1,092,740	429.8	246.9	342.4	433.3
1992	3,705	1,686	5,391	1,126,970	456.7	227.2	347.1	441.8
1993	3,699	1,950	5,649	1,135,610	456.9	265.4	365.8	440.3
1994	4,398	2,104	6,502	1,113,180	539.5	284.4	418.1	427.6
1995	5,015	2,019	7,034	1,099,210	609.5	272.0	449.4	418.3
1996	4,596	1,948	6,544	1,029,810	553.5	260.1	414.3	388.2

Notes: (1) Metropolitan Statistical Area - see Appendix A for areas included; (2) calculated by the editors using the following formula: (number of crimes in the MSA minus number of crimes in the city); (3) calculated by the editors using the following formula: ((number of crimes in the MSA minus number of crimes in the city) ÷ (population of the MSA minus population of the city)) x 100,000; n/a not avail.
Source: U.S. Department of Justice, FBI Uniform Crime Reports, 1977 - 1996

Burglaries and Burglary Rates: 1977 - 1996

Year	Number				Rate per 100,000 population			
	City	Suburbs[2]	MSA[1]	U.S.	City	Suburbs[3]	MSA[1]	U.S.
1977	12,027	10,367	22,394	3,071,500	2,063.0	1,627.8	1,835.8	1,419.8
1978	13,749	10,291	24,040	3,128,300	2,318.5	1,622.3	1,958.7	1,434.6
1979	12,042	10,045	22,087	3,327,700	1,990.4	1,546.8	1,760.7	1,511.9
1980	13,955	11,622	25,577	3,795,200	2,221.8	1,754.6	1,982.0	1,684.1
1981	14,932	10,710	25,642	3,779,700	2,315.7	1,575.0	1,935.5	1,649.5
1982	12,593	8,974	21,567	3,447,100	1,908.3	1,289.5	1,590.7	1,488.8
1983	10,104	7,806	17,910	3,129,900	1,503.8	1,101.7	1,297.4	1,337.7
1984	9,457	6,847	16,304	2,984,400	1,379.0	982.1	1,178.9	1,263.7
1985	9,359	7,376	16,735	3,073,300	1,325.5	1,046.0	1,185.8	1,287.3
1986	7,663	6,748	14,411	3,241,400	1,060.5	935.0	997.8	1,344.6
1987	6,434	6,016	12,450	3,236,200	881.3	851.0	866.4	1,329.6
1988	6,560	5,484	12,044	3,218,100	896.1	773.7	835.9	1,309.2
1989	6,318	5,676	11,994	3,168,200	833.5	797.3	816.0	1,276.3
1990	5,752	5,165	10,917	3,073,900	735.3	722.0	729.0	1,235.9
1991	7,403	5,618	13,021	3,157,200	927.1	769.4	851.7	1,252.0
1992	6,776	5,737	12,513	2,979,900	835.2	773.3	805.6	1,168.2
1993	6,014	5,792	11,806	2,834,800	742.9	788.4	764.6	1,099.2
1994	5,823	5,075	10,898	2,712,800	714.3	686.0	700.8	1,042.0
1995	5,477	4,745	10,222	2,593,800	665.6	639.3	653.1	987.1
1996	4,700	4,222	8,922	2,501,500	566.0	563.7	564.9	943.0

Notes: (1) Metropolitan Statistical Area - see Appendix A for areas included; (2) calculated by the editors using the following formula: (number of crimes in the MSA minus number of crimes in the city); (3) calculated by the editors using the following formula: ((number of crimes in the MSA minus number of crimes in the city) ÷ (population of the MSA minus population of the city)) x 100,000; n/a not avail.
Source: U.S. Department of Justice, FBI Uniform Crime Reports, 1977 - 1996

Larceny-Thefts and Larceny-Theft Rates: 1977 - 1996

Year	Number				Rate per 100,000 population			
	City	Suburbs[2]	MSA[1]	U.S.	City	Suburbs[3]	MSA[1]	U.S.
1977	21,064	22,316	43,380	5,905,700	3,613.0	3,504.1	3,556.1	2,729.9
1978	21,731	22,222	43,953	5,991,000	3,664.6	3,503.2	3,581.2	2,747.4
1979	24,019	25,810	49,829	6,601,000	3,970.1	3,974.3	3,972.3	2,999.1
1980	29,608	28,972	58,580	7,136,900	4,713.9	4,373.9	4,539.4	3,167.0
1981	31,708	27,103	58,811	7,194,400	4,917.3	3,985.7	4,439.1	3,139.7
1982	32,199	26,597	58,796	7,142,500	4,879.4	3,821.9	4,336.6	3,084.8
1983	26,959	23,254	50,213	6,712,800	4,012.3	3,281.8	3,637.3	2,868.9
1984	24,296	20,855	45,151	6,591,900	3,542.8	2,991.4	3,264.8	2,791.3
1985	24,331	22,768	47,099	6,926,400	3,446.0	3,228.7	3,337.4	2,901.2
1986	24,241	23,713	47,954	7,257,200	3,354.9	3,285.8	3,320.4	3,010.3
1987	22,259	22,306	44,565	7,499,900	3,048.8	3,155.2	3,101.2	3,081.3
1988	23,118	21,908	45,026	7,705,900	3,158.1	3,090.7	3,125.0	3,134.9
1989	23,656	21,559	45,215	7,872,400	3,121.0	3,028.2	3,076.1	3,171.3
1990	23,435	21,242	44,677	7,945,700	2,995.9	2,969.5	2,983.3	3,194.8
1991	25,663	23,328	48,991	8,142,200	3,213.7	3,194.7	3,204.6	3,228.8
1992	23,806	23,430	47,236	7,915,200	2,934.2	3,158.0	3,041.1	3,103.0
1993	21,398	23,665	45,063	7,820,900	2,643.3	3,221.4	2,918.3	3,032.4
1994	20,300	20,986	41,286	7,879,800	2,490.1	2,836.7	2,655.0	3,026.7
1995	19,745	20,317	40,062	7,997,700	2,399.6	2,737.4	2,559.8	3,043.8
1996	19,793	20,200	39,993	7,894,600	2,383.6	2,696.9	2,532.2	2,975.9

Notes: (1) Metropolitan Statistical Area - see Appendix A for areas included; (2) calculated by the editors using the following formula: (number of crimes in the MSA minus number of crimes in the city); (3) calculated by the editors using the following formula: ((number of crimes in the MSA minus number of crimes in the city) ÷ (population of the MSA minus population of the city)) x 100,000; n/a not avail.
Source: U.S. Department of Justice, FBI Uniform Crime Reports, 1977 - 1996

Motor Vehicle Thefts and Motor Vehicle Theft Rates: 1977 - 1996

Year	Number				Rate per 100,000 population			
	City	Suburbs[2]	MSA[1]	U.S.	City	Suburbs[3]	MSA[1]	U.S.
1977	3,447	2,452	5,899	977,700	591.3	385.0	483.6	451.9
1978	3,596	2,748	6,344	1,004,100	606.4	433.2	516.9	460.5
1979	4,012	2,854	6,866	1,112,800	663.1	439.5	547.3	505.6
1980	4,480	2,966	7,446	1,131,700	713.3	447.8	577.0	502.2
1981	3,752	2,598	6,350	1,087,800	581.9	382.1	479.3	474.7
1982	3,373	2,186	5,559	1,062,400	511.1	314.1	410.0	458.8
1983	2,784	1,928	4,712	1,007,900	414.3	272.1	341.3	430.8
1984	2,770	1,715	4,485	1,032,200	403.9	246.0	324.3	437.1
1985	3,064	1,938	5,002	1,102,900	434.0	274.8	354.4	462.0
1986	3,055	1,866	4,921	1,224,100	422.8	258.6	340.7	507.8
1987	3,447	2,102	5,549	1,288,700	472.1	297.3	386.1	529.4
1988	4,039	2,297	6,336	1,432,900	551.8	324.1	439.7	582.9
1989	4,426	2,429	6,855	1,564,800	583.9	341.2	466.4	630.4
1990	4,205	2,458	6,663	1,635,900	537.6	343.6	444.9	657.8
1991	4,512	2,499	7,011	1,661,700	565.0	342.2	458.6	659.0
1992	3,793	2,366	6,159	1,610,800	467.5	318.9	396.5	631.5
1993	4,014	2,669	6,683	1,563,100	495.8	363.3	432.8	606.1
1994	4,521	2,517	7,038	1,539,300	554.6	340.2	452.6	591.3
1995	4,225	2,303	6,528	1,472,400	513.5	310.3	417.1	560.4
1996	3,719	1,985	5,704	1,395,200	447.9	265.0	361.2	525.9

Notes: (1) Metropolitan Statistical Area - see Appendix A for areas included; (2) calculated by the editors using the following formula: (number of crimes in the MSA minus number of crimes in the city); (3) calculated by the editors using the following formula: ((number of crimes in the MSA minus number of crimes in the city) ÷ (population of the MSA minus population of the city)) x 100,000; n/a not avail.
Source: U.S. Department of Justice, FBI Uniform Crime Reports, 1977 - 1996

HATE CRIMES

Criminal Incidents by Bias Motivation

Area	Race	Ethnicity	Religion	Sexual Orientation
San Jose	14	2	0	5

Notes: Figures include both violent and property crimes. Law enforcement agencies must have submitted data for at least one quarter of calendar year 1995 to be included in this report, therefore figures shown may not represent complete 12-month totals; n/a not available
Source: U.S. Department of Justice, FBI Uniform Crime Reports, Hate Crime Statistics 1995

ILLEGAL DRUGS

Drug Use by Adult Arrestees

Sex	Percent Testing Positive by Urinalysis (%)				
	Any Drug[1]	Cocaine	Marijuana	Opiates	Multiple Drugs
Male	48	16	27	5	15
Female	53	21	19	9	23

Notes: The catchment area is the entire county; (1) Includes cocaine, opiates, marijuana, methadone, phencyclidine (PCP), benzodiazepines, methaqualone, propoxyphene, barbiturates & amphetamines
Source: National Institute of Justice, 1996 Drug Use Forecasting, Annual Report on Adult and Juvenile Arrestees (released June 1997)

LAW ENFORCEMENT

Full-Time Law Enforcement Employees

Jurisdiction	Police Employees			Police Officers per 100,000 population
	Total	Officers	Civilians	
San Jose	1,706	1,300	406	156.6

Notes: Data as of October 31, 1996
Source: U.S. Department of Justice, FBI Uniform Crime Reports, 1996

Number of Police Officers by Race

Race	Police Officers				Index of Representation[1]		
	1983		1992				
	Number	Pct.	Number	Pct.	1983	1992	% Chg.
Black	20	2.2	50	4.1	0.46	0.85	84.8
Hispanic[2]	159	17.4	240	19.6	0.78	0.74	-5.1

Notes: (1) The index of representation is calculated by dividing the percent of black/hispanic police officers by the percent of corresponding blacks/hispanics in the local population. An index approaching 1.0 indicates that a city is closer to achieving a representation of police officers equal to their proportion in the local population; (2) Hispanic officers can be of any race
Source: Bureau of Justice Statistics, Sourcebook of Criminal Justice Statistics, 1994

CORRECTIONS

Federal Correctional Facilities

Type	Year Opened	Security Level	Sex of Inmates	Rated Capacity	Population on 7/1/95	Number of Staff
None listed						

Notes: Data as of 1995
Source: Bureau of Justice Statistics, Sourcebook of Criminal Justice Statistics Online

City/County/Regional Correctional Facilities

Name	Year Opened	Year Renov.	Rated Capacity	1995 Pop.	Number of COs[1]	Number of Staff	ACA[2] Accred.
Santa Clara Co Dept of Corrections	n/a	--	n/a	n/a	n/a	n/a	No
Santa Clara County Women's Residential Center	1963	1987	34	n/a	n/a	n/a	No

Notes: Data as of April 1996; (1) Correctional Officers; (2) American Correctional Assn. Accreditation
Source: American Correctional Association, 1996-1998 National Jail and Adult Detention Directory

Private Adult Correctional Facilities

Name	Date Opened	Rated Capacity	Present Pop.	Security Level	Facility Construct.	Expans. Plans	ACA[1] Accred.
None listed							

Notes: Data as of December 1996; (1) American Correctional Association Accreditation
Source: University of Florida, Center for Studies in Criminology and Law, Private Adult Correctional Facility Census, 10th Ed., March 15, 1997

Characteristics of Shock Incarceration Programs

Jurisdiction	Year Program Began	Number of Camps	Average Num. of Inmates	Number of Beds	Program Length	Voluntary/ Mandatory
California	1993	3[a]	350	200[b]	4 months[c]	Voluntary

Note: Data as of July 1996; (a) One boot camp; two work training and parole camps; (b) 200 program beds at San Quentin shock incarceration facility. Work training beds vary with each facility; (c) Shock incarceration and intensive parole programs: 4 months; Work training program: 2 months
Source: Sourcebook of Criminal Justice Statistics Online

INMATES AND HIV/AIDS

HIV Testing Policies for Inmates

Jurisdiction	All Inmates at Some Time	All Convicted Inmates at Admission	Random Samples While in Custody	High-risk Groups	Upon Inmate Request	Upon Court Order	Upon Involvement in Incident
Santa Clara Co.	Yes	No	No	No	Yes	Yes	No

Source: HIV in Prisons and Jails, 1993 (released August 1995)

Inmates Known to be Positive for HIV

Jurisdiction	Number of Jail Inmates in Facilities Providing Data	Type of HIV Infection/AIDS Cases				HIV/AIDS Cases as a Percent of Tot. Custody Pop.
		Total	Asymptomatic	Symptomatic	Confirmed AIDS	
Santa Clara Co.	4,237	25	7	18	0	0.6

Source: HIV in Prisons and Jails, 1993 (released August, 1995)

DEATH PENALTY

Death Penalty Statistics

State	Prisoners Executed		Prisoners Under Sentence of Death					Avg. No. of Years on Death Row[4]
	1930-1995	1996[1]	Total[2]	White[3]	Black[3]	Hisp.	Women	
California	294	2	420	251	160	61	8	7.0

Notes: Data as of 12/31/95 unless otherwise noted; (1) Data as of 7/31/97; (2) Includes persons of other races; (3) Includes people of Hispanic origin; (4) Covers prisoners sentenced 1974 through 1995
Source: Bureau of Justice Statistics, Capital Punishment 1995 (released 12/96); Death Penalty Information Center Web Site, 9/30/97

Capital Offenses and Methods of Execution

Capital Offenses in California	Minimum Age for Imposition of Death Penalty	Mentally Retarded Excluded	Methods of Execution[1]
First-degree murder with special circumstances; train-wrecking; treason; perjury causing execution.	18	No	Lethal injection; lethal gas

Notes: Data as of 12/31/95 unless otherwise noted; (1) Data as of 7/31/97
Source: Bureau of Justice Statistics, Capital Punishment 1995 (released 12/96); Death Penalty Information Center Web Site, 9/30/97

LAWS

Statutory Provisions Relating to the Purchase, Ownership and Use of Handguns

Jurisdiction	Instant Background Check	Federal Waiting Period Applies[1]	State Waiting Period (days)	License or Permit to Purchase	Regis-tration	Record of Sale Sent to Police	Concealed Carry Law
California	No	No	15	No	No	Yes	Yes[a]

Note: Data as of 1996; (1) The Federal 5-day waiting period for handgun purchases applies to states that don't have instant background checks, waiting period requirements, or licensing procedures exempting them from the Federal requirement; (a) Restrictively administered discretion by local authorities over permit issuance, or permits are unavailable and carrying is prohibited in most circumstances
Source: Sourcebook of Criminal Justice Statistics Online

Statutory Provisions Relating to Alcohol Use and Driving

Jurisdiction	Drinking Age	Blood Alcohol Concentration Levels as Evidence in State Courts[1]		Open Container Law[1]	Anti-Consump-tion Law[1]	Dram Shop Law[1]
		Illegal per se at 0.10%	Presumption at 0.10%			
California	21	(a)	(a)	Yes	Yes	Yes[b]

Note: Data as of January 1, 1997; (1) See Appendix C for an explanation of terms; (a) 0.08%; (b) Applies only to the actions of intoxicated minors
Source: Sourcebook of Criminal Justice Statistics Online

Statutory Provisions Relating to Curfews

Jurisdiction	Year Enacted	Latest Revision	Age Group(s)	Curfew Provisions
San Jose	1994	-	16 and 17 15 and under	11:30 pm to 5 am every night 10 pm to 5 am every night

Note: Data as of February 1996
Source: Sourcebook of Criminal Justice Statistics Online

Statutory Provisions Relating to Hate Crimes

Jurisdiction	Bias-Motivated Violence and Intimidation						Institutional Vandalism
	Civil Action	Criminal Penalty					
		Race/ Religion/ Ethnicity	Sexual Orientation	Mental/ Physical Disability	Gender	Age	
California	Yes	Yes	Yes	Yes	Yes	No	Yes

Source: Anti-Defamation League, 1997 Hate Crimes Laws

Seattle, Washington

OVERVIEW

The total crime rate for the city increased 31.4% between 1977 and 1996. During that same period, the violent crime rate decreased 0.9% and the property crime rate increased 35.3%.

Among violent crimes, the rates for: Murders decreased 4.2%; Forcible Rapes decreased 36.1%; Robberies increased 0.9%; and Aggravated Assaults increased 4.1%.

Among property crimes, the rates for: Burglaries decreased 33.5%; Larceny-Thefts increased 63.9%; and Motor Vehicle Thefts increased 84.9%.

ANTI-CRIME PROGRAMS

The city was among the six selected for a nationwide city project to examine the effects of "intense, all-out intervention into the lives of impoverished young people." The idea is to change the child's behavior by taking care of the family's problems. Preliminary results suggest that the approach can have a dramatic effect on juvenile crime in a particular neighborhood.

Families and Schools Together (FAST TRACK), a highly regarded violence-prevention program is being used in selected schools. The program combines training for parents and special enrichment classes for selected students, the 10% as seen as most troubled.
New York Times, 12/30/94

CRIME RISK

Your Chances of Becoming a Victim[1]

Area	Any Crime	Violent Crime					Property Crime			
		Any	Murder	Forcible Rape[2]	Robbery	Aggrav. Assault	Any	Burglary	Larceny -Theft	Motor Vehicle Theft
City	1:10	1:119	1:14,584	1:1,060	1:275	1:236	1:11	1:69	1:15	1:85

Note: (1) Figures have been calculated by dividing the population of the city by the number of crimes reported to the FBI during 1996 and are expressed as odds (eg. 1:20 should be read as 1 in 20).
(2) Figures have been calculated by dividing the female population of the city by the number of forcible rapes reported to the FBI during 1996. The female population of the city was estimated by calculating the ratio of females to males reported in the 1990 Census and applying that ratio to 1996 population estimate.
Source: FBI Uniform Crime Reports 1996

CRIME STATISTICS

Total Crimes and Total Crime Rates: 1977 - 1996

Year	Number				Rate per 100,000 population			
	City	Suburbs[2]	MSA[1]	U.S.	City	Suburbs[3]	MSA[1]	U.S.
1977	38,378	53,021	91,399	10,984,500	7,848.3	5,629.4	6,387.7	5,077.6
1978	44,084	57,574	101,658	11,209,000	9,089.5	5,791.8	6,873.2	5,140.3
1979	46,339	63,395	109,734	12,249,500	8,884.2	6,300.3	7,182.5	5,565.5
1980	53,294	72,555	125,849	13,408,300	10,834.4	6,543.4	7,862.0	5,950.0
1981	55,764	71,481	127,245	13,423,800	11,070.9	6,295.5	7,763.0	5,858.2
1982	53,401	66,233	119,634	12,974,400	10,519.4	5,788.0	7,241.9	5,603.6
1983	53,039	64,248	117,287	12,108,600	10,312.5	5,542.8	7,008.7	5,175.0
1984	56,019	63,809	119,828	11,881,800	11,257.9	5,337.7	7,077.7	5,031.3
1985	63,102	70,391	133,493	12,431,400	12,743.0	5,770.5	7,783.7	5,207.1
1986	67,740	73,361	141,101	13,211,900	13,513.4	5,941.6	8,128.0	5,480.4
1987	72,937	76,983	149,920	13,508,700	14,751.9	5,986.9	8,421.1	5,550.0
1988	72,694	80,094	152,788	13,923,100	14,384.0	6,058.5	8,361.0	5,664.2
1989	66,396	77,508	143,904	14,251,400	12,907.5	5,568.7	7,549.1	5,741.0
1990	65,053	74,931	139,984	14,475,600	12,600.8	5,146.1	7,097.4	5,820.3
1991	65,208	80,282	145,490	14,872,900	12,247.5	5,347.4	7,153.8	5,897.8
1992	65,400	73,986	139,386	14,438,200	12,001.3	4,907.0	6,790.4	5,660.2
1993	62,679	80,303	142,982	14,144,800	11,797.9	5,198.8	6,887.6	5,484.4
1994	57,905	83,277	141,182	13,989,500	10,717.8	4,997.2	6,397.8	5,373.5
1995	55,507	n/a	n/a	13,862,700	10,482.4	n/a	n/a	5,275.9
1996	55,636	n/a	n/a	13,473,600	10,310.8	n/a	n/a	5,078.9

Notes: (1) Metropolitan Statistical Area - see Appendix A for areas included; (2) calculated by the editors using the following formula: (number of crimes in the MSA minus number of crimes in the city); (3) calculated by the editors using the following formula: ((number of crimes in the MSA minus number of crimes in the city) ÷ (population of the MSA minus population of the city)) x 100,000; n/a not avail.
Source: U.S. Department of Justice, FBI Uniform Crime Reports, 1977 - 1996

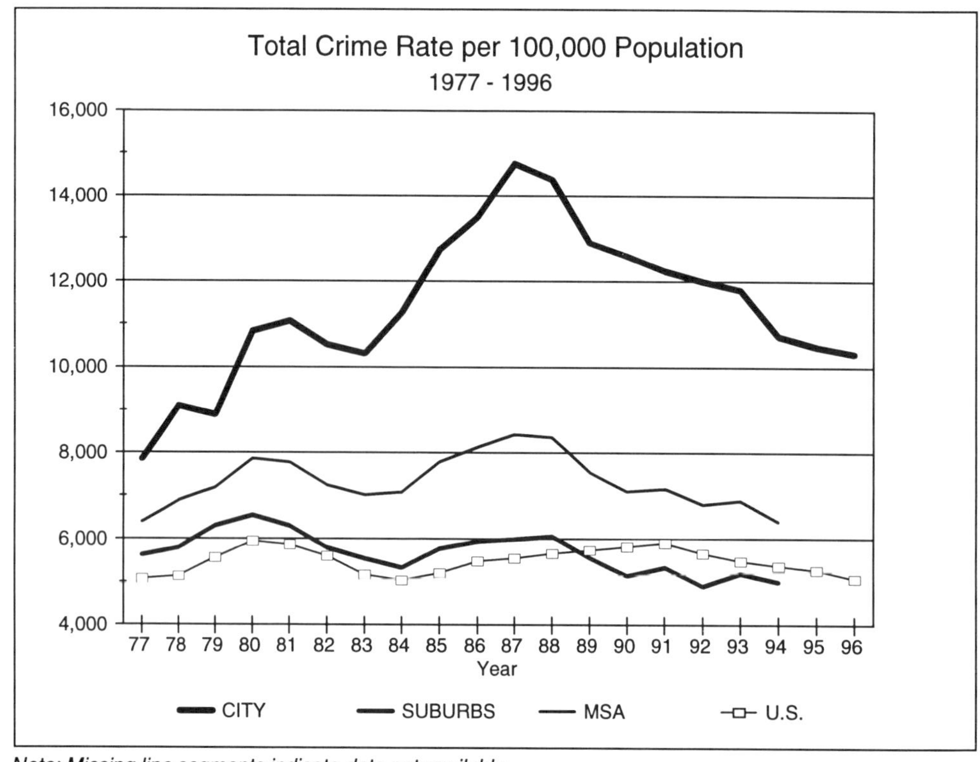

Note: Missing line segments indicate data not available.

Violent Crimes and Violent Crime Rates: 1977 - 1996

Year	Number				Rate per 100,000 population			
	City	Suburbs[2]	MSA[1]	U.S.	City	Suburbs[3]	MSA[1]	U.S.
1977	4,156	2,696	6,852	1,029,580	849.9	286.2	478.9	475.9
1978	4,900	2,963	7,863	1,085,550	1,010.3	298.1	531.6	497.8
1979	4,857	3,085	7,942	1,208,030	931.2	306.6	519.8	548.9
1980	5,201	3,752	8,953	1,344,520	1,057.3	338.4	559.3	596.6
1981	5,414	3,644	9,058	1,361,820	1,074.9	320.9	552.6	594.3
1982	5,120	3,060	8,180	1,322,390	1,008.6	267.4	495.2	571.1
1983	4,818	2,677	7,495	1,258,090	936.8	230.9	447.9	537.7
1984	5,553	3,020	8,573	1,273,280	1,116.0	252.6	506.4	539.2
1985	6,523	3,135	9,658	1,328,800	1,317.3	257.0	563.1	556.6
1986	6,790	2,964	9,754	1,489,170	1,354.5	240.1	561.9	617.7
1987	7,096	2,905	10,001	1,484,000	1,435.2	225.9	561.8	609.7
1988	6,879	3,332	10,211	1,566,220	1,361.2	252.0	558.8	637.2
1989	6,878	3,624	10,502	1,646,040	1,337.1	260.4	550.9	663.1
1990	7,780	4,061	11,841	1,820,130	1,507.0	278.9	600.4	731.8
1991	7,221	4,909	12,130	1,911,770	1,356.3	327.0	596.4	758.1
1992	7,327	4,491	11,818	1,932,270	1,344.6	297.9	575.7	757.5
1993	7,437	4,929	12,366	1,926,020	1,399.8	319.1	595.7	746.8
1994	6,538	5,429	11,967	1,857,670	1,210.1	325.8	542.3	713.6
1995	4,904	n/a	n/a	1,798,790	926.1	n/a	n/a	684.6
1996	4,543	n/a	n/a	1,682,280	841.9	n/a	n/a	634.1

Notes: Violent crimes include murder, forcible rape, robbery and aggravated assault; n/a not available; (1) Metropolitan Statistical Area - see Appendix A for areas included; (2) calculated by the editors using the following formula: (number of crimes in the MSA minus number of crimes in the city); (3) calculated by the editors using the following formula: ((number of crimes in the MSA minus number of crimes in the city) ÷ (population of the MSA minus population of the city)) x 100,000
Source: U.S. Department of Justice, FBI Uniform Crime Reports, 1977 - 1996

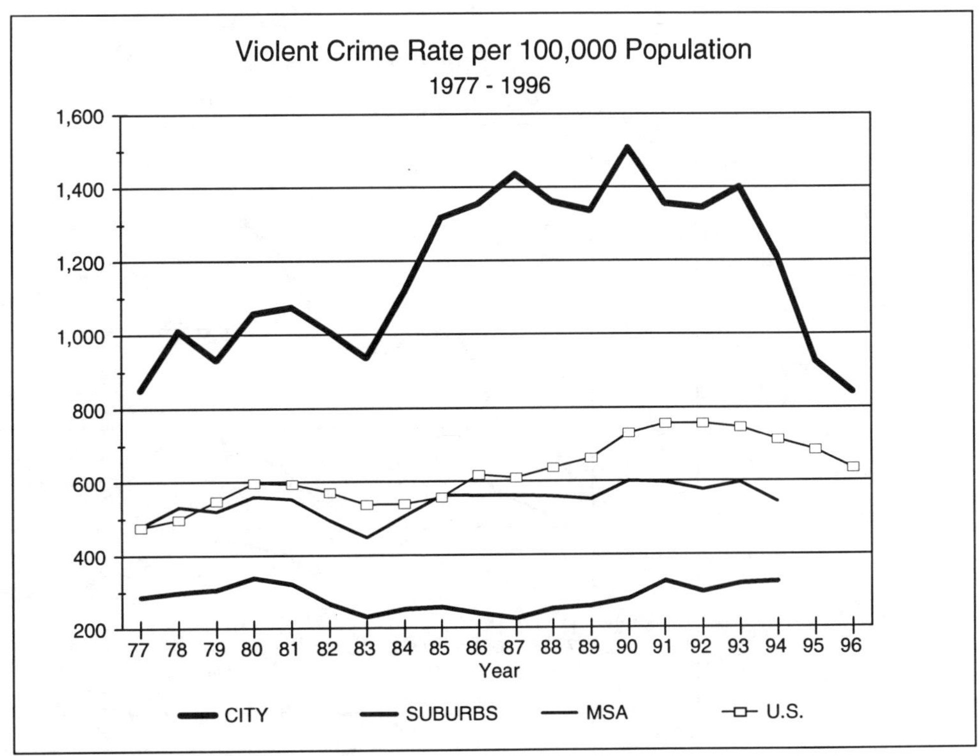

Note: Missing line segments indicate data not available.

Property Crimes and Property Crime Rates: 1977 - 1996

Year	Number				Rate per 100,000 population			
	City	Suburbs[2]	MSA[1]	U.S.	City	Suburbs[3]	MSA[1]	U.S.
1977	34,222	50,325	84,547	9,955,000	6,998.4	5,343.2	5,908.8	4,601.7
1978	39,184	54,611	93,795	10,123,400	8,079.2	5,493.8	6,341.6	4,642.5
1979	41,482	60,310	101,792	11,041,500	7,953.0	5,993.8	6,662.6	5,016.6
1980	48,093	68,803	116,896	12,063,700	9,777.0	6,205.0	7,302.7	5,353.3
1981	50,350	67,837	118,187	12,061,900	9,996.1	5,974.6	7,210.4	5,263.9
1982	48,281	63,173	111,454	11,652,000	9,510.8	5,520.6	6,746.7	5,032.5
1983	48,221	61,571	109,792	10,850,500	9,375.7	5,311.8	6,560.8	4,637.4
1984	50,466	60,789	111,255	10,608,500	10,141.9	5,085.1	6,571.3	4,492.1
1985	56,579	67,256	123,835	11,102,600	11,425.7	5,513.5	7,220.6	4,650.5
1986	60,950	70,397	131,347	11,722,700	12,158.9	5,701.5	7,566.2	4,862.6
1987	65,841	74,078	139,919	12,024,700	13,316.7	5,761.0	7,859.3	4,940.3
1988	65,815	76,762	142,577	12,356,900	13,022.9	5,806.5	7,802.2	5,027.1
1989	59,518	73,884	133,402	12,605,400	11,570.4	5,308.3	6,998.2	5,077.9
1990	57,273	70,870	128,143	12,655,500	11,093.9	4,867.2	6,497.1	5,088.5
1991	57,987	75,373	133,360	12,961,100	10,891.3	5,020.5	6,557.4	5,139.7
1992	58,073	69,495	127,568	12,505,900	10,656.8	4,609.2	6,214.6	4,902.7
1993	55,242	75,374	130,616	12,218,800	10,398.0	4,879.7	6,291.9	4,737.6
1994	51,367	77,848	129,215	12,131,900	9,507.7	4,671.5	5,855.5	4,660.0
1995	50,603	n/a	n/a	12,063,900	9,556.3	n/a	n/a	4,591.3
1996	51,093	n/a	n/a	11,791,300	9,468.8	n/a	n/a	4,444.8

Notes: Property crimes include burglary, larceny-theft and motor vehicle theft; n/a not available; (1) Metropolitan Statistical Area - see Appendix A for areas included; (2) calculated by the editors using the following formula: (number of crimes in the MSA minus number of crimes in the city); (3) calculated by the editors using the following formula: ((number of crimes in the MSA minus number of crimes in the city) ÷ (population of the MSA minus population of the city)) x 100,000
Source: U.S. Department of Justice, FBI Uniform Crime Reports, 1977 - 1996

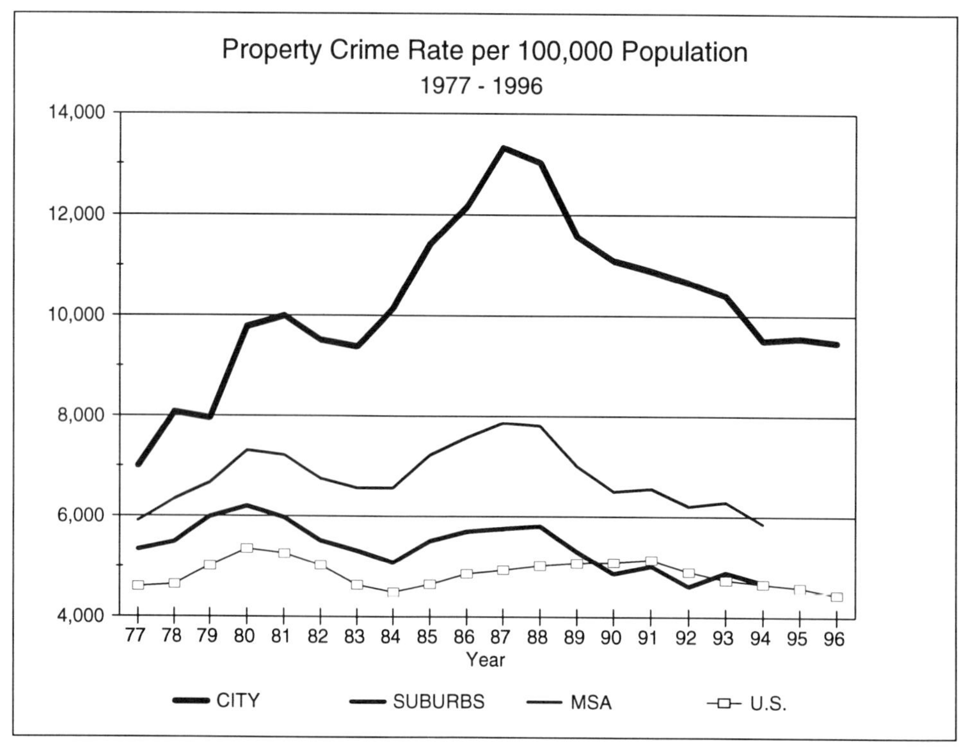

Note: Missing line segments indicate data not available.

Murders and Murder Rates: 1977 - 1996

Year	Number				Rate per 100,000 population			
	City	Suburbs[2]	MSA[1]	U.S.	City	Suburbs[3]	MSA[1]	U.S.
1977	35	26	61	19,120	7.2	2.8	4.3	8.8
1978	54	32	86	19,560	11.1	3.2	5.8	9.0
1979	37	41	78	21,460	7.1	4.1	5.1	9.7
1980	63	44	107	23,040	12.8	4.0	6.7	10.2
1981	59	35	94	22,520	11.7	3.1	5.7	9.8
1982	31	41	72	21,010	6.1	3.6	4.4	9.1
1983	61	44	105	19,310	11.9	3.8	6.3	8.3
1984	50	40	90	18,690	10.0	3.3	5.3	7.9
1985	61	39	100	18,980	12.3	3.2	5.8	7.9
1986	50	46	96	20,610	10.0	3.7	5.5	8.6
1987	54	37	91	20,100	10.9	2.9	5.1	8.3
1988	56	39	95	20,680	11.1	3.0	5.2	8.4
1989	38	34	72	21,500	7.4	2.4	3.8	8.7
1990	53	42	95	23,440	10.3	2.9	4.8	9.4
1991	43	39	82	24,700	8.1	2.6	4.0	9.8
1992	60	40	100	23,760	11.0	2.7	4.9	9.3
1993	67	47	114	24,530	12.6	3.0	5.5	9.5
1994	69	56	125	23,330	12.8	3.4	5.7	9.0
1995	41	n/a	n/a	21,610	7.7	n/a	n/a	8.2
1996	37	n/a	n/a	19,650	6.9	n/a	n/a	7.4

Notes: (1) Metropolitan Statistical Area - see Appendix A for areas included; (2) calculated by the editors using the following formula: (number of crimes in the MSA minus number of crimes in the city); (3) calculated by the editors using the following formula: ((number of crimes in the MSA minus number of crimes in the city) ÷ (population of the MSA minus population of the city)) x 100,000; n/a not avail.
Source: U.S. Department of Justice, FBI Uniform Crime Reports, 1977 - 1996

Forcible Rapes and Forcible Rape Rates: 1977 - 1996

Year	Number				Rate per 100,000 population			
	City	Suburbs[2]	MSA[1]	U.S.	City	Suburbs[3]	MSA[1]	U.S.
1977	370	324	694	63,500	75.7	34.4	48.5	29.4
1978	360	372	732	67,610	74.2	37.4	49.5	31.0
1979	421	448	869	76,390	80.7	44.5	56.9	34.7
1980	512	573	1,085	82,990	104.1	51.7	67.8	36.8
1981	485	569	1,054	82,500	96.3	50.1	64.3	36.0
1982	435	561	996	78,770	85.7	49.0	60.3	34.0
1983	434	491	925	78,920	84.4	42.4	55.3	33.7
1984	448	600	1,048	84,230	90.0	50.2	61.9	35.7
1985	441	682	1,123	88,670	89.1	55.9	65.5	37.1
1986	443	581	1,024	91,460	88.4	47.1	59.0	37.9
1987	465	594	1,059	91,110	94.0	46.2	59.5	37.4
1988	439	678	1,117	92,490	86.9	51.3	61.1	37.6
1989	478	754	1,232	94,500	92.9	54.2	64.6	38.1
1990	481	857	1,338	102,560	93.2	58.9	67.8	41.2
1991	398	1,098	1,496	106,590	74.8	73.1	73.6	42.3
1992	353	969	1,322	109,060	64.8	64.3	64.4	42.8
1993	356	1,158	1,514	106,010	67.0	75.0	72.9	41.1
1994	318	1,127	1,445	102,220	58.9	67.6	65.5	39.3
1995	260	n/a	n/a	97,470	49.1	n/a	n/a	37.1
1996	261	n/a	n/a	95,770	48.4	n/a	n/a	36.1

Notes: (1) Metropolitan Statistical Area - see Appendix A for areas included; (2) calculated by the editors using the following formula: (number of crimes in the MSA minus number of crimes in the city); (3) calculated by the editors using the following formula: ((number of crimes in the MSA minus number of crimes in the city) ÷ (population of the MSA minus population of the city)) x 100,000; n/a not avail.
Source: U.S. Department of Justice, FBI Uniform Crime Reports, 1977 - 1996

Robberies and Robbery Rates: 1977 - 1996

Year	Number				Rate per 100,000 population			
	City	Suburbs[2]	MSA[1]	U.S.	City	Suburbs[3]	MSA[1]	U.S.
1977	1,764	595	2,359	412,610	360.7	63.2	164.9	190.7
1978	2,257	661	2,918	426,930	465.4	66.5	197.3	195.8
1979	2,071	771	2,842	480,700	397.1	76.6	186.0	218.4
1980	2,253	1,017	3,270	565,840	458.0	91.7	204.3	251.1
1981	2,344	961	3,305	592,910	465.4	84.6	201.6	258.7
1982	2,271	782	3,053	553,130	447.4	68.3	184.8	238.9
1983	2,032	677	2,709	506,570	395.1	58.4	161.9	216.5
1984	2,386	834	3,220	485,010	479.5	69.8	190.2	205.4
1985	2,843	865	3,708	497,870	574.1	70.9	216.2	208.5
1986	2,792	853	3,645	542,780	557.0	69.1	210.0	225.1
1987	2,959	866	3,825	517,700	598.5	67.3	214.9	212.7
1988	2,709	1,016	3,725	542,970	536.0	76.9	203.8	220.9
1989	2,448	1,074	3,522	578,330	475.9	77.2	184.8	233.0
1990	2,695	1,060	3,755	639,270	522.0	72.8	190.4	257.0
1991	2,761	1,436	4,197	687,730	518.6	95.6	206.4	272.7
1992	2,577	1,290	3,867	672,480	472.9	85.6	188.4	263.6
1993	2,670	1,485	4,155	659,870	502.6	96.1	200.2	255.9
1994	2,536	1,695	4,231	618,950	469.4	101.7	191.7	237.7
1995	2,213	n/a	n/a	580,510	417.9	n/a	n/a	220.9
1996	1,963	n/a	n/a	537,050	363.8	n/a	n/a	202.4

Notes: (1) Metropolitan Statistical Area - see Appendix A for areas included; (2) calculated by the editors using the following formula: (number of crimes in the MSA minus number of crimes in the city); (3) calculated by the editors using the following formula: ((number of crimes in the MSA minus number of crimes in the city) ÷ (population of the MSA minus population of the city)) x 100,000; n/a not avail.
Source: U.S. Department of Justice, FBI Uniform Crime Reports, 1977 - 1996

Aggravated Assaults and Aggravated Assault Rates: 1977 - 1996

Year	Number				Rate per 100,000 population			
	City	Suburbs[2]	MSA[1]	U.S.	City	Suburbs[3]	MSA[1]	U.S.
1977	1,987	1,751	3,738	534,350	406.3	185.9	261.2	247.0
1978	2,229	1,898	4,127	571,460	459.6	190.9	279.0	262.1
1979	2,328	1,825	4,153	629,480	446.3	181.4	271.8	286.0
1980	2,373	2,118	4,491	672,650	482.4	191.0	280.6	298.5
1981	2,526	2,079	4,605	663,900	501.5	183.1	280.9	289.7
1982	2,383	1,676	4,059	669,480	469.4	146.5	245.7	289.2
1983	2,291	1,465	3,756	653,290	445.4	126.4	224.4	279.2
1984	2,669	1,546	4,215	685,350	536.4	129.3	249.0	290.2
1985	3,178	1,549	4,727	723,250	641.8	127.0	275.6	302.9
1986	3,505	1,484	4,989	834,320	699.2	120.2	287.4	346.1
1987	3,618	1,408	5,026	855,090	731.8	109.5	282.3	351.3
1988	3,675	1,599	5,274	910,090	727.2	121.0	288.6	370.2
1989	3,914	1,762	5,676	951,710	760.9	126.6	297.8	383.4
1990	4,551	2,102	6,653	1,054,860	881.5	144.4	337.3	424.1
1991	4,019	2,336	6,355	1,092,740	754.9	155.6	312.5	433.3
1992	4,337	2,192	6,529	1,126,970	795.9	145.4	318.1	441.8
1993	4,344	2,239	6,583	1,135,610	817.7	145.0	317.1	440.3
1994	3,615	2,551	6,166	1,113,180	669.1	153.1	279.4	427.6
1995	2,390	n/a	n/a	1,099,210	451.3	n/a	n/a	418.3
1996	2,282	n/a	n/a	1,029,810	422.9	n/a	n/a	388.2

Notes: (1) Metropolitan Statistical Area - see Appendix A for areas included; (2) calculated by the editors using the following formula: (number of crimes in the MSA minus number of crimes in the city); (3) calculated by the editors using the following formula: ((number of crimes in the MSA minus number of crimes in the city) ÷ (population of the MSA minus population of the city)) x 100,000; n/a not avail.
Source: U.S. Department of Justice, FBI Uniform Crime Reports, 1977 - 1996

Burglaries and Burglary Rates: 1977 - 1996

Year	Number				Rate per 100,000 population			
	City	Suburbs[2]	MSA[1]	U.S.	City	Suburbs[3]	MSA[1]	U.S.
1977	10,712	15,752	26,464	3,071,500	2,190.6	1,672.4	1,849.5	1,419.8
1978	11,476	18,135	29,611	3,128,300	2,366.2	1,824.3	2,002.0	1,434.6
1979	11,508	18,200	29,708	3,327,700	2,206.3	1,808.8	1,944.5	1,511.9
1980	13,780	20,684	34,464	3,795,200	2,801.4	1,865.4	2,153.0	1,684.1
1981	14,567	21,154	35,721	3,779,700	2,892.0	1,863.1	2,179.3	1,649.5
1982	13,273	18,287	31,560	3,447,100	2,614.6	1,598.1	1,910.4	1,488.8
1983	12,999	17,680	30,679	3,129,900	2,527.4	1,525.3	1,833.3	1,337.7
1984	14,406	18,050	32,456	2,984,400	2,895.1	1,509.9	1,917.0	1,263.7
1985	16,262	19,606	35,868	3,073,300	3,284.0	1,607.3	2,091.4	1,287.3
1986	16,215	19,931	36,146	3,241,400	3,234.7	1,614.2	2,082.2	1,344.6
1987	17,254	20,799	38,053	3,236,200	3,489.7	1,617.5	2,137.5	1,329.6
1988	16,880	20,144	37,024	3,218,100	3,340.1	1,523.7	2,026.1	1,309.2
1989	14,162	17,006	31,168	3,168,200	2,753.1	1,221.8	1,635.0	1,276.3
1990	11,181	14,548	25,729	3,073,900	2,165.8	999.1	1,304.5	1,235.9
1991	10,639	15,242	25,881	3,157,200	1,998.2	1,015.2	1,272.6	1,252.0
1992	9,250	13,297	22,547	2,979,900	1,697.4	881.9	1,098.4	1,168.2
1993	9,247	13,840	23,087	2,834,800	1,740.5	896.0	1,112.1	1,099.2
1994	8,186	14,129	22,315	2,712,800	1,515.2	847.8	1,011.2	1,042.0
1995	7,689	n/a	n/a	2,593,800	1,452.1	n/a	n/a	987.1
1996	7,855	n/a	n/a	2,501,500	1,455.7	n/a	n/a	943.0

Notes: (1) Metropolitan Statistical Area - see Appendix A for areas included; (2) calculated by the editors using the following formula: (number of crimes in the MSA minus number of crimes in the city); (3) calculated by the editors using the following formula: ((number of crimes in the MSA minus number of crimes in the city) ÷ (population of the MSA minus population of the city)) x 100,000; n/a not avail.
Source: U.S. Department of Justice, FBI Uniform Crime Reports, 1977 - 1996

Larceny-Thefts and Larceny-Theft Rates: 1977 - 1996

Year	Number				Rate per 100,000 population			
	City	Suburbs[2]	MSA[1]	U.S.	City	Suburbs[3]	MSA[1]	U.S.
1977	20,396	30,934	51,330	5,905,700	4,171.0	3,284.4	3,587.4	2,729.9
1978	24,177	32,537	56,714	5,991,000	4,984.9	3,273.2	3,834.5	2,747.4
1979	26,161	37,436	63,597	6,601,000	5,015.6	3,720.5	4,162.6	2,999.1
1980	30,483	43,325	73,808	7,136,900	6,197.0	3,907.3	4,610.9	3,167.0
1981	32,835	42,944	75,779	7,194,400	6,518.8	3,782.2	4,623.1	3,139.7
1982	32,321	41,707	74,028	7,142,500	6,366.9	3,644.7	4,481.2	3,084.8
1983	32,910	41,078	73,988	6,712,800	6,398.8	3,543.9	4,421.3	2,868.9
1984	33,771	39,926	73,697	6,591,900	6,786.8	3,339.8	4,352.9	2,791.3
1985	37,534	44,210	81,744	6,926,400	7,579.7	3,624.3	4,766.3	2,901.2
1986	41,625	46,661	88,286	7,257,200	8,303.8	3,779.1	5,085.7	3,010.3
1987	43,586	48,138	91,724	7,499,900	8,815.5	3,743.6	5,152.2	3,081.3
1988	43,196	51,282	94,478	7,705,900	8,547.2	3,879.1	5,170.1	3,134.9
1989	39,540	50,702	90,242	7,872,400	7,686.7	3,642.8	4,734.0	3,171.3
1990	39,522	50,393	89,915	7,945,700	7,655.5	3,460.9	4,558.8	3,194.8
1991	40,502	53,808	94,310	8,142,200	7,607.2	3,584.1	4,637.3	3,228.8
1992	41,125	50,140	91,265	7,915,200	7,546.7	3,325.5	4,446.1	3,103.0
1993	39,176	54,690	93,866	7,820,900	7,374.0	3,540.6	4,521.6	3,032.4
1994	36,758	56,272	93,030	7,879,800	6,803.7	3,376.7	4,215.7	3,026.7
1995	35,970	n/a	n/a	7,997,700	6,792.9	n/a	n/a	3,043.8
1996	36,883	n/a	n/a	7,894,600	6,835.4	n/a	n/a	2,975.9

Notes: (1) Metropolitan Statistical Area - see Appendix A for areas included; (2) calculated by the editors using the following formula: (number of crimes in the MSA minus number of crimes in the city); (3) calculated by the editors using the following formula: ((number of crimes in the MSA minus number of crimes in the city) ÷ (population of the MSA minus population of the city)) x 100,000; n/a not avail.
Source: U.S. Department of Justice, FBI Uniform Crime Reports, 1977 - 1996

Motor Vehicle Thefts and Motor Vehicle Theft Rates: 1977 - 1996

Year	Number				Rate per 100,000 population			
	City	Suburbs[2]	MSA[1]	U.S.	City	Suburbs[3]	MSA[1]	U.S.
1977	3,114	3,639	6,753	977,700	636.8	386.4	472.0	451.9
1978	3,531	3,939	7,470	1,004,100	728.0	396.3	505.1	460.5
1979	3,813	4,674	8,487	1,112,800	731.0	464.5	555.5	505.6
1980	3,830	4,794	8,624	1,131,700	778.6	432.3	538.8	502.2
1981	2,948	3,739	6,687	1,087,800	585.3	329.3	408.0	474.7
1982	2,687	3,179	5,866	1,062,400	529.3	277.8	355.1	458.8
1983	2,312	2,813	5,125	1,007,900	449.5	242.7	306.3	430.8
1984	2,289	2,813	5,102	1,032,200	460.0	235.3	301.4	437.1
1985	2,783	3,440	6,223	1,102,900	562.0	282.0	362.9	462.0
1986	3,110	3,805	6,915	1,224,100	620.4	308.2	398.3	507.8
1987	5,001	5,141	10,142	1,288,700	1,011.5	399.8	569.7	529.4
1988	5,739	5,336	11,075	1,432,900	1,135.6	403.6	606.1	582.9
1989	5,816	6,176	11,992	1,564,800	1,130.6	443.7	629.1	630.4
1990	6,570	5,929	12,499	1,635,900	1,272.6	407.2	633.7	657.8
1991	6,846	6,323	13,169	1,661,700	1,285.8	421.2	647.5	659.0
1992	7,698	6,058	13,756	1,610,800	1,412.6	401.8	670.1	631.5
1993	6,819	6,844	13,663	1,563,100	1,283.5	443.1	658.2	606.1
1994	6,423	7,447	13,870	1,539,300	1,188.9	446.9	628.5	591.3
1995	6,944	n/a	n/a	1,472,400	1,311.4	n/a	n/a	560.4
1996	6,355	n/a	n/a	1,395,200	1,177.7	n/a	n/a	525.9

Notes: (1) Metropolitan Statistical Area - see Appendix A for areas included; (2) calculated by the editors using the following formula: (number of crimes in the MSA minus number of crimes in the city); (3) calculated by the editors using the following formula: ((number of crimes in the MSA minus number of crimes in the city) ÷ (population of the MSA minus population of the city)) x 100,000; n/a not avail.
Source: U.S. Department of Justice, FBI Uniform Crime Reports, 1977 - 1996

HATE CRIMES

Criminal Incidents by Bias Motivation

Area	Race	Ethnicity	Religion	Sexual Orientation
Seattle	14	1	4	21

Notes: Figures include both violent and property crimes. Law enforcement agencies must have submitted data for at least one quarter of calendar year 1995 to be included in this report, therefore figures shown may not represent complete 12-month totals; n/a not available
Source: U.S. Department of Justice, FBI Uniform Crime Reports, Hate Crime Statistics 1995

LAW ENFORCEMENT

Full-Time Law Enforcement Employees

Jurisdiction	Police Employees			Police Officers per 100,000 population
	Total	Officers	Civilians	
Seattle	1,776	1,238	538	229.4

Notes: Data as of October 31, 1996
Source: U.S. Department of Justice, FBI Uniform Crime Reports, 1996

Number of Police Officers by Race

Race	Police Officers				Index of Representation[1]		
	1983		1992				
	Number	Pct.	Number	Pct.	1983	1992	% Chg.
Black	42	4.2	105	8.5	0.43	0.84	95.3
Hispanic[2]	18	1.8	32	2.6	0.65	0.69	6.2

Notes: (1) The index of representation is calculated by dividing the percent of black/hispanic police officers by the percent of corresponding blacks/hispanics in the local population. An index approaching 1.0 indicates that a city is closer to achieving a representation of police officers equal to their proportion in the local population; (2) Hispanic officers can be of any race
Source: Bureau of Justice Statistics, Sourcebook of Criminal Justice Statistics, 1994

CORRECTIONS

Federal Correctional Facilities

Type	Year Opened	Security Level	Sex of Inmates	Rated Capacity	Population on 7/1/95	Number of Staff
None listed						

Notes: Data as of 1995
Source: Bureau of Justice Statistics, Sourcebook of Criminal Justice Statistics Online

City/County/Regional Correctional Facilities

Name	Year Opened	Year Renov.	Rated Capacity	1995 Pop.	Number of COs[1]	Number of Staff	ACA[2] Accred.
King Co Dept of Adult Det	1986	1991	1,623	2,334	432	585	No

Notes: Data as of April 1996; (1) Correctional Officers; (2) American Correctional Assn. Accreditation
Source: American Correctional Association, 1996-1998 National Jail and Adult Detention Directory

Private Adult Correctional Facilities

Name	Date Opened	Rated Capacity	Present Pop.	Security Level	Facility Construct.	Expans. Plans	ACA[1] Accred.
Seattle Processing Ctr	7/89	150	150	Min/Med	Renov.	None	Yes-9/91

Notes: Data as of December 1996; (1) American Correctional Association Accreditation
Source: University of Florida, Center for Studies in Criminology and Law, Private Adult Correctional Facility Census, 10th Ed., March 15, 1997

Characteristics of Shock Incarceration Programs

Jurisdiction	Year Program Began	Number of Camps	Average Num. of Inmates	Number of Beds	Program Length	Voluntary/ Mandatory
Washington	1993	1	150	180	4 months	Voluntary

Note: Data as of July 1996;
Source: Sourcebook of Criminal Justice Statistics Online

INMATES AND HIV/AIDS

HIV Testing Policies for Inmates

Jurisdiction	All Inmates at Some Time	All Convicted Inmates at Admission	Random Samples While in Custody	High-risk Groups	Upon Inmate Request	Upon Court Order	Upon Involvement in Incident
King Co.	No	No	No	Yes	Yes	Yes	Yes

Source: HIV in Prisons and Jails, 1993 (released August 1995)

Inmates Known to be Positive for HIV

Jurisdiction	Number of Jail Inmates in Facilities Providing Data	Type of HIV Infection/AIDS Cases				HIV/AIDS Cases as a Percent of Tot. Custody Pop.
		Total	Asymptomatic	Symptomatic	Confirmed AIDS	
King Co.	2,125	3	0	0	3	0.1

Source: HIV in Prisons and Jails, 1993 (released August, 1995)

DEATH PENALTY

Death Penalty Statistics

State	Prisoners Executed		Prisoners Under Sentence of Death					Avg. No. of Years on Death Row[4]
	1930-1995	1996[1]	Total[2]	White[3]	Black[3]	Hisp.	Women	
Washington	49	0	9	8	1	0	0	n/c

Notes: Data as of 12/31/95 unless otherwise noted; n/c not calculated on fewer than 10 inmates; (1) Data as of 7/31/97; (2) Includes persons of other races; (3) Includes people of Hispanic origin; (4) Covers prisoners sentenced 1974 through 1995
Source: Bureau of Justice Statistics, Capital Punishment 1995 (released 12/96); Death Penalty Information Center Web Site, 9/30/97

Capital Offenses and Methods of Execution

Capital Offenses in Washington	Minimum Age for Imposition of Death Penalty	Mentally Retarded Excluded	Methods of Execution[1]
Aggravated first-degree murder.	18	No	Lethal injection; hanging

Notes: Data as of 12/31/95 unless otherwise noted; (1) Data as of 7/31/97
Source: Bureau of Justice Statistics, Capital Punishment 1995 (released 12/96); Death Penalty Information Center Web Site, 9/30/97

LAWS

Statutory Provisions Relating to the Purchase, Ownership and Use of Handguns

Jurisdiction	Instant Background Check	Federal Waiting Period Applies[1]	State Waiting Period (days)	License or Permit to Purchase	Regis-tration	Record of Sale Sent to Police	Concealed Carry Law
Washington	No	Yes	5[a]	No	No	Yes	Yes[b]

Note: Data as of 1996; (1) The Federal 5-day waiting period for handgun purchases applies to states that don't have instant background checks, waiting period requirements, or licensing procedures exempting them from the Federal requirement; (a) May be extended by police to 30 days in some circumstances. An individual not holding a driver's license must wait 90 days; (b) "Shall issue" permit system, liberally administered discretion by local authorities over permit issuance, or no permit required
Source: Sourcebook of Criminal Justice Statistics Online

Statutory Provisions Relating to Alcohol Use and Driving

Jurisdiction	Drinking Age	Blood Alcohol Concentration Levels as Evidence in State Courts[1]		Open Container Law[1]	Anti-Consump-tion Law[1]	Dram Shop Law[1]
		Illegal per se at 0.10%	Presumption at 0.10%			
Washington	21	Yes	No	Yes	Yes	(a,b)

Note: Data as of January 1, 1997; (1) See Appendix C for an explanation of terms; (a) Adopted via case law decisions; (b) Applies only to the actions of intoxicated minors and/or adults who have lost their will to stop drinking
Source: Sourcebook of Criminal Justice Statistics Online

Statutory Provisions Relating to Hate Crimes

Jurisdiction	Bias-Motivated Violence and Intimidation						Institutional Vandalism
	Civil Action	Criminal Penalty					
		Race/ Religion/ Ethnicity	Sexual Orientation	Mental/ Physical Disability	Gender	Age	
Washington	Yes	Yes	Yes	Yes	Yes	No	Yes

Source: Anti-Defamation League, 1997 Hate Crimes Laws

Sioux Falls, South Dakota

OVERVIEW

The total crime rate for the city increased 1.8% between 1977 and 1996. During that same period, the violent crime rate increased 157.7% and the property crime rate decreased 3.8%.

Among violent crimes, the rates for: Murders decreased 83.0%; Forcible Rapes increased 73.1%; Robberies increased 158.1%; and Aggravated Assaults increased 209.2%.

Among property crimes, the rates for: Burglaries decreased 7.9%; Larceny-Thefts increased 0.9%; and Motor Vehicle Thefts decreased 42.4%.

ANTI-CRIME PROGRAMS

Programs include:

- Neighborhood Watch, Realtor Watch, Civilian Watch
- Crime Free Multi-Housing
- Crime Stoppers
  Police Department, 7/97

CRIME RISK

Your Chances of Becoming a Victim[1]

Area	Any Crime	Violent Crime					Property Crime			
		Any	Murder	Forcible Rape[2]	Robbery	Aggrav. Assault	Any	Burglary	Larceny -Theft	Motor Vehicle Theft
City	1:21	1:234	1:110,891	1:707	1:1,706	1:341	1:23	1:128	1:29	1:531

Note: (1) Figures have been calculated by dividing the population of the city by the number of crimes reported to the FBI during 1996 and are expressed as odds (eg. 1:20 should be read as 1 in 20).
(2) Figures have been calculated by dividing the female population of the city by the number of forcible rapes reported to the FBI during 1996. The female population of the city was estimated by calculating the ratio of females to males reported in the 1990 Census and applying that ratio to 1996 population estimate.
Source: FBI Uniform Crime Reports 1996

CRIME STATISTICS

Total Crimes and Total Crime Rates: 1977 - 1996

Year	Number				Rate per 100,000 population			
	City	Suburbs[2]	MSA[1]	U.S.	City	Suburbs[3]	MSA[1]	U.S.
1977	3,553	394	3,947	10,984,500	4,741.9	1,671.5	4,007.1	5,077.6
1978	3,775	468	4,243	11,209,000	5,033.3	1,770.9	4,183.3	5,140.3
1979	4,325	614	4,939	12,249,500	5,761.8	2,193.4	4,792.5	5,565.5
1980	4,630	587	5,217	13,408,300	5,711.0	2,027.1	4,741.5	5,950.0
1981	4,328	600	4,928	13,423,800	5,369.1	2,076.1	4,500.0	5,858.2
1982	4,237	391	4,628	12,974,400	5,205.2	1,344.8	4,189.2	5,603.6
1983	3,751	291	4,042	12,108,600	4,546.5	988.0	3,610.3	5,175.0
1984	3,866	313	4,179	11,881,800	4,569.1	1,057.6	3,659.2	5,031.3
1985	4,080	231	4,311	12,431,400	4,809.8	688.0	3,641.0	5,207.1
1986	4,443	300	4,743	13,211,900	5,046.0	984.8	4,002.1	5,480.4
1987	4,163	241	4,404	13,508,700	4,265.0	948.8	3,580.2	5,550.0
1988	4,485	333	4,818	13,923,100	4,530.9	1,292.8	3,862.3	5,664.2
1989	4,491	306	4,797	14,251,400	4,496.6	1,178.7	3,812.1	5,741.0
1990	4,474	485	4,959	14,475,600	4,437.9	2,109.2	4,005.4	5,820.3
1991	5,184	441	5,625	14,872,900	5,088.1	1,898.8	4,496.0	5,897.8
1992	4,596	664	5,260	14,438,200	4,460.2	1,629.4	3,658.0	5,660.2
1993	4,875	824	5,699	14,144,800	4,585.4	1,959.9	3,841.4	5,484.4
1994	5,317	791	6,108	13,989,500	4,957.2	1,865.9	4,081.5	5,373.5
1995	5,766	917	6,683	13,862,700	5,223.5	2,068.2	4,319.3	5,275.9
1996	5,354	1,187	6,541	13,473,600	4,828.2	2,516.8	4,138.4	5,078.9

Notes: (1) Metropolitan Statistical Area - see Appendix A for areas included; (2) calculated by the editors using the following formula: (number of crimes in the MSA minus number of crimes in the city); (3) calculated by the editors using the following formula: ((number of crimes in the MSA minus number of crimes in the city) ÷ (population of the MSA minus population of the city)) x 100,000; n/a not avail.
Source: U.S. Department of Justice, FBI Uniform Crime Reports, 1977 - 1996

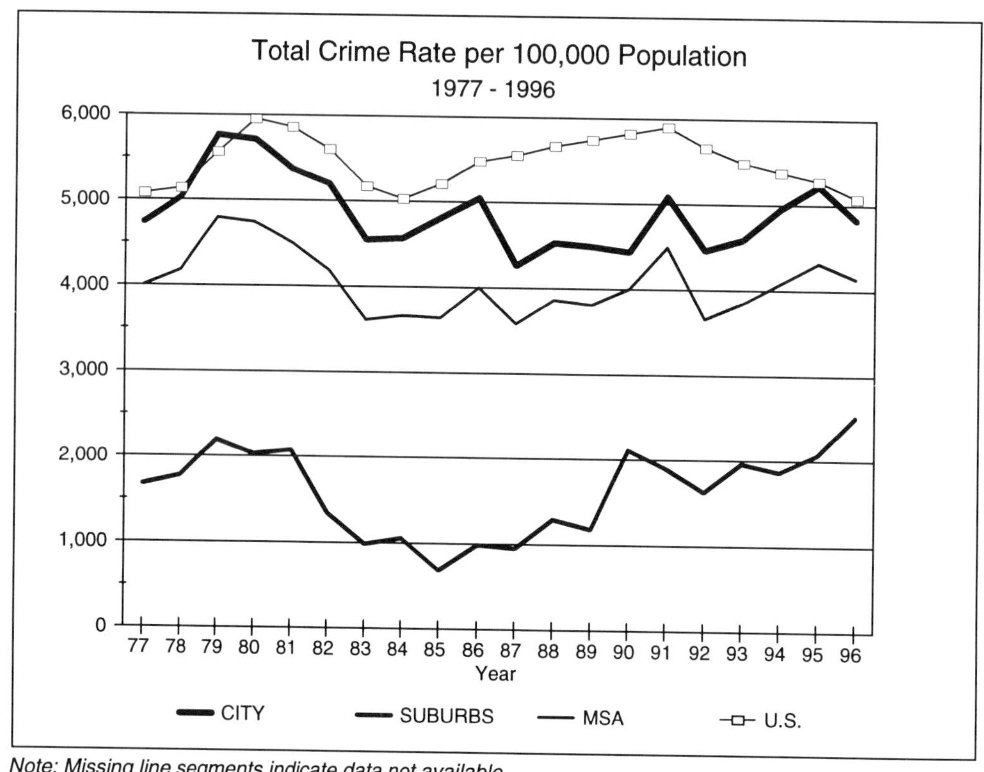

Note: Missing line segments indicate data not available.

Violent Crimes and Violent Crime Rates: 1977 - 1996

Year	Number				Rate per 100,000 population			
	City	Suburbs[2]	MSA[1]	U.S.	City	Suburbs[3]	MSA[1]	U.S.
1977	124	32	156	1,029,580	165.5	135.8	158.4	475.9
1978	126	28	154	1,085,550	168.0	106.0	151.8	497.8
1979	165	29	194	1,208,030	219.8	103.6	188.2	548.9
1980	130	26	156	1,344,520	160.4	89.8	141.8	596.6
1981	132	21	153	1,361,820	163.8	72.7	139.7	594.3
1982	148	20	168	1,322,390	181.8	68.8	152.1	571.1
1983	150	26	176	1,258,090	181.8	88.3	157.2	537.7
1984	164	28	192	1,273,280	193.8	94.6	168.1	539.2
1985	192	14	206	1,328,800	226.3	41.7	174.0	556.6
1986	193	17	210	1,489,170	219.2	55.8	177.2	617.7
1987	201	14	215	1,484,000	205.9	55.1	174.8	609.7
1988	235	17	252	1,566,220	237.4	66.0	202.0	637.2
1989	320	21	341	1,646,040	320.4	80.9	271.0	663.1
1990	310	25	335	1,820,130	307.5	108.7	270.6	731.8
1991	378	22	400	1,911,770	371.0	94.7	319.7	758.1
1992	431	53	484	1,932,270	418.3	130.1	336.6	757.5
1993	475	57	532	1,926,020	446.8	135.6	358.6	746.8
1994	487	59	546	1,857,670	454.0	139.2	364.8	713.6
1995	501	76	577	1,798,790	453.9	171.4	372.9	684.6
1996	473	99	572	1,682,280	426.5	209.9	361.9	634.1

Notes: Violent crimes include murder, forcible rape, robbery and aggravated assault; n/a not available; (1) Metropolitan Statistical Area - see Appendix A for areas included; (2) calculated by the editors using the following formula: (number of crimes in the MSA minus number of crimes in the city); (3) calculated by the editors using the following formula: ((number of crimes in the MSA minus number of crimes in the city) ÷ (population of the MSA minus population of the city)) x 100,000
Source: U.S. Department of Justice, FBI Uniform Crime Reports, 1977 - 1996

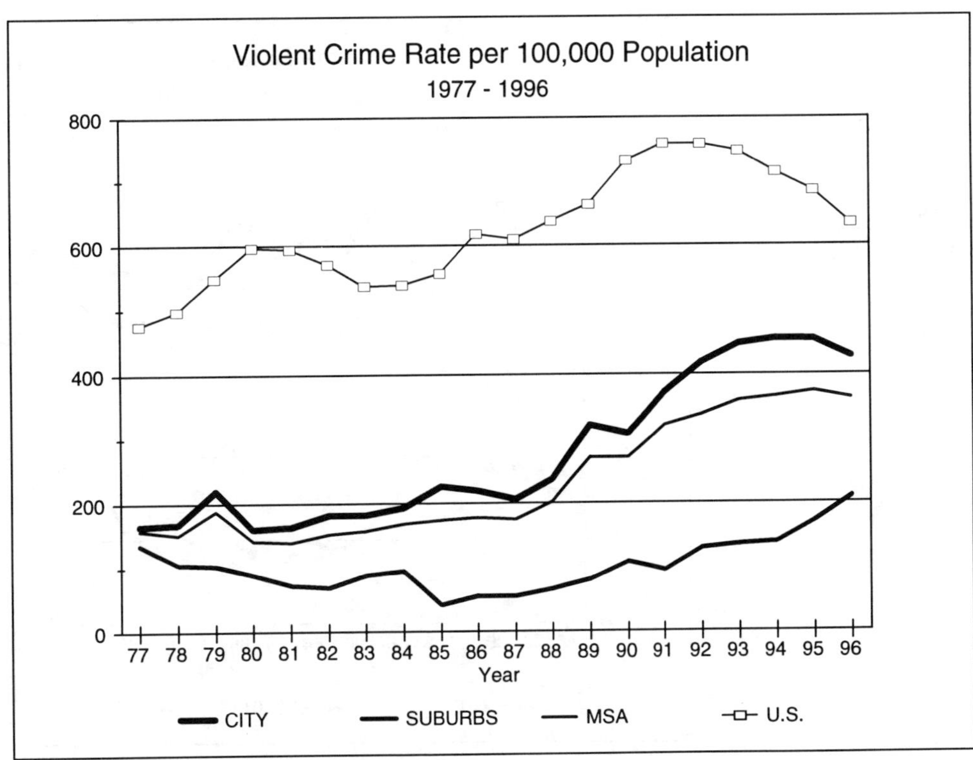

Note: Missing line segments indicate data not available.

Property Crimes and Property Crime Rates: 1977 - 1996

Year	Number				Rate per 100,000 population			
	City	Suburbs[2]	MSA[1]	U.S.	City	Suburbs[3]	MSA[1]	U.S.
1977	3,429	362	3,791	9,955,000	4,576.5	1,535.7	3,848.8	4,601.7
1978	3,649	440	4,089	10,123,400	4,865.3	1,665.0	4,031.5	4,642.5
1979	4,160	585	4,745	11,041,500	5,542.0	2,089.8	4,604.3	5,016.6
1980	4,500	561	5,061	12,063,700	5,550.7	1,937.3	4,599.7	5,353.3
1981	4,196	579	4,775	12,061,900	5,205.4	2,003.4	4,360.3	5,263.9
1982	4,089	371	4,460	11,652,000	5,023.4	1,276.0	4,037.1	5,032.5
1983	3,601	265	3,866	10,850,500	4,364.7	899.7	3,453.1	4,637.4
1984	3,702	285	3,987	10,608,500	4,375.3	963.0	3,491.1	4,492.1
1985	3,888	217	4,105	11,102,600	4,583.4	646.3	3,467.0	4,650.5
1986	4,250	283	4,533	11,722,700	4,826.8	929.0	3,824.9	4,862.6
1987	3,962	227	4,189	12,024,700	4,059.1	893.7	3,405.4	4,940.3
1988	4,250	316	4,566	12,356,900	4,293.5	1,226.8	3,660.3	5,027.1
1989	4,171	285	4,456	12,605,400	4,176.2	1,097.8	3,541.1	5,077.9
1990	4,164	460	4,624	12,655,500	4,130.4	2,000.4	3,734.8	5,088.5
1991	4,806	419	5,225	12,961,100	4,717.1	1,804.1	4,176.3	5,139.7
1992	4,165	611	4,776	12,505,900	4,042.0	1,499.3	3,321.4	4,902.7
1993	4,400	767	5,167	12,218,800	4,138.6	1,824.3	3,482.8	4,737.6
1994	4,830	732	5,562	12,131,900	4,503.2	1,726.7	3,716.6	4,660.0
1995	5,265	841	6,106	12,063,900	4,769.7	1,896.8	3,946.4	4,591.3
1996	4,881	1,088	5,969	11,791,300	4,401.6	2,306.8	3,776.5	4,444.8

Notes: Property crimes include burglary, larceny-theft and motor vehicle theft; n/a not available; (1) Metropolitan Statistical Area - see Appendix A for areas included; (2) calculated by the editors using the following formula: (number of crimes in the MSA minus number of crimes in the city); (3) calculated by the editors using the following formula: ((number of crimes in the MSA minus number of crimes in the city) ÷ (population of the MSA minus population of the city)) x 100,000
Source: U.S. Department of Justice, FBI Uniform Crime Reports, 1977 - 1996

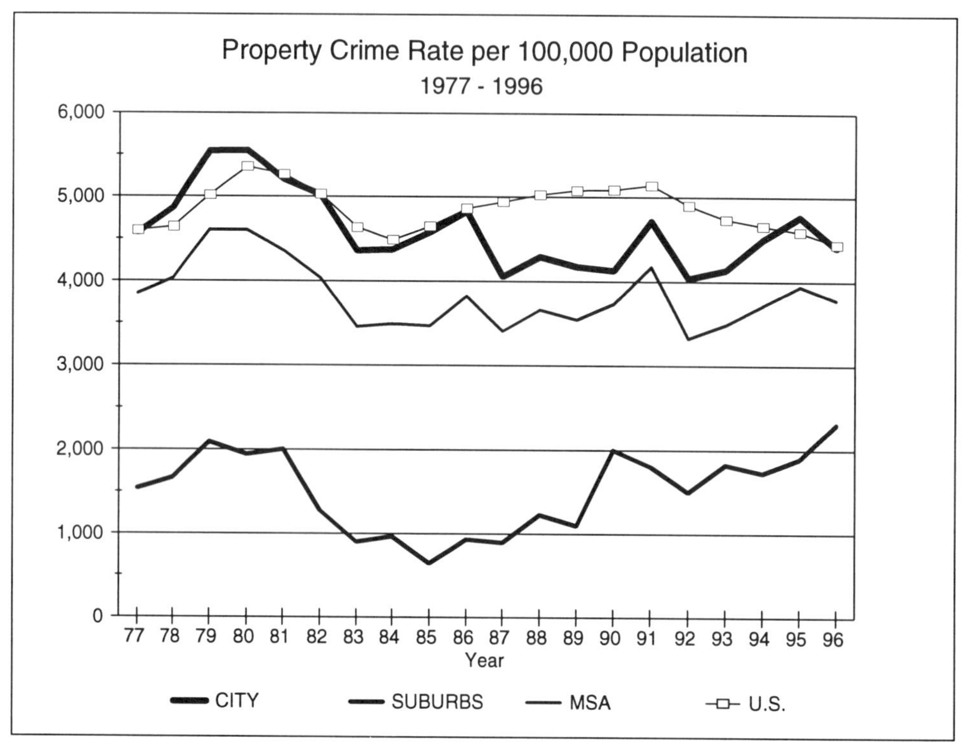

Note: Missing line segments indicate data not available.

Murders and Murder Rates: 1977 - 1996

Year	Number				Rate per 100,000 population			
	City	Suburbs[2]	MSA[1]	U.S.	City	Suburbs[3]	MSA[1]	U.S.
1977	4	0	4	19,120	5.3	0.0	4.1	8.8
1978	3	1	4	19,560	4.0	3.8	3.9	9.0
1979	2	0	2	21,460	2.7	0.0	1.9	9.7
1980	0	0	0	23,040	0.0	0.0	0.0	10.2
1981	2	1	3	22,520	2.5	3.5	2.7	9.8
1982	1	0	1	21,010	1.2	0.0	0.9	9.1
1983	1	0	1	19,310	1.2	0.0	0.9	8.3
1984	3	0	3	18,690	3.5	0.0	2.6	7.9
1985	1	2	3	18,980	1.2	6.0	2.5	7.9
1986	3	1	4	20,610	3.4	3.3	3.4	8.6
1987	1	1	2	20,100	1.0	3.9	1.6	8.3
1988	4	0	4	20,680	4.0	0.0	3.2	8.4
1989	2	0	2	21,500	2.0	0.0	1.6	8.7
1990	4	0	4	23,440	4.0	0.0	3.2	9.4
1991	2	0	2	24,700	2.0	0.0	1.6	9.8
1992	0	0	0	23,760	0.0	0.0	0.0	9.3
1993	2	0	2	24,530	1.9	0.0	1.3	9.5
1994	3	1	4	23,330	2.8	2.4	2.7	9.0
1995	5	0	5	21,610	4.5	0.0	3.2	8.2
1996	1	0	1	19,650	0.9	0.0	0.6	7.4

Notes: (1) Metropolitan Statistical Area - see Appendix A for areas included; (2) calculated by the editors using the following formula: (number of crimes in the MSA minus number of crimes in the city); (3) calculated by the editors using the following formula: ((number of crimes in the MSA minus number of crimes in the city) ÷ (population of the MSA minus population of the city)) x 100,000; n/a not avail.
Source: U.S. Department of Justice, FBI Uniform Crime Reports, 1977 - 1996

Forcible Rapes and Forcible Rape Rates: 1977 - 1996

Year	Number				Rate per 100,000 population			
	City	Suburbs[2]	MSA[1]	U.S.	City	Suburbs[3]	MSA[1]	U.S.
1977	32	5	37	63,500	42.7	21.2	37.6	29.4
1978	17	2	19	67,610	22.7	7.6	18.7	31.0
1979	25	4	29	76,390	33.3	14.3	28.1	34.7
1980	21	5	26	82,990	25.9	17.3	23.6	36.8
1981	14	3	17	82,500	17.4	10.4	15.5	36.0
1982	17	3	20	78,770	20.9	10.3	18.1	34.0
1983	25	2	27	78,920	30.3	6.8	24.1	33.7
1984	38	10	48	84,230	44.9	33.8	42.0	35.7
1985	56	3	59	88,670	66.0	8.9	49.8	37.1
1986	39	4	43	91,460	44.3	13.1	36.3	37.9
1987	39	3	42	91,110	40.0	11.8	34.1	37.4
1988	63	3	66	92,490	63.6	11.6	52.9	37.6
1989	93	3	96	94,500	93.1	11.6	76.3	38.1
1990	81	4	85	102,560	80.3	17.4	68.7	41.2
1991	88	8	96	106,590	86.4	34.4	76.7	42.3
1992	97	9	106	109,060	94.1	22.1	73.7	42.8
1993	103	12	115	106,010	96.9	28.5	77.5	41.1
1994	70	3	73	102,220	65.3	7.1	48.8	39.3
1995	70	15	85	97,470	63.4	33.8	54.9	37.1
1996	82	40	122	95,770	73.9	84.8	77.2	36.1

Notes: (1) Metropolitan Statistical Area - see Appendix A for areas included; (2) calculated by the editors using the following formula: (number of crimes in the MSA minus number of crimes in the city); (3) calculated by the editors using the following formula: ((number of crimes in the MSA minus number of crimes in the city) ÷ (population of the MSA minus population of the city)) x 100,000; n/a not avail.
Source: U.S. Department of Justice, FBI Uniform Crime Reports, 1977 - 1996

Robberies and Robbery Rates: 1977 - 1996

Year	Number				Rate per 100,000 population			
	City	Suburbs[2]	MSA[1]	U.S.	City	Suburbs[3]	MSA[1]	U.S.
1977	17	7	24	412,610	22.7	29.7	24.4	190.7
1978	32	1	33	426,930	42.7	3.8	32.5	195.8
1979	32	7	39	480,700	42.6	25.0	37.8	218.4
1980	36	2	38	565,840	44.4	6.9	34.5	251.1
1981	30	2	32	592,910	37.2	6.9	29.2	258.7
1982	32	1	33	553,130	39.3	3.4	29.9	238.9
1983	23	2	25	506,570	27.9	6.8	22.3	216.5
1984	23	2	25	485,010	27.2	6.8	21.9	205.4
1985	31	2	33	497,870	36.5	6.0	27.9	208.5
1986	28	1	29	542,780	31.8	3.3	24.5	225.1
1987	32	0	32	517,700	32.8	0.0	26.0	212.7
1988	25	2	27	542,970	25.3	7.8	21.6	220.9
1989	33	1	34	578,330	33.0	3.9	27.0	233.0
1990	33	1	34	639,270	32.7	4.3	27.5	257.0
1991	32	3	35	687,730	31.4	12.9	28.0	272.7
1992	34	0	34	672,480	33.0	0.0	23.6	263.6
1993	44	3	47	659,870	41.4	7.1	31.7	255.9
1994	56	3	59	618,950	52.2	7.1	39.4	237.7
1995	82	5	87	580,510	74.3	11.3	56.2	220.9
1996	65	2	67	537,050	58.6	4.2	42.4	202.4

Notes: (1) Metropolitan Statistical Area - see Appendix A for areas included; (2) calculated by the editors using the following formula: (number of crimes in the MSA minus number of crimes in the city); (3) calculated by the editors using the following formula: ((number of crimes in the MSA minus number of crimes in the city) ÷ (population of the MSA minus population of the city)) x 100,000; n/a not avail.
Source: U.S. Department of Justice, FBI Uniform Crime Reports, 1977 - 1996

Aggravated Assaults and Aggravated Assault Rates: 1977 - 1996

Year	Number				Rate per 100,000 population			
	City	Suburbs[2]	MSA[1]	U.S.	City	Suburbs[3]	MSA[1]	U.S.
1977	71	20	91	534,350	94.8	84.8	92.4	247.0
1978	74	24	98	571,460	98.7	90.8	96.6	262.1
1979	106	18	124	629,480	141.2	64.3	120.3	286.0
1980	73	19	92	672,650	90.0	65.6	83.6	298.5
1981	86	15	101	663,900	106.7	51.9	92.2	289.7
1982	98	16	114	669,480	120.4	55.0	103.2	289.2
1983	101	22	123	653,290	122.4	74.7	109.9	279.2
1984	100	16	116	685,350	118.2	54.1	101.6	290.2
1985	104	7	111	723,250	122.6	20.8	93.7	302.9
1986	123	11	134	834,320	139.7	36.1	113.1	346.1
1987	129	10	139	855,090	132.2	39.4	113.0	351.3
1988	143	12	155	910,090	144.5	46.6	124.3	370.2
1989	192	17	209	951,710	192.2	65.5	166.1	383.4
1990	192	20	212	1,054,860	190.4	87.0	171.2	424.1
1991	256	11	267	1,092,740	251.3	47.4	213.4	433.3
1992	300	44	344	1,126,970	291.1	108.0	239.2	441.8
1993	326	42	368	1,135,610	306.6	99.9	248.0	440.3
1994	358	52	410	1,113,180	333.8	122.7	274.0	427.6
1995	344	56	400	1,099,210	311.6	126.3	258.5	418.3
1996	325	57	382	1,029,810	293.1	120.9	241.7	388.2

Notes: (1) Metropolitan Statistical Area - see Appendix A for areas included; (2) calculated by the editors using the following formula: (number of crimes in the MSA minus number of crimes in the city); (3) calculated by the editors using the following formula: ((number of crimes in the MSA minus number of crimes in the city) ÷ (population of the MSA minus population of the city)) x 100,000; n/a not avail.
Source: U.S. Department of Justice, FBI Uniform Crime Reports, 1977 - 1996

Burglaries and Burglary Rates: 1977 - 1996

Year	Number				Rate per 100,000 population			
	City	Suburbs[2]	MSA[1]	U.S.	City	Suburbs[3]	MSA[1]	U.S.
1977	634	129	763	3,071,500	846.2	547.3	774.6	1,419.8
1978	741	207	948	3,128,300	988.0	783.3	934.7	1,434.6
1979	766	168	934	3,327,700	1,020.5	600.2	906.3	1,511.9
1980	893	188	1,081	3,795,200	1,101.5	649.2	982.5	1,684.1
1981	856	187	1,043	3,779,700	1,061.9	647.0	952.4	1,649.5
1982	827	111	938	3,447,100	1,016.0	381.8	849.1	1,488.8
1983	701	87	788	3,129,900	849.7	295.4	703.8	1,337.7
1984	679	108	787	2,984,400	802.5	364.9	689.1	1,263.7
1985	719	63	782	3,073,300	847.6	187.6	660.5	1,287.3
1986	912	67	979	3,241,400	1,035.8	219.9	826.1	1,344.6
1987	780	92	872	3,236,200	799.1	362.2	708.9	1,329.6
1988	807	109	916	3,218,100	815.3	423.2	734.3	1,309.2
1989	694	77	771	3,168,200	694.9	296.6	612.7	1,276.3
1990	579	148	727	3,073,900	574.3	643.6	587.2	1,235.9
1991	800	149	949	3,157,200	785.2	641.6	758.5	1,252.0
1992	621	218	839	2,979,900	602.7	535.0	583.5	1,168.2
1993	735	242	977	2,834,800	691.3	575.6	658.5	1,099.2
1994	874	217	1,091	2,712,800	814.9	511.9	729.0	1,042.0
1995	904	269	1,173	2,593,800	819.0	606.7	758.1	987.1
1996	864	311	1,175	2,501,500	779.1	659.4	743.4	943.0

Notes: (1) Metropolitan Statistical Area - see Appendix A for areas included; (2) calculated by the editors using the following formula: (number of crimes in the MSA minus number of crimes in the city); (3) calculated by the editors using the following formula: ((number of crimes in the MSA minus number of crimes in the city) ÷ (population of the MSA minus population of the city)) x 100,000; n/a not avail.
Source: U.S. Department of Justice, FBI Uniform Crime Reports, 1977 - 1996

Larceny-Thefts and Larceny-Theft Rates: 1977 - 1996

Year	Number				Rate per 100,000 population			
	City	Suburbs[2]	MSA[1]	U.S.	City	Suburbs[3]	MSA[1]	U.S.
1977	2,550	210	2,760	5,905,700	3,403.3	890.9	2,802.1	2,729.9
1978	2,695	205	2,900	5,991,000	3,593.3	775.7	2,859.2	2,747.4
1979	3,133	369	3,502	6,601,000	4,173.8	1,318.2	3,398.2	2,999.1
1980	3,388	346	3,734	7,136,900	4,179.1	1,194.8	3,393.7	3,167.0
1981	3,138	354	3,492	7,194,400	3,892.9	1,224.9	3,188.7	3,139.7
1982	3,115	237	3,352	7,142,500	3,826.8	815.1	3,034.2	3,084.8
1983	2,746	152	2,898	6,712,800	3,328.4	516.1	2,588.5	2,868.9
1984	2,884	150	3,034	6,591,900	3,408.5	506.9	2,656.6	2,791.3
1985	3,028	138	3,166	6,926,400	3,569.6	411.0	2,674.0	2,901.2
1986	3,208	198	3,406	7,257,200	3,643.4	650.0	2,873.9	3,010.3
1987	3,045	120	3,165	7,499,900	3,119.6	472.4	2,573.0	3,081.3
1988	3,264	188	3,452	7,705,900	3,297.4	729.8	2,767.2	3,134.9
1989	3,305	192	3,497	7,872,400	3,309.1	739.6	2,779.0	3,171.3
1990	3,450	299	3,749	7,945,700	3,422.1	1,300.3	3,028.1	3,194.8
1991	3,837	260	4,097	8,142,200	3,766.0	1,119.5	3,274.7	3,228.8
1992	3,414	375	3,789	7,915,200	3,313.1	920.2	2,635.0	3,103.0
1993	3,470	497	3,967	7,820,900	3,263.9	1,182.1	2,673.9	3,032.4
1994	3,742	491	4,233	7,879,800	3,488.8	1,158.2	2,828.6	3,026.7
1995	4,136	513	4,649	7,997,700	3,746.9	1,157.0	3,004.7	3,043.8
1996	3,808	730	4,538	7,894,600	3,434.0	1,547.8	2,871.2	2,975.9

Notes: (1) Metropolitan Statistical Area - see Appendix A for areas included; (2) calculated by the editors using the following formula: (number of crimes in the MSA minus number of crimes in the city); (3) calculated by the editors using the following formula: ((number of crimes in the MSA minus number of crimes in the city) ÷ (population of the MSA minus population of the city)) x 100,000; n/a not avail.
Source: U.S. Department of Justice, FBI Uniform Crime Reports, 1977 - 1996

Motor Vehicle Thefts and Motor Vehicle Theft Rates: 1977 - 1996

Year	Number				Rate per 100,000 population			
	City	Suburbs[2]	MSA[1]	U.S.	City	Suburbs[3]	MSA[1]	U.S.
1977	245	23	268	977,700	327.0	97.6	272.1	451.9
1978	213	28	241	1,004,100	284.0	106.0	237.6	460.5
1979	261	48	309	1,112,800	347.7	171.5	299.8	505.6
1980	219	27	246	1,131,700	270.1	93.2	223.6	502.2
1981	202	38	240	1,087,800	250.6	131.5	219.2	474.7
1982	147	23	170	1,062,400	180.6	79.1	153.9	458.8
1983	154	26	180	1,007,900	186.7	88.3	160.8	430.8
1984	139	27	166	1,032,200	164.3	91.2	145.4	437.1
1985	141	16	157	1,102,900	166.2	47.7	132.6	462.0
1986	130	18	148	1,224,100	147.6	59.1	124.9	507.8
1987	137	15	152	1,288,700	140.4	59.1	123.6	529.4
1988	179	19	198	1,432,900	180.8	73.8	158.7	582.9
1989	172	16	188	1,564,800	172.2	61.6	149.4	630.4
1990	135	13	148	1,635,900	133.9	56.5	119.5	657.8
1991	169	10	179	1,661,700	165.9	43.1	143.1	659.0
1992	130	18	148	1,610,800	126.2	44.2	102.9	631.5
1993	195	28	223	1,563,100	183.4	66.6	150.3	606.1
1994	214	24	238	1,539,300	199.5	56.6	159.0	591.3
1995	225	59	284	1,472,400	203.8	133.1	183.6	560.4
1996	209	47	256	1,395,200	188.5	99.7	162.0	525.9

Notes: (1) Metropolitan Statistical Area - see Appendix A for areas included; (2) calculated by the editors using the following formula: (number of crimes in the MSA minus number of crimes in the city); (3) calculated by the editors using the following formula: ((number of crimes in the MSA minus number of crimes in the city) ÷ (population of the MSA minus population of the city)) x 100,000; n/a not avail.
Source: U.S. Department of Justice, FBI Uniform Crime Reports, 1977 - 1996

HATE CRIMES

Criminal Incidents by Bias Motivation

Area	Race	Ethnicity	Religion	Sexual Orientation
Sioux Falls	n/a	n/a	n/a	n/a

Notes: Figures include both violent and property crimes. Law enforcement agencies must have submitted data for at least one quarter of calendar year 1995 to be included in this report, therefore figures shown may not represent complete 12-month totals; n/a not available
Source: U.S. Department of Justice, FBI Uniform Crime Reports, Hate Crime Statistics 1995

LAW ENFORCEMENT

Full-Time Law Enforcement Employees

Jurisdiction	Police Employees			Police Officers per 100,000 population
	Total	Officers	Civilians	
Sioux Falls	182	154	28	138.9

Notes: Data as of October 31, 1996
Source: U.S. Department of Justice, FBI Uniform Crime Reports, 1996

CORRECTIONS

Federal Correctional Facilities

Type	Year Opened	Security Level	Sex of Inmates	Rated Capacity	Population on 7/1/95	Number of Staff
None listed						

Notes: Data as of 1995
Source: Bureau of Justice Statistics, Sourcebook of Criminal Justice Statistics Online

City/County/Regional Correctional Facilities

Name	Year Opened	Year Renov.	Rated Capacity	1995 Pop.	Number of COs[1]	Number of Staff	ACA[2] Accred.
Minnehaha County Jail	1977	--	188	n/a	n/a	n/a	No

Notes: Data as of April 1996; (1) Correctional Officers; (2) American Correctional Assn. Accreditation
Source: American Correctional Association, 1996-1998 National Jail and Adult Detention Directory

Private Adult Correctional Facilities

Name	Date Opened	Rated Capacity	Present Pop.	Security Level	Facility Construct.	Expans. Plans	ACA[1] Accred.
None listed							

Notes: Data as of December 1996; (1) American Correctional Association Accreditation
Source: University of Florida, Center for Studies in Criminology and Law, Private Adult Correctional Facility Census, 10th Ed., March 15, 1997

Characteristics of Shock Incarceration Programs

Jurisdiction	Year Program Began	Number of Camps	Average Num. of Inmates	Number of Beds	Program Length	Voluntary/ Mandatory
South Dakota	1996[a]	n/a	n/a	48	4 months	Voluntary

Note: Data as of July 1996; (a) Planned to open late 1996
Source: Sourcebook of Criminal Justice Statistics Online

DEATH PENALTY

Death Penalty Statistics

State	Prisoners Executed		Prisoners Under Sentence of Death					Avg. No. of Years on Death Row[4]
	1930-1995	1996[1]	Total[2]	White[3]	Black[3]	Hisp.	Women	
South Dakota	1	0	2	2	0	0	0	n/c

Notes: Data as of 12/31/95 unless otherwise noted; n/c not calculated on fewer than 10 inmates; (1) Data as of 7/31/97; (2) Includes persons of other races; (3) Includes people of Hispanic origin; (4) Covers prisoners sentenced 1974 through 1995
Source: Bureau of Justice Statistics, Capital Punishment 1995 (released 12/96); Death Penalty Information Center Web Site, 9/30/97

Capital Offenses and Methods of Execution

Capital Offenses in South Dakota	Minimum Age for Imposition of Death Penalty	Mentally Retarded Excluded	Methods of Execution[1]
First-degree murder with 1 of 10 aggravating circumstances.	None[2]	No	Lethal injection

Notes: Data as of 12/31/95 unless otherwise noted; (1) Data as of 7/31/97; (2) Juveniles may be transferred to adult court. Age can be a mitigating factor.
Source: Bureau of Justice Statistics, Capital Punishment 1995 (released 12/96); Death Penalty Information Center Web Site, 9/30/97

LAWS

Statutory Provisions Relating to the Purchase, Ownership and Use of Handguns

Jurisdiction	Instant Background Check	Federal Waiting Period Applies[1]	State Waiting Period (days)	License or Permit to Purchase	Regis-tration	Record of Sale Sent to Police	Concealed Carry Law
South Dakota	No	Yes[a]	2	No	No	Yes	Yes[b]

Note: Data as of 1996; (1) The Federal 5-day waiting period for handgun purchases applies to states that don't have instant background checks, waiting period requirements, or licensing procedures exempting them from the Federal requirement; (a) The Federal waiting period does not apply to a person holding a valid permit or license to carry a firearm, issued within 5 years of proposed purchase; (b) "Shall issue" permit system, liberally administered discretion by local authorities over permit issuance, or no permit required
Source: Sourcebook of Criminal Justice Statistics Online

Statutory Provisions Relating to Alcohol Use and Driving

Jurisdiction	Drinking Age	Blood Alcohol Concentration Levels as Evidence in State Courts[1]		Open Container Law[1]	Anti-Consump-tion Law[1]	Dram Shop Law[1]
		Illegal per se at 0.10%	Presumption at 0.10%			
South Dakota	21	Yes	Yes	Yes	No	(a)

Note: Data as of January 1, 1997; (1) See Appendix C for an explanation of terms; (a) Adopted via case law decisions
Source: Sourcebook of Criminal Justice Statistics Online

Statutory Provisions Relating to Curfews

Jurisdiction	Year Enacted	Latest Revision	Age Group(s)	Curfew Provisions
Sioux Falls	1957	1994	17 and under	11 pm to 4 am every night

Note: Data as of February 1996
Source: Sourcebook of Criminal Justice Statistics Online

Statutory Provisions Relating to Hate Crimes

Jurisdiction	Bias-Motivated Violence and Intimidation						Institutional Vandalism
	Civil Action	Criminal Penalty					
		Race/ Religion/ Ethnicity	Sexual Orientation	Mental/ Physical Disability	Gender	Age	
South Dakota	No	Yes	No	No	No	No	No

Source: Anti-Defamation League, 1997 Hate Crimes Laws

Springfield, Missouri

OVERVIEW

The total crime rate for the city decreased 6.9% between 1977 and 1996. During that same period, the violent crime rate increased 69.7% and the property crime rate decreased 10.0%.

Among violent crimes, the rates for: Murders decreased 50.0%; Forcible Rapes increased 141.5%; Robberies increased 4.5%; and Aggravated Assaults increased 105.7%.

Among property crimes, the rates for: Burglaries decreased 40.9%; Larceny-Thefts increased 2.3%; and Motor Vehicle Thefts increased 29.6%.

ANTI-CRIME PROGRAMS

The Crime Prevention/D.A.R.E. unit offers free programs to various civic clubs, churches, schools, businesses and other groups. These programs include burglary prevention, commercial crime prevention, crime prevention for the home, rape prevention, robbery prevention, shoplifting prevention and vacation security.

Other programs include:

- D.A.R.E. (Drug Abuse Resistance Education)—officers provide classroom drug awareness training in the grade schools.
- Neighborhood Watch—designed to organize neighborhoods into Watch Groups that report suspicious circumstances to the Police.
- Operation Identification—involves the inventory and marking of property with an identifying number as a means of discouraging theft.
- Security Surveys—provided to the business and residential community. It consists of an on-site examination of physical facilities and surrounding property, with the intent of recognizing, appraising and anticipating loss potential, along with recommendations to minimize criminal opportunity.
- Senior Citizens—addresses home security and those crimes commonly committed against the elderly, such as thefts, swindles and con games.
- Child Identification—provides parents with fingerprints of their children over the age of 3.
- Child Safety Programs—McGruff the Crime Dog teaches children in preschool through grade 3 and their parents about safety.
- McGruff House Program—in cooperation with the local PTA and Springfield Public Schools, this program consists of adults who are willing to allow their homes or businesses to become safe havens for youngsters who have an emergency while in the neighborhood.
- Gang and Drug Awareness and Prevention—this presentation, for ages nine to adult, discusses drugs, crime and gangs, in terms of being a "game in which no one wins." *Springfield Police Department, 6/97*

CRIME RISK

Your Chances of Becoming a Victim[1]

Area	Any Crime	Violent Crime					Property Crime			
		Any	Murder	Forcible Rape[2]	Robbery	Aggrav. Assault	Any	Burglary	Larceny -Theft	Motor Vehicle Theft
City	1:13	1:191	1:38,006	1:1,056	1:879	1:280	1:14	1:70	1:19	1:225

Note: (1) Figures have been calculated by dividing the population of the city by the number of crimes reported to the FBI during 1996 and are expressed as odds (eg. 1:20 should be read as 1 in 20). (2) Figures have been calculated by dividing the female population of the city by the number of forcible rapes reported to the FBI during 1996. The female population of the city was estimated by calculating the ratio of females to males reported in the 1990 Census and applying that ratio to 1996 population estimate.
Source: FBI Uniform Crime Reports 1996

CRIME STATISTICS

Total Crimes and Total Crime Rates: 1977 - 1996

Year	Number				Rate per 100,000 population			
	City	Suburbs[2]	MSA[1]	U.S.	City	Suburbs[3]	MSA[1]	U.S.
1977	10,978	1,182	12,160	10,984,500	8,131.9	2,374.2	6,580.6	5,077.6
1978	11,032	1,775	12,807	11,209,000	7,824.1	3,700.7	6,777.5	5,140.3
1979	12,504	1,941	14,445	12,249,500	9,177.1	2,817.4	7,041.3	5,565.5
1980	13,472	1,789	15,261	13,408,300	10,127.9	2,449.5	7,406.3	5,950.0
1981	13,414	1,914	15,328	13,423,800	10,009.3	2,601.2	7,383.5	5,858.2
1982	11,996	1,667	13,663	12,974,400	8,927.7	2,259.5	6,564.2	5,603.6
1983	10,973	1,442	12,415	12,108,600	8,135.2	1,947.1	5,941.9	5,175.0
1984	9,689	1,013	10,702	11,881,800	7,122.0	1,315.5	5,023.2	5,031.3
1985	9,591	1,355	10,946	12,431,400	6,974.5	1,681.2	5,018.5	5,207.1
1986	11,470	1,630	13,100	13,211,900	8,279.6	2,007.0	5,961.3	5,480.4
1987	10,243	1,701	11,944	13,508,700	7,296.7	1,964.9	5,262.9	5,550.0
1988	11,277	1,923	13,200	13,923,100	7,954.9	2,166.6	5,726.2	5,664.2
1989	12,907	2,051	14,958	14,251,400	9,015.0	2,231.3	6,362.6	5,741.0
1990	12,549	2,138	14,687	14,475,600	8,932.1	2,135.9	6,104.5	5,820.3
1991	11,905	2,041	13,946	14,872,900	8,406.5	2,022.8	5,750.5	5,897.8
1992	10,916	2,649	13,565	14,438,200	7,656.2	2,107.6	5,056.5	5,660.2
1993	10,907	2,475	13,382	14,144,800	7,437.8	1,885.6	4,815.4	5,484.4
1994	13,096	2,312	15,408	13,989,500	8,856.1	1,746.8	5,498.2	5,373.5
1995	12,092	2,460	14,552	13,862,700	8,006.3	1,751.2	4,992.0	5,275.9
1996	11,505	3,070	14,575	13,473,600	7,567.9	1,814.4	4,537.3	5,078.9

Notes: (1) Metropolitan Statistical Area - see Appendix A for areas included; (2) calculated by the editors using the following formula: (number of crimes in the MSA minus number of crimes in the city); (3) calculated by the editors using the following formula: ((number of crimes in the MSA minus number of crimes in the city) ÷ (population of the MSA minus population of the city)) x 100,000; n/a not avail.
Source: U.S. Department of Justice, FBI Uniform Crime Reports, 1977 - 1996

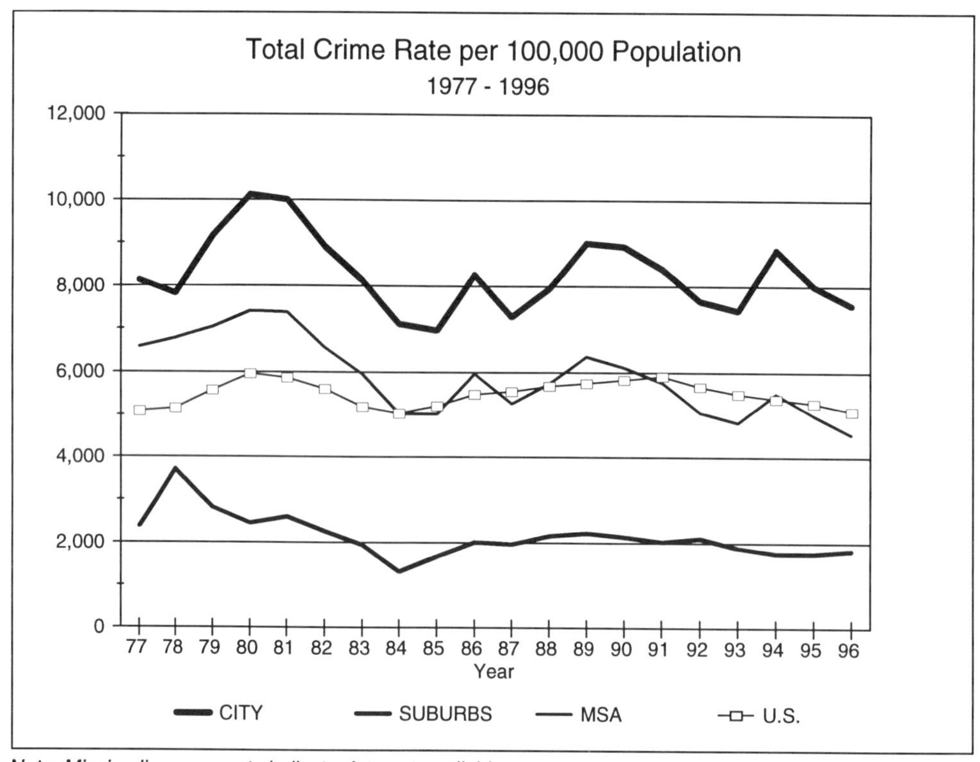

Note: Missing line segments indicate data not available.

Violent Crimes and Violent Crime Rates: 1977 - 1996

Year	Number				Rate per 100,000 population			
	City	Suburbs[2]	MSA[1]	U.S.	City	Suburbs[3]	MSA[1]	U.S.
1977	416	80	496	1,029,580	308.1	160.7	268.4	475.9
1978	489	100	589	1,085,550	346.8	208.5	311.7	497.8
1979	601	108	709	1,208,030	441.1	156.8	345.6	548.9
1980	427	77	504	1,344,520	321.0	105.4	244.6	596.6
1981	366	134	500	1,361,820	273.1	182.1	240.9	594.3
1982	417	128	545	1,322,390	310.3	173.5	261.8	571.1
1983	363	102	465	1,258,090	269.1	137.7	222.6	537.7
1984	354	107	461	1,273,280	260.2	138.9	216.4	539.2
1985	306	138	444	1,328,800	222.5	171.2	203.6	556.6
1986	377	173	550	1,489,170	272.1	213.0	250.3	617.7
1987	439	165	604	1,484,000	312.7	190.6	266.1	609.7
1988	514	162	676	1,566,220	362.6	182.5	293.3	637.2
1989	605	140	745	1,646,040	422.6	152.3	316.9	663.1
1990	571	77	648	1,820,130	406.4	76.9	269.3	731.8
1991	635	94	729	1,911,770	448.4	93.2	300.6	758.1
1992	649	144	793	1,932,270	455.2	114.6	295.6	757.5
1993	669	131	800	1,926,020	456.2	99.8	287.9	746.8
1994	812	146	958	1,857,670	549.1	110.3	341.9	713.6
1995	829	106	935	1,798,790	548.9	75.5	320.7	684.6
1996	795	250	1,045	1,682,280	522.9	147.8	325.3	634.1

Notes: Violent crimes include murder, forcible rape, robbery and aggravated assault; n/a not available; (1) Metropolitan Statistical Area - see Appendix A for areas included; (2) calculated by the editors using the following formula: (number of crimes in the MSA minus number of crimes in the city); (3) calculated by the editors using the following formula: ((number of crimes in the MSA minus number of crimes in the city) ÷ (population of the MSA minus population of the city)) x 100,000
Source: U.S. Department of Justice, FBI Uniform Crime Reports, 1977 - 1996

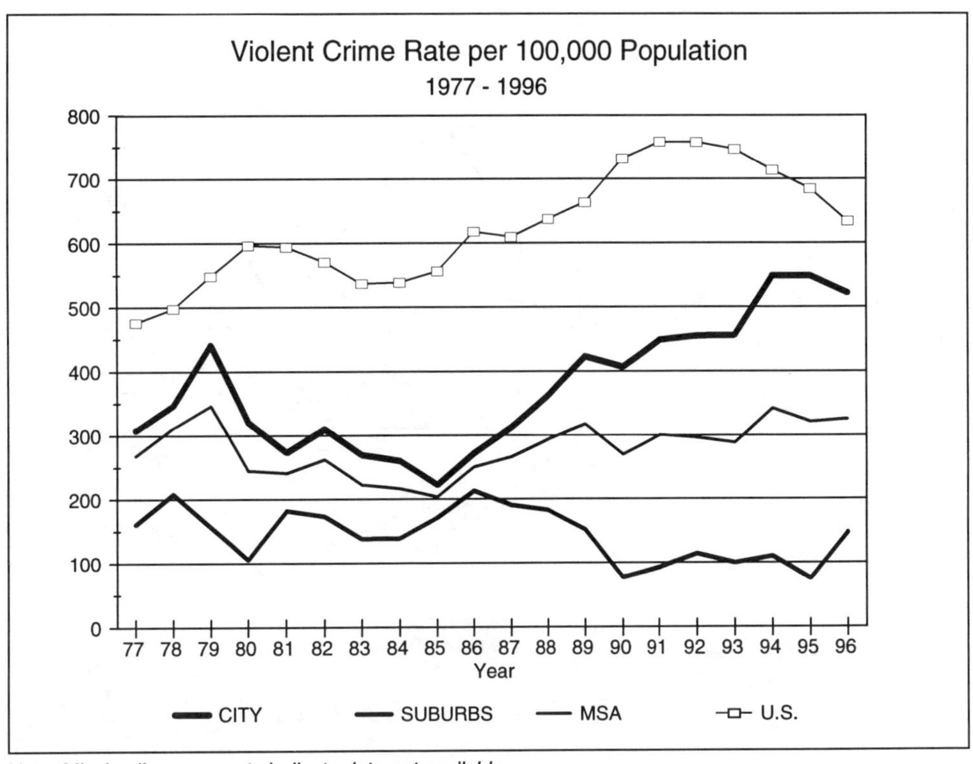

Note: Missing line segments indicate data not available.

Property Crimes and Property Crime Rates: 1977 - 1996

Year	Number				Rate per 100,000 population			
	City	Suburbs[2]	MSA[1]	U.S.	City	Suburbs[3]	MSA[1]	U.S.
1977	10,562	1,102	11,664	9,955,000	7,823.7	2,213.5	6,312.2	4,601.7
1978	10,543	1,675	12,218	10,123,400	7,477.3	3,492.2	6,465.8	4,642.5
1979	11,903	1,833	13,736	11,041,500	8,736.0	2,660.6	6,695.7	5,016.6
1980	13,045	1,712	14,757	12,063,700	9,806.9	2,344.1	7,161.7	5,353.3
1981	13,048	1,780	14,828	12,061,900	9,736.2	2,419.1	7,142.7	5,263.9
1982	11,579	1,539	13,118	11,652,000	8,617.4	2,086.0	6,302.4	5,032.5
1983	10,610	1,340	11,950	10,850,500	7,866.1	1,809.4	5,719.3	4,637.4
1984	9,335	906	10,241	10,608,500	6,861.8	1,176.5	4,806.8	4,492.1
1985	9,285	1,217	10,502	11,102,600	6,751.9	1,509.9	4,814.9	4,650.5
1986	11,093	1,457	12,550	11,722,700	8,007.4	1,794.0	5,711.1	4,862.6
1987	9,804	1,536	11,340	12,024,700	6,984.0	1,774.3	4,996.8	4,940.3
1988	10,763	1,761	12,524	12,356,900	7,592.3	1,984.1	5,433.0	5,027.1
1989	12,302	1,911	14,213	12,605,400	8,592.4	2,079.0	6,045.7	5,077.9
1990	11,978	2,061	14,039	12,655,500	8,525.6	2,059.0	5,835.2	5,088.5
1991	11,270	1,947	13,217	12,961,100	7,958.1	1,929.7	5,449.9	5,139.7
1992	10,267	2,505	12,772	12,505,900	7,201.0	1,993.0	4,760.9	4,902.7
1993	10,238	2,344	12,582	12,218,800	6,981.6	1,785.8	4,527.5	4,737.6
1994	12,284	2,166	14,450	12,131,900	8,307.0	1,636.4	5,156.4	4,660.0
1995	11,263	2,354	13,617	12,063,900	7,457.4	1,675.7	4,671.2	4,591.3
1996	10,710	2,820	13,530	11,791,300	7,044.9	1,666.7	4,212.0	4,444.8

Notes: Property crimes include burglary, larceny-theft and motor vehicle theft; n/a not available; (1) Metropolitan Statistical Area - see Appendix A for areas included; (2) calculated by the editors using the following formula: (number of crimes in the MSA minus number of crimes in the city); (3) calculated by the editors using the following formula: ((number of crimes in the MSA minus number of crimes in the city) ÷ (population of the MSA minus population of the city)) x 100,000
Source: U.S. Department of Justice, FBI Uniform Crime Reports, 1977 - 1996

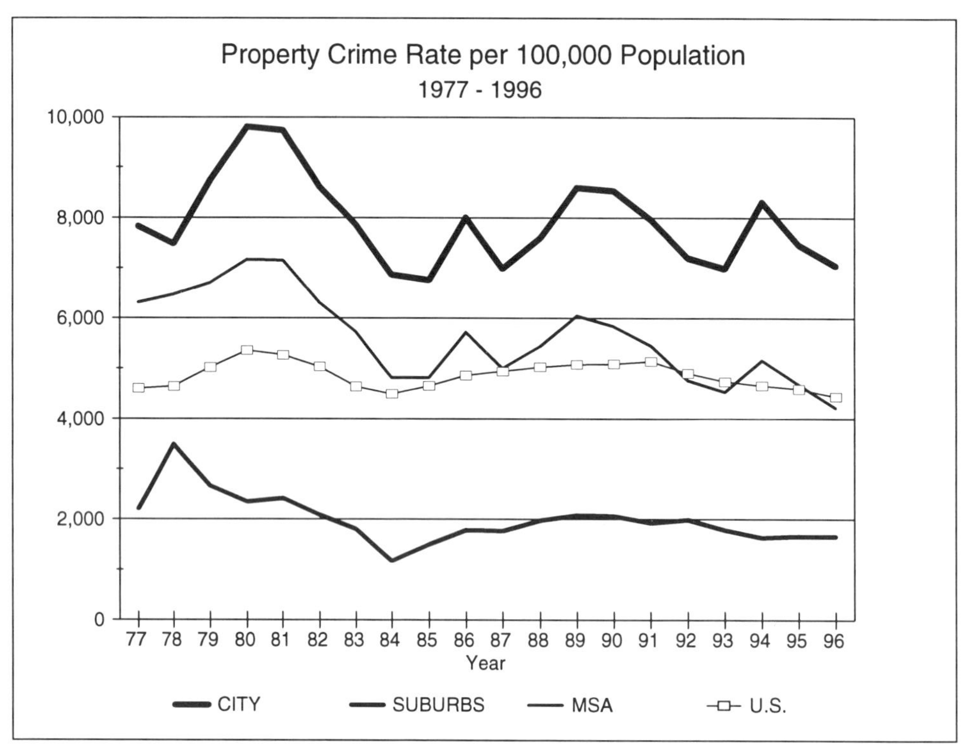

Note: Missing line segments indicate data not available.

Murders and Murder Rates: 1977 - 1996

Year	Number				Rate per 100,000 population			
	City	Suburbs[2]	MSA[1]	U.S.	City	Suburbs[3]	MSA[1]	U.S.
1977	7	3	10	19,120	5.2	6.0	5.4	8.8
1978	8	1	9	19,560	5.7	2.1	4.8	9.0
1979	12	2	14	21,460	8.8	2.9	6.8	9.7
1980	6	4	10	23,040	4.5	5.5	4.9	10.2
1981	8	3	11	22,520	6.0	4.1	5.3	9.8
1982	6	2	8	21,010	4.5	2.7	3.8	9.1
1983	5	3	8	19,310	3.7	4.1	3.8	8.3
1984	13	0	13	18,690	9.6	0.0	6.1	7.9
1985	6	5	11	18,980	4.4	6.2	5.0	7.9
1986	5	3	8	20,610	3.6	3.7	3.6	8.6
1987	1	3	4	20,100	0.7	3.5	1.8	8.3
1988	5	0	5	20,680	3.5	0.0	2.2	8.4
1989	7	1	8	21,500	4.9	1.1	3.4	8.7
1990	7	1	8	23,440	5.0	1.0	3.3	9.4
1991	4	1	5	24,700	2.8	1.0	2.1	9.8
1992	8	2	10	23,760	5.6	1.6	3.7	9.3
1993	7	1	8	24,530	4.8	0.8	2.9	9.5
1994	3	3	6	23,330	2.0	2.3	2.1	9.0
1995	5	3	8	21,610	3.3	2.1	2.7	8.2
1996	4	0	4	19,650	2.6	0.0	1.2	7.4

Notes: (1) Metropolitan Statistical Area - see Appendix A for areas included; (2) calculated by the editors using the following formula: (number of crimes in the MSA minus number of crimes in the city); (3) calculated by the editors using the following formula: ((number of crimes in the MSA minus number of crimes in the city) ÷ (population of the MSA minus population of the city)) x 100,000; n/a not avail.
Source: U.S. Department of Justice, FBI Uniform Crime Reports, 1977 - 1996

Forcible Rapes and Forcible Rape Rates: 1977 - 1996

Year	Number				Rate per 100,000 population			
	City	Suburbs[2]	MSA[1]	U.S.	City	Suburbs[3]	MSA[1]	U.S.
1977	28	8	36	63,500	20.7	16.1	19.5	29.4
1978	38	6	44	67,610	27.0	12.5	23.3	31.0
1979	60	19	79	76,390	44.0	27.6	38.5	34.7
1980	63	4	67	82,990	47.4	5.5	32.5	36.8
1981	41	3	44	82,500	30.6	4.1	21.2	36.0
1982	56	13	69	78,770	41.7	17.6	33.2	34.0
1983	42	7	49	78,920	31.1	9.5	23.5	33.7
1984	42	8	50	84,230	30.9	10.4	23.5	35.7
1985	54	4	58	88,670	39.3	5.0	26.6	37.1
1986	40	7	47	91,460	28.9	8.6	21.4	37.9
1987	41	13	54	91,110	29.2	15.0	23.8	37.4
1988	67	6	73	92,490	47.3	6.8	31.7	37.6
1989	61	13	74	94,500	42.6	14.1	31.5	38.1
1990	58	8	66	102,560	41.3	8.0	27.4	41.2
1991	54	14	68	106,590	38.1	13.9	28.0	42.3
1992	61	21	82	109,060	42.8	16.7	30.6	42.8
1993	77	19	96	106,010	52.5	14.5	34.5	41.1
1994	74	20	94	102,220	50.0	15.1	33.5	39.3
1995	82	28	110	97,470	54.3	19.9	37.7	37.1
1996	76	29	105	95,770	50.0	17.1	32.7	36.1

Notes: (1) Metropolitan Statistical Area - see Appendix A for areas included; (2) calculated by the editors using the following formula: (number of crimes in the MSA minus number of crimes in the city); (3) calculated by the editors using the following formula: ((number of crimes in the MSA minus number of crimes in the city) ÷ (population of the MSA minus population of the city)) x 100,000; n/a not avail.
Source: U.S. Department of Justice, FBI Uniform Crime Reports, 1977 - 1996

Robberies and Robbery Rates: 1977 - 1996

Year	Number				Rate per 100,000 population			
	City	Suburbs[2]	MSA[1]	U.S.	City	Suburbs[3]	MSA[1]	U.S.
1977	147	8	155	412,610	108.9	16.1	83.9	190.7
1978	164	20	184	426,930	116.3	41.7	97.4	195.8
1979	156	19	175	480,700	114.5	27.6	85.3	218.4
1980	112	12	124	565,840	84.2	16.4	60.2	251.1
1981	126	11	137	592,910	94.0	14.9	66.0	258.7
1982	160	10	170	553,130	119.1	13.6	81.7	238.9
1983	148	8	156	506,570	109.7	10.8	74.7	216.5
1984	135	3	138	485,010	99.2	3.9	64.8	205.4
1985	109	9	118	497,870	79.3	11.2	54.1	208.5
1986	133	11	144	542,780	96.0	13.5	65.5	225.1
1987	157	6	163	517,700	111.8	6.9	71.8	212.7
1988	137	11	148	542,970	96.6	12.4	64.2	220.9
1989	192	10	202	578,330	134.1	10.9	85.9	233.0
1990	139	16	155	639,270	98.9	16.0	64.4	257.0
1991	151	12	163	687,730	106.6	11.9	67.2	272.7
1992	165	19	184	672,480	115.7	15.1	68.6	263.6
1993	136	24	160	659,870	92.7	18.3	57.6	255.9
1994	184	21	205	618,950	124.4	15.9	73.2	237.7
1995	145	17	162	580,510	96.0	12.1	55.6	220.9
1996	173	22	195	537,050	113.8	13.0	60.7	202.4

Notes: (1) Metropolitan Statistical Area - see Appendix A for areas included; (2) calculated by the editors using the following formula: (number of crimes in the MSA minus number of crimes in the city); (3) calculated by the editors using the following formula: ((number of crimes in the MSA minus number of crimes in the city) ÷ (population of the MSA minus population of the city)) x 100,000; n/a not avail.
Source: U.S. Department of Justice, FBI Uniform Crime Reports, 1977 - 1996

Aggravated Assaults and Aggravated Assault Rates: 1977 - 1996

Year	Number				Rate per 100,000 population			
	City	Suburbs[2]	MSA[1]	U.S.	City	Suburbs[3]	MSA[1]	U.S.
1977	234	61	295	534,350	173.3	122.5	159.6	247.0
1978	279	73	352	571,460	197.9	152.2	186.3	262.1
1979	373	68	441	629,480	273.8	98.7	215.0	286.0
1980	246	57	303	672,650	184.9	78.0	147.0	298.5
1981	191	117	308	663,900	142.5	159.0	148.4	289.7
1982	195	103	298	669,480	145.1	139.6	143.2	289.2
1983	168	84	252	653,290	124.6	113.4	120.6	279.2
1984	164	96	260	685,350	120.5	124.7	122.0	290.2
1985	137	120	257	723,250	99.6	148.9	117.8	302.9
1986	199	152	351	834,320	143.6	187.2	159.7	346.1
1987	240	143	383	855,090	171.0	165.2	168.8	351.3
1988	305	145	450	910,090	215.1	163.4	195.2	370.2
1989	345	116	461	951,710	241.0	126.2	196.1	383.4
1990	367	52	419	1,054,860	261.2	51.9	174.2	424.1
1991	426	67	493	1,092,740	300.8	66.4	203.3	433.3
1992	415	102	517	1,126,970	291.1	81.2	192.7	441.8
1993	449	87	536	1,135,610	306.2	66.3	192.9	440.3
1994	551	102	653	1,113,180	372.6	77.1	233.0	427.6
1995	597	58	655	1,099,210	395.3	41.3	224.7	418.3
1996	542	199	741	1,029,810	356.5	117.6	230.7	388.2

Notes: (1) Metropolitan Statistical Area - see Appendix A for areas included; (2) calculated by the editors using the following formula: (number of crimes in the MSA minus number of crimes in the city); (3) calculated by the editors using the following formula: ((number of crimes in the MSA minus number of crimes in the city) ÷ (population of the MSA minus population of the city)) x 100,000; n/a not avail.
Source: U.S. Department of Justice, FBI Uniform Crime Reports, 1977 - 1996

Burglaries and Burglary Rates: 1977 - 1996

Year	Number				Rate per 100,000 population			
	City	Suburbs[2]	MSA[1]	U.S.	City	Suburbs[3]	MSA[1]	U.S.
1977	3,281	398	3,679	3,071,500	2,430.4	799.4	1,991.0	1,419.8
1978	2,930	656	3,586	3,128,300	2,078.0	1,367.7	1,897.7	1,434.6
1979	3,034	681	3,715	3,327,700	2,226.8	988.5	1,810.9	1,511.9
1980	3,488	628	4,116	3,795,200	2,622.2	859.9	1,997.5	1,684.1
1981	4,037	745	4,782	3,779,700	3,012.3	1,012.5	2,303.5	1,649.5
1982	3,288	544	3,832	3,447,100	2,447.0	737.4	1,841.0	1,488.8
1983	2,663	430	3,093	3,129,900	1,974.3	580.6	1,480.3	1,337.7
1984	2,177	286	2,463	2,984,400	1,600.2	371.4	1,156.1	1,263.7
1985	2,168	379	2,547	3,073,300	1,576.5	470.2	1,167.7	1,287.3
1986	2,716	466	3,182	3,241,400	1,960.5	573.8	1,448.0	1,344.6
1987	2,528	501	3,029	3,236,200	1,800.9	578.7	1,334.7	1,329.6
1988	2,274	465	2,739	3,218,100	1,604.1	523.9	1,188.2	1,309.2
1989	2,612	573	3,185	3,168,200	1,824.4	623.4	1,354.8	1,276.3
1990	2,354	645	2,999	3,073,900	1,675.5	644.4	1,246.5	1,235.9
1991	2,560	679	3,239	3,157,200	1,807.7	673.0	1,335.6	1,252.0
1992	1,961	712	2,673	2,979,900	1,375.4	566.5	996.4	1,168.2
1993	2,094	611	2,705	2,834,800	1,428.0	465.5	973.4	1,099.2
1994	2,369	554	2,923	2,712,800	1,602.0	418.6	1,043.1	1,042.0
1995	2,123	679	2,802	2,593,800	1,405.7	483.4	961.2	987.1
1996	2,182	768	2,950	2,501,500	1,435.3	453.9	918.4	943.0

Notes: (1) Metropolitan Statistical Area - see Appendix A for areas included; (2) calculated by the editors using the following formula: (number of crimes in the MSA minus number of crimes in the city); (3) calculated by the editors using the following formula: ((number of crimes in the MSA minus number of crimes in the city) ÷ (population of the MSA minus population of the city)) x 100,000; n/a not avail.
Source: U.S. Department of Justice, FBI Uniform Crime Reports, 1977 - 1996

Larceny-Thefts and Larceny-Theft Rates: 1977 - 1996

Year	Number				Rate per 100,000 population			
	City	Suburbs[2]	MSA[1]	U.S.	City	Suburbs[3]	MSA[1]	U.S.
1977	6,817	689	7,506	5,905,700	5,049.6	1,384.0	4,062.0	2,729.9
1978	7,017	900	7,917	5,991,000	4,976.6	1,876.4	4,189.7	2,747.4
1979	8,243	1,002	9,245	6,601,000	6,049.8	1,454.4	4,506.5	2,999.1
1980	9,035	952	9,987	7,136,900	6,792.3	1,303.5	4,846.8	3,167.0
1981	8,592	933	9,525	7,194,400	6,411.2	1,268.0	4,588.2	3,139.7
1982	7,871	893	8,764	7,142,500	5,857.8	1,210.4	4,210.5	3,084.8
1983	7,525	829	8,354	6,712,800	5,578.9	1,119.4	3,998.3	2,868.9
1984	6,744	581	7,325	6,591,900	4,957.2	754.5	3,438.1	2,791.3
1985	6,728	783	7,511	6,926,400	4,892.5	971.5	3,443.6	2,901.2
1986	7,951	917	8,868	7,257,200	5,739.4	1,129.1	4,035.5	3,010.3
1987	6,849	961	7,810	7,499,900	4,879.0	1,110.1	3,441.3	3,081.3
1988	8,045	1,202	9,247	7,705,900	5,675.0	1,354.3	4,011.4	3,134.9
1989	9,151	1,266	10,417	7,872,400	6,391.6	1,377.3	4,431.0	3,171.3
1990	9,193	1,330	10,523	7,945,700	6,543.3	1,328.7	4,373.8	3,194.8
1991	8,275	1,184	9,459	8,142,200	5,843.2	1,173.5	3,900.4	3,228.8
1992	7,842	1,662	9,504	7,915,200	5,500.1	1,322.3	3,542.8	3,103.0
1993	7,690	1,584	9,274	7,820,900	5,244.1	1,206.8	3,337.2	3,032.4
1994	9,317	1,454	10,771	7,879,800	6,300.6	1,098.5	3,843.6	3,026.7
1995	8,440	1,515	9,955	7,997,700	5,588.2	1,078.5	3,415.0	3,043.8
1996	7,851	1,831	9,682	7,894,600	5,164.3	1,082.1	3,014.1	2,975.9

Notes: (1) Metropolitan Statistical Area - see Appendix A for areas included; (2) calculated by the editors using the following formula: (number of crimes in the MSA minus number of crimes in the city); (3) calculated by the editors using the following formula: ((number of crimes in the MSA minus number of crimes in the city) ÷ (population of the MSA minus population of the city)) x 100,000; n/a not avail.
Source: U.S. Department of Justice, FBI Uniform Crime Reports, 1977 - 1996

Motor Vehicle Thefts and Motor Vehicle Theft Rates: 1977 - 1996

Year	Number				Rate per 100,000 population			
	City	Suburbs[2]	MSA[1]	U.S.	City	Suburbs[3]	MSA[1]	U.S.
1977	464	15	479	977,700	343.7	30.1	259.2	451.9
1978	596	119	715	1,004,100	422.7	248.1	378.4	460.5
1979	626	150	776	1,112,800	459.4	217.7	378.3	505.6
1980	522	132	654	1,131,700	392.4	180.7	317.4	502.2
1981	419	102	521	1,087,800	312.6	138.6	251.0	474.7
1982	420	102	522	1,062,400	312.6	138.3	250.8	458.8
1983	422	81	503	1,007,900	312.9	109.4	240.7	430.8
1984	414	39	453	1,032,200	304.3	50.6	212.6	437.1
1985	389	55	444	1,102,900	282.9	68.2	203.6	462.0
1986	426	74	500	1,224,100	307.5	91.1	227.5	507.8
1987	427	74	501	1,288,700	304.2	85.5	220.8	529.4
1988	444	94	538	1,432,900	313.2	105.9	233.4	582.9
1989	539	72	611	1,564,800	376.5	78.3	259.9	630.4
1990	431	86	517	1,635,900	306.8	85.9	214.9	657.8
1991	435	84	519	1,661,700	307.2	83.3	214.0	659.0
1992	464	131	595	1,610,800	325.4	104.2	221.8	631.5
1993	454	149	603	1,563,100	309.6	113.5	217.0	606.1
1994	598	158	756	1,539,300	404.4	119.4	269.8	591.3
1995	700	160	860	1,472,400	463.5	113.9	295.0	560.4
1996	677	221	898	1,395,200	445.3	130.6	279.6	525.9

Notes: (1) Metropolitan Statistical Area - see Appendix A for areas included; (2) calculated by the editors using the following formula: (number of crimes in the MSA minus number of crimes in the city); (3) calculated by the editors using the following formula: ((number of crimes in the MSA minus number of crimes in the city) ÷ (population of the MSA minus population of the city)) x 100,000; n/a not avail.
Source: U.S. Department of Justice, FBI Uniform Crime Reports, 1977 - 1996

HATE CRIMES

Criminal Incidents by Bias Motivation

Area	Race	Ethnicity	Religion	Sexual Orientation
Springfield	21	1	0	6

Notes: Figures include both violent and property crimes. Law enforcement agencies must have submitted data for at least one quarter of calendar year 1995 to be included in this report, therefore figures shown may not represent complete 12-month totals; n/a not available
Source: U.S. Department of Justice, FBI Uniform Crime Reports, Hate Crime Statistics 1995

LAW ENFORCEMENT

Full-Time Law Enforcement Employees

Jurisdiction	Police Employees			Police Officers per 100,000 population
	Total	Officers	Civilians	
Springfield	302	233	69	153.3

Notes: Data as of October 31, 1996
Source: U.S. Department of Justice, FBI Uniform Crime Reports, 1996

CORRECTIONS

Federal Correctional Facilities

Type	Year Opened	Security Level	Sex of Inmates	Rated Capacity	Population on 7/1/95	Number of Staff
Federal Medical Center	1933	Admin.	Male	874	921	681

Notes: Data as of 1995
Source: Bureau of Justice Statistics, Sourcebook of Criminal Justice Statistics Online

City/County/Regional Correctional Facilities

Name	Year Opened	Year Renov.	Rated Capacity	1995 Pop.	Number of COs[1]	Number of Staff	ACA[2] Accred.
Greene County Jail	1936	1988	214	177	53	62	No

Notes: Data as of April 1996; (1) Correctional Officers; (2) American Correctional Assn. Accreditation
Source: American Correctional Association, 1996-1998 National Jail and Adult Detention Directory

Private Adult Correctional Facilities

Name	Date Opened	Rated Capacity	Present Pop.	Security Level	Facility Construct.	Expans. Plans	ACA[1] Accred.
None listed							

Notes: Data as of December 1996; (1) American Correctional Association Accreditation
Source: University of Florida, Center for Studies in Criminology and Law, Private Adult Correctional Facility Census, 10th Ed., March 15, 1997

Characteristics of Shock Incarceration Programs

Jurisdiction	Year Program Began	Number of Camps	Average Num. of Inmates	Number of Beds	Program Length	Voluntary/ Mandatory
Missouri	1994	1	40 to 45	50	90 days	Mandatory

Note: Data as of July 1996;
Source: Sourcebook of Criminal Justice Statistics Online

DEATH PENALTY

Death Penalty Statistics

State	Prisoners Executed		Prisoners Under Sentence of Death					Avg. No. of Years on Death Row[4]
	1930-1995	1996[1]	Total[2]	White[3]	Black[3]	Hisp.	Women	
Missouri	79	6	92	51	41	0	2	6.1

Notes: Data as of 12/31/95 unless otherwise noted; (1) Data as of 7/31/97; (2) Includes persons of other races; (3) Includes people of Hispanic origin; (4) Covers prisoners sentenced 1974 through 1995
Source: Bureau of Justice Statistics, Capital Punishment 1995 (released 12/96); Death Penalty Information Center Web Site, 9/30/97

Capital Offenses and Methods of Execution

Capital Offenses in Missouri	Minimum Age for Imposition of Death Penalty	Mentally Retarded Excluded	Methods of Execution[1]
First-degree murder (565.020 RSMO).	16	No	Lethal injection; lethal gas

Notes: Data as of 12/31/95 unless otherwise noted; (1) Data as of 7/31/97
Source: Bureau of Justice Statistics, Capital Punishment 1995 (released 12/96); Death Penalty Information Center Web Site, 9/30/97

LAWS

Statutory Provisions Relating to the Purchase, Ownership and Use of Handguns

Jurisdiction	Instant Background Check	Federal Waiting Period Applies[1]	State Waiting Period (days)	License or Permit to Purchase	Regis-tration	Record of Sale Sent to Police	Concealed Carry Law
Missouri	No	No	7	Yes[a]	No	Yes	Yes[b]

Note: Data as of 1996; (1) The Federal 5-day waiting period for handgun purchases applies to states that don't have instant background checks, waiting period requirements, or licensing procedures exempting them from the Federal requirement; (a) A purchase permit is required for a handgun, must be issued to qualified applicants within 7 days, and is valid for 30 days; (b) No permit system exists and concealed carry is prohibited
Source: Sourcebook of Criminal Justice Statistics Online

Statutory Provisions Relating to Alcohol Use and Driving

Jurisdiction	Drinking Age	Blood Alcohol Concentration Levels as Evidence in State Courts[1]		Open Container Law[1]	Anti-Consump-tion Law[1]	Dram Shop Law[1]
		Illegal per se at 0.10%	Presumption at 0.10%			
Missouri	21	Yes	No	No	(a)	(b)

Note: Data as of January 1, 1997; (1) See Appendix C for an explanation of terms; (a) Applies to drivers only; (b) Cause of action limited to licensees who have been convicted of selling alcoholic beverages to minors or intoxicated individuals
Source: Sourcebook of Criminal Justice Statistics Online

Statutory Provisions Relating to Curfews

Jurisdiction	Year Enacted	Latest Revision	Age Group(s)	Curfew Provisions
Springfield	1946	-	14 and under	9 pm to 5 am every night Oct - May 10 pm to 5 am every night June - Sept.

Note: Data as of February 1996
Source: Sourcebook of Criminal Justice Statistics Online

Statutory Provisions Relating to Hate Crimes

Jurisdiction	Bias-Motivated Violence and Intimidation						Institutional Vandalism
		Criminal Penalty					
	Civil Action	Race/ Religion/ Ethnicity	Sexual Orientation	Mental/ Physical Disability	Gender	Age	
Missouri	Yes	Yes	No	No	No	No	Yes

Source: Anti-Defamation League, 1997 Hate Crimes Laws

Stamford, Connecticut

OVERVIEW

The total crime rate for the city increased 5.5% between 1977 and 1996. During that same period, the violent crime rate increased 97.3% and the property crime rate increased 0.9%.

Among violent crimes, the rates for: Murders increased 16.7%; Forcible Rapes increased 17.5%; Robberies increased 38.4%; and Aggravated Assaults increased 309.6%.

Among property crimes, the rates for: Burglaries decreased 64.8%; Larceny-Thefts increased 83.0%; and Motor Vehicle Thefts decreased 26.8%.

ANTI-CRIME PROGRAMS

Some programs include:

- Community Based Policing—specially trained officers are assigned to specific areas in an effort to address almost any situation whether related to crime, traffic or quality of life issues.
- CAT—individuals voluntarily register their vehicles with the police department. This allows police to stop and check their autos in an attempt to deter the theft of the vehicle.
- Neighborhood Watch.

The police also offer anti-robbery and shoplifting seminars to businesses. They will go to church groups and others and teach the groups how to avoid becoming victims.
Stamford Police Department, 7/97

CRIME RISK

Your Chances of Becoming a Victim[1]

Area	Any Crime	Violent Crime					Property Crime			
		Any	Murder	Forcible Rape[2]	Robbery	Aggrav. Assault	Any	Burglary	Larceny -Theft	Motor Vehicle Theft
City	1:22	1:243	1:17,861	1:3,113	1:505	1:523	1:24	1:152	1:32	1:224

Note: (1) Figures have been calculated by dividing the population of the city by the number of crimes reported to the FBI during 1996 and are expressed as odds (eg. 1:20 should be read as 1 in 20).
(2) Figures have been calculated by dividing the female population of the city by the number of forcible rapes reported to the FBI during 1996. The female population of the city was estimated by calculating the ratio of females to males reported in the 1990 Census and applying that ratio to 1996 population estimate.
Source: FBI Uniform Crime Reports 1996

CRIME STATISTICS

Total Crimes and Total Crime Rates: 1977 - 1996

Year	Number				Rate per 100,000 population			
	City	Suburbs[2]	MSA[1]	U.S.	City	Suburbs[3]	MSA[1]	U.S.
1977	4,601	n/a	n/a	10,984,500	4,381.9	n/a	n/a	5,077.6
1978	n/a	n/a	n/a	11,209,000	n/a	n/a	n/a	5,140.3
1979	7,703	n/a	n/a	12,249,500	7,323.0	n/a	n/a	5,565.5
1980	7,371	n/a	n/a	13,408,300	7,252.4	n/a	n/a	5,950.0
1981	7,817	n/a	n/a	13,423,800	7,600.8	n/a	n/a	5,858.2
1982	7,664	n/a	n/a	12,974,400	7,402.5	n/a	n/a	5,603.6
1983	7,165	2,628	9,793	12,108,600	6,953.6	2,719.5	4,904.5	5,175.0
1984	6,866	2,424	9,290	11,881,800	6,597.6	2,485.0	4,607.8	5,031.3
1985	6,118	2,595	8,713	12,431,400	5,965.5	2,643.7	4,341.0	5,207.1
1986	7,076	2,545	9,621	13,211,900	6,867.2	2,649.8	4,832.6	5,480.4
1987	7,095	2,921	10,016	13,508,700	6,970.4	3,085.8	5,098.6	5,550.0
1988	6,596	2,508	9,104	13,923,100	6,490.2	2,653.6	4,641.5	5,664.2
1989	7,136	2,303	9,439	14,251,400	7,104.3	2,496.7	4,898.6	5,741.0
1990	6,625	2,587	9,212	14,475,600	6,131.1	2,737.5	4,547.9	5,820.3
1991	6,503	2,371	8,874	14,872,900	6,011.1	2,506.1	4,375.9	5,897.8
1992	5,970	7,925	13,895	14,438,200	5,535.3	3,578.6	4,219.4	5,660.2
1993	5,872	7,534	13,406	14,144,800	5,461.1	3,392.0	4,066.9	5,484.4
1994	6,433	7,302	13,735	13,989,500	5,986.5	3,289.6	4,169.3	5,373.5
1995	6,051	6,941	12,992	13,862,700	5,644.6	3,092.7	3,917.6	5,275.9
1996	4,955	7,410	12,365	13,473,600	4,623.7	3,302.8	3,729.8	5,078.9

Notes: (1) Metropolitan Statistical Area - see Appendix A for areas included; (2) calculated by the editors using the following formula: (number of crimes in the MSA minus number of crimes in the city); (3) calculated by the editors using the following formula: ((number of crimes in the MSA minus number of crimes in the city) ÷ (population of the MSA minus population of the city)) x 100,000; n/a not avail.
Source: U.S. Department of Justice, FBI Uniform Crime Reports, 1977 - 1996

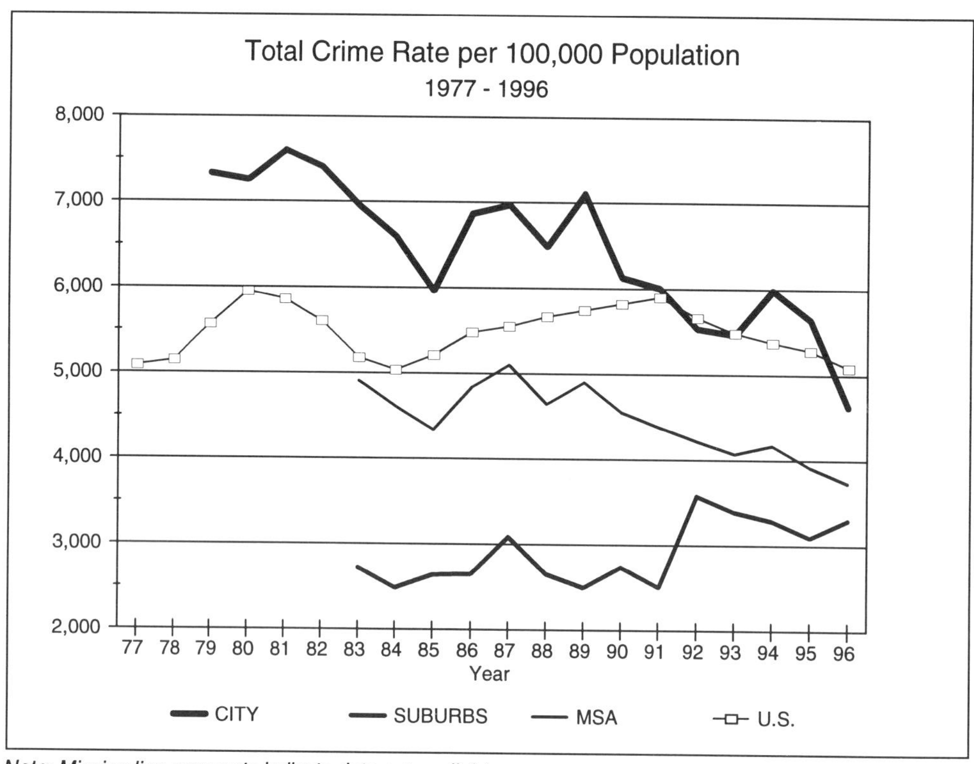

Note: Missing line segments indicate data not available.

Violent Crimes and Violent Crime Rates: 1977 - 1996

Year	Number				Rate per 100,000 population			
	City	Suburbs[2]	MSA[1]	U.S.	City	Suburbs[3]	MSA[1]	U.S.
1977	219	n/a	n/a	1,029,580	208.6	n/a	n/a	475.9
1978	n/a	n/a	n/a	1,085,550	n/a	n/a	n/a	497.8
1979	399	n/a	n/a	1,208,030	379.3	n/a	n/a	548.9
1980	420	n/a	n/a	1,344,520	413.2	n/a	n/a	596.6
1981	646	n/a	n/a	1,361,820	628.1	n/a	n/a	594.3
1982	620	n/a	n/a	1,322,390	598.8	n/a	n/a	571.1
1983	531	43	574	1,258,090	515.3	44.5	287.5	537.7
1984	411	47	458	1,273,280	394.9	48.2	227.2	539.2
1985	499	39	538	1,328,800	486.6	39.7	268.0	556.6
1986	816	43	859	1,489,170	791.9	44.8	431.5	617.7
1987	588	50	638	1,484,000	577.7	52.8	324.8	609.7
1988	525	47	572	1,566,220	516.6	49.7	291.6	637.2
1989	576	40	616	1,646,040	573.4	43.4	319.7	663.1
1990	538	54	592	1,820,130	497.9	57.1	292.3	731.8
1991	567	50	617	1,911,770	524.1	52.8	304.2	758.1
1992	493	360	853	1,932,270	457.1	162.6	259.0	757.5
1993	537	414	951	1,926,020	499.4	186.4	288.5	746.8
1994	636	420	1,056	1,857,670	591.9	189.2	320.6	713.6
1995	511	385	896	1,798,790	476.7	171.5	270.2	684.6
1996	441	383	824	1,682,280	411.5	170.7	248.6	634.1

Notes: Violent crimes include murder, forcible rape, robbery and aggravated assault; n/a not available; (1) Metropolitan Statistical Area - see Appendix A for areas included; (2) calculated by the editors using the following formula: (number of crimes in the MSA minus number of crimes in the city); (3) calculated by the editors using the following formula: ((number of crimes in the MSA minus number of crimes in the city) ÷ (population of the MSA minus population of the city)) x 100,000
Source: U.S. Department of Justice, FBI Uniform Crime Reports, 1977 - 1996

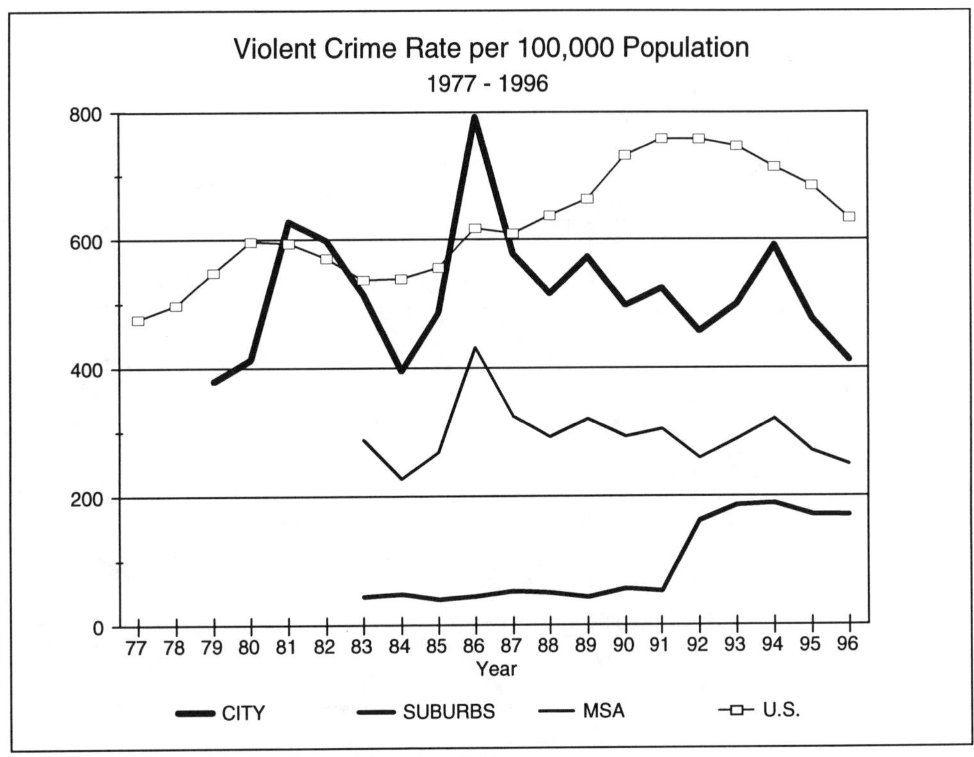

Note: Missing line segments indicate data not available.

Property Crimes and Property Crime Rates: 1977 - 1996

Year	Number				Rate per 100,000 population			
	City	Suburbs[2]	MSA[1]	U.S.	City	Suburbs[3]	MSA[1]	U.S.
1977	4,382	n/a	n/a	9,955,000	4,173.3	n/a	n/a	4,601.7
1978	n/a	n/a	n/a	10,123,400	n/a	n/a	n/a	4,642.5
1979	7,304	n/a	n/a	11,041,500	6,943.7	n/a	n/a	5,016.6
1980	6,951	n/a	n/a	12,063,700	6,839.1	n/a	n/a	5,353.3
1981	7,171	n/a	n/a	12,061,900	6,972.7	n/a	n/a	5,263.9
1982	7,044	n/a	n/a	11,652,000	6,803.6	n/a	n/a	5,032.5
1983	6,634	2,585	9,219	10,850,500	6,438.3	2,675.0	4,617.0	4,637.4
1984	6,455	2,377	8,832	10,608,500	6,202.7	2,436.8	4,380.7	4,492.1
1985	5,619	2,556	8,175	11,102,600	5,478.9	2,604.0	4,072.9	4,650.5
1986	6,260	2,502	8,762	11,722,700	6,075.3	2,605.1	4,401.1	4,862.6
1987	6,507	2,871	9,378	12,024,700	6,392.8	3,033.0	4,773.9	4,940.3
1988	6,071	2,461	8,532	12,356,900	5,973.6	2,603.9	4,349.9	5,027.1
1989	6,560	2,263	8,823	12,605,400	6,530.9	2,453.4	4,578.9	5,077.9
1990	6,087	2,533	8,620	12,655,500	5,633.2	2,680.4	4,255.6	5,088.5
1991	5,936	2,321	8,257	12,961,100	5,487.0	2,453.2	4,071.6	5,139.7
1992	5,477	7,565	13,042	12,505,900	5,078.2	3,416.0	3,960.4	4,902.7
1993	5,335	7,120	12,455	12,218,800	4,961.7	3,205.6	3,778.4	4,737.6
1994	5,797	6,882	12,679	12,131,900	5,394.7	3,100.4	3,848.7	4,660.0
1995	5,540	6,556	12,096	12,063,900	5,168.0	2,921.2	3,647.4	4,591.3
1996	4,514	7,027	11,541	11,791,300	4,212.2	3,132.1	3,481.2	4,444.8

Notes: Property crimes include burglary, larceny-theft and motor vehicle theft; n/a not available; (1) Metropolitan Statistical Area - see Appendix A for areas included; (2) calculated by the editors using the following formula: (number of crimes in the MSA minus number of crimes in the city); (3) calculated by the editors using the following formula: ((number of crimes in the MSA minus number of crimes in the city) ÷ (population of the MSA minus population of the city)) x 100,000
Source: U.S. Department of Justice, FBI Uniform Crime Reports, 1977 - 1996

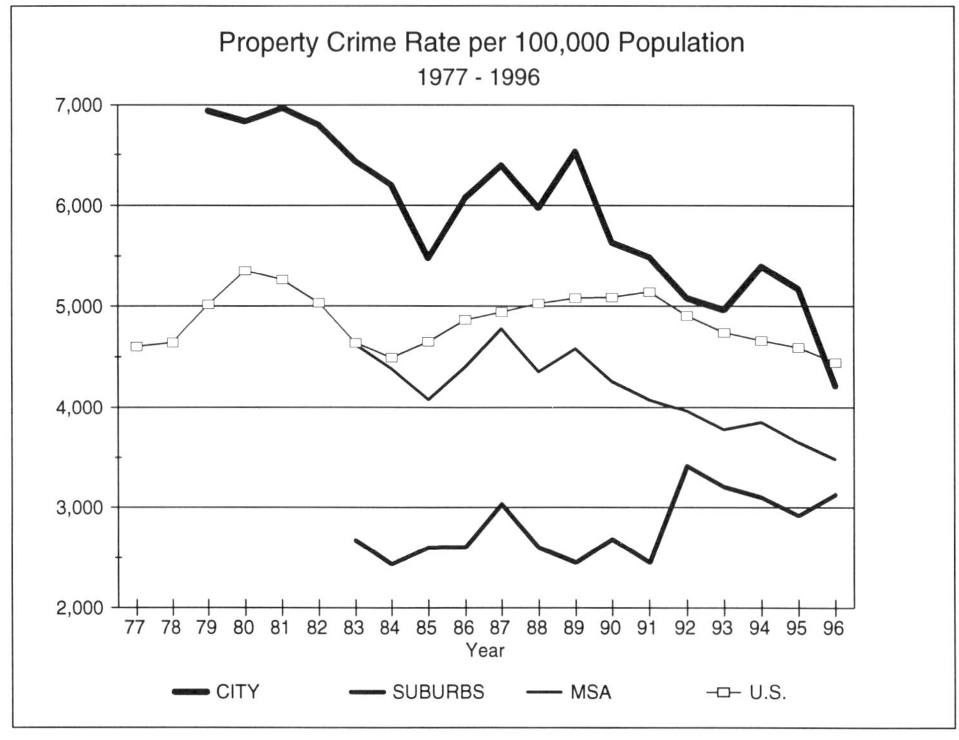

Note: Missing line segments indicate data not available.

Murders and Murder Rates: 1977 - 1996

Year	Number				Rate per 100,000 population			
	City	Suburbs[2]	MSA[1]	U.S.	City	Suburbs[3]	MSA[1]	U.S.
1977	5	n/a	n/a	19,120	4.8	n/a	n/a	8.8
1978	n/a	n/a	n/a	19,560	n/a	n/a	n/a	9.0
1979	5	n/a	n/a	21,460	4.8	n/a	n/a	9.7
1980	5	n/a	n/a	23,040	4.9	n/a	n/a	10.2
1981	3	n/a	n/a	22,520	2.9	n/a	n/a	9.8
1982	6	n/a	n/a	21,010	5.8	n/a	n/a	9.1
1983	6	1	7	19,310	5.8	1.0	3.5	8.3
1984	8	1	9	18,690	7.7	1.0	4.5	7.9
1985	5	2	7	18,980	4.9	2.0	3.5	7.9
1986	6	2	8	20,610	5.8	2.1	4.0	8.6
1987	4	2	6	20,100	3.9	2.1	3.1	8.3
1988	6	1	7	20,680	5.9	1.1	3.6	8.4
1989	9	0	9	21,500	9.0	0.0	4.7	8.7
1990	10	0	10	23,440	9.3	0.0	4.9	9.4
1991	10	0	10	24,700	9.2	0.0	4.9	9.8
1992	7	7	14	23,760	6.5	3.2	4.3	9.3
1993	8	10	18	24,530	7.4	4.5	5.5	9.5
1994	6	7	13	23,330	5.6	3.2	3.9	9.0
1995	4	5	9	21,610	3.7	2.2	2.7	8.2
1996	6	7	13	19,650	5.6	3.1	3.9	7.4

Notes: (1) Metropolitan Statistical Area - see Appendix A for areas included; (2) calculated by the editors using the following formula: (number of crimes in the MSA minus number of crimes in the city); (3) calculated by the editors using the following formula: ((number of crimes in the MSA minus number of crimes in the city) ÷ (population of the MSA minus population of the city)) x 100,000; n/a not avail.
Source: U.S. Department of Justice, FBI Uniform Crime Reports, 1977 - 1996

Forcible Rapes and Forcible Rape Rates: 1977 - 1996

Year	Number				Rate per 100,000 population			
	City	Suburbs[2]	MSA[1]	U.S.	City	Suburbs[3]	MSA[1]	U.S.
1977	15	n/a	n/a	63,500	14.3	n/a	n/a	29.4
1978	n/a	n/a	n/a	67,610	n/a	n/a	n/a	31.0
1979	19	n/a	n/a	76,390	18.1	n/a	n/a	34.7
1980	13	n/a	n/a	82,990	12.8	n/a	n/a	36.8
1981	16	n/a	n/a	82,500	15.6	n/a	n/a	36.0
1982	19	n/a	n/a	78,770	18.4	n/a	n/a	34.0
1983	22	2	24	78,920	21.4	2.1	12.0	33.7
1984	26	3	29	84,230	25.0	3.1	14.4	35.7
1985	16	2	18	88,670	15.6	2.0	9.0	37.1
1986	17	3	20	91,460	16.5	3.1	10.0	37.9
1987	29	2	31	91,110	28.5	2.1	15.8	37.4
1988	13	2	15	92,490	12.8	2.1	7.6	37.6
1989	19	1	20	94,500	18.9	1.1	10.4	38.1
1990	18	3	21	102,560	16.7	3.2	10.4	41.2
1991	25	7	32	106,590	23.1	7.4	15.8	42.3
1992	22	18	40	109,060	20.4	8.1	12.1	42.8
1993	22	13	35	106,010	20.5	5.9	10.6	41.1
1994	15	18	33	102,220	14.0	8.1	10.0	39.3
1995	14	21	35	97,470	13.1	9.4	10.6	37.1
1996	18	28	46	95,770	16.8	12.5	13.9	36.1

Notes: (1) Metropolitan Statistical Area - see Appendix A for areas included; (2) calculated by the editors using the following formula: (number of crimes in the MSA minus number of crimes in the city); (3) calculated by the editors using the following formula: ((number of crimes in the MSA minus number of crimes in the city) ÷ (population of the MSA minus population of the city)) x 100,000; n/a not avail.
Source: U.S. Department of Justice, FBI Uniform Crime Reports, 1977 - 1996

Robberies and Robbery Rates: 1977 - 1996

Year	Number				Rate per 100,000 population			
	City	Suburbs[2]	MSA[1]	U.S.	City	Suburbs[3]	MSA[1]	U.S.
1977	150	n/a	n/a	412,610	142.9	n/a	n/a	190.7
1978	n/a	n/a	n/a	426,930	n/a	n/a	n/a	195.8
1979	229	n/a	n/a	480,700	217.7	n/a	n/a	218.4
1980	279	n/a	n/a	565,840	274.5	n/a	n/a	251.1
1981	385	n/a	n/a	592,910	374.4	n/a	n/a	258.7
1982	362	n/a	n/a	553,130	349.6	n/a	n/a	238.9
1983	306	17	323	506,570	297.0	17.6	161.8	216.5
1984	228	19	247	485,010	219.1	19.5	122.5	205.4
1985	273	16	289	497,870	266.2	16.3	144.0	208.5
1986	364	18	382	542,780	353.3	18.7	191.9	225.1
1987	307	20	327	517,700	301.6	21.1	166.5	212.7
1988	204	27	231	542,970	200.7	28.6	117.8	220.9
1989	269	32	301	578,330	267.8	34.7	156.2	233.0
1990	237	30	267	639,270	219.3	31.7	131.8	257.0
1991	297	19	316	687,730	274.5	20.1	155.8	272.7
1992	241	170	411	672,480	223.5	76.8	124.8	263.6
1993	270	237	507	659,870	251.1	106.7	153.8	255.9
1994	348	204	552	618,950	323.8	91.9	167.6	237.7
1995	231	158	389	580,510	215.5	70.4	117.3	220.9
1996	212	204	416	537,050	197.8	90.9	125.5	202.4

Notes: (1) Metropolitan Statistical Area - see Appendix A for areas included; (2) calculated by the editors using the following formula: (number of crimes in the MSA minus number of crimes in the city); (3) calculated by the editors using the following formula: ((number of crimes in the MSA minus number of crimes in the city) ÷ (population of the MSA minus population of the city)) x 100,000; n/a not avail.
Source: U.S. Department of Justice, FBI Uniform Crime Reports, 1977 - 1996

Aggravated Assaults and Aggravated Assault Rates: 1977 - 1996

Year	Number				Rate per 100,000 population			
	City	Suburbs[2]	MSA[1]	U.S.	City	Suburbs[3]	MSA[1]	U.S.
1977	49	n/a	n/a	534,350	46.7	n/a	n/a	247.0
1978	n/a	n/a	n/a	571,460	n/a	n/a	n/a	262.1
1979	146	n/a	n/a	629,480	138.8	n/a	n/a	286.0
1980	123	n/a	n/a	672,650	121.0	n/a	n/a	298.5
1981	242	n/a	n/a	663,900	235.3	n/a	n/a	289.7
1982	233	n/a	n/a	669,480	225.0	n/a	n/a	289.2
1983	197	23	220	653,290	191.2	23.8	110.2	279.2
1984	149	24	173	685,350	143.2	24.6	85.8	290.2
1985	205	19	224	723,250	199.9	19.4	111.6	302.9
1986	429	20	449	834,320	416.3	20.8	225.5	346.1
1987	248	26	274	855,090	243.6	27.5	139.5	351.3
1988	302	17	319	910,090	297.2	18.0	162.6	370.2
1989	279	7	286	951,710	277.8	7.6	148.4	383.4
1990	273	21	294	1,054,860	252.6	22.2	145.1	424.1
1991	235	24	259	1,092,740	217.2	25.4	127.7	433.3
1992	223	165	388	1,126,970	206.8	74.5	117.8	441.8
1993	237	154	391	1,135,610	220.4	69.3	118.6	440.3
1994	267	191	458	1,113,180	248.5	86.0	139.0	427.6
1995	262	201	463	1,099,210	244.4	89.6	139.6	418.3
1996	205	144	349	1,029,810	191.3	64.2	105.3	388.2

Notes: (1) Metropolitan Statistical Area - see Appendix A for areas included; (2) calculated by the editors using the following formula: (number of crimes in the MSA minus number of crimes in the city); (3) calculated by the editors using the following formula: ((number of crimes in the MSA minus number of crimes in the city) ÷ (population of the MSA minus population of the city)) x 100,000; n/a not avail.
Source: U.S. Department of Justice, FBI Uniform Crime Reports, 1977 - 1996

Burglaries and Burglary Rates: 1977 - 1996

Year	Number				Rate per 100,000 population			
	City	Suburbs[2]	MSA[1]	U.S.	City	Suburbs[3]	MSA[1]	U.S.
1977	1,958	n/a	n/a	3,071,500	1,864.8	n/a	n/a	1,419.8
1978	n/a	n/a	n/a	3,128,300	n/a	n/a	n/a	1,434.6
1979	2,544	n/a	n/a	3,327,700	2,418.5	n/a	n/a	1,511.9
1980	2,542	n/a	n/a	3,795,200	2,501.1	n/a	n/a	1,684.1
1981	2,576	n/a	n/a	3,779,700	2,504.8	n/a	n/a	1,649.5
1982	2,033	n/a	n/a	3,447,100	1,963.6	n/a	n/a	1,488.8
1983	1,873	699	2,572	3,129,900	1,817.7	723.3	1,288.1	1,337.7
1984	1,463	431	1,894	2,984,400	1,405.8	441.8	939.4	1,263.7
1985	1,230	453	1,683	3,073,300	1,199.3	461.5	838.5	1,287.3
1986	1,637	499	2,136	3,241,400	1,588.7	519.6	1,072.9	1,344.6
1987	1,508	445	1,953	3,236,200	1,481.5	470.1	994.2	1,329.6
1988	1,458	377	1,835	3,218,100	1,434.6	398.9	935.5	1,309.2
1989	1,602	354	1,956	3,168,200	1,594.9	383.8	1,015.1	1,276.3
1990	1,512	532	2,044	3,073,900	1,399.3	563.0	1,009.1	1,235.9
1991	1,236	425	1,661	3,157,200	1,142.5	449.2	819.1	1,252.0
1992	1,037	2,542	3,579	2,979,900	961.5	1,147.8	1,086.8	1,168.2
1993	1,105	1,411	2,516	2,834,800	1,027.7	635.3	763.3	1,099.2
1994	1,078	1,208	2,286	2,712,800	1,003.2	544.2	693.9	1,042.0
1995	935	1,220	2,155	2,593,800	872.2	543.6	649.8	987.1
1996	704	1,398	2,102	2,501,500	656.9	623.1	634.0	943.0

Notes: (1) Metropolitan Statistical Area - see Appendix A for areas included; (2) calculated by the editors using the following formula: (number of crimes in the MSA minus number of crimes in the city); (3) calculated by the editors using the following formula: ((number of crimes in the MSA minus number of crimes in the city) ÷ (population of the MSA minus population of the city)) x 100,000; n/a not avail.
Source: U.S. Department of Justice, FBI Uniform Crime Reports, 1977 - 1996

Larceny-Thefts and Larceny-Theft Rates: 1977 - 1996

Year	Number				Rate per 100,000 population			
	City	Suburbs[2]	MSA[1]	U.S.	City	Suburbs[3]	MSA[1]	U.S.
1977	1,784	n/a	n/a	5,905,700	1,699.0	n/a	n/a	2,729.9
1978	n/a	n/a	n/a	5,991,000	n/a	n/a	n/a	2,747.4
1979	3,917	n/a	n/a	6,601,000	3,723.8	n/a	n/a	2,999.1
1980	3,593	n/a	n/a	7,136,900	3,535.2	n/a	n/a	3,167.0
1981	3,858	n/a	n/a	7,194,400	3,751.3	n/a	n/a	3,139.7
1982	4,365	n/a	n/a	7,142,500	4,216.0	n/a	n/a	3,084.8
1983	4,122	1,703	5,825	6,712,800	4,000.4	1,762.3	2,917.2	2,868.9
1984	4,344	1,764	6,108	6,591,900	4,174.2	1,808.4	3,029.6	2,791.3
1985	3,778	1,901	5,679	6,926,400	3,683.8	1,936.7	2,829.4	2,901.2
1986	3,912	1,805	5,717	7,257,200	3,796.5	1,879.3	2,871.6	3,010.3
1987	4,081	2,195	6,276	7,499,900	4,009.4	2,318.9	3,194.8	3,081.3
1988	3,811	1,884	5,695	7,705,900	3,749.9	1,993.4	2,903.5	3,134.9
1989	3,993	1,703	5,696	7,872,400	3,975.3	1,846.3	2,956.1	3,171.3
1990	3,586	1,768	5,354	7,945,700	3,318.6	1,870.9	2,643.2	3,194.8
1991	3,741	1,596	5,337	8,142,200	3,458.0	1,686.9	2,631.7	3,228.8
1992	3,538	4,141	7,679	7,915,200	3,280.4	1,869.9	2,331.8	3,103.0
1993	3,503	4,865	8,368	7,820,900	3,257.9	2,190.3	2,538.6	3,032.4
1994	4,005	4,911	8,916	7,879,800	3,727.0	2,212.4	2,706.5	3,026.7
1995	3,999	4,738	8,737	7,997,700	3,730.4	2,111.1	2,634.6	3,043.8
1996	3,332	5,099	8,431	7,894,600	3,109.2	2,272.7	2,543.1	2,975.9

Notes: (1) Metropolitan Statistical Area - see Appendix A for areas included; (2) calculated by the editors using the following formula: (number of crimes in the MSA minus number of crimes in the city); (3) calculated by the editors using the following formula: ((number of crimes in the MSA minus number of crimes in the city) ÷ (population of the MSA minus population of the city)) x 100,000; n/a not avail.
Source: U.S. Department of Justice, FBI Uniform Crime Reports, 1977 - 1996

Motor Vehicle Thefts and Motor Vehicle Theft Rates: 1977 - 1996

Year	Number				Rate per 100,000 population			
	City	Suburbs[2]	MSA[1]	U.S.	City	Suburbs[3]	MSA[1]	U.S.
1977	640	n/a	n/a	977,700	609.5	n/a	n/a	451.9
1978	n/a	n/a	n/a	1,004,100	n/a	n/a	n/a	460.5
1979	843	n/a	n/a	1,112,800	801.4	n/a	n/a	505.6
1980	816	n/a	n/a	1,131,700	802.9	n/a	n/a	502.2
1981	737	n/a	n/a	1,087,800	716.6	n/a	n/a	474.7
1982	646	n/a	n/a	1,062,400	624.0	n/a	n/a	458.8
1983	639	183	822	1,007,900	620.1	189.4	411.7	430.8
1984	648	182	830	1,032,200	622.7	186.6	411.7	437.1
1985	611	202	813	1,102,900	595.8	205.8	405.1	462.0
1986	711	198	909	1,224,100	690.0	206.2	456.6	507.8
1987	918	231	1,149	1,288,700	901.9	244.0	584.9	529.4
1988	802	200	1,002	1,432,900	789.1	211.6	510.9	582.9
1989	965	206	1,171	1,564,800	960.7	223.3	607.7	630.4
1990	989	233	1,222	1,635,900	915.3	246.6	603.3	657.8
1991	959	300	1,259	1,661,700	886.5	317.1	620.8	659.0
1992	902	882	1,784	1,610,800	836.3	398.3	541.7	631.5
1993	727	844	1,571	1,563,100	676.1	380.0	476.6	606.1
1994	714	763	1,477	1,539,300	664.4	343.7	448.3	591.3
1995	606	598	1,204	1,472,400	565.3	266.5	363.1	560.4
1996	478	530	1,008	1,395,200	446.0	236.2	304.1	525.9

Notes: (1) Metropolitan Statistical Area - see Appendix A for areas included; (2) calculated by the editors using the following formula: (number of crimes in the MSA minus number of crimes in the city); (3) calculated by the editors using the following formula: ((number of crimes in the MSA minus number of crimes in the city) ÷ (population of the MSA minus population of the city)) x 100,000; n/a not avail.
Source: U.S. Department of Justice, FBI Uniform Crime Reports, 1977 - 1996

HATE CRIMES

Criminal Incidents by Bias Motivation

Area	Race	Ethnicity	Religion	Sexual Orientation
Stamford	0	0	0	0

Notes: Figures include both violent and property crimes. Law enforcement agencies must have submitted data for at least one quarter of calendar year 1995 to be included in this report, therefore figures shown may not represent complete 12-month totals; n/a not available
Source: U.S. Department of Justice, FBI Uniform Crime Reports, Hate Crime Statistics 1995

LAW ENFORCEMENT

Full-Time Law Enforcement Employees

Jurisdiction	Police Employees			Police Officers per 100,000 population
	Total	Officers	Civilians	
Stamford	306	281	25	262.2

Notes: Data as of October 31, 1996
Source: U.S. Department of Justice, FBI Uniform Crime Reports, 1996

CORRECTIONS

Federal Correctional Facilities

Type	Year Opened	Security Level	Sex of Inmates	Rated Capacity	Population on 7/1/95	Number of Staff
None listed						

Notes: Data as of 1995
Source: Bureau of Justice Statistics, Sourcebook of Criminal Justice Statistics Online

City/County/Regional Correctional Facilities

Name	Year Opened	Year Renov.	Rated Capacity	1995 Pop.	Number of COs[1]	Number of Staff	ACA[2] Accred.
None listed							

Notes: Data as of April 1996; (1) Correctional Officers; (2) American Correctional Assn. Accreditation
Source: American Correctional Association, 1996-1998 National Jail and Adult Detention Directory

Private Adult Correctional Facilities

Name	Date Opened	Rated Capacity	Present Pop.	Security Level	Facility Construct.	Expans. Plans	ACA[1] Accred.
None listed							

Notes: Data as of December 1996; (1) American Correctional Association Accreditation
Source: University of Florida, Center for Studies in Criminology and Law, Private Adult Correctional Facility Census, 10th Ed., March 15, 1997

Characteristics of Shock Incarceration Programs

Jurisdiction	Year Program Began	Number of Camps	Average Num. of Inmates	Number of Beds	Program Length	Voluntary/ Mandatory
Connecticut did not have a shock incarceration program as of July 1996						

Source: Sourcebook of Criminal Justice Statistics Online

DEATH PENALTY

Death Penalty Statistics

State	Prisoners Executed		Prisoners Under Sentence of Death					Avg. No. of Years on Death Row[4]
	1930-1995	1996[1]	Total[2]	White[3]	Black[3]	Hisp.	Women	
Connecticut	21	0	5	2	3	0	0	n/c

Notes: Data as of 12/31/95 unless otherwise noted; n/c not calculated on fewer than 10 inmates; (1) Data as of 7/31/97; (2) Includes persons of other races; (3) Includes people of Hispanic origin; (4) Covers prisoners sentenced 1974 through 1995
Source: Bureau of Justice Statistics, Capital Punishment 1995 (released 12/96); Death Penalty Information Center Web Site, 9/30/97

Capital Offenses and Methods of Execution

Capital Offenses in Connecticut	Minimum Age for Imposition of Death Penalty	Mentally Retarded Excluded	Methods of Execution[1]
Capital felony with 9 categories of aggravated homicide (C.G.S. 53a-54b).	18	No	Lethal injection

Notes: Data as of 12/31/95 unless otherwise noted; (1) Data as of 7/31/97
Source: Bureau of Justice Statistics, Capital Punishment 1995 (released 12/96); Death Penalty Information Center Web Site, 9/30/97

LAWS

Statutory Provisions Relating to the Purchase, Ownership and Use of Handguns

Jurisdiction	Instant Background Check	Federal Waiting Period Applies[1]	State Waiting Period (days)	License or Permit to Purchase	Regis- tration	Record of Sale Sent to Police	Concealed Carry Law
Connecticut	No	No	14[a,b]	No	No	Yes	Yes[c]

Note: Data as of 1996; (1) The Federal 5-day waiting period for handgun purchases applies to states that don't have instant background checks, waiting period requirements, or licensing procedures exempting them from the Federal requirement; (a) The state waiting period does not apply to a person holding a valid permit or license to carry a firearm; (b) Purchases from licensed dealers only; (c) "Shall issue" permit system, liberally administered discretion by local authorities over permit issuance, or no permit required
Source: Sourcebook of Criminal Justice Statistics Online

Statutory Provisions Relating to Alcohol Use and Driving

Jurisdiction	Drinking Age	Blood Alcohol Concentration Levels as Evidence in State Courts[1]		Open Container Law[1]	Anti- Consump- tion Law[1]	Dram Shop Law[1]
		Illegal per se at 0.10%	Presumption at 0.10%			
Connecticut	21	Yes	No	No	No	Yes[a]

Note: Data as of January 1, 1997; (1) See Appendix C for an explanation of terms; (a) Connecticut has a statue that places a monetary limit on the amount of damages that can be awarded in dram shop liability actions
Source: Sourcebook of Criminal Justice Statistics Online

Statutory Provisions Relating to Hate Crimes

Jurisdiction	Bias-Motivated Violence and Intimidation						Institutional Vandalism
		Criminal Penalty					
	Civil Action	Race/ Religion/ Ethnicity	Sexual Orientation	Mental/ Physical Disability	Gender	Age	
Connecticut	Yes	Yes	Yes	Yes	Yes	No	Yes

Source: Anti-Defamation League, 1997 Hate Crimes Laws

Tacoma, Washington

OVERVIEW

The total crime rate for the city increased 29.6% between 1977 and 1996. During that same period, the violent crime rate increased 123.8% and the property crime rate increased 21.4%.

Among violent crimes, the rates for: Murders increased 9.3%; Forcible Rapes decreased 12.4%; Robberies increased 76.7%; and Aggravated Assaults increased 195.4%.

Among property crimes, the rates for: Burglaries decreased 34.9%; Larceny-Thefts increased 33.8%; and Motor Vehicle Thefts increased 232.4%.

ANTI-CRIME PROGRAMS

Among their programs:

- CARES (Cleanup and Revitalization Efforts)—joins local government, business, grassroots organizations, non-profit agencies and private citizens in a partnership to reduce litter, debris, blight, contamination and associated crime. The team approach facilitates and streamlines the cleanup process, eliminating the traditional need to go from one agency to another to address multiple concerns. *Tacoma Police Department, 7/97*

CRIME RISK

Your Chances of Becoming a Victim[1]

Area	Any Crime	Violent Crime					Property Crime			
		Any	Murder	Forcible Rape[2]	Robbery	Aggrav. Assault	Any	Burglary	Larceny -Theft	Motor Vehicle Theft
City	1:9	1:68	1:9,478	1:714	1:239	1:103	1:11	1:58	1:17	1:67

Note: (1) Figures have been calculated by dividing the population of the city by the number of crimes reported to the FBI during 1996 and are expressed as odds (eg. 1:20 should be read as 1 in 20).
(2) Figures have been calculated by dividing the female population of the city by the number of forcible rapes reported to the FBI during 1996. The female population of the city was estimated by calculating the ratio of females to males reported in the 1990 Census and applying that ratio to 1996 population estimate.
Source: FBI Uniform Crime Reports 1996

CRIME STATISTICS

Total Crimes and Total Crime Rates: 1977 - 1996

Year	Number				Rate per 100,000 population			
	City	Suburbs[2]	MSA[1]	U.S.	City	Suburbs[3]	MSA[1]	U.S.
1977	12,631	11,635	24,266	10,984,500	8,201.9	4,357.6	5,763.8	5,077.6
1978	13,463	13,822	27,285	11,209,000	8,575.2	4,839.8	6,164.8	5,140.3
1979	14,324	15,254	29,578	12,249,500	8,699.6	5,261.7	6,507.0	5,565.5
1980	16,516	15,818	32,334	13,408,300	10,446.5	4,869.9	6,695.6	5,950.0
1981	16,193	18,076	34,269	13,423,800	10,002.2	5,434.7	6,930.1	5,858.2
1982	17,183	16,757	33,940	12,974,400	10,531.3	4,999.0	6,810.2	5,603.6
1983	18,733	16,921	35,654	12,108,600	11,334.4	4,983.5	7,062.8	5,175.0
1984	19,135	17,366	36,501	11,881,800	11,680.0	4,896.9	7,040.3	5,031.3
1985	21,002	18,283	39,285	12,431,400	12,994.3	5,056.0	7,508.1	5,207.1
1986	22,365	19,613	41,978	13,211,900	13,669.4	5,356.9	7,924.2	5,480.4
1987	23,674	20,107	43,781	13,508,700	14,646.2	5,275.8	8,066.4	5,550.0
1988	23,603	22,183	45,786	13,923,100	14,284.6	5,693.8	8,252.2	5,664.2
1989	23,225	21,027	44,252	14,251,400	13,829.1	5,187.9	7,719.4	5,741.0
1990	20,805	20,580	41,385	14,475,600	11,776.6	5,017.3	7,052.2	5,820.3
1991	20,560	21,672	42,232	14,872,900	11,287.0	5,124.3	6,979.6	5,897.8
1992	19,991	21,855	41,846	14,438,200	10,722.5	5,047.8	6,755.9	5,660.2
1993	21,046	21,797	42,843	14,144,800	11,200.9	4,887.7	6,759.2	5,484.4
1994	22,408	23,557	45,965	13,989,500	11,729.4	5,195.5	7,132.4	5,373.5
1995	21,766	25,247	47,013	13,862,700	11,697.5	5,446.9	7,237.4	5,275.9
1996	20,143	25,638	45,781	13,473,600	10,625.7	5,429.4	6,917.9	5,078.9

Notes: (1) Metropolitan Statistical Area - see Appendix A for areas included; (2) calculated by the editors using the following formula: (number of crimes in the MSA minus number of crimes in the city); (3) calculated by the editors using the following formula: ((number of crimes in the MSA minus number of crimes in the city) ÷ (population of the MSA minus population of the city)) x 100,000; n/a not avail.
Source: U.S. Department of Justice, FBI Uniform Crime Reports, 1977 - 1996

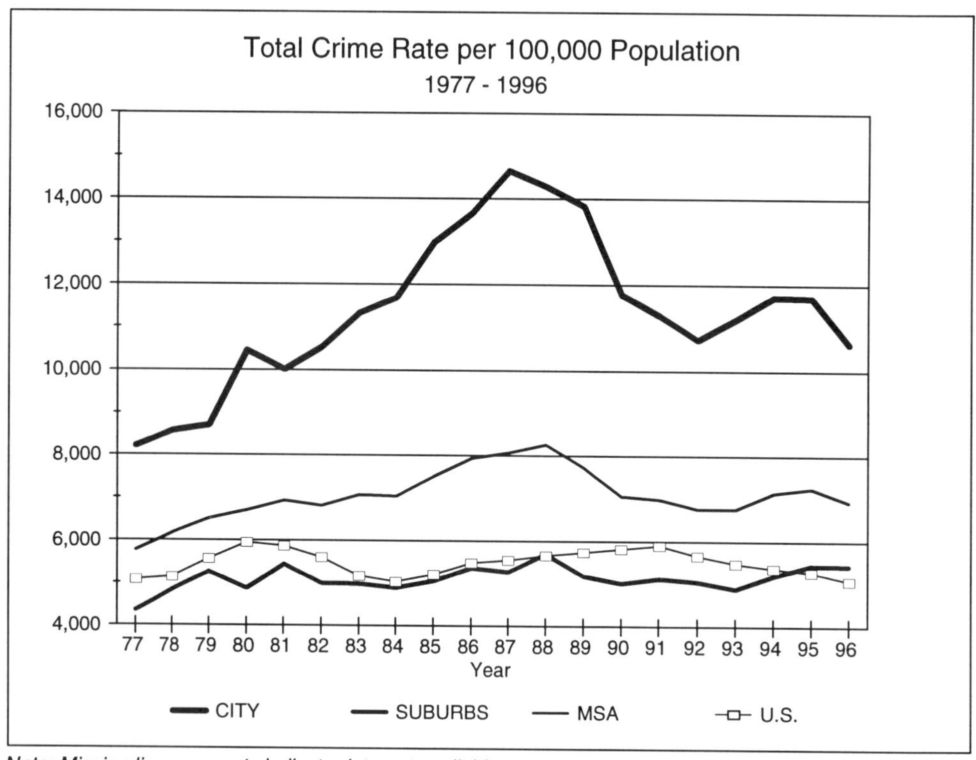

Note: Missing line segments indicate data not available.

Violent Crimes and Violent Crime Rates: 1977 - 1996

Year	Number				Rate per 100,000 population			
	City	Suburbs[2]	MSA[1]	U.S.	City	Suburbs[3]	MSA[1]	U.S.
1977	1,011	857	1,868	1,029,580	656.5	321.0	443.7	475.9
1978	962	976	1,938	1,085,550	612.7	341.7	437.9	497.8
1979	1,117	1,131	2,248	1,208,030	678.4	390.1	494.5	548.9
1980	1,408	1,381	2,789	1,344,520	890.6	425.2	577.5	596.6
1981	1,356	1,503	2,859	1,361,820	837.6	451.9	578.2	594.3
1982	1,357	1,300	2,657	1,322,390	831.7	387.8	533.1	571.1
1983	1,651	1,244	2,895	1,258,090	998.9	366.4	573.5	537.7
1984	1,846	1,476	3,322	1,273,280	1,126.8	416.2	640.7	539.2
1985	2,010	1,400	3,410	1,328,800	1,243.6	387.2	651.7	556.6
1986	2,204	1,405	3,609	1,489,170	1,347.1	383.7	681.3	617.7
1987	2,381	1,464	3,845	1,484,000	1,473.0	384.1	708.4	609.7
1988	2,781	1,708	4,489	1,566,220	1,683.1	438.4	809.1	637.2
1989	3,078	1,737	4,815	1,646,040	1,832.8	428.6	839.9	663.1
1990	3,096	1,804	4,900	1,820,130	1,752.5	439.8	835.0	731.8
1991	3,583	2,150	5,733	1,911,770	1,967.0	508.4	947.5	758.1
1992	3,425	2,297	5,722	1,932,270	1,837.1	530.5	923.8	757.5
1993	3,441	2,148	5,589	1,926,020	1,831.3	481.7	881.8	746.8
1994	3,522	2,432	5,954	1,857,670	1,843.6	536.4	923.9	713.6
1995	3,223	2,449	5,672	1,798,790	1,732.1	528.4	873.2	684.6
1996	2,785	2,106	4,891	1,682,280	1,469.1	446.0	739.1	634.1

Notes: Violent crimes include murder, forcible rape, robbery and aggravated assault; n/a not available; (1) Metropolitan Statistical Area - see Appendix A for areas included; (2) calculated by the editors using the following formula: (number of crimes in the MSA minus number of crimes in the city); (3) calculated by the editors using the following formula: ((number of crimes in the MSA minus number of crimes in the city) ÷ (population of the MSA minus population of the city)) x 100,000
Source: U.S. Department of Justice, FBI Uniform Crime Reports, 1977 - 1996

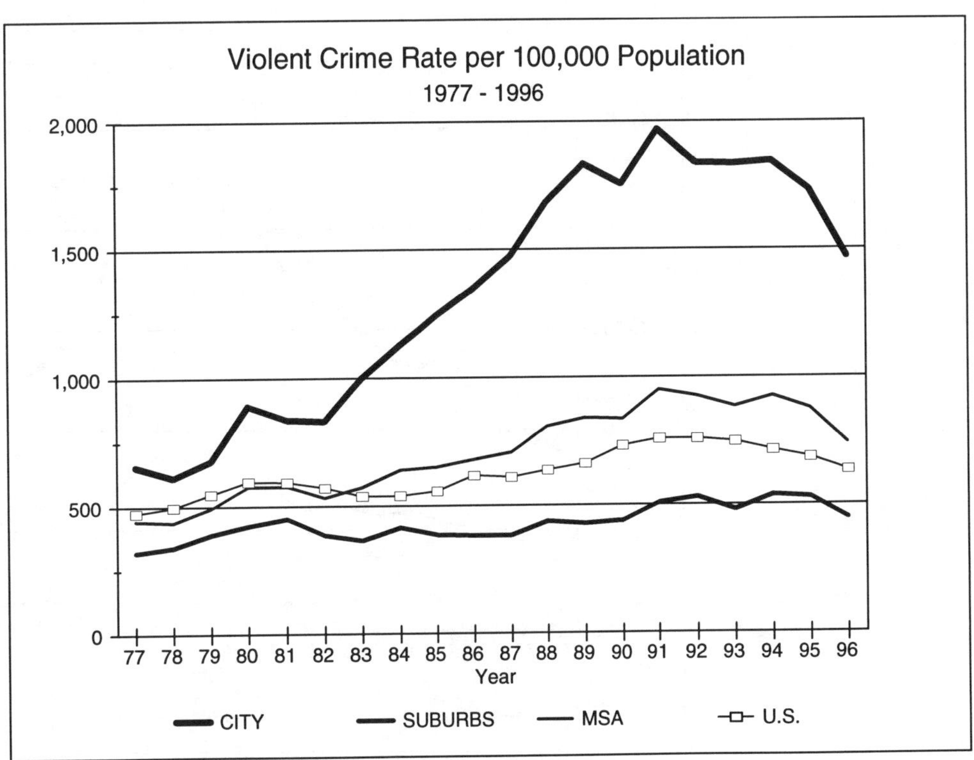

Note: Missing line segments indicate data not available.

Property Crimes and Property Crime Rates: 1977 - 1996

Year	Number				Rate per 100,000 population			
	City	Suburbs[2]	MSA[1]	U.S.	City	Suburbs[3]	MSA[1]	U.S.
1977	11,620	10,778	22,398	9,955,000	7,545.5	4,036.6	5,320.1	4,601.7
1978	12,501	12,846	25,347	10,123,400	7,962.4	4,498.0	5,727.0	4,642.5
1979	13,207	14,123	27,330	11,041,500	8,021.2	4,871.6	6,012.5	5,016.6
1980	15,108	14,437	29,545	12,063,700	9,555.9	4,444.7	6,118.1	5,353.3
1981	14,837	16,573	31,410	12,061,900	9,164.6	4,982.8	6,351.9	5,263.9
1982	15,826	15,457	31,283	11,652,000	9,699.6	4,611.2	6,277.1	5,032.5
1983	17,082	15,677	32,759	10,850,500	10,335.5	4,617.1	6,489.3	4,637.4
1984	17,289	15,890	33,179	10,608,500	10,553.2	4,480.7	6,399.6	4,492.1
1985	18,992	16,883	35,875	11,102,600	11,750.7	4,668.9	6,856.4	4,650.5
1986	20,161	18,208	38,369	11,722,700	12,322.3	4,973.1	7,243.0	4,862.6
1987	21,293	18,643	39,936	12,024,700	13,173.2	4,891.6	7,357.9	4,940.3
1988	20,822	20,475	41,297	12,356,900	12,601.5	5,255.4	7,443.1	5,027.1
1989	20,147	19,290	39,437	12,605,400	11,996.3	4,759.3	6,879.5	5,077.9
1990	17,709	18,776	36,485	12,655,500	10,024.1	4,577.5	6,217.2	5,088.5
1991	16,977	19,522	36,499	12,961,100	9,320.0	4,616.0	6,032.1	5,139.7
1992	16,566	19,558	36,124	12,505,900	8,885.4	4,517.3	5,832.1	4,902.7
1993	17,605	19,649	37,254	12,218,800	9,369.6	4,406.1	5,877.4	4,737.6
1994	18,886	21,125	40,011	12,131,900	9,885.8	4,659.1	6,208.5	4,660.0
1995	18,543	22,798	41,341	12,063,900	9,965.4	4,918.6	6,364.2	4,591.3
1996	17,358	23,532	40,890	11,791,300	9,156.6	4,983.4	6,178.8	4,444.8

Notes: Property crimes include burglary, larceny-theft and motor vehicle theft; n/a not available; (1) Metropolitan Statistical Area - see Appendix A for areas included; (2) calculated by the editors using the following formula: (number of crimes in the MSA minus number of crimes in the city); (3) calculated by the editors using the following formula: ((number of crimes in the MSA minus number of crimes in the city) ÷ (population of the MSA minus population of the city)) x 100,000
Source: U.S. Department of Justice, FBI Uniform Crime Reports, 1977 - 1996

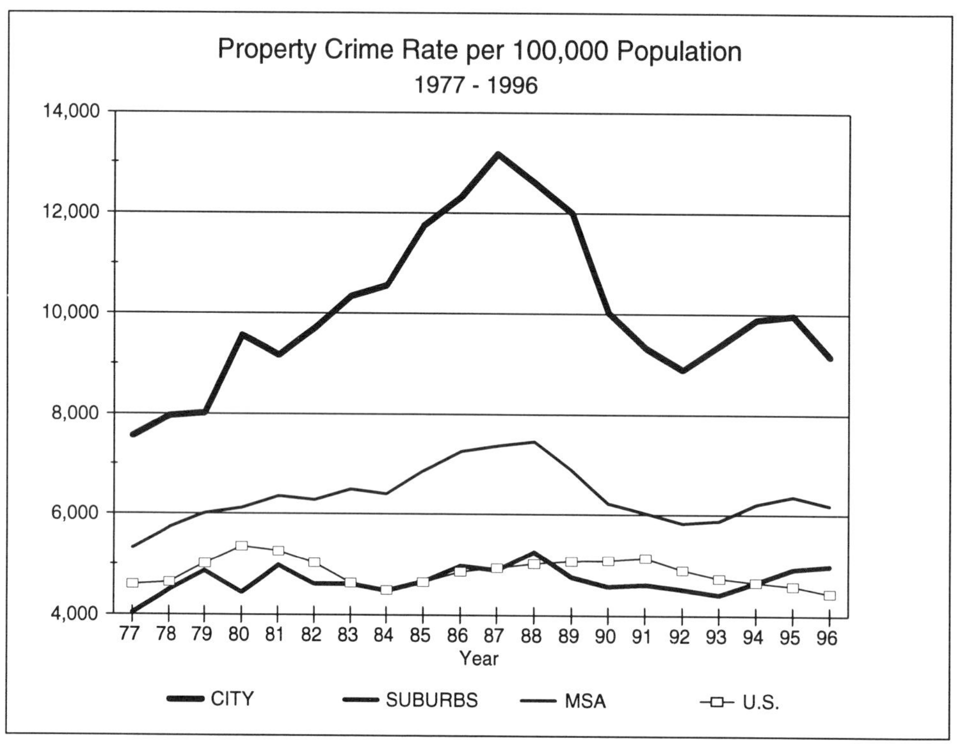

Note: Missing line segments indicate data not available.

Murders and Murder Rates: 1977 - 1996

Year	Number				Rate per 100,000 population			
	City	Suburbs[2]	MSA[1]	U.S.	City	Suburbs[3]	MSA[1]	U.S.
1977	15	13	28	19,120	9.7	4.9	6.7	8.8
1978	10	10	20	19,560	6.4	3.5	4.5	9.0
1979	10	13	23	21,460	6.1	4.5	5.1	9.7
1980	13	12	25	23,040	8.2	3.7	5.2	10.2
1981	10	13	23	22,520	6.2	3.9	4.7	9.8
1982	16	10	26	21,010	9.8	3.0	5.2	9.1
1983	14	11	25	19,310	8.5	3.2	5.0	8.3
1984	15	22	37	18,690	9.2	6.2	7.1	7.9
1985	13	19	32	18,980	8.0	5.3	6.1	7.9
1986	17	16	33	20,610	10.4	4.4	6.2	8.6
1987	24	9	33	20,100	14.8	2.4	6.1	8.3
1988	33	25	58	20,680	20.0	6.4	10.5	8.4
1989	21	25	46	21,500	12.5	6.2	8.0	8.7
1990	25	20	45	23,440	14.2	4.9	7.7	9.4
1991	31	23	54	24,700	17.0	5.4	8.9	9.8
1992	31	25	56	23,760	16.6	5.8	9.0	9.3
1993	31	26	57	24,530	16.5	5.8	9.0	9.5
1994	33	31	64	23,330	17.3	6.8	9.9	9.0
1995	28	25	53	21,610	15.0	5.4	8.2	8.2
1996	20	25	45	19,650	10.6	5.3	6.8	7.4

Notes: (1) Metropolitan Statistical Area - see Appendix A for areas included; (2) calculated by the editors using the following formula: (number of crimes in the MSA minus number of crimes in the city); (3) calculated by the editors using the following formula: ((number of crimes in the MSA minus number of crimes in the city) ÷ (population of the MSA minus population of the city)) x 100,000; n/a not avail.
Source: U.S. Department of Justice, FBI Uniform Crime Reports, 1977 - 1996

Forcible Rapes and Forcible Rape Rates: 1977 - 1996

Year	Number				Rate per 100,000 population			
	City	Suburbs[2]	MSA[1]	U.S.	City	Suburbs[3]	MSA[1]	U.S.
1977	127	102	229	63,500	82.5	38.2	54.4	29.4
1978	110	151	261	67,610	70.1	52.9	59.0	31.0
1979	142	157	299	76,390	86.2	54.2	65.8	34.7
1980	165	196	361	82,990	104.4	60.3	74.8	36.8
1981	174	206	380	82,500	107.5	61.9	76.8	36.0
1982	151	182	333	78,770	92.5	54.3	66.8	34.0
1983	194	184	378	78,920	117.4	54.2	74.9	33.7
1984	208	174	382	84,230	127.0	49.1	73.7	35.7
1985	279	201	480	88,670	172.6	55.6	91.7	37.1
1986	245	213	458	91,460	149.7	58.2	86.5	37.9
1987	240	247	487	91,110	148.5	64.8	89.7	37.4
1988	279	285	564	92,490	168.9	73.2	101.7	37.6
1989	252	312	564	94,500	150.1	77.0	98.4	38.1
1990	245	282	527	102,560	138.7	68.8	89.8	41.2
1991	277	331	608	106,590	152.1	78.3	100.5	42.3
1992	309	350	659	109,060	165.7	80.8	106.4	42.8
1993	191	224	415	106,010	101.7	50.2	65.5	41.1
1994	204	240	444	102,220	106.8	52.9	68.9	39.3
1995	171	216	387	97,470	91.9	46.6	59.6	37.1
1996	137	172	309	95,770	72.3	36.4	46.7	36.1

Notes: (1) Metropolitan Statistical Area - see Appendix A for areas included; (2) calculated by the editors using the following formula: (number of crimes in the MSA minus number of crimes in the city); (3) calculated by the editors using the following formula: ((number of crimes in the MSA minus number of crimes in the city) ÷ (population of the MSA minus population of the city)) x 100,000; n/a not avail.
Source: U.S. Department of Justice, FBI Uniform Crime Reports, 1977 - 1996

Robberies and Robbery Rates: 1977 - 1996

Year	Number				Rate per 100,000 population			
	City	Suburbs[2]	MSA[1]	U.S.	City	Suburbs[3]	MSA[1]	U.S.
1977	364	206	570	412,610	236.4	77.2	135.4	190.7
1978	385	282	667	426,930	245.2	98.7	150.7	195.8
1979	468	229	697	480,700	284.2	79.0	153.3	218.4
1980	566	305	871	565,840	358.0	93.9	180.4	251.1
1981	494	324	818	592,910	305.1	97.4	165.4	258.7
1982	502	278	780	553,130	307.7	82.9	156.5	238.9
1983	534	241	775	506,570	323.1	71.0	153.5	216.5
1984	689	314	1,003	485,010	420.6	88.5	193.5	205.4
1985	640	321	961	497,870	396.0	88.8	183.7	208.5
1986	665	305	970	542,780	406.4	83.3	183.1	225.1
1987	781	315	1,096	517,700	483.2	82.7	201.9	212.7
1988	1,104	479	1,583	542,970	668.1	122.9	285.3	220.9
1989	1,262	426	1,688	578,330	751.4	105.1	294.5	233.0
1990	969	352	1,321	639,270	548.5	85.8	225.1	257.0
1991	1,100	536	1,636	687,730	603.9	126.7	270.4	272.7
1992	1,011	540	1,551	672,480	542.3	124.7	250.4	263.6
1993	1,015	431	1,446	659,870	540.2	96.6	228.1	255.9
1994	1,004	445	1,449	618,950	525.5	98.1	224.8	237.7
1995	925	480	1,405	580,510	497.1	103.6	216.3	220.9
1996	792	437	1,229	537,050	417.8	92.5	185.7	202.4

Notes: (1) Metropolitan Statistical Area - see Appendix A for areas included; (2) calculated by the editors using the following formula: (number of crimes in the MSA minus number of crimes in the city); (3) calculated by the editors using the following formula: ((number of crimes in the MSA minus number of crimes in the city) ÷ (population of the MSA minus population of the city)) x 100,000; n/a not avail.
Source: U.S. Department of Justice, FBI Uniform Crime Reports, 1977 - 1996

Aggravated Assaults and Aggravated Assault Rates: 1977 - 1996

Year	Number				Rate per 100,000 population			
	City	Suburbs[2]	MSA[1]	U.S.	City	Suburbs[3]	MSA[1]	U.S.
1977	505	536	1,041	534,350	327.9	200.7	247.3	247.0
1978	457	533	990	571,460	291.1	186.6	223.7	262.1
1979	497	732	1,229	629,480	301.9	252.5	270.4	286.0
1980	664	868	1,532	672,650	420.0	267.2	317.2	298.5
1981	678	960	1,638	663,900	418.8	288.6	331.2	289.7
1982	688	830	1,518	669,480	421.7	247.6	304.6	289.2
1983	909	808	1,717	653,290	550.0	238.0	340.1	279.2
1984	934	966	1,900	685,350	570.1	272.4	366.5	290.2
1985	1,078	859	1,937	723,250	667.0	237.5	370.2	302.9
1986	1,277	871	2,148	834,320	780.5	237.9	405.5	346.1
1987	1,336	893	2,229	855,090	826.5	234.3	410.7	351.3
1988	1,365	919	2,284	910,090	826.1	235.9	411.7	370.2
1989	1,543	974	2,517	951,710	918.8	240.3	439.1	383.4
1990	1,857	1,150	3,007	1,054,860	1,051.1	280.4	512.4	424.1
1991	2,175	1,260	3,435	1,092,740	1,194.0	297.9	567.7	433.3
1992	2,074	1,382	3,456	1,126,970	1,112.4	319.2	558.0	441.8
1993	2,204	1,467	3,671	1,135,610	1,173.0	329.0	579.2	440.3
1994	2,281	1,716	3,997	1,113,180	1,194.0	378.5	620.2	427.6
1995	2,099	1,728	3,827	1,099,210	1,128.0	372.8	589.1	418.3
1996	1,836	1,472	3,308	1,029,810	968.5	311.7	499.9	388.2

Notes: (1) Metropolitan Statistical Area - see Appendix A for areas included; (2) calculated by the editors using the following formula: (number of crimes in the MSA minus number of crimes in the city); (3) calculated by the editors using the following formula: ((number of crimes in the MSA minus number of crimes in the city) ÷ (population of the MSA minus population of the city)) x 100,000; n/a not avail.
Source: U.S. Department of Justice, FBI Uniform Crime Reports, 1977 - 1996

Burglaries and Burglary Rates: 1977 - 1996

Year	Number				Rate per 100,000 population			
	City	Suburbs[2]	MSA[1]	U.S.	City	Suburbs[3]	MSA[1]	U.S.
1977	4,095	4,470	8,565	3,071,500	2,659.1	1,674.1	2,034.4	1,419.8
1978	4,293	5,114	9,407	3,128,300	2,734.4	1,790.7	2,125.4	1,434.6
1979	4,738	5,060	9,798	3,327,700	2,877.6	1,745.4	2,155.5	1,511.9
1980	5,119	5,167	10,286	3,795,200	3,237.8	1,590.8	2,130.0	1,684.1
1981	4,855	6,180	11,035	3,779,700	2,998.9	1,858.1	2,231.6	1,649.5
1982	5,116	5,787	10,903	3,447,100	3,135.5	1,726.4	2,187.7	1,488.8
1983	5,727	5,582	11,309	3,129,900	3,465.1	1,644.0	2,240.2	1,337.7
1984	6,138	6,125	12,263	2,984,400	3,746.6	1,727.2	2,365.3	1,263.7
1985	7,137	6,421	13,558	3,073,300	4,415.8	1,775.7	2,591.2	1,287.3
1986	6,167	6,649	12,816	3,241,400	3,769.2	1,816.0	2,419.3	1,344.6
1987	6,561	6,682	13,243	3,236,200	4,059.0	1,753.2	2,439.9	1,329.6
1988	6,123	7,253	13,376	3,218,100	3,705.7	1,861.7	2,410.8	1,309.2
1989	5,080	5,796	10,876	3,168,200	3,024.8	1,430.0	1,897.2	1,276.3
1990	3,956	4,308	8,264	3,073,900	2,239.3	1,050.3	1,408.2	1,235.9
1991	3,752	4,405	8,157	3,157,200	2,059.8	1,041.6	1,348.1	1,252.0
1992	3,430	4,352	7,782	2,979,900	1,839.7	1,005.2	1,256.4	1,168.2
1993	3,915	4,488	8,403	2,834,800	2,083.6	1,006.4	1,325.7	1,099.2
1994	3,653	4,276	7,929	2,712,800	1,912.1	943.1	1,230.3	1,042.0
1995	3,655	4,745	8,400	2,593,800	1,964.3	1,023.7	1,293.1	987.1
1996	3,284	4,752	8,036	2,501,500	1,732.4	1,006.3	1,214.3	943.0

Notes: (1) Metropolitan Statistical Area - see Appendix A for areas included; (2) calculated by the editors using the following formula: (number of crimes in the MSA minus number of crimes in the city); (3) calculated by the editors using the following formula: ((number of crimes in the MSA minus number of crimes in the city) ÷ (population of the MSA minus population of the city)) x 100,000; n/a not avail.
Source: U.S. Department of Justice, FBI Uniform Crime Reports, 1977 - 1996

Larceny-Thefts and Larceny-Theft Rates: 1977 - 1996

Year	Number				Rate per 100,000 population			
	City	Suburbs[2]	MSA[1]	U.S.	City	Suburbs[3]	MSA[1]	U.S.
1977	6,836	5,595	12,431	5,905,700	4,439.0	2,095.5	2,952.7	2,729.9
1978	7,371	6,868	14,239	5,991,000	4,694.9	2,404.8	3,217.2	2,747.4
1979	7,592	8,107	15,699	6,601,000	4,611.0	2,796.4	3,453.7	2,999.1
1980	9,095	8,470	17,565	7,136,900	5,752.7	2,607.7	3,637.3	3,167.0
1981	9,103	9,542	18,645	7,194,400	5,622.8	2,868.9	3,770.5	3,139.7
1982	9,835	8,902	18,737	7,142,500	6,027.8	2,655.7	3,759.7	3,084.8
1983	10,490	9,274	19,764	6,712,800	6,347.0	2,731.3	3,915.1	2,868.9
1984	10,322	9,045	19,367	6,591,900	6,300.5	2,550.5	3,735.5	2,791.3
1985	10,943	9,662	20,605	6,926,400	6,770.6	2,671.9	3,938.0	2,901.2
1986	12,963	10,675	23,638	7,257,200	7,922.9	2,915.7	4,462.2	3,010.3
1987	13,548	10,955	24,503	7,499,900	8,381.6	2,874.4	4,514.5	3,081.3
1988	13,170	12,022	25,192	7,705,900	7,970.5	3,085.7	4,540.5	3,134.9
1989	12,991	12,224	25,215	7,872,400	7,735.4	3,016.0	4,398.6	3,171.3
1990	11,975	12,982	24,957	7,945,700	6,778.4	3,165.0	4,252.8	3,194.8
1991	11,677	13,864	25,541	8,142,200	6,410.4	3,278.1	4,221.1	3,228.8
1992	11,291	13,801	25,092	7,915,200	6,056.1	3,187.6	4,051.0	3,103.0
1993	11,355	13,676	25,031	7,820,900	6,043.3	3,066.7	3,949.1	3,032.4
1994	11,971	14,727	26,698	7,879,800	6,266.2	3,248.0	4,142.7	3,026.7
1995	12,250	15,781	28,031	7,997,700	6,583.4	3,404.7	4,315.2	3,043.8
1996	11,255	16,460	27,715	7,894,600	5,937.2	3,485.8	4,188.0	2,975.9

Notes: (1) Metropolitan Statistical Area - see Appendix A for areas included; (2) calculated by the editors using the following formula: (number of crimes in the MSA minus number of crimes in the city); (3) calculated by the editors using the following formula: ((number of crimes in the MSA minus number of crimes in the city) ÷ (population of the MSA minus population of the city)) x 100,000; n/a not avail.
Source: U.S. Department of Justice, FBI Uniform Crime Reports, 1977 - 1996

Motor Vehicle Thefts and Motor Vehicle Theft Rates: 1977 - 1996

Year	Number				Rate per 100,000 population			
	City	Suburbs[2]	MSA[1]	U.S.	City	Suburbs[3]	MSA[1]	U.S.
1977	689	713	1,402	977,700	447.4	267.0	333.0	451.9
1978	837	864	1,701	1,004,100	533.1	302.5	384.3	460.5
1979	877	956	1,833	1,112,800	532.6	329.8	403.3	505.6
1980	894	800	1,694	1,131,700	565.5	246.3	350.8	502.2
1981	879	851	1,730	1,087,800	542.9	255.9	349.9	474.7
1982	875	768	1,643	1,062,400	536.3	229.1	329.7	458.8
1983	865	821	1,686	1,007,900	523.4	241.8	334.0	430.8
1984	829	720	1,549	1,032,200	506.0	203.0	298.8	437.1
1985	912	800	1,712	1,102,900	564.3	221.2	327.2	462.0
1986	1,031	884	1,915	1,224,100	630.1	241.4	361.5	507.8
1987	1,184	1,006	2,190	1,288,700	732.5	264.0	403.5	529.4
1988	1,529	1,200	2,729	1,432,900	925.4	308.0	491.9	582.9
1989	2,076	1,270	3,346	1,564,800	1,236.1	313.3	583.7	630.4
1990	1,778	1,486	3,264	1,635,900	1,006.4	362.3	556.2	657.8
1991	1,548	1,253	2,801	1,661,700	849.8	296.3	462.9	659.0
1992	1,845	1,405	3,250	1,610,800	989.6	324.5	524.7	631.5
1993	2,335	1,485	3,820	1,563,100	1,242.7	333.0	602.7	606.1
1994	3,262	2,122	5,384	1,539,300	1,707.5	468.0	835.4	591.3
1995	2,638	2,272	4,910	1,472,400	1,417.7	490.2	755.9	560.4
1996	2,819	2,320	5,139	1,395,200	1,487.1	491.3	776.5	525.9

Notes: (1) Metropolitan Statistical Area - see Appendix A for areas included; (2) calculated by the editors using the following formula: (number of crimes in the MSA minus number of crimes in the city); (3) calculated by the editors using the following formula: ((number of crimes in the MSA minus number of crimes in the city) ÷ (population of the MSA minus population of the city)) x 100,000; n/a not avail.
Source: U.S. Department of Justice, FBI Uniform Crime Reports, 1977 - 1996

HATE CRIMES

Criminal Incidents by Bias Motivation

Area	Race	Ethnicity	Religion	Sexual Orientation
Tacoma	26	4	10	5

Notes: Figures include both violent and property crimes. Law enforcement agencies must have submitted data for at least one quarter of calendar year 1995 to be included in this report, therefore figures shown may not represent complete 12-month totals; n/a not available
Source: U.S. Department of Justice, FBI Uniform Crime Reports, Hate Crime Statistics 1995

LAW ENFORCEMENT

Full-Time Law Enforcement Employees

Jurisdiction	Police Employees			Police Officers per 100,000 population
	Total	Officers	Civilians	
Tacoma	425	370	55	195.2

Notes: Data as of October 31, 1996
Source: U.S. Department of Justice, FBI Uniform Crime Reports, 1996

CORRECTIONS

Federal Correctional Facilities

Type	Year Opened	Security Level	Sex of Inmates	Rated Capacity	Population on 7/1/95	Number of Staff
None listed						

Notes: Data as of 1995
Source: Bureau of Justice Statistics, Sourcebook of Criminal Justice Statistics Online

City/County/Regional Correctional Facilities

Name	Year Opened	Year Renov.	Rated Capacity	1995 Pop.	Number of COs[1]	Number of Staff	ACA[2] Accred.
Pierce Co Detention and Corrections Ctr	1955	1984	996	1,198	226	259	No

Notes: Data as of April 1996; (1) Correctional Officers; (2) American Correctional Assn. Accreditation
Source: American Correctional Association, 1996-1998 National Jail and Adult Detention Directory

Private Adult Correctional Facilities

Name	Date Opened	Rated Capacity	Present Pop.	Security Level	Facility Construct.	Expans. Plans	ACA[1] Accred.
None listed							

Notes: Data as of December 1996; (1) American Correctional Association Accreditation
Source: University of Florida, Center for Studies in Criminology and Law, Private Adult Correctional Facility Census, 10th Ed., March 15, 1997

Characteristics of Shock Incarceration Programs

Jurisdiction	Year Program Began	Number of Camps	Average Num. of Inmates	Number of Beds	Program Length	Voluntary/ Mandatory
Washington	1993	1	150	180	4 months	Voluntary

Note: Data as of July 1996;
Source: Sourcebook of Criminal Justice Statistics Online

DEATH PENALTY

Death Penalty Statistics

State	Prisoners Executed		Prisoners Under Sentence of Death					Avg. No. of Years on Death Row[4]
	1930-1995	1996[1]	Total[2]	White[3]	Black[3]	Hisp.	Women	
Washington	49	0	9	8	1	0	0	n/c

Notes: Data as of 12/31/95 unless otherwise noted; n/c not calculated on fewer than 10 inmates; (1) Data as of 7/31/97; (2) Includes persons of other races; (3) Includes people of Hispanic origin; (4) Covers prisoners sentenced 1974 through 1995
Source: Bureau of Justice Statistics, Capital Punishment 1995 (released 12/96); Death Penalty Information Center Web Site, 9/30/97

Capital Offenses and Methods of Execution

Capital Offenses in Washington	Minimum Age for Imposition of Death Penalty	Mentally Retarded Excluded	Methods of Execution[1]
Aggravated first-degree murder.	18	No	Lethal injection; hanging

Notes: Data as of 12/31/95 unless otherwise noted; (1) Data as of 7/31/97
Source: Bureau of Justice Statistics, Capital Punishment 1995 (released 12/96); Death Penalty Information Center Web Site, 9/30/97

LAWS

Statutory Provisions Relating to the Purchase, Ownership and Use of Handguns

Jurisdiction	Instant Background Check	Federal Waiting Period Applies[1]	State Waiting Period (days)	License or Permit to Purchase	Regis-tration	Record of Sale Sent to Police	Concealed Carry Law
Washington	No	Yes	5[a]	No	No	Yes	Yes[b]

Note: Data as of 1996; (1) The Federal 5-day waiting period for handgun purchases applies to states that don't have instant background checks, waiting period requirements, or licensing procedures exempting them from the Federal requirement; (a) May be extended by police to 30 days in some circumstances. An individual not holding a driver's license must wait 90 days; (b) "Shall issue" permit system, liberally administered discretion by local authorities over permit issuance, or no permit required
Source: Sourcebook of Criminal Justice Statistics Online

Statutory Provisions Relating to Alcohol Use and Driving

Jurisdiction	Drinking Age	Blood Alcohol Concentration Levels as Evidence in State Courts[1]		Open Container Law[1]	Anti-Consump-tion Law[1]	Dram Shop Law[1]
		Illegal per se at 0.10%	Presumption at 0.10%			
Washington	21	Yes	No	Yes	Yes	(a,b)

Note: Data as of January 1, 1997; (1) See Appendix C for an explanation of terms; (a) Adopted via case law decisions; (b) Applies only to the actions of intoxicated minors and/or adults who have lost their will to stop drinking
Source: Sourcebook of Criminal Justice Statistics Online

Statutory Provisions Relating to Curfews

Jurisdiction	Year Enacted	Latest Revision	Age Group(s)	Curfew Provisions
Tacoma	1995	-	17 and under	Midnight to 6 am every night

Note: Data as of February 1996
Source: Sourcebook of Criminal Justice Statistics Online

Statutory Provisions Relating to Hate Crimes

Jurisdiction	Bias-Motivated Violence and Intimidation						Institutional Vandalism
		Criminal Penalty					
	Civil Action	Race/ Religion/ Ethnicity	Sexual Orientation	Mental/ Physical Disability	Gender	Age	
Washington	Yes	Yes	Yes	Yes	Yes	No	Yes

Source: Anti-Defamation League, 1997 Hate Crimes Laws

Tallahassee, Florida

OVERVIEW

The total crime rate for the city increased 39.7% between 1977 and 1996. During that same period, the violent crime rate increased 35.5% and the property crime rate increased 40.3%.

Among violent crimes, the rates for: Murders decreased 19.1%; Forcible Rapes decreased 5.5%; Robberies increased 47.1%; and Aggravated Assaults increased 38.0%.

Among property crimes, the rates for: Burglaries decreased 26.5%; Larceny-Thefts increased 71.9%; and Motor Vehicle Thefts increased 91.0%.

ANTI-CRIME PROGRAMS

Information not available at time of publication.

CRIME RISK

Your Chances of Becoming a Victim[1]

Area	Any Crime	Violent Crime					Property Crime			
		Any	Murder	Forcible Rape[2]	Robbery	Aggrav. Assault	Any	Burglary	Larceny -Theft	Motor Vehicle Theft
City	1:10	1:88	1:13,800	1:761	1:380	1:126	1:11	1:64	1:15	1:174

Note: (1) Figures have been calculated by dividing the population of the city by the number of crimes reported to the FBI during 1996 and are expressed as odds (eg. 1:20 should be read as 1 in 20).
(2) Figures have been calculated by dividing the female population of the city by the number of forcible rapes reported to the FBI during 1996. The female population of the city was estimated by calculating the ratio of females to males reported in the 1990 Census and applying that ratio to 1996 population estimate.
Source: FBI Uniform Crime Reports 1996

CRIME STATISTICS

Total Crimes and Total Crime Rates: 1977 - 1996

Year	Number				Rate per 100,000 population			
	City	Suburbs[2]	MSA[1]	U.S.	City	Suburbs[3]	MSA[1]	U.S.
1977	5,693	3,733	9,426	10,984,500	7,269.2	6,061.2	6,737.4	5,077.6
1978	6,771	3,867	10,638	11,209,000	8,556.7	6,663.0	7,755.5	5,140.3
1979	7,883	3,707	11,590	12,249,500	9,860.5	5,715.7	8,004.0	5,565.5
1980	9,696	4,555	14,251	13,408,300	12,006.1	5,968.5	9,072.7	5,950.0
1981	9,783	4,082	13,865	13,423,800	11,400.2	5,033.7	8,307.0	5,858.2
1982	8,158	3,071	11,229	12,974,400	9,278.4	3,696.1	6,566.2	5,603.6
1983	7,253	3,854	11,107	12,108,600	8,045.2	3,268.5	5,338.2	5,175.0
1984	8,406	4,156	12,562	11,881,800	7,828.1	4,007.1	5,950.8	5,031.3
1985	11,013	4,316	15,329	12,431,400	9,473.4	4,371.3	7,130.2	5,207.1
1986	12,365	4,707	17,072	13,211,900	10,355.1	4,639.4	7,729.5	5,480.4
1987	14,261	5,586	19,847	13,508,700	11,593.2	5,504.1	8,840.5	5,550.0
1988	n/a	n/a	n/a	13,923,100	n/a	n/a	n/a	5,664.2
1989	14,974	5,958	20,932	14,251,400	11,602.3	5,633.3	8,913.9	5,741.0
1990	n/a	n/a	n/a	14,475,600	n/a	n/a	n/a	5,820.3
1991	19,927	7,289	27,216	14,872,900	15,562.7	6,527.0	11,353.3	5,897.8
1992	19,300	7,228	26,528	14,438,200	14,837.4	6,371.3	10,893.4	5,660.2
1993	19,426	7,340	26,766	14,144,800	14,688.6	6,295.7	10,756.3	5,484.4
1994	17,363	7,239	24,602	13,989,500	12,870.9	6,087.2	9,692.6	5,373.5
1995	16,611	6,328	22,939	13,862,700	12,235.7	5,209.3	8,917.6	5,275.9
1996	14,018	n/a	n/a	13,473,600	10,157.9	n/a	n/a	5,078.9

Notes: (1) Metropolitan Statistical Area - see Appendix A for areas included; (2) calculated by the editors using the following formula: (number of crimes in the MSA minus number of crimes in the city); (3) calculated by the editors using the following formula: ((number of crimes in the MSA minus number of crimes in the city) ÷ (population of the MSA minus population of the city)) x 100,000; n/a not avail.
Source: U.S. Department of Justice, FBI Uniform Crime Reports, 1977 - 1996

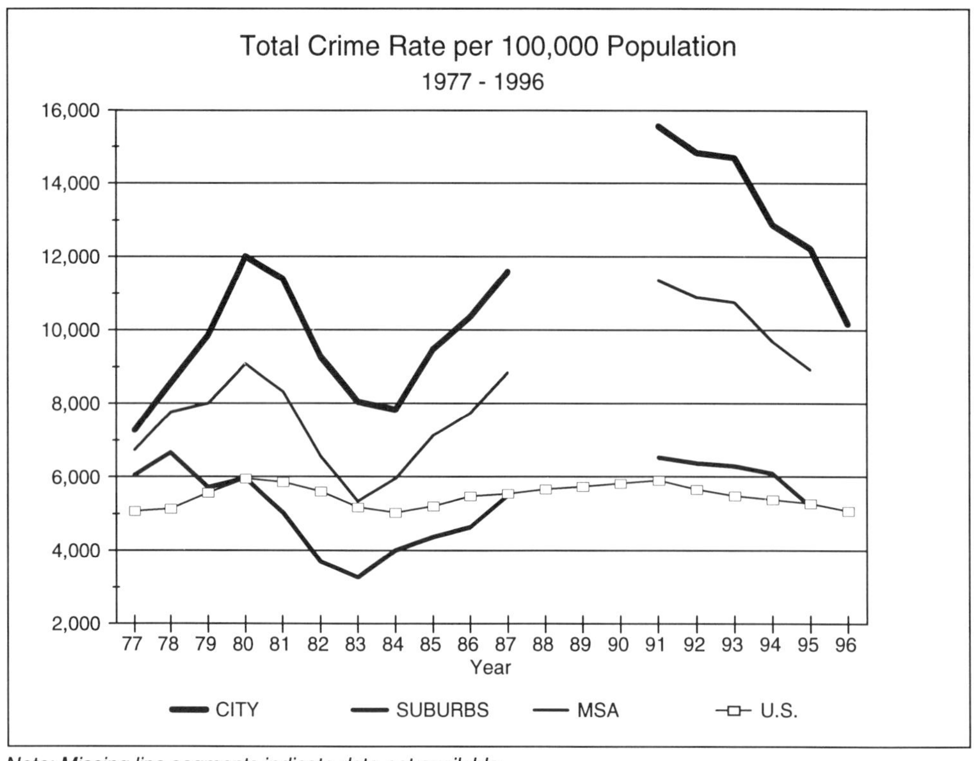

Note: Missing line segments indicate data not available.

Violent Crimes and Violent Crime Rates: 1977 - 1996

Year	Number				Rate per 100,000 population			
	City	Suburbs[2]	MSA[1]	U.S.	City	Suburbs[3]	MSA[1]	U.S.
1977	654	340	994	1,029,580	835.1	552.1	710.5	475.9
1978	675	325	1,000	1,085,550	853.0	560.0	729.0	497.8
1979	757	339	1,096	1,208,030	946.9	522.7	756.9	548.9
1980	931	358	1,289	1,344,520	1,152.8	469.1	820.6	596.6
1981	1,013	383	1,396	1,361,820	1,180.5	472.3	836.4	594.3
1982	786	245	1,031	1,322,390	893.9	294.9	602.9	571.1
1983	722	321	1,043	1,258,090	800.9	272.2	501.3	537.7
1984	805	463	1,268	1,273,280	749.7	446.4	600.7	539.2
1985	1,194	580	1,774	1,328,800	1,027.1	587.4	825.2	556.6
1986	1,246	578	1,824	1,489,170	1,043.5	569.7	825.8	617.7
1987	1,515	774	2,289	1,484,000	1,231.6	762.7	1,019.6	609.7
1988	n/a	n/a	n/a	1,566,220	n/a	n/a	n/a	637.2
1989	1,979	989	2,968	1,646,040	1,533.4	935.1	1,263.9	663.1
1990	n/a	n/a	n/a	1,820,130	n/a	n/a	n/a	731.8
1991	2,825	1,181	4,006	1,911,770	2,206.3	1,057.5	1,671.1	758.1
1992	2,596	1,324	3,920	1,932,270	1,995.7	1,167.1	1,609.7	757.5
1993	2,690	1,157	3,847	1,926,020	2,034.0	992.4	1,546.0	746.8
1994	2,350	1,103	3,453	1,857,670	1,742.0	927.5	1,360.4	713.6
1995	1,929	1,035	2,964	1,798,790	1,420.9	852.0	1,152.3	684.6
1996	1,562	n/a	n/a	1,682,280	1,131.9	n/a	n/a	634.1

Notes: Violent crimes include murder, forcible rape, robbery and aggravated assault; n/a not available; (1) Metropolitan Statistical Area - see Appendix A for areas included; (2) calculated by the editors using the following formula: (number of crimes in the MSA minus number of crimes in the city); (3) calculated by the editors using the following formula: ((number of crimes in the MSA minus number of crimes in the city) ÷ (population of the MSA minus population of the city)) x 100,000
Source: U.S. Department of Justice, FBI Uniform Crime Reports, 1977 - 1996

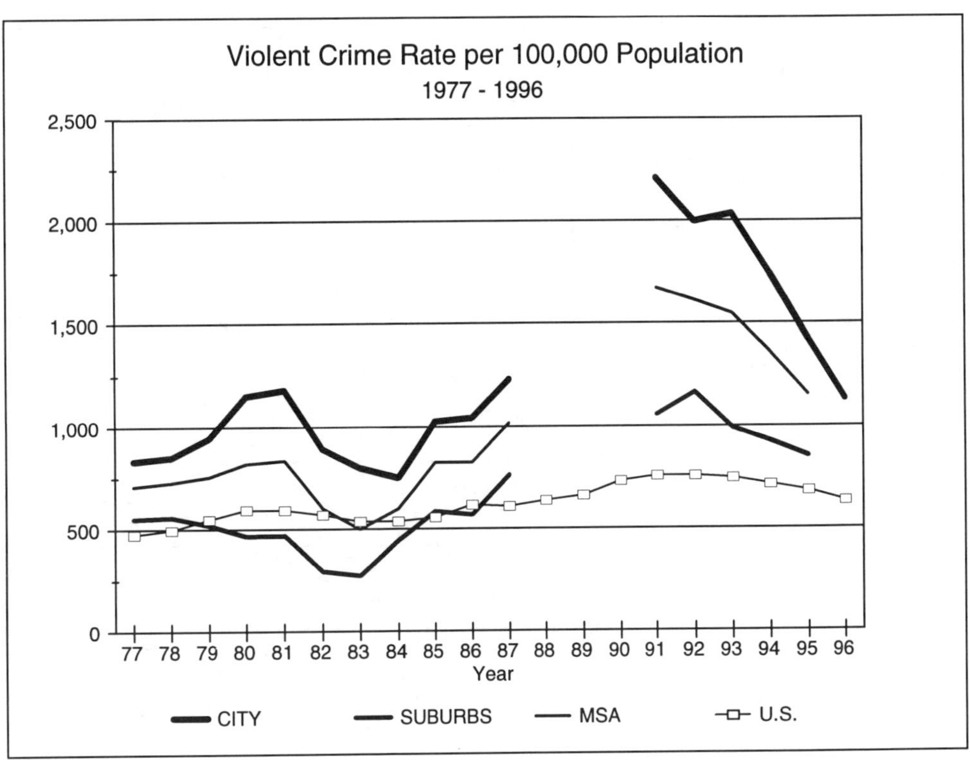

Note: Missing line segments indicate data not available.

Property Crimes and Property Crime Rates: 1977 - 1996

Year	Number				Rate per 100,000 population			
	City	Suburbs[2]	MSA[1]	U.S.	City	Suburbs[3]	MSA[1]	U.S.
1977	5,039	3,393	8,432	9,955,000	6,434.1	5,509.2	6,026.9	4,601.7
1978	6,096	3,542	9,638	10,123,400	7,703.7	6,103.0	7,026.4	4,642.5
1979	7,126	3,368	10,494	11,041,500	8,913.6	5,193.0	7,247.1	5,016.6
1980	8,765	4,197	12,962	12,063,700	10,853.3	5,499.4	8,252.1	5,353.3
1981	8,770	3,699	12,469	12,061,900	10,219.8	4,561.4	7,470.6	5,263.9
1982	7,372	2,826	10,198	11,652,000	8,384.4	3,401.2	5,963.3	5,032.5
1983	6,531	3,533	10,064	10,850,500	7,244.4	2,996.2	4,836.9	4,637.4
1984	7,601	3,693	11,294	10,608,500	7,078.5	3,560.7	5,350.1	4,492.1
1985	9,819	3,736	13,555	11,102,600	8,446.3	3,783.9	6,305.0	4,650.5
1986	11,119	4,129	15,248	11,722,700	9,311.6	4,069.7	6,903.7	4,862.6
1987	12,746	4,812	17,558	12,024,700	10,361.6	4,741.4	7,820.9	4,940.3
1988	n/a	n/a	n/a	12,356,900	n/a	n/a	n/a	5,027.1
1989	12,995	4,969	17,964	12,605,400	10,068.9	4,698.2	7,650.0	5,077.9
1990	n/a	n/a	n/a	12,655,500	n/a	n/a	n/a	5,088.5
1991	17,102	6,108	23,210	12,961,100	13,356.5	5,469.4	9,682.2	5,139.7
1992	16,704	5,904	22,608	12,505,900	12,841.6	5,204.2	9,283.7	4,902.7
1993	16,736	6,183	22,919	12,218,800	12,654.6	5,303.3	9,210.3	4,737.6
1994	15,013	6,136	21,149	12,131,900	11,128.9	5,159.7	8,332.2	4,660.0
1995	14,682	5,293	19,975	12,063,900	10,814.8	4,357.3	7,765.3	4,591.3
1996	12,456	n/a	n/a	11,791,300	9,026.0	n/a	n/a	4,444.8

Notes: Property crimes include burglary, larceny-theft and motor vehicle theft; n/a not available; (1) Metropolitan Statistical Area - see Appendix A for areas included; (2) calculated by the editors using the following formula: (number of crimes in the MSA minus number of crimes in the city); (3) calculated by the editors using the following formula: ((number of crimes in the MSA minus number of crimes in the city) ÷ (population of the MSA minus population of the city)) x 100,000
Source: U.S. Department of Justice, FBI Uniform Crime Reports, 1977 - 1996

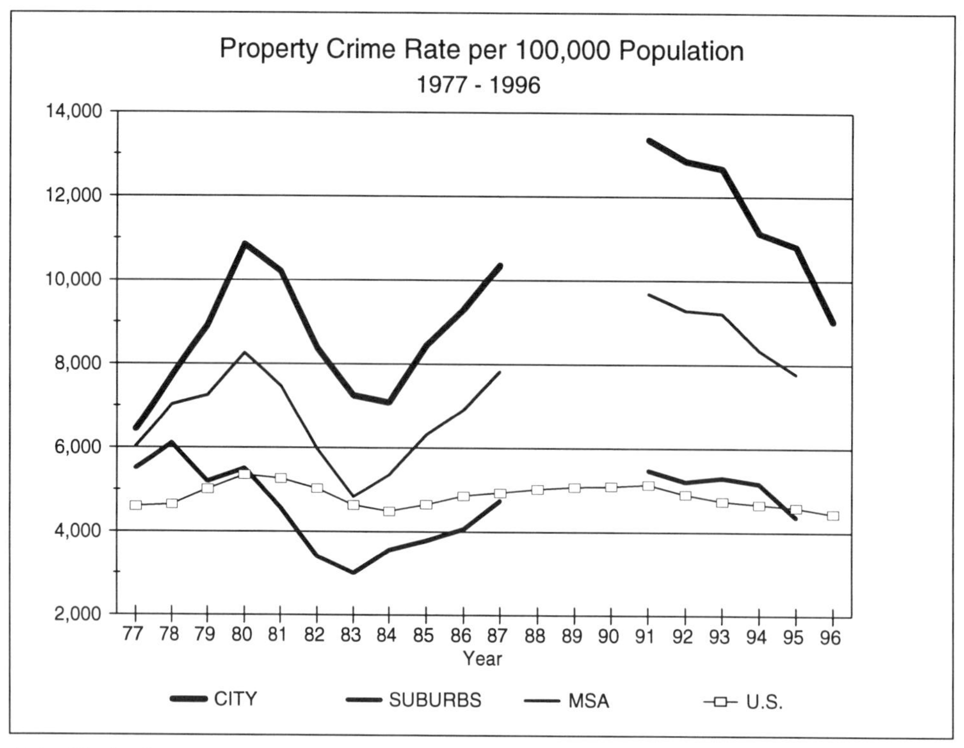

Note: Missing line segments indicate data not available.

Murders and Murder Rates: 1977 - 1996

Year	Number				Rate per 100,000 population			
	City	Suburbs[2]	MSA[1]	U.S.	City	Suburbs[3]	MSA[1]	U.S.
1977	7	1	8	19,120	8.9	1.6	5.7	8.8
1978	4	6	10	19,560	5.1	10.3	7.3	9.0
1979	1	2	3	21,460	1.3	3.1	2.1	9.7
1980	8	5	13	23,040	9.9	6.6	8.3	10.2
1981	8	5	13	22,520	9.3	6.2	7.8	9.8
1982	9	7	16	21,010	10.2	8.4	9.4	9.1
1983	4	10	14	19,310	4.4	8.5	6.7	8.3
1984	4	7	11	18,690	3.7	6.7	5.2	7.9
1985	3	6	9	18,980	2.6	6.1	4.2	7.9
1986	8	13	21	20,610	6.7	12.8	9.5	8.6
1987	8	14	22	20,100	6.5	13.8	9.8	8.3
1988	n/a	n/a	n/a	20,680	n/a	n/a	n/a	8.4
1989	7	10	17	21,500	5.4	9.5	7.2	8.7
1990	n/a	n/a	n/a	23,440	n/a	n/a	n/a	9.4
1991	14	10	24	24,700	10.9	9.0	10.0	9.8
1992	15	7	22	23,760	11.5	6.2	9.0	9.3
1993	9	9	18	24,530	6.8	7.7	7.2	9.5
1994	9	9	18	23,330	6.7	7.6	7.1	9.0
1995	12	7	19	21,610	8.8	5.8	7.4	8.2
1996	10	n/a	n/a	19,650	7.2	n/a	n/a	7.4

Notes: (1) Metropolitan Statistical Area - see Appendix A for areas included; (2) calculated by the editors using the following formula: (number of crimes in the MSA minus number of crimes in the city); (3) calculated by the editors using the following formula: ((number of crimes in the MSA minus number of crimes in the city) ÷ (population of the MSA minus population of the city)) x 100,000; n/a not avail.
Source: U.S. Department of Justice, FBI Uniform Crime Reports, 1977 - 1996

Forcible Rapes and Forcible Rape Rates: 1977 - 1996

Year	Number				Rate per 100,000 population			
	City	Suburbs[2]	MSA[1]	U.S.	City	Suburbs[3]	MSA[1]	U.S.
1977	57	30	87	63,500	72.8	48.7	62.2	29.4
1978	60	43	103	67,610	75.8	74.1	75.1	31.0
1979	86	32	118	76,390	107.6	49.3	81.5	34.7
1980	98	49	147	82,990	121.3	64.2	93.6	36.8
1981	92	32	124	82,500	107.2	39.5	74.3	36.0
1982	68	28	96	78,770	77.3	33.7	56.1	34.0
1983	82	44	126	78,920	91.0	37.3	60.6	33.7
1984	70	46	116	84,230	65.2	44.4	55.0	35.7
1985	72	38	110	88,670	61.9	38.5	51.2	37.1
1986	80	50	130	91,460	67.0	49.3	58.9	37.9
1987	96	70	166	91,110	78.0	69.0	73.9	37.4
1988	n/a	n/a	n/a	92,490	n/a	n/a	n/a	37.6
1989	129	63	192	94,500	100.0	59.6	81.8	38.1
1990	n/a	n/a	n/a	102,560	n/a	n/a	n/a	41.2
1991	119	67	186	106,590	92.9	60.0	77.6	42.3
1992	147	92	239	109,060	113.0	81.1	98.1	42.8
1993	137	82	219	106,010	103.6	70.3	88.0	41.1
1994	114	61	175	102,220	84.5	51.3	68.9	39.3
1995	119	57	176	97,470	87.7	46.9	68.4	37.1
1996	95	n/a	n/a	95,770	68.8	n/a	n/a	36.1

Notes: (1) Metropolitan Statistical Area - see Appendix A for areas included; (2) calculated by the editors using the following formula: (number of crimes in the MSA minus number of crimes in the city); (3) calculated by the editors using the following formula: ((number of crimes in the MSA minus number of crimes in the city) ÷ (population of the MSA minus population of the city)) x 100,000; n/a not avail.
Source: U.S. Department of Justice, FBI Uniform Crime Reports, 1977 - 1996

Robberies and Robbery Rates: 1977 - 1996

Year	Number				Rate per 100,000 population			
	City	Suburbs[2]	MSA[1]	U.S.	City	Suburbs[3]	MSA[1]	U.S.
1977	140	45	185	412,610	178.8	73.1	132.2	190.7
1978	140	41	181	426,930	176.9	70.6	132.0	195.8
1979	135	28	163	480,700	168.9	43.2	112.6	218.4
1980	217	65	282	565,840	268.7	85.2	179.5	251.1
1981	280	58	338	592,910	326.3	71.5	202.5	258.7
1982	174	31	205	553,130	197.9	37.3	119.9	238.9
1983	172	39	211	506,570	190.8	33.1	101.4	216.5
1984	189	78	267	485,010	176.0	75.2	126.5	205.4
1985	260	84	344	497,870	223.7	85.1	160.0	208.5
1986	289	73	362	542,780	242.0	72.0	163.9	225.1
1987	429	117	546	517,700	348.7	115.3	243.2	212.7
1988	n/a	n/a	n/a	542,970	n/a	n/a	n/a	220.9
1989	445	176	621	578,330	344.8	166.4	264.5	233.0
1990	n/a	n/a	n/a	639,270	n/a	n/a	n/a	257.0
1991	833	142	975	687,730	650.6	127.2	406.7	272.7
1992	648	163	811	672,480	498.2	143.7	333.0	263.6
1993	790	227	1,017	659,870	597.3	194.7	408.7	255.9
1994	740	218	958	618,950	548.6	183.3	377.4	237.7
1995	607	219	826	580,510	447.1	180.3	321.1	220.9
1996	363	n/a	n/a	537,050	263.0	n/a	n/a	202.4

Notes: (1) Metropolitan Statistical Area - see Appendix A for areas included; (2) calculated by the editors using the following formula: (number of crimes in the MSA minus number of crimes in the city); (3) calculated by the editors using the following formula: ((number of crimes in the MSA minus number of crimes in the city) ÷ (population of the MSA minus population of the city)) x 100,000; n/a not avail.
Source: U.S. Department of Justice, FBI Uniform Crime Reports, 1977 - 1996

Aggravated Assaults and Aggravated Assault Rates: 1977 - 1996

Year	Number				Rate per 100,000 population			
	City	Suburbs[2]	MSA[1]	U.S.	City	Suburbs[3]	MSA[1]	U.S.
1977	450	264	714	534,350	574.6	428.7	510.3	247.0
1978	471	235	706	571,460	595.2	404.9	514.7	262.1
1979	535	277	812	629,480	669.2	427.1	560.8	286.0
1980	608	239	847	672,650	752.9	313.2	539.2	298.5
1981	633	288	921	663,900	737.6	355.1	551.8	289.7
1982	535	179	714	669,480	608.5	215.4	417.5	289.2
1983	464	228	692	653,290	514.7	193.4	332.6	279.2
1984	542	332	874	685,350	504.7	320.1	414.0	290.2
1985	859	452	1,311	723,250	738.9	457.8	609.8	302.9
1986	869	442	1,311	834,320	727.7	435.6	593.6	346.1
1987	982	573	1,555	855,090	798.3	564.6	692.7	351.3
1988	n/a	n/a	n/a	910,090	n/a	n/a	n/a	370.2
1989	1,398	740	2,138	951,710	1,083.2	699.7	910.5	383.4
1990	n/a	n/a	n/a	1,054,860	n/a	n/a	n/a	424.1
1991	1,859	962	2,821	1,092,740	1,451.9	861.4	1,176.8	433.3
1992	1,786	1,062	2,848	1,126,970	1,373.0	936.1	1,169.5	441.8
1993	1,754	839	2,593	1,135,610	1,326.3	719.6	1,042.0	440.3
1994	1,487	815	2,302	1,113,180	1,102.3	685.3	906.9	427.6
1995	1,191	752	1,943	1,099,210	877.3	619.1	755.3	418.3
1996	1,094	n/a	n/a	1,029,810	792.7	n/a	n/a	388.2

Notes: (1) Metropolitan Statistical Area - see Appendix A for areas included; (2) calculated by the editors using the following formula: (number of crimes in the MSA minus number of crimes in the city); (3) calculated by the editors using the following formula: ((number of crimes in the MSA minus number of crimes in the city) ÷ (population of the MSA minus population of the city)) x 100,000; n/a not avail.
Source: U.S. Department of Justice, FBI Uniform Crime Reports, 1977 - 1996

Burglaries and Burglary Rates: 1977 - 1996

Year	Number				Rate per 100,000 population			
	City	Suburbs[2]	MSA[1]	U.S.	City	Suburbs[3]	MSA[1]	U.S.
1977	1,665	863	2,528	3,071,500	2,126.0	1,401.2	1,806.9	1,419.8
1978	1,928	1,006	2,934	3,128,300	2,436.5	1,733.4	2,139.0	1,434.6
1979	2,157	1,056	3,213	3,327,700	2,698.1	1,628.2	2,218.9	1,511.9
1980	2,684	1,355	4,039	3,795,200	3,323.5	1,775.5	2,571.4	1,684.1
1981	2,808	1,175	3,983	3,779,700	3,272.2	1,448.9	2,386.3	1,649.5
1982	2,191	862	3,053	3,447,100	2,491.9	1,037.5	1,785.2	1,488.8
1983	1,919	931	2,850	3,129,900	2,128.6	789.6	1,369.7	1,337.7
1984	2,057	1,007	3,064	2,984,400	1,915.6	970.9	1,451.5	1,263.7
1985	2,876	1,002	3,878	3,073,300	2,473.9	1,014.8	1,803.8	1,287.3
1986	3,248	1,340	4,588	3,241,400	2,720.0	1,320.7	2,077.3	1,344.6
1987	3,608	1,522	5,130	3,236,200	2,933.0	1,499.7	2,285.1	1,329.6
1988	n/a	n/a	n/a	3,218,100	n/a	n/a	n/a	1,309.2
1989	3,623	1,753	5,376	3,168,200	2,807.2	1,657.5	2,289.4	1,276.3
1990	n/a	n/a	n/a	3,073,900	n/a	n/a	n/a	1,235.9
1991	4,889	2,414	7,303	3,157,200	3,818.2	2,161.6	3,046.5	1,252.0
1992	4,446	2,003	6,449	2,979,900	3,418.0	1,765.6	2,648.2	1,168.2
1993	3,970	2,067	6,037	2,834,800	3,001.8	1,772.9	2,426.1	1,099.2
1994	3,293	1,887	5,180	2,712,800	2,441.0	1,586.8	2,040.8	1,042.0
1995	2,800	1,619	4,419	2,593,800	2,062.5	1,332.8	1,717.9	987.1
1996	2,157	n/a	n/a	2,501,500	1,563.0	n/a	n/a	943.0

Notes: (1) Metropolitan Statistical Area - see Appendix A for areas included; (2) calculated by the editors using the following formula: (number of crimes in the MSA minus number of crimes in the city); (3) calculated by the editors using the following formula: ((number of crimes in the MSA minus number of crimes in the city) ÷ (population of the MSA minus population of the city)) x 100,000; n/a not avail.
Source: U.S. Department of Justice, FBI Uniform Crime Reports, 1977 - 1996

Larceny-Thefts and Larceny-Theft Rates: 1977 - 1996

Year	Number				Rate per 100,000 population			
	City	Suburbs[2]	MSA[1]	U.S.	City	Suburbs[3]	MSA[1]	U.S.
1977	3,138	2,404	5,542	5,905,700	4,006.8	3,903.4	3,961.3	2,729.9
1978	3,872	2,391	6,263	5,991,000	4,893.2	4,119.8	4,565.9	2,747.4
1979	4,661	2,188	6,849	6,601,000	5,830.3	3,373.6	4,729.9	2,999.1
1980	5,693	2,688	8,381	7,136,900	7,049.4	3,522.2	5,335.6	3,167.0
1981	5,568	2,378	7,946	7,194,400	6,488.5	2,932.4	4,760.7	3,139.7
1982	4,831	1,844	6,675	7,142,500	5,494.5	2,219.3	3,903.2	3,084.8
1983	4,337	2,453	6,790	6,712,800	4,810.7	2,080.3	3,263.4	2,868.9
1984	5,251	2,537	7,788	6,591,900	4,890.0	2,446.1	3,689.3	2,791.3
1985	6,495	2,567	9,062	6,926,400	5,587.0	2,599.9	4,215.1	2,901.2
1986	7,306	2,595	9,901	7,257,200	6,118.4	2,557.7	4,482.8	3,010.3
1987	8,352	3,063	11,415	7,499,900	6,789.6	3,018.1	5,084.6	3,081.3
1988	n/a	n/a	n/a	7,705,900	n/a	n/a	n/a	3,134.9
1989	8,627	2,958	11,585	7,872,400	6,684.4	2,796.8	4,933.5	3,171.3
1990	n/a	n/a	n/a	7,945,700	n/a	n/a	n/a	3,194.8
1991	10,882	3,300	14,182	8,142,200	8,498.7	2,955.0	5,916.1	3,228.8
1992	10,226	3,436	13,662	7,915,200	7,861.5	3,028.7	5,610.1	3,103.0
1993	10,701	3,395	14,096	7,820,900	8,091.4	2,912.0	5,664.7	3,032.4
1994	10,436	3,634	14,070	7,879,800	7,736.0	3,055.8	5,543.2	3,026.7
1995	10,751	3,206	13,957	7,997,700	7,919.2	2,639.2	5,425.8	3,043.8
1996	9,505	n/a	n/a	7,894,600	6,887.6	n/a	n/a	2,975.9

Notes: (1) Metropolitan Statistical Area - see Appendix A for areas included; (2) calculated by the editors using the following formula: (number of crimes in the MSA minus number of crimes in the city); (3) calculated by the editors using the following formula: ((number of crimes in the MSA minus number of crimes in the city) ÷ (population of the MSA minus population of the city)) x 100,000; n/a not avail.
Source: U.S. Department of Justice, FBI Uniform Crime Reports, 1977 - 1996

Motor Vehicle Thefts and Motor Vehicle Theft Rates: 1977 - 1996

Year	Number				Rate per 100,000 population			
	City	Suburbs[2]	MSA[1]	U.S.	City	Suburbs[3]	MSA[1]	U.S.
1977	236	126	362	977,700	301.3	204.6	258.7	451.9
1978	296	145	441	1,004,100	374.1	249.8	321.5	460.5
1979	308	124	432	1,112,800	385.3	191.2	298.3	505.6
1980	388	154	542	1,131,700	480.4	201.8	345.1	502.2
1981	394	146	540	1,087,800	459.1	180.0	323.5	474.7
1982	350	120	470	1,062,400	398.1	144.4	274.8	458.8
1983	275	149	424	1,007,900	305.0	126.4	203.8	430.8
1984	293	149	442	1,032,200	272.9	143.7	209.4	437.1
1985	448	167	615	1,102,900	385.4	169.1	286.1	462.0
1986	565	194	759	1,224,100	473.2	191.2	343.6	507.8
1987	786	227	1,013	1,288,700	639.0	223.7	451.2	529.4
1988	n/a	n/a	n/a	1,432,900	n/a	n/a	n/a	582.9
1989	745	258	1,003	1,564,800	577.2	243.9	427.1	630.4
1990	n/a	n/a	n/a	1,635,900	n/a	n/a	n/a	657.8
1991	1,331	394	1,725	1,661,700	1,039.5	352.8	719.6	659.0
1992	2,032	465	2,497	1,610,800	1,562.2	409.9	1,025.4	631.5
1993	2,065	721	2,786	1,563,100	1,561.4	618.4	1,119.6	606.1
1994	1,284	615	1,899	1,539,300	951.8	517.1	748.2	591.3
1995	1,131	468	1,599	1,472,400	833.1	385.3	621.6	560.4
1996	794	n/a	n/a	1,395,200	575.4	n/a	n/a	525.9

Notes: (1) Metropolitan Statistical Area - see Appendix A for areas included; (2) calculated by the editors using the following formula: (number of crimes in the MSA minus number of crimes in the city); (3) calculated by the editors using the following formula: ((number of crimes in the MSA minus number of crimes in the city) ÷ (population of the MSA minus population of the city)) x 100,000; n/a not avail.
Source: U.S. Department of Justice, FBI Uniform Crime Reports, 1977 - 1996

HATE CRIMES

Criminal Incidents by Bias Motivation

Area	Race	Ethnicity	Religion	Sexual Orientation
Tallahassee	2	0	0	0

Notes: Figures include both violent and property crimes. Law enforcement agencies must have submitted data for at least one quarter of calendar year 1995 to be included in this report, therefore figures shown may not represent complete 12-month totals; n/a not available
Source: U.S. Department of Justice, FBI Uniform Crime Reports, Hate Crime Statistics 1995

LAW ENFORCEMENT

Full-Time Law Enforcement Employees

Jurisdiction	Police Employees			Police Officers per 100,000 population
	Total	Officers	Civilians	
Tallahassee	478	328	150	237.7

Notes: Data as of October 31, 1996
Source: U.S. Department of Justice, FBI Uniform Crime Reports, 1996

CORRECTIONS

Federal Correctional Facilities

Type	Year Opened	Security Level	Sex of Inmates	Rated Capacity	Population on 7/1/95	Number of Staff
Federal Correctional Inst.[1]	1938	Low/Admin.	Male	850	1,529	362

Notes: Data as of 1995; (1) A minimum security satellite camp is operated adjacent to this facility.
Source: Bureau of Justice Statistics, Sourcebook of Criminal Justice Statistics Online

City/County/Regional Correctional Facilities

Name	Year Opened	Year Renov.	Rated Capacity	1995 Pop.	Number of COs[1]	Number of Staff	ACA[2] Accred.
Leon County Detention Center	1993	--	744	766	208	289	No

Notes: Data as of April 1996; (1) Correctional Officers; (2) American Correctional Assn. Accreditation
Source: American Correctional Association, 1996-1998 National Jail and Adult Detention Directory

Private Adult Correctional Facilities

Name	Date Opened	Rated Capacity	Present Pop.	Security Level	Facility Construct.	Expans. Plans	ACA[1] Accred.
None listed							

Notes: Data as of December 1996; (1) American Correctional Association Accreditation
Source: University of Florida, Center for Studies in Criminology and Law, Private Adult Correctional Facility Census, 10th Ed., March 15, 1997

Characteristics of Shock Incarceration Programs

Jurisdiction	Year Program Began	Number of Camps	Average Num. of Inmates	Number of Beds	Program Length	Voluntary/ Mandatory
Florida	1987	1	94	112	120 days min.	n/a

Note: Data as of July 1996;
Source: Sourcebook of Criminal Justice Statistics Online

DEATH PENALTY

Death Penalty Statistics

State	Prisoners Executed		Prisoners Under Sentence of Death					Avg. No. of Years on Death Row[4]
	1930-1995	1996[1]	Total[2]	White[3]	Black[3]	Hisp.	Women	
Florida	206	2	362	228	134	35	6	6.9

Notes: Data as of 12/31/95 unless otherwise noted; (1) Data as of 7/31/97; (2) Includes persons of other races; (3) Includes people of Hispanic origin; (4) Covers prisoners sentenced 1974 through 1995
Source: Bureau of Justice Statistics, Capital Punishment 1995 (released 12/96); Death Penalty Information Center Web Site, 9/30/97

Capital Offenses and Methods of Execution

Capital Offenses in Florida	Minimum Age for Imposition of Death Penalty	Mentally Retarded Excluded	Methods of Execution[1]
First-degree murder; felony murder; capital drug-trafficking.	16	No	Electrocution

Notes: Data as of 12/31/95 unless otherwise noted; (1) Data as of 7/31/97
Source: Bureau of Justice Statistics, Capital Punishment 1995 (released 12/96); Death Penalty Information Center Web Site, 9/30/97

LAWS

Statutory Provisions Relating to the Purchase, Ownership and Use of Handguns

Jurisdiction	Instant Background Check	Federal Waiting Period Applies[1]	State Waiting Period (days)	License or Permit to Purchase	Regis-tration	Record of Sale Sent to Police	Concealed Carry Law
Florida	Yes[a]	No	3[b,c]	No	No	No	Yes[d]

Note: Data as of 1996; (1) The Federal 5-day waiting period for handgun purchases applies to states that don't have instant background checks, waiting period requirements, or licensing procedures exempting them from the Federal requirement; (a) Concealed firearm carry permit holders are exempt from Instant Check; (b) The State waiting period does not apply to a person holding a valid permit or license to carry a firearm; (c) Purchases from licensed dealers only; (d) "Shall issue" permit system, liberally administered discretion by local authorities over permit issuance, or no permit required
Source: Sourcebook of Criminal Justice Statistics Online

Statutory Provisions Relating to Alcohol Use and Driving

Jurisdiction	Drinking Age	Blood Alcohol Concentration Levels as Evidence in State Courts[1]		Open Container Law[1]	Anti-Consump-tion Law[1]	Dram Shop Law[1]
		Illegal per se at 0.10%	Presumption at 0.10%			
Florida	21	(a)	(a,b)	Yes	No	Yes[c]

Note: Data as of January 1, 1997; (1) See Appendix C for an explanation of terms; (a) 0.08%; (b) Constitutes prima facie evidence; (c) Applies only to the actions of intoxicated minors or persons known to be habitually addicted to alcohol
Source: Sourcebook of Criminal Justice Statistics Online

Statutory Provisions Relating to Hate Crimes

Jurisdiction	Bias-Motivated Violence and Intimidation						Institutional Vandalism
	Civil Action	Criminal Penalty					
		Race/ Religion/ Ethnicity	Sexual Orientation	Mental/ Physical Disability	Gender	Age	
Florida	Yes	Yes	Yes	No	No	No	Yes

Source: Anti-Defamation League, 1997 Hate Crimes Laws

Tampa, Florida

OVERVIEW

The total crime rate for the city increased 50.6% between 1977 and 1996. During that same period, the violent crime rate increased 144.6% and the property crime rate increased 37.2%.

Among violent crimes, the rates for: Murders increased 24.8%; Forcible Rapes increased 21.7%; Robberies increased 126.1%; and Aggravated Assaults increased 169.5%.

Among property crimes, the rates for: Burglaries decreased 6.1%; Larceny-Thefts increased 31.6%; and Motor Vehicle Thefts increased 372.3%.

ANTI-CRIME PROGRAMS

Programs include:

- CHOICE—students who have been suspended for three to 10 days from school are referred to the program along with their parents. These students are exposed to a curriculum that includes English, writing, reading and mathematics, decision making, and physical education. Subjects such as teen pregnancy, drugs, alcohol abuse, gun violence, gangs, auto theft, AIDS, and others are discussed during a 10-day stay.
- C.O.P. (Community Oriented Policing) Firehouse Program—48 officers are assigned to twenty-four fire stations throughout the city. The officers have been trained as Community Oriented Policing and Crime Prevention Practitioners. Their primary responsibility is proactive law enforcement, targeting crime and "quality of life" problems that affect the communities served by the fire houses. *Police Department, 7/97*

CRIME RISK

Your Chances of Becoming a Victim[1]

Area	Any Crime	Violent Crime					Property Crime			
		Any	Murder	Forcible Rape[2]	Robbery	Aggrav. Assault	Any	Burglary	Larceny -Theft	Motor Vehicle Theft
City	1:7	1:34	1:6,853	1:579	1:110	1:52	1:9	1:40	1:14	1:49

Note: (1) Figures have been calculated by dividing the population of the city by the number of crimes reported to the FBI during 1996 and are expressed as odds (eg. 1:20 should be read as 1 in 20). (2) Figures have been calculated by dividing the female population of the city by the number of forcible rapes reported to the FBI during 1996. The female population of the city was estimated by calculating the ratio of females to males reported in the 1990 Census and applying that ratio to 1996 population estimate.
Source: FBI Uniform Crime Reports 1996

CRIME STATISTICS

Total Crimes and Total Crime Rates: 1977 - 1996

Year	Number				Rate per 100,000 population			
	City	Suburbs[2]	MSA[1]	U.S.	City	Suburbs[3]	MSA[1]	U.S.
1977	25,606	63,651	89,257	10,984,500	9,662.6	5,665.2	6,428.1	5,077.6
1978	27,002	68,988	95,990	11,209,000	10,228.0	6,005.7	6,794.7	5,140.3
1979	31,687	75,449	107,136	12,249,500	11,431.0	6,465.8	7,418.9	5,565.5
1980	38,903	86,202	125,105	13,408,300	14,477.7	6,727.6	8,071.1	5,950.0
1981	40,856	86,626	127,482	13,423,800	14,308.8	6,362.4	7,739.9	5,858.2
1982	38,532	82,187	120,719	12,974,400	13,171.0	5,891.5	7,153.4	5,603.6
1983	33,159	81,294	114,453	12,108,600	11,054.3	5,495.4	6,432.6	5,175.0
1984	33,959	82,681	116,640	11,881,800	11,736.1	5,467.9	6,474.7	5,031.3
1985	41,770	96,344	138,114	12,431,400	14,641.8	6,059.2	7,364.8	5,207.1
1986	48,294	109,774	158,068	13,211,900	16,480.9	6,721.1	8,205.8	5,480.4
1987	49,350	117,203	166,553	13,508,700	17,263.9	6,953.9	8,449.0	5,550.0
1988	n/a	n/a	n/a	13,923,100	n/a	n/a	n/a	5,664.2
1989	45,329	130,199	175,528	14,251,400	15,659.7	7,397.8	8,564.7	5,741.0
1990	44,660	n/a	n/a	14,475,600	15,949.1	n/a	n/a	5,820.3
1991	47,576	127,880	175,456	14,872,900	16,556.6	6,969.7	8,267.9	5,897.8
1992	46,131	125,062	171,193	14,438,200	15,802.6	6,708.8	7,940.1	5,660.2
1993	45,373	117,472	162,845	14,144,800	15,706.7	6,353.2	7,617.1	5,484.4
1994	51,510	121,940	173,450	13,989,500	17,481.0	6,465.4	7,953.9	5,373.5
1995	41,112	114,948	156,060	13,862,700	14,182.3	6,051.2	7,127.8	5,275.9
1996	42,873	n/a	n/a	13,473,600	14,549.5	n/a	n/a	5,078.9

Notes: (1) Metropolitan Statistical Area - see Appendix A for areas included; (2) calculated by the editors using the following formula: (number of crimes in the MSA minus number of crimes in the city); (3) calculated by the editors using the following formula: ((number of crimes in the MSA minus number of crimes in the city) ÷ (population of the MSA minus population of the city)) x 100,000; n/a not avail.
Source: U.S. Department of Justice, FBI Uniform Crime Reports, 1977 - 1996

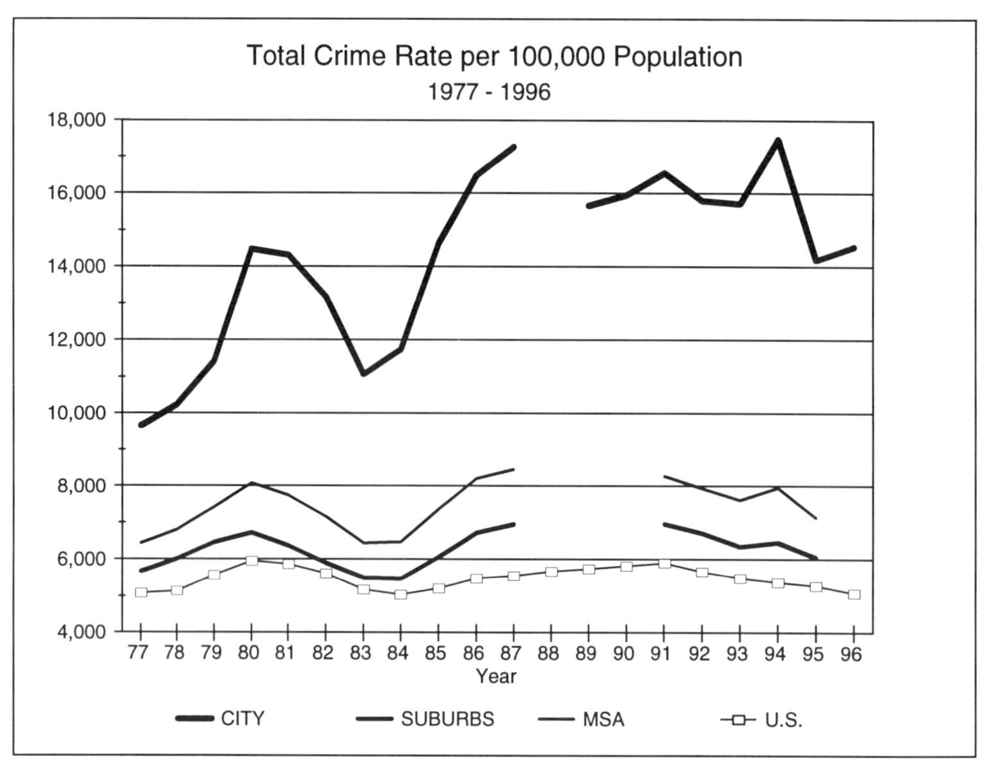

Note: Missing line segments indicate data not available.

Violent Crimes and Violent Crime Rates: 1977 - 1996

Year	Number				Rate per 100,000 population			
	City	Suburbs[2]	MSA[1]	U.S.	City	Suburbs[3]	MSA[1]	U.S.
1977	3,194	5,477	8,671	1,029,580	1,205.3	487.5	624.5	475.9
1978	3,510	6,431	9,941	1,085,550	1,329.5	559.8	703.7	497.8
1979	4,206	7,113	11,319	1,208,030	1,517.3	609.6	783.8	548.9
1980	5,089	8,213	13,302	1,344,520	1,893.9	641.0	858.2	596.6
1981	5,674	8,294	13,968	1,361,820	1,987.2	609.2	848.1	594.3
1982	5,736	9,100	14,836	1,322,390	1,960.7	652.3	879.1	571.1
1983	5,053	8,430	13,483	1,258,090	1,684.5	569.9	757.8	537.7
1984	5,852	8,871	14,723	1,273,280	2,022.4	586.7	817.3	539.2
1985	6,855	10,194	17,049	1,328,800	2,402.9	641.1	909.1	556.6
1986	8,147	11,855	20,002	1,489,170	2,780.3	725.8	1,038.4	617.7
1987	8,899	11,926	20,825	1,484,000	3,113.1	707.6	1,056.4	609.7
1988	n/a	n/a	n/a	1,566,220	n/a	n/a	n/a	637.2
1989	7,910	14,947	22,857	1,646,040	2,732.6	849.3	1,115.3	663.1
1990	8,608	n/a	n/a	1,820,130	3,074.1	n/a	n/a	731.8
1991	10,362	16,473	26,835	1,911,770	3,606.0	897.8	1,264.5	758.1
1992	9,864	17,482	27,346	1,932,270	3,379.0	937.8	1,268.3	757.5
1993	9,379	16,776	26,155	1,926,020	3,246.7	907.3	1,223.4	746.8
1994	10,262	16,740	27,002	1,857,670	3,482.6	887.6	1,238.2	713.6
1995	8,735	15,796	24,531	1,798,790	3,013.3	831.6	1,120.4	684.6
1996	8,689	n/a	n/a	1,682,280	2,948.7	n/a	n/a	634.1

Notes: Violent crimes include murder, forcible rape, robbery and aggravated assault; n/a not available; (1) Metropolitan Statistical Area - see Appendix A for areas included; (2) calculated by the editors using the following formula: (number of crimes in the MSA minus number of crimes in the city); (3) calculated by the editors using the following formula: ((number of crimes in the MSA minus number of crimes in the city) ÷ (population of the MSA minus population of the city)) x 100,000
Source: U.S. Department of Justice, FBI Uniform Crime Reports, 1977 - 1996

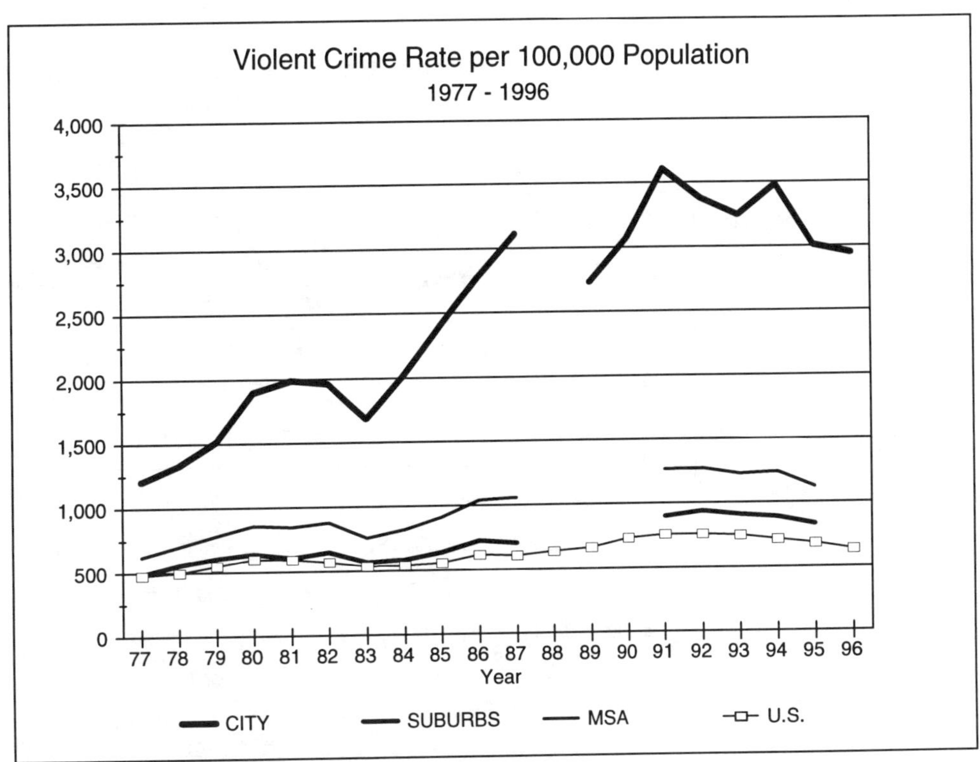

Note: Missing line segments indicate data not available.

Property Crimes and Property Crime Rates: 1977 - 1996

Year	Number				Rate per 100,000 population			
	City	Suburbs[2]	MSA[1]	U.S.	City	Suburbs[3]	MSA[1]	U.S.
1977	22,412	58,174	80,586	9,955,000	8,457.4	5,177.7	5,803.6	4,601.7
1978	23,492	62,557	86,049	10,123,400	8,898.5	5,445.8	6,091.0	4,642.5
1979	27,481	68,336	95,817	11,041,500	9,913.7	5,856.3	6,635.1	5,016.6
1980	33,814	77,989	111,803	12,063,700	12,583.9	6,086.6	7,212.9	5,353.3
1981	35,182	78,332	113,514	12,061,900	12,321.6	5,753.2	6,891.9	5,263.9
1982	32,796	73,087	105,883	11,652,000	11,210.4	5,239.1	6,274.3	5,032.5
1983	28,106	72,864	100,970	10,850,500	9,369.8	4,925.6	5,674.8	4,637.4
1984	28,107	73,810	101,917	10,608,500	9,713.7	4,881.2	5,657.4	4,492.1
1985	34,915	86,150	121,065	11,102,600	12,238.9	5,418.1	6,455.7	4,650.5
1986	40,147	97,919	138,066	11,722,700	13,700.6	5,995.3	7,167.4	4,862.6
1987	40,451	105,277	145,728	12,024,700	14,150.8	6,246.3	7,392.6	4,940.3
1988	n/a	n/a	n/a	12,356,900	n/a	n/a	n/a	5,027.1
1989	37,419	115,252	152,671	12,605,400	12,927.0	6,548.5	7,449.4	5,077.9
1990	36,052	n/a	n/a	12,655,500	12,875.0	n/a	n/a	5,088.5
1991	37,214	111,407	148,621	12,961,100	12,950.6	6,071.9	7,003.3	5,139.7
1992	36,267	107,580	143,847	12,505,900	12,423.6	5,771.0	6,671.8	4,902.7
1993	35,994	100,696	136,690	12,218,800	12,460.0	5,445.9	6,393.7	4,737.6
1994	41,248	105,200	146,448	12,131,900	13,998.4	5,577.8	6,715.6	4,660.0
1995	32,377	99,152	131,529	12,063,900	11,169.0	5,219.7	6,007.4	4,591.3
1996	34,184	n/a	n/a	11,791,300	11,600.8	n/a	n/a	4,444.8

Notes: Property crimes include burglary, larceny-theft and motor vehicle theft; n/a not available; (1) Metropolitan Statistical Area - see Appendix A for areas included; (2) calculated by the editors using the following formula: (number of crimes in the MSA minus number of crimes in the city); (3) calculated by the editors using the following formula: ((number of crimes in the MSA minus number of crimes in the city) ÷ (population of the MSA minus population of the city)) x 100,000
Source: U.S. Department of Justice, FBI Uniform Crime Reports, 1977 - 1996

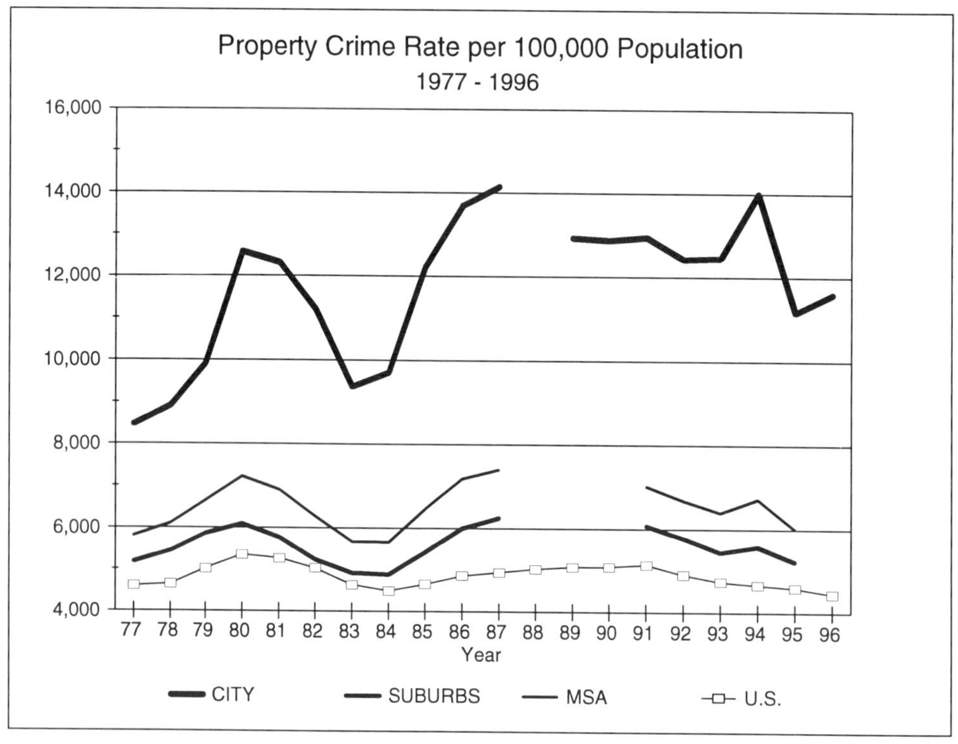

Note: Missing line segments indicate data not available.

Murders and Murder Rates: 1977 - 1996

Year	Number				Rate per 100,000 population			
	City	Suburbs[2]	MSA[1]	U.S.	City	Suburbs[3]	MSA[1]	U.S.
1977	31	66	97	19,120	11.7	5.9	7.0	8.8
1978	41	78	119	19,560	15.5	6.8	8.4	9.0
1979	37	70	107	21,460	13.3	6.0	7.4	9.7
1980	44	82	126	23,040	16.4	6.4	8.1	10.2
1981	69	89	158	22,520	24.2	6.5	9.6	9.8
1982	59	88	147	21,010	20.2	6.3	8.7	9.1
1983	58	97	155	19,310	19.3	6.6	8.7	8.3
1984	52	103	155	18,690	18.0	6.8	8.6	7.9
1985	70	110	180	18,980	24.5	6.9	9.6	7.9
1986	79	121	200	20,610	27.0	7.4	10.4	8.6
1987	61	88	149	20,100	21.3	5.2	7.6	8.3
1988	n/a	n/a	n/a	20,680	n/a	n/a	n/a	8.4
1989	57	124	181	21,500	19.7	7.0	8.8	8.7
1990	60	n/a	n/a	23,440	21.4	n/a	n/a	9.4
1991	64	112	176	24,700	22.3	6.1	8.3	9.8
1992	49	108	157	23,760	16.8	5.8	7.3	9.3
1993	43	87	130	24,530	14.9	4.7	6.1	9.5
1994	62	77	139	23,330	21.0	4.1	6.4	9.0
1995	47	98	145	21,610	16.2	5.2	6.6	8.2
1996	43	n/a	n/a	19,650	14.6	n/a	n/a	7.4

Notes: (1) Metropolitan Statistical Area - see Appendix A for areas included; (2) calculated by the editors using the following formula: (number of crimes in the MSA minus number of crimes in the city); (3) calculated by the editors using the following formula: ((number of crimes in the MSA minus number of crimes in the city) ÷ (population of the MSA minus population of the city)) x 100,000; n/a not avail.
Source: U.S. Department of Justice, FBI Uniform Crime Reports, 1977 - 1996

Forcible Rapes and Forcible Rape Rates: 1977 - 1996

Year	Number				Rate per 100,000 population			
	City	Suburbs[2]	MSA[1]	U.S.	City	Suburbs[3]	MSA[1]	U.S.
1977	195	454	649	63,500	73.6	40.4	46.7	29.4
1978	253	507	760	67,610	95.8	44.1	53.8	31.0
1979	308	466	774	76,390	111.1	39.9	53.6	34.7
1980	348	565	913	82,990	129.5	44.1	58.9	36.8
1981	409	583	992	82,500	143.2	42.8	60.2	36.0
1982	411	639	1,050	78,770	140.5	45.8	62.2	34.0
1983	288	530	818	78,920	96.0	35.8	46.0	33.7
1984	277	634	911	84,230	95.7	41.9	50.6	35.7
1985	288	648	936	88,670	101.0	40.8	49.9	37.1
1986	375	609	984	91,460	128.0	37.3	51.1	37.9
1987	297	652	949	91,110	103.9	38.7	48.1	37.4
1988	n/a	n/a	n/a	92,490	n/a	n/a	n/a	37.6
1989	175	740	915	94,500	60.5	42.0	44.6	38.1
1990	343	n/a	n/a	102,560	122.5	n/a	n/a	41.2
1991	347	801	1,148	106,590	120.8	43.7	54.1	42.3
1992	303	904	1,207	109,060	103.8	48.5	56.0	42.8
1993	247	897	1,144	106,010	85.5	48.5	53.5	41.1
1994	298	846	1,144	102,220	101.1	44.9	52.5	39.3
1995	277	736	1,013	97,470	95.6	38.7	46.3	37.1
1996	264	n/a	n/a	95,770	89.6	n/a	n/a	36.1

Notes: (1) Metropolitan Statistical Area - see Appendix A for areas included; (2) calculated by the editors using the following formula: (number of crimes in the MSA minus number of crimes in the city); (3) calculated by the editors using the following formula: ((number of crimes in the MSA minus number of crimes in the city) ÷ (population of the MSA minus population of the city)) x 100,000; n/a not avail.
Source: U.S. Department of Justice, FBI Uniform Crime Reports, 1977 - 1996

Robberies and Robbery Rates: 1977 - 1996

Year	Number				Rate per 100,000 population			
	City	Suburbs[2]	MSA[1]	U.S.	City	Suburbs[3]	MSA[1]	U.S.
1977	1,062	1,283	2,345	412,610	400.8	114.2	168.9	190.7
1978	1,080	1,398	2,478	426,930	409.1	121.7	175.4	195.8
1979	1,312	1,538	2,850	480,700	473.3	131.8	197.4	218.4
1980	1,877	1,829	3,706	565,840	698.5	142.7	239.1	251.1
1981	2,314	2,146	4,460	592,910	810.4	157.6	270.8	258.7
1982	1,842	2,145	3,987	553,130	629.6	153.8	236.3	238.9
1983	1,529	1,768	3,297	506,570	509.7	119.5	185.3	216.5
1984	1,843	1,915	3,758	485,010	636.9	126.6	208.6	205.4
1985	2,657	2,567	5,224	497,870	931.4	161.4	278.6	208.5
1986	3,512	3,464	6,976	542,780	1,198.5	212.1	362.1	225.1
1987	3,427	3,653	7,080	517,700	1,198.9	216.7	359.2	212.7
1988	n/a	n/a	n/a	542,970	n/a	n/a	n/a	220.9
1989	3,137	4,666	7,803	578,330	1,083.7	265.1	380.7	233.0
1990	2,915	n/a	n/a	639,270	1,041.0	n/a	n/a	257.0
1991	3,094	4,239	7,333	687,730	1,076.7	231.0	345.5	272.7
1992	2,999	3,826	6,825	672,480	1,027.3	205.2	316.6	263.6
1993	2,965	3,657	6,622	659,870	1,026.4	197.8	309.7	255.9
1994	3,378	3,589	6,967	618,950	1,146.4	190.3	319.5	237.7
1995	2,626	3,409	6,035	580,510	905.9	179.5	275.6	220.9
1996	2,671	n/a	n/a	537,050	906.4	n/a	n/a	202.4

Notes: (1) Metropolitan Statistical Area - see Appendix A for areas included; (2) calculated by the editors using the following formula: (number of crimes in the MSA minus number of crimes in the city); (3) calculated by the editors using the following formula: ((number of crimes in the MSA minus number of crimes in the city) ÷ (population of the MSA minus population of the city)) x 100,000; n/a not avail.
Source: U.S. Department of Justice, FBI Uniform Crime Reports, 1977 - 1996

Aggravated Assaults and Aggravated Assault Rates: 1977 - 1996

Year	Number				Rate per 100,000 population			
	City	Suburbs[2]	MSA[1]	U.S.	City	Suburbs[3]	MSA[1]	U.S.
1977	1,906	3,674	5,580	534,350	719.2	327.0	401.9	247.0
1978	2,136	4,448	6,584	571,460	809.1	387.2	466.1	262.1
1979	2,549	5,039	7,588	629,480	919.5	431.8	525.5	286.0
1980	2,820	5,737	8,557	672,650	1,049.5	447.7	552.1	298.5
1981	2,882	5,476	8,358	663,900	1,009.4	402.2	507.4	289.7
1982	3,424	6,228	9,652	669,480	1,170.4	446.4	571.9	289.2
1983	3,178	6,035	9,213	653,290	1,059.5	408.0	517.8	279.2
1984	3,680	6,219	9,899	685,350	1,271.8	411.3	549.5	290.2
1985	3,840	6,869	10,709	723,250	1,346.0	432.0	571.0	302.9
1986	4,181	7,661	11,842	834,320	1,426.8	469.1	614.8	346.1
1987	5,114	7,533	12,647	855,090	1,789.0	447.0	641.6	351.3
1988	n/a	n/a	n/a	910,090	n/a	n/a	n/a	370.2
1989	4,541	9,417	13,958	951,710	1,568.8	535.1	681.1	383.4
1990	5,290	n/a	n/a	1,054,860	1,889.2	n/a	n/a	424.1
1991	6,857	11,321	18,178	1,092,740	2,386.3	617.0	856.6	433.3
1992	6,513	12,644	19,157	1,126,970	2,231.1	678.3	888.5	441.8
1993	6,124	12,135	18,259	1,135,610	2,119.9	656.3	854.1	440.3
1994	6,524	12,228	18,752	1,113,180	2,214.1	648.3	859.9	427.6
1995	5,785	11,553	17,338	1,099,210	1,995.6	608.2	791.9	418.3
1996	5,711	n/a	n/a	1,029,810	1,938.1	n/a	n/a	388.2

Notes: (1) Metropolitan Statistical Area - see Appendix A for areas included; (2) calculated by the editors using the following formula: (number of crimes in the MSA minus number of crimes in the city); (3) calculated by the editors using the following formula: ((number of crimes in the MSA minus number of crimes in the city) ÷ (population of the MSA minus population of the city)) x 100,000; n/a not avail.
Source: U.S. Department of Justice, FBI Uniform Crime Reports, 1977 - 1996

Burglaries and Burglary Rates: 1977 - 1996

Year	Number				Rate per 100,000 population			
	City	Suburbs[2]	MSA[1]	U.S.	City	Suburbs[3]	MSA[1]	U.S.
1977	7,061	18,507	25,568	3,071,500	2,664.5	1,647.2	1,841.4	1,419.8
1978	7,532	20,362	27,894	3,128,300	2,853.0	1,772.6	1,974.5	1,434.6
1979	8,640	20,620	29,260	3,327,700	3,116.8	1,767.1	2,026.2	1,511.9
1980	11,950	25,609	37,559	3,795,200	4,447.2	1,998.6	2,423.1	1,684.1
1981	12,575	26,866	39,441	3,779,700	4,404.1	1,973.2	2,394.6	1,649.5
1982	11,208	23,299	34,507	3,447,100	3,831.1	1,670.2	2,044.8	1,488.8
1983	9,513	22,849	32,362	3,129,900	3,171.4	1,544.6	1,818.8	1,337.7
1984	9,196	22,226	31,422	2,984,400	3,178.1	1,469.9	1,744.2	1,263.7
1985	12,117	25,913	38,030	3,073,300	4,247.4	1,629.7	2,027.9	1,287.3
1986	14,634	30,524	45,158	3,241,400	4,994.0	1,868.9	2,344.3	1,344.6
1987	13,245	31,530	44,775	3,236,200	4,633.5	1,870.8	2,271.4	1,329.6
1988	n/a	n/a	n/a	3,218,100	n/a	n/a	n/a	1,309.2
1989	11,694	30,353	42,047	3,168,200	4,039.9	1,724.6	2,051.6	1,276.3
1990	11,400	n/a	n/a	3,073,900	4,071.2	n/a	n/a	1,235.9
1991	11,239	28,182	39,421	3,157,200	3,911.2	1,536.0	1,857.6	1,252.0
1992	10,005	27,877	37,882	2,979,900	3,427.3	1,495.4	1,757.0	1,168.2
1993	8,987	25,362	34,349	2,834,800	3,111.0	1,371.6	1,606.7	1,099.2
1994	8,734	24,649	33,383	2,712,800	2,964.1	1,306.9	1,530.8	1,042.0
1995	6,622	22,244	28,866	2,593,800	2,284.4	1,171.0	1,318.4	987.1
1996	7,373	n/a	n/a	2,501,500	2,502.1	n/a	n/a	943.0

Notes: (1) Metropolitan Statistical Area - see Appendix A for areas included; (2) calculated by the editors using the following formula: (number of crimes in the MSA minus number of crimes in the city); (3) calculated by the editors using the following formula: ((number of crimes in the MSA minus number of crimes in the city) ÷ (population of the MSA minus population of the city)) x 100,000; n/a not avail.
Source: U.S. Department of Justice, FBI Uniform Crime Reports, 1977 - 1996

Larceny-Thefts and Larceny-Theft Rates: 1977 - 1996

Year	Number				Rate per 100,000 population			
	City	Suburbs[2]	MSA[1]	U.S.	City	Suburbs[3]	MSA[1]	U.S.
1977	14,204	37,059	51,263	5,905,700	5,360.0	3,298.4	3,691.9	2,729.9
1978	14,653	39,242	53,895	5,991,000	5,550.4	3,416.2	3,815.0	2,747.4
1979	17,152	44,398	61,550	6,601,000	6,187.5	3,804.8	4,262.2	2,999.1
1980	20,034	48,734	68,768	7,136,900	7,455.6	3,803.4	4,436.5	3,167.0
1981	20,554	47,902	68,456	7,194,400	7,198.5	3,518.2	4,156.2	3,139.7
1982	19,668	46,609	66,277	7,142,500	6,722.9	3,341.1	3,927.4	3,084.8
1983	16,998	46,667	63,665	6,712,800	5,666.7	3,154.7	3,578.2	2,868.9
1984	17,190	47,866	65,056	6,591,900	5,940.8	3,165.5	3,611.2	2,791.3
1985	20,570	55,803	76,373	6,926,400	7,210.5	3,509.5	4,072.5	2,901.2
1986	23,172	62,687	85,859	7,257,200	7,907.7	3,838.1	4,457.2	3,010.3
1987	24,261	67,809	92,070	7,499,900	8,487.1	4,023.3	4,670.6	3,081.3
1988	n/a	n/a	n/a	7,705,900	n/a	n/a	n/a	3,134.9
1989	20,515	75,250	95,765	7,872,400	7,087.3	4,275.7	4,672.8	3,171.3
1990	18,484	n/a	n/a	7,945,700	6,601.1	n/a	n/a	3,194.8
1991	20,072	72,983	93,055	8,142,200	6,985.1	3,977.7	4,385.0	3,228.8
1992	18,923	69,982	88,905	7,915,200	6,482.3	3,754.1	4,123.5	3,103.0
1993	18,534	66,517	85,051	7,820,900	6,415.9	3,597.4	3,978.3	3,032.4
1994	21,503	70,325	91,828	7,879,800	7,297.5	3,728.7	4,210.9	3,026.7
1995	19,773	68,517	88,290	7,997,700	6,821.1	3,607.0	4,032.5	3,043.8
1996	20,787	n/a	n/a	7,894,600	7,054.3	n/a	n/a	2,975.9

Notes: (1) Metropolitan Statistical Area - see Appendix A for areas included; (2) calculated by the editors using the following formula: (number of crimes in the MSA minus number of crimes in the city); (3) calculated by the editors using the following formula: ((number of crimes in the MSA minus number of crimes in the city) ÷ (population of the MSA minus population of the city)) x 100,000; n/a not avail.
Source: U.S. Department of Justice, FBI Uniform Crime Reports, 1977 - 1996

Motor Vehicle Thefts and Motor Vehicle Theft Rates: 1977 - 1996

Year	Number				Rate per 100,000 population			
	City	Suburbs[2]	MSA[1]	U.S.	City	Suburbs[3]	MSA[1]	U.S.
1977	1,147	2,608	3,755	977,700	432.8	232.1	270.4	451.9
1978	1,307	2,953	4,260	1,004,100	495.1	257.1	301.5	460.5
1979	1,689	3,318	5,007	1,112,800	609.3	284.3	346.7	505.6
1980	1,830	3,646	5,476	1,131,700	681.0	284.5	353.3	502.2
1981	2,053	3,564	5,617	1,087,800	719.0	261.8	341.0	474.7
1982	1,920	3,179	5,099	1,062,400	656.3	227.9	302.2	458.8
1983	1,595	3,348	4,943	1,007,900	531.7	226.3	277.8	430.8
1984	1,721	3,718	5,439	1,032,200	594.8	245.9	301.9	437.1
1985	2,228	4,434	6,662	1,102,900	781.0	278.9	355.2	462.0
1986	2,341	4,708	7,049	1,224,100	798.9	288.3	365.9	507.8
1987	2,945	5,938	8,883	1,288,700	1,030.2	352.3	450.6	529.4
1988	n/a	n/a	n/a	1,432,900	n/a	n/a	n/a	582.9
1989	5,210	9,649	14,859	1,564,800	1,799.9	548.2	725.0	630.4
1990	6,168	n/a	n/a	1,635,900	2,202.7	n/a	n/a	657.8
1991	5,903	10,242	16,145	1,661,700	2,054.3	558.2	760.8	659.0
1992	7,339	9,721	17,060	1,610,800	2,514.0	521.5	791.3	631.5
1993	8,473	8,817	17,290	1,563,100	2,933.1	476.8	808.7	606.1
1994	11,011	10,226	21,237	1,539,300	3,736.8	542.2	973.9	591.3
1995	5,982	8,391	14,373	1,472,400	2,063.6	441.7	656.5	560.4
1996	6,024	n/a	n/a	1,395,200	2,044.3	n/a	n/a	525.9

Notes: (1) Metropolitan Statistical Area - see Appendix A for areas included; (2) calculated by the editors using the following formula: (number of crimes in the MSA minus number of crimes in the city); (3) calculated by the editors using the following formula: ((number of crimes in the MSA minus number of crimes in the city) ÷ (population of the MSA minus population of the city)) x 100,000; n/a not avail.
Source: U.S. Department of Justice, FBI Uniform Crime Reports, 1977 - 1996

HATE CRIMES

Criminal Incidents by Bias Motivation

Area	Race	Ethnicity	Religion	Sexual Orientation
Tampa	7	1	1	0

Notes: Figures include both violent and property crimes. Law enforcement agencies must have submitted data for at least one quarter of calendar year 1995 to be included in this report, therefore figures shown may not represent complete 12-month totals; n/a not available
Source: U.S. Department of Justice, FBI Uniform Crime Reports, Hate Crime Statistics 1995

LAW ENFORCEMENT

Full-Time Law Enforcement Employees

Jurisdiction	Police Employees			Police Officers per 100,000 population
	Total	Officers	Civilians	
Tampa	1,200	915	285	310.5

Notes: Data as of October 31, 1996
Source: U.S. Department of Justice, FBI Uniform Crime Reports, 1996

CORRECTIONS

Federal Correctional Facilities

Type	Year Opened	Security Level	Sex of Inmates	Rated Capacity	Population on 7/1/95	Number of Staff
None listed						

Notes: Data as of 1995
Source: Bureau of Justice Statistics, Sourcebook of Criminal Justice Statistics Online

City/County/Regional Correctional Facilities

Name	Year Opened	Year Renov.	Rated Capacity	1995 Pop.	Number of COs[1]	Number of Staff	ACA[2] Accred.
Hillsborough Co Orient Rd Jail	1990	--	1,714	1,456	377	677	Yes
Hillsborough Co Work Rel Ctr	1957	1990	54	n/a	n/a	n/a	No
Hillsborough Co Morgan Street Jail	1964	1981	508	432	134	182	Yes

Notes: Data as of April 1996; (1) Correctional Officers; (2) American Correctional Assn. Accreditation
Source: American Correctional Association, 1996-1998 National Jail and Adult Detention Directory

Private Adult Correctional Facilities

Name	Date Opened	Rated Capacity	Present Pop.	Security Level	Facility Construct.	Expans. Plans	ACA[1] Accred.
None listed							

Notes: Data as of December 1996; (1) American Correctional Association Accreditation
Source: University of Florida, Center for Studies in Criminology and Law, Private Adult Correctional Facility Census, 10th Ed., March 15, 1997

Characteristics of Shock Incarceration Programs

Jurisdiction	Year Program Began	Number of Camps	Average Num. of Inmates	Number of Beds	Program Length	Voluntary/ Mandatory
Florida	1987	1	94	112	120 days min.	n/a

Note: Data as of July 1996;
Source: Sourcebook of Criminal Justice Statistics Online

INMATES AND HIV/AIDS

HIV Testing Policies for Inmates

Jurisdiction	All Inmates at Some Time	All Convicted Inmates at Admission	Random Samples While in Custody	High-risk Groups	Upon Inmate Request	Upon Court Order	Upon Involvement in Incident
Hillsborough Co.[1]	No	No	No	No	Yes	Yes	Yes

Notes: (1) All facilities reported following the same testing policy or authorities reported the policy to be jurisdiction-wide
Source: HIV in Prisons and Jails, 1993 (released August 1995)

Inmates Known to be Positive for HIV

Jurisdiction	Number of Jail Inmates in Facilities Providing Data	Type of HIV Infection/AIDS Cases				HIV/AIDS Cases as a Percent of Tot. Custody Pop.
		Total	Asymptomatic	Symptomatic	Confirmed AIDS	
Hillsborough Co.	2,126	40	33	2	5	1.9

Source: HIV in Prisons and Jails, 1993 (released August, 1995)

DEATH PENALTY

Death Penalty Statistics

State	Prisoners Executed		Prisoners Under Sentence of Death					Avg. No. of Years on Death Row[4]
	1930-1995	1996[1]	Total[2]	White[3]	Black[3]	Hisp.	Women	
Florida	206	2	362	228	134	35	6	6.9

Notes: Data as of 12/31/95 unless otherwise noted; (1) Data as of 7/31/97; (2) Includes persons of other races; (3) Includes people of Hispanic origin; (4) Covers prisoners sentenced 1974 through 1995
Source: Bureau of Justice Statistics, Capital Punishment 1995 (released 12/96); Death Penalty Information Center Web Site, 9/30/97

Capital Offenses and Methods of Execution

Capital Offenses in Florida	Minimum Age for Imposition of Death Penalty	Mentally Retarded Excluded	Methods of Execution[1]
First-degree murder; felony murder; capital drug-trafficking.	16	No	Electrocution

Notes: Data as of 12/31/95 unless otherwise noted; (1) Data as of 7/31/97
Source: Bureau of Justice Statistics, Capital Punishment 1995 (released 12/96); Death Penalty Information Center Web Site, 9/30/97

LAWS

Statutory Provisions Relating to the Purchase, Ownership and Use of Handguns

Jurisdiction	Instant Background Check	Federal Waiting Period Applies[1]	State Waiting Period (days)	License or Permit to Purchase	Registration	Record of Sale Sent to Police	Concealed Carry Law
Florida	Yes[a]	No	3[b,c]	No	No	No	Yes[d]

Note: Data as of 1996; (1) The Federal 5-day waiting period for handgun purchases applies to states that don't have instant background checks, waiting period requirements, or licensing procedures exempting them from the Federal requirement; (a) Concealed firearm carry permit holders are exempt from Instant Check; (b) The State waiting period does not apply to a person holding a valid permit or license to carry a firearm; (c) Purchases from licensed dealers only; (d) "Shall issue" permit system, liberally administered discretion by local authorities over permit issuance, or no permit required
Source: Sourcebook of Criminal Justice Statistics Online

Statutory Provisions Relating to Alcohol Use and Driving

Jurisdiction	Drinking Age	Blood Alcohol Concentration Levels as Evidence in State Courts[1]		Open Container Law[1]	Anti-Consumption Law[1]	Dram Shop Law[1]
		Illegal per se at 0.10%	Presumption at 0.10%			
Florida	21	(a)	(a,b)	Yes	No	Yes[c]

Note: Data as of January 1, 1997; (1) See Appendix C for an explanation of terms; (a) 0.08%; (b) Constitutes prima facie evidence; (c) Applies only to the actions of intoxicated minors or persons known to be habitually addicted to alcohol
Source: Sourcebook of Criminal Justice Statistics Online

Statutory Provisions Relating to Curfews

Jurisdiction	Year Enacted	Latest Revision	Age Group(s)	Curfew Provisions
Tampa	1993	-	17 and under	11 pm to 6 am weekday nights midnight to 6 am weekend nights

Note: Data as of February 1996
Source: Sourcebook of Criminal Justice Statistics Online

Statutory Provisions Relating to Hate Crimes

Jurisdiction	Bias-Motivated Violence and Intimidation						Institutional Vandalism
		Criminal Penalty					
	Civil Action	Race/ Religion/ Ethnicity	Sexual Orientation	Mental/ Physical Disability	Gender	Age	
Florida	Yes	Yes	Yes	No	No	No	Yes

Source: Anti-Defamation League, 1997 Hate Crimes Laws

Topeka, Kansas

OVERVIEW

The total crime rate for the city increased 83.1% between 1977 and 1996. During that same period, the violent crime rate increased 118.0% and the property crime rate increased 79.9%.

Among violent crimes, the rates for: Murders increased 30.8%; Forcible Rapes increased 57.0%; Robberies increased 156.1%; and Aggravated Assaults increased 109.8%.

Among property crimes, the rates for: Burglaries increased 58.2%; Larceny-Thefts increased 88.2%; and Motor Vehicle Thefts increased 99.7%.

ANTI-CRIME PROGRAMS

Information not available at time of publication.

CRIME RISK

Your Chances of Becoming a Victim[1]

Area	Any Crime	Violent Crime					Property Crime			
		Any	Murder	Forcible Rape[2]	Robbery	Aggrav. Assault	Any	Burglary	Larceny -Theft	Motor Vehicle Theft
City	1:8	1:81	1:7,147	1:718	1:228	1:141	1:9	1:34	1:13	1:181

Note: (1) Figures have been calculated by dividing the population of the city by the number of crimes reported to the FBI during 1996 and are expressed as odds (eg. 1:20 should be read as 1 in 20). (2) Figures have been calculated by dividing the female population of the city by the number of forcible rapes reported to the FBI during 1996. The female population of the city was estimated by calculating the ratio of females to males reported in the 1990 Census and applying that ratio to 1996 population estimate.
Source: FBI Uniform Crime Reports 1996

CRIME STATISTICS

Total Crimes and Total Crime Rates: 1977 - 1996

Year	Number				Rate per 100,000 population			
	City	Suburbs[2]	MSA[1]	U.S.	City	Suburbs[3]	MSA[1]	U.S.
1977	8,444	1,571	10,015	10,984,500	6,921.3	1,907.5	4,900.7	5,077.6
1978	9,111	1,736	10,847	11,209,000	7,468.0	2,031.8	5,228.9	5,140.3
1979	10,008	1,786	11,794	12,249,500	8,032.7	2,808.4	6,267.2	5,565.5
1980	9,595	1,856	11,451	13,408,300	8,268.4	2,723.8	6,217.2	5,950.0
1981	10,742	1,705	12,447	13,423,800	9,154.9	2,474.7	6,683.5	5,858.2
1982	8,927	1,316	10,243	12,974,400	7,522.7	1,888.6	5,438.4	5,603.6
1983	8,350	1,056	9,406	12,108,600	6,987.2	1,940.5	5,408.1	5,175.0
1984	8,449	1,014	9,463	11,881,800	6,956.8	1,877.4	5,393.3	5,031.3
1985	9,277	923	10,200	12,431,400	7,760.6	1,641.3	5,802.8	5,207.1
1986	10,430	1,077	11,507	13,211,900	8,687.0	1,906.3	6,517.3	5,480.4
1987	10,941	1,164	12,105	13,508,700	9,168.6	1,986.7	6,803.6	5,550.0
1988	11,473	1,484	12,957	13,923,100	9,540.8	2,503.2	7,216.9	5,664.2
1989	11,808	1,059	12,867	14,251,400	9,583.0	2,477.9	7,753.3	5,741.0
1990	11,416	1,269	12,685	14,475,600	9,522.6	3,088.1	7,880.1	5,820.3
1991	12,598	1,262	13,860	14,872,900	10,435.3	3,049.8	8,550.0	5,897.8
1992	12,225	1,265	13,490	14,438,200	10,014.0	3,023.3	8,229.6	5,660.2
1993	n/a	n/a	n/a	14,144,800	n/a	n/a	n/a	5,484.4
1994	n/a	n/a	n/a	13,989,500	n/a	n/a	n/a	5,373.5
1995	15,931	n/a	n/a	13,862,700	13,148.2	n/a	n/a	5,275.9
1996	15,394	n/a	n/a	13,473,600	12,670.5	n/a	n/a	5,078.9

Notes: (1) Metropolitan Statistical Area - see Appendix A for areas included; (2) calculated by the editors using the following formula: (number of crimes in the MSA minus number of crimes in the city); (3) calculated by the editors using the following formula: ((number of crimes in the MSA minus number of crimes in the city) ÷ (population of the MSA minus population of the city)) x 100,000; n/a not avail.
Source: U.S. Department of Justice, FBI Uniform Crime Reports, 1977 - 1996

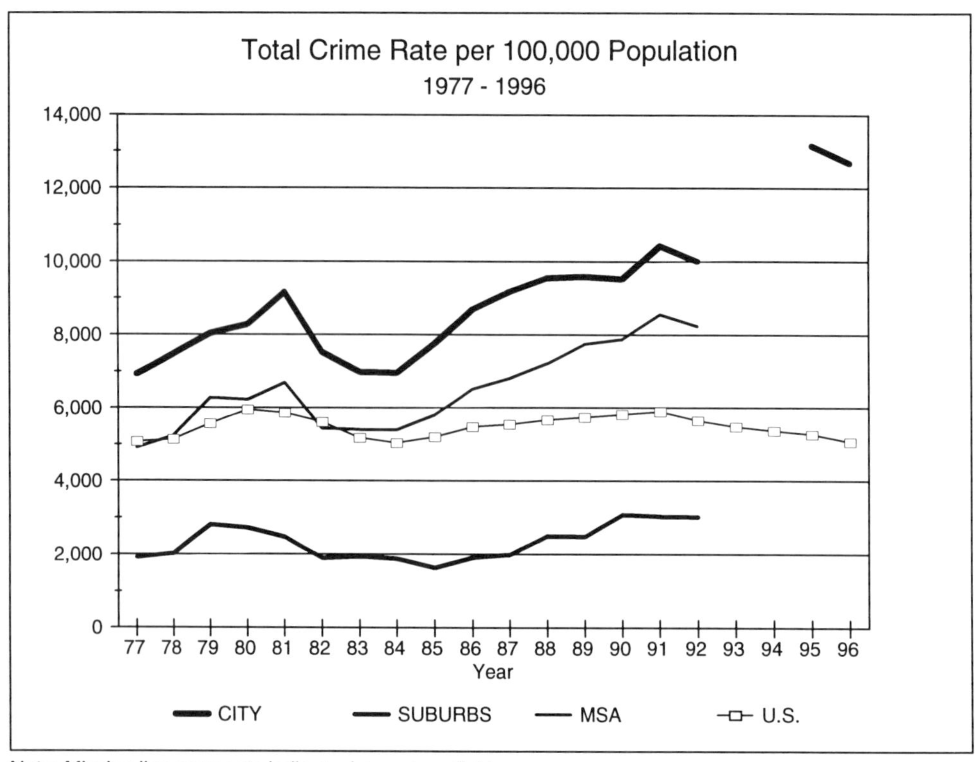

Note: Missing line segments indicate data not available.

Violent Crimes and Violent Crime Rates: 1977 - 1996

Year	Number				Rate per 100,000 population			
	City	Suburbs[2]	MSA[1]	U.S.	City	Suburbs[3]	MSA[1]	U.S.
1977	692	94	786	1,029,580	567.2	114.1	384.6	475.9
1978	698	110	808	1,085,550	572.1	128.7	389.5	497.8
1979	903	148	1,051	1,208,030	724.8	232.7	558.5	548.9
1980	745	165	910	1,344,520	642.0	242.1	494.1	596.6
1981	753	125	878	1,361,820	641.7	181.4	471.4	594.3
1982	594	116	710	1,322,390	500.6	166.5	377.0	571.1
1983	686	70	756	1,258,090	574.0	128.6	434.7	537.7
1984	703	117	820	1,273,280	578.8	216.6	467.3	539.2
1985	694	124	818	1,328,800	580.6	220.5	465.4	556.6
1986	800	78	878	1,489,170	666.3	138.1	497.3	617.7
1987	881	65	946	1,484,000	738.3	110.9	531.7	609.7
1988	888	64	952	1,566,220	738.4	108.0	530.3	637.2
1989	980	77	1,057	1,646,040	795.3	180.2	636.9	663.1
1990	1,162	108	1,270	1,820,130	969.3	262.8	788.9	731.8
1991	1,427	80	1,507	1,911,770	1,182.0	193.3	929.6	758.1
1992	1,627	93	1,720	1,932,270	1,332.7	222.3	1,049.3	757.5
1993	n/a	n/a	n/a	1,926,020	n/a	n/a	n/a	746.8
1994	n/a	n/a	n/a	1,857,670	n/a	n/a	n/a	713.6
1995	1,507	n/a	n/a	1,798,790	1,243.8	n/a	n/a	684.6
1996	1,502	n/a	n/a	1,682,280	1,236.3	n/a	n/a	634.1

Notes: Violent crimes include murder, forcible rape, robbery and aggravated assault; n/a not available; (1) Metropolitan Statistical Area - see Appendix A for areas included; (2) calculated by the editors using the following formula: (number of crimes in the MSA minus number of crimes in the city); (3) calculated by the editors using the following formula: ((number of crimes in the MSA minus number of crimes in the city) ÷ (population of the MSA minus population of the city)) x 100,000
Source: U.S. Department of Justice, FBI Uniform Crime Reports, 1977 - 1996

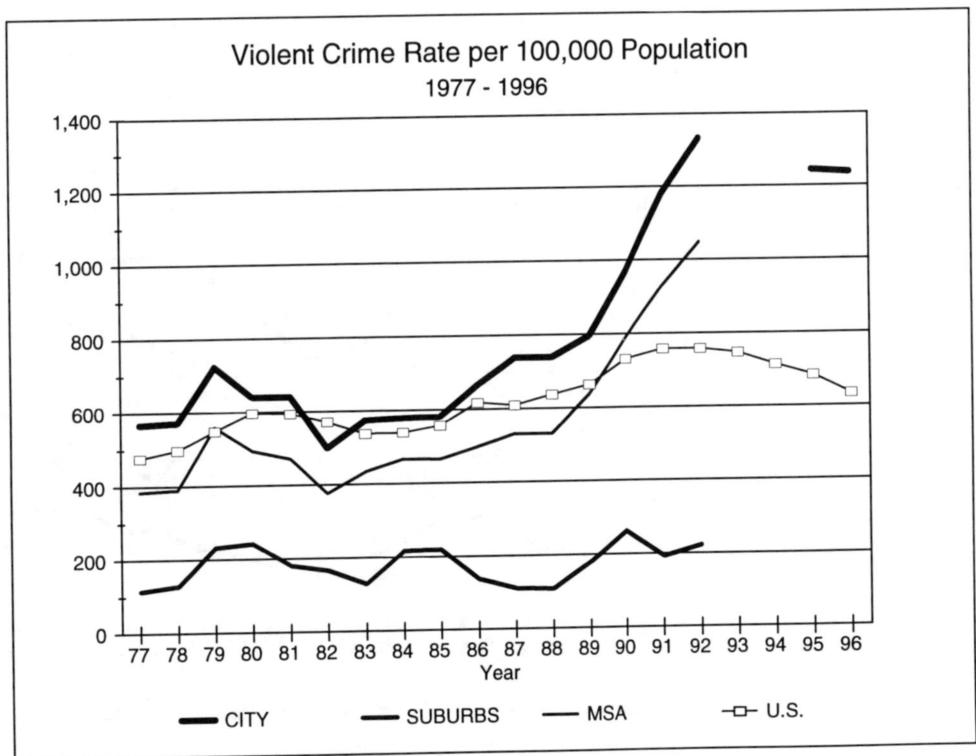

Note: Missing line segments indicate data not available.

Property Crimes and Property Crime Rates: 1977 - 1996

Year	Number				Rate per 100,000 population			
	City	Suburbs[2]	MSA[1]	U.S.	City	Suburbs[3]	MSA[1]	U.S.
1977	7,752	1,477	9,229	9,955,000	6,354.1	1,793.3	4,516.1	4,601.7
1978	8,413	1,626	10,039	10,123,400	6,895.9	1,903.0	4,839.4	4,642.5
1979	9,105	1,638	10,743	11,041,500	7,307.9	2,575.7	5,708.7	5,016.6
1980	8,850	1,691	10,541	12,063,700	7,626.4	2,481.7	5,723.1	5,353.3
1981	9,989	1,580	11,569	12,061,900	8,513.2	2,293.2	6,212.1	5,263.9
1982	8,333	1,200	9,533	11,652,000	7,022.2	1,722.2	5,061.4	5,032.5
1983	7,664	986	8,650	10,850,500	6,413.2	1,811.8	4,973.4	4,637.4
1984	7,746	897	8,643	10,608,500	6,378.0	1,660.8	4,925.9	4,492.1
1985	8,583	799	9,382	11,102,600	7,180.0	1,420.8	5,337.5	4,650.5
1986	9,630	999	10,629	11,722,700	8,020.7	1,768.2	6,020.0	4,862.6
1987	10,060	1,099	11,159	12,024,700	8,430.3	1,875.7	6,271.9	4,940.3
1988	10,585	1,420	12,005	12,356,900	8,802.3	2,395.2	6,686.6	5,027.1
1989	10,828	982	11,810	12,605,400	8,787.7	2,297.7	7,116.3	5,077.9
1990	10,254	1,161	11,415	12,655,500	8,553.3	2,825.3	7,091.1	5,088.5
1991	11,171	1,182	12,353	12,961,100	9,253.3	2,856.5	7,620.4	5,139.7
1992	10,598	1,172	11,770	12,505,900	8,681.3	2,801.0	7,180.3	4,902.7
1993	n/a	n/a	n/a	12,218,800	n/a	n/a	n/a	4,737.6
1994	n/a	n/a	n/a	12,131,900	n/a	n/a	n/a	4,660.0
1995	14,424	n/a	n/a	12,063,900	11,904.4	n/a	n/a	4,591.3
1996	13,892	n/a	n/a	11,791,300	11,434.2	n/a	n/a	4,444.8

Notes: Property crimes include burglary, larceny-theft and motor vehicle theft; n/a not available; (1) Metropolitan Statistical Area - see Appendix A for areas included; (2) calculated by the editors using the following formula: (number of crimes in the MSA minus number of crimes in the city); (3) calculated by the editors using the following formula: ((number of crimes in the MSA minus number of crimes in the city) ÷ (population of the MSA minus population of the city)) x 100,000
Source: U.S. Department of Justice, FBI Uniform Crime Reports, 1977 - 1996

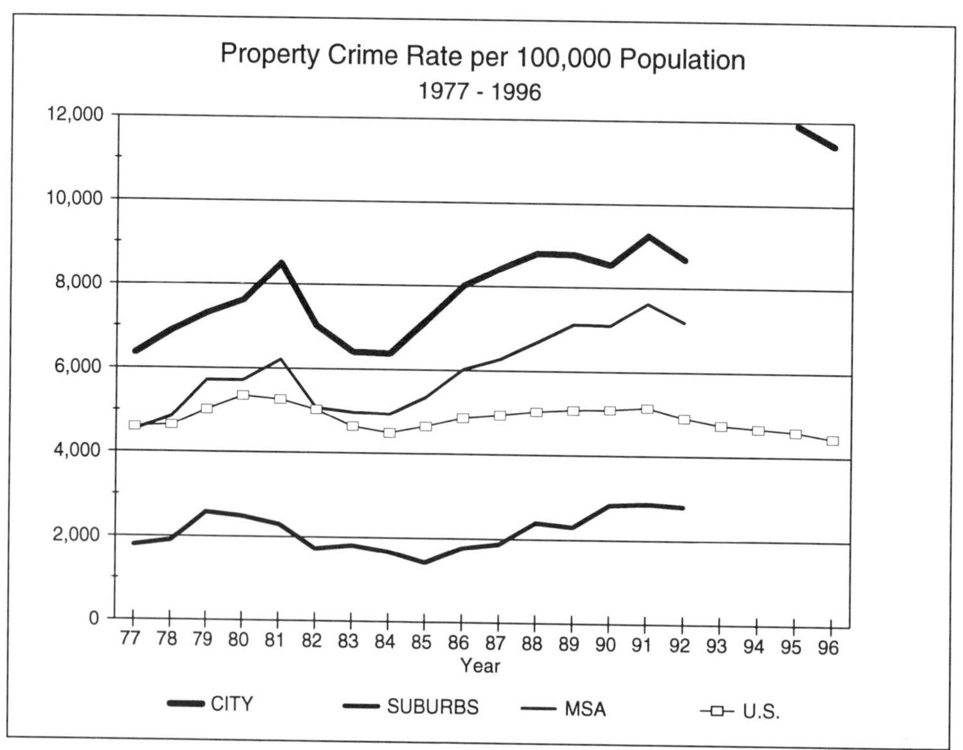

Note: Missing line segments indicate data not available.

Murders and Murder Rates: 1977 - 1996

Year	Number				Rate per 100,000 population			
	City	Suburbs[2]	MSA[1]	U.S.	City	Suburbs[3]	MSA[1]	U.S.
1977	13	0	13	19,120	10.7	0.0	6.4	8.8
1978	13	3	16	19,560	10.7	3.5	7.7	9.0
1979	9	2	11	21,460	7.2	3.1	5.8	9.7
1980	15	6	21	23,040	12.9	8.8	11.4	10.2
1981	13	3	16	22,520	11.1	4.4	8.6	9.8
1982	6	1	7	21,010	5.1	1.4	3.7	9.1
1983	5	3	8	19,310	4.2	5.5	4.6	8.3
1984	3	2	5	18,690	2.5	3.7	2.8	7.9
1985	6	1	7	18,980	5.0	1.8	4.0	7.9
1986	12	0	12	20,610	10.0	0.0	6.8	8.6
1987	4	1	5	20,100	3.4	1.7	2.8	8.3
1988	7	1	8	20,680	5.8	1.7	4.5	8.4
1989	11	0	11	21,500	8.9	0.0	6.6	8.7
1990	11	0	11	23,440	9.2	0.0	6.8	9.4
1991	16	1	17	24,700	13.3	2.4	10.5	9.8
1992	8	4	12	23,760	6.6	9.6	7.3	9.3
1993	n/a	n/a	n/a	24,530	n/a	n/a	n/a	9.5
1994	n/a	n/a	n/a	23,330	n/a	n/a	n/a	9.0
1995	9	n/a	n/a	21,610	7.4	n/a	n/a	8.2
1996	17	n/a	n/a	19,650	14.0	n/a	n/a	7.4

Notes: (1) Metropolitan Statistical Area - see Appendix A for areas included; (2) calculated by the editors using the following formula: (number of crimes in the MSA minus number of crimes in the city); (3) calculated by the editors using the following formula: ((number of crimes in the MSA minus number of crimes in the city) ÷ (population of the MSA minus population of the city)) x 100,000; n/a not avail.
Source: U.S. Department of Justice, FBI Uniform Crime Reports, 1977 - 1996

Forcible Rapes and Forcible Rape Rates: 1977 - 1996

Year	Number				Rate per 100,000 population			
	City	Suburbs[2]	MSA[1]	U.S.	City	Suburbs[3]	MSA[1]	U.S.
1977	57	8	65	63,500	46.7	9.7	31.8	29.4
1978	63	6	69	67,610	51.6	7.0	33.3	31.0
1979	74	6	80	76,390	59.4	9.4	42.5	34.7
1980	66	3	69	82,990	56.9	4.4	37.5	36.8
1981	60	6	66	82,500	51.1	8.7	35.4	36.0
1982	41	6	47	78,770	34.6	8.6	25.0	34.0
1983	51	6	57	78,920	42.7	11.0	32.8	33.7
1984	59	3	62	84,230	48.6	5.6	35.3	35.7
1985	56	0	56	88,670	46.8	0.0	31.9	37.1
1986	57	9	66	91,460	47.5	15.9	37.4	37.9
1987	71	5	76	91,110	59.5	8.5	42.7	37.4
1988	55	3	58	92,490	45.7	5.1	32.3	37.6
1989	62	15	77	94,500	50.3	35.1	46.4	38.1
1990	80	7	87	102,560	66.7	17.0	54.0	41.2
1991	79	6	85	106,590	65.4	14.5	52.4	42.3
1992	82	8	90	109,060	67.2	19.1	54.9	42.8
1993	n/a	n/a	n/a	106,010	n/a	n/a	n/a	41.1
1994	n/a	n/a	n/a	102,220	n/a	n/a	n/a	39.3
1995	89	n/a	n/a	97,470	73.5	n/a	n/a	37.1
1996	89	n/a	n/a	95,770	73.3	n/a	n/a	36.1

Notes: (1) Metropolitan Statistical Area - see Appendix A for areas included; (2) calculated by the editors using the following formula: (number of crimes in the MSA minus number of crimes in the city); (3) calculated by the editors using the following formula: ((number of crimes in the MSA minus number of crimes in the city) ÷ (population of the MSA minus population of the city)) x 100,000; n/a not avail.
Source: U.S. Department of Justice, FBI Uniform Crime Reports, 1977 - 1996

Robberies and Robbery Rates: 1977 - 1996

Year	Number				Rate per 100,000 population			
	City	Suburbs[2]	MSA[1]	U.S.	City	Suburbs[3]	MSA[1]	U.S.
1977	209	14	223	412,610	171.3	17.0	109.1	190.7
1978	207	10	217	426,930	169.7	11.7	104.6	195.8
1979	262	10	272	480,700	210.3	15.7	144.5	218.4
1980	193	13	206	565,840	166.3	19.1	111.8	251.1
1981	249	7	256	592,910	212.2	10.2	137.5	258.7
1982	214	13	227	553,130	180.3	18.7	120.5	238.9
1983	257	4	261	506,570	215.1	7.4	150.1	216.5
1984	216	5	221	485,010	177.9	9.3	126.0	205.4
1985	226	3	229	497,870	189.1	5.3	130.3	208.5
1986	244	4	248	542,780	203.2	7.1	140.5	225.1
1987	261	9	270	517,700	218.7	15.4	151.8	212.7
1988	252	9	261	542,970	209.6	15.2	145.4	220.9
1989	259	3	262	578,330	210.2	7.0	157.9	233.0
1990	290	14	304	639,270	241.9	34.1	188.8	257.0
1991	332	9	341	687,730	275.0	21.7	210.4	272.7
1992	369	11	380	672,480	302.3	26.3	231.8	263.6
1993	n/a	n/a	n/a	659,870	n/a	n/a	n/a	255.9
1994	n/a	n/a	n/a	618,950	n/a	n/a	n/a	237.7
1995	504	n/a	n/a	580,510	416.0	n/a	n/a	220.9
1996	533	n/a	n/a	537,050	438.7	n/a	n/a	202.4

Notes: (1) Metropolitan Statistical Area - see Appendix A for areas included; (2) calculated by the editors using the following formula: (number of crimes in the MSA minus number of crimes in the city); (3) calculated by the editors using the following formula: ((number of crimes in the MSA minus number of crimes in the city) ÷ (population of the MSA minus population of the city)) x 100,000; n/a not avail.
Source: U.S. Department of Justice, FBI Uniform Crime Reports, 1977 - 1996

Aggravated Assaults and Aggravated Assault Rates: 1977 - 1996

Year	Number				Rate per 100,000 population			
	City	Suburbs[2]	MSA[1]	U.S.	City	Suburbs[3]	MSA[1]	U.S.
1977	413	72	485	534,350	338.5	87.4	237.3	247.0
1978	415	91	506	571,460	340.2	106.5	243.9	262.1
1979	558	130	688	629,480	447.9	204.4	365.6	286.0
1980	471	143	614	672,650	405.9	209.9	333.4	298.5
1981	431	109	540	663,900	367.3	158.2	290.0	289.7
1982	333	96	429	669,480	280.6	137.8	227.8	289.2
1983	373	57	430	653,290	312.1	104.7	247.2	279.2
1984	425	107	532	685,350	349.9	198.1	303.2	290.2
1985	406	120	526	723,250	339.6	213.4	299.2	302.9
1986	487	65	552	834,320	405.6	115.0	312.6	346.1
1987	545	50	595	855,090	456.7	85.3	334.4	351.3
1988	574	51	625	910,090	477.3	86.0	348.1	370.2
1989	648	59	707	951,710	525.9	138.1	426.0	383.4
1990	781	87	868	1,054,860	651.5	211.7	539.2	424.1
1991	1,000	64	1,064	1,092,740	828.3	154.7	656.4	433.3
1992	1,168	70	1,238	1,126,970	956.8	167.3	755.2	441.8
1993	n/a	n/a	n/a	1,135,610	n/a	n/a	n/a	440.3
1994	n/a	n/a	n/a	1,113,180	n/a	n/a	n/a	427.6
1995	905	n/a	n/a	1,099,210	746.9	n/a	n/a	418.3
1996	863	n/a	n/a	1,029,810	710.3	n/a	n/a	388.2

Notes: (1) Metropolitan Statistical Area - see Appendix A for areas included; (2) calculated by the editors using the following formula: (number of crimes in the MSA minus number of crimes in the city); (3) calculated by the editors using the following formula: ((number of crimes in the MSA minus number of crimes in the city) ÷ (population of the MSA minus population of the city)) x 100,000; n/a not avail.
Source: U.S. Department of Justice, FBI Uniform Crime Reports, 1977 - 1996

Burglaries and Burglary Rates: 1977 - 1996

Year	Number				Rate per 100,000 population			
	City	Suburbs[2]	MSA[1]	U.S.	City	Suburbs[3]	MSA[1]	U.S.
1977	2,262	459	2,721	3,071,500	1,854.1	557.3	1,331.5	1,419.8
1978	2,374	550	2,924	3,128,300	1,945.9	643.7	1,409.5	1,434.6
1979	2,436	521	2,957	3,327,700	1,955.2	819.3	1,571.3	1,511.9
1980	2,943	585	3,528	3,795,200	2,536.1	858.5	1,915.5	1,684.1
1981	3,759	624	4,383	3,779,700	3,203.6	905.7	2,353.5	1,649.5
1982	2,593	468	3,061	3,447,100	2,185.1	671.6	1,625.2	1,488.8
1983	1,985	364	2,349	3,129,900	1,661.0	668.9	1,350.6	1,337.7
1984	1,918	392	2,310	2,984,400	1,579.3	725.8	1,316.5	1,263.7
1985	2,245	368	2,613	3,073,300	1,878.0	654.4	1,486.6	1,287.3
1986	4,038	384	4,422	3,241,400	3,363.2	679.7	2,504.5	1,344.6
1987	2,866	402	3,268	3,236,200	2,401.7	686.1	1,836.8	1,329.6
1988	2,900	485	3,385	3,218,100	2,411.6	818.1	1,885.4	1,309.2
1989	3,047	349	3,396	3,168,200	2,472.9	816.6	2,046.3	1,276.3
1990	2,878	417	3,295	3,073,900	2,400.7	1,014.8	2,046.9	1,235.9
1991	3,524	418	3,942	3,157,200	2,919.0	1,010.1	2,431.8	1,252.0
1992	3,627	449	4,076	2,979,900	2,971.0	1,073.1	2,486.6	1,168.2
1993	n/a	n/a	n/a	2,834,800	n/a	n/a	n/a	1,099.2
1994	n/a	n/a	n/a	2,712,800	n/a	n/a	n/a	1,042.0
1995	5,894	n/a	n/a	2,593,800	4,864.4	n/a	n/a	987.1
1996	3,563	n/a	n/a	2,501,500	2,932.6	n/a	n/a	943.0

Notes: (1) Metropolitan Statistical Area - see Appendix A for areas included; (2) calculated by the editors using the following formula: (number of crimes in the MSA minus number of crimes in the city); (3) calculated by the editors using the following formula: ((number of crimes in the MSA minus number of crimes in the city) ÷ (population of the MSA minus population of the city)) x 100,000; n/a not avail.
Source: U.S. Department of Justice, FBI Uniform Crime Reports, 1977 - 1996

Larceny-Thefts and Larceny-Theft Rates: 1977 - 1996

Year	Number				Rate per 100,000 population			
	City	Suburbs[2]	MSA[1]	U.S.	City	Suburbs[3]	MSA[1]	U.S.
1977	5,153	963	6,116	5,905,700	4,223.8	1,169.3	2,992.8	2,729.9
1978	5,699	1,009	6,708	5,991,000	4,671.3	1,180.9	3,233.7	2,747.4
1979	6,279	1,024	7,303	6,601,000	5,039.7	1,610.2	3,880.8	2,999.1
1980	5,552	1,033	6,585	7,136,900	4,784.4	1,516.0	3,575.2	3,167.0
1981	5,880	894	6,774	7,194,400	5,011.2	1,297.6	3,637.4	3,139.7
1982	5,472	671	6,143	7,142,500	4,611.2	963.0	3,261.5	3,084.8
1983	5,415	595	6,010	6,712,800	4,531.2	1,093.3	3,455.5	2,868.9
1984	5,586	471	6,057	6,591,900	4,599.5	872.0	3,452.1	2,791.3
1985	6,039	406	6,445	6,926,400	5,051.9	722.0	3,666.6	2,901.2
1986	5,233	569	5,802	7,257,200	4,358.5	1,007.1	3,286.1	3,010.3
1987	6,795	640	7,435	7,499,900	5,694.2	1,092.3	4,178.8	3,081.3
1988	7,270	878	8,148	7,705,900	6,045.6	1,481.0	4,538.3	3,134.9
1989	7,311	597	7,908	7,872,400	5,933.4	1,396.9	4,765.1	3,171.3
1990	6,948	712	7,660	7,945,700	5,795.7	1,732.7	4,758.5	3,194.8
1991	7,148	725	7,873	8,142,200	5,920.9	1,752.1	4,856.7	3,228.8
1992	6,523	697	7,220	7,915,200	5,343.3	1,665.8	4,404.6	3,103.0
1993	n/a	n/a	n/a	7,820,900	n/a	n/a	n/a	3,032.4
1994	n/a	n/a	n/a	7,879,800	n/a	n/a	n/a	3,026.7
1995	7,535	n/a	n/a	7,997,700	6,218.8	n/a	n/a	3,043.8
1996	9,659	n/a	n/a	7,894,600	7,950.1	n/a	n/a	2,975.9

Notes: (1) Metropolitan Statistical Area - see Appendix A for areas included; (2) calculated by the editors using the following formula: (number of crimes in the MSA minus number of crimes in the city); (3) calculated by the editors using the following formula: ((number of crimes in the MSA minus number of crimes in the city) ÷ (population of the MSA minus population of the city)) x 100,000; n/a not avail.
Source: U.S. Department of Justice, FBI Uniform Crime Reports, 1977 - 1996

Motor Vehicle Thefts and Motor Vehicle Theft Rates: 1977 - 1996

Year	Number				Rate per 100,000 population			
	City	Suburbs[2]	MSA[1]	U.S.	City	Suburbs[3]	MSA[1]	U.S.
1977	337	55	392	977,700	276.2	66.8	191.8	451.9
1978	340	67	407	1,004,100	278.7	78.4	196.2	460.5
1979	390	93	483	1,112,800	313.0	146.2	256.7	505.6
1980	355	73	428	1,131,700	305.9	107.1	232.4	502.2
1981	350	62	412	1,087,800	298.3	90.0	221.2	474.7
1982	268	61	329	1,062,400	225.8	87.5	174.7	458.8
1983	264	27	291	1,007,900	220.9	49.6	167.3	430.8
1984	242	34	276	1,032,200	199.3	63.0	157.3	437.1
1985	299	25	324	1,102,900	250.1	44.5	184.3	462.0
1986	359	46	405	1,224,100	299.0	81.4	229.4	507.8
1987	399	57	456	1,288,700	334.4	97.3	256.3	529.4
1988	415	57	472	1,432,900	345.1	96.1	262.9	582.9
1989	470	36	506	1,564,800	381.4	84.2	304.9	630.4
1990	428	32	460	1,635,900	357.0	77.9	285.8	657.8
1991	499	39	538	1,661,700	413.3	94.2	331.9	659.0
1992	448	26	474	1,610,800	367.0	62.1	289.2	631.5
1993	n/a	n/a	n/a	1,563,100	n/a	n/a	n/a	606.1
1994	n/a	n/a	n/a	1,539,300	n/a	n/a	n/a	591.3
1995	995	n/a	n/a	1,472,400	821.2	n/a	n/a	560.4
1996	670	n/a	n/a	1,395,200	551.5	n/a	n/a	525.9

Notes: (1) Metropolitan Statistical Area - see Appendix A for areas included; (2) calculated by the editors using the following formula: (number of crimes in the MSA minus number of crimes in the city); (3) calculated by the editors using the following formula: ((number of crimes in the MSA minus number of crimes in the city) ÷ (population of the MSA minus population of the city)) x 100,000; n/a not avail.
Source: U.S. Department of Justice, FBI Uniform Crime Reports, 1977 - 1996

HATE CRIMES

Criminal Incidents by Bias Motivation

Area	Race	Ethnicity	Religion	Sexual Orientation
Topeka	n/a	n/a	n/a	n/a

Notes: Figures include both violent and property crimes. Law enforcement agencies must have submitted data for at least one quarter of calendar year 1995 to be included in this report, therefore figures shown may not represent complete 12-month totals; n/a not available
Source: U.S. Department of Justice, FBI Uniform Crime Reports, Hate Crime Statistics 1995

LAW ENFORCEMENT

Full-Time Law Enforcement Employees

Jurisdiction	Police Employees			Police Officers per 100,000 population
	Total	Officers	Civilians	
Topeka	353	272	81	223.9

Notes: Data as of October 31, 1996
Source: U.S. Department of Justice, FBI Uniform Crime Reports, 1996

CORRECTIONS

Federal Correctional Facilities

Type	Year Opened	Security Level	Sex of Inmates	Rated Capacity	Population on 7/1/95	Number of Staff
None listed						

Notes: Data as of 1995
Source: Bureau of Justice Statistics, Sourcebook of Criminal Justice Statistics Online

City/County/Regional Correctional Facilities

Name	Year Opened	Year Renov.	Rated Capacity	1995 Pop.	Number of COs[1]	Number of Staff	ACA[2] Accred.
Shawnee Co Jail	1987	1990	220	n/a	n/a	n/a	No

Notes: Data as of April 1996; (1) Correctional Officers; (2) American Correctional Assn. Accreditation
Source: American Correctional Association, 1996-1998 National Jail and Adult Detention Directory

Private Adult Correctional Facilities

Name	Date Opened	Rated Capacity	Present Pop.	Security Level	Facility Construct.	Expans. Plans	ACA[1] Accred.
None listed							

Notes: Data as of December 1996; (1) American Correctional Association Accreditation
Source: University of Florida, Center for Studies in Criminology and Law, Private Adult Correctional Facility Census, 10th Ed., March 15, 1997

Characteristics of Shock Incarceration Programs

Jurisdiction	Year Program Began	Number of Camps	Average Num. of Inmates	Number of Beds	Program Length	Voluntary/ Mandatory
Kansas	1991	1	95	95	180 days	Mandatory

Note: Data as of July 1996;
Source: Sourcebook of Criminal Justice Statistics Online

DEATH PENALTY

Death Penalty Statistics

State	Prisoners Executed		Prisoners Under Sentence of Death					Avg. No. of Years on Death Row[4]
	1930-1995	1996[1]	Total[2]	White[3]	Black[3]	Hisp.	Women	
Kansas	15	0	0	0	0	0	0	0.0

Notes: Data as of 12/31/95 unless otherwise noted; (1) Data as of 7/31/97; (2) Includes persons of other races; (3) Includes people of Hispanic origin; (4) Covers prisoners sentenced 1974 through 1995
Source: Bureau of Justice Statistics, Capital Punishment 1995 (released 12/96); Death Penalty Information Center Web Site, 9/30/97

Capital Offenses and Methods of Execution

Capital Offenses in Kansas	Minimum Age for Imposition of Death Penalty	Mentally Retarded Excluded	Methods of Execution[1]
Capital murder with 7 aggravating circumstances.	18	Yes	Lethal injection

Notes: Data as of 12/31/95 unless otherwise noted; (1) Data as of 7/31/97
Source: Bureau of Justice Statistics, Capital Punishment 1995 (released 12/96); Death Penalty Information Center Web Site, 9/30/97

LAWS

Statutory Provisions Relating to the Purchase, Ownership and Use of Handguns

Jurisdiction	Instant Background Check	Federal Waiting Period Applies[1]	State Waiting Period (days)	License or Permit to Purchase	Regis-tration	Record of Sale Sent to Police	Concealed Carry Law
Kansas	No	Yes	(a)	(a)	(a)	No	Yes[b]

Note: Data as of 1996; (1) The Federal 5-day waiting period for handgun purchases applies to states that don't have instant background checks, waiting period requirements, or licensing procedures exempting them from the Federal requirement; (a) Local ordinance in certain cities or counties; (b) No permit system exists and concealed carry is prohibited
Source: Sourcebook of Criminal Justice Statistics Online

Statutory Provisions Relating to Alcohol Use and Driving

Jurisdiction	Drinking Age	Blood Alcohol Concentration Levels as Evidence in State Courts[1]		Open Container Law[1]	Anti-Consump-tion Law[1]	Dram Shop Law[1]
		Illegal per se at 0.10%	Presumption at 0.10%			
Kansas	21	(a)	(a,b)	Yes	Yes	No

Note: Data as of January 1, 1997; (1) See Appendix C for an explanation of terms; (a) 0.08%; (b) Constitutes prima facie evidence
Source: Sourcebook of Criminal Justice Statistics Online

Statutory Provisions Relating to Hate Crimes

Jurisdiction	Bias-Motivated Violence and Intimidation						Institutional Vandalism
		Criminal Penalty					
	Civil Action	Race/ Religion/ Ethnicity	Sexual Orientation	Mental/ Physical Disability	Gender	Age	
Kansas	No	No	No	No	No	No	Yes

Source: Anti-Defamation League, 1997 Hate Crimes Laws

Tucson, Arizona

OVERVIEW

The total crime rate for the city decreased 7.7% between 1977 and 1996. During that same period, the violent crime rate increased 109.9% and the property crime rate decreased 13.8%.

Among violent crimes, the rates for: Murders decreased 16.4%; Forcible Rapes increased 55.1%; Robberies increased 49.3%; and Aggravated Assaults increased 160.3%.

Among property crimes, the rates for: Burglaries decreased 60.6%; Larceny-Thefts increased 2.5%; and Motor Vehicle Thefts increased 100.3%.

ANTI-CRIME PROGRAMS

Information not available at time of publication.

CRIME RISK

Your Chances of Becoming a Victim[1]

Area	Any Crime	Violent Crime					Property Crime			
		Any	Murder	Forcible Rape[2]	Robbery	Aggrav. Assault	Any	Burglary	Larceny -Theft	Motor Vehicle Theft
City	1:10	1:91	1:10,269	1:862	1:367	1:132	1:11	1:70	1:17	1:79

Note: (1) Figures have been calculated by dividing the population of the city by the number of crimes reported to the FBI during 1996 and are expressed as odds (eg. 1:20 should be read as 1 in 20).
(2) Figures have been calculated by dividing the female population of the city by the number of forcible rapes reported to the FBI during 1996. The female population of the city was estimated by calculating the ratio of females to males reported in the 1990 Census and applying that ratio to 1996 population estimate.
Source: FBI Uniform Crime Reports 1996

CRIME STATISTICS

Total Crimes and Total Crime Rates: 1977 - 1996

Year	Number				Rate per 100,000 population			
	City	Suburbs[2]	MSA[1]	U.S.	City	Suburbs[3]	MSA[1]	U.S.
1977	32,025	9,624	41,649	10,984,500	10,639.5	7,421.6	9,670.6	5,077.6
1978	29,111	8,902	38,013	11,209,000	9,639.4	5,794.3	8,342.9	5,140.3
1979	30,799	9,543	40,342	12,249,500	9,747.2	5,798.0	8,394.6	5,565.5
1980	35,947	11,077	47,024	13,408,300	10,843.5	5,527.7	8,840.8	5,950.0
1981	37,241	10,688	47,929	13,423,800	10,921.6	5,185.3	8,760.5	5,858.2
1982	35,925	10,147	46,072	12,974,400	10,288.8	4,807.5	8,223.8	5,603.6
1983	34,963	9,468	44,431	12,108,600	9,665.3	4,330.0	7,655.2	5,175.0
1984	35,616	10,328	45,944	11,881,800	9,570.4	4,541.0	7,662.6	5,031.3
1985	38,249	10,630	48,879	12,431,400	10,026.7	4,439.3	7,871.9	5,207.1
1986	38,840	12,112	50,952	13,211,900	9,782.8	4,859.5	7,884.0	5,480.4
1987	42,316	12,864	55,180	13,508,700	11,297.9	5,239.1	8,898.8	5,550.0
1988	48,699	13,674	62,373	13,923,100	12,709.4	5,443.5	9,832.3	5,664.2
1989	n/a	n/a	n/a	14,251,400	n/a	n/a	n/a	5,741.0
1990	48,158	14,771	62,929	14,475,600	11,879.4	5,648.8	9,436.3	5,820.3
1991	43,139	13,931	57,070	14,872,900	10,400.8	5,207.1	8,364.3	5,897.8
1992	44,133	14,647	58,780	14,438,200	10,412.8	5,357.7	8,430.6	5,660.2
1993	48,945	16,418	65,363	14,144,800	11,480.2	5,809.9	9,219.9	5,484.4
1994	54,093	19,625	73,718	13,989,500	12,254.8	6,707.9	10,043.8	5,373.5
1995	54,706	19,268	73,974	13,862,700	12,157.4	6,271.8	9,769.5	5,275.9
1996	46,385	16,043	62,428	13,473,600	9,819.3	4,974.4	7,853.6	5,078.9

Notes: (1) Metropolitan Statistical Area - see Appendix A for areas included; (2) calculated by the editors using the following formula: (number of crimes in the MSA minus number of crimes in the city); (3) calculated by the editors using the following formula: ((number of crimes in the MSA minus number of crimes in the city) ÷ (population of the MSA minus population of the city)) x 100,000; n/a not avail.
Source: U.S. Department of Justice, FBI Uniform Crime Reports, 1977 - 1996

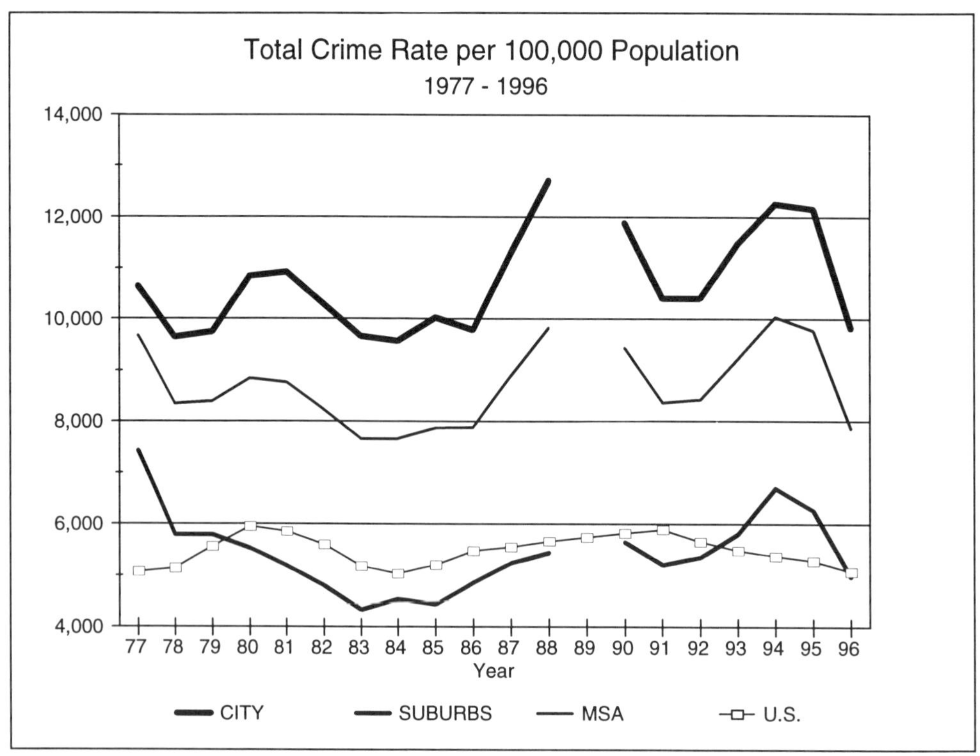

Note: Missing line segments indicate data not available.

Violent Crimes and Violent Crime Rates: 1977 - 1996

Year	Number				Rate per 100,000 population			
	City	Suburbs[2]	MSA[1]	U.S.	City	Suburbs[3]	MSA[1]	U.S.
1977	1,578	607	2,185	1,029,580	524.3	468.1	507.3	475.9
1978	1,654	624	2,278	1,085,550	547.7	406.2	500.0	497.8
1979	2,029	667	2,696	1,208,030	642.1	405.2	561.0	548.9
1980	2,584	693	3,277	1,344,520	779.5	345.8	616.1	596.6
1981	2,810	682	3,492	1,361,820	824.1	330.9	638.3	594.3
1982	2,925	672	3,597	1,322,390	837.7	318.4	642.1	571.1
1983	2,776	735	3,511	1,258,090	767.4	336.1	604.9	537.7
1984	2,959	702	3,661	1,273,280	795.1	308.7	610.6	539.2
1985	3,713	723	4,436	1,328,800	973.3	301.9	714.4	556.6
1986	3,644	1,026	4,670	1,489,170	917.8	411.6	722.6	617.7
1987	3,523	944	4,467	1,484,000	940.6	384.5	720.4	609.7
1988	3,527	949	4,476	1,566,220	920.5	377.8	705.6	637.2
1989	n/a	n/a	n/a	1,646,040	n/a	n/a	n/a	663.1
1990	3,680	928	4,608	1,820,130	907.8	354.9	691.0	731.8
1991	3,896	804	4,700	1,911,770	939.3	300.5	688.8	758.1
1992	4,327	920	5,247	1,932,270	1,020.9	336.5	752.6	757.5
1993	4,363	984	5,347	1,926,020	1,023.4	348.2	754.2	746.8
1994	4,882	1,077	5,959	1,857,670	1,106.0	368.1	811.9	713.6
1995	5,427	1,215	6,642	1,798,790	1,206.1	395.5	877.2	684.6
1996	5,199	1,233	6,432	1,682,280	1,100.6	382.3	809.2	634.1

Notes: Violent crimes include murder, forcible rape, robbery and aggravated assault; n/a not available; (1) Metropolitan Statistical Area - see Appendix A for areas included; (2) calculated by the editors using the following formula: (number of crimes in the MSA minus number of crimes in the city); (3) calculated by the editors using the following formula: ((number of crimes in the MSA minus number of crimes in the city) ÷ (population of the MSA minus population of the city)) x 100,000
Source: U.S. Department of Justice, FBI Uniform Crime Reports, 1977 - 1996

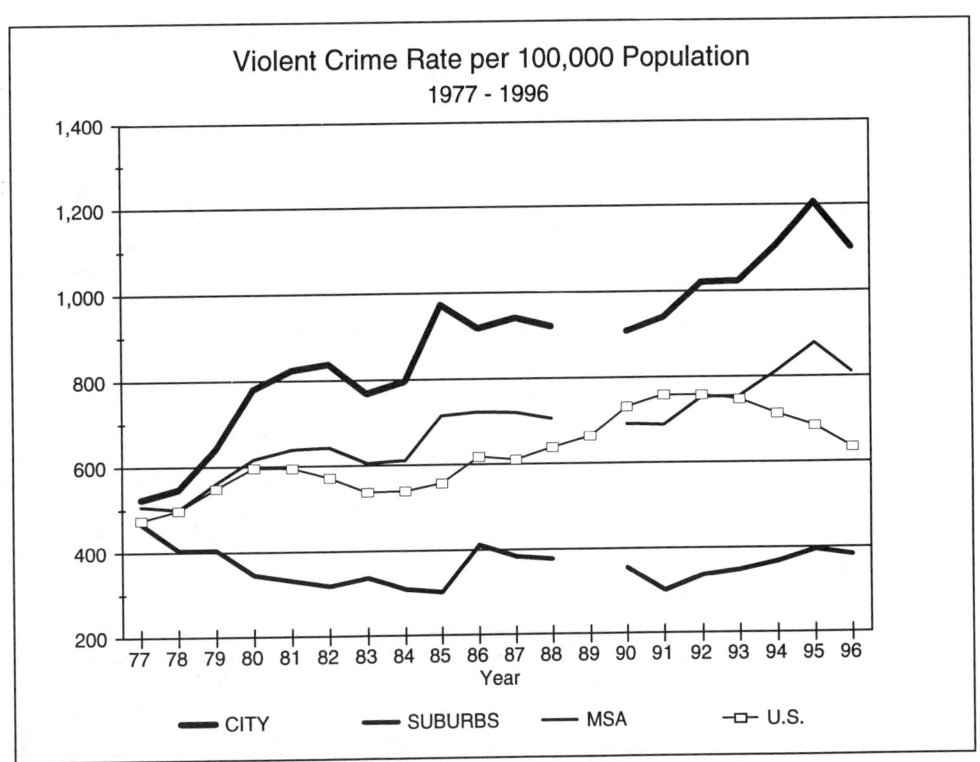

Note: Missing line segments indicate data not available.

Property Crimes and Property Crime Rates: 1977 - 1996

Year	Number				Rate per 100,000 population			
	City	Suburbs[2]	MSA[1]	U.S.	City	Suburbs[3]	MSA[1]	U.S.
1977	30,447	9,017	39,464	9,955,000	10,115.3	6,953.5	9,163.3	4,601.7
1978	27,457	8,278	35,735	10,123,400	9,091.7	5,388.1	7,842.9	4,642.5
1979	28,770	8,876	37,646	11,041,500	9,105.1	5,392.7	7,833.6	5,016.6
1980	33,363	10,384	43,747	12,063,700	10,064.1	5,181.9	8,224.7	5,353.3
1981	34,431	10,006	44,437	12,061,900	10,097.5	4,854.5	8,122.2	5,263.9
1982	33,000	9,475	42,475	11,652,000	9,451.1	4,489.2	7,581.7	5,032.5
1983	32,187	8,733	40,920	10,850,500	8,897.9	3,993.8	7,050.3	4,637.4
1984	32,657	9,626	42,283	10,608,500	8,775.3	4,232.3	7,052.0	4,492.1
1985	34,536	9,907	44,443	11,102,600	9,053.3	4,137.3	7,157.5	4,650.5
1986	35,196	11,086	46,282	11,722,700	8,865.0	4,447.8	7,161.4	4,862.6
1987	38,793	11,920	50,713	12,024,700	10,357.3	4,854.6	8,178.4	4,940.3
1988	45,172	12,725	57,897	12,356,900	11,788.9	5,065.7	9,126.7	5,027.1
1989	n/a	n/a	n/a	12,605,400	n/a	n/a	n/a	5,077.9
1990	44,478	13,843	58,321	12,655,500	10,971.7	5,293.9	8,745.4	5,088.5
1991	39,243	13,127	52,370	12,961,100	9,461.5	4,906.6	7,675.5	5,139.7
1992	39,806	13,727	53,533	12,505,900	9,391.8	5,021.1	7,678.1	4,902.7
1993	44,582	15,434	60,016	12,218,800	10,456.8	5,461.7	8,465.7	4,737.6
1994	49,211	18,548	67,759	12,131,900	11,148.8	6,339.8	9,231.9	4,660.0
1995	49,279	18,053	67,332	12,063,900	10,951.4	5,876.4	8,892.3	4,591.3
1996	41,186	14,810	55,996	11,791,300	8,718.7	4,592.1	7,044.5	4,444.8

Notes: Property crimes include burglary, larceny-theft and motor vehicle theft; n/a not available; (1) Metropolitan Statistical Area - see Appendix A for areas included; (2) calculated by the editors using the following formula: (number of crimes in the MSA minus number of crimes in the city); (3) calculated by the editors using the following formula: ((number of crimes in the MSA minus number of crimes in the city) ÷ (population of the MSA minus population of the city)) x 100,000
Source: U.S. Department of Justice, FBI Uniform Crime Reports, 1977 - 1996

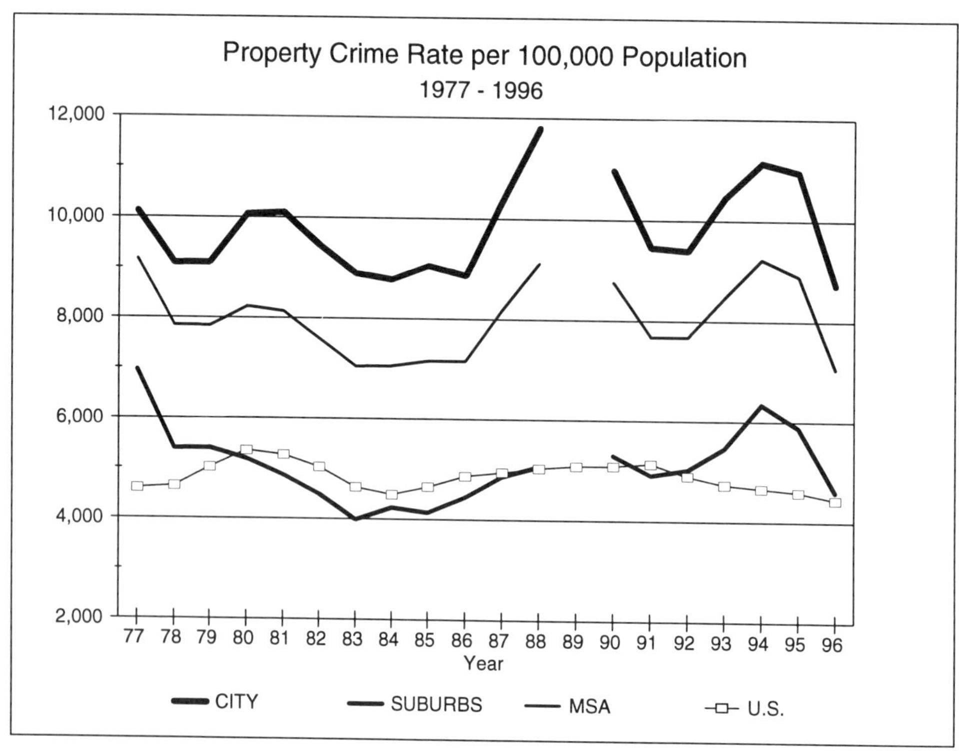

Note: Missing line segments indicate data not available.

Murders and Murder Rates: 1977 - 1996

Year	Number				Rate per 100,000 population			
	City	Suburbs[2]	MSA[1]	U.S.	City	Suburbs[3]	MSA[1]	U.S.
1977	35	13	48	19,120	11.6	10.0	11.1	8.8
1978	26	11	37	19,560	8.6	7.2	8.1	9.0
1979	14	14	28	21,460	4.4	8.5	5.8	9.7
1980	38	12	50	23,040	11.5	6.0	9.4	10.2
1981	28	10	38	22,520	8.2	4.9	6.9	9.8
1982	31	22	53	21,010	8.9	10.4	9.5	9.1
1983	26	14	40	19,310	7.2	6.4	6.9	8.3
1984	25	20	45	18,690	6.7	8.8	7.5	7.9
1985	32	19	51	18,980	8.4	7.9	8.2	7.9
1986	41	22	63	20,610	10.3	8.8	9.7	8.6
1987	23	15	38	20,100	6.1	6.1	6.1	8.3
1988	31	25	56	20,680	8.1	10.0	8.8	8.4
1989	n/a	n/a	n/a	21,500	n/a	n/a	n/a	8.7
1990	30	21	51	23,440	7.4	8.0	7.6	9.4
1991	24	20	44	24,700	5.8	7.5	6.4	9.8
1992	42	18	60	23,760	9.9	6.6	8.6	9.3
1993	44	21	65	24,530	10.3	7.4	9.2	9.5
1994	37	19	56	23,330	8.4	6.5	7.6	9.0
1995	65	27	92	21,610	14.4	8.8	12.2	8.2
1996	46	29	75	19,650	9.7	9.0	9.4	7.4

Notes: (1) Metropolitan Statistical Area - see Appendix A for areas included; (2) calculated by the editors using the following formula: (number of crimes in the MSA minus number of crimes in the city); (3) calculated by the editors using the following formula: ((number of crimes in the MSA minus number of crimes in the city) ÷ (population of the MSA minus population of the city)) x 100,000; n/a not avail.
Source: U.S. Department of Justice, FBI Uniform Crime Reports, 1977 - 1996

Forcible Rapes and Forcible Rape Rates: 1977 - 1996

Year	Number				Rate per 100,000 population			
	City	Suburbs[2]	MSA[1]	U.S.	City	Suburbs[3]	MSA[1]	U.S.
1977	116	60	176	63,500	38.5	46.3	40.9	29.4
1978	155	53	208	67,610	51.3	34.5	45.7	31.0
1979	184	60	244	76,390	58.2	36.5	50.8	34.7
1980	174	72	246	82,990	52.5	35.9	46.2	36.8
1981	163	81	244	82,500	47.8	39.3	44.6	36.0
1982	236	76	312	78,770	67.6	36.0	55.7	34.0
1983	253	88	341	78,920	69.9	40.2	58.8	33.7
1984	282	83	365	84,230	75.8	36.5	60.9	35.7
1985	297	62	359	88,670	77.9	25.9	57.8	37.1
1986	251	103	354	91,460	63.2	41.3	54.8	37.9
1987	281	86	367	91,110	75.0	35.0	59.2	37.4
1988	281	88	369	92,490	73.3	35.0	58.2	37.6
1989	n/a	n/a	n/a	94,500	n/a	n/a	n/a	38.1
1990	290	97	387	102,560	71.5	37.1	58.0	41.2
1991	332	95	427	106,590	80.0	35.5	62.6	42.3
1992	386	95	481	109,060	91.1	34.7	69.0	42.8
1993	314	113	427	106,010	73.6	40.0	60.2	41.1
1994	289	114	403	102,220	65.5	39.0	54.9	39.3
1995	292	104	396	97,470	64.9	33.9	52.3	37.1
1996	282	97	379	95,770	59.7	30.1	47.7	36.1

Notes: (1) Metropolitan Statistical Area - see Appendix A for areas included; (2) calculated by the editors using the following formula: (number of crimes in the MSA minus number of crimes in the city); (3) calculated by the editors using the following formula: ((number of crimes in the MSA minus number of crimes in the city) ÷ (population of the MSA minus population of the city)) x 100,000; n/a not avail.
Source: U.S. Department of Justice, FBI Uniform Crime Reports, 1977 - 1996

Robberies and Robbery Rates: 1977 - 1996

Year	Number				Rate per 100,000 population			
	City	Suburbs[2]	MSA[1]	U.S.	City	Suburbs[3]	MSA[1]	U.S.
1977	550	156	706	412,610	182.7	120.3	163.9	190.7
1978	584	172	756	426,930	193.4	112.0	165.9	195.8
1979	697	166	863	480,700	220.6	100.9	179.6	218.4
1980	655	142	797	565,840	197.6	70.9	149.8	251.1
1981	872	162	1,034	592,910	255.7	78.6	189.0	258.7
1982	910	152	1,062	553,130	260.6	72.0	189.6	238.9
1983	766	152	918	506,570	211.8	69.5	158.2	216.5
1984	809	155	964	485,010	217.4	68.1	160.8	205.4
1985	1,051	149	1,200	497,870	275.5	62.2	193.3	208.5
1986	1,042	171	1,213	542,780	262.5	68.6	187.7	225.1
1987	911	154	1,065	517,700	243.2	62.7	171.8	212.7
1988	768	152	920	542,970	200.4	60.5	145.0	220.9
1989	n/a	n/a	n/a	578,330	n/a	n/a	n/a	233.0
1990	902	180	1,082	639,270	222.5	68.8	162.2	257.0
1991	889	188	1,077	687,730	214.3	70.3	157.8	272.7
1992	970	201	1,171	672,480	228.9	73.5	168.0	263.6
1993	894	190	1,084	659,870	209.7	67.2	152.9	255.9
1994	1,012	223	1,235	618,950	229.3	76.2	168.3	237.7
1995	1,192	262	1,454	580,510	264.9	85.3	192.0	220.9
1996	1,288	278	1,566	537,050	272.7	86.2	197.0	202.4

Notes: (1) Metropolitan Statistical Area - see Appendix A for areas included; (2) calculated by the editors using the following formula: (number of crimes in the MSA minus number of crimes in the city); (3) calculated by the editors using the following formula: ((number of crimes in the MSA minus number of crimes in the city) ÷ (population of the MSA minus population of the city)) x 100,000; n/a not avail.
Source: U.S. Department of Justice, FBI Uniform Crime Reports, 1977 - 1996

Aggravated Assaults and Aggravated Assault Rates: 1977 - 1996

Year	Number				Rate per 100,000 population			
	City	Suburbs[2]	MSA[1]	U.S.	City	Suburbs[3]	MSA[1]	U.S.
1977	877	378	1,255	534,350	291.4	291.5	291.4	247.0
1978	889	388	1,277	571,460	294.4	252.5	280.3	262.1
1979	1,134	427	1,561	629,480	358.9	259.4	324.8	286.0
1980	1,717	467	2,184	672,650	517.9	233.0	410.6	298.5
1981	1,747	429	2,176	663,900	512.3	208.1	397.7	289.7
1982	1,748	422	2,170	669,480	500.6	199.9	387.3	289.2
1983	1,731	481	2,212	653,290	478.5	220.0	381.1	279.2
1984	1,843	444	2,287	685,350	495.2	195.2	381.4	290.2
1985	2,333	493	2,826	723,250	611.6	205.9	455.1	302.9
1986	2,310	730	3,040	834,320	581.8	292.9	470.4	346.1
1987	2,308	689	2,997	855,090	616.2	280.6	483.3	351.3
1988	2,447	684	3,131	910,090	638.6	272.3	493.6	370.2
1989	n/a	n/a	n/a	951,710	n/a	n/a	n/a	383.4
1990	2,458	630	3,088	1,054,860	606.3	240.9	463.1	424.1
1991	2,651	501	3,152	1,092,740	639.2	187.3	462.0	433.3
1992	2,929	606	3,535	1,126,970	691.1	221.7	507.0	441.8
1993	3,111	660	3,771	1,135,610	729.7	233.6	531.9	440.3
1994	3,544	721	4,265	1,113,180	802.9	246.4	581.1	427.6
1995	3,878	822	4,700	1,099,210	861.8	267.6	620.7	418.3
1996	3,583	829	4,412	1,029,810	758.5	257.0	555.0	388.2

Notes: (1) Metropolitan Statistical Area - see Appendix A for areas included; (2) calculated by the editors using the following formula: (number of crimes in the MSA minus number of crimes in the city); (3) calculated by the editors using the following formula: ((number of crimes in the MSA minus number of crimes in the city) ÷ (population of the MSA minus population of the city)) x 100,000; n/a not avail.
Source: U.S. Department of Justice, FBI Uniform Crime Reports, 1977 - 1996

Burglaries and Burglary Rates: 1977 - 1996

Year	Number				Rate per 100,000 population			
	City	Suburbs[2]	MSA[1]	U.S.	City	Suburbs[3]	MSA[1]	U.S.
1977	10,841	3,293	14,134	3,071,500	3,601.7	2,539.4	3,281.8	1,419.8
1978	8,460	2,461	10,921	3,128,300	2,801.3	1,601.8	2,396.9	1,434.6
1979	7,793	2,357	10,150	3,327,700	2,466.3	1,432.0	2,112.1	1,511.9
1980	9,392	3,417	12,809	3,795,200	2,833.1	1,705.2	2,408.2	1,684.1
1981	10,521	3,009	13,530	3,779,700	3,085.5	1,459.8	2,473.0	1,649.5
1982	9,481	2,973	12,454	3,447,100	2,715.3	1,408.6	2,223.0	1,488.8
1983	9,568	2,662	12,230	3,129,900	2,645.0	1,217.4	2,107.2	1,337.7
1984	9,909	3,291	13,200	2,984,400	2,662.7	1,447.0	2,201.5	1,263.7
1985	9,914	3,386	13,300	3,073,300	2,598.9	1,414.1	2,142.0	1,287.3
1986	9,577	3,604	13,181	3,241,400	2,412.2	1,446.0	2,039.6	1,344.6
1987	7,954	3,084	11,038	3,236,200	2,123.6	1,256.0	1,780.1	1,329.6
1988	8,230	2,654	10,884	3,218,100	2,147.8	1,056.5	1,715.7	1,309.2
1989	n/a	n/a	n/a	3,168,200	n/a	n/a	n/a	1,276.3
1990	7,909	2,664	10,573	3,073,900	1,951.0	1,018.8	1,585.4	1,235.9
1991	7,493	2,636	10,129	3,157,200	1,806.6	985.3	1,484.5	1,252.0
1992	6,815	2,659	9,474	2,979,900	1,607.9	972.6	1,358.8	1,168.2
1993	7,363	2,638	10,001	2,834,800	1,727.0	933.5	1,410.7	1,099.2
1994	7,205	2,766	9,971	2,712,800	1,632.3	945.4	1,358.5	1,042.0
1995	5,995	2,766	8,761	2,593,800	1,332.3	900.3	1,157.0	987.1
1996	6,710	2,646	9,356	2,501,500	1,420.5	820.4	1,177.0	943.0

Notes: (1) Metropolitan Statistical Area - see Appendix A for areas included; (2) calculated by the editors using the following formula: (number of crimes in the MSA minus number of crimes in the city); (3) calculated by the editors using the following formula: ((number of crimes in the MSA minus number of crimes in the city) ÷ (population of the MSA minus population of the city)) x 100,000; n/a not avail.
Source: U.S. Department of Justice, FBI Uniform Crime Reports, 1977 - 1996

Larceny-Thefts and Larceny-Theft Rates: 1977 - 1996

Year	Number				Rate per 100,000 population			
	City	Suburbs[2]	MSA[1]	U.S.	City	Suburbs[3]	MSA[1]	U.S.
1977	17,692	5,250	22,942	5,905,700	5,877.7	4,048.6	5,327.0	2,729.9
1978	17,126	5,279	22,405	5,991,000	5,670.9	3,436.1	4,917.3	2,747.4
1979	19,009	5,976	24,985	6,601,000	6,015.9	3,630.8	5,199.0	2,999.1
1980	21,976	6,424	28,400	7,136,900	6,629.1	3,205.7	5,339.4	3,167.0
1981	22,126	6,491	28,617	7,194,400	6,488.8	3,149.1	5,230.6	3,139.7
1982	21,803	6,000	27,803	7,142,500	6,244.3	2,842.7	4,962.8	3,084.8
1983	20,954	5,612	26,566	6,712,800	5,792.6	2,566.5	4,577.2	2,868.9
1984	20,292	5,810	26,102	6,591,900	5,452.7	2,554.5	4,353.3	2,791.3
1985	22,586	5,983	28,569	6,926,400	5,920.7	2,498.6	4,601.0	2,901.2
1986	23,510	6,901	30,411	7,257,200	5,921.6	2,768.8	4,705.6	3,010.3
1987	28,888	8,242	37,130	7,499,900	7,712.8	3,356.7	5,987.9	3,081.3
1988	34,878	9,410	44,288	7,705,900	9,102.4	3,746.1	6,981.4	3,134.9
1989	n/a	n/a	n/a	7,872,400	n/a	n/a	n/a	3,171.3
1990	34,101	10,372	44,473	7,945,700	8,411.9	3,966.5	6,668.8	3,194.8
1991	28,281	9,531	37,812	8,142,200	6,818.5	3,562.5	5,541.8	3,228.8
1992	28,629	9,700	38,329	7,915,200	6,754.7	3,548.1	5,497.4	3,103.0
1993	32,076	11,469	43,545	7,820,900	7,523.5	4,058.6	6,142.3	3,032.4
1994	35,209	14,288	49,497	7,879,800	7,976.6	4,883.7	6,743.8	3,026.7
1995	37,235	13,807	51,042	7,997,700	8,274.8	4,494.3	6,740.9	3,043.8
1996	28,460	10,285	38,745	7,894,600	6,024.7	3,189.1	4,874.2	2,975.9

Notes: (1) Metropolitan Statistical Area - see Appendix A for areas included; (2) calculated by the editors using the following formula: (number of crimes in the MSA minus number of crimes in the city); (3) calculated by the editors using the following formula: ((number of crimes in the MSA minus number of crimes in the city) ÷ (population of the MSA minus population of the city)) x 100,000; n/a not avail.
Source: U.S. Department of Justice, FBI Uniform Crime Reports, 1977 - 1996

Motor Vehicle Thefts and Motor Vehicle Theft Rates: 1977 - 1996

Year	Number				Rate per 100,000 population			
	City	Suburbs[2]	MSA[1]	U.S.	City	Suburbs[3]	MSA[1]	U.S.
1977	1,914	474	2,388	977,700	635.9	365.5	554.5	451.9
1978	1,871	538	2,409	1,004,100	619.5	350.2	528.7	460.5
1979	1,968	543	2,511	1,112,800	622.8	329.9	522.5	505.6
1980	1,995	543	2,538	1,131,700	601.8	271.0	477.2	502.2
1981	1,784	506	2,290	1,087,800	523.2	245.5	418.6	474.7
1982	1,716	502	2,218	1,062,400	491.5	237.8	395.9	458.8
1983	1,665	459	2,124	1,007,900	460.3	209.9	366.0	430.8
1984	2,456	525	2,981	1,032,200	660.0	230.8	497.2	437.1
1985	2,036	538	2,574	1,102,900	533.7	224.7	414.5	462.0
1986	2,109	581	2,690	1,224,100	531.2	233.1	416.2	507.8
1987	1,951	594	2,545	1,288,700	520.9	241.9	410.4	529.4
1988	2,064	661	2,725	1,432,900	538.7	263.1	429.6	582.9
1989	n/a	n/a	n/a	1,564,800	n/a	n/a	n/a	630.4
1990	2,468	807	3,275	1,635,900	608.8	308.6	491.1	657.8
1991	3,469	960	4,429	1,661,700	836.4	358.8	649.1	659.0
1992	4,362	1,368	5,730	1,610,800	1,029.2	500.4	821.8	631.5
1993	5,143	1,327	6,470	1,563,100	1,206.3	469.6	912.6	606.1
1994	6,797	1,494	8,291	1,539,300	1,539.9	510.7	1,129.6	591.3
1995	6,049	1,480	7,529	1,472,400	1,344.3	481.7	994.3	560.4
1996	6,016	1,879	7,895	1,395,200	1,273.5	582.6	993.2	525.9

Notes: (1) Metropolitan Statistical Area - see Appendix A for areas included; (2) calculated by the editors using the following formula: (number of crimes in the MSA minus number of crimes in the city); (3) calculated by the editors using the following formula: ((number of crimes in the MSA minus number of crimes in the city) ÷ (population of the MSA minus population of the city)) x 100,000; n/a not avail.
Source: U.S. Department of Justice, FBI Uniform Crime Reports, 1977 - 1996

HATE CRIMES

Criminal Incidents by Bias Motivation

Area	Race	Ethnicity	Religion	Sexual Orientation
Tucson	2	1	2	0

Notes: Figures include both violent and property crimes. Law enforcement agencies must have submitted data for at least one quarter of calendar year 1995 to be included in this report, therefore figures shown may not represent complete 12-month totals; n/a not available
Source: U.S. Department of Justice, FBI Uniform Crime Reports, Hate Crime Statistics 1995

LAW ENFORCEMENT

Full-Time Law Enforcement Employees

Jurisdiction	Police Employees			Police Officers per 100,000 population
	Total	Officers	Civilians	
Tucson	1,071	813	258	172.1

Notes: Data as of October 31, 1996
Source: U.S. Department of Justice, FBI Uniform Crime Reports, 1996

Number of Police Officers by Race

Race	Police Officers				Index of Representation[1]		
	1983		1992				
	Number	Pct.	Number	Pct.	1983	1992	% Chg.
Black	17	3.1	25	3.2	0.81	0.74	-8.6
Hispanic[2]	95	17.3	151	19.6	0.69	0.67	-2.9

Notes: (1) The index of representation is calculated by dividing the percent of black/hispanic police officers by the percent of corresponding blacks/hispanics in the local population. An index approaching 1.0 indicates that a city is closer to achieving a representation of police officers equal to their proportion in the local population; (2) Hispanic officers can be of any race
Source: Bureau of Justice Statistics, Sourcebook of Criminal Justice Statistics, 1994

CORRECTIONS

Federal Correctional Facilities

Type	Year Opened	Security Level	Sex of Inmates	Rated Capacity	Population on 7/1/95	Number of Staff
Federal Correctional Inst.	1982	Med./Admin.	Male/Both	389	772	242

Notes: Data as of 1995
Source: Bureau of Justice Statistics, Sourcebook of Criminal Justice Statistics Online

City/County/Regional Correctional Facilities

Name	Year Opened	Year Renov.	Rated Capacity	1995 Pop.	Number of COs[1]	Number of Staff	ACA[2] Accred.
Pima Co Adult Detention Ctr	1984	–	1,680	931	352	456	No

Notes: Data as of April 1996; (1) Correctional Officers; (2) American Correctional Assn. Accreditation
Source: American Correctional Association, 1996-1998 National Jail and Adult Detention Directory

Private Adult Correctional Facilities

Name	Date Opened	Rated Capacity	Present Pop.	Security Level	Facility Construct.	Expans. Plans	ACA[1] Accred.
None listed							

Notes: Data as of December 1996; (1) American Correctional Association Accreditation
Source: University of Florida, Center for Studies in Criminology and Law, Private Adult Correctional Facility Census, 10th Ed., March 15, 1997

Characteristics of Shock Incarceration Programs

Jurisdiction	Year Program Began	Number of Camps	Average Num. of Inmates	Number of Beds	Program Length	Voluntary/ Mandatory
Arizona did not have a shock incarceration program as of July 1996						

Source: Sourcebook of Criminal Justice Statistics Online

DEATH PENALTY

Death Penalty Statistics

State	Prisoners Executed		Prisoners Under Sentence of Death					Avg. No. of Years on Death Row[4]
	1930-1995	1996[1]	Total[2]	White[3]	Black[3]	Hisp.	Women	
Arizona	42	2	117	97	14	18	1	7.2

Notes: Data as of 12/31/95 unless otherwise noted; (1) Data as of 7/31/97; (2) Includes persons of other races; (3) Includes people of Hispanic origin; (4) Covers prisoners sentenced 1974 through 1995
Source: Bureau of Justice Statistics, Capital Punishment 1995 (released 12/96); Death Penalty Information Center Web Site, 9/30/97

Capital Offenses and Methods of Execution

Capital Offenses in Arizona	Minimum Age for Imposition of Death Penalty	Mentally Retarded Excluded	Methods of Execution[1]
First-degree murder accompanied by at least 1 of 10 aggravating factors.	None	No	Lethal injection; lethal gas

Notes: Data as of 12/31/95 unless otherwise noted; (1) Data as of 7/31/97
Source: Bureau of Justice Statistics, Capital Punishment 1995 (released 12/96); Death Penalty Information Center Web Site, 9/30/97

LAWS

Statutory Provisions Relating to the Purchase, Ownership and Use of Handguns

Jurisdiction	Instant Background Check	Federal Waiting Period Applies[1]	State Waiting Period (days)	License or Permit to Purchase	Regis-tration	Record of Sale Sent to Police	Concealed Carry Law
Arizona	Yes[a]	Yes[b]	No	No	No	No	Yes[c]

Note: Data as of 1996; (1) The Federal 5-day waiting period for handgun purchases applies to states that don't have instant background checks, waiting period requirements, or licensing procedures exempting them from the Federal requirement; (a) Concealed firearm carry permit holders are exempt from Instant Check; (b) The Federal waiting period does not apply to a person holding a valid permit or license to carry a firearm, issued within 5 years of proposed purchase; (c) "Shall issue" permit system, liberally administered discretion by local authorities over permit issuance, or no permit required
Source: Sourcebook of Criminal Justice Statistics Online

Statutory Provisions Relating to Alcohol Use and Driving

Jurisdiction	Drinking Age	Blood Alcohol Concentration Levels as Evidence in State Courts[1]		Open Container Law[1]	Anti-Consumption Law[1]	Dram Shop Law[1]
		Illegal per se at 0.10%	Presumption at 0.10%			
Arizona	21	Yes	Yes	No	Yes	Yes

Note: Data as of January 1, 1997; (1) See Appendix C for an explanation of terms
Source: Sourcebook of Criminal Justice Statistics Online

Statutory Provisions Relating to Curfews

Jurisdiction	Year Enacted	Latest Revision	Age Group(s)	Curfew Provisions
Tucson	1969	-	16 and 17 15 and under	Midnight to 5 am every night 10 pm to 5 am every night

Note: Data as of February 1996
Source: Sourcebook of Criminal Justice Statistics Online

Statutory Provisions Relating to Hate Crimes

Jurisdiction	Bias-Motivated Violence and Intimidation						Institutional Vandalism
	Civil Action	Criminal Penalty					
		Race/ Religion/ Ethnicity	Sexual Orientation	Mental/ Physical Disability	Gender	Age	
Arizona	No	No	No	No	No	No	Yes

Source: Anti-Defamation League, 1997 Hate Crimes Laws

Washington, DC

OVERVIEW

The total crime rate for the city increased 63.5% between 1977 and 1996. During that same period, the violent crime rate increased 71.9% and the property crime rate increased 61.4%.

Among violent crimes, the rates for: Murders increased 161.1%; Forcible Rapes decreased 18.4%; Robberies increased 22.2%; and Aggravated Assaults increased 206.9%.

Among property crimes, the rates for: Burglaries increased 7.0%; Larceny-Thefts increased 54.2%; and Motor Vehicle Thefts increased 358.9%.

ANTI-CRIME PROGRAMS

The police consider their most innovative program to be the Youth Trauma Services Team which "provides intervention, crisis debriefing, therapy, victim assistance services, prevention services and follow-up to the victim and witnesses....Primary clients have been children and young adults who are often parents themselves." *Metropolitan Police Department, 7/97*

The city instituted a program which the National League of Cities (1993) considers among those which are innovative for combatting crime and violence:

- Third Party Custodians in Superior Court where custodians supervise pretrial defendants into whose custody they have been released. Defendants must check in regularly with custodians who help them enroll in substance abuse, vocational, educational or other programs. The program has resulted in an impressive track record for ensuring that defendants appear at court proceedings. It effectively eliminates the need to post bond. *Exemplary Programs in Criminal Justice, National League of Cities, 1994*

CRIME RISK

Your Chances of Becoming a Victim[1]

Area	Any Crime	Violent Crime					Property Crime			
		Any	Murder	Forcible Rape[2]	Robbery	Aggrav. Assault	Any	Burglary	Larceny -Theft	Motor Vehicle Theft
City	1:8	1:40	1:1,368	1:1,115	1:84	1:86	1:11	1:55	1:17	1:54

Note: (1) Figures have been calculated by dividing the population of the city by the number of crimes reported to the FBI during 1996 and are expressed as odds (eg. 1:20 should be read as 1 in 20). (2) Figures have been calculated by dividing the female population of the city by the number of forcible rapes reported to the FBI during 1996. The female population of the city was estimated by calculating the ratio of females to males reported in the 1990 Census and applying that ratio to 1996 population estimate.
Source: FBI Uniform Crime Reports 1996

CRIME STATISTICS

Total Crimes and Total Crime Rates: 1977 - 1996

Year	Number				Rate per 100,000 population			
	City	Suburbs[2]	MSA[1]	U.S.	City	Suburbs[3]	MSA[1]	U.S.
1977	49,821	127,534	177,355	10,984,500	7,273.1	5,408.0	5,827.8	5,077.6
1978	50,950	130,671	181,621	11,209,000	7,593.1	5,525.5	5,982.5	5,140.3
1979	56,430	141,954	198,384	12,249,500	8,602.1	6,027.3	6,588.2	5,565.5
1980	63,668	147,405	211,073	13,408,300	10,022.8	6,124.8	6,938.8	5,950.0
1981	67,910	147,301	215,211	13,423,800	10,677.7	6,013.9	6,975.3	5,858.2
1982	65,692	130,054	195,746	12,974,400	10,410.8	5,278.1	6,324.5	5,603.6
1983	57,776	121,149	178,925	12,108,600	9,273.8	4,517.1	5,413.7	5,175.0
1984	53,524	120,476	174,000	11,881,800	8,591.3	4,352.4	5,131.1	5,031.3
1985	50,075	128,125	178,200	12,431,400	7,999.2	4,515.3	5,145.0	5,207.1
1986	52,159	132,416	184,575	13,211,900	8,332.1	4,596.3	5,263.2	5,480.4
1987	52,519	137,543	190,062	13,508,700	8,443.6	4,600.6	5,262.5	5,550.0
1988	61,423	149,282	210,705	13,923,100	9,906.9	4,839.0	5,687.1	5,664.2
1989	62,118	145,411	207,529	14,251,400	10,284.4	4,597.1	5,509.0	5,741.0
1990	65,389	157,687	223,076	14,475,600	10,774.3	4,754.4	5,685.5	5,820.3
1991	64,319	169,761	234,080	14,872,900	10,755.7	5,036.9	5,898.6	5,897.8
1992	67,134	172,828	239,962	14,438,200	11,398.0	4,648.5	5,571.5	5,660.2
1993	67,946	172,349	240,295	14,144,800	11,755.4	4,510.5	5,462.4	5,484.4
1994	63,144	174,992	238,136	13,989,500	11,077.9	4,540.6	5,382.9	5,373.5
1995	67,401	183,408	250,809	13,862,700	12,166.2	4,664.0	5,590.4	5,275.9
1996	64,557	180,896	245,453	13,473,600	11,889.0	4,567.9	5,450.7	5,078.9

Notes: (1) Metropolitan Statistical Area - see Appendix A for areas included; (2) calculated by the editors using the following formula: (number of crimes in the MSA minus number of crimes in the city); (3) calculated by the editors using the following formula: ((number of crimes in the MSA minus number of crimes in the city) ÷ (population of the MSA minus population of the city)) x 100,000; n/a not avail.
Source: U.S. Department of Justice, FBI Uniform Crime Reports, 1977 - 1996

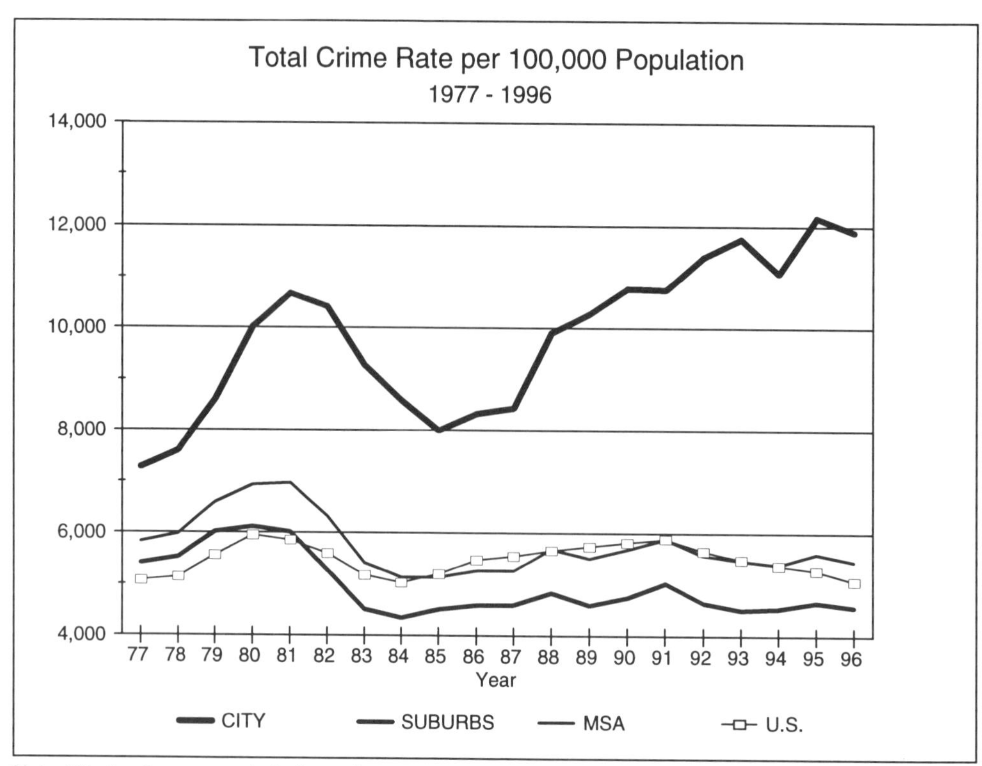

Note: Missing line segments indicate data not available.

Violent Crimes and Violent Crime Rates: 1977 - 1996

Year	Number				Rate per 100,000 population			
	City	Suburbs[2]	MSA[1]	U.S.	City	Suburbs[3]	MSA[1]	U.S.
1977	9,843	8,554	18,397	1,029,580	1,436.9	362.7	604.5	475.9
1978	9,515	9,394	18,909	1,085,550	1,418.0	397.2	622.9	497.8
1979	10,553	10,313	20,866	1,208,030	1,608.7	437.9	693.0	548.9
1980	12,772	11,647	24,419	1,344,520	2,010.6	483.9	802.8	596.6
1981	14,468	12,380	26,848	1,361,820	2,274.8	505.4	870.2	594.3
1982	13,397	11,503	24,900	1,322,390	2,123.1	466.8	804.5	571.1
1983	11,933	11,517	23,450	1,258,090	1,915.4	429.4	709.5	537.7
1984	10,725	11,650	22,375	1,273,280	1,721.5	420.9	659.8	539.2
1985	10,171	12,027	22,198	1,328,800	1,624.8	423.9	640.9	556.6
1986	9,422	12,421	21,843	1,489,170	1,505.1	431.1	622.9	617.7
1987	10,016	12,256	22,272	1,484,000	1,610.3	409.9	616.7	609.7
1988	11,913	13,476	25,389	1,566,220	1,921.5	436.8	685.3	637.2
1989	12,936	14,270	27,206	1,646,040	2,141.7	451.1	722.2	663.1
1990	14,919	15,843	30,762	1,820,130	2,458.2	477.7	784.0	731.8
1991	14,665	16,491	31,156	1,911,770	2,452.3	489.3	785.1	758.1
1992	16,680	16,694	33,374	1,932,270	2,831.9	449.0	774.9	757.5
1993	16,888	17,047	33,935	1,926,020	2,921.8	446.1	771.4	746.8
1994	15,177	16,431	31,608	1,857,670	2,662.6	426.3	714.5	713.6
1995	14,744	17,398	32,142	1,798,790	2,661.4	442.4	716.4	684.6
1996	13,411	17,196	30,607	1,682,280	2,469.8	434.2	679.7	634.1

Notes: Violent crimes include murder, forcible rape, robbery and aggravated assault; n/a not available; (1) Metropolitan Statistical Area - see Appendix A for areas included; (2) calculated by the editors using the following formula: (number of crimes in the MSA minus number of crimes in the city); (3) calculated by the editors using the following formula: ((number of crimes in the MSA minus number of crimes in the city) ÷ (population of the MSA minus population of the city)) x 100,000
Source: U.S. Department of Justice, FBI Uniform Crime Reports, 1977 - 1996

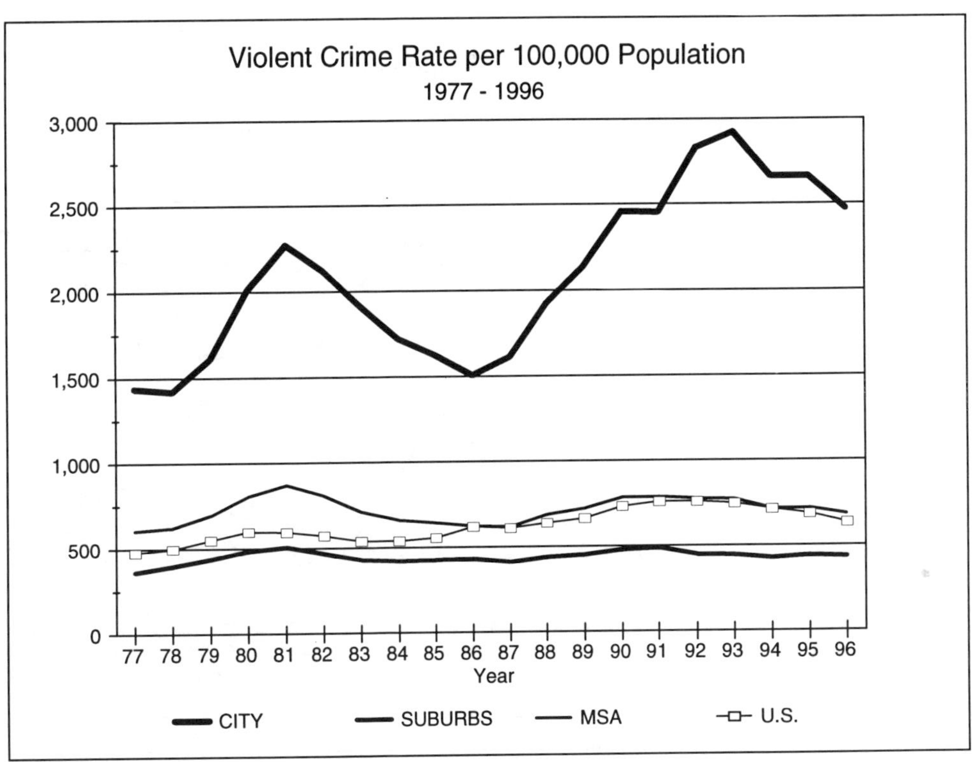

Note: Missing line segments indicate data not available.

Property Crimes and Property Crime Rates: 1977 - 1996

Year	Number				Rate per 100,000 population			
	City	Suburbs[2]	MSA[1]	U.S.	City	Suburbs[3]	MSA[1]	U.S.
1977	39,978	118,980	158,958	9,955,000	5,836.2	5,045.3	5,223.3	4,601.7
1978	41,435	121,277	162,712	10,123,400	6,175.1	5,128.3	5,359.7	4,642.5
1979	45,877	131,641	177,518	11,041,500	6,993.4	5,589.4	5,895.3	5,016.6
1980	50,896	135,758	186,654	12,063,700	8,012.2	5,640.9	6,136.1	5,353.3
1981	53,442	134,921	188,363	12,061,900	8,402.8	5,508.5	6,105.1	5,263.9
1982	52,295	118,551	170,846	11,652,000	8,287.6	4,811.3	5,520.0	5,032.5
1983	45,843	109,632	155,475	10,850,500	7,358.4	4,087.7	4,704.2	4,637.4
1984	42,799	108,826	151,625	10,608,500	6,869.8	3,931.5	4,471.3	4,492.1
1985	39,904	116,098	156,002	11,102,600	6,374.4	4,091.5	4,504.1	4,650.5
1986	42,737	119,995	162,732	11,722,700	6,827.0	4,165.2	4,640.3	4,862.6
1987	42,503	125,287	167,790	12,024,700	6,833.3	4,190.7	4,645.8	4,940.3
1988	49,510	135,806	185,316	12,356,900	7,985.5	4,402.2	5,001.8	5,027.1
1989	49,182	131,141	180,323	12,605,400	8,142.7	4,146.0	4,786.8	5,077.9
1990	50,470	141,844	192,314	12,655,500	8,316.0	4,276.7	4,901.5	5,088.5
1991	49,654	153,270	202,924	12,961,100	8,303.3	4,547.6	5,113.5	5,139.7
1992	50,454	156,134	206,588	12,505,900	8,566.0	4,199.5	4,796.6	4,902.7
1993	51,058	155,302	206,360	12,218,800	8,833.6	4,064.4	4,691.0	4,737.6
1994	47,967	158,561	206,528	12,131,900	8,415.3	4,114.3	4,668.5	4,660.0
1995	52,657	166,010	218,667	12,063,900	9,504.9	4,221.6	4,874.0	4,591.3
1996	51,146	163,700	214,846	11,791,300	9,419.2	4,133.7	4,771.0	4,444.8

Notes: Property crimes include burglary, larceny-theft and motor vehicle theft; n/a not available; (1) Metropolitan Statistical Area - see Appendix A for areas included; (2) calculated by the editors using the following formula: (number of crimes in the MSA minus number of crimes in the city); (3) calculated by the editors using the following formula: ((number of crimes in the MSA minus number of crimes in the city) ÷ (population of the MSA minus population of the city)) x 100,000
Source: U.S. Department of Justice, FBI Uniform Crime Reports, 1977 - 1996

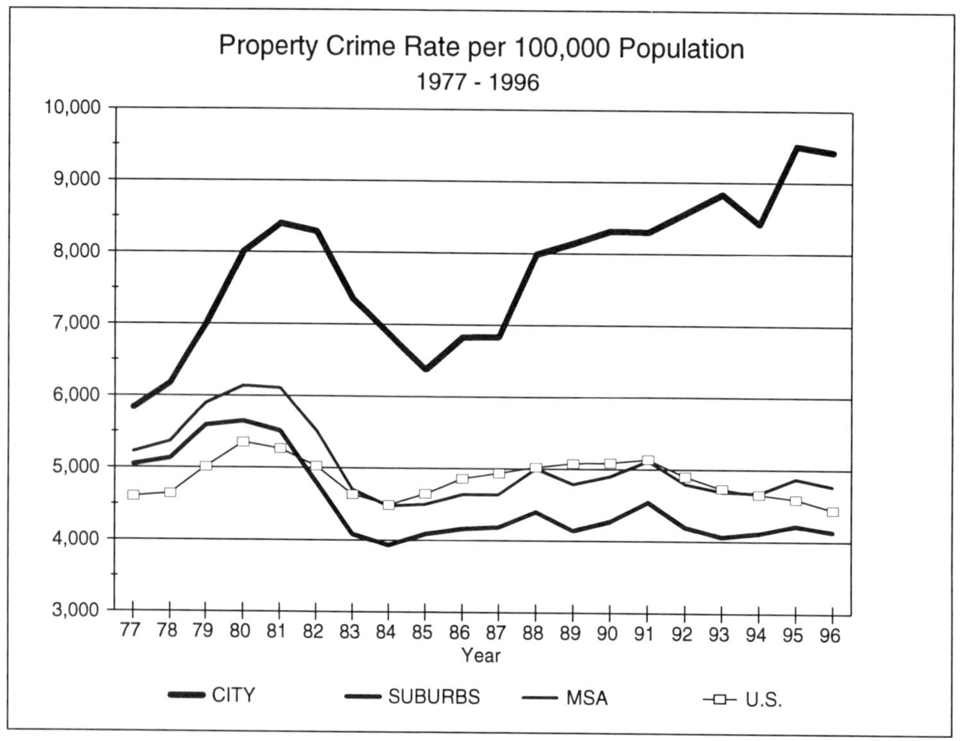

Note: Missing line segments indicate data not available.

Murders and Murder Rates: 1977 - 1996

Year	Number				Rate per 100,000 population			
	City	Suburbs[2]	MSA[1]	U.S.	City	Suburbs[3]	MSA[1]	U.S.
1977	192	121	313	19,120	28.0	5.1	10.3	8.8
1978	189	106	295	19,560	28.2	4.5	9.7	9.0
1979	180	101	281	21,460	27.4	4.3	9.3	9.7
1980	200	126	326	23,040	31.5	5.2	10.7	10.2
1981	223	127	350	22,520	35.1	5.2	11.3	9.8
1982	194	140	334	21,010	30.7	5.7	10.8	9.1
1983	183	115	298	19,310	29.4	4.3	9.0	8.3
1984	175	110	285	18,690	28.1	4.0	8.4	7.9
1985	147	96	243	18,980	23.5	3.4	7.0	7.9
1986	194	104	298	20,610	31.0	3.6	8.5	8.6
1987	225	142	367	20,100	36.2	4.7	10.2	8.3
1988	369	178	547	20,680	59.5	5.8	14.8	8.4
1989	434	206	640	21,500	71.9	6.5	17.0	8.7
1990	472	212	684	23,440	77.8	6.4	17.4	9.4
1991	482	237	719	24,700	80.6	7.0	18.1	9.8
1992	443	234	677	23,760	75.2	6.3	15.7	9.3
1993	454	242	696	24,530	78.5	6.3	15.8	9.5
1994	399	236	635	23,330	70.0	6.1	14.4	9.0
1995	360	240	600	21,610	65.0	6.1	13.4	8.2
1996	397	224	621	19,650	73.1	5.7	13.8	7.4

Notes: (1) Metropolitan Statistical Area - see Appendix A for areas included; (2) calculated by the editors using the following formula: (number of crimes in the MSA minus number of crimes in the city); (3) calculated by the editors using the following formula: ((number of crimes in the MSA minus number of crimes in the city) ÷ (population of the MSA minus population of the city)) x 100,000; n/a not avail.
Source: U.S. Department of Justice, FBI Uniform Crime Reports, 1977 - 1996

Forcible Rapes and Forcible Rape Rates: 1977 - 1996

Year	Number				Rate per 100,000 population			
	City	Suburbs[2]	MSA[1]	U.S.	City	Suburbs[3]	MSA[1]	U.S.
1977	402	698	1,100	63,500	58.7	29.6	36.1	29.4
1978	447	756	1,203	67,610	66.6	32.0	39.6	31.0
1979	489	875	1,364	76,390	74.5	37.2	45.3	34.7
1980	439	925	1,364	82,990	69.1	38.4	44.8	36.8
1981	414	916	1,330	82,500	65.1	37.4	43.1	36.0
1982	421	884	1,305	78,770	66.7	35.9	42.2	34.0
1983	406	797	1,203	78,920	65.2	29.7	36.4	33.7
1984	366	837	1,203	84,230	58.7	30.2	35.5	35.7
1985	337	786	1,123	88,670	53.8	27.7	32.4	37.1
1986	328	857	1,185	91,460	52.4	29.7	33.8	37.9
1987	245	828	1,073	91,110	39.4	27.7	29.7	37.4
1988	165	919	1,084	92,490	26.6	29.8	29.3	37.6
1989	186	858	1,044	94,500	30.8	27.1	27.7	38.1
1990	303	1,076	1,379	102,560	49.9	32.4	35.1	41.2
1991	214	1,069	1,283	106,590	35.8	31.7	32.3	42.3
1992	215	1,106	1,321	109,060	36.5	29.7	30.7	42.8
1993	324	1,145	1,469	106,010	56.1	30.0	33.4	41.1
1994	249	1,062	1,311	102,220	43.7	27.6	29.6	39.3
1995	292	1,073	1,365	97,470	52.7	27.3	30.4	37.1
1996	260	983	1,243	95,770	47.9	24.8	27.6	36.1

Notes: (1) Metropolitan Statistical Area - see Appendix A for areas included; (2) calculated by the editors using the following formula: (number of crimes in the MSA minus number of crimes in the city); (3) calculated by the editors using the following formula: ((number of crimes in the MSA minus number of crimes in the city) ÷ (population of the MSA minus population of the city)) x 100,000; n/a not avail.
Source: U.S. Department of Justice, FBI Uniform Crime Reports, 1977 - 1996

Robberies and Robbery Rates: 1977 - 1996

Year	Number				Rate per 100,000 population			
	City	Suburbs[2]	MSA[1]	U.S.	City	Suburbs[3]	MSA[1]	U.S.
1977	6,655	4,085	10,740	412,610	971.5	173.2	352.9	190.7
1978	6,333	4,462	10,795	426,930	943.8	188.7	355.6	195.8
1979	6,920	4,843	11,763	480,700	1,054.9	205.6	390.6	218.4
1980	8,897	6,015	14,912	565,840	1,400.6	249.9	490.2	251.1
1981	10,399	6,811	17,210	592,910	1,635.1	278.1	557.8	258.7
1982	9,137	5,689	14,826	553,130	1,448.0	230.9	479.0	238.9
1983	7,698	5,034	12,732	506,570	1,235.6	187.7	385.2	216.5
1984	6,087	4,710	10,797	485,010	977.0	170.2	318.4	205.4
1985	5,230	4,899	10,129	497,870	835.5	172.6	292.4	208.5
1986	4,719	4,724	9,443	542,780	753.8	164.0	269.3	225.1
1987	4,462	4,748	9,210	517,700	717.4	158.8	255.0	212.7
1988	5,689	5,420	11,109	542,970	917.6	175.7	299.8	220.9
1989	6,541	6,073	12,614	578,330	1,082.9	192.0	334.8	233.0
1990	7,365	6,625	13,990	639,270	1,213.5	199.7	356.6	257.0
1991	7,265	7,055	14,320	687,730	1,214.9	209.3	360.9	272.7
1992	7,456	6,677	14,133	672,480	1,265.9	179.6	328.1	263.6
1993	7,107	7,144	14,251	659,870	1,229.6	187.0	324.0	255.9
1994	6,311	6,705	13,016	618,950	1,107.2	174.0	294.2	237.7
1995	6,864	7,330	14,194	580,510	1,239.0	186.4	316.4	220.9
1996	6,444	7,010	13,454	537,050	1,186.7	177.0	298.8	202.4

Notes: (1) Metropolitan Statistical Area - see Appendix A for areas included; (2) calculated by the editors using the following formula: (number of crimes in the MSA minus number of crimes in the city); (3) calculated by the editors using the following formula: ((number of crimes in the MSA minus number of crimes in the city) ÷ (population of the MSA minus population of the city)) x 100,000; n/a not avail.
Source: U.S. Department of Justice, FBI Uniform Crime Reports, 1977 - 1996

Aggravated Assaults and Aggravated Assault Rates: 1977 - 1996

Year	Number				Rate per 100,000 population			
	City	Suburbs[2]	MSA[1]	U.S.	City	Suburbs[3]	MSA[1]	U.S.
1977	2,594	3,650	6,244	534,350	378.7	154.8	205.2	247.0
1978	2,546	4,070	6,616	571,460	379.4	172.1	217.9	262.1
1979	2,964	4,494	7,458	629,480	451.8	190.8	247.7	286.0
1980	3,236	4,581	7,817	672,650	509.4	190.3	257.0	298.5
1981	3,432	4,526	7,958	663,900	539.6	184.8	257.9	289.7
1982	3,645	4,790	8,435	669,480	577.7	194.4	272.5	289.2
1983	3,646	5,571	9,217	653,290	585.2	207.7	278.9	279.2
1984	4,097	5,993	10,090	685,350	657.6	216.5	297.5	290.2
1985	4,457	6,246	10,703	723,250	712.0	220.1	309.0	302.9
1986	4,181	6,736	10,917	834,320	667.9	233.8	311.3	346.1
1987	5,084	6,538	11,622	855,090	817.4	218.7	321.8	351.3
1988	5,690	6,959	12,649	910,090	917.7	225.6	341.4	370.2
1989	5,775	7,133	12,908	951,710	956.1	225.5	342.7	383.4
1990	6,779	7,930	14,709	1,054,860	1,117.0	239.1	374.9	424.1
1991	6,704	8,130	14,834	1,092,740	1,121.1	241.2	373.8	433.3
1992	8,566	8,677	17,243	1,126,970	1,454.3	233.4	400.4	441.8
1993	9,003	8,516	17,519	1,135,610	1,557.6	222.9	398.2	440.3
1994	8,218	8,428	16,646	1,113,180	1,441.8	218.7	376.3	427.6
1995	7,228	8,755	15,983	1,099,210	1,304.7	222.6	356.3	418.3
1996	6,310	8,979	15,289	1,029,810	1,162.1	226.7	339.5	388.2

Notes: (1) Metropolitan Statistical Area - see Appendix A for areas included; (2) calculated by the editors using the following formula: (number of crimes in the MSA minus number of crimes in the city); (3) calculated by the editors using the following formula: ((number of crimes in the MSA minus number of crimes in the city) ÷ (population of the MSA minus population of the city)) x 100,000; n/a not avail.
Source: U.S. Department of Justice, FBI Uniform Crime Reports, 1977 - 1996

Burglaries and Burglary Rates: 1977 - 1996

Year	Number				Rate per 100,000 population			
	City	Suburbs[2]	MSA[1]	U.S.	City	Suburbs[3]	MSA[1]	U.S.
1977	11,590	30,622	42,212	3,071,500	1,692.0	1,298.5	1,387.1	1,419.8
1978	12,497	30,692	43,189	3,128,300	1,862.4	1,297.8	1,422.6	1,434.6
1979	13,452	32,931	46,383	3,327,700	2,050.6	1,398.2	1,540.4	1,511.9
1980	16,260	37,509	53,769	3,795,200	2,559.7	1,558.5	1,767.6	1,684.1
1981	16,832	35,219	52,051	3,779,700	2,646.5	1,437.9	1,687.1	1,649.5
1982	14,774	28,708	43,482	3,447,100	2,341.4	1,165.1	1,404.9	1,488.8
1983	12,483	26,275	38,758	3,129,900	2,003.7	979.7	1,172.7	1,337.7
1984	10,954	25,201	36,155	2,984,400	1,758.3	910.4	1,066.2	1,263.7
1985	10,005	25,852	35,857	3,073,300	1,598.2	911.1	1,035.3	1,287.3
1986	10,814	25,421	36,235	3,241,400	1,727.5	882.4	1,033.2	1,344.6
1987	11,241	25,549	36,790	3,236,200	1,807.2	854.6	1,018.6	1,329.6
1988	12,295	26,481	38,776	3,218,100	1,983.1	858.4	1,046.6	1,309.2
1989	11,778	23,939	35,717	3,168,200	1,950.0	756.8	948.1	1,276.3
1990	12,035	24,918	36,953	3,073,900	1,983.0	751.3	941.8	1,235.9
1991	12,403	25,472	37,875	3,157,200	2,074.1	755.8	954.4	1,252.0
1992	10,719	25,340	36,059	2,979,900	1,819.9	681.6	837.2	1,168.2
1993	11,532	24,723	36,255	2,834,800	1,995.2	647.0	824.2	1,099.2
1994	10,037	24,874	34,911	2,712,800	1,760.9	645.4	789.1	1,042.0
1995	10,184	25,533	35,717	2,593,800	1,838.3	649.3	796.1	987.1
1996	9,828	23,690	33,518	2,501,500	1,809.9	598.2	744.3	943.0

Notes: (1) Metropolitan Statistical Area - see Appendix A for areas included; (2) calculated by the editors using the following formula: (number of crimes in the MSA minus number of crimes in the city); (3) calculated by the editors using the following formula: ((number of crimes in the MSA minus number of crimes in the city) ÷ (population of the MSA minus population of the city)) x 100,000; n/a not avail.
Source: U.S. Department of Justice, FBI Uniform Crime Reports, 1977 - 1996

Larceny-Thefts and Larceny-Theft Rates: 1977 - 1996

Year	Number				Rate per 100,000 population			
	City	Suburbs[2]	MSA[1]	U.S.	City	Suburbs[3]	MSA[1]	U.S.
1977	25,646	79,027	104,673	5,905,700	3,743.9	3,351.1	3,439.5	2,729.9
1978	25,744	81,107	106,851	5,991,000	3,836.7	3,429.7	3,519.6	2,747.4
1979	28,819	88,001	116,820	6,601,000	4,393.1	3,736.5	3,879.5	2,999.1
1980	31,068	87,926	118,994	7,136,900	4,890.8	3,653.4	3,911.8	3,167.0
1981	32,845	89,585	122,430	7,194,400	5,164.3	3,657.5	3,968.1	3,139.7
1982	33,435	80,582	114,017	7,142,500	5,298.7	3,270.3	3,683.9	3,084.8
1983	29,405	74,462	103,867	6,712,800	4,719.9	2,776.3	3,142.7	2,868.9
1984	27,471	73,907	101,378	6,591,900	4,409.5	2,670.0	2,989.6	2,791.3
1985	24,874	78,356	103,230	6,926,400	3,973.5	2,761.4	2,980.5	2,901.2
1986	25,818	80,264	106,082	7,257,200	4,124.3	2,786.0	3,024.9	3,010.3
1987	24,965	83,199	108,164	7,499,900	4,013.7	2,782.9	2,994.9	3,081.3
1988	28,582	89,437	118,019	7,705,900	4,610.0	2,899.1	3,185.4	3,134.9
1989	29,113	87,343	116,456	7,872,400	4,820.0	2,761.3	3,091.4	3,171.3
1990	30,326	97,603	127,929	7,945,700	4,996.9	2,942.8	3,260.5	3,194.8
1991	29,119	108,118	137,237	8,142,200	4,869.4	3,207.9	3,458.3	3,228.8
1992	30,618	110,919	141,537	7,915,200	5,198.3	2,983.3	3,286.3	3,103.0
1993	31,466	111,920	143,386	7,820,900	5,443.9	2,929.0	3,259.5	3,032.4
1994	29,673	114,535	144,208	7,879,800	5,205.8	2,971.9	3,259.7	3,026.7
1995	32,281	119,010	151,291	7,997,700	5,826.9	3,026.4	3,372.2	3,043.8
1996	31,343	118,018	149,361	7,894,600	5,772.2	2,980.2	3,316.8	2,975.9

Notes: (1) Metropolitan Statistical Area - see Appendix A for areas included; (2) calculated by the editors using the following formula: (number of crimes in the MSA minus number of crimes in the city); (3) calculated by the editors using the following formula: ((number of crimes in the MSA minus number of crimes in the city) ÷ (population of the MSA minus population of the city)) x 100,000; n/a not avail.
Source: U.S. Department of Justice, FBI Uniform Crime Reports, 1977 - 1996

Motor Vehicle Thefts and Motor Vehicle Theft Rates: 1977 - 1996

Year	Number				Rate per 100,000 population			
	City	Suburbs[2]	MSA[1]	U.S.	City	Suburbs[3]	MSA[1]	U.S.
1977	2,742	9,331	12,073	977,700	400.3	395.7	396.7	451.9
1978	3,194	9,478	12,672	1,004,100	476.0	400.8	417.4	460.5
1979	3,606	10,709	14,315	1,112,800	549.7	454.7	475.4	505.6
1980	3,568	10,323	13,891	1,131,700	561.7	428.9	456.7	502.2
1981	3,765	10,117	13,882	1,087,800	592.0	413.1	449.9	474.7
1982	4,086	9,261	13,347	1,062,400	647.5	375.8	431.2	458.8
1983	3,955	8,895	12,850	1,007,900	634.8	331.7	388.8	430.8
1984	4,374	9,718	14,092	1,032,200	702.1	351.1	415.6	437.1
1985	5,025	11,890	16,915	1,102,900	802.7	419.0	488.4	462.0
1986	6,105	14,310	20,415	1,224,100	975.2	496.7	582.1	507.8
1987	6,297	16,539	22,836	1,288,700	1,012.4	553.2	632.3	529.4
1988	8,633	19,888	28,521	1,432,900	1,392.4	644.7	769.8	582.9
1989	8,291	19,859	28,150	1,564,800	1,372.7	627.8	747.3	630.4
1990	8,109	19,323	27,432	1,635,900	1,336.1	582.6	699.2	657.8
1991	8,132	19,680	27,812	1,661,700	1,359.9	583.9	700.8	659.0
1992	9,117	19,875	28,992	1,610,800	1,547.9	534.6	673.1	631.5
1993	8,060	18,659	26,719	1,563,100	1,394.5	488.3	607.4	606.1
1994	8,257	19,152	27,409	1,539,300	1,448.6	497.0	619.6	591.3
1995	10,192	21,467	31,659	1,472,400	1,839.7	545.9	705.7	560.4
1996	9,975	21,992	31,967	1,395,200	1,837.0	555.3	709.9	525.9

Notes: (1) Metropolitan Statistical Area - see Appendix A for areas included; (2) calculated by the editors using the following formula: (number of crimes in the MSA minus number of crimes in the city); (3) calculated by the editors using the following formula: ((number of crimes in the MSA minus number of crimes in the city) ÷ (population of the MSA minus population of the city)) x 100,000; n/a not avail.
Source: U.S. Department of Justice, FBI Uniform Crime Reports, 1977 - 1996

HATE CRIMES

Criminal Incidents by Bias Motivation

Area	Race	Ethnicity	Religion	Sexual Orientation
Dist. of Columbia	2	0	1	1

Notes: Figures include both violent and property crimes. Law enforcement agencies must have submitted data for at least one quarter of calendar year 1995 to be included in this report, therefore figures shown may not represent complete 12-month totals; n/a not available
Source: U.S. Department of Justice, FBI Uniform Crime Reports, Hate Crime Statistics 1995

ILLEGAL DRUGS

Drug Use by Adult Arrestees

Sex	Percent Testing Positive by Urinalysis (%)				
	Any Drug[1]	Cocaine	Marijuana	Opiates	Multiple Drugs
Male	66	33	40	9	17
Female	58	40	23	11	17

Notes: The catchment area is the entire city; (1) Includes cocaine, opiates, marijuana, methadone, phencyclidine (PCP), benzodiazepines, methaqualone, propoxyphene, barbiturates & amphetamines
Source: National Institute of Justice, 1996 Drug Use Forecasting, Annual Report on Adult and Juvenile Arrestees (released June 1997)

LAW ENFORCEMENT

Full-Time Law Enforcement Employees

Jurisdiction	Police Employees			Police Officers per 100,000 population
	Total	Officers	Civilians	
Dist. of Columbia	4,369	3,611	758	665.0

Notes: Data as of October 31, 1996
Source: U.S. Department of Justice, FBI Uniform Crime Reports, 1996

Number of Police Officers by Race

Race	Police Officers 1983		Police Officers 1992		Index of Representation[1]		
	Number	Pct.	Number	Pct.	1983	1992	% Chg.
Black	1,931	50.1	2,980	67.8	0.71	1.03	45.1
Hispanic[2]	40	1.0	132	3.0	0.36	0.56	55.6

Notes: (1) The index of representation is calculated by dividing the percent of black/hispanic police officers by the percent of corresponding blacks/hispanics in the local population. An index approaching 1.0 indicates that a city is closer to achieving a representation of police officers equal to their proportion in the local population; (2) Hispanic officers can be of any race
Source: Bureau of Justice Statistics, Sourcebook of Criminal Justice Statistics, 1994

CORRECTIONS

Federal Correctional Facilities

Type	Year Opened	Security Level	Sex of Inmates	Rated Capacity	Population on 7/1/95	Number of Staff
None listed						

Notes: Data as of 1995
Source: Bureau of Justice Statistics, Sourcebook of Criminal Justice Statistics Online

City/County/Regional Correctional Facilities

Name	Year Opened	Year Renov.	Rated Capacity	1995 Pop.	Number of COs[1]	Number of Staff	ACA[2] Accred.
DC Department of Corrections	n/a	--	n/a	n/a	n/a	n/a	No
DC Detention Center	1976	--	1,681	645	n/a	646	No

Notes: Data as of April 1996; (1) Correctional Officers; (2) American Correctional Assn. Accreditation
Source: American Correctional Association, 1996-1998 National Jail and Adult Detention Directory

Private Adult Correctional Facilities

Name	Date Opened	Rated Capacity	Present Pop.	Security Level	Facility Construct.	Expans. Plans	ACA[1] Accred.
Corr Treatment Facil	3/97	866	n/a	Med.	Take-over	None	Will be sought

Notes: Data as of December 1996; (1) American Correctional Association Accreditation
Source: University of Florida, Center for Studies in Criminology and Law, Private Adult Correctional Facility Census, 10th Ed., March 15, 1997

Characteristics of Shock Incarceration Programs

Jurisdiction	Year Program Began	Number of Camps	Average Num. of Inmates	Number of Beds	Program Length	Voluntary/ Mandatory
The District of Columbia did not have a shock incarceration program as of July 1996						

Source: Sourcebook of Criminal Justice Statistics Online

INMATES AND HIV/AIDS

HIV Testing Policies for Inmates

Jurisdiction	All Inmates at Some Time	All Convicted Inmates at Admission	Random Samples While in Custody	High-risk Groups	Upon Inmate Request	Upon Court Order	Upon Involvement in Incident
Dist. of Columbia[1]	No	No	Yes	No	Yes	Yes	No

Notes: (1) All facilities reported following the same testing policy or authorities reported the policy to be jurisdiction-wide
Source: HIV in Prisons and Jails, 1993 (released August 1995)

Inmates Known to be Positive for HIV

Jurisdiction	Number of Jail Inmates in Facilities Providing Data	Type of HIV Infection/AIDS Cases: Total	Asymptomatic	Symptomatic	Confirmed AIDS	HIV/AIDS Cases as a Percent of Tot. Custody Pop.
Dist. of Columbia[1]	1,687	169	0	0	0	10.0

Note: (1) Detail does not add to total.
Source: HIV in Prisons and Jails, 1993 (released August, 1995)

DEATH PENALTY

The District of Columbia did not have the death penalty as of July 31, 1997.
Source: Death Penalty Information Center Web Site, 9/30/97

LAWS

Statutory Provisions Relating to the Purchase, Ownership and Use of Handguns

Jurisdiction	Instant Background Check	Federal Waiting Period Applies[1]	State Waiting Period (days)	License or Permit to Purchase	Regis-tration	Record of Sale Sent to Police	Concealed Carry Law
Dist. of Columbia	No	No	No	Yes[a]	Yes[a]	Yes	Yes[b]

Note: Data as of 1996; (1) The Federal 5-day waiting period for handgun purchases applies to states that don't have instant background checks, waiting period requirements, or licensing procedures exempting them from the Federal requirement; (a) No handgun may be possessed unless it was registered prior to Sept. 23, 1976 and re-registered by Feb. 5, 1977; (b) No permit system exists and concealed carry is prohibited
Source: Sourcebook of Criminal Justice Statistics Online

Statutory Provisions Relating to Alcohol Use and Driving

Jurisdiction	Drinking Age	Blood Alcohol Concentration Levels as Evidence in State Courts[1]		Open Container Law[1]	Anti-Consump-tion Law[1]	Dram Shop Law[1]
		Illegal per se at 0.10%	Presumption at 0.10%			
Dist. of Columbia	21	Yes	(a)	Yes	Yes	(b)

Note: Data as of January 1, 1997; (1) See Appendix C for an explanation of terms; (a) Prima facie evidence at greater than 0.05% blood alcohol concentration; (b) Adopted via case law decisions
Source: Sourcebook of Criminal Justice Statistics Online

Statutory Provisions Relating to Curfews

Jurisdiction	Year Enacted	Latest Revision	Age Group(s)	Curfew Provisions
Dist. of Columbia	1995	-	16 and under	Midnight - 6 am during July/August 11 pm - 6 am all other weekday nights Midnight - 6 am all other weekend nights

Note: Data as of February 1996
Source: Sourcebook of Criminal Justice Statistics Online

Statutory Provisions Relating to Hate Crimes

Jurisdiction	Bias-Motivated Violence and Intimidation						Institutional Vandalism
		Criminal Penalty					
	Civil Action	Race/ Religion/ Ethnicity	Sexual Orientation	Mental/ Physical Disability	Gender	Age	
Dist. of Columbia	Yes	Yes	Yes	Yes	Yes	Yes	Yes

Source: Anti-Defamation League, 1997 Hate Crimes Laws

Worcester, Massachusetts

OVERVIEW

The total crime rate for the city decreased 27.8% between 1977 and 1996. During that same period, the violent crime rate increased 106.5% and the property crime rate decreased 35.5%.

Among violent crimes, the rates for: Murders increased 75.0%; Forcible Rapes increased 122.7%; Robberies increased 25.5%; and Aggravated Assaults increased 174.5%.

Among property crimes, the rates for: Burglaries decreased 45.9%; Larceny-Thefts increased 2.6%; and Motor Vehicle Thefts decreased 72.3%.

ANTI-CRIME PROGRAMS

Information not available at time of publication.

CRIME RISK

Your Chances of Becoming a Victim[1]

Area	Any Crime	Violent Crime					Property Crime			
		Any	Murder	Forcible Rape[2]	Robbery	Aggrav. Assault	Any	Burglary	Larceny -Theft	Motor Vehicle Theft
City	1:17	1:107	1:23,826	1:808	1:407	1:161	1:20	1:75	1:32	1:150

Note: (1) Figures have been calculated by dividing the population of the city by the number of crimes reported to the FBI during 1996 and are expressed as odds (eg. 1:20 should be read as 1 in 20). (2) Figures have been calculated by dividing the female population of the city by the number of forcible rapes reported to the FBI during 1996. The female population of the city was estimated by calculating the ratio of females to males reported in the 1990 Census and applying that ratio to 1996 population estimate.
Source: FBI Uniform Crime Reports 1996

CRIME STATISTICS

Total Crimes and Total Crime Rates: 1977 - 1996

Year	Number				Rate per 100,000 population			
	City	Suburbs[2]	MSA[1]	U.S.	City	Suburbs[3]	MSA[1]	U.S.
1977	13,762	15,296	29,058	10,984,500	8,340.6	3,185.6	4,504.0	5,077.6
1978	12,577	14,368	26,945	11,209,000	7,668.9	2,991.9	4,182.5	5,140.3
1979	12,573	15,666	28,239	12,249,500	7,621.8	3,266.3	4,381.0	5,565.5
1980	12,978	16,927	29,905	13,408,300	8,041.7	3,507.6	4,643.9	5,950.0
1981	n/a	n/a	n/a	13,423,800	n/a	n/a	n/a	5,858.2
1982	12,689	13,415	26,104	12,974,400	7,790.9	2,754.5	4,016.7	5,603.6
1983	12,361	5,321	17,682	12,108,600	7,608.0	2,183.6	4,353.5	5,175.0
1984	10,281	4,801	15,082	11,881,800	6,334.7	1,952.2	3,694.5	5,031.3
1985	11,701	5,343	17,044	12,431,400	7,289.5	2,140.2	4,155.3	5,207.1
1986	11,662	5,030	16,692	13,211,900	7,252.8	2,022.6	4,076.4	5,480.4
1987	10,908	5,025	15,933	13,508,700	6,886.6	1,974.4	3,858.8	5,550.0
1988	12,036	4,643	16,679	13,923,100	7,563.9	1,816.0	4,021.0	5,664.2
1989	n/a	n/a	n/a	14,251,400	n/a	n/a	n/a	5,741.0
1990	n/a	n/a	n/a	14,475,600	n/a	n/a	n/a	5,820.3
1991	n/a	n/a	n/a	14,872,900	n/a	n/a	n/a	5,897.8
1992	11,791	n/a	n/a	14,438,200	6,967.1	n/a	n/a	5,660.2
1993	n/a	n/a	n/a	14,144,800	n/a	n/a	n/a	5,484.4
1994	11,426	7,399	18,825	13,989,500	6,936.5	2,399.9	3,979.7	5,373.5
1995	11,386	7,310	18,696	13,862,700	6,847.1	2,330.7	3,895.6	5,275.9
1996	10,043	6,401	16,444	13,473,600	6,021.6	2,035.0	3,416.4	5,078.9

Notes: (1) Metropolitan Statistical Area - see Appendix A for areas included; (2) calculated by the editors using the following formula: (number of crimes in the MSA minus number of crimes in the city); (3) calculated by the editors using the following formula: ((number of crimes in the MSA minus number of crimes in the city) ÷ (population of the MSA minus population of the city)) x 100,000; n/a not avail.
Source: U.S. Department of Justice, FBI Uniform Crime Reports, 1977 - 1996

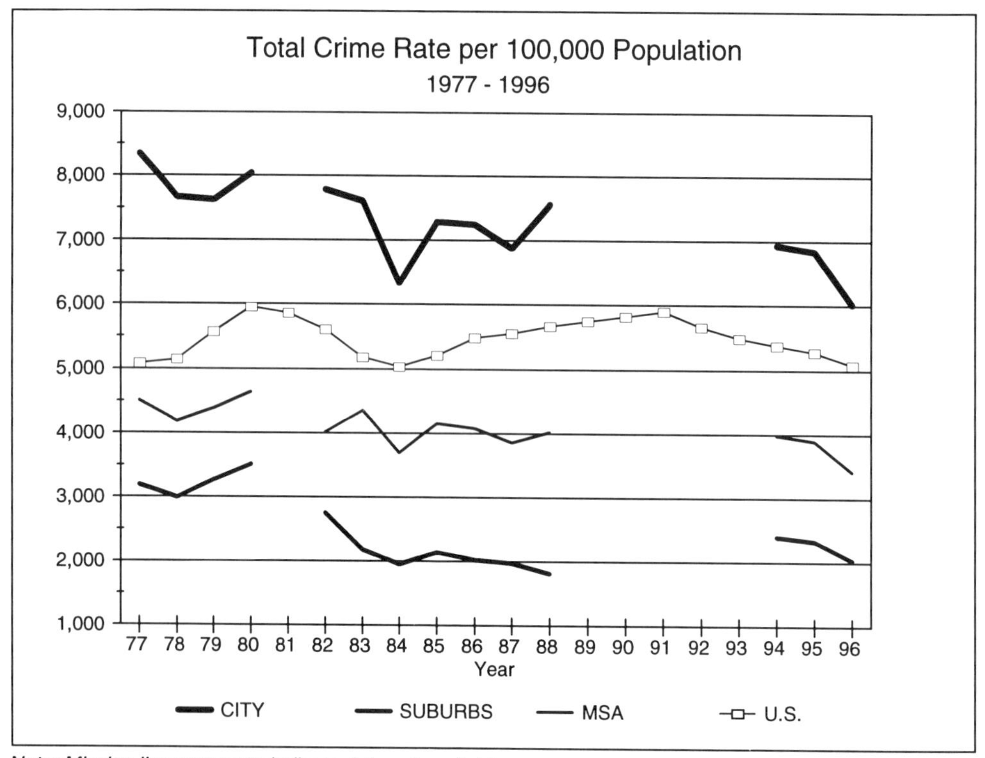

Note: Missing line segments indicate data not available.

Violent Crimes and Violent Crime Rates: 1977 - 1996

Year	Number				Rate per 100,000 population			
	City	Suburbs[2]	MSA[1]	U.S.	City	Suburbs[3]	MSA[1]	U.S.
1977	749	762	1,511	1,029,580	453.9	158.7	234.2	475.9
1978	807	878	1,685	1,085,550	492.1	182.8	261.6	497.8
1979	955	903	1,858	1,208,030	578.9	188.3	288.2	548.9
1980	1,169	1,043	2,212	1,344,520	724.4	216.1	343.5	596.6
1981	n/a	n/a	n/a	1,361,820	n/a	n/a	n/a	594.3
1982	1,273	859	2,132	1,322,390	781.6	176.4	328.1	571.1
1983	1,150	349	1,499	1,258,090	707.8	143.2	369.1	537.7
1984	1,343	322	1,665	1,273,280	827.5	130.9	407.9	539.2
1985	1,521	425	1,946	1,328,800	947.6	170.2	474.4	556.6
1986	1,794	387	2,181	1,489,170	1,115.7	155.6	532.6	617.7
1987	1,463	373	1,836	1,484,000	923.6	146.6	444.7	609.7
1988	1,464	445	1,909	1,566,220	920.0	174.0	460.2	637.2
1989	n/a	n/a	n/a	1,646,040	n/a	n/a	n/a	663.1
1990	n/a	n/a	n/a	1,820,130	n/a	n/a	n/a	731.8
1991	n/a	n/a	n/a	1,911,770	n/a	n/a	n/a	758.1
1992	1,291	n/a	n/a	1,932,270	762.8	n/a	n/a	757.5
1993	n/a	n/a	n/a	1,926,020	n/a	n/a	n/a	746.8
1994	1,697	1,310	3,007	1,857,670	1,030.2	424.9	635.7	713.6
1995	1,782	1,366	3,148	1,798,790	1,071.6	435.5	655.9	684.6
1996	1,563	1,257	2,820	1,682,280	937.2	399.6	585.9	634.1

Notes: Violent crimes include murder, forcible rape, robbery and aggravated assault; n/a not available; (1) Metropolitan Statistical Area - see Appendix A for areas included; (2) calculated by the editors using the following formula: (number of crimes in the MSA minus number of crimes in the city); (3) calculated by the editors using the following formula: ((number of crimes in the MSA minus number of crimes in the city) ÷ (population of the MSA minus population of the city)) x 100,000
Source: U.S. Department of Justice, FBI Uniform Crime Reports, 1977 - 1996

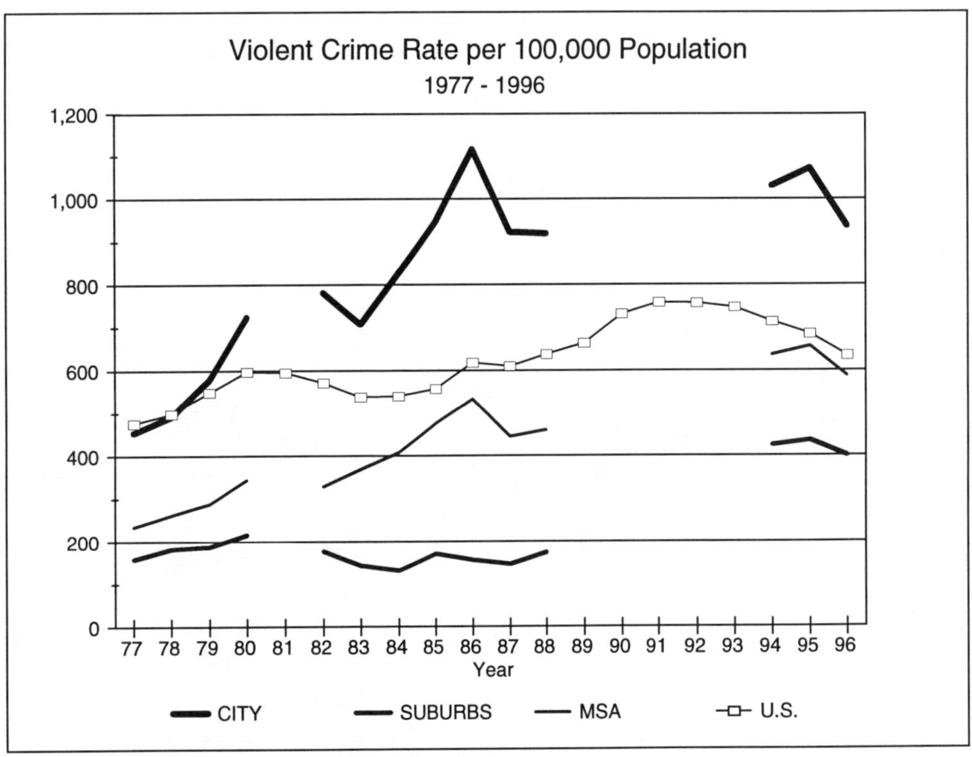

Note: Missing line segments indicate data not available.

Property Crimes and Property Crime Rates: 1977 - 1996

Year	Number				Rate per 100,000 population			
	City	Suburbs[2]	MSA[1]	U.S.	City	Suburbs[3]	MSA[1]	U.S.
1977	13,013	14,534	27,547	9,955,000	7,886.7	3,026.9	4,269.8	4,601.7
1978	11,770	13,490	25,260	10,123,400	7,176.8	2,809.1	3,921.0	4,642.5
1979	11,618	14,763	26,381	11,041,500	7,042.9	3,078.0	4,092.7	5,016.6
1980	11,809	15,884	27,693	12,063,700	7,317.3	3,291.4	4,300.4	5,353.3
1981	n/a	n/a	n/a	12,061,900	n/a	n/a	n/a	5,263.9
1982	11,416	12,556	23,972	11,652,000	7,009.3	2,578.1	3,688.6	5,032.5
1983	11,211	4,972	16,183	10,850,500	6,900.2	2,040.4	3,984.4	4,637.4
1984	8,938	4,479	13,417	10,608,500	5,507.2	1,821.3	3,286.7	4,492.1
1985	10,180	4,918	15,098	11,102,600	6,342.0	1,969.9	3,680.9	4,650.5
1986	9,868	4,643	14,511	11,722,700	6,137.1	1,867.0	3,543.8	4,862.6
1987	9,445	4,652	14,097	12,024,700	5,962.9	1,827.9	3,414.2	4,940.3
1988	10,572	4,198	14,770	12,356,900	6,643.9	1,641.9	3,560.8	5,027.1
1989	n/a	n/a	n/a	12,605,400	n/a	n/a	n/a	5,077.9
1990	n/a	n/a	n/a	12,655,500	n/a	n/a	n/a	5,088.5
1991	n/a	n/a	n/a	12,961,100	n/a	n/a	n/a	5,139.7
1992	10,500	n/a	n/a	12,505,900	6,204.3	n/a	n/a	4,902.7
1993	10,317	6,435	16,752	12,218,800	6,293.5	2,097.2	3,558.4	4,737.6
1994	9,729	6,089	15,818	12,131,900	5,906.3	1,975.0	3,344.0	4,660.0
1995	9,604	5,944	15,548	12,063,900	5,775.5	1,895.2	3,239.6	4,591.3
1996	8,480	5,144	13,624	11,791,300	5,084.5	1,635.4	2,830.5	4,444.8

Notes: Property crimes include burglary, larceny-theft and motor vehicle theft; n/a not available; (1) Metropolitan Statistical Area - see Appendix A for areas included; (2) calculated by the editors using the following formula: (number of crimes in the MSA minus number of crimes in the city); (3) calculated by the editors using the following formula: ((number of crimes in the MSA minus number of crimes in the city) ÷ (population of the MSA minus population of the city)) x 100,000
Source: U.S. Department of Justice, FBI Uniform Crime Reports, 1977 - 1996

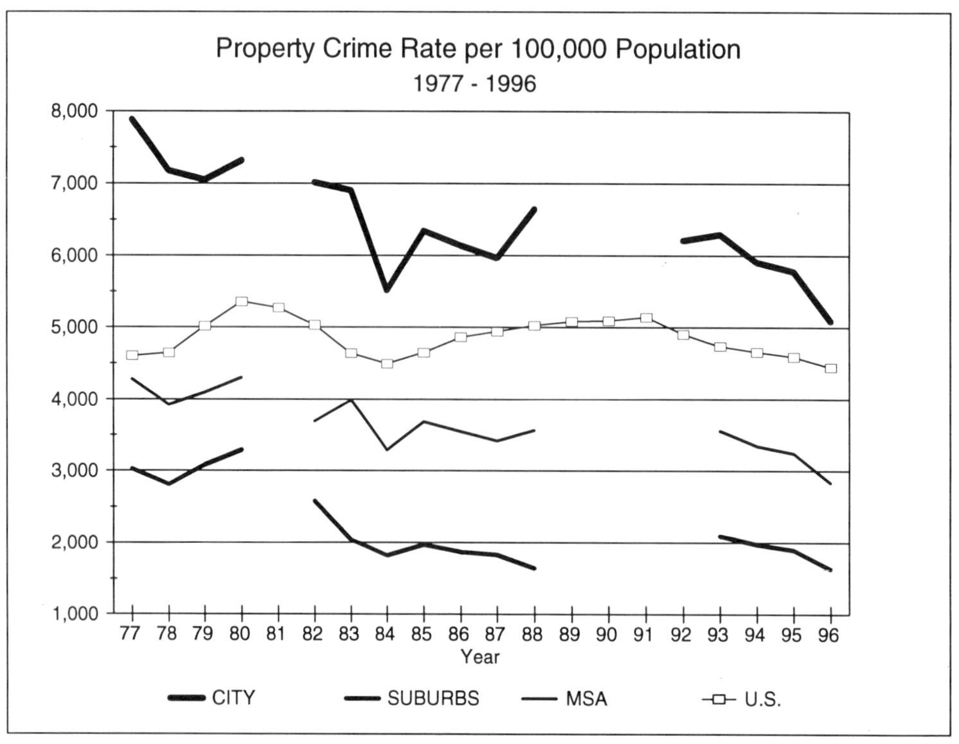

Note: Missing line segments indicate data not available.

Murders and Murder Rates: 1977 - 1996

Year	Number				Rate per 100,000 population			
	City	Suburbs[2]	MSA[1]	U.S.	City	Suburbs[3]	MSA[1]	U.S.
1977	4	11	15	19,120	2.4	2.3	2.3	8.8
1978	6	3	9	19,560	3.7	0.6	1.4	9.0
1979	16	10	26	21,460	9.7	2.1	4.0	9.7
1980	6	8	14	23,040	3.7	1.7	2.2	10.2
1981	n/a	n/a	n/a	22,520	n/a	n/a	n/a	9.8
1982	8	9	17	21,010	4.9	1.8	2.6	9.1
1983	9	3	12	19,310	5.5	1.2	3.0	8.3
1984	8	1	9	18,690	4.9	0.4	2.2	7.9
1985	6	5	11	18,980	3.7	2.0	2.7	7.9
1986	4	8	12	20,610	2.5	3.2	2.9	8.6
1987	13	0	13	20,100	8.2	0.0	3.1	8.3
1988	11	1	12	20,680	6.9	0.4	2.9	8.4
1989	n/a	n/a	n/a	21,500	n/a	n/a	n/a	8.7
1990	n/a	n/a	n/a	23,440	n/a	n/a	n/a	9.4
1991	n/a	n/a	n/a	24,700	n/a	n/a	n/a	9.8
1992	13	n/a	n/a	23,760	7.7	n/a	n/a	9.3
1993	12	3	15	24,530	7.3	1.0	3.2	9.5
1994	13	5	18	23,330	7.9	1.6	3.8	9.0
1995	5	5	10	21,610	3.0	1.6	2.1	8.2
1996	7	0	7	19,650	4.2	0.0	1.5	7.4

Notes: (1) Metropolitan Statistical Area - see Appendix A for areas included; (2) calculated by the editors using the following formula: (number of crimes in the MSA minus number of crimes in the city); (3) calculated by the editors using the following formula: ((number of crimes in the MSA minus number of crimes in the city) ÷ (population of the MSA minus population of the city)) x 100,000; n/a not avail.
Source: U.S. Department of Justice, FBI Uniform Crime Reports, 1977 - 1996

Forcible Rapes and Forcible Rape Rates: 1977 - 1996

Year	Number				Rate per 100,000 population			
	City	Suburbs[2]	MSA[1]	U.S.	City	Suburbs[3]	MSA[1]	U.S.
1977	48	63	111	63,500	29.1	13.1	17.2	29.4
1978	37	58	95	67,610	22.6	12.1	14.7	31.0
1979	85	65	150	76,390	51.5	13.6	23.3	34.7
1980	59	89	148	82,990	36.6	18.4	23.0	36.8
1981	n/a	n/a	n/a	82,500	n/a	n/a	n/a	36.0
1982	74	91	165	78,770	45.4	18.7	25.4	34.0
1983	65	37	102	78,920	40.0	15.2	25.1	33.7
1984	87	35	122	84,230	53.6	14.2	29.9	35.7
1985	109	40	149	88,670	67.9	16.0	36.3	37.1
1986	82	30	112	91,460	51.0	12.1	27.4	37.9
1987	83	34	117	91,110	52.4	13.4	28.3	37.4
1988	91	38	129	92,490	57.2	14.9	31.1	37.6
1989	n/a	n/a	n/a	94,500	n/a	n/a	n/a	38.1
1990	n/a	n/a	n/a	102,560	n/a	n/a	n/a	41.2
1991	n/a	n/a	n/a	106,590	n/a	n/a	n/a	42.3
1992	112	n/a	n/a	109,060	66.2	n/a	n/a	42.8
1993	77	68	145	106,010	47.0	22.2	30.8	41.1
1994	68	51	119	102,220	41.3	16.5	25.2	39.3
1995	82	39	121	97,470	49.3	12.4	25.2	37.1
1996	108	56	164	95,770	64.8	17.8	34.1	36.1

Notes: (1) Metropolitan Statistical Area - see Appendix A for areas included; (2) calculated by the editors using the following formula: (number of crimes in the MSA minus number of crimes in the city); (3) calculated by the editors using the following formula: ((number of crimes in the MSA minus number of crimes in the city) ÷ (population of the MSA minus population of the city)) x 100,000; n/a not avail.
Source: U.S. Department of Justice, FBI Uniform Crime Reports, 1977 - 1996

Robberies and Robbery Rates: 1977 - 1996

Year	Number				Rate per 100,000 population			
	City	Suburbs[2]	MSA[1]	U.S.	City	Suburbs[3]	MSA[1]	U.S.
1977	323	170	493	412,610	195.8	35.4	76.4	190.7
1978	380	170	550	426,930	231.7	35.4	85.4	195.8
1979	420	208	628	480,700	254.6	43.4	97.4	218.4
1980	605	228	833	565,840	374.9	47.2	129.4	251.1
1981	n/a	n/a	n/a	592,910	n/a	n/a	n/a	258.7
1982	554	184	738	553,130	340.2	37.8	113.6	238.9
1983	525	63	588	506,570	323.1	25.9	144.8	216.5
1984	524	53	577	485,010	322.9	21.6	141.3	205.4
1985	638	70	708	497,870	397.5	28.0	172.6	208.5
1986	550	60	610	542,780	342.1	24.1	149.0	225.1
1987	515	73	588	517,700	325.1	28.7	142.4	212.7
1988	422	33	455	542,970	265.2	12.9	109.7	220.9
1989	n/a	n/a	n/a	578,330	n/a	n/a	n/a	233.0
1990	n/a	n/a	n/a	639,270	n/a	n/a	n/a	257.0
1991	n/a	n/a	n/a	687,730	n/a	n/a	n/a	272.7
1992	448	n/a	n/a	672,480	264.7	n/a	n/a	263.6
1993	628	85	713	659,870	383.1	27.7	151.5	255.9
1994	668	88	756	618,950	405.5	28.5	159.8	237.7
1995	431	77	508	580,510	259.2	24.6	105.8	220.9
1996	410	56	466	537,050	245.8	17.8	96.8	202.4

Notes: (1) Metropolitan Statistical Area - see Appendix A for areas included; (2) calculated by the editors using the following formula: (number of crimes in the MSA minus number of crimes in the city); (3) calculated by the editors using the following formula: ((number of crimes in the MSA minus number of crimes in the city) ÷ (population of the MSA minus population of the city)) x 100,000; n/a not avail.
Source: U.S. Department of Justice, FBI Uniform Crime Reports, 1977 - 1996

Aggravated Assaults and Aggravated Assault Rates: 1977 - 1996

Year	Number				Rate per 100,000 population			
	City	Suburbs[2]	MSA[1]	U.S.	City	Suburbs[3]	MSA[1]	U.S.
1977	374	518	892	534,350	226.7	107.9	138.3	247.0
1978	384	647	1,031	571,460	234.1	134.7	160.0	262.1
1979	434	620	1,054	629,480	263.1	129.3	163.5	286.0
1980	499	718	1,217	672,650	309.2	148.8	189.0	298.5
1981	n/a	n/a	n/a	663,900	n/a	n/a	n/a	289.7
1982	637	575	1,212	669,480	391.1	118.1	186.5	289.2
1983	551	246	797	653,290	339.1	101.0	196.2	279.2
1984	724	233	957	685,350	446.1	94.7	234.4	290.2
1985	768	310	1,078	723,250	478.5	124.2	262.8	302.9
1986	1,158	289	1,447	834,320	720.2	116.2	353.4	346.1
1987	852	266	1,118	855,090	537.9	104.5	270.8	351.3
1988	940	373	1,313	910,090	590.7	145.9	316.5	370.2
1989	n/a	n/a	n/a	951,710	n/a	n/a	n/a	383.4
1990	n/a	n/a	n/a	1,054,860	n/a	n/a	n/a	424.1
1991	n/a	n/a	n/a	1,092,740	n/a	n/a	n/a	433.3
1992	718	n/a	n/a	1,126,970	424.3	n/a	n/a	441.8
1993	n/a	n/a	n/a	1,135,610	n/a	n/a	n/a	440.3
1994	948	1,166	2,114	1,113,180	575.5	378.2	446.9	427.6
1995	1,264	1,245	2,509	1,099,210	760.1	397.0	522.8	418.3
1996	1,038	1,145	2,183	1,029,810	622.4	364.0	453.5	388.2

Notes: (1) Metropolitan Statistical Area - see Appendix A for areas included; (2) calculated by the editors using the following formula: (number of crimes in the MSA minus number of crimes in the city); (3) calculated by the editors using the following formula: ((number of crimes in the MSA minus number of crimes in the city) ÷ (population of the MSA minus population of the city)) x 100,000; n/a not avail.
Source: U.S. Department of Justice, FBI Uniform Crime Reports, 1977 - 1996

Burglaries and Burglary Rates: 1977 - 1996

Year	Number				Rate per 100,000 population			
	City	Suburbs[2]	MSA[1]	U.S.	City	Suburbs[3]	MSA[1]	U.S.
1977	4,076	4,890	8,966	3,071,500	2,470.3	1,018.4	1,389.7	1,419.8
1978	3,707	4,700	8,407	3,128,300	2,260.4	978.7	1,305.0	1,434.6
1979	3,641	4,721	8,362	3,327,700	2,207.2	984.3	1,297.3	1,511.9
1980	4,294	5,747	10,041	3,795,200	2,660.7	1,190.9	1,559.2	1,684.1
1981	n/a	n/a	n/a	3,779,700	n/a	n/a	n/a	1,649.5
1982	4,430	4,071	8,501	3,447,100	2,720.0	835.9	1,308.1	1,488.8
1983	4,336	1,696	6,032	3,129,900	2,668.7	696.0	1,485.1	1,337.7
1984	3,202	1,466	4,668	2,984,400	1,972.9	596.1	1,143.5	1,263.7
1985	3,408	1,628	5,036	3,073,300	2,123.1	652.1	1,227.8	1,287.3
1986	2,942	1,434	4,376	3,241,400	1,829.7	576.6	1,068.7	1,344.6
1987	3,252	1,411	4,663	3,236,200	2,053.1	554.4	1,129.3	1,329.6
1988	3,378	1,180	4,558	3,218,100	2,122.9	461.5	1,098.8	1,309.2
1989	n/a	n/a	n/a	3,168,200	n/a	n/a	n/a	1,276.3
1990	n/a	n/a	n/a	3,073,900	n/a	n/a	n/a	1,235.9
1991	n/a	n/a	n/a	3,157,200	n/a	n/a	n/a	1,252.0
1992	4,333	n/a	n/a	2,979,900	2,560.3	n/a	n/a	1,168.2
1993	3,404	1,712	5,116	2,834,800	2,076.5	557.9	1,086.7	1,099.2
1994	3,234	1,647	4,881	2,712,800	1,963.3	534.2	1,031.9	1,042.0
1995	2,523	1,633	4,156	2,593,800	1,517.2	520.7	866.0	987.1
1996	2,230	1,256	3,486	2,501,500	1,337.1	399.3	724.2	943.0

Notes: (1) Metropolitan Statistical Area - see Appendix A for areas included; (2) calculated by the editors using the following formula: (number of crimes in the MSA minus number of crimes in the city); (3) calculated by the editors using the following formula: ((number of crimes in the MSA minus number of crimes in the city) ÷ (population of the MSA minus population of the city)) x 100,000; n/a not avail.
Source: U.S. Department of Justice, FBI Uniform Crime Reports, 1977 - 1996

Larceny-Thefts and Larceny-Theft Rates: 1977 - 1996

Year	Number				Rate per 100,000 population			
	City	Suburbs[2]	MSA[1]	U.S.	City	Suburbs[3]	MSA[1]	U.S.
1977	4,955	7,464	12,419	5,905,700	3,003.0	1,554.5	1,925.0	2,729.9
1978	4,866	6,986	11,852	5,991,000	2,967.1	1,454.7	1,839.7	2,747.4
1979	5,284	8,117	13,401	6,601,000	3,203.2	1,692.4	2,079.0	2,999.1
1980	5,446	8,481	13,927	7,136,900	3,374.6	1,757.4	2,162.7	3,167.0
1981	n/a	n/a	n/a	7,194,400	n/a	n/a	n/a	3,139.7
1982	5,605	7,229	12,834	7,142,500	3,441.4	1,484.3	1,974.8	3,084.8
1983	5,622	2,767	8,389	6,712,800	3,460.2	1,135.5	2,065.5	2,868.9
1984	4,786	2,552	7,338	6,591,900	2,948.9	1,037.7	1,797.5	2,791.3
1985	5,579	2,762	8,341	6,926,400	3,475.6	1,106.3	2,033.5	2,901.2
1986	5,817	2,683	8,500	7,257,200	3,617.7	1,078.9	2,075.8	3,010.3
1987	5,021	2,687	7,708	7,499,900	3,169.9	1,055.8	1,866.8	3,081.3
1988	6,022	2,538	8,560	7,705,900	3,784.5	992.7	2,063.7	3,134.9
1989	n/a	n/a	n/a	7,872,400	n/a	n/a	n/a	3,171.3
1990	n/a	n/a	n/a	7,945,700	n/a	n/a	n/a	3,194.8
1991	n/a	n/a	n/a	8,142,200	n/a	n/a	n/a	3,228.8
1992	4,774	n/a	n/a	7,915,200	2,820.9	n/a	n/a	3,103.0
1993	5,221	3,983	9,204	7,820,900	3,184.9	1,298.1	1,955.1	3,032.4
1994	5,108	3,975	9,083	7,879,800	3,101.0	1,289.3	1,920.2	3,026.7
1995	5,790	3,815	9,605	7,997,700	3,481.9	1,216.4	2,001.3	3,043.8
1996	5,137	3,436	8,573	7,894,600	3,080.1	1,092.4	1,781.1	2,975.9

Notes: (1) Metropolitan Statistical Area - see Appendix A for areas included; (2) calculated by the editors using the following formula: (number of crimes in the MSA minus number of crimes in the city); (3) calculated by the editors using the following formula: ((number of crimes in the MSA minus number of crimes in the city) ÷ (population of the MSA minus population of the city)) x 100,000; n/a not avail.
Source: U.S. Department of Justice, FBI Uniform Crime Reports, 1977 - 1996

Motor Vehicle Thefts and Motor Vehicle Theft Rates: 1977 - 1996

Year	Number				Rate per 100,000 population			
	City	Suburbs[2]	MSA[1]	U.S.	City	Suburbs[3]	MSA[1]	U.S.
1977	3,982	2,180	6,162	977,700	2,413.3	454.0	955.1	451.9
1978	3,197	1,804	5,001	1,004,100	1,949.4	375.7	776.3	460.5
1979	2,693	1,925	4,618	1,112,800	1,632.5	401.4	716.4	505.6
1980	2,069	1,656	3,725	1,131,700	1,282.0	343.2	578.4	502.2
1981	n/a	n/a	n/a	1,087,800	n/a	n/a	n/a	474.7
1982	1,381	1,256	2,637	1,062,400	847.9	257.9	405.8	458.8
1983	1,253	509	1,762	1,007,900	771.2	208.9	433.8	430.8
1984	950	461	1,411	1,032,200	585.3	187.5	345.6	437.1
1985	1,193	528	1,721	1,102,900	743.2	211.5	419.6	462.0
1986	1,109	526	1,635	1,224,100	689.7	211.5	399.3	507.8
1987	1,172	554	1,726	1,288,700	739.9	217.7	418.0	529.4
1988	1,172	480	1,652	1,432,900	736.5	187.7	398.3	582.9
1989	n/a	n/a	n/a	1,564,800	n/a	n/a	n/a	630.4
1990	n/a	n/a	n/a	1,635,900	n/a	n/a	n/a	657.8
1991	n/a	n/a	n/a	1,661,700	n/a	n/a	n/a	659.0
1992	1,393	n/a	n/a	1,610,800	823.1	n/a	n/a	631.5
1993	1,692	740	2,432	1,563,100	1,032.1	241.2	516.6	606.1
1994	1,387	467	1,854	1,539,300	842.0	151.5	391.9	591.3
1995	1,291	496	1,787	1,472,400	776.4	158.1	372.3	560.4
1996	1,113	452	1,565	1,395,200	667.3	143.7	325.1	525.9

Notes: (1) Metropolitan Statistical Area - see Appendix A for areas included; (2) calculated by the editors using the following formula: (number of crimes in the MSA minus number of crimes in the city); (3) calculated by the editors using the following formula: ((number of crimes in the MSA minus number of crimes in the city) ÷ (population of the MSA minus population of the city)) x 100,000; n/a not avail.
Source: U.S. Department of Justice, FBI Uniform Crime Reports, 1977 - 1996

HATE CRIMES

Criminal Incidents by Bias Motivation

Area	Race	Ethnicity	Religion	Sexual Orientation
Worcester	0	1	1	1

Notes: Figures include both violent and property crimes. Law enforcement agencies must have submitted data for at least one quarter of calendar year 1995 to be included in this report, therefore figures shown may not represent complete 12-month totals; n/a not available
Source: U.S. Department of Justice, FBI Uniform Crime Reports, Hate Crime Statistics 1995

LAW ENFORCEMENT

Full-Time Law Enforcement Employees

Jurisdiction	Police Employees			Police Officers per 100,000 population
	Total	Officers	Civilians	
Worcester	524	464	60	278.2

Notes: Data as of October 31, 1996
Source: U.S. Department of Justice, FBI Uniform Crime Reports, 1996

CORRECTIONS

Federal Correctional Facilities

Type	Year Opened	Security Level	Sex of Inmates	Rated Capacity	Population on 7/1/95	Number of Staff
None listed						

Notes: Data as of 1995
Source: Bureau of Justice Statistics, Sourcebook of Criminal Justice Statistics Online

City/County/Regional Correctional Facilities

Name	Year Opened	Year Renov.	Rated Capacity	1995 Pop.	Number of COs[1]	Number of Staff	ACA[2] Accred.
None listed							

Notes: Data as of April 1996; (1) Correctional Officers; (2) American Correctional Assn. Accreditation
Source: American Correctional Association, 1996-1998 National Jail and Adult Detention Directory

Private Adult Correctional Facilities

Name	Date Opened	Rated Capacity	Present Pop.	Security Level	Facility Construct.	Expans. Plans	ACA[1] Accred.
None listed							

Notes: Data as of December 1996; (1) American Correctional Association Accreditation
Source: University of Florida, Center for Studies in Criminology and Law, Private Adult Correctional Facility Census, 10th Ed., March 15, 1997

Characteristics of Shock Incarceration Programs

Jurisdiction	Year Program Began	Number of Camps	Average Num. of Inmates	Number of Beds	Program Length	Voluntary/ Mandatory
Massachusetts did not have a shock incarceration program as of July 1996						

Source: Sourcebook of Criminal Justice Statistics Online

DEATH PENALTY

Massachusetts did not have the death penalty as of July 31, 1997.
Source: Death Penalty Information Center Web Site, 9/30/97

LAWS

Statutory Provisions Relating to the Purchase, Ownership and Use of Handguns

Jurisdiction	Instant Background Check	Federal Waiting Period Applies[1]	State Waiting Period (days)	License or Permit to Purchase	Regis-tration	Record of Sale Sent to Police	Concealed Carry Law
Massachusetts	No	No	7	Yes[a]	No	Yes	Yes[b]

Note: Data as of 1996; (1) The Federal 5-day waiting period for handgun purchases applies to states that don't have instant background checks, waiting period requirements, or licensing procedures exempting them from the Federal requirement; (a) Firearm owners must possess a Firearms Owner's ID Card (FID) or a license to carry.; (b) Restrictively administered discretion by local authorities over permit issuance, or permits are unavailable and carrying is prohibited in most circumstances
Source: Sourcebook of Criminal Justice Statistics Online

Statutory Provisions Relating to Alcohol Use and Driving

Jurisdiction	Drinking Age	Blood Alcohol Concentration Levels as Evidence in State Courts[1]		Open Container Law[1]	Anti-Consump-tion Law[1]	Dram Shop Law[1]
		Illegal per se at 0.10%	Presumption at 0.10%			
Massachusetts	21	No	(a)	No	Yes[b]	(c)

Note: Data as of January 1, 1997; (1) See Appendix C for an explanation of terms; (a) 0.08%; (b) Applies to drivers only; (c) Adopted via case law decisions
Source: Sourcebook of Criminal Justice Statistics Online

Statutory Provisions Relating to Hate Crimes

Jurisdiction	Bias-Motivated Violence and Intimidation						Institutional Vandalism
	Civil Action	Criminal Penalty					
		Race/ Religion/ Ethnicity	Sexual Orientation	Mental/ Physical Disability	Gender	Age	
Massachusetts	Yes	Yes	No	No	No	No	Yes

Source: Anti-Defamation League, 1997 Hate Crimes Laws

Appendix A

Metropolitan Statistical Areas

Abilene, TX

1977–1982
Includes Callahan, Jones and Taylor Counties

1983–1996
Includes Taylor County

Albuquerque, NM

1977–1982
Includes Bernalillo and Sandoval Counties

1983–1991
Includes Bernalillo County

1992–1996
Includes Bernalillo, Sandoval and Valencia Counties

Amarillo, TX

1977–1996
Includes Potter and Randall Counties

Ann Arbor, MI

1977–1992
Includes Washtenaw County

1993–1996
Includes Lenawee, Livingston and Washtenaw Counties

Atlanta, GA

1977–1982
Includes Butts, Cherokee, Clayton, Cobb, DeKalb, Douglas, Fayette, Forsythe, Fulton, Gwinnett, Henry, Newton, Paulding, Rockdale and Walton Counties

1983–1991
Includes Barrow, Butts, Cherokee, Clayton, Cobb, Coweta, DeKalb, Douglas, Fayette, Forsythe, Fulton, Gwinnett, Henry, Newton, Paulding, Rockdale, Spalding and Walton Counties

1992
Includes Barrow, Bartow, Carroll, Cherokee, Clayton, Cobb, Coweta, DeKalb, Douglas, Fayette, Forsythe, Fulton, Gwinnett, Henry, Newton, Paulding, Pickens, Rockdale, Spalding and Walton Counties

1993–1996
Includes Barrow, Bartow, Carroll, Cherokee, Cobb, Coweta, DeKalb, Douglas, Fayette, Forsythe, Fulton, Gwinnett, Henry, Newton, Paulding, Pickens, Rockdale, Spalding and Walton Counties

Austin-San Marcos, TX

1977–1991
Includes Hays, Travis and Williamson Counties

1992–1996
Includes Bastrop, Caldwell, Hays, Travis and Williamson Counties

Baltimore, MD

1977–1982
Includes Baltimore City; Anne Arundel, Baltimore, Carroll, Harford and Howard Counties

1983–1996
Includes Baltimore City; Anne Arundel, Baltimore, Carroll, Harford, Howard and Queen Anne's Counties

Boston, MA-NH

1977–1982
Includes Essex, Middlesex, Norfolk and Suffolk Counties

1983–1991
Includes parts of Bristol, Essex, Middlesex, Norfolk, Plymouth and Worcester Counties, MA; and all of Suffolk County, MA

1992
Includes all of Essex and Suffolk County, MA; parts of Bristol, Hampden, Middlesex, Norfolk, Plymouth and Worcester Counties, MA; all of Strafford County, NH; parts of Hillsborough, Merrimack and Rockingham County, NH; all of Windham County, CT; all of York County, ME

1993–1996
Includes parts of Bristol, Essex, Middlesex, Plymouth, Suffolk and Worcester Counties, MA; part of Rockingham County, NH

Charlotte-Gastonia-Rock Hill, NC-SC

1977–1982
Includes Gaston, Mecklenburg and Union Counties, NC

1983–1996
Includes Cabarrus, Gaston, Lincoln, Mecklenburg, Rowan and Union Counties, NC; York County, SC

Chicago, IL

1977–1982
Includes Cook, DuPage, Grundy, Kane, Lake, McHenry and Will Counties

1983–1991
Includes Cook, DuPage and McHenry Counties

1992–1996
Includes Cook, DeKalb, DuPage, Grundy, Kane, Kendall, Lake, McHenry and Will Counties

Cincinnati, OH-KY-IN

1977–1991
Includes Clermont, Hamilton and Warren Counties, OH; Boone, Campbell and Kenton Counties, KY; Dearborn County, IN

1992–1996
Includes Brown, Clermont, Hamilton and Warren Counties, OH; Boone, Campbell, Gallatin, Grant, Kenton and Pendleton Counties, KY; Dearborn and Ohio Counties, IN

Cleveland, OH

1977–1991
Includes Cuyahoga, Geauga, Lake and Medina Counties

1992–1996
Includes Ashtabula, Cuyahoga, Geauga, Lake, Lorain and Medina Counties

Colorado Springs, CO

1977–1982
Includes El Paso and Teller Counties

1983–1996
Includes El Paso County

Columbus, OH

1977–1982
Includes Delaware, Fairfield, Franklin, Madison and Pickaway Counties

1983–1991
Includes Delaware, Fairfield, Franklin, Licking, Madison, Pickaway and Union Counties

1992–1996
Includes Delaware, Fairfield, Franklin, Licking, Madison and Pickaway Counties

Dallas, TX

1977–1982
Dallas was part of the Dallas-Ft. Worth MSA which included Collin, Dallas, Denton, Ellis, Hood, Johnson, Kaufman, Parker, Rockwall, Tarrant and Wise Counties

1983–1991
Includes Collin, Dallas, Denton, Ellis, Kaufman and Rockwall Counties

1992
Includes Collin, Dallas, Denton, Ellis, Henderson, Hunt, Kaufman and Rockwall Counties

1993–1996
Includes Collin, Dallas, Denton, Ellis, Henderson, Kaufman and Rockwall Counties

Denver, CO

1977–1982
Includes Adams, Arapahoe, Boulder, Denver, Douglas, Gilpin and Jefferson Counties

1983–1996
Includes Adams, Arapahoe, Denver, Douglas and Jefferson Counties

Detroit, MI

1977–1982
Includes Lapeer, Livingston, Macomb, Oakland, St. Clair and Wayne Counties

1983–1991
Includes Lapeer, Livingston, Macomb, Monroe, Oakland, St. Clair and Wayne Counties

1992–1996
Includes Lapeer, Macomb, Monroe, Oakland, St. Clair and Wayne Counties

Durham, NC

See Raleigh-Durham-Chapel Hill, NC

Eugene-Springfield, OR

1977–1996
Includes Lane County

Flint, MI

1977–1982
Includes Genesee and Shiawassee Counties

1983–1996
Includes Genesee County

Ft. Lauderdale, FL

1977–1996
Includes Broward County

Ft. Wayne, IN

1977–1982
Includes Adams, Allen, DeKalb and Wells Counties

1983–1992
Includes Allen, DeKalb and Whitley Counties

1993–1996
Includes Adams, Allen, DeKalb, Huntington, Wells and Whitley Counties

Ft. Worth-Arlington, TX

1977–1982
Ft. Worth was part of the Dallas-Ft. Worth MSA which included Collin, Dallas, Denton, Ellis, Hood, Johnson, Kaufman, Parker, Rockwall, Tarrant and Wise Counties

1983–1996
Includes Johnson, Parker and Tarrant Counties

Grand Rapids-Muskegon-Holland, MI

1977–1991
Includes Kent and Ottawa Counties

1992–1996
Includes Allegan, Kent, Muskegon and Ottawa Counties

Greensboro–Winston-Salem–High Point, NC

1977–1982
Includes Davidson, Forsyth, Guilford, Randolph, Stokes and Yadkin Counties

1983–1991
Includes Davidson, Davie, Forsyth, Guilford, Randolph, Stokes and Yadkin Counties

1992–1996
Includes Alamance, Davidson, Davie, Forsyth, Guilford, Randolph, Stokes and Yadkin Counties

Honolulu, HI

1977–1996
Includes Honolulu County

Houston, TX

1977–1982
Includes Brazoria, Fort Bend, Harris, Liberty, Montgomery and Waller Counties

1983–1991
Includes Fort Bend, Harris, Liberty, Montgomery and Waller Counties

1992–1996
Includes Chambers, Fort Bend, Harris, Liberty, Montgomery and Waller Counties

Indianapolis, IN

1977–1991
Includes Boone, Hamilton, Hancock, Hendricks, Johnson, Marion, Morgan and Shelby Counties

1992–1996
Includes Boone, Hamilton, Hancock, Hendricks, Johnson, Madison, Marion, Morgan and Shelby Counties

Jacksonville, FL

1977–1982
Includes Baker, Clay, Duval, Nassau and St. Johns Counties

1983–1996
Includes Clay, Duval, Nassau and St. Johns Counties

Kansas City, KS-MO

1977–1982
Includes Cass, Clay, Jackson, Platte and Ray Counties, MO; Johnson and Wyandotte Counties, KS

1983–1991
Includes Cass, Clay, Jackson, Lafayette, Platte and Ray Counties, MO; Johnson, Leavenworth, Miami and Wyandotte Counties, KS

1992–1996
Includes Cass, Clay, Clinton, Jackson, Lafayette, Platte and Ray Counties, MO; Johnson, Leavenworth, Miami and Wyandotte Counties, KS

Knoxville, TN

1977–1982
Includes Anderson, Blount, Knox and Union Counties

1983–1996
Includes Anderson, Blount, Grainger, Jefferson, Knox, Sevier and Union Counties

Lansing, MI

1977–1982
Includes Clinton, Eaton, Ingham and Ionia Counties

1983–1996
Includes Clinton, Eaton and Ingham Counties

Las Vegas, NV-AZ

1977–1991
Includes Clark County

1992–1996
Includes Clark and Nye Counties, NV; Mohave County, AZ

Lexington-Fayette, KY

1977–1992
Includes Bourbon, Clark, Fayette, Jessamine, Scott and Woodford Counties

1993–1996
Includes Bourbon, Clark, Fayette, Jessamine, Madison, Scott and Woodford Counties

Los Angeles-Long Beach, CA

1977–1996
Includes Los Angeles County

Lubbock, TX

1977–1996
Includes Lubbock County

Madison, WI

1977–1996
Includes Dane County

Manchester, NH

1977–1982
Includes Hillsborough County

1983–1996
Includes parts of Hillsborough, Merrimack and Rockingham Counties

Miami, FL

1977–1996
Includes Dade County

Milwaukee-Waukesha, WI

1977–1996
Includes Milwaukee, Ozaukee, Washington and Waukesha Counties

Mobile, AL

1977–1996
Includes Baldwin and Mobile Counties

Minneapolis-St. Paul, MN-WI

1977–1982
Includes Anoka, Carver, Chisago, Dakota, Hennepin, Ramsey, Scott, Washington and Wright Counties, MN; St. Croix County, WI

1983–1991
Includes Anoka, Carver, Chisago, Dakota, Hennepin, Isanti, Ramsey, Scott, Washington and Wright Counties, MN; St. Croix County, WI

1992–1996
Includes Anoka, Carver, Chisago, Dakota, Hennepin, Isanti, Ramsey, Scott, Sherburne, Washington, Wright and Pierce Counties, MN; St. Croix County, WI

Nashville, TN

1977–1996
Includes Cheatham, Davidson, Dickson, Robertson, Rutherford, Sumner, Williamson and Wilson Counties

New Orleans, LA

1977–1982
Includes Jefferson, Orleans, St. Bernard and St. Tammany Parishes

1983–1991
Includes Jefferson, Orleans, St. Bernard, St. Charles, St. John the Baptist and St. Tammany Parishes

1992–1996
Includes Jefferson, Orleans, Plaquemines, St. Bernard, St. Charles, St. James, St. John the Baptist and St. Tammany Parishes

New York, NY

1977–1982
Includes Bronx, Kings, New York, Putnam, Queens, Richmond, Rockland and Westchester Counties, NY; Bergen County, NJ

1983–1991
Includes Bronx, Kings, New York, Putnam, Queens, Richmond, Rockland and Westchester Counties

1992
Includes Bronx, Kings, Nassau, New York, Putnam, Queens, Richmond, Rockland, Suffolk and Westchester Counties, NY; Bergen, Essex, Hudson, Hunterdon, Middlesex, Monmouth, Morris, Ocean, Passaic, Somerset, Sussex, Union and Warren Counties, NJ; Pike County, PA

1993–1996
Includes Bronx, Kings, New York, Putnam, Queens, Richmond, Rockland and Westchester Counties

Norfolk-Virginia Beach-Newport News, VA-NC

1977–1982
Includes Chesapeake, Norfolk, Portsmouth, Suffolk and Virginia Beach Cities, VA; Currituck County, NC

1983–1991
Includes Chesapeake, Hampton, Newport News, Norfolk, Poquoson, Portsmouth, Suffolk, Virginia Beach and Williamsburg Cities, VA; Gloucester, James City and York Counties, VA

1992–1996
Includes Chesapeake, Hampton, Newport News, Norfolk, Poquoson, Portsmouth, Suffolk, Virginia Beach and Williamsburg Cities, VA; Gloucester, Isle of Wright, James City, Mathews and York Counties, VA; Currituck County, NC

Oakland, CA

1977–1982
Oakland was part of the San Francisco-Oakland MSA which included Alameda, Contra Costa, Marin, San Francisco and San Mateo Counties

1983–1996
Includes Alameda and Contra Costa Counties

Omaha, NE-IA

1977–1982
Includes Douglas and Sarpy Counties, NE; Pottawattamie County, IA

1983–1996
Includes Douglas, Sarpy and Washington Counties, NE; Pottawattamie County, IA

Orlando, FL

1977–1991
Includes Orange, Osceola and Seminole Counties

1992–1996
Includes Lake, Orange, Osceola and Seminole Counties

Philadelphia, PA-NJ

1977–1991
Includes Bucks, Chester, Delaware, Montgomery and Philadelphia Counties, PA; Burlington, Camden and Gloucester Counties, NJ

1992–1996
Includes Bucks, Chester, Delaware, Montgomery and Philadelphia Counties, PA; Burlington, Camden, Gloucester and Salem Counties, NJ

Phoenix-Mesa, AZ

1977–1991
Includes Maricopa County

1992–1996
Includes Maricopa and Pinal Counties

Pittsburgh, PA

1977–1983
Includes Allegheny, Beaver, Washington and Westmoreland Counties

1984–1991
Includes Allegheny, Fayette, Washington and Westmoreland Counties

1992–1996
Includes Allegheny, Beaver, Butler, Fayette, Washington and Westmoreland Counties

Portland-Salem, OR-WA

1977–1982
Includes Clackamas, Multnomah and Washington Counties, OR; Clark County, WA

1983–1991
Includes Clackamas, Multnomah, Washington and Yamhill Counties, OR

1992–1996
Includes Clackamas, Columbia, Multnomah, Washington and Yamhill Counties, OR; Clark County, WA

Raleigh-Durham-Chapel Hill, NC

1977–1982
Includes Durham, Orange and Wake Counties

1983–1991
Includes Durham, Franklin, Orange and Wake Counties

1992–1996
Includes Chatham, Durham, Franklin, Johnston, Orange and Wake Counties

Reno, NV

1977–1996
Includes Washoe County

Richmond-Petersburg, VA

1977
Includes Richmond City; Charles City, Chesterfield, Goochland, Hanover, Henrico and Powhatan Counties

1978–1982
Includes Richmond City; Charles City, Chesterfield, Goochland, Hanover, Henrico, New Kent and Powhatan Counties

1983–1996
Includes Colonial Heights, Hopewell, Petersburg and Richmond Cities; Charles City, Chesterfield, Dinwiddie, Goochland, Hanover, Henrico, New Kent, Powhatan and Prince George Counties

Sacramento, CA

1977–1982
Includes Placer, Sacramento and Yolo Counties

1983–1991
Includes El Dorado, Placer, Sacramento and Yolo Counties

1992–1996
Includes El Dorado, Placer and Sacramento Counties

St. Louis, MO-IL

1977–1982
Includes St. Louis City and Franklin, Jefferson, St. Charles, St. Louis Counties, MO; Clinton, Madison, Monroe and St. Clair Counties, IL

1983–1985
Includes St. Louis City and Franklin, Jefferson, St. Charles, St. Louis Counties, MO; Monroe County, IL

1986–1988
Includes St. Louis City and Franklin, Jefferson, St. Charles and St. Louis Counties, MO; Clinton, Jersey, Madison, Monroe and St. Clair Counties, IL

1989–1991
Includes St. Louis and Sullivan Cities; Franklin, Jefferson, St. Charles and St. Louis Counties, MO; Clinton, Jersey, Madison, Monroe and St. Clair Counties, IL

1992–1996
Includes St. Louis City and Franklin, Jefferson, Lincoln, St. Charles, St. Louis and Warren Counties, MO; Jersey, Madison, Monroe and St. Clair Counties, IL

St. Paul, MN

See Minneapolis-St. Paul, MN-WI

Salt Lake City-Ogden, UT

1977–1982
Includes Davis, Salt Lake, Tooele and Weber Counties

1983–1996
Includes Davis, Salt Lake and Weber Counties

San Antonio, TX

1977–1991
Includes Bexar, Comal and Guadalupe Counties

1992–1996
Includes Bexar, Comal, Guadalupe and Wilson Counties

San Diego, CA

1977–1996
Includes San Diego County

San Francisco, CA

1977–1982
San Francisco was part of the San Francisco-Oakland MSA which included Alameda, Contra Costa, Marin, San Francisco and San Mateo Counties

1983–1996
Includes Marin, San Francisco and San Mateo Counties

San Jose, CA

1977–1996
Includes Santa Clara County

Seattle-Bellevue-Everett, WA

1977–1991
Includes King and Snohomish Counties

1992–1996
Includes Island, King and Snohomish Counties

Sioux Falls, SD

1977–1991
Includes Minnehaha County

1992–1996
Includes Lincoln and Minnehaha Counties

Springfield, MO

1977–1991
Includes Christian and Greene Counties

1992–1996
Includes Christian, Greene and Webster Counties

Stamford-Norwalk, CT

1977–1982
Was not classified as being in an MSA

1983–1996
Includes part of Fairfield County

Tacoma, WA

1977–1996
Includes Pierce County

Tallahassee, FL

1977–1982
Includes Leon and Wakulla Counties

1983–1996
Includes Gadsden and Leon Counties

Tampa-St. Petersburg-Clearwater, FL

1977–1982
Includes Hillsborough and Pinellas Counties

1983–1996
Includes Hernando, Hillsborough, Pasco and Pinellas Counties

Topeka, KS

1977–1982
Includes Shawnee County

1983–1996
Includes Jefferson, Osage and Shawnee Counties

Tucson, AZ

1977–1996
Includes Pima County

Washington, DC-MD-VA-WV

1977–1982
Includes District of Columbia; Charles, Montgomery and Prince George Counties, MD; Alexandria, Fairfax, Falls Church, Manassas and Manassas Park Cities and Arlington, Fairfax, Loudoun and Prince William Counties, VA

1983–1991
Includes District of Columbia; Calvert, Charles, Frederick, Montgomery and Prince George Counties, MD; Alexandria, Fairfax, Falls Church, Manassas and Manassas Park Cities and Arlington, Fairfax, Loudoun, Prince William and Stafford Counties, VA

1992–1996
Includes District of Columbia; Calvert, Charles, Frederick, Montgomery and Prince George Counties, MD; Alexandria, Fairfax, Falls Church, Fredericksburg, Manassas and Manassas Park Cities and Arlington, Clarke, Culpeper, Fairfax, Fauquier, King George, Loudoun, Prince William, Spotsylvania, Stafford and Warren Counties, VA; Berkeley and Jefferson Counties, WV

Worcester, MA-CT

1977–1982
Includes Worcester County

1983–1991
Includes part of Worcester County

1992–1996
Includes parts of Hampden and Worcester Counties, MA; Part of Windham County, CT

Appendix B

Police Departments

Abilene, TX

Police Department
PO Box 60
Abilene, TX 79604
(915) 676-6601

Albuquerque, NM

Police Department
400 Roma, NW
Albuquerque, NM 87102
(505) 768-2200

Amarillo, TX

Police Department
200 SE Third Ave.
Amarillo, TX 79101
(806) 378-3038

Ann Arbor, MI

Police Department
City Hall
100 N. Fifth Ave.
Ann Arbor, MI 48107
(313) 994-2855

Atlanta, GA

Police Department
675 Ponce de Leon Avenue, NE
9th Floor, City Hall East
Atlanta, GA 30308
(404) 817-6900

Austin, TX

Police Department
715 E. Eighth Street
Austin, TX 78701
(512) 480-5000

Baltimore, MD

Police Department
601 E. Fayette Street
Baltimore, MD 21202
(410) 396-2020

Boston, MA

Police Department
154 Berkeley Street
Boston, MA 02116
(617) 343-4500

Charlotte, NC

Police Department
601 E. Trade Street
Charlotte, NC 28202
(704) 336-2337

Chicago, IL

Police Department
1121 S. State Street
Chicago, IL 60605
(312) 747-5501

Cincinnati, OH

Police Department
310 Ezzard Charles Drive
Cincinnati, OH 45214
(513) 352-3536

Cleveland, OH

Police Department
Justice Center
1300 Ontario Street
Cleveland, OH 44113
(216) 623-5005

Colorado Springs, CO

Police Department
705 S. Nevada Ave.
Colorado Springs, CO 80903
(719) 444-7401

Columbus, OH

Public Safety Department
Police Division
120 Marconi Blvd.
Columbus, OH 43215-0009
(614) 645-4600

Dallas, TX

Police Department
2014 Main Street, Room 506
Dallas, TX 75201-5203
(214) 670-4402

Denver, CO

Police Department
1331 Cherokee Street
Denver, CO 80204
(303) 640-3875

Detroit, MI

Police Department
1300 Beaubien Street
Detroit, MI 48226
(313) 596-1800

Durham, NC

Police Department
101 City Hall Plaza
Durham, NC 27701
(919) 560-4322

Eugene, OR

Public Safety Department
Police Division
777 Pearl St.
Eugene, OR 97401
(541) 687-5467

Flint, MI

Police Department
210 E. Fifth Ave.
Flint, MI 48502
(810) 766-7313

Fort Lauderdale, FL

Police Department
1300 W. Broward Blvd.
Fort Lauderdale, FL 33312
(305) 761-5590

Fort Worth, TX

Police Department
350 W. Belknap Street
Fort Worth, TX 76102
(817) 877-8385

Ft. Wayne, MI

Police Department
1320 E. Creighton
Ft. Wayne, MI 48603
(219) 427-1230

Grand Rapids, MI

Police Department
333 Monroe Avenue, NW
Grand Rapids, MI 49503
(616) 456-3364

Greensboro, NC

Police Department
PO Box 3136
Greensboro, NC 27402-3136
(910) 373-2450

Honolulu, HI

Police Department
801 S. Beretania Street
Honolulu, HI 96813
(808) 943-3163

Houston, TX

Police Department
61 Riesner Street
PO Box 1562
Houston, TX 77251
(713) 247-5500

Indianapolis, IN

Public Safety Department
Police Division
50 N. Alabama St., Room E211
Indianapolis, IN 46208
(317) 327-3580

Jacksonville, FL

Police Department
501 E. Bay Street
Jacksonville, FL 32202
(904) 630-2120

Kansas City, MO

Police Department
1125 Locust
Kansas City, MO 64106
(816) 234-5010

Knoxville, TN

Police Department
800 E. Church Ave.
Knoxville, TN 37915
(615) 521-1229

Lansing, MI

Police Department
120 W. Michigan Ave.
Lansing, MI 48933
(517) 483-4600

Las Vegas, NV

Detention/Enforcement Services
3300 E. Stewart Avenue
Las Vegas, NV 89101
(702) 229-6617

Lexington, KY

Public Safety Department
Police Division
150 E. Main Street
Lexington, KY 40507
(606) 258-3574

Los Angeles, CA

Police Department
150 N. Los Angeles St., Room 615
Los Angeles, CA 90012
(213) 485-3202

Lubbock, TX

Police Department
PO Box 2000
Lubbock, TX 79457
(806) 767-2750

Madison, WI

Police Department
211 S. Carroll Street
Madison, WI 53703-3303
(608) 266-4020

Manchester, NH

Police Department
351 Chestnut Street
Manchester, NH 03101
(603) 668-8711

Miami, FL

Police Department
400 NW Second Avenue
Miami, FL 33128
(305) 579-6565

Milwaukee, WI

Police Department
Police Administration Building
749 W. State Street
Milwaukee, WI 53201-0531
(414) 935-7200

Minneapolis, MN

Police Department
350 S. 5th Street, Room 130
City Hall
Minneapolis, MN 55415-1389
(612) 673-2853

Mobile, AL

Police Department
2460 Government Bldg.
Mobile, AL 36618
(334) 434-1700

Nashville, TN

Police Department
200 James Robertson Parkway
Nashville, TN 37201-5110
(615) 862-7301

New Orleans, LA

Police Department
715 S. Broad Street
New Orleans, LA 70119
(504) 826-2727

New York, NY

Police Department
1 Police Plaza
New York, NY 10038
(212) 374-6710

Norfolk, VA

Police Department
100 Brooke Avenue
Norfolk, VA 23510
(804) 441-2261

Oakland, CA

Police Department
455 7th Street
Oakland, CA 94607
(510) 238-3365

Omaha, NE

Police Department
505 S. 15th Street
Omaha, NE 68102
(404) 444-5666

Orlando, FL

Police Department
100 S. Hughey Avenue
Orlando, FL 32801
(407) 246-2401

Philadelphia, PA

Police Department
Police Administration Building
8th & Race Streets
Philadelphia, PA 19106
(215) 686-3358

Phoenix, AZ

Police Department
620 W. Washington Street
Phoenix, AZ 85003
(602) 262-6747

Pittsburgh, PA

Police Bureau
200 Ross Street
Pittsburgh, PA 15219
(412) 255-2814

Portland, OR

Police Bureau
1111 SW 2nd Avenue
Portland, OR 97204
(503) 823-0000

Raleigh, NC

Police Department
110 S. McDavell Street
PO Box 590
Raleigh, NC 27602
(919) 890-3385

Reno, NV

Police Department
PO Box 1900
Reno, NV 89505
(702) 334-2100

Richmond, VA

Police Department
Safety Building
501 N. Ninth Street
Richmond, VA 23219
(804) 780-6700

Sacramento, CA

Police Department
Hall of Justice
813 6th Street
Sacramento, CA 95814
(916) 264-5121

Saint Louis, MO

Police Department
1200 Clark St.
Saint Louis, MO 63103
(314) 444-5624

Saint Paul, MN

Police Department
100 E. 11th Street
Saint Paul, MN 55101
(612) 292-1111

Salt Lake City, UT

Police Department
315E 200 South
Salt Lake City, UT 84111
(801) 799-3100

San Antonio, TX

Police Department
PO Box 839966
San Antonio, TX 78283
(210) 207-7360

San Diego, CA

Police Department
1401 Broadway
San Diego, CA 92101
(619) 531-2000

San Francisco, CA

Police Department
Hall of Justice, Room 505
850 Bryant Street
San Francisco, CA 94103
(415) 553-1551

San Jose, CA

Police Department
201 W. Mission Street
San Jose, CA 95110
(408) 277-4212

Seattle, WA

Police Department
1001 Public Safety Building
610 3rd Avenue
Seattle, WA 98104
(206) 684-5577

Sioux Falls, SD

Police Department
Public Safety Building
501 N. Dakota Avenue
Sioux Falls, SD 57104
(605) 367-7259

Springfield, MO

Police Department
PO Box 8368
Springfield, MO 65801
(417) 864-1782

Stamford, CT

Police Department
PO Box 10152
Stamford, CT 06904
(203) 977-4681

Tacoma, WA

Police Department
930 Tacoma Ave., South
Tacoma, WA 98402
(206) 591-5900

Tallahassee, FL

Police Department
234 E. Seventh Ave.
Tallahassee, FL 32303
(904) 891-4242

Tampa, FL

Police Department
1710 Tampa Street
Tampa, FL 33602
(813) 223-1515

Topeka, KS

Police Department
204 SW Fifth St.
Topeka, KS 66603
(913) 368-9551

Tucson, AZ

Police Department
270 S. Stone Ave.
Tucson, AZ 85701-1917
(520) 791-4441

Washington, DC

Metropolitan Police Department
300 Indiana Avenue NW
Municipal Center, Room 5080
Washington, DC 20001
(202) 727-4220

Worcester, MA

Police Department
9-11 Lincoln Square
Worcester, MA 01608
(508) 799-8600

Appendix C

Crime Definitions

Aggravated Assault

Aggravated assault is an unlawful attack by one person upon another for the purpose of inflicting severe or aggravated bodily injury. This type of assault is usually accompanied by the use of a weapon or by means likely to produce death or great bodily harm. Attempts are included since it is not necessary that an injury result when a gun, knife, or other weapon is used which could and probably would result in serious personal injury if the crime were successfully completed.

Burglary

Burglary is defined as the unlawful entry of a structure to commit a felony or theft. The use of force to gain entry is not required to classify an offense as burglary. Burglary is categorized into three subclassifications: forcible entry, unlawful entry where no force is used, and attempted forcible entry.

Forcible Rape

Forcible rape is the carnal knowledge of a female forcibly and against her will. Assaults or attempts to commit rape by force or threat of force are also included; however, statutory rape (without force) and other sex offenses are excluded.

Larceny-Theft

Larceny-theft is the unlawful taking, carrying, leading, or riding away of property from the possession or constructive possession of another. It includes crimes such as shoplifting, pocket-picking, purse-snatching, thefts from motor vehicles, thefts of motor vehicle parts and accessories, bicycle thefts, etc., in which no use of force, violence, or fraud occurs. In the Uniform Crime Reporting Program, this crime category does not include embezzlement, "con" games, forgery, and worthless checks. Motor vehicle theft is also excluded from this category inasmuch as it is a separate Crime Index offense.

Motor Vehicle Theft

Defined as the theft or attempted theft of a motor vehicle, this offense category includes the stealing of automobiles, trucks, buses, motorcycles, motorscooters, snowmobiles, etc. The definition excludes the taking of a motor vehicle for temporary use by those persons having lawful access.

Murder and Nonnegligent Manslaughter

Murder and nonnegligent manslaughter, as defined in the Uniform Crime Reporting Program, is the willful (nonnegligent) killing of one human being by another. Not included in the count for this offense classification are deaths caused by negligence, suicide, or accident; justifiable homicides; and attempts to murder or assaults to murder, which are scored as aggravated assaults.

Property Crime

Property crime includes the offenses of burglary, larceny-theft, motor vehicle theft, and arson (not included in this book). The object of these offenses is the taking of money or property, but there is no force or threat of force against the victims.

Robbery

Robbery is the taking or attempting to take anything of value from the care, custody, or control of a person or persons by force or threat of force or violence and/or putting the victim in fear.

Violent Crime

Violent crime is composed of four offenses: murder and nonnegligent manslaughter, forcible rape, robbery and aggravated assault. All violent crimes involve force or threat of force.

Statutory Provisions Relating to Alcohol Use and Driving

Blood Alcohol Concentration

The evidentiary weight given to blood alcohol concentration levels generally falls into one of two categories. "Illegal per se at 0.10%" indicates that such a level of blood alcohol concentration is considered conclusive evidence of intoxication in a court of law. "Presumption at 0.10%" indicates that such a level of blood alcohol concentration creates a presumption of intoxication in a court of law. Statutory provisions of several jurisdictions treat the 0.10% level as both presumptive and illegal per se evidence of driving under the influence. This appears to be the result of States having adopted one of the standards without amending statutes that had previously authorized the other standard. In such cases, the actual statutes should be consulted for clarification.

Open Container Law

Refers to laws prohibiting the possession of open containers of alcoholic beverages in the passenger compartment of a motor vehicle.

Anti-consumption Law

Refers to laws prohibiting the consumption of alcoholic beverages in the passenger compartment of a motor vehicle.

Dram Shop Law

Refers to laws that make owners of drinking establishments civilly liable for serving alcohol to an intoxicated patron who then goes out and injures another individual in a motor vehicle accident.

In the table, "Yes" indicates that such a provision is provided expressly by statute. In all jurisdictions, use of a controlled substance or use of a controlled substance in conjunction with alcohol also constitutes the basis for a driving while intoxicated charge. Most jurisdictions have established more stringent blood alcohol concentration levels for operators of commercial motor vehicles, as well as juvenile motor vehicles operators. Statutes should be consulted for the full text and meaning of specific provisions.